THE SIEGE OF
KHE SANH
1967-1968

The Most Famous Battle of the Vietnam War
[21st January 1968 to 6th April 1968]

Military History

Historical Dramatisation of the
77 Day Siege of Khe Sanh

By
Lieutenant David Peter EHRLICH
(Royal Australian Navy Reserves)

A LEVANTER BOOK

The right of David Peter EHRLICH to be identified as author of this work has been asserted by him in accordance with the Copyright Act 1968 (Commonwealth of Australia) and the common law and international treaty appertaining to such copyright.

Printed in United States of America by Createspace (An Amazon Company)
Typeset by Createspace

EHRLICH, David Peter, 1959 –

VIETNAM WAR: The Siege of KHE SANH 1967 – 1968

I. Title

A823.3
All Rights Reserved.

No part of this publication may be reproduced, stored in a retrieval system, or transmitted in any form or by any means without the prior permission in writing of the publisher and the author jointly, nor be otherwise circulated in any form of binding or cover other than that in which it is herein published and without a similar condition including this condition being imposed on the subsequent purchaser.

Published by Createspace an Amazon Company
Copyright (C) David Peter EHRLICH, 2012
ISBN – 13:978-0646323022
ISBN – 10:0646323024

I First & Foremost Dedicate this Book to,

NGUYEN CAO KY
[8th September 1930 - 23rd July 2011]

Prime Minister of South Vietnam
[1965 to 1967]

Vice President of South Vietnam
[1968 to 1971]

Air Marshal of the South Vietnamese Air Force [VNAF]

'Quotes' of the Late & Sadly Missed Air Marshal Nguyen Cao Ky

"Many times, I asked President Johnson and other people to stop this war. To win, you have to go offensive."

"The US was and is the world's leading naval power, but, fearing to offend the Soviets, failed to blockade Haiphong. A river of munitions flowed through that port to be used against South Vietnam and its allies."

"After Watergate, America was a ship without a rudder. Vietnam was left to its own devices, drifting along towards its fate."

This Book is Also Dedicated to,

Colonel David E. Lownds USMC (retired)
Sergeant David Charles Dolby US Army (retired)
Robert William *(Blowtorch Bob)* Komer
Chief of Civil Operations & Rural Development Support [CORDS]
& National Security Adviser

Lieutenant General Phillip Buford Davidson Jr.
(Chief of US Army Intelligence J-2 for
Military Assistance Command Vietnam)

And

All the men and women of the **United States Marine Corps,
United States Army, United States Air Force, United States Navy** and the **Armed Forces of the Republic of Vietnam [ARVN]** who fought in the Vietnam War from 1959 to 1975

As Well as,

The **Armed Forces of the French Union** who fought in the First Indochina War from 19th December 1946 to 1st August 1954

And to the memory of,

General Henri Eugene Navarre
(Commander of the French Union Forces from May 1953 to August 1954)

And to my Wife

Authors Preface

There is a considerable volume of work, perhaps as many as fifty or more, being mostly military histories, on the Siege of Khe Sanh which lasted for 77 days from the night of 21st January 1968 to 6th April 1968 when the Marine Combat base was relieved during Operation Pegasus by the 1st Cavalry Division (Airmobile). There is also a collection of oral histories and eyewitness accounts of men who were actually there on the ground at Khe Sanh, Old and New Lang Vei and the surrounding areas during the critical months both before and after the siege. However, to the best of my knowledge and as far as I am aware there is no historical dramatisation or work of historically accurate fiction mixed with a solid military history basis that deals with the entire siege of Khe Sanh from start to finish. This book attempts to cover that void and thus to be not only entertaining but as far as I could make it historically accurate to the events that unfolded. The work by Chaplain Ray Stubbe who was the religious minister at KSCB is one such excellent eyewitness account in his book, 'Valley of Decision: The Siege of Khe Sanh.'

As a child growing up in the 1960's (I was 9 years old in 1968) I had little or no understanding of the Second Vietnam War and frankly no interest in it nor the daily radio news broadcasts and black and white television coverage of the war which always went on about this thing called *'body counts'* and the tally of our wounded and killed which included of course the Australian contingent to Vietnam in Phuoc Tuy Province. It was only when I joined the Royal Australian Navy in 1986 as a Lieutenant Legal Officer and when I specialised in public international law, the laws of war and rules of engagement did my interest in the Vietnam conflict awaken. I undertook more than 3 years of solid research into the history of not only the Khe Sanh engagement but the entire French Indochina War and the second American Vietnam War initiated under the Eisenhower and then Kennedy Administrations starting with the first military advisers in the period 1959 to 1962.

I have tried to remain as historically accurate to the actual events at Khe Sanh during 1967 and 1968 and they are told in an approximate chronological order.

It is with much sadness that I learnt of the recent passing of Colonel David E. Lownds in Florida who was the commander of the 26th Marine Regiment at Khe Sanh which constituted the bulk of the garrison along with the 1st Battalion, 9th Marine Regiment and the 37th ARVN Rangers. This book is dedicated to Colonel David E. Lownds and all the men and women of all the United States Armed Forces that served in Vietnam.

I was also saddened by the recent passing of Sergeant David Charles Dolby on 6th August 2010 and even though he was not involved in the Khe Sanh action I nevertheless dedicate this book to him as well.

Being a work of historical fiction the main protagonist is of course fictitious along with several other characters. The rest of the description of the siege of Khe Sanh is as accurate and as precise as I could make it to be and any errors in the chronological sequence of events is my responsibility. I hope that some people may find this book an entertaining read as well as giving an insight into that momentous battle that occurred along National Route 9 near the Laotian border with South Vietnam. Thank you.

David Peter EHRLICH
[Attorney-at-Law] (Sydney, Australia) October, 2012

Table of Contents

Chapter 1   Brinks Hotel Saigon 1

Chapter 2   Conference at the Tan Son Nhut Air Base 19

Chapter 3   General William Childs Westmoreland 35

Chapter 4   US Special Forces Camp at Lang Vei 57

Chapter 5   The Battle for Thonthamkhe 85

Chapter 6   Arrival at Khe Sanh 115

Chapter 7   325thC North Vietnamese Division 151

Chapter 8   January 20th 1968 D Day Minus 1 at Khe Sanh 187

- Final Plea to COMUSMACV for the Use of Nuclear Weapons at Khe Sanh

Chapter 9   January 21st 1968 D Day at Khe Sanh 247

- Mightiest Corporal in the World: Corporal Robert J. Arrotta [1/3/26th Marines]
- The Beginning

  Attack on Hill 861A 0035 hours, 21st January 1968
- The Detonation of Khe Sanh's Ammunition Dump [ASP 1]
- The PAVN Attack on Khe Sanh Village: 21st January 1968

Chapter 10   Another DIEN BIEN PHU? 311

- History of the Khe Sanh Combat Base Prior to the Advent of the Siege on night of 20th to 21st January 1968

Chapter 11   The Onslaught - Destruction of US Special Forces at Lang Vei 341

- The Vulnerability of Khe Sanh's Water Supply and the *Rao Quan River*
- Prelude to the TET OFFENSIVE 1968

- The Viet Cong Sapper Attack on the US Embassy Saigon: 30th to 31st January 1968
- The PAVN Attack on Hills 881 South and 861A: 5th February 1968
- The Destruction of US Special Forces at Lang Vei: 7th February 1968
- Lieutenant Colonel Howard M. Dallman (United States Air Force) – AFSN:0-823814 Hero of the United States of America

Chapter 12 OPERATION NIAGARA 441

- Captain Frank C. Willoughby's Escape from Lang Vei: 7th to 8th February 1968
- Conference at MACV FORWARD
- Major George Quamo [ASN:0-5307391] FOB3, 5th Special Forces Group (Airborne), 1st Special Forces Command.
- Captain Edward Kufeldt [MCSN:0-89361] VMO-6, Marine Aircraft Group Sixteen, First Marine Aircraft Wing, United States Marine Corps
- The 304th PAVN Division Attack the 1st Battalion, 9th Marines on Hill 64: 8th February 1968
- OPERATION S.L.I.C.E. [8th & 9th February 1968] (Search. Locate. Identify. Crush. & Exterminate.)
- B-52 Arc Light Raids on General Vo Nguyen Giap's Suspected Headquarters in Laos: 10th to 18th February 1968

Chapter 13 THE STORM ABATES.. 637

- The Hazards of Aerial Supply at Khe Sanh
- The Heaviest PAVN Artillery Barrage of the Siege: 1,307 Incoming Rounds on the 23rd February 1968
- The PAVN's Last Major Ground Assault Against Khe Sanh: 29th February to 1st March 1968
- The First Attack Against the 37th ARVN Rangers: 2130 hours, 29th February 1968
- The Second Attack Against the 37th ARVN Rangers: 2330 hours On 29th February 1968
- The Third Attack Against the 37th ARVN Rangers: 0315 hours On 1st March 1968

Chapter 14   OPERATION PEGASUS 685

- The Withdrawal of the PAVN (North Vietnamese) from Khe Sanh: 6th to 31st March 1968
- What was the North Vietnamese Strategy at Khe Sanh?
- The Creation of Landing Zone STUD: 25th March 1968
- Operational Plans for PEGASUS

Chapter 15   The Relief of Khe Sanh 713

- D DAY: 1st April 1968: The 3rd Brigade, 1st Cavalry Division (Airmobile) Attacks West of CA LU
- D Plus 2: 2nd/3rd April 1968: The 2nd Brigade, 1st Cavalry Division (Airmobile) Attacks Towards LZ TOM and LZ Wharton
- The 1st Battalion, 5th Cavalry Attack the Old French Fort
- The 1st Battalion, 9th Marines Attack Hill 471 : 4th to 5th April 1968
- The 66th North Vietnamese Army Regiment Launch a Counter-Attack Against Hill 471 on 5th April 1968
- The Relief of Khe Sanh : 6th April 1968
  84th Company, 8th ARVN Airborne Battalion Lands at Khe Sanh
- Elements of the 3rd Brigade, 1st Cavalry Division (Airmobile) Arrive at Khe Sanh on 8th April 1968
- 1st Battalion, 8th Cavalry Regiment, 1st Airborne Brigade Recapture the US Special Forces Camp at Lang Vei : 10th April 1968
- The Final Act of Khe Sanh
  3rd Battalion, 26th Marines Attack Hill 881 North: 14th April 1968

Chapter 16   Presidential Unit Citations 761

- Farewell Gathering at MACV Headquarters, Pentagon East
- The Tomb of the Unknown Soldier : Arlington National Cemetery
- Presidential Unit Citations   The White House

Further Suggested Reading 775

Map 1: Map of the Republic of South Vietnam

Showing the 4 Military Operational Corps Zones I to IV

Northern I Corps & Quang Tri Province

[Note: Khe Sanh & Lang Vei not shown on this map.]

I Corps is primarily the responsibility of 3rd Marine Amphibious Force or III MAF

III MAF is made up of 1st & 3rd Marine Divisions plus elements of 2nd Marine Division after 1968

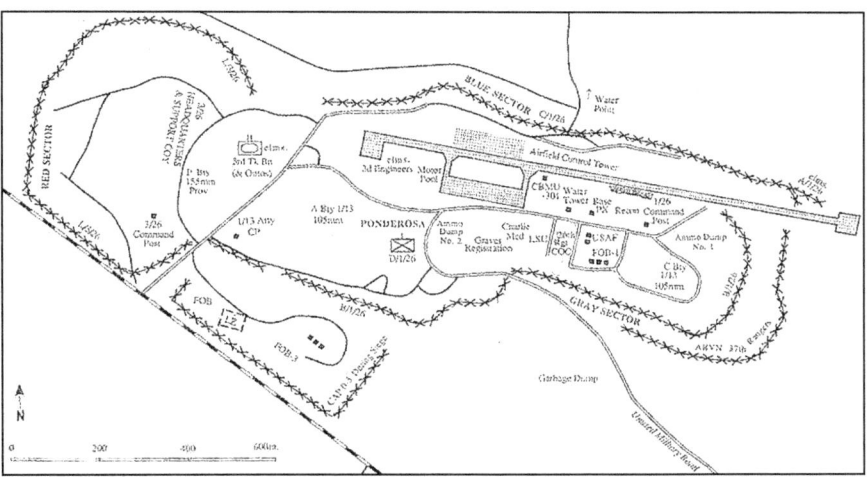

Map 2: Khe Sanh Combat Base

during the 77 Day Siege from 21st January 1968 to 6th April 1968:- Showing the; Red Sector, Gray Sector, Blue Sector, KSCB Airstrip 3,895 feet in length, Forward Operating Base 3 and 1, 105mm and 155mm howitzer positions, ONTOS positions, PONDEROSA, positions of the various companies and battalions of the 26th Marine Regiment, drop zone which is north of the positions of the L/3/26, MATU/MATCU bunker, garbage dump, ammunition dumps 1 and 2, United States Air Force Forward Operating Base 1 (where Captain Mirza Baig did most of his fire control work organising SUPERGAGGLES and running Operation Combat SKYSPOT), motor pool, 3rd Engineers detachment, positions of the 37th ARVN Ranger Battalion in the Gray Sector, the water tower and the PX building, the Reconnaissance Command Post, airfield control tower, the Rock Quarry is not on this map but is west of the Red Sector, TA CON Village is west of Forward Operating Base 3 also not shown on this map, military service roads running south, north-west and east south-east of the base leading to National Route 9 and Lang Vei (Old & New) and Khe Sanh Village. Hill 471 not shown on this map is approximately 1 mile due south of the Gray Sector.

The LAPES [Low Altitude Parachute Extraction System] and GPES [Ground Proximity Extraction System] operations were carried out by

C-123 Providers; C-130/C-130E Hercules transports and 14,356 tons were dropped by USAF; 8,120 tons by Para-drop & 4,661 tons by 1st Marine Aircraft Wing with 465 tons dropped by helicopters to the Hill Outposts just in the month of February 1968 using SUPERGAGGLE.

North Vietnamese 304th Division Attacks

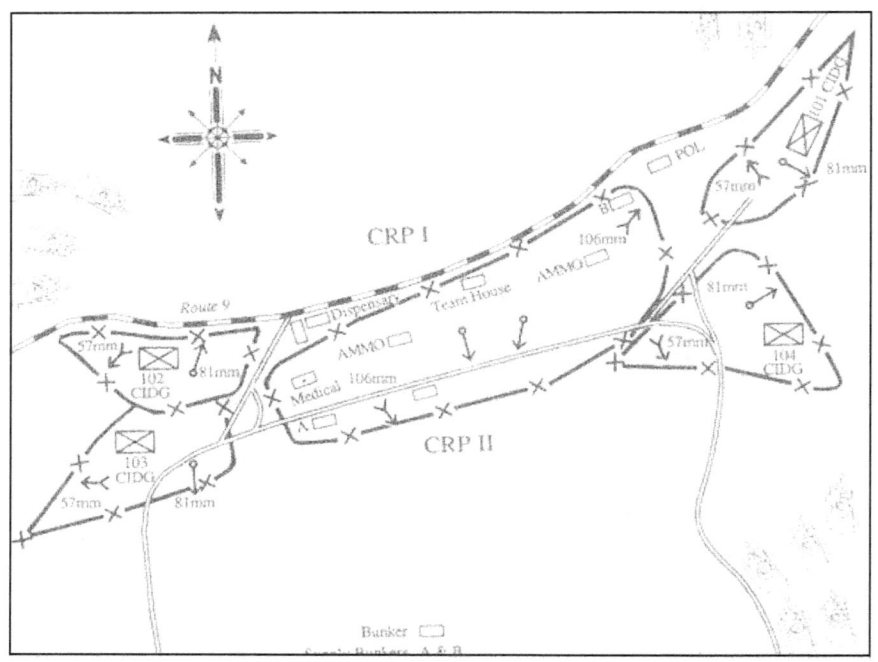

500 CIDG troops plus 24 Green Berets

Map 3: New Lang Vei Special Forces Camp

showing dispositions of; Detachment A-101 of the 5th Special Forces Group plus CIDG Irregular Forces Being mostly Bru and Hre Montagnard Tribesmen. Approximately 500 CIDG troops plus 24 US Army Green Berets commanded by Captain Frank C. Willoughby. Lieutenant Colonel Daniel Schungel arrived at Lang Vei about 2 days prior to 7th February 1968 when PT-76 Communist amphibious tanks supplied courtesy of the Soviets made their assault. New Lang Vei also included a detachment of ARVN Rangers.

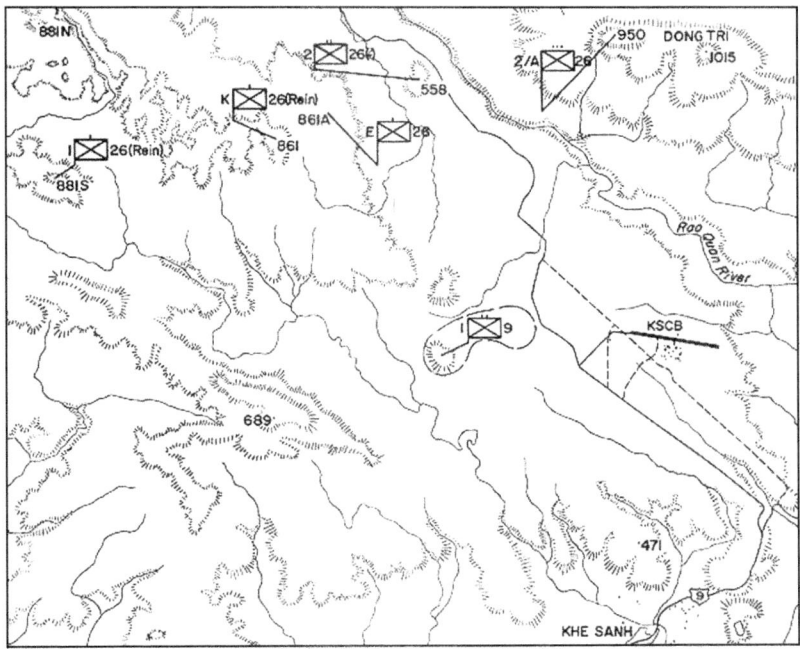

Map 4: Dispositions of the Marine Forces around the Hill Outposts

being; **Hills 881 South, Hill Complex 861 and 861A, Hill 558, Hill 564 (aka 64)**, Hill 950 and Hill 1015 Hill 881 North was assaulted during the April and May 1967 Khe Sanh Hill battles but was lost again to the North Vietnamese Imperialist Aggressor Forces prior to the outbreak of the renewed hostilities that commenced the so-called 'Siege' on the night of 20th to 21st January 1968.

List of Units on the Hill Outposts:

Hill 881 South: I/3/26 plus two platoons and M/3/26 Command Group (400 troops)
Hill 861: K/3/26 plus two platoons A/1/26 (300 troops)
Hill 861A: E/2/26 (200 troops) – occupied on 5th February 1968
Hill 558: 2/26 and E/2/26 being in total 1,000 troops approximately
Hill 950: 2nd Platoon A/1/26 (50 troops)
Hill 1015 – No troops stationed there.
Hill 564 or (aka) Hill 64: 1st Battalion, 9th Marine Regiment (1,192 troops)

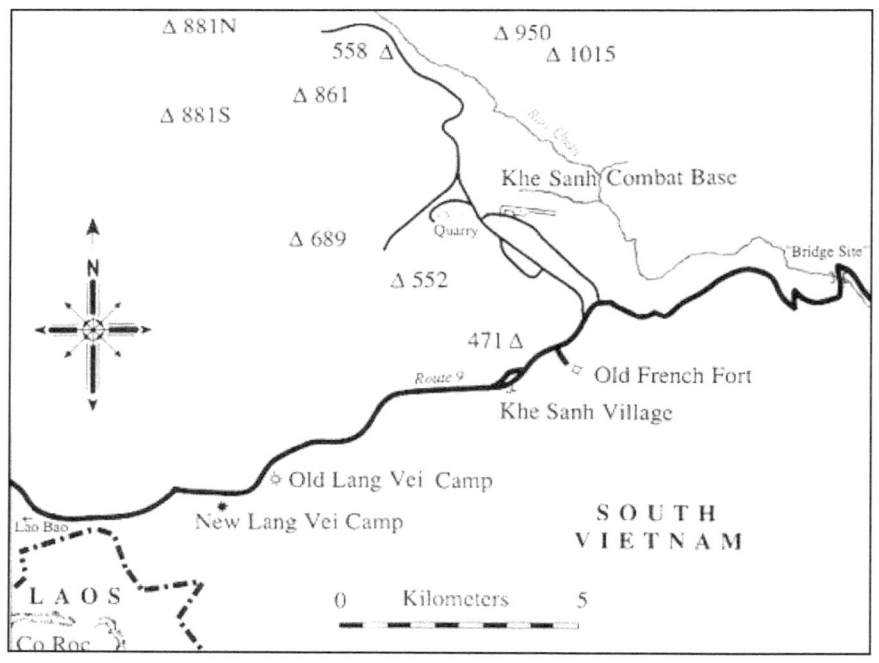

Map 5: Khe Sanh

Old and New Lang Vei, Khe Sanh Village, Old French Fort, the Communist Aggressor Forces 'Co Roc' Artillery Position and the Hill Outposts at the time of the 'Siege' from January 1968 to April 1968.

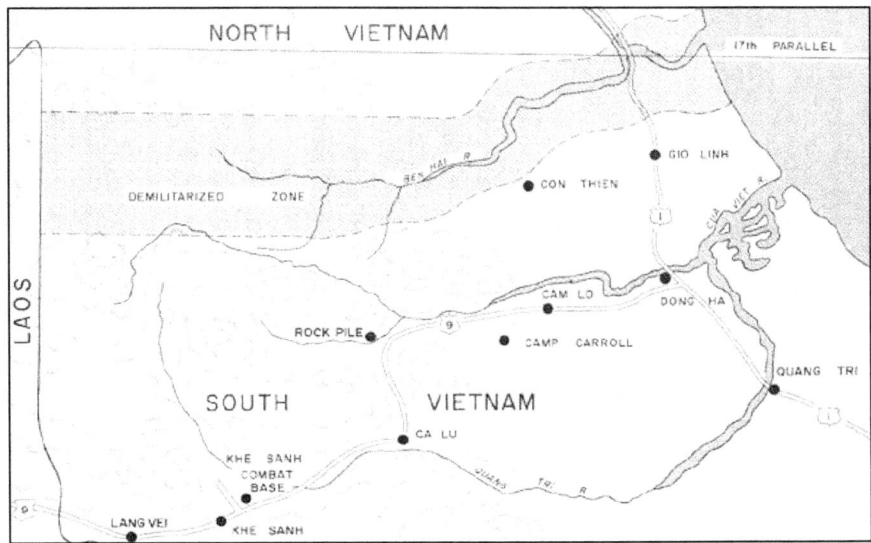

Map 6:

Khe Sanh Combat Base (KSCB), Lang Vei, Camp Carroll [from where the 175mm M107 self-propelled guns were fired in support of KSCB throughout the siege], Cam Lo, Dong Ha, Quang Tri City, Con Thien, Ca Lu and the Rock Pile where further USA artillery was stationed in support of KSCB.

[Note: Map shows only part of Northern I Corps Operational Zone.]

Inside the Khe Sanh base was the organic Marine artillery consisting of; 60mm M19 mortars, 81mm M29 mortars, 4.2 inch M30 mortars, 105mm M101A1 howitzers, 155mm M114A1 howitzers plus the ONTOS with 4 recoilless rifles mounted on each tracked vehicle.

There were also several M48 Patton tanks in dug-in positions at several strategic points inside KSCB.

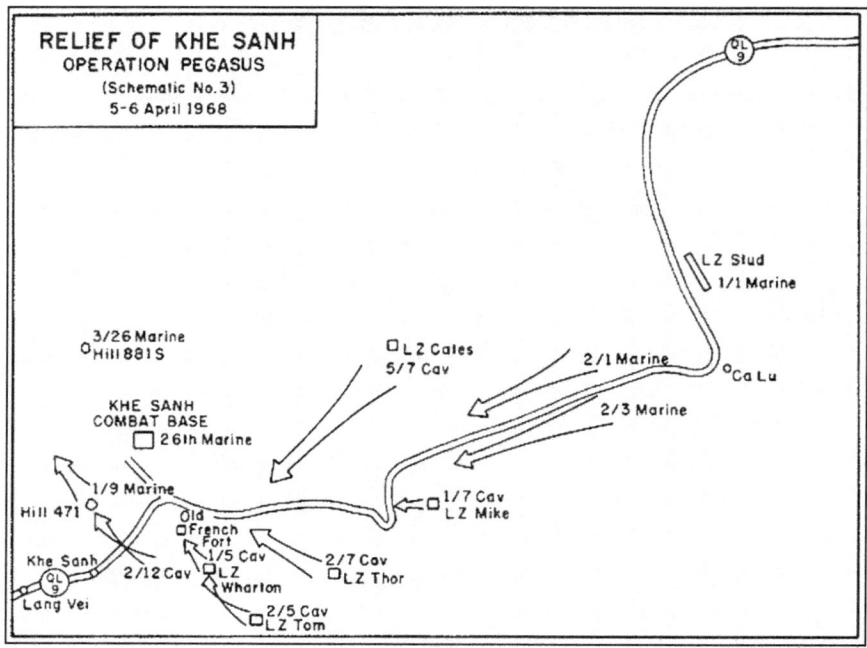

Map 7: Operation PEGASUS

by the 1st Cavalry Division (Airmobile) to Counter-Attack and relieve the besieged Khe Sanh Combat base launched against The North Vietnamese Imperialist Aggressor Forces with great success.

First elements of the ARVN Airborne Forces reached KSCB on 6th April 1968 with elements of the 3rd Brigade, 1st Cavalry Division (Airmobile) reaching KSCB on the 8th April 1968.

The PAVN (North Vietnamese) Forces suffered a Crushing Defeat at Khe Sanh.

Operation NIAGARA

air offensive launched by MACV proved instrumental in this momentous Victory for the Free World Forces against Communist Aggression and Imperialism.

Entire Vietnam War (1959 – 1975)

Force	KIA	WIA	MIA	CIA
US Forces	47,378 [1]	304,704 [2]	2,338 [3]	766 [4]
ARVN	223,748	1,169,763	NA	NA
South Korea	4,407	17,060	NA	NA
Australia	469	2,940	6	NA
Thailand	351	1,358	NA	NA
New Zealand	55	212	NA	NA
NVA/VC	1,100,000	600,000	NA	26,000 [5]

Table 1:

Note 1: there were an additional 10,824 non-hostile deaths for a total of 58,202
Note 2: of the 304,704 WIA, 153,329 required hospitalization
Note 3: this number decreases as remains are recovered and identified
Note 4: 114 died in captivity
Note 5: Does not include 101,511 *Hoi Chanh*

Legend: KIA = *Killed In Action* WIA = *Wounded In Action*
MIA = *Missing In Action* CIA = *Captured In Action*

Table 2: 1968 Tet Offensive

Force	KIA	WIA	MIA	CIA
US Forces	1,536	7,764	11	unknown
ARVN	2,788	8,299	587	unknown
NVA/VC	45,000	unknown	unknown	6,991

Legend: KIA = *Killed In Action* WIA = *Wounded In Action*
MIA = *Missing In Action* CIA = *Captured In Action*

Table 3: Troop Levels as of 1 January 1968

Force	Total Strength	Support	Combat Arms
US Forces	409,111	346,260	62,850
ARVN	Not Avail	Not Avail	Not Avail
NVA/VC	420,000	unknown	unknown

Troop Levels as of 1 January 1969

Force	Total Strength	Support	Combat Arms
US Forces	440,029	372,429	67,600
ARVN	Not Avail	Not Avail	Not Avail
NVA/VC	332,000	unknown	unknown

The figures for relative strengths assume the following: On January 1, 1969 there were 110 battalions in Vietnam (98 Infantry, 3 tank, and 9 artillery). An Infantry battalion had 656 infantrymen (4 companies per battalion with 164 men per company). An armour battalion had 204 tankers (3 companies per battalion with 68 tankers per company). An artillery battalion had approximately 300 men. Therefore, the number of actual "trigger pullers" added up to 67,600. Note that this was "authorized strength". Most battalions were not even close to their TO&E strength during the war, with many infantry companies operating with 80 men. This was true despite the fact that the parent divisions reported being at, or slightly over, authorized strength.

***There were a large number of REMFs in Vietnam.
[Rear Echelon Motherfuckers = REMFs]
[The US ARMY in Vietnam had a small Head with teeth but a HUGE TAIL]

Table 4: United States Troop Strength in South Vietnam from 1960 to 1972

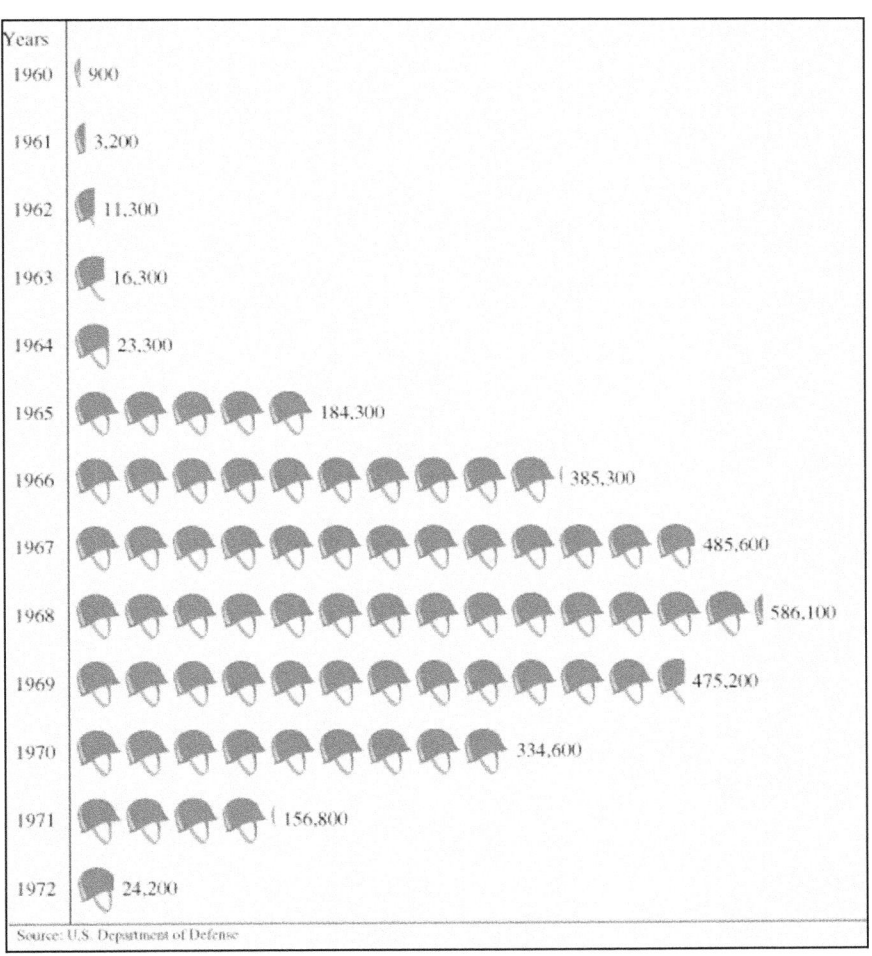

Figure 29.1 U.S. Troop Levels in Vietnam, 1960-1972

PROLOGUE

The United States of America did **Not** lose the war in Vietnam.

Anybody who could suggest even remotely that America *'lost'* the war in South Vietnam is displaying their ignorance of the subject matter and the facts. What can you expect? For this widely held and erroneous view has been nurtured and promulgated by the irresponsibility and disinformation of the media and the press/television not only inside the United States but also the international media.

The United States Armed Forces never lost a single engagement in the period 1959 to 1972 when it withdrew all but its Air Force from South Vietnam (with a few minor exceptions such as the *Lang Vei* assault and some minor Fire Support Base engagements).

Even in the period March to May 1972 during the Communist Easter Offensive when the United Sates had only 24,200 troops left in South Vietnam and almost no ground combat troops as most of these personnel were United States Air Force did the Army of the Republic of South Vietnam [ARVN] successfully halt and defeat the PAVN largely on their own albeit with US air and logistical support.

I would ask the question how can the United States *'lose'* a war in South Vietnam when the end came in 1975 when it did not have any army, navy or air force units of any significance in South Vietnam to so lose?

The younger generations, those people born after 1975, have nobody to blame for this ridiculous misconception that America lost the war in South Vietnam other than the international and domestic media which has traditionally been of a 'dovish' persuasion.

It is also a total fallacy and ludicrous to suggest that the people of the United States of America did not on the whole support the Vietnam War at least until 1968 – 1969.

The fact is that the majority of citizens in the United States of America (despite the domestic media) did support the American Peace and Security efforts in Vietnam to assist our ally the Republic of Vietnam [South Vietnam].

It is a tragedy that the Ford Administration from 1974 onwards and Congress decided after the Watergate fiasco to 'pull-the-plug' on our beleaguered ally who in the period 1974 to 1975 were facing the full might of not only the entire conventional forces of North Vietnam but also the massive logistical and material support provided to them by the Soviet Union and the Chicoms (Communist Chinese) without, virtually, any further assistance from the United States.

The United States Congress on 19th June 1973 passed the *Case-Church Amendment* which brought into law and into effect the complete cessation of all military activities in Southeast Asia with a deadline for 15th August 1973. This brought to an end the 12 years of the United States involvement in the war in Vietnam. In addition, after the Watergate debacle when Richard Nixon resigned and Gerald Ford took over the reins of power in Washington in the fall of 1974 the US Congress decided to cut funding to South Vietnam for the next fiscal year from 1.26 billion US dollars to only 700 million US dollars. This was a clear signal to the coterie of imperialist aggressors and madmen in Hanoi that now the time was ripe to go in for 'the kill.' And they did so mercilessly planning an all-out military war of conquest against South Vietnam when all United States Forces had already long gone.

We only have to listen to what the war criminal, Party Secretary of the North Vietnamese Communist Party, Le Duan said in December 1974, and I quote;

"The Americans have withdrawn......this is what marks the opportune moment."

Yes indeed! An opportune moment for the North Vietnamese to embellish and to perpetuate their litany of war crimes and military aggression against the free democratic country of South Vietnam. The PAVN (People's Army of North Vietnam) began its horrendous assault in March 1975 in the Central Highlands targeting *Ban Me Thout* which was a strategically important hamlet that was the lynch-pin between the north and south of South Vietnam.

On 13th March 1975 President Thieu ordered a strategic withdrawal of the ARVN forces which resulted in the Communist capture of *Pleiku* and *Kontum* which virtually left the rolling rice paddies and open ground of the south and Mekong Delta wide open to the PAVN. President Thieu rightly criticised the cutting to a trickle of United States economic and material aid. He said that if full aid would have been granted as was originally intended then most of South Vietnam could be held and that if only half the aid was forthcoming then only half of South Vietnam could be held. This is what happened.

It should be noted that the initial reason for the entry of the United States into Vietnam under the Eisenhower and then Kennedy Administrations in the period 1959 to 1963 namely, 'guerrilla warfare' was now, in 1975, totally irrelevant.

North Vietnam launched a full-scale war of imperial aggression with all the organic weapons of a modern standing army using tanks, heavy artillery, high-powered machine guns and even their fledgling air force supplied and equipped by the Bolshevik Empire and the Chicoms. It should also be noted that the Soviet Union's denial of helping to any substantial degree the North Vietnamese Communists is total and unmitigated garbage. It is a fact that Soviet fighter pilots actually flew the vastly inferior Mig-17's, Mig-19's and Mig-21's against the United States Air Force and its pilots in South Vietnam face-to-face through their respective cockpits and actually shot some US planes down.

The United States forces won every major engagement against the Main Force Viet Cong and then later the PAVN. By the time the so-called 'TET' offensive was over in April 1968 the Main Force Viet Cong had been virtually wiped out as an effective fighting force. Of the 84,000 estimated troops in the Viet Cong at the start of TET once the US forces had finished with them they had suffered a staggering 45,000 either killed, wounded or captured. That is 53.6% of their entire force structure.

The Cambodian raids from 1st to 3rd May 1970 put the finishing touches to the Viet Cong as their border sanctuaries were no longer inviolate and the US went in to dismantle and crush and exterminate their nefarious logistics and supply lines along the Ho Ch Minh complex of trails that led into War Zones C & D and the 'Parrot's Beak.'

The situation was so bad that the regular forces of the PAVN actually disguised themselves as the black pyjama'd Viet Cong in order to keep up the appearance that the Southern Communists could still fight and still had the majority of support from the ordinary peasants in the South.

I want to make it absolutely clear that at No time did the Viet Cong ever have the majority of support from the peasants nor the city dwellers of South Vietnam. To verify this you only have to look at the unclassified documents and statistics from the PHOENIX Program and the Strategic Hamlet Program.

To say that the population of South Vietnam were solidly behind the Viet Cong is a stupidity and a farce.

The United States had to fight this war with one hand tied behind its back and one leg shackled to the other with just enough slack so that it could hobble along like the giant it was in terms of its superior technology and firepower. Who do we have to thank for this? I do not need to tell you, surely?

For most of the Vietnam War the bombing of the most important targets in North Vietnam was off-limits to the USAF. Is this the manner in which to 'win' a war?

The objective of the war never was and was never contemplated to be the overthrow of the North Vietnamese government. Many in the US intelligence and military communities as well as the CIA would have relished such an objective. But it was never United States policy to do this. The renewed B-52 an B-52D Arc Light

bombing of the North was designed firstly as a response to the April and May 1972 Easter Offensive and then later in 1973 to bring the cabal of Communist henchmen in Hanoi back to the Geneva conference table when Operations LINEBACKER I and II were initiated.

One simple task could have brought the war to an end in favour of the United States and South Vietnam as far back as 1968-1969 and that would have been the bombing and destruction of the Red River dykes that would have crippled the entire food and distribution apparatus of North Vietnam. It was never done.

In terms of the military destruction of the insurrection in the South by the Viet Cong and its political cadres the United States won the war hands down. In terms of defeating the regular armed forces and main force units of the North Vietnamese Army the United States also won a clear and decisive victory while it was still there on the ground until 1971. By 1972, as I said above, only 24,200 US personnel were left in the Republic and they were mostly USAF for air support and logistics.

Nobody in all honesty could say that America 'lost' the war in Vietnam.

By 1975 when the US Congress refused to provide any more aid to South Vietnam other than a trickle of money it was too late. Millions of innocent South Vietnamese civilians were torn from their homes, brutalised, imprisoned, tortured and sent to Communist re-education and concentration camps.

The betrayal of South Vietnam was a shocking and irreversible mistake by the Administration at the time as well as the US Congress. Vice-President Nguyen Cao Ky fled to California and became the owner of liquor store. He passed away just recently in 2011. If you ever would have wanted to hear the 'truth' of what happened in this most unfortunate chain of events then you should have asked him while he was still with us. I was very sad when I heard of his passing. He was a great visionary, with charm and charisma and he had his countries' best interests always at the forefront of his actions.

Where would America be today if we had stated and announced that it was our policy not to aid our allies against external aggression? Where would that have left us in the Cold War from 1945 to 1991? And where would that leave us today in 2012-2013 and post 9/11 where we are supporting Iraq and Afghanistan and fighting the War Against Terror and the continued efforts of rogue states such as North Korea and Iran to acquire and to stock-pile WMD's [Weapons of Mass Destruction]?

The war that North Vietnam won in 1975 was not the Vietnam War that the United States had been involved in which ended effectively in 1972.

It was a separate war between the Republic of South Vietnam standing alone with virtually no significant aid from the US against the well experienced and battle hardened PAVN Communist aggressor main force units. The Viet Cong had virtually ceased to exist by 1975.

Lieutenant David Peter EHRLICH

Just as an example of the fighting resilience and bravery of the ARVN [South Vietnamese Army] whom we deserted, it was not until the onslaught in 1974 that Phuoc Binh, the capital of Phuoc Long province about 60 miles north of Saigon fell to the PAVN. It was the first provincial capital to fall since the PAVN took Quang Tri City on 1st May 1972 – a gap of 2 years in which the ARVN held on grimly and with exemplary determination against the Communist aggressors. During the entire war the PAVN were never able to capture nor to hold onto even one of the 44 provincial capitals in South Vietnam. In 1972 the ARVN successfully held and defeated the Communist Easter Offensive of that year much to their credit.

In terms of public support in the United States for the war in the South it is a fact that the majority of Americans supported the peace and security efforts of Military Assistance Command [MACV] right up until 1969-1970. In 1967 the support for the security efforts in South Vietnam was extremely high. In a Gallup poll in February 1968, 25% of Americans wanted to broaden and intensify the military operations; 28% wanted to start an all-out and massive effort to bring the war to a speedy conclusion despite the chance of China or Russia entering the war and just 24% wanted to discontinue and pull out in the near future. Also 10% wanted to continue the war at its present level in 1967. Peak support for the war was in 1965 to 1967 when 75% of people under 30 years of age and 57% over 49 years thought the war was not a mistake. When US troops were virtually gone in May 1971 still 34% under 30 years and 23% over 49 years thought that the war was correct in its initiation. The Gallup poll revealed that more people were dissatisfied that President Johnson was too timid! Rather than that he was too vigorous in the conduct of the war.

In conclusion, the battle of *Khe Sanh* was a stupendous victory for the armed forces of the United States of America. It was, in those 77 critical days of the engagement, the most lethal and concentrated application of tactical air power in support of ground forces in the entire recorded history of human warfare. Operation NIAGARA dropped more bombs in the siege of that beleaguered Marine combat base than all the bombs dropped in World War Two in the European theatre of operations. Credit for this magnificent effort goes to the men and women of the United States Air Force, United States Marine 1st Air Wing and the personnel of Task Force 77 of the US Navy in the Gulf of Tonkin as well as of course Strategic Air Command that provided the strategic bombing with its B-52's.

The battle of *Khe Sanh* demonstrated vividly in the words of President Lyndon Baines Johnson, the utter futility of the Communist imperialist aggressor's hopes of every winning a military victory in South Vietnam, or anywhere else for that matter.

The North Vietnamese asked for trouble at *Khe Sanh* and the United States gave them what for.

It will be a victory that will be relished, studied and admired by future generations of Americans. It demonstrated beyond a shadow of a doubt the enormous technological and firepower superiority of the United States Armed Forces over any other nation on earth. It was in some sense the most glorious pinnacle of achievement in the Vietnam War for the Free World Forces. To this day and into the future period of conflicts that await us from 2013-2018 we shall continue to see the development of American military technological superiority in weaponry, space gathered intelligence and remote-piloted war machines that do not require a human operator that will leave the rest of the world's nations appearing as if they were back in the Stone Age fighting with sticks and shards of animal bones. The gap between the technology of today's Chicoms and Russians is at least 20 years and that gap will not diminish in the future but increase in scope and in the quality difference between force structures.

Some have said that the strategy of General Vo Nguyen Giap was successful at *Khe Sanh* in that it was designed as a 'diversion' of US manoeuvre battalions away from the cities and into the Central Highlands and Northern I Corps to allow the 'TCK-TKN' (*Tong Cong Kich – Tong Khoi Nghia*) or General Offensive, General Uprising to be successful in the cities. If that is the case it was one of the most expensive diversions in the history of warfare where you had the better part of 3 North Vietnamese Divisions that could have created untold havoc in the South being pinned down in a remote area near the Laotian border by merely one reinforced Marine regiment. If this *really* was General Giap's plan then it was idiotic and moronic and it failed anyway. It failed because the TCK-TKN failed miserably. *Khe Sanh* was a failure for the Communists. The TET Offensive was another failure and debacle for the Communists of biblical proportions resulting in the virtual destruction of their Viet Cong stooges and gangsters in the South.

The mistakes have been made and we cannot turn back the clock after 38 years since the tragic fall of Saigon.

The United States of America was fully justified under both Public International Law and *customary international law* in invoking the principle of 'Collective-Self-Defence' under *Article 2(4)* of the United Nations Charter and in abiding by *Article 51* of the U.N. Charter being the inherent right of South Vietnam to its self-defence against external aggression.

In the United Nations *General Assembly Resolution 2131* Part XX, Article 21 on 21st December 1965 it was decided [with only one abstaining vote] that it was to be condemned on the part of any member nation to use 'armed intervention and all other forms of interference or attempted threats against the personality of the State or against its political, economic and cultural elements.'

Clearly the North Vietnamese had breached *General Assembly Resolution 2131 Part XX and Article 21.*

Vice-President Nguyen Cao Ky of the Republic of Vietnam said in a television interview back in the 1980's that it was the **'duty' of America** to come to the aid of South Vietnam, its ally, then under threat.

The United States of America did come to the rescue of South Vietnam and our Nation **did its 'Duty'** as best as we could with *bona fide* intentions.

David Peter EHRLICH
[Attorney-at-Law] (Sydney, Australia) October, 2012

Chapter 1
Brinks Hotel Saigon

It was Christmas Eve in December 1967. The air was almost suffocatingly hot and the humidity was unbearable. But he was used to it. Taking a standard issue handkerchief he wiped the sweat off his brow but could not reach the beads of salty liquid that had dribbled down the spine of his camouflage shirt. The room that United States Marine Lieutenant Colonel Richard Vortex was sitting in was quite sparse but nevertheless comfortable. At least for Saigon standards. It was in the top floor of the *Brinks Hotel* in downtown Saigon. A floor which was reserved exclusively for officers.

Lieutenant Colonel Richard Vortex had a telegram in his moist palm but he did not like it. It was in fact his Christmas present from his wife. The telegram told him that she wanted a divorce.

Happy Christmas! He thought to himself. Perhaps it was just as well. His most painful concern at this moment was how it was going to affect his daughter Peggy. He loved her very much and wanted to ensure that she would understand the reason for the divorce. Or, failing that, at least to take it in her stride. He knew also that she was a smart girl, much more mature than her nineteen years.

Over the next twenty minutes Richard Vortex put pen to paper and wrote his daughter a long letter. His communication was considerably overdue.

The overhead ceiling fan whirred and thudded like the blades of a *Jolly Green Giant*. That enormous helicopter that had saved his ass on more than one occasion in the jungles near the DMZ line.

Suddenly the phone next to his double bed rang shrilly.

"Hello?" said the Vietnamese accented voice on the other end.

"This is Lieutenant Colonel Vortex."

"Oh! Yes! Colonel!" It was the familiar voice of the proprietor of the *Brinks Hotel*. "Sorry to bother you Colonel."

"What is it?" he asked as he folded the letter into a yellow envelope.

"Sergeant Major Leonard Crighton is here to see you Colonel."

Vortex told the manager to send him up immediately. Command Sergeant Major [E-9] Leonard Crighton from Georgia was one of the toughest, most dedicated soldiers that Colonel Vortex knew. The Sergeant Major's loyalty to him was unshakable. He had been his orderly NCO for nearly two years now.

With letter to daughter Peggy in one hand and the divorce telegram from his wife in the other, he waited for the Sergeant Major to knock on the door.

Colonel Vortex knew that something was brewing at US Army Supreme Headquarters in Saigon *[Pentagon East- Headquarters of MACV (Military Assistance Command Vietnam – Headed by COMUSMACV – Four Star General William Childs Westmoreland – Hero of the United States of America; (Date of Birth: March 26, 1914 – Date of Death: July 18, 2005)]* but he didn't know what, although he had a feeling that he would soon be enlightened.

Richard Vortex was 41 years old and stood six foot two and a half inches tall. He weighed all of 204.6 lbs [93 kilograms] and it was only bone and muscle. Not an ounce of fat adorned his extremely fit body. He had graduated from the Marine Academy in 1950 [*Officer's School at Camp Pendleton and Camp Lejeune*] a year after his marriage.

However Richard Vortex joined the Marines in 1944 at age 18 years as an enlisted man first and was just about to be sent to the *Battle of Okinawa* before those orders were cancelled in 1945 as the United States had already won the war after dropping the two fission bombs, *Fat Boy* and *Little Boy* on Hiroshima and Nagasaki on the 6th August and 9th August 1945 respectively, culminating in the glorious and magnificent victory of the gallant and heroic Armed Forces of the United States of America against the pernicious and evil aggression of the Japanese Imperial Empire and their coterie of sycophantic samurai madmen in Tokyo.

Vortex was a career soldier and the Marine Corps was his whole life. He had no intention of leaving it until he would be kicked out by the maximum retiring age. Lieutenant Colonel Vortex was currently commander of the 9th Marine Regiment which consisted of three fully equipped Marine Infantry Battalions totalling some 3,000 men. The 9th Marine Regiment [*Nicknamed: 'The Walking Dead' for their stay in Vietnam had so far been the longest in duration*] was one of three making up the 3rd Marine Division under the command of Major General Rathvon C. Tompkins. Tompkins' superior was Lieutenant General Robert E. Cushman commanding the III Marine Amphibious Force or III MAF. Vortex had light brown hair and azure blue eyes. He had grown up in San Diego but his parents had died in a car accident in Roswell, New Mexico when he was only eighteen years old. He had no brothers or sisters. It was then that he had decided to join the US Marine Corps. There was nothing left in his life and his only desire was to serve his country in the best way he knew how. By supreme war and fanatical aggression against anybody or anything that stood in the way of America's vital national security interests. He was

no lover of intellectual bleeding hearts and he hated Communists with a burning passion. Vortex's only desire was to see them annihilated in an inferno of superior US firepower and weaponry. He firmly believed in the motto of; *"Peace through Superior Firepower."*

His loyalty to the Marine Corps was fanatical. He was also deeply religious and spoke to Almighty God and to Jesus everyday in his prayers asking for the wherewithal and the guidance to provide him the moral and intellectual strength to combat all enemies of the United States of America be they foreign or domestic.

"Good afternoon sir!" said Command Sergeant Major Crighton as he knocked and then entered the room.

Vortex smiled, "Sit down Sergeant Major. Can I offer you a glass of beer?"

"Thank you sir," the Sergeant Major thirstily consumed the *Budweiser* imported from the United States.

"What's the news?" asked Vortex as he fiddled with the yellow envelope in his hand.

"Oh! I heard that those hippies back in the States tried to block the armed forces induction centre in Oakland and over two hundred and fifty of them were arrested."

Vortex chuckled, "So what else is new?" He took a beer and looked out the window into the busy Saigon Street. Rickshaws, scooters and cars jammed the downtown area. Vietnamese women and girls traded shoddy goods in their corner stalls and he noticed a group of US Air Force NCOs' walking into a nearby bistro.

Vortex was clean shaven and his face was rugged with a chiselled appearance. His nose was sharp and his lips seemed thin and pale. Sergeant Major Crighton thought he had a touch of malaria as the Colonel was sweating profusely and his pallor was almost anaemic.

"Are you alright sir? You don't look completely Co-Percentic!"

Vortex stepped away from the window and clapped his Sergeant affectionately on the shoulder.

"I'm fine! As fit as an ox!"

"Glad to hear it Colonel!" the Sergeant Major took out a packet of Pal Mals and Vortex helped himself to one as well.

Command Sergeant Major Crighton was even bigger and beefier than the Lieutenant Colonel. He had black hair and brown eyes and stood six foot four inches in his socks. He was a lean 142 kilograms of rippling, Communist crushing muscle and venom. Crighton hated *'Charlie'* even more than his commander. He had not gone to University in Georgia but he was not a typical career senior NCO either. Vortex thought that with some classical education, Crighton could step out of the working class mould and even be an academic. Yet he also had no intention of leaving the Marines.

"I have a letter here for my daughter Peggy. I was wondering if you could post it for me Sergeant Major?"

"It is already done sir," Crighton took the yellow envelope and neatly pocketed it into his camouflage army shirt. His three stripes were immaculately sown on both sleeves. He wore a 7.92mm VBR Glock Pistol around his waist in a leather holster.

"And how is she sir?" asked Crighton.

"Fine, thank you Sergeant Major."

"Isn't she at Berkeley University in San Francisco?"

"That's right – doing a psychology degree with a double major in Forensic Psychiatry."

Crighton whistled, "She must make you proud sir? Very proud!"

"Yes. She does," Vortex decided to stop there and not mention anything about his wife to the Sergeant Major.

There were a few moments of silence as both men drank their beer and tried to ignore the heavy traffic noise coming up from the street.

"I want you to inform the staff here in Saigon that there will be a Regimental Staff meeting here at the Brinks Hotel at 1900 hours. The battalion commanders and their 2-IC's only."

The Sergeant Major barked, "Understood sir."

"I shall inform Major Thrush myself as he is also here in this hotel."

The Sergeant Major nodded. "Is that all sir?"

Richard Vortex nodded and Sergeant Major Crighton asked, "When do you think we shall be getting back to the Regiment at *Quang Tri*?"

"I don't know Sergeant. But not before my situation conference with General Tompkins at the air base at *Tan Son Nhut*."

Crighton saluted and walked out after Vortex ordered him to attend the meeting of his battalion commanders and their staffs that same evening.

It was 1700 hours before Lt. Colonel Vortex walked down to the lobby of the Brinks Hotel. His mind was so numb with pain that he didn't even think about his wife's request for a divorce. But he knew the reasons for it. She was having an affair with a used car salesman from Detroit. What he didn't know was how long her extra-curricular sexual escapades had been going on. He suspected that she had been carrying on multiple affairs for at least seven years with over a dozen different men. At least he had been honest about his affair here in Saigon. He had been absent from the States for one year and as a result he had fallen in love with a beautiful 29 year old Asian girl named Susie Ky.

Susie Ky was the daughter of a fabulously rich South Vietnamese business man who had large factories in Saigon and in the provincial city of *Hue* in the north of the country. Susie Ky's father was also a junior Minister for Foreign Trade in the South

Vietnamese Government. Currently, the latest President of South Vietnam was Thieu. President Lyndon B. Johnson had tried to persuade President Thieu to include at least a few of the defeated civilian candidates in the latest election in his 19 member Cabinet to form a Government of so-called national unity. However President Thieu only placed his own handpicked cronies to fill in the Cabinet positions. One of these cronies was going to be his future father-in-law. When his wife had been informed she had screamed over the phone to him like a raving bitch-in-heat. Vortex had nothing left to give his wife and the more he thought about it, the more he came to realise that divorce was probably the best solution for the impasse. Just as he was about to step outside into the maddening Saigon traffic, the proprietor of the Brinks Hotel called him from behind the reception counter.

"Colonel!" Vortex spun around on his heels, "Yes?"

"Telephone for you sir!"

"Thank you," Vortex went to the desk and snatched the receiver out of the man's hands.

"Hello?"

"It's me!" said the soft, feminine voice. Vortex's heart missed a beat. He was amazed that at the age of 41 he could still feel intoxicated by the aroma of desire.

"Oh! Susie! I was just leaving the hotel to come and see you!"

"I'm glad Richard. I've missed you so much!"

Richard could hear the trembling emotion in Susie Ky's voice. It was almost tearful with longing and love.

"Where are you Susie?" Vortex felt his legs wanted to explode in an avalanche of movement. His only thought was to run to her. To embrace and to kiss this sweet girl who was 12 years his junior but who cared nothing for such artificial barriers.

"I'm at home Richard! Oh! Please come quickly! Come right away!"

Susie's voice was sweet and melodic to his ears. He knew exactly where *'home'* was. It was the splendid mansion where Susie, her mother and father lived not far from the US Embassy Compound in Saigon. It was one of the best quarters of the city. Vortex was also concerned about Susie's safety as many explosions continually rocked Saigon city from Viet Cong infiltrators and sappers. Nobody's safety could be guaranteed.

"I'll be there in ten minutes Susie! I love you!" said Vortex.

"I love you too!" cried Susie and then she started to cry with a mixture of pain and joy.

Lt. Colonel Vortex found it agonizing to put down the telephone receiver. He bolted out of the lobby and into the bright Saigon sunshine. Flagging down the first scooter he paid the Vietnamese driver triple the fare, asking him to drive as fast as he could to Susie Ky's home.

Vortex took the stairs to the front door three at a time and the maid opened the door.

"Good evening Colonel Vortex," she said in her broken English.

He brushed past the elderly woman and as he started up the staircase he met Susie coming down.

"Oh! There you are at last!"

Vortex could see that her delicate, deep brown eyes were red with tears. He held her close to his body with one swift, agile movement. They kissed deeply and passionately. Susie was trembling in his powerful arms and he held her finely like a rare China doll.

It seemed like minutes that they stood there, kissing and embracing but it was only seconds. Both of them were in a feverish state of longing and anticipation.

"I haven't seen you for more than two months! My sweety!" Vortex spoke from the heart and he was amazed at his genuine passion which had been lying dormant for so long amidst the chaos of war and the reflections of his inner fear.

It was the beautiful and delicate Susie Ky, a flower from South Vietnam who had awakened within him powerful forces of caring and love which he had never realised that he possessed.

Both of them were almost intoxicated with each other's presence. Vortex felt that he would die if anything would happen to Susie. Even the Marine Corps would mean nothing to him if he lost her. When they walked up to the top floor of Susie's palatial home and were inside her bedroom Vortex asked, "I forgot how you felt, how you smiled, your sweet fragrance."

Susie unzipped her long, silk Chinese style dress and let it fall to the floor.

"Well my love! Don't forget any longer. Taste that which you have savoured before," as Susie spoke she shook her head from side to side allowing the long strands of her fine, silky black hair to fall over her firm breasts. Richard took a step forward and kissed that luxurious hair. He smelt the fragrance of her milky white almost alabaster skin.

So soft, so tender.

"Come!" he said as he gently lifted her naked body onto the large four poster bed which had netting hanging from all sides. Susie undressed Vortex and watched as the shoulder boards with the silver oak leaves fell to the floor. He was her officer. All hers.

They made love passionately for some considerable time and as Vortex felt himself engulfed by her he remembered how he had met Susie more than a year ago. It was at an Embassy party held by the US Ambassador to South Vietnam. Henry Cabot Lodge was the Ambassador at the time and the other dignitaries present were; Admiral Ulysses S. Grant Sharp Jr. the Commander-in-Chief of Pacific Forces as well as President Thieu of South Vietnam and William Putnam Bundy an expert in Asian Affairs

with the State Department. In addition there were a host of senior officers from the United States military and the South Vietnamese Army High Command.

Vortex held Susie on top of his pleasantly exhausted torso and ran his hands slowly up and down the smooth naked back of the girl. Susie had firm breasts with beautiful pink nipples. Her mouth was dainty and her lips had an indescribable sensuousness about them. Her face was extremely attractive and her figure was a gorgeous five feet four inches, slim but still with inviting curves in all the right places.

"I haven't finished yet!" laughed Susie Ky.

"Neither have I my darling," moaned Richard.

He gently eased Susie onto her stomach and slid into her from the rear. He could feel the soft, moist flesh of her womb as it enclosed around him like a suction of love.

Susie reached backwards and placed his hands under her organ so that Vortex could stimulate her as he performed his love making. It was exquisite.

Vortex had to be careful not to apply his full weight onto Susie's body because of the large size difference.

They both drank from the same glass of whisky as Vortex alternated his love making from her front to her seldom used rear avenue. The constriction he felt from her rectum was beautiful and they climaxed together several times.

An hour or so later when they had rested and were satiated she asked, "When do you have to go back to your Regiment?"

"I'm not sure yet Susie," said Vortex honestly.

Then he added as he kissed the nape of her neck, her nipples and her mouth, "I have received a telegram from my wife."

Susie's expression changed suddenly, "Oh! What did she say?"

Vortex did not beat about the bush, "She wants a divorce."

Susie lit a cigarette, "You have been expecting something like this to happen for a long time haven't you? I mean – it is not really a surprise?"

"No."

Vortex rested his head on Susie Ky's small, soft shoulder, "Don't worry my darling," began Susie, "I am sure everything will turn out alright in the end."

Vortex sighed, "Yes." He paused for a moment and then lifted himself up off the luxurious silk pillows, "I want to take you back to New York with me when my tour of duty has expired. After the divorce from my wife, Alice, I want you to be my wife!"

Susie felt her heart leap in her chest as she pounced on Vortex with undiluted enthusiasm. As she smothered him with kisses, she asked, "Do you really mean it?"

"Well of course I do! I love you!"

Susie started to cry with a mixture of joy and surprise, "And what about your daughter Peggy?"

Vortex chuckled as he slid Susie off the bed and they both started to wash and dress after their heated and succulent love making, "Don't worry about her! She's 19 years old and a university student at Berkeley!"

Susie clapped her hands in front of her face in a feminine gesture, "Oh! I have a daughter-in-law!"

Vortex held her by the waist and bounced her up and down in his powerful arms.

"Hold on! Hold on my Vietnamese flower! We're not married yet! I'm not even divorced yet!"

They both laughed and walked downstairs to eat and talk with Susie Ky's mother. Some time later a distinguished guest arrived while Susie and Colonel Vortex were in the dining room. It was Nguyen Cao Ky, the Vice-President of South Vietnam.

"Hello Mr Vice-President!" said Susie excitedly.

"I have come to see your father. Where is he?" asked Air Marshal Nguyen Cao Ky.

Colonel Vortex jumped to his feet and saluted the Vice-President.

"He is at the presidential palace I think," she answered.

"I know you," said Marshal Ky as he smiled and shook Vortex's hand.

"Now let me think! I have an excellent memory! Don't introduce yourself yet."

Nguyen Ky rubbed his chin thoughtfully and stared at Lt. Colonel Vortex. The Vice-President was a good looking, slim and athletic man. He had a black moustache and dark hair as all Asians do. His eyes were dark and piercing and he was one of the most flamboyant characters in the whole of Saigon, or the whole of South Vietnam for that matter. He was President Thieu's right hand man. As the Vice-President he had regular meetings with President Lyndon B. Johnson, Secretary of Defence MacNamara and William Bundy, the Special Adviser to the National Security Council.

Marshal Nguyen Cao Ky was the Commander of the South Vietnamese Air Force and was also Prime Minister. In 1964 Ky became famous when he threatened to bomb the headquarters of the arguing generals of the Khanh Regime. However, the then US Ambassador, Maxwell Taylor (a veteran soldier from World War II and Korea), had severely admonished both Khanh and Ky for their ludicrous and irresponsible behaviour. After that regrettable incident Ky assisted Khanh in thwarting a coup attempt in 1965. But later, to save his own skin and to increase his chances of seizing the Presidency later on, Ky supported the banishment of Khanh. The Lieutenant Colonel knew of Nguyen Ky and all he had done, though this was the first time that he had met the Vice-President in person. Vortex further recalls as he stood like a bean pole in front of such a high ranking official – the Number 2 man in all South Vietnam, that in the spring of 1965 Ky became Prime Minister and shared power with Nguyen Van Thieu. In an amazing speech in Hawaii in 1966 before President Lyndon B. Johnson and the Joint Chiefs of Staff, Marshal Ky had assured the Johnson Administration of a complete and total *social revolution* in South Vietnam which would destroy the power

of the Viet Cong at the grass roots level. Yet, cynically Vortex knew that the master of Ky's interests and priorities lay solely in himself and thus the Vice-President did not want to interfere with the established order of corruption in the South Vietnamese hierarchy. In addition to this Richard Vortex could not agree with Marshal Ky's policy of crushing the Buddhists which he continued with even greater zeal than the previous President Diem who had been assassinated in November 1963.

Suddenly, General Ky slapped Colonel Vortex on the shoulder with a beaming smile, "You are the Commander of the 9th Marine Regiment! A part of the 3rd Marine Division currently stationed at Quang Tri!" Then Vice-President Ky mentioned Vortex's name.

"You have an excellent memory sir!" barked out Colonel Vortex as Susie Ky giggled.

"One day I hope that peace will come to a strong and independent South Vietnam!" mentioned Ky as he waved his hands to five large South Vietnamese Military police officers indicating to them to wait outside where his limousine and ten motorcycle escorts were waiting.

"That is my hope also Marshal Ky," said Vortex as Susie handed Ky a glass of beer.

"Now off the record Colonel Vortex! What is your opinion as to how the war is being run by the Pentagon and President Johnson?"

Vortex immediately felt uneasy.

"It is not my place to say, sir."

Vortex looked to Susie and she looked to Ky, grinning.

"Come on now! I said off the record!" he admonished.

"Are you sure sir? I won't be quoted on this?" Vortex felt a surge of panic grip him. If Major General Rathvon Tompkins ever found out that he had talked so freely with the Vice-President he would be chewed out severely.

"I give you my word! Come on! You are a senior field commander! You must have a military opinion."

Vortex hesitated and then let loose.

"In my opinion the war is *not* being waged as it should be."

Nguyen Cao Ky started to smile with glee as Vortex continued, "We have nearly half a million US combat troops here not counting the South Vietnamese military and other allies. And all we are doing is reacting to the Viet Cong movements and offensives! It is we who should be taking the offensive against them! The initiative lies with us! We have the superior firepower! The superior mobility! I advocate a massive all out offensive into Laos and Cambodia to cut the lines of communication of the *Ho Chi Minh Trail*! This is what we must do and it will not be easy but it will create the window of opportunity for a quick and crushing victory against the North Vietnamese regular army and their Viet Cong collaborators! By cutting the spine of the *Ho Chi*

Minh Trail we will paralyse their whole re-supply effort to the South. The two truncated halves will then wither on the vine as we apply massive and unceasing air strikes to pulverise their heavy armor and equipment. But this cutting of the enemies' spine cannot be achieved by air power alone! We must drive a multi-divisional force, probably six to seven infantry divisions supported by at least seven brigades of air cavalry and armor into Laos to sever the back of the Viet Cong monster."

Nguyen Cao Ky was entranced by Colonel Vortex's speech. He sat down at the elegant mahogany table and said, "Please continue!"

Susie and her mother brought in tea and biscuits for them all as Vortex finished what he was saying.

"In addition to this massive ground offensive we must annihilate the industrial and social infrastructure of North Vietnam by saturation bombing! Hanoi, Haiphong and the other major cities must be treated to a firestorm of B-52 Arc Light raids. I would advocate, as does Senator Barry Goldwater, the selective and surgical use of low yield tactical nuclear weapons to take out key industrial centres in North Vietnam!"

Marshal Ky whistled with disbelief as he sipped on his tea, "You seriously think we should go for the nuclear option?"

Colonel Vortex nodded as he said, "Sir! I am convinced of it! But it is not as bad as you think! As a senior officer in the Marine Corps I am privy to certain highly secret information. I cannot disclose the precise content of that information but suffice it to say that our technology is now working on a nuclear device that produces the normal amount of blast effect but with minimal radiation fallout. I advocate that this weapon, when ready for deployment, would be ideal in taking out large formations of the Viet Cong and North Vietnamese regulars with minimal impact upon the natural environment. They could be easily delivered by the B-52 *Stratofortress* or alternatively, by tactical missiles with a range of 300 to 950 miles."

Vice-President Ky jumped to his feet and affectionately slapped Colonel Vortex on the shoulder, saying, "I like you Colonel!"

"Thank you sir!"

"It was not meant as a vacuous compliment but as an expression of my sincere feelings! I should like to have further meetings with you and your superiors, Generals Tompkins and Cushman."

Vortex nodded, "Looking forward to it sir." He snapped to attention and saluted as the Vice-President, flanked by his military police bodyguards made for the door.

"But I must be off now for a meeting with President Thieu and the rest of the Cabinet at the Palace."

Nguyen Cao Ky turned and stepped out the front door but swung his head around for a second and said before he disappeared, "Oh! Colonel Vortex! You have excellent taste!" He winked as he spoke and his purple scarf wafted in the warm breeze.

As he spoke, Marshal Ky gave a mischievous smirk to Susie Ky checking her curves out from top to bottom, making her blush deeply to a crimson hue.

A few moments later Susie said, "He's a funny man isn't he darling?"

Vortex kissed her and laughed, "He is one of the most intelligent men in the whole of South Vietnam. He already knows before hand when the shit is about to hit the fan."

After the meeting of battalion commanders at the Brinks Hotel, Lt. Colonel Vortex, Sergeant Major Crighton and Major Thrush as well as Major Lansdale who commanded 2nd Battalion 9th Marine Regiment jumped into their army jeeps and drove to Susie Ky's home. From there they all went to a lively nightclub in the Cholon District of Saigon to celebrate Christmas Eve.

The Cholon District was populated mainly by Chinese Vietnamese and it was a prosperous and commercial centre for the Republic of South Vietnam.

Vortex signalled the Vietnamese waitress to take their orders and he shouted everybody a round of drinks.

Major Lansdale remarked, "So I hear that Johnson has ordered a cessation of hostilities and air attacks for a Christmas truce?"

"That's right Major," and Susie Ky mentioned, "I am sure that the Viet Cong are going to break the truce."

Major Thrush said, "They already have. I have heard of attacks in the Mekong Delta and in II Corps Operational Zone."

Vortex scoffed, "There is no real truce! There can't be! We must fight *'Charlie'* to the end. Until he is smashed and annihilated! That must be our sole and only objective!"

Susie said, "Anyway gentlemen. Let's lighten up! As you say in the States. It's Christmas Eve!"

Sergeant Major Crighton smiled, "She's right. Come let's dance!"

Both of the Majors and the Sergeant Major had their girlfriends with them and they moved out onto the dance floor which was already crowded. The music was loud and everybody seemed excited. The whole of Saigon was in a festive atmosphere.

"I want to ring my daughter Peggy in San Francisco. Will you come with me and you can speak to her. But don't mention anything yet Susie."

Susie kissed Richard and he took her hand gently. They squeezed into a long distance phone booth and after ten minutes finally managed to get a line through to the States.

"Hello? Who's this?" asked Vortex.

"It's Peggy! Who's calling?"

As she heard her father's voice crackling over the long distance underwater cable line she became very elated and happy.

"Oh! Dad! I'm so glad you called! I love you!"

"I love you too. How are you keeping and Merry Christmas!"

"Merry Christmas to you too Dad!"

Susie put her ear up to the receiver as Vortex held it to his.

"Have you spoken to your mother?" asked Vortex as the music and the dancing in the Saigon nightclub became louder.

"Yes! Oh! Yes Dad! She's fine."

Vortex was a little nervous, "Listen Peggy! I want you to say hello to one of my very good friends here in Saigon. Her name is Susie Ky. OK darling?"

Peggy laughed, "Oh sure Dad. Put her on."

Vortex could hear pop music from his daughter's end. He thought that she must be having a party as well. He had set her up in her own apartment very close to the Berkeley Campus in San Francisco.

Vortex coughed into the telephone anxiously, "Actually I already told you about her."

Susie snatched the phone away from Richard and spoke to Peggy for some five or six minutes. She asked her how her studies were progressing and told her a little of whom she was here in Saigon and that one day soon she hoped to visit her in the United States.

"Well! You two seemed to have gotten along quite well." exclaimed Vortex after Susie had hung up.

Susie laughed as they resumed their seats at the dining table, "I am sure that the two of us will get on famously! But I hope to have children of our own and soon!"

Vortex smiled, "I think I can manage that."

Suddenly everybody in the nightclub heard the rumble of distant artillery fire. But it was such a common occurrence it hardly interrupted the pre-Christmas festivities.

The girlfriend's of Majors Thrush and Lansdale as well as his Sergeant Major were all small and attractive. The Vietnamese women had her own special and delicate beauty which Colonel Vortex had come to love and appreciate.

He was determined never to let Susie Ky out of his sight. If he could he wished he could get her to the States and to safety while his tour in Vietnam came to a close. His officers returned to the table as Susie said, "I am going to the bathroom for a second darling."

Vortex nodded and watched as Susie Ky walked gracefully to the other side of the nightclub and down a dark corridor to the 'powder room'.

Major Thrush commented, "Did you hear the latest news?"

As he spoke, Thrush reached down under the table and caressed lubriciously the naked thigh of his girlfriend. She was wearing a mini-skirt but she had no underpants

on. Thrush dipped his fingers into the sweet, moist mound of her mons pubis. He could almost smell the fragrance of her reproductive organ.

"What fucking news?" asked Major Lansdale as Vortex looked vacantly about the sea of sweating, contorting bodies dancing to the latest *'Beatles'* music which he considered as offensive to the ears. He was an ultra-conservative despite his Ph.D. in Law and Jurisprudence and his two Masters degrees from the Marine Academy in Nuclear Physics.

Major Thrush said, "About two weeks ago – around the 4th or 5th of December, the 9th Infantry Division's Riverine force launched an attack in the Mekong Delta."

Vortex asked as he looked at his watch wondering where Susie had been for more than ten minutes, "What happened then?"

Thrush added in response, "The 9th Infantry Division joined up with ARVN battalions and attacked several Viet Cong battalions on and near the River Delta. An air cavalry battalion of the 9th Infantry Division dropped in on top of *'Charlie's'* head and fucked him good and proper. About 235 Viet Cong were killed for minimal casualties on our side."

Lt. Colonel Vortex smiled, "That's a good body count."

Sergeant Major Crighton had gone up to one of the private rooms above the nightclub which you could rent for a small fee, taking his beautiful Vietnamese girl with him. She was only 18 years old. For the next two hours they made love until the sheets they were lying on were soaked with sweat, semen and vaginal juices.

"I'm going to see where Susie is!" said Vortex feeling annoyed. "She's been gone far too long."

Thrush said to Lansdale when Vortex was out of earshot, "Our glorious leader is head over heels with that Susie Ky!"

Lansdale smirked, "That's for sure!" and added, "I hope his craze for pussy does not overcome his craze for killing Communists! Then we are all fucked!"

As Richard Vortex walked down the passageway looking for his beloved Susie he had a strange feeling in his guts as if something was about to rip him apart. The corridor was narrow, with the men's toilet on the left and the ladies on the right. He smacked out his fist and pushed away a Vietnamese civilian who was spaced out on drugs of some sort. The man grabbed Colonel Vortex's arms as he walked past and tried to say something. With the agility of a vicious snake Vortex gripped the arm of the civilian and wrenched it so far backwards that he could feel the ligaments and tendons snapping. With his other hand, Vortex grabbed a fistful of the man's hair and slammed his head into the concrete wall, breaking his nasal septum with a sweet clicking noise. The man groaned as Vortex smashed his fist into the left temple for the *coup de grace*. The man crumpled to the floor with blood streaming from his nostrils.

"You can't fucking walk to the men's room in peace anymore!" said Vortex to himself with great anger and frustration. A little further down the corridor, where the light was almost non-existent, he could see an Asian man standing up against the wall. He had his hands on the head of a teenage girl who was kneeling before him and performing fellatio on his organ with swift movements of her head.

Vortex snarled, "Get out of here you degenerates!" As he spoke he head-butted the Vietnamese drug pusher and the man screamed and ran down the corridor with his pants around his ankles.

Colonel Vortex was now starting to lose his patience. He kicked open the door to the Ladies' Privy with brutal and savage force. The blood was starting to seep into his brain and from there like a hammer-blow to his fists and feet.

Lieutenant Colonel Vortex was a master at Japanese Karate. He had been the self defence instructor for more than a year at the United States Marine Academy at Annapolis when he was a First Lieutenant on duty there in the early 1950's. Vortex received his Shodan or 1st Dan Black belt in Karate when he was only 16 years old. When he reached the age of 22 he was already a sensei with a 7th Dan Black belt. He was also the Marine Corps martial arts champion as well as the foremost boxer in his 3rd Marine Division. And, as he weighed 93 kilograms of solid, rock hard and rippling, Communist pulverizing muscle he was a match for any man or beast.

"Susie! Susie Ky! My honey! Are you there? Where are you for God's sake?" as he spoke Vortex began to look under the toilet doors one at a time. He hated to do this. He detested walking into the women's lavatories but he didn't have any choice. He had to find his future wife, his sweetheart, his Susie Ky. There was no answer. The toilets were huge. There must have been a row of at least thirty cubicles.

"Ahhh!" came a sound from the far end of the toilet heads. It was like a muffled scream. It was a feminine scream. Vortex's heart sank like the *USS Indianapolis* in World War 2 after it delivered the atomic bomb to the island of Tinian.

"Oh! My Susie! What has happened?"

As Vortex bolted forward he saw three Vietnamese men all gripping Susie Ky's throat, shoulders and breasts. They had her pinned up against the concrete wall and one of the men had already stripped off her skirt and was pushing his fingers into her sweet delicate vagina.

"You bastards! Stop that! How dare you hit a woman! How dare you violate an innocent girl!" screamed Vortex.

"Fuck off!" said the nearest Vietnamese in his own language. Colonel Vortex spoke fluent and excellent Vietnamese as well as French, German and Italian and a spattering of Spanish. Vortex knew that he would have to fight for Susie's life. Already he could see one of the men had three fingers inserted into her vagina as the other

man was exploring her anal passage. Her panties and bra had been completely ripped off. Her dress was a shambles.

Colonel Vortex screamed, "I am a United States Marine Officer and as such I must give you a warning to desist from molesting that innocent girl! If you do not then I shall have to use deadly and unremitting force to prevent you from carrying out this illegal and criminal assault. I shall also have to perform an arrest and take you to the nearest Vietnamese civilian Police authorities to be charged!"

The three men who wore black pantaloons and black tunics all laughed so hard that they nearly choked on their mirth.

Colonel Vortex was wearing his duty camouflage shirt and trousers with his Lieutenant Colonel's silver oak leaves clearly visible on his shoulder boards. He also wore shiny black general purpose combat boots. But the Vietnamese criminals did not seem to care. One of them pulled out a stiletto and lunged towards him.

Vortex said, "I am afraid I shall have to cripple all of you!" As he spoke Vortex side-stepped the dagger lunges and lashed out a knife hand strike to the man's carotid artery. The criminal seemed to hover in the air motionless for a few moments.

Vortex said calmly, "Let the girl go."

As he spoke he slipped out his silver handled Marine dagger and falling to his knees he sliced the blade through the septum of the third man's testicles as he head-butted him simultaneously. The first and second Vietnamese criminals froze where they stood. Vortex shifted the blade from left to right and easily cut off the man's testicles right through his black pantaloons. The horrendous scream from the man was indescribable. Next, Vortex quickly withdrew the blood drenched knife from the mutilated gonads and threw the blade at the second man. It impaled itself inside his left eye but Vortex did not wait. He spun on his heels and side-kicked the third man who had just been castrated. Then, as the first man froze in sheer terror, Vortex smashed both his fists into the third man's skull simultaneously. One fist into the right temple and the other into the left in a textbook Karate manoeuvre.

"I am going to destroy you all!" was all that Vortex screamed.

And he screamed like a raving beast in the jungle. Vortex literally picked up the third man and crashed him through the nearest toilet door, then gripping his head he buried it inside the toilet cistern and flushed the toilet so that the man drowned in pieces of shit and urine.

Next, Vortex moved like greased lightning and head-butted the second Vietnamese whose head was knocked backwards into the skull of the first man.

Susie Ky was crying and crawling on her hands and knees away from the whole fiasco. She was not hurt – just bruised mildly in a couple of places.

Vortex grabbed the hair of both men and slammed their skulls together with unbelievable force and power so that terrible compression fractures resulted.

As Susie staggered to her feet and said, "Smash them to pieces!" Vortex nodded and held both of them up against the concrete wall with their noses to the bathroom tiles.

"I am going to rearrange their facial structure!" he chuckled to Susie Ky.

The Colonel slammed his upper arm in a Karate elbow strike into the back of their skulls. The momentum crushed their noses and cheek bones into the hard wall and caused additional fractures. Just then Sergeant Major Crighton, who was even bigger and more vicious than Colonel Vortex bolted into the toilets.

"My God sir! What has happened here?" asked the Sergeant Major with horror and some considerable anger.

"These criminals tried to rape and bash my Susie!" cried Vortex as he jabbed his fingers into both men in an expert and lethal eye gouge. White foam and yellow pus was oozing out of the mouths of both rapists.

"I shall crush their bodies!" screamed Sergeant Major Crighton who weighed 142 kilograms of lethal muscle and pure vicious venom which was mostly directed against Communists.

"Here then!" laughed Vortex as he smashed his skull into the crushed face of the first rapist and then threw his limp body to Crighton who punched forward into the man's solar plexus as his body came towards him. With that one massive punch the whole of the man's chest and rib cage collapsed into his lungs. Blood vomited from his mouth as Crighton picked him up over his head and slammed him downwards into another of the toilet doors which splintered like toothpicks.

"This bastard is finished!"

Next Crighton and Vortex both set to work on the first and remaining man. Vortex held him in a head lock from behind while Crighton rained more than three hundred and forty punches and kicks into every part of his body. The gruesome bashing was so severe that blood and pieces of broken flesh sprayed into Vortex's face as Susie sat down on a nearby chair to rest and watch the hideous spectacle.

"Give me your knife!" screamed Vortex.

Crighton threw him his Marine blade and Vortex severed off both ears and hacked out the tongue of the Vietnamese criminal. At that second as they dumped the limp body into another toilet cistern, Majors Thrush and Lansdale, together with about twenty South Vietnamese Military Police entered the toilets.

"Are you alright Colonel?" asked Major Thrush.

"Don't fucking worry about me! I can handle myself! Worry about Susie!"

Vortex helped Susie to her feet.

"I'm alright my darling!" she said with surprising vigour.

"They didn't hurt me or penetrate me in any way! You came just in time!"

Vortex sighed a breath of relief, "I am so glad!"

The South Vietnamese Major in charge of the military police department came up and saluted smartly to Vortex.

"Thank you very much sir!"

Vortex returned the salute and asked with a scowl on his face, "Thank you? Thank you for what?"

The Vietnamese Major smiled, "For catching these Viet Cong infiltrators for us! We believe that they were trying to abduct Susie Ky because of her highly placed family in the South Vietnamese Government."

"Oh! Really!" said Vortex.

"Yes indeed!" confirmed the Major.

Majors Thrush and Lansdale prodded the limp but still living bodies of the three badly mutilated Viet Cong.

"What are you going to do with them now?" asked Vortex.

"We have just received new standing orders from President Thieu himself that all Viet Cong saboteurs and infiltrators that are caught inside Saigon or any other South Vietnamese city are to be summarily executed on the spot where they are found."

Sergeant Major Crighton looked to Vortex in amazement.

Vortex looked to his two officers in greater amazement.

"I don't agree with extra-judicial executions Major!" said Vortex to the Vietnamese Military Police Officer.

"I understand Lieutenant Colonel Vortex but I'm sorry! It's out of your hands now. Out of your jurisdiction."

Vortex did not give up as he held Susie close to his body, protecting her.

"I believe in the due process of the law. These men, or rather Viet Cong, must be brought before a Court and sentenced by a competent judge free from executive interference."

The Major laughed, "This is South Vietnam Colonel, not the United States! We are fighting for our very survival here as you can well imagine!"

Vortex shrugged his shoulders, "It is true that I don't have any authority over the running of the internal affairs of your government."

The Major saluted to Colonel Vortex and nodded to nine of his military police guards. Three men with large calibre .45 Magnum hand guns stepped up to each wounded Viet Cong in the toilet cubicles. That is nine men altogether to carry out the executions. Each of these nine men carried the .45 Magnum hand gun, one of the most powerful in the world. When the men were in position with their guns pointed at each Viet Cong the Major stepped backwards and raised his arm high in the air.

Vortex whispered to Major Thrush, "This is due process in South Vietnam."

Thrush chuckled and watched with glee.

The Major lowered his arm like a flag and three hand guns into each Viet Cong body exploded like mini artillery pieces. The shots could be heard all over the Saigon nightclub. Screams from some of the Vietnamese girls outside could be heard. A large crowd had gathered outside the toilets but they were held back by the military police.

The heads of the three Viet Cong infiltrators exploded like ripe watermelons. In fact as Vortex and Susie peeped into the toilet cubicles they saw that the cadavers were almost headless. It was as if the men had been decapitated by the shots. Then a second round of shots bombed through the air. This time the bullets were directed against the bodies.

The Vietnamese Major smiled to Vortex and said, "At least they died in an appropriate setting."

Vortex was already walking out with Susie and his men when he asked cheekily, "What the fuck do you mean?"

The Major lit up a cigarette, "Well? They died surrounded by shit and piss! Didn't they?"

Vortex said with disgust in his voice, "Good night Major!"

When they were outside in the street and the ominous light of tracer fire could be seen on the horizon, Vortex said to Susie, "Let's go back to your home. I've had enough for one day!"

Susie nodded silently as she was held close by Vortex. They all climbed into their army jeep and drove away to the sound of rumbling explosions in the distance.

There was no such thing as a truce in Vietnam. Not even on Christmas Eve.

Chapter 2
Conference at the Tan Son Nhut Air Base

Lieutenant General Robert E. Cushman Jr. was in excellent spirits. Part of the reason for his elated mood was that he was going to get married in about 3 months time. Cushman was 56 years old and his fiancée was a beautiful girl of 27 years. This fact alone also added to his happiness.

Lt. General Cushman was the Commander of the III MAF or 3rd Marine Amphibious Force. The United States 3rd Marine Division was part of this elite and professional outfit. They had met *'Charlie'* many times on his own ground and under his own conditions and had whipped the Viet Cong's ass severely. The body counts had always been high. Especially for the 1st and 3rd Marine Divisions which Cushman considered to be the two best units in the Vietnam theatre.

He arose from his desk and lay down on a luxurious sofa, fixing himself a whisky and tonic. Lt. General's were provided with five star opulent accommodation. This suite that he was currently occupying was in the middle of one of the largest air bases in South Vietnam, the *Tan Son Nhut Jet Air Base*. This installation alone housed at any one time at least 7 squadrons of F-4E Phantoms; a wing of F-105 Thunderchiefs and a host of transport aircraft such as the C-130 Hercules and the C-123 Providers as well as the C-7A Caribou Transports. In addition to this there were upwards of 400 to 500 Bell UH-1D Helicopters, wide-bodied Boeing-Vertol CH-47 Chinooks and HH-53C Sikorsky Jolly Green Giants fitted with in-flight refuelling probes and two jettison able 450 gallon fuel tanks and rescue hoists.

Suddenly the telephone next to his plush silk bed rang shrilly. General Cushman picked up the receiver, "Yes?"

"There is a Lieutenant Caroline Henderson from the Air Force G-2 Section waiting outside to see you sir. Shall I let her in?"

Cushman barked back with anger, "Well of course I fucking want you to show her in to my quarters! Didn't I already give you orders to that affect? Whenever she wants access to me you are to immediately usher her into my presence!"

The orderly warrant officer at the other end of the receiver quaked in his boots.

"Yes sir! Sorry Sir! At once Sir! She is on her way in Sir!"

Cushman slammed down the receiver as he took another stiff shot of whisky. He was going to meet the Supreme Commander in Vietnam, General William C. Westmoreland later that evening for a *'situation conference'*. He needed to unwind and relax before that meeting. Westmoreland, he knew, was going to chew his ass over the conduct of Marine Operations in I Corps Operational Zone. He was thinking of the fiasco when on 1st February this year US Marine artillery and planes accidentally hit a South Vietnamese hamlet 12 miles southwest of *Da Nang* which resulted in the deaths of 8 innocent civilians.

There was a soft knocking on the door.

Cushman arose from the bed and walked half-way across the room and then stopped. He could feel the adrenalin surging through his body.

"Come!" he said.

Cushman who was five foot eleven inches tall and weighed 86 kilograms was solidly built. For an American he was only of average height but his body was solid muscle. He had not an ounce of fat anywhere on his torso. He was clean shaven and had piercing, brutal and vicious black eyes that now seemed to mellow in front of the gorgeous white American female officer that walked into the room.

She closed the door behind her and without saluting at all, she placed her hands on her hips waiting for General Cushman to say something.

Lieutenant Caroline Henderson was General Cushman's fiancé. The General had met her while on his first tour of duty in 1966. They immediately started having discreet sexual meetings which turned into something much more than mere lust in the jungle hot house of South Vietnam. General Cushman discarded his ugly, bitching and pestering wife at the beginning of 1967 and let his two sons run amok in the family used car business which he ran as a side-line. A few weeks ago Caroline and he decided that it was best to get married as Cushman wanted to retain an aura of respectability as he was still bucking for the position of Commandant of the United States Marine Corps.

"What took you so long?" asked General Cushman as he greedily slung his arm around the shapely waist of Caroline.

"There was a fire-fight north of Saigon," she began as she undid the band in her blonde hair, letting the long strands fall beautifully over her shoulders.

"I had to wait in my escort convoy until a battalion from the 9th Infantry and some ARVN Rangers came in and murdered those fucking Viet Cong infiltrators."

Cushman laughed, "Did they get the gooks?"

Caroline ran her tongue inside Cushman's mouth and sucked his saliva into her throat, saying, "I saw 150 dead on the roadside. I spat on their stinking bodies as my armoured car drove by. They caused me to be late for our delicious rendezvous."

The General laughed as Caroline stripped off her blouse and skirt which was regular deep blue Air Force uniform.

Cushman was already naked as he gripped the rear of Caroline's buttocks pushing her vagina close to his crotch.

"Let me suck it!" she said.

Cushman lay back on the bed and the girl performed fellatio on the General with the expertise of a cheap Danish prostitute.

Caroline Henderson was a succulent five foot seven inches tall. She had firm and large breasts with dark nipples that stood out like pencils when aroused. She had fucked many officers in her career, sometimes two or three at a time but never one as senior as Cushman. She was planning to rise up the Air Force ranks with the help of her future husband to be.

General Cushman was hoping that General Westmoreland would not arrive just at this moment. He needed at least another two hours to satisfy his lust and empty his aching loins.

The Warrant Officer had promised to give Cushman at least an advance warning of half an hour if Westmoreland's plane or helicopter approached the *Tan Son Nhut Air Base*. He did not want to be caught in *flagrante delicto*.

As Caroline moaned, struggling to retain his organ in her mouth, Cushman heard artillery fire rumbling about fifty miles away. He knew it was the 9th Infantry Division in action against *'Charlie.'*

Cushman wrestled the 27 year old woman onto her belly as he licked and sucked her hair and breasts.

"My organ is aching!" screamed Caroline.

"Then I'll fill it nicely and succulently for you," laughed General Cushman.

Their love making was hot, wet and intense. Cushman entered her vagina from the rear as she gripped and almost crushed his gonads. Then he spreadeagled her legs wide and performed anal intercourse while rubbing *KY* jelly into her clitoris and eating it with gusto. They then ate each other out in the sixty-nine position while Caroline inserted her entire fist inside the General's rectum.

Suddenly as Cushman exploded his semen over her bouncing breasts to the sounds of the explosions outside, the phone rang.

"What is it?" snarled General Cushman.

It was the Warrant Officer on the line, "Sir. General Westmoreland will be here in less than half an hour!"

Cushman slammed down the receiver without answering and turned to Caroline who was panting, naked on the bed.

"Fucking shit!" he yelled.

"What is it?" she asked.

Cushman jumped into the shower and then started to dress in his immaculate general service uniform with his three stars shining like beacons from his shirt collar.

"Westmoreland is on his way here!"

"What shall I do?" she asked as she grabbed her uniform from the floor.

"Make yourself scarce!" Then Cushman added, "Wait for me in the Officer's Mess at the other side of the air base until this fucking situation conference is over. Then we can continue our extracurricular love-play."

Major General Rathvon C. Tompkins was driving with 200 of his men in a thirty jeep convoy north and then west from Saigon. He liked to travel with only the minimum of staff.

It was late afternoon as they approached the *Tan Son Nhut Air Base*.

"Where is Lieutenant Colonel Vortex?" asked General Tompkins.

His Chief-of-Staff, a full bird Colonel answered, "He's already on his way sir. I spoke to Lieutenant Colonel Vortex in Saigon this morning. He is proceeding to the conference with his battalion commanders and about 100 of his regimental headquarters staff."

The Major General seemed satisfied, "Good! He better be on time because General Westmoreland and Admiral Ulysses S. Grant Sharp will be heading the conference."

The Chief of Staff assured Major General Tompkins that Vortex would indeed be on time when the two officers plus their three Master Sergeants sitting in the front of the large jeep were seared with a lightning flash of fire and tremendous explosions that ripped them from their car seats and threw them high into the air.

Major General Rathvon C. Tompkins was thrown head-first with his legs pointing to the sky, into a ditch by the side of the road. The jeep launched itself into the air and did two summersaults, crushing the head of one of the Master Sergeants like a ripe watermelon. Blood and grey brain matter splattered over Tompkins' face. The jeep then landed on another jeep behind it, killing two Corporals and then bursting into flames as its seventy gallon fuel tank ignited like a bomb.

"Fuck!" was all that the dazed Major General could say. This was the first time that the Commander of the US 3rd Marine Division had had his jeep blown from underneath him. He knew that it was a shoulder launched RPG-7 Soviet made anti-tank missile. He also knew that a Viet Cong infiltration cell was nearby.

Tompkins looked sideways and saw his Chief of Staff, the Colonel, lying face down in the mud. His shirt was torn away as was one of his ears. A bloody hole replaced it in the side of his head. But what was worse, the Colonel's right foot and been blown completely off by the blast and blood was pouring out of the stump of his lacerated ankle. Ants were already crawling into his severed veins and shattered arteries. The Colonel was screaming like a young teenage girl who had been fucked for the first time, her hymen torn into two delicious pieces.

"Medic! Fuck you Medic for the Colonel!" screamed Major General Tompkins.

Just then three of his officers arrived. The men of his 200 strong Divisional Headquarters company had already opened fire across the road and into a thick patch of jungle about 200 metres away. The Viet Cong were returning fierce and continuous fire with AK-47's, light mortars and Soviet made machine guns.

"Jesus fuck!" screamed a Major from the Staff headquarters. Tompkins looked to him as he clicked his fingers and a corporal came over with a radio telephone unit strapped to his back.

"Surprised Major?" asked Tompkins as the corporal presented his back to the General so that Tompkins could pick up the receiver of the radio telephone.

"How did *'Charlie'* get in so close to Saigon and the air base?"

"Fucked if I know!" screamed back Major General Tompkins as he yelled over the roar of M-60 machine gun fire coming from his troops. "Probably from the *'Iron Triangle'*.

A Captain said to Tompkins, "We are caught out on this road with only 200 men! The Viet Cong over there must have upwards of 500 at least."

Major General Tompkins screamed, "Bullshit! Crap! They don't have more than a 100 or so."

"What are you going to do sir?" asked the Major. More NCO's and junior officers crowded around their commanding General in a protective cordon as the automatic rifle and machine gun fire became more intense.

"Take care of the Colonel!" screamed Rathvon Tompkins.

Three medics had picked up the officer and were applying bandages to the stump where his foot used to be. They also gave him seven powerful injections of morphine and plugged a hole in his head where his ear was sheared off. The Colonel was covered in blood and was unconscious from the shock of the blast and the hideous mutilation to his body.

Tompkins said, "I'm going to call in an airstrike!"

He snatched the radio telephone receiver and talked to the air operations officer at *Tan Son Nhut Air Base*.

"These are our coordinates! I want a napalm strike on *'Charlie's'* position."

The Major General then read out the exact Latitude and Longitude from his map that he held in front of him. At that second two more of his jeeps were blown high into the air, showering his men with burning metal splinters and glass.

"Christ! Don't they ever give up!" shouted a 2nd Lieutenant.

"Look! Up there! At eleven o'clock. They are coming in low but fast!" shouted General Tompkins.

All his men continued to fire their machine guns but watched as nine F-105 Republic Thunderchiefs came roaring in behind them in formation. The *THUD's* as

they were affectionately called were travelling sub-sonic at about 690 mph. As they approached the target coordinates they slowed to 420 mph to give the napalm blast the best and most destructive affect upon human flesh. This is what Major General Tompkins loved. He loved the napalm cocktail which he could serve up to the enemy any time he liked by just calling in on the two-way radio. This was real power, he thought to himself. It was better than sex.

The F-105 *Thunderchiefs* were about 4 miles away.

"It's only seconds now!" screamed General Tompkins.

His 200 men, minus about two dozen who had already been killed or wounded, lowered their heads. Their sweating bodies almost became one with the side of the ditches they were slammed up against for about 300 yards in both directions. The rumbling sound of the supersonic engines developing in total some half a million horsepower was like a spine-crushing avalanche behind them.

The Major General and his staff saw the Thunderchiefs banking and then coming in low for the kill. They had a mixed payload of high explosives and napalm.

The roar and flash were deafening. A wall of fire rose up like Armageddon in front of his troops and the jungle seemed to smoulder like black ash. Hideous screams could be heard like muffled groans coming from the Viet Cong.

Major General Tompkins liked to kill with a knife. Whenever he had the chance to engage the enemy in hand-to-hand combat, which was very seldom, he would use his Marine bayonet or a specially crafted dagger to strip the flesh off the Viet Cong.

He despised *'Charlie'*.

Now! He thought to himself, was pay back time! He would have an opportunity to use his blade on fresh Viet Cong meat.

"It's unbelievable!" screamed the Major crouching next to Major General Tompkins.

"It's nothing of the sort!" laughed Tompkins who clapped the officer affectionately on the back and added, "It's simply gut-crunching American airpower! If there is one thing in this whole fucking, stinking Vietnam War that will defeat *'Charlie'* and that is our awesome firepower! I would advocate blowing North Vietnam back into the Stone Age! And turning the rubble into smaller rubble!"

The Major, a young man from Iowa as well as a dozen other officers nodded and grunted in solemn agreement with their Divisional Commander.

"Give me that radio again son!" said Tompkins to the Corporal.

"I want you to strafe that fucking *'Charlie'* concentration to death!" shouted Tompkins to the leader of the F-105 Thunderchief squadron.

The Major who was the squadron leader high above then confirmed the orders and the jets screamed around in a tight arc with after-burners blazing ten miles to their east.

"Here they come again!" said the Major who was commander of the Headquarters Company.

Tompkins and his men watched as the *THUD's* came in low and slow. About 350 mph this time to increase their time over the target. Like a chattering roar the machine guns of the Thunderchief's opened up like an irresistible tide of destruction. Each plane could fire in excess of five hundred rounds per minute.

The jungle was being ripped to shreds like a mix master shredding vegetables. Palm trees, undergrowth and small trees were torn up and then catapulted into the air.

"Fuck! Do you hear that!" said a Lieutenant in the military police.

Horrible screams and groans could be heard coming from the jungle. Mutilated bodies started staggering and falling out of the jungle and into the open rice field next to the road.

"Open fire!" shouted Tompkins.

His men let loose a torrent of M-60 Machine gun and M-16 fire that cut down the already wounded Viet Cong.

"Show them no mercy! For they deserve none!" screamed the General. "Follow me Major!" he said breathlessly.

"What are we going to do?" asked the officer.

Tompkins snarled, "We are going to attack! Attack Major!"

"But – but! Don't you think we should call in another air strike and wait for reinforcements?"

General Tompkins ushered the Major to his feet, saying with brutal sarcasm, "What's the matter with you Major? Don't you want to kick *'Charlie's'* ass?"

The Major knew it was useless to argue with the General. He gave the orders down the line. Seconds later the whole company of about 170 survivors rushed forward and into the jungle line abreast. They fired their machine guns all the way and headed directly into the undergrowth.

"You men. Over there. And this squad flank over to the right." Shouted Tompkins. The Major General loved to give constant and detailed commands to his men while in action. It gave him a sense of power. He also felt that he was like a father to his troops and many of his 3rd Marine Division felt likewise as if they were his children. Minutes later the General was advancing into thick jungle. The rest of his men had spread out. Only two Sergeants and three Corporals were directly behind him when suddenly a ripping sheet of bullets came out of nowhere and sliced into two of the men behind him.

"Jesus! Take Cover!" screamed Tompkins.

But it was too late. One of his Staff Sergeants caught an AK-47 bullet in his left eyeball. The side of his head bulged out with grotesque blood and severed flesh. His screams filled the jungle with a type of surrealistic nightmare or as a chorus from hell.

Another Corporal had lost his legs from the knees down. Bullets had sliced his calves into pulp and his kneecaps were shattered. Tompkins rushed forward and saw about six Viet Cong rushing towards him. The men behind just froze were they lay in a state of stupefaction.

"Get up and follow me!" shouted the Major General. But they did nothing. A punch smashed into Tompkins' jaw from the right and then another hand crushed his midsection. He was surrounded by the Viet Cong all wearing their black pyjama-like pantaloons and tunics.

"Fuck you! You think you can take me out? You Gook bastards!" screamed Tompkins. He grabbed the nearest Viet Cong with his powerful fists and wrenched the man's ears forward. At the same time he head butted the man until his nose was crushed into a yellow-red stream of pus and blood. At that same second two men on his right swung their machetes and tried to decapitate him. But Tomkins, moving with the grace and skill of a Bengal tiger ducked both swipes. His right hand caught one of the machetes and in the same graceful movement he wrenched the huge sword out of the Viet Cong's hand and brought it down on the head of the second one while kicking a third.

"Oh My God!" said Tompkins to himself. The sight was gruesome even for his eyes to behold. He could see the grey matter of the Viet Cong's brain come oozing out from his skull. The machete was already buried half-way through his entire head with the haft of the blade at the level of the eyes.

But Tompkins had no time to think. Two more Viet Cong had grabbed him in a headlock when one of his Sergeants' bolted forward and drove his bayonet into the spine of one of them.

"Thank you Sergeant!" barked Tompkins whose face and shirt were richly splashed with blood and entrails. Tompkins threw his head backwards and smashed the skull of the other Viet Cong. The headlock was loosened slightly but not completely broken.

"Fuck you get off of me!" yelled Tompkins as he stumbled backwards. Being much larger than the Viet Cong assailant, Tompkins reached backwards with his huge arms and managed to grip the ass of the man. Tompkins could feel that his body was skinny though muscular. It also stank rankly of body odour. In a decisive movement Tompkins dropped down on one knee and as he grabbed onto the buttocks of the Viet Cong he catapulted the man over his head and head butted his skull as he fell to the ground in front of the General.

The Viet Cong shouted something unintelligible as now Tompkins swung his arm around the man's neck and commenced to strangle him with brutal force.

"I'm going to teach you a lesson *Charlie*!" shouted the General in a mad frenzy. As he spoke he gouged his fingers into both of the Viet Cong's eyes. Slowly the flesh of the eyeballs were crushed and mutilated as Tompkins pushed deeper and deeper into

the man's skull. Finally, the man stopped struggling and Tompkins withdrew his fingers from the bloodied sockets, wiping the crushed eyes onto the tunic of their owner.

"Watch out General!" screamed a Warrant Officer who had come running up from behind a large tree. A second later that same Warrant Officer was knifed in the back by two Viet Cong. Tompkins saw them twisting the blade inside his man's spine as blood gushed out of his mouth in a crimson shower. The General bolted forward and threw his dagger into the heart of one Viet Cong. The other Gook grabbed General Tompkins and they did a deadly quadrille of homicidal struggle all across the thick and luxurious undergrowth.

"You bastard!" screamed Tompkins as he punched the Viet Cong viciously in the midsection and in both temples. The much smaller man started to crumple. Tompkins was a big American weighing all of 126 kilograms of pure muscle. The Viet Cong he was struggling with was barely 63 kilograms. Tompkins lifted the man off the ground and into the air above his head like a rag doll. He saw a jagged branch sticking up into the air a few steps away. The General ran forward with the Viet Cong in his arms and then brought his hands crashing down thus impaling the man's body on the sharp branch.

A Sergeant came running up behind the General, "Oh! My God!" The edge of the branch pierced right through the lungs and emerged from the Viet Cong's chest cavity like a bloody stump covered with intestines and human tissue.

Tompkins too his Marine dagger and plunged it into the impaled man's neck severing the carotid and jugular arteries. They were both splashed with hot, sticky blood.

"Fuck you Charlie!" as the General screamed he smashed down with his fist onto the root of the branch. Both the Viet Cong and the blood smeared branch came tumbling down to earth. As Tompkins turned to the Sergeant the latter had his mouth open as if to speak. The General waited for a few moments but no words came out. Then to his horror, he saw the flesh around the lips and teeth of the Sergeant erupt like a red volcano. He was splashed with blood as a stray bullet blew open the skull of his man like a watermelon crushed under the wheels of a truck.

"Jesus!" moaned Tompkins as more of his men came running up behind him and they all opened up with M-60 Machine guns. The Major arrived covered in his own blood and said, "It looks like the air strike didn't get them all General."

"Of course it didn't!" Tompkins spat back, "It only softens them up! It is the infantry that has to go in and finish them off! Occupy the land physically."

The Major nodded as Tompkins waved his hand towards his officers and men.

"Come on Marines! What are we?"

All the men shouted without exception, "We are Marines sir!"

"And what are we going to do?" asked Tompkins in a wild frenzy.

"We're going to fuck'n kick *'Charlie's'* ass!" they all shouted back with wild enthusiasm.

"Then let's go!" screamed the Major General. His remaining men charged forward and for the next ninety minutes flushed out the surviving Viet Cong troops. Tompkins charged through the jungle and found himself confronted by three Viet Cong brandishing machetes. He faced them squarely and let them attack. The first one swiped his blade but missed. The General took out his hand gun and blew the side of his face clean off with a tremendous amount of force. Tompkins didn't carry the standard issue Colt .45 pistol but preferred to use the 500 Magnum 0.50 calibre with dumb-dumb bullets. He found it had greater stopping power. The second Viet Cong's arm and shoulder were torn off his chest as the General took aim and fired. The third gook screamed at the top of his lungs and waved his machete in the air like a circus clown.

"Come on! You motherfucker!" shouted Tompkins as he waved the man towards him with the palm of his hands. The Viet Cong lunged but Tompkins struck sideways with an elbow strike knocking out several teeth. He then dropped down on his knees and sliced his Marine dagger into the crotch of the Viet Cong's trousers. He could feel the blade slicing deliciously through the septum of the penis and into the gonads of the enemy attacker. A terrible howl of dogs in hell emanated forth.

Tompkins ran his fist into the mutilated man's mouth and at the same time buried deliciously his Marine dagger into the Asian's chest. It pierced the myocardial tissue of the heart with a sweet suction sound. In the next second the man vomited blood and bits of lung tissue directly onto Tompkins open mouth as the General was shouting obscenities at his opponent. The Major General found himself vomiting from fright and disgust directly back into the Viet Cong's gullet. The whole scene was horrid and macabre to a 2nd Lieutenant who came bolting up to the aid of his commanding officer.

"Quickly!" ordered Tompkins, "Finish the bastard off! My arm is wounded."

Tompkins staggered back and clutched the brachialis muscle of his upper arm. It was severed in two places. It must have been one of the machete attacks. Medics arrived as the 2nd Lieutenant grabbed the Viet Cong around the mouth and cheeks. This young American boy from Arkansas was so huge and his fist so large that his hand almost completely smothered the enemy's face. Then with a powerful twisting motion he clicked the Asian's head around so hard and viciously that his spine broke like an egg. The junior officer then unloaded a whole magazine of pistol shots into the body. Red geysers of blood erupted from the flesh like sprinkles from hell.

Tompkins snatched his knife out of the dead heart and ran back to a UH-1D helicopter.

Within minutes his surviving headquarters company was onboard about 25 helicopters that had swooped down to extract them from the deadly but successful melee.

"Let's get the fuck out of here!" ordered Tompkins.

With a thudding roar of rotor blades and humming engines his troops were lifted high and aloft to safety.

Back in Saigon Lieutenant Colonel Richard Vortex was relaxing in Susie Ky's bedroom. They sat at a large table sipping whisky.

"Do you have to go my darling?" asked Susie with a tear in her eye.

"I'm afraid so Susie," Vortex leant over and kissed Susie passionately. She reciprocated that ardour by giving her lover a succulent French kiss so that Vortex could hold her soft, delicious tongue between his teeth. Her flesh seemed to him as fragrant as oleander and as bright as alabaster.

"Have some of this opium," she offered. Both of them stripped naked and smoked the opium as they made love. Vortex slid beautifully into her vagina and he allowed himself to luxuriate in the feel and tenderness of her flesh.

She sucked his gonads and then his nipples as he penetrated first one orifice leading to her womb and then the other leading to her rectum and bowels. Both were heavenly and soon the pair of copulators were drenched in their own sweat, semen and vaginal slime as they slid like eels across the bed's silken sheets.

Suddenly there was a loud knocking on the door. The punches on the wooden frame were so loud and indelicate that Vortex thought there was a madman outside.

"Oh! Shit!" exclaimed Susie Ky as she pulled a bed sheet over her be-slimed bosoms.

"Who the fuck is that?" asked Vortex, the blood starting to seep in a torrent of adrenalin to his mad, frenzied skull.

"I hope it is not who I think it is!" whispered Susie to her military and jingoistic lover.

"I'll go and see," said Vortex viciously as the knocking grew louder and even more persistent.

Suddenly Susie Ky jumped off the bed and grabbed Vortex by the arm. Her small but beautiful breasts bobbled in the humid night air.

"Don't worry. My gorgeous," exclaimed Vortex as he took another sniff of opium to electrify his senses and add strength to his awesome musculature.

"I can handle this cock-sucking bastard, whoever he is or thinks he is!"

Susie sank back onto the bed horrified at the coming encounter. Vortex swung open the door with such force that it almost came off its hinges. A five foot six inch Vietnamese man was standing at the doorway. Without any invitation he pushed past Vortex's massive body and confronted Susie Ky.

"What the fuck is going on here?" asked Vortex as he closed the door behind the impudent man.

"Let me explain," said Susie not to Vortex but to the well dressed Vietnamese who was about 30 years of age and was wearing a tuxedo.

"You bet I want you to fucking explain!" he shouted, "I thought that we were going to go away with each other?"

Vortex watched as Susie Ky shook her head, "Impossible! I don't love you! I love this man! You are nothing compared to him! Now get the fuck out of here before I throw you out!"

Vortex was dumbfounded, "Who is this jackanapes?"

Before Vortex could stop him the Asian man stepped forward and slapped Susie across the face with terrible power and accuracy. Her naked body fell back onto the bed in a daze.

"What the hell?" asked Vortex, livid.

The smaller Vietnamese man did not seem to be awed by Vortex's massive size and powerful physique. The Lieutenant Colonel despite being stark naked and high on copious quantities of opium bounded forward and gave the little man such a powerful blow to the right temple that blood splashed like a crimson shower across his features. He was catapulted into the air and onto the bed with the naked Susie.

Vortex screamed, "I am going to teach you not to hit a lady! And not my fiancé!" Vortex snarled like a wild animal and lunged onto the man's neck as he pushed Susie out of the way. The Colonel at first bit into the man's carotid artery and actually managed to pierce the flesh and epidermal layer to sever the arterial vessel. Blood gushed like a small and delightful fountain over Susie's naked bosoms and crotch. It ran in rivulets across the silken bed sheets of their recent and frenzied copulation. But in that instant the little man seemed to find his last reserves of strength. With a skilful Karate strike he kicked Vortex backwards so that he crashed into a nearby dressing table.

"Jesus! You fuck-meister!" cried the Colonel.

In the next second the Vietnamese man head butted the Colonel and smashed his fist with an eagle strike into Vortex's testicles. But the Colonel shouted, "I'll eviscerate you!" As he raved he bit off the lower portion of the smaller man's ear including the lobe. Susie Ky scrambled off the bed and opened her writing table drawer frantically searching for something.

The Vietnamese man yelled, "Die you bastard!"

A head punch and then another and another smashed into Vortex's skull so that he became dizzy and almost punch drunk. Yet the Colonel was not so easily beaten. His left hand found a can of insecticide on the dressing table. Head butting the attacker backwards he sprayed almost half the can into his eyes and face.

"You fucker! I'll rip out your living guts and use them to grease the wheels of my tanks!" shouted the enraged Colonel. To his amazement, as the Colonel staggered back across the room to take a rest and to regroup for the next punching bout, he saw Susie take something long, thin and sharp from her writing table. As the man fell backwards she plunged a small rapier into his spine with savage force.

"Oh! My God!" screamed Vortex, "Susie? What have you done?"

The Colonel was deeply shocked as blood vomited out from the Vietnamese man's mouth. Susie lunged again and again, plunging the dagger into his heart, neck and chest.

"You've murdered him Susie! How could you do such a thing?" asked Vortex as he cupped his hand to his mouth.

"What else could I do my darling?" she started to cry and then fell into Vortex's arms with deep sorrow.

"I just wanted to give him a beating for hitting you but I had no idea that you would stab him in the back like that? Usually that is what English Colonialists do, especially to their own people. It is also part of the English Navy's tradition – back stabbing and jealousy, I mean."

Susie started to explain, "Listen my love! This man is Nguyen Van Tran Thong. He used to be my extracurricular lover while I was dating the son of the Japanese Ambassador here in Saigon. Our affair lasted only three months and he thought that he owned me, the fucking prick! I used to fuck him three days a week after school. I was only nineteen then. He kept insisting that I go to America with him. He told me that he already had US citizenship because his parents were so rich that they bought visas and permanent residency by following business migration for half a million US dollars. Anyway, I kept refusing his insidious advances and I had no desire to make love to him anymore as I was already sharing the beds of two other men at that stage. However he had a beautiful sister who was sixteen and we experimented with each other by sleeping together. I had never experienced a lesbian sexual encounter but I found it smooth, succulent and delicious. We usually made a point to meet late at night while both our parent's were sleeping. We undressed each other and then had a hot bath. She would rub rare oils and spices into my body and then we would perform cunnilingus on each other's organs. It was so sweet and delicious, her vagina I mean."

Vortex laughed with glee, "Oh! Susie! I don't care if you have made love to a dozen girls. You don't need to confess to me. I am not a priest. But I do respect and revere the Catholic religion and all its most excellent institutions including the Vatican and the Papacy. I must tell you that I am a firm believer in the Church of Rome and the fact that you are a solid Buddhist does not bother me at all."

Susie put on her pink panties as Vortex kissed the firm nipples on her breast that stood out at him with fright and brazen effrontery.

"But you must understand that I am a high ranking officer. I must set an example to my men. I can't be involved in any stinking or sordid murders in Saigon involving dissatisfied lovers. My job is simply to butcher the enemy on a large scale which is completely legal and sanctioned by the United States Government and the Government of President Thieu."

Susie took a deep sniff of opium, "I fully understand my love. As you say you must be honest and true to the glorious US military war machine and the Administration of the President Lyndon B. Johnson. I am the one who has committed this foul and treacherous murder. It was a moment of haste and unthinking brutality. I am so sorry!"

She started to cry again and Colonel Vortex seemed lost for words.

"It's alright. It's alright my sweet and gentle dove," as he spoke Vortex put his arm around Susie and added, "This unfortunate little episode has made absolutely no difference to my love and adoration for you."

Susie asked as she wiped away the tears from her eyes with the shirt sleeve of the man she had just knifed to death, "Does that mean that you still want to marry me?"

Vortex chuckled heartily as he lifted his head to the ceiling showing his brilliant and perfectly formed teeth, "Of course I want to marry you!"

Susie continued, "Does that mean that as a married couple you are still willing to take me to the United States to live?"

Vortex smiled, "Again the answer is affirmative my sweetheart."

Susie breathed a sigh of genuine relief, "Oh! I love you so! I know that the United States is a land of milk and honey. Every opportunity exists for people who are willing to work hard and long hours. It is the quintessential capitalist system at work. The great and mighty dollar and the pursuit of more of the same is the single most important goal in life. We must strive after this filthy war is over, to make more and more money no matter what. And the United States is our meal ticket to that end. It doesn't matter that there are millions living in poverty in America and the whole façade of the democratic system is a foul deception to pander to the interests of huge multinational corporations and the lobby groups in the upper echelons of US Government and industry. It even doesn't matter that the United States oppresses and subjugates the whole of Central and Latin America to its economic ends and at the same time marginalising the poor and the black disadvantaged people in its own country, for the history of white settlement in the America's is a bloody catalogue of horrors that extends to the limits of one's imagination. I don't give a fucking rat's ass about all or any of that!"

Vortex lifted up his hand, "That's enough Susie! It is not my place to comment on vaporous politics. I am a military man and an officer. My only concern is to obey the orders of the President like an unthinking automaton."

Susie reached up and ran her tongue inside Vortex's mouth, kissing and sucking as she fondled his gonads. He reciprocated that ardour and totally ignoring the bloodied and mutilated corpse on the bed, lay down naked next to it and copulated afresh, both feverishly and with intoxicating dreams of social justice spinning in their heads for another thirty minutes.

When Susie had ejaculated with a bitching scream she asked, "What are we going to do with this foul and rancid corpse? This ex-lover fucker of mine?"

Vortex looked at the body as he ripped off its clothes and rolled them in a bundle. "How the fuck should I know? You killed the shithead! Not I!"

Susie put her finger to her chin and thought deeply for some moments. Then she asked in wonderment, "What are you doing with his clothes?"

"I am going to burn them of course! Or rather you are going to burn them my sexy queen of Vietnam."

They both laughed and took up a large glass of straight whisky which they consumed in less than a minute.

"I'm going to need some alcohol for what we are going to do next."

"And what is that?" asked Vortex as he dressed back in his camouflage uniform.

Susie began, "I just had an idea. Downstairs in the concrete basement which is two stories below ground, there is a huge vat of quicklime. It's pH is only 2.5 and thus extremely acidic."

Vortex was amazed, "What does this house need a vat of quicklime for?"

Susie robed in her dressing gown and slippers, "We do a lot of entertaining and cooking in this house as my father is a high ranking Minister in the Thieu Government. Therefore we have a lot of refuse and chicken waste to dispose of. My mother thought that a vat of quicklime would be the most efficient way of dissolving flesh and other organic garbage."

"I know what you have in mind!"

Susie continued, "Let's take the body of my impudent and selfish ex-lover fucker and throw it into that vat of quicklime. In less than six hours the whole corpse including the skeleton will be completely dissolved."

"Excellent idea!" cried Vortex as he tongue kissed his lover. An hour passed and the job was done. As soon as the dead flesh touched the quicklime it started to sizzle and fizz. Just as they ascended the stairs from the basement the telephone rang.

"Who could that be?" asked Lieutenant Colonel Vortex. Susie shrugged her shoulders and nonchalantly picked up the receiver. She listened intently and then said to her lover, "I think it's for you."

"For me?" asked Vortex incredulously.

"Yes, that's right!"

"Who would call me here?"

Susie smiled, "Its Westmoreland!"

Vortex nearly fell over backwards, "Did you say Westmoreland? You mean General Westmoreland?"

"That's correct," giggled Susie Ky.

With trembling hands Vortex picked up the receiver and looked at it as if it was an alien creature in his sweating palm.

"This is Lieutenant Colonel Richard Vortex."

His voice trembled. He had only met William Childs Westmoreland on three previous occasions.

"Richard? Is that you?" asked the familiar voice.

His throat almost choked with excitement, "Yes sir! General Westmoreland!"

"What are you doing still in Saigon? Aren't you coming to the situation conference at *Tan Son Nhut* ?"

"I was just about to get underway sir!" said Vortex apologetically.

"Good. I'll be pleased to see you again Vortex!" The Supreme Commander in Vietnam sounded as if he was in a jovial mood.

"Thank you sir! It is always a privilege to serve!" shouted back Vortex in his best parade ground voice.

"There is something very big building up around *Khe Sanh*."

Vortex knew about that Marine base in the far north of South Vietnam very close to the Laos border and that with the North.

"*Khe Sanh*?" repeated Vortex.

"That's right Vortex. And I want you to play a big part in any possible future operations up there. I want you to be *my man* in that sector. You will report confidentially back to me at all times."

Vortex barked, "Understood sir!"

"That's all for now. See you at the conference in three hours." General William C. Westmoreland hung up.

The troops knew him as '*Westy*'.

Vortex turned to Susie Ky, "I've got to get going at once! I'm already late!"

Susie asked as she grabbed the Colonel's arm, "What is it?"

Vortex thought for a few seconds and then said as he made for the door, "I think the whole bottom is going to fall out from under us here in Vietnam!"

Chapter 3
General William Childs Westmoreland

Four star General William Childs Westmoreland strode into the underground bunker conference room like an Imperial Roman imperator. He was the King Pin and he knew it. Yet he had compassion and genuine concern for his troops. In many ways he was the perfect *GI General*.

"Where is Lieutenant General Robert E. Cushman?" he asked one of the army military police Lieutenants standing like a ramrod in front of the conference room door. With quaking voice the junior officer answered, "He is already in the situation room sir! With Major General Rathvon C. Tompkins, sir!"

Westmoreland nodded, "Thank you Lieutenant!"

The four star general and his small party walked in through the doors that the military police opened for them with mathematical precision.

General Westmoreland was the Deputy Commander under General Paul Harkins until he took over in June 1964. He was a decorated combat hero from World War 2 and Korea and prior to arriving in Vietnam was the Superintendent at West Point where he had previously earned his army commission. Of the utmost importance to Westmoreland was organisation, discipline and efficiency but not necessarily in that order. It was he who urged the Johnson Administration to supply more and more troops to the effort in Vietnam. By the middle of 1967 there were upwards of 536,000 troops supporting the South Vietnamese Government. As soon as General Westmoreland entered the room everybody snapped to attention and stood as if they had a broom stick stuffed up their backsides.

The overall strategic plan envisioned by Westmoreland was to use the South Vietnamese Army [ARVN] to protect population centres while the US and its associated allied forces such as the Australians and New Zealanders would secure the coastline, block Viet Cong infiltration to the south and then conduct a war of attrition against the enemy by "search and destroy" missions into the countryside. Helicopters and air

power were vital to this plan to provide mobility and support to the ground forces. General Cushman was the first to step forward and salute.

"Good evening sir," said Cushman.

"Good to see you General," said Westmoreland cheerily.

General *'Westy'* as he was affectionately known by his men always carried with him a personnel staff that was not overly large but was sufficient in numbers to meet any eventuality.

He had a Brigadier General in charge of his Headquarters and two Colonels with one light Colonel as liaison officer between him and Task Force 77 in the Gulf of Tonkin. In addition there was an Air Force Brigadier General to coordinate land and air bombing operations and of course a whole retinue of Marine officers headed by Lieutenant General Cushman. All of these officers were currently present and standing behind Westmoreland at a respectful distance as he conferred with General Cushman.

"Listen Robert," he began as he rubbed his chin thoughtfully, "There is something serious brewing up in the far North-West corner of I Corps Operational Zone. But I don't want to begin the briefing until your field commanders are here."

General Cushman nodded, "You mean Lieutenant Colonel Richard Vortex? Commander of the 9th Marine Regiment?"

General Westmoreland nodded, "Yes. I spoke to him on the phone in Saigon. He should be here shortly."

Then Westmoreland hesitated for a moment and looked about the room. With a polite gesture he curled his finger and signalled to Major General Rathvon C. Tompkins to come over.

The three Generals then conferred with each other while the other officers in the large circular room talked quietly and helped themselves to tea, coffee and cakes that were laid out in a large and lavish spread.

"I heard you ran into a fire-fight on the way here?" asked Westmoreland.

"That's right sir," began General Tompkins. "I lost 12 of my headquarters staff killed and 19 wounded. We counted over 300 Viet Cong bodies. We left them to rot where they fell."

"Good effort. But I heard that they caught you by surprise on the road here from Saigon," commented General Cushman.

"Yes sir," answered Tomkins.

General Westmoreland broke in, "I want to send Colonel Vortex up to the *Lang Vei Special Forces Camp* and the Marine Support base at *Khe Sanh*. We have some latest intelligence from G-2 section that the North Vietnamese are building up massive reinforcements in that area. Two complete North Vietnamese Divisions are concentrating there. It seems that they intend to take the base or at least to split and turn our flank and drive onto Highway 9 to the coast at *Quang Tri*."

"That is very disturbing sir," said General Cushman as he looked to General Tompkins.

Westmoreland added, "If they succeed in doing that! Well gentlemen, that would be a disaster of the first magnitude! The North Vietnamese could roll up our entire I Corps Operational Area and come smashing down into central South Vietnam!"

Both of the lower ranking generals nodded gravely.

Then Tompkins said, "Lieutenant Colonel Vortex is the best field commander that I have in the 3rd Marine Division. And I say that without any reservations whatsoever."

Westmoreland nodded, "I agree. That is why I want him up there as my eyes and ears."

General Cushman asked, "Are you going to relieve Colonel David E. Lownds of command at *Khe Sanh*?"

"Hell no!" riposted Westmoreland angrily, "Colonel Lownds has my complete confidence. I just want another senior officer up there to report developments to me as they come to hand."

General Tompkins asked, "And what about the 9th Marine Regiment? Do you want to send all three battalions into *Khe Sanh* as reinforcements?"

Westmoreland hesitated for a few moments, "I am not sure yet. But I don't want to over-stack the support base with troops. I don't think it will add any great defensive value. On the contrary it might just lay us open to more unnecessary casualties. But I will order that Colonel Vortex take up at least one of his battalions. It would be ludicrous to send him up there without any operational combat troops. Colonel Lownds would have him running errands instead of killing the enemy. Something which Vortex does extremely well."

Just at that second Lieutenant Colonel Richard Vortex himself entered the conference room with Majors Thrush, Lansdale, Sergeant Major Crighton and about half a dozen other regimental staff officers trailing behind his huge and muscular frame.

"Ah! There you are!" exclaimed General Westmoreland.

Vortex bolted up to the Supreme Commander of the Military Assistance Command in Vietnam [MACV] and saluted like a pistol shot. Westmoreland returned the salute with fanatical precision.

"You will be pleased to know," began General Westmoreland as he took Vortex off to one side, "……That you're promotion to full bird Colonel just came through."

Richard Vortex smiled as Generals Cushman and Tomkins offered their congratulations.

"Here is the official confirmation of your promotion to full Colonel," said General Cushman as he handed Vortex a yellow teletex sheet of paper. Then he added, "It has come direct from the Chairman of the Joint Chiefs of Staff."

"Thank you sir," said Vortex as he snapped his fingers to Sergeant Major Crighton who scurried up and took the piece of paper, filing it in his gold handled leather attaché case which he carried for Vortex everywhere they went.

"Listen, I have something for you," said General William Westmoreland as he signalled to one of his aides, a Captain, to come over.

The Captain handed Westmoreland a small black box like the type that is used to house rings or cuff-links.

"This used to be mine during World War 2. I want you to have it."

"What is it sir?" asked Vortex who looked to the Supreme Commander in amazement.

"Well! Open it and find out! Its yours Richard!" said General Westmoreland with genuine enthusiasm.

Colonel Vortex opened the small black jewellery box carefully and with reverent awe. Inside he found a set of four highly polished eagles. The insignia for a full Colonel in the United States Marine Corps, Navy, Army or Air Force. There were four eagles making up two pairs for his uniform shirts.

"Oh! Sir!" exclaimed Vortex his heart brimming over with undiluted emotion.

"I can't accept these! They must be very special to you!"

General Westmoreland laughed and clapped Vortex affectionately on the back.

"I insist! I can't think of any other officer I would rather give them to," replied the Supreme Commander.

Colonel Vortex picked up one pair of eagles with religious submission.

"Come here!" said General Westmoreland, "Let me put them on you now without delay!"

Lieutenant General Robert Cushman said in a loud voice to all the staff officers in the situation room, which included some South Vietnamese generals, "Listen up! Listen up everybody!"

Immediately all the officers in the room snapped to attention like automatons.

"Lieutenant Colonel Richard Vortex has just been promoted to full Colonel!"

There was a loud and boisterous thunder of applause and hoorahs as General Westmoreland held up the shiny eagles. He then removed the silver oak leaves from Vortex's shirt collar and replaced them with the eagles.

"There! How do you feel?" asked General Westmoreland.

Vortex replied, "Deeply honoured and privileged sir!"

"Now this is what you know. Now I have something to give you which you did not know about."

"What do you mean sir?" asked Colonel Vortex respectfully.

General Westmoreland said directly, "For your gallant action in pursuing and killing Viet Cong irregulars in and near the *DMZ* (Demilitarised Zone) last fall. You have…been awarded the *Congressional Medal of Honour!*"

Everybody in the room applauded loudly. The clapping continued for nearly five minutes as the Supreme Commander handed Colonel Vortex the brilliant and beautiful "*Congressional Medal of Honour.*"

General Westmoreland went on, "Also the 9th Marine Regiment of the 3rd Marine Division has received five unit citations for its actions at *Quang Tri* earlier this year."

Again there was applause and loud cheering.

"Colonel Vortex has also been awarded the *Bronze Star* and the *Silver Star* for his action at the *Dakto Highlands* from the 3rd to the 22nd November where he killed thirteen North Vietnamese regulars with only knives and machetes after his gallant team ran out of ammunition." As General Westmoreland spoke, General Tompkins and Cushman shook hands with Colonel Vortex and then each officer in the 'situation room' came up one after the other to offer their congratulations and felicitations.

After the pleasantries were over and when Admiral Ulysses S. Sharp arrived with his staff from Task Force 77 and the US 7th Fleet, the conference proper began.

General Westmoreland opened and lead the conference.

"Now listen up! Quiet! Quiet! Listen up! And I don't want any interruptions!"

Everybody in the room became deathly silent. You could hear a pin drop and nobody dared to cough or let out any other bodily noise.

A large map was placed on the huge circular table and General Westmoreland started to point and wave his hands about the contours of the country they were trying to save from Communist infiltration and their incessant campaign to murder and intimidate innocent South Vietnamese civilians.

Westmoreland began, "As you know on the 8th January 1967 *Operation Cedar Falls* was executed. This involved 16,000 US and 14,000 South Vietnamese troops. Its aim was to stop Viet Cong insurgency in and around the Saigon area. The main concentration of the enemy was in the "*Iron Triangle*" and the *Thanhdien Forest Preserve* which is a 60 square mile area of jungle, swamps and other mangrove filled areas believed to contain base camps and supply dumps for the enemy murderers. We annihilated a massive tunnel complex in this "*Iron Triangle*" thus circumventing any further infiltration into the Saigon centre. The village of *Bensuc* was wiped off the face of the earth using napalm and high explosives because it was a fucking breeding ground for dirty scum-sucking Viet Cong guerrillas!"

As General William Westmoreland talked with great power and eloquence, everybody in the room inwardly smiled and approved of the colourful metaphors he was using. They always thoroughly enjoyed '*Westy's*' speeches. It filled their hearts and lungs with the sweet hatred and lust for vengeance against the Viet Cong enemy who was faceless and merciless.

Westmoreland continued after he was handed a pointing baton by his Chief of Staff, a Brigadier General by the name of Schweiz.

Brigadier Schweiz had been a veteran of the Second World War but had served in the 3rd Panzer Corps of the German Wehrmacht. At that time his rank was Obersturmbannfuhrer [Lieutenant Colonel in the Schierheitsdienst]. He had emigrated after

the war to the United States attaining citizenship there and immediately enlisted in the US Army as war was the only profession that he knew, relishing in it.

"The end result of this magnificent operation, which by the way was my unique brainchild, was a body count of 711 enemy killed and 488 captured. We flew in over 1,229 bombing sorties against the Viet Cong enemy. Our airpower is magnificent!"

General Westmoreland then shifted his baton to another point on the South Vietnamese map.

"On or about the 25th January 1967 I assigned the 3rd Battalion of the 9th Infantry Division to permanently patrol and flush out the Viet Cong from the *Mekong Delta* area. Since then the operations of this battalion and its associated South Vietnamese allies have been highly successful. I have commenced to follow up this initiative by bringing in what will in the end amount to 2 Divisions of troops or 30,000 US men to gain full control of the *Mekong Delta* from the enemy.

On the 2nd and 3rd of February I ordered elements of the 4th and 25th Infantry Divisions to undertake *"Operation Gadsden"* inside *War Zone C* near the Cambodian border to halt or at least interrupt the flow of supplies through the rotten *Ho Chi Minh Trail* named after that ruthless Communist cocksucker. This operation consisted of 8,000 of our boys and on the 3rd of February *"Operation Big Spring"* is launched against a Viet Cong stronghold near the Cambodian border."

Brigadier General/Obersturmbannfuhrer Schweiz interrupts the briefing by whispering in General Westmoreland's ear. Nobody knows or could hear exactly what he said but Admiral Sharp already knew what was going on. General Westmoreland cleared his throat noisily and went on.

"On the 11th of February 1967 I ordered that *"Operation Lam Son 67"* be commenced. It involved substantial elements of the 1st Infantry Division, the *"Big Red One"*. Their job was to clear the enemy from numerous villages in an area 13 miles south of Saigon. It was highly successful and the body count was high. While this was going on the 1st Marine Division began *"Operation Stone"* in the southern sector below *Da Nang*. Shortly after this *"Operation Thayer II"* which began back in October 1966 in *Binhdinh* ends with the death of 1,744 of the enemy. At the end of February 1967 I ordered *"Operation Junction City"* to commence. It involved a multi-divisional force of over 25,000 US troops and was the biggest and most brilliant operation that I have devised so far. Its aim was to crush, smash and annihilate with savage force *War Zone C* of the Viet Cong and their strongholds there. It sucked in 34 US Battalions and 2 ARVN battalions."

Admiral Sharp cuts in, "On the 26th February 1967 I ordered cruisers and destroyers of the US 7th Fleet to shell North Vietnamese supply routes along a 250 mile stretch between the DMZ and *Thanhhoa*."

Westmoreland nods to the Admiral and says, "On the 27th February 1967 the Viet Cong shell our airbase at *Da Nang*. We suffer 12 casualties and the base is heavily

damaged. Then as "*Operation Junction City*" continues, the 1st Infantry Division suffers heavy losses as well as the 173rd Airborne Brigade which is ambushed near the Cambodian border. On the 20th March "*Operation Prairie III*" the 1st Battalion of the 4th Marines goes in at *Gio Linh* and they bush-wack the Viet Cong guerrillas in a highly successful operation. Then, on the 6th April about 2,500 of the enemy make a coordinated attack on the city of *Quang Tri*, 15 miles south of the DMZ. Heavy casualties are suffered by them as we repulse this move with the excellent fighting prowess of the 9th Marine Regiment of the 3rd Marine Division…"

As Westmoreland speaks he nods and smiles approvingly to Colonel Vortex and adds, "Then the North Vietnamese make their first attack across the bridge spanning the *Benhai River* at the 17th Parallel. But we push them back without pity for their suicide stupidity! The Communists blow to smithereens 2 bridges between *Da Nang* and *Quang Tri* on the North-South Highway Number 2. However, I ordered the quick rebuilding of the bridges with 7 Seabee battalions. In the middle of April 1967 I fly back to the Pentagon and request an additional 4 and one half Divisions to bolster our strength to 671,616 men from our present level of over 485,600. I am still waiting for the President's decision. On the 20th April jets from *Kitty Hawk* and the *Ticonderoga* hit power plants in the *Haiphong* area. The raid was successful but I urged the National Security Council and the President to allow me to increase the level of bombing to include all industrial areas regardless of the '*collateral damage*' to the civilian areas which I could not give a fuck about. I would have liked to pulverise the entire city by three months of constant air attack using B-52 Arc Light raids of full duration and with the utmost strength. However…..anyway, it was not to be."

General Westmoreland resented the way his hands were being tied in the conduct of the war by Washington. But now was not the time or the place to criticise the Administration, especially not in front of the officer corps.

He continued, "Then in the period 24th April to 5th May 1967, our US Marines of the 3rd Division defeat North Vietnamese regulars on the hills surrounding the support base at *Khe Sanh* near the DMZ border in the *Quang Tri* province. This support base is less than 10 miles from the Laos border and is thus a highly sensitive area. We suffered about 160 dead and 764 wounded but the enemy suffered much more. On the 5th of May the last hill is wrested from the dogs and jackals of the Viet Cong and NVA. Simultaneously another enemy force attacked the Special Forces Camp at *Lang Vei* about 7 miles west of *Khe Sanh* but we repulsed them there as well."

Suddenly another Brigadier General interrupts the four star supremo and steps up to the table. His name is Brigadier General Joseph A. McChristian who is Westmoreland's Chief of Intelligence.

McChristian adds, "During the middle of this year I presented a report to the President and the National Security Council indicating that the strength of the

combined North Vietnamese and Viet Cong guerrillas was in excess of 400,000 troops. The CIA did not believe this estimate from my G-2 Section."

Westmoreland interrupted and waved the G-2 Chief back behind the table, "I think gentlemen that we can simply forget what the CIA think! They tried to poison that lickspittle Castro and couldn't even do that! The simplest thing in the world!"

Everybody in the room roared with laughter.

Colonel Vortex looked to Lieutenant General Cushman and they smirked happily to each other. All of the officers appreciated '*Westy's*' jokes and considered it to be light entertainment.

"On the 8th of May….," continues Westmoreland, "…the North Vietnamese attack the base at *Con Thien* with troops and mortars but are repulsed after 179 of the enemy are killed. Attacks are also fended off at *Giolinh* and *Camp Carroll*. Also, in further developments at *Khe Sanh* which I shall deal with in more detail in just a moment, the Marines of the 3rd Marine Regiment repulse the enemy about 9 miles northwest of that support base. In the period 15 to 23 May the enemy again attack our forces south of the DMZ with artillery fire. Casualties are taken at *Dongha* and *Con Thien* as well as *Camp Carroll* and *Cam Lo*. I then ordered nearly 6,000 troops as well as a battalion of ARVN Rangers to go into the south-eastern section of the DMZ and disrupt enemy troop concentrations and infiltration routes there. The operation was a great success thanks to the 9th Marine Regiment and Colonel Vortex."

Westmoreland nods to Vortex and the latter bows with respect and admiration for the Supreme Commander.

"The North Vietnamese protest the invasion of the DMZ buffer zone but those rascal hypocrites are the ones who violated the zone in the first place! So we piss on their impudent protests!" said '*Westy*' with anger.

"Then the gallant men of the 26th Marine Regiment under Colonel David Lownds begin, under my brilliant plan, "*Operation Prairie IV*" east of *Khe Sanh*. The object of my plan is to clear the enemy out of the DMZ south of the *Ben Hai River*. Helping the 26th Marines are 5 battalions of the 1st ARVN Division who work their way along the axis of Highway 1 between *Giolinh* and the *Ben Hai River*. The 26th operates along the river itself. Then I order in 7 more Marine Battalions to attack Hill 174 southwest of *Con Thien*. The whole operation masterminded by me and conceived by me is a great and unqualified success! We suffer only 164 dead and 999 wounded which is small compared to the enemy disposed of. In June, "*Operation Union II*" is highly successful in rooting out the Viet Cong from their bunkers in *Quong Tin Province*. In the period 12 to 17 June I order in the *Big Red One* (1st Infantry Division) to smash its way into the heart of *War Zone D* which as you know is 50 miles north of Saigon. We annihilate four Viet Cong battalions with a correspondingly high body count. At the end of June the 9th Infantry Division smashes the enemy on the *Rach-hui River* which is

19 miles south of Saigon. Our losses are minimal while the enemies are substantial. Unfortunately we then suffered a setback in *Dakto* in the *Kontum Province* at the end of June. One of our companies in the 173rd Airborne Brigade is severely mauled and we lose 80 dead when they are ambushed. However the enemy losses were higher. At the beginning of July one of the Platoon's of the 9th Marine Regiment, Colonel Vortex's outfit, is ambushed by the Viet Cong around *Con Thien* just south of the DMZ. Colonel Vortex and I order in massive reinforcements and the battle intensifies to the detriment of the enemy. The *90th Viet Cong Regiment* is involved and we kick their ass severely as they retreat. We lose only 96 dead. Again the enemy attack the valiant 9th Marine regiment in the first two weeks of July and Colonel Vortex's brilliant field leadership saves the day once again with my overall supervision as the inspiring force. The battle takes place at *Con Thien* once more and we helicopter in the 3rd Battalion while the reinforced 1st Battalion bush-wack the enemies flank. Two more battalions of the 3rd Marine Division of Major General Tompkins are flown in by a fleet of over 300 helicopters and the fighting continues until the middle of July. We suffer only 159 dead while the enemy lose about 1,301 dogs. They never really learn do they?" said General Westmoreland half to himself and half to the assembled room of staff officers. They will never be able to defeat us on the battlefield!"

Colonel Vortex adds, "I can assure you sir!" He was talking directly to General Westmoreland, "When my unit is in a fire-fight with the enemy then I go straight for the jugular. My only aim is to kill and annihilate as many of the Viet Cong as I possibly can with all the firepower at my disposal!"

Westmoreland nods to Vortex and continues, "Then in the Central Highlands around the 10th and 11th of July a heavy battle erupts. In the first action the 173rd Airborne Brigade comes under machine gun and mortar attack while sweeping the *Dakto* area near *Kontum*. In the second action the 4th Infantry Division pulverises the Viet Cong near *Ducco* with only 35 dead on our side. I then ordered Major General Tompkins and his 3rd Marine Division to initiate "*Operation Kingfisher*" from July to the end of October in the I Corps Operational Zone south of the DMZ. It was a highly successful operation with only 340 dead on our side and 3,086 wounded. The 4th Infantry Division smashes a Viet Cong battalion near *Ducco* in the Central Highlands around the 23rd of July. On the 9th August the *1st Cavalry Airmobile Division* lands near the *Songre Valley* about 25 miles west of *Ducpho* and we hit the enemy hard with the loss of only 5 helicopters. During the week of 13 to 19 August I order Arc Light B-52 raids over the north of the DMZ in North Vietnam proper. We hit and smash enemy installations, supply depots and coastal shipping and other infiltration traffic."

Westmoreland then signals his aides and they usher forth a Captain by the name of Stephen Pless.

"Now listen up! I hereby award the *Congressional Medal of Honour*, the *Silver Star*, two *Distinguished Service Crosses* and the *Purple Heart* to Captain Stephen Pless!"

Suddenly a gigantic roar of applause and approval thunders through the conference room.

General Westmoreland smiles to Captain Pless, shakes his hand and awards him the bundle of sacred medals that illustrates the heroic tradition, honour and gallantry of the armed forces of the United States.

"You all know the gallant and brave actions of Captain Pless. He is the epitome of the superior American fighting man. In him shines all the great qualities of sacrifice and heroism upon which this great country of ours is built. The quintessential elements of the American military tradition are exemplified and shine like a magnificent aura of wonder and grace through the firmament of the galaxy of stars which is the victory of American arms. Not only over the brutal and sadistic Asiatic foe but also all the other degenerate enemies that the United States has had to fight in the past and defeat in an orgy of blood and monumental sacrifice caused by foreign aggression, foreign suppression, foreign brutality and foreign lust for war and savage retribution against the heroic forces of the free world and the democratic system which is epitomized in the '*American Way*' of truth and justice. America which is the home of the brave and the land of the free!"

The whole gathering burst into another round of applause and Colonel Vortex swelled his chest out with pride and a savage determination to crush the Viet Cong like they had never been crushed to death before. He promised to himself that in the coming campaign at *Khe Sanh* he would slice the living guts out of the North Vietnamese and the filthy scum that made up the dirty cowards in the Viet Cong gang of murdering rapists and thieves in *COSVN*.

All this he thought silently to himself as General Westmoreland, one of the greatest Generals America has ever produced continues his speech.

"Never in my more than thirty years of service during World War 2 and in Korea from September 1950 to 1952 have I seen an action so brave and heroic as that of Captain Stephen Pless! From his helicopter gunship he spots four of our men who have landed on a remote beach on the coast after their helicopter was shot down. These men were being beaten to a pulp and bayoneted by a cowardly force of 30 Viet Cong gangsters and pimps. That is the way the Viet Cong attack. They murder like dogs the innocent who are outnumbered by them. They would never attack an equal or superior force but like jackals they run away and hide. They fight like putrid homosexuals. Always they creep up on a man when his back is turned! That is why the ambush is their favourite method of attack! It is the tactics of cowardly pimps and gangsters! Anyway! Captain Pless was only one man and there were more than thirty jackals down there on the beach murdering innocent and defenceless Americans who

had already surrendered! The swine in the Viet Cong are so pig ignorant that they haven't even heard of the *1949 Geneva Convention III* Relative to the Treatment of Prisoners of War in Time of Armed Conflict. Neither have they heard of the *1949 Geneva Convention I* for the Amelioration of the Condition of the Wounded and Sick in Armed Forces in the Field. Or, if they have heard about these binding instruments which have now become crystallised into *customary international law* they did not read them or follow their humanitarian edicts for conduct in the pursuance of hostilities! The Bastards! They were murdering these brave men of ours and what does Captain Pless do? You would probably think that being one man he would radio in for help and hope for the best. But no! Captain Pless takes his lone aircraft into the fray and fires his machine guns and rockets at the scoundrels and murdering jackals of the Viet Cong as they typically run away like the yellow cowards they are, into the trees after bayoneting our poor boys! He lands his helicopter under intense fire from the pitiless and gutless enemy and manages to save three of our wounded men as he takes off again in his overloaded helicopter gunship! What a miraculous and fantastic feat of bravery and sacrifice! I salute you Captain Pless!"

As Westmoreland spoke he jumped to attention at his full six foot one inches and ricocheted a brilliant salute to the Captain. Everybody in the conference room including Colonel Vortex shot up like bean poles and saluted the magnificent *Captain of America*. For the next couple of minutes Captain Pless was congratulated by everyone and then he made a short speech.

"To the Supreme Commander General William Westmoreland and to our great President, I thank you! I accept with honour and a deep sense of loyalty these medals that symbolise the greatness of our United States of America over all the other countries in the world. The tradition of our fighting men is surpassed by no other except perhaps the *Wehrmacht*. I know in my heart that we have the wherewithal to utterly annihilate and crush the enemy until their blood flows greater and mightier than any river on this globe. I know also that the United States will lead the world of free nations in pulverising the filthy, rancid scourge of Communism in a tornado of military destruction. Before this incident came to pass I had the intention of going back into civilian lifer after my tour of duty was over in Vietnam. But now I have only one desire! And that is to remain in the Army and kill the pimps and stooges of the North Vietnamese regime as well as their cocksucking, motherfucking Chinese keepers!"

Westmoreland clapped enthusiastically as did everyone else at Captain Pless's words.

"Thank you Captain!" said Westmoreland as Brigadier General A. McChristian of the G-2 Section ushered the officer and hero back to the rear of the room. The conference continued.

General Westmoreland prodded with his fingers from one corner of the large map on the table to the other.

"For most of September the North Vietnamese regular army *(NVA)* attacks the *Con Thien* Marine base with heavy artillery. The other bases of *Cam Lo*, *Camp Carroll* and *Dongha* are also hammered by artillery. I then ordered in counter barrages with our artillery and with B-52 raids that were successful. From the 4th to the 7th of September a large and brutal engagement is fought in the *Queson Valley* which is 25 miles south of *Da Nang*. The 5th Marine Regiment takes some 114 casualties but we hit back hard and drive the enemy back into his stinking tunnel complexes. The Viet Cong are worse than rats! They always burrow and hide in their foul tunnels when we try to stand up and fight them like men! They are nothing but dirty, stinking, stupid cowards!"

Everybody in the room murmured their tacit approval at General Westmoreland's words of wisdom.

He continued, "In the middle of September I order that *"Operation Coronado 5"* be implemented. This involved the 9th Infantry Division supported by ARVN battalions on its right and left flanks. The battle took place 47 miles southwest of Saigon and I ordered in massive air strikes supported by artillery. Then, after consultation with the US 7th Air Force and its excellent commanders I order that the *Thatkhe Bridge* in North Vietnam be blown to smithereens. This bridge is only 7 miles away from our gangster friends in mainland Communist China. The bridge is totally annihilated in a heart-warming operation of pure success. On the 19th September I had the privilege of welcoming in a marvellous battalion of Thai troops as they disembarked in Saigon. I am pleased to say that now six other allied countries have supplied troops to this great enterprise besides the United States and South Vietnam. On the 30th September I instruct the F-105 Thunderchief squadrons of the 7th Air Force to bomb the *Loidong* transhipment point on the *Cua Cam* estuary. Navy bombers from Task Force 77 are also used. This target is only 4 miles northeast from Haiphong. Other squadrons smash the *Kienan MiG base* and the *Kepha* army barracks as well as the *Phucloi* petroleum storage area near the stinking city of *Vinh* in North Vietnam. Then on 4th October I order the 1st Cavalry Division Airmobile and specifically the 3rd Brigade thereof to fly to the northern part of South Vietnam. They are flown to *Quangtin* and *Quangngai* to relieve the heavy pressure that the Viet Cong gangsters are putting on *Quang Tri* as well as *Thauthien* and *Quangngai*. Therefore I have shifted the 1st Cavalry Division Airmobile to that area to allow Marine units to move closer to the DMZ. On the 13th October the North Vietnamese gangsters shelled our base at *Giolinh* just below the DMZ. They let loose nearly 400 rounds of heavy calibre shells and then tried to penetrate the defences of *Con Thien* nearby. But Colonel Vortex and a battalion of his valiant and brave troops beat them back with savage hand-to-hand combat."

Colonel Vortex stepped forward and interrupted. He knew that on this occasion General Westmoreland would not mind.

"Yes sir. The fighting was vicious and brutal," began Colonel Vortex, "I ploughed into more than a dozen of the enemy by myself. I used Karate tactics as well as small arms training. I am a superlative expert in both. My favourite weapon is the long clasped Marine dagger which is 18 inches long and razor sharp on both sides. This is an excellent weapon for cutting open the intestines of the Viet Cong and the North Vietnamese! On that day I personally eviscerated more than ten men and their rancid and bleeding guts were smeared in a horrific miasma across my uniform, face and hands. I urged my men not to take any prisoners but to cut out the living guts of these vermin with the praise and the sanction of Almighty God!"

General Westmoreland nodded with approval as Colonel Vortex finished his dissertation.

"Thank you Colonel Vortex, winner of the Congressional Medal of Honour! I congratulate you and your magnificent troops who have done so much in the eyes of God to crush the Viet Cong anti-Christ!"

Everybody in the huge conference room applauded with loud cheers. Just at that second Nguyen Cao Ky, the Vice-President of South Vietnam and Air Marshal of the whole South Vietnamese Air Force entered the room with about 20 men from his General Staff Headquarters. All of them were wearing a multitude of brilliant medals but none more than Nguyen Cao Ky himself. It seemed that Ky's chest was one huge smorgasbord of colourful medals. His uniform was made of the finest silk and it looked immaculate. He wore a purple scarf around his neck and was holding a cigarette.

"Good evening gentlemen! Good evening!" shouted Nguyen Cao Ky with great mirth and happiness. His brilliant and vivacious eyes glowing with their black intensity. He, it seemed, was thoroughly enjoying the war that was ripping the fabric of his 3rd World country apart.

General Westmoreland smiled and beamed. He jumped to a solid salute and shook hands with the South Vietnamese supremo and the number two man in the Republic after President Thieu. Suddenly Vice-President Ky turned to Colonel Vortex, "Ah! Congratulations on your promotion Colonel Vortex!"

Vortex snapped up a pistol-like salute, "Thank you sir! Good to see you again so soon!"

Marshal Ky beamed, "And congratulations on winning the *Congressional Medal of Honour* as well as the *Distinguished Service Cross*!"

Vortex thanked the Vice-President and then the latter went over to Captain Pless to offer his heartfelt congratulations.

"Sorry to interrupt General Westmoreland," began Ky, "Please continue with the situation conference."

Westmoreland nodded and went on, "In consultation with the 7th Air Force and Task Force 77 in the Gulf of Tonkin I ordered massive air strikes against the huge *Phucyen* airfield about 18 miles north-west of Hanoi. This rotten base is supposed to be the biggest MiG base in North Vietnam. The attack lasted two days and we bushwacked the bastards destroying many of their jets while they sat like fat ducks on the tarmac! I then ordered additional attacks on multiple targets in the Hanoi-Haiphong area on the 25th October. The *Longbien Bridge* is smashed into dust and it is the only rail link from Hanoi to Haiphong and the Chinese border. The 32,000 kilowatt thermal power plant inside Hanoi is also obliterated in a wherewithal of firepower from our magnificent fly-boys. Our air force units in Thailand hit targets such as *Kieana, Kep* and *Hoalac* MiG bases and the *Yenbai* airfield. The Viet Cong's 273rd Regiment attacks our Special Forces Camp at *Locninh* but I order two battalions of the 1st Infantry Division in to provide support. The fighting is the best possible kind! Hand to hand! We slowly drive the motherfuckers out of *Locninh* street by bloody street! We confirm a body count of 900 Viet Cong killed and countless more wounded."

Westmoreland took a deep sigh and gathered his strength. After reorganising the maps on the table he continued with seeming effortless patience.

"In the period 3rd to 22nd November one of the largest and most gruesome battles of the war took place in the Central Highlands near *Dakto*. *Dakto* as you know is about 280 miles north of Saigon near the Cambodian border. We have large installations at *Dakto* including an ammunition dump, an airfield and a South Vietnamese militia camp. Before the battle commences we have only 1,000 troops in the immediate area. I immediately order in reinforcements of 4,500 men from the 4th Infantry Division and the 173rd Airborne Brigade. The enemy numbers about 6,000 jackals made up into 4 regiments. The fighting centres around *Hill 875* during the 19th to 22nd November which is 12 miles south-west of *Dakto*. The 173rd Airborne Brigade performs magnificently and forces the enemy to abandon its last line of defence on the ridge to *Hill 875*. We kill about 1,455 of the North Vietnamese oppressors for the loss of only 285 men. It is a brilliant victory for American Arms and illustrates our superlative military prowess and dedication. On the 6th November I order the Air Force base at *Korat* in Thailand to strike heavily the *Giathuoung* storage complex three miles from the centre of Hanoi. I urged President Johnson to take this storage facility off the restricted list of targets and he acquiesced after realising the wisdom of my advice. On the 7th November I order jets to bomb rail facilities 21 miles from the Chinese border. The shipyard at *Anninhgoai* and the repair facilities west of Haiphong are cut to pieces. As you know on the 22nd November I returned to Washington to report to the President and the National Security Council and the Pentagon. I informed the President that the battle around *Dakto* was the beginning of a great defeat for the enemy. We also found intelligence from one of the dead Viet Cong that this build up around *Dakto* was to

be the beginning of a massive winter-spring offensive in the *B-3 Front*. But as you can see we smashed this plan and nipped the offensive in the bud before it could get off the ground. On the 6th of December and up until the 8th of this month the 3rd North Vietnamese Division attacked our troops near *Bongson* which is 140 miles south of Da Nang. A fierce battle ensues which ends with the rout of this 3rd Division for minimal casualties on our side. Then on the 10th December our gallant South Vietnamese allies trap two Viet Cong battalions near *Vithanh* which is 100 miles south-west of Saigon. Another body count indicates 365 Communist dead. Then I masterminded a plan just a few days ago to thwart the enemies' winter-spring offensive by launching a powerful drive in and around the DMZ. The strength of the enemy in this area is conservatively estimated at 35,000 to 45,000 troops. I ordered 1,000 Marines to land by boat and helicopter along the coast of *Quangngai Province*. They exchanged fire with the North Vietnamese who were entrenched there. Then B-52 Arc Light raids were ordered by me into the DMZ itself and they are highly successful. Also a destroyer from the 7th Fleet has succeeded in pulverising a Communist bunker five miles east of *Giolinh*."

Westmoreland brushed back his greying hair as he said, "Well gentlemen! That is the position at the moment. Of course this is only a brief overview of the main engagements during 1967. But I would like to say that in 1968 I plan to urge the President and the Pentagon to make an all out offensive to crush the North Vietnamese and their Viet Cong stooges by a massive land, sea and air offensive. I intend to ask the President to increase troop numbers to over 750,000 men not including our allies. I have also asked for the deployment of more powerful weapons to smash, crush, kill and eviscerate the putrid and evil enemy that is the Viet Cong pimps and their North Vietnamese keepers."

Quickly General Westmoreland looked to Vice-President Ky and he smiled back cheekily to the American Supreme Commander. Only the two of them knew exactly what General Westmoreland was talking about and what he was going to ask the President at a future secret meeting. Westmoreland continued after blowing his nose, "Also to increase the number of fighter and fighter-bomber squadrons to 95 from their present level of 67. But at this juncture with the approval of Vice-President Nguyen Cao Ky…" Westmoreland nodded to Ky who nodded back and waved his hand upwards with a gesture of confirmation,"…I would like to hand the briefing over to Brigadier General A. McChristian the Chief of my *G-2 Section*. We have gathered the very latest intelligence which indicates disturbing developments up in the zone immediately south of the DMZ. Specifically, in the area around the Marine support base at *Khe Sanh*. It appears that the North Vietnamese Army is massing 2 and perhaps 3 whole Divisions around that northern area of South Vietnam which is only a few miles from the Laos border. But I will now hand you over to Brigadier General McChristian."

Westmoreland walked over and stood next to Vice-President Ky. The Supreme Commander had a rugged face with thick, black eyebrows and was about six foot one inches tall and solidly built. He was 53 years old and a magnificent soldier. One of the finest officers that America has ever produced. He had a keen grasp of detail, a photographic memory and a brilliant tactical and strategic military mind. His understanding of the complexities of logistics for large armies in the field was almost computer-like in its superlative accuracy and precision. Everyone watched as Brigadier General McChristian stepped up to the table and pointed with the long, thin baton that Westmoreland had given him.

"Gentlemen! We have used the high altitude reconnaissance *SR-71 Blackbird* aircraft as well as spy satellites and routine air patrols to monitor the massive and gigantic build-up of North Vietnamese and Viet Cong forces around the north-western tip of South Vietnam near the Laos border. We have identified at least 2 complete North Vietnamese divisions assembling there near the base at *Khe Sanh*. They are the *304th North Vietnamese Division* and the *325th North Vietnamese Division* each comprising about 12,000 men. The 304th enemy division has taken up positions along the Laos border directly west of the US Special Forces camp at *Lang Vei*. The commander of the *Lang Vei* camp is Captain Frank C. Willoughby. He has requested increased air strikes with F-105 Thunderchiefs and F-4E Phantoms to crush the continued advance in the build-up of the 304th Division. We have acceded to that request and the Supreme Commander has issued appropriate orders to the 7th Air Force and Task Force 77 in the Gulf of Tonkin. The second division as I have just indicated is the 325th. It has taken up positions north by north-west of *Khe Sanh*. This puts it directly next to the following hills."

As he spoke Brigadier General McChristian pointed with his baton to each hill which was clearly marked on the large scale map. Everyone in the conference room, including Colonel Vortex craned their necks forward to take a good look at where the G-2 Chief was pointing. There were now over 100 high ranking officers from both armies present in the situation room.

"Here is Hill 881-North! And to the east of it is Hill 558!" As he spoke Brigadier General McChristian waved his pointing baton around like a performing prima donna.

"…and here is Hill 881-South which as you can see is south of Hill 881-North! And to the east of 881-South is Hill 861. Now as you can see from the position of these high points they are and will be crucial to any possible large-scale engagement at *Khe Sanh*. These hills are currently defended by battalions from the 26th Marine regiment under Colonel David E. Lownds. If the North Vietnamese and their Viet Cong conspirators manage to capture these strategic high points in the terrain then they will move up artillery and mortars and their…"

Colonel Vortex interrupted, "If they do that they will blow the fucking hell out of *Khe Sanh*. Our 155mm howitzers and 81mm mortars will have to aim upwards at them which is almost an impossible task and they can shoot down on us with a clear field of vision. It will be a slaughter and a God-damn turkey shoot!"

Brigadier McChristian did not like to be interrupted in his moment of glory, especially not in front of Vice-President Ky. But since it was Colonel Vortex he said nothing but simply continued.

"Yes! That's right! Thank you Colonel." Then he turned to the rest of the conference.

"As the Colonel has indicated the control and possession of these hills is vital. Now! Further north and east is the 320th North Vietnamese Division. It is continually receiving fresh supplies and troops directly across from the DMZ. Our bases at *Ca Lu* on Highway 9 and *Camp Carroll* and the base at *Cam Lo* are directly opposite the 325th Division's field of operations. On the north-western side of the DMZ sits the fully equipped and powerful *324th North Vietnamese Division* which can be called in to support either the 325th Division facing *Khe Sanh* or, alternatively, the 320th Division facing our other Marine positions along the DMZ frontier. I would also like to add that the control of the *Cua Viet River* which runs from east to west along the southern edge of the DMZ is vital for our troops. General Westmoreland has indicated to me that he is going to bring in more riverine patrol boats and heavy artillery to maintain control of the river and its multitude of tributaries."

Brigadier General McChristian paused for a moment as he fiddled with a large stack of maps and aerial photographs and then added, "We are not sure yet what the intentions of these 4 North Vietnamese Divisions are. They may not attack the base at *Khe Sanh*. They may instead try to by-pass it altogether and simply cut Highway 9 on the road to *Quang Tri*. If they do that then they could roll up the entire northern flank of I Corps Operational Zone."

General Westmoreland waved his hands to Brigadier McChristian as you wave off a pet poodle. The G-2 Chief stepped back from the table and Vice-President Ky and Lieutenant General Cushman walked forwards to take over.

"Now Listen up! Gentlemen!" began Westmoreland, "In the light of these massive troop reinforcements by the North Vietnamese in the *Khe Sanh* area I am going to take a series of steps to bolster our forces in that operational zone."

He looked to Lieutenant General Cushman and to Major General Tompkins and they nodded.

Westmoreland continued excitedly but with a measured pace and a controlled voice that did not falter, "I am going to send Colonel Vortex and one of his Marine Battalions of the 9th Marine Regiment into *Khe Sanh* as reinforcements. The other two

battalions of Colonel Vortex's command will be kept in reserve at *Quang Tri*. When the time is right these units will be helicopter'd in to relieve *Khe Sanh*."

"My men are ready sir! They are eager to grapple with the enemy criminals!" shouted Vortex.

Vice-President Ky smiled, "And I have a suggestion General Westmoreland!"

The Supreme Commander of the Vietnam Military Assistance Command looked up from the coloured map, "And what is that sir?"

Vice-President Ky said, "I would like to bring in the *37th ARVN Ranger Battalion* to support your magnificent and professional Marines at *Khe Sanh*."

Westmoreland rubbed his chin thoughtfully and remarked, "The 37th ARVN Rangers! Now wait a minute! Yes! I remember that superlative outfit! They were the ones who surrounded and decimated three entire Viet Cong battalions in the Mekong Delta just a few months ago!"

Vice-President Ky confirmed Westmoreland's memory.

Lieutenant General Cushman added, "It would be an honour and a privilege to have those fine fighting men of the 37th alongside our Marines in the 26th and the 9th!"

Westmoreland said, "Then it shall be so! Give the orders Brigadier General Schweiz to mobilise and airlift the 37th ARVN Ranger Battalion and the 1st Battalion of the 9th Marines into *Khe Sanh* within the next 48 hours max!"

Brigadier General Schweiz who was an expert marksman and a superb fencer came forward with a notepad and started taking down copious quantities of notes and field instructions as they were issued. As the Chief of Staff for the Supreme Commander he was one of the prime movers in the organisational efficiency of the American forces in South Vietnam.

"It is already under way sir!" he said with determination.

Colonel Vortex ordered, "Major Thrush! You will go in with the 1st Battalion of my Regiment and set up defences there with Colonel David E. Lownds. I will be following shortly."

Major Thrush barked, "Yes sir!"

Without waiting for the situation conference to end, Major Thrush, at the tacit nod of Colonel Vortex and General Westmoreland, left the room with three Captains and a 1st Lieutenant from Vortex's 2nd Battalion Staff Headquarters. They were on their way to *Quang Tri* by *Jolly Green Giant* helicopter to pick up the 1,500 men of the 1st Battalion and from there onwards to *Khe Sanh* where they would reinforce defences and await Colonel Vortex's arrival.

"Well gentlemen?" said General Westmoreland as he waved his hands across the huge map.

"I think that is all for now. Does anyone have any questions?"

Colonel Vortex looked to Vice-President Nguyen Cao Ky who looked to Lieutenant General Cushman and then Major General Tompkins glanced with a wary eye at the host of medal adorned officers of the South Vietnamese Army. Tompkins knew that they looked impressive but he was sceptical of their fighting ability against the North Vietnamese, especially when it involved large scale operations. He always tried to use ARVN troops in a support role whenever he could.

"I have a question sir," said Colonel Vortex as he placed his finger on the label which read *Khe Sanh*.

"What is it Richard?" asked William Westmoreland with interest.

"I have been thinking…, what if this is a prelude to an all out offensive by General Vo Nguyen Giap?"

Westmoreland asked, "You mean the gathering of the 4 North Vietnamese Divisions so close to the DMZ?"

Vortex nodded, "Yes."

Vice-President Nguyen Cao Ky cut in, "With respect Colonel Vortex, I think you are wrong."

"Why – sir?" asked Vortex as he received a stern look from his immediate superior, Major General Rathvon Tompkins.

Vice-President Ky continued, "I don't think that Giap is ready for an all out strike. His supply lines are not well established enough. His troops are still waiting for more equipment from the lime-sucking pigs in Communist China. In addition my own intelligence unit has briefed me on the situation. They don't think that General Giap can launch an offensive in 1968. He will probably need another 12 months to attempt such a strike."

Brigadier General Joseph A. McChristian spoke to General Westmoreland while looking at Ky, "I have to agree with Colonel Vortex sir. My whole intelligence network and the spies that I have planted inside General Giap's own Supreme Headquarters tell me that the North Vietnamese are indeed preparing for an all out offensive operation. These 4 Divisions in the north are just one portion of the troops they are massing for the attack. We estimate that they are readying not less than ten divisions!"

General Westmoreland shouted, "Ten divisions!"

Lieutenant General Cushman scoffed, "That's impossible!"

Major General Tompkins added, "That's more than the entire reserves of the North Vietnamese Army!"

"Nevertheless that is the opinion of the G-2 Section," said Brigadier McChristian adamantly.

"I agree with Brigadier McChristian sir," said Vortex as he picked up the pointing baton, "My estimation of General Giap is that he can never be underestimated!"

"But!…" cut in Vice-President Ky, "…in the same manner you should not overestimate him!"

"I don't think I am overestimating him!" said Colonel Vortex.

"Anyway, let us just wait and see what develops," finalised General Westmoreland.

Brigadier General Schweiz stepped forward and waved his hands like an orchestra conductor to the assembled room of officers.

"Thank you gentlemen! That will be all for now."

As the officers started to file out of the room, Westmoreland turned to Lieutenant General Cushman and Major General Tompkins.

"Could you gentlemen follow me please. I have some further things to say to you."

Colonel Vortex turned to leave with the other officers when General Westmoreland grabbed hold of his arm, "And you too Colonel."

Adjoining the conference room was a smaller suite that was sumptuously furnished with red carpet and ornate chandeliers hanging from the ceiling.

Vortex thought that it looked like a high-class bordello and expected the whores to make their appearance at any moment.

Into this room strode General Westmoreland followed by Generals Cushman, Tompkins, Schweiz and McChristian. Vice-President Ky and three of his most senior generals also followed. Colonel Vortex brought up the rear. A brace of huge American military police bolted the door when everyone was inside.

The nine men waited for the Supreme Commander to speak. They were curious to know what he had to say. Only Vice-President Ky already knew what the contents of his speech would be.

"Gentlemen!" began Westmoreland with a sly smile, "Last month when I visited the Pentagon and spoke to President Johnson, I asked the President to allow me to increase the firepower we have here in Vietnam."

The commander of the 3rd Marine Amphibious Force *[3rd MAF]*, Lieutenant General Cushman asked, "Increase our firepower? What do you mean sir?"

General Westmoreland said, without changing the expression on his rugged face, "I have asked the President to allow me to employ low yield tactical *nuclear weapons* on our B-52's and our fighter bomber jets such as the F-105 and the F-4E."

The mouths of the men in the room, except for Ky, fell open like gates.

There was stunned silence for a few moments. Nobody knew what to say.

Cushman said in a comatose voice, "Nuclear weapons?"

Vice-President Ky said cheerily, "Yes! Nuclear weapons! I fully support General Westmoreland's request. I don't see that surgical strikes by low yield nuclear weapons could have that much of a deleterious affect on the environment. Besides it would allow us to decimate the North Vietnamese army formations as they concentrated."

General Westmoreland added enthusiastically, "If I could use tactical strikes with nuclear weapons I could win this war in less than 6 months!"

Colonel Vortex rubbed his chin asking, "What exactly do you mean by low yield sir?"

Brigadier Schweiz answered, "We have recommended to the President that weapons of between 5 and 50 kilotons be used."

Vortex said, "I see! 50 kilotons would be roughly equivalent to the Hiroshima and Nagasaki bombs. And would that be the maximum kilotonage you would dare to use?"

General Westmoreland said, "Absolutely no greater than 50 kilotons! I assured the President! Many of them would be much less than that anyway. We could fire most of them from artillery pieces using our *Atomic Cannon* developed by the *ACME Corporation*, the same company that makes cornflakes and artificial sweeteners. They are atomic shells that could take out, say, two to three square miles in a single blast. Just what we need for annihilating the North Vietnamese divisions as they concentrated."

Vice-President Ky said, "I have also spoken to President Johnson and in addition to the request for nuclear weapons I put forward the view that we should commence *Unrestricted* and large scale bombing of Hanoi and Haiphong and all the North Vietnamese industry and transport infrastructure."

Colonel Vortex said, "I agree with taking off the restrictions for conventional bombing and I have absolutely no reservations about the use of even large yield nuclear weapons such as atomic artillery."

General Westmoreland smiled, "I knew that you would support the idea Vortex!" The Colonel answered as he looked to the Supreme Commander, "Sir! I would advocate that much higher yield nuclear weapons be used! Even *Strategic ICBM's* against Hanoi. Yes! Absolutely now that I have considered it! That is the only way to go sir!"

General Westmoreland beamed, "Excellent! I knew that you would agree Richard!"

"But sir?" asked Colonel Vortex as he fiddled with his hands not knowing where to put them.

"What is it?" snapped Westmoreland as he murmured something to Vice-President Ky.

"What did President Johnson say?"

"He refused but said he would give it further consideration at the next meeting of the National Security Council and take it under advisement."

Vice-President Nguyen Cao Ky slapped Vortex affectionately on the back, "As soon as President Johnson gives the green light for their employment I know that we can win this sorry conflict and drive the Communist fuck-assed stooges and their Viet Cong lackeys out of our country. I then propose that we should launch a full scale ground invasion of North Vietnam!"

Westmoreland started to walk out of the room followed by his staff, "I concur with those plans Vice-President Ky! And I shall see you in Saigon tomorrow for our joint meeting with President Thieu."

When only Vortex and his immediate superior, Lieutenant General Robert Cushman were left in the room, Vortex asked, "What do you think sir?"

General Cushman picked up his briefcase and stuffed a bundle of telex papers into it with great frustration.

"What do I think about what?"

"About the possible use of nuclear weapons?" asked the Colonel as he spotted the beautiful Lieutenant Caroline Henderson waiting for him at the entrance. Even though she was now going to marry Lieutenant General Cushman, Vortex had known her for some 3 years previously. They had enjoyed a steamy and torrid sexual affair which lasted 4 months while Vortex was stationed at *Fort Benning* in Georgia. Susie Ky and Caroline had even joined Vortex in a delicious ménage a trios while in Saigon without the knowledge of Cushman. General Cushman answered, "I fully support the use of nuclear weapons as you do Vortex!"

But then Cushman added as he lasciviously clapped eyes on his beloved Caroline, "I am also afraid its going to fucking start World War 3 with the Chinese and then the Russians!"

The two men immediately left for *Quang Tri* and the US 3rd Marine Division which was stationed there.

General Tompkins said, "I think the fucking shit is really going to hit the proverbial fan up near the DMZ!"

Chapter 4
US Special Forces Camp at LANG VEI

Captain Frank C. Willoughby was a tremendously efficient soldier. He was a Special Forces Green Beret with the United States Army. In addition he was commander of the Special Forces Camp at *Lang Vei* at the beginning of 1968.

Among his other decorations he held the Congressional Medal of Honour, three Bronze Stars, two Silver Stars, the Distinguished Service Cross and for his action recently at the gruesome and vicious battle of *Dakto* from the 3rd to 22nd November 1967 in the Central Highlands where he single handed killed with a knife twelve Viet Cong criminals after he had run out of ammunition, he was awarded the Purple Heart – the US Forces most celebrated award for gallantry above and beyond the call of duty.

Captain Frank Willoughby's Detachment A-101 forces numbered only 24 American *Green Berets* and approximately 900 *Montagnard* tribesmen who were fanatically anti-Communist and anti-Viet Cong. Willoughby knew that he could trust the *Montagnards* just as much as he could trust his own US Army personnel.

The base camp at *Lang Vei* was half a kilometre long and 900 metres wide. It had several helicopter landing pads constructed by a Seabee battalion early in 1967. There were no solid buildings at the camp but instead they had dug in deeply using sandbag emplacements, tents and *Montagnard* huts. The *Montagnard* village was only a mile away from the *Lang Vei* camp encapsulated in deep jungle.

Captain Willoughby was only 25 years old and a graduate of West Point Military Academy. He was the purest killing machine that the US Army had ever manufactured. He loved hand-to-hand combat. Knives, daggers, swords, spiked clubs, knuckledusters, steel pincers and techniques of brutal interrogation of Communists were his speciality. He was only five feet eleven inches tall but he weighed in at 119 kilograms of rippling, gut-crunching, brain-splitting muscle. He was, like Colonel Vortex, a Black Belt expert in Karate and Kendo. His marksmanship was unbelievable. His superiors had also informed him that his promotion to Major was already being processed.

"Get me a cup of coffee!" screamed Captain Willoughby to his Sergeant.

The Captain and a dozen of his Green Berets were sitting underground in the main bunker of the *Lang Vei* Camp. The roof was made of steel girders and the earth walls were reinforced with sandbags and wooden beams. It was quite a cosy little dugout.

"My job here is to monitor the movement of the Viet Cong as they infiltrate men and supplies through the *Ho Chi Minh Trail*," said Captain Willoughby to Lieutenant Max Reinhardt, his 2nd in command. Lieutenant Reinhardt and Captain Willoughby were attached to the 1st Air Cavalry Division (Airmobile) as part of the 3rd Force Reconnaissance Battalion, B Company as well as being part of 5th Special Forces Group.

"But sir!" protested Reinhardt, "I think we should attack the Viet Cong encampment which we spotted 3 miles from the *Montagnard* village."

"Are you crazy? That's *Charlie's* point! He has over 1,000 men there! How can we attack them with only 24 Green Berets?" asked Captain Frank Willoughby in a lather.

"But isn't that our job?" asked Lieutenant Reinhardt.

"It fucking is not our mission here!" screamed back Willoughby.

As soon as he raised his voice several Sergeants and Warrant Officers who were playing cards at a nearby table looked apprehensively in their direction.

Willoughby continued, "Didn't you hear what Colonel David Lownds told us? We have to conserve our men and simply monitor the build up of forces in and around the DMZ and the territory from here to the Laos border. That's all! We are not supposed to mount any attacks."

Max Reinhardt nodded sheepishly and took a sip of his coffee.

"Jesus! Fuck!" screamed one of the Sergeants.

Suddenly the whole bunker they were in shuddered with a tremendous series of explosions.

"North Vietnamese heavy artillery!" screamed Willoughby as he threw himself to the floor.

"It must be 130mm shells!" groaned Lieutenant Reinhardt as his body swung sideways and hit a pile of sandbags.

The table that the other Green Berets were sitting and playing cards at was lifted into the air. The bodies of the six men had been flung through the atmosphere from the explosive concussion wave and then slammed back into the table, splintering it into toothpicks.

"Ahiee!" screamed one Sergeant as he lay next to Willoughby.

The left side of his face had been ripped away. The commander could see the contours of the severed blood vessels and the muscle tissue that was hanging in lacerated pieces from his features. A hot, sweet trickle of blood pulsed with each faint heartbeat over Willoughby's camouflage uniform as he tried to comfort the mutilated NCO.

"Medic! Medic! Over fucking here!" screamed Lieutenant Reinhardt.

The shelling intensified as their eardrums were hammered by the roar of high explosives.

Willoughby could smell the cordite of the munitions outside.

"I'll take care of him sir!" said a Corporal in the medical team as he scrambled on his hands and knees to the wounded man in Willoughby's arms.

"Do that!" remarked Willoughby as he grabbed Reinhardt's arm, "Come with me!"

The two officers scrambled up the wooden stairs and out of the makeshift bunker. The smell of burning flesh and hot blood mixed with cordite assailed their nostrils like a scent from hell itself.

Just as they were scrambling down towards a twin mortar emplacement manned by seven of their Green Berets, the earth erupted in a geyser of blood in front of them. At first Willoughby was blinded by the heavy artillery shell as his body was smacked to the ground. Then he saw bits of steel from jerry cans, a severed human hand, showers of intestines and a decapitated *Montagnard* head with its eyes rolled back, shoot up in front of him. The flotsam of the explosion then settled back to the earth as yet another explosion ripped the camp a hundred yards away.

Reinhardt managed to throw himself into the mortar emplacement.

"Fire you bastards! Fire!" screamed the Lieutenant.

"We haven't got the range yet sir," apologised a Sergeant who was still fiddling with the range finder.

"Give it here!" screamed Willoughby who just then threw himself headfirst into the mortar ditch as another shell exploded behind them while a wall of eruptions spewed the earth upwards in front of them near to the edge of the jungle.

"Do you think that this could be the Viet Cong's main assault on the *Lang Vei* camp?" asked Reinhardt over the deafening roar of 200 pound shells smashing into their dugouts and earth moving machinery in the camp.

Willoughby opened his mouth to speak but he couldn't find the words as he watched with horror as one of the five ton *Rome ploughs* nearby was catapulted into the air and then smashed down onto its steel tray. A second later, as diesel fuel spewed from a ruptured tank, it burst into flames.

"Cover! Take cover!" screamed Captain Willoughby.

But it was too late. The force of the explosion had disconnected the steel tray of the bulldozer and sent it flying towards their mortar emplacement.

"Oh! My Jesus!" was all that Willoughby had time to say as it struck. The two ton piece of steel cut into the ground as it flew and then bounced into the trench. The leading jagged saw edge of the monstrous piece of steel missed Captain Willoughby by inches. Everyone watched however, as it sliced into the cervical vertebrae of the mortar sergeant, neatly decapitating him with a smooth, oozing, blood lubricated movement.

Lieutenant Reinhardt stepped back with horror as the headless trunk of the Green Beret Sergeant fell limply into his outstretched arms, the tray of the bulldozer continuing to career out of control into the jungle foliage beyond.

Captain Willoughby screamed at the top of his lungs as he punched a nearby Corporal in the mouth. A tooth and blood mixed with saliva vomited outwards into his face.

"Didn't I tell you Corporal!" began Captain Willoughby as he yelled at the top of his lungs over the continuous roar of Viet Cong artillery fire, "…didn't I tell you,… you fuck-faced moron! To secure that bulldozer away from the compound over in the artillery park!"

The Corporal raised his arms over his face as Captain Willoughby smashed his fists from both left and right into his skull in a merciless rain of punches. The officer's hands were streamed with NCO blood.

Finally Captain Willoughby kicked the Corporal savagely in the crack of his ass, "Get the fuck out of here! Go back to the *COMMO* (communication) bunker. I shall decide whether to recommend you for your court martial!"

Willoughby watched as the Corporal scurried away. As the NCO was half way to the dugout he caught a piece of metal shrapnel in the side of his face. A geyser of blood erupted from his facial flesh as he twirled in the air like a martinet and then fell to the ground.

"Look sir!" yelled Lieutenant Reinhardt as he grabbed his commanding officer.

Willoughby wrenched a pair of binoculars out of a nearby soldier's hand. The mortar team was now pumping 81mm shells into both mortar devices as fast as their hands could move. The American shells were a mixture of high explosive and incendiary. The mortar blasts were detonating over 2 miles away into the jungle and where Captain Willoughby thought the North Vietnamese gun emplacements were.

"What the deuce is it Lieutenant?" asked the commander.

"Over there sir!" pointed Lieutenant Reinhardt, "…in the jungle just beyond the cleared killing zone."

As the heavy artillery shells crashed all around them, Willoughby could make out a group of *Montagnard* women and children scrambling through the jungle. The constant chatter of machine gun fire could be heard not only from his own M-60 machine guns but also from North Vietnamese machine gun emplacements in the jungle.

"Jesus Christ!" was all that Captain Frank Willoughby could say as he saw through his eyepiece a group of innocent *Montagnard* women and children being cut to pieces by a hail of Communist machine gun fire.

"Isn't there anything we can do to help them sir?" asked a Warrant Officer standing behind Captain Willoughby.

"I'm afraid not soldier!" yelled back the commander.

"But they will all be killed sir!" screamed back Lieutenant Reinhardt.

Willoughby thrust his finger into Reinhardt's chest, "Listen! I am not sparing any more of my men out there! It's a suicide mission to pull them back into the camp's perimeter. We wouldn't make it to the edge of the *'killing zone'*."

The so called *'killing zone'* was a circular expanse of ground that had been completely levelled and flattened free from jungle by heavy *Rome plough* bulldozers. This gave the Allied forces a clear field of fire as the North Vietnamese approached the base for a full frontal assault.

Willoughby saw what looked like a half-naked *Montagnard* woman running towards them out of the jungle. She had a baby in her left arm and a small infant in the other. Her belly was swollen and she looked pregnant. Suddenly, through his binoculars, Willoughby saw red points erupt through the women's flesh all around her abdomen. They looked like spots of paint. Then the points became holes and the holes spread out into ghastly mutilated cauldrons of vivisected human flesh and intestines. The North Vietnamese had plunged more than a hundred heavy calibre rounds into the pregnant *Montagnard* female. Her organs exploded upwards as her legs were cut in two. The blood and miasma of her own foetus was splashed into her eyes and nose. The child in her arms had had its entire body quartered by the North Vietnamese machine gun fire and the small infant tripped over the loose strands of it's mother's unwinding intestines.

"That does it!" screamed Willoughby. He could feel the rage and the anger boil in his arteries like an unquenchable tornado of hot, vicious blood lust. He wanted to murder every Viet Cong stooge. Bomb Hanoi to the oblivion of the *Triassic Age*.

"Get me the radio telephone!" he screeched.

"What?" asked a nearby Lance Corporal with surprise.

With a powerful movement of his cougar-like body, Captain Willoughby lashed around and slapped the soldier in the face so that the imprint of his palm was clearly visible on the man's features.

"The fucking radio telephone! Can't you understand plain dumb-assed English you insipid moron!" screamed the commanding officer.

Just then 155mm shells started to boom out from the Green Berets' howitzers of which they had five at the *Lang Vei* Camp. It took all of Captain Willoughby's 24 men to handle the five heavy howitzers. And that is exactly where they were now.

Five minutes later the telephone receiver was in Willoughby's hands and he was speaking to the Air Force Command duty officer at *Chu Lai* which had a large jet air base as well as tankers and C-130's.

"I want an air strike near the *Lang Vei Camp*," began Captain Willoughby.

"Copy that!" came back the methodical, almost robot-like voice of the air control officer.

"Here are the exact coordinates!" Willoughby read out the Latitude and Longitude and added, "If you have any napalm then I'd like to apply a heavy dosage."

The *Chu Lai* controller confirmed that a flight of F-4E's were in the area and that they should be able to execute a sortie in approximately five to six minutes.

"They are on their way!"

"Good!" answered Lieutenant Reinhardt.

Just then a Warrant Officer who had been feeding the mortar with shells was arched back in a whiplash action as if his spine was a bow with an arrow in it.

"What the fuck?" screamed Willoughby as the man struck him in the head with his back as he keeled over. An eruption of blood like the Captain had never seen vomited in a crimson sheet from the senior NCOs' mouth.

Reinhardt screeched, "He's been hit!"

"Jesus motherfucker!" yelled Willoughby, "…they are behind us! The North Vietnamese have encircled the camp!"

A buzz and a whirr of bullets streamed through the atmosphere as another Green Beret had the lower portion of his mouth severed off by an exploding dumb-dumb bullet. The tongue and the bottom row of teeth splashed Willoughby's face as he tried to pull the Warrant Officer into his arms.

"He's fucking dead sir!" screamed Reinhardt as the barrage of North Vietnamese heavy artillery seemed to intensify rather than diminish.

"I've lost another two men."

The private with the missing mouth was caught in a frenzied seizure on the ground. His hands and legs were whiplashing backwards and forwards like a Spitfire piston.

"God be screwed! Where is that lousy airstrike?" asked Willoughby. He knew that if they did not come soon his camp would be obliterated in a smorgasbord of death and utter destruction.

"There they are!" shouted one Corporal who had already given up on the mortars.

As if God himself had answered Captain Willoughby's call for help, out of the sky, like bread and fish from heaven itself came the resurrection and the light. It was a Godsend. It was the living son of God that Christ of pure, vicious, blood bursting firepower.

"It's come! Take cover! Take cover!" screamed the Captain.

The roar was awesome and it was beautiful to the ears of the American soldiers. This was justice! This was might! This was the roar of victory in Vietnam. This was the heaven opening up like a thunder of sacramental retribution upon the heads of the brutal North Vietnamese foe. From out of the afternoon sun came a flock of 12 F-4E *Phantom* fighter bombers. The Green Berets at the *Lang Vei* camp crouched low in their fox holes and bunkers and plugged their ears with their fingers so that the eardrums and the tympanic membranes of their middle ears would not be broken,

first by the roar of the engines and second by the even louder cacophony of the high explosives.

"It's pay back time!" said the Captain to Reinhardt. The Lieutenant simply watched as more than 2 million horsepower bore down upon the Communist positions at a speed of 500 mph.

"It's fantastic!" said a Corporal next to Reinhardt as he watched with awe.

Reinhardt clasped the crucifix that was strung around his neck. He watched and waited for the coming of the light. The 12 *Phantoms* split formation with the precision of a fine Swiss watch. Six fighter bombers peeled off to the left in a gentle arc of massive horsepower. They would come in for the second round. The first group of six came in low and started to reduce their speed from 500 to barely 300 mph. They took up line abreast positions.

"They've got it right this time!" shouted the Captain over the heart wrenching roar.

The noses of the *Phantoms* seemed to bob backwards and forwards like thoroughbred stallions jockeying for position. And then it came.

A brilliant flash and a sound like ripping thunder shuddered the earth and all the creatures large and small upon it.

Willoughby could see a wall of flame that was napalm rise up like the Armageddon of God. It was exactly where the Green Beret officer had wanted the airstrike to be.

"The whole jungle is on fire!" said Reinhardt as he let his fingers out of his ears.

As the first row of six *Phantoms* arched up and went vertical they increased their speed to supersonic. As they came around again they had no bombs left but their sonic boom ripped the very fabric of the atmosphere above the heads of the North Vietnamese and their Viet Cong stooges. The blast of the million horsepower travelling at 850 mph tore at the very flesh of the enemy. His guts exploded, his eyes turned to jelly, his spleen was eviscerated and his liver became a miasma of blood. The American pilots then dropped their 1 ton empty fuel drop tanks into the Viet Cong positions. As they plummeted earthwards like blocks of steel, whole rows of trees were battered down by the beautiful sight of the impact.

"It's the second attack coming in!" said Captain Willoughby as he ordered his 155mm howitzers to cease firing.

Above even the roar of fire and the crackling of jungle debris, the Captain could hear what sounded like a deep and sorrowful cry. It grew and grew in intensity and was like the cry of a child, muffled and agonised in the last minutes of its life. Then Willoughby realised that it was not the cry of a single child but the wall of an entire community of adults. It was the Viet Cong bodies that had once been so strong and proud just a few moments ago. These bodies that were now dripping flesh like rivulets

of molasses. It was the hot, sweet sting of petrochemical napalm that washed over them like the veil of merciful death. The Captain knew that already this enemy battalion was finished. It was done. The resurrection of Christ and his vengeance had come to pass.

It had been ordained by God for the Victory of the West over the Communist Oriental scourge and pestilence.

"Listen?" said Reinhardt with amazement.

Captain Willoughby asked, "What?" As he turned in the mortar trench he noticed that two more of his men had died. One had the left side of his head avulsed by a flying piece of metal. Brain matter was slowly and gracefully oozing out from his cerebrum. The second man had lost his right arm from the shoulder down. The severed limb was nowhere to be seen but the soldier was in deep shock from loss of blood and mutilation trauma.

"The artillery! Its stopped!" noticed Reinhardt.

It was true. Like a tap that had been suddenly turned off. The rain of enemy shells was no more.

"It's a miracle," said one Sergeant as he started to cry like a maladjusted child.

The Captain scoffed and slapped him on the back, "Its not a fucking miracle! Its American firepower!"

And then all of Willoughby's Green Berets as well as the 900 *Montagnard* ragtag band of CIDG men could hear it.

"Oh! My Jesus! Have mercy on them!" said one nameless soldier.

It was a hideous screaming noise coming out of the jungle. The sound of it was worse than any animal could make. Now that the barrage had lifted and their own guns had stopped firing everybody could make it out.

"The second air strike is coming in!" said Lieutenant Reinhardt as he shook his head.

A Warrant officer asked the Captain, "Sir! Do you think we should call the second strike off? The VC are already finished. We would just be slaughtering the wounded."

Willoughby turned around in a fit of rage as he struck the cheeks of the NCO with his brutal fists.

"You fucking sanctimonious idiot! How do you know that? How do you know that all the VC are dead or wounded? I guarantee you that not even 20% of the fuckers have been taken out!"

The Warrant Officer retreated back and said nothing more.

"Here they go!" screamed the Captain. And just before the second row of *Phantoms* struck, *Charlie* recommenced his machine gun fire from the jungle beyond. Even some Soviet and Chinese made RPG rocket launchers slammed into the COMMO bunker behind them.

"See you fuck-heads! *'Charlie'* isn't finished! He's just taken a coffee break!"

Reinhardt and the Captain laughed until their sides split. The other Green Berets, however, just cringed morosely in their trenches. They waited for the merciful end. And it came with the second napalm strike. After it was all over and the enemy shelling had ceased, all was quiet except for occasional and sporadic machine gun fire and tracer shells that streaked across the red-orange glow of the dusk that was almost upon them. Later that night when it was over, the Captain was summing up the day's losses.

"Five men killed and three wounded. That means I have only 16 able-bodied men left."

Lieutenant Reinhardt asked, "What do you think we should do? Do you think we should get Colonel Lownds on the blower and ask him to abandon our position here at *Lang Vei*?"

Willoughby growled with disgust, "What are you Lieutenant? A fucking yellow bellied coward?"

"No sir!"

"Then why do you say we should abandon our position here?"

The Lieutenant stammered and spluttered – caught off guard by the stinging rebuke from his fanatical commanding officer.

Reinhardt was scared of no one, except Captain blood and guts Willoughby.

"So why don't we call up Colonel Lownds and ask him to abandon *his* position at *Khe Sanh* as well? Just in case," continued Captain Willoughby sarcastically.

"Or for that matter why don't we speak to General Westmoreland and tell him that the whole 3rd Marine Amphibious Force, including the 3rd Division, is abandoning its position in I Corps Operational Zone. Let's leave the Army boys to take care of things here! We Marines and Green Berets can abandon our position in the whole of South Vietnam and go fucking home for New Years!"

Some of the Sergeants and senior NCOs' laughed as Captain Willoughby spoke. Lieutenant Reinhardt felt humiliated and shut his mouth.

"Anyway! I'm going out! I think its time I did another reconnaissance of the *Montagnard* village and our friends there."

A Corporal by the name of Jameison jumped up and saluted the Captain.

"Pardon me sir!" Jameison was only five foot seven inches and weighed about 81 kilograms. But he was an exceptional Green Beret and had already clocked up 7 Viet Cong kills to his credit in hand-to-hand combat. Captain Willoughby knew him and trusted his abilities.

"What do you want Corporal?"

Jameison cringed forward in a submissive stance, "Permission to accompany the Captain on his reconnaissance and provide assistance sir!"

Willoughby clapped Jameison on the shoulders affectionately, "You are a good man Corporal. But this time I'm going by myself."

Lieutenant Reinhardt said, "Good luck sir."

"I should be back by dawn Lieutenant. But if I'm not then send a search party for me."

"Will do Captain."

Willoughby was deep in the jungle and already past the cleared *'killing zone'* of the *Lang Vei* camp. He knew that the Viet Cong were everywhere. They never rested or slept. Sometimes Willoughby thought that they were superhuman. But after careful consideration he knew that *'Charlie'* was just super-scum.

They were oppressors and stinking vermin trying to subjugate a free and independent South Vietnam.

The Milky Way was clearly visible and it shone through the jungle leaves like a plethora of beautiful and variegated points of light.

"Like a thousand points of light."

The Captain looked up at the spangled firmament. The air was hot and tepid. His body coursed with sweat that meandered down the crevice in his spine and washed uncomfortably inside the cheeks of his ass.

"Fuck it!" whispered Willoughby to himself as he slapped his hand to his neck. A large, black leech had attached itself to his skin. He could feel the sting of the bite as it sucked his blood through the thin epidermal layer of his flesh and then into the arterioles and venules of his circulatory system. Leeches carried malaria and other unsavoury diseases such as *Dengy* fever. Just in case, the Captain popped a quinine tablet in his mouth to counteract these scourges of the Third World and their grinding, relentless poverty.

But the Captain cursed to himself. He should not even have whispered. The North Vietnamese were everywhere. There could be a whole platoon of them just yards away from him at this very second.

The Green Beret officer knew all the booby traps that the Viet Cong loved to use. His feet stepped across the jungle slowly and with reverent awe and caution. Any false movement, a carless twinge of his tired body could mean sudden and terrible death.

The Viet Cong delighted in causing unnecessary suffering and trauma to the liberating and protecting American solider. They used tin-can grenades which were ordinary grenades placed in appropriately sized tin cans. The only difference was that the safety pin was removed. The tin-cans were tied to trees, usually two at a time with a wire attached from one tree to the other. The more effective trap had tin-can grenades attached to both trees. A pull on the wire by a human body extracts the grenade which then primes itself and explodes. Serious injury or death is the result. But Captain Willoughby was especially cautious of the *'Spiked Ball.'*

The Spiked Ball was a heavy mud ball which had *punji* stakes embedded into it. This gruesome medieval device was then attached to a tree by an apparently innocuous jungle vine that blended in with the jungle undergrowth. A trip-wire was installed so that when the young American GI stepped forward breaking the wire, the spiked ball would swing out and savagely arc across the track impaling the soldier on the razor sharp *punji* stakes in a nightmarish mutilation of flesh and blood.

The *Punji* stake traps used the sharpened stake of that name which was placed in a shallow pit in the vertical position. Many *punji* stakes were used and embedded upright in the floor of the pit. The man sized pit was then covered with camouflage twigs, leafs and foliage so that it would hide the treacherous pit and look seemingly innocent. The depth of the pit was sufficient so that when the soldier stepped into it, enough force was applied to drive the stakes through his boot and into his flesh. The mutilation was horrifying. Some traps had *punji* stakes attached to the walls of the pit as well, facing downwards. Thus when the soldier attempted to pull his mutilated foot out of the trap he was given additional mutilation from the sides which cut into his calves and thighs for added horror. All these devices Captain Willoughby knew well. His eyes and ears were on full alert for these nasty practical jokes of the enemy.

After half an hour of careful manoeuvring through a hardly visible jungle path the Captain came upon the small *Montagnard* village. It had been constantly raided by the Viet Cong and North Vietnamese but now most of the 900 men were stationed in the *Lang Vei* camp for protection.

The moon was out and it was eerily quiet. Willoughby could hear his own breath come in short, spasmodic gasps. He tried to soothe his lungs, slow them, relax his sweat drenched torso. His eyes circled around like a hawk as he almost bent double and scurried into the largest straw hut which was in the middle of the village.

He opened the rickety straw door and immediately felt the keen edge of a dagger at his back.

He froze in terror. Then a voice spoke. It was female and it was in Vietnamese. Captain Willoughby could speak perfect Vietnamese as he relaxed slightly.

He knew the voice well.

"It's Frank!" he whispered with urgency.

The tip of the dagger was drawn back from his flesh.

The Captain turned around as the female voice said, "What took you so long? We've been waiting for you!"

"I'm sorry darling! But you heard the attack today."

Frank Willoughby felt the keen, razor sharp blade being withdrawn from his spine and in its place he could feel the warm, soft hand of a very pretty South Vietnamese girl.

"Are you alright?" she asked as she clasped her arms around Frank's huge shoulders.

"I think so," he smirked and added, "...but I almost got killed today by the shelling. A *Rome plough* bulldozer blew up in my face."

The 19 year old Vietnamese girl cried, "Oh! Frank! I would die if anything happened to you!"

His lips sucked on hers in a passionate kiss. Their tongues intertwined in a miasma of loving. He could feel the cool elixir of her young saliva. The Captain was so tall at six foot two that even when the girl was on her toes she could barely reach his neck with her arms.

"Nothing is going to happen to me! Don't worry your pretty little head about that – Monica!"

The South Vietnamese girl's name was Monica Thang. She was five foot three inches tall and she had a lovely cute and cuddly appearance. Her hair was jet black but she had warm green eyes. Her figure was slim and athletic with fine curves all around. Her breast invited caressing and fondling with a fine degree of tactility. Her buttocks had a beautiful cleavage in them and her skin was like marble as it shone with a radiant glow of health.

"I've fixed you some rice, come!" she said as they hugged.

"I'm only hungry for your flesh!"

They both laughed. The straw hut was dark and quiet.

They stripped off each other's clothes and lay naked in the humid air upon an old mattress.

"I've missed you so much Frank!" she cried and the clear droplets of lachrymal fluid coursed over the beauty of her naked breasts.

The Captain held her right breast and licked the tear drops off her flesh by stroking his long, coarse tongue around her ruby coloured nipples. Monica grasped his stiffened penis in her hand and rubbed it with expert aplomb.

"I want you to make love to me," she moaned.

With a swift, agile movement he rolled her body on-top of his and placed her pelvis over his face. Monica glued her lips to the red ridge of his glistening penis while he drove his hungry tongue into the orifice of her *mons labia*.

"Oh! Move your tongue in deeper!" she cried.

The Captain held his seed in check as Monica's gorgeous face pumped up and down on his gargantuan reproductive device.

The lovemaking was hot and sweet.

They could not give a fuck about the war at that moment only about fucking each other.

"Move over here!" grunted Willoughby.

He put one hand on her head and guided it to his testicular organs.

She licked them with savage lust.

Suddenly he could feel the warm liquid of her vaginal excretions over his face and lips as she climaxed while he probed into the realm of her rectum with first one and then two fingers like an exploratory surgeon.

"Sodomise me deeper!" Monica yelled as she bucked to yet another delicious and heart-warming orgasm.

"I want your womb to fuck!" grunted Willoughby.

"Then take it my gorgeous American lover! Liberator of our country – the Republic of South Vietnam!" screamed Monica as she smothered kisses over the Captain's bearded face.

He flipped her onto her back and slid his hands underneath her warm, soft ass cheeks. Her vagina was moist and slippery with genuine desire and he slid into her easily and deliciously.

"Oh! Monica! It feels so good!" moaned the Captain.

"I want you to enjoy my forbidden organs my love!" she whispered as she nibbled on his ear and licked his neck.

They fucked beautifully in the missionary position for more than thirty minutes and while they copulated so serenely they could hear the distant sound of machine gun fire and mortar explosions, coupled with the shrieks of the dying.

Captain Willoughby had met Monica Thang when he was on *R & R* in Saigon. Monica had been a 3rd year medical student at Saigon University in 1966. The war, however, had forced her to return home to *Lang Vei* to care for her younger sister and her parents. She had watched one night in January 1967 when the Viet Cong had come into her village and pack raped her sixty year old mother. She was forced to witness her mother being disembowelled by the Communists as they fucked and then sodomised her simultaneously. Her father, much to her growing suspicions, was not in the village at the time. It was a miracle she escaped with her life. Monica and her 14 year old sister, Susan, had fled into the jungle. They lived on wild berries and juniper until they finally thought it was safe enough to go back to the village. When they returned they saw a field of naked and mutilated corpses that used to be their friends and relatives in the forlorn and devastated community centre. It was from that moment onwards that the Chief of their *Montagnard* village had sworn to fight the Viet Cong and the North Vietnamese unto the death.

Earlier in Saigon, Captain Willoughby originally met Monica at a dinner reception organised by the American Embassy and Ambassador Ellsworth Bunker. They were immediately attracted to each other physically. Their emotions blossomed with the delicious physical enjoyment they gave one another in copious quantities and at the dead of night.

As the Captain gently pumped in and out of Monica's fine and succulent womb, he remembered how they had sneaked out of the Embassy reception back to his hotel in the *Cholon District*. The lovemaking then was intense and supremely gratifying. That first night of their affair they tried every possible variation and combination of positions for copulation that bordered on the extreme envelopes of what was physically and manually possible. The bed-sheets were soaked with sweat, semen and female juices as they collapsed in the morning out of sheer exhaustion from their extracurricular activities.

A week later Monica abandoned her medical course and devoted her full time to Captain Willoughby. She cooked for him, shared his bed and did shopping for him until he had to return to duty.

"Let me sit on top of you my darling," said Monica softly, her lovely green eyes flashing in the darkness of the pathetic and rat infested straw hut that smelled of pig shit.

The Captain did not ejaculate but lifted Monica's slim and perspiring body over his groin. She pinched the head of his penis between her thumb and forefinger and sucked it energetically before sliding it inside her fundament once more. As Monica rode her American lover the Captain gorged himself on her firm and dainty breasts.

"Oh! Fucking Jesus! I'm coming!" groaned the officer.

As her lover exploded his viscous semen in her womb, Monica gripped his testicles from behind and squeezed until every last ounce of juice was evacuated from his groin sacks.

"Do you think you can take me to America?" asked Monica when they lit up a cigarette and lay peacefully on a pile of cushions on the mattress.

Before answering her the Captain looked at the slim, brown and immaculately shaped legs that were entwined around his own.

He didn't need any time at all to make up his mind.

"Of course I want to take you back with me! I love you Monica!"

"I love you too Frank!" she answered as they kissed.

Then she pursed her lips, "And my little sister, Susan?"

The Captain held her small attractive head in his hands and said softly, "Do you think if I am going to marry you I would leave your pretty sister here alone?"

Monica shook her head and took a sip of whisky which Willoughby had in a small flask.

"Of course I love your sister Susan as well," said the Green Beret as he caressed his lover's breasts and the delicate mound of her vagina.

"She will have a room right next to ours with an adjoining door."

"What is life like in America?" she asked full of excitement and joy.

"It is wonderful as long as you have plenty of money," began Willoughby.

He gulped down some whisky and continued, "America is the land of the free and the home of the brave! It is God's country. And the more money you have – the freedom and the bravery comes easier to you. There is no other country like it. It is the beacon for democracy around the world. America is the peacemaker. America is always willing to help a less advantaged people and come to their aid in the face of dirty and murderous Communist aggression and subversion. It also allows the *US War Machine* to try out its new weaponry and technology, which is even better!"

Monica asked with wonder, "Is that why you are here in South Vietnam? To help us with new technology?"

The Captain said with total conviction, "Of course! We are here to maintain the American way of life. It is the American way. The path of truth, justice, democracy and opportunity for all. Those are the ingredients for society we are trying to protect in South Vietnam for the good of all people in this Asian continent. We want to make South Vietnam a carbon copy of the United States."

"It is an admirable quest that your President has embarked on," commented Monica as her pretty face beamed with a beautiful smile.

The Captain spoke with ardour, "I am proud to be an American! I am proud to be an American soldier. And I can assure you right now that we shall never let South Vietnam fall into the hands of the Viet Cong and their North Vietnamese masters!" Then he added, "But the President didn't decide this by himself, the *Military-Industrial Complex* call the shots in America."

"I'm so glad to hear your reassurances," said Monica as she stroked her hands lovingly through the hair on the Captain's chest.

"Do you want to know where we shall live?" asked Willoughby.

"Where?" exploded Monica with great joy in her heart.

"I have bought a house in Florida. It is a fine three storey house. It has many rooms, three bathrooms…"

Monica interrupted, "Three bathrooms!"

He laughed, "Yes! It is in St. Petersburg in Florida."

Monica asked, "Where is Florida?"

"Florida is in the south-east of the United States. It is one of the warmest parts of America. The life is peaceful and happy there and more so if you have plenty of money. After all! I am not going to be a soldier all my life."

Monica giggled and kissed the Captain's chest with lust and passion.

"The three of us can all be happy here! You, Susan and I. I will initiate her myself into the pleasures and sensual ways of our Western Society so that her flesh and desire will want for nothing but be totally satiated with lubricious excess. I will do the rites myself."

"I can't wait to go to Florida with you! Wherever that fucking place is on the map. Geography was never my strong point at school. I blame it on the Communist swine. We can have our wedding there!"

Suddenly, in the darkness of the squalid and shitty straw hut the Captain heard a noise outside. He froze. He put his finger on Monica's lips.

"What is it? I can't hear anything," whispered Monica as her luscious breasts rested languidly on Willoughby's massive chest. In the next second the door to the straw hut opened and a figure walked in.

The Captain jumped to his feet and was at the door with the speed of lightning. He clasped the intruder to his naked body, a knife to its throat. But the body was small and female.

"Oh! Its you Susan!"

The little five foot zero South Vietnamese girl smiled up at the naked Captain and he bent down, kissing her with as much passion as he had Monica, with tongue to tongue.

"Come here you little thing!" said Monica to her fourteen year old sister.

Susan was extremely attractive with a small round face and delicate features. Like Monica she was slim but slightly smaller, with budding breasts and a finely contoured body.

"I've got you!" laughed the Captain as he picked Susan up in his arms and carried her over to the mattress.

"I'm glad you came Frank. Will you take us to America now?"

Willoughby and Monica laughed heartily as the three of them lay down on the bed. Susan took off her blouse and her skirt as the Captain ran his hands across her naked legs and buttocks.

"I love you too Frank!" said Susan excitedly.

"Yes! We both love and adore you Frank," said Monica as she guided her sister's body so that Frank lay in-between them.

"Is it allowed in America for you to have two wives?" asked the fourteen year old girl.

The Captain smirked, "No! But don't worry! You can both share my bed! There is no law against that once Susan turns sixteen! But out here you don't have to give a fuck about the law because there is none."

Susan kissed the Captain as he held her body right up against his massive torso. He could feel the sweat from both girls run over his muscles. The body odour of the females was like rose petals in full bloom or the scent of a tropical garden in the lush forests of Sumatra.

Monica moaned with delight and performed fellatio on the officer and *Captain of America* as he kissed the fourteen year old. Her tongue was sweet and fragrant.

"Let Susan try," said Willoughby as he guided Susan's mouth to his member. Both sisters then licked and savoured that long, red shaft as they alternately sucked on the head which was glistening with engorged blood.

"This is supreme! Its delicious!" screamed the *Captain of America*.

The threesome was hot and energetic. Only lust prevailed.

Willoughby lay Susan on her back and encunted her with relish.

Surprisingly the hymen was already broken from stretching and daily work. Her womb was tight but delightfully warm and moist. Untrammelled as yet by any other.

"Do you like it?" asked Monica as she kissed her sister while Frank kissed her own breasts as he made love to Susan.

The three of them kissed each other in rotation, their three tongues intertwining in a ménage of affection and physical enjoyment. This was the first time for more than two years that the Captain had made love to two girls at once. Then Willoughby had Monica sit on his face and he performed cunnilingus on her while anchoring her down by inserting three fingers into her rectum. The gorgeous little Susan was re-fucked as she sat on the officer's pelvis, his device embedded deeply inside her small organ. In that position the three of them climaxed with a profusion of kissing, sucking, caressing and licking. The entire straw hut seemed to simmer with their illicit lovemaking.

"I want to see you love each other," said Willoughby.

"What do you mean?" asked Monica as she wiped the ejaculate off her face.

The *Captain of America* placed the two girls in the sixty-nine position and they eagerly ate each other in-between kisses and giggles.

The Green Beret master soldier then penetrated both girls in the *doggie style* as well as alternating from normal to sodomitical sex. First he would kneel behind Monica as the sisters sucked each other and then he would mount the tiny Susan from the other end of their delicious battle formation. This went on for more than an hour until Monica ran outside and came back with some savoury Mangoes.

"That was beautiful," exclaimed Frank as his body was saturated with the sweat of all three of them.

"Ooooh!" was all that Susan giggled as she cuddled up to the *Captain of America*. As he ate the wonderful fruit of temptation he placed Susan over his groin and slid into her once more to the pits of her fundament.

"Here my little darling, have some of this," he handed the fourteen year old the tempting fruit while Monica entwined her arms around both of them.

"I have something serious to tell you Frank," said the older sister.

Willoughby looked at Monica with a mixture of curiosity and suspicion.

"What is that?" he asked as he licked the mango juice from his tongue onto Susan's small breasts as he grew stiffer inside her womb.

"It's my father," answered Monica.

"And what about your fucking father?" replied Willoughby brutally.

Monica said with anger and defiance in her voice, "He is a fucking spy and a traitor to democracy! To the magnificence of freedom that the United States represents! The leader of the Free World as we know it! He is a Communist pig!"

The Captain's mouth fell open while his hands gripped the slim, sweet ass of the teenager, forcing her deeper into his projectile.

"You mean for the stinking Viet Cong?"

Monica laughed, "Of course! Who else?"

Then the *Captain of America* said, "How do you know he is a traitor to the Capitalist system that we adore?"

Monica riposted, "I know!"

"You must be sure that he is guilty of being an enemy to the free market supply and demand system of the Western economies! After all he is your own father! Even though that in itself means less than pig's shit to me."

Monica jeered, "He is my father but he is also a Viet Cong pig and a *Scheißkerl*."

Willoughby asked, "What did you say? A what…?"

"*Er ist ein Scheißstich*"

Monica translated from the German, "I said he is a fucking prick!"

"Oh! I see!" then Willoughby added, "I did not know that you speak German?"

Monica replied, "I am a woman of many talents. I learnt German because I am a student of military history and in my opinion the *Wehrmacht* is the only army in the world that can attack simultaneously in opposite directions with less than 24 hours notice."

"But what about the American Army?"

"I am talking about the period 1939 to 1945."

The *Captain of America* conceded at once, "Oh! Yes of course! The German Army was far superior to any other army in the world at that time which included our freedom fighters in the US Army of that period."

Monica nodded as if it was common knowledge.

The Green Beret asked, "Alright he is a traitor. But what do you want me to do about it?"

Monica looked surprised and said without hesitation, "I want you to kill him! What do you think?"

Willoughby rubbed his chin as he threw the half-finished mango into the corner of the straw hut where it was immediately set upon by rats that scurried out of nowhere. Monica thought that they must be Communist rats.

"Kill him?" said the *Captain of America*, "I… I'm, not sure about that."

"What the fuck do you mean?" said Monica viciously as she ran her tongue across the face of Willoughby, trying to soften him up for some gratuitous murder.

"I am not an assassin Monica! I have to follow military law. I have to obey the code of conduct of the United States Army," he said with exasperation.

He added, "I can't go around killing non-combatants just because you ask me to!"

Monica interjected immediately, "But he is a combatant!" Willoughby pricked up his ears, "He is?"

"Yes!"

Susan was oblivious to their conversation as Willoughby continued to make love to her as she sucked his nipples.

"Did you see him with a gun?"

Monica threw her head back and explained, "About three months ago when I was hiding in the jungle about three miles from the *Lang Vei* camp, I saw my father with a large number of Viet Cong, perhaps 400 to 500 men. He was carrying an AK-47 Soviet assault rifle and he was interrogating a group of South Vietnamese peasants who had refused to supply the Viet Cong swine with food and supplies."

Willoughby was fascinated, "What did he do then?"

Monica slapped him playfully on the thigh and pinched her sister's naked buttocks, "If you fuck'n shut up and let me finish I'll tell you!"

The Captain nodded and moaned as he was close to coming into the delightful Asian fourteen year old.

"My father was punching several old women and asking them a lot of foolish questions. He then brought out the sons of these women and their grandchildren. The other Viet Cong questioned them as well. I was hiding up in a tree about 100 yards away. The questioning went on for the whole morning. My stinking pig of a father then took out his knife and he started to slice slivers of flesh off the women's face, neck and breasts. He was soon covered in blood. Then he would begin punching and kicking the women. He threatened them that if they would not tell him of American troop movements in the region he would begin raping them and cutting off the testicles of their sons and grandsons. The old women did not believe him. So they were all brutally raped by about fifty of the Viet Cong including my father."

The Green Beret said, "This sounds very disagreeable and disturbing!"

Monica continued, "My father then grabbed the youngest boy who was about six years old. The child was the grandson of one of the old women who were now lying naked in the mud and still being continually raped by endless lines of Viet Cong bastards. My father used a rusty knife and severed off the testicles of the young child right in front of the grandmother's face.

Es war ein Totalmisserfolg!"

Willoughby interjected, "What? What was that last thing you said?"

"I said it was a total fiasco! You better learn some German yourself so that you don't keep asking me stupid language questions!" She scoffed as she spoke and went

on, "The old woman cried with horror and pain in her shrieking wails for mercy for her children. But my father simply laughed and spat into her face. He then forced the grandmother to eat the mutilated gonads which he himself stuffed into her mouth. Then he gathered the blood from the emasculated boy and…"

Captain Willoughby was horrified, "That's enough! I've heard enough! Stop! I feel sick to my guts!"

Monica smiled and asked, "Shall we continue our lovemaking instead?"

"No!" yelled the Captain as he ejaculated into Susan.

"So you see he is a combatant and a spy against the American liberators here in Vietnam."

Willoughby dressed back in his camouflage uniform and general purpose boots. The twin sliver Captain's bars shining on his epaulettes.

"In my opinion he is not *de jure* but a *de facto* enemy of the state according to *Public International Law*. However, pursuant to the *Geneva Conventions of 1949* and the *Hague Conventions* on the Laws of War he may be properly classified as a combatant as you say. Thus, I have come to the conclusion that he must be liquidated, killed! Your father is a homicidal maniac! My killing cannot be classified as such as my combat is State sanctioned whereas his killing is clearly not and thus in contravention of the international statute law and also *customary international law* as I have just postulated."

"I told you so!" jeered Monica with delight.

"Where is the disagreeable person. The bastard? This Viet Cong pimp that is your father?" asked the Captain as he took out his Special Forces dagger and checked its razor sharpness. Willoughby's knife was over 18 inches long and it had a serrated edge on one side and a gutting groove in the middle to suck out the innards of his hapless victims. But no victim was going to be so deserving as this individual who happened to be the father of the two girls he had just fornicated with.

"You are in luck my darling!" cried Monica sweetly as she dressed with Susan and then started for the door to the decrepit little hut.

"He's here?" asked Willoughby, the blood pulsing through his musculature.

"Yes! I'll show you. I noticed the scum-sucker come into the village just before you arrived."

"Let's go then!" said Willoughby as he picked up his M-60 machine gun which he always carried with him on solitary patrol. Even though the M-60 was exceedingly heavy at about 28 pounds, Willoughby loved to have the firepower to back up his missions. As they emerged from the stinking hut that was surrounded with pig manure and bird droppings as well as Communist rats, the Captain suddenly turned in his tracks.

"Susan! You better stay here in the hut and hide. This is not going to be pleasant."

Monica grabbed Susan as she started away.

"No! I want her to witness the death of her father. It will be edifying for her. The stinking, motherfucking traitor and Viet Cong pimping coward!"

"As you wish," said Willoughby as he shrugged his shoulders nonchalantly and added, "Don't blame me if she gets *post-traumatic stress syndrome* because I am not going to pay for her treatment in Florida. I need the money for booze and cocaine and a new plasma television."

The three of them crawled in the shadows through the village which was almost deserted. The Viet Cong had almost taken everything there was to take including the village girls and boys whom they had raped and sodomised respectfully as a form of terror against other villages they subjugated. The *'Pacification Program'* run by the Central Intelligence Agency [CIA] was going extremely well and 90% of South Vietnamese villages detested the hated Viet Cong murderers and pimps.

"What is a plasma television?" asked Monica suddenly.

Willoughby told her to shut-the-fuck-up.

Captain America could see by the romantic moonlight, several dozen half decomposed bodies strewn around the huts and animal pens of the village enclosure that smelled like shit as did the rest of the country.

"Did the Viet Cong do this?" asked the *Captain of America*.

"Of course! Who the fuck else do you think could have done it?" said Monica laughing and wiping a tear of hilarity from her eye as she spoke.

"They didn't even have the decency to bury their poor victims!"

Susan gripped both of them suddenly and signalled them to be quiet.

The Captain could see a villager coming towards them from a large hut. It was not clear whether he was a Viet Cong or not. The three of them walked out from the shadows and confronted him directly.

"Who are you?" asked the Vietnamese man in his own language.

He looked surprised when Willoughby answered in his native tongue.

"Get the fuck out of my way!"

The man said, "You leave this village!"

Willoughby pushed him roughly aside with his fist.

Then the man erupted into a fit of berserk rage. He started shouting Vietnamese obscenities at the Captain and the two girls.

He grabbed Willoughby around by the neck and strangled him.

"You prick!" shouted the Captain.

The Green Beret inserted his arms in-between the outstretched limbs of his attacker and gripped them so hard that he could feel the humerus cracking under his vice-like grip. He then head butted the Asian man with terrible force. A second and a third head butt smashed into the much smaller man's skull until he was reeling. With his grip broken, Willoughby arched forward and punched the man directly into his

nasal septum. The blow was so devastating and accurate that the man's skull cracked from his brow to his cervical spine.

"Watch this!" said Willoughby to Monica and Susan.

Taking out his Special Forces dagger, the Captain sliced deliciously into the liver of the suspected Viet Cong. He drove his knife downwards and then sideways while biting the Asian man's tongue in-between his teeth. He used all his massive power until he could feel the blade mutilating horizontally, the colon, large intestines and then left kidney. The abdominal aorta was severed at the level of *thoracic 9* and the man drowned cruelly in his own blood as the Captain gave him one final crushing blow into his testicles.

"Fuck you!" screamed Willoughby as he tore the Asian's tongue clean from the roots of his mouth, spitting the organ into the mud.

"That was excellent!" began Monica, "I have never seen such a professional kill! You are a superlative and magnificent warrior! I love you so much *Captain America*!"

Monica was brimming with undiluted enthusiasm as the Captain asked, "So where is your murdering, motherfucking father?"

"He is in a large hut where this pig just came from."

Willoughby slowly walked up the dirt incline and peeped through the cracks in the bamboo walls of the structure.

Turning his head from side to side through the angle of the crack he could see three men and a woman. The female was kneeling on the floor and performing fellatio on one of the men who was sitting on a chair and eating chicken while he talked to the other two. They were all talking excitedly and gesticulating with their arms. All three of them were Viet Cong infiltrators.

Willoughby could tell by the black pyjama-like pantaloons and tunics they were wearing.

"Do you see anything?" asked Monica as he moved away from the wall.

"Yes!" The Captain ushered his lover forward, "Take a look. Tell me which one is your father."

Monica and Susan both crept up to the exterior wall like small mice. They took a peep and nodded to each other.

"Well?" asked the Captain.

"The one being sucked by that Viet Cong whore is my father. The dirty lime-sucking traitor."

"I see!" whistled Willoughby.

Susan said with hatred in her eyes, "Make him suffer horribly!"

The Captain looked surprised, "So you are sure you want me to perform patricide for you by proxy?"

Monica said seriously, "If you kill the son-of-a-bitch for us then it won't be patricide at all!"

The Captain laughed softly as he tongue kissed both gorgeous girls.

"It will be a type of summary justice as you said validated by your interpretation of *customary international law* and the exigencies of battlefield conditions."

All three of them held back their mirth.

Willoughby put his forefinger to his lips indicating silence.

The two girls slunk back into the shadows at the bottom of the straw hut as the Green Beret Captain bounded forward up the stairs.

"Here goes!" whispered Captain Willoughby under his hot, acrid breath. He could still taste the bodily juices of the two sisters in his mouth as he savagely kicked open the door to the filthy hut.

The four people inside froze as the figure ripped viciously into the room. Monica's father allowed the piece of chicken in his mouth to drop to the floor as Willoughby flung a dagger into the nearest man's chest. The blade pierced the heart of the Viet Cong and he fell limply to the floor.

"Prepare to die!" screamed Willoughby.

"Who are you?" asked Monica's father in utter bewilderment.

The woman who was kneeling reared back in shock. Her greasy mouth slid off the man's still rigid organ, saliva and semen dribbling from the corners of her mouth in a delicious cocktail of love making and debauchery.

"I am your executioner according to international law! You stinking traitor!" shouted Willoughby as he lunged forward over the carcass of the first Viet Cong grabbing the second in a headlock.

Unexpectedly Monica and Susan burst into the room.

"I told you to stay outside!" screamed the Captain as he rammed the head of the man in his arms against a steel spike.

"Ahiee!" the victim shouted.

The Captain whirled the skinny Viet Cong soldier around the room and slammed his body from left to right into all the furniture he could find. Blood gushed out from every conceivable pore.

"So there you are father," said Monica with disgust. She stepped up to her seated father and slapped him hard across the face. In a few seconds he lost his erection as the whore who had sucked him made for the door.

But the Captain was too quick and agile in his expert homicidal movements.

"No you don't!"

He bounded towards the naked Vietnamese whore and sliced the tip of his steel boot into her crotch with horrible affect.

The woman doubled over with a terrible shriek as the boot penetrated the soft flesh of her fury vagina. Blood oozed out from the skin next to the clitoris. Willoughby took hold of the woman's breasts and almost pulling them out of her chest, he flung her onto the wooden table and head butted her in the forehead. She was smashed into unconsciousness.

Susan screamed, "Watch out my darling!"

The warning was directed at Willoughby as the second Viet Cong soldier staggered to his feet and lunged at the Green Beret with his stiletto. He missed.

"Fuck you to hell!" smirked the Captain as he caught the knife wielding wrist in his hands and snapped the whole arm backwards and through 180 degrees. The humerus and ulna bones broke like twigs.

As the soldier fell to the ground, Willoughby fell with him as he wrenched the knife out of his hands. In a swift movement that comes only with dedicated training and some courage, the Captain sliced the Viet Cong's blade into its owner's neck, heart and eyes. Stabbing relentlessly the Green Beret gouged out both eyeballs in a fountain of blood that seemed like an indescribable orgy of mutilation.

"Oh! My God!" said Monica's father as he started to crawl on all fours towards the door. His pants still hung loosely around his ankles, his penis drooping forlornly.

Monica grabbed a bayonet knife from the dead Viet Cong next to her and leapt after her progenitor.

"Trying to get away are you?" she asked in a fury.

"Mercy!" screamed her father as he held his hands out imploringly to his daughter.

"Fuck your mercy!" shrieked Monica.

As she spoke she deliciously drove the full length of the bayonet inside her father's anal passage and rectum so that the leading point actually punctured the bladder and small intestines. The cry that emanated forth from the mutilated man was indescribable.

Even the Captain shrank back with horror as he saw Monica's father roll to left and right on the mud floor with this huge blade impaled up the inside of his sweating, bleeding ass.

Monica took out her own knife and bent down, severing off both of her father's ears.

One hand of the man went for his ass. The other limb tried to comfort the gaping holes in the side of his head where his ears used to be.

"Here my lover!" said Monica as she threw her father's severed ears to Captain Willoughby.

"My father is all ears!"

The Green Beret Captain laughed with a mixture of joy and horror at his lover's pure biblical viciousness. He thought that she would have made an excellent concubine for the ancient Emperor Tiberius.

The gorgeous little Susan jumped up onto the table where the Viet Cong prostitute was lying and with her own knife she started to peel the flesh off the woman's mammary glands one layer at a time.

"I've got him," said Willoughby calmly as he grabbed her father and slammed him back onto the chair where he was originally sitting.

"I'm not going to provide a fellatio service for you! You dirty Viet Cong traitor and pimp!" As the Captain shouted he grabbed the left hand of the Asian man and started to break each finger and thumb one at a time.

"Ahiee! Ahiee!" screamed the victim.

Monica stood behind her father and spat into his bloodied face as she cut off his nipples with a small dagger.

The Captain, when he had broken every digit in the man's hands, stripped the Viet Cong naked and using a steel hammer he started to crush all the toes in Monica's father's feet. The blood and eviscerated tissue was splashed all across the room.

Monica spoke, "My father. I would like to explain to you what we are doing here. You are a Viet Cong. I trusted you to lead my sister Susan and myself to the promised land of the United States of America. The land of milk and honey and if you have money then all is good and if not – you're fucked! I wanted a better life with plenty of money and unbelievable luxuries and fuck everything and everybody else! I wanted an existence that would be uplifted by the greatest country on this earth. The land of the free and the home of the brave that is the magnificent continent of America. This one nation in its superlative power and magnificence is the guiding light for all the free world. But what do I find? My own father has become a stinking, putrid coward and pimp for the rabid North Vietnamese Communists and their fuck-faced Chinese masters! You are a rabid and unadulterated disgrace to all the valiant heroes in the South Vietnamese Army who are fighting for our survival with the brave and gallant American troops! You make me sick!"

As Monica spoke she punched her father in the testicles and ripped at his penis with her razor sharp finger nails.

"What do you want me to do now?" asked Captain Willoughby as he surveyed his gruesome and bloody handiwork. The entire surface of the man's feet had been reduced to a crushed pulp of flesh, blood and broken, splintered bone. It was incapable of being repaired even by the most skilled micro surgeon.

Monica answered, "I want you to interrogate him!"

The Captain leaned over the terrified man and head butted him several times with brutal force. Blood splashed over all three of them as Monica licked her lips greedily, tasting the life fluid of her progenitor.

"When is General Vo Nguyen Giap planning an offensive against the DMZ? How many troops are the North Vietnamese going to commit to the offensive? Which North Vietnamese Divisions are going to be used? Is *Khe Sanh* a major objective in General Giap's strategy? How many artillery pieces do the Viet Cong troops have? How many tanks, if any?"

The Green Beret Captain shooted question after question at Monica's father but only groans were his response.

Monica grabbed a fistful of her father's hair as she warned with venom, "If you do not tell us what we want to know I shall have this brave *Captain of America* inflict upon you what you have so mercilessly inflicted upon others! I am the lover of this magnificent hero of America. We have fucked each other without your permission in every conceivable combination and permutation of love making. I spit on your authority and your position as my father. You are a traitor and as such you forfeit any right to have control over my actions. You also abrogate your rights as a result of your contravention of *customary international law*. Your youngest daughter, Susan, is also the illicit, under-age lover of this gallant soldier of the *Reich* – sorry, I mean America!"

When Monica's father heard those words he squirmed with fury despite his mutilated state.

Captain Willoughby smashed his fist into the man's eye and then used his thumb and forefinger to gouge out that eyeball.

"How dare you show your fury at us!" screamed the Green Beret.

"I am the only one who has the right and the power to illustrate my anger at you - you contemptible little Viet Cong bastard! You think that you can win the war here against *Captain America* and the *United States War Machine*? But we are just toying with you so far! We haven't even used a small fraction of our available firepower. I will see that the guts and intestines of your North Vietnamese pimping allies will be swirled and churned like a mix master of destruction and death! Nothing can escape the wherewithal of our power and force against you dirty scum!"

Monica slapped her father's face as she spoke and he slipped into unconsciousness.

"Give that prick here to me!" said the Captain in a furious lather of sheer, murderous rage.

Willoughby picked up the ragged body of the Viet Cong and threw him like a doll into the table where the prostitute was being cut open by Susan.

"I'll give you one last chance to speak!" said the Green Beret.

"Are the North Vietnamese going to attack *Khe Sanh*?"

There was no reply as Monica kicked her father's naked ass viciously.

"Right! You've had it!" barked the officer.

In a split second his head swooped down on the Viet Cong infiltrator and his teeth gripped into the Asian man's tongue. At the same time Willoughby's hand lunged over and clasped around the testicles and penis. As he crushed the tongue with his teeth, he pulverised the testicles with his fist for double horror.

"Oh! My lover! This is beautiful!" shouted Monica with joy as she caressed Frank's shoulders and arms while he continued with the torture. She could feel the rippling muscles of the trapezium and the biceps as they worked heatedly in their devious assault upon the enemies flesh.

Monica leapt around her dying father throwing heinous insults and jibes at his mutilated and dying body. She pinched his ass and cheeks but he was already expiring slowly and hideously.

The Captain finally tore out the bloodied tongue with his teeth and spat it on top of the naked breasts of the Viet Cong whore.

Susan exclaimed, "Oh! Frank! What did you do that for?"

As the fourteen year old girl spoke she picked up the severed organ and threw it into a corner of the hut where it was immediately set upon by large, black rats that seemed to infest every corner of Vietnam.

For the *coup de grace*, Willoughby ordered his sensual lover to enact the last act of Christian revenge upon the Viet Cong. For this Green Beret believed in that brand of Christianity which did not and would never, *'turn the other cheek'* in order that it be slapped by the pitiless enemy.

"As I pull out his groin I want you to sever it off!"

Monica nodded and seconds later as Willoughby yanked out the testicles with all his massive and vicious power, she sliced and slivered that very organ that had 19 years before given life unto her and to her sister. Now it was the avenging and spiteful child that crushed out that seed which had spawned the evil that was responsible for its destruction and violation.

But God and Christ knew in their infinite power and mercy that this was the right path, for Communism was an affront to God and his invincible Son and as such it must be extirpated from the nucleus of the Universe.

"Our job is nearly complete!" riposted Willoughby with joy.

He then arose from the carcass and sliced his dagger three times into the heart of the Viet Cong. Monica picked up a meat cleaver and decapitated her father with a violent but elegant manoeuvre.

"Praise be to Jesus and his illustrious Father! The task has come to fruition!" As Monica spoke she crossed herself and bowed for she was a devout Catholic.

"Tell me the number of North Vietnamese that are going to attack?" screamed Captain Willoughby as he leant over the mutilated prostitute on the table. She made

no reply as Susan punched her vagina and sliced her dagger into the crease of the bitch's *mons labia*.

"Fuck the whore!" began Monica, "…we shall elicit nothing from her no matter how hard we try by the grace of Almighty God."

"I agree with you. It is useless," as the Captain spoke he slid down his camouflage trousers and raped the Viet Cong bitch for more than ten minutes as Susan and Monica caressed his body from both sides. When he had ejaculated into the enemy he arose and sighed.

"Let us return quickly to the *Lang Vei* camp for I fear that a major North Vietnamese offensive is on the way!"

Just before they walked out the door the Captain pumped five rounds from his M-60 machine gun into the prostitute's heart, ripping it open like a burst watermelon.

As they crouched back into the jungle they set fire to the entire village and exulted in the smell of burning and decomposed flesh that assailed their nostrils.

To them it was the scent of pure Victory.

Chapter 5
THE BATTLE For THONTHAMKHE

On the night of the 26th December 1967 after the conference at the *Tan Son Nhut* Air Base, Colonel Richard Vortex and his regimental headquarters staff numbering 256 men and 17 officers helicopter'd into the Marine base at the provincial capital of *Quang Tri*. The population of *Quang Tri* was approximately 120,000 civilians. The headquarters of the US 3rd Marine Division and the III Marine Amphibious Force was also stationed there.

Quang Tri was a vital link and anchor base for the American and ARVN forces in the I Corps Operational Zone in the northern portion of South Vietnam. It was from here that Route 9 extended westwards along the *Quang Tri River* right up to the Laos border and the Marine base at *Khe Sanh* and then finally to the US Special Forces Camp at *Lang Vei* commanded by Captain Frank C. Willoughby.

Also Route 1 branched out southwards from *Quang Tri* leading all the way down to *Da Nang* and *Chu Lai* on the coast. The *Cua Viet River* ran northwards from *Quang Tri* starting at the Gulf of Tonkin and meandering its way into the middle of the DMZ just below the 17th Parallel.

The tremendous roar of 112 UH-1D helicopters burst through the air above *Quang Tri*.

Major Lansdale was sitting next to his commanding officer Colonel Vortex in the lead helicopter. The Colonel was not sitting in the back seat for passengers but was personally manning twin M-60 machine gun pods that were mounted on both sides of the UH-1D. He had his finger on the trigger and was itching to fire at something – anything.

In addition to the twin M-60's there was a seven tube pod for rockets on the left side of the helicopter.

"We're nearly there sir," said the helicopter pilot who was a Warrant Officer 1st Class from New Jersey.

Colonel Vortex nodded and looked to Sergeant Major Crighton. The Sergeant Major glanced at his map and made some quick calculations.

"We are only 15 miles from *Quang Tri*!" The senior NCO had to shout over the continuous thunder of the rotor blades to make himself heard to the Colonel.

"That's the fucking village! Isn't it? Sergeant Major?" asked Vortex.

As he spoke he primed the awesome power of four M-60 machine guns which together could let loose 7,000 rounds per minute into the unsuspecting Viet Cong enemy at a speed of over 150 mph. This was a whirlwind of destructive mayhem at his fingertips. Then Richard Vortex knew that if you multiplied this by the 112 helicopters in his formation, you had an avalanche of firepower which was simply unstoppable.

Colonel Vortex did the math and came up with 784,000 bullets spewing into the enemy simultaneously per minute.

"That's *Charlie's* village sir!" smiled Sergeant Major Crighton.

"I know," answered Colonel Vortex.

Major Lansdale lit up a cigarette and protested to the Colonel.

"Sir! Our orders are to join Major General Rathvon C. Tompkins in *Quang Tri* ASAP! Sir!"

"Relax Major," began the Colonel as he swung the machine gun pods to left and right testing their manoeuvrability and agility to his touch. They were working excellently.

"You'll get to *Khe Sanh* soon enough. I promise you that! But first I have some unfinished business to take care of in this Viet Cong village."

Suddenly, as if on queue, heavy machine gun fire burst upwards from the small village below them. One of the helicopters to the starboard of Colonel Vortex's lead ship was hit and started to trail smoke. The pilot had a hard time trying to keep it airborne.

"Shit!" screamed Vortex's pilot, "Colonel! I think we should make a detour around this village and the next one. We have had reports of heavy concentrations of Viet Cong forces in this area just south of *Quang Tri*."

Colonel Vortex looked to Major Lansdale and to another one of his Captains. They smirked.

"On the contrary Warrant Officer!" barked Vortex over the din of more than 100 sets of rotor blades.

"I want you to go right in there. Signal all the other birds for the attack."

The pilot looked frazzled, "But sir! I…"

"Just do it! That's an order pilot!" screamed Vortex as he slapped the soldier on the shoulders.

Major Lansdale asked, "That's the village of *Thonthamkhe*."

"Yes," the Colonel answered as he put on his flak jacket and tied the buckles firmly.

"I'm going to fucking chew their asses for what they did to our battalion!"

Major Lansdale continued, "You mean sir when you had Major Thrush and the 1st Battalion on manoeuvres during a search and destroy mission out of *Quang Tri*? I remember that you and the 1,500 men of 1st Battalion were ambushed down there last year?"

Richard Vortex corrected, "It wasn't last year. It was in February this year. I lost 147 men killed in this fuck-assed village! We were ambushed by 5 Viet Cong battalions and 2 regular North Vietnamese regiments. I lost a lot of good boys down there! Now I'm going to eviscerate the bastards!"

The pilot asked, "I've told the 12 double rotor Chinooks to return to base at *Quang Tri* sir. They don't have any armament on them. It would be useless to keep them with us."

Colonel Vortex nodded, "Good!"

The Major asked, "Are the other birds ready?"

The pilot answered in the affirmative.

The village of *Thonthamkhe* was situated in a clearing with thick jungle on all four sides. It was about 16 miles from the coast and 15 miles south of the provincial capital. As the 100 helicopter gunships roared in at 165 mph Colonel Vortex noticed that the population centre was comprised of about 300 to 400 huts and other ramshackle structures such as corrugated iron sheds and outhouses. Here and there were anti-aircraft emplacements bristling with heavy calibre weapons. As they swooped in closer to within 2 miles he could see men and women carrying children and screaming in every direction.

The Viet Cong were preparing their defences.

"Give me the microphone and patch me in to all the other gunships," said Colonel Vortex calmly.

"Yes sir," the pilot handed him the command helmet. It had an eagle on the front to signify Vortex's rank and blue and red stripes running from front to back to illustrate that he was the Command and Coordinating officer.

"Now listen up!" shouted Vortex into the microphone.

Major Lansdale also put on a command helmet with a golden oak leaf in front to signify his rank as 2-I-C.

"We are going to attack in five waves," as Colonel Vortex spoke Sergeant Major Crighton and the other men in their helicopter loaded and cocked their M-16's and M-60 machine guns, pointing them out of the open hatchway.

"I will lead the first wave of 20 helicopters line abreast.

I want the other four waves also in line abreast formation 20 gunships wide. I'll give the order to land when I consider it time to do so. I don't want any ship to land in the village without my express orders! Is that clear!"

The 100 pilots through their squadron leaders signalled in their confirmation of Colonel Vortex's orders.

The lead 20 gunships carrying the 9th Marine regiment headquarters company as well as one regular company of the 3rd battalion swooped in towards the village at tree top level. Colonel Vortex gripped the handle bars of his quad M-60's and remembered the glory days of World War 2 when the magnificent and heroic *German Wehrmacht* held out against the pestilential murderers and cowardly pimps in the Communist Bolshevik army in Berlin in April 1945 at such overwhelming odds dying in a blaze of Wagnerian glory for the *Fuhrer*.

Beads of sweat and ripples of excitement coursed through his arterial system. He could feel the thrill of death tugging at his shoulders.

"Fire! Fire! Fire!" screamed Colonel Vortex.

Then he added, "Or as the lime-sucking British would say, "Shoot! Shoot! Shoot my good man!"

No sooner had the words escaped his mouth than a horrendous eruption of gunfire burst forth in a sea of orange-yellow flame from the lead 20 gunships. Tens of thousands of rounds spewed into the Viet Cong every second as they were still running for cover.

In Vortex's wild and sentimental imagination he imagined that he was coming to the rescue of the *4th Panzer Army* struggling in the defence of Berlin against the Bolshevik rats.

Vortex swung his M-60's around and fired into a schoolyard as his ship flew to portside of the position. A large anti-aircraft emplacement was set up next to the school building.

Colonel Vortex could see the bullets tearing three Viet Cong torsos into a bloody shambles. Unfortunately the endless spray of munitions pelted a group of women carrying infants. The flesh of the children and the women were mutilated into a single mass of blood and intestines by the eruption of firepower.

"Wheel around to the left!" screamed Vortex to the pilot.

Major Lansdale and Sergeant Major Crighton were leaning out of the hatch and firing their machine guns into a group of running people who were making their way towards the jungle along a small stream.

"Kill them before they get to cover!" screamed the Major.

The Captain and two Lieutenants unpinned half a dozen grenades from their camouflage belts and dropped them into the people below. The gunship swerved upward and away as the blasts tore through the atmosphere.

"This is fantastic!" yelled Vortex as he cried with joy and nudged Major Lansdale with affection.

Major Lansdale looked at him with bewilderment and Vortex repeated this time in German.

"Das ist fantastisch! Bumsen Sie den Viet Cong tot in ihren Spuren!"

"It's the second wave coming in! Watch them!" cried Sergeant Major Crighton.

As Colonel Vortex's wave reached the edge of the jungle at the far side of the village the second wave came streaking in along the path they had just annihilated.

"Oh fucking Shit!" expostulated the pilot.

Vortex looked around with horror.

"They are finished. There is nothing we can do for them now,"

He said as he saw one of his gunships burst into flames from inside the cockpit.

A platoon of Viet Cong below had fired several *RPG* rocket launchers into the gunship. They had been deadly accurate. The munitions exploded directly in front of the dashboard of the gunship, incinerating the pilot and the co-pilot. The force of the blast had belted the other four men belonging to his HQ detachment straight out of the hatchway with their clothes on fire. Then men had fallen over 200 yards to the ground. A group of Viet Cong were knifing them to death with long daggers.

"Come around in front of the chopper!" roared Vortex, "I want to see if we can assist them!"

Vortex's gunship tried to keep up with the doomed helicopter as it swayed in the air before him. Just then more explosions were heard and yet another gunship from the first wave was detonated with the melodious shrieks of dying Americans.

"Jesus! Watch it!" screamed Sergeant Major Leonard Crighton.

Before Vortex could realise what was happening a broken piece of helicopter rotor blade shot into the hatchway at incredible speed. It missed him but with a hot, sweet spray of blood and severed tissue it neatly decapitated the Captain sitting next to him.

"Oh! Fuck! Save him!" cried Vortex as their gunship swerved crazily in the atmosphere before the other sinking *UH-1D*. The headless cadaver of his Captain slumped into Vortex's arms. The head rolled heavily to the metal skirting planks of the ship and the open wound in the neck pulsed blood directly into the Colonel's lips and nostrils as the corpse still had its heart beating.

"Get it off me! *Bekommen Sie es von mir!*" screamed Vortex as he scrambled forwards into the cockpit.

Sergeant Major Crighton grabbed hold of the body and laid it gently onto the floor of the chopper, next to its head.

"Look!" laughed one of the Lieutenant's, "…the Captain's lips are still quivering!"

Major Lansdale scowled at the junior officer as he fired his M-60 into the village.

"Shut up! You idiot! Have some respect for our dead comrades-in-arms!"

The Lieutenant dropped his head and then threw a satchel charge into a group of huts where Viet Cong women were scurrying about and firing their *SKS* rifles into the American warbirds.

"Oh! My Jesus! Have mercy on them!" cried Colonel Vortex. As their gunship wheeled around in the air he could see out of the cockpit windshield as the faces of the

two other pilots were red-black with burnt blood and melting flesh. Terrible shrieks emanated forth from their tortured bodies.

Suddenly a bullet ricocheted inside their ship and pierced the glass. It penetrated directly into the brain of Vortex's pilot from the left temple. Blood spewed in a fine trickle onto Vortex's legs and waist. The chopper, without a pilot, dived out of control at over 150 mph. It was heading straight for the jungle.

"Motherfucking hell! What's going on up there?" screamed Major Lansdale as he scrambled forwards.

"The pilot's dead!" shouted back Vortex as he manhandled the controls and yaw stick.

"Can you fly?" asked the Major.

"Of course I can fucking fly!" screamed back Vortex as he pushed the corpse of the pilot backwards and out of the flying hot seat.

Vortex added proudly, "I was taught to fly by *Hanna Reitsch* herself!"

Lansdale asked confused, "Who is *Hanna Reitsch*?"

The Colonel looked upwards in disgust and rolled his crazed eyes in their sockets, "You ignorant simpleton! Don't you know anything? I'll tell you later you numbskull!"

Gripping the controls with all his might, Vortex lifted the chopper out of its death dive with superhuman strength. He thought the tail blade was going to be shorn off by the stress. The bottom edge of the helicopter brushed the tree tops as it skimmed dangerously over the jungle foliage.

Sergeant Major Crighton handed Vortex a map of the village of *Thonthamkhe* just as the third, fourth and fifth waves of gunships were finishing off their attack run.

"Now listen up! All squadron leaders! All gunships!"

As Vortex spoke a flurry of *RPG* rocket fire came up at them from the Viet Cong village. Four more helicopters were hit as they exploded and started to tumble out of the atmosphere. The losses in men and material were starting to get extremely heavy.

"I will go in with the first and second waves. We'll land to the east of the village just near the stream and at the edge of the jungle clearing. I want the remaining 60 gunships to maintain their positions over the Viet Cong and give us intense fire support! My men will sweep through the entire expanse of the village. Then our 40 gunships will lift off and meet us at the other side to the west. I intend to crush them completely gentlemen!"

As Vortex finished speaking the gunship squadron leaders called in their confirmation of the orders and the strategy.

"Here we go again Colonel!" screamed Sergeant Major Crighton.

Major Lansdale and the other men held onto their seats as Vortex led the remaining 36 helicopters out of the original 40 into the drop zone.

"Jesus!" said one Corporal, "Sir! The fire is pretty intense down there! I think there is more of *Charlie* than we imagined!"

Major Lansdale waved his hands up in despair, "I know Corporal! We should be in *Quang Tri* by now breaking out the Budweiser! It's the Colonel's idea!"

The junior NCO rolled up his eyes and clutched his M-16 to his chest like it was a precious baby essential for his survival. They went in as more gunships were damaged by the withering Viet Cong fire.

Colonel Vortex began to think that the whole thing was a mistake. Originally, as he landed his chopper and the others plonked heavily to the ground east of the main village complex, he estimated that there would be no more than 500 to 600 Viet Cong irregulars here. But now he was not so sure. A terrible fear crashed through his body as he leapt out of the cockpit, that perhaps they had run into a whole Viet Cong regiment of upwards of 5,000 men.

"Major! Take *C Company* with about 250 men and work your way around the village to the north! I'll take the *HQ Company* and work southwards. We'll meet at the other end of this Viet Cong cesspool!"

"Right sir!" The Major fell to the ground as a hail of bullets greeted them from the direction of the village of *Thonthamkhe*. A Lance Corporal/Bombardier in front of Vortex had the side of his head blown away by intense fire from several Chinese made *Type 24 7.92mm* heavy machine guns.

"Take cover!" screamed the Colonel. As soon as Vortex's 500 men had left the helicopters they found themselves pinned to the ground. The resistance from the village was fierce. Now mortar shells were landing amongst his troops. A brace of American bodies were blown into the air in a mutilated heap. Severed arms, legs and other body parts landed all around them like rain drops.

"Oh! Jesus shit!" Vortex looked backwards and saw one of his helicopters as its tail rotor blade was blown off. The craft swung 360 degrees in a wild spin of death and then crashed into three of his upright men cutting them to pieces even before they could fire their weapons at the Viet Cong. A second and a third helicopter was blown from the sky. The 60 gunships above them were also suffering heavy and continual losses.

A Captain next to Vortex protested, "Sir! We can't advance on the village until we get reinforcements!"

Vortex scoffed as he pumped a full belt of M-60 shells into the village, "This is all we've got! We're going to crush that village!"

The Captain reluctantly nodded and stood up to direct his men for the advance. A second later as the Colonel was running another belt of ammunition into his weapon, he felt a stream of hot blood pouring over his shoulders. The Captain had swung around in an arc. Vortex could see multiple geysers of blood erupting from his chest.

"Captain!" he shouted as the junior officer's hand slapped down on Vortex's nose and lips. The man was dead even before his body hit the ground.

Colonel Vortex was staggering to his feet as the corpse knocked him back into the mud.

"Help the Colonel up! Get him up!" screamed a Corporal. A staff Sergeant and two Lance Corporals pulled the Captain's cadaver off Vortex and dumped it unceremoniously into a ditch.

"Are the men ready?" asked the Colonel.

Another Captain arrived and said, "The men are in position sir! Major Lansdale's troops are already making their way around the other flank of the Viet Cong position."

Vortex gave the signal to advance and his 250 or so men crawled on their bellies towards the village.

The eruption of earth and mud as the bullets pelted them from every direction was horrifying. In three lines abreast Vortex's men advanced suffering severe casualties.

By the time they reached the village perimeter Vortex could see that the Viet Cong were dug in deep and there were not hundreds of them but about two thousand.

"Oh! Sweet Jesus!" said Vortex to himself, "I've made a big mistake!"

Before the Captain and the 2nd Lieutenant next to him could ask what he was talking about a thundering explosion ripped through the molecules of atmosphere above their heads. It was a heavy artillery shell from a *Soviet 130mm M-46* Field gun.

Vortex knew this weapon well. It could fire a *73.61 lb HE* projectile to a distance of 33,000 yards. And with this capability it outranged the American *M102 105mm* howitzer.

"Take cover! Incoming! Incoming!" screamed Colonel Vortex.

A deadly rain of shells pounded the 250 Americans as their bodies erupted in a miasma of blood and intestines.

The Captain turned around and had his spine vivisected out of his back as a shell spliced and diced two men in front of him. Vortex was flung into the air for a distance of 12 yards and landed on his skull, tumbling into a ditch inside the Viet Cong stronghold.

Moments passed and everything was a circular whirl. Vortex struggled to raise his arms but he had no control over his nervous system. He tried forlornly to raise his head but couldn't.

More minutes passed. He only recognised masses of bodies swirling first one way and then changing direction as they streamed past in the opposite direction. It was utter chaos.

The 500 American troops were being cut to pieces by a Viet Cong regiment of over 2,000 men with heavy artillery and mortars. When Vortex finally staggered to his feet he saw that he had been covered over by the dead body of one of his Corporals.

"Captain! Major Lansdale!" he shouted.

Vortex flung himself around 360 degrees but could not see any of his men. There were village huts all around. Some were in flames as plumes of thick black smoke etched skywards. Some had corpses flung over them and from others intense machine gun fire could be heard.

Then he realised that his men had been routed and had been driven back to the edge of the jungle. There were dead and dying GI and Viet Cong bodies strewn all around.

Colonel Vortex picked up his M-60 and ran for cover as he heard Vietnamese voices behind him. He just managed to propel himself into a half demolished straw hut when a group of about 70 Viet Cong ran past. He peeped through the bamboo walls and saw that the enemy was bayoneting and robbing all the American wounded they could find in the most horrific manner imaginable. Shrieks, cries for mercy and gut-wrenching groans could be heard from his murdered men.

Something cold and hard pierced his flesh as the Colonel was totally preoccupied with his idiotic defeat here in this village of *Thonthamkhe*. He swung sideways and lashed out with his fist. He hit the face of a delicate Viet Cong girl of about 13 years. She had stabbed the Colonel just above his 11th floating rib. The blood oozed out of his torso but he could feel it was only a superficial wound.

The girl said something to the effect of, "Die! You American Imperialist swine!"

Vortex sighed with grief at the pain and struck the girl to the floor. She started screaming but he gagged her mouth with his huge fist and punched her so viciously in the guts that he could feel her backbone. Outside stern voices could be heard, the gruesome voices of the enemy that had once more defeated the Colonel in this minor engagement. He realised now that he had underestimated the Viet Cong. This was a multi-brigade job. Not the chore of a half-strength battalion.

"How many of you are there here?" asked Vortex to the 13 year old girl under his massive body. He spoke in perfect Vietnamese.

The girl did not answer but swore obscenities at him.

Richard Vortex realised that more Viet Cong could burst into this hut at any second. But equally, he knew that he must tear out this information from the child. He would return with most of the US 3rd Division of 15,000 men, 560 M1 tanks and armoured personnel carriers and the Division's Air Mobile Brigade of 850 *Cobra* and UH-1D gunships and totally obliterate *Thonthamkhe* once and for all.

He said to the violent child, "*Ich bin Gong, um Sie leck mich am Arsch! Kleines Schlampe-Weibchen zu lieben!*"

When Vortex was enraged he always reverted to his second language of German for he thought it was the true language of the Gods and of the purity of the Western world.

He whispered the words in the girl's ear as he pinned her to the floor.

Explosions and machine gun fire intensified outside instead of abating. The Vietnamese Communist teenager understood what was going to happen to her and she shrieked even through the Colonel's crushing fist. Her body squirmed and wriggled to be free.

"You little bitch!" laughed Vortex, "I'm going to ask you one more time! How many Viet Cong troops are here in *Thonthamkhe?*"

As he interrogated Vortex slapped the girl across the chin and soft flesh of her face leaving the red imprint of his vicious strikes.

The 13 year old spat in his face and then started to shriek and cry all at once.

"You've asked for it!"

Vortex gripped the flimsy black tunic with his right hand and tore it off revealing a very beautiful and slim adolescent body. The girl was almost fully developed with small, firm breasts topped with a pair of delicious pink nipples. But it was lower down that caused Vortex to become electrified with desire.

"Beautiful! *Das ist Fantastisch!*" he said as he ran his course and blood stained fingers through the soft, luxuriant pubic hair of the girl's olive vagina.

He sniffed it and it smelt as sweet as honey. It was almost as good as his fiancées, Susie Ky.

The girl grabbed a clump of Vortex's hair and pulled it apart, forcing his head away from her. But at his nearly 205 lbs of solid muscle it was no contest.

"I'm going to make savage love to you until you reveal to me the precise information that I require."

As he spoke Vortex licked the child's breasts and nibbled on her soft and pliant nipples. Catching them between his teeth he bit down hard causing her to scream. But still no information was revealed.

Pulling his camouflage pants down to his ankles, Vortex ran his tongue inside the moist flesh of her young vagina. The clitoris and *mons labia* were delicious. His cunnilingus continued as he drove his three fingers into the girl's mouth while ramming another three fingers of his other hand into the vaginal orifice as he sucked, licked and teated that gorgeous shrine of physical enjoyment.

"Now its pay back time!" whispered the Colonel.

His rigid device slid deliciously into the young child's womb. The sensation was indescribable and beautiful. The skin of her womb was soft and wet and he ejaculated into her within seconds. His tongue intertwined around hers as they sucked, one passive and resisting and the other aflame with heated and debauched lust and anger.

"Tell me where the main body of the North Vietnamese troops are? How many Viet Cong are there in *Thonthamkhe?* How many heavy artillery pieces do you have? How many mortars?"

The questions kept coming and as Vortex deliciously fucked and re-fucked her he started to pinch and bite small pieces of flesh out of her face with his brutal teeth.

The girl screamed when she could but her naked body was streaked with sweat and utterly exhausted.

After the second explosion of his rich and viscous seed into her, the Colonel flipped the girl over and inserted a steel bar 12 inches long and 2 inches in diameter up her vagina's opening. The massive device stretched her reproductive flesh to the limit as he prepared her rectum for sodomy.

Vortex could hear the machine gun fire getting closer as he caressed the girl's breasts and yanked her head backwards, whispering, "If you don't give me the information I need I'm going to sodomise you! You Viet Cong slut!"

There was no reply.

Vortex eased his penis into the crack of her ass and after several attempts he breached the opening to her sanctified bowels. The fucking was fast and furious. Sweat poured off the Colonel as he used one free hand to plunge the steel bar deeper into the girl's womb. So far inside was it that his penis could feel the hard wall of steel from the other side of the girl's womb tissue.

Her anal passage was so tight that even after two previous exertions he climaxed again. His hands gripping those slender legs and shapely buttocks and plunging them backwards and forwards from his body as he fucked her delightfully.

The girl's head drooped in front of him as he was still inside her when suddenly the door to the mangy hut burst open.

The Colonel's mouth fell down like a sack of potatoes with an admixture of terror and surprise.

Instinctively the Marine Colonel threw the girl's body closer up in front of him as a type of human shield. He was also wearing a flak jacket over his camouflage shirt. It was this that saved him.

The Viet Cong had fired his Chinese made *Type 56-1* assault rifle with its 7.62mm bullets directly at Vortex's head. But the Colonel had ducked just in time and covered himself with the naked girl's living body. The bullets sprayed into her in a myriad eruption of fantastic blood geysers.

"Shit!" exclaimed Vortex as he felt the bullets piercing right through the teenager's flesh and impacting against his flak jacket.

The Viet Cong man was the girl's father. He groaned with agony when he saw that he had hit the wrong target. For a few seconds the Communist suffered from shock and hesitation. This was all that Vortex needed. This was the window of opportunity. Lunging like a maniac with his trousers still ridiculously hanging around his ankles, the Colonel caught hold of his Marine dagger and with one elegant movement that was almost feline in appearance, he launched it at the father.

"Ahiieee!" screamed the Communist.

The blade found its mark as it pierced the carotid artery and exited through the neck behind the cervical spine. Blood gushed across the room in a fine arch. Whipping up his pants the Colonel kicked the rifle out of the Viet Cong's arms and slashed his legs under those of the enemy. As the mutilated man fell to the floor, Vortex drove his bayonet directly into the myocardial tissue of the heart.

He rushed over to the mortally wounded girl and held her in his arms, screaming, "How many Viet Cong regiments are there here?" Vortex grabbed her cheeks in his hands and shook her whole head from side to side with vicious and murderous force.

He had not one iota of pity in him for the Viet Cong just as he remembered the words of history when the *Fuhrer* swore to eradicate the scourge and pestilence of Bolshevism. He dreamed of being present at the *Parteitagesversammlung*.

In a delirious state the 13 year old child thought that the man in front of her was her Asian father. She answered.

"Four regiments." As she spoke her eyes rolled backwards and she died silently in Vortex's arms.

The Colonel had the information he needed. He worked quickly. Finding a jerry can full of gasoline in the corner of the decrepit straw hut he splashed its full contents over the naked body of the girl and the father as well as the walls and floor. As soon as he jumped outside he threw a grenade into the structure and it burst into red-orange flames that arched, spiked and raced to heaven and beyond. To Vortex is was like the angels of victory heralding the triumph of God almighty.

A heavy slap hit the back of Vortex's head. He spun around on the balls of his feet and lashed out with a butcher's axe that he had found in the rat infested hut. The blade buried itself inside the face of an old woman.

"You fucking geriatric cow!" screamed the Colonel. He could see that the edge of the blade had dissected the mandible and cheeks of the Viet Cong woman and the meat cleaver was embedded so far horizontally that it was right into the bridge of the nose below the eyes. He kicked her body into a ditch when he felt a hand descend onto his shoulders.

"Jesus fuck Colonel! Where have you been?"

It was the voice of Major Lansdale. He had a Lieutenant and twenty Marines with him including the radio telephone.

Vortex looked up and could see his gunships continuing to blast the main body of the village about half a mile away.

"Where are the rest of the men?" asked Vortex, his face red with rage.

"I sent them back to the choppers! At least what's left of them! We got creamed Colonel!"

The Major was watching the edge of the forest for any sign of their rescue transport.

"How dare you counteract my orders!" shouted Vortex as he brought his face right up to Lansdale's eyeballs.

"But sir......"

Vortex interrupted, "I gave you the order to attack! How dare you compromise my directives by yourself?"

The Major spluttered and was about to say something when their small detachment was suddenly and expertly ambushed by over 50 Viet Cong irregulars.

"Take cover!" screamed Vortex as he hit the dirt.

Bullets sprayed in every direction. Three Marines were dropped in the initial fusillade.

Three Viet Cong came running towards the Colonel. Major Lansdale jumped up and fired. He cut one Asian in half with his M-16 but collected an 18 inch bayonet in his guts that severed his colon and punctured his stomach. It was a mortal wound.

Vortex grabbed Lansdale and was almost impaled by the same blade which pointed out of the officer's spine. He handed him over to a Medic who pulled him over to a chopper that had just landed 200 yards away. More gunships were now landing to pull them out.

"Fuck you!" barked out Vortex as he took out his Colt .45 and pumped a full magazine into one, two and then three Viet Cong who charged at him. With his ammunition exhausted and his M-16 blown away, Vortex slashed, hacked and gouged with the unwieldy butcher's axe that he brandished with expert venom. He grabbed one Viet Cong in his early twenties and tore off his ears and facial flesh with a single blow of the axe. As the man arched backwards in horrific agony clutching that part of his skull where his flesh used to be, the Colonel swung upwards into the testicles. The axe impaled itself inside the crotch and then into the pelvis bone almost splitting the man in half. Another Viet Cong crunched his fist into Vortex's spine. Frantically extricating the axe from one body, Vortex buried it inside another. This time he hacked off an arm and decapitated another soldier who tried to clasp him in a headlock from the rear. A spray of M-60 bullets flowered the VC in front of them. It was coming from the rescue gunships to their rear. Slowly the Communists retreated temporarily allowing the Colonel and his ragged survivors to clamber onto their escape craft. Eleven out of the twenty men originally with Major Lansdale lay dead or wounded on the field. Their bodies would later be stripped naked and dismembered by the Viet Cong in an orgy of blood lust.

"Lift off! Lift off!" screamed the Colonel.

Seven choppers roared into the air as a tide of Viet Cong swept forward. Vortex manned the quad M-60 and pulverised the wave of enemy humanity that rolled forward like a *King Tide*.

His men watched as Vortex swung the tripod from back to front, from left to right and upwards and then earthwards, firing all the time. It was sheer madness.

"I'll kill all the fuckers!"

The pilot was joining the remaining gunships and the survivors, about 73 of the original 100 choppers, glided past the village and on to *Quang Tri*.

"How is he?" asked Vortex as they flew out of range of the anti-aircraft fire coming from *Thonthamkhe*.

"Not good sir," said the medical Warrant Officer as he placed an oxygen mask over Major Lansdale's face.

"Here! Let me see," said Vortex.

He looked at the large and festering wound that severed the liver and small intestines.

Vortex shook his head, "I don't think we can save the Major in time."

The medics nodded but nevertheless gave the officer three injections of morphine, one of tryptanol and another of nor-epinephrine to stimulate his withering and traumatised heart.

"Major can you hear me?" asked Colonel Vortex.

The officer mumbled something incoherently.

"Speak if you can Major," repeated Vortex.

After a few moments, as blood and yellow pus oozed out of the Major's mouth he said, "My wife."

Vortex saw that his intestines were starting to spill out onto the metal floor of the helicopter.

"Jesus! You fucking idiots! Can't you see his innards are spewing out?" Vortex grabbed a Corporal and yanked him over to his enraged face, "Put some gauze dressing over it or I'll fucking throw you out of the chopper and feed you to the dirty Viet Cong pimps and whore-masters myself!"

The junior NCO was terrified and started to stuff large quantities of dressing into the wound even though it was entirely useless.

"What did you say Major Lansdale?" asked Vortex as he pulled the dying man's face up to his own.

"Did you want me to give a message to your wife?"

"My wife!" repeated the Major as his body started to convulse with horrible twitching and contortions as if he was being conveyed into everlasting hell itself.

Vortex looked up to one of the Captains, "I can't make any fucking sense out of him!"

The Captain leaned over the Major and again he heard, "My wife!"

Vortex lost his patience and grabbed the officer up off the stretcher by his shirt collar.

"What about your fucking wife Major?"

Major Lansdale sighed one terrible sigh, "Tell her I want a divorce!"

In the next second, as Vortex looked dumbfounded at his second in command, the Major rolled up his eyes and died without a sound.

"He's finished sir," said the Medic checking his pulse and then covering the officer with an army issue blanket.

Vortex sighed as he looked to Sergeant Major Crighton, "He must have been delirious?"

"Yes sir," answered the NCO as he wiped Viet Cong blood from his M-16 bayonet.

The remainder of the journey to *Quang Tri* took about 20 minutes.

Not much was said as the Colonel and his men were exhausted. Their helicopter fleet landed at the *Quang Tri* air base. The body disposal unit of the US Army Medical Corps swung into action.

Each dead American soldier was placed in a black, heavy duty plastic body bag with a tough zipper that ran from the ankles to the scalp. The cadavers of Colonel Vortex's command were dragged off the helicopters, tagged, placed in the body bags and then flown back to the United States in a C-130 Hercules transport aircraft via the Philippines and Hawaii.

"Good afternoon Colonel Vortex," said Major General Rathvon C. Tompkins who had arrived earlier that day.

"Good afternoon sir," said Vortex as he gave a stream of personal commands to his subordinates during the unloading of their dead and wounded.

"Is the 1st Battalion and Major Thrush in *Khe Sanh* yet, sir?" asked Vortex.

"Yes," began General Tompkins as he lit up a cigarette, "They were flown in this morning. The 37th ARVN Ranger Battalion should get their by the 27th January."

"Good," was all that Vortex said as he ran the palm of his hands across Major Lansdale's eyes.

"Your Major has been killed?" asked General Tompkins.

"Yes sir. It was a fire-fight at the village of *Thonthamkhe*. We were outnumbered and outmanoeuvred!"

"I'm sorry to hear that Colonel!" said the General laughing.

"What's so God-dam funny sir?" asked Vortex, his face purple with rage.

The two star General continued to snigger and smirk ludicrously.

"I lost a lot of good men this afternoon!"

General Tomkins waved his hands up nonchalantly, "So I should have warned you not to go into that meat-grinder."

Vortex walked up to the General commanding the 3rd Marine Division. His eyes beamed directly into the General's eyes. But Vortex realised that it was like looking into the black, limitless vaults of hell. There was no light reflecting from his gaze, no compassion, no pity and no remorse.

"And why didn't you?" asked Vortex.

The General shrugged his shoulders, "I didn't think you were stupid enough to go in there with only 2 Companies."

Vortex snarled and took one last look at the dead Major. He brushed the man's eyelids shut and flung the plastic body bag over the corpse's head, zipping it up himself.

"Take him now," said Vortex to one of the medical orderlies.

The Major disappeared into the deep vaults of one of the many C-130's on the *Quang Tri* tarmac.

General Tompkins led Colonel Vortex away to the sumptuous Marine Officers Quarters at the *Quang Tri* base complex. The Officer's building was in fact a series of seven large apartment buildings on the edge of the air base. At any one time there were usually 2 fully equipped battalions guarding the entire grounds as well as the air base perimeter from possible Viet Cong infiltration and sabotage.

The Marine Officer's Mess itself had three indoor heated swimming pools, five saunas, two gymnasiums, four spa's, twelve tennis courts, a solarium, sixteen squash courts and three five star standard restaurants to choose from. All officers from the rank of 2nd Lieutenant or Sub-Lieutenant in the Navy upwards were allowed to stay in these opulent and luxurious surroundings. However, only officers from the rank of Lieutenant Colonel or Commander in the Navy, were allowed access to certain parts of the living quarters and facilities. These areas contained all the little extra luxuries that senior officers came to expect such as a personal massage service by highly attractive South Vietnamese girls.

"I have a surprise for you Colonel!" expostulated General Tompkins.

"A surprise?" queried Vortex as he waved to Sergeant Major Crighton to hurry up with his luggage.

"Yes."

"I've already had enough fucking surprises for one day sir!" barked Vortex with annoyance.

Tompkins laughed, "But you'll like this one!"

Jumping into a jeep they drove to the entrance of the Officer's Quarters which had a large fountain in the driveway. Manicured gardens edged their way all around the buildings.

"Its waiting for you in your rooms." With those words General Tompkins left, followed by a retinue of junior officers. But he told Vortex to meet him in the *'Las Vegas Restaurant'* at 1900 hours for dinner.

"Its all here sir," said Sergeant Major Crighton as he gently placed the Colonel's luggage in front of his suite.

"Thank you Sergeant Major. You better take a rest now. I'll see you tomorrow."

Crighton nodded and left as Vortex gingerly opened the door to his suite on the 3rd Floor of the concrete and steel reinforced building.

As a full bird Colonel he was entitled to a suite measuring 200 square yards. It had three bathrooms, a large lounge and bar, two bedrooms, a laundry and ante-room and a very expansive balcony overlooking the *Quang Tri* air base. It was, he thought, most comfortable. Above him were the penthouses of the one, two and three star Generals. Lieutenant General Robert E. Cushman Jr. had a permanent suite on the top floor with his own heated swimming pool and sauna.

"The privileges of rank," said Colonel Vortex softly to himself. No sooner had he entered the room than he found a familiar pair of female arms surrounding his massive chest.

"Oh! Jesus!" exclaimed Vortex with pleasant shock.

"It's you!"

Susie Ky tongue kissed her lover and they fell onto the queen sized bed.

"I had to come and see you Richard my love! I had to embrace you once more before you went to *Khe Sanh*!" Susie Ky started to wipe the tears from her eyes.

"Please forgive me!"

"You're forgiven my delicious girl," said Vortex as he unbuttoned her pink blouse and ripped offer her miniskirt.

"Come let us make love avidly!"

The two fell into each other and started to exchange bodily fluids *'in flagrante delicto.'*

Suddenly Vortex lifted his head from Susie's smooth and luxuriant vaginal hair, "How did you know about *Khe Sanh*?"

She laughed and gripped the Colonel's gonads in her small fingers, massaging them with ardour.

"Remember, I am the daughter of a Minister in President Thieu's Government."

Colonel Vortex smiled at his lover suspiciously and bent his head sideways.

Susie Ky giggled, "Actually it was Vice-President Nguyen Cao Ky who mentioned that you may be expecting an attack there from North Vietnamese regular army formations."

"Oh!" was all that Vortex said.

For the next hour and a half they made love in a number of differing and novel positions. Colonel Vortex mounted Susie doggie-style and slid alternately into her womb and rectum, mixing the pink with the brown. He couldn't decide which was more gratifying. They drank copious quantities of Red Label Scotch whisky to relax and then Susie sat on Richard's face so that he could dine on her flesh before the real repast would begin.

She mouthed his penis until it was red-purple and glistening.

"Kiss my face!" moaned Vortex as he clutched Susie's juicy buttocks and fingered her asshole as he performed cunnilingus on her.

"What the devil did you say?" she asked, her little breasts bobbing up and down like a doll.

"I said kiss my face," repeated Vortex.

Susie shrugged her shoulders, "You didn't tell me before Richard that you craved for these simple pleasures?"

"I do. Jesusfuck! I do!"

Susie enclosed her small delicate mouth over his massive engine and sucked for all she was worth. Her tongue ran deliciously up and down the engorged shaft of his member as she climaxed into Vortex's awaiting orifice.

The excretions had a pungent odour to it as it streamed in unhealthy rivulets across the silken bed sheets supplied by the American taxpayer.

Vortex swallowed those waste products and then sodomised Susie afresh.

"I want you to defecate in my mouth!" he cried, sweat pouring off his face in a lather of raw lust.

Susie yelled, "You are insane Richard! I've never done that before!"

"There is always a first time. Now come on! I haven't got all the time in the world. Because the whole fucking world is going to hell! We must present ourselves to General Tompkins for dinner in less than thirty minutes."

Susie pushed her sphincter over Vortex's beslimed features and the black mards of shit slid into his mouth. He chewed on them with relish as Susie sucked him to a gigantic and explosive ejaculation that shot his rich fuck all over her delicious breasts and face.

Turning her around they savagely tongue kissed, mixing the sweet shit with the fuck until they collapsed in a devilish heap. The love making over they dressed and went downstairs to the luxury five star *Las Vegas Restaurant*.

Colonel Vortex was wearing his most immaculate dress blues with the newly awarded "*Purple Heart*" shining resplendently on his chest above his fifteen rows of multi-coloured ribbons. He was the most highly decorated Colonel in the entire US Marine Corps. Susie Ky was wearing a purple chiffon evening dress and a medal of *Distinguished Civilian Service* awarded by the South Vietnamese Government. Her

father had also arranged that Susie was to have a seat in the South Vietnamese Government from 1969 onwards. The *Las Vegas Restaurant* was reserved for senior officers and their families only.

"Good evening sir," said the *maitre d'hôtel* who was a Warrant Officer E13 in the Marine Supply Section.

"Good evening Chief," answered Vortex cheerily.

As the Colonel sat down to a sumptuously set dining table for six, he looked about the restaurant and saw that it was already half full. Apart from Marine officers there were officers from all the other services, including the US Coast Guard and the Royal Australian Army, Navy and Air Force.

Five minutes later Brigadier General William McBride strode up. This officer was in command of sensor operations in I Corps Operational Zone. Accompanying him was Colonel William Walker who was Director of the G-2 Intelligence Section of the entire III Marine Amphibious Force. Generals Cushman and Tompkins brought up the rear.

After the introductions were over the conversation began in earnest.

General Cushman said to Brigadier General McBride, "Colonel Vortex is going up to *Khe Sanh* to join Colonel David Lownds in the defence of that all important Marine base."

McBride smirked, "Good luck Colonel. Better you than me!"

Colonel Vortex snarled, "That is why I am a superlative combat field commander and not just a pen pusher, a REMF [rear echelon motherfucker] and intelligence gatherer. We Marines are always the ones who have to do the dirty work and clean up your fiascos while you pansies in the Air Force sit in your bucket seats and play with your fancy aeroplanes!"

General Tompkins winced, "Colonel Vortex! May I remind you that you are speaking to a superior officer?"

Brigadier General McBride raised his hands in a conciliatory gesture, "Its alright General! I realise that Colonel Vortex, even though he has just been awarded the *Purple Heart* and another *Congressional Medal of Honour*, is under a lot of stress."

Vortex spat out with venom as he snarled viciously, "You! General! Don't know the meaning of the word stress! So how can you judge when others are being subjected to it?"

General McBride was now starting to lose his temper as he leaned forward in his chair and spluttered something. Saliva sprinkled from his lips but the words did not usher forth. His chest was heaving up and down uncontrollably as Colonel Walker whispered something in his ear to placate him. Lieutenant General Cushman was just about to severely scold Colonel Vortex when the *maitre d'hôtel* came up to take their orders.

Susie Ky ordered first, "I would like to have for entrée a Caesar salad with Italian dressing and six dim sims. Also could you bring some tomato soup and onion soup… you know? With the extra melted cheese on top. For main course I would have Baron of Beef well done, suckling pig, boiled gammon, sweetbread and sausages, porterhouse prime frankfurts, salami as well as fish cakes, soused fish, bouillabaisse, minestrone soup and fricassee salami."

The waiter was furiously writing everything down, "And for desert madam?"

Susie Ky giggled and looked to Colonel Vortex mischievously, "I haven't finished my main course order yet! Do you mind?"

The Marine waiter bowed his head apologetically.

Susie Ky continued with her order, "In addition I would add to that Russian salad, *specialite de la maison*, *consomme* soup, mackerel plaice with kipper and oh! yes! Langouste with scallops and green cheese and a side plate of Beluga caviar."

The waiter scribbled frantically and looked flustered as the other Generals looked at Susie with amazement. General Cushman whispered in Vortex's ear and the Colonel smirked as Susie went on.

"For desert I would like you to bring me, Yorkshire pudding, sugar plum candy, Turkish delight with ice cream but it must be vanilla flavoured and no other, Orange Jaffa fruit, mangosteen fruit with maraschino cherry on top and lashings of rich dairy cream. Also do you have any whortleberry pies?"

The waiter wiped the sweat off his brow and looked with stupefaction to the other officers repeating stupidly, "Whortleberry pie? I don't know madam?"

Susie Ky admonished as she waved her hands impatiently for him to go away.

"Well? Don't just stand there! Go and see!"

"Yes Madam!" The Warrant Officer scurried off and came back in four minutes.

"Yes madam, we have whortleberry pie."

The *maitre d'hôtel* turned to Lieutenant General Cushman Jr.

"May I take your order sir?"

Susie Ky cut in abruptly, as she smacked the NCOs' arm, "What's the matter with you? I haven't given you my wine order yet nor my cheese and coffee order!"

The waiter was almost beside himself, "Sorry madam!"

"Give me some *Zweibach* cake and English muffins as well. For wine I'll have a 1959 *Bollinger* champagne, Vin du pays but not later than a 1948 vintage, Burgundy white and Rheinish red, some Vin Rose and Spumante as well, say two bottles of each of those. For cocktails with my entrée I'll have a glass of the following; Highball, a Shandy, hippocras, *posset* and a stingo mixed drink with cherries on top, and on all of them a touch of lemon. But not too much mind you! I'll have a cup of Turkish coffee as well as one of Irish to round it all up with. For cheese with the coffee I want Camembert, Roquefort, Parmesan, ripe cheese, Edam in thick slices and Dutch cheese in

thin slices as well as Stilton cheese in medium slices with savoury crackers but not with pepper on top but with salt."

The waiter's hand started to get writers' cramp, "Will that be all madam?"

Susie Ky fiddled with the napkin on her lap, "Yes! I think so."

She pursed her lips and corrected, "No! Wait! I want some gefilte fish and matzo ball dumpling chicken soup as part of my entrée. Do you understand waiter?"

The Marine *maitre d'hôtel*, nodded ludicrously, "Yes. I understand. You want gefilte fish. I think we have that available although it is not the most popular dish on the Marine officer's menu."

The waiter turned to the Generals and took their orders briskly and succinctly. All three of them, including Colonel William Walker, simply ordered a de luxe hamburger with French fries and American mustard.

"And you sir?" the waiter asked as he twirled his pen over the yellow menu pad.

Colonel Vortex stretched his back and cracked the joints in his fingers by flexing his digits in the interlocking position.

"The gefilte fish sounds good. Give me that and the matzo ball dumpling chicken soup. For main course I'll have the delicious Vienna Schnitzel with tomato sauce and French fries. Oh!..."

The Colonel paused and thought carefully, "I'd like some fried onion rings on the Vienna Schnitzel as well."

The waiter nodded and asked, "Anything for desert sir?"

Colonel Vortex riposted, "You know what I want for desert!"

The Warrant Officer's mouth fell open with stupefaction.

"I beg your pardon sir?"

Vortex snarled, "I've been here before. Don't you remember what I ordered for desert on that previous occasion?"

The senior NCO blushed red, "No. I'm sorry sir. I don't."

"That's why I'm a Colonel and your still a Warrant Officer."

Then he added as he smirked at Susie Ky and lit a cigarette, "I want vanilla, chocolate, raspberry, pistachio, lemon, strawberry, coffee, hazelnut, lime, mango, passion fruit and cherry flavoured ice cream. I want it served in double cones on silver goblets."

The waiter smiled, "Yes sir!"

Vortex growled, "I haven't finished yet!"

The waiter suddenly had a depressed expression spread across his face.

Vortex continued, "Each cone must be exactly 2 and one half inches in diameter and the ice cream must be firm when you bring it out. I want those little chocolate crackers or wafers edged into the top right hand corner of each ice cream cone. But they should not be inserted into the desert more than one quarter of an inch. All these dishes should be served to me simultaneously. Do you understand that?"

The waiter was becoming extremely nervous.

Do you mean sir that you want all the ice cream flavours served to you simultaneously?"

Vortex waved his arms up in despair and slapped the waiter across his forearm.

"No! You moron! I want everything served to me simultaneously! The entrée, the salad, the main course and the desert and the coffee but excepting for the after dinner mints."

"I understand sir. But…"

Vortex brutally interrupted the harassed waiter, "What is it now?"

"Is it alright if we bring another portable table on wheels up to the main dining table? As I don't think there will be enough room on this table?"

Vortex beamed with delight, "Of course!"

General Cushman asked as the waiter finally left, "I didn't know that you liked matzo ball chicken soup and gefilte fish?"

Vortex said briskly, "Well I do."

"Why do you?" asked Cushman.

"I don't know. I just do."

"Its bizarre," said General Cushman as he handed Brigadier General William McBride the tasty garlic bread and pickles.

"I suppose…." began Vortex, "I like matzo ball soup because even though it can't do you any good – at least it can't hurt!"

Everybody at the table chuckled as the brass band started playing some martial music to set the romantic atmosphere.

The substantial and sumptuously delicious dinner went on for more than three hours. Second helpings were ordered and Susie Ky who had not yet sated herself with her original order also asked for an entire suckling pig to be roasted on a spit and served with gravy. It was 2300 hours before the coffee and cheese was served. Five waiters brought in three huge plates of the most exotic and rare cheeses from all over Europe and the world while the rank and file Marines guarding the base outside were on dry C rations.

Finally, as Lieutenant General Cushman secretly undid one notch in his Marine belt to ease the pressure on his stomach, he asked, "Colonel Vortex? Would you be interested in a small interrogation?"

Vortex pricked up his ears as he massaged the inside of Susie's thigh under the table.

"Did you say an interrogation?"

Cushman repeated, "Yes. I did. A very important interrogation and it has to do with *Khe Sanh*."

"Then of course I am interested. You know that I am an expert in the art of extracting information from spies and prisoners of war. I undertook a special course as part of my Marine Academy training."

"Excellent," cut in Brigadier McBride.

"Yes!" added Colonel William Walker, "I have tried to question the young cur as to the troop strength which is now building up around *Khe Sanh*. But the little bastard refused to divulge anything."

Vortex scoffed, "I'm not surprised! What methods did you use?"

"I beg your pardon?" asked the other Colonel.

Vortex rolled his eyes to the ceiling, "I said! Colonel! What methods of interrogation did you use? Did you inject the prisoner with scopolamine? Or any other truth serum? Did you use electric shock treatment? Or perhaps simple physical punishment and discomfort? Did you threaten this young cur with any harm to his family members if he did not divulge the required information?"

Colonel Walker blustered and turned red with embarrassment.

"I didn't do any of those things Colonel Vortex. I am an intelligence officer not a crude and vulgar prison officer!"

Vortex laughed as Susie Ky ran her hands over his burgeoning crotch under the table.

"Then its no wonder that you got nothing out of him! If you want to deal with these pieces of shit then you have to dish out a little bit of shit! A little vulgarity goes a long way with these Viet Cong motherfucking pimps!"

Lieutenant General Cushman echoed, "I couldn't agree more."

He munched on a huge slice of Camembert cheese and added, "You must use a fair degree of force to achieve success."

"I have always thought so," confirmed Vortex, his brilliant blue eyes shining with the prospect of delights to come.

Brigadier McBride asked, "And why is this particular prisoner so important?"

"I'll tell you why!" began Major General Tompkins, "…he is the nephew of none other than General Vo Nguyen Giap!"

Colonel Vortex stammered, "General Giap's nephew? Marvellous. How did you catch him? How old is he?"

General Cushman answered, "The bastard is 18 years of age and he is a volunteer in the North Vietnamese 304th Division. We had a search and destroy mission out from Hill 881 North which is just above *Khe Sanh*. Our 26th Marine Regiment brought the little rat in. Good job don't you think? They were on the attack trying to take Hill 881 North but Colonel Lownds and his men stopped them. This nephew of his is a platoon commander."

Colonel Vortex asked, "He's a bit young isn't he?"

Brigadier McBride answered, "We know for a fact that they are scrapping the bottom of the barrel. We have seen battalion commanders who are only 25 years old."

Susie Ky cut in as she arose from her chair, "Come my love! Let us dance!"

Colonel Vortex nodded to the other officers, "Excuse me gentlemen."

General Cushman said, "Enjoy your dancing. I have promised my partner that I would not dance until this war is finally over."

Colonel Walker chuckled as he sipped on a glass of Bollinger RD, "Then it looks like your dance floor technique is going to get pretty rusty General!"

As Vortex and Susie walked out to the parquetted floor General McBride said angrily to General Cushman, "This Vortex fellow is a rude and arrogant bastard! I'm surprised General that you do not discipline him further than you have."

Cushman answered with venom, "Why don't you mind your own fucking business Brigadier General! You are an Air Force General Officer! Don't presume to tell me or to attempt to instruct me on how to deal with my own Marine field commanders! I would have thought that you had enough trouble dealing with your Air Force personnel! You leave us Marines to ourselves! We look after our own and we don't stab each other in the back like the stinking English Navy! That bunch of lime-sucking stooges!"

There was a few moments of stony silence. Then everyone turned their attention to the dance floor.

The whole restaurant laughed as Susie Ky and Richard Vortex slid like greased eels onto the dance floor. There were about a dozen couples doing the honours.

Vortex requested the band leader to play the appropriate music and they showed their ballroom prowess with one fantastic routine after the other. Vortex spun the giddy Susie through the, Lambeth Walk, the Charleston, the samba, the conga line, the hornpipe, the Irish jig, the Hamilton House, the Gay Gordon's, the rumba, the mambo, the *cha cha cha*, the *Palais Glide*, the foxtrotter, the gavotte, the polka and the fandango.

"Bravo! Bravo! Bravo magnificent display!" screamed Lieutenant General Cushman. Everyone in the large restaurant put their hands together in rapturous applause.

"You two are a sensation!" expostulated Colonel William Walker.

"Thank you! answered Vortex.

"I am an expert dancer," said Susie Ky as she fluffed her chiffon evening dress and brushed back her luxurious black hair. Vortex looked at his watch, "Oh! Its 1am already. I'd like to see this nephew of the great General Giap. The one who is trying to take *Khe Sanh* away from us."

"Of course Colonel Vortex. After splendiferous dancing like that your request is my immediate command!"

They arose from the dining table and the American taxpayer picked up the bill for their enormous and succulent repast – half of which was left rotting on the tables uneaten.

They bid Brigadier General McBride and Colonel Walker a good evening and left them for the main building in the centre of the Marine complex at *Quang*

Tri. This was the Supreme Headquarters of the III Marine Amphibious Force and contained the Divisional Headquarters Staff for the 1st Marine Division as well as the 2nd and 3rd Marine Divisions. Of course these three Divisions also had alternate Headquarters in the field when they were on the move and at *Phu Bai* and *Dong Ha*.

After traversing a maze of corridors that led through the centre of the building they came to the bunker entrance. Six swarthy Marine Military police guards checked their ID's and then gave the three officers a whiplash salute.

"Thank you," said Cushman as he led the way after returning the salute.

They walked down a concrete stairway for some 350 steps deep into the bowels of the earth. Everything was reinforced steel and concrete from 12 to 21 inches thick.

"This place can withstand a direct nuclear blast," mentioned Major General Rathvon Tompkins.

Colonel Vortex laughed, "Sir! I don't think the North Vietnamese have nuclear weapons!"

Lieutenant General Cushman quipped back, "No! But the Chinese Chicom motherfuckers and the Soviet-Bolshevik cunts do!"

Vortex was immediately sobered by this thought.

But then he became filled with joy at the prospect of a nuclear war with the Soviets as he was sure it would accelerate his career path.

On the right was the underground communications centre and the fire control and coordination centre. It was a hive of constant activity. From here the assets of US *Task Force 77* off the Gulf of Tonkin together with the US 7th Air Force and Strategic Air Command with its fleets of B-52's and the combined firepower of the US Army and the US Marine Corps were coordinated and intermeshed to achieve maximum destructive power.

"Here we are. The maximum security detention and interrogation centre for the III MAF and I Corps Operational Zone," said General Cushman as five sturdy Marine guards swung back an enormous titanium steel door. They walked on.

Major General Tompkins said, "We are so far underground here that the only thing bringing air into these chambers and cells is a highly efficient air ventilation system powered by 10,000 Watts of electricity. It supplies all our power requirements from computers to kitchen stoves."

"Very impressive!" cried Colonel Vortex.

Then he asked as he smirked at his lover, Susie Ky, "How far down are we here?"

Tompkins answered without embellishment, "Four hundred feet below the surface of the earth."

"This way," ushered Cushman.

Vortex noticed that there were two rows of cells on each side of the concrete corridor. The ceiling was about 10 feet high but the corridor itself was massive stretching 25 feet wide and going on in a straight line for one and a half miles.

"How many prison cells are there here in this God-awful place?" asked Vortex as Susie Ky looked around with macabre fascination.

General Cushman answered, "We have 2,350 concrete cells in this prison complex. Each cell is 8 feet wide by 8 feet deep and 5 feet high. It has no bed, no toilet and no furniture. It is just a concrete box where the Viet Cong or other political prisoners reside 24 hours a day except when he or she is brought into the larger interrogation rooms where we are going now. The prisoner, when he is not being questioned, is kept in perpetual darkness even at meal times. He is given a bowel to shit in and this must be emptied twice a day. He or she uses the same bowl to eat from. He or she sleeps on the concrete floor and the temperature is maintained at 50 degrees Fahrenheit. This is just warm enough to keep the prisoner alive. No blankets or clothing other than his orange tunic is supplied. While in his cell the prisoner is manacled with steel chains at all times. There is absolutely no sound inside the cell as they are sound proof as well as light proof."

Major General Tompkins interrupted his superior as he laughed, "Sometimes we have kept Viet Cong prisoners in total darkness and total silence without letting them out of their concrete box for seven, even eight months at a stretch!"

Vortex giggled, "That is very illuminating. I suspect then that your method here is to break them down psychologically before you begin the gruesome physical torture?"

Cushman answered, "That's absolutely right! We have kept General Giap's nephew in solitary now for 10 days. And it is good that you are here to begin the physical interrogation of this young cur."

Vortex said modestly as he caressed Susie Ky's buttocks while the two Generals were looking in the other direction, "I am the most superlative expert available in these subtle methods and techniques of interrogation."

General Tompkins beamed with delight, "We are here!"

Two muscular and vicious looking Marine guards, each over six foot six inches in height, snapped a salute to the senior officers and checked ID's even though everybody knew Cushman and Tompkins by sight.

General Cushman ordered, "Open interrogation room 7-D!"

At his command the Marine guard on the left moved like a robot and pressed a red button in the side of the wall. Immediately a 12 inch thick steel titanium door slid sideways revealing what looked like a large and expansive room. Vortex noticed that it was about forty feet long, fifty feet wide and twenty feet high. All sorts of tools and devices were sitting on steel trolleys in the middle of the chamber. But one thing in particular caught Vortex's eye.

"This is the prisoner?" As he spoke Susie Ky gasped with shock and then with delight as Cushman switched on the lights to the underground chamber.

The Viet Cong youth was in a steel chair unlike anything that Vortex had seen before. There were steel manacles built into the chair to lock around the ankles and the wrists. The seat of the chair was hollow so that Vortex could see that the naked buttocks of the Viet Cong was exposed, allowing implements and other devices to be inserted into the rectum from below.

"This is the first light that this bastard has seen for 10 days," said General Cushman.

"He looks very thin? I don't think that he'll be able to stand up to my physical interrogation General," mentioned Vortex as he went up to the youth and pinched his nipples savagely drawing blood as he did so.

Cushman said with mock hilarity, "This is not a five star hotel! This is an intensive and high security interrogation centre! We feed the Viet Cong and North Vietnamese one bowl of drain water and a hot soup made of raw pig's intestines and gruel. That's all that these bastards need in my opinion!"

Vortex chuckled, "Who am I to disagree with you General?"

Major General Rathvon Tompkins interrupted, "But I think we should leave Colonel Vortex so that he can get on with the interrogation."

General Cushman nodded, "If you find out anything from this Viet Cong cur you make sure that you let me know in precise detail."

Vortex snapped up a salute, "Absolutely General!"

As Cushman and Tompkins walked out of the interrogation room, two large Marine guards entered briskly. One had a plate of caviar and cheese refreshments which he placed on the writing table in the middle of the room. The other wheeled in a steel trolley that looked like a portable barbecue. It was in fact a charcoal brazier which had several iron pokers and pincers heating in its glowing flames.

"Excellent!" exclaimed Susie Ky, "I see that they have brought the tools and devices of special and ordinary questioning."

Vortex sniggered, "Yes! They are fine implements for persuasion and illumination!"

The young boy who was manacled to the steel chair by his four limbs was completely naked as he started to scream and shriek with horror. He blathered a torrent of words in Vietnamese.

Vortex understood that they were cries for mercy.

"If you reveal to me everything you know…" began Vortex as he gripped the black hair of the 18 year old, "…I shall make it easier on you. Perhaps I won't find it necessary to use all these terrible instruments."

Susie Ky took off her chiffon evening dress until she was naked except for her silk panties. Her luscious breasts bobbed up in front of her brazenly. But the young boy was too terrified to take any notice.

"You are a lovely young boy," she began as she sat on the naked child's lap, "…why did you become a Communist? Is it because your uncle is the infamous and brilliant General Giap?"

There was no answer from the youth as he looked in terror at the red hot steel pincers and tongs residing languidly in the glowing charcoal brazier.

"It looks like we shall have to show this young man that we mean business!" screamed Vortex as he slapped the youth across the face with a savage blow. Two more slaps hit his face as Susie Ky bit into his left ear, tearing, nibbling and scratching until blood flowed. She then licked the blood off the child's face with gentle lust and indecency.

The shrieks of the boy increased audibly as Vortex chuckled, "You can scream as much as you like you little prick! Nobody can hear you down here in this concrete and steel bunker."

The Colonel walked slowly over to the charcoal brazier and picked up one of the steel pincers gingerly. Its end was red hot and glowing like a match.

"Bring it over here!" laughed Susie Ky.

"How should I commence my lover?" asked the Colonel.

Susie said as she caressed the boy's gonads in her fingers, "Why don't you extricate his teeth and fingernails?"

Vortex sniggered, "That's indeed a fine starting point."

The red hot pincer was wielded expertly by the Colonel. The boy's hands struggled, twisted and wrenched in the steel manacles that held his arms to the titanium chair. But it was useless. The more he struggled the deeper were the laceration wounds in his wrists and ankles.

Vortex screamed, "Give it here!"

As he spoke he caught the first finger of the man's right hand in the poker and gouged the device underneath the nail into the very quick of the digit, tearing and pulling. Blood erupted from the flesh as the nail was easily ripped out of its roots. Vortex worked slowly and deliberately until every nail had been vivisected free from its base. The blood from the man's hands streamed in a fine film across his legs and gonads onto the concrete floor.

Susie Ky and her lover took a break for refreshments.

"This cheese and liqueur is delicious!" began Vortex, "I'll have to order some up to my room this evening before we continue our licentious love making."

They both sniggered as they gorged themselves on the food. Then Vortex placed Susie Ky onto his lap and slid himself into her in full view of the suffering Communist

cur. The rear of Susie's vagina was clearly visible to Giap's nephew as they fucked. The semen burst forth in another ejaculation as they tongue kissed, mixing the food into their own comingled saliva.

Five minutes later when they had eaten their fill of the fine Swiss and Italian delicacies, they began in earnest.

"Why don't you make love to this rascal as I proceed with his toes?"

Susie nodded and Vortex snapped the head brace into position around the Viet Cong's skull. This steel frame had the shape of a head so that it encapsulated the victim's skull neatly and completely. There were openings in the steel for the ears, the nose, the mouth and tongue and the eyes. Each of these organs could thus be mutilated at leisure while the rest of the skull was held in place.

"I shall tongue kiss this boy while you mutilate his toes!" laughed Susie Ky.

Vortex mentioned, "Give him his last enjoyment in this life my lover."

"I shall! Don't you worry about that!" the beautiful woman laughed.

Vortex tore into the boy's feet with all his strength. He gripped each toe and closed the burning pincer around it. At first it took him more than half an hour to wrench out the toenails but he decided that it was not enough.

Susie Ky inserted her mouth and tongue through the aperture in the head-vice and tongue kissed the boy with relish. She sucked, cavorted, licked, teased and kissed the youth until he was almost suffocating for air. In-between her kisses the horrific screams would escape in the foul gasps from his tortured features. It was an unbelievable sight to behold.

Vortex asked, "Hand me that surgical blade on the writing table!
I think they call it a dermatome."

Susie complied and the Marine officer proceeded to sever off each toe completely.

"There! It is well done!" he commented.

The two of them stood back and surveyed their savage handiwork. The man's screams were slightly softer now as he had lost a tremendous amount of blood.

"I want you to answer my questions Viet Cong," said Vortex as he leaned into the man's face.

"I want you to reveal to me how many Viet Cong divisions are concentrating around *Khe Sanh*? Which divisions are they? What are General Vo Nguyen Giaps' plans? How many artillery pieces do the North Vietnamese have? When do they plan to launch the attack? What is the objective? *Khe Sanh*? Or multiple incursions into the DMZ and I Corps?"

Vortex slapped the youth as he proceeded with the brutal and unrelenting interrogation.

Susie Ky heard only muffled screams, blathering and incomprehensible mutterings that told them nothing.

"It is useless!" she screamed, "He won't tell us anything!"

Vortex grabbed the man's hair and took an electric clipper. He shaved until the man was bald and poured gasoline over the scalp, igniting it. Still there was no answer to the questions as the flames licked and flowed gracefully across the burning, screaming flesh.

"I think…," began Susie Ky as she picked up a small, surgical knife, "I think that what we need now is an enema of boiling oil."

The Colonel said with surprise, "All the necessary tools and hoses are here."

He pointed over to an aluminium trolley at the far end of the room which had; hammers, tongs, thumbscrews, needles, steel spikes, rubber hoses and clubs arrayed over its surface.

"I shall prepare the concoction," said Vortex.

Susie Ky knelt before the man and took each sac of his groin into her mouth, sucking them for one last divine moment of sexual revelation. She tried to suck the shaft of the penis to an erection but it was impossible due to the Viet Cong's suffering and torment at the hideous mutilation. He was now fingerless and toeless.

"It is prepared!" announced the Colonel as he stuffed a rubber hose inside the rectum and pushed it directly into the bowels of the man. The burning hot oil was pumped upwards and the new shrieks of horror were unfathomable. Even Susie winced at the noise of the divine suffering. Vortex severed off the man's ears, slit his nose, and cut out his lips as Susie castrated him simultaneously. The man died in Susie's arms as she tried to revive him with smelling salts, revealing nothing of the Viet Cong and NVA offensive against *Khe Sanh*.

Richard Vortex stepped back as his lover dressed into her chiffon evening dress and lit up a cigarette.

Then he prayed, "Oh! Lord! Our Merciful God and His Almighty and Gracious Son! Give us the strength this day to combat those that you have matched against us. Let Jesus in his power and his mercy bring us with everlasting salvation to a quick and speedy victory over the Communists and the Asian anti-Christ that has many false faces and is so surfeit with malice and deception.

Unto your Trust Oh Lord! We bequeath our struggle for victory in Vietnam!"

Chapter 6
Arrival at Khe Sanh

General William C. Westmoreland was in a foul mood on that morning of the 18th January 1968. The new year was not auguring well for American troops in Vietnam. The enemy, thought the General, as he sipped on his strong, black Hungarian coffee at the Officers Mess of the III MAF Supreme Headquarters in *Quang Tri*, seemed to bounce back with remarkable resilience even after the most devastating defeats and despite the massive firepower of the US Military Assistance Command [US-MACV].

General Westmoreland also knew that time was running out.

American public opinion was at best critical of the conflict and at worst downright hostile to the extent of being almost revolutionary in its condemnation of President Lyndon B. Johnson and the Military Establishment. The US media were like vultures, trying to exaggerate every set back and belittle every success. Westmoreland was reaching exasperation point. He knew that he could not afford to suffer even one minor battlefield defeat by the Viet Cong. If that happened the press would have a field day. But what was worse, President Johnson might panic and pull the entire plug on the continual build-up of US manpower and machinery in South East Asia.

Lieutenant General Cushman, who was sitting opposite, could see the look of bewilderment and concern on General Westmoreland's face as he ate a delicious Hungarian cheese pocket which had been warmed up by the Marine kitchen.

"Are you alright sir?" asked Cushman.

General Westmoreland grunted something that Cushman couldn't make out. He didn't bother to ask again.

In fact General Westmoreland was thinking about the shock resignation of Secretary of Defence Robert S McNamara who had quit out of growing disillusionment with the conduct of the conflict. His appointment as President of the World Bank would at least allow him to pursue the war with slightly more vigour than previously.

In addition he was not reassured by his superior General Earle G. Wheeler, the Chairman of the Joint Chiefs of Staff, when he said that the single most important

factor in the prolongation of the war was Hanoi's belief that the Americans would crumple and cave in before the Viet Cong irregular forces were obliterated in a whirlwind of firepower.

On 1st January 1968 Westmoreland had a meeting with Admiral Ulysses Grant Sharp, Commander in Chief Pacific, *(CinPAC)*, who told him that Operation Rolling Thunder had been a great success so far. The Admiral claimed that massive amounts of Communist materiel had been annihilated as well as forcing the North Vietnamese to divert manpower from civilian construction and agriculture to military tasks. It had also, the Admiral claimed, forced North Vietnam to rely more heavily on military and economic aid from their Chinese and Soviet masters.

However General Westmoreland, as he watched the sun go up on the horizon, knew that he could not rely entirely on these fanciful and over optimistic predictions. He believed only in hard realities and what his guts told him. And his guts said that the Viet Cong were getting stronger while his troops were struggling to maintain their own.

Suddenly Colonel Vortex sauntered into the breakfast room of the Officers Mess, followed by Major General Rathvon Tompkins and Susie Ky.

"Good morning Colonel!" beamed General Westmoreland. The Supreme Commander's spirits were automatically lifted at the sight of this brutal, efficient and deadly field commander. Westmoreland had the utmost faith in Colonel Vortex. All the other worries and tribulations seemed to evaporate from his consciousness as the Colonel walked in.

"And a very good morning to you too sir!" as Vortex spoke he jumped in front of General Westmoreland's breakfast table like a gazelle and snapped up such a vicious salute that General Cushman sitting nearby thought that Vortex's arm was going to be pulled out of its *humero-scapular* ball and socket joint.

Susie Ky, who knew Westmoreland well, walked over gracefully and kissed William Westmoreland modestly on the cheek. The Supreme Commander was touched.

"Please! Miss Ky! Colonel Vortex! And you too, Tompkins! Sit down and have some of this delicious Hungarian cheese cake. Its simply divine!"

"I don't mind if I do sir," laughed Vortex. Everybody sat down and the Marine waiters brought on fresh coffee and more pastries. The presence of General William Westmoreland at the *Quang Tri* headquarters was always a special treat. A line of six Marine chefs and waiters stood at a discreet distance from the breakfast table ready to fulfil the slightest culinary wish or desire. Vortex noticed that behind the Supreme Commander were members of his personal staff. There were six Captains, four Majors, two Lieutenant Colonels and of course Brigadier General Joseph A. McChristian, the Chief of the G-2 Section. They murmured softly to each other and went through that morning's telex and field command reports as well as coordinating the air strikes into North Vietnam proper for the next 24 hours.

"Its delicious sir," said Vortex as he finished one cheese pocket and gorged himself on a second.

"How is your father Miss Ky?" asked Westmoreland as he clicked his fingers indicating that he wanted Brigadier McChristian.

"Very good. Thank you General." Susie partook of some cornflakes and coffee as she fiddled with her coiffure.

Brigadier McChristian whispered something into Westmoreland's ear and the Supreme Commander nodded calmly.

Lieutenant General Cushman asked, "Are you ready sir? The helicopters are standing by."

General Westmoreland took a telex paper marked Top Secret in red capital letters that were emblazoned both vertically and horizontally across the A4 sheet from Brigadier McChristian who stood like a vulture behind the breakfast table.

He read the contents of the page and then pursed his lips.

Waving his arms in a contemptuous yet graceful manner he handed the telex sheet back to his G-2 Chief.

"Well! That is that!" sighed General Westmoreland.

"Anything the matter sir?" asked Lieutenant General Cushman as Major General Tompkins leaned forward on the breakfast table, obviously not much interested in Hungarian cheese cakes.

"I've just had word from the President," began the Supreme Commander.

"About?" asked Cushman in monosyllables.

"Nuclear weapons," answered General Westmoreland tersely.

General Cushman asked excitedly, "The President has approved their use?" His eyes almost popped out of their skull.

Major General Tomkins added, almost beside himself with the joy of anticipation.

"Sir! I can have atomic artillery shells flown into *Khe Sanh* today! They have a yield of between 5 to 25 kilotons each! The dirty Viet Cong won't know what hit them! Now we can pulverise their troop concentrations around *Khe Sanh* even before they begin the attack! If they are indeed going to attack."

"No," was all Westmoreland said as he lifted his coffee cup to his lips.

"I beg your pardon sir?" asked General Cushman already dreaming about the North Vietnamese *body counts* he was going to have when the Marine Corps unleashed their tactical nuclear arsenal.

"No!" said Westmoreland again.

"No?" asked Cushman, his face crestfallen.

"You mean – No?" repeated Major General Tomkins.

"It can't be – No?" asked Colonel Vortex as he dropped his Hungarian cheese pocket onto the plate in front of him, suddenly losing his appetite.

Susie Ky laughed, "It must be that 'No' means 'Yes', eventually."

"No means No," repeated Westmoreland as he felt all the demons in his mind emerging once more.

"It's impossible!" blustered Vortex as he jumped up and threw back his chair in anger.

"It's absolutely No!" expostulated Brigadier McChristian who stepped forward into the fray and waved the Top Secret telex in front of Vortex's vicious, blistering gaze.

Westmoreland continued to sip his coffee calmly.

"Here! Let me see that!" screamed Vortex as he snatched the Top Secret telex out of the Brigadier's hands.

General Cushman stood up and peered over Vortex's shoulders as he read the telex. He stood on his toes as he was only nearly six foot tall while Vortex was six foot two and a half inches tall in his bare socks.

"Shit!" exclaimed Vortex in bitter disappointment.

"Fuck!" said General Cushman in a state of manic depression.

"It can't be?" admonished Major General Tompkins as he slapped his coffee cup onto the table.

"It is gentlemen," said Brigadier McChristian with resignation.

Everybody looked to the Supreme Commander.

General Westmoreland finished his coffee and straightened his khaki shirt collar. The four stars on both sides of his shirt shone like brilliant lights in a dark and foreboding firmament.

"I'm sorry gentlemen! I'm truly sorry!"

Colonel Vortex resumed his seat painfully as Susie Ky wiped a tear from her eye, "I am sorry too sir. I was so looking forward to using atomic shells at *Khe Sanh*. It would have helped us enormously."

"It is a filthy betrayal of the South Vietnamese people!" cried Susie Ky, then she added, "Does President Thieu know yet?"

"Has anybody told Vice-President Nguyen Cao Ky?" asked Tompkins.

"He will be here shortly. He is going to accompany us on the inspection tour of *Khe Sanh's* defences," said General Westmoreland who had suddenly developed a terrible migraine.

Then the Supreme Commander added, "The President has ordered that under no circumstances will nuclear weapons ever be used, regardless of their yield or method of delivery."

Colonel Vortex protested, "That may be sir! But couldn't we just sneak in a few small atomic artillery shells into *Khe Sanh*? Say, the smallest yield weapons we have in our inventory,…"

Vortex rubbed his chin as he said with a whining voice, "…only, say, 5 or 10 kilotons?"

General Westmoreland thought severely for a moment as General Cushman almost willed the Supreme Commander to say '*Yes.*'

"It's out of the question, I'm sorry," repeated General Westmoreland.

Major General Tompkins, whose face now appeared ashen with grief, said, "Part of the *37th ARVN Ranger Battalion* will be flying in with us sir."

"Good," said Westmoreland as he wiped the brilliantly clean napkin across his lips and chin.

"These Hungarian cheese cakes are magnificent!"

Then the Supreme Commander added, "Pack some for me in the helicopter."

At his command a Marine Warrant Officer gave the orders with a snap of his fingers. A picnic hamper was prepared.

Colonel Vortex took Susie Ky aside as the Supreme Commander and the rest of the high ranking officers, including South Vietnamese general staff officers, made their way out of the building and into the *Quang Tri* air base where 357 UH-1D helicopters, 59 CH-47 Chinook helicopters and elements of the 1st Air Cavalry Division comprising 120 of the latest *Cobra* attack gunships were warming up in a forest of spinning rotor blades. The roar of over 500 aircraft was deafening.

On board were the men of the 37th ARVN Ranger Battalion numbering 1,500 troops, 3 batteries of 105mm howitzers, 1 battery of 155mm howitzers and 18 guns of 175mm calibre to provide the '*big punch*' if and when *Khe Sanh* would be attacked. In addition to this, hundreds of tons of ammunition, recoilless rifles, grenades, 0.50 cal machine guns, *Rome plough* bulldozers, tractors to clear the jungle, steel pipes, *Bangalore torpedoes* and a host of other equipment were due to be airlifted into *Khe Sanh* by C-130 Hercules transports over the next few days.

"Well this is goodbye then?" asked Susie Ky.

"Not really," said Vortex as he took the beautiful South Vietnamese girl in his arms and lavished kisses over her smooth and succulent flesh, tasting her aroma and sweetness.

They tongue kissed for some minutes in the corridor that led down to the subterranean interrogation chambers. Nobody was in the immediate vicinity.

As they embraced and groped like love-sick teenage fornicators they could hear the groans and shrieks of Viet Cong prisoners being questioned below them.

It didn't bother them in the slightest as Vortex massaged Susie's vagina over her well tailored pants.

His lover got down on her knees and started to unzip the Colonel's camouflage trousers which had been freshly starched and ironed to perfection by a retinue of servants. But he stopped her.

"No! It's not possible my sensuous lover! Not here! Not now! They are waiting for me in the helicopters!"

Susie started to cry with anger, "They can wait for you a little longer!"

"They can't," said Vortex as he lifted her to her dainty feet.

Then he added, "We can make love when I get back!"

Susie slapped him on the chest with playful frustration.

"You always spoil my fun!"

"I do not!"

"Yes you do!"

"I can't fuck you here in the fucking corridor! Anyone could burst in!"

"Who gives a fucking rat's ass!"

"I do!" admonished Vortex as he added, "What if Westmoreland walks in on us?"

"So? Big deal!" she screamed.

Then they both started to giggle as the hideous shrieks from under the earth became more audible and more terrifying.

"Go then! But don't get yourself killed. You hear me?" cried Susie as she took out her handkerchief and wiped the concourse of tears from her eyes and cheeks.

"I suggest that you go back to Saigon my love," said Vortex as he turned to go.

"Why?" asked Susie Ky.

"I think it will be safer for you there."

They embraced once more as Vortex said, "I don't know how long I'll be in *Khe Sanh* for. It could be a month, perhaps two. Who knows? It all depends on General Vo Nguyen Giap's plans."

They kissed and the last Susie saw of Vortex was his muscular spine and shoulders disappearing behind a door at the end of the corridor leading to the tarmac.

The 536 assorted helicopters were all revving up and standing by ready to go. They were all waiting on Colonel Vortex himself.

"Glad you could make it Colonel!" laughed General Westmoreland facetiously, as Vortex sprinted across the open expanse of the huge concrete and steel tarmac at *Quang Tri.*

"Sorry sir!" said Vortex as he threw his duffel bag into the pit of the Cobra gunship.

His breath came in deep gasps from the exertion.

As soon as the Colonel's feet left the tarmac the 536 gunships started to lift into the air.

General Westmoreland, Lieutenant General Cushman, Major General Tompkins, Colonel Vortex, Brigadier General McChristian, Brigadier General Schweiz and the Lieutenant Colonel commanding the 37th ARVN Ranger Battalion were all in the lead gunship.

Lieutenant David Peter EHRLICH

The 105mm, 155mm and 175mm howitzers were carried behind the *Cobras* and UH-ID's by the CH-47 Chinooks. Further behind were 7 *CH-54 Tarhe Sky Cranes* carrying the heavy equipment such as the *Rome plough* bulldozers and tractors.

"We have an escort of 12 F-4E *Phantoms* from the *USS Midway* in the Gulf of Tonkin, sir," said General Cushman.

General Westmoreland nodded and as if on queue the jets could be seen streaking past the lead formation of Cobra gunships.

Major General Tompkins informed, "We will be flying over the *Quang Tri River* along Route 9 straight into *Khe Sanh*, sir!"

Everybody had to shout because of the roar of the multitude of rotor blades, engines and now jet aircraft.

"Give me a run down on the history of the Marine Combat base at *Khe Sanh* Colonel Vortex!" screamed the Supreme Commander.

"Yes sir!" began Richard Vortex as he sat down on the helicopter bench seat next to the four star General.

One of the most experienced pilots in the US Army was flying their *Cobra*. His name was Major Saunders and he was a veteran of countless battles with the Viet Cong. He had won the Distinguished Service Cross in 1966 for machine gunning more than 20 Viet Cong snipers single handed when his chopper had crashed near *Dakto* after running out of petrol.

Colonel Vortex began, "The *Khe Sanh* base, as you well know sir, is located some 6 miles from the border with Laos and about 14 miles south of the DMZ. Our base is a tangible threat to the stinking and rancid *Ho Chi Minh trail* which links the North Vietnamese supply depots and rail yards with the Viet Cong and regular North Vietnamese divisions (PAVN) deployed in South Vietnam. It was the Special Forces that originally set up the nucleus of the current base at *Khe Sanh*. Their objective in those early days was to use it as a staging post for patrolling the maze of roads and tracks nearby that made up the *Ho Chi Minh* trail. The first attack by the Viet Cong pimps came in January 1966 when they shelled the base with long range artillery. They failed to cause any lasting damage. However, from January 1966 to December 1966 the North Vietnamese and their cocksucking Viet Cong stooges increased pressure on *Khe Sanh* by endless spoiling attacks and harassment. However, our magnificent men in the Special Forces repulsed all of these stupid attacks with minimal losses. So, in January 1967 our boys in the Marines arrived and took over from Army Special Forces. The first commander as you know General, was Colonel John Lanigan and his 3rd Marine Regiment. The Special Forces boys moved deeper into Viet Cong territory by moving westwards to the Montagnard village at *Lang Vei*.

Captain Frank Willoughby is now commanding that superlative outfit."

General William Westmoreland interrupted as General Cushman handed out some steaming Jasmine tea which they all appreciated immensely.

"I know Captain Willoughby very well! He is an excellent man!" said the Supreme Commander with enthusiasm.

General Tompkins cut in, "You will meet him sir at *Khe Sanh* in a few minutes. He is going to report developments at *Lang Vei* to you in person!"

"Excellent!" beamed Westmoreland, and then he added, "Please continue Colonel Vortex."

Vortex sipped on his tea and went on, "Last year a Seabee battalion built a 1,500 foot runway made of pierced steel planking so that we could bring in the big C-130's. By May last year Colonel Lanigan had succeeded in throwing back the Viet Cong pimps from the various strategically placed hills north and north-east of *Khe Sanh*."

General Westmoreland interrupted once more,"…and they would be Hill 881 North, Hill 881 South, Hill 558 and 861/861A and Hill 1015 to the north-east."

Colonel Vortex nodded, "That's absolutely right sir! And in May of last year Colonel John Padley's boys in the 26th Marine Regiment replaced the 3rd Marines. During the later half of last year the constant flow of C-130 Hercules transports beefed up the base defences but it took its toll on the runway. The extreme weight of the Hercules which could be up to 135,000 lbs fully loaded, caused the wet clay beneath the steel planking of the airstrip to shift continuously. While the Seabee's were making repairs we ordered the lighter transports such as the *C-7A Caribou's* to fly in."

Lieutenant General Cushman who was now munching on a chocolate bar added, "Yes. But the *Caribou's* could not bring in all the heavy material needed to fix the runway. This included the matting made of steel as a foundation for the airstrip."

General Westmoreland asked, "What did you do then?"

Colonel Vortex continued as he noticed the deep and melodic boom of artillery fire in the distance. It seemed to be coming from the Marine bases at *Cam Lo* and Camp Carroll which were to the north of their formation as they flew westwards to *Khe Sanh* and *Lang Vei*.

"At first we started to para-drop some of the heavy supplies needed by the Seabee's to fix the airstrip while it was closed. However, since the aluminium matting needed for the steel planking of the runway could not be para-dropped we devised the method of *'Parachute extraction.'*"

Major General Tompkins explained, "Yes. It was an ingenious method. Our riggers on the aircraft lashed the strips of aluminium to metal pallets and loaded them onto the C-130's. As the Hercules transports flew very low over the runway with its rear cargo bay open, the pilot would signal the boys in the cargo compartment to release the bonds holding in the pallet. Immediately, a parachute which was filled by

the flow of the plane's slipstream opened like a whiplash and pulled the metal pallet with its cargo out the rear hatch. This pallet then sailed through the air for say 30 to 40 feet until it hit the ground and slid to a halt."

General Westmoreland said, "Very impressive!"

Colonel Vortex picked up the briefing, "Thus the Seabee boys extended the airstrip to a length of 3,900 feet. But we had other problems."

"What?" asked the Supreme Commander.

"Well sir," he continued, "...*Khe Sanh* is built on a small plateau which is overlooked by those hills that we just mentioned. This gave the Viet Cong and their North Vietnamese keepers a very good expanse of high ground upon which to bombard the living shit out of us in *Khe Sanh*. In addition, the stream that supplied water to the base had its origins in enemy held territory further towards the Laos border. Thus they could fuck with our vital water supply as they pleased. Even poison it. On top of all that the weather in the early months of the year is pitiful. Dense fog shrouds the base and the nearby hills making air operations difficult and defence of those hills a sheer nightmare! It limits our artillery spotting visibility almost to zero on some days. And the rest of the situation you already know sir."

General Westmoreland leaned out of the gunship hatch. He was still strapped in by a seatbelt however.

"Thank you Colonel Vortex!"

Brigadier McChristian said as he frowned at Colonel Vortex, "I think all these preparations are more than adequate sir."

"Really?" replied Westmoreland.

"I don't think that the enemy are going to attack within the next few weeks. Especially not so soon after the new year and their upcoming *Tet Lunar Festivities* which is such an important date on the Buddhist calendar."

Colonel Vortex lost his patience, "Oh! Come on! General! That is, I believe, one reason why they are most likely to make a surprise attack! They think that most of the South Vietnamese Army will be on leave during the *Tet Lunar New Year* holiday. And they will be right! It is the perfect time for the North Vietnamese to launch an offensive."

General Westmoreland said as their formation of gunships filled the air at over 170mph.

"I tend to agree with Colonel Vortex."

"What do you mean sir?" asked Lieutenant General Cushman.

"I mean that I can feel it in my guts that they are up to something. I don't know exactly what – yet! But I had this premonition or feeling during my service in the Korean War of 1950 -1952. It happened just before the scum-sucking Chinese Chicoms attacked across the *Yalu River* causing our American home town boys to be

massacred by those Communist fanatics. It resulted in the biggest *'Bug Out'* I have ever seen in my entire and illustrious military career!"

Everybody in the chopper fell silent for a few moments. Finally it was Colonel Richard Vortex who spoke as he tapped the pilot on the shoulder indicating to him to speed up the formation's descent into *Khe Sanh*.

"Let me assure you sir that whatever happens over the next few months – *Khe Sanh* will NOT! Fall!"

Vortex took out his huge, razor sharp Marine dagger and brandished it in front of General William Westmoreland's face.

"I give a guarantee of blood! My blood! That *Khe Sanh* will indeed be held! We Marines of the 9th Marine Regiment, the 26th Marine Regiment and the 37th ARVN battalion will pledge our blood and our honour in the defence of *Khe Sanh*. We shall give you General Westmoreland a sterling, top class performance. My whole body and mind is geared up and ripping with revenge for the destruction of the Viet Cong malingerers and whore-masters and the magnificent defence of *Khe Sanh*. I shall cut out the living guts of the North Vietnamese imperialist cocksuckers and use them to grease the treads of our bulldozers and tractors. I shall use their livers to oil our 175mm artillery pieces. The only regret that I shall have is that I haven't been able to kill, butcher, eviscerate and annihilate enough of the putrid vermin!"

Lieutenant General Cushman looked in amazement at Major General Tompkins who looked to Brigadier General McChristian and General Schweiz and all of them looked to General William Westmoreland who was brimming with pride.

Colonel Vortex's face was flustered red and purple with uncontrollable patriotic zeal and homicidal fervour as he continued.

"I don't give a fucking rat's ass what the defeatist media back in the States say about this war! I don't care how many times they lampoon and degrade our heroic efforts here in this titanic struggle in the Republic of South Vietnam! They can talk and report all the twisted crap and putrid vomit they like but *we know* General! We know in our hearts the truth of what is happening out here in Vietnam! Our magnificent American boys will show once more the superiority of their training and their dedication in combat that has earned the United States Marine Corps the prestige of being the finest fighting force the world has ever produced – of course, along with our German brethren in the *Wehrmacht* during their efforts in World War 2 against the Bolshevik scourge and pestilence.

My Marine Corps is more precious to me than even the firmaments of heaven itself.

God! Corps! And Country! That is our motto and nothing on this fucking earth will change our will to win! We shall pulverise those stinking Viet Cong pimps and

by the time we have finished with them they will wish that they were back in their mother's womb, never having been born in the first place!"

Brigadier General Schweiz added, "*Wir werden sie wie zerschlagen wir zerquetschten die Bolschewiken im Weltkrieg 2!*" [Translated: We will smash them as we crushed the Bolsheviks in World War 2.]

By the time Colonel Vortex had finished his speech his voice had ascended into a high pitched shriek of pure vicious venom.

General Westmoreland leaned over and clasped Colonel Vortex's hand with both of his own in a desperate show of sincere gratitude.

"Let me tell you Colonel,..." began the Supreme Commander as the other Generals looked on, "I have in you an absolute and unqualified trust! You are one of the best, if not *the best* field commander I have. I am glad to have you on board and with us so wholeheartedly. Your unbounded enthusiasm and dedication is a primal force that dispels all the darker angels from my subconscious fears,...you know – Colonel?"

General Westmoreland took out his handkerchief and slowly and deliberately wiped the beads of sweat from his brow. His movements were slow and methodical, as if he was trying to search for the right expressions.

"When I lie awake at night and try to sleep before the next day's duty, I think of all those fine American boys from Kansas, from Iowa, Kentucky, Arkansas, Alabama and Georgia and all the other States of our great American nation. I think of them and how they have sacrificed their lives in the ultimate defence of our glorious, God-fearing and just United States of America and in the containment of this evil and pernicious force of world communism and the international Communist conspiracy for total world domination. I weighed up the grains of sand and try to decide what has been gained as opposed to what has been lost. I torture my mind in endless, circular thought. Should we continue here in Vietnam? Or, should I advise the President to scale down our effort and prepare to pull out? When I hear you speak Colonel Vortex, then all my doubts and fears, all my remorse and feelings of guilt, my inner demons and my hesitation are dispelled. Your words are as a beacon of redeeming light. Your single minded devotion to the destruction of our enemies is a sacred force that must be nurtured and cherished. I wish I had the unshakable will, the '*der unerschütterliche Wille, um zu rasen,*' that you seem to possess in abundance. The stamina of your pursuit against the Viet Cong and PAVN is breathtaking!"

Colonel Vortex's chest swelled with the sweet atmosphere of the hills around *Khe Sanh.*

"I thank you sir for those kind words. Your confidence in me has redoubled my strength and tripled my determination to exterminate the enemy around *Khe Sanh* and its strategic hills!"

General Westmoreland added, "I shall give you all the support I am able to muster!"

Brigadier General McChristian added, "Colonel Vortex. We are making contingency plans for something called *Operation Niagara*."

"*Operation Niagara*?" repeated the Colonel with curiosity.

"Yes,…" continued the Supreme Commander, "*Operation Niagara* is a contingency plan that the US 7th Air Force and Task Force 77 in the Gulf of Tonkin have drawn up. It involves the heaviest concentration of air power the world has ever seen. Even our new Aggressor Squadrons will be involved. But the biggest punch will come from the B-52 *Stratofortress*."

Vortex was impressed. "*Khe Sanh* will receive direct support from the B-52's?"

"Absolutely!" beamed General Westmoreland.

Then he added, "We have incorporated all the latest technology in ground control and radar surveillance into the package as well. It will be the showcase of our digital tracking technology and the new computerisation of command and control. Something hitherto never attempted in the annals of air warfare."

Major Saunders leaned backwards in his cockpit seat and said, "There is *Khe Sanh*."

All the Generals craned their necks forward to see through the bullet proof Plexiglass helicopter window.

Khe Sanh lay majestically before them on a small plateau. The 3,900 foot runway was clearly visible with two taxiing roads coming out at right angles to form a small box at its western end. The concrete pillboxes, sandbag emplacements, dugouts, the *Direct Air Support Centre* and the *Marine Air Traffic Control Unit* buildings were all visible.

Suddenly machine gun fire erupted all around them as they approached from the east along Route 9. Bullets sprayed everywhere. Immediately the lead group of 100 *Cobra* gunships opened fire with their quad 0.50 cals. The noise was deafening.

Lieutenant General Cushman shouted to Westmoreland, "It's the North Vietnamese troops sir! Their 304th Division! Every time we fly in the anti-aircraft fire becomes more and more intense!"

General Westmoreland nodded, "I want the *Phantoms* to lay down a high explosive and napalm carpet as the Task Force lands."

Major General Tompkins nodded and spoke to the Major commanding the F-4E squadron.

"Understood sir! We shall blow them to hell!" answered the Marine officer from the cockpit of his *Phantom* fighter-bomber.

Everybody heard his voice over the radio-telephone.

The 12 *Phantoms* were from the 390th Tactical Fighter Squadron based in *Da Nang*.

"Here they come! Block your ears!" screamed Colonel Vortex.

The *Phantoms* came in line abreast at 650mph. The gut-busting, heart-wrenching sound could easily implode a man's eardrums if they were unprotected. They swooped in like huge vultures or birds of prey at tree top level as the CH-47 Chinooks and the heavy CH-54 *Tarhe Sky Cranes* landed first at the eastern end of the runway near the 81mm mortar battery emplacements.

The Generals put their fingers in their ears while the helicopter pilot and co-pilot and the three gunners had their helmets to protect them.

General Westmoreland's guts seemed to wrench into two diagonal frames of nausea as the first spread of napalm hit their targets to the north of *Khe Sanh* just ahead of Hill 881 North. This area was known to have a heavy concentration of North Vietnamese troops and anti-aircraft batteries.

"Land us immediately!" screamed General Cushman. The 120 *Cobra's* followed by the 357 UH-1D's and 1E's landed in wave after wave. As soon as the helicopters had divulged their cargo and troops they took off at once and headed back to *Quang Tri*. Only the 120 *Cobra's* would stay for an extra 30 minutes while General Westmoreland completed his inspection tour.

"We are out of the firing sphere sir!" yelled Colonel Vortex as their gunship touched down very near to the *Ground Controlled Approach Headquarters* and bunker complex, abbreviated to [GCA], which was roughly in the very centre of the *Khe Sanh* defences.

The airstrip control tower was nearby at the edge of the runway. It was fully manned and the staff were frantically directing the inflow of scores of helicopters. Other personnel were seeing to the disembarking of the 1,500 men of the *37th ARVN Ranger Battalion* of the South Vietnamese Army. These were the elite troops of President Thieu's government and they were well received by the rest of the Marines at the base.

The General Staff officers piled out of the helicopter as they followed the Supreme Commander. A small brass band was playing martial music as Colonel David E. Lownds came running up with his own staff.

Major General Tompkins strode up to Colonel Lownds, "Colonel? We shall want a full report later!"

Colonel Lownds was about five feet eleven inches tall and he weighed 188lbs. Thus compared to Colonel Vortex he was quite small and did not have the same huge musculature or barrel chest.

"Yes sir!" shouted back Colonel Lownds. The commander of the 26th Marine Regiment had blue eyes and his hair was already greying as he was in his mid-forties. Colonel Vortex who had just turned 41 years had climbed the ladder faster than Lownds and was already earmarked for a meteoric rise once he returned to the Pentagon in Washington D.C.

General Westmoreland shook hands with Lownds after saluting.

The Supreme Commander said, "I want to congratulate you on the fine work that you have done here at *Khe Sanh* so far!"

"Thank you sir!" beamed back Colonel Lownds.

"You know Colonel Vortex, commander of the 9th Marine Regiment?" asked Westmoreland.

Vortex stepped forward and shook hands tentatively with the other Colonel. They did not like each other much as a few years back Colonel Lownds' son had been dating Vortex's daughter. Vortex did not like it. What both father's had never found out, however, was that Peggy, Vortex's daughter, had become pregnant at the age of 14 years and she had secretly organised an abortion in a dirty backyard clinic run by a de-registered doctor from the backwaters of the Crimea who had emigrated to the United States. The unwanted foetus was flushed out unceremoniously but at the price of an infection which Peggy had to keep hidden from her father for several months due to the doctor using unsterilized surgical blades.

"Of course sir! We know each other well!"

Colonel Lownds scowled at Vortex, "What are you doing here Colonel Vortex? I am the ground commander at *Khe Sanh*! Not you!"

Lieutenant General Cushman and the 3rd Marine Division commander winced with embarrassment. They were terrified least the two Colonel's would start an argument in front of General Westmoreland right before the inspection tour. It would be an unforgivable fiasco.

"Ah! That is not exactly correct Colonel Lownds," began the Supreme Commander.

"Sir?" asked Lownds with a fever of apprehension as he added, "Am I being relieved of my command sir!" His face turned crimson and then ashen with hatred for Colonel Vortex. He knew that Vortex was Westmoreland's personal pet and he was just another faceless regimental commander without any special standing.

Major General Tompkins gave a stern look to Colonel Lownds as if to tell him by eye contact alone, to shut-the-fuck-up and to do so at once.

General Westmoreland laughed as he slapped the Colonel affectionately on the shoulders, "No! No! Whatever gave you that idea? Colonel Vortex has just joined you in joint command of *Khe Sanh*."

"Joint Command?" asked Colonel David E. Lownds as wind blustered out of his open mouth in gasps.

"That's right Colonel," added Vortex who lit up a cigarette after using his lighter to ignite the Supreme Commander's. General Westmoreland spoke in deliberate tones as he watched the stream of men from the 37th ARVN Ranger Battalion walk off the

airstrip and into their accommodation bunkers as they were directed by NCOs' from the 26th Marines.

"I have appointed Colonel Vortex to be your joint command and duty officer here at *Khe Sanh*. He has my full and utmost confidence! You will both direct the forces here after consultation with Major General Tompkins and Lieutenant General Cushman. Orders will be given according to how the tactical and strategic developments will unfold. The day to day running of the base, of course, will be entirely up to you and Colonel Vortex."

As the Supreme Commander spoke Lownds straightened up his spine and thrust out his chest, "Sir. With all due respect to Colonel Vortex. I can't carry on this sort of joint command. It will interfere with the efficiency of the base and its operations."

General Westmoreland looked angrily to Lieutenant General Cushman who was standing to his right. He then spoke to Lownds without mincing words and in a frustrated tone of voice.

"Either you are in joint command with Colonel Vortex or I *will* relieve you of command of *Khe Sanh* altogether!"

Colonel Lownds turned yellow as his guts felt like putrid shit, "Of course sir! It will be no problem at all! Joint command as you say sir! Absolutely! The best way to go about it sir! I am sure Colonel Vortex and I shall put up a sterling service for you and the Marine Corps!"

General Westmoreland nodded sarcastically at this sudden cave-in and back-flip.

Colonel Lownds was terrified of being relieved of his command. Especially since this engagement that he could feel was coming, might earn him a promotion and the *Distinguished Service Cross* as well as a unit citation for his 26th Marines.

"Where is Lieutenant Colonel Tran?" asked Westmoreland.

A South Vietnamese officer came running up from the direction of the airstrip. Colonel Tran was the commander of the 37th ARVN Rangers.

"Are all your men disembarked – or should I say *de-planed*?" asked General Westmoreland.

"Just about sir!" answered the South Vietnamese battalion commander.

"Good! Then come with us!"

"Ah! Sir! Good to see you again sir." The voice came from a Marine Major General who walked out of the (DASC) or *Direct Air Support Centre* which was slightly behind the GCA and further away from the airstrip.

General Westmoreland spun around on his heels, "Who is that?"

The Major General who approached with several other Marine officers was well known to everyone. His name was Major General Norman J. Anderson and

he commanded the 1st MAW or First Marine Air Wing. He had succeeded Major General Robert Shaw on the 2nd June 1967. The Marine Air Wing would supply about 50% of the total jet and fighter-bomber air support for the battle that everybody expected would come soon.

"General Anderson? I didn't know you were here?" said the Supreme Commander.

Suddenly a tremendous thundering roar came from the direction of Hill 881 North which was about 3 miles away.

"It's the Squadron of *Phantoms* that escorted us sir. They are just finishing off their final attack on the North Vietnamese positions and anti-aircraft batteries that constantly harass us." As Colonel Vortex spoke the whole ground shuddered underneath them. It felt like a small tremor. In the distance a wall of flame could be seen rising slowly at tree top level and then dispersing into black, odious clouds of pure destruction. Melted Viet Cong flesh mixed with the uprising black clouds seemed to have the stench of *Bergen Belsen*.

"That should keep them quiet for awhile!" said Major General Tompkins.

"Everything is ready for the start of the inspection tour sir," beamed General Cushman enthusiastically.

"Let us begin!" said Westmoreland as the 12 *Phantoms* screamed overhead like frightened banshees. The jets would fly subsonic over American positions but would increase their speed to supersonic when traversing known Viet Cong territory. In that way they could cause additional damage to the enemy from the shock of the sound wave boom trailing behind the aircraft's engines. Many Viet Cong eardrums had been ripped apart in this way.

"If you please sir," ushered Colonel Lownds, "The *Guard of Honour* is ready for inspection."

Lined up along the internal roadway in front of the (DASC) was 1,000 handpicked men of the 1st Battalion 26th Marine Regiment. They stood in ranks 200 wide and five deep. They were immaculately dressed in their camouflage greens. The senior NCOs' stood behind the phalanx and the junior officers in front. General Westmoreland reviewed the ranks and stopped occasionally to talk to the rank and file.

"Where are you from son?" he asked one soldier who was only five feet seven but was extremely muscular.

"From Los Angeles sir!" shouted back the Pfc.

"And what did you do there before you joined the Marines son?" asked the Supreme Commander.

"I was a law student at UCLA, sir!" shouted back the soldier.

"Do you want to return to your legal career?" asked Westmoreland as he placed his hand on the man's shoulder in a gesture of friendship.

"No sir!" answered the Pfc.

"No?" asked Westmoreland as he looked around at General Cushman and Colonel Vortex in surprise.

"Why not? Son?" asked the Supreme Commander.

The private answered as he threw out his chest with pride.

"Because sir! I want to stay here in Vietnam and kill Communists! Sir!"

Colonel David E. Lownds' face almost fell into two pieces and Vortex had difficulty holding back a chuckle that he hoped was not audible to the other Generals.

As Westmoreland moved along the ranks he turned to Colonel Lownds, "The enthusiasm of your troops is heartening Colonel!"

"Thank you sir!" smiled the commander of the 26th Marines.

"And what is your name son?" asked General Westmoreland as he looked up at a huge Corporal who was six foot seven inches tall and must have weighed approximately 245 lbs of solid muscle. Even Colonel Vortex, at six foot two and a half was dwarfed by this monster Marine man.

Corporal Heinrich Totenkopf sir! Marine Number 34987002 Sir!" screamed the beefy Marine at the top of his lungs.

"You are a very impressive soldier Corporal Totenkopf," said Westmoreland. Then he added, "Have you always been this tall since age 17 years?"

The Corporal answered, "No Sir! I was only six foot tall when I had my 12th birthday sir!"

Major General J. Anderson smiled, "Colonel Lownds has a battalion of supermen here General Westmoreland."

"It seems so," replied the Supreme Commander.

"Totenkopf?" repeated Westmoreland, "…that is not a common name is it? Where do your parents come from son? Before they immigrated to the United States?"

The Corporal answered, "From the Ukraine sir!"

"That's part of the Soviet Union isn't it?" asked Westmoreland.

"No sir! It is an occupied independent country subjugated by the Soviet Union! Our country is closely allied and shares a common heritage with the great German Reich!" shouted back the Marine NCO.

"Why did your parents come to the United States soldier?"

The Corporal screamed back with venom in his voice, "Because sir! My grandmother was pack raped and mutilated to death by the Soviet pigs during World War II sir! They found out that she was a *White Russian* supporter during the civil war from 1917 to 1921 when the *White Russian* armies supported by the United States, France, Germany and the other Western Allies failed to bring back the Tsar! That was after the fall of the *Kerensky Government* that wanted to continue the fight in World War I. Sir! My grandfather was killed by Bolshevik troops in the 1930's at *Yekaterinburg* sir! My mother was imprisoned by Stalin after she was found to be

supporting and providing sustenance to the glorious liberating German Army as they freed our country during the launch of Operation *Barbarossa* on 22nd June 1941. She was imprisoned from 1941 to 1957 for this and also for accidentally dropping bread crumbs on Stalin's picture in the newspaper sir! I hate the Bolsheviks sir! That is why I relish my duty in the rock-crushing United States Marine Corps where I get to kill Communists and the chance to murder the sub-human North Vietnamese Communists rats in Vietnam sir! They are nothing but stinking, lime-sucking lackeys of the Bolshevik swine and Chinese barbarians sir! Thank you sir!"

General Westmoreland felt his heart go out to this valiant Corporal who was a member of the magnificent United States Marine Corps.

"I have every sympathy for you Corporal! Every thought is that of solidarity with you and the ideals of freedom and justice and equality for all of us! Made possible by our Superior Firepower! That is what our great United States of America represents! Firepower to crush our enemies and detractors! It is people like you that have made our nation great and that is why America is the Peacemaker in this world! After having taken that role from Germany."

"Thank you sir!" shouted the Corporal as he beamed with pride.

"Our mission here," continued General Westmoreland, "…is to make peace through uncompromising destruction of those that do not wish for peace! To gain a just *status quo* that can be accepted by both South Vietnam and the United States after the North is crushed."

Lieutenant General Cushman stepped forward, "Sir?"

"What is it?" asked Westmoreland.

"Time is running short sir. Time is of the essence. I suggest we continue with our tour of the rest of *Khe Sanh* before the afternoon."

Just then as Colonel Vortex stood behind Colonel Lownds and Major General Tompkins, Major Thrush came sneaking up from (GCA) or *Ground Controlled Approach Centre* at the edge of the airstrip. He had to scream in Vortex's ear because three C-130 Hercules transports were landing on the runway, bringing in much needed 155mm artillery ammunition.

"Sir!" screamed Major Thrush.

"Good to see you Major!" answered Vortex.

"I'm sorry about Major Lansdale sir!"

"Yes! Me too! His body is already on its way back to the States."

"I have a surprise for you sir!" said Major Thrush with a sly grin on his face.

"A surprise?" asked Vortex as he watched Westmoreland continue to walk up and down the ranks like a peacock as they followed from behind.

"What fucking surprise?" asked Vortex viciously under his breath, "I don't need any more surprises today. Besides, I have to figure out how to deal with this pompous

ass, Colonel David E. Lownds. I think he is going to try to usurp my authority here at *Khe Sanh!*"

Major Thrush added in confirmation, "Yes sir, I never liked that mangy son-of-a-bitch!"

As they whispered to each other Colonel Lownds glanced backward and gave Vortex and Thrush a dirty look.

Major General Tompkins was simply amused at the intense rivalry among his subordinate regimental commanders and he did nothing to intervene. As long as his subordinates fought amongst themselves then his position as Divisional Commander was secure.

"You two, - shut-the-fuck-up!" said Tompkins to Vortex and Thrush, "Can't you see that the Supreme Commander is talking to the troops! Our men need all the morale boosting that they can get! Now pipe down! And listen up!"

Colonel Vortex saluted to Major General Tompkins like a crazed automaton and said nothing more.

General Westmoreland inspected all the ranks, talked to several more of the Marines and then the whole party filed into the *Ground Controlled Approach Centre* for a briefing by Major General Norman J. Anderson of the 1st MAW (Marine Air Wing).

All the 6,000 or so men on the base and at the Hill outposts were extremely excited at the visit by the Supreme Commander.

The building and bunker complex of the GCA Centre had sandbag stairs leading down into the earth which continued for about fifty yards until it reached the steel door that guarded the entrance. General Westmoreland followed Colonel Lownds who led the way in. After them trooped Lieutenant General Cushman, Major General Tompkins, Colonel Vortex, Major Thrush, Lieutenant Colonel Tran, Brigadier General McChristian, Brigadier General Schweiz, Major Saunders the Army pilot and Captain Mirza Baig who was *Khe Sanh's* officer in charge of the *Base Fire Support Coordination Centre* as well as Captain Frank Willoughby, the commander of the US Special Forces [Green Berets] at *Lang Vei* who had just arrived by *Cobra* gunship only a few moments before.

A host of 2nd Lieutenants, Captains and Majors who were the officers commanding the various Companies and Battalions of the 26th Marines,

9th Marines, the artillery battalion and the 37th ARVN Rangers also followed and took up their positions in the rear of the room while the senior officers stood close to the briefing table. On the left side of the GCA Centre were a dozen NCOs' who sat in front of radar screens and other electronic equipment that monitored every incoming and outgoing flight of all types of aircraft from the USAF *Fairchild AC-119G SHADOW* gunship to the mammoth B-52D *Stratofortress* that was used in the devastating Arc Light raids on North Vietnam's industrial-military infrastructure.

"Right!" yelled General Westmoreland, "…Major General Anderson! I want you to give me a briefing on your plans for employing the 1st MAW at *Khe Sanh* and I also want to know every detail about the *"Super Gaggle" technique* that you are going to use here at this Marine Fire Support base!"

Major General Anderson looked around the room at the host of senior and junior officers and he felt the heavy pressure of high command weigh upon his broad and muscular shoulders. Major General Anderson was a distinguished looking man with brilliant, azure blue eyes and greying hair. His physique was slim and powerful for its medium stature of five foot nine and 178 lbs.

"It will be my pleasure to conduct the briefing General Westmoreland!" answered the 1st MAW Chief.

"Then get on with it!" barked back Westmoreland, his thick, black and bushy eyebrows raised and fell with the swings in his mood and the endurance of his patience.

Colonel Vortex grinned stupidly to Major Thrush as the later poked his fingers into Vortex's kidney for fun. Major General Tompkins glared at them to be still.

"Yes sir!" as he spoke Major General Anderson took up his leather briefcase from the large mahogany briefing table and pulled out a thick bundle of red and orange telex papers and briefing notes. You could hear a pin drop in the conference room as the officer's and NCOs' numbering nearly two hundred dared not even breath too heavily in front of the Supreme Commander.

Anderson coughed to clear his throat, placed his two palms flat on the table and looked intensely at the large scale map of the I Corps Operational Zone with *Khe Sanh* and its surroundings clearly standing out in coloured relief.

"As you know sir! The complex operation for the resupply and defence of *Khe Sanh* with aerial assets is a bottom to top operation!"

General Westmoreland slammed his fist down upon the table so hard that all the junior officers at the rear of the bunker briefing room jumped up with fright. Colonel Vortex merely laughed to himself. He was not afraid. He knew that he was William Westmoreland's favourite. He could do nothing wrong. The Supreme Commander had not even admonished him for the fiasco at *Thonthamkhe*.

"What the hell do you mean by that?" barked General Westmoreland, "What is bottom to top?"

The two star General quivered slightly, "Sir! Bottom to top signifies the lucid integration of all aerial assets into a cohesive mixture of continuous and unidirectional attack based on synchronised timing and radar and computer controlled accuracy which is termed *Combat SKYSPOT*."

General Westmoreland smiled and relaxed completely, "Oh! Of course! Yes! Why didn't you say that at the beginning! I understand now! Please continue!"

All the junior officers in the rear were able to loosen their cramped muscles for a few moments.

"Thank you sir," said Major General Anderson as his two brilliant stars flashed like gold teeth on his shirt collar which was starched to perfection so that it seemed as stiff as an ironing board. Anderson always wore his thirteen rows of ribbons. Even on his camouflage fatigues. The colour splashed out from his chest into everyone's eyes as he spoke.

He clicked his fingers and one of the 2nd Lieutenant's on his staff scurried forward with a white ivory pointing baton which he gently handed to the two star prima donna.

Anderson continued, "With the build up of the North Vietnamese 304th and 325th Divisions around *Khe Sanh* and its strategic hills, we, in the 1st MAW, and with of course your approval sir! Intend to use the full spectrum of tactical air support to obliterate the enemy both as they move and as they dig in. There will be nowhere for the forces of General Vo Nguyen Giap to hide. They think that because of their numerical superiority they can and will crush *Khe Sanh* over the coming weeks. But they are wrong. The more they concentrate their forces for the attack the easier it will be for us to pulverise them with an orgy of massive air strikes controlled by *Combat Skyspot*."

Suddenly the whole bunker complex reverberated with hideous explosions. Outside screaming voices could be heard as more detonations ripped and erupted through the delicate, moist and nauseating 3rd World atmosphere that reeked of decaying jungle and human shit.

General Westmoreland said, "Jesus! My Gracious God! What is that?"

Lieutenant General Cushman replied, "Just the usual mortar attack by the PAVN and their Viet Cong dogs. They control about 80% of the entire perimeter around *Khe Sanh*. Only Route 9 is still open. But enemy pressure is increasing daily to seal off that final escape route as well."

"Oh! I see! Will we be safe in here during the briefing?" asked Westmoreland as more thunderous explosions caused the ground to tremble beneath them. Dust from the steel reinforced ceiling of the bunker fell gently in a weird mist onto the mahogany briefing table.

"Perfectly safe sir," replied Cushman.

Colonel Vortex joked, "I feel like *Gruppenfuhrer Hermann Fegelein* in *Der Bunker* with the *Fuhrer* beneath the *Reich Chancellery* building in those last days of April 1945."

General Westmoreland said with indignation, "But *Gruppenfuhrer Fegelein* was a traitor! He tried to desert from the Bunker with his mistress and a stash of jewels and false passports! He thought that just because he was *Eva Braun's* brother-in-law as he was married to her sister, *Gretel*, that he could get away with such an outrage.

But Martin Borman had other plans for Fegelein. You are no traitor Vortex! I would equate myself more with *Gruppenfuhrer Mohnke* who valiantly took charge of the Berlin defence and fought to the death and to the last man in defence of the Reich!"

Colonel Vortex sheepishly nodded his apologies in silence.

Then added, "Sir, I actually met *Wilhelm Mohnke* when I was stationed at *Ramstein* for a few months back in 1963."

"Oh? Really? That's fascinating Richard. What does *Wilhelm* do these days now that he is out of *that* uniform?" asked Westmoreland.

Vortex smiled, "He has gone into the trucking business in West Germany sir."

"Oh well, good luck to him then," answered Westmoreland.

Anderson looked up with the whites of his eyes and continued the briefing, "As I was saying – all assets will be used from the United States Air Force, the US Navy, Vietnamese Air Force under Marshal Ky and the Marine Air Wing, as well as Strategic Sir Command using the B-52 *Stratofortress* which will take off from our overseas bases; namely, *Anderson AFB* in Guam, *Kadena AFB* in Okinawa and the *Korat Air Base* in Thailand. The *SuperGaggle* technique has been devised to co-ordinate air power to resupply and support the strategic hills around *Khe Sanh*. Each *SuperGaggle* applies to one operational mission. The heavy concentrations of anti-aircraft fire coming from the enemy, as you witnessed this morning sir, is a serious problem. The 1st MAW has devised the *SuperGaggle* to reduce the risks of our UH-1D helicopters and *Cobra* gunships from being shot down every time they fly in or out of the strategic hills. The weather is also a nuisance, especially in the early months of the year when fog and mist make it necessary to fly by instruments. With our *SuperGaggle* we send in a flight of transport helicopters with an escort of A-4 jets and UH-1E gunships which are under the control of a TAC(A) who flies in a *TA-4F*. The TAC commander coordinates any break in the weather and then orders all aircraft to rendezvous over the designated target or drop zone at the same time. The DASC or *Direct Air Support Centre* here in *Khe Sanh* will give the orders for the *SuperGaggle* to get underway. Therefore it will be Colonel David Lownds' responsibility to decide when to initiate air support and strike activities."

General Westmoreland interrupted again, "It will be Colonel Vortex's responsibility, General Anderson!"

"Oh! Sorry! Of course! Colonel Vortex!"

Colonel Lownds' face turned crimson with fury.

Vortex giggled.

Anderson went on, "We will resupply the formation by in-flight refuelling from KC-130 tankers that will lift off from *Da Nang*. The A-4's will come from our air base at *Chu Lai*, the UH-1E's from *Quang Tri* and the CH-46's from *Dong Ha*. It usually takes about 30 minutes for all elements to rendezvous over *Khe Sanh* at the

command of the TAC(A). Because of the stinking mist and foul weather, *'instrument climb outs'* will often be required by our pilots and even the CH-46's with their external loads will have to climb out on a *tacan bearing* until they fly on top of the target. If the putrid weather breaks then the TAC(A) can order the target area around *Khe Sanh* to be worked over with a cocktail of napalm, rockets and 20mm cannon fire as well as smoke if required by the ground commander at *Khe Sanh*. The CH-46's then come down in a spiral descent and drop their loads onto *Khe Sanh's* airstrip and the strategic hill outposts. This all takes less than five minutes. They spiral back up to the operational ceiling as well as the jets who immediately hook up to the KC-130 tankers for in-flight refuelling. Then our assets head back to *Da Nang* and *Chu Lai* while the choppers return to *Quang Tri*."

General Westmoreland said, "Thank you General Anderson for that illuminating and erudite insight into our air operational techniques!"

The Supreme Commander turned to Lieutenant General Cushman, "Could you give us a short briefing on the ground situation please."

"Certainly sir," said Cushman as he stepped up to the table. General Cushman was lean and tall with an intense demeanour. His grey eyes sparkled. He was one of those General Staff officers who loved every minute of his service in Vietnam. He had supreme confidence in himself and was fanatically loyal to General Westmoreland and the Pentagon Administration.

"Sir! Officers at *Khe Sanh*!" he began as he took the ivory pointing baton away from Major General Anderson.

"As you are well aware, the North Vietnamese have been building up their forces south of the DMZ and around *Khe Sanh* since November to December 1967. The central G-2 Section has identified no less than four enemy divisions in the area. They are the 304th which is just west of our Special Forces unit at *Lang Vei*…"

Suddenly Lieutenant General Robert Cushman asked as he peered around the bunker room, "Oh! Where is Captain Frank Willoughby? Is he here?"

Colonel Vortex nudged Major Thrush, "Have you seen the Captain?"

Then everyone's eyes swung towards the bunker entrance of the GCA complex they were in.

"I'm sorry I'm late!" saluted the US Green Beret Special Forces officer. It was Captain Willoughby himself who walked in with immaculate timing. He was dusty and his general purpose boots were caked in mud.

General Cushman scowled at the Captain through his glasses that fell onto the bridge of his nose.

"So! You have deemed to grace us with your presence Captain!"

Captain Willoughby whiplashed into a fearsome salute. First to General Westmoreland and then to the 3rd Marine Amphibious Force Commander.

"It's alright Captain. Come! Join the conference. I will want your input in a few moments." As General Westmoreland spoke he shook hands with the junior officer and ushered him to stand next to Major General Tompkins and Colonel Vortex.

Vortex knew Willoughby well from their previous 12 month tour in Vietnam. The two men smiled and nodded to each other. Richard Vortex looked on the 25 year old Willoughby as a younger brother. They had developed a special camaraderie.

General Cushman continued, "As I was saying, the 304th and 325th PAVN Divisions are west and north of *Khe Sanh* respectively. The 320th is opposite the *'Rockpile'* on the *Cua Viet River* and the 324th Division is inside the DMZ. We presume that this division is a strategic reserve for the other three and can be moved in any direction inside the I Corps Operational Zone to engage us as General Giap orders and sees fit."

"Overall, I have to say gentlemen…" Cushman hesitated for a few moments as he looked apprehensively over to General Westmoreland, "…overall I think the situation is becoming critical. Our 4 battalions and 1 artillery battalion here at *Khe Sanh* are already heavily outnumbered. We estimate that Communist strength must be at least 20,000 troops and possibly as high as 50,000 men. In addition Brigadier General McChristian estimates that about 11 to 12 Viet Cong Regiments are supporting the PAVN divisions bringing total enemy strength close to 86,000 troops plus auxiliary personnel and transport troops."

General Westmoreland asked, "So what do you think is the strategic objective of the PAVN?"

"I fear sir,…that Giap wants to encircle *Khe Sanh* and then roll up the entire front of I Corps from here to *Dong Ha. Ca Lu, Camp Carroll, Cam Lo* and *Quang Tri* itself are all in danger. I believe that the PAVN want to occupy the northern portion of South Vietnam as a bargaining chip if and when peace negotiations commence. Also if they are successful in rolling up I Corps then that would pave the way for them to initiate a general offensive to drive into the *Central Highlands* capture *Dak To* and threaten Saigon itself."

Westmoreland studied the colour map and ran his fingers along the *Khe Sanh* perimeter. He was oblivious to everyone for a few seconds.

"Thank you General Cushman," he said at last.

Without lifting up his head from the map he said bluntly, "And you Colonel Lownds! Report!"

The Commander of the 26th Marine Regiment stepped forward. He put his field glasses down on the briefing table, took a deep sigh and began.

"I have to agree with the assessment of General Cushman and the G-2 Section. Frankly! I think the PAVN are going to attack us. But I don't know when. That is the problem. Everyday I send out 200 man patrols from *Khe Sanh*. Some days I send 3 and on others 4 or 5. The most important patrol and reconnaissance that I organise is for

a 200 man Company to head out north from Hill 881 South. Each time my men go out there they get bushwhacked! But I have no choice! I have to know what the hell is going on! How many troops the PAVN are bringing up, how many VC irregulars there are – how many pieces of 130mm *M-46 artillery* they bring in and so on."

Westmoreland at last stood up straight from the briefing table with great effort. A million things were weighing down upon him. He knew that if *Khe Sanh* would fall his military career would be over. He would be sent home on a mail plane in utter disgrace. He would be the laughing stock of the entire military establishment and people would spit at him on the street, even in his own home town. That is why he ordered Colonel Vortex into *Khe Sanh*, his *angel of death*. Even though Westmoreland knew that the Colonel could be somewhat extreme in his political views and in some situations use a slight amount of excessive force, he also knew that if any officer could galvanise the men under him into an effective fighting force then it was Vortex. The Supreme Commander always believed in having an insurance policy to back himself up in case of an unmitigated disaster. And Colonel Vortex was his insurance policy at *Khe Sanh*.

"Where do you send the other patrols, Colonel Lownds?" asked Westmoreland.

Pointing with his finger, Lownds continued his report, "I send another patrol west from Hill 881 South and from *Khe Sanh* itself towards Route 9. These two patrols, each 200 men strong, link up south-west of *Khe Sanh* after reconnoitring the area north of *Lang Vei* and the *Khe Sanh* Village itself. They tell me what is going on in the village and how many enemy troops are harassing our Special Forces boys at *Lang Vei*. The rest of the patrols I send out east from Hill 558 and Hill 1015. These reconnaissance manoeuvres tell me what is happening on my northern flank where the NVA 325th Division is dug in."

Major General Tompkins interrupted, "If the *big push* does come. What is going to happen to the civilians in *Khe Sanh Village*?"

Colonel Lownds answered, "We have made contingency plans for the entire population to be airlifted to *Da Nang*."

"I see!" said the commander of the 3rd US Marine Division.

General Westmoreland turned to their gallant South Vietnamese allies.

"Colonel Tran? How are your men?"

The South Vietnamese officer commanding the 37th ARVN Rangers stepped forward.

"Ready for action sir! We are itching to grapple with the dirty VC! And their stinking North Vietnamese keepers!"

Lieutenant Colonel Tran was short at five foot seven but he was massively built with wide shoulders and arms like steel girders. He was an expert marksman and a martial arts fanatic. He weighed in at 190 lbs of rock hard muscle that loved to dismember Viet Cong traitors. This was his 9th year in the ARVN.

Major General Tompkins said, "It is good to have your men on board."

The South Vietnamese officer nodded and then asked General Westmoreland a question.

"Sir! Some of my men have expressed their wish to attack the enemy while on patrol."

"What do you mean?" asked Westmoreland.

Lieutenant Colonel Tran continued, "They want to launch a series of suicide attacks by driving trucks filled with high explosives into the PAVN ammunition dumps which we have located north of Hill 881 South. They will then detonate the trucks once they have driven them into the centre of the storage areas."

Colonel Vortex looked flabbergasted as he glanced sideways to Major Thrush. The latter simply rolled up his eyes in a mock gesture of disbelief.

"I am afraid that that is utterly impossible!" screamed General Westmoreland almost beside himself with a mixture of rage and pity.

"But sir!..." protested Lieutenant Colonel Tran. But the South Vietnamese 37th ARVN commander was cut brutally off in mid-sentence. He could see the orange-crimson fire in Westmoreland's eyes.

"Don't think that we Americans don't appreciate the gesture Colonel Tran! But your men are much too valuable, too precious an asset to sacrifice in such reckless attacks. Let our airpower smash their supply dumps, incinerate their flesh and crush their bloody bones into a pulp. We need every man here at *Khe Sanh*! Do you understand me?"

Colonel Tran nodded sheepishly as Westmoreland's voice rose to fever pitch and then fell off again.

Noises from outside indicated that a flight of 10 *Cobra* gunships were landing from *Quang Tri*. Inside one of the metal birds of prey was Brigadier General Burl McLaughlin USAF, the commander of aerial supply at *Khe Sanh*. In a few minutes he was inside the bunker briefing room and shaking hands with the Supreme Commander.

McLaughlin began, "The air supply of *Khe Sanh*, even under attack, is something that I can fairly well guarantee for you General Westmoreland."

"That is very reassuring Brigadier," smiled Westmoreland.

Lieutenant General Cushman asked the Air Force Brigadier, "But can you arrange for the Vietnamese civilians at *Khe Sanh* village as well as the Montagnard families at *Lang Vei* to be evacuated when the time comes?"

McLaughlin said without hesitation, "No problem!"

Westmoreland put his hands on Captain Frank Willoughby's shoulders with a hint of genuine affection, "And finally! Give us the current situation at *Lang Vei*, Captain. How are you Green Berets holding up?"

The young Captain stepped forward and ran his hands through his grimy hair. He seemed exhausted. Willoughby put his dirt streaked palms flat on the briefing table, smudging the immaculate coloured relief map of *Khe Sanh* and its environs.

"It's not good sir. The North Vietnamese are pushing, sniping, murdering and probing every hour of every day. I lost 12 Montagnard warriors yesterday. They were ambushed by the NVA not 500 yards from my camp. I found their mutilated bodies this morning. One of my Green Beret Sergeants was knifed in the back while on patrol. The others came under murderous fire and were lucky to escape. Its my opinion that there are much more than 20,000 PAVN out there. I would put the figure at more than 100,000 at least!"

Lieutenant General Cushman asked, "How long do you think you can hold out?"

Captain Willoughby coughed and tried to straighten his body, "I don't know. Perhaps a week or two, the way things are going. Less, if things get worse!"

General Westmoreland clapped the officer on the back, "You are performing magnificently! I heard about your successful ambush of a Viet Cong battalion a few weeks ago. Keep in close contact with Colonels Vortex and Lownds here at *Khe Sanh*. They have to know what is happening in front of the 304th Division."

"Will do sir!" saluted Willoughby.

General Cushman stepped forward, "Time is running short sir. I think its best if we proceed with the full tour of the base now."

Westmoreland nodded and addressed the whole retinue of staff officers and ARVN personnel.

"Thank you gentleman! I don't have to remind you how important nor how critical the situation is here at *Khe Sanh*! I know that all of you will do your utmost. All I ask is that you chew the VC's ass and eviscerate the NVA bastards! Don't let them catch their breath. We will provide you with a tornado of air power such as the world has never before witnessed. And I know that some of you who have been misguided by the defeatist media at home think that this could turn out badly for us. But you must trust in American technology and American ingenuity! We are the best army in the world. We have the finest equipment. The most sophisticated tactics, the most competent commanders and above all, we have a superlative will and a dedication to duty that only the American fighting man and woman can equal! God bless our United States of America! And good luck to you all! Thank you!"

Applause rose up from the conference room like a roaring tide before the storm that was about to unleash itself on the unsuspecting men of the valiant United States Marine Corps.

But the American nation always arose to the challenge with dignity, courage and valour.

Twelve wide bodied jeeps were lined up and waiting outside the GCA complex. Westmoreland, Cushman, Tompkins, Vortex and Lownds piled into the lead vehicle.

The rest of the entourage filled the others. As the jeeps drove off they could hear the intense machine gun fire in the distance as well as mortar explosions and heavy artillery. Huge mounds of dirt and sand were erupting into the air about 400 yards past the *Khe Sanh* perimeter wire.

Colonel Lownds said as everyone put on their helmets, "It's the NVA again sir! They are starting up another artillery barrage. The machine gun fire is coming from our boys over at Hill 881 South and Hill 558. The VC and NVA are probing our hill defences. It's a daily occurrence now."

Westmoreland nodded, "You must hang on to those hills! Do you understand me?"

As he spoke the Supreme Commander leaned backwards in the front seat of the jeep as Sergeant Major Crighton drove it. He looked intensely at the two Colonels.

"Those hills are your eyes and ears! If you lose them the enemy has captured the initiative. They will climb up those prominences, bring in their heavy artillery and blast your *Khe Sanh* plateau to smithereens!"

Colonel Vortex answered with a look of fanatical determination, "Don't worry sir! Those hills will be held! There is no possibility for retreat! No option for compromise! We shall defend them to the last man, the last bullet, the last artillery shell!"

General Cushman could almost feel the surging hate and venom in Vortex's blood whenever he fantasised about coming up against the North Vietnamese Imperialists and their war mongering Viet Cong stooges.

The jeeps drove slowly up the airstrip itself and started the tour of *Khe Sanh* working in an anti-clockwise direction. Westmoreland inspected the Headquarters bunker of the 26th Marines which now had the 9th Marine component as well. This bunker and mortar emplacement was at the western end of the base situated at the end of the airstrip. About 9 *Jolly Green Giant* helicopters and 7 C-130 Hercules transport planes were parked along the side taxi road of the runway. *Khe Sanh's* drop zone was close to the western edge of the perimeter. This is where the *Caribou's* and other planes would parachute drop supplies in if necessary. The TAFDS or *Tactical Airfield Fuel Dispensing System* was located just before the 26th Marine HQ bunker. Driving around to the south they came into the Forward Operating Base 3, which is where the 26th Marines had set up a full battalion who guarded the outer perimeter of *Khe Sanh*. Slightly in from these troops and their dugouts and bunkers was the ASRT or *Air Support Radar Team*. These men operated the radar systems to coordinate the air supply as well as the air strikes by tactical jets and the *SuperGaggle* missions to reinforce and supply the hill outposts around *Khe Sanh* which was manned by men from the 9th and 26th Marine regiments. As Westmoreland drove on he was cheered by all the 6,000 men at the base. The next bunker to be inspected was the MATU or *Marine Air Traffic Control Unit* which coordinated operations of the 1st Marine Air Wing operating out of

Quang Tri and *Chu Lai* as well as *Da Nang*. Next to this was the FSCC or *Fire Support Coordination Centre* headed by Captain Mirza Baig.

General Westmoreland and his entourage stretched their legs for a bit at this point. Then COMUSMACV, which was the other official title of General Westmoreland signifying, *'The Commander of the United States Military Assistance Command Vietnam'*, went into the FSCC and spoke to Captain Mirza Baig, the officer in charge.

"Is everything in order Captain?" asked COMUSMACV.

"Yes sir!" replied the fire support officer as he stood to attention like a stuffed bean pole.

Captain Mirza Baig was a career officer. He was 27 years old, of medium height with brown eyes and ash blonde hair. His physique was stocky and extremely muscular. His biceps alone measured 22 inches of steel, Viet Cong ripping flesh.

The NCOs' and men of Captain Baig's command also shot upwards to attention as the senior officers entered the FSCC.

"Could you please give me a quick briefing on the function and operation of this fire support centre?" asked COMUSMACV.

"Certainly sir!" barked back Captain Mirza Baig.

"You men get on with what you were doing! Don't mind me!" said Westmoreland as he waved his hand in a majestic sweep to the troops in the communication bunker.

Colonel Vortex and Major Thrush leaned over one of the radar screens out of simple curiosity.

The NCOs' plonked down into their seats as rapidly as they had jumped to attention.

Captain Baig began, "Sir! The foul and stinking weather is our major problem here at *Khe Sanh*."

Lieutenant General Cushman looked up from his bundle of teletype reports concerning the rest of the US 3rd Marine Division as it battled the PAVN and VC along the perimeter of the DMZ all the way from *Khe Sanh* to the coast adjacent to *Gio Linh*. He nodded in agreement and gave Major General Tompkins a piece of paper to look at.

Captain Baig explained, "Radar is an invaluable tool for guiding tactical fighters as well as heavy bombers such as the B-52 and B-52D. In addition, it is essential for the resupply and maintenance of *Khe Sanh* by transport aircraft such as the Hercules and the C-123 Fairchild Providers. We have now perfected a technique using both radar and computers which we call *'Combat Skyspot'*. This revolutionary method of radar guidance allows the ground operators here in this bunker as well as others all over the theatre of operations, to give a pilot, say in a B-52, the exact coordinates and timing for the unleashing of his munitions to hit a preselected target. We here in the

26th Marine regiment have our own radar for controlling both supply drops into *Khe Sanh* as well as tactical air strikes."

General Westmoreland interrupted, "It sounds excellent!"

Colonel Vortex added, "It is the most efficient way so far for coordinating our tornado of firepower. The bloody PAVN are going to die like vermin under a cascade of our bombs and a virtual molten torrent of napalm!"

COMUSMACV smiled at Vortex and turned back to Captain Mirza Baig as he continued his illuminating dissertation.

"We here at the FSCC or *Fire Support Coordination Centre* utilise data from the ground sensors that have been laid in the surrounding jungle. From that information we deduce the likely avenues of attack of the PAVN and the VC. On those lines of thrust used by the enemy we pile on artillery barrages, mortar bombardments and tactical air strikes which can devastate an area up to 125 acres! However the biggest punch comes from our magnificent *'Arc Light'* raids by the B-52 Stratofortress! This stupendous war machine when flying in groups or cells of three aircraft, can unleash 150,000 lbs of *HE* bombs from 25,000 feet and annihilate whole formations of the war mongering and murdering PAVN and their VC puppets!"

General Westmoreland smiled, "Thank you Captain Baig for that most illuminating briefing."

The entourage followed COMUSMACV back into the jeeps and the final leg of the tour was enacted. The DASC or *Direct Air Support Centre* and the GCA or *Ground Controlled Approach Centres* were inspected by the Supreme Commander.

Major General Tompkins then suggested that COMUSMACV have a look at the 81mm mortar emplacements that ran parallel to the airstrip and stretched almost the full length of the 1.5 mile long *Khe Sanh* perimeter. It took nearly an hour for General Westmoreland to make his way through the 26th Marines and some of the 37th ARVN Rangers who had already deployed forward. He chatted and gave morale boosting speeches to the rank and file troops who affectionately referred to the four star General as *'Westy'*.

The final points to look at were the huge ammunition dump which was situated right next to the western side of the airstrip and the water point.

"Our main problem sir," began Colonel David E. Lownds as he wiped the sweat off his brow while lifting up the brim of his steel combat helmet, "…is that the Viet Cong regularly attempt to poison our water supply."

"How so?" asked Westmoreland.

"Because the stream from which our water is drawn commences inside the jungle surrounds controlled by the PAVN troops."

"Is there anything that you can do to stop this perfidious sabotage?" asked the 3rd Marine Division commander.

"I'm afraid that all we can do is run the water through our water purifying pumps and filtration system that we have set up here," Colonel Lownds pointed to a large piece of machinery with hoses and valves proliferating in every direction.

Suddenly everyone looked skyward as from the east a flight of six *F-105 Republic Thunderchiefs* screamed over the base with a deafening roar.

Westmoreland asked, "What is the objective of those *Thunderchiefs*?"

Colonel Vortex roughly grabbed the field telephone out of a Lieutenant's hands who was standing behind Major Thrush.

"Captain Baig?" he asked.

The FSCC officer answered and informed Vortex that the jets were going to strike PAVN positions in the valley between Hill 881 North and Hill 558. Vortex informed Westmoreland of the fact as relayed to him.

"Do you mean to tell me Colonel Lownds? That we don't control the valleys between our Hill positions?" asked Westmoreland as his face turned purple with rage.

"I'm afraid that is correct sir," said Colonel Lownds.

"And why the hell haven't you attempted to push the 304th and 325thC divisions out of there?" Lieutenant General Cushman asked savagely as he backed up COMUSMACV.

Colonel Lownds turned ashen white and then red with adrenalin as his anger, intermixed with fear, could be easily seen upon his harassed features.

"We simply don't have enough men to hold the low points in between our Hill outposts! Its utterly impossible!" And then Lownds added, "Sir!"

COMUSMACV looked unimpressed as he put his hands to his waist and looked over to General Cushman as if to say, *'what type of officers do you have in your 3rd Marine Division?'*

Westmoreland barked out, "I am not interested in what is impossible! I am only concerned with what is possible and achievable! And it is officers like Colonel Vortex who are the prime movers of the possible and the credible and sometimes even the impossible!"

Major General Rathvon Tompkins felt ashamed and swore under his breath that he would castigate Colonel Lownds at a later point when they were in private.

General Tompkins knew and followed the cardinal rule of command that you never ridicule or dress down your subordinates in front of the troops or other more junior officers that were now crowded all around with their mouths agape.

Colonel Vortex stepped forward briskly and actually elbowed Colonel Lownds out of the way so that he faced COMUSMACV.

"I can prepare and launch an attack by 0500 hours on the 20th sir!"

Westmoreland beamed with pleasure.

"I shall use my own 1st Battalion 9th Marines. I don't need any of the 26th Marines or the 37th ARVN Ranger unit. I shall gather an attack force of 1,000 men from my 1,500 man battalion and then push forward from Hill 881 South to Hills 881 North and 558, thus linking the two strong points!"

Colonel Lownds said angrily, "That's impossible!"

General Tompkins lashed out, "Shut up Colonel Lownds!"

"I'm going to order that Colonel Vortex undertake his assault as just indicated," added General Cushman.

"Excellent!" expostulated COMUSMACV.

Westmoreland clapped both his hands onto Vortex's shoulders and smiled, "I knew I could count on you Richard!"

But Colonel Lownds did not give up so easily as he stepped in between Westmoreland and Vortex.

"And how long do you think you will be able to hold that position? The PAVN and VC outnumber us at least 5 to 1 or maybe even more! For Jesus sake! They have upwards of 35,000 men out there! Their *M-46 130mm* artillery and RPG's will blow you to smithereens. You'll be retreating back to the hill outposts before you even finish your moronic assault!"

Colonel Lownds turned to Westmoreland in an imploring gesture, his hands outstretched and palms facing upwards to the sky.

"Sir! Please! The 9th Marines will be cut to pieces! I've been here for quite a few months now. With all due respect to Colonel Vortex and his men, they have just arrived. He doesn't know what we are up against. What Colonel Vortex proposes is a job for a whole Brigade or even a Division! Not half a battalion. If you would bring up the *199th Light Infantry Brigade* then perhaps the plan could succeed!"

"Bullshit! Colonel!" spat out Vortex as he looked down at Lownds from his 6 feet 2.5 inches. "I don't need a whole brigade! The 199th is a fine unit but let them continue to operate in the *Iron Triangle* west of Saigon where they are needed more! My boys can handle the job!"

Lownds never gave in, "But sir! I protest!, I…"

Major General Tompkins cut in brutally, "That's enough Colonel Lownds!"

COMUSMACV turned his head and back on Lownds and smiled at Vortex, "Good luck in your assault!"

"I think its time to be getting underway sir," said General Cushman, "You have to inspect the 1st and 2nd Marine Divisions along the DMZ tomorrow."

COMUSMACV nodded and his theatre staff started to pile into the four dozen *Cobra* gunships that were now warming up their engines, their rotor blades

a forest of whirling, spinning steel. Brigadier Generals McChristian and Schweiz shook hands with the two Colonels and boarded the choppers with the rest of the personnel.

General Westmoreland signalled Cushman, Tompkins, Vortex and Lownds to come over for a final briefing. They stood on *Khe Sanh's* airstrip shouting to each other over the host of supercharged helicopter engines.

"I leave *Khe Sanh* in your competent hands gentlemen!" began COMUSMACV.

"I don't have to tell you how vital this Marine base is to our whole effort in this Republic. You must hold it at all costs. I am going to have an additional briefing in the next few days with General William M. Momyer the commander of the US 7th Air Force in Saigon as well as Vice-President Nguyen Cao Ky, to see what extra air power we can organise for the defence and supply of *Khe Sanh*."

Then General Westmoreland turned mostly to Colonel Vortex, almost ignoring Lownds totally, to the latter's immense chagrin.

"I shall be in my *Tran Quy Cap Street* villa in Saigon or in the MACV Headquarters at the *Tan Son Nhut Air Base* over the next couple of weeks if you need anything urgently," said the COMUSMACV.

The MACV HQ was a huge, two-story, concrete and steel building which had air-conditioned office space for 4,000 officers and men. It was the nerve centre for the entire allied effort in South Vietnam. It was nicknamed *Pentagon East*.

"Thank you sir!" began Colonel Vortex.

Then the Colonel drew the Supreme Commander over to one side.

"Sir?"

"Yes?" asked Westmoreland.

"Can you do me a favour?" asked Vortex his eyes ablaze with intense concern.

"If it is in my power to perform it, yes, certainly," replied General Westmoreland.

Vortex sucked in a breath of air and continued, "Could you please make sure that Susie Ky is alright? She is back in Saigon now. As the daughter of a Minister in President Thieu's government I told her to go and live in the *Tan Son Nhut Air Base* next to the MACV HQ if anything happens."

Westmoreland clicked his fingers to his Marine Corps aide and nodded to Colonel Vortex.

Captain Charles W. Sampson came running over from one of the *Cobra* gunships with a notepad in hand.

"Yes sir?" he asked. The Captain was a blonde, blue eyed, lean and handsome career officer. He was a dedicated and fanatical soldier who would gladly risk his life for the safety of COMUSMACV.

General Westmoreland made Colonel Vortex's request an order and gave it to Captain Sampson who scribbled it down dutifully.

"I'll be in touch by radio-telephone each day for the situation reports." With those words Westmoreland jumped sprightly into the *Cobra* gunship.

Lieutenant General Cushman went up to Vortex, "Chew them out as best as you are able Colonel! I want you to bleed the bloody fucking PAVN pigs and VC pimps until they are as white as vampires in the driven snow of desolation. We shall do the rest!"

Vortex snarled, "Sir! I will kill, crush, annihilate, vivisect, destroy, pulverise, mutilate and incinerate the stinking Communist motherfuckers and cocksuckers! They shall never take *Khe Sanh*! Never! I guarantee that they won't make it within 500 yards of the perimeter concertina wire!"

Colonel Lownds simply rolled up the white's of his eyes and looked to heaven in an attitude of prayer as if to ask God Almighty if he was the only sane soldier in this fanatical and murderous cabal of military homicidal lunatics.

Cushman and Tompkins both said, "Good!" They practically ignored the forlorn Colonel Lownds except for nodding at him with a sarcastic countenance and saluting him as they left.

Major Thrush and Captain Frank C. Willoughby came up behind Vortex and they watched COMUSMACV and his entourage lift into the air and disappear in the direction of *Camp Carroll* and *Quang Tri*.

"Well!" laughed Major Thrush as Sergeant Major Crighton clambered out of the command jeep and joined them, "We are on our own!"

Captain Willoughby smacked Colonel Vortex on the chest playfully and asked, "So Richard! How about I buy you a beer in the officer's mess!"

"Good idea!" chuckled back Vortex.

"Care to join us?" asked Willoughby to Lownds. The commander of the 26th Marines looked extremely tired as he ran his fingers through his dirt slimed hair.

"I suppose so. I can't see anything better to do at the moment."

Vortex went over and put his arm around Lownds' shoulders, "You just let me handle things here Colonel. Relax! We have the finest men of any army in the world. America has never been beaten in any conflict in its entire 200 year history. With the only exception being the *Confederate States of America* in 1865 – but that was excused because they were beaten by fellow Americans. So that does not count – for the only people that can beat Americans are other Americans!"

Colonel Lownds gave a sad laugh, "Maybe Vietnam will be our first and greatest defeat?"

Captain Willoughby was enraged but said nothing. He simply spat his thick yellow sputum into the tarmac of *Khe Sanh's* airstrip in utter disgust. It was hard to determine who was more vicious and fanatical, him or Vortex. The Green Beret officer was already prepared to fight the PAVN to the bloody and violent death of himself and all

his men in Detachment A-101 of the 5th Special Forces Group. And if it came to that, he had decided to shoot any of his troops who showed the least hint of cowardice or disobedience to his orders, or even pity or mercy to the enemy, including the *Montagnard* tribesman under his *Lang Vei* command.

Major Thrush interrupted as Lieutenant Colonel Tran, the small but lively commander of the 37th ARVN Rangers came up after overseeing the delivery of munitions from several C-130 Hercules transports at the other end of the runway.

"But you have to come and see my surprise!" Vortex remembered as Lownds asked, "What fucking surprise?"

Major Thrush chuckled, "You'll see!"

The officers moved off and walked into the 9th Marine HQ bunker complex and dugout which was right next to the *Fire Support Coordination Centre*.

As they entered Lieutenant Colonel Tran said in a whisper to Sergeant Major Crighton so that the others would not hear, "You know Sergeant Major? The Allies may indeed be defeated here in Vietnam. If that happens you Americans can simply go home to your Kentucky Fried Chicken Shops and your McDonalds outlets, your steel belted radials and your coloured television sets! But we South Vietnamese! – we are fighting for our very existence! Our very survival!"

Sergeant Major Crighton whispered back as he saw Vortex speaking excitedly to Major Thrush and Captain Willoughby inside the bunker HQ.

"I too have my doubts Lieutenant Colonel Tran. But I dare not mention them to anyone, especially not to Colonel Vortex! He would court martial me for defeatist sentiments!"

Colonel Tran nodded as he put down his M16 rifle and picked up a cup of coffee instead.

"I understand fully. Vortex is remarkable. He has an unshakable will and a fanatical determination. He cannot even conceive of the word – *defeat!* His only passion is to exterminate the filthy PAVN and VC in a miasma of complete destruction!"

Sergeant Major Crighton indicated that he must go over to Vortex but he said quickly under his breath, "I only know one thing!"

Colonel Tran asked, "What is that?"

"*Khe Sanh* will be the litmus test for American success or failure in Vietnam!"

Chapter 7
325thC North Vietnamese Division

"So where is this surprise?" asked Vortex as he broke open a can of *Budweiser* beer.

Major Thrush led the small party into an underground bunker room at the rear of the complex housing the 1st Battalion 9th Marine Headquarters.

"Here sir!" said Thrush as he swung open the steel door. Sitting in the middle of the room was a young woman wearing black pantaloons and a dark grey blouse of coarse canvas-like material.

"So what do we have here?" asked Vortex as he sniggered with glee.

Vortex, Thrush, Lownds, Willoughby, Sergeant Major Crighton and Lieutenant Colonel Tran sauntered into the interrogation room and closed the door after the three huge military police guards left at a click of the fingers from Colonel Vortex.

Major Thrush explained as he took off his flak jacket and ammunition belt and placed them on the only piece of furniture in the room, a wooden table. Overhead was a single 100 watt globe that provided a bright light for the underground chamber.

"We captured this Viet Cong murdering slut on a patrol west of Hill 881 North on the 16th January 1968," Thrush also drank a *Budweiser* in-between his explanations. "I lost one man killed and three wounded when we ran into a Viet Cong company. This bitch launched an RPG into my men. She is responsible for the casualties. But we called in an airstrike, manoeuvred around the VC company and blew it to hell. We caught her as she tried to make it back to the PAVN lines."

Colonel Lownds stepped up to the girl and loosened the gag of cloth that was tied around her mouth. A steel ball was rammed into her throat to prevent her from screaming. Lownds withdrew the device and threw it onto the floor.

"She has to be sent to *Quang Tri* for proper interrogation. I'll arrange a chopper within the hour."

As Lownds spoke, Vortex yelled back, "No!" He then walked up to the Viet Cong girl and placed his hand under her chin, lifting her face up to his own. Her hands were still tied behind her back as she sat on the bamboo chair.

"What do you mean? No?" screamed back Colonel Lownds as he grabbed Vortex's left arm and brutally pushed him away from the Viet Cong girl.

"It means exactly what I said!" spitted back Vortex as he leaned into Lownds and then thrust his chest in an arrogant manner into the 26th Marine commander.

Sergeant Major Crighton who was standing behind the girl and running his fingers through her black hair, giggled to himself.

"I won't allow any unauthorised interrogations at *Khe Sanh*!" yelled back Lownds.

Vortex ignored him for a few seconds and took a close look at the Viet Cong girl. She was 19 years old with long black hair and beautiful, smooth, white skin. Her eyes were intelligent and glistening in their dark brown colour. She had a small attractive face, shapely legs and delicious breasts that stood up firmly through her blouse. Vortex licked his lips as he could see that her nipples were stiff and erect with fear.

Speaking perfect Vietnamese, Vortex asked, "And what is your name?"

The girl threw back her head and shouted in her own language, "Mẹ mày! Bạn dâm máu Mỹ Đế quốc bastard motherfucker, đi đến địa ngục!"

[Fuck you! You American imperialist motherfucker. Go to hell!]

She then spat in Vortex's face.

Stunned, Vortex reeled backwards and watched the yellow sphere of sputum trickle down his shirt. His blue eyes were afire with a lust for revenge.

In a slithery movement Vortex took out his handkerchief and wiped the spit from his shirt. He then greased it back into the girl's cheeks.

"Sergeant Major Crighton! Pick up this girl and take her to the chopper!" ordered Colonel David Lownds in a shrill voice.

Sergeant Major Crighton did not move a muscle at the command of the other Colonel. He obeyed only commands from Colonel Vortex.

"Did you hear what I said?" asked Lownds.

"Yes," came back the unenthusiastic reply from the huge Marine Sergeant Major.

"Then do as you are ordered!" screamed Lownds, his face now purple and crimson.

"No sir!" shouted back Sergeant Major Crighton.

Vortex pointed his finger into Lownds' chest, "My men obey me! Not you!"

Lownds laughed nervously, "This is outrageous!"

Vortex spoke to Sergeant Major Crighton in German so that nobody else could understand his frustration with Colonel Lownds.

"Dieser Mann versteht nicht, was es genau ist, dass wir versuchen zu tun. Er hat den Magen für die unwohlschmeckenderen Methoden nicht, die manchmal mit diesen Gefangenen verwendet werden müssen, um zu ellicit von ihnen die Lebensintelligenz, die für das Überleben unserer Basis hier an Khe Sanh erforderlich ist."

Translated:-

[This man does not understand what it is exactly that we are trying to do. He does not have the stomach for the more unsavoury methods that sometimes must be employed with these prisoners in order to illicit from them the vital intelligence that is required for the survival of our base here at Khe Sanh.]

Sergeant Major Crighton replied, *"Ich treffe mit Ihnen Herr zusammen. Geben Sie mir gerade die Ordnungen, das Quälen dieser Schlampe zu blutigen Stücken anzufangen, und ich werde so mit dem Geschmack tun, während Sie sich Oberst Lownds verpissen und ihn das Bumsen aus hier bekommen, bumsen die stummen-assed Kopf, der Clown zwischenbeschneidet."*

Translated:-

[I concur with you sir. Just give me the orders to commence torturing this slut to bloody pieces and I will do so with relish while you fuck off Colonel Lownds and get him the fuck out of here, the dumb-assed fuck-head interloping clown.]

Lownds laughed nervously, "This is outrageous! What are you two talking about in that gibberish behind my back?"

Vortex riposted, "If you had ever bothered to learn German, you nit-wit! You would understand exactly what we are saying! You spend too much time with your chicken-coops and roosters back in the *Mid-West*!"

Vortex added, "General Westmoreland has put me in charge of all interrogations here at *Khe Sanh*. You can send this viperous slut back to *Quang Tri* or wherever else you like – but only after I have interrogated her myself first!"

Colonel Lownds started to waver as Captain Frank Willoughby added, "Listen Colonel! She has to be interrogated here at *Khe Sanh*. This could be a golden opportunity for finding out what the 325thC North Vietnamese Division is up to! What there objective is. When they are preparing to attack. How they are going to coordinate with the 304th PAVN Division and the 320th and 324th Divisions."

Vortex nodded, "Be reasonable Colonel Lownds!"

"Alright! Alright!" screamed back Lownds as he strode up to Colonel Vortex and grabbed his camouflage shirt collar pulling the officer closer to himself.

"But if you mistreat this enemy soldier in any way, I'll…"

"You'll what?" screamed back Vortex as he inserted his arms in-between Lownds' grip and then whiplashed the 26th commander viciously away from his body.

"I'll do whatever the fuck I please with this enemy bitch!" screamed Vortex in a white lather of rage.

Lownds and Lieutenant Colonel Tran walked out of the room in a huff.

"They don't understand what we are trying to achieve here," said Captain Willoughby.

"He is a man of very little foresight or ability," added Vortex.

Only the Colonel, Sergeant Major Crighton, Major Thrush and Captain Willoughby were left in the room with the Viet Cong woman.

A few minutes later several Marines from the 9th regiment brought in some fried chicken, steak and a 12 pack carton of *Budweiser* beer.

"Great! I'm famished!" said Sergeant Major Crighton. They all started eating with gusto as Vortex walked over to the woman and gripped her blouse with both hands. With a brutal ripping motion he ruthlessly tore off her blouse while Sergeant Major Crighton grabbed her pants and pulled them down across her ankles. The girl was not wearing any bra and her beautiful breasts popped out brazenly at the four large and powerful men.

Vortex took hold of her white cotton panties and tore them off, running his fingers easily across the moist black hairs of her vagina. He then lowered his head and kissed the sweet smelling *mons pubis* of her reproductive organ.

"Delicious slut!" he smiled with joy.

"Its hard to believe that this succulent girl killed one of your men?" giggled Captain Willoughby.

Vortex said nonplussed, "It is. But nevertheless she is going to pay!"

The girl screamed, "Don't you touch me you American imperialist bastard!"

The men laughed. Vortex took out his razor sharp Marine dagger and brandished it close to her naked vagina and then up to her breasts, tickling them with the point of his knife. He then walked to her rear and cut loose the rope that tied her arms. Immediately the 19 year old girl leapt to her feet and made for the door, even though completely naked. Vortex could see the sweat cover her delicious body in a fine film. She was a lovely specimen.

"No you don't!" said Captain Willoughby as he moved easily to the door to cut her off. She punched the Green Beret with all her might but her tiny fist seemed to bounce harmlessly off the soldier's massive chest.

Willoughby hooked his thick, hairy arm around her expertly and held her securely in a head-vice.

Vortex grabbed both her breasts in his hands and squeezed them lubriciously.

"What is the objective of the 325thC Division?" he screamed as he stroked her smooth skin. Catching the nipples in-between his fingers he ran his coarse tongue over them, licking and sucking with savage lust.

At the same instant Sergeant Major Crighton walked over and tongue kissed the girl as her head was viced by Willoughby.

"When is *Khe Sanh* going to be attacked? What are General Vo Nguyen Giap's plans?" screamed Vortex as he inserted three of his fingers into her vagina, pushing them upwards until he could feel the beautiful slime of her moist womb.

She screamed back, "You are all going to die! You fucking American pigs!"

Vortex pushed Sergeant Willoughby away from his tongue kissing of the girl and then ran his own tongue over her cheeks, nose and lips. He could taste the sweet perspiration of the Asian girl inside his mouth as he swallowed. It was delicious.

"Fuck you!" said Vortex in a clam voice. He slapped her across the breasts and then the face with every ounce of power in his body. The savagery of the blow was such that it left red imprints on her body where the epidermis was traumatised. He then punched her once in the vagina. She shrieked with excruciating pain.

"Bring her onto the table!"

Captain Willoughby lifted her off the ground and slammed the female body onto the wooden table where Major Thrush held her two ankles. She writhed, contorted and wiggled to be free as Willoughby held her wrists. But it was useless.

She spat once more into Sergeant Major Crighton's eyes but he slammed his fist into her belly knocking out the oxygen from her lungs. The Viet Cong female gasped for air as Vortex wheeled in a steel trolley from another room in the bunker. Upon this trolley were knives of all shapes and sizes, a large battery with positive and negative steel terminals, thumbscrews, pincers, steel tongs, pliers, hammers and oil.

Sergeant Major Crighton also pulled in a charcoal brazier which was already red hot from its glowing coal fire. He placed two pairs of tongs and a pincer into the fire.

"This is going to be indescribable!" said the Marine Sergeant Major with joy and savage enthusiasm.

Colonel Vortex then began to speak to the girl as he climbed up on-top of the table and sat on her stomach, his two legs on either side of her torso. As he spoke he held her face in a vice-like grip and began by tongue kissing her savagely. Despite her hatred of the Americans the Viet Cong girl seemed to sexually respond to Vortex's perfidious ministrations.

"Now listen up!" Vortex spoke in fluent Vietnamese and the other three men in the room also had a good command of the language.

"I am going to interrogate you and you must know that no pity or remorse, no leniency or tolerance can be found in my heart for it is devoid of any sentimentality for the enemies of the State. As far as I am concerned you are the enemy. And that fact alone frees my mind, my will and my conscience, what little I have remaining, from all possible guilt for the things that I am going to perform on you without hesitation and without compunction that are still conducive of the maxims of public international law guidelines. I have studied the case law of the international legal system and I have found cogent precedents to condone and to justify my actions if not *de jure* then at least *de facto*. I wash my hands of your blood for my Government has sanctioned all types of action against you. An example of this uncircumscribed action is the *'Pacification Program'* run by Mr William Colby in the villages and hamlets of South Vietnam to awaken the ordinary people to the murderous treachery of the savage Viet Cong

pimps and gangsters to whom you belong. You are the one who has butchered my men and who is trying to subjugate a free and valiant people who want to retain their magnificent and free democratic government of South Vietnam. The people of South Vietnam have chosen the right path, the American model of a free and just society. Your regime, on the other hand, is nothing but a stinking cesspool of corruption and dictatorship. It is a blight upon the nations of the world and that is why we are going to exterminate you with an avalanche of firepower for America is the peacemaker! We alone, bring peace and security to the world through our strength and fortitude! Of course, don't be afraid to scream during this lawful interrogation under the law. It is no shame to scream, to cry, to writhe in hideous agony! Because I assure you that the torture I am about to unleash upon your smooth and delicate flesh will be, even though it is strictly within the set guidelines of operational procedure, going to be horrific! After several hours you will beg me to kill you! But I will refuse to release you from the excruciating agony. You see? My young Viet Cong maiden…" as he spoke Vortex stroked his fingers inside the girl's vagina until they were deliciously be-slimed with her juices. He then smelt his fingers and rubbed the bodily excretions back onto the girl's lips after which he tongue kissed her.

"You must realise that I am an expert in the subtle and not so subtle techniques of interrogation. I proceed by slow and gradual stages. Your body will gradually accustom itself to the grades of ever increasing and terrible physical mutilation. And of course you shall tell me everything you know about the stinking, motherfucking North Vietnamese troops, your impudent and sickening General Giap who is nothing but a pimping coward and your bum boys in the idiotic Viet Cong. And after all avenues of physical destruction have been wrought upon you I shall use mind altering substances and narcotic drugs and truth serums such as *Scopolamine* which I shall inject into your eyes and your carotid artery for maximum affect."

The girl started to shriek with terror at Vortex's words. She cried and shook her head from side to side. But her mind was too delirious with fear for her to construct comprehensible words.

"Hold her down!" Ordered Vortex as he stripped off his camouflage trousers. With Thrush at one end and Willoughby at the other, Vortex slid himself beautifully into the girl's reproductive organ. The lovemaking was energetic and wondrous with Vortex's savage power.

"As I enjoy her Sergeant Major Crighton!" gasped Vortex with delight, "I want you to use those steel pliers and break each of her ten fingers one by one and slowly!"

"It will be my pleasure sir!" beamed back Vortex's NCO.

Taking up the pair of pliers Crighton grabbed hold of the girl's index finger and snapped it around while twisting. The gleaming, splintered bone could be seen coming

out of the flesh as blood erupted all over her hands and onto the table. He proceeded in the same fashion with the other nine digits.

Each time the girl screamed Vortex thrust into her womb so that her naked ass was splintered in a hundred places by the rough wood of the table they were fornicating on so nonchalantly.

Captain Willoughby laughed, "Now I can see why you want to perform all the interrogations yourself!"

Vortex ejaculated into the girl and screamed at the same time, "Shut up! This is no laughing matter! I am trying to wrench information out of this stinking, foul bitch! It may be critical for the survival of *Khe Sanh*! And if you think I am enjoying myself then you are wrong!"

Willoughby did not make any further flippant comments after that rebuke by his superior but engrossed himself wholeheartedly in the hideous interrogation procedure that was unfortunately quite necessary so that only officers of the highest moral dedication and sacrifice to service could perform them.

Vortex dug his hands underneath the girl's shapely buttocks and clawed at her ass flesh with savagery. He used this leverage to drive himself deeper into her womb until he exploded his ejaculate into the Communist female for a second time. But as he knelt upwards from the table she managed to scratch the Colonel with one of her mangled hands. Blood escaped from his left cheek as a result of a superficial wound.

"You disagreeable slut!" screamed Vortex. Like a wild beast he tore at the girl's left ear with his teeth. In a few minutes as he lacerated the flesh by swinging his head from side to side the whole ear came off in the commander's jaws. He thereupon spat it onto the floor while Sergeant Major Crighton finished breaking all her digits.

"Bring her up and give me those scissors!" said Vortex. The girl was then punched in the stomach, head and vagina by Major Thrush and Captain Willoughby as Vortex tied her wrists with rope and hauled her body up from a pulley contraption attached to the ceiling. Lead weights were then chained to her ankles to increase the pressure on her spine. The girl's body was thus stretched so that she dangled only four inches from the floor.

"Let's see how she looks bald?" said Vortex as he removed all her long, black hair with the scissors. Oil was then poured over her freshly cut scalp and ignited with a match.

"Ahiiee!" she screamed as the flesh turned black and started to wrinkle horribly from the burns.

"Now tell me where the 325thC Division intends to attack? Is it *Khe Sanh*? How many troops are the PAVN preparing for the offensive? How many 130mm artillery pieces will be used?"

As Vortex questioned the girl, Major Thrush walked up behind her with a leather whip and started to flog her naked ass mercilessly. Bits of flesh and blood splattered across the room as she screamed with agony.

Vortex then picked up the steel sphere that Colonel Lownds had thrown to the floor earlier. He rammed it into the girl's mouth breaking several teeth so that she almost choked.

"Where is General Giap? Where can we find him? Is he encamped inside the DMZ?" Vortex slapped her across the breasts and legs with a steel whip while Thrush flogged her buttocks with a leather one.

The girl shrieked but gave no answer at all.

"You little unsavoury bitch!" screamed Major Thrush as he lost his temper.

Sergeant Major Crighton handed him a steel pair of tongs. The gouging pincers of which were red hot from the charcoal brazier.

"May I sir?" asked Thrush to Vortex.

"Be my guest!" replied the 9th Marine Commander and interrogation maestro.

Major Thrush held up the burning steel tongs and first kissed and licked the bare buttocks of the girl, nuzzling his nose like a pig at the trough, inside the crack of her ass cheeks. He then applied the tongs to her buttocks and *gluteus maximus* and *minimus* muscles so that it sizzled like bacon on a frying pan and all to the tune of her horrendous shouts and gurgled cries for mercy.

Simultaneously Colonel Vortex with Sergeant Major Crighton's help, inserted a heavy duty steel tube right up the confines of her vagina and drove it deep into her womb. The Sergeant Major then pumped hot oil into her flesh through the tube which seared her pink reproductive flesh horribly. The steel tube was removed and Vortex continued to lash her belly, breasts and thighs until a puddle of blood formed upon the floor of the bunker interrogation room.

"Do you know who this is?" asked Vortex as he grabbed the girl's nose in-between his fingers while pinching her nipples. The photograph was that of General Vo Nguyen Giap, the Defence Minister and senior General of the North Vietnamese Army. The girl nodded with indescribable agony as blood oozed from almost every pore of her mutilated body.

She answered in-between gasps of pain, "General Giap!"

Vortex asked, "Where can we find him? I want to know where he is so that we can arrange an assassination squad to exterminate that evil and pernicious jackal!"

The girl's head was held up by Sergeant Major Crighton who was sodomising the girl with his fingers.

Finally she shook her head again and again. Vortex slapped her across the face six or seven times. He asked again but she refused once more. Using his Marine dagger, Vortex sliced off her remaining ear but still she refused to talk.

"Now we shall begin with the second grade of torture," said Vortex calmly as he stopped for a few minutes to have a glass of red wine and some delicious Kentucky Fried Chicken flown in directly from California. The other men ate cheese and steak that was cooked to perfection with mint sauce and a side dish of *Thousand Island* salad.

Vortex threw his half chewed chicken bones into the girl's bloodied face as he laughed with glee and joy in his heart.

"She's not as easy as I first thought. Never mind. I enjoy and relish a challenging interrogation!"

Major Thrush finished eating and picked up his knife using it to slit open the nasal septum of the Viet Cong woman. The flesh of the girl peeled off exactly as the layers of an onion are removed.

"I want her raised and dropped!" ordered Vortex to his Sergeant Major.

"Absolutely sir," said Crighton.

The once attractive girl was pulled higher into the air by the pulley system attached to the ceiling and then dropped five or six feet. One could almost hear her spine cracking under the added pressure of the lead weights attached to her ankles. The raising and dropping continued for about an hour. With each whiplash fall the girl groaned with agony.

"That's enough for now!" said Vortex.

The Colonel unhooked the stubborn Viet Cong girl and laid her on the floor.

"Bring me that piece of wood and some long steel nails and a hammer."

Sergeant Major Crighton could feel the warm slush of blood surging through his loins. He knew what his commander was going to do next.

Captain Willoughby carried over a heavy beam of wood that was eight feet long by one foot wide by four inches thick.

Vortex spread out her arms against the grain of the wood so that her palms were facing upwards.

"Give me that hammer," as Major Thrush complied Vortex placed the sharp point of a long, industrial sized nail against the soft flesh of the girl and lifting the hammer above his head, he smashed it down into her *interphalangeal* joints.

The sight was unbelievable in its ferocity.

"Beautiful!" laughed Vortex.

"She is a female martyr!" expostulated Frank Willoughby.

The eerie crunching sounds of splintered, shattered bone could be heard as Vortex held the girl down by placing his knee onto her neck and then savagely striking the second nail into her remaining hand.

The Viet Cong prisoner was thus impaled onto the wooden beam, her hands a miasma of broken human flesh as her fingers had already been splintered to pieces by Sergeant Major Crighton.

"Tell me where the 325thC North Vietnamese Division is going to attack? What is its objective? Is it *Khe Sanh*? Where is General Giap? Answer me!" screamed Vortex.

The girl opened her mouth as Sergeant Major Crighton decided to cut off her hands with a machete. As he did this she uttered almost incomprehensibly, "The 325th Division is going to attack at…"

Just at that second the door to the bunker room burst open and Colonel David E. Lownds burst in.

"Jesus Christ!" he rushed forward and grabbed Vortex by his shirt collar.

"What the fuck is going on in here?"

"Not now!" spat out Vortex.

He turned to the girl and as he lifted her blood soaked chest her head fell back limp, the eyes staring to infinity like sad black pearls.

"No!..." Vortex was beside himself with frustration.

Sergeant Major Crighton who was also a trained medic examined her with a stethoscope. He felt her carotid artery, examined her eyes and listened to her cardio-vascular and respiratory systems.

"She's dead Colonel," said Crighton as he packed away his first aid kit.

"You moron! You imbecile!" screamed Vortex in a white-hot lather of rage.

Colonel Lownds was thrust backwards so that he fell over the naked girl's mutilated corpse. Vortex shook off his hold and instead grabbed the other Colonel by the throat, dragging him half way across the room.

Lownds asked sheepishly, "Did I do anything wrong?"

"She was just about to tell me the objective of the expected PAVN attack!"

Colonel Lownds asked, stupefied, "She was?..She!..."

"Yes!" Vortex slammed the 26th Marine Commander up against the wall so hard that you could hear the air escaping from his lungs in a violent outrush.

"But you burst in and spoiled everything! We have just spent four hours getting to this point and you ruined it for us! The safety of *Khe Sanh* may have been jeopardised by your interruption!"

Colonel Lownds was speechless as he surveyed the grisly mess of human destruction on the floor.

Vortex allowed his grip to slacken as Lownds just shook his head and walked out.

Later that evening a party was held for the arrival of Colonel Vortex and his staff. It was held in the 9th Marine Regiment HQ bunker. A large dining room combination bar had been constructed on the upper level of the complex next to the communications and fire control room. Colonel Lownds, his battalion commanders from the 26th Regiment and Lieutenant Colonel Tran were also in attendance.

Sergeant Major Crighton and Lieutenant Donald Shanley, one of Vortex's Company commanders supervised the barbecue. Prime ribs, chicken roast, pork chops,

sausages, grilled fish, French fries, caviar, smoked cheese, garlic bread, bouillabaisse, custard pie, seasoned prawns, lobster mornay, *pom frets*, jugged hare, whortleberry pie, coleslaw, Irish coffee and sauerkraut were served up in huge quantities.

"Boy!" exclaimed Colonel Vortex as he feasted until his guts were about to explode. "The food here is more succulent and delicious than the kitchen at Pentagon East in the *Tan Son Nhut Air Base*!"

"I'm glad you like it Colonel," answered Lownds as he sipped on a glass of sherry.

The party was for officers only. A conveyer line of 30 men passed the food down into the HQ bunker from the barbecue above. Only Sergeant Major Crighton was allowed by Vortex to sit with the commissioned personnel for the feast.

"I'll have to be on my way back to *Lang Vei*," mentioned Captain Willoughby.

Vortex had a barbecue pork rib hanging out of his mouth.

"Good! I'll go with you. I want to reconnoitre the entire area from here to the *Khe Sanh* Village and onwards to your Special Forces Camp."

Colonel Lownds asked, "Do you think that is wise Colonel? Enemy troop concentrations and activity have increased markedly over the past few days."

As he spoke the 100 or so officers who were feasting with an avaricious appetite heard the distant thunder of heavy artillery and the whirr of tracer fire about 3 or 4 miles away.

"Is that *Lang Vei*?" asked Vortex with a worried look.

Captain Willoughby was even more concerned. He had left his two lovers, Susan and Monica Thang at the Green Beret Camp. His subordinate Lieutenant Max Reinhardt was looking after them.

"It could well be!" answered Willoughby as he tucked into a chicken pie and sirloin steak that was extremely well done.

"Then we better get over there ASAP!"

Just then Lieutenant Shanley walked in and sat down next to Lieutenant Colonel Tran, a large plate of sausages before him with lashings of caviar and red wine to boot.

"Forget about eating now!" said Vortex as he was already fully sated with delicious sustenance.

"I beg your pardon sir?" asked the thunderstruck junior officer.

"I said get on your feet! We're moving out now! I want your 250 man B Company of my 1st Battalion ready and fully loaded for extreme battle combat within ten minutes! Now get off your fucking ass and hop to it!" screamed Colonel Vortex with undiluted rage.

"But sir!" protested Lieutenant Donald Shanley, "I…I haven't finished my dinner yet."

Vortex grabbed the junior officer by his lapels and dragged him to his feet, "I don't give a fuck about your dinner! For all I care you can eat tomorrow or the day after!

That is if you survive this reconnaissance. Now get moving before I court martial your dumb ass!"

The dazed Lieutenant Shanley barked, "Yes sir!"

Lieutenant Colonel Tran stepped up to Vortex and picked his mouth with his index finger, trying to dislodge a piece of marinated chicken breast from between his teeth, "I'd like to come with you Colonel."

Vortex looked down at the stocky South Vietnamese elite Ranger commando, "If you like."

Vortex shrugged his shoulders with complete and utter nonchalance. He knew that he could kill North Vietnamese like chickens without the help of their South Vietnamese enemies.

Colonel Lownds protested, "I don't think that's a good idea."

Lieutenant Colonel Tran whipped his head around as he finished a can of *Budweiser* courtesy of the Quarter Master General of I Corps Operational Zone who had made it a point to fly in only the very best rations and gourmet food for the Marines at *Khe Sanh*.

"Why not sir?" asked Tran as one of his Majors came up and handed him a modified *7.62mm MAT-49 Mod SMG* machine gun.

"You are needed here with the 37th Rangers. I can't afford to have you blown away on the first night of your arrival."

As Lownds spoke he poured himself a small shot of Kentucky Bourbon, finishing it with a single swipe of his head as he thrust it backwards like a flouncing peacock.

"But what about Colonel Vortex? Can you risk losing him?" asked the beefy little Lieutenant Colonel Tran.

Colonel Lownds decided not to answer that question as Vortex asked,""Hey! Tran! Why do you carry that putrid Communist weapon? Why don't you use a M60 or M16?"

Tran laughed as he threw down his unfinished plate of salad and sausages.

"Because I find that this weapon, the *MAT-49 Mod SMG* which was originally left behind by our French allies during the First Vietnamese Conflict from 1948 to 1954, has a better accuracy at long range than your Yankee devices."

Vortex scoffed, "Is that so?"

Major Thrush giggled as he brandished a dagger at another Viet Cong prisoner who was lashed in a supine position on a steel rack in front of the dining area.

Tran nodded sheepishly and made for the exit.

Colonel Vortex grabbed his arm, "Let me tell you that that *frog* shit can't compare with our unique and fine workmanship in the United States!"

Before they left Vortex took out a map and indicated to Colonel Lownds that he would take his B Company only up to the *Khe Sanh* Village itself. Then Captain

Willoughby and the three Green Berets he had with him would continue on to the Special Forces Camp at *Lang Vei*.

Reluctantly David E. Lownds approved of the plan only because valuable information might be gleaned from probing the PAVN strength in and around the village of *Khe Sanh* which was only a statute mile away to the south south-west.

"You better stay here with the rest of the battalion Major Thrush," said Vortex as he stepped up to the foul smelling VC prisoner tied to the steel contraption.

"Who the fuck is this?" asked Vortex as he spat on the naked and bruised body of the man and then gripped his puny testicles inside his massive fist.

Colonel Lownds walked up to the rack and ran the palm of his hand over the Viet Cong's face. Then suddenly he slapped the VC across his chin and punched him savagely in the kidneys and the side of his head.

Vortex was taken aback with a surge of pleasant surprise.

"So you too can be angry at the Communist enemy? Colonel?" asked Vortex as he tightened his vice-like grip around the man's gonads.

The man screamed horribly and chafed his wrists against the iron manacles that tied him to the rack.

"In this case I am very angry!" admonished Colonel David E. Lownds as he grabbed a fistful of the VC's hair and then slammed his skull with a sickening thud onto the iron head of the interrogation rack.

"What did he do?" asked Vortex as Major Thrush moved to the end of the steel device and using a steel hammer he commenced to break the man's toes without mercy or compassion believing that none was due or warranted under *public international law* because the man was not a recognised combatant and thus not covered by the Geneva nor Hague Conventions of 1949.

Captain Willoughby meanwhile, stripped the flesh off the VC's thighs using a surgical dermatome.

The officers were soon drenched with blood as they continued their feasting.

"Let me tell you what this pig did," began Colonel David E. Lownds.

"We had arranged to pick up three innocent Montagnard families from the *Khe Sanh* village about a week ago. I sent a platoon from my 3rd Battalion to go out and give them safe passage to the base and from there they were going to be airlifted by *Sikorsky* to *Quang Tri*. But what did my Lieutenant find when he arrived at their thatched huts? This VC pimp had murdered the three mother's of the families, one of which was pregnant. He had cut out the foetus of the Montagnard mother while raping her. The other children he dismembered with a group of other regular PAVN soldiers. We could catch only this one."

Vortex leaned into the Viet Cong's face and asked in Vietnamese, "Are you afraid to die?"

There was no answer as the man merely screamed while his toes were crushed and his thighs mutilated.

"I asked you a question you motherfucking imperialist Viet Cong murderer and child molester!" screamed Vortex as he tightened even further his crushing hold on the man's testicles.

Still no answer came forth from the thin, almost feminine looking lips that contorted in twisted agony.

Vortex thought that the Viet Cong had an inherently evil appearance and demeanour in their black pyjama-like garb. He thought that they looked like something out of a Halloween festival.

A crunching head butt from Vortex caved-in the man's nose until it was spread flat across his face in a jellied miasma of suffering.

"I shall have to deal with this Viet Cong rat when I come back!" said Vortex.

"Keep him on ice for me will you, Colonel?"

Lownds answered as he punched the VC in the stomach several times, "Don't worry! This homicidal hound is not going anywhere!"

Before Vortex walked outside he unsheathed his Marine dagger and with expert skill severed the fine tissue between the two testicles and then cut into both sacks like a surgeon from the medieval inquisition. Using his fingers he gouged out both gonads and crushed them under his general purpose combat boots. The screeches were only stopped when the VC prisoner became unconscious from the torture and all attempts to revive him with injections of adrenalin and smelling salts had failed.

By the time Colonel Vortex emerged from the HQ bunker, his B Company were already on the hop and lined up in three neat ranks between the *Marine Air Traffic Control Unit* and the *Fire Support Coordination Centre*.

The rest of Vortex's battalion, some 1,200 men, were manning the concertina wire perimeter of the *Khe Sanh* combat base along its western side near the *Red Sector* and the *Rock Quarry*. The B/1/26 were manning the *Gray Sector*; the 37th ARVN Rangers were East on the far end of the *Khe Sanh* airstrip with the B/1/26 battalion; A/1/26 were on the other side of the airstrip being the northern side; *Blue Sector* was occupied by C/1/26 and the northern drop zone was protected by L/3/26. The 9th Marines also occupied the water point behind the Airfield Control Tower.

"Now listen up!" said Vortex as he was followed by Lieutenant Colonel Tran and Captain Hoang Pho (who would later take over the 37th ARVN Rangers when Tran would be called back to *Pentagon East*), as well as Major Thrush, Sergeant Major Crighton and Lieutenant Donald Shanley.

"We are going to make a reconnaissance into the *Khe Sanh* village itself. The usual scouting formation will be used. We shall form up in three columns of staggered file. About 80 men in each column and we shall keep a separation between the lines of

about 100 yards. That way each column can herringbone to the right or the left to support the other if attacked. Be wary and watchful for an ambush!"

Just then Captain Willoughby and his three accompanying NCOs' stepped up behind Vortex.

Willoughby whispered in Vortex's ear, "What about bayonets?"

Colonel Vortex smiled and clapped Frank affectionately on the right shoulder.

"Oh! Yes!" Everyone attach bayonets to their M16's now!"

A massive tinkling noise could be discerned as each of the 250 men in B Company 1st Battalion took their razor sharp and gleaming bayonets out of their knapsacks and clicked them onto the rifle barrels of their automatic weapons.

"If you see any dirty VC or PAVN troops that are lying about, whether they appear to be dead or not I want you to run them through with your bayonets or with your knifes! I don't have to tell you that the VC love to play dead and then bolt up behind you and shoot you in the back before you realise what has happened! Also they booby-trap their dead with grenades so that when moved they blow up in your face so use ropes to drag the dead motherfuckers out of the way."

Captain Willoughby interrupted Vortex, "Also men! When you reach the *Khe Sanh* village don't automatically think that every Montagnard villager you see is friendly. Some of the villagers may be Viet Cong traitors or saboteurs! So watch your back and keep your eyes open!"

Colonel Vortex motioned to Captain Hoang Pho who came running forward with a crack platoon of South Vietnamese Rangers. There were 40 men in the unit and they carried 4 heavy M60 machine guns and 6 portable mortars as well as their usual equipment.

"What is this?" asked Vortex as he looked at the immaculate platoon.

"I'd like to bring a few of my Rangers along for the experience Colonel!" said Captain Hoang Pho (ARVN) excitedly.

"Ok! You and your men can stay with me in the centre column. I'll keep them in reserve as a reaction force if anything goes wrong. Ok?"

Captain Hoang Pho smiled, "Ok! Sir!"

Vortex turned to Major Thrush, "I'll see you at sun-up Major."

Major Thrush saluted, "Take care Colonel!"

Vortex turned to his troops, "Alright! Lock and load your weapons! Now move out!"

B Company made their way out of the *Khe Sanh* perimeter through the *Gray Sector* towards the village as they were watched by the rest of the 6,000 strong garrison. It was 2330 hours and the night was moonless. It was pitch black and extraordinarily silent as they slid into the hot, humid and uninviting jungle.

Captain Willoughby said, "I'll take point Colonel with my three Green Berets."

Vortex nodded, "Take one of the field telephones and keep in touch with me."

Willoughby moved off to the front of the 290 man formation. He was a superlative expert in jungle warfare and knife combat as well as assassination by cunning, silence and stealth. The four Green Berets kept about 60 yards in front of the three columns as they traversed the jungle.

The 1 to 2 statute miles was traversed slowly and carefully in about 30 minutes of crawling through the thick vines and undergrowth. The only thing that could be heard was the insects and birds.

Vortex was positioned in the middle of the central column with the ARVN Ranger platoon.

Captain Willoughby reached the outside edge of *Khe Sanh* village and crouched to the ground behind some thick jungle undergrowth with his three Green Berets.

"Hand me those infra-red binoculars and the rangefinder!" whispered Willoughby.

A large, beefy Texan Master Sergeant handed them over and the Captain strained his eyes to watch for anything unusual. The village of *Khe Sanh* had about 120 hooch's and straw huts scattered over an area of about one quarter of a square mile. The *Old French Fort* was just to the east of the village. Hill 471 was directly north of the village about half a mile away. The old roadway *'QL9'* ran through the village that lead about 3 miles further down to the *Old Lang Vei* Camp and a little further on the *New Lang Vei Special Forces Camp*. About one and half miles north of the *New Lang Vei Special Forces Camp* was Hill 527.

The vitally important Route 9 ran straight through the centre of the hamlet. Captain Willoughby knew that if and when the North Vietnamese 304th Division was going to attack, it would have to obliterate and take *Khe Sanh* Village before launching its assault on the *Khe Sanh* combat base proper.

"It seems quiet sir," said the Texan Sergeant who had two lovely daughters and a wife waiting for him in San Antonio.

"Everything is not always what it seems Sergeant!" whispered back the Green Beret Captain.

Willoughby could make out the silhouettes of the huts clearly with the *AN/PVS-2 Starlight Star-bright* infra-red lens but it was so dark that with the naked eye almost nothing could be discerned.

"Wait!" the Captain put his hand in front of the other three soldiers.

"What is it sir? Do you see something?" asked the Texan sergeant.

"Yes!"

Willoughby pushed forward his M16 and aimed it at a large group of huts situated in the middle of the village.

"Do you hear that?" asked the officer to his men.

As they listened they could hear the sound of loud talking, almost screaming, coming from the huts. Then a few single rifle shots could be heard echoing through the jungle night.

"Jesus!" said Willoughby, "Something is going down in the village!"

One of his men handed him the field telephone which the Captain wrenched towards himself.

"Did you hear that sir?" asked Willoughby as he spoke to Colonel Vortex who was about 200 yards behind with the rest of B Company.

"I certainly did Captain! You stay put and I'll come up with the central column. The other two columns will swing around in a flanking movement to the north and south of the village to surround it. I think this is worth investigating!"

The Special Forces Captain said excitedly, "Right you are sir! Over and out!"

Vortex gave the hand signals for the manoeuvring into position of the elite Marine B Company.

"Captain Hoang Pho and Lieutenant Colonel Tran – you are the anchor men. Your platoon will stay right here while my central column advances on the village perimeter. If anything goes wrong then this is the position where the whole unit will fall back and converge to. Understood?"

The South Vietnamese officers confirmed the order and Vortex moved off.

A few moments later Vortex crawled up beside Captain Willoughby.

"Ok! Captain! Lets see what we shall see!"

As Vortex spoke he told Lieutenant Shanley to stay with the column.

"Sergeant Major Crighton, you Willoughby and your three men come with me. Let's take a look at that group of hooch's up ahead where the noise and rifle shots are coming from," said Vortex.

The six men crawled forward on their bellies as Lieutenant Shanley felt the sweat pouring down the crease in his spine. The Colonel had told him only to move forward upon his order. The 80 men lay flat to the moist earth as their commander inched ever closer to potential danger.

The other two columns were already in position to the north and south of the village about 150 yards from the perimeter. The crack unit of Marines had *Khe Sanh* village totally surrounded. But what they did not realise was that a much larger unit of the enemy was already taking up positions *around them*.

Even now a 3,000 man Viet Cong Regiment was approaching the *Khe Sanh* village from the direction of Hill 527 in total silence.

Vortex and his group came up to the first hut.

"You stay here," said the Colonel. Willoughby nodded as he watched the senior officer slowly tiptoe up the bamboo stairs. Vortex could feel the adrenalin cascading

through his veins. Suddenly he saw a black garbed man walking around from the other side of the hut. Immediately he dropped to the floor in front of the entrance.

He had to think quickly. If he stayed in this position the man would walk right on top of him.

Vortex unsheathed his 18 inch Marine dagger and jumped up like a cougar. The Vietnamese man was so startled that he literally froze in his tracks. But it was too late. Vortex lunged forward and covered the man's mouth with his fists and at the same time he drove his dagger deliciously into the chest bone while clutching the man's ass from behind.

A soft gurgle of death could be heard as the victim fell into Vortex's arms. The knife pierced the cartilage of the manubriums and sucked wondrously into the heart tissue. The man died instantly as his left ventricle was cut to pieces.

Vortex laid the corpse gently on the ground so as not to make any noise. The Colonel could see immediately that the man was a Viet Cong infiltrator. The whole village must be full of them he thought.

Sergeant Major Crighton and the Green Berets could see everything that had happened.

Vortex made his way slowly to a window in the hut and in the pitch darkness he peered over the ledge. There was a dim light coming from inside. Voices could be heard. Some of them were speaking excitedly.

What Vortex saw caused a tremor of horror to shudder through his nerves. Three naked villagers lay on the floor with their throats cut. Another four Vietnamese women were hanging from the ceiling by ropes. They were being sexually abused and mutilated by about five PAVN soldiers and Viet Cong and also some Laotian Communists who were probably from the 304th Division. A group of children, also naked, were tied together in the middle of the hut with steel wire. They were being punched and kicked as well as having been lasciviously raped and sodomised by the PAVN regulars. The girls especially were crying horribly and clutching their bruised and violated reproductive organs. Vortex gave a hand signal to come quickly to his position. Immediately, Sergeant Major Crighton, Captain Willoughby and the others tiptoed up the stairs and onto the landing. They crouched next to the Colonel.

Vortex moved first after telling his men not to use firearms because it might alert other Communist forces in the village. Standing up in front of the window Vortex threw his dagger into the throat of the nearest PAVN soldier. The man clutched his neck as blood shot out in a hot stream. The other five men launched themselves into the room and hand to hand fighting erupted amidst the shrieks and cries of the mutilated South Vietnamese civilians.

Vortex grabbed the head of one Viet Cong and thrust it into a steel spike nearby. The grey brain matter was impaled in a slush of blood and yellow tissue that vomited disgustingly all over his camouflage fatigues. As he did this Crighton head-butted one PAVN soldier and smashed him into the torso of a Viet Cong wearing their standard black pantaloon-like pyjamas.

Captain Willoughby sliced his knife into the buttocks of a PAVN soldier as he rushed towards him while looping a thin steel garrotting wire around the head of another. As the Captain tightened the noose around the Communists' neck, the wire dug cruelly into the flesh until it reached the spinal cord. With a final yank and backwards thrust the shrieking skull was decapitated in a shower of sticky, viscous blood that spurted its way down Willoughby's camouflage tunic.

"Watch out!" screamed Vortex to one of Captain Willoughby's Green Berets. The man had just crushed the skull of one Viet Cong when another came up behind him and drove a large machete through his chest. The other Americans watched in horror as the tip of the blade broke open the chest of their comrade-in-arms like a ripe watermelon bursting.

The Green Beret walked strangely forward with a mesmerised expression on his face as his fingers played with the tip of the blade that had vivisected him into two half spheres.

Vortex stepped forward as if to help the forlorn man but was caught in a headlock by one of the two remaining NVA regulars.

It was Captain Willoughby and the Texan Master Sergeant who came up behind the initial attacker and drove both their knives into his left kidney and liver respectively. Crighton leapt forward simultaneously and punched the guts and gonads of the man who had his Colonel in a head-vice.

"Fuck you stinking VC!" roared Vortex as he gripped the Communist's hair from behind and dropped to his knees. As he levered forward he catapulted the enemy over his head and commenced to gouge out his eyes with his fingers as Crighton tore at the man's testicles and then sliced them off with his Marine dagger.

Willoughby and his special forces troops finished off the last NVA soldier by sliding his chest onto a razor sharp steel spike that was sticking vertically up from the floor. This was the Viet Cong's favourite instrument of torture. They would insert the delicate anus of an innocent South Vietnamese civilian onto the steel spike after stripping him or her naked. Using oil which they smeared over the buttocks and genitalia they would force the body of the victim further and further inside the spike by wrenching down the arms until the impalement was complete. Sometimes the spike would drive itself straight through the entire length of the viscera and emerge horribly from the mouth.

"Free the children first!" screamed Vortex as he lifted up the last Viet Cong soldier and slammed his head into the side of the wall. Sergeant Major Crighton said, "Stand him up vertical!"

One of the Green Berets complied and Vortex's NCO deliciously drove his bayonet into the man's guts.

"He's dead," said Captain Willoughby with sorrow. The Green Beret who was impaled so excruciatingly with the machete just at that moment died in the Captain's arms.

Vortex knelt before the dead man and prayed;

"The Lord killeth, and maketh alive; he bringeth down to the grave and bringeth up. But the adversaries of the Lord shall be broken to pieces; out of heaven shall be thunder upon them: the Lord shall judge the ends of the earth; and he shall give strength unto his King, and exalt the horn of his anointed!

Oh! Lord our God! Give us strength this day to combat thine enemies, the Viet Cong and their devilish minions. Give us the strength to carry your eternal light which shall be like a burning sacrament to cleanse and purify the earth from these Communist jackals and demons of Leviathan! Give mercy unto this fallen soul and raise him up to heaven so that he may sit at your right hand! For he hath fought for your son, Jesus! And unto Jesus he shall return in everlasting and redeeming peace!"

Captain Willoughby and the others said with dignified sorrow, "Amen!"

Vortex freed the children and gathered them around him like a gallant and heroic protector. A few of the adult women were still alive and they were cut down also.

By this time Lieutenant Donald Shanley was getting quite apprehensive. He had heard nothing from Colonel Vortex's group for more than 30 minutes.

Then, it seemed that his guts were ripped apart with fear as a fusillade of fire hit into his column from both the west and the east. A Corporal in front of him was cut in half by fire from a Chinese *Type 24 7.92mm heavy machine gun* which could fire 400 rounds per minute. Even before he could open his mouth, his 80 men returned fire from both sides.

"Shit!" screamed Lieutenant Shanley as a tracer bullet tore open his left thigh. Blood splashed his face.

Colonel Vortex's group had just emerged from the hut when he heard the outbreak of fighting. As if from nowhere, scores of innocent *Khe Sanh* villagers started running from their straw dwellings, screaming, shouting and waving their arms about like crazed delinquents.

Vortex grabbed the field telephone, "Shanley! Lieutenant Shanley? What the fuck is going on?"

The dazed Lieutenant replied from the other end of the line, "I don't know sir! We started getting incoming fire from both sides! We must be surrounded by the PAVN and VC!"

Before Colonel Vortex could answer the junior officer he heard fresh gunfire coming from the west and the east.

Sergeant Major Crighton stumbled over one of the naked children as he screamed, "Sir! They have opened up on our other two columns as well! We are totally surrounded! The village is encircled!"

Vortex watched as dark pyjama clad figures came running out of the jungle towards the village from all sides.

"Shit! Give me that field telephone!" barked Vortex as 7.62mm bullets started pelting into the naked children ahead of them.

"Lieutenant Colonel Tran! Captain Hoang Pho! Pho! Pho! Fuck you Pho! Are you there?"

The South Vietnamese commanders and their men, 40 strong, were also under fire. However their platoon had not yet been ambushed.

The Texan Master Sergeant screamed, "Watch it Colonel! Behind you!"

Vortex ducked as three Viet Cong guerrillas came up from the rear. Each one of them was about five feet six inches tall and they brandished machetes and *AK-47* assault rifles.

"Oh! Boy!" grunted the Colonel.

Sergeant Major Crighton was holding the hands of two small South Vietnamese girls as he was trying to move them to a position of safety. But there was nowhere to run.

Vortex spun on his heels and slapped his dagger into the neck of one VC as he ran past. A second guerrilla jumped onto Vortex's back but the Colonel shot him forward and crushed his skull with the butt of his M16.

The Texan Master Sergeant gripped the third Communist and cracked open his chest with a field axe. He then threw the axe to Vortex who sliced it neatly into the man's intestines. They were showered in blood and mutilated tissue as the group of children they were shielding were ripped apart by PAVN machine gun fire. Almost half the naked infants were cut to pieces by the cruel Communist fusillade.

Captain Willoughby saw little hands and small limbs splatter through the air. A ten year old girl's ear hit his face and then a severed foot smacked into his back. His camouflage fatigues were splashed with infant blood. His two surviving Green Berets tried to cover the children from the murderous fire but it was no use.

"Colonel Vortex! Are you there?" It was the hysterical voice of Captain Hoang Pho coming in over the field telephone.

Crighton threw the handset to Vortex as he fired his M60 into the jungle foliage.

"What's happening back there?" asked the 9th Marine Commander.

Captain Hoang Pho informed, "We are coming under heavy fire Colonel! I've already taken several casualties! What do you want me to do?"

Vortex screamed back over the din of hot, flying metal and RPG explosions.

"I want you to hold your position! Do you hear me Captain Pho? We will work our way back to you and then the whole unit will retreat back to *Khe Sanh*! We're completely outnumbered. It's a bloody effective ambush the cocksucking PAVN have brought down on us!"

Captain Pho answered, "Understood! Will hold until you link up with us!"

Vortex crawled on his belly to Captain Willoughby who had three surviving children cradled under his arm.

"You better get back to *Lang Vei* Captain!"

Willoughby had a broken nose that was oozing blood after one Viet Cong had struck him with a rifle butt. The Special Forces officer glanced sideways.

"Yes Colonel! This could be my last chance to break out of the village!"

Sergeant Major Crighton crawled up behind them as *AK-47* fire raked the huts to the rear and kept a constant stream of burning metal flying over their skulls.

"Go now and good luck Captain!" yelled Vortex over the screams of dying South Vietnamese villagers who were falling all around them.

"But what about you? Sir?" asked Willoughby as his two Green Berets picked up their M60's and made ready to go.

"Don't worry Frank!" sighed Vortex, "I'll make it! When I get back to the *Khe Sanh* perimeter I'll order in an airstrike to flatten the whole area around this village."

Willoughby nodded and ran with his men into the jungle past the village clearing. It was another 3 or 3.5 miles of tortuous jungle to the *Lang Vei Camp*.

Sergeant Major Crighton retorted, "Poor bastard! He'll never make it!"

Vortex clapped his NCO on the shoulder, "I wouldn't be too sure about that Sergeant Major! He's an extremely resourceful and cunning man!"

Vortex raised his head and fired his M60 like a crazed lunatic. He unleashed a torrent of bullets and did not stop until he had exhausted 12 belts of ammunition.

Meanwhile Lieutenant Donald Shanley was in bad shape. His central column had lost 3 dead and 17 wounded already. What was worse there was no helicopters so the wounded would have to be dragged back to the *Khe Sanh* perimeter through the *Gray Sector*.

A Corporal at the head of Shanley's column was firing into the jungle when they were rushed by over two hundred regular PAVN. A Communist bayonet was driven viciously through the back of his neck as he lay firing on his stomach. The enemy soldier drove the tip of the blade through the cervical spine and out of the Corporal's throat from in front, splitting his trachea. Thus the bayonet pinned him to the ground

while a second Viet Cong stove in his skull as he groped in his own suffocating blood. More than a dozen men around the Corporal panicked and stood up to run to the rear. They were mowed down by merciless PAVN and VC fire. The Communists tore into the group and used their bayonets to empty the guts of another 7 of the elite squad of Marines.

"Help! Help!" screamed one private as he ran towards Lieutenant Shanley. He never made it. Three Viet Cong jumped up and emptied their AK-47's into the retreating American, literally tearing his head off so that a piece of his mutilated mouth went flying through the air.

Of the forty men at the front of the central column almost all were killed or wounded.

"Lieutenant Shanley! Shanley! Come in!" screamed the voice of Colonel Vortex.

Shanley and more than twenty of his men had separated from their main group. They retreated and slid into a gulley that was 200 yards to the east of where their comrades were being cut to pieces.

A Sergeant had the field telephone and hearing the Colonel's voice he handed it to Shanley.

"Come in? Who's this?" said Shanley in a daze.

Vortex snapped back, "Who do you think it is? You imbecile!"

"Sir?" said Shanley as the PAVN started firing into the prostrate Americans lying in terror at the bottom of the mud filled gulley of red dust and slush.

"Sir! Help us! We need reinforcements!" screamed back Shanley.

The enemy force which was a mixed Regiment of PAVN and a battalion of Viet Cong sappers had already, unknown to the Colonel, pinned down and ambushed the other two columns to the east and west of *Khe Sanh* village.

"What are you talking about you idiot?" spat back the Colonel, "How can I help you? I have just Sergeant Major Crighton with me!"

Shanley gripped the field phone until his fingers were bled white with terror inspired pressure.

"Sir! We had to fall back!"

"Where are you now Lieutenant?"

"About 200 yards east of where we were – in a ditch or something!"

As Shanley spoke the Warrant Officer next to him holding the field telephone received a bullet one inch above his left eye. The big man seemed to arch backwards in a spasmodic movement and then crumple into the mud face down.

"That's insane!" roared back Colonel Vortex, "Get back to your original position. The Sergeant Major and I shall work our way around to the west and see if we can find the other column. Then we'll make our way back to you."

Lieutenant Shanley said, "We'll try sir! Out!"

Vortex said to Crighton, in German, *"Dieser Idiot Shanley ist bereits zurückgewichen und hat seine Säule in zwei gespalten. Ich bin dabei, seinen Esel auszuschimpfen, wann und wenn wir zu Khe Sanh zurückkommen."*

[Translated:- That idiot Shanley has already fallen back and split his column in two. I am going to chew out his ass when and if we get back to Khe Sanh.]

Sergeant Major Crighton looked to Vortex with disbelief and commented, also answering in German as when the two comrades were in extreme stress they always reverted back to the language that gave them the most comfort and which allowed them to collect their mental state of mind, *"Warum brachten Sie ihm mit uns? Sie sollten Kommandanten des Oberstleutnants Johns F. Mitchell des 1. Bataillons gebracht haben. Er kann sein kühles besser unter dem intensiven Feuer behalten und weiß, wie man sich und seine Männer von einer unmöglichen Situation befreit. Ich mochte nie Shanley auch. Er ist unfähig, und er ist ein bafoon und ein Hohlkopf, der ein ROTC Offizier ist."*

[Translated:- Why did you bring him with us? You should have brought Lieutenant Colonel John F. Mitchell commander of the 1st Battalion. He can keep his cool better under intense fire and knows how to extricate himself and his men from an impossible situation. I never liked Shanley either. He's incompetent and he is a buffoon and a simpleton being an ROTC officer.]

Vortex shrugged his shoulders in apology as Crighton asked further, *"So sind wir dabei, zwei von uns selbstständig vorwärts zu gehen und dass andere Säule zu finden?"*

[Translated:- So are we going to advance, the two of us on our own and find that other column?]

Vortex kept his head down as he watched three Montagnard men and two women being erupted into the air by Communist RPG rockets. Their limbs disassembled in a shower of gore.

"There is nothing else we can do!" moaned Vortex.

"And the children?" asked Sergeant Major Crighton, "There are three still alive?"

Vortex looked at the three naked girls aged between 7 and 12 years.

"We can't take them with us. I can't carry them and run through the Viet Cong at the same time while firing my weapon. Its impossible!"

The Sergeant Major had them all under his chest like a *Fairy God Mother* to protect them from the withering fire, "So what do we do sir?"

Vortex threw two hand grenades into the jungle from where the enemy fire was coming from. The explosions sent foliage and branches flying everywhere.

"We have to let them go Sergeant Major."

"But sir! They will be raped and dismembered by the stinking VC when they take this village!"

"I know that Sergeant Major. But there is nothing we can do to prevent it except perhaps to hide them."

Crighton left the naked children in a nearby thatched hut, hoping they would be spared by the VC. He gave them his field rations from his knapsack and told them in fluent Vietnamese to run away with their parents, if they could find them, before the VC came into the village in force. The children cried hysterically amidst the sound of gunfire and erupting munitions but nodded their understanding.

Vortex and Crighton ran to the edge of the *Khe Sanh* village perimeter and disappeared like phantoms in the night into the thick and luxurious jungle surrounding *Khe Sanh*.

It seemed that bullets, tracer fire and RPG explosions were coming from a full 360 degree circle wherever they went.

"Jesus! Colonel!" expostulated Sergeant Major Crighton as the two men rolled on their bellies down a steep ravine and into a stream.

"How did the fucking PAVN and VC get in so close? And where are the other 160 men of B Company?"

Vortex led the way up the stream as they waded in the stagnant water up to their chests.

"Fucked if I know Sergeant Major! But what we have to do now is get back to Shanley and then find the rest of my men."

Vortex felt something nibbling at the corner of his crotch just inside his right thigh. He reached down into the water and put his hand inside his pants. What he feared was there, eating and burrowing into his flesh, sucking his blood. A huge black leech.

"Fuck! Leeches!" whispered Vortex.

The Sergeant Major also had some eating into his anal orifice and his buttocks and one had crawled right up inside his anus and was making its way into his putrid, beer and whisky soaked bowels.

"I've got them too sir!" The Sergeant Major moaned with agony and asked Vortex if they could stop for a second so that he could gouge them out of his flesh with a knife.

A few minutes passed and when the Sergeant was ready they heard Vietnamese voices coming from the stream behind them.

Vortex held the Sergeant Major's shoulder and put his finger to his mouth. Both men lowered themselves into the stinking water until only their eyes and scalps were above the waterline.

Crighton could see a squad of 10 or 12 PAVN regulars with camouflage pith helmets wading up the stream from the direction they had come.

Vortex gave the signal to attack them once they had passed. As soon as the last enemy soldier had passed the two Americans swung into action. Vortex glided up to one NVA and grabbing him around the mouth with his right hand he plunged into

his right kidney and then upwards into his heart with an 18 inch Marine dagger. Crighton did the same for a second NVA who was level with the one that Vortex had killed so deliciously. The two Marines were so silent that the other 10 NVA did not hear a thing.

Vortex nodded and raised his M60 machine gun. He had a clear field of fire to exterminate the remaining 10 NVA. Crighton took out 4 hand grenades and unpinned all of them simultaneously. He waited long enough so that as soon as he would throw the grenades they would explode over the NVA troops. This took years of experience and acquired expertise in death-dealing. At the same time Vortex would open up with the *M60*. The 10 men would fall quickly under a hail of bullets.

It was done. The grenades burst above the pith helmeted skulls and the bullets from Vortex felled them all like ninepins.

"One of them is getting away!" screamed Vortex.

Crighton was already after him. He cascaded through the water like a huge venomous snake and chased the black pyjama'd figure onto the bank of the stream. Vortex followed.

With a single leap Crighton brought the enemy down in a vicious headlock, the *AK-47* rifle flying through the air.

But the body felt unusually soft, eerily succulent and tactile.

"What is this?" asked Vortex as he kicked off the NVA pith helmet. To both Marines it was an incredible surprise.

The PAVN soldier was a young girl of about 22 years of age.

"The fucking bitch!" said Colonel Vortex as he slapped the North Vietnamese woman soldier across the breasts, into her vagina and then ripped at her face with his hands.

Sergeant Major Crighton asked as he looked with unabated fury at the girl, "Do we have enough time to give her a good going over?"

"We certainly do!" said Vortex as they heard constant machine gun fire and screams nearby.

Sergeant Major Crighton searched her pockets and blouse.

"Hey! Oh! My God! My dear God! Oh! No! Sweet Jesus!" exclaimed the Sergeant Major.

Vortex thought that his NCO was having a mild heart attack as he clutched his chest with indescribable agony.

"What is it Crighton? Are you hit? Are you hurt? Did you catch a piece of hot shrapnel?"

"This fucking murdering bitch, slut!" was all that Crighton could utter with rage.

He lifted his hand towards Vortex, "I found this in her tunic! The rapacious murdering whore!"

Vortex took the object out of the NCOs' hand as he knelt down and head-butted the woman, causing blood to cascade upwards into his face.

The object was a solid 22 carat gold cigarette lighter. On the back was the inscription;

"For my beloved Green Beret from your adoring wife, Monique. For our seventh Wedding Anniversary."

And under that was the name of the soldier;

"Master Sergeant Thomas Lucas Hendrickson."

Vortex let out a terrible, heart wrenching yell.

"I knew Sergeant Hendrickson well! He was a fine man! And he was an excellent soldier! He belongs to Captain Willoughby's outfit! And this bitch killed him!"

Sergeant Major Crighton stripped the Communist woman naked and beat her breasts and savaged his hands inside her reproductive organ while inserting his Marine dagger up the crevice of her buttocks and into her anus. Blood gushed in a torrent from the white, smooth and soft female flesh.

Colonel Vortex dropped his camouflage pants and in the thick jungle fornicated ferociously with the enemy woman until he ejaculated his discarded seed into her. He continued for a second climax as he ripped the girl's ears off by biting her flesh and then having Sergeant Major Crighton use his knife for the final operative process.

"Tell me where you stole this cigarette lighter! From whom?" screamed Vortex in perfect Vietnamese.

The enemy woman spat in his face and screamed hysterically.

Now it was Sergeant Major Crighton who mounted her in the doggie position and fucked her with savage and malevolent force while Vortex, kneeling in front, used his fingers to gouge out both her eyes.

Taking up a steel rod, Vortex smashed her thighs and fibula until you could see the white splintered bone protruding in a hideous mixture from her crushed limbs.

"I'll fuck you to death you slut and murdering she-devil!"

Crighton gripped her head in-between his hands and crushed her skull with unbelievable force by ramming his hands together with all his might and *Christian power* of righteous revenge.

The Viet Cong girl's head practically imploded from the suppressive kinetic force of those two massive fists.

"She's dead praise be to the Lord!" remarked Colonel Vortex as he winced at *AK-47* fire that was flying everywhere around them.

Sergeant Major Crighton picked up the mangled body of the girl and threw it head first into the small stream. It joined the other corpses in the water all of which floated gently with the tide away from the *Khe Sanh* village to be consumed by leeches and other assorted aquatic vermin.

"Colonel Vortex? Where are you? This is *Tango-Charlie*. Out."

Vortex answered his field telephone. It was the voice of Lieutenant Colonel Tran. "What's happening at your position Tran?"

The South Vietnamese officer sounded agitated as gunfire could be heard through the radio from his position.

"The PAVN and VC are everywhere Colonel Vortex. I can't hold on much longer. I have taken 5 KIA (killed in action) and 9 WIA (wounded in action) already. The Communists have almost totally surrounded my position as it is."

Vortex looked at Sergeant Major Crighton and barked into the handset, "Listen Tran! Hang on! I'll be there soon. But I've got to find the other two columns."

Lieutenant Colonel Tran answered, "One of them is already here with us Colonel! And Lieutenant Shanley's group as well. Both groups have suffered many killed, many wounded.! Out!"

Vortex looked to Sergeant Major Crighton and covered his handset, "Tran says that two columns have already joined up with his Ranger platoon."

Crighton beamed, "That's good sir!"

Vortex nodded. Then added, "At least one good thing came out of this sortie that went pear shaped."

"What the fuck is that sir?" asked Crighton in surprise.

"At least I can return the cigarette lighter to Mrs Hendrickson so that she knows that her husband was murdered by these fiends from the bowels of hell. It would be her keepsake as the body of her husband was never recovered."

Crighton nodded with heartfelt sorrow and a tear came to his eye.

"Listen Tran! Stay where you are. When I find the third column I'm going to call *Khe Sanh FSCC* and order in a full barrage of 175mm fire to blast these fucking gooks to kingdom come!"

The South Vietnamese officer confirmed these instructions and told them to Captain Hoang Pho before going off the air.

"Come on! Let's get the rat's fuck out of here before the whole place is swarming with PAVN forces from the 304th Division!" blurted out Vortex in a fit of rage.

The two men could hardly see through the jungle foliage as there was no moonlight. Only tracer fire in the distance illuminated the terrain ahead for a few seconds at a time. As Crighton leapt behind a tree and Vortex fired into the foliage ahead of them, a large and venomous snake curled itself around the Colonel's left ankle.

"Watch out sir!" screamed the Sergeant Major.

Just at that second three camouflage pith helmeted PAVN regulars came screaming out of the trees to their left. Vortex had his M16 with bayonet attached and he fired. One PAVN soldier dropped immediately but the other two knifed Vortex with

their *AK-47* bayonets. Both blades just skimmed the surface of the Colonel's thigh and right forearm.

Crighton, axe in hand, swung viciously in the desperate defence of his beloved Colonel. The razor sharp axe ate into the flesh of one NVA. His head was disconnected from his trunk as the axe cut the cervical vertebrae and sliced the carotid and jugular arteries in a shower of brilliant coloured blood.

Vortex gripped the remaining NVA soldier as the snake made its way up his legs to bite at his testicles.

"Fuck you! *Bumsen Sie Sie!*" screamed Vortex as he swiped the *AK-47* out of the NVA's hands and head butted the soldier while gripping his camouflage tunic.

Sergeant Major Crighton acted quickly. He grabbed the snake that was threatening Colonel Vortex and ripping it clean off his commander's leg, he thrust it into the screaming face of the North Vietnamese soldier.

The snake's huge fangs, its dribbling and venomous jaws hissed like a beast from hell as it snapped shut across the ugly pock-marked face of the Communist assassin.

Vortex unsheathed his Marine dagger as he watched the reptile's fangs puncture the left eye and right cheek of the agonized Communist trooper.

"Give it to him sir!" screamed Crighton as the Sergeant Major picked up the fallen field telephone.

Vortex shouted, "Eat this!" The Marine officer deliciously plunged his dagger into the soft guts of the NVA as his face was mauled by the snake. The beast curled its forty foot trunk around the man and started to crush him in a hideous bear hug while Vortex stabbed the enemy simultaneously in his liver, spleen and intestines with savage abandon.

When it was done and the snake had half swallowed the entire skull of the NVA soldier, Vortex stepped back with his M16 and pumped three full magazines into both man and beast killing them both.

"Fucking beautiful Sergeant Major!" sighed Vortex as he lay back on the grass for a few moments to catch his breath.

"Thank you sir," said Crighton who reloaded the M60.

"It was smart thinking to use that grotesque snake as a weapon against the NVA motherfuckers."

Crighton answered back with some wit, "You should always use one reptile to destroy another!"

The two men laughed but soon stopped as a figure stumbled out of the trees in front of them.

Vortex swung to the ground and was about to open fire when he saw that it was one of his men. A Captain.

"Jesus!" screamed the Colonel as he ran towards the man. The officer was Captain Jellico, who was in command of the missing third column.

Sergeant Major Crighton managed to catch the Captain as he collapsed. The sight was hideous.

Captain Jellico had, moments before, been mutilated by an RPG rocket launched by the NVA who had surrounded his 80 Marines. His right arm was missing up to the level of the shoulder. Vortex could see that only a white, charred stump of bone and blackened, mangled flesh was hanging in bloodied strips from his shoulder stump. That was all that was left of his once proud and powerful arm.

"Can you give him something to ease the hellish pain?" asked Vortex.

Crighton gently lowered him to the ground, "Yes sir. I have an ampoule of *Morphine*."

Vortex watched as the paramedical trained Crighton expertly injected 250ml of morphine into the *ante-cubital vein* of the Captain's remaining arm.

"Tell me what happened to you?" asked Vortex as he shook the Captain back to consciousness.

"The gooks…, they bushwhacked us!"

As the Captain spoke blood vomited from his mouth and he was almost incoherent.

"Where are your men Captain?" asked Vortex as the machine gun fire seemed to be getting closer.

There was no answer.

"Your men Captain? Where the fuck are they? How many killed? How many wounded?"

"Its no use sir," began Sergeant Major Crighton, "He's not going to make it. He's going into shock!"

Vortex shook the Captain viciously and finally he pointed to the west from the direction he had come.

"We can't leave him here Sergeant Major. Do you think you can carry him on your back?"

Crighton replied, "I don't have to."

Vortex took his Starlight infrared binoculars and started to comb through the jungle from west to east as he asked, "What do you mean?"

"The Captain's dead sir."

Vortex turned around and could see the lifeless form of his Company Commander.

"Then we shall have to leave him here I'm afraid."

The two men moved off after covering the dead officer with a plastic ground sheet.

They scurried up embankments, down gulley's and into the thick foliage until they came to the source of the gunfire.

"Look Sergeant Major!" Vortex handed Crighton the night field glasses. They could see hundreds of NVA and VC troops crawling through the jungle ahead of them. Captain Jellico's men had been ambushed but a small group still held out as the enemy forces continued to lay down a heavy stream of suppressive fire in preparation for an all out attack to wipe the Marines out.

"If we work our way around to the south we might be able to reach the survivors," said Vortex.

Crighton said, "We totally underestimated the strength of the gooks in this area sir."

Vortex ran in front with Crighton behind. They moved through the jungle like swift gazelles. They had covered nearly a half mile when they were forced to hit the ground due to intense 0.50 cal fire.

"Shit!" whispered Vortex. "The gooks have gotten around behind us!"

Vortex took out his flare gun and shot two *slap flares* into the inky black night to illuminate their opponents.

As he spoke two NVA came rushing at them from the thick and luxurious undergrowth. One Communist managed to string piano wire around Vortex's neck, strangling him as the steel thread started to cut into his flesh and spinal ligaments.

Sergeant Major Crighton swung around and let a M60 burst cut the other NVA into two pieces. He watched as the stomach and erupting intestines separated from the chest cavity.

But a hideous blow smacked into Crighton's skull as he fired forwards. Another NVA regular had sneaked up from behind and slammed his *AK-47* butt into the NCOs' head.

"Ahiiee!" screamed Crighton as he fell forwards, his face burying itself into the mutilated intestines of the enemy corpse.

Vortex swung his torso from left to right in a maniacal frenzy, trying to shake off the much lighter NVA man. Finally he dropped forward on his knees and catapulted the Communist over his head as he hung on to the sharp piano wire so as to prevent it from decapitating him by accident. Vortex then slid out his knife and thrust it into the gaping mouth of the screaming NVA soldier. The blade managed to travel right through the trachea and down into the oesophagus itself causing unheard of mutilation of the internal viscera.

Crighton, without Vortex's help, reached backwards in a frantic bid to survive the hand to hand combat. His massive fists grabbed a tuft of the NVA's hair. But yet another Communist bolted out of the jungle and jumped onto the six foot four and a half Marine Sergeant Major.

Before Vortex could do anything for his gallant NCO, Crighton roared like a majestic lion with two stinking Communist rats hanging to his spine, neck and mane.

He arose to his feet lifting the two North Vietnamese with him. With supreme violence and savagery, Crighton swung his body into a nearby tree so that the head of one NVA was dismembered upon the spike of a sharp edged branch.

"I've got the other one Sergeant Major!" screamed Vortex as spittle came out of his mouth.

The Colonel ran forward and knifed the second Communist in the buttocks as he hung onto Crighton's neck. The Sergeant Major reached backwards in a curvature that was amazing for his bulk and ripped into the NVA's nose with his teeth, savaging the man until his face was a mutilated mess.

Vortex withdrew the dagger as he could feel that it struck clear through to the pelvic bone and reinserted it into the man's right and left lungs. Blood erupted like a beautiful shower onto his tunic.

Then in a synchronized manoeuvre, both Vortex and Crighton grabbed hold of the NVA's skull from each ear and slammed the head sideways into a tree trunk. The skull was impaled by a horizontal branch and the left eye of the Communist was weirdly separated from his nose and mouth as it was gouged upwards.

"Jesus! The gooks are everywhere sir!" moaned Crighton.

"Yes," said Vortex picking up the field telephone and the M60, "…we must continue on to our men and extract them from this hot zone."

As they proceeded to the sounds of the battle they came upon many corpses, some belonging to Vortex's B Company and others were PAVN or VC.

Sergeant Major Crighton pumped several bullets into each dead PAVN/VC soldier that he came across because his experience at the *'Battle of Dakto'* told him that the VC and PAVN loved to play dead and then arise suddenly like some resuscitated anti-Christ from the pits of hell behind the advancing and heroic Americans throwing a grenade or letting loose with an *AK-47*.

"Over here sir!" shouted a voice through the jungle.

Vortex ran forward and grabbed hold of a 2nd Lieutenant from his third column.

"Jesus Mary mother of our Lord!" expostulated the Lieutenant, "Where did you come from sir?"

"Never mind that Lieutenant!" said Vortex angrily, "Are these all the men that are left?"

The Colonel looked to a row of about fifty men lying behind a gulley and firing continuously at the invisible PAVN who were very close by.

"Yes sir!" said the junior officer as he fired his M60 into the jungle ahead of them.

Crighton was horrified in that instant as he ran up and down the line of men giving them encouragement and directing their fire, when a wall of PAVN regulars burst out of the undergrowth directly in front of their position.

"Take cover!" shouted Vortex. The Lieutenant he was speaking to caught a round directly through the centre of his midbrain. He slumped against the Colonel's left arm,

dying instantly. Approximately 700 PAVN and 300 VC advanced towards the handful of stoic Marines.

Vortex watched with horror as men whiplashed backwards with bullet wounds, some crawled forwards trying to shield themselves deeper into the mud, while others were blown to bits by RPG rockets which tore into them, sending chunks of roasted flesh flying through the air.

Vortex truly thought that this was the end. He had, surely, only moments to live.

And then a miracle came to pass.

Vortex thought that he heard something behind him. Swinging his head to the rear he saw no less than five huge *Sikorsky S-65*; *HH-53B Jolly Green Giant* helicopters of the 1st Marine Air Wing. He knew that these helicopters had just flown the 1 or so miles from *Khe Sanh* to their rescue. Each of the five helicopters had a six-man crew, 3 *Miniguns* at front and from the side hatch, armour plating, flight refuelling and a rescue hoist. Each chopper could carry at least 40 men.

"We're saved!" screamed Colonel Vortex to Sergeant Major Crighton as his NCO came running up with some of the wounded. Immediately the 15 *Miniguns* from the five giant *Sikorsky's* opened up with a maelstrom of fire at the advancing NVA and VC troops that were almost on top of Vortex. Each *Minigun* could fire 2,000 rounds per minute. Thus 30,000 rounds per minute, a veritable avalanche of streaking hot steel and tracers, was slamming into the Viet Cong and their PAVN masters.

Vortex watched with awe filled joy as the front rank of Communists, nearly 100 men, were ripped apart in a mutilated eruption of human flesh and intestines. Blood fell over the surviving Americans like an inhuman shower of death.

"It's beautiful to watch sir!" screamed Crighton over the roar of the five huge *Sikorsky's* as they unleashed an avalanche of firepower into the PAVN/Viet Cong. About 230 of the survivors, including Shanley's group and Captain Hoang Pho and Lieutenant Colonel Tran's ARVN Rangers were already inside the choppers. They had been picked up a few minutes earlier when Colonel Tran had radioed *Khe Sanh* for a quick helicopter extraction from a precariously dangerous situation.

"Let's go! Move it men! Able-bodied take one wounded each to the choppers!" screamed Vortex.

As the host of *Miniguns* kept the PAVN heads down, the 50 survivors of the third column scrambled into the helicopters. The men moved like greased lightning.

"They are all in sir," said Crighton over the roar of munitions and the deafening thud thud thud of the 72 foot rotor blades that spun to invisible speed.

"Good work Sergeant Major!" said Vortex as he clapped the NCO on the back.

The pilot of the lead *Sikorsky* asked the Colonel, "Sir! I have the *390th Tactical Fighter Squadron* on the horn. Do you want me to call in an airstrike? There are 9 *Republic F-105 Thunderchiefs* circling about 3 miles away to the east of *Khe Sanh*?"

Vortex held the pilot's shoulder gently.

"Yes! Send them in. Blast the rat-fuckers to hell! And let's get out of here and back to *Khe Sanh*!"

The pilot nodded and like huge majestic birds, the five *Sikorskys* banked away to the north towards Hill 471 and headed for the *Khe Sanh* airstrip as they crossed over the *'Gray Sector'* and *Ta Con Village* as well as the *Rock Quarry* and *'Red Sector.'*

Vortex watched with delight as a minute later, the formation of *THUDS [F-105 Republic Thunderchiefs* (fighter-bombers/Century Fighters) came screeching in at 400mph just above tree top level.

The whole sky was ignited in a cataclysm of sweet gasoline/petrochemical aluminium-jelly smelling napalm and roasting Communist flesh.

Colonel Vortex smiled to Sergeant Major Crighton inside the crowded chopper.

Richard Vortex dreamed and said to himself as he prayed;

"That America's devastating and righteous firepower, its speed, accuracy and awesome magnificence, would provide him with every battlefield Victory just as the Lord God had ordained it in the name of his Son, Jesus Christ."

Chapter 8
January 20th 1968 D Day Minus 1 at KHE SANH

As the five *Sikorskys* landed on the *Khe Sanh* airstrip, Colonel David E. Lownds was in the COMMO bunker of the 26th Marine HQ complex. Artillery fire had started up as the PAVN used their *130mm M-46* field guns. Shells were erupting inside the perimeter sending clumps of earth, steel girders, aluminium planking from the airstrip and sandbags flying through the air.

The 6,000 men of the *Khe Sanh* garrison [approximately 3,000 were at the Hill outposts; 881 South, 861/861A, 558, 950 and 564 (aka hill 640)] were out of their hammocks and joining the duty squads on the concertina wire perimeter.

The whole base was a hive of frantic activity.

Just then a flight of 4 *Fairchild C-123 Providers* came swooping into the airstrip. They used *'Parachute Extraction'* [LAPES] to drop their loads of ammunition and food and then took off immediately back to the mammoth *Da Nang Air Base* on the South Vietnamese coast.

Major Thrush said, "This could be the *big push*, sir!"

Colonel Lownds was handed the field telephone by a Master Sergeant from the 26th Marines signal company.

"I don't think so Major," answered Lownds.

"What then?" asked Major Thrush.

"This is just a warm up Major. A dress rehearsal."

As Colonel Lownds was speaking into the field phone, Colonel Vortex and Lieutenant Colonel Tran had just run from the choppers and burst into the COMMO bunker. The seriously wounded were already being medevacked to *Quang Tri* by 3 additional *Sikorskys* that were fuelled up and ready to go.

"Jesus! They were all over us not more than 2 miles from the perimeter!" expostulated Colonel Vortex.

Colonel Lownds turned to the 9th Marine commander, "Just a minute Colonel. I have Captain Willoughby on the horn."

"Did he make it back to *Lang Vei*?" asked Vortex.

Colonel Lownds held up his hand for silence.

The voice of the super-aggressive and brilliant 5th Special Forces Captain could be clearly heard over the field phone.

"Listen sir!" began Willoughby, "…we have hundreds, perhaps thousands of gooks all around the perimeter! I just barely made it back to *Lang Vei*. The whole jungle area between the *Khe Sanh* perimeter, Hill 527, Hill 471, Hill 552, Hill 689, Hill 564 (aka64) and the *Lang Vei* camp is infested with both regular North Vietnamese troops as well as numerous crack regiments of main force Viet Cong. I need artillery support from your base. You know the coordinates Colonel Lownds! Can you start up a six hour barrage around the *Lang Vei* perimeter to help us hold on?"

Colonel Lownds was just about to speak into the handset when Vortex stepped forward and ripped it away from the other Colonel.

"Now listen up! Captain Willoughby! This is Vortex."

The Captain asked, "Sir? Are you alright?"

Vortex snapped back with venomous rage, "Don't fucken worry about me Captain! Your only concern is our camp at *Lang Vei*. You must hold it to the last man, the last bullet and the last satchel charge and claymore mine! Do you hear me?"

Willoughby shouted back with equal enthusiasm, "Yes sir! Those PAVN pimps and VC motherfuckers won't get inside the *Lang Vei* perimeter! I guarantee it!"

Vortex shouted back through the handset, "Good!"

Colonel Lownds angrily snatched the handset back from Vortex.

"Captain? We shall commence the artillery barrage ASAP! Ok?"

"Ok!" yelled back Willoughby as you could hear screams and gunfire coming down the other end of the line.

"Major Thrush! You come with me! I want to see personally to the commencement of the artillery barrage!" said Vortex.

Just as Vortex and Thrush made for the exit tunnel to the HQ bunker, Colonel Lownds roared, "Colonel!"

Vortex ignored Lownds for a few moments which enraged the 26th Marine commander even further.

Lownds rushed up to Colonel Vortex and grabbed him by his field webbing that had straps running vertically from his broad shoulders.

"You bastard!" shouted Lownds in a frenzy as he tore Vortex off the sand bagged stairs and back into the COMMO bunker.

The other officers in the complex; Lieutenant Colonel Tran, Captain Hoang Pho, Major Thrush, Captain Mirza Baig, Lieutenant Colonel John F. Mitchell (Commander

1st Battalion 9th Marines), Lieutenant Colonel John A. Hennelly (Commander 1st Battalion 13th Marines artillery), Lieutenant Colonel Francis J. Heath (Commander 2nd Battalion 26th Marines), Lieutenant Colonel Harry L. Aderman (Commander 3rd Battalion 26th Marines), Major Lucius J. Campbell (Commander Forward Operating Base 3) and Lieutenant Shanley watched in amazement as the two senior Colonels in command of *Khe Sanh* became enraged with animal-like frenzy.

Vortex looked genuinely surprised, "What's the matter with you Lownds?"

The 26th Commander shrieked, "How dare you? How dare you do that!"

Vortex half laughed as Lownds swung him by his webbing all around the COMMO bunker, knocking Major Thrush sideways with the Colonel's body.

"Do what?" asked Vortex as he slid his right foot expertly in-between Lownds' feet and tripped the other Colonel so that he landed flat on his ass.

Vortex asked again as Lownds jumped back to his feet, "Do what? What did I do? You fucking moron!"

Upon hearing those words Colonel Lownds struck out and his fist slammed into Vortex's left temple, causing him to lose his balance for a few moments. He fell heavily onto a wooden table behind two Master Sergeants and cracked the furniture into a dozen pieces with his massive body. Maps, pencils and teletype sheets flew everywhere.

"I'm sick of you interrupting me when I am speaking to other junior officers who are under my command!" shrieked Lownds.

"I'll speak to any officer that I feel like addressing!" said Vortex back with equal stubbornness, "And I'll do so whenever and wherever I like!"

"Oh! Is that so?" said Lownds who put his hands on his hips and stared back into Vortex's face from a close distance.

"Yes it is," replied Vortex as he glanced sideways to Major Thrush and also Major Lucius Campbell who ran the Forward Operating Base 3 and while looking at them sniggered at the whole farce that was being enacted.

"I am the Field Commander at *Khe Sanh*! Not you!" replied Lownds.

"No you are not!" barked back Colonel Vortex.

Colonel Lownds turned purple and then crimson as he blustered and blew hot air out of his mouth, "I am so!"

Vortex explained, "Didn't you hear General Westmoreland? I have joint command of *Khe Sanh* with you."

Lownds scoffed, "*Joint Command?* That's ridiculous! How can I operate this Marine Support Base when I have to risk every order that I give being countermanded by you?"

Vortex laughed and simply shrugged his shoulders. "That's the way it is Colonel Lownds," he said flippantly.

"Its preposterous!" rankled back Lownds.

"Preposterous or not, that is the way that COMUSMACV wants it. And that's the way it shall be!"

Lownds was just about to answer back furiously when one 130mm NVA shell made a direct hit on the roof of the COMMO bunker. Every man in the complex was thrown off his feet and slammed like swatted flies against the walls. The concussion wave from the blast was tremendous.

Five minutes later Vortex picked himself up off the floor, stunned and dazed. Everyone also staggered to their feet covered in dust and debris except for one Master Sergeant.

"Medic! Medic!" shouted Colonel Lownds.

Already troops from outside had come running in with stretchers. The Sergeant who had been hit, was lying on his back in a pool of blood. The concussion blast had driven a 12 inch splinter of wood directly into his right eyeball. The point of the projectile had also entered his brain tissue behind the optic chiasm. Both his ear drums had also burst.

"Ahiiee! Ahiiee!" he screamed in excruciating agony.

Colonel Vortex ordered to the Medics, "Get him prepped up with saline and plasma and load him onto one of the choppers for medivac to *Quang Tri* ASAP!"

"Yes sir!" answered a Specialist Fourth class paramedic.

"Come on Major Thrush. Let's see to that artillery, and calling to Lieutenant Colonel John A. Hennelly (Commander 1st Battalion 13th Marines artillery), "You are needed Colonel."

Vortex and his retinue walked out and made their way past the *Air Support Radar Team* bunker to the 155mm howitzer emplacements.

Colonel Lownds and his staff from the 26th Regiment went out to the northern perimeter at the *'Blue Sector'* and checked the defences there where the C/1/26 and A/1/26 were dug in.

"Are you loaded and primed up?" asked Vortex to the Captain in charge of the 155mm howitzers.

"Yes sir. You want us to lay down a field of fire around the *Lang Vei* perimeter?"

"That's right Captain," answered Vortex who had his command jeep brought up with his briefcase full of tactical maps. As the Colonel examined them carefully the tremendous boom of the entire 3 batteries of 155's started up under the direction of Lieutenant Colonel John A. Hennelly (Commander 1st Battalion 13th Marines artillery). The noise was deafening. The shells could be seen in the night air as they streaked like rockets to the west and south-west, trailing a blaze of orange-red tracer streams which looked like *Thor's lightning* behind them. Shell after shell was launched and catapulted into the traumatized atmosphere. Illumination rounds were also fired.

The PAVN shells were also continuing to pound the base. It was the classical high explosive and incendiary artillery duel and Colonel Vortex loved it.

"Do you know what Napoleon said about artillery?" he asked Lieutenant Colonel John Hennelly.

"What?" asked the artillery commander.

"Napoleon said, *'Artillery is the God of War.'*"

Vortex added, "Napoleon won his General's commission at the Battle of Toulon in 1796 using artillery to blast the British Navy to hell."

Major Thrush drove the jeep up to a high point in *Khe Sanh* so that Colonel Vortex could get a better look at the action with his high powered *Starlight* infrared field glasses.

Seven company commanders, the Regimental Chief of Staff and Major Thrush accompanied Vortex onto the flat roof of the ASRT *(Air Support Coordination Centre)*. From that building you could see almost to *Lang Vei* which was about 5 to 6 miles west to south-west near the Laos border and the PAVN sanctuaries located along the *Ho Chi Minh Trail*.

Suddenly the field telephone came to life as it was strapped to the back of the 1st Battalion 9th Marines Master Sergeant supremo. This soldier was a veteran of the Korean War and had taken part in General MacArthur's *Inchon Landings* which eventually dislocated the North Koreans and drove them back behind the 38th Parallel until the Chinese Communists crossed the Yangtze River to turn the conflict into a major world confrontation. Vortex always loved to have both Sergeant Major Crighton and this Master Sergeant with him for added morale and to bolster his own personnel security.

"Incoming message for you sir," said the Master Sergeant whose name was Max Richter.

Vortex took the handset and spoke to Captain Willoughby. The Special Forces officer wanted the support fire to close in tighter around the *Lang Vei* perimeter. He informed Vortex that several thousand PAVN regulars seemed to be preparing to storm the concertina wire but were hugging close to the base wire and defences in order to escape the artillery offensive by the 13th Marines.

"Ok! Willoughby! I'll give the batteries the updated fire coordinates," said Vortex as he continued to survey the thick jungle to the west through his binoculars.

The Captain continued, "…and sir? Do you think you can give us something a little heavier than the 155's? How about the 175mm? Can you let them loose for us?"

Vortex answered, "I'll see what I can do Captain, Tango-Alpha, Over and Out."

Richter took the handset as Major Thrush shot some *slap flares* across the *Khe Sanh* western perimeter in the *'Red Sector'* to see if anything was moving in the jungle that edged up close to the base.

"Master Sergeant Richter," began Vortex as he pointed to the enormous batteries of 155mm howitzers which were emplaced just south of the DASC *(Direct Air Support Centre).*

"Yes sir!" Richter made Vortex and Sergeant Major Crighton look like puny weasels. Even though the Sergeant was only six foot five inches tall in his socks he was also an amateur weight lifter in his spare time. His musculature was awesome as he tipped the scales at just over 265lbs of rock hard flesh and bone.

His chest expanded to 71 inches and he could crush an ordinary man's skull like an eggshell.

"I want you to go over to that son-of-a-bitch in charge of the 155's and tell him to crank up his outfit and be firing faster in support of *Lang Vei* in no less than five minutes. If he doesn't I'm going to chew his ass out!" screamed Vortex to Richter.

"Yes sir," beamed the Master Sergeant as he double timed it all the way to the heavy batteries.

Crighton handed the field phone back to Colonel Vortex who called up the additional batteries which were emplaced in the American bases at the *Rockpile* and *Camp Carroll*.

The artillery commanders at both support bases were delighted to oblige with fire support missions. C Battery of the 2/94th Artillery Regiment opened up first from *Camp Carroll*. *Camp Carroll* was 15 miles east of *Khe Sanh* along Route 9 leading to *Quang Tri*.

"Do you see that? Isn't it magnificent?" shouted Colonel Vortex.

Major Thrush swung around as he was standing upright in the command jeep. Without his field glasses he could see the arcs of light sweeping across the night sky as it flew over *Khe Sanh* from *Camp Carroll*. The sound of the incoming shells was like a constant high pitched droning noise, or the sound of a screeching ramjet engine. Each of the 6,000 men at *Khe Sanh* could feel the vibrations in the air as the heavy artillery streaked about 3,000 feet above the base ripping apart the night atmosphere.

"Awesome!" was all Colonel Vortex could say. The enormous 175mm shells were propelled out of their barrels at over 2,500mph. They reached *Lang Vei* in less than a minute. When they struck the deep thunder of the explosions could be easily heard from *Khe Sanh* which was 5 to 6 miles away to the east north-east.

Major Thrush remarked as the *Khe Sanh* batteries of 105mm guns also started up to add to the din of the 155's, "Captain Willoughby can't complain now! He's getting a whirlwind of fire to suppress any breach in the *Lang Vei* perimeter."

Vortex nodded, "I'm exhausted Major. I'm going to get some shut-eye for about 3 or 4 hours."

Then he turned to Master Sergeant Max Richter, "Wake me up at 0500 hours will you? Master Sergeant."

Richter was lackadaisically sharpening his Marine dagger as most of the 6,000 men at *Khe Sanh* were watching the awesome display of firepower. A cordon of 100 men of the 1st/9th Marines were positioned around Vortex's lookout and they had set up some 106mm recoilless rifles in case any NVA emerged out of the jungle. For at their vantage point they would probably spot them first before the rest of the 5 battalions manning the perimeter of *Khe Sanh*.

Colonel Vortex fell asleep as soon as his head touched the pillow. A room had been set aside for him in the main HQ bunker complex of the 9th and 26th Marines west of the airstrip near the *'Red Sector.'* It was quite generously furnished for combat field standards, with a private bathroom, a lounge and several chairs. Colonel Lownds had the same set up nearby at the southern end of the HQ complex.

At 0530 hours another conference of battalion and regimental commanders was held in the conference room at the DASC. All the company commanders were also present as well as the regimental staffs and the fire support people who organised *'Operation Combat Skyspot'* and the *'SuperGaggle'* missions to the hill outposts surrounding *Khe Sanh*. These radar and coordination troops all belonged to Captain Mirza Baig at FSCC.

It was the morning of the 20th January 1968. Everyone in the room and indeed the entire base at *Khe Sanh*, had an eerie feeling that this was the last calm period before the storm they had all been expecting and suspecting, would break loose atop their heads.

Colonel Vortex took charge of the conference as usual, "Now listen up everyone! As I discussed with COMUSMACV only two days ago, I am going to try to retake the valley between Hill 881 South and Hill 861A. I'll take half of the 1st Battalion of the 9th Marines."

Colonel Lownds said with frustration, "Listen Vortex! Even if you manage to cross over the valley what do you hope to achieve? We don't need the low ground between the hill outposts. I have a fully equipped company of 220 men on each of those hill positions from my Regiment. From there they have a commanding view of any major PAVN or VC movement towards the *Khe Sanh* perimeter. If you go down into those small valleys you are going to get bushwhacked unnecessarily."

Vortex waved the palm of his hand up and down, "Yes! Yes! I know that Colonel Lownds! I just want to hold the area for a day. I want to see what the gooks have down there. How much artillery, how many men and the quantity of supplies they are amassing."

Then Vortex chuckled to everyone in the room, "Who knows? I might run into that cocksucking fiend, General Vo Nguyen Giap! And rip out his guts so that I can use them to grease the barrels of our 175's!"

All the men laughed at that jibe.

Major Thrush joined in, "The 500 men of C and D Companies are ready, loaded and itching to go sir."

Vortex smiled and spoke to Captain Baig, "Listen. I want you to have TAC air strikes and artillery ready for us if I call in for them."

Captain Mirza Baig was a blue eyed, slim and intelligent looking officer, "No problem sir. I have the 1st Marine Air Wing on the boil. And the artillery crews here in the perimeter and at *Camp Carroll* and the *Rockpile* are all primed up and rearing to go. You'll have all the fire support you need. Lashings of it. In fact, it will be difficult for me to coordinate so much incoming munitions. It will be wave after wave of different types of bombs, rockets, mortars, 20mm cannon, *Miniguns*, napalm and the awesome *AC-47 "SPOOKY" Gunships* which can let loose an avalanche of 18,000 rounds per minute from 3 *Miniguns* in its nose and cargo hatches."

Vortex clapped Captain Baig affectionately on the shoulder.

"Excellent! You are a fine officer! And I'm counting on you!"

Colonel Lownds asked Captain Baig, "Which tactical air units are standing by for *Khe Sanh*?"

The FSCC officer answered, "At *Da Nang* we have the *390th Tactical Fighter Squadron* and the *4th AC Squadron* with the AC-47 gunships.

At *Nha Trang* we have the 5th ACS, at *Bien Hoa* north of Saigon we have available jets from the *308th Tactical Fighter Squadron* as well as the *351st* and *510th Squadrons*. These units have F-100D and F Type Super Sabres being the best of the *Century Fighters*. Also at *Bien Hoa* we have the *4503rd Tactical Fighter Squadron* with F-5's. At *Tan Son Nhut Air Base* the *416th Tactical Fighter Squadron* also with F-100's and the excellent *F-105 THUDS* or Republic Thunderchiefs which came in to assist us only last night. In addition the *433rd Tactical Fighter Squadron* at the UBON Air Base in Thailand and the *497th Squadron* also stationed there have been made available to us.

Operation NIAGARA is almost ready to roll if we need it, which will see a flight of 6 B-52's over *Khe Sanh* every 90 minutes day and night, seven days a week, for as long as we need them. That all depends if and when the PAVN and VC are going to attack and where they launch their long awaited offensive. At the Korat Air Base also in Thailand, the *421st* and *469th Tactical Fighter Squadrons* are standing by for *Khe Sanh* among other duties. In addition to this we have Task Force 77 of the US 7th Fleet on station in the Gulf of Tonkin. The Navy can supply us with 4 Squadrons of *F-4 Phantoms* as well as the *A-4 Grunmman Intruders* as well as *Skyraiders* from the VNAF based at *Tan Son Nhut Air Base*."

Colonel Lownds seemed satisfied, "That sounds good to me."

Colonel Vortex picked up his field pack and M60 machine gun and was almost ready to go.

"Oh! One more thing Colonel Lownds."

Lownds asked, "Yes? What is it?"

Vortex explained, "I'm going to try to bring back some fresh prisoners, especially of officer rank. Maybe we can tear some flesh and thus information out of the gooks before they come down on us."

Colonel Lownds smiled, "Good luck!"

"Oh! You have an outpost just across the *Quang Tri River?*'

'That's right Vortex. It's a platoon of about 45 men. I placed them there to the north of the river just to cover my field of vision. If the PAVN are going to attack from that direction I'll want to know about it."

"Then that is where I shall finish my sweep. With any luck I should be there by dawn on the 21st January. That's tomorrow."

Colonel Lownds said, "Ok Vortex. I'll keep in touch with you by AN/PRC-41 field telephone."

Minutes later the 500 men of Vortex's C and D Companies moved out of the *Khe Sanh* perimeter from the north, directly towards Hills 881S and 861A. Company C was in staggered formation on the right and D Company on the left, separated by about 150 yards. In this way each company column could come to the support of the other if needed.

The company sized units on Hills 881S and 861A already knew that Vortex was coming and they were glad. They felt like a small band of boy scouts surrounded by a sea of North Vietnamese regulars.

Major Thrush, Sergeant Major Crighton and the Herculean Master Sergeant Max Richter were all walking with Colonel Vortex in the centre of C Company.

In less than 100 yards, as the Marines moved past the *Khe Sanh* northern perimeter through the *'Drop Zone'* area and the *'Blue Sector'*, the men of Vortex's command were sucked in by the jaws of a vast and inhospitable jungle. It was like being enveloped by green quicksand. Once you were inside its grasp, entwined in the jungle's deathly embrace with the PAVN and Main Force VC swirling all around for an ambush, it was extremely difficult to extricate yourself and your men without a bloodbath of destruction.

"Major Thrush!" said Vortex softly, "You better take one field telephone and ride point for D Company. I need you out there on the left as my eyes and ears."

The Major gave hand instructions and his signals squad scurried up from the rear of the column and went with him.

"Right sir!" Major Thrush moved off with his men and quickly disappeared behind lush jungle foliage. The vegetation was so thick that you could not see more than 5 to 10 yards in front of you.

"Give me the handset," said Vortex to Richter.

"This is Charlie-Bravo Over?" said Vortex as the humidity in the jungle surrounds was devastating. Vortex could see that both Richter and Crighton were wiping streaks

of grimy sweat from their face and necks. The Colonel was calling the company sized unit at Hill 881 South. They were from Colonel Lownds' 26th Marines.

At first there was only static across the field telephone. Vortex repeated the call. Still no answer.

Master Sergeant Richter whispered as they continued to walk warily through the jungle, "Perhaps they have their AN/PRC-41 field radio turned off, sir?"

Vortex snapped back, "That's impossible Richter!"

Finally a voice came through but it was not from Hill 881 South, it was the Captain in command at Hill 861A.

"This is Hill 861A! Is that you sir?" asked the Captain's voice.

Vortex barked back angrily, "Yes! Is everything alright up there?"

The Captain responded, "All quiet over here, sir."

Vortex asked, "Why doesn't Hill 881 South answer Captain?"

Just at that second the commander of Hill 881 South came in over the two-way radio.

Vortex castigated him brutally, "Wake up you son-of-a-bitch! I've been trying to call you for the last five minutes! What the fuck is the matter with you?"

"I'm sorry sir. It won't happen again sir," responded the terrified voice of the other Captain.

"If you sleep on watch," began Vortex, "I'll relieve your ass from command and have you court martialled!"

The awestruck Captain gave his apologies once more over the field radio.

Vortex then tapped into the outposts at Hills 881 North, 64 and 558. The Lieutenant in command at Hill 881N had some perturbing news.

"What did you say?" asked Vortex as his 500 men inched their way closer to the *Khe Sanh* outposts.

"Sir," began the junior officer, "We have been watching all last night and this morning. The PAVN seem to be up to something! They seem to be on the move."

Vortex cupped the handset and spoke to Master Sergeant Richter, "He says the gooks are on the move!"

Richter was waving the men forward as Vortex and his party stopped for a few moments to talk.

Sergeant Major Crighton took Vortex's M60 away from him for a second so that the Colonel could catch his breath.

"It doesn't surprise me sir," said Richter as he stopped one private and adjusted his webbing for him. Master Sergeant Max Richter was the ideal veteran soldier. He was professional, fair and had a deep affection for the men under his command. This senior NCO was always ready to protect the more inexperienced men of his battalion from basic errors that could be fatal in the face of the unrelenting enemy.

Vortex asked, "You have a gut feeling?"

Richter smiled with the knowledge of countless previous engagements and fire fights, "I do indeed sir. My guts tell me that the gooks are gearing up for an all out offensive. I don't know exactly when! Maybe tomorrow, next week? Could be today, at lunch time? But its coming!"

Vortex grunted. He rubbed his chin and could not help but agree with his NCO.

Grabbing the AN/PRC-41 field phone he asked the commander at Hill 881N, "Tell me what you have observed?"

The Lieutenant answered, "I sent out a patrol to reconnoitre the jungle north of my hill. I lost three KIA (killed in action) and four seriously wounded only an hour ago. The survivors from the squad indicated that hundreds, perhaps thousands of PAVN and Main Force VC are streaming south towards us. The sniper fire is pretty heavy also. If you ask me Colonel, I think the whole bloody 325thC PAVN Division is about to attack. I have also seen some *PT-76 light amphibious* tanks!"

"The Communists have tanks as well? I see!" said Vortex and then the Colonel added as machine gun fire from his forward troops at the head of the column suddenly erupted to everybody's surprise.

"Hold! Hold on! Lieutenant!" screamed Vortex as the men around him all dived into the slush and mud of the jungle.

"We are now under attack as well! I'm bringing in two Companies to Hill 881 South. You hold 881 North! Do you hear me? If the gooks attack you resist and counter-attack. I'll call in air strikes and artillery if necessary. But under no circumstances shall you abandon your position is that clear?"

The Marine Lieutenant yelled back, "We won't budge an inch from here sir! I'll tie my men to trees if necessary! But they're good men – they're itching to grapple with the fucking NVA and their cuntsucking VC stooges! Sir!"

Vortex shouted back with one finger in his ear, "Good man! Good man! I'm counting on you to delay the enemy attack if it comes so that I can arrange for a *SuperGaggle* mission to reinforce the hill outposts, Over and Out!"

Master Sergeant Richter grabbed Vortex's shoulder as a tracer round flew inches above the commander's skull.

"Thanks," bellowed the Colonel and then, "What the fuck is going on? Who's firing?"

Sergeant Major Crighton came running back from the head of the column. He threw Vortex's M60 back into the Colonel's hands.

"Sir! It's a bloody shambles! The head of the column has run into a NVA patrol. I reckon that its about company strength at least. Could be more! Maybe a battalion?"

Vortex replied as he waved his men forward, "We're going to attack! Fucken attack! I want to annihilate the motherfuckers!"

Master Sergeant Richter replied, "They are positioned directly between us and Hill 881 South. Sir."

Vortex said as he clapped the massive shoulders of Richter, "We're going to steamroll them back!"

"Yes sir!" answered Richter.

The Colonel took out his map and studied it for a few moments.

Crighton, Richter and the Captain in command of C Company peered over his shoulders.

Vortex explained, "Listen men! We are about here. Half way between the *Khe Sanh* north-west perimeter and Hill 881 South. Hill 700 is just over there. I'm going to instruct Major Thrush and D Company to swing around the gooks from the east and cut their line of retreat. We will then move forward and annihilate them in an encircling manoeuvre. Give me the field phone!"

Crighton handed Vortex the radio and the Colonel gave the Major the appropriate orders. D Company was also under fire from its right flank.

As Vortex and his entourage moved forward through the foliage a Marine to their right caught a 7.62mm round right between his eyes. Blood splashed sideways over the Colonel's camouflage tunic.

"Scheiße bumst das lächerlich! Fuck! Shit!" screamed the Colonel, "I told you men to advance in the prone position!"

Vortex crawled up to the dying private, "Medic! Medic!"

The soldier's skull had separated along its longitudinal axis. It was a ghastly mess of broken blood vessels and exploded flesh. The Sergeant paramedic looked up at Vortex, "Its no use sir! He's dead."

Vortex was already inching forward, "Leave the body here. We'll pick it up later."

Sergeant Major Crighton and Vortex reached the head of the column as D Company was already swinging around the enemy's rear to the east.

Using his field glasses Vortex could see that the NVA fire was coming from an entrenched position that extended for nearly half a mile.

"I'll take the 1st Platoon and attack head on," said Vortex to the company commander. "You will take the rest of the company and follow me when I give the word. Do you understand Captain? Is that clear?"

The young 26 year old Marine officer saluted with savage precision and replied, "Crystal! Sir!"

"Good! Crighton and Richter come with me!"

Vortex waved his men forward and they strove to the attack. The Colonel had hardly advanced 100 yards when two of his men fell into a pit of punji stakes. Their screams were horrific.

"Help me! Help me!"

Vortex snarled, "Shut up! Shut your fucking face soldier! Suck up the pain like a man! What are you? Are you a defeatist hippy or are you a gallant Marine with a capital 'M'? Take it, the pain! Take the horror! Swallow the agony like a Marine! Remember the glory and heroism of *Iwo Jima* and *Okinawa*! Remember the deeds of your forefathers at *Inchon* and at *Bastogne*! Remember and take the horror of that pain of mutilation with pride and courage and make it your everlasting friend! You are a United States Marine! The whole world looks to you as an example of what a superlative combat soldier is supposed to be! There is no other Army and Marine Corps in the history of the world – with the exception of the German *Wehrmacht* – which is more stupendous, more magnificent, more heroic than our men of the United States of America! So take the pain!"

A medic crawled up as gunfire whistled all about them. To the left of the punji stake trap two more Marines were bulldozed by *AK-47* slugs that cut open their bellies. Vortex watched as their green-red intestines split and oozed out over the jungle floor.

"So can you do anything for him?" asked Vortex to the Medic NCO. But the Sergeant with medical kit in hand slumped to his knees at the edge of the trap and started vomiting out his guts. The horrendous sight of mutilated, vivisected human flesh was too much for him. His sticky, foul smelling vomit cascaded in a shower over the mutilated flesh of the shredded Marines. It was not intended – it just happened.

Vortex slapped the Corpsman/Medic Sergeant on his back as the Sergeant Major came running up from the front.

"Get on with it!" The two Marines could not be extricated from the punji stakes while the unit was under fire. They had been caught in the most evil version of this cruel VC contraption with stakes running down from the walls of the pit as well as up vertically from the floor. This made it impossible to withdraw the limb or torso without ripping the whole human trunk to pieces. Their screams mingled with the groans of fallen Marines and the shrieks of the Communists who were being slowly pushed back by the American fire from both front and rear. The whole cacophony made for an eerie orchestral chorus of hideous suffering. The mayhem was unbelievable.

Bodies erupted into crimson pots of death from both sides.

Richter led Vortex up to the edge of the action but the Colonel, his face crimson with adrenalin pumped rage and a lust for sweet revenge, ran forward directly into the NVA fire. Sergeant Major Crighton and the Master Sergeant had no choice but to follow their over-stressed leader. The rest of the platoon hugged the earth and gave suppressive fire in support. Colonel Vortex leapt into the deep gulley where the *1st Battalion* of the *PAVN 29th Regiment* of the 325thC Division were entrenched.

Immediately two NVA soldiers jumped on Vortex, one grabbed the Colonel's groin while the other strangled his neck. A third was just about to drive his *AK-47*

bayonet into the 9th Marine commander's guts. But Vortex was a dynamo of martial arts prowess. He slammed his body forwards and kicked the bayonet sideways. Using his fingers he ripped his hands into the eyes of the Communist who was strangling him. The hold was loosened sufficiently so that Vortex was bequeathed those vital seconds in which he could swing around and plunge his Marine dagger into the man's heart tissue.

The Marine Colonel looked into the NVA soldier's eyes and said in perfect Vietnamese, "I am going to crush your 325th C Golden Star Division into a mound of mutilated flesh! You fucking Communist rat!"

Even with the knife tickling his heart the Communist managed to spit into Vortex's eyes, saying, "We shall mercilessly fuck you American Imperialists to death until there is no colour of blood left in your flesh or soul!"

Vortex punched the NVA, splitting his nose down the septum and then twisted the dagger as he viced it into the enemy's chest, first to the left and then to the right thus ripping asunder the myocardial tissue.

The remaining two NVA staggered to their feet with bayonets. Vortex, through his peripheral vision, saw the menace.

"Die! Communists!" screamed the Colonel. In the next second he twisted his dagger out of the cadaver and arced it across and through the face of the advancing NVA. It slit the NVA's lips away from his nose and eyes and the whole head seemed to flap apart like a torn sheet of red-stained paper.

Several bullets blew past Vortex, one of them grazing his thigh with a superficial wound as the third NVA emptied his magazine.

"No you don't Communist motherfucker!" It was the voice of Master Sergeant Richter who catapulted himself into the gulley and using his field axe he splintered the third NVA down the middle of his spine. The leading edge of the razor sharp axe burst through the chest in a shower of blood and lung tissue that covered Vortex's combat uniform.

"Thank you Richter!" shouted Vortex as he picked up his M60 machine gun and let loose on the second NVA who was clutching his blood soaked features. The burst of steel and lead cut the torso of the Communist apart, his legs separating from his chest. The three Marines crawled on their bellies under a hail of fire. Their platoon stormed over the gulley and down the embankment. Vicious hand-to-hand fighting erupted. Hundreds of men were screaming, groaning, yelling, diving, shooting, hacking, gouging and knifing each other in a delirious orgy of destruction.

"Follow me!" said Vortex to his NCOs as the rest of C Company advanced on the lone battalion of the *29th PAVN Regiment*.

Vortex crushed the skull of one PAVN soldier who jumped out from some foliage behind them. As the Colonel pressed the sides of the man's temples until blood pis-

sed out of his eyes and nose, Richter stood behind and drove his bayonet through the base of the cervical spine so that the edge burst forth from the enemy's mouth orifice. It was a classic stab-in-the-back manoeuvre that the British Navy would have been proud of.

Vortex slammed the body to the dirt while Sergeant Major Crighton cut down another NVA with M16 fire.

"They are all around us!" screamed the Captain in command of C Company.

As those words left his mouth an RPG rocket streaked in with the sound of a banshee, obliterating the Captain's body in a delicious shower of sliced and diced flesh. The jungle foliage all around them was covered with blood streaked human tissue. The only thing left of the Captain was his empty general purpose combat boots that stood exactly where his body was blown out of them, side by side with smoke emanating from their interiors.

"Jesus!" screamed Crighton. Vortex set up the M60 and poured fire into the foliage where the enemy was still sending a sheet of burning metal into his men.

C Company had already suffered horrendous casualties but the PAVN Regiment seemed to be hovering on the verge of retreat. And this is the moment when Major Thrush and D Company struck the *29th PAVN Regiment* from the rear.

The Major leapt forward with his 250 men and set up M60 positions as well as 106mm recoilless rifles all around the 29th Regiment. Tracer fire, streaming sheets of bullets and erupting blood washed through the once peaceful jungle.

The Major was leapt upon by three NVA soldiers who were all about five feet eight or nine inches tall. [This was tall for North Vietnamese males as the race was on average short. It also explained why they used tunnel warfare as it suited their diminutive stature. General Westmoreland having called them an;

"Army of Moles."]

He knew that only the very cream of North Vietnam's fighting men were picked for service with this elite Division of 12,000 men. Major Thrush also knew that the 29th Regiment was the elite of the elite.

"Fuck you, you gook bastard!" screamed Thrush as one of the Communists knocked his M60 out of his sweating grasp.

The others circled him like crazed vultures intent on consuming human flesh. Their Asian eyes were like red points of savagery.

These were General Giap's finest assassins.

But Major Thrush also realised as he spoke to himself, "That scheming fiend General Vo Nguyen Giap is too much of a fucking, rat-stinking Communist coward to lead his own *29th PAVN Regiment* into battle! He hides with his headquarters troops in some lime cave near the DMZ!"

The NVA soldiers overheard these words which Thrush uttered in Vietnamese and it sent them into a frenzy.

The brilliant glint of a bayonet streaked in front of the Major's eyes but he rammed his Marine dagger into the chin of the Communist. The knife end sucked deliciously upwards through the trachea in an orgy of blood.

Pivoting on his toes the Major whipped out his Colt 0.45 and detonated the skull of another NVA that had gripped him by the throat. The Captain in command of D Company had materialised behind them and quickly penetrated the NVA's buttocks and testicles with a jagged edged gutting knife that he kept handy for close encounters.

"Jesus! Be Praised!" screamed Major Thrush. It was his way of saying thank you to the Captain. More men of D Company streamed through the jungle and fell onto the NVA positions.

The *29th PAVN Regiment* started to execute a fighting withdrawal. Meanwhile Colonel Vortex and his men were closing in on Major Thrush's position.

Master Sergeant Richter was crawling forward with two platoons on the left flank while Vortex led the right.

Suddenly Richter felt a multitude of hands groping around the back of his spine.

"What the fuck!" screamed the enormous NCO.

Three NVA soldiers had leapt out of the foliage and were strangling the behemoth of a man. They ripped, gouged, tore with their nails and lashed punches into the gargantuan body of the Marine.

Richter emptied his M16 into several more NVA that were running across his field of fire. Then, rushing backwards he crushed the bodies of the NVA against a tree trunk.

Colonel Vortex came running up with more men and drove his field axe into the skull of an enemy soldier as he bounced off the tree trunk. Richter swivelled around and pushed another Communist hard up against a branch that had entered his spinal cord. The piece of wood erupted out of the chest cavity in a grotesque display of internal anatomy.

"Come on Sergeant Major! Let's finish the motherfuckers off!" screamed Colonel Vortex. C Company advanced slowly towards D Company thus engaging the PAVN in a murderous cross-fire that smothered them sideways and squeezed them into a full retreat.

Colonel Vortex stepped over a wounded NVA soldier as he was raising his arms to throw a grenade in a die-hard gesture of defiance.

"No you don't!" said the Colonel as he kicked the grenade sideways and bayoneted the NVA directly threw his eyeballs and then sliced into his kidney's and groin. Sergeant Major Crighton was right behind his commander as he finished off seven more wounded NVA with his Marine dagger and then bayonet. His arms and fists were like pistons in an engine, ramming the blade back and forth, up and down, into the Communist flesh so that he was smothered in blood.

The right flank of C Company met the left flank of D Company as the 1ˢᵗ Battalion of the *29ᵗʰ PAVN Regiment* was sucked out in retreat.

"There you are sir!" said Major Thrush as he linked up with Colonel Vortex.

"Tell your men to spread out and begin mopping up! I'm going to call in choppers to medivac out our wounded to *Khe Sanh*."

Vortex reloaded his M60 as he spoke.

Major Thrush asked, "Are we still going to advance to Hill 881 South - Sir?"

Vortex snapped back, "Of course!"

Major Thrush saluted and directed the two Companies forward. In ten minutes 7 UH-1D and E Huey helicopters came roaring in at tree top level.

"I'm going to get a ride in to *Khe Sanh*! Major Thrush. You are in command until I get back."

Major Thrush answered through the field phone as he was already 400 yards forward, driving the PAVN back to their main concentration areas beyond the hill outposts.

"Co-percentic sir!" came back the Major's reply.

"I'll rejoin the formation in about two or three hours. There's some things I have to clear up with Colonel Lownds."

Again Major Thrush's confirmation came through the AN/PRC-41 radio.

The wounded were loaded onto the choppers and Vortex took Sergeant Major Crighton and Master Sergeant Richter with him. Just at the same time that Colonel Vortex was air lifted out of the fire fight halfway between the *Khe Sanh* perimeter and the hill outposts, a C-130 Hercules transport with three *Miniguns* attached to its port and starboard hatches made a smooth landing and two high ranking officers walked out looking for Colonel Lownds and Colonel Vortex.

They were Brigadier General Phillip B. Davidson the Chief of *G-2 Intelligence Section* for the entire MACV, designated J-2 and a Colonel Kenneth Houghton who was the G-2 counterpart for the III MAF (Marine Amphibious Force) commanded by Lieutenant General Cushman.

"Where is Colonel Lownds and Colonel Vortex?" asked Brigadier General Davidson. The General was of medium height with blue eyes and he had an unusually gentle appearance.

The Warrant Officer who was also the Air Control Officer, led General Davidson and Colonel Houghton past the *Tactical Airfield Fuel Dispensing System* and into the bustling HQ bunker complex of the 26ᵗʰ Marines.

Colonel Lownds was just speaking to Lieutenant General Cushman and Major General Tompkins by radio telephone when Brigadier General Davidson walked in.

"Oh! Sir! Its good to see you," said Lownds.

Lieutenant Colonel Tran and Captain Hoang Pho of the 37ᵗʰ ARVN Rangers were also in the room.

"How is it going?" asked Colonel Houghton.

"Its getting pretty hairy here sir!" answered Lieutenant Colonel Tran as he offered both senior intelligence officers some coffee and biscuits.

General Davidson turned to the 37th Ranger commander, "How do you mean?"

Colonel Tran explained that Colonel Vortex had taken half the battalion of the 1st/9th to make a patrol sweep between the hill outposts to the north. He told the General that intense fire could be heard from *Khe Sanh* coming from Vortex's position but that they had not opened up with 155mm from *Khe Sanh* and 175mm artillery from *Camp Carroll* because Vortex had wanted to get in close and grapple with the PAVN face to face. Tran also informed that Vortex was coming in right this minute with the medivacked wounded.

"I see!" said General Davidson who peered over the map of the *Khe Sanh* area that lay on a large conference table.

Colonel Lownds put down the handset of the telephone, "Sir! I've just been on the horn to Major General Tompkins and Lieutenant General Cushman. They have indicated to me that COMUSMACV is extremely concerned about the build-up of two PAVN Divisions around us. The *304th* and the *Golden Star 325thC Divisions*. In addition to that Pentagon East at *Tan Son Nhut* has identified the North Vietnamese *24th Artillery Regiment* as well as the *68thB* and *164th Artillery regiments*. They have about 96 heavy guns in all."

General Davidson asked, "Has there been any other activity?"

Colonel Lownds answered, "Yes sir. Last night at approximately 2330 hours which was the 19th January, Vortex made a sortie into *Khe Sanh* village and ran into heavy PAVN fire. Probably from the 304th Division. We had to send in *Sikorsky* gunships to extract him. However, Captain Frank Willoughby, the Special Forces commander at *Lang Vei* managed to get back to his outpost."

Suddenly choppers could be heard coming in over *Khe Sanh's* landing strip.

General Davidson asked, "I presume that is Colonel Vortex coming in now with the wounded?"

"I am sure of it sir," replied Lownds.

"I want to know first hand what is going on out there on the hill outposts because I am flying back to Saigon this very afternoon to confer with General Westmoreland about the entire situation up here in I Corps Operational Zone."

Brigadier General Davidson as well as Colonel Lownds and the others went outside to meet Vortex.

The wounded were in a shocking state. Many of them had mutilations and knife wounds that would disfigure them for life. Some of Vortex's Marines even had their arms or legs hacked off by the NVA soldiers in the bloody and horrific melee and intense fighting.

Colonel Vortex jumped out of the lead chopper with NCOs' Richter and Crighton.

Brigadier General Phillip Davidson did not wait for Vortex to come to the bunker but walked out to meet him half way. They met in the middle of *Khe Sanh's* airstrip just as three C-123 *Providers* were lifting off at the far end past the water point which commenced from the *Rao Quan River* held by the PAVN forces.

"Colonel Vortex!" he smiled, "I am glad to see you in one piece!"

The two men chuckled. But Colonel Lownds did not find anything amusing about the nepotism shown to the 9th Marine Commander by all the General Staff officers as well as Vice-President Nguyen Cao Ky and the commander of the *ARVN 1ST Infantry Division*, General Ngoi Quang Truong. The latter being a close and personal friend of Colonel Vortex as well as his lover, Susie Ky who used to engage in extracurricular activities with the 1st Division Commander prior to committing herself to Vortex.

Vortex shook hands with Colonel Houghton and the whole entourage trouped back into the HQ bunker.

"I am convinced that the North Vietnamese are going to attack within the next 48 to 72 hours!" said Colonel Vortex to the J-2 General Staff officer.

"I tend to agree with you Colonel," replied General Phillip B. Davidson. Colonel Lownds interrupted and disagreed, "I don't think it will be that soon. My estimation is that it will take them another 2 or 3 weeks to build up enough supplies and munitions to launch an offensive as well as to position their troops properly before they attack."

Colonel Kenneth Houghton commented, "I disagree with you Lownds. I think General Giap wants to attack us now!"

As he spoke Colonel Vortex slammed his fist on the table.

Vortex said, "I just ran into the *29th PAVN Regiment*. Or at least the best part of one of its battalions. By the look of those gooks I think that *Charlie* is on the boil. How can you be so stupid Lownds? How can you be such a moron? To say that the PAVN are not ready to attack? What about the massive fire fight at *Khe Sanh* village last night?"

Colonel Lownds' face turned crimson and then purple with rage as he tried to control himself from punching Vortex out in front of the General. He wanted to leap across the map table and strangle him once and for all.

Brigadier General Davidson said, "Anyway gentlemen! What we must do is to get more seismic and acoustic sensors laid all around the *Khe Sanh* area. All the way from here to the Ho Chi Minh supply depot and communication centre at *Tchepone*."

Colonel Vortex added, "General. I would also like you to have the Air Force deploy those new chemical sniffers that can pick up the stale urine and sweat and body odour of those motherfucking gooks and their scum-sucking PAVN Officer Corps of pimps and bandits as they march down the blasted Ho Chi Minh Trail."

Colonel Houghton answered, as he couldn't help but let out a small giggle at Vortex's colourful metaphors, "We are already working on it. They should be in place within 7 days."

Colonel Vortex drew Brigadier General Davidson aside to one corner of the bunker while the other senior officers talked amongst themselves at the map table.

"What is it Colonel?" asked Davidson.

"Sir! I've been thinking about the whole situation here at *Khe Sanh*. Frankly I don't think that we can hold out if Giap attacks with more than four full Divisions. I am sure, however, that we can beat them back if they attack with three Divisions or less."

Brigadier General Davidson said seriously, "I doubt very much Colonel Vortex, whether they can commit four Divisions to *Khe Sanh*. If Giap did that it would be the largest conventional battle so far in America's involvement in South East Asia since the Korean War 1950 – 1953."

Colonel Vortex nodded as he watched Colonel Lownds looking their way with suspicion and jealousy.

"Well! Actually! What I meant to ask you General was whether you would do me a favour?"

General Davidson held Vortex's shoulder affectionately, "Of course Colonel! Hell! That's the least that I can do! You are out here in the middle of a nightmare that is just about to happen. What is it you want me to do?"

Vortex pursed his lips and then cracked the inter-phalangeal joints in his hands like a naughty schoolboy who was going to ask his teacher for something he shouldn't.

"I know that I spoke to General Westmoreland about this topic only last December 1967 when intelligence reports started to come in about Giap's build-up around *Khe Sanh*."

Vortex paused and then came out with it, his blue eyes sparkling.

"Sir? Couldn't you ask COMUSMACV to reconsider the possibility of allowing us here at *Khe Sanh* to use Nuclear Weapons?"

Brigadier General Davidson sucked in his breath for a few moments and looked surprised.

The General repeated, "Nuclear weapons?"

Vortex nodded and smiled with hopeful anticipation as he rubbed his hands together in a servile gesture.

"Yes sir! Just a few? What do you think? Can you persuade COMUSMACV to release them to us? The nuclear weapons I mean?"

Colonel Vortex's eyes were almost popping out of his head.

General Davidson rubbed his chin and said angrily, "But Colonel Vortex! You know very well that it is not up to COMUSMACV. A decision like that, involving nuclear munitions and their use, has to be made by the President himself!"

Vortex glanced sideways at Colonel Lownds who was edging ever closer to the two men, trying to overhear what they were saying.

"I know sir! But what I mean was – could you ask COMUSMACV to ask the President again. I know that initially the President had refused. But perhaps if President Johnson sees the situation here at *Khe Sanh* – well? He might just reconsider?"

Now it was Brigadier General Phillip Davidson's turn to surprise Colonel Vortex as Colonel Lownds was becoming exasperated with frustration at not being able to eavesdrop on the private little conference.

General Davidson said in a hushed voice, his blue eyes sparkling with excitement in the dull light of the HQ bunker, "COMUSMACV has informed me only a few days ago that if and when *Khe Sanh* is surrounded. If that happens! Mind you! Then COMUSMACV wants to form a secret staff group at Pentagon East HQ in Saigon to discuss and evaluate such a countermeasure!"

Vortex was dumbfounded as he sank back into a chair while General Davidson continued, "COMUSMACV wants to make a feasibility study concerning the use of low yield nuclear munitions such as atomic artillery shells or bombs dropped from B-52's. These weapons would have no more than 5 to 50 kilotons of explosive delivery power. The main reason that COMUSMACV thinks that the use of small yield nuclear weapons around *Khe Sanh* would be efficacious is that it could annihilate the PAVN troop concentrations while at the same time causing minimal civilian casualties and collateral damage to non-military buildings and infrastructure in general. This is because *Khe Sanh* and its surrounding area is so remote and isolated from the main population centres. In other words *Khe Sanh* is *expendable* to the use of nuclear weapons."

Colonel Vortex nodded, "Oh! Yes sir! Then *Khe Sanh* would be the ideal place to employ atomic munitions! We must try to persuade COMUSMACV and the President to take that bold step!"

Brigadier General Phillip B. Davidson was gripped gently at the elbow by Colonel Kenneth Houghton.

"Sir? Its time to go to Saigon, sir. You're meeting with General Westmoreland and the *Deputy* COMUSMACV, General Creighton Abrams."

Brigadier General Davidson looked to Colonel Houghton, "Ok! Kenneth. I'm coming in just a minute."

Colonel Houghton moved back to speak with Lieutenant Colonel Tran and Captain Hoang Pho of the *37th ARVN Rangers* and also Colonel Lownds.

"Does this Colonel Houghton know about the MACV secret study to employ nuclear weapons sir?" asked Colonel Vortex.

"No! He does not Richard. You are the only tactical field commander that I have revealed this plan to. Apart from us, only General Westmoreland, General Creighton

Abrams, Vice-President Nguyen Cao Ky and President Thieu as well as three or four Army Generals and of course General William Momyer the commanding general of the US 7th Air Force know about it."

Vortex said flippantly, "Oh! I see sir! That means everybody in the whole of fucking Vietnam knows about it then?"

Both men laughed heartily as a Master Sergeant brought up a succulent tray of caviar and sweetmeats for the senior officers. Colonel Vortex was starting to feel a great affection towards Brigadier General Phillip B. Davidson. He realised that this was a man he could count on in pushing his cause for the use of nuclear weapons at *Khe Sanh*. There was indeed some chance of success, thought Colonel Vortex, if only President Johnson would ignore the idiotic and sanctimonious doves in Congress and listen to the Chairman of the Joint Chiefs of Staff, General Earle Wheeler as well as COMUSMACV and himself. He was willing to cut across the chain of command and talk direct to the President if necessary. The employment of atomic munitions would devastate General Giap's strategy, thought Vortex. It would have immense shock value that would send the whole stinking North Vietnamese Politburo into a death spin. Vortex was also convinced that the Communist Superpowers, China and Bolshevik Russia would not risk a World War 3 simply because America decided to use a few low yield atomic shells at *Khe Sanh* to obliterate four rat-fucking North Vietnamese Divisions in the backwaters of a filthy flea-infested 3rd World Country like South Vietnam. Nor if they were used to take out the devilish fiend, General Vo Nguyen Giap himself.

Vortex thought that if the United States could kill Giap in the battlefield under a cascade of atomic shells, then at least it would go some way to avenging the pride and prestige of the Western Nations in the face of the entire world. And especially to avenge the humiliating defeat of the glorious French forces 14 years earlier at *Dien Bien Phu.*

All these thoughts were rushing through Colonel Vortex's mind when Brigadier General Davidson took him by the arm and said, "I must go now Colonel."

Vortex replied, "I have enjoyed your visit General. I know that in your heart you believe as I do that we must use all the wherewithal and military might at our disposal to crush and totally exterminate these Viet Cong vermin and their disgusting NVA masters."

As General Davidson and Colonel Houghton were making their way to the airstrip, Colonel Lownds came up angrily behind Vortex and demanded, "What was all that about Vortex?"

Vortex turned to Lownds and said, "You don't have to know everything!"

Lownds was furious.

"Listen to me Colonel Vortex!" began the 26th Marine Commander, "I am just about fucking fed up with your constant interference in my command of *Khe Sanh!*"

Vortex grabbed Lownds by the shirt collars as Sergeant Major Crighton and Master Sergeant Richter looked on with awe.

"Its not only your command but mine as well!"

Lownds changed his line of attack as Vortex pushed the other Colonel away from him as they were half way up the bunker steps to the airstrip beyond and the Central *'Ponderosa'* area in the middle of the *Khe Sanh* base [KSCB].

Luckily Brigadier General Davidson did not notice the ridiculous fracas that was taking place between the two most important men who were supposed to be responsible for the Marine base at *Khe Sanh*.

"I want you to know Vortex....," began Lownds, "...that I have written up a report concerning your unnecessary and exceedingly brutal and vicious interrogation techniques against enemy combatants. I am sending this critical report not only to COMUSMACV at *Pentagon East* in Saigon but also to the Pentagon in Washington D.C. It may mean an investigation of your activities by the Judge Advocate General's Corps of the Army and a possible court martial for you!"

Now Vortex found it difficult to control his rage against Lownds. But with a supreme effort he merely added, "Oh! Colonel Lownds! You are so naïve! My interrogation techniques are no different to anyone else's here in South Vietnam. I follow to the letter the edicts of *public international law* and the *Geneva Conventions on the Treatment of Prisoners of War (1949)*. You forget that I studied Law at the US Army Staff College and obtained my B.Juris. in that discipline. I know the Law and I follow that Law to the letter both by statute and by the general principles of both domestic common law and the Law of Treaties as codified in the Geneva and Hague Conventions of 1949."

Lownds scoffed, "Is that so?"

"Yes that is so!" replied Vortex as he continued, "You can make as many reports about me as you like! Frankly Colonel Lownds!" and Vortex moved right up to the other Colonel's face as he spoke with pure animal-like venom, "I don't give a fucking rat's ass who you report me to! I should like to remind you Lownds, that you are a member of the United States Marine Corps! The most superlative fighting unit the world has ever produced in its 5,000 years of recorded civilisation – with perhaps the exception of the *Wehrmacht* in World War 2 which was equally proficient in the arts of war on a multi-divisional and multi-theatre strain of operations. This is not the lime-sucking British Royal Navy where fellow officers go around stabbing their comrades in the back like cowards. We in the Marine Corps do not have that English habit. Marine officers are supposed to support and help each other at all times!"

Colonel Lownds' face dropped suddenly and he seemed to be having a change of heart.

Vortex could see this and softened a little, placing his hands on Colonel Lownds' shoulder.

"My dear Colonel. I know, I realise that you have been placed under a lot of stress lately. Your command of the 26th Marine Regiment is, despite the differences we have had, stupendous. In my opinion you are a superb tactical commander on the battlefield!"

Colonel Lownds was completely taken aback, "Why thank you Colonel Vortex. Its only that I didn't understand why COMUSMACV split the command structure here at *Khe Sanh*. But now, I realise the brilliance and superb planning of General Westmoreland that did not really have any planning involved with it at all – that's what makes it so like a stroke of genius, without thought merely like an instinct of what is best for us here in the KSCB. He truly is a magnificent genius of command and logistics! We are fortunate indeed to have him as COMUSMACV! Instead of having only one excellent Marine Colonel here to see to *Khe Sanh* he appointed two top class commanders. That would double his chances of defeating the foul, stinking rat-fucker General Vo Nguyen Giap!"

Vortex smiled and the two men laughed with relief.

Colonel Lownds beamed with satisfaction as he ushered Vortex up the bunker steps to catch up with General Davidson and his entourage.

"I'll have that report that I made about you immediately withdrawn Colonel Vortex. I shall utterly destroy it. You are correct when you say that this is not the British Navy. Certainly we officers in the Marine Corps are not in the habit of stabbing each other in the back to further our promotional prospects or to torpedo the career of another commissioned officer."

Vortex said, "Thank you Lownds."

They made their way to the C-130 Hercules transport that had all four massive turbo-prop engines warming up. The roar was deafening. In addition 25 *Cobra* gunships had just come in from *Da Nang* and were going to make a strafing run against the *29th PAVN Regiment* at the request of Major Thrush who was mercilessly pushing the PAVN soldiers back from around the hill outposts, past 881 North and away from Hill 881 South.

The choppers buzzed directly over their heads.

"Goodbye sir!" said Colonel Vortex and Colonel Lownds almost simultaneously.

"Good afternoon gentlemen! And good hunting!" Davidson returned their salutes and climbed into the Hercules followed by Colonel Houghton.

"I shall let you know about the outcome of my meeting with COMUSMACV and General Creighton Abrams this afternoon."

With those final words the General disappeared into the vaults of the massive 2.5 million dollar aircraft. The C-130 taxied to the start of the runway and then roared to full throttle. It was in the air in less than a minute.

"Hey! What's going on over there!" pointed Colonel Vortex to the very end of the *Khe Sanh* aluminium planked airstrip.

"I don't know?" muttered Colonel Lownds.

The two Colonels and their entourage ran to the concertina wire perimeter which was manned by men of the 26th Marines.

As Vortex moved closer he could see that several PAVN soldiers were walking towards the *Khe Sanh* outer perimeter at the eastern end of *'Blue Sector'* with their hands high in the air.

The Marines manning the perimeter were armed with M60 machine guns and were about to open fire. They thought that it was just another dirty Communist trick.

"It's a suicide squad with explosives!" screamed a 2nd Lieutenant in command of the platoon on that sector of the perimeter.

"Fire!" he screamed.

Some rounds were let loose when Colonel Vortex came running up with the others.

"Stop firing! Stop firing!" Vortex brushed aside the startled 2nd Lieutenant and jumped through the gate at the perimeter.

With his Colt 0.45 handgun out in front of him he rushed at three PAVN soldiers coming towards *Khe Sanh*. They were screaming for mercy in Vietnamese and their arms were ramrod straight above their skulls.

Vortex could see that one of them was an officer.

"We surrender! We surrender!" they shouted with terrified expressions.

Vortex reached the Communists and pistol whipped the two enlisted men. Master Sergeant Richter grabbed hold of the officer and head butted him with savage force and power. With a single vicious blow he burst the man's nose and caused a terrible haemorrhage in his left eye.

"Fuck you bastard gooks!" screamed Vortex as Sergeant Major Crighton and 24 other Marines ran up and grabbed the PAVN soldiers. With much, punching, kicking, tearing, gouging and all around rough and unsavoury handling the PAVN prisoners were manhandled into three separate interrogation bunkers in the 9th Marine headquarters complex near the *Ponderosa* [the Old *Khe Sanh* Special Forces Camp].

"Listen Colonel Vortex. I'll give you full slather and acquiescence to interrogate the prisoners in any way that you see fit," said Colonel Lownds.

"Thank you Colonel," smiled Vortex and then he added, "Please join us for the interrogation. I think you will find it most entertaining as well as illuminating!"

Lownds nodded as Vortex said, "I am going to work on the PAVN officer first."

As Vortex and the others were grabbing the Communist defectors at the *Khe Sanh* perimeter, Brigadier General Davidson's C-130 Hercules was just banking into a steep climb over the airstrip.

General Davidson was sipping on a can of *Budweiser* when he looked out of the fuselage window.

"Hey! What's going on down there?" he queried with excitement.

Colonel Kenneth Houghton peered over the General's shoulder and tried to see through the low swirling clouds.

"It looks like some sort of fire fight or engagement at the *Khe Sanh* southern perimeter."

Brigadier General Davidson barked, "No it isn't!"

"No?" asked Colonel Houghton as another Major from the General's staff also came up to look out of the aircraft window.

"No!" Its some Communist soldiers surrendering! I'm sure of it!"

General Davidson dropped his *Budweiser* onto the metal floor of the plane and rushed up to the cockpit.

"Pilot!" he shouted.

The USAF pilot turned around with a frightened look. He thought the General was going to tell him that an engine was on fire or that they were being shot at by an NVA anti-aircraft fusillade from the jungle below.

"Yes sir!" screamed back the 1st Lieutenant over the roar of the engines.

"I want you to land this plane back at *Khe Sanh*! Now!"

The pilot was dumbfounded.

"Land? Are you sure sir?" he asked as the co-pilot just grinned with a wild look of exasperation.

"Of course I'm sure! Land immediately!"

The C-130 did a graceful banking turn and headed west again towards *Khe Sanh*.

Meanwhile Colonel Vortex was with the PAVN defector, a 1st Lieutenant by his uniform insignia.

"Strip the gook!" said Vortex calmly.

Sergeant Major Crighton and Master Sergeant Richter were in the room. The only other person present was Colonel Lownds who sat on a chair in the background as he smoked a *Salem*. Twenty Marine Military Police (MP's) armed with carbines were guarding the outer door.

The other two enlisted PAVN had already been stripped naked and tied to chairs in two other rooms. They were being kicked, punched and suffocated with wet rags across their mouths and noses as a preliminary softening up exercise before the real questioning would begin.

Richter took off his shirt and wheeled in an electric battery with two large terminals, both positive and negative, which he placed next to the Communist's head.

The PAVN officer seemed to shiver in his chair as he saw the bulging muscles of Richter's massive 265lb body of sheer steel and sinewed flesh.

"You may begin the preliminary softening up Richter," said Vortex with joy in his voice. Vortex glanced back to Colonel Lownds and smiled.

Richter stepped up to the North Vietnamese soldier and slammed his fist like a whiplash across the man's cheeks. Another punch was delivered in his trachea. Suddenly the NVA started to suffocate as the cartilage in the trachea had been crushed with that one devastating blow.

Colonel Vortex knew exactly what to do. He took a surgical blade called a dermatome and sliced open the flesh above the tracheal cartilage to allow air to be sucked in through the neck tissue.

"Be more careful Richter," said Vortex. "We have to keep the rat fucker alive for as long as possible."

"Sorry sir!"

Foul smelling urine started to escape from the NVA's penis as the man was almost beside himself with terror.

"Mercy! Have mercy! I defected!" said the officer as he cried.

Richter, his hairy sweating chest thrust into the NVA's face shouted, "Give us your name! Your rank and unit!"

As he spoke the Master Sergeant clapped the NVA's head in-between his massive paws and smashed his skull into the Communist's teeth, shattering them all in a bloody mess of broken enamel. He then gripped the Communist's nose in-between his teeth and tore off chunk after chunk of flesh until blood flowed like a sweet river of revenge all over the naked body of the NVA.

"So! What do we have here?" asked Vortex as he found the identity papers of the Communist.

"You are Lieutenant La Than Tonc? You command the 14th Anti-Aircraft Company of the *95thC Infantry Regiment* of the *325thC Golden Star Division* of the North Vietnamese Army of imperialists and rat fucking warmongers? Is that right?"

The PAVN officer nodded with hideous agony as Richter grabbed the man's testicles and started to crush them within his vice-like grip. At the same time Sergeant Major Crighton knelt down before the chair in which the NVA was tied and started to prepare two large steel vices with turning handles to control the pressure applied at any given moment. He placed them next to the NVA's ankles and toes.

"I didn't hear you?" screamed Vortex with savagery as he punched the Communist in the belly, the kidney's and the temples.

"Yes! Mercy! I am Lieutenant La Than Tonc! Please I seek political asylum! I am a defector!"

Colonel Vortex laughed, "Defector? Bullshit! You are a dirty rat fucking scum-sucking Communist spy!" As he screamed he ripped his nails down the full length of the Communist's face, creating deep flesh wounds which bled profusely.

Richter started to rip and tear the man's penis and testicles with his fingers in an orgy of savagery.

Sergeant Major Crighton prepared a charcoal brazier of hot coal and placed steel pincers and tongs into the fire in preparation for the beautiful delights yet to come. He then brought up a bowel of boiling oil and some steel tubes that were the correct diameter for a man's anus.

"Listen to me Communist spy," began Vortex in a surprisingly soft tone of voice.

"I really am quite a reasonable man you see? I don't want to cause you any more discomfort than what is absolutely necessary for this interrogation. But you must realise that we Americans are going to exterminate the whole fucking North Vietnamese nation because you are a disgusting, lawless, imperialistic, warmongering race of devils who want to subjugate the free and democratic people of South Vietnam. We shall never allow the government of President Thieu to fall! I don't understand why you bastards and mental defectives in Hanoi don't understand that simple fact! It really is quite elementary!"

Master Sergeant Richter and Sergeant Major Crighton chuckled as Colonel Vortex continued, "I simply want to ask you a few questions and then send you to our prisoner of war facilities in Saigon where you will be incarcerated for the duration of your life – or at least until this war is over. But if you do not answer all my queries then I am afraid I shall have to hand you over to these men here…" Vortex pointed to Richter and Crighton as they prepared their implements and fiendish tools to render apart the NVA's flesh, "…and these gentlemen are not as kind hearted nor as lenient as I am in my subtle interrogation techniques."

La Than Tonc vomited out pieces of red lung tissue with fear as Vortex finished his speech but said nothing.

Vortex asked, "When are the PAVN going to attack? How many troops will General Giap commit to the battle? How many artillery pieces do you have? Have you contaminated *Khe Sanh's* water supply yet from the *Rao Quan River*?"

But La Than Tonc, half out of fear and partly out of stubbornness, said nothing.

Colonel Vortex shrugged his shoulders, "I warned you! You stupid Communist pig! Now you must face the consequences of your intransigence."

Master Sergeant Richter picked out a red hot steel pincer from the charcoal brazier and brought it up to La Than Tonc's left eye.

"Sir?" he asked Colonel Vortex.

"You may proceed Richter," said Vortex calmly. All the while this was happening Colonel David Lownds was sitting impassively at the back of the room, smoking *Salem* after *Salem* with nervous rapidity.

A horrific scream reverberated through the small bunker room as the steel pincer started to sizzle like fried bacon as it was inserted into the NVA's eye. The cornea and iris almost liquefied in seconds as the burning steel cut through the soft flesh like a knife through melted butter. Blood pulsed with each heartbeat onto the floor as it escaped from the eye socket.

"What the devil is going on here?"

Everyone in the room turned around as two Marine officers walked in. It was the voice of Brigadier General Phillip B. Davidson. Colonel Kenneth Houghton was right behind him.

Colonel Vortex explained, "This PAVN officer claims that he is a defector sir. But we think he is a stinking, motherfucking spy!"

General Davidson said hurriedly, "Listen Vortex! I have to get back to Saigon for a meeting with General Westmoreland. But I can't leave until you tear all the requisite information out of this Communist. So hurry up and use all the means at your disposal! I want to know when Giap is going to attack, where and with how many troops and which Divisions of the PAVN are concentrated around KSCB?"

Vortex saluted like a pistol shot, "Yes sir! Immediately sir!"

Sergeant Major Crighton placed the steel vices around both ankles. The contraption was so designed that it had slots for the toes as well. Crighton progressively tightened the vice until blood and splintered bone burst forth from the mutilated feet. Master Sergeant Richter applied an enema of boiling sulphur and oil which he flushed into the bowels with a set of steel tubes while Vortex smashed punch after punch into La Than Tonc's face with a knuckle-duster. The PAVN Lieutenant was revived by a Marine Corpsman with smelling salts and kept alive with regular injections of adrenalin to keep his heart going despite the shock to the nervous system. He was then flipped over onto his stomach. Crighton used a pair of pliers to break open every finger until the splintered bone protruded grotesquely from the severed flesh.

A steel rod was inserted into the rectum and then twisted by both Richter and Crighton as they grasped one end of it. As they heaved, the other end of the rod tore up the internal viscera of the Communist officer.

Finally La Than Tonc squealed like a man on the last vestiges of his human endurance, "Giap is going to attack *Khe Sanh* tonight! He has 25,000 troops around the base made up of the 304th and 325thC Divisions. There are 96 heavy guns of the *68th*, *24th* and *164th PAVN Artillery Regiments* around *Khe Sanh*."

Vortex was not satisfied as General Davidson stood impatiently behind him. The Colonel slammed his fist into La Than Tonc's genitalia and the man squirmed with hellish agony.

"I know that you know more! Spit it out you foul bastard!" screamed Vortex, "Or I'll instruct my men to continue the dissection of your body!"

But the stubborn Communist refused to say anything further.

Vortex nodded as he slapped Richter on the back, urging him on. The Master Sergeant used the surgical dermatome to sever off both ears, slit the nose and hack off both hands of the PAVN Lieutenant. This was enough to force the Communist to regurgitate all the remaining information needed.

La Than Tonc further divulged that the 325thC Division was going to attack Hills 881 North and 861, as well as the *Khe Sanh* base itself that very night. He also told Vortex that the PAVN plan was to take *Khe Sanh* and then drive on to *Quang Tri* and *Hue* [Imperial City of Ancient Vietnam], destroying the American bases on the way such as *Camp Carroll, Ca Lu, Cam Lo* and the *Rockpile*.

General Davidson, Colonels Vortex, Lownds and Houghton and the others walked out into the sunshine near the *Ponderosa* and the edge of the airstrip.

"Do you think he is telling the truth sir?" asked Vortex, "…it could be simply disinformation designed to trick us and the real attack may come somewhere else entirely."

Brigadier General Phillip B. Davidson rubbed his chin thoughtfully and looked at the three Colonels from left to right.

"No! I think that this La Than Tonc bastard is telling the truth. His story sounds very logical and very convincing. All the signs of the PAVN preparations so far have indicated the veracity of his admissions."

Colonel Lownds added, "I agree with you sir. I am sure that this rat stinking scum has told us the true situation and intentions of the fiend General Giap."

Then Colonel Lownds asked, "Do you have any suggestions sir? I mean if the attack is going to happen tonight?"

General Davidson and Colonel Houghton looked around the messy *Khe Sanh* base that was a hive of activity with hundreds of Marines scurrying hither and thither trying to get the supplies and ammunition underground and to position the M50A1 ONTOS tanks [Greek for '*The Thing*'] in their correct battle positions on the perimeter.

The Marines simply called it *The Pig*. It mounted six 106mm recoilless rifles, four with spotting rifles plus a 0.30cal M191A4 machine gun. The vehicle weighed 8.5 tons and carried three crew. It fired both '*flechette*' and high explosive *(H & E)* rounds. Any massed attack on the *Khe Sanh* perimeter would be met by all ten ONTOS on the base and they would prove to be devastating to the Communist enemy.

"I would suggest Colonel Lownds! That you start to dig in deeper. And at once! All these tents, fuel ammunition dumps, storage areas, the headquarters bunkers and command complexes are too exposed and too much above ground and thus conducive to PAVN artillery fire! Dig! Dig! Start digging in as deep as you can go!"

Colonel Lownds saluted like a madman possessed with some urgent crusade, "Yes sir!"

He barked at three Captains and seven Lieutenants from the 26th Marines and gave them a plethora of the appropriate orders as they had just been relayed to him by the one star general.

"I also suggest Colonel Lownds, that you place the ARVN 37th Ranger Battalion to the south south-west, about 200 metres from the concertina wire perimeter in the *'Gray Sector'*. In that way Lieutenant Colonel Tran and Captain Hoang Pho can block any PAVN advance from *Khe Sanh* village."

Colonel Vortex stepped forward with the AN/PRC-41 radio telephone and called in to each of the Hill outposts telling them of the new information and to expect a full scale attack from the PAVN and Main Force VC that very night.

"Are you absolutely sure?" screamed back Captain Dabney who was the commanding officer at Hill 881 South. Dabney had 400 men of the 3rd Battalion 26th Marines with him as well as some fire-control officers belonging to Captain Mirza Baig, most notable of which was the soon to be famous Corporal Robert J. Arrotta who would be dubbed; *"The Mightiest Corporal in the World."*

Vortex looked at the handset with mock anger and handed Captain Dabney over to his superior, Colonel Lownds.

"Dabney! I want you to prepare for a full scale assault! Is that clear? Dig in! Dig in and fight to the death! That's an order! Do not even contemplate a withdrawal! The gooks are coming tonight! That's what we think after interrogating a captured PAVN soldier and officer!"

Captain Dabney barked back his confirmation of the orders and told Colonel Vortex before signing off that Major Thrush and his 2 Company force had just arrived on his Hill as they had withdrawn from Hill 881 North.

Captain Jasper on Hill 861 South was the next to be informed along with his 200 Marines, also from the 3/26th being K Company. The Captains at Hill 558 and at the Rock Quarry west of the *Khe Sanh* perimeter were also informed. There were 1,000 marines at all of these positions.

Finally Vortex phoned in to the signallers on Hill 950 which was east of Captain Jasper and next to the unmanned Hill 1015. About 50 Marines were stationed there and they helped to coordinate the fire coming from the 2 batteries of 175mm guns at *Camp Carroll* which was 17 miles to the east along Route 9.

"I think that's about everyone!" said Colonel Vortex.

Colonel Lownds was now catapulted into a frenzy of activity. He gave hundreds of orders by frantic hand signals, field telephone and face to face. The 3,000 Marines inside the *Khe Sanh* base proper were scurrying, running and falling over each other with a nervous excitement that was propelled by their own adrenalin. Every man knew that the crunch was about to come. This was to be the litmus test of American involvement in Vietnam.

Colonel Vortex drew Brigadier General Davidson aside and beseeched, "Sir! I implore you! I must go with you to Saigon and talk to COMUSMACV! I must plead the case for the immediate release and employment of nuclear weapons at *Khe Sanh*!"

General Davidson smiled as they walked to the waiting C-130 Hercules on the airstrip. Its immense engines were at full taxi idling throttle.

"I think you are wasting your time but if you insist Colonel! Its alright by me."

Vortex informed Colonel Lownds and Major Thrush that he would try to be back from *Pentagon East* by 1900 hours that same evening.

Colonel Lownds said before Vortex left, "Good luck Colonel. We sure could use atomic shells in those 175mm howitzers at *Camp Carroll*. That would make all the difference!"

Vortex and General Davidson nodded their unqualified agreement as the three PAVN prisoners were hauled onto the Hercules manacled by leg and wrist chains and with a steel neck collar and tongue restraint attached to their mutilated skulls. They were stuffed into the depressurised cargo hold for the entire 50 minute flight to Saigon. They would be sent to the *LBJ Ranch* whose proper name was the *Long Binh Jail* for an exhausting and thorough interrogation, where every form of grotesque physical experimentation and mind altering drugs such as *Scopolamine* would be administered and performed upon their bodies until they would become living vegetables devoid of emotion or reason with pre-frontal lobotomies' being conducted once all possible intelligence had been extracted.

The *Long Binh* prison was north-east of Saigon next to the *Bien Hoa Air Base*, the II FFV (Field Force Vietnam Headquarters) commanded by General Weyand, the 199th Light Infantry Brigade Headquarters and the III Corps Operational Zone Headquarters.

The C-130 Hercules roared as the pilot pulled the throttle lever back to maximum take-off thrust. It was the *'K' version* of the aircraft that had rocket assisted thrust for take-off and steep ascent to avoid the intense Communist anti-aircraft fire. In less than a minute the aircraft lifted gracefully off the *Khe Sanh* airstrip and flew over the 800 feet deep ravine at the southern end of the runway.

Colonel Vortex and General Davidson cracked open two cans of *Budweiser* and a packet of cashews as they headed south for Saigon.

Final Plea to COMUSMACV for the Use of Nuclear Weapons at Khe Sanh

Colonel Vortex radioed ahead from the cockpit of the C-130 and spoke to his personal friend and colleague, Major General Olinto M. Barsanti. General Barsanti was the commander of the elite *101ˢᵗ Airborne Division*.

[To the Communists they were known as the *'Chicken Men.'* Standing orders were given to all PAVN forces to avoid contact with the Chicken Men as they were told that invariably they would loose].

The nickname for the Division was the *"Screaming Eagles"*. This was signified by their eagle shoulder flashes.

Major General Barsanti was a newcomer to the conflict in Vietnam. He and his staff had just arrived from Fort Campbell, Kentucky on the 13th December 1967. Colonel Vortex had known Barsanti since the Korean War when Vortex was a platoon commander. General Barsanti had achieved an ROTC commission in 1940. He was a battalion commander at the Normandy invasion and a regimental commander in the Korean conflict where his unit was part of the 2nd Division. Like Vortex he was highly decorated with a Distinguished Service Cross, three Silver Stars and no less than five Purple Hearts.

Vortex loved the way that Major General Barsanti would blow his stack and chew out his subordinates. He had the most vicious temper that Vortex had ever seen. The General was a real "Patton-like" prima Dona. He would growl, swear, scream, stamp his feet and blow steam like a pressure cooker. But like General Westmoreland, General Barsanti had a soft spot for the awesome, savage and almost primeval presence of Colonel Richard Vortex.

Vortex was leaning against the co-pilot of the C-130 as he spoke into the handset, "Hello?"

A voice answered, "Who's this?"

Vortex replied giving his name and rank and indicating that he wanted to speak to Major General Barsanti.

The officer on the other end of the line at the *101ˢᵗ Airborne Division HQ* near *Bien Hoa Air Base* was Colonel William P. Tallon, Chief of Staff of the *'Screaming Eagles.'*

"The General is busy in a staff meeting Colonel Vortex. You have to radio in later," said the Chief of Staff.

"I don't have time later, Colonel! I have to speak to General Barsanti now! Go and get him please!"

"I'll see what I can do," said Colonel Tallon.

A few minutes later as the Hercules streaked towards Saigon, having just over flown *Dak To* in the Central Highlands, the familiar shrieking voice of the Major General echoed through the handset.

"Is that you Richard?" asked General Barsanti.

"It sure is sir!" answered Vortex enthusiastically as he grinned at the pilot.

"So its Colonel Vortex! You son of a gun! How the hell are you Colonel?" asked General Barsanti.

"I'm fine sir! And how are you? And Oh!...Welcome to Vietnam! I heard you only just arrived last month sir!"

General Barsanti laughed, "Yea! Its been pretty hectic so far Vortex."

"I'm Ok General. I'm at *Khe Sanh* with my unit, the 9th Marine Regiment."

General Barsanti's voice became more serious, "Oh! Yes! *Khe Sanh*! COMUSMACV tells me that something serious is brewing up there Colonel."

Vortex replied, "That's right sir. But we better not discuss it over the airwaves."

"Yes. You're right. So when can we see each other? Its been three years since I had dinner with you and your lovely wife and daughter, her name is Peggy I think? It was in New York wasn't it Colonel?" asked Barsanti.

Vortex laughed, "Yes sir. I remember you had lobster thermidor and it damned near killed you afterwards. I had to carry you back to the hotel from *'Sardi's Restaurant'* – you remember sir?"

"How can I forget that?" screamed back the Major General.

Vortex could hear other voices in the background belonging to staff officers of the 101st Airborne Division.

"Listen sir. I need your help and besides that I'd like to see you before I have to return to *Khe Sanh* this very evening."

General Barsanti said without hesitation, "Absolutely Colonel Vortex. I had a staff meeting of my battalion commanders but I can postpone that for a few hours."

Vortex continued, "I am having a meeting with General Westmoreland and the Deputy COMUSMACV at *Pentagon East* next to the *Tan Son Nhut Air Base*. Brigadier General Phillip Davidson the J-2 for MACV is with me as well as Colonel Houghton, the J-2 for III MAF. I was wondering if you can join us at the meeting. The subject of the meeting is *Khe Sanh*."

Major General Barsanti barked back, "I'll be there Richard!"

Colonel Vortex asked, "And sir. Can you do me one more favour?"

Barsanti asked, "Just name it Richard."

"Can you contact Susie Ky, the daughter of Mr Ky, Minister in the government of President Thieu and tell her to meet me at *Pentagon East* in the Officer's Mess? Her number is kept at the central switch of MACV HQ. I should be there in about an hour from now."

Major General Barsanti agreed and they signed off.

A short time later the C-130 Hercules landed on the main east-west runway of *Tan Son Nhut* and Vortex together with General Davidson and the rest of his entourage sped into the massive two-storey complex of offices that was *Pentagon East*.

They were ushered into a huge and luxurious conference room with crystal chandeliers hanging above a mahogany table covered in maps that was 70 feet long by 35 feet wide. The whole floor was carpeted by plush red velvet carpet and the walls were of panelled oak from France. There were beautiful tapestries on the wall in gold frames that had been imported from Venice. COMUSMACV liked to work and think in comfort. At the far end of the gargantuan table was General Westmoreland seated in a lounge chair and sipping a cup of piping hot coffee and standing next to him with a plate of Beluga caviar was the Deputy COMUSMACV, General Creighton Abrams.

Both General's were in a foul mood.

General Abrams said to General Westmoreland, "This caviar is lousy! What's the matter with the Officer's Mess in this place? They don't even know how to make a decent *Vienna Schnitzel*."

General Abrams threw the caviar along with the whole silver plated dish into a waste paper basket a few feet away.

COMUSMACV said with annoyance, "Can you forget about the fucking caviar and the *Vienna Schnitzel* for a minute? We have other more pressing problems to attend to at the moment General!"

General Creighton Abrams nodded sullenly as Brigadier General Phillip B. Davidson and Colonel Vortex entered and proceeded up the length of the seemingly endless table. The rest of Davidson's entourage were left standing outside the conference room like ducks in thunder.

As soon as General Westmoreland saw Colonel Vortex he jumped to his feet, his face turning crimson with rage, "What are you doing here Vortex?"

General Abrams mimicked, "Yes! What are you doing at Pentagon East Colonel?"

General Westmoreland asked with fury in his eyes, "I thought you were supposed to be at *Khe Sanh* with Colonel Lownds?"

Colonel Vortex said quickly, "I am returning to *Khe Sanh* in about three hours sir! I just flew down from there. We have to report some serious developments. Also some latest intelligence that we have received concerning the expected attack at the Marine Combat Base KSCB."

COMUSMACV said as he waved his hands for the two men to take a seat in the red leather lounge chairs opposite, "Go ahead gentlemen. What latest intelligence reports do you have?"

Brigadier General Davidson began. He did not want Colonel Vortex to get all the credit for this intelligence coup. This was so even though the two men liked each other, because they had to consider their respective careers in the military.

"Just as I was leaving *Khe Sanh* Colonel Vortex and his Marines captured an NVA spy. The man, who is an officer in the *325thC Golden Star Division* claims that he is a defector. He is at the *Long Binh Jail* now undergoing a more thorough interrogation. But what we have learned from him so far is that the Communists are going to attack *Khe Sanh* tonight! And the NVA defector indicates that the attack will be the main offensive thrust to capture the base and then drive onwards to *Quang Tri* and *Hue*, rolling up the entire Northern I Corps Operational Zone."

General Creighton Abrams interrupted, "Yes! Yes! But you realise General Davidson that this cock-and-bull story could be just simple disinformation? That rat, General Giap, could have ordered this PAVN officer to play at defecting to give us this misleading information. This *disinformation*."

Colonel Vortex interrupted, "With respect sir! I don't think this is disinformation. I think that this gook was telling the truth."

General Creighton Abrams said, "Oh? Really? Well let me tell you Colonel Vortex that I,…"

General Westmoreland cut in, "It doesn't matter Creighton! Whether this spy or defector, or whatever the fucken hell he is, was giving accurate information or not, it doesn't matter! We must assume that his information is indeed accurate and therefore all precautions must be immediately implemented."

General Abrams looked sullen, "Yes sir. I suppose you are right."

Colonel Vortex added, "The gook said that his division was going to attack Hills 881 South and North and Hill 861 South as well as the *Khe Sanh* base proper."

General Westmoreland nodded seriously as he raised the coffee cup to his lips.

"What do you think we should do sir?" asked General Creighton Abrams.

"We must prepare to deploy all our aerial assets and get ready to commence Operation NIAGARA. That is what we must do," said General Westmoreland as he looked sideways to the Deputy COMUSMACV.

Brigadier General Davidson added, "It seems to me sir,…" the J-2 officer shifted uneasily in his chair as Vortex looked on with amusement, "…That this Colonel Lownds is living in a dream world."

COMUSMACV asked incredulously, "What do you mean?"

General Davidson explained, "He doesn't think that the PAVN are going to attack tonight."

Vortex added, "But I told him to prepare *Khe Sanh* for all contingencies sir. Before leaving I ordered the Officer's Mess closed and all the cinemas, of which there are six at *Khe Sanh*, to stop screening their selection of movies."

Brigadier General Davidson continued, "We notified the hill outposts and warned Captains Jasper, Dabney and Willoughby, who is in charge of our Green Berets and *Montagnard* [CIDG] irregulars at *Lang Vei* to be on full alert."

COMUSMACV said, "That's good."

"But…," Davidson added, "The whole base at *Khe Sanh* seems to me to be unprepared for a heavy artillery or mortar bombardment. Colonel Lownds has failed to order his troops to dig in deep enough. All the buildings, ammunition dumps, storage areas and the like are too exposed to the PAVN heavy guns."

COMUSMACV was getting visibly annoyed, "Is that so?"

Vortex said, "Yes! I only arrived there a couple of days ago as you know sir, when we conducted our inspection tour. I'm sure you also could see the general state of unpreparedness!"

General Westmoreland became quite agitated by this as he looked to General Abrams.

"I should have told Lieutenant General Cushman and Major General Tompkins to put somebody more capable in command of *Khe Sanh*."

COMUSMACV seemed to be on the verge of exploding as he jumped up from his chair, brushing past Colonel Vortex. Westmoreland then started to pace up and down in front of the three seated officers, rubbing his chin and muttering to himself with excited whispers.

Finally the Supreme Commander said as he stood in front of the two Generals and the Colonel, his hands on his hips in a determined gesture, "It is not entirely Colonel Lownds' fault. I should castigate Lieutenant General Cushman. He is the one who should have organised the command structure more effectively. He is the one who should have insured that *Khe Sanh* was fully prepared. Anyway! I am going to create! As of this moment! The new command structure of **MACV Forward**!"

General Abrams looked dumbfounded at Brigadier General Davidson who glanced sideways at the grinning Colonel Vortex.

"MACV Forward?" said General Davidson nervously running his fingers through his grey hair.

"Who do you want to put in charge of MACV Forward?" asked General Creighton Abrams as he leaned back in his lounge chair almost instinctively trying to duck for cover at any new operational set up.

"You!" said General Westmoreland.

"Me!" cried General Abrams, "Why me sir?" The four star General seemed to be on the edge of a nervous fit.

"Because you are the Deputy COMUSMACV Creighton," said Westmoreland as he affectionately placed his hands on the other man's shoulders.

"Who else should be the forward Supreme Commander but you?"

General Abrams said trying to wriggle his way out, "But the Marines won't like it sir!"

COMUSMACV scoffed, "I don't give a fig whether they like it or not! This is not a popularity contest. I should have known that General Cushman in command of III MAF could not properly keep hold of the whole scenario of operations up in I Corps Operational Zone. The whole thing is too complex for just one command."

Colonel Vortex added, "Sir. I think the idea of MACV Forward is an excellent concept!"

"There! You see Creighton? Some of the Marines like the idea," said General Westmoreland.

"When do I go up to *Quang Tri*?" asked General Abrams nervously.

COMUSMACV said emphatically, "Within the next 48 hours."

Just at that second the double oak doors of the plush conference room opened quickly and then closed even more rapidly. A single general officer stalked in like a tiger.

It was Major General Olinto M. Barsanti.

He saluted COMUSMACV and his Deputy, then Brigadier General Davidson. Each of his movements was like a pistol shot.

He turned to Colonel Vortex and after the military niceties the two men shook hands warmly.

"Good to see you Vortex!" shouted General Barsanti, the 101st Airborne Commander.

"A pleasure to have you in Vietnam sir!" bellowed back Vortex, grinning with joy.

"So? Are we going to kick some gook ass!" screamed General Barsanti as he paced up and down in front of the table.

"We sure are sir," replied Vortex.

General Westmoreland said, "General Barsanti. Can you have a seat for a moment. We are just in the middle of appointing General Abrams as the new MACV Forward."

General Barsanti whistled, "I was wondering when you were going to finally take that important step sir."

General Westmoreland said to Abrams, "When you get up to *Quang Tri* I want you to report to me directly on every facet of the Marine Operations up there near the DMZ and the *A Shau Valley* which is heavily infiltrated with PAVN and Main Force Viet Cong.

And especially all developments at *Khe Sanh*!"

Abrams reluctantly nodded as Colonel Vortex interrupted them.

"Sir?"

"What is it Vortex?" asked COMUSMACV.

"There was something else I wanted to ask you sir."

COMUSMACV said, "Then get on with it Colonel. You have to get back to *Khe Sanh* and I,…" Westmoreland looked at his watch, "…have to attend a meeting with General William M. Momyer. I am going to appoint him as the single manager in charge of all air operations and tactical air strikes in and around *Khe Sanh* and the DMZ."

Vortex took a deep breath and continued, "I am primarily here sir! To request again that we be allowed to use nuclear weapons at *Khe Sanh*. Particularly the employment of atomic artillery shells in our 155mm howitzers and low yield fission bombs on the fighter bombers as well as the B-52 Arc Light strikes to annihilate the PAVN troop concentrations as they form up. Sir!"

General Barsanti grew an enormous grin that stretched from one side of his face to the other. He slapped his hands on his knees, "You son of a gun! Vortex my main man! Nuclear weapons? Jesus! And I thought I was the stomping, steaming loon around here!"

General Westmoreland waved his hands up and down at the loud, shrieking and almost comical voice of General Barsanti.

"Listen Vortex!" began COMUSMACV. "We've been over this ground before. I told you that it is not up to me to release nuclear weapons to our operational forces. That decision is reserved for the President and the National Security Council in Washington."

Vortex protested, "But sir! I,…"

COMUSMACV interrupted again, "Listen, I sympathise with you Colonel! If it was up to me I would already be bombing the PAVN and Viet Cong back to the Stone Age with tactical atomic warheads! And that includes Hanoi and Haiphong as well! But my hands are tied!"

General Davidson looked to Vortex as the latter said, "Sir! This morning part of my battalion ran up against the *29th PAVN Regiment*. The colossal weight of the Communist forces demands that the President at least reconsider the use of nuclear and atomic munitions at *Khe Sanh*. The area is lightly populated being mostly jungle surrounds. The villagers at *Khe Sanh* can be evacuated along with the few French missionaries that are there. Thus the detonation of atomic warheads will cause minimal *collateral damage* to non-combatants."

Brigadier General Davidson asked, "Colonel Vortex? Have you considered what happens after you annihilate the PAVN build-up areas with fission weapons?"

Vortex asked, "What do you mean sir?"

General Davidson said wryly, "The radioactivity fallout consequences! Surely you know that even the smallest tactical atomic shells, including artillery shells result in radioactive fallout. If the winds change direction as they do, then the pollution from the radioactivity will waft all over the *Khe Sanh* base! And for that matter the whole

of I Corps Operational Zone! What then? With danger from radioactivity that could threaten our troops as well as the ARVN, not to mention the countless civilians in the area – the whole I Corps Tactical Zone may have to be abandoned! Thus the PAVN will simply step into the vacuum!"

"Fuck the radioactivity! Who gives a shit! That's a small price to pay for victory in *Khe Sanh* and eventually in the whole of South Vietnam!"

General Davidson said to Colonel Vortex, "Are you not familiar with the works of *Tacitus*?"

"Of course I am! He wrote, amongst other things about the 2nd Punic War between Rome and Carthage."

"Then you know what he said when the Roman Empire subjugated and destroyed Carthage?"

"What! What the fuck did he say?" asked Vortex in a lather.

"*You have made a desert! And you call it Peace!*" answered Brigadier General Phillip B. Davidson.

Vortex just threw up his arms in the air in exasperation.

General Westmoreland listened to both arguments as Vortex continued addressing him and not General Davidson.

"Sir! If you could persuade President Johnson yourself! I am sure that he would see the light. In 1953 the M65 Atomic Cannon was developed by the *Picatinny Arsenal* upon orders from the Pentagon to provide a viable battlefield tactical nuclear delivery system. This M65 Atomic Cannon was named *'Atomic Annie.'*

The design was based on the excellent K5 German Railroad Gun from World War 2. The Germans are brilliant at designing the latest technology. It was the Germans in World War 2 that developed the world's first jet fighter the Me262, the first rocket being the V1 and V2 and they were the first to use camouflage uniforms of any army in the world. It was Werner Von Braun that developed the V2 which was the father of America's Space Rocket program today. Without German scientists we would, America would, be nowhere! So it was that Robert Schwartz from *Picatinny Arsenal Industries* developed the awesome 280mm Atomic Annie. It was tested in the Nevada desert in 1953 and was a great success story firing successfully a 15 kiloton shell some 7 miles with great affect. It was marvellous! These tests in the deserts of Nevada were part of the *"Upshot-Knothole" Program* to deliver viable battlefield nuclear weapons to our forces and to reinforce NATO in Europe. Of course we know that the 280mm M65 Atomic Cannon was retired in 1963. But we have developed the W48 nuclear warhead for use with our existing 155mm howitzers and also the W33 nuclear warhead for use with our 203mm artillery pieces. If you explain all this to President Johnson and also the limited risk to civilians and our military alike with negligible col-

lateral damage then I am sure that Washington and President Johnson would change his mind."

General Davidson riposted, "The danger of using nuclear munitions is still too great sir!"

Major General Barsanti thundered his disapproval as he leapt to his feet and started to smack his fists down violently on the mahogany conference table.

"Begging your pardon sir! But what a load of crud!" he screamed like a madman at Brigadier General Davidson who cowered backwards in his lounge chair as the 101st Airborne Divisional commander fumed like a volcano.

Barsanti continued, "I have seen other reports by the DoD (Department of Defence) which indicates that the fallout from low yield fission weapons is practically negligible!"

General Westmoreland cut in, "Listen! Gentlemen! I told you I don't have time for this now! We can argue until we are blue in the face. The decision is not ours to make. All I can do is to report to President Johnson and ask him once more to release those atomic munitions to us. The W33 and W48 warheads to use with our existing artillery pieces."

Colonel Vortex spoke directly to COMUSMACV, "Please do not misunderstand me sir. *Khe Sanh* will be held. It will be held no matter what happens down to the last man, the last bullet and the last artillery shell. However, the use of atomic weapons such as the W48/W33 warheads would undoubtedly shorten the battle and save American lives! The lives of our precious young boys."

General Barsanti cried, "Here! Here! I agree absolutely!"

The five senior officers turned around dazed as yet another person entered the huge conference room.

It was Vice-President Nguyen Cao Ky who was also Air Marshal of the VNAF (South Vietnamese Air Force). His dark, immaculately manicured moustache shimmered in the neon light. He walked as if he had a broom stick embedded in his bowels, wearing his customary purple scarf and flight suit.

Vice-President Ky saluted to COMUSMACV and then nodded to the others.

Ky began, "General Westmoreland. I have just emerged from a Cabinet meeting with President Thieu and General Lom of the ARVN. The discussion was nuclear weapons."

COMUSMACV almost fell back in his chair. Major General Barsanti laughed, "That's security for you!"

Blustering until his face turned crimson and then purple, *'Westy'* spluttered, "How?...when?..."

Ky laughed, "Relax General! We have been informed about your well considered plans to use thermonuclear weapons in our country by the Special Advisor to your President, a Mr William Bundy!"

"I see!" said General Westmoreland.

Colonel Vortex swivelled around in his chair and waited anxiously for Vice-President Ky's response.

The Vice-President smiled, "Both President Thieu and myself as well as the whole Supreme Command of the ARVN fully support the immediate use of thermonuclear weapons in the Republic of South Vietnam."

COMUSMACV said with surprise, "You do?"

Vortex corrected, "Not thermonuclear Marshal Ky. Its atomic fission weapons."

Ky waved his hands, "Oh? Yes? Whatever you say?"

General Barsanti sniggered as Ky repeated beaming, "Yes General! When can you hit the North Vietnamese in the *A Shau Valley* and around *Khe Sanh* with nuclear weapons?"

COMUSMACV could see the comical side to the interchange as he said sitting down heavily in the plush red leather lounge chair, "We can't."

Vice-President Ky screeched like a teenage girl, "What?"

Then COMUSMACV started to explain to the flamboyant Vice-President that President Johnson had not yet given permission for their use. That it was unlikely that such permission would ever be granted but that the whole issue was going to be reconsidered during the next few weeks.

The meeting quickly broke up after that.

Brigadier General Davidson, General Creighton Abrams, the new MACV Forward, walked out with Vice-President Ky to have a sumptuous late lunch in the senior officer's mess which was adjacent to the huge Pentagon East complex in the *Tan Son Nhut* Air Base.

COMUSMACV closed the doors with only Colonel Vortex and Major General Barsanti in attendance.

"Listen up gentlemen!" said Westmoreland. He brushed aside a pile of detailed maps and teletype sheets on the mahogany conference table and studied an inch thick report that was bound in red plastic and marked *'Top Secret.'*

General Westmoreland began, "We have been studying satellite reconnaissance photographs as well as aerial pictures taken over the Laotian Hills, *Tiger Peak* and a network of limestone caves just on the Laos side of the border north-west of *Khe Sanh*. There appears to be heavy vehicular traffic and radio communications coming from those underground caves. PAVN personnel are driving in and out as well as there being a considerable amount of other Communist traffic and activity that we can't

explain. It is our estimation that this particular site could be a new headquarters for General Vo Nguyen Giap!"

Major General Barsanti said, "Then why don't you pulverise the site with a massive B-52 Arc Light raid sir?"

COMUSMACV said, "We are. But only when the time is right. We have contacts in Hanoi who will indicate to us when General Giap might be leaving the capital. That is when we shall strike!"

Colonel Vortex smiled, "I see!"

Westmoreland continued, "But if the strike fails to kill General Giap we have another option."

Major General Barsanti asked as he lit up a *Salem*, "What option is that sir?"

COMUSMACV looked to Colonel Vortex and asked, "Would you be willing to lead a crack force of super commandos from the *Khe Sanh* base when the time is right, to attempt a battlefield assassination of this virulent and brutal North Vietnamese Defence minister and senior general?"

Colonel Vortex looked to Major General Barsanti, the latter clapping Vortex on the back with pride and joy.

Vortex's face lit up like a Christmas tree. Tears of wonder and delight shimmered in the corners of his bright blue eyes.

"It would be the greatest pleasure of my military career sir!" shouted back Vortex with savage venom in his voice.

General Barsanti asked, "And which unit are you calling super commandos?"

COMUSMACV smiled dryly, "They are the 3rd Force Reconnaissance Company attached to the 3rd Marine Division. They used to be part of the 3rd Reconnaissance Battalion which was at the disposal of the divisional commander. But now I have direct control over all of their operations."

Colonel Vortex interrupted, "I know that unit sir. It was the brainchild of Major General Herman Nickerson Jr. Or *'Herman the German'* as we call him in the Marine Corps. General Nickerson made possible this elite unit of marines whose responsibility was, and still is extremely Long Range patrolling way in excess and beyond our long range artillery support fan. Other functions of this unit are the deep penetration into enemy held territory to assess the extent of our B-52 bombing raids as well as rescue of downed helicopter personnel and of course our fly-boys. These reconnaissance super commandos also have laser range finding equipment and target acquisition devices which they can use to coordinate accurate bombing raids on the enemy with our new generation of *'SMART'* bombs or laser guided munitions."

Major General Barsanti whistled with awe. He was flabbergasted at the incredible depth and precision of knowledge which Colonel Vortex possessed about every facet of military and technological endeavour.

Colonel Vortex continued to speak as COMUSMACV stood at the window and watched a flight of 9 F-100D Super Sabres taking off from the nearby east-west runway of *Tan Son Nhut*. Even through the bullet and rocket proof Plexiglas of the enormous MACV HQ you could hear the deep growling thunder of almost 5 million horsepower ascending into the atmosphere to wreck havoc against the indomitable PAVN and their Main Force VC allies who never seemed to give up.

"Isn't that unit, the 3rd Force Reconnaissance Company, headed by Major Alex Lee? I think he just came over from Quantico, Virginia where the Special Marine Development and Test Centre is located?"

COMUSMACV said, "Yes! You are right on the button again Colonel Vortex. What do you do at night? Don't you sleep? Do you stay up and read all the operations and field manuals or something?"

General Westmoreland was truly impressed as he smiled at Major General Barsanti.

COMUSMACV continued, "This is the unit I am going to assign to you to assist you in the attempted assassination of this brutal PAVN commander. Normally the 3rd Force Recon guys don't carry out hit and run assassinations of this type but I have added one extra operative from Operation Phoenix to help you out. But as I said, it is only in the planning stage at the moment. We don't even know if we can get the thing off the ground. It all depends on the movements of General Giap and his scurvy bum-sucking hangers on. But if these guys are unavailable I have arranged for another unit from General Barsanti's outfit to take their place. They are two officers of the 101st Airborne Division that were veterans in the French Union Forces and who both fought at *Dien Bien Phu*. One is a Brigadier General and the other is a Colonel. Also one highly decorated Sergeant will accompany them if the other unit I mentioned can't make it."

"I see!" said Vortex.

"But now I really must be getting over to 7th Air Force HQ across the road to speak to General Momyer about air support for *Khe Sanh* and the implementation of Operation NIAGARA, and you…"

COMUSMACV spoke directly to Vortex, "…you better be getting back there. I want detailed reports from you by field phone every 24 hours."

Colonel Vortex snapped up a vicious salute and then walked out with Major General Barsanti.

The 101st Airborne Commander sighed, "Boy! Brother! You really have your hands full Richard! Hell! I am just a division commander!"

Both men laughed as they walked into the plush senior officer's mess on the base.

The restaurant was well appointed and Vortex immediately saw his lover Susie Ky chatting with the wife of Vice-President Nguyen Cao Ky.

When she saw Vortex, Susie jumped to her feet and ran over hugging him with delicious ardour.

"Oh! My love! I never expected to see you again so soon!"

Susie Ky smothered kisses onto the Colonel's lips.

"Unfortunately I have to go back to *Khe Sanh* in about 2 or 3 hours my sweetheart."

Vortex was torn between his duty to the Marine Corps and his adoration for the beautiful and slim South Vietnamese flower that was Susie Ky.

Her black eyes sparkled and shone with genuine love and affection for her handsome American officer.

Major General Barsanti sat down to the dining table and kissed the hand of the equally delectable Mrs Nguyen Cao Ky. As the four of them ordered a succulent repast of fried chicken, caviar, Russian eggs, gefilte fish, smoked salmon, bouillabaisse, French onion soup, Peking Duck, Mongolian Lamb and seven bottles of vintage white and red from the 1940's and 1930's together with three bottles of Bollinger R.D. champagne from 1916, they could see the sweating and nauseated bodies of American Seabee's from the 3rd Construction Battalion who had been assigned to work in the blistering sun to extend the runway at *Tan Son Nhut*.

Colonel Vortex and the others watched the perspiration pour down their backs as they feasted in the air-conditioned luxury of the senior officer's mess.

"So! I hear you are in command of the base at *Khe Sanh*?" asked Mrs Nguyen Cao Ky.

"That's right Madame," answered Colonel Vortex politely.

"And you General? You are in command of the 101st Airborne Division?" Mrs Ky asked General Barsanti.

Barsanti answered in the affirmative and added, "Mrs Ky! It is a pleasure to be able to meet you in the flesh. I saw your handsome pictures in the Newsweek Magazine back in the States. It was after your husband threatened to blow up that group of military officers who planned a coup against General Khanh. You and your husband, the Vice-President make a very handsome couple."

"Why! Thank you Major General Barsanti. I appreciate those kind words!" Mrs Ky lit up a *Salem* and said, "Colonel Vortex, Susie and you General are invited to my home near the Presidential Palace here in Saigon for dinner when this *Khe Sanh* business is concluded."

Colonel Vortex held Susie's hand under the table and stroked her smooth, soft thighs.

"That's very kind of you! Mrs Ky. I appreciate it!" said Vortex.

Susie leant over and kissed Mrs Ky on the cheek and they both giggled like schoolgirls. The two young women had known each other since they were infants.

The wife of the Vice-President was only 4 or 5 years older than Susie, being in her early thirties. She was also devastatingly attractive.

"Listen Richard," began Barsanti, "…I have to get back to Division HQ. But if there is anything you need up there at *Khe Sanh* you just let me know. Ok?"

Vortex thanked Major General Barsanti who bid his farewells to the two ladies and he walked out of MACV HQ with his entourage of 17 officers from the 101st Airborne Division. They filed into a waiting convoy of six jeeps and drove off towards the HQ complex adjacent to the *Bien Hoa Air Base* where the Headquarters of the 199th Light Infantry Brigade, the Command Centre of the II FFV (2nd Field Force Vietnam Command – CO: General Weyand) was situated.

As Vortex and his lovely companions were finishing their sumptuous lunch, Vice-President Nguyen Cao Ky sauntered into the Restaurant dressed in a purple flying jump suit with two pearl handled revolvers hanging from holsters around his hips. Vortex thought he looked absolutely ridiculous in those garish costumes that he persistently wore. But despite that he had great admiration for the head of the VNAF (South Vietnamese Air Force).

General Ngoi Quang Truong, the commander of the elite 1st ARVN Infantry Division also accompanied Air Marshal Ky but the General and the entourage of officers filed off to the bar for the *'happy hour.'* Only Vice-President Ky walked up and kissed his wife as he leant over her.

Sitting down and ordering two dozen oysters Kilpatrick and Beluga caviar he said to Vortex, "Very interesting meeting Colonel!"

Vortex nodded as he wiped his lips with a gold embroidered serviette.

"Yes sir."

"I want you to know Vortex," began the Vice-President, "…that my South Vietnamese Air Force will be right there with you at *Khe Sanh*. We shall provide at least 20 air sorties every 24 hours if needed."

Colonel Vortex thanked, "It is always a reassurance to me to know that our gallant South Vietnamese allies are in the air to protect us with their superlative umbrella of air power."

Air Marshal Ky took out his pearl handled revolvers and started to play with them by twirling them threw his fingers as he ate oyster after delicious oyster.

"Bring me some chilli sauce as well." screamed Ky.

Vortex whispered to the radiant Susie as she gossiped and giggled with Mrs Ky, "My darling!"

"Yes my love?" asked Susie as she sipped on some Bollinger champagne.

"I have good news for you. I have organised your permanent residency papers and visa for the United States. You should pick them up at the US Embassy here in Saigon on the 30th January."

Susie was delighted as she kissed and hugged her lover.

"I have also arranged visa's for your parents any time they wish to travel to the United States."

"Come! You only have a few hours left in Saigon! I want to spend them with you in private my darling!" said Susie tugging at his arm under the table.

Susie Ky was feverish with love and longing.

"Excuse me Vice-President Ky," said Vortex as he arose from the table with Susie.

The Vice-President was showing General Ngoi Quang Truong as well as several other American general staff officers, how quickly he could draw his revolvers from their holsters just like in the American cowboy pictures that he loved to watch, especially the ones starring Ronald Reagan.

Nguyen Cao Ky was standing on top of one of the large dining tables after telling the waiters to clear it. A large group of laughing, grinning American and South Vietnamese generals and colonels were watching as the Vice-President shot out his wrists and catapulted the pistols into the air in front of him. He had General Truong time him with a sports Seiko stopwatch to see how fast his draw was and to try to match it with *Buffalo Bill's* speed draw. Nguyen Cao Ky never heard Vortex's farewell as the Colonel left the restaurant with the beautiful and dainty Susie.

All he could hear was the hilarious laughter in the background as the Vice-President continued his American Wild West impersonation and did not stop even when General Westmoreland entered the dining area with some very surprised Senators and Congressmen from Washington D.C.

Vortex led Susie into a plush private suite reserved for field ranking officers in the accommodation block.

"Come my darling! Mrs Ky gave me some hashish!"

As Susie spoke she stripped off her silk dress and underclothes while Vortex snuffled at her vagina that smelt like rose petals.

"What?" he asked, "Hashish? I can't touch that stuff! I'm on duty! And even if I was not I wouldn't consume drugs! I am an officer in the United States Marine Corps and I have to set an example to my men! Its against the law anyway!"

Susie Ky giggled as she consumed the hashish through a special pipe, "Fuck the Law! Do you think anyone gives a rat's ass about the *Law* here in South Vietnam?"

Colonel Vortex shrugged his shoulders, "I do! I try to follow the edicts and maxims of *Public International Law* at all times. In that way all my actions both on and off the battlefield are fully justified! Whatever I do no matter how horrible or upsetting it is to me is justified by the Principles of *Customary International Law.*"

Vortex undressed. When they were naked on the bed he rubbed oil into Susie's buttocks, back and reproductive organ until her smooth white flesh was glimmering like an incandescent light.

Vortex then fucked her to perfection in the missionary position until his first discharge growled from his loins.

Susie then flipped herself onto her stomach and raised her ass so that Vortex could deliciously sodomise her with savage power. He sprayed his second climax onto the small of her back and then gave her the hashish while he sipped on a can of *Budweiser*. The lovemaking continued for another hour in a multitude of differing and novel positions.

Susie became adventurous and greased Vortex's penis with marmalade jam and then chewed, licked and sucked his shaft to a third delectable orgasm.

Suddenly there was a knocking on the door.

Vortex put on his bathrobe and answered the interruption.

It was a Marine Warrant Officer who had a message from Lieutenant General Cushman. The message was simply to telephone the commander of the III MAF as soon as possible.

Vortex drank another glass of *Budweiser* as Susie tried on some silk lingerie that Mrs Ky had given her.

The wife of the Vice-President liked to think of herself as the premier fashion plate for the whole of South Vietnam.

"Do you like it my darling?" said Susie as she pranced delicately up and down the length of the bed.

"Its marvellous my sweet!" exclaimed Vortex.

The Colonel had already picked up the telephone and the military exchange had patched him through to III MAF HQ in *Quang Tri*. The extremely angry voice of Lieutenant General Cushman came roaring through at the other end.

"Is it true?"

"Is what true sir?" asked Vortex taken aback as Susie threw her arms around the huge shoulders of the Marine officer, licking and kissing his face with her luscious tongue.

"You dolt! The news about creating this ludicrous MACV Forward! That's what I'm fucking talking about Colonel!" screamed Cushman in a rage that frightened even the savage Vortex.

Susie giggled in the background at the loud voice.

Richard put his finger to his lips to signal Susie to be quiet as he playfully and gently slapped her on her curvaceous buttocks.

"Well there is nothing I can do about it sir!" answered back Vortex with frustration.

General Cushman barked, "What did COMUSMACV say? And what did this Brigadier General Davidson say to make COMUSMACV come to this crazy and irresponsible decision to wrest control of my Marines away from me and into the hands of a four star Army General? Mind you I have nothing against General Creighton Abrams. He's a professional soldier and a man of great honour and courage. But hell! Vortex! My command is for a three star general and not a four star general officer of Abram's standing!"

Colonel Vortex sucked in a deep breath as his lover lay on her stomach and switched on the television. Susie never missed an episode of the American series; *'Rin Tin Tin.'* She loved it and the cute German Shepherd dog.

"You won't like what Brigadier General Davidson said sir!" said Vortex with dread in his voice.

"Give it to me straight Vortex! I want to know who my enemies are!"

"Ok! Sir!" Vortex sipped on a can of *Budweiser* and explained.

"General Davidson and Colonel Houghton came to inspect the *Khe Sanh* base. They told *'Westy'* that Colonel Lownds had failed to adequately prepare *Khe Sanh* for a full scale bombardment. When COMUSMACV heard this he blew his stack. He started to blame the inefficiency of Colonel Lownds and then he started to lay the blame on you. He said that you couldn't handle the III MAF and the whole I Corps situation. Then he decided to put General Abrams in charge."

General Cushman cursed, "Shit it!"

Vortex continued, "COMUSMACV told Abrams to set up MACV Forward at the old Imperial city of *Hue* and at *Phu Bai* no later than the first week of February! Sir!"

"That's just great! Wait till General Chapman hears about this!" blustered General Cushman, "The commandant of the Marine Corps is going to go ape shit about this one! I bet you he goes straight to General Earle Wheeler the CJCS [Chairman of the Joint Chiefs of Staff]!"

Vortex cleared his throat, "But that's not the worst of it sir!"

Cushman screeched, "There's more?"

"Yes sir." Said Vortex as he massaged Susie's naked ass with his fingers, "General Westmoreland has also taken direct operational control of the 1st Marine Air Wing away from Major General Norman J. Anderson."

Cushman sounded like a lunatic over the long distance field phone.

Vortex snapped, "Yes sir. He has placed General William Momyer the CG (Commanding General) of the 7th Air Force in charge of all tactical sorties in and around *Khe Sanh*. That includes not only the Marines but the Navy, the Army Air and the VNAF."

"I honestly can't believe this is happening!" said General Cushman.

Then the III MAF commander said, "Listen Vortex! You get your ass back to *Khe Sanh* and stay there! Keep an eye on developments and report everything to me. OK?"

Vortex saluted to the telephone handset as if it was a living creature, "Yes sir!"

The he added, "You have heard sir, about the latest intelligence?"

Cushman said, "You mean about that PAVN Lieutenant you interrogated who said that the big attack is coming tonight? Yes, I heard all about it from Colonel Kenneth Houghton. That is why I want you back at *Khe Sanh* as soon as possible! The story may indeed be true!"

General Cushman went on, "I have to call General Chapman in Washington D.C. and see if I can't get this whole thing reversed."

Vortex said as he laughed, "General Chapman is going to go through the overhead on this one. He'll be screaming direct to the President."

Cushman said before hanging up, "Its no laughing matter!"

A few moments of silence passed as Vortex thought deeply. Then he said as he gathered Susie in his arms, "I have to go now my delicious Queen."

Susie held her lover and started to cry, "I am so worried Richard!"

"Worried about what my Vietnamese flower?"

"About you!" she cried as she slapped his chest half crying now and partly laughing. The tears streamed down her lovely smooth cheeks as Vortex wiped them off with his kisses.

"I don't want you to go and get yourself killed up there at *Khe Sanh*! Do you hear me?"

Vortex lifted Susie into the air and bounced her up and down like a pet poodle.

"Don't you worry about me my gorgeous! I am really relishing the chance to teach those North Vietnamese cousins of yours a lesson!"

Susie said with hysteria, "But how can you be so sure that you won't get hurt?"

Vortex laughed, "Because my dear girl! I have God on my side! And besides that I am invincible when my cause is a righteous one!"

The two lovers caressed each other once more and then dressed. Within half an hour they were driven out to *Tan Son Nhut* airfield where rows upon rows of jet fighters were lined up. Some of the F-4 *Phantoms*, F-100 *Super Sabres* and F-105 *Thunderchiefs* were in neat rows, parked along the main east-west runway. Other jets were already in their dome shaped concrete and reinforced steel revetments for the evening. A USAF Warrant Officer came running up and pointed to a gleaming, silver coloured F-100D *Super Sabre* of the *416th Tactical Fighter Squadron*.

"Your jet is ready and fuelled sir!" The Air Force NCO beamed a welcoming smile.

"Thanks Warrant Officer," said Vortex. He turned to Susie who looked flabbergasted.

"But darling?"

"Yes?" asked Vortex grinning as he led Susie up to the iron ladder leading to the cockpit.

"Where is the pilot?" she asked putting her hands to her beautiful mouth.

"I am the pilot darling!" Vortex answered as he kissed her.

"You never told me that you can fly?" she screamed with delight.

"It was a surprise sweety!"

They kissed fervently and Vortex said just before closing the cockpit canopy, "I'll keep in touch each day by radio field phone so keep you're AN/PRC-41 with you at all times. Do you hear me?"

"Take care!" she screamed over the increasing roar of the turbofan engines. Tears flowed freely from her eyes. Susie Ky feared for the safety of Colonel Vortex. Also, deep down in her secret wishes she knew that he was her express ticket out of Vietnam forever and she did not want to loose that free pass to freedom in the United States.

The engines of the gleaming *Super Sabre* roared to life as Vortex pressed all the right buttons and activated his HUD [Head-Up-Display Console] and pulled back the throttle. The last thing he could see was his beautiful Susie waving to him from the beginning of the runway.

Vortex spoke to the control tower and was instructed to take off to the east after a flight of Phantoms were launched towards North Vietnam as part of *Operation Rolling Thunder.*

The sleek, silver titanium bird, one of the best of the *Century Fighters*, edged its nose along the east-west runway.

Vortex could feel the droplets of sweat meandering down the crease of his spine. He yanked the throttle back. Immediately his torso was slammed rearwards into the flight chair. He felt the G forces steadily building. His stomach was eased back onto the rear of his spine.

Seconds crawled past that felt like hours. Finally the *Super Sabre* lifted gracefully off the tarmac. Its wheels spinning even though they were in the air.

Vortex adjusted the flaps and the trim of the aircraft to make a steep, banking climb towards the *Cholon District* of Saigon. Within 3 minutes he was cruising at 550 knots and had reached the first cloud layer at 4,500 feet.

Saigon past rapidly below him. To the west of the capital lay the 'IRON TRIANGLE' and *War Zone C.* These were the Communist's strongest positions. And despite all American efforts they were still entrenched well within the borders of South Vietnam.

Vortex used the onboard computer to check the status of his weapons load. The *Super Sabre* was armed with ASROC missiles. The Colonel did not believe that he would come up against any MIG-17's or even the superior MIG-21's but he asked the air force boys to load them on all the same.

But what Vortex really loved on the Super Sabre was his munitions' load of flechette bombs. Each one weighed 1,000 lbs. The common troops in Vietnam called them 'NAILS.'

NAILS was absolutely devastating against the human body. It literally tore human and animal flesh apart like diced mince meat.

NAILS was a cluster bomb with many bomblets each containing about 300 pellets. The whole bomb could dispense 200,000 pellets or flechettes. The flechettes were tiny darts made of steel and they looked like arrows or needles. The detonation flung these arrows or needles at 900 metres per second into the human body or anything else that got in the way.

The high-velocity effect of flechettes thus caused extensive destruction of human tissues, adjacent blood vessels, nerves and other organs. The number of wounds inflicted were enormous and hard to treat. They were hard to locate and difficult to remove surgically as it would only aggravate the damage and intensify the excruciating suffering of the victim.

Colonel Richard Vortex cherished these flechette bombs and as he streaked north towards the *A Shau Valley* he was itching to expend his jets' ordinance on the PAVN and Main Force Viet Cong in an orgy of destruction.

He had already passed the Central Highlands and the village of *Dakto* where tremendous battles had been fought with the PAVN the year before.

"Not long now!" screamed Vortex to himself.

Suddenly a call came in for all tactical jets in the *A Shau Valley* area.

Vortex acknowledged the call sign of the ground control operator. He told the infantry air control and support coordinator that he was approaching the *A Shau Valley* from the south and was about 10 minutes away.

"Roger that!" bellowed back the voice of the infantry officer far below in the heat of the merciless jungle.

Vortex was talking to a Lieutenant Colonel Patrick Stewart who was the XO (Executive Officer) of the elite *US 173rd Airborne Brigade*.

"This is Apocalypse -7" said Vortex.

"Apocalypse-7. We need your assistance ASAP," came back the cool calm voice of Lieutenant Colonel Stewart. Vortex was surprised in that the voice carried a slight English accent.

"What is the problem XO?"

"We have heavy fire coming from two *Charlie* held hills in our vicinity. Over."

Vortex smiled. Now he would have a chance to unleash his flechette bombs before reaching *Khe Sanh*.

"No problem XO! I'll be there shortly with some NAILS!"

Colonel Stewart looked to his battalion commander and said as he cupped the radio-telephone handset, "We are going to get some NAILS!"

The Major next to Stewart almost cried with joy, "Excellent sir!"

Vortex called back as his *Super Sabre* had now increased to a supersonic speed of 980 knots. The thick and forbidding *A Shau Valley* jungle below was dark and foreboding. The PAVN infested this murderous valley where so many valiant Americans had died trying to protect the principles of freedom and democracy for which the United States stood for.

"Just give me your exact coordinates Colonel Stewart."

The latitude and longitude were relayed and Vortex banked his jet in the appropriate direction punching in the coordinates into his NAV computer system.

The *Super Sabre* flew over the friendly positions of the *173rd Airborne Brigade* and reduced speed as it approached the two PAVN held hills.

Colonel Vortex pressed the release button as he suddenly wrenched the nose of the jet upwards. The flechette bombs detached from their cradles and swam through the air at over 300 mph.

Colonel Stewart could see them glide into the hills from his position on the *A Shau Valley* floor.

He thought it was beautiful to watch.

A few seconds past as Vortex banked away. His *Super Sabre* screamed like a banshee as it accelerated back to attack altitude.

Then it happened.

Weeks after the event Lieutenant Colonel Patrick Stewart could swear an oath to his fellow officers in the 173rd. He told them that he could actually hear the screams and horrendous cries of the mutilated PAVN and Main Force Viet Cong as the flechettes were detonated in a lethal spray of hot steel.

As Vortex streaked away the white concussion waves spread outwards from the multiple detonations. The humid air slowed down the shower of death by mere fractions of a second. PAVN bodies were torn open. They were gouged free of their intestines. They were eviscerated. Then vivisected in a bloody orgy of mutilation as their screams were cut off by the cruel steel of righteous and God bequeathed United States firepower against the evil Communists below.

This was what Vortex thought as he got back on the horn to Lieutenant Colonel Patrick Stewart.

"Listen Colonel. I'm leaving the area for I Corps. But I've got some unexpended 20mm cannon and three 2,000 lbs napalm bombs still under my wings."

The XO answered back without hesitation.

"We sure could use them on those hills Apocalypse-7!"

"Roger that," confirmed Colonel Vortex.

The *Super Sabre* had received some heavy anti-aircraft fire from the gulley's that ran parallel to those hills. So Vortex decided to strafe those PAVN positions first with

his 20mm forward and side mounted cannon. Then he would drop the petro-jelly napalm munitions on the peak of both hills. *Charlie* would be fried up there like roast chicken, he thought. Swooping down into the Communist trenches at 350 mph, Vortex emptied his 20mm cannons in a violent spray of death. As he streaked past he saw bodies being cut in half as they aimed at his jet in vain. A group of Viet Cong women were all decapitated by the cannon shells as they tried to take cover in the jungle.

"Now its time for the jelly fire!" laughed Vortex to himself through his oxygen mask.

The *Super Sabre*, its afterburner glowing red and orange with flames, dived for the attack. The long, cigar-shaped napalm incendiary bombs flew like beautiful white doves of peace into the humid air and struck the Regimental Headquarters of the harassing PAVN force on top of the hills.

A wall of fire and bursting gas rushed over the Communists turning their flesh into charred molasses.

"Well done Apocalypse-7!" came back the excited voice of light Colonel Stewart.

"Its my pleasure!" said Vortex as he swung his aircraft around the battalion positions of the 173rd Brigade.

"I'm on my way home."

Colonel Stewart signed off and resumed operations of his Brigade in moping up the remains of the opposing PAVN Regiment.

As Vortex passed over the hills one last time he felt a sudden ripping impact in his left wing and in the fuselage behind it near the engine.

"Fuck this!" he screamed as he checked his gauges.

Everything appeared normal at first. Then suddenly the whole titanium frame of the aircraft started to shudder and shake as he tried to increase speed beyond the 746 mph sound barrier. Then, horrified, Vortex noticed that his left fuel tank gauge was dropping fast. He had only 650 lbs of fuel left in that tank.

"Oh! Jesus! Fuck me dead!" he screamed as he tore off his oxygen mask to take a better look.

Then he saw that his hydraulic fuel pressure and his engine oil pressure were also falling rapidly.

"What fucking next!" screamed the Marine Colonel.

"It must have been a hit from the gooks anti-aircraft fire," he said to himself again. Talking to himself helped to calm Vortex. Especially when he was flying.

Fuel pressure was now down to 590 lbs in both tanks. The turbofan engine started to make grinding noises as Vortex throttled back to a crawl of 436 mph.

The sun was already setting as its long shadows covered the murderous and infamous jungle of the *A Shau Valley*.

Vortex studied his map and checked his position. He just might be able to make it to the *Khe Sanh* airstrip. He was only 57 miles away.

The *Super Sabre* jolted violently. The throttle stick seemed to be in rebellion as it tried to shake off Vortex's huge, muscular arms. The jet continued to lose both altitude and speed.

It was heartbreaking.

"Only 39 miles to go to *Khe Sanh*," whispered Vortex with a sweated breath.

"Come on baby! You can make it!"

No sooner had Vortex uttered those words than more Communist 37mm anti-aircraft fire belted up at him from below. Several shells hit his undercarriage bay.

"Oh! No! The wheels!" screamed Vortex.

A few minutes later he was only 3 miles from *Khe Sanh* but his undercarriage wouldn't open. Vortex pressed the button frantically but he could not feel the familiar thudding of the wheels and their pylons locking into place below him.

Getting *Khe Sanh's* FSCC (Fire Support Coordination Centre) on the horn, Vortex spoke to Captain Mirza Baig.

"What's the problem Colonel?" asked Baig.

Vortex told the zealous FSCC control officer his problem.

"Well sir? All I can suggest is that you crash your plane near the concertina wire perimeter and I'll inform Colonel Lownds. A rescue squad will be sent out to collect you and bring you safely back inside the perimeter.

Colonel Vortex scoffed, "Thanks!"

The *Super Sabre* was shaking and rattling like a bucket full of bolts.

"Shit! Fuels out!" screamed Vortex as both tanks showed zero.

The 800 foot ravine that bordered the southern edge of *Khe Sanh* was rushing up to Vortex's nose like the speed of light.

"I'm not going to make it!" screamed Vortex as he now cranked a lever to jettison the plexiglass cockpit canopy. The canopy rushed backwards with a sucking sound and crashed unceremoniously into the trees below breaking them in half.

A wall of humid air travelling at 290 mph slammed into the Colonel's face and chest.

His altimeter showed only 987 feet. The ravine ledge was about 800 feet. But he was dropping like a stone. Vortex wanted to close his eyes. But they remained comatose in the open-locked position.

"Here we go motherfuckers!" groaned Vortex.

The *Super Sabre* danced in the air before the ravine ledge. It hit it once on the underbelly. The upward thrust of the impact gave the F-100D *Super Sabre* just enough kinetic energy and height to catapult behind *Khe Sanh*.

Colonel Vortex was thankful that the jet was bone dry of fuel. If he was carrying even half capacity that impact would have detonated the jet like a fireball. He would have been roasted into a juicy Shish-Keb-Ab.

"Oh! Hell!" Vortex screamed and covered his face with his arms as the *Super Sabre* slid on its belly like a swan but completely out of control. The airframe was ripped apart as the fuselage hit tree branches, rocks, undergrowth and finally it struck a large tree at the edge of the jungle surrounding *Khe Sanh*. The plane broke in half and Vortex was catapulted out of the cockpit. He flew through the air and landed in a thick mattress of jungle undergrowth right on the padding of his muscular ass. The *Khe Sanh* base was approximately 1.5 miles from his position. He could see the southern edge of the airstrip and the bunkers and sandbag emplacements of the *'Gray Sector'* and the 37th ARVN Rangers. At that instant heavy machine gun fire opened up both behind Vortex and to his south-west.

"Jesus!" he groaned, "…they are on to me already!"

The North Vietnamese had seen the jet crash and they were bringing in hundreds of troops closer to the *Khe Sanh* perimeter.

Vortex took out his field phone and spoke to Colonel Lownds.

"Don't worry Vortex," began Lownds, "I've sent a twenty man team from your 9th Marines to haul your ass in."

Both men chuckled.

"When I get back to base I'll shout you to a can of *Budweiser*!" said Colonel Vortex.

Colonel Lownds asked, "Only one can?"

It was already a deep violet-blue twilight over the jungle. The humidity caused Vortex to ooze yellow liquid perspiration. His hands could hardly grip the 0.45 Colt handgun that was his only weapon. He had to wipe the sweat from his palms onto his camouflage pants.

Vortex crept away from the sizzling *Super Sabre* that was now just a pile of junk.

The Colonel crawled on his belly to a distance of 300 yards away from the downed aircraft. He was just inside the jungle perimeter that surrounded *Khe Sanh*.

Then movement was detected on his left. The PAVN were slowly combing the jungle searching for the pilot.

Vortex dared not breathe as he slid under some large jungle leaves. The PAVN were now all around him. He could see their feet barely 20 feet away as they patrolled.

Vortex crept up to within 10 feet of one NVA squad. He watched and waited. The squad started to move. Like greased lightning Vortex pounced on the NVA straggler who brought up the rear of the column. Using his Marine dagger the Colonel slit open the NVA's throat as he smothered the mouth with his other hand. Not a sound escaped as warm blood flowed beautifully over his arm and chest. A few minutes later

heavy *AK-47* and *M-16* fire erupted from every direction. Bullets whizzed past Vortex's head as he knew that now the rescue squad were on their way.

Three UH-1H helicopter gunships were thudding overhead and laying down a murderous field of suppressive fire to support the extraction.

Vortex, however, was not content at being idle. He worked his way around to the south edge of the ravine that he had just flown over. He was itching for fresh victims. The Viet Cong and regular PAVN soldiers were already climbing all over the *Super Sabre*. As they did so the Huey's came over and blasted them with stupendous *Minigun* fire. Intestines, severed heads and showers of bloodied flesh sprayed all about as they were annihilated.

Towards the southern edge of the ravine that bordered *Khe Sanh*, Vortex spotted an enemy anti-aircraft position. Slowly crawling through the jungle undergrowth Colonel Vortex positioned himself to the west of the emplacement. He was barely 10 yards away. Peeping through some leaves he saw that the heavy machine gun was Russian made and that three Viet Cong women were operating the weapon.

Vortex was crazed with fury as these women had fired at his *Super Sabre* as he glided in over the ravine for that indelicate crash landing. He was foaming at the mouth for revenge.

Taking his only weapon, the Colt 0.45 handgun, Vortex aimed for the head of the tallest of the three Viet Cong girls. The sound of the pistol shot echoed through the *Khe Sanh* valley.

The Colonel never missed. The bullet erupted the skull of the woman who was just about to load fresh ammunition into the breach of the heavy calibre 37mm weapon.

Vortex watched with glee as her head came apart like a ripe watermelon. Blood gushed onto her two companions even before they could scream.

In the next few seconds Colonel Vortex put all his homicidal prowess into fast forward.

As the two women swirled on their toes to face him, Vortex rushed up to the gun emplacement and leaping with a homogeneous action of pure viciousness he drove his steel dagger into the bosom of the girl nearest to him.

The Viet Cong girl was quite pretty and slim as she groaned with agony. Her right breast had been impaled by the 18 inch blade so that the nipple on that breast had been slivered onto the face of the blade itself. The actual point of the knife was embedded in her heart as it passed through her ribcage.

"You Viet Cong fucking bitch!" screamed Vortex as he grabbed the second girl by her long black hair.

The Colonel head butted her with such power that her nose was collapsed inwards across her face.

"You dirty American bastard!" said the girl in Vietnamese.

Answering in perfect Vietnamese Colonel Vortex laughed, "I am going to consume the heat of your womb!"

Deliciously slithering out the blade from the second girl's mutilated heart, Vortex threw the other Viet Cong woman to the jungle floor.

With surprising eloquence the Communist female said to the handsome Vortex, "You can kill me you filthy American pig! But you are all going to die here at *Khe Sanh*! All of you!"

Vortex fell to his knees and stripped off the girl's blouse as machine gun fire rattled all about them. Her two lovely, pink and soft breasts popped out brazenly in front of the Colonel's salivating mouth.

"You PAVN dogs will never be able to defeat our crushing American firepower! We have the righteous might of *Almighty God* to bear witness to our valiant struggle against you! – you! the Anti-Christ!"

The girl shrieked as she clawed her nails into Vortex's face drawing blood. Her naked body twisted like a slippery eel. Vortex held her head down with his right hand and then ripped off her pantaloons with the other. In a few moments he was kissing her blood stained features and had successfully penetrated into the moist and smooth confines of her slick vagina.

Colonel Vortex believed in screwing the enemy with more than just firepower. Anything was sanctioned in war against your opponent and upon the Colonel's reading of case law he was convinced that the maxims of public international law were exonerative of his actions.

It was Colonel Richard Vortex's opinion that the *'1949 Geneva Convention I for the Amelioration of the Condition of the Wounded and Sick in Armed Forces in the Field'* did not apply to hostilities in South Vietnam as the enemy combatants were *de facto* and not *de jure* and thus not recognised as *'combatants'* under the customary international law principles. His actions, so he thought, were immune to that international instrument giving him open slather to prosecute the conflict in any way, shape or by whatever means that he considered necessary or expedient for the facilitation of the conflict.

As he made delicious love to the screaming Viet Cong girl [a *de facto* irregular subversive and hence not a *de jure* combatant], beneath him, he realised that it had been the gross torture and brutalisation of American POW's by the Main Force Viet Cong units that had abrogated the *Geneva Convention of 1949*.

Colonel Vortex did not believe that the Geneva Conventions had as yet crystallised into edicts of *customary international law*. And as such the United States and its magnificent men and women in uniform were not bound to follow its provisions in any case even if the Viet Cong irregulars could be considered as *'de jure.'*

As he climaxed into the girl's womb he felt her body relaxing under the sweat that he had slimed onto her flesh during his orgasm.

What happened next was almost indescribable.

Vortex had just risen to his feet as he zipped up his camouflage pants. Before he could do anything the naked girl staggered upright.

Vortex saw the beauty of her slim and curvaceous body despite the blood and the grime that ordained it.

Semen was still dribbling from her organ.

In a cat-like movement she ran over to the Soviet designed twin *37mm AA M38/39* gun. A long sharp stake of bamboo was resting against one of the barrels.

The girl spat with pure hatred in Vortex's direction as she grabbed the bamboo stake and placed the sharp edge against the open slit of her moist vagina.

In the next second she drove her body weight onto the long piece of bamboo so that the point thrust right up into her womb and bowels.

Vortex calmly walked over to the Viet Cong girl and raised her impaled body up against a tree.

The bamboo stake was pinned inside her internal organs as blood flowed down the insides of her legs.

"Why did you do that?" asked Vortex as he lasciviously licked and kissed the face of the dying girl.

Her words were sheer agony to utter.

"Because I wanted to destroy your filthy American seed! Destroy it before it impregnates my body with the stench of your evil!"

Vortex chuckled with a mixture of awe and disbelief.

The girl spat into the Colonel's face and said, "All you American imperialist swine are going to die at *Khe Sanh*! Die just as we destroyed the French at *Dien Bien Phu*!"

Vortex simply shrugged his shoulders as he buried his Marine knife into the girl's throat.

As he walked away towards the Marine rescue team he thought secretly, "What if this Viet Cong bitch is right?

What then?"

Chapter 9
January 21st 1968 D Day at Khe Sanh

Colonel David E. Lownds greeted Colonel Vortex as he was escorted into the *Khe Sanh* perimeter through the *'Gray Sector'* by men of his own 9th Regiment.

It was now 2030 hours. Vortex had been away from *Khe Sanh* for only 11 hours in total. A deep moonless and gruesome blackness had veiled *Khe Sanh*. It felt eerie and foreboding.

"How was your meeting with COMUSMACV?" asked Lownds as he offered Vortex a can of *Budweiser*.

"It was not fruitful," answered Vortex with frustration.

"You mean that General Westmoreland again refused to release nuclear weapons to us?"

Vortex nodded and continued, "Not only that but the 1st Marine Air Wing has been placed under the control of the CG for the 7th Air Force, General William Momyer!"

Colonel Lownds looked flabbergasted, "Major General Anderson will be spitting chips!"

Vortex chuckled, "I haven't finished yet! COMUSMACV has also decided to create an MACV Forward at *Phu Bai* and *Quang Tri* to replace operational control of the III MAF from Lieutenant General Cushman."

The only thing that Lownds could do was whistle with surprise. They were both whistling *Dixie*.

"Who will be in command of this MACV Forward?" asked Lownds.

Vortex mentioned the name of General Creighton Abrams.

"Anyway Colonel," continued Vortex as he finished off his beer with a single gulp. "I better get back up to Hill 861 South and see how Major Thrush is doing."

Colonel Lownds informed, "I have put the whole base on full alert. Captain Dabney who is in charge of India Company on Hill 881 South has reported increased PAVN movement all along the hill positions."

Vortex said, "Then it looks like the big attack is indeed coming tonight or before dawn."

Colonel Lownds agreed and as Vortex made his way over to the *Khe Sanh* airstrip and the *Ponderosa* he stopped over at the FSCC to talk to Captain Mirza Baig.

The Captain had already prepared the operational orders to put Operation NIAGARA into action at the first inkling of a major PAVN offensive. In fact Captain Baig told Colonel Vortex that NIAGARA had in fact commenced already on the 15th January 1968.

"Are you ready for Operation *Combat Skyspot*?" asked Vortex. Captain Baig always wore a huge cheesy grin as he saluted smartly to the Colonel.

"Yes sir!" Then he added, "I have also requested the Air Force to place 250 additional sensors around the *Ho Chi Minh Trail* in Laos and around the jungle environs leading up to *Khe Sanh*."

Vortex commented, "That's excellent Captain! Which sensors?"

Captain Baig informed, "We are using the full array of seismic, electronic and acoustic sensors. In addition there is the new *Chemical Sniffer* sensors that can be dropped from aircraft. These devices can monitor the smell of human perspiration and urine. That should give an accurate indication of any build-up in the movement of PAVN and Main Force Viet Cong men and materiel into South Vietnam from the trail.

All the incoming data from these sensors is fed into the computers at *Nakhon Phanom* in Thailand where the *'Infiltration Surveillance Centre'* is located. Their analysis and results at *Nakhon Phanom* is immediately relayed to us here at *Khe Sanh*. We then request tactical air strikes from the vast air armada that we have at our disposal. Also the ARC LIGHT B-52 raids are planned from these sources to hit the PAVN as they move for the offensive."

Vortex was truly impressed with Captain Baig's professionalism.

"Well done! Excellent Captain! Keep up the good work!"

Just then heavy mortar fire could be heard in the distance. It was coming from the hill outposts.

"If I order a tactical air strike in support of my troops on the perimeter. How long will it take for the air assets to get here?" asked the Colonel.

Captain Baig answered confidently, "If the *Phantoms* or THUDS come from *Da Nang* or *Quang Tri* it will take less than 10 minutes sir. If *Super Sabre's* or *OV-10 Bronco's* from VMO-6 come from further afield, like *Tan Son Nhut* or *Bien Hoa*, then it could take up to 25 minutes."

Vortex nodded. Before he left he got Captain Frank Willoughby on the secondary tactical frequency.

"Have you heard Captain?"

Willoughby answered smartly, "I have heard sir. I understand that the spy you captured has indicated that the offensive is coming tonight before dawn. And I am ready!"

Colonel Vortex then spoke severely.

"Now listen up! This is an order!"

"I'm tuned in sir!" answered back Captain Willoughby.

Vortex gave the *suicide command*, "You will not retreat from *Lang Vei*! You will hold the position until the last man! The last bullet! If any of the 900 Montagnards attempt to run away you will ruthlessly shoot them in the back!"

"Understood sir!" answered Willoughby.

"Get any idea of retreat or surrender out of your head!" screamed Vortex in a frenzy. Then he added, "I promise you that everything is sanctioned by the Law. By that I mean the edicts and maxims of *Public International Law*. Forget about concepts of quarter or mercy for the enemy for they deserve none. I have read international case law and our enemies are *'de facto'* combatants and thus not recognised as proper armed forces. Therefore the restraints in the 1949 Geneva and Hague Conventions do not apply to them. You have open slather to exterminate them as you see fit. That is what the Law says."

"I'm going to rip out the living guts of those PAVN bastards sir!" shouted back the Green Beret Captain with venom.

Vortex wished the junior officer good luck and signed off. Thirty minutes later Vortex was dropped off at Hill 861 South by a flight of 3 UH-1H helicopter gunships.

Sergeant Major Creighton and Master Sergeant Richter came running up through the rocks and undergrowth of that bleak, bomb-blasted and desolate hilltop. They saluted and the former said, "Good to see you back sir."

Vortex asked, "Anything happen while I was away?"

Richter informed, "We took another 5 WIA's and killed four gooks. But sir. I have a feeling in my guts! The PAVN are going to attack at any moment!"

Sergeant Major Crighton added his say, "I agree with Richter sir! We have been detecting large scale movement all along the valley. Using our AN/PVS-2 *Starlight Starbright* scopes for infrared night vision we have watched the North Vietnamese bring up hundreds if not thousands of fresh troops. They have also positioned extra 130mm howitzers about 2,000 yards away from us here at Hill 861. The guns are in a type of natural depression in the shape of a horseshoe."

Vortex licked his lips, "It sounds very interesting."

Then the Colonel turned to Major Thrush who just appeared from the jungle foliage along with the battalion staff officers and the radiomen.

"Who's in charge of the 26th Marine component?" asked Vortex.

Major Thrush saluted like a pistol shot, "Its Captain Jasper of K Company. The 3/26th. He has 200 men excluding our 500 troops."

Vortex snapped as he slapped Major Thrush affectionately on the shoulders, "Bring me to him!"

A few moments later the circle of Marines were making their way through the line of trenches and sandbag emplacements that Captain Jasper's men had constructed over the past weeks. In addition to the M60 the Marines had 106mm recoilless rifles, M79 grenade launchers, 60mm M19 mortars, 81mm M29 mortars, 4.2 inch M30 mortars, 105mm M101A1 howitzers, 155mm M114A1 howitzers and 175mm M107 self-propelled guns.

"Report Captain Jasper!" said Colonel Vortex in a gruff and superior manner.

The Captain dropped his cold ration C pack in surprise and jumped to his feet inside the damp, wet and leech infested trench that they were standing in.

"Sir! The PAVN are all around us!"

The Captain then paused and waited for Colonel Vortex to speak. Instead the Colonel slapped the Captain's chest with his open palm in disgust.

"I said give me a full report Captain! I know that the fucking PAVN are all around our positions! My teenage daughter could have told me that! And she's not even here!"

Captain Jasper was humiliated in front of Major Thrush, Richter, Crighton and the others.

Taking a deep breath and cursing Vortex in his thoughts he started to explain to the commander of the 9th Marines the direction of the avenue of retreat of the 29th PAVN Regiment from the action that morning. The PAVN seemed to have totally encircled the approaches around *Khe Sanh*. Hills 881 North and South were surrounded on all sides. The wedge that had been opened by Colonel Vortex's two Companies in the morning engagement had already been shut by fresh PAVN troops from the *325thC Golden Star Division*.

The 1,000 Marines on Hill 558 comprising the 2/26th and the E/2/26th and the equal number of US troops at the *Rock Quarry* and Forward Operating Base 3 [558 troops] were also surrounded.

Only National Route 9 to the east and Hill 950 with its 50 Marines from the A/1/26th and their signallers and combat air spotters were free to move to the east without obstruction. Thus they were only closed on three sides. The *Khe Sanh* village itself was still in communication with the combat base (KSCB) but even this link was tenuous.

Vortex clicked his fingers for a signaller to give him his back upon which was strapped a AN/PRC-41 field radio.

"Is that you Captain Dabney?" asked Vortex.

The commander of India Company on Hill 881 South replied, "Yes sir!"

"What's your status over there?"

Captain Dabney answered, "We are getting sniper fire and harassment all along the line sir. An attack is imminent!"

Vortex grunted. He then grabbed Captain Jasper's flak jacket and pulled the junior officer right up to him so that his spittle tickled the man's face as he spoke.

"We are going out for a patrol!"

"Now Sir?" asked Captain Jasper with trepidation.

"Yes now!" barked back Vortex.

Minutes later Vortex and his party were on the move yet again.

The Colonel had informed Captain Dabney that they would be coming over for a *'coffee.'*

Captain Jasper and Colonel Vortex took point. Master Sergeant Richter and 10 Marines were in the centre. Sergeant Major Crighton and 4 signallers along with the M60 machine gun squad brought up the rear.

The patrol had just bottomed out into the lowest point of the valley between Hills 861/861A and 881 South when it came under a murderous cross fire.

The PAVN *325thC Golden Star Division* had watched Vortex and his group crawl expertly out of the trenches of Hill 861 and 861A. In response they brought up a full battalion of 1,000 men plus a commando company from the *95thC Regiment*. These Communist troops had now enveloped the small patrol.

"Jesus Christ!" shouted Master Sergeant Richter as bullets and the clatter of AK-47 fire buzzed all around him. Two Marines had already been hit. Blood covered their faces.

In the next second Colonel Vortex was blown off his feet by an RPG rocket explosion not 12 yards ahead. Captain Jasper received *frag* wounds (fragmentation wounds) in his cheeks and left testicle.

"Ahie! Ahie!" screamed the junior officer.

Colonel Vortex let loose with his M16 and slapped Captain Jasper across his bloodied features.

"Take the pain! Take it! Like a man! You are a Marine! Suck it up!"

Captain Jasper cried like a baby as blood and pus escaped from his ripped jaw.

"Take up your weapon Captain!" screamed Vortex brutally.

"But!...But I'm wounded sir!" cried Jasper with tears of blood flowing from his eyes.

"Bullshit!" screamed the Colonel as he yanked Captain Jasper into the nearest ditch alongside him.

"That's just a scratch! I expect you to do your duty! Remember the *Chosin Reservoir*! Remember *Iwo Jima* and *Guadalcanal*! You are a Marine! Behave like one! Remember our motto.

Unit! Corps! God! And Country!"

Upon hearing those words Captain Jasper suddenly came alive and gripped his M60 machine gun with renewed fervour.

Even Colonel Vortex was surprised at how rapidly and viciously the Captain was now pumping rounds into the unseen NVA who were crouching in the jungle ahead of them like dirty rats – as Vortex thought and watched.

Master Sergeant Richter and his men were caught in the open when the shooting started. As he ran forward the man on his right was tripped by jungle vine that noosed itself around his ankle. Richter watched in horror as the Marine was lifted into the air by the medieval *'spiked ball'* trap.

"Help me!" shouted the young trooper.

But it was too late as his inverted body was slammed against the razor sharp spikes of the *punji* sticks.

A hail of AK-47 bullets ripped open the stomach of the Marine in front of Richter as they tumbled through the stinking jungle. A piece of liver and a slither of large intestines covered in blood and half digested food splashed across Richter's face.

But it did not affect him at all.

Master Sergeant Richter pumped a full magazine into several PAVN regulars who had launched themselves out of the jungle foliage. They crumpled like sacks of potatoes as blood erupted from their chests like small geysers.

"Help that man on the *punji* sticks!" yelled Richter.

Two Marines rushed up and tried to suck the skull of the man off three *punji* sticks that had passed through the flesh of his face and scalp.

But as they did so NVA regulars appeared behind the Marines. One of the helpers was stabbed in the back of his spine with a bayonet from an AK-47. The other had the side of his head blown away by several bullets.

Richter with a swift and powerful movement pounced on the attackers. Using his trench spade he stoved open the skull of the nearest NVA soldier. The Communists' brains splashed out over Richter's tunic in a collage of horrible colour. A Corporal from the Master Sergeant's squad leapt forward and knifed the other NVA in his buttocks. The Communist grabbed the Corporal's hair and tried to twirl the American away from his body.

The two struggling men were almost snapping their fangs at each other when another NVA regular came up and machine gunned both of them in a spray of blood. Richter then shot that man in the left eye with his Colt 0.45.

A few dozen yards behind the Master Sergeant and his men, Sergeant Major Crighton was reaching for the field phone that was strapped onto the back of one of his signallers. As the Lance Corporal took a step backwards Crighton could feel a rush of wind below his knees. There was also a sharp explosion.

"Ahiiee!" screamed the Lance Corporal. Sergeant Major Crighton watched as the man's left foot and part of his ankle was blown off by a Viet Cong anti-personnel mine.

The specie of mine was called a *'toe-popper.'*

Two other Marines ran up to catch the falling Lance Corporal as his left leg was pouring blood from the hideous stump where his foot used to be. Shreds of lacerated flesh and broken arteries were hanging from it loosely.

But both these men were hit by AK-47 fire as well as rounds from the Chinese *Type 24 7.92mm* heavy machine gun.

Sergeant Major Crighton could only leap into a ditch as he saw their faces literally explode in a shower of blood and tissue.

Colonel Vortex screamed into his field phone, "Captain Dabney! Dabney!"

The commander of India Company answered, "Colonel! Jesus! Get out of there! My men up here are watching through their *Starlight Starbright* infrared scopes. There are hundreds of gooks all over the valley. My men are also returning fire from every position we hold on Hill 881 South!"

Colonel Vortex answered, "We are trying to make it to your hill outpost. But I have already lost more than half of my patrol!"

Captain Dabney screamed as mortars started to detonate around his HQ emplacement.

"Listen Colonel! Hold your current position! I'm calling in 3 AH-1 *Cobra* gunships to extract you out of the valley floor!"

Vortex clipped his handset, "Roger that. Out."

Captain Jasper was firing his M60 but had now run out of ammunition. He was using slap flares to illuminate the jungle around them.

"Watch it Colonel!" screamed the Captain.

Several dozen PAVN regulars came bursting through the foliage.

They rushed at Vortex's position like demons.

The Colonel felled six of them with his M16 but they kept coming. Out of the corner of his eye Vortex could see that several NVA soldiers had pounced on Captain Jasper. They were beating him to a pulp with the butt end of their AK-47's. Vortex blew two of them away with his rifle. He then knew instinctively what to do.

"Get off him you Communist scoundrels!" screamed Vortex as he withdrew his double edged hunting axe from his knapsack. The nearest NVA soldier was strangling Captain Jasper as the others were punching him in the groin, neck and chest. Vortex clubbed the axe into the exact centre of the NVA's skull. Surprisingly enough the man, who was quite large for a Vietnamese, stopped his throttling of the Captain. That one blow was all that was needed. Vortex watched as his brain peeled apart into two neat hemispheres. The left side of the mouth and the nose

was separated from the right. And the eyes parted company in a hideous display of mutilation *par excellence*.

"*Gehen Sie Sie zum Teufel Scheißkerl!*" screamed Vortex in a lather, reverting to his German in times of stress and when an altercation was being enacted before him which was to his dissatisfaction.

Jasper regained his balance as he kicked another NVA back from his torso and knifed a third in the guts. Vortex used his axe like *Gotz Von Berlichigen* to strike upwards into the man's testicles and pelvis. His legs came apart with a sickly sloshing sound.

"Let's get to cover!" screamed Vortex as he unpinned one of the grenades attached to his webbing.

Captain Jasper scurried into a thicker section of the jungle floor while Vortex followed counting to three. At the very last instant before detonation the Colonel threw the grenade into an advancing squad of PAVN, blowing them to smithereens.

"Jesus! Hell!" exclaimed Jasper as a severed leg covered in blood and slime fell onto his face from above.

Disgustingly lacerated body parts were strewn everywhere. Entrails were hanging in loops from the jungle leaves.

Meanwhile Sergeant Major Crighton had joined up with Master Sergeant Richter. The 3 AH-1 *Cobra* gunships had appeared overhead. They had made the short hop from *Khe Sanh* in a matter of minutes. The pilots were well trained as Colonel Vortex spoke to them through the AN/PRC-41 field radio from the valley floor.

"When you are ready come in to get us the fuck out of here! But if you judge the PAVN fire too hot then pull back for awhile. We can hold out a little longer!"

The pilot Warrant Officer of the lead *Cobra* answered, "Yes sir! We should be coming up to your position shortly sir."

Two of the *Cobra's* started to circle the large numbers of PAVN in a *Wagon Wheel* formation. As they rotated they fired their Miniguns, 20mm cannon and rockets into the Communists.

The fire was truly hellish. The jungle was turned into a bonfire as secondary explosions erupted from the PAVN's destroyed ammunition and combustible supplies.

"I can hear them now sir!" groaned Captain Jasper as he picked hot pieces of metal fragments from his bleeding face.

Colonel Vortex grabbed the junior officer and ran with him towards the sounds of the rotor blades.

Master Sergeant Richter watched as the third *Cobra* slowly eased down below tree top level to extract them.

"What the fuck is this?" screamed Richter to Sergeant Major Crighton.

Crighton could see the problem, "That one chopper is not enough to lift us off the valley floor!"

Master Sergeant Richter admonished, "I have seven wounded men here! Five KIA's for body bags and there is still another nine of us operational! The Cobra can't lift more than six extra men not counting the crew!"

"We'll have to get the wounded on first and wait for more choppers," said Sergeant Major Crighton.

The AH-1A *Cobra* landed on a small clearing in front of them. The wounded Marines were piled onto the helicopter as the other two *Cobras* continued to pound the whole area surrounding their defensive perimeter.

But the PAVN troops were savage and relentless. They were determined to wipe out Vortex's small and valiant patrol of Americans. And they were going to do so regardless of their casualties just as the human wave attacks of the Bolsheviks against the heroic *Wehrmacht* defenders during the war on the Eastern front in *Operation Barbarossa*.

The overall control of the 325thC and 304th PAVN Divisions was exercised by the evil genius of General Vo Nguyen Giap himself – the nemesis of the Free World and the butcher of *Dien Bien Phu* against the magnificent French Colonial Forces. This General Officer had a complete and brutal disregard for the unnecessary suffering and casualties of not only the enemy but of his own Communist troops. It was to his foul discredit.

General Giap never gave a second thought to how useless an attack might be or how costly to his own men in the face of overwhelming American firepower and superior tactics on the ground. Colonel Vortex believed that if there was any repugnant war criminal in the Vietnam theatre of operations then first place would be awarded to this sink-hole rat-bastard General Giap whose hands were covered in the blood of hundreds of thousands.

But now Master Sergeant Richter and Sergeant Major Crighton, the valiant *Knight Templars* of the Free World Forces started to run into terrible trouble. As the last WIA (wounded-in-action) were hurriedly manhandled onto the steel floor of the chopper the PAVN fire intensified despite the gunship support.

Several bullets smashed into the bodies of the already wounded men in the *Cobra*, killing two of them.

Richter and the others fired in wide sweeping arcs all around and in front of the *Cobra* to suppress the PAVN onslaught just long enough for the aircraft to make its escape.

Then the *Cobra* co-pilot collected an AK-47 bullet in his right eyeball. The plexiglass canopy of the chopper splintered as his blood erupted onto it from the inside.

"Jesus Christ!" shouted Master Sergeant Richter as he saw what had happened.

Some of the WIA's in the Cobra panicked and frantically climbed over their screaming comrades as they came tumbling back out of the chopper.

The pilot screamed at them to get back in because now he could not lift off even though he had achieved a sufficient rotor speed and power level.

It was then that dozens of PAVN infantrymen started to charge out of the jungle foliage directly at the chopper.

"Get back! Back!" screamed Master Sergeant Richter as his men fired their weapons into the enemy as well as trying to herd the wounded back to the *Cobra*.

By this stage the pilot was in a comatose frenzy. He had angry PAVN troopers rushing towards his broken plexiglass canopy and a seriously wounded co-pilot sprawled over the controls.

Sergeant Major Crighton whipped his head up from the ditch he was lying in and saw several bullets rip into the engine turbofan of the AH-1A *Cobra*. Flames and horrific crunching sounds emanated from the helicopter. Three PAVN soldiers had also leapt into the hatchway and they were ruthlessly knifing the wounded Marines with long curved daggers. The door gunners had already been killed by the merciless PAVN fire.

"Oh! My God!" was all that Master Sergeant Richter could utter.

The *Cobra* pilot was screaming through the plexiglass as he began to lift the *Cobra* off the ground with the murdering PAVN jackals still inside. The aircraft managed to rise about 12 feet off the jungle turf when one of the Communist soldiers knifed the pilot in the back of his throat. Flames were spreading over the entire fuselage when heavy calibre slugs from a Chinese *Type 42* machine gun smashed into the furiously spinning rotor blades. Richter and Crighton watched in horror as the *Cobra* tilted violently out of control, throwing some of the wounded Marines out of the hatchway.

The rotor blades made a screeching noise and then detached from the pinion with awesome power and speed. The steel blades shattered and flew through the air with their incredible kinetic energy.

And then the worst came to pass.

One of the rotor blades flew diagonally, faster than the eye could discern and hacked its way into 5 able-bodied Marines who were standing behind Sergeant Major Crighton. The knife edge of the rotor blade shaved Crighton's short hair even shorter and literally vivisected the 5 Marine bodies in half. Richter was horrified as five pairs of legs slumped into the mud followed by their screaming torsos.

At that second Colonel Vortex and Captain Jasper staggered out of the jungle.

"Jesus! What the fuck is happening here?" screamed the Colonel.

Before anybody could answer the rotor-less *Cobra* crashed into the jungle mud and burst into flames.

Crighton, incensed with fury, saw two of the murdering PAVN scamper free. He machine gunned them down.

Colonel Vortex whistled, "This is a bloody fiasco!"

But they had no time to discuss the niceties of tactics.

"Get down sir!" screamed Richter as a hail of fire belted at their bodies from every conceivable direction.

"Armageddon 6! This is Apocalypse 7! Over!" Vortex spoke into the AN/PRC-41 field phone to the two remaining *Cobras* in the air above them.

"Armageddon 4 is down; all hands lost; Charlie holds the perimeter!"

The pilot above answered, "Roger that Apocalypse 7! Have expended all munitions and returning to base. Will send 3 additional *Sikorsky* gunships. Over."

Vortex answered, "Armageddon 6! Be sure to send a CH-47 for extraction and lift to 881S!"

The Cobras peeled away from the triple layered jungle canopy after confirming that request.

However the PAVN surrounding Vortex had not given up yet. In fact their determination to annihilate the survivors had redoubled.

Vortex watched with horror as his wounded men crawled all around him in the mud. There were no medics or Corpsmen on hand to give them even the most rudimentary treatment. Shrieks and groans filled the bullet infested air. It was a cacophony of horror. The *Cobra* gunship was a blackened, burning hulk.

"Sir! Look!" yelled Sergeant Major Crighton.

The body of the Marine pilot staggered out of the burning wreck. It was a human torch. Orange flames licked over the entire torso as the charred face of the aviation Warrant Officer tried to scream unsuccessfully.

Mercifully the PAVN machine gun fire cut the man to pieces before he could die of his burns.

"They are coming in again!" groaned Master Sergeant Max Richter.

Now the fighting was hand to hand. The NVA had leapt on Vortex and his few survivors before they could fire what ammunition they had left.

Captain Jasper bayoneted two black pyjama'd Viet Cong irregulars who came screeching towards him.

Vortex threw one NVA over his back as the Communist tried to slice open his guts with a machete.

Master Sergeant Richter tripped one running NVA and then sliced his knife into the man's testicles, ripping vertically until he cut open the internal viscera that slid out beautifully.

Sergeant Major Crighton was surrounded by three NVA all of whom were scowling and screaming with fury. A torrent of Vietnamese abuse pouring from their orifices. The Sergeant Major head butted the closest assailant and then shot the other two with his Colt 0.45 having expended all his M16 ammo.

"Watch it!" screamed Vortex as a six foot North Vietnamese slammed his AK-47 butt into Richter's spine.

"Aahh! Ahie!" the senior NCO screamed as Vortex proceeded to cut that man to pieces with his trench axe.

Miraculously the 3 *Sikorsky S-65 HH-53B Super Jolly Green* helicopters swooped directly over their dazed heads just at the most opportune moment.

Each gunship had 3 Miniguns and a 20mm cannon. Thus 9 Miniguns and 3 cannon were immediately brought to bear on the vastly superior PAVN forces that had surrounded the small group. They belched forth an awesome avalanche of hot steel into the enraged PAVN attackers. The Communists temporarily backed off in a spray of mutilation and blood.

The centre HH-53B dropped down and Vortex and his exhausted survivors clambered aboard. As many of the WIA's that could be grabbed were also wrenched onto the gunship. The losses were terrible. Apart from Vortex, Jasper, Richter, Crighton and two others, the rest of the 27 man patrol were either killed or wounded.

"We can't leave those men down there sir!" screamed Master Sergeant Richter as he pointed to several wounded and dead Marines. Vortex was crazed with frustration, "I'll have to retrieve them later! This chopper could be blown out of the sky at any moment!"

As if to confirm his words, bullets were already slamming into the gunship from the relentless PAVN fire below. The 3 *Sikorsky's* peeled off rapidly from the valley floor and deposited Vortex's badly mauled party right onto the crown of Hill 881 South.

Captain Dabney of India Company was there to meet them. He was none too pleased either. Several of his Marines had been wounded in the last 30 minutes.

"Sir! I think the big attack is coming!" said Captain Dabney as he motioned for his India Company medics and Corpsmen to treat the wounded as best as they were able before the *Sikorsky's* would lift them over to the *Khe Sanh* base hospital.

Vortex nodded, "I want you to put your men on full alert Captain."

Dabney responded, "They already are sir."

The junior officer ushered Colonel Vortex and his NCOs' into the Company HQ bunker dug into the side of Hill 881S. It was more like a large foxhole which had been dug 12 feet underground and which was shielded by an overhanging escarpment.

"You are very exposed to PAVN fire up here," said Colonel Vortex as they filed into the HQ foxhole.

"I know sir," began Captain Dabney as he ran his fingers threw his short greying hair.

"But what can I do? My men are dug in as deep as they can go. The PAVN have been spotted all around this hill. They are also bringing up 81mm mortars and 75mm recoilless rifles."

As they spoke a tremendous explosion could be heard in the distance. It was followed shortly after by screams.

"What the hell?" yelled Captain Dabney as he ran outside with Colonel Vortex.

A First Lieutenant from India Company came running up. His face was covered in blood. The webbing under his flak jacket was torn by fragmentation debris.

"Sir! The PAVN are homing in on us with their 81mm mortars!"

Captain Dabney turned to Colonel Vortex, "You see Colonel. It has begun!"

Vortex took the handset of a field phone and got on the horn to Captain Mirza Baig.

"Listen Captain! I want you to scramble a flight of F-4E's from the hot pad at *Da Nang* and bring them over to these coordinates between 881 South and 861. I want the TAC air to pound the whole valley with napalm and cluster bombs!"

The Conscientious FSCC officer was happy to oblige.

Vortex clicked off the phone and said, "You see Captain Dabney. That is why I was begging General Westmoreland and MACV to release battlefield FROGS to us!"

Captain Dabney looked with surprise and asked, "You mean tactical nuclear ordnance?"

"I do," said Vortex calmly.

Dabney ran his hands through his hair with exasperation saying, "That would have saved a lot of my boys and yours!"

Vortex grunted with approval spitting out with fury, "One W48 shell from our 155mm howitzers could have evaporated that entire valley floor below us and stopped the PAVN offensive on these two Hills dead in their tracks!"

Vortex threw his hands up into the air with exasperated futility and said, "I want a full inspection tour of your entrenched positions."

Vortex and his entourage walked all around the perimeter. The night was hot, stinking and very black. The smell of rotting human flesh seemed to be permeating out of the dense jungle around them like a veil of foulness.

"You see that?" asked Vortex as he pointed with his finger towards the distant jungle to the north of Hill 881 South. The Colonel was holding a *Starlight* infrared scope up to his eyes as he expertly scanned the contours of the PAVN infested jungle.

Dabney, Richter, Crighton, Jasper and the others were standing behind him with their *Starlights*.

"The PAVN are moving up heavy artillery!"

"Let me see!" said Captain Dabney excitedly.

The India Company commander took Vortex's *Starlight* and peered through the scope. He could see large black objects moving slowly past the tree lines. These objects were pointed at the front and much larger than men.

"You are right sir!"

Vortex swung around to the south-east in the direction of the Marine position at the *Rock Quarry* and FOB3 [Forward Operating Base 3]. Looking past that strong point he saw the same thing. The PAVN were moving in hundreds of men and 130mm Soviet designed artillery pieces.

"I estimate that the *'horseshoe'* is about 2,000 yards from our position here," said the Colonel.

Master Sergeant Richter turned to the Captain, "Sir. You must keep a close watch on the incoming PAVN fire from this *horseshoe* position. Because once the gooks start up with their heavy guns *Khe Sanh* will have barely 30 seconds to dive for cover!"

Vortex grunted his agreement, "I estimate, Master Sergeant, that it would be closer to 20 seconds before *Khe Sanh* would be blasted by those 130mm howitzers!"

The group of officers were standing in a trench line along with the men of India Company.

Mightiest Corporal in the World: Corporal Robert J. Arrotta [1/3/26th Marines]

Colonel Vortex stepped up to a boyish looking Corporal who was manning one of the many M60 machine gun positions.

"What is your name son?" asked Vortex as he put his hands on the young man's shoulders.

The junior NCO looked up at the 41 year old, 6ft 2.5 inch, 205 lb mountain of military, Christian-Right muscle and pure viciousness to the enemies of the righteous – the defender of Christ.

He was shaking in his general purpose boots that were caked in mud and slime. The air was acrid with the stench of cordite.

"Corporal Robert J. Arrotta! Sir!" answered the youthful Marine smartly as he saluted.

His comrades also inched up along the trench line to overhear what the famous Colonel Vortex would ask of him.

"Where are you from Corporal Robert Arrotta?"

"From San Diego sir."

Vortex looked to Richter and Crighton and then asked, "And what do you think of the American effort here in the Republic of South Vietnam?"

The Corporal answered back without hesitation, "I think our Government is doing the right thing sir."

Vortex allowed a bemused grin to slide across his features, "What do you mean Corporal Arrotta?"

Arrotta answered, "It is the duty of the United States to uphold democracy and freedom anywhere in the world. Especially when it is threatened by the evil and pernicious Communist forces of North Vietnam. But sir!..."

Vortex asked, "Yes Corporal? What is your question?"

Corporal Arrotta bit his lip and hesitated but then asked with courage, "Why are we fighting this war according to the lousy Communist rules? Why do we simply react to every Viet Cong and PAVN offensive? Why doesn't President Johnson order us to go on the attack? We should be launching a full scale invasion of North Vietnam and Laos and Cambodia as well! The total infrastructure and economy of North Vietnam must be wiped from the face of this earth! I am dying here in this stinking, fucking trench at *Khe Sanh*! But I would be happy to die for my country if I knew that my country would do all that can be done to achieve victory against the murdering PAVN pigs! Its crazy sir! I simply don't understand it sir!"

Colonel Vortex nodded his head and the other officers behind him were aghast at hearing the truth so candidly expressed and so resolutely determined.

"I guarantee you Corporal!" began Vortex, "That *Khe Sanh* will be held! We shall smite the PAVN offensive in a sea of their own blood and entrails! They will be pulverised before they reach the concertina wire surrounding our magnificent base at *Khe Sanh*! We shall unleash such an avalanche of hot steel and explosive firepower upon their rat-fucking heads that they will be annihilated in a whirlwind of destruction!

It will be like a waterfall of fire and brimstone!

The NIAGARA of their utter destruction!"

Corporal Arrotta added as he saluted to Colonel Vortex, "I look forward to the orgy of their total annihilation! My only wish is to kill and mutilate as many of those motherfucking Communist pigs as I can get my hands on!"

And then he added, "Sir!"

The dozens of other Marines standing behind Corporal Arrotta shouted their agreement.

Colonel Vortex was delighted to see that the morale of the troops was so high.

But he bitterly cursed the MACV High Command at *Pentagon East* in Saigon and the Executive Government in Washington D.C. for not allowing him to use nuclear weapons at *Khe Sanh*.

Colonel Vortex was convinced that if the 175mm howitzers at Camp Carroll would be allowed to fire the W48 atomic shells at the merciless and murdering PAVN troops then he could smash the Communist offensive even before it would begin. The lackeys of General Vo Nguyen Giap and the rest of his coterie of criminals would be vaporised in a series of beautiful mushroom clouds that would pop up like beacons of American victory all over the stinking jungle surrounding *Khe Sanh*.

But it was not to be!

Colonel Vortex shook his head and tried to forget these beautiful dreams that would never come to fruition.

All the Marines on Hill 881 South suddenly looked skyward as a deep full throated roar came out of the jungle blackness from the east.

"It's the Phantoms from *Da Nang*," remarked Colonel Vortex.

Sergeant Major Crighton handed Vortex the field phone and he spoke to the TAC(A) who then spoke to the flight leader over a secure VHF tactical frequency. The Colonel simply told the USAF through the TAC(A) who told the pilots to hammer the area between 881S and 861A with everything they have.

The *Phantoms* went quickly into action as they swooped in four abreast. The Marines put their fingers into their ears as a brace of 24 napalm bombs glided through the eerie darkness cutting the humid atmosphere open like a scythe.

The F-4 *Phantom II* could carry up to 24 *'iron bombs'* which was twice the load of a World War 2 *B-17G Superfortress* while an A-6A *Intruder* could deliver 30 of the 500lb bombs.

The standard munitions that Vortex now watched with glee dropping over the enemy that gave him a weird form of almost sexual excitement was the *Snake-Eye* bomb weighing 500lb. This was the Standard Mark 82 general-purpose bomb fitted with large Mk 15 folding fins that opened when released to retard the bomb's fall. This allowed low-flying fighter-bombers to exit the target area before the bomb string impacted and prevented collateral damage to the aircraft from its own bombs' fragmentation and out-flying debris. Usually secondary explosions erupted after the bombs hit their targets as the enemy material and ammunition was ignited in a satisfying, to Vortex, conflagration of destruction.

The iron bombs included the 250lb Mk 81, the 500lb Mk 82, the 750lb M117, the 1,000lb Mk 83 and the beautiful in Vortex's eyes, 2,000lb Mk 84. Usually as the Colonel knew well, a 500lb Mk 82 was filled with 192lb of *Tritonal*. Another bomb that Vortex approved of immensely was the BLU-27/B 750lb *fire bomb* filled with 100 gallons of gasoline enhanced and thickened with benzene and polystyrene – Napalm-B for an actual bomb weight of 873lb. This was Vortex's favourite as it would most assuredly incinerate the PAVN and Main Force Viet Cong so that their flesh peeled off their bones.

Colonel Vortex and his entourage watched with delight as the jungle floor where they had been bush-wacked by the PAVN came alight in an awesome pyrotechnic display.

The thick and highly incendiary liquid consisted of petrol which had been gelled with aluminium soaps or *Palmitate*.

The magnificent napalm weapon was a triumph for American technology and ingenuity.

The black void became, for a few moments, an artificial day of illuminating destruction. The concussion waves spread out concentrically from the 24 detonation points which had been right on target. The awesome display even allowed Colonel Vortex and his entourage to see the men on Hill 861A and 861 with high powered binoculars, the Navy 20-power binoculars as if it was the middle of a cloudless day.

Sergeant Major Crighton said, "Look Sir! There are the secondary explosions!"

Colonel Vortex knew that the napalm had ignited PAVN ammunition and other combustible equipment. This meant that they had hit the Communists hard. The flames spread forward and outwards from the point of impact at roughly the same speed as the advancing jets. The petro-jelly turned the jungle foliage into charred slush and the smell of gasoline mixed with burning human flesh assaulted all their nostrils. It almost made Captain Jasper vomit.

From below the hill designated 881 South shrieks and shouts of frenzied Vietnamese gibberish could be heard over the lessening roar.

The *Phantom II's* then made a wide arc with their locus of flight being 4 to 5 miles west of 881S/861. At this distance their ramjet engines sounded like a deep thunder from the very caverns of hell itself.

"They are coming in for the cluster bomb strike," said Vortex as Captain Dabney indicated to the Colonel to look through his *Starlight* scopes far to the west.

"We have yet another problem sir," began Dabney as Vortex sweeped the horizon with his precise military eyes. He was using a technique called *'strip scanning'*. This involved moving your eyes from left to right starting from the foreground and then gradually shifting your search pattern further and further back towards the distant horizon.

"Continue!" said Vortex tersely as Master Sergeant Richter and Sergeant Major Crighton also strip scanned methodically.

"Just across the border on the Laotian side, the PAVN have emplaced even heavier artillery,…"

Vortex interrupted as he said, "I know what you are talking about Captain Dabney. I have seen the aerial reconnaissance photographs from *Nakhon Phanom* that have been produced by our Surveillance Centre there. The 68th PAVN artillery regiment has been spotted at the *'Co Roc'* formation which is about 17 miles from the base. They have nearly 100 152mm howitzers. They can blast *Khe Sanh* in less than a minute once the shells leave their barrels."

The Captain nodded seriously as the *Phantoms* came in for their final bomb run. The Marines watched as the cluster munitions detonated inside the valley. The jungle was devastated by these *flechette* weapons that sent hundreds of thousands of hot, razor sharp steel darts flying into human flesh at over 900 metres per second.

Colonel Vortex and his troop of followers jumped into two UH-1E helicopters and flew over to Hill 881 North which was defended by another Company of Marines.

They then made a quick battlefield inspection. Vortex ordered the company commander there to reposition his 106mm recoilless rifles. He also ordered the troops to dig in deeper and prepare for the worst.

Colonel Vortex then took the choppers back to Hills 861 and 861A. Captain Jasper saw to the disposition of his men and issued them with increased loads of ammunition.

"As soon as the major push by the PAVN begins," began Vortex as he spoke to Colonel Lownds over the VHF tactical frequency.

"I want you to send a flash encrypted message to III MAF and MACV in Saigon ordering the immediate implementation of Operation NIAGARA."

[In fact Operation NIAGARA had already commenced on 15th January 1968 – but Vortex was asking for an intensification of the aerial bombardment]

"I understand Colonel Vortex," said Lownds. Then the commander of the 26th Marines added, "I have put the Marines on the *Rock Quarry* and Hill 558 on full alert."

Colonel Lownds was in the DASC (Direct Air Support Centre) at KSCB.

Lieutenant Colonel Tran and Captain Hoang Pho commanding the ARVN 37th Rangers were standing next to him along with upwards of 30 other officers and NCOs'. The tension at *Khe Sanh* was electric. Hundreds of Marines were peering into the dark and eerie jungle through the concertina wire perimeter.

They watched. They waited. And they held their breath.

The time was now 0025 hours.

The 21st January 1968 had arrived.

Colonel Vortex knew that the climax of his savage wish for retribution would soon be unleashed upon them all. As he waited with Richter, Crighton, Major Thrush and the others in that stinking foxhole on Hill 861A he prayed to Almighty God to give him strength for the coming conflict with the forces of the Communist Anti-Christ.

THE BEGINNING
Attack on Hill 861A 0035 hours, 21st January 1968

An ear splitting roar of absolute savagery awakened Colonel Vortex as he lay with his face resting on the table of Captain Jasper's HQ.

Before Vortex had time to fully lift his head into the upright position it seemed that his skull was thrust downwards again. The roof of the bunker disintegrated under the impact of three 81mm mortar shells that came streaming down like hammers of death.

Sergeant Major Crighton was blown sideways and crushed against the sandbag walls of the foxhole/bunker.

Master Sergeant Richter was so stunned that he fell backwards onto his skull as his chair was flung over by the blast.

"Its started!" screamed Captain Jasper as he had just descended the sandbagged stairs leading into the bunker. The Captain and three of his Warrant Officers were flung into the middle of the dirt floor of the bunker.

"Outside! Everyone outside!" yelled Colonel Vortex as he grabbed Sergeant Major Crighton by his webbing and pulled him unceremoniously to his feet.

The huge Marine grinned down at Colonel Vortex from his 6 feet 4.5 inches and said, "Sorry Sir!"

Vortex asked with surprise, "What do you mean?"

"For allowing myself to doze off for a few seconds. I am a United States Marine! The finest fighting force in the world! I cannot afford the luxury of sleep in combat!"

Colonel Vortex chuckled as he patted his beefy Sergeant Major.

"I forgive you Crighton! Besides! I also fell asleep!"

The two men laughed and Vortex asked his friend if he was alright. The Sergeant Major seemed to be relatively unscathed. The officers and NCOs' tumbled out of the foxhole and were greeted by a hail of fire.

The 200 men of K Company 26th Marines were returning fire with everything they had. M60's, mortars and 106mm recoilless rifles boomed out into the jungle below them. But the incoming PAVN fire was even more savage. Hill 861A had trench lines around the crown of the position. Vortex's 2 companies had reinforced Captain Jasper's men to a strength of approximately 650 troops.

Colonel Vortex and his entourage jumped into the trench that was facing north towards the heaviest concentration of Communist fire.

"We should be able to hold out long enough for TAC(A) air support to reach us!" said Captain Jasper.

Vortex grabbed the Captain in a frenzy, "We are going to hold this position with or without fucking air support! Or any other fire support! Do you hear me Captain!"

Captain Jasper looked at the Colonel with a comatose face etched in terror.

"There will be no retreat! No withdrawal whatsoever!"

As Vortex screamed Captain Dabney and Major Thrush crawled together along the trench mud and grabbed one of the 106mm recoilless rifles manhandling it into position towards the valley between 881S and 861A/861. Major Thrush then grabbed his leader by the sleeve.

"Sir!" he yelled over the machine gun and mortar fire.

Before Vortex could answer the battalion commander, an 81mm shell landed directly inside their trench line less than 20 yards away.

The resulting carnage was unbelievable. A young 2nd Lieutenant from K Company was decapitated. His broken arteries twitched grotesquely as they streamed blood from the stump of his neck. The body continued to stand weirdly upright but the head was nowhere to be found.

The Corporal next to him had his right arm severed off at the shoulder. Another Marine was catapulted out of the trench and onto the exposed portion of the hill. He was immediately cut to pieces by AK-47 fire.

Several other men received flash burns and concussion.

Vortex screamed as he fired his M60 into the jungle, "What is it Major?"

"We've spotted the PAVN mortar position. Corporal Arrotta has with his Navy 20-power binoculars using infrared. Or at least one of them."

Major Thrush pointed with his bayonet, "Over there to the north-east. About 300 yards away at the base of 861."

Vortex nodded and clicked his fingers to Richter and Crighton.

"We are going to take it out!"

Major Thrush was bleeding from his chest. He had received several fragmentation wounds under his epidermal layer of skin. But as a Marine – one of America's finest, he simply ignored the excruciating pain and continued to fight for freedom and democracy and the American way of life.

"Who do you want to go with you?" asked Thrush.

The Colonel loaded additional grenades and M16 magazine clips to his webbing.

"I'll take ten of your men from C Company as well as Richter and Crighton. You stay here and take command with Dabney. Take over this hill [861A]. I don't trust Captain Jasper!"

Major Thrush nodded and screamed over the intense fire, "We shall hold here until our guts are ripped out in a sea of blood!"

Vortex clapped the Major on the shoulders, "I knew that I could count on you!"

Vortex and his troop of Marines made their way through the trench lines on the northern perimeter of Hill 861. There was a small gulley at the eastern end which opened out into the dense jungle below. This is the route that Vortex chose. His men had painted camouflage markings on their features. They moved swiftly and expertly behind their Colonel. Each Marine was handpicked and deadly.

Vortex gave hand signals for the men to move into the jungle spaced about 10 yards abreast. AK-47 fire was coming at them from every direction. As they crawled on their bellies they could see the moving figures of the PAVN. There were hundreds if not thousands of them all wearing camouflaged pith helmets with leaves and shrubs attached.

Suddenly the Marines on Hill 861 let off some slap flares. It illuminated the earth and exposed Vortex and his squad as they crouched in the jungle. Shots rang out and

one of the Marines was mortally wounded in the chest and head. The AK-47 bullets ripped away his mouth and nose in an orgy of blood.

"Fire! Fire!" screamed Vortex.

[He thought to himself at that second that if he would have been in the British Army he would have said – 'Shoot! Shoot!']

The automatic fire erupted from a full 360 degrees field of destruction.

"Shit! There are gooks all around us!" shouted Master Sergeant Richter.

Two NVA came bursting out of the dense foliage of the jungle and Sergeant Major Crighton shot them through the eyes before they could reach Richter. A piece of one Communist eyeball actually splashed inside Richter's mouth as he swung around in fright. Vortex could see that the PAVN were caught off balance by his movement right up to their forward positions. The fire was chaotic. Vortex and his squad was sandwiched in the middle with hundreds of enemy troops firing willy-nilly in every conceivable direction. The bullets were thicker in the air than the mosquitoes were at sunset in the *Shunderbun* forest.

"Dive for cover! Here! Here!" shouted the Colonel.

His squad ran for their lives right into the teeth of the PAVN mortar positions. Since there were PAVN behind them as well as in front the fighting became hand-to-hand.

Crighton ducked as one scowling Communist tried to bayonet his skull. Reaching under the NVA's groin he struck upwards with his field knife and severed open the man's gonads in a delicious slime of blood.

Richter saved Colonel Vortex by shooting one NVA who had crept up behind the commanding officer and was about to bayonet him in the spine. A Marine running behind Master Sergeant Richter was cut down by heavy machine gun fire from a Chinese 7.92mm. His hands and body whiplashed outwards as if begging for help.

Richter was sprinkled with the Marine's blood as a horde of PAVN came up and drove their multiple bayonets into the dying body.

The Communists aimed for the face and heart, mutilating it beyond recognition.

"To the mortars! Get the mortars!" screamed Vortex as he ran through the jungle. Richter and Crighton were right behind him.

The whole attack was a fiasco. Colonel Vortex stumbled in the mud and slush as a large punji trap yawned in front of him. Richter avoided it and Crighton managed to jump over the side of it. But a Marine coming up from behind was running too fast.

"No! Stop!" shouted Colonel Vortex.

But it was too late. The Marine leapt right into the gruesome pit and his heart was impaled by the punji razors. Richter could see his legs twitching like the beak of a small bird. Sergeant Major Crighton felt two pairs of hands strangling him as he lay in the mud. One of the PAVN soldiers throttling him had dropped his RPG-7 rocket launcher.

Colonel Vortex arched backwards and stabbed one of the NVA directly into his mouth and throat with his 18 inch Marine dagger. As the blood vomited out from the enemies' mouth, Crighton savagely head butted the second attacker.

"You fucken gook!" groaned Richter. The Master Sergeant had bolted up behind the NVA soldier and proceeded to crush his skull with his trench spade. Small bits of cerebrum splashed onto Vortex's lips as he tore at the throat of another Communist with his teeth.

"Pick it up!" yelled Master Sergeant Richter.

The Colonel lunged for the fallen RPG rocket launcher and used the Communists' weapon against them. With an elegant locus of movement, the Colonel aimed the RPG at the PAVN mortar pit in front of them. The explosive head streaked away with a high pitched wail. Seconds later the whole jungle seemed to detonate. There were screams. There was blood. And severed limbs showered the battered Marine squad.

Bloody PAVN soldiers came hurtling away from their mortar positions as the Marines threw multiple grenades into the enemy pits.

Colonel Vortex stood up and met the North Vietnamese soldiers head on as they charged him. He smashed his M16 butt into the skull of one man causing the forehead to collapse in a gruesome mess. He knifed two others in the heart and strangled an NVA trooper in a headlock while Crighton plunged his Marine dagger into the man from behind.

Master Sergeant Richter moved his huge body with the ease of a fencing master. He slashed, cut, shot and hacked his way through five Communist bodies. Two more of Vortex's men were blown away behind them by increasing numbers of enemy troops.

The PAVN were everywhere.

"Its no use sir!" cried Sergeant Major Crighton.

Master Sergeant Richter pointed upwards to Hill 861. The PAVN were already streaming up that bleak, bomb blasted and desolate hill in large numbers. Gunfire and mortar rounds could also be heard from Hills 881 South and Hill 558 where 1,000 Marines from 2/26th and E/2/26th were defending the northern approaches to KSCB along QL9 effectively blocking the route to the Marine base.

"Give me the AN/PRC-41 field phone!" shouted Vortex.

He grabbed the handset but could not make himself heard over the terrible screaming of one of his wounded men. The Marine lying at their feet was the only survivor of the 10 man squad. Sergeant Major Crighton was trying to comfort him while Richter pumped vast quantities of morphine and adrenalin into his carotid artery with hastily prepared syringes. Some of the broken needles had stuck in his throat.

The man had lost both arms at the shoulder level. Two disgusting, slime and blood covered stumps gazed out at them where his limbs should have been.

Vortex fell to his knees and cupped the screaming mouth of the mutilated man.

"Shut up! Shut-the-fuck-up! You idiot! You fucking! Fucken idiot!"

The Colonel was beside himself with rage. He was worried that this Marine's screaming would bring the whole PAVN regiment down upon their heads. And as if to legitimise his fears a solitary PAVN soldier appeared out of the green foliage behind them. Sergeant Major Crighton cupped the man's mouth with his right hand and buried his dagger into both kidney's and the liver in quick succession.

"Keep quiet! Do your duty soldier!" said Vortex with vicious power as he stared into the man's horribly contorted face. The Master Sergeant just kept up the morphine injections until the Marine fell into a drug induced coma.

"Colonel Lownds! Lownds? Are you there?" whispered Vortex.

The three men lay in a ditch as platoon after platoon of fresh PAVN soldiers filed past their position in that bloody first night of the *Khe Sanh* battle.

Seconds that seemed like hours passed by before Colonel Lownds answered through the VHF tactical frequency.

"What's happening over there Vortex?" asked the 26th Marine commander.

"Hill 861 and 861A are under full-scale attack by the PAVN! Its started Colonel! The big push is on! Alert III MAF headquarters and MACV in Saigon! Now!" screamed Vortex.

"I've already done that Colonel! Also TAC(A) air and an AC-47 SPOOKY gunship is on its way to you."

"Good! Have you alerted the 7th Air Force and General Momyer to commence Operation NIAGARA to maximum level from its initial alert level on 15th January?" asked Vortex.

The cool and calm voice of Colonel Lownds answered, "I have."

Vortex seemed satisfied as he signed off.

"We better get back up to Major Thrush as soon as possible," said Vortex as he looked at the wounded Marine.

Sergeant Major Crighton said, "There is no way that we can carry him with us. Poor bastard!"

The Master Sergeant sighed, "You won't have to!"

"What do you mean?" asked the Colonel.

"He's dead," came back the stoic voice of Richter as he covered the dead man with a plastic poncho ground sheet. The three men weaved their way back to the top of Hill 861 along the gulley that led into the trench line. When they jumped into the sandbagged foxholes they were surprised to discover that the trenches had been abandoned. Only dead Marines littered the ground.

"Shit! I'll kill that son-of-a-bitch Jasper!" admonished Colonel Vortex.

Suddenly they heard the gibberish of Vietnamese voices behind them. As Vortex understood every word he realised that the PAVN were shouting to kill them.

Hundreds of PAVN were all around. It appeared that they had taken the northern half of the hill. Vortex and his NCOs' ran for their lives across the top of 861 and down to the southern side of the outpost. They were chased by the regular PAVN forces who had already begun to strip the American dead of their uniforms. Naked bodies began to rot in the stinking humidity of the jungle pre-dawn.

"Over there!" groaned Vortex as they threw themselves into the last line of trenches held by the Marines.

"Jesus Colonel! We thought you were dead!" It was the voice of Major Thrush whose face was covered in a veil of blood and grime. His left eye was lacerated shut with a mutilation that was unbelievable. But the Major was as tough as nails. Ignoring his battalion commander and livid with fury, Colonel Vortex spotted Captain Jasper cowering under the merciless PAVN mortar fire. The *horseshoe* artillery emplacement of the Communists had also begun to pound all the hill outposts including the *Rock Quarry* and FOB3. The Marines there had also suffered casualties.

"You bastard! You abandoned your position!" screeched Vortex as he pounced on the flabbergasted Captain Jasper. Vortex was speechless with rage. Instead he rained punches into the Captain's guts and chest. His blows were so vicious that Master Sergeant Richter thought that Jasper's heart muscle might be stopped by the power of the trauma inflicted.

Richter and Crighton had to physically tear their Colonel away from the junior officer. Mercifully, as the Captain staggered backwards, a mortar fragment cut open his spine at the thoracic level. He collapsed into the mud of the trenches and was carried away my medics.

Colonel Vortex regained his composure and was soon giving instructions to Colonel Lownds who was still hunkered down in the DASC at *Khe Sanh*. Captain Mirza Baig had already called in a series of TAC(A) air strikes, including the A-6 Intruder aircraft that used the RABFAC-offset-bombing beacon, as well as F-4E *Phantoms* and THUDS from the hot pad at *Da Nang* that had been scrambled immediately after Hill 861/861A were hit.

The whole *Khe Sanh* base was a hive of activity and the concertina wire perimeter was manned by every last Marine who did not have some specific function to perform in the communication and fire control bunkers. Even now, C-130 Hercules transports and Fairchild C-123 Providers were flying in supplies in the hazy pre-dawn light. Their wheels thudded on the aluminium and steel reinforced planking of the 1,190 metre *Khe Sanh* airstrip that the Seabee battalion had constructed so efficiently.

Just then Vortex looked upwards and heard the familiar droning noise of a heavily laden AC-47 SPOOKY gunship. A murmur of approval arose from the battle weary Marines on Hill 861/861A as almost immediately the six 7.62mm *Miniguns* of the AC-47 belched forth an avalanche of unbelievable firepower upon the heads of the PAVN. The SPOOKY hit the northern half of the hill outpost. 18,000 rounds per minute pulverised the exposed PAVN regulars. Dozens of Communists were cut to pieces by the shower of hot steel.

But Colonel Vortex knew that this would only give them a few moments of respite. As much as he hated to admit it. The PAVN were a brutal, vicious and relentless foe. They never seemed to give up no matter how many casualties they suffered at the hands of withering American firepower.

The US War Machine was a Juggernaut but it had been caught in a quicksand of ruthless North Vietnamese determination.

Colonel Vortex assisted Major Thrush in applying gauze bandages to his wounded eye.

"Thank you sir! But I am alright now," said Major Thrush as he swivelled an M-55 Quad 0.50 calibre mounted on a 2.5 ton M35A2 truck right at the incoming line of PAVN soldiers. The combined rate of fire of the four M2 machine guns was 2,000 to 2,600 rounds per minute with a 1,825 metre maximum effective range. As Thrush aimed the quad Vortex opened fire like a madman spraying a torrent of bullets into the enemy, swinging right then left and back upwards to the tree line. Vortex's mouth was foaming as white pus escaped and he was oblivious to the trauma to his middle ear at the horrendous cacophony of the weapon as it spewed its death all around.

Vortex was loving every second of it. He believed himself to be invincible.

He knew that God was on *his* side.

"Jesus sir!" screamed Sergeant Major Crighton.

"The AC-47 SPOOKY killed hundreds of the gook bastards but they are still coming!"

As Major Thrush continued to bleed profusely he worked the 0.50 calibre over the direction of the Communists with the determination of a crazed loon as Vortex fired till his hands were bleeding. Bullets sprayed out of the four breaches of that weapon like a veritable shower of death.

Colonel Vortex was immensely proud of Major Thrush and had already made up his mind to recommend the officer for the Distinguished Service Cross.

Vortex said as he cupped his ears due to the ferocity of the heavy fire, "I am going to organise a counter-attack to retake this Hill!"

"How sir?" asked Master Sergeant Richter.

Vortex explained, "By putting together a MIC Force at *Khe Sanh* made up of what is left of my 1st Battalion!"

Then Vortex screamed at Major Thrush, "I wish that Lieutenant General Cushman would have allowed me to bring up the rest of my 9th Regiment and the 3rd Battalion, all of the *'Walking Dead.'"*

The Major nodded his agreement as he frantically loaded fresh belts of ammunition into the quad 0.50 M-55.

The PAVN had reached the apex of Hill 861 and were now cascading down to the last trench positions held by K Company on the reverse slope.

The few hundred Marines fired straight into the oncoming tide of bodies of Giap's soldiers. Blood erupted like geysers, bits of human tissue and severed organs splashed before them in the eerie pre-dawn light.

"Here they come! Brace yourselves!" ordered Colonel Vortex.

A full line abreast of nearly 600 PAVN regulars leaped into the American trench lines. Man tore and hacked at his fellow man with gruesome and hellish savagery.

Vortex caught one NVA who tried to crawl into the trench with them and stove in his skull with the butt of his M16.

Master Sergeant Richter did not wait for the gooks to come to him. He went after them.

Leaping out of the trench like an Olympic athlete at the *1936 Berlin Olympics* he swung his M60 machine gun around in wide arcs, hosing down the PAVN in a bloodbath of destruction.

Sergeant Major Crighton directed dozens of other Marines in the trench to let off the claymore mines that had already been put in place. The ordnance went off like a series of thunder-strikes. The Communists were blown into the air behind the tip of their advance.

A reinforced sapper company of PAVN troops then pierced the eastern end of the Marine positions and rushed up the trench lines like a torrent of free flowing lava.

Vortex and his men fought tooth and nail to drive them back. The Colonel was gripped around the throat by a large pimple faced Communist.

"Fuck you imperialist dog!" screamed the NVA soldier.

Vortex swivelled his arms in-between the limbs of the enemy and crushed his open fists against the man's skull. Turning 90 degrees Vortex head butted the attacker and drove his dagger deliciously into the man's spleen and lungs. Blood vomited sweetly into the Colonel's face as Richter stepped up from behind and cut open the Communist's throat.

At that second another NVA appeared behind Richter. Only Vortex could see that his Master Sergeant was about to receive a frontal lobotomy.

Whipping out his Colt 0.45 handgun, Vortex calmly took aim and blew away about 3 inches from the top of the man's skull. Turning around Richter could see the

exposed cerebellum and brain stem of the man as it quivered free in the air like blood soaked jelly.

"Thank you sir! I appreciate it!"

Vortex nodded as he flung grenades into more enemy troops as they ran parallel to the trenches.

Just then another deep throated roar could be heard from the sky.

"What is the time?" asked Vortex.

"Its 0400 hours sir!" answered Sergeant Major Crighton.

The sturdy NCO had strangled two gooks with some piano wire as they attempted to bayonet him. He then cut open their intestines which slithered in a slimy organic mess upon the trench floor. Grinning at his commander, Colonel Vortex told the Sergeant Major to look to the east.

The orange-red glow of the sun's rays were permeating through the fog that surrounded *Khe Sanh*. The sun's disk had yet to break the horizon.

But what did break it was a flight of 7 A-6 *Grumman Intruder's* each carrying thirty 500lb bombs.

These aircraft were from the 308th Tactical Fighter Squadron based at *Nha Trang*.

"Where do you want the surprise package?"

The question came from the flight leader as it was transmitted through the VHF secondary frequency from TAC(A) to Vortex.

Vortex picked up the handset of the AN/PRC-41 field phone, "Right on top of this fucking hill!"

The Colonel then carefully read out the exact latitude and longitude of 861/861A. He then called Captain Dabney on 881S to warn him of the impending air strike.

As the Grumman A-6's lazily swung around in a wide arc to line up for the attack run, Colonel Vortex got Colonel David E. Lownds on the horn.

"I want you to prepare a MIC Force of 2 companies. I want them heli-lifted by a SUPERGAGGLE formation of AH-1 *Cobra's*, CH-47 Chinooks and TAC Air Support with F-105 THUDS from *Da Nang*!"

Colonel Lownds had already proceeded halfway with the request for counter-attack preparations.

Colonel Lownds answered, "The THUDS are already en route to your position. They are crossing over from the coast at Mach 1.3. The 2 companies are on the *Khe Sanh* ready pad near the *Ponderosa* and are being loaded onto the transport helicopters. The *Cobras* won't be far behind."

Vortex was pleased as he asked, "Anything cooking over at the *Khe Sanh Village* itself?'

Lownds replied, "Nothing yet Vortex. But I sent a company sized patrol of the ARVN 37th Rangers to check it out."

Colonel Vortex looked skyward as the A-6's made their bomb run.

"I want the SUPERGAGGLE over here by 0445 hours. Copy?"

Lownds answered confidently, "Copy that."

The beautiful sight of 7 by 30 *flechette* cluster bombs gliding through the air gave a warm feeling of security to Colonel Vortex.

"Incoming! Incoming!" screamed Master Sergeant Richter.

The senior NCO had kicked several mutilated NVA bodies back out of the trench. The 600 surviving Marines on Hill 861/861A plastered themselves onto the slimy floor of their trenches. The PAVN were already ransacking the HQ bunker of K Company at the apex when the *flechette* munitions struck. Their affect on human tissue is indescribable.

Vortex watched as the detonation points ripped huge chunks of earth out of the side of the hill. PAVN bodies were literally sheared apart in layers of shredded flesh and intestines. Shrieks and screams mingled with the high explosive eruptions. The smell of cordite mixed with burning sulphur added to the olfactory overload experienced by the defenders of 861/861A. The A-6's peeled off and then swung back to work over the entire northern side of 861 with 20mm cannon.

Even the 3 *Sikorsky* gunships from *Khe Sanh* joined in with their 7.62mm *Miniguns*.

This assault broke the back of the initial PAVN onslaught. However hundreds of Communists were still dug in deep on the crown of the hill. To make matters worse, the 130mm heavy artillery from the PAVN held *horseshoe* erupted afresh. The shells were landing directly on Hill 881 South and Hill 558 as well as the *Khe Sanh* combat base.

Vortex knew that when the MIC Force arrived, he would have to lead his men on a bloody retaking of lost ground. There would be many more casualties before the day was out.

As the concussion waves of the *flechette* cluster bombs spread out and dissipated, Major Thrush organised several 106mm recoilless rifles. He had them pointing up to 861 to the K Company HQ which he proceeded to pound mercilessly.

At 0443 precisely, the MIC Force arrived and the CH-47 Chinooks deposited the fresh troops behind them. The landing insertion was supported by yet further airstrikes from the SUPERGAGGLE mission.

The F-4E *Phantom II's* and the THUDS appeared from the east and hammered not only 861 but the lower slopes of enemy held 881 South as well.

The AH-1 *Cobra's* hovered behind until the TAC air strikes were completed. They would then sweep up the face of Hill 861/861A and proceed to lay down a murderous suppressive fire while rotating around the PAVN in a wagon wheel formation.

"Major Thrush! I want you to take charge of the MIC Force!" yelled Colonel Vortex.

"Yes sir!" answered the Major.

The Chinooks had just finished unloading the last of the 500 man MIC Force when a Communist RPG-7 rocket launcher streaked out from the hill facing them.

The rear of the two rotor blades on the lead CH-47 disintegrated in a shower of broken steel. The flying fragments cut into several Marines who shrieked horribly as the jagged metal ripped open their flesh in an orgy of blood.

The Chinook seemed to hover there about 20 feet off the ground as it slowly came apart at the seams.

Major Thrush was screaming at the MIC Force. The 500 reinforcements charged up Hill 861 as the AH-1 *Cobra's* continued their suppressive fire ahead of them.

Colonel Vortex and his NCOs' brought up the original force comprising K Company and his own C and D Companies.

It was an excruciating ascent to the apex.

The PAVN fought like possessed demons. They clung onto every inch of ground fanatically.

Colonel Vortex was impressed by the enemies' sheer gut-wrenching determination.

The Chinook finally slumped backwards onto the earth as if it was doing the fandango. The fuselage cracked and burst into an awesome fireball as three more RPG's plunged into it. The whole crew was incinerated into a charred abomination of flesh and steel.

Master Sergeant Richter led 250 Marines up the north-west side of 861 while Colonel Vortex and Sergeant Major Crighton took charge of 350 men moving up the north-east face and the intersection of 861 and 861A slightly to the north-east.

Major Thrush had already reached the crown of the hill where a tremendous battle was taking place between the PAVN and the MIC Force.

With an M16 rifle in one hand and a machete in the other, Vortex was shooting and slashing at anything that moved. The Colonel cut to pieces wounded NVA men who were bleeding and contorting in agony on the bleak earth of that unforgiving hill.

Sergeant Major Crighton ordered the men to bayonet every Communist whether they appeared dead or alive.

The PAVN were well known for throwing grenades in the rear of advancing US troops even when they were mortally wounded or booby trapping the bodies of their dead.

"Watch out sir!" yelled a 2nd Lieutenant who was firing an M60 behind Colonel Vortex.

One North Vietnamese soldier had jumped to his feet just as Vortex had walked past. The Communist was about to drive his AK-47 bayonet into the Colonel's spine.

Vortex swung around and expertly head butted the NVA trooper. Dropping his M16 that was out of ammunition, Vortex placed his whole hand inside the Communist's mouth and tore downwards ripping the muscles of the throat and larynx open in a gruesome display of savagery.

The Colonel simultaneously plunged his Marine dagger into the testicles of the Communist. As he ripped upwards he could hear the tissues splitting all the way up to the pelvis. The left and right scrotal sacs had been viced apart in a bloody interlineation.

"He's mine sir!" said Sergeant Major Crighton.

The NCO came over and cracked open the man's skull with a trench spade spilling blood and brains over the Colonel's camouflage tunic and even a few drops of blood landed on one of his colonel's *eagles*.

Vortex gave the treacherous NVA a savage elbow strike to the heart which caused the body to summersault backwards.

Crighton punched the dead body to the earth and stepped all over the mutilated face as the advance up the hill continued.

Major Thrush stormed the K Company HQ bunker at the top of 861. He led 100 Marines of the MIC Force into the foxhole complex that was interconnected with the six foot deep trenches. The F-4's and F-105's continued to pound the jungle below the hill with napalm and folding-fin rockets. This prevented any further reinforcements reaching the embattled PAVN who were dug in on 861 itself.

"Advance! Follow me!" shouted Major Thrush to his troops.

Vortex's number 2 man leapt into the main bunker. Inside were 37 PAVN soldiers from the *325thC Golden Star Division*.

A PAVN Lieutenant Colonel and two of his Captains were trying to call their Communist comrades over the Marine radio set. Major Thrush realised at once that they were trying to call in reinforcements.

"No you don't!" screamed the Major.

The PAVN officers were so surprised that the Marines had already stormed their positions that they were caught off balance. Major Thrush drove his machete clean through the throat of the PAVN Lieutenant Colonel, severing the trachea like a chicken at a slaughter house.

Blood streaked out rhythmically with each heart pulse.

Another Marine shot the Captains at point blank range. A collage of their intestines was splattered across the sandbagged walls of the bunker.

"Trying to call your rat-fuck Communist bastards? Were you?" shouted Major Thrush with animal fury. His eyes were bloodshot with rage.

He gripped the head of the Communist Lieutenant Colonel and drove it into a steel spike that jutted out of the bunker wall. The tip of the spike pierced his left eye-

ball and entered the brain. The officer died suffocating on his own blood. The remaining Communists in the bunker were torn to pieces by the MIC Force as they used daggers and machetes in a macabre orgy of mutilation as well as their side-arms.

Captain Jasper redeemed himself by blowing the brains out of three Communists who tried to scamper out of the HQ bunker by climbing through the demolished roof.

The MIC Force were finally gaining the upper hand as the PAVN were driven off the apex of Hill 861. As they retreated the TAC air and AH-1 *Cobras* pounded them all the way down the northern slope and into the valley beyond with Hill 561 directly north of the battle about 1 mile away.

By the time Colonel Vortex arrived with the rest of the Marines the battle was raging back at the jungle perimeter at the base of the hill.

"Sir!" called out Sergeant Major Crighton as he held the field phone in front of him.

"Its Lieutenant General Cushman from III MAF!"

Surprised, Vortex gave orders for the continued advance and then fell to his knees, quite exhausted with the morning's exertions, to speak to the General in the retaken trench lines.

"I have heard from Colonel Lownds that it has started," said General Cushman.

"That's right sir. The PAVN managed to overrun part of Hill 861 but we drove them back with the assistance of a SUPERGAGGLE and several TAC air strikes," answered Colonel Vortex as Communist mortar rounds were still falling all over 861 and 881 South nearby to the west.

"Have they attacked the *Khe Sanh* base proper?" asked General Cushman.

"Not yet sir. But we expect that attack at any moment," answered Vortex.

As he spoke to the commanding General of the III MAF, the flight of 6 *Phantoms* and 4 F-105 THUDS came streaking over the hill outpost.

The time was now 0515 hours.

Colonel Vortex could smell the AVGAS from the 10 jet engines and could see the afterburners flaming a hellish trail of fire that ignited the cool dawn air.

The lead F-4E *Phantom* dipped its wings in a signal that it was returning to *Da Nang*, all its munitions having been expended.

General Cushman continued, "I want reports from you Colonel at least every 12 hours."

"Understood sir," replied Vortex and then he asked, "How do you think you are going to handle this new MACV Forward setup with General Abrams in command. It will be a gross interference with Marine Corps control over III MAF."

General Cushman grunted with Vortex's comments when something happened that knocked the handset of the field phone out of Vortex's sturdy grip.

A wounded NVA Lieutenant had been lying in the mud face down behind Vortex. He had been knocked unconscious by the air strikes and was covered in bloody fragmentation wounds.

Suddenly, the Communist had regained consciousness and seeing the high ranking American kneeling in front of him had decided to strangle the enemy officer.

Vortex was gripped around the throat by the maniacal Lieutenant who punched the Colonel with savage power in his liver and kidneys.

"What the hell is going on Vortex?" asked the impatient voice of General Cushman through the handset.

Only grunts and screams answered the commander.

Vortex reached backwards as he was being strangled and managed to grip the ears of the NVA attacker with each hand. He ripped the left one clean off and then head butted the Communist by slamming his skull backwards into the man's nose. The Communist screamed obscenities at Colonel Vortex as the latter swivelled on his knees and proceeded to throttle the enemy for a change.

"Colonel Vortex! Are you there? Did you hang up on me or what?"

screamed General Cushman through the handset that was lying in the mud.

"Sir! Are you having trouble?"

It was the voice of Sergeant Major Leonard Crighton. He had about 50 Marines with him. They had just come running up from the base of Hill 861.

"Glad you could make it Sergeant Major," said Vortex as he wrestled with the PAVN officer.

"Anything that you would like me to do?" asked the Sergeant Major cheekily.

Vortex tore at the enemy's throat with his teeth, drawing blood.

The Colonel answered as he tried to reach the field phone.

"Could you smash this bastard's skull in for me so that I can continue my conversation with Lieutenant General Cushman?"

Sergeant Major Crighton chuckled, "Happy to sir!"

The NCO jumped into the trench with more than twenty other Marines. In an elegant movement Sergeant Major Leonard Crighton swung his trench spade and collected the skull of the PAVN officer. Blood and brain matter splashed out in all directions as the man was decapitated. The headless torso quivered spasmodically in the mud. But the Marines were not taking any chances.

One Corporal and a Warrant Officer stepped up and bayoneted the twitching headless corpse fifteen times in the stomach and groin.

"Thanks!" grinned Colonel Vortex as he staggered to his feet. They all laughed heartily. It was a rare moment of joviality in an otherwise taxing morning of endeavours.

Picking up the handset he said, "Sorry General! Just had to take care of a minor disturbance."

General Cushman told Vortex to make full use of the 1st Marine Air Wing. He informed the Colonel that he had ordered Major General Norman J. Anderson to give *Khe Sanh* first priority in every mission request as part of Operation NIAGARA.

"I'm going back to *Khe Sanh* now sir," informed Vortex, "…just in case the PAVN and their Viet Cong puppets launch their full scale attack."

"Good!" was all that General Cushman said.

Two AH-1 *Cobra* gunships landed on 861 and Colonel Vortex, Sergeant Major Crighton and Master Sergeant Richter jumped onboard. Several minutes later they were back in the DASC (Direct Air Support Centre) at *Khe Sanh*. It was just south of the Airfield Control Tower next to the runway and the helicopter parking area.

Colonel David E. Lownds and Captain Mirza Baig were speaking to Major General Rathvon C. Tompkins who was currently at Camp Carroll about 15 miles to the east along National Route 9 (QL9).

"What's cooking?" asked Vortex as he sauntered into the room. His camouflage uniform was hanging in shreds from his body covered in blood, mud and bits of the unimaginable. Vortex's orderly, a Sergeant by the name of Urlich ran for a new uniform and a new pair of combat boots so that the Colonel could freshen up. The smart and highly organised Captain Baig replied, "Just fine tuning the 175mm M107 fire from *Camp Carroll*, sir."

"That's good," answered Vortex.

"Did you suffer heavy casualties on Hill 861/861A?" asked Colonel David E. Lownds as he sipped on a cup of tea while pouring over several fire control maps.

"We did. I don't know yet exactly how many. But we've retaken most of the hill. The PAVN are back at the base of the outpost licking their wounds and I have put Major Thrush in command for the moment."

Colonel Lownds nodded as a continual stream of Marine NCOs' and officers filed in and out of the DASC bunker. They carried important acoustic, seismic and electronic sensor information which Captain Baig analysed and fed into the fire control computers using the *'Thin Client'* setup with the Mainframe at Pentagon East in Saigon.

This analysis was then used to coordinate Operation Combat SKYSPOT. Hitting the PAVN units as they concentrated for the attack.

"What is the time now?" asked Lownds.

Captain Baig replied, "0530 hours, sir."

Just as the last word escaped the Fire Control Officer's lips a tremendous roar came up from the jungle all around *Khe Sanh*.

"Jesus Christ!" yelled Colonel Vortex.

"Oh! My God!" expostulated Colonel Lownds.

"This is what we feared!" added Master Sergeant Richter as he picked up his 7.62 *Minigun* as if it was a feather pen.

It seemed like the whole earth around the Marine combat base shook and shuddered with the force of an earthquake.

But it was not a force of nature that had been unleashed. It was the beginning of the PAVN artillery and rocket bombardment of the *Khe Sanh* base proper. This signalled the start of General Vo Nguyen Giap's offensive.

The Detonation of Khe Sanh's Ammunition Dump [ASP 1]

Vortex, Lownds and the others streamed out of the DASC bunker to watch the spectacle.

It was awesome.

Almost as soon as they emerged into the morning air, 152mm shells from the PAVN heavy artillery at the *'Co Roc'* pounded into the aluminium and steel planking of the *Khe Sanh* airstrip now maintained by the 301st Seabees whose bunkers were immediately adjacent to the western end of the runway.

The 68th PAVN artillery Regiment obviously knew the range and their objective was to put the airstrip out of action as soon as possible.

This would prevent the resupply of *Khe Sanh* and thus eventually doom its 5,772 Marines, 228 sailors from the 301st Seabee Mobile Construction Battalion and the handful of USAF personnel who operated the Combat SKYSPOT computers that Captain Baig used so efficiently. As well as the 37th ARVN Ranger Battalion.

"Oh! My Jesus! Look at that!" screamed Colonel Lownds.

Vortex and the others watched as streaks of orange flame and tracer fire lit up the early morning sky.

The pyrotechnics supplied more light on that fateful morning than the sun itself.

The PAVN rockets, artillery and mortars came down on the base like an avalanche from every section of the surrounding jungle. The PAVN juggernaut of firepower hit *Khe Sanh* from a full 360 degree ambit.

It was now life in the V-RING, thought Colonel Vortex to himself.

Colonel Vortex ordered the 26th Marine artillery officer to open up with the three batteries of 105mm howitzers for counter-battery fire as well as the 106mm recoilless rifles and the 4.2 inch mortars on every inch of known PAVN positions surrounding the hill outposts. Within minutes the American guns boomed out in response.

The artillery duel at dawn had begun.

Vortex remembered the history of the Wild-West, as he watched, the *'Duel at the OK Corall.'*

But the PAVN bombardment was heavier at this opening salvo of the *Khe Sanh* battle.

"I don't understand where the PAVN obtained so much firepower!" screamed Master Sergeant Richter.

Colonel Vortex replied as he spoke to the Forward Control Officers for the artillery through his AN/PRC-41 field phone, "General Giap has been preparing this attack for months! And you can thank the Russians and the Chinese as well!"

The group of Command Officers started to run towards the FSCC bunker.

Just then a 152mm shell burst directly into a foxhole nearby. Two Marines were vivisected into a shower of blood by the horrendous blast.

Colonel Vortex could only see a torn pair of combat boots flying crazily through the air above them.

Inside one of the boots was the foot and leg portion of the dead Marine. The limb was sheared off and ended just below the knee.

That was all that was left of that soldier.

Colonel Lownds watched with horror as the boot with half its resident leg hit the ground in front of him. It poured with blood from the grisly open stump. The white splinters of bone clearly visible through the miasma of mutilated flesh. Approximately half the total force of Marines from the 26th and the 9th were inside the main *Khe Sanh* base. This amounted to slightly over 2,500 men.

The commanding officer of the *Rock Quarry* and FOB3, Major Lucius J. Campbell, where 1,000 Marines were stationed called Colonel Lownds.

"Sir! We are receiving heavy fire!" It was the voice of a steadfast and reliable officer coming through the field phone. Colonel Lownds answered as the group continued to run across the open ground between the DASC and the FSCC.

"Hold on to your position Major!" screamed Lownds over the deafening roar of the incoming fire.

Colonel Vortex snatched the handset away from Colonel Lownds.

"Listen Major! I want you to warn us of the PAVN's fire preparation from now on! Do you copy that?"

The Major shouted back as Vortex could hear explosions coming through the two-way radio itself. The *Rock Quarry* and the FOB3 was receiving a merciless hammering.

"Roger that sir!"

The 2,500 Marines inside the base ran, ducked, jumped, leaped and scurried into every available foxhole, bunker, dugout and reinforced building at *Khe Sanh*.

It was the beginning of the daily performance of the *'Khe Sanh shuffle.'*

Colonel Vortex let Captain Baig and his retinue of staff officers go inside the FSCC bunker to organise a series of air strikes on the known PAVN positions.

Colonel Lownds and his group remained outside, braving the intense fire.

"Those howitzer crews of the 1st Battalion, 13th Marines are doing a splendid job!" remarked Vortex as he looked over to the 105mm and 155mm gun emplacements.

The Marines there practically ignored the deadly rain of shells as they worked frantically pumping round after round into the heavy guns that boomed back counter-battery fire at the Communist barrage.

Very soon a veritable mountain of spent and smouldering cartridge shells piled up high next to each artillery piece. The smell of cordite and sulphur reeked through the humid atmosphere.

Master Sergeant Richter and Sergeant Major Crighton led the way up the stairs of the *Khe Sanh* control tower adjacent to the airstrip.

From here the officers could survey the entire base.

"Oh! Hell! What timing!" cried Colonel Vortex.

Colonel Lownds was standing next to him peering through his field binoculars. Lieutenant Colonel Tran from the 37th ARVN Rangers was also up there with them, as well as a dozen staff officers from the HQ's of both regiments.

"It looks like that crazy son-of-a-bitch is still going to land!" shouted Colonel Lownds in amazement.

The subject of their consternation was a C-130 Hercules transport plane that was gliding in from the south-east. It had just reached the 800 ft escarpment and was reducing altitude for a textbook landing.

Then a murderous hail of incoming PAVN fire started to shred the aluminium and steel planking of the runway.

Bombs and rockets tore great chunks out of the 301st Seabee Battalion's pride and joy. The airstrip that they had so meticulously crafted over the past weeks and months was being ripped apart.

In the DASC bunker, the air control officers were speaking to the C-130 pilot. They were instructing him to abort the landing and head back for *Da Nang* or *Nha Trang*.

But the pilot said he was committed to a landing and was running out of fuel. He would have to gas up from *Khe Sanh's* TAFDS (Tactical Airfield Fuel Dispensing System).

When Colonel Vortex heard this he looked at Colonel Lownds and screamed, "That crazy son of a gun! He says he has to fuel up! That lunatic is going to be blown away even before he reaches the end of the runway!"

Colonel Lownds shouted back, "Well? What can I do about it?" Vortex clicked his fingers indicating for Master Sergeant Richter and Sergeant Major Leonard Crighton to follow him. They scrambled like scorched cats down the stairs of the control tower. When they were half way down Vortex was vindicated by the heaviest concentration of PAVN fire yet suffered by KSCB. Huge 152mm shells were detonating the airstrip planking. Vortex saw with undiluted horror that the C-130 had just slammed its wheels onto the far end of the airstrip.

The centre section of the runway was at that moment being catapulted into the air.

Huge silvery chunks of aluminium girders, steel sheets and bolts sprayed into the atmosphere.

A hole the size of a ten ton truck was gaping at the C-130 Hercules as the aircraft sped towards it at over 140 mph. The pilot no longer had control over his bladder as he slammed on the foot brakes of the huge airplane and brought up the flaps.

Colonel Vortex and his two NCOs' ran down the edge of the airstrip each carrying a pair of fire extinguishers. It was like trying to prevent a massive oil fire with three cups of water.

However Vortex was determined that the C-130 should not reach the AVGAS storage cylinder near the TAFDS.

Blue smoke that had an unbelievable smell of poignant rubber burned from the enormous maze of wheels under the C-130 Hercules. The brake pads were sizzling up and the tread of the huge wheels came off in strips.

The plane veered to the right as it slowed to 90 mph.

But it was too late.

Vortex screamed, "She's going to tip over!"

Richter and Crighton were almost level with the speeding plane.

They did not know whether to run towards it or run away from the out of control juggernaut.

"Shit!" was all that Colonel Vortex could say.

The left set of wheels caught the huge hole in the airstrip. The fuselage of the Hercules shuddered as the entire undercarriage was ripped away. Huge pieces of metal and individual aircraft wheels catapulted through the sky above their heads.

Colonel Lownds in the control tower becoming catatonic with fury at the sheer stupidity of the USAF pilot. But Colonel Vortex realised that there was not much the pilot could do.

The C-130 Hercules was divested of its portside undercarriage system and the huge plane crashed with its left wing hitting the tarmac. The nose of the aircraft also smashed into the airstrip. More explosions erupted to the left and right of the plane as it skidded directly for the AVGAS cylinders near the TAFDS.

"Oh! My God!" shouted Colonel Vortex.

His worst fears were coming to fruition.

Colonel Lownds and his staff in the control tower watched helplessly as the portside wing of the C-130 sheared off. The rest of the fuselage slammed into the AVGAS cylinder detonating it seconds later. A plume of orange-red fire shot up into the sky. The black clouds from the burning gasoline intermixed with the smoke and debris of the continuing PAVN bombardment.

Colonel Vortex ran to the stricken C-130 and wrenched open one of the side fuselage hatches. He used the manual override on the exterior of the plane. Master Sergeant Richter kicked his way through the burning hulk and grabbed the two pilots in the cockpit.

They were both unconscious after having concussed their skulls against the cockpit Plexiglass.

"Have you got them?" shouted Colonel Vortex.

Sergeant Major Leonard Crighton was hosing down the entrance to the hatch with the fire extinguishers.

The white foam spread out like a huge bubble bath.

"Can you give me a hand sir!" screamed Richter.

Vortex bounded inside and assisted his NCO in dragging the bodies out by the scruff of their necks.

The MATU (Marine Air Traffic Control Unit) medics just managed to stretcher the pilots away before the whole C-130 burst into flames.

The *Khe Sanh* (KSCB) airstrip was now out of action to fixed wing aircraft.

Colonel Lownds scurried up and cried, "Well done Colonel!"

Vortex nodded and surveyed the destruction.

AVGAS, oil, pieces of aluminium planking and steel girders littered the airstrip in a blazing inferno.

As each PAVN mortar round or artillery shell impacted upon the sea of liquid fuel the secondary fires intensified.

One of the HH-53B *Sikorsky's* parked along the edge of the runway received a mortar round on its starboard side.

"Jesus! Take cover!" screamed Vortex.

The gaggle of more than 30 officers and NCOs standing around the MATU bunker dived for cover.

A large chunk of the *Sikorsky's* rotor blade had been blown off by the detonation. It was heading straight for them.

A sea of skulls plastered themselves to the ground as the silvery blade hit a sandbagged wall outside the MATU bunker. The sandbags were severed open like a knife through hot butter. As the rotor blade ricocheted backwards it severed the left arm clean off a Master Sergeant crouching next to Colonel Lownds. The face of the 26th Marine Regiment commander was sprinkled with blood as the NCO let out a horrific scream of agony.

Several other Marines nearby were peppered with hot fragmentation projectiles that tore open their flesh. Marines were falling to the ground everywhere inside *Khe Sanh* due to the PAVN pounding.

"I'm worried about all our UH-1E and UH-1H Huey's parked along the edge of the runway," said Colonel Vortex to Colonel Lownds.

Lownds replied, "And what about the *Sikorsky's* and the AH-1 *Cobras* parked here next to the MATU bunker and the *Ponderosa*?"

A second later Master Sergeant Richter shouted, "Incoming!"

The unmistakable whine of an incoming 152mm shell from the PAVN held *'Co Roc'* position came blasting down upon their heads.

A UH-1H Huey parked at the southern end of the devastated airstrip was lifted into the air skids over rotors. The whole machine then disintegrated before them.

The time was now 0615 hours.

The PAVN barrage was intensifying.

Captain Mirza Baig emerged from the FSCC bunker and gave instructions to the Marine artillery officer, Lieutenant Colonel John A. Hennelly, who was in charge of the 1st Battalion, 13th Marines (Artillery) and the teams of gunners as they frantically fed their heavy artillery counter-battery fire.

KSCB possessed 18 pieces of 105mm artillery and 6 of the heavier 155mm guns from the 1st Provisional 155mm Howitzer battery and the 1st Searchlight Battery Detachment. The other units inside *Khe Sanh* for counter battery fire support were; Section, Battery A, 1st Battalion (Automatic Weapons, Self-Propelled); 44th Artillery, Section, Battery G (0.50 cal Machine Gun) 65th Artillery; Detachment, 238th Artillery Detachment (Counter-mortar Radar); Detachment, 1st Platoon, 25th Chemical Company (Smoke); 544th Signal Detachment (Tactical Communications); Mobile Advisory Team 4 (*Huong Hoa* District); Battalion Advisory Team (37th Ranger Battalion ARVN) and the 834th Air Division Detachment A.

The Seabees from the US Navy scrambled around like frustrated chooks in a chicken coop trying, already, to fix the mangled KSCB airstrip. They were from; Naval Mobile Construction Battalion 5 and 10 and 53 as well as Detachment Bravo, Naval Mobile Construction Battalion Unit 301. They were supported by; Detachment, 5th Communication Battalion; 7th Communication Battalion; Logistics Support Unit, Force Logistics Command; Sub-Team No:1, 17th Interrogator-Translator Team (*a team that Colonel Richard Vortex was particularly found of as it assisted him with his forceful and unconventional interrogation techniques that he liked to carry out personally against the Communist scourge and pestilence (as Vortex saw them)*; and the HQ and Maintenance Squadron, MAG 16 being Detachment 01 designated.

Colonel Richard Vortex and Colonel David E. Lownds stood by as Captain Mirza Baig gave the artillery batteries the exact latitude and longitude of the latest PAVN positions as spotted by the *'Mightiest Corporal in the World'* Corporal Robert J. Arrotta of the 1/3/26 Marines who was itching with enthusiasm up on Hill 881 South spotting

the infernal Communists (*as he considered them*) with his Navy 20 Power binoculars with the assistance of *'Pineapple Chunk'* a Lance Corporal of American-Samoan extraction by the name of Molimao Niuatoa. He was known by this nickname because of his diminutive size which was made up for by boundless Communist-despising enthusiasm. The muzzle flashes were spotted by these two *heroes* on Hill 350 and continuous corrections and coordinates were then radioed in to Captain Mirza Baig.

In addition the coordinates were amplified, confirmed and enhanced by the information provided from the multitude of seismic, acoustic and chemical sensors placed by the USAF in the triple canopy jungle around *Lam Son* and the *'Co Roc'* as well as all the way up and down the stinking *Ho Chi Minh Trail* that was such a bloody pain-in-the-ass to the MACV (*in the opinion of Colonels Lownds and Vortex*).

Captain Baig had fed the data through the Marine computers at the base and at the Infiltration Surveillance Centre in *Nakhon Phanom* in Thailand.

The computers had then worked out a mathematical probability analysis of the likeliest PAVN/VC ground dispositions.

As the *Khe Sanh* howitzers adjusted their field of fire, Captain Baig called up the US base at Camp Carroll using the VHF (Very High Frequency) wavelengths.

The battery of 175mm howitzers at Camp Carroll thus also thundered to the latest intelligence.

"It's happening!" cried Colonel Richard Vortex as a tremendous and jaw breaking explosion erupted all over the base at KSCB.

Khe Sanh, at that moment, felt as if it was undergoing a *'subterranean revolution'*.

The first of the PAVN 152mm shells and mortar bombs had hit the *Khe Sanh* ammunition dump.

The Marine ammunition storage facility was colossal. It was stacked in steel containers, in barrels and boxes to a height of 45 feet at the southern end of the airstrip. More than 2,000 tons of ordnance was stored there.

It was like a small Atomic Bomb ready to be ignited by the slightest spark.

The PAVN provided that spark much to their discredit.

Colonel Vortex sighed with defeat, "Oh! No! *Scheisse!*"

Colonel Lownds put his hands to his head in a gesture of hopelessness.

"Take cover! Take cover! The ammunition dump is going to blow!" screamed Vortex as Master Sergeant Richter made to run towards the huge stockpile of ammunition and artillery shells.

Colonel Vortex grabbed him by the arm and yanked him back, saying, "What the infernal ass-fuck are you thinking Sergeant?"

Then he added, "There is nothing you can do!"

"But sir!" admonished the Master Sergeant.

Colonel Vortex watched with awe as he screamed, pushing the NCO back with the others, "Its finished!"

The initial 152mm shell did not have that much of an affect. Some of the petrol barrels blew in the air and burst into flames. They fell heavily onto the ground in front of the huge ammunition mountain.

But the main stockpile was still intact.

"Its not so bad sir!" screamed Sergeant Major Crighton and Master Sergeant Richter in unison.

The oil and petrol washed along the dirty ground on the portside of the *Khe Sanh* airstrip. Ominously the flames of that first blast licked teasingly at the ammunition dump.

Then a second and a third PAVN heavy artillery shell arrived. As the Communist bombs exploded into the sea of petrol the first of the ammunition containers was affected.

A large wooden box containing 4.2 inch mortar shells exploded as the burning petrol washed over it.

This box was at the base of the ammunition mountain. The 4.2 inch shells detonated with a thump. As the ordnance fell onto the ammo dump from above it ignited several thousand rounds of 7.62mm bullets for the M16 and M60 rifles and machine guns.

This was the beginning of the chain reaction.

The standard M16 bullets whizzed past in every direction.

"Jesus Christ!" yelled Colonel Lownds.

Captain Mirza Baig grabbed Colonel Vortex and pulled him to the mud as a wall of ammunition streaked towards them. There were not dozens of bullets, not hundreds but literally thousands and thousands of rounds that went off in an uncontrolled maelstrom of undirected firepower.

A Corporal in the 26th Marine signal company who was standing behind Sergeant Major Crighton received a 7.62mm bullet directly into his midbrain.

The man died instantly as blood trickled down his nose and into his gaping mouth.

Vortex, Lownds and the whole entourage leapt into a foxhole next to the MATU bunker complex. Some Marines ran out of the MATU bunker but Colonel Lownds screamed at them to get back inside.

Miraculously the 105mm and 155mm howitzer crews kept working continuously despite the coming inferno.

Colonel Vortex who watched them with pride was determined to award each man a *Bronze Star* at least.

Now the PAVN were using 130mm shells from the *'Horseshoe'* position near Hill 861/861A. These bombs together with the already exploding 7.62mm rounds ignited the main body of the ammunition dump.

The first to blow was the heavy 155mm artillery shells. Several hundred shells weighing in excess of 300 tons exploded like a mini atomic blast.

The concussion wave spread outwards from the airstrip and blew the wooden and corrugated iron *Khe Sanh Post Office* to smithereens.

Vortex watched in horror as three young Marine privates were catapulted off their feet and thrown 20 yards through the air.

All of them fell heavily into a sandbagged wall, breaking bones and lacerating their flesh into a bloody mess.

As the huge mountain of ordnance started to come apart even the flight activity was affected.

Three AH-1 *Cobras* were coming in from the south-west. They had just returned from a fire support mission at Hill 558. When the shells rocketed into the air in front of them the pilots peeled off to the west to escape the destruction. Flying debris and columns of flame narrowly missed the rotors of the choppers.

Blast after blast boomed out across the *Khe Sanh* plateau. The noise and the blast waves were so intense that the seemingly endless reverberations bounced off the hills surrounding the KSCB base.

"There is nothing we can do Colonel Vortex," said Colonel Lownds with utter resignation.

More ordnance containers ricocheted into the air like thunderballs of mayhem.

Men were scrambling for cover all over the plateau as the shells, rockets, mortars and grenades from their own dump rained down on them like the coming of Armageddon.

This was the *'Khe Sanh Shuffle'* par excellence.

Vortex watched, his face in the mud, as a Marine 2nd Lieutenant from Lownds' regiment was hit as he was running from the PX to the FSCC bunker. The man was lifted into the air and then his whole body seemed to come apart in a shower of blood and splintered bone. When the sulphur and cordite lifted, Vortex could see nothing left of the officer except for a puddle of blood and mashed flesh.

"Its coming apart!" screamed Colonel Lownds as he was talking to the aircrews on the other side of the *Khe Sanh* airstrip.

Vortex saw the structure of the ammunition dump disintegrate as the central mass of artillery shells and grenades blew 500 feet into the air.

More than a thousand tons of ordnance lifted majestically into the humid atmosphere.

Grown men were screaming like children and crying.

Three UH-1E helicopters were blown onto their sides as the blast wave hit them at the speed of sound. A sonic boom shattered the ear drums of the *Khe Sanh* Marines.

But they hung on valiantly.

Never before had American military valour and bravery shone so brilliantly as the eternal stars in heaven as it did at *Khe Sanh* on that miserable January day in 1968.

Colonel Vortex watched as an avalanche from the sky came crashing down onto the PX building.

"Shit! Sir!" said Sergeant Major Crighton.

Major Thrush who was looking through his *Zeiss* field binoculars on the apex of Hill 861 saw the catastrophe. He was frantically trying to reach either of the Colonel's.

But they were too busy dodging the rain of death.

Just as the last words left Sergeant Major Crighton's mouth the *Khe Sanh* ammunition hit the PX.

Fortunately for the Marines, the Laws of Physics were working on their side.

Most of the falling US ammunition did not explode upon impact with the *Khe Sanh* earth, foxholes and bunkers.

The reason was that the safety devices in the projectiles needed the enormous G forces of acceleration in the tube of a mortar or the barrel of a gun to prime and ignite the fuses.

The PX building crumpled and disintegrated in a cloud of smoke.

"There are men inside there!" shouted Vortex to Colonel Lownds.

The 9th Marine commander rushed up from his foxhole and ran to the pile of rubble that seconds before had been the PX building.

"No! Vortex! Stop!" yelled Colonel Lownds.

But Vortex ignored him and plunged into the annihilated mess of broken wood and smouldering debris.

Sergeant Major Crighton and Master Sergeant Richter were close behind.

In a miraculous display of heroism the three Marines pulled five of their wounded comrades out of the tangled ruins.

Colonel Lownds made a mental note that he would personally recommend his fellow Colonel and Regimental commander for the *Distinguished Service Cross* and *Medal of Honour*. He would later also slate both Richter and Crighton for *Silver Stars*.

Colonel Vortex shouted, "Over here! Medics! Medics!"

A medical team from the MATU bunker braved the fire and pulled the wounded men underground.

A few moments later the tear gas canisters that had been sitting to the right of the ammunition dump exploded with a thrump. Clouds of tear gas bellowed across the *Khe Sanh* plateau.

Colonel Vortex took a squad of men from a nearby foxhole and began to run around the artillery positions handing out gas masks and facial respirators to the heroic artillery crews.

Nothing would stop *Khe Sanh's* heavy artillery.

Those men who had already succumbed to the choking tear gas were carried into the main MEDEVAC bunker close to the FSCC. Suddenly, high above the continuing explosions that rippled across the terra firma of *Khe Sanh* came one of the largest TAC air sorties so far.

Using the RABFAC-offset-bombing beacon and the *Khe Sanh* computers that guided *'Operation Combat Skyspot'* the American airpower descended onto the PAVN positions like the *Hammer of Thor*.

Most of the aircraft were from Task Force 77 off the Gulf of Tonkin and from the 308th Tactical Fighter Squadron based at *Nha Trang*.

No less than fifteen F-4E *Phantoms* from the US 7th Fleet and eighteen A-6 Grumman Intruders from *Nha Trang* struck the PAVN held *'Horseshoe.'*

This awesome display was provided courtesy of Captain Mirza Baig.

The jets screamed almost as loud as the explosions as they swooped in line abreast. They carried a lethal cocktail of cluster bombs, napalm, high explosive 500lb incendiary bombs and heavy duty 1,000lb demolition bombs.

The A-6's also carried the full complement of 'NAILS.'

A rain of ordnance crushed onto the 130mm PAVN guns.

Bodies were erupted into showers of blood.

Whole Communist platoon and company sized headquarters were wiped out where they stood.

Many of the attacking PAVN guns were put out of action.

However, the jets could not strike the *'Co Roc'* position just across the border in Laos where most of the Communist fire was coming from. These 152mm guns were spared because President Johnson would not allow the use of American firepower over Laotian territory.

So the pounding of *Khe Sanh* continued. It continued all morning and all the rest of that day and into the night.

It was truly the fire and brimstone unleashed by the forces of hell, thought Colonel Vortex as he staggered into the COMMO bunker. His camouflage uniform was torn and shredded. But his body and mind were resilient.

He was thirsting for Communist blood.

Awaiting the moment of brutal and swift revenge against General Vo Nguyen Giap and his coterie of criminals and stooges.

Both Colonel's and their whole regimental staffs, including the USAF personnel who interpreted the incoming sensor information, convened a meeting at 1535 hours

in the FSCC bunker. By the afternoon the PAVN fire had settled down to a punishing barrage of approximately 100 rounds per hour.

That day at *Khe Sanh*, D Day for the stalwart Americans and the gallant ARVN, more than 1,000 Communist artillery and mortar shells would rocket the base.

Colonel Vortex spoke to the Marine commander at Hill 558.

"What is the position there?"

The tough sounding Major from the 26th Regiment answered, "We are holding firm sir. I sent out two 100 man patrols this morning. We ran into heavy PAVN fire. The gooks ambushed both of my patrols but with the help of AH-1 *Cobra* gunships and fire support from Camp Carroll I managed to exfiltrate my men. And the whole perimeter of Hill 558 is uncompromised sir!"

Colonel Lownds asked his officer, "What are your casualties Major?"

"We lost 7 KIA (killed in action) and 19 WIA's (wounded in action) sir!"

Vortex shook his head, "We can't afford to continuously sustain casualties like that!"

He was speaking to Colonel Lownds and Captain Baig.

Both men nodded sullenly as Vortex signed off with the words, "I expect you Major! To hold on to Hill 558 at all costs! There will be no retreat! No surrender!"

The Major barked back angrily, "Sir! I would rather die a thousand deaths by a thousand cuts each in medieval fashion before surrendering my position to the root-fucking gooks!"

"Good man!" exclaimed Vortex.

Captain Baig looked to Colonel Lownds and then Vortex. His face was stressed with concern.

"We have two major problems, sirs!"

Vortex gave a deathly grin.

"Yes! Our first major problem is the *Khe Sanh* airstrip. It must be repaired at all costs and ASAP! The second problem is our ammunition dump. It has been annihilated in a grotesque pyrotechnic display. We need replacement artillery shells, 81mm mortar bombs, 7.62mm rounds and everything else!"

Colonel Lownds agreed and called for the commander of the Seabees to present himself.

The Navy Captain in charge of the 228 men of the Mobile Construction battalion appeared.

He was tall and powerfully built with sparkling blue eyes.

Vortex said, "I want you Captain, to start work on repairing the *Khe Sanh* airstrip immediately! And I mean right now!"

The Seabee Captain was thunderstruck.

"But sir? The Communist shells are still falling all around us!"

Vortex pounded his fist down on the map table.

"I know that! And I don't give a flying fuck! You will start work right now!"

The Captain nodded grumpily. Then he made another excuse.

"We will have to cease work at 1800 hours. The repair of the aluminium planking and the tarmac cannot proceed in darkness after sunset. Sir."

Colonel Lownds rolled his eyes up into his sockets and wished that he could have had a Marine Construction unit at *Khe Sanh*.

Colonel Vortex was beside himself with fury.

"Listen to me! You will work 24 hours a day and 7 days a week until *Khe Sanh's* airstrip is operational again!"

Then Vortex turned to Lieutenant Colonel Tran of the 37th ARVN Rangers.

"You Colonel! Will get your Rangers to set up large flood lights all around the airstrip perimeter."

Then turning to the Seabee Captain, "This will allow your Seabees to work around the clock! Dismissed!"

The Seabee commander and Lieutenant Colonel Tran looked to each other, saluted and bolted out of the bunker to carry out their orders.

Colonel Vortex sighed and put his hands on his hips.

Master Sergeant Richter could see that his leader was almost fainting with exhaustion. But Sergeant Major Leonard Crighton who had brought up a fresh and starched uniform for his beloved commander, knew that Colonel Vortex was kept standing by the force of his indomitable will alone. His desire to utterly destroy, smash and kill the PAVN even though they were out to destroy him gave him a nuclear reserve of inner strength.

It mattered little to Vortex that his 6,000 Marines were surrounded by up to 45,000 PAVN soldiers. In fact it only increased his vicious will to resist.

Colonel Vortex's only concern as an officer was the safety and security of his troops. Sergeant Major Crighton had seen Colonel Vortex put his life on the cutting edge many times so that his men might have a better chance of surviving.

This was the true test of a sterling field officer.

Master Sergeant Richter looked up at his Colonel and smiled with pride and honour. Everything about Colonel Richard Vortex was exemplary.

This Colonel, he thought, epitomised the bravery and integrity of the glorious United States Military tradition par excellence.

"Give me a VHF frequency to *Da Nang*. I want to get General Burl McLaughlin on the horn!" screamed Vortex as he sipped on a glass of icy water.

Master Sergeant Richter then handed Vortex 12 aspirins with 30mg of Codeine in each one which he took in with one gulp.

Vortex loved the soothing effect of the Codeine coursing through his overheated veins and arteries. He swallowed all 360mg of Codeine in a single swipe. An ordinary man would have keeled over. But not Vortex, it just took the 'edge' off the Colonel of death to bring his maniacal fanaticism back to life.

Brigadier General Burl McLaughlin was the United States Air Force officer in charge of aerial supply for *Khe Sanh*. Technically though, he was now under the command of General Momyer, the commanding General of the US 7th Air Force with its HQ at *Pentagon East*.

"Is that you Vortex?" asked the one star General.

His voice sounded professional but it had a hint of alarm in it. He obviously knew that it had started at *Khe Sanh* in a big way.

Before Vortex could open his mouth into the handset, tremendous explosions erupted above the reinforced ceiling of the FSCC bunker.

In the next few seconds a large slab of steel girding and piles of sandbags came crashing down onto the skulls of both Colonel Lownds and Vortex.

Both men were smothered to the ground. They were also concussed by the heavy blow to their heads.

"Jesus wept! Are you alright sir?" asked Master Sergeant Richter as he and a dozen other NCOs' and officers helped the two Colonel's to their feet.

Vortex laughed and slapped Colonel Lownds on the back.

"That was a close one wasn't it Lownds?"

However, Lownds could not see the humour in it as he brushed himself off of the crap that was all over his immaculate uniform.

Saying simply, "I'm too fucking old for this shit! I should be back in Washington in a desk job with a Brigadier's star on my collar, not fucking around here in this putrid shit hole fighting against impossible odds!"

Vortex sniggered, "Well Lownds? We all have our own personal crosses to bear!"

"Yeah! And I have a fuck'n trunk full of them so that I don't know which one to take out and strap onto my shoulders first!"

"Are you still there?" asked Vortex.

The PAVN bombardment continued unabated. The burning *Khe Sanh* ammunition dump was shaken with constant secondary explosions much to the gory delight of the Communists perched in their hilltop sanctuaries like putrid vultures watching the poor hapless Americans fighting for their lives.

Each new detonation was triggered when another container of ordnance had reached its critical temperature of 136.57 degrees Celsius.

"Colonel Vortex! What the hell-in-fuck blazes is going on there?" asked Brigadier General Burl McLaughlin.

"Oh! Its nothing sir! Just a minor disturbance in the atmosphere while we were sipping on our iced teas here in the FSCC bunker."

Then in a more serious tone of voice, "Listen sir!" began Vortex, "We have serious problems here at *Khe Sanh* besides the spilling of our iced tea!"

"No shit!" General McLaughlin answered, "I know. I've just been in communication with General Westmoreland and the new MACV Forward, General Creighton Abrams. Both men assured me that Operation NIAGARA will intensify at first light on the 22nd January 1968. You will have at least 6

B-52 *Stratofortresses* over *Khe Sanh* every 90 minutes to pulverise the enemy gook-fucked formations on the ground as they concentrate."

Vortex nodded, "Yes. I realise that sir. But we have more immediate problems that require urgent attention and rectification by you."

Colonel Lownds then took over the conversation and explained the situation regarding the ruined airstrip and the sudden shortage of ammunition.

Brigadier McLaughlin answered as he worked everything out in his head like a human abacus.

"Ok! I understand gentlemen. I shall immediately start diverting Fairchild C-123 *Providers* to *Da Nang*. They will take on ammunition there and fly to *Khe Sanh* to unload. The first aircraft should arrive tomorrow afternoon on the 22nd January 1968. I realise that the C-123's can only carry 16,000lbs of cargo which is less than half that of the C-130's. But they do have pod-mounted jet engines under each wing. This gives the C-123's a STOL (Short Take Off and Landing) capability. Do you think that they will be able to land at *Khe Sanh*? How badly is the airstrip damaged?"

Colonel Lownds answered without hesitation, "The C-123's will be able to land General. I guarantee it! The Seabees are working on the airstrip already and when night comes in this rat-fuck hell-of-a-pissing hole they will be working by floodlights."

Colonel Vortex added, "Sir! It is essential that we receive additional ammunition. We need the full spectrum from 7.62mm rounds to the heavy 155mm shells."

General McLaughlin said, "Don't worry! Your supply replenishment will begin tomorrow in a steady and unceasing stream that should drown in blood those Communist motherfuckers!"

Both Colonel's were satisfied with the arrangements as elucidated to them as Vortex smiled and said, "I shall use flares to illuminate the runway because the landing lights have been knocked out."

As soon as Colonel Vortex had finished speaking to Brigadier General Burl McLaughlin one of the radio operators in the FSCC bunker held up another handset.

"Sirs! Its Lieutenant General Cushman."

Vortex and Lownds listened as their commander spoke.

"I have just been in consultation with COMUSMACV and MACV Forward. General Westmoreland and I have decided that it is not possible to relieve *Khe Sanh* by road. Our forces are spread too thinly along National Route 9. You will have to rely solely on air drops and the LAPES (*Low Altitude Parachute Extraction System*) and GPES (*Ground Proximity Extraction System*) to replenish *Khe Sanh's* stores and ordnance."

Colonel Lownds said, "I am sure we can hold out for as long as it takes sir."

Colonel Vortex asked, "General Cushman. I have estimated that *Khe Sanh* requires at least 200 TAC air strikes (sorties) per day to pound the PAVN and the Main Force Viet Cong positions. This will help us greatly in the defence of the base."

General Cushman answered, "I can do better than that for you Colonel Vortex! I have also been in conference with General William Momyer. He has assured me that at least 400 TAC (tactical sorties) per day will be launched against the PAVN positions in and around the whole *Khe Sanh* area. Wherever those bastards are crouching and hiding and leering we shall fuck them up good and proper! That is one sortie every 5 minutes, day and night without interruption. Let that cunt-sucking bastard Giap deal with that!"

Colonel Lownds smiled as Vortex said, "That is excellent General! My conscience is clear because I have consulted my texts on Public International Law, the Laws of War and the *Geneva and Hague Conventions of 1949* and we are fully justified under the Law to exercise the fair and reasonable degree of force that this Operation shall exemplify. We are within our rights and I can sleep easy at night knowing that the *customary international law* principles are on our side as per the case-law of the *Law of State Sovereignty*."

And as if to verify the words of Lieutenant General Cushman, the 100 NCOs' and staff officers inside the FSCC bunker could hear the roar of yet another flight of *Sky-Hawks* and *Intruders* which were right at that moment swooping down on the PAVN held *'Horseshoe'* position.

Another flight of F-4E *Phantom II's* were attacking the valley that lay between Hills 881 South and 861A.

This noise added with the continuing detonations of the now ruined *Khe Sanh* ammunition dump produced a terrible cacophony of sound that blasted the eardrums of every Marine on the base.

General Cushman continued, "But we have had some disturbing intelligence."

Colonel Lownds took a bundle of maps from Captain Mirza Baig and asked, "What is that sir?"

"The G-2 section of III MAF has been monitoring the movement of the PAVN 320th Division which is just south of the DMZ near the *Rockpile*. It appears that General Giap may order this formation, supported by the 324th PAVN Division, to attack and overrun our base at *Camp Carroll*."

Vortex immediately shouted, "But that would be absolutely disastrous sir!"

Cushman sighed, "Yes. Of course it would."

There was a pause over the VHF tactical frequency as both Colonel's looked at each other and at Captain Mirza Baig with sheer horror. Vortex commented, "If that happens sir. Two things will immediately come to pass. The first is that our heavy fire support from the 175mm M107 howitzers will be gone. The second is that Giap will have succeeded in driving a wedge into our positions which will cut the Marine forces in I Corps into two and simultaneously prevent any ground relief from reaching *Khe Sanh* in the future. They could then roll-up the entire I Corps front from east to west and there is nothing that could stop them – short of course, of tactical nuclear weapons which I have been begging for but which request of mine falls onto deaf ears back at Washington with the powers-to-be!"

Vortex sounded almost hysterical.

Then he asked, "What are you going to do about it sir?"

General Cushman Jr. answered confidently, "Don't lose your cool Colonel Vortex! And you too Colonel Lownds! I have already prepared contingency plans for thwarting any possible Communist advance on *Camp Carroll*."

"What is that sir?" asked Vortex as he fiddled nervously with a bull-hide riding whip that he was lashing about in front of the conference table.

"I have devised *Plan B*," answered Lieutenant General Cushman.

"*Plan B*?" asked Vortex.

"Yes, that's right - *Plan B*," repeated Cushman.

"And what pray tell is that sir?" asked Colonel Lownds.

Cushman said confidently, "*Plan B* is the plan that will be implemented when *Plan A* does not work or in the alternative becomes unviable to implement."

Vortex looked to the ruined ceiling of the FSCC bunker, asking, "Yes sir. It is usual for B to come after A but that does not exactly tell us what is involved with *Plan B*?"

Cushman replied, "It is the Plan that will work when *Plan A* does not."

Vortex threw the bull whip to the floor.

He asked, as he watched Sergeant Major Crighton scamper to pick it dutifully up from the dust, "Are you trying to be funny sir?"

"Not in the least Colonel," answered Cushman flippantly.

Colonel Lownds whispered to Vortex so that Cushman could not pick it up on the VHF frequency, "I think the General is serious!"

"And when is this *Plan B* to be implemented sir?" asked Vortex.

"Soon Vortex," the General answered.

"How soon?"

"Very soon Colonel," said Cushman.

"May I ask what *Plan B* involves sir?"

"You may ask," answered Cushman.

Vortex waited with Colonel Lownds for an answer as they both had their ears to the handset.

But no answer came.

"Are you still there sir?" asked Vortex.

"Yes, I am still here Colonel."

"We are waiting, sir, for an answer, sir?" asked Vortex.

"Answer to what?" asked Lieutenant General Cushman.

"About *Plan B* sir," said Vortex now becoming agitated.

"Oh! I see!" began Cushman, then he added, "I can't tell you about the why's and wherefore's of *Plan B*. Sorry Colonel Vortex."

"But don't you think that we have a '*need to know*' basis for an answer, sir?" asked Vortex as he looked to Lownds with exasperation.

"That may well be Colonel but I can only tell you about the Plan – *Plan B* that is, when I am about to execute it."

Vortex was immediately enlightened, "Oh! That explains everything! Sir!"

Cushman said, "Good!"

Colonel Lownds scratched his head as Lieutenant General Cushman revealed, "But since you are so interested in *Plan B* I can tell you that it involves '*Body Counts*'."

Vortex looked puzzled, "Body Counts? What do you mean sir?"

"Well you remember when General Westmoreland introduced his *Master Plan* which simply said, '*Kill more of the enemy than they can kill of you and you can slowly bleed them to death, bleach them white of blood so that they must come to the negotiating table in due course?*'"

Vortex smiled, "I remember that well sir. But I thought we were already doing that?"

Cushman answered, "Its not that simple. *Plan B* involves, at least part of it, the super-acceleration of that policy."

Vortex laughed, "Well now that you have explained that sir, it illuminates everything for me!"

The III MAF commander then explained that he had ordered 7 battalions of Marines from the 1st Marine Division at *Hue* to be transferred to the *Camp Carroll* sector.

Colonel Vortex knew that the magnificent 1st Marine Division of the United States was commanded by Major General Herman Nickerson Jr. He was affectionately called, '*Herman the German*' by his loyal troops.

Colonel Lownds also knew that if General Nickerson's troops had reinforced *Camp Carroll* and its surroundings then there was indeed nothing to worry about.

Vortex asked, "Sir! Could you please convey my sincere greetings to Major General Nickerson."

Cushman replied, "Will do Colonel!"

Just at that second Lieutenant Colonel Tran, who had been trying to douse the fires from *Khe Sanh's* ammunition dump with a 200 man squad, came tumbling down the bunker stairs.

Colonel Tran was so excited that he lost his footing at the entrance to the FSCC bunker and his short but immensely muscular body went head-over-heels.

The ARVN officer landed heavily into the spine of Master Sergeant Richter who helped the battalion commander back to his feet.

General Cushman was speaking but Vortex dropped the handset and asked, "What is it Colonel?"

Screaming at the top of his lungs, the 37th ARVN Ranger commander said, "The Communists are attacking the *Khe Sanh Village*! The Ville!

They are attacking in force!"

The PAVN Attack on Khe Sanh Village: 21st January 1968

"What is that? What is going on at the *Khe Sanh Village*?" asked Lieutenant General Cushman who had overheard a few of the words on the VHF tactical frequency.

Colonel Lownds spoke hastily through the handset, "The PAVN are attacking the village sir!"

Vortex signed off, "Got to go sir! I am going to make the PAVN pay in blood for every square foot that they violate in that village!"

Vortex had already dropped the AN/PRC-41 field phone and did not hear General Cushman's voice wishing them good luck.

The 500 man MIC Force that had reinforced Hill 861 and 861A that morning was back inside the *Khe Sanh* perimeter, having taken up positions next to FOB3 (Forwarding Operating Base 3).

Colonel Vortex ordered it to be resupplied with what little ammunition there was left. The elite attack force made up of several companies from the 9th and 26th Marines piled into 20 UH-1E Huey's and 7 *Sikorsky's*.

The choppers peeled off from *Khe Sanh's* smouldering airstrip near the *'Ponderosa'*.

Rockets and mortar shells were still streaking skyward from the blazing ammunition dump.

Eighteen Marines had been killed and forty wounded when the stockpile detonated. But Colonel Vortex was satisfied to see that the sailors of the Seabee battalion had already started repairs on the runway despite the continuing NVA barrage.

The 2 mile distance from the *Khe Sanh* combat base to the village (*The Ville*) was covered by the choppers in about 2 to 3 minutes.

Colonel Vortex was in command while Colonel Lownds directed operations at the Marine base (KSCB) now under siege.

Intense mortar and machine gun fire was erupting out of the jungle to the west of the Ville.

Unknown to Colonel Vortex was the fact that the patrol from the 37th ARVN Rangers sent there in the morning, had already been ambushed by the Main Force Viet Cong and PAVN elements in the area and cut to pieces 300 yards from the Route 9 highway (really a mud track infested with vermin).

There were few survivors.

As the MIC Force was deposited onto National Route 9 just east of *Khe Sanh Village* it was greeted by a hail of fire from a Communist fan of 270 degrees ambit.

"Hit the dirt! Take cover!" screamed Colonel Vortex.

The MIC Force spread out line abreast and fought their way into the Village centre. The bloody and mutilated bodies of South Vietnamese civilians already littered the landscape.

On the other side of the Ville the North Vietnamese soldiers were stripping and looting the bodies of the fallen ARVN Rangers. This disgraceful conduct by the North Vietnamese Armed Forces was not the exception but rather the rule in Vietnam. In addition, the PAVN did not confine themselves to defiling ARVN and US troops only as well as the Australians and New Zealanders. The Communists also relished in the torture and butchering of South Vietnamese civilians who did not support the Viet Cong or the coterie of psychopathic criminals and madmen in Hanoi.

All these facts passed through Colonel Vortex's mind as he crouched in the jungle with Master Sergeant Richter and Sergeant Major Crighton.

"We cannot allow the *Khe Sanh* village to fall!" admonished Vortex.

Master Sergeant Richter answered, "If that happens sir, then the Green Berets and Captain Frank Willoughby in *Lang Vei* will be surrounded and cut off from *Khe Sanh*!"

"That's right Master Sergeant!" said Vortex as he fired grenades from a M79 launcher into the jungle around them.

Vortex added as he spoke to Crighton and Richter, "I made sure that everything is co-percentic before this mission began. I consulted my Law text books while running to the helicopters just a few minutes ago. I wanted to make sure that all was above board as far as the principles of *public international law* go and that we abide by the ROE (Rules of Engagement)."

Leonard Crighton who had not studied law as Vortex had done at North Western University gaining a Bachelor of Jurisprudence which he completed part-time over 5 years while in the Marines asked, "What is ROE sir?"

"What's the matter with you? Are you a retard or something?"

Crighton looked to Richter who just shrugged his shoulders in dumbfounded ignorance not knowing what to say.

"ROE stands for *Rules of Engagement* Sergeant Major Crighton. You should get up to speed with the Law. After all you are the highest ranking non commissioned officer in the whole of the Marine Corps."

"Sir? I still don't understand what *Rules of Engagement* mean sir. Sorry about that. I never went to Law School like you did."

Vortex laughed and slapped the Sergeant Major affectionately on the back, saying, "Rules of Engagement are the pre-defined set of tactical parameters that are elucidated before a specific or non-identified limited engagement are initiated between two or more opposing forces in the field whereby the force that sets its pre-determined locus of reactive actions and counter-actions set forth a strict guideline or set of non-deviatory parameters which describe the options available to counter or react to each initiation of force or provocative action from the opposing force or forces on a tactical but not strategic level."

Richter said, "Oh! Now that you put it in layman's terms like that sir, I understand fully."

Vortex quipped, "Good!"

Crighton asked, "And in this tactical situation as we attempt to re-take *Khe Sanh Village* what do the ROE prescribe for our forces sir?"

Vortex said simply as he threw two more grenades into the jungle before them without even looking where they were going to fall, "It means in this particular case to blast to hell every North Vietnamese and Viet Cong we see or don't see, killing them in the fastest possible way without thought for any chance of capitulation by them. Fuck them all to hell and back. That's what it means for us now."

Crighton pumped three rockets into the tree line before them from an RPG that he had captured back at Hill 881 South, saying, "Sounds good to me!"

The MIC Force were already embroiled in a fire-fight with the PAVN all along the eastern perimeter of the *Khe Sanh ville*.

About half the thatched huts were on fire.

Screams and shrieks mingled with the steady stream of gunfire as the civilians were caught in the middle in a *collateral damage* smorgasbord.

Vortex pointed to several hooch's to their left.

"Let's clear this side of the ville!" he screamed.

The Marines rushed forward as they fired their weapons.

As soon as they cleared the edge of the jungle they ran into a veritable wall of AK-47 fire from the 8th Battalion of the 66th Regiment of the 304th PAVN Division.

This unit was storming in on every side of the MIC Force. Seven Marines dropped to the ground with hideous wounds before Colonel Vortex reached the first hut.

Master Sergeant Richter kicked in the bamboo door. Vortex leapt inside followed by Sergeant Major Crighton.

Immediately Vortex could see the gleaming edge of a bayonet thrusting towards his kidneys and spleen. But Richter threw his Marine dagger into the NVA soldier. The razor sharp point impaled the Communist's heart and he died instantly, vomiting up his own blood and lung tissue.

Three other PAVN soldiers were inside. They were mutilating to death a South Vietnamese grandmother, three children and their screaming parents.

Sergeant Major Crighton blew two of them away with his M16. Vortex could see that the third was copulating with the mother and simultaneously stripping slices of skin off a 7 year old girl's thighs.

Richter pulled him away from the raped woman and buried his bayonet into the man's stomach and testicles in alternate piston strikes. But the NVA grabbed Richter's throat and started to strangle him as he died.

"No you don't!" shouted Vortex who came up behind the Communist and crushed his brains open with the butt of his M16.

Trickles of blood and oozing brain tissue spread out across the dirt floor of the hut.

The children screamed and the violated mother fainted.

"Get them out of here!" ordered Colonel Vortex.

A platoon of Marines entered the hut and evacuated the South Vietnamese civilians to the designated LZ (landing zone). From there they were helicopter'd back to the KSCB.

As the family were leaving the hut, the eldest child who was almost a woman gave emotional thanks to Colonel Vortex. She spoke only Vietnamese and Vortex reciprocated her gratitude in his own fluent Vietnamese.

The girl was extremely beautiful with a shapely body and a delicate, attractive face. She reminded Colonel Vortex of his fiancée, Susie Ky.

The girl held Vortex's face in-between her palms and kissed him on the cheek.

Master Sergeant Richter continued the advance through the village as Vortex escorted the young woman and her family into a *Sikorsky* HH-53B which lifted into the air.

By the time the Colonel returned to the huts and straw hooch's his Marines had been sucked into a massive fire-fight all along the village perimeter.

The MIC Force had hooked up with the survivors of the 37th ARVN patrol but they were being squeezed on all sides by a vastly superior PAVN force being the 8th Battalion of the 66th Regiment.

"Form a defensive perimeter!" shouted Colonel Vortex.

Master Sergeant Richter and a Captain organised the Marines into a cigar shaped wedge that lay across most of the village.

But Colonel Vortex could see that it was impossible to hold the *Khe Sanh ville* for much longer.

At 1750 hours he ordered in the choppers to evacuate his men.

"Shit! We can't hold!" said the Colonel to Richter and Crighton.

The NCOs' were also bitterly disappointed.

They knew that the Combat base KSCB could not spare any more troops to hold onto the ville. They were stretched to the limit as it was.

It was then that the PAVN 8th Battalion charged the American positions. The whole Communist force advanced, screaming, all down the defensive perimeter.

The Marines fired back as it was now the Communists who laid down a murderous suppressive fire.

The 68th PAVN Artillery Regiment at the 'Co Roc' co-ordinated with their ground troops and pounded the Marines with their 152mm shells.

As Vortex blasted away with his M60 a whole squad of 8 Marines nearby were blown into the air. The hut behind which they had been crouching was disintegrated. Pieces of human debris and blood soaked limbs fell from the sky as the Marines were annihilated.

The whole MIC Force was wavering on the brink of collapse. Then the gruesome and savage hand-to-hand fighting commenced.

Colonel Vortex screamed into the AN/PRC-41 field phone to Captain Mirza Baig who was now in the MATU bunker.

"Get us out of here! We're being cut to pieces!"

Captain Baig replied, "The *Sikorsky's* are already on their way sir!"

Master Sergeant Richter felt a bayonet pierce the flesh of his left thigh. About 50 NVA had rushed the MIC Force LZ.

Vortex head butted the Communist and grabbing his skull he catapulted the man over his head. Sergeant Major Crighton then cut open his chest with a field axe.

"Do you see that?" asked the Colonel.

His Marines watched in awe as the broken rib cage revealed a beating heart that was clearly visible through the horrific mutilation. With each compression of the heart muscle blood spurted upwards from the corpse.

Vortex stabbed five more PAVN troops with his sacred Marine dagger *'Sempre Fi'*, then jumped back onto the M60. He wiped the blood from his knife onto the face of a dead PAVN soldier and then kicked the carcass away with disgust.

He fired like the devil himself. Bullets cut down dozens of the Communists but still they came on in an evil and toxic tide.

"Now that's what I mean by following the *Rules of Engagement*!" Vortex blustered to Richter and Crighton.

The HH-53B *Sikorsky's* had swooped over the MIC Force position and were saturating the attackers with an avalanche of *Minigun* fire.

The 8th Battalion started firing into the large *Jolly Green Giants* with Chinese *Type 42* machine guns.

One of the *Sikorsky's* started to trail a plume of black smoke as its turbofan engine on the portside was disintegrated by large calibre rounds.

Even the *Minigun* fire was not enough to force back the PAVN 8th Battalion.

This time the Communists were determined to take the village. And they did so within the next 10 minutes.

The stricken *Sikorsky* lost power and crashed to the ground right on top of the roof of one of the huts. Several Marines and a few Communists were crushed to death by the fuselage.

As Vortex and his men rushed forward to save the helicopter crew a 75mm recoilless rifle from the PAVN battalion detonated the chopper.

The pilot staggered out of the cockpit trying to brush flames off his body. But he was turned to charred flesh within seconds. The other men in the aircraft were cut in half by the murderous fire.

As Colonel Vortex reached out a hand to one of the door gunners the entire machine blew apart in a shower of steel and plexiglass.

"Jesus Christ!" screamed Vortex.

Now five AH-1 *Cobras* came in and started to extract some of the MIC Force.

A Communist soldier took a swipe at Master Sergeant Richter with his machete. Expertly the NCO ducked the blow and knifed the Communist directly into his groin. Vortex jumped up from behind and sliced the man's head off with his field axe.

"Good work! Sir!" exclaimed the Master Sergeant.

"To the choppers! Get to the choppers!" cried Colonel Vortex as he shepherded his courageous men onto the waiting HH-53B's. The *Sikorsky's* having landed right on the Route 9 roadway, such as it was, just east of the village now in Communist hands.

Now the 155mm guns from *Khe Sanh* blasted the village as Vortex gave the orders from his field phone. The intense artillery fire kept the North Vietnamese ducking and weaving just long enough for the battered MIC Force and ARVN Rangers to scramble aboard.

Vortex said bitterly to Master Sergeant Richter, "We've lost the ville! Damn it! Fuck it! Shit this fucking war! If only MACV would have given me nuclear weapons! We could have held that village by blasting it with nukes right off the fucking map and the PAVN with it! I could have wiped the village out and thus saved it!"

"I know sir. But we'll get it back eventually," said Richter as he fired a mounted *Minigun* from the hatch of the HH-53B like a madman with his toy of Armageddon.

Sergeant Major Crighton said, "Sir! Now *Lang Vei* is cut off! The Green Beret Base is surrounded on four sides!"

Vortex nodded as the formation of helicopters made the short hop back to the combat base.

"I have to inform Captain Willoughby immediately."

As they landed on the *Khe Sanh* airstrip the smoke obscured sun was just setting on the horizon.

Tear gas and the poignant smell of gasoline filled the air and small explosions continued from the black heap of smouldering rubbish that used to be the *Khe Sanh* ammunition dump.

"Let's get inside and make some calls," said Vortex to his two senior NCOs' and one of his Captain's who was the Deputy Battalion commander under Major Thrush.

Both the 9th and the 26th Marine Regiments had suffered severe casualties that day. Over 35 Marines had died since morning defending the seven separate US positions.

Apart from KSCB itself there was; Hill 861A/861, Hill 881 South, Hill 881 North, Hill 558, Hill 950 and *Lang Vei* six miles to the west.

Hill 881 South was the most westerly position held by US Forces in Vietnam.

It was literally the end of the line.

Vortex knew that this line had to be refused to the enemy.

Colonel Vortex and his entourage staggered into the FSCC bunker. Colonel Lownds had received a minor flesh wound that was bleeding profusely.

"What happened to you?" asked Vortex as he collapsed into the nearest chair.

Colonel Lownds grinned, "Oh! Its nothing. Just a fragmentation wound. I was standing too close to the ammunition dump when a box full of 81mm mortar rounds went up."

Captain Mirza Baig handed the weary Colonel a cup of steaming Jasmine tea.

"Oh! Thanks Captain."

Vortex rested his head on the map table. The clear and precise voices of the fire control personnel could be heard as they sat at their computer consoles, radios and radar screens. Every five minutes they directed a fresh TAC air strike against known PAVN positions in the hills and valleys around *Khe Sanh*.

The mobilisation of American Air Power that was now underway was awesome.

In the coming 77 days at *Khe Sanh* the United States air armada would drop the equivalent of 5 Hiroshima sized bombs on the Communist forces in the 77 day period of the momentous siege. Colonel Vortex thought that this was not nearly enough. In his opinion with the use of the *W48* nuclear shells for the 155mm howitzers in the KSCB it would be possible to drop the equivalent of 5 Hiroshima sized fission bombs on the four PAVN Divisions not in 77 days but in one day and each day unrelenting until the Communist forces were pulverised and totally annihilated. Secret negotiations were taking place between Colonel Vortex and an undisclosed Major General in the Ordnance Department of the Pentagon in Washington to *'accidentally'* release to the KSCB a number of *W48* shells on the sly for use by Vortex under his own responsibility to deliciously nuke the Communists to oblivion where he personally believed that they belonged along with their cabal of lunatics and sycophants' back in Hanoi. If Colonel Vortex would have had his way he would have nuked Hanoi itself without a moment's hesitation giving him a satisfaction far more exquisite even than the sexual act with desirous women.

That was equivalent to approximately 70,000 tons metric of Tri-Nitro-Toluene (TNT).

Captain Mirza Baig offered Colonel Vortex the field phone as he stood behind the senior officer.

"Who is that?"

"Its Captain Frank Willoughby from *Lang Vei* sir."

"Oh! Good! I was just about to get him on the horn."

The voice of the Green Beret Captain and ultimate 'killing machine' was excited but still professional despite the horrendous setbacks suffered by the gallant and heroic United States forces. His lover, Monica Thang and her sister Susan were also sheltering with the US forces at the base.

The Main Force Viet Cong had them on the death list and Captain Willoughby was determined to get them to safety at any cost.

He had already interrogated three Main Force Viet Cong sappers who tried to breach the *Lang Vei* concertina wire in order to murder his twin lovers and Monica's sister, the beautiful young vixen that took delight in her first torture session by cutting off the testicles of the Viet Cong sappers with a rusted razor blade in extreme slow motion.

Captain Willoughby subjected them to an intense physical beating and then slowly electrocuted their genitals (before Monica's sister did her handiwork) until they offered up the required information. The torture then continued unabated just for the sheer pleasure of Monica and her sibling.

"Sir!" commenced the Green Beret *Captain of America*, "We have seen the tremendous explosions at the base! What has happened?"

Vortex told the *Captain of America* the current situation. The attacks on the hill outposts and the condition of the airstrip and ammunition dump.

"Do you think you can hold out sir?"

Colonel Vortex ignored the question, "Fuck! Don't worry about us here at *Khe Sanh*. I have to inform you that the *Khe Sanh ville* has fallen to the PAVN less than an hour ago. We tried to counterattack but it was useless. We could have saved the *Khe Sanh Village* by blowing it to smithereens with nuclear weapons. But they wouldn't give me any. I have nightmares about our lack of nukes! It drives me crazy! They outnumbered us at least five to one."

There was a few moments of stony silence.

Captain Willoughby tried to digest the full horror of his position.

"You mean sir? That my position at *Lang Vei* is now completely surrounded by the PAVN and thus untenable?"

"I'm afraid so Captain."

Vortex sighed and then added, "We shall try to give you as much air support as possible."

Captain Willoughby grunted, "What are my orders now sir?"

Colonel Lownds stepped over and took the handset, "Hang on! Hang on as long as possible Captain! Remember that you have God and Jesus on your side!"

Willoughby asked, "And what if we are overrun?"

Vortex answered, "First you pray to God and then you try to make it back to *Khe Sanh* with as many men as possible. And kill any fucking Communist prisoners before you go – and slowly at that!"

Willoughby chuckled with a sense of doom, "It doesn't give us many options sir."

Colonel Lownds said, "I know. But do your best Captain!

Jesus is counting on you!"

The Green Beret officer acknowledged the orders and signed off after telling both Colonels that the Communist pressure around his base was increasing by the minute.

PAVN sappers were constantly trying to breach the perimeter of the small base.

Colonel Vortex immediately ordered Captain Mirza Baig and the FSCC personnel to direct a series of TAC air strikes for the support of *Lang Vei*.

Ten minutes later a flight of six Crusaders and four A-6's could be heard screeching like banshees over *Khe Sanh*. They were heading west to *Lang Vei*.

The deep rumble of cluster and fragmentation bombs could be heard from 6 miles away as the PAVN around that small US outpost were blasted mercilessly.

One of Colonel Lownds' battalion commanders, a Major, came sauntering into the FSCC bunker.

"You better take a look outside sirs," he said as he ran his fingers through his dark brown hair.

"What is it?" asked Colonel Lownds.

"It's the civilians sir. They have panicked due to the intense bombardment by the NVA and they want refuge inside the base."

Vortex grinned up to Master Sergeant Richter who was cleaning his M60 machine gun with oil and a pull through.

"I don't blame them." Then he turned to Lownds, "Come! Let us take a look Colonel. If they are anti-Communist then we must protect them!"

When the two Colonels and their entourage of 30 NCO's and junior officers arrived at the main gate of the *Khe Sanh* base, the sight that greeted them was one of pure chaos. Hundreds of civilians had panicked and fled from the surrounding countryside.

They all congregated in a great swirling mass outside the concertina wire.

About 100 Marines were trying to supervise them and to reassure them. But it was no use.

Mothers holding their babies were crying and screaming. Refugees from Laos were begging the Marines to let them inside the base.

Ca tribesmen and their wives were also beseeching the soldiers for mercy. They had been involved in a fire fight with the PAVN on the Laos side of the border. They were now afraid that the PAVN and the Main Force Viet Cong were going to hunt them down and kill them without pity or remorse.

The *Ca tribesmen* hated and despised the Viet Cong. The Communists had regularly tortured and raped their wives and daughters, stolen their crops and burned their villages. They had also impressed their young men into service with the local VC units despite their opposition.

In addition there were *Bru families* who had fled the Communists. They had nothing to eat and nowhere to go.

They were in a hopeless state of sheer frenzied panic.

"How many civilians are there?" asked Colonel Lownds.

A First Lieutenant standing near the main gates answered, "About 1,400 or so, sir."

Then the junior officer asked, "What do you want me to do with them sir? Shall I let them all in?"

Colonel Vortex barked back, "Don't be ridiculous! We can't accommodate them all! Its impossible!"

Colonel Lownds scratched his head, "I don't know what to do? We have to transport them out of here."

As well as the indigenous population there were also French expatriates who had homes in the *Khe Sanh Village* as well as the European missionaries and the nuns.

Colonel Vortex whispered to Colonel Lownds, "Listen! Some of them may be Viet Cong or NVA spies. We can't take the chance of exposing our base defences to them."

"I agree absolutely Vortex."

Above the tumult of their cries and entreaties, Vortex added, "But what about the Europeans? The French families and the missionaries? I suppose we can let them in?"

Colonel Lownds agreed and gave the orders to a Military Police Captain next to him.

The white Europeans and the missionaries were given temporary shelter inside a confined portion of the *Khe Sanh* combat base. However even they were kept under close guard by a large detachment of Marines.

The rest of the indigenous refugees remained outside. Within a couple of hours they had set up a squalid camp of tents and other makeshift structures right alongside the main gate. When it was clear to the native refugees that they would not be allowed into the base perimeter Colonel Lownds made an announcement to them with the use of a loudspeaker. He told them that they would be evacuated by air in the next few days.

Clearly, many of them were relieved to hear this.

As Colonel Lownds spoke, Colonel Vortex, Richter and Crighton walked through the throng of people.

Vortex watched and examined all the tribesmen. He was hoping to identify some Viet Cong spies for interrogation. Then suddenly, he saw one South Vietnamese who was clearly not a *Ca* or *Bru tribesman*.

"Sergeant Major! Over here!" screamed Vortex.

The Colonel leapt over a muddy ditch and grabbed the man, asking in perfect Vietnamese, "Are you VC?"

The man trembled and tried to shake off Colonel Vortex's hold on his neck.

Sergeant Major Crighton jumped behind the man and caught him in a vicious headlock.

Vortex slammed a punch into the Vietnamese man's stomach and then head-butted him with savagery. Blood sprinkled out over some nearby *Bru* children who were playing in the mud and laughing at the spectacle.

A large crowd of refugees formed a circle around Colonel Vortex and the Viet Cong suspect.

"Are you VC?" screamed the Colonel.

A squad of Marines came running up with M60 machine guns at the ready.

"Strip the bastard naked and check his clothes!" yelled Colonel Vortex as he slapped the man across the face. The Colonel then swung his right foot and kicked the man savagely in the testicles. Both sacs were crushed in a slime of blood.

As the suspect doubled over in unbelievable pain, Sergeant Major Crighton ripped off his black tunic and pantaloons. Even his underwear was torn off his body.

It started to rain in that dark twilight over *Khe Sanh* and the man shivered as he was viced in a headlock by the huge Sergeant Major. Master Sergeant Richter checked his pockets.

"He's a Viet Cong alright sir! Look!" screamed Master Sergeant Richter.

The NCO produced some maps and written material that indicated the US positions in the hills. Then Vortex noticed some deep scars on the man's back and thighs.

"How did you get these scars?" barked the Colonel as he punched the Vietnamese man in the groin, spine and then the kidney's. Richter started to gouge his fingers into the man's eyes, drawing blood and dislodging the left eyeball.

"Take him away for a thorough interrogation!" ordered Vortex.

The squad of Marines grabbed the Viet Cong infiltrator and kicked and punched his naked body all the way to the 26th Marine HQ bunker.

As Colonel Vortex turned to go back inside the base, he felt a soft hand hold his wrist. Turning, he was surprised to see the beautiful young South Vietnamese girl whom he had saved along with her family only a couple of hours before in the *Khe Sanh village*.

"Hello!" said Vortex as he caressed her long black hair. The girl had beautiful skin, as smooth as marble, and her eyes sparkled brilliantly.

"Take care of me!" she said to Vortex with tears in her eyes.

Vortex took her hand and held it softly.

Her body was slim and exquisite. She stood about five feet five inches tall and had already entered womanhood.

"Why? Where is your family?" asked Vortex in his fluent Vietnamese.

"They are all dead! A Communist bomb. They were killed as we climbed off the helicopters."

Vortex could see that the girl was visibly shaken.

He took her gently by the hand and they entered the base along with the French families and the missionaries.

"What is your name?"

She replied as she gently squeezed the Colonel's palm, "Ngo Nhu."

"You are beautiful Ngo Nhu!"

The young girl blushed as Vortex took her to the 26th Marine HQ bunker complex where he had a private room set aside.

"How old are you Ngo?"

"Seventeen Colonel," she smiled up at Vortex.

"My name is Richard Vortex," as he spoke the Colonel closed the door and lay down on the bunk in utter exhaustion. He was almost at the end of his strength and his mental resilience was shattered.

"I understand how tired you must be Richard," said Ngo in her native tongue. Only the two of them were in the small bedroom.

Ngo said, "I will be forever grateful to you for saving me."

As she spoke the continued roar of PAVN artillery fire could be heard in the night air. Explosions still rocked the *Khe Sanh* base every few minutes.

Marines and civilians continued to be wounded and killed. Master Sergeant Richter and three other Marine officers were beating the Viet Cong infiltrator with their fists and with iron bars in another part of the bunker. They would not stop until they had reduced the Communist's legs to a pile of splintered bone and mutilated flesh.

Ngo Nhu kissed Vortex on the lips and lay down beside him on the tiny bunk. She took off her clothes and wrapped her delicious body around the exhausted Colonel.

He had no strength left with which to move. Vortex's head swam in a sea of pain. Images washed through his mind. Images of suffering and death. Only punctuated by the relieving dreams of nuclear weapons arriving at *Khe Sanh* in the nick of time, as if by some unforetold miracle of providence.

"Can you give me those tablets over there?" asked Vortex as he held the girl in his arms.

She helped him to swallow 15 30mg Codeine Pain killers and the 10 100mg Valium tablets with a glass of water.

In less than half an hour both Vortex and the beautiful South Vietnamese girl had fallen asleep together. Their bodies intertwined as one.

Vortex was unable to copulate with the girl even though she was willing and ready for it because of the massive injection of Valium and Codeine into his bloodstream.

In his deepest unconsciousness, Vortex had already decided to look after Ngo Nhu whatever happened. He lay there and dreamed of having sexual liaisons with her and also of embracing the much awaited W48 nuclear artillery shells, not knowing in his dreams which to caress first, the girl or the atom bombs, in his delirious and frenzied state. His first task was to fly her to safety as soon as the C-123's would land at *Khe Sanh*.

As the clock above their heads slithered past the midnight hour the first tempestuous day of the *Battle for Khe Sanh* was over.

There would be seventy-six more days of the siege.

Chapter 10
ANOTHER DIEN BIEN PHU?

Lady Bird Johnson was shifting and turning uneasily in her bed at the White House.

That night of the 23rd to 24th January 1968 seemed to go on forever.

She couldn't get to sleep no matter how hard she tried. Uppermost in her mind was the torment, both mental and physical, that her husband, the President, was going through.

She looked at the clock that lay on her mahogany bedside table.

It was 3.15am.

But where was her husband?

Lady Bird Johnson reached over in the dark and felt for Lyndon's arm or chest. He was not in the bed.

Then she knew that he was on one of his nocturnal strolls through the corridors and basements of the White House.

Lady Bird Johnson arose from the sumptuous, silk covered bed and made her way to the bathroom. She took a mild pain killer and another sleeping tablet and went back to bed.

She sighed and spoke softly to herself.

"Its useless to try to find Lyndon. He wouldn't come back to bed anyway."

But Lady Bird Johnson had a pretty good idea of exactly where the President of the United States would be at this very moment. Lyndon was in the basement situation room of the White House. He had informed her the day before that something new had been built for him, at his own orders, by the Pentagon boys in that dingy underground bunker.

Suddenly the phone rang. Its bell screeched loudly in the otherwise still night.

"Hello?" answered Lady Bird Johnson.

"Oh! Is that you Mrs Johnson?"

The male voice at the other end of the line was mature and respectful.

The gentleman knew how to behave when speaking to the First Lady of the United States of America.

"It is," she replied.

"I'm sorry to bother you at this late hour Mrs Johnson."

There was a few moments lull in the conversation before the gentleman identified himself.

"Sorry Madame. This is Walt Rostow speaking. I am the National Security Adviser for the President."

Lady Bird Johnson chuckled as she sat up in bed. She pulled the magnificent silk sheets up around her neck. It was cold in Washington on that winter January night.

"Of course! Mr Rostow! I immediately recognised your voice."

Walt Rostow thanked the First Lady and asked whether he could speak to the President.

Lady Bird Johnson answered, "You could if he was here. But Lyndon has gone for his usual nightly stroll through the White House corridors Mr Rostow."

The National Security Advisor thanked Lady Bird Johnson for her patience and said, "I think I know where the President might be Madame."

Lady Bird Johnson asked, "The basement?"

"Yes Madame," he answered.

When Mr Rostow had put down the telephone Lady Bird Johnson reached over for a glass that contained some Bourbon whisky. As she sipped it slowly she wondered and said aloud to herself, "What the hell is going on in that basement?"

President Lyndon B. Johnson took the security elevator down into the White House basement that served as a makeshift 'Situation Room.'

The Secret Service minders were everywhere.

Each time the President crossed a doorway or went down a flight of steps there would be a tall, massive and imposing figure of a young man in the Secret Service Protection detail.

All of them would stiffen upright at the approach of the President. This would be followed by a dignified, "Good evening Mr President!"

But Lyndon Baines Johnson was in a hurry. A hurry to get to the basement and gloat over his new plaything.

Finally he sauntered into the huge underground complex. Massive steel and titanium doors greeted the entrance. There were six Marine Guards standing at attention on the outside of the bunker in the neon lit corridor.

Then a familiar face appeared.

"Good evening Mr President!"

Johnson nodded and asked, "Where is it?"

General Robert Ginsburg of the *G-2 Army Intelligence Directorate* at the Pentagon ushered the President inside.

There was a large, specially constructed table standing in the middle of the room. George Christian, the President's Press Secretary, leapt out from behind the table.

"It is finally ready sir!" he exclaimed as he looked at the surface of the table.

"It looks very realistic George!" said Johnson.

General Ginsburg assured, "It is exact down to the very minutest detail Mr President!"

A few moments of silence ensued as President Johnson poured over the large table. He peeped here and there, surveyed, inspected and examined the hole thing with great fervour.

Then finally as General Ginsburg and George Christian held their breath, the President stood upright and clapped his hands together loudly.

General Ginsburg watched the huge figure of President Johnson as he was dressed in his bathrobe and black leather slippers.

Johnson said, "So this is the *Khe Sanh* plateau!"

"It is a perfect sand-table reconstruction sir!" said Ginsburg.

Johnson barked back, "It better be General!"

Ginsburg nodded nervously.

"Mr President. The National Security Advisor called," said George Christian.

President Johnson ordered, "I want you to call him in this morning. I want him in the Oval Office by 9am sharp!"

"Yes sir, Mr President!"

The President continued, "I want you to also call in Dean Rusk, General Earle Wheeler, Robert Komer, Clark Clifford, William Bundy and Henry Kissinger."

The Press Secretary acknowledged the President's orders as Johnson walked out. His bathrobe flapped in the air behind him like a large albatross.

Exactly on time the President's private secretary announced that the Chairman of the Joint Chief's of Staff, General Earle Wheeler was waiting outside the Oval Office.

"Show him in please," said President Johnson as he watched the television that was built into one of the Oval Office wall units.

The President did not like what he was hearing and seeing. The American press were having a field day with the sudden outbreak of fighting around *Khe Sanh*.

Already the lugubrious Walter Cronkite from the CBS was informing the American public that disaster was about to befall the defenders at *Khe Sanh*.

Walter Cronkite and the vast majority of the United States media were already likening *Khe Sanh* to the disastrous defeat of the French Colonial Forces at *Dien Bien Phu* in 1954.

As General Wheeler walked in with a crisp military style President Johnson jumped to his feet behind the Oval Office desk.

"Earle! Have you heard this?" exclaimed President Johnson as he pointed to the face of Walter Cronkite on national television.

General Wheeler answered, trying to conceal his undiluted rage, "I have Mr President! And I must say I don't like it!"

Johnson nodded vigorously, "You bet your cotton picking boots we don't like it!"

President Johnson stepped over and turned the volume down on the T.V. set.

He looked at General Wheeler with his features twisted in a type of hysterical panic. Johnson's eyes were almost bulging out of his head.

"Is it as serious as they say General?"

"You mean about the developments at *Khe Sanh*?"

"No! I meant about the possibility of an Alien invasion from Mars!"

Of course that's what I mean!" said Johnson in a loud voice.

"Well sir. It is serious but its nothing that we can't handle. My boys are on the job. And they know how to finish it!"

Johnson grunted and sat down again.

The President had a pile of telex sheets in front of him marked *'Top Secret.'*

They were from the MACV Headquarters in Saigon and from General Westmoreland.

General Earle Wheeler had been appointed Army Chief of Staff in 1962 under the Kennedy Administration. He was also a protégé of the famous World War II officer, General Maxwell Taylor.

Both the then Secretary of Defence Robert McNamara and General Wheeler had made great strides in modernizing the United States War Machine.

Wheeler had become the CJCS (Chairman of the Joint Chiefs of Staff) in 1964. Since then he had advised President Johnson on continuing the build-up of American combat troops and air support to the South Vietnamese government.

He was a strong adherent to President Johnson's war policy in South-East-Asia.

"Sir! With all due respect and before the others arrive," began General Wheeler, "I must request that you reconsider the option of a full scale and unrestricted bombing of the North!"

Johnson looked up at Wheeler and scowled. He said nothing but kept reading the telex sheets.

He did not like what he was reading either.

Last November, General Westmoreland had requested that 206,000 additional American combat troops be sent to Vietnam. This meant that the President would have to call up the Reserves at a time when public opinion was steadily moving against the war.

Johnson had refused to take this step.

Actually it was General Wheeler who had coerced or manoeuvred General Westmoreland into making this request.

"I can't decide on something like that now! General!" shouted Johnson.

His private secretary walked in and served coffee to the two men.

"Besides!" began Johnson, "Our lunch today with the Joint Chiefs and the National Security Council is already totally booked out with picking out a long list of bombing targets! I can't add any more targets to the list – besides our soup would get cold! And the deserts would spoil!"

"But Mr President! I don't suggest this action lightly. I propose that we increase the bombing of North Vietnam and at the same time we should launch a full scale invasion not only of Laos and Cambodia to cut off and interdict the *Ho Chi Minh Trail* at places like *Tchepone* but also a direct ground assault on the North itself with at least six additional combat divisions!"

The President started to lose his patience even before the full meeting had begun.

"Christ! Earle! And I thought I was conservative about the War! Shit! Do you know what you are asking for?"

Wheeler simply said, "Victory!"

"Listen Earle! You know I can't sanction any such escalation at the moment. Everything depends on this *Khe Sanh* business. What if we loose too many boys out there? What if our air support proves to be inadequate? What happens if, God forbid! The Communists overrun the *Khe Sanh* base?"

General Wheeler chuckled, "Mr President! That is impossible!"

Johnson glared back, "Are you so sure?"

Wheeler repeated as he flourished his hands in a wide sweeping gesture, "Absolutely sir! I have prepared a full report on the situation at *Khe Sanh*."

Just then Walt Rostow, the National Security Advisor and Clark Clifford, the Secretary of Defence entered the Oval Office.

"Good morning gentlemen," said Johnson.

Both men greeted the President and sat down.

"It seems that we have a crisis on our hands Mr President?" said Walt Rostow.

The National Security Advisor was a Yale educated Rhodes Scholar. He had been a lecturer at MIT during the 1950's and was an aggressive member of the Ivy League alumni who dominated the CIA.

Previously he had been an assistant to McGeorge Bundy, the then National Security Advisor under Kennedy.

Walt Rostow had called the North Vietnamese *"scavengers of the modernization process."*

Colonel Richard Vortex was a close friend of Walt Rostow whom he had met during a tour of duty at the Pentagon while a Major in the Marine Corps G-2 Directorate.

"I must reiterate Mr President! That only increased American firepower and more combat troops will solve problems like *Khe Sanh* and other situations that will almost certainly arise in the Vietnam Theatre of Operations!" remarked the National Security Advisor.

"I also strongly support the use of tactical nuclear weapons at this remote *Khe Sanh* base. We must show and demonstrate to the criminals and war mongers in Hanoi, such as Pham Van Dong and this leech, General Vo Nguyen Giap that we Americans mean business!"

The Secretary of Defence, Clark Clifford, burst into the conversation.

"Now wait a minute Walt! Can you imagine what the ramifications and repercussions would be if we used nuclear weapons in any part of the Vietnam Theatre?"

Clark Clifford bent over in his chair and rested his elbow on the President's table.

General Wheeler looked to the President as Walt Rostow asked, "What do you mean? What ramifications?"

Clark Clifford appeared agitated as he said, "Well? For one thing! Have you thought about what the Russians and the Chinese would do if we used nuclear weapons to smash one of their small satellite states?"

Walt Rostow laughed a little and sipped on a cup of herbal tea that had just been served.

"I have thought about it," he answered with a mock grin on his face.

"And?" asked the Defence Secretary again.

Walt Rostow barked back angrily, "And! And it is my opinion that the Russian Imperialists will do nothing! Absolutely nothing! They won't risk going to war over an economic basket case such as North Vietnam! What is there anyway? Just stinking rice paddies and putrid fish markets!"

Clark Clifford threw up his hands into the air and looked forlornly at the President. General Wheeler cut in with a sombre and calculative voice.

"Mr President. I am also of the opinion that the Chinese and the Soviets will not intervene if and when we decide to use nuclear weapons in Vietnam. I know that General Westmoreland has ordered his staff in the MACV to prepare a feasibility study on exactly this option. The study should be presented to you in a matter of days."

President Johnson slammed his fist down on the Oval Office table.

"Listen gentlemen! I did not call this meeting to discuss the possibility of using nuclear weapons! That decision is a long way off as far as I am concerned. And I am the one who has the final say. The buck stops with me here in this room! I want to evaluate how we are going to hose down this media hype about the *Khe Sanh* battle

that has blown up in our faces. I also want to make sure that we are going to hold this plateau in the stinking hills of South Vietnam at all costs! Of course I realise that this one miserable combat base is of no value either militarily or otherwise. But it has immense importance in how the American public *perceive* my Administration's handling of the war."

Then Johnson took a deep breath as he stood to his feet, "I am afraid that the whole bottom is going to fall out of our Vietnam policy if this base falls to the Communists!"

Just at that second Dean Rusk, the Secretary of State, William P. Bundy, a member of the National Security Council as well as XCOM [Executive Committee of the NSC] and a close advisor to the President, as well as Henry Kissinger and Robert Komer entered the Oval Office.

All were now present for the appointed meeting.

"Mr President! I can assure you that *Khe Sanh* will not fall!"

The voice was that of Dean Rusk.

Secretary of State Rusk was a Rhodes Scholar who had served in the military in World War II. He was a firm advocate of halting the threat of Chinese Communist expansion. He was also a qualified lawyer much to his credit.

Colonel Richard Vortex was also a close friend of Dean Rusk as well as Walt Rostow. Before Vortex was married he had dated the eldest daughter of Dean Rusk almost becoming engaged to her. After those times Colonel Vortex and Dean Rusk had kept in touch mainly because of their common profession, both being qualified Attorneys-at-Law, as well as their interest in military history and war games which they both attended at the *Washington Naval Yard* from time to time.

Rusk placed his hands on the back of Clark Clifford's chair and continued as the other men took their seats in the Oval Office.

"I would advocate Mr President a dramatic increase in troop commitments to Vietnam coupled with a renewed and more vigorous application of the bombing campaign that was initiated with Operation ROLLING THUNDER to encompass the entire North Vietnamese infrastructure. We should not confine ourselves to hitting only primary military targets but should include secondary targets such as raw material supplies, commercial shipping and railroads, rolling stock, hospitals, political indoctrination schools, police stations, kindergartens and the shopping centres of the main cities. Our aim should be to utterly smash the population centres such as Hanoi and Haiphong so that they can no longer support human, animal or plant life nor even that of microbes and bacteria."

William P. Bundy interjected, "You realise Mr Secretary that bombing purely civilian targets is contrary to the *1949 Geneva Conventions on Land Warfare*. It is a maxim of international humanitarian law that a military mission should not cause

unnecessary and superfluous collateral damage, injury to the civilian population or to civilian structures. In other words excessive, as I just said, *'collateral damage'* should be avoided at all costs."

Rusk laughed, "That is what another lawyer, Colonel Richard Vortex keeps telling me!"

President Johnson asked curiously, "Who is this Colonel Vortex?"

"Didn't you know sir?" replied General Earle Wheeler, adding, "He's in command of the *Khe Sanh* base along with Colonel David E. Lownds."

"What the deuce is a lawyer doing in command of *Khe Sanh*? Are you all crazy?" asked President Johnson. Then saying, "Do you want him to sell the base to the Communists! Or put it into his Trust Account for them!"

"No sir you don't understand. Colonel Vortex is commander of the 9th Marine Regiment. Being a lawyer is just one his hobbies shall we say. A sideline!"

"Oh!" was all President Johnson blurted.

William Bundy had been one of the close advisors to President John F. Kennedy.

His brother, McGeorge Bundy had also been an advisor.

Both of them persuaded Kennedy, along with others, to broaden the US involvement in Vietnam as well as, earlier, to launch the *Bay of Pigs* invasion that was not entirely satisfactory in terms of its expected outcome for the *anti-Castro League* in Florida.

William Bundy had 10 years experience in the CIA [Central Intelligence Agency] as well as being the Assistant Defence Secretary for International Security Affairs under President Kennedy from 1960 to 1963.

Dean Rusk yelled back angrily, "I know that! I know my International Law! Don't presume to teach me Law! What I meant was that we should destroy all civilian installations that give aid or sustenance to the North Vietnamese military apparatus and its coterie of criminals! I didn't mean to bomb these Asian civilians willy nilly!"

William Bundy grunted.

"Alright! Alright! Then!" His voice was extremely angry.

However Bundy was no dove either. For he was the principal architect of the *Gulf of Tonkin Resolution*. This Resolution gave President Johnson almost limitless powers to wage a war in South-East-Asia.

William Bundy had also devised the idea of 'SURGICAL BOMBING' and the Theory of 'GRADUATED RESPONSE.'

It was this theory of Graduated Response which governed the 'ROLLING THUNDER' Campaign from 1964 to 1967.

The United States would under this theory inform the Communists in Hanoi that such and such a structure, building or bridge would be blown up. This would give Giap

and his cronies and sycophants time to evacuate civilians from the area. Not that Giap was particularly concerned about casualties even amongst his own people.

In that regard Senior General Giap who was also the Defence Minister was unusually brutal and callous.

When the air strike had been concluded the United States Government would ask the Communist Politburo in Hanoi whether it wished to enter into meaningful negotiations for a settlement. If Hanoi refused then the process would be repeated. To *ad nauseam* if necessary as the United States had a plentiful supply of bombs and the capacity to make more.

Another set of targets would be hit and another cooling off period would ensue.

The Theory of Graduated Response and its concomitant technique of surgical bombing predicted that eventually the air strikes would force the North Vietnamese to the bargaining table. Unfortunately the Theory of Graduated Response proved to be wrong.

The Communists were absolutely intransigent in their refusal to negotiate or to compromise.

The Secretary of Defence Clark Clifford interrupted.

"Mr President. I think it is time that we proceed with the main briefing. Specifically *Khe Sanh* and the threat to that Marine combat base."

President Johnson said as he dropped the military reports on the table in front of him, "I agree."

Clark Clifford had only just been appointed as the Secretary of Defence.

He was a distinguished Washington lawyer who was also a close personal friend of the President. Clifford supported most of Johnson's war policies in the Vietnam Theatre.

However in the weeks ahead, Clifford would gradually shift away from his support of increasing troop commitments in Vietnam.

His disillusionment with the conflict would actually see him engage in a conspiracy against the President to extricate the United States from the war.

Clifford, would in the next few weeks, convene a council of *'wise men'* to debate continued American involvement in the war. They would include General Omar Bradley, former Ambassador Henry Cabot Lodge and former Secretary of State Dean Acheson among others.

President Johnson picked up a piece of paper and almost screamed.

"Have you seen this!"

"What is it sir?" asked General Wheeler.

Johnson continued as his face turned purple.

"This! This CBS correspondent in the State Department!"

Henry Kissinger asked, "You mean Marvin Kalb?"

"I do!"

"What did he say?" asked Walt Rostow.

President Johnson explained, "This Kalb fellow said that, and I quote;

"...the historical ghost of the French disaster was casting a long shadow over Washington!"

Robert Komer laughed, "You mean he is referring to the French defeat at *Dien Bien Phu?*"

The President nodded as Walt Rostow scowled viciously.

"That's preposterous Mr President!" added Robert Komer.

Robert Komer was a graduate of Harvard University. Under the Kennedy Administration and then Johnson's he became a CIA analyst.

Komer was a superlative expert on the French colonial period in Indochina. He had read practically every book or article ever written on Western intervention in South-East-Asia.

He had a superb analytical mind that dissected every problem with the precision of a brain surgeon.

Komer advocated and masterminded the 'PHOENIX Operation.'

This CIA run covert operation in Vietnam attempted to win over the Vietnamese people and paralleled the *'Pacification' Program* to subdue the hamlets and villages in South Vietnam.

Komer also started the CORDS Program which stood for *Civil Operations and Rural Development Support.*

The White House staff often called Komers' messages as *'Komergrams'* because of their easy and free wheeling style that was not afraid to get straight to the point.

The troops in Vietnam called him the *'Blowtorch.'*

Komer set up the *Accelerated Pacification Program* (APC). He realised that the ordinary people and peasants in Vietnam had to be brought over to the Thieu and Nguyen Cao Ky government as quickly as possible.

"Do you think so?" asked Johnson.

Komer replied, "I do Mr President! The French situation in 1954 at *Dien Bien Phu* is totally different to the current scenario at *Khe Sanh*. Or for that matter in the whole Vietnam Theatre of operations!"

President Johnson grunted his approval and said, "But I want to know more about this *DINBINPHOO* engagement that defeated the French!"

General Wheeler said smartly, "I have anticipated that request sir. And I have prepared a small briefing for you before we get on with the *Khe Sanh* business."

"Excellent!" said President Johnson, "Get on with it then!"

General Earl Wheeler pressed the intercom button on the President's desk.

"Bring it in now!" he ordered in a stern military voice.

A few moments later two officers walked into the Oval Office carrying a large map approximately 6 feet high by 4 feet wide. It was an extremely detailed map with arrows and circles and other insignia on it.

President Johnson could clearly see that it was a battle map of some kind.

"Will there be anything else sir?" asked one of the aides who was a USAF Major.

The map was placed on a portable stand in front of the President's desk.

"No. You may leave," said General Wheeler.

Then the Chairman of the Joint Chiefs of Staff turned to the President and said, "This, Mr President, is *Dien Bien Phu*."

Henry Kissinger approved as he studied the relief map.

Kissinger was a student of Harvard and later taught there on subjects such as government policy and foreign affairs.

In the middle of 1967 he was contacted by several French acquaintances to serve as liaison between President Johnson and Ho Chi Minh.

"It is good Mr President that you study the lessons of military history. Such knowledge will hopefully prevent the repetition of the *Dien Bien Phu* fiasco," said Kissinger.

President Johnson nodded and said, "I remember when I was on the Senate Armed Services Committee in 1954. I was at that time opposed to any American operation to rescue the French forces at *Dinbinphoo*."

Walt Rostow added, "If I remember correctly sir. There was a plan by Admiral Radford which was called Operation *VULTURE*."

President Johnson asked as he shifted in his luxurious leather armchair, "Operation *Vulture*? What the hell was that?"

The National Security Advisor explained.

"Operation *Vulture* was a contingency plan drawn up by the Pentagon War Plans Directorate. It proposed saving the French forces at *Dien Bien Phu* by dropping at least 20 Atomic Fission bombs on the encircling *VietMinh* forces.

Each of those weapons would have had ten times the explosive power of the Hiroshima bomb."

Dean Rusk interjected, "It sounded like an excellent idea to me!"

Walt Rostow nodded to the Secretary of State, "It was a magnificent plan! It would have not only saved the beleaguered French forces from the clutches of Giap but it would have decimated the better part of 5 North Vietnamese (Viet Minh) front line divisions.

That would probably have turned the tide of the war back in favour of the French!"

Dean Rusk said as he looked to the President, "Sir! I am convinced that if Operation *Vulture* would have been executed back in 1954 then we here today would not have the problem of the Vietnam War to contend with.

The French would probably still be in control of Indochina. The Communists would have been smashed!"

The President said, "You may be right gentlemen. But let us examine the strategy and tactics of this General Vo Nguyen Giap at *Dinbinphoo* that is such a thorn in our proverbial backsides now. This analysis may give us some fresh insight into how to deal with Giap's dastardly and cowardly attack on *Khe Sanh* now."

General Wheeler nodded and looked to President Johnson.

"May I begin sir?" he asked.

President Johnson nodded and lit up a cigarette.

General Wheeler took up a long ivory pointing baton with a pearl handled top from the map stand.

He was like a task master at some strict English grammar school.

"Gentlemen!" he began, "*Dien Bien Phu* was a French fortress on the Laotian border.

It was created when 2 French parachute battalions were dropped into the Nam Yum River Valley near the village of *Dien Bien Phu* on the morning of the 20th November 1953. The battlefield commander was General de Division Rene Cogny."

Clark Clifford interrupted as General Wheeler pointed to the map.

"Who was the overall commander?"

"It was General Henri Navarre," answered General Wheeler.

Then he continued, "His main aim in setting up the base was to create an 'airhead' for future offensive operations near the Laotian border.

The 2 French parachute battalions had a brief battle with the Viet Minh troops who occupied the village.

The Communists were caught by surprise.

In the next 4 days the French dropped in 3 additional parachute battalions and a Headquarters field Regiment.

The whole exercise was called '*Operation Castor*.'"

General Cogny then began to lengthen and improve the *Dien Bien Phu* airstrip and ordered his elite parachute troops to begin digging earthworks and field defences.

Then General Navarre appointed a new commander.

Colonel Christian de la Croix de Castries. This new commander had orders to turn *Dien Bien Phu* into a fortress.

Navarre told him not to even contemplate the notion of a retreat or withdrawal from *Dien Bien Phu*.

He would use half his troops to defend the base.

The other half of his paratroopers would launch offensive raids into the Nam Yum River Valley.

The objective of General Navarre was to push the Viet Minh out of the lower foothills near the Laotian border and thus make possible a link up with other French

units inside Laos itself. Additional French battalions were dropped into *Dien Bien Phu* by C-47's and other aircraft until the troop strength reached 10,814 men.

The overall French strength consisted of 4 Foreign Legion battalions, 1 Moroccan, 3 Algerian and 2 native T'ai battalions.

However General Giap ordered an intense bombardment of the *Dien Bien Phu* airstrip with his 105mm howitzers.

Over the coming weeks the Viet Minh would bring in the equivalent of 3 Artillery Regiments to support their 49,000 assault troops and sappers."

As General Earle Wheeler spoke he indicated all the salient points of interest on the battle map.

Everyone, including the President, listened avidly.

The Chairman of the Joint Chiefs of Staff continued, "Week by week the Viet Minh artillery fire increased in intensity and in accuracy.

The French down in the valley were a very exposed and concentrated target.

The Viet Minh forces also held the hill positions around the *Dien Bien Phu* bastion [*which was not the case in the Khe Sanh scenario*]. Thus they could use this advantage to direct their artillery fire with greater precision and deadliness.

The French paratroopers also had to cut down most of the vegetation and wood on the valley floor to use for fuel and for camouflage. This made them even more conspicuous to Giap's forces. The Viet Minh knew the entire disposition of the French garrison.

By the beginning of March 1954 General Vo Nguyen Giap had massed 3 Viet Minh Infantry Divisions around the perimeter of *Dien Bien Phu*.

In addition, the 351st Heavy Division with its 48 105mm howitzers, 48 75mm guns and 120mm mortars were also committed into the coming battle by the Viet Minh. The Communists also had large numbers of anti-aircraft weapons brought in to interdict the aerial resupply of *Dien Bien Phu* by the French.

Most of the transport aircraft were supplied *gratis* to the French by the United States as per President Truman's orders.

The air space above *Dien Bien Phu* was called the '*chamber-pot.*'

The battle began in earnest on the night of 13th March 1954.

General Giap attacked the 5 separate but interconnected French strongholds. These defensive positions were called…"

As General Wheeler spoke he pointed to the French positions on the relief battle map.

"…*Gabrielle* to the north; *Beatrice* to the north-east; *Anne-Marie* to the north-west; and in the centre; *Huguette, Dominique, Eliane, Claudine* and *Francoise*. The central defensive positions formed the main *Dien Bien Phu* base with its main airstrip.

About a mile to the south was '*Isabelle*' which had an auxiliary French airstrip.

General Giap launched a massive artillery bombardment on that night of the 13th March 1954.

The intense fire blew apart almost every French plane on the airstrip. The bunkers, foxholes and trenches were smashed in a sea of French blood.

The Viet Minh came forward in suicide attacks all along the barbed wire perimeter of *Dien Bien Phu*. They had explosive charges attached to their bodies and when the Communists reached the concertina wire they blew apart that section of the French defence perimeter."

Walt Rostow exclaimed with horror, "They are absolutely fanatical!"

General Wheeler nodded and continued, "By the morning of the 14th March 1954 the north-eastern stronghold of *Beatrice* had fallen to the Viet Minh.

The French paratroopers were stunned and in a state of utter shock. They had never expected the Communist attack to be so vicious and so strong.

49,000 Communist troops faced only 10,800 French paratroopers. The overall strategy of Giap was to reduce and crush each stronghold one by one.

The heavy artillery possessed by the French was all situated in the central position around the village of *Dien Bien Phu*. But during the Communist bombardment these field pieces had almost been totally destroyed.

The outposts held by the French had thus almost no artillery support except for the recoilless rifles and mortars they had with them.

The Viet Minh slowly closed the noose ever tighter around the French bastion in the coming weeks.

Giap used siege tactics such as the digging of trenches and employing forward sappers to gradually encroach upon the French defensive positions.

Then a remarkable thing happened!"

President Johnson interrupted, "What was that?"

General Wheeler smiled ingratiatingly, "There was a mutiny in the French forces!"

Dean Rusk, "Oh! My God!"

Wheeler informed, "The French parachute *'Mafia'* of battalion commanders conspired together and replaced Colonel Castries. They considered him no longer fit to lead the besieged French forces at *Dien Bien Phu*!"

Clark Clifford uttered, "Unbelievable!"

General Wheeler continued, "On the night of the 6th May 1954 General Giap brought up some Soviet-made *Katyusha* rocket-launchers. These weapons devastated the remaining French strongholds.

The merciless and brutal bombardment continued all night and into the morning of the 7th May 1954. The French were squeezed into one last remaining pocket of resistance around the southern end of the main airstrip.

It was Colonel de Castries who called General Navarre and General Cogny in Hanoi by field phone. Castries told them that the battle was lost.

The Colonel then informed Giap that the remaining French troops consisting of about 1,000 men would lay down their arms at 1730 hours on the 7th May 1954.

Thus ended the vicious *Battle of Dien Bien Phu!*"

President Johnson was visibly shaken at this accurate description of the French humiliation at *Dien Bien Phu*.

He turned livid and seemed to perspire profusely.

"Are you alright sir?" asked Walt Rostow who noticed the unhealthy appearance of the President.

Johnson opened his mouth but could not find any words. His mind was filled with visions of American troops being slaughtered and blown to pieces by North Vietnamese PAVN troops in a *Dien Bien Phu* type scenario.

He felt like vomiting.

Johnson knew that if *Khe Sanh* would fall his Vietnam policy would shatter into a million pieces.

He also knew that he would lose the Presidency and be disgraced in the eyes of the American people.

But what he worried about more was that he would be vilified as an incompetent idiot in the History Books of the future.

He was so terrified that images of nuclear bombs with angel's wings floating down as saviours from heaven started to fill his mind and he was having second thoughts about not using them immediately at *Khe Sanh*. It was only the spectre of a World War III with the Imperialist Russians and the Mongoloid Chinese that held him back.

Johnson came to the realisation at that moment that extraordinary measures would have to be taken by him to prevent an *'American' Dien Bien Phu* at *Khe Sanh*.

He wished that cruddy, miserable, fucking little base had never been built in the first place out in the middle of the boon-docks.

Walt Rostow could see the President's mind ticking over.

The National Security Advisor knew the President well enough to recognise that his boss was in a state of panic and might at any moment with his *finger on-the-button* order United States Forces worldwide up from DEFCON-4 to an immediate DEFCON-3 or even DEFCON-2 status. If that would happen then the employment of tactical nuclear weapons at *Khe Sanh* was only days away. Once that would happen the Strategic nuclear arsenal of the *Strategic TRIAD* would be poised for an all out assault on the Bolsheviks in Moscow and the Chinese. Vietnam would turn into a side-show just as the *Africa Corps* Campaign in Tunis and Libya was a side-show during World War II where the Eastern Front decided the

fate of the valiant and gallant *Tripartite Pact* led by the National Socialist Government in Germany under the Fuhrer.

Rostow jumped to his feet to take advantage of the moment.

He wanted to push his views forward and transform them into solid policy action.

"Mr President!" he exclaimed.

Johnson took out his handkerchief and wiped the sweat off his brow.

"Mr President! We must ensure that all military steps are taken to pre-empt any possibility of a similar disaster befalling our American boys who are gallantly defending *Khe Sanh*."

Walt Rostow took a deep breath and looked at Dean Rusk before he spoke.

Dean Rusk nodded silently.

"I must insist Mr President that you give the orders for the immediate deployment of tactical nuclear weapons at *Khe Sanh*!"

Dean Rusk said, "It is the paramount option sir!"

General Wheeler added, "I assure you Mr President that it will be completely safe and our nuclear response will be measured and fully controlled!"

Johnson leaned back in his sumptuous leather chair.

He gazed vacantly about the Oval Office as if looking for something visible.

Walt Rostow and Dean Rusk could see that the President was wavering.

General Wheeler's description of the *Dien Bien Phu* fiasco was having a profound effect.

The eerie silence in the Oval Office continued for a few more moments.

Finally the President said, "I'll have to look at the nuclear option in more detail.

I must examine it thoroughly.

Particularly, I must know what the Soviets and the Chinese may do or how they will react if we choose the nuclear option."

General Wheeler said confidently, "Sir! As was mentioned before. I am sure the Soviets and the Chinese will do nothing."

Clark Clifford jumped to his feet and walked over to the map of *Dien Bien Phu*.

The Secretary of Defence studied the battle map and then swung on the balls of his feet to face the President.

"I think any possible use of nuclear weapons will be a mistake! A fatal mistake!"

Dean Rusk waved his hands at Clifford.

"Oh! Rubbish!"

Clark Clifford persisted, "Sir! If we smash the PAVN with nuclear weapons we risk escalating the conflict. The response of the Soviets would be immediate and deadly.

The North Atlantic Treaty Organisation (NATO) would find itself under terrible pressure.

The Soviets would put their Warsaw Pact forces on a higher state of alert. The likelihood of an all out war with the Russians would increase!"

Walt Rostow snapped back, "I simply can't agree with you Clifford!"

President Johnson started to gather himself together.

"Now listen up gentlemen. I am not going to make any decision about the use of atomic shells from 175mm howitzers or atomic bombs dropped from B-52's without first consulting the Pentagon War Plans Directorate.

I also want input from General Westmoreland and the MACV staff in Saigon."

The President put his hand to his face, trying to rub the creases of worry and anxiety from his leather-like skin, adding, "And for that matter I would like the opinion of this Lawyer you put in charge of *Khe Sanh* – this Colonel of Marines, what's his name, …"

Henry Kissinger answered to help, "Its Colonel Richard Vortex sir."

Johnson continued, "Yes, Colonel Vortex and Colonel David E. Lownds. If I decide to unleash hell over there I want to have at least the input of the two senior field commanders actually on the ground. Not just a boutique of Ivy League pen-pushers here in Washington D.C. and yourselves for that matter. And any final decision has to be considered by the National Security Council and also XCOM. I also want, before I press that damned red button, the opinion of Dean Acheson as well. I greatly respect his wisdom and experience in the early Cold War period when he served under the Truman and Eisenhower Administrations."

Then President Johnson put out his hands to the men in the Oval Office in a gesture of entreaty.

"And please! I do not want anything said in this room to be leaked to the press or to anybody else!"

Everyone nodded their heads sullenly.

"Now! General Wheeler! I want to know what can be done for the *Khe Sanh* garrison on the ground. In terms of purely conventional weaponry."

President Johnson, General Wheeler and all the others trooped out of the Oval Office and made their way down to the White House basement situation room.

As they assembled around the sand-table model of the *Khe Sanh* plateau, General Wheeler began the briefing.

"As you know sir, *Khe Sanh* was attacked on the night of the 20th to 21st January 1968.

The North Vietnamese have massed 4 front line divisions around the Marine base termed KSCB.

The 304th and the 325thC *Golden Star* Divisions are directly north and west of the Marine bastion.

In addition the 320th and 324th enemy divisions are poised along the DMZ [Demilitarised Zone]."

Henry Kissinger interrupted General Wheeler, "Earle, I think it would be a good idea to let the President know how the base at *Khe Sanh* first came to be and the early history of the engagements that took place there and in the surrounding hills and along Route 9 which leads to the Laos border and Tchepone. Without filling the President in on that background it would not be possible for the President to understand how this current crisis at *Khe Sanh* came about.

Don't you think so?"

General Earle Wheeler nodded to Kissinger, "Yes of course! No problem."

Robert Komer interjected, "Do you want me to give the President the early history of how the base at *Khe Sanh* came to be? As you know I am the number one superlative and unchallenged expert on all of the History of South-East-Asia and Indochina Wars 1 and 2."

Clark Clifford scoffed, "Yes, and modest too!"

The men in the room chuckled, all except of course, Robert Komer, who looked at Clark Clifford as if he could scratch his eyes out.

General Wheeler said, "By all means Robert. You take over – if you like."

Robert Komer stepped up to the sand table relief model of the KSCB and began as President Johnson and the others listened with avid and undiluted attention. They were right in believing that Robert Komer was the world's number one expert on the Indochina conflicts and their social and economic backgrounds in all their myriad facets and nuances.

Komer began, as he snatched the pointing baton away from General Wheeler,

"General Westmoreland is of the opinion that the PAVN are attempting a repetition of their triumph over the French at *Dien Bien Phu*. However I am not so sure about that. Whether General Giap thinks that *Khe Sanh* itself is strategically important as it stands alone is also debatable. The other theory is that the North Vietnamese may be using *Khe Sanh* as a trap or bait to draw our forces away from the populated areas of the coast. Our manoeuvre battalions that is."

History of the Khe Sanh Combat Base Prior to the Advent of the Siege on night of 20th to 21st January 1968

Robert Komer continued after lighting up a Pal Mal, "The real strategic importance of *Khe Sanh* lies in the geography of Vietnam itself. And by this I mean of course that pain-in-the-ass *Ho Chi Minh Trail*. This trail or road network or whatever you want to call it has been used as a communication link between the north and the south since the conflict began between the Viet Minh Communists

and the French, during the First Indochina War. It is in fact a highly sophisticated interlacing of road paths and tracks that began in North Vietnam and entered Laos through the various mountain passes. As several of the trails penetrated South Vietnam at points while others crossed into Laos and Cambodia. The position of *Khe Sanh* is at a stricture point or intersection between the junction where North Vietnam, Laos and South Vietnam come together geographically. Thus for the Viet Minh and now the PAVN *Khe Sanh* was and is a major artery for their entry into the Northern I Corp area or northern South Vietnam.

It is obvious that a US military foothold at *Khe Sanh* would allow us to observe and monitor the Communist movement from North to South and for that matter the other way as well as they rotate troops and bring out their wounded and prisoners captured in the South.

As far back as July 1962 our forces made an initial presence at *Khe Sanh* being an Army Special Forces detachment. This unit moved into the Old French Fort next to the *Khe Sanh* village.

The ARVN, such as it was at the time, created a basic low grade runway or airstrip at *Khe Sanh*. One of their sapper/engineer teams were responsible for this. During 1962 and 1963 the Marine Corps deployed air assets to *Khe Sanh* such as helicopters to back up our Green Beret boys at the French Fort as well as the few ARVN units in the area.

Then in April 1964 the Marines inserted a communications intelligence unit to the area to keep a close eye on the Viet Cong and PAVN radio communications.

It was in April 1964 that General Westmoreland first inspected the base to see for himself how successful or otherwise these intelligence gathering operations had been.

It was not just '*Westy's*' opinion but that of most of the Pentagon boys and our own boys over at CIA in Langley that *Khe Sanh* could be used as a patrol base for the interdiction of enemy personnel and supplies coming down this infernal *Ho Chi Minh Trail* from Laos into northern South Vietnam. We could also harass them from there via covert operations and use the airstrip for aerial reconnaissance of the trail. *Khe Sanh* would also be the western-most terminus of the defensive line along the DMZ and a jumping off point for a full scale invasion of Laos to cut the trail.

Thus simply leaving *Khe Sanh* unattended would take away this buffer and knife at the throat of the *Ho Chi Minh Trail* allowing Giap and the PAVN to roll forward and take the initiative right into the coastal cities such as *Hue, Quang Tri, Da Nang* and *Dong Ha*."

"So what happened after April 1964?" asked President Johnson.

"Well sir, I am getting to that now," Robert Komer swept his hands over the sand table map like a maestro conducting a Wagnerian Opera, "In the Spring of 1966 this toad, General Giap, began to deploy large numbers of PAVN troops within the DMZ

in direct contravention of *public international law*. I have spoken to Colonel Richard Vortex about it during my last visit to Vietnam. We had lunch at the officer's club of the *25th Tropic Lightning Division* at *Cu Chi*. Vortex was there giving advice to the 25th Division boys on how to smoke out those midget rats, the Viet Cong, from their stinking tunnel complexes around the *'Iron Triangle'* as well as *War Zone C*. Well, to get on with it Mr President, we thought that Giap's rationale, if indeed he was capable of any, was to frustrate the U.S. Pacification Program. That was my *'baby'* as you know. I am talking about the *'Strategic Hamlet Program'*. The propaganda cretins in Hanoi said that the Strategic Hamlet Program was no better than the concentration camps of World War II as they accused us of putting the average South Vietnamese peasant behind barbed wire in confined pre-determined village locations."

Henry Kissinger said, "But you did and you are now still putting them behind barbed wire, Komer?"

Robert Komer became highly agitated as he riposted to Henry Kissinger, "Yes! We did! But it was for their own good! We placed them in *'protective villages'* and a safe environment secure from harassment and intimidation from the Viet Cong puppets and stooges of the North. It was for their own good."

Kissinger said calmly, "It still sounds a lot like concentration camps to me?"

Komer said sarcastically, "Whose side are you on anyway Kissinger. Don't go on harping about some ridiculous analogy about what happened in Europe some 23 years and more ago to what we at the CIA were doing to better the lives of the average South Vietnamese citizen then and now."

President Johnson interjected, "That's enough gentlemen! I did not come down into this drafty basement to hear you guys engage in a slanging match!"

Turning to Komer the President said, "Get on with it! I have to take my morning constitutional before lunch when we start all over again with that damned list of bombing targets that I have to choose while eating my soup and roast chicken."

Komer continued, "Well. Giap's plan was to suck US troops away from the populated areas of the South by opening a new strategic front away from central I Corps and II Field Force Vietnam [II FFV]. Giap thought, and of course in this respect he was right, that the North would have shorter supply lines and their movements would be more difficult for our forces to detect. Also that by drawing us ever deeper into the *'boon-docks'* it would prove more difficult for us to bring our massive firepower to bear on the enemy because of the geographically inhospitable terrain. And he was right to a certain extent.

Our computers were fed with every scrap of INTEL that we could hanker-up, from spies on the ground, from deserters, prisoners and from our sophisticated sensors, both acoustic/chemical and seismic that we placed by air insertion into the triple canopied jungle around the DMZ and the *A Shau Valley* all the way to *Quang Tri* and

the coast. The Pentagon boys came to the conclusion that this concentration of PAVN and Main Force Viet Cong forces was the encore to launch a major attack across the DMZ. General Westmoreland moved, in response to this, further units up to the north being mainly Marine assets under Lieutenant General Cushman and Major General Herman J. Nickerson Jr.

So, during the passing of 1966 and 1967 the skirmishes along the DMZ intensified. I can accurately report that, according to CIA and Pentagon analysis that, we lost 541 KIA while the PAVN/Viet Cong lost 3,492 KIA. But in my opinion these losses were not that debilitating for Giap and his gang of war criminals. Though, some in the War Plans Directorate of the Pentagon would beg to differ.

So what did Giap do in response to this increased velocity and intensity of fighting head-to-head along the DMZ?

He acted like any coward would. He turned volte-face and skirted around the DMZ like a rat and went for a flanking movement to *Tchepone* in Laos and then sweeping across the border towards *Khe Sanh* and our Green Beret camp at *Lang Vei*.

This, thought the PAVN was a much easier avenue of entry. And indeed it was!

In March 1967, we had only one Company of our Marine boys at the *Khe Sanh* base and surrounding areas being the Hills 881 South and North, Hills 861 and its sister Hill 861A, Hill 558 and Hill 950 which was used and still is, as a radio beacon outpost and communications interdiction point.

Much to the, I admit, poor planning of MACV, we did not have the capability then, for a mobile defence and offensive posture due to lack of air assets, troops, artillery and logistics and supply points nor Fire Bases whose interlocking field of fire parameters, one covering the other covering the next in the line could have severely thwarted the plans of Giap for this concentration of forces around the *Khe Sanh* area and down into the *A Shau Valley*.

We, at the time, could only maintain a static, billboard-type of defence around *Khe Sanh* by the usual patrolling and aerial reconnaissance and the use of counter-batter fire and artillery interdiction. This posture was simply to prevent PAVN infiltration.

Then in April 1967, the PAVN increased their attacks against the *Khe Sanh* base. The Communists used sappers to blow up critical points along Route 9 to cut the road link between *Khe Sanh* and *Lang Vei* to the West and to the east with Camp Carroll, the Rockpile and on to *Ca Lu* and *Quang Tri*.

Giap assigned one PAVN Regiment to permanently occupy positions around the KSCB.

At the same time Giap ordered other battalions and regiments of the PAVN to step-up diversionary rocket, sapper, artillery and mortar attacks at the surrounding Fire Support Bases such as *Camp Carroll* and the *Rockpile*. Our helicopter staging areas were also hit.

The Siege of Khe Sanh 1967-1968

In April 1967 the PAVN with their puppet VC launched a major attack to capture the KSCB and the airfield with secondary attacks against the French Fort and *Lang Vei* Green Beret forces.

However I am happy to say that Giap and the PAVN fucked-up and we kicked them back with heavy losses.

In order to do this General William Westmoreland moved two Marine manoeuvre battalions by air to the *Khe Sanh* area. This was the end of *Khe Sanh* Stage 1.

The powers-to-be in Hanoi then did a back-flip in strategic policy and planning. They decided in their wisdom or rather lack of it, to try to destroy my *'Strategic Hamlet Program'* and Pacification Program, to expand their tentacles into the countryside and to try to end what they saw as our imminent plans to invade the North proper, which we never had but which we should have had, and to destroy our *'will'* to resist with the aim of dragging us to the peace conference table. To do this they decided to bring the war into the cities and large towns of South Vietnam where hitherto we had the predominance.

So, in October 1967, Giap ordered more troops and supplies to be brought down the stinking *Ho Chi Minh Trail* to be infiltrated across the border areas of *Khe Sanh*. These units, as was already mentioned by Earle, included the 304th Division, the first large formation of the PAVN to enter South Vietnam proper, followed by the 325th C *Golden Star* Division and the 320th Division. This brought Communist strength up to 22,000 men plus the Main Force Viet Cong units if counted in would bring their numbers up to approximately 35,000 to 40,000 troops plus supporting arms.

On the other side of the coin, we had at *Khe Sanh*, one Marine infantry battalion reinforced with Marine tanks and artillery.

Now, in December 1967 and January 1968, General Westmoreland bolstered our forces with three more Marine Battalions, including Colonel Vortex's 9th Marines, plus the 37th ARVN Ranger battalion being one of the best units in the forces of the South. We now have about 6,053 troops in and round KSCB and the Hills I just mentioned.

At this moment 50% of our strength is deployed on those hills with the rest in KSCB itself.

In terms of geography KSCB is on a slight plateau while the Hills provide a good observation point for infiltration and artillery spotting around the environs of KSCB.

On those hills we have all the organic infantry weapons that we could muster such as mortars, recoilless rifles, light artillery like the 105mm howitzer, the heavier medium howitzer being the 155mm and the ONTOS tracked anti-tank vehicle, the M50A1 which we call the 'PIG'.

We now have 50% of all our manoeuvre battalions in I Corps. This is not an ideal situation as its strips a lot of our firepower from II, III and IV Corp Operational Areas and especially from II Field Force Vietnam [II FFV] under General Weyand.

We have ordered Colonel David E. Lownds and Colonel Richard Vortex to dig in at the KSCB and expect the worst.

That's how the situation sums up at this point in time."

Henry Kissinger asked, "And what about those prisoners or spies that you captured at KSCB in the last couple of months?"

President Johnson added, "Yes! I want to know about those prisoners from the North?"

Robert Komer answered, "Well. I was just getting to that Mr President."

Komer took a sip of water and continued, "On 17th January 1968, just one week ago, one of our reconnaissance patrols was ambushed by a PAVN force near Hill 881 South. On the early morning of 20th January 1968 the I Company,

3rd Battalion, 26th Marines under the command of Captain William H. Dabney set out to find the ambush site to recover possible lost classified INTEL and other communications intercepts. Captain Dabney ran into a very stiff east-west defensive line north of 881 South and half-way to Hill 881 North. The fighting continued for hours with all the organic infantry weapons of both sides. Colonel Vortex and Colonel Lownds ordered Captain Dabney to disengage and withdraw back to Hill 881 South.

Then as we know, on 21st January 1968 the PAVN launched a full-phase artillery/mortar bombardment of KSCB destroying the ammunition dump. Colonel Lownds' quarters were obliterated as well as the PX, the Mess Hall, some UH-1B's and other air assets. We lost 16,000 artillery shells and a large quantity of C.S. tear gas that spread around the KSCB much to the discomfort of our troops. This pile of ordnance 'cooked-off' for more than 48 hours.

It was a fucking fiasco.

These attacks brought the whole media circus down on our heads.

In response the 7th Air Force and the Marine Air Wing brought in C-124's and C-130's and we resupplied the lost ordnance.

Now, it is my opinion and that of General Westmoreland that this is no diversion. General Philip Davidson head of J-2 for MACV also believes that this is not a diversion but a genuine attempt by the PAVN to make *Khe Sanh* into another *Dien Bien Phu*.

This was our golden opportunity to at last pin the enemy down in large concentrations as they massed for the *Khe Sanh* attack allowing us to bring the meat grinder of our massive air power and infantry firepower to bear on the enemy thus allowing us to annihilate them in an orgy of destruction.

We have been waiting for this moment for 3 years now since late 1964.

I just wish I could be there to see it.

This is the problem that the French Army had as well in Indochina War One. The French Generals were frustrated at never being able to lure the large divisional

and corps sized formations of the Viet Minh into large set-piece battles, where they thought, that superior French tactics and firepower could crush and kill them.

Basically, General Westmoreland and we too at Langley want to use the coming *Khe Sanh* battle as a 'killing ground' to inflict a massive and humiliating defeat on that asshole, Giap.

I have spoken also to Captain Mirza Baig at the MATU and FSCC facilities and he believes, and I agree, that we must allow the enemy to mass around the perimeter of the KSCB, to expose their supply lines and staging areas, siege works, communication and anti-air assets and then using Combat SKYSPOT and Arc-Light raids along with TAC air we can cut them to pieces. This is the whole rationale behind Operation NIAGARA.

We in the United States have the best high technology killing machine in the world.

And I personally want to see it used to fucking annihilate those Communist bastards!

This *Khe Sanh* confrontation is without a doubt the heaviest concentration of opposing forces so far in the entire Vietnam Conflict to date and I mean as far back as 1959-1960 when President Kennedy sent in our first advisors to President Diem.

Then on 2nd January 1968 a sentry dog at the base perimeter discovered a group of six PAVN infiltrators. They were challenged in English. No answer came. So they were fired upon. Five out of six were killed. They were no ordinary PAVN soldiers. Amongst the dead were a Regimental Commander, the Operations officer, Communications officer and NCO's.

Then on 20th January, just 3 days ago, we captured a PAVN officer at the eastern end of the KSCB airstrip. His name was Lieutenant La Thanh Tonc. It is believed that he is the commander of the 14th Anti-aircraft Company of the 325thC *Golden Star* Division.

This fucking Lieutenant Tonc spilled out his guts to us.

Colonel Vortex personally interrogated Tonc with his usual zeal and unconventional methods eliciting a lot of useful information which could turn out to be the biggest intelligence coup of the war to date.

This Tonc claimed that he defected because he was angry at being passed over for promotion and of being constantly told a croc-of-shit from his Communist superiors. He also cited the terrible casualties suffered by his men due to our superlative and God sanctioned firepower against the Communist heathens.

Tonc told Vortex under persuasive pressure applied by Richard, who happens to be a good friend of mine, that the main attack was to come that very evening of 20th to 21st January 1968 just 3 days ago. And he was correct as we know.

The plan, according to Tonc, was for Giap to capture Hill 861/861A and then move in on KSCB itself. The action called for interdicting the aerial supply, blasting the airstrip and the Marine artillery emplacements. Tonc even claimed that Giap had tanks in reserve just across the DMZ to support this action.

This intelligence seemed to indicate that the whole thrust of the PAVN attack was to capture our bases along the east-west axis of the DMZ and I Corps in order to put Pham Van Dong and his criminals in a better bargaining position at the conference table.

I should mention that Robert Brewer our boy in *Quang Tri* and one of our CIA operatives captured a Communist communication indicating this very sequence of events.

As you know all came to pass just after midnight on the 21st January 1968 when the bombardment began and the ammunition dump went sky high along with everything else I have just stipulated to you Mr President including the attack on Hill 861/861A.

So as it stands we believe that from 21st January 1968 onwards it is Giap's plan to capture KSCB."

As Robert Komer finished he felt quite satisfied with his debriefing of the President.

President Johnson asked, "But I still don't understand why the 320th and 324th Divisions of Giap are back at the DMZ? What are they doing there? Why aren't they threatening *Khe Sanh* with the other two, the 325th C and the 304th?"

General Wheeler reached into his leather attaché case and fumbled with a set of aerial photographs.

"Well sir. I have been speaking with Brigadier General Davidson and General Westmoreland this morning. I rang them in Saigon at about 5am our time.

It is the opinion of the MACV J-2 Intelligence Directorate that Giap is holding these divisions in reserve.

We think that he may try to bring in the 324th and 320th to crush *Khe Sanh* in the final stages of the battle."

Henry Kissinger asked, "Or, the North Vietnamese may launch another strike upon a totally different target while the *Khe Sanh* battle is in progress."

Walt Rostow nodded, "Yes Henry. I think that the Communists may attack the ancient Imperial city of *Hue* on the coast along the Perfume River."

Johnson asked, "Why Hue? Does it have any strategic importance?"

Dean Rusk answered as he looked at Robert Komer, "Absolutely Mr President! This city straddles the north-south highway. They call it *National Route 1*. In Bernard Fall's excellent book about the French Indochina War he called it, '*The Street Without*

Joy'. If the Communists took Hue it would dislocate the entire logistical structure of our forces in the I Corps Operational Zone."

General Wheeler pointed with his pearl handled ivory baton to the American bases at the *Rockpile* and *Camp Carroll*.

"Sir. What the Secretary of State says may be a possibility. But we in the Joint Chiefs of Staff think that the North Vietnamese may assault our bases here. At the Rockpile and Camp Carroll."

Clark Clifford said as he leaned over the sand-table model, "Doesn't *Camp Carroll* give heavy artillery support to *Khe Sanh*?"

General Wheeler answered in the affirmative and went on.

"If the PAVN take the *Rockpile* and *Camp Carroll* then it would drive a wedge in-between our III MAF [Marine Amphibious Force] in the I Corps Operational Zone. It would wipe out the heavy artillery support for *Khe Sanh* from our 175mm howitzers at *Camp Carroll*. And most importantly it would prevent any relief operation from being mounted to lift the siege of *Khe Sanh*."

Robert Komer added as he looked to the President, "It would also put Giap in a position of being able to 'roll up' the whole I Corps front and drive us back to the coast and the Perfume River outlet to the sea!"

Dean Rusk added, "And if that would happen Mr President. Then it would be an even bigger disaster than simply losing the *Khe Sanh* base!"

President Johnson said, "Then you must not allow these bases to be taken. What steps have you initiated to prevent this?"

General Wheeler said, "MACV has moved up two battalions from the 1st Marine Division, as Komer said, and an airborne brigade from the 101st Airborne Division. These units will reinforce our positions all along the DMZ."

Clark Clifford rubbed his chin.

"I disagree Mr President," began the Secretary of Defence.

"It is my opinion that the enemy are massing for an attack against *Con Thien* and *Gio Linh* further to the east and near the coast."

General Wheeler scoffed with disdain and asked, "Why do you think that Mr Secretary?"

Clifford explained, "Because that is where the PAVN hit us early last year."

Walt Rostow laughed, "And what do you know about military tactics? Especially battlefield tactics? You only became the Secretary of Defence a few days ago! You're just a lawyer for Christ's sake!"

Clark Clifford slammed his fist against the edge of the sand-table reconstruction so that some of the toy American flags on the model jumped up into the air.

His face was purple with rage.

"And what do *you* know about military strategy? You are not a General!"

Walt Rostow stammered back with fury, "I am an expert in military and strategic affairs!"

Clifford laughed, "Says who? You?"

President Johnson intervened, "That is enough gentlemen! I would appreciate a modicum of decorum thank you. Let's keep the fighting confined to these North Vietnamese jackals!"

The men grunted their assent.

Henry Kissinger just shook his head in disbelief.

Then Johnson asked Wheeler, "Earle? I don't understand something. You said there were how many Marines at *Khe Sanh*?"

The Chairman answered, "Approximately 6,000 Marines sir. Including a battalion of Vietnamese Rangers. The final elements of that ARVN unit will arrive at the base on the 27th January 1968."

President Johnson ran his fingers through his hair and mumbled to himself.

He said, "Six thousand. That is a sizeable force. Why don't the Marines just retreat down this National Route 9 and link up with our forces to the east at, say, *Camp Carroll*?"

General Wheeler answered, "Mr President. It is not as simple as that. One reinforced Marine Regiment of 6,000 men cannot simply pack up its equipment and walk away from two enemy divisions! Perhaps three.

One regiment cannot fight its way through territory for some 20 to 30 miles when it is surrounded by such overwhelming enemy forces."

President Johnson asked, "What would happen if they tried?"

Walt Rostow pre-empted the General, "They would be cut to pieces sir!"

Wheeler hated to be upstaged by the cocky National Security Advisor and said calmly, "They would be ambushed by the regular PAVN forces and decimated."

President Johnson asked, "Even with our awesome air superiority?"

General Wheeler nodded, "Even with that."

President Johnson shook his head with despair.

"So? What is Westmoreland doing?"

General Wheeler said, "COMUSMACV has decided to hold the base at all costs. And as you know, Operation NIAGARA is already underway."

Johnson remarked, "Operation NIAGARA will saturate the Communists with enough firepower so that they will not be able to overrun the base?"

General Wheeler said, "Absolutely! There will be two cells of six B-52 bombers over *Khe Sanh* every 90 minutes. They will pound the storage areas, troop concentrations and artillery emplacements of the enemy. In addition to that there will be a TAC air strike by fighter bombers over *Khe Sanh* every 5 minutes around the clock and regardless of weather conditions."

President Johnson nodded and said grimly, "I want to know the bottom line gentlemen! Is there any possibility that *Khe Sanh* will turn into another *Dinbinphoo*?"

Walt Rostow said, "That is impossible sir!"

Dean Rusk added, "Totally out of the question Mr President!"

Robert Komer said, "It is a totally different situation."

Johnson asked, "Tell me how it is different!"

Walt Rostow was just about to cut in to answer the President's question when General Wheeler beat him to it.

"Well! For one thing sir! The French as I said were caught in a small and inaccessible valley. The French had only a few artillery pieces. And these guns were smashed up early in the battle.

We have a formidable array of howitzers at *Khe Sanh*. In addition we have our heavy guns at *Camp Carroll* and the *Rockpile*. They can blast the enemy from outside the defensive perimeter. The French never had that.

The French also did not control the hills around the base.

We control all the important hill outposts."

Wheeler pointed with his baton, "Here! Mr President! Hills 881 South and North, Hills 558 and 861/861A and the Rock Quarry as well as Hill 950. This gives us an advantage in seeing the enemy as he approaches and denying the enemy his eyes to see us. The French never had that either.

What is more important is that the French troops lacked air support. The *Legionnaires* had only a few aircraft for resupply and a handful of fighters.

On the other hand we have a vast air armada of over 2,500 jet fighter-bombers to interdict enemy movement and annihilate troop concentrations as well as thousands of transport aircraft to fly in supplies and over 2,000 helicopters including the *Jolly Green Giants* and the *Tarhe* H-54 *Sky Crane* that can bring in M-1 Battle tanks if necessary.

The 2,000 helicopters are used to lift troops in and medevack wounded out of *Khe Sanh*.

The French had virtually no helicopters.

We have a fleet of deadly B-52 strategic bombers that can pound the PAVN at will from 35,000 feet with 500lb and 750lb iron bombs. They are guided onto their targets by electronic and seismic sensors using computers to analyse the information digitally.

This is called 'Operation COMBAT SKYSPOT.'

The French had no strategic bombers at all!"

President Johnson was nervously touching the small American Toy Flags on the sand-table model and as he held them he thought that he was holding the vestiges of his Presidency for if these flags were to be captured he would be a total disgrace in the

eyes of the American people and a putrid laughing stock in the eyes of the rest of the hostile world outside NATO.

He tried to wipe the nightmare visions of an American defeat at *Khe Sanh* out of his mind.

Wheeler continued, "Our reinforcements are quite close by along Route 9. The French had no other units around *Dien Bien Phu*."

President Johnson said gravely, "Alright gentlemen. That is the conventional scenario.

Now what about the possibility of using tactical nuclear weapons?"

Walt Rostow immediately jumped in as he rubbed his hands with glee.

The National Security Advisor jealously grabbed the pointing baton away from General Wheeler as he began to speak.

"Mr President! It is the most excellent tactic to use here at *Khe Sanh*!"

President Johnson asked sceptically, "Why?"

Rostow answered, "Because sir! The whole area around the *Khe Sanh* plateau is almost completely uninhabited. These conditions would be ideal for the employment of atomic munitions as there would be no civilians in the way to get accidentally nuked.

No chance of unnecessary *collateral damage* as we say.

It would pulverise the Communist troop concentrations as they formed up for the attack.

We could use the small 15 to 30 kiloton atomic W48 artillery shells as well as the slightly larger yield weapons."

President Johnson asked, "What larger yield weapons?"

General Wheeler answered, "He means the 300 kiloton to 1 million ton (1 Megaton) Fusion Bombs. It can be delivered by the B-52 or alternatively launched from our nuclear submarines on station in the *Gulf of Tonkin*."

President Johnson was aghast, "One million ton Fusion Bomb! Are you mad? You will blow away not only the fucking North Vietnamese but the whole of fucking I Corps as well! This is insane!"

Walt Rostow said flippantly, "No sir! But using these higher yield weapons would demonstrate to the North Vietnamese Politburo and to Prime Minister Pham Van Dong our '*Firmness Of Purpose*.'"

Henry Kissinger repeated as he rolled his eyes towards the ceiling of the decrepit little basement, "*Our Firmness Of Purpose*! Yes!"

Rostow scowled at Kissinger and Wheeler just shrugged his shoulders, saying, "You realise Mr President that a one million ton Fusion Bomb might sound a little bit big but we have much larger weapons in our arsenal that would definitely not have to be used at *Khe Sanh*."

President Johnson asked, "And you said that a one Megaton Fusion Bomb would have a minimal impact on the environment?"

Dean Rusk said, "Absolutely minimal Mr President. That's right."

Walt Rostow went on, "I have been speaking to General Westmoreland. He tells me that he is convinced that if we use nuclear weapons at *Khe Sanh* it would likely not have to be more than 15 kiloton up to a maximum of 300 kiloton fission bombs and it would demonstrate to the North Vietnamese that we mean business. Just as in World War II when we dropped the two atomic bombs, *Little Boy* and *Fat Boy* on Hiroshima and Nagasaki using *Enola Gay* and the other B-29 the *Boxcar*, with the resultant surrender of the Japanese Empire in Tokyo Bay on the *Battleship Missouri*. [Big Moe].

You may remember Mr President that the use of nuclear weapons at the end of World War II saved countless American lives, estimated at 1,000,000 troop casualties alone.

It negated our having to launch 'OPERATION OLYMPIC' the ground invasion of the Japanese mainland."

President Johnson thought for a few moments and then sat down in a luxurious red leather armchair that had been set up behind the sand-table model with the toy American battle flags of the 9th and 26th Marines.

Finally he said, "I shall tell you gentlemen what I want at this moment.

The loss of *Khe Sanh* would be the ultimate catastrophe not only for my Administration and my Presidency but also for the American God-fearing and righteous peoples as a whole.

Our natural superiority in the world would be undermined.

It would be a disaster for the United States on a biblical level and Jesus would be angry with us!

What is at stake here is our national pride and prestige and our current position as the *A One Number One* God-fearing righteous country in the whole damned world! Which we are!"

President Johnson turned to General Earle Wheeler and said with a frenzied look in his eyes.

"General! I want from you and the other Joint Chiefs a signed statement guaranteeing me that you are sure that General Westmoreland has the ability and the wherewithal to hold *Khe Sanh*!"

Stunned silence roared across the White House bunker.

Everybody in the room was flabbergasted.

Chapter 11
The Onslaught - Destruction of US Special Forces at LANG VEI

Colonel Richard Vortex was in the control tower adjacent to the *Khe Sanh* airstrip as the first of the *Fairchild* C-123 Providers came swooping in with the badly needed ammunition. It was 1230 hours on the 22nd January 1968.

Ngo Nhu was standing next to Vortex.

Her slim and beautiful body was leaning against him.

She felt comforted and at ease when in the Colonel's presence.

Colonel David E. Lownds walked up the stairs of the control tower as several PAVN artillery shells landed near the TAFDS [Tactical Airfield Fuel Dispensing System].

"Jesus!" exclaimed Lownds.

Debris from the explosions rocked the Marine bunkers nearby.

A ruined UH-1E helicopter that was lying on its side was hit again. Pieces of metal, rotor blades and Plexiglas flew through the air above the control tower.

It narrowly missed the officers standing there and fell back to earth right on top of the bunker ceiling of the MATU [Marine Air Traffic Control Unit].

"The bombardment is much less today!" said Vortex to Colonel Lownds.

The 26th commander nodded, "I wish it would stop altogether!"

Vortex laughed, "Fat fucking chance!"

Lownds asked, "Who's this?" He pointed to Ngo Nhu.

"I'm evacuating her along with the other 1,432 civilian refugees."

Vortex made his way down the tower and started to supervise the unloading of the badly needed ammunition.

A whole company of the 26th was detailed to man-handle the crates and boxes into a specially prepared bunker near the 155mm howitzer emplacements.

The Marines were returning fire into the valleys around *Khe Sanh*.

Everyday they fired 5 rounds for each incoming Communist shell or mortar bomb. But the Marines were the more visible, more concentrated target.

The PAVN constantly shifted back and forth through the jungle attempting to avoid the American TAC air strikes.

"Hurry up! Get a move on!" screamed Colonel Vortex to the Marines.

"We don't want that ammunition to blow up in our faces again before it is stored in the bunkers."

Master Sergeant Richter ran up and saluted.

"I'll make sure it is all packed away ASAP sir!"

"Good man," said Vortex as he slapped the huge Senior NCO on the back.

"Do I have to go now?" asked Ngo Nhu.

The beautiful South Vietnamese girl looked up at the six foot two and a half inch Vortex.

"It is best for you. You will be safe in *Quang Tri*," began Vortex.

He wiped away a few tears from her cheeks and from the corner of her eyes.

She put her arms around the Colonel's neck and kissed him on the lips.

Vortex could feel that her mouth was warm and soft. Her breath had a sweet fragrance. It electrified him.

"I want you to go to the 9th Marine Regiment Headquarters at the *Quang Tri* base. My 2nd and 3rd battalions are stationed there. That is the rest of my regiment."

Vortex handed Ngo Nhu a piece of paper with a name on it and some instructions which he signed at the bottom.

"I want you to go and see this officer. His name is Major Coffman. He is the Chief of Staff of my regiment. He will look after you, just give him this! OK!"

Ngo Nhu squeezed Vortex's hand with passion.

"I will do exactly as you say!" she said in Vietnamese.

Vortex led her to a taxiing C-123 and personally put her on the aircraft along with the French missionaries and their nuns.

She was one of the first civilians to be airlifted out of *Khe Sanh*.

As the C-123 lifted safely into the air and headed east along National Route 9, Vortex felt a sense of relief, almost satisfaction.

Captain Mirza Baig walked up behind him.

Without turning around Vortex knew it was the Fire Control Officer. He had memorised the sound and rhythm of the Captain's own particular footfalls.

Just then a flight of Navy A-1 *Skyraiders* came screeching in from the east.

There were six aircraft and they came in at subsonic speed at around 2,000 feet.

"Did you order that air strike?" asked Vortex as he turned to Captain Baig.

Before Baig could answer another flight of US jets were streaking in from the south. They had come from *Bien Hoa*. Four F-4E *Phantom II's* thundered in across the 800 foot deep escarpment at the southern fringe of the *Khe Sanh* airstrip.

Vortex looked at the fighter-bombers with his Navy Power 20 field binoculars.

The Colonel loved *Phantoms*.

They were his favourite aircraft. The sleek lines, the twin ramjet engines and the incredible punch that they packed were absolutely devastating to the enemy.

When the *Phantom II's* came in it was called a *'MICRO-Arc Light'* strike. The power approached that of the B-52 Arc Light raids.

"I ordered both TAC air strikes Colonel," answered Baig.

"Why? What's happening?"

Captain Baig informed, "The Lieutenant Colonel in command over at Hill 558 with the 2/26th and E/2/26th, Lieutenant Colonel Francis J. Heath Jr. requested them. He called up saying there was heavy PAVN pressure on his Hill 558 perimeter where about 1,000 Marines are hunkered down blocking the northern link of the QL9 [Route 9] into KSCB.

One of his patrols was ambushed this morning at 0345 hours.

The unit suffered 7 WIA's and 1 KIA."

Colonel Vortex followed the 450 mph flight locus of the *Phantom II's* as they headed north. The Navy *Skyraiders* fell in behind the USAF jets and together they descended onto the jungle surrounding Hill 558.

The massive thunder of explosions could be heard seconds later.

Even inside the *Khe Sanh* combat base, the earth vibrated as the cluster bombs peeled off the ammunition racks of the planes.

Napalm was also unleashed as well as HE 250lb iron bombs.

Captain Baig and three other officers joined Vortex as they peered through their field glasses.

A wall of petro-jelly flame burst into the atmosphere both north and west of Hill 558.

"Excellent!" exclaimed Colonel Vortex,"…the pilots are extremely accurate and professional. Those munitions landed within only 100 yards of the Marine forward positions."

Captain Baig smiled, "I try to do my best sir!"

Hill 558 was approximately 1.5 to 2 miles from the *Khe Sanh* northern perimeter.

Vortex arched his spine backwards as he watched the *Phantoms* go ballistic. Their sonic boom rocked the base as they smashed the 743 mph sound barrier.

The effect of the sonic boom would be devastating to the Communist troops directly under it. Eardrums would be burst open in a sweet mushroom of warm blood.

The Navy *Skyraiders* worked over the target area with 20mm cannon and rockets. When they had finished the F-4's came back from high altitude and strafed the PAVN yet again. But this time with 7.62mm *Miniguns*.

"You haven't seen anything yet!" said Captain Baig excitedly.

Vortex watched the *Phantoms* streak directly over *Khe Sanh* airstrip. They were heading back to *Bien Hoa*. All their ordnance expended.

As the afterburners glowed like fiery pits from hell, the multitude of Marines inside the base cheered as their USAF comrades returned to the nest.

"What do you mean?" asked Colonel Vortex.

Captain Baig asked his assistant, a young 1st Lieutenant with golden hair and green eyes, what the time was.

"Its 1303 hours sir."

Captain Baig nodded with glee and answered the Colonel.

"You are about to see the first B-52 Arc Light strike for today that is part of Operation NIAGARA!"

The Fire Control Officer rubbed his hands together in a state of feverish excitement. Baig's eyes were almost popping out of his skull.

Vortex grinned, "Magnificent!"

Colonel Lownds and his retinue of 35 staff officers and NCO's came jogging up.

They had just left the FSCC bunker where they were informed about the days schedule for Operation NIAGARA.

Colonel Lownds did not want to miss the show either.

"Its about to start?" he asked Baig.

"Yes sir!" As the Captain answered another 3 Fairchild C-123 Providers came swooping down on top of the runway.

Are they going to land?" asked Vortex.

Colonel Lownds said, "No. They are going to use the LAPES (Low Altitude Parachute Extraction System)."

The retinue of officers watched as the first C-123 came in at 155 mph. As it was one third of the way down the airstrip, a red and white parachute billowed out from the back of the plane. The chute was detonated open by the jet stream and air wash behind the C-123. The parachute was attached by steel cables to the ammunition pallet.

As the parachute slowed relative to the plane, the ammunition pallet was sucked out of the rear hatch.

The C-123 built up speed as the pilot never allowed the aircraft to descend more than 15 feet from the ground. The pallet slid along the runway and finally came to a stop as the C-123 headed back to cruising altitude.

"Very skilful indeed!" exclaimed Vortex, and then he asked Baig, "Where is the Arc Light going to hit?"

The Captain answered, "Our sensors picked up heavy movement around the PAVN held 'horseshoe'. We believe as does the G-2 section of III MAF, that the *24th PAVN Artillery Regiment* is there with its 130mm M46 Soviet designed howitzers.

The B-52's are going to soften them up a little.

There will be a cell of six bombers on this mission."

Colonel Vortex said as he turned to Colonel Lownds, "You can't see them and you can't hear them."

Colonel Lownds asked, "You mean the B-52's?"

"Yes! They travel too high – over 30,000 feet to be seen or heard from the ground. This adds to the shock effect upon the enemy! The bombs are falling on their heads even before they know what is happening!" continued Vortex and then he explained Arc Light to the group of officers standing before him.

As the 9th Marine commander spoke the C-123's continued their LAPES run over the *Khe Sanh* airstrip.

In addition, CH-47 Chinooks were medevacking the wounded back to *Da Nang* and *Nha Trang*.

Colonel Vortex explained the history of the Arc Light raids to the assembled officers of the 26th Regimental staff headquarters company.

"The SAC [Strategic Air Command] Bomb Scoring Team arrived in South Vietnam in early 1966. These teams provided the flexibility and precision for the *Stratofortress* to be used in close-in ground support operations.

The advent of the new '*Big Belly*' B-52D meant that a larger payload could be delivered to the targets.

The aircraft carried radar transponders and together with the radars of the SAC bomb scoring teams on the ground, could accurately direct bombing out to 100 nautical miles.

Seven SAC radar sites were established in March 1966. The first was at the *Bien Hoa* air base.

This was the nucleus of what we know as 'Combat SKYSPOT'.

In the middle of 1966 the Third Air Division placed six B-52's on permanent 10 hour alert status.

This was called the '*Quick Reaction Force*'. It would prove invaluable to field commanders such as Colonel Lownds and myself.

The B-52 usually hits a target box about 1 mile by 2 miles.

This 2 square mile box allows for maximum destructive effect against the target. However it was not possible for the bombers to strike any closer than within 2 to 2.5 miles of our own forces for danger of hurting them with 'friendly fire'. SAC then created what we call 'SLAM' Zones."

Master Sergeant Richter asked, "What are they sir?"

Colonel Vortex continued as the excitement intensified.

Everyone was waiting for Operation NIAGARA for that 22nd January 1968 to commence.

Colonel Vortex Continued, "SLAM Zones are 'Seek, Locate, Annihilate and Monitor' areas.

These are areas where the enemy is located.

The tactical field commander on the ground usually requests that one of these SLAM Zones be acted upon by the B-52's.

Free Fire Zones were also set up for all aerial assets.

When the *U-Tapao Base* was set up at *Sattahip* in Thailand, the B-52's could reach their targets without aerial refuelling.

MACV in Saigon is now asking for an increase in the sortie rate from 800 per month to 1,200 per month for Operation NIAGARA.

In the last few months, the PAVN have been shelling our bases at *Con Thien*, *Camp Carroll* and *Dong Ha*.

COMUSMACV then gave the orders for 'Operation NEUTRALISE' to begin in September and October of last year."

The Seabee Commander and Forward Operations Base 3 Commander, Major Lucius J. Campbell asked, "What was the result of *'Operation Neutralise'* sir?"

Vortex looked at the officer and smiled.

The sailors of the Mobile Construction battalion had made great progress in fixing the *Khe Sanh* airstrip from the pounding it received the day before.

However the C-130's could not land as yet but the repair work was proceeding at a frantic pace.

Also MACV had temporarily halted C-130 landings at *Khe Sanh* due to the PAVN bombardment as these aerial assets at $2,500,000 each were too expensive to lose in large numbers.

Colonel Vortex answered, "The full spectrum of firepower was used in *Operation Neutralise*.

We pounded the PAVN artillery emplacements with TAC air, naval gunfire, concentrated heavy artillery and B-52's. The fire was non-stop and around-the-clock. It proved effective as the Communist guns were almost completely silenced.

Operation Neutralise involved 2 Arc Light sorties per day. Nearly 1,000 sorties for the entire operation.

Then in November an event happened which forced us to reappraise the B-52 bombing tactics.

During an Arc Light raid on PAVN positions near the perimeter of *Con Thien*. One B-52 accidentally dropped its payload inside the 2.5 mile 'buffer zone' between the target and our friendly forces. This attack sparked 'secondary explosions' which indicated that the enemy were 'hugging' the defensive perimeters of our troops in an attempt to avoid the effects of the air strike.

Consequently the B-52's now routinely hit up to 1 mile from our troop lines and fortified positions instead of the 2.5 mile limit as previously."

Suddenly Captain Baig pointed to the north-west and screamed, "It's started! And right on time too! 1327 hours precisely."

The gathering of officers watched with awe as a deep throated roar echoed up from across the *Khe Sanh* plateau.

The noise was monstrous and evil.

The PAVN held *'horseshoe'* was about 4 miles from the base. The ground seemed to shift and tremble under the feet of the Marines.

Everyone inside *Khe Sanh* stopped what they were doing and listened and felt the tremendous surge of explosive power as it ripped across the jungle floor.

Hundreds of acres of jungle foliage were annihilated in a vaporised inferno of destruction.

"Give me your field binoculars," said Lownds to one of his Captains, "They are more powerful than mine."

Vortex too, watched the horizon. He could see streams of earth and black clouds shooting into the air. Each eruption from the surface of the planet was followed by a string of further detonations.

As the 750lb and 500lb iron bombs fell in formation it had a sort of cataclysmic effect. Each B-52D could carry 84 500lbs iron bombs or a total of 42,000lbs of ordnance. Thus 252,000lbs of explosive power was now being unleased.

The Marines on Hill 861A had a much closer viewpoint.

Major Thrush and Captain Jasper, who was recovering from his spinal wounds, had to retreat inside their bunkers.

The men of K Company plastered themselves to the ground behind their sandbag walls as the concussion waves from the detonations slammed into them with terrible force.

Marine Corporal Mike Brown, who was with his squad in the trenches defending Hill 861A, could not believe his eyes. Each time a 500lb bomb detonated whole layers of sandbags in front of him rose into the air a few inches.

The concussion and blast effect of the B-52's was indescribable.

Hill 861A was only 2,000 yards from the target.

"Jesus Christ!" exclaimed Major Thrush as the B-52's came in.

"It's started!"

The Major and his staff took what shelter they could inside the battered HQ bunker on top of Hill 861A.

K Company was still engaged in a vicious fire-fight with the PAVN all along their northern perimeter.

The 325th C *Golden Star* Division never eased off the pressure on the besieged Marines despite the torrential downpour of US firepower.

Back at *Khe Sanh*, Colonel Vortex lowered his field binoculars and said to Lownds, "Well? It looks like another successful mission."

Lownds replied, "We don't know that yet Vortex. Not for sure."

Vortex nodded, "You're right! I am going to send one of my force reconnaissance teams of six men into the *'horseshoe'* to assess the bomb damage."

Colonel Lownds mentioned that a bomb damage assessment mission was a good idea.

Vortex added, "I'll have to send them at night. That way they can observe with their Starlight Scopes and get in a little closer to the gooks."

Captain Baig mentioned, "From our aerial reconnaissance photographs we have detected that the Communists always try to move their artillery and other heavy equipment back into well fortified and camouflaged positions.

In that way they can try to avoid our air strikes."

Lownds said, "And when the air strike is over they pull them right out again and start firing!"

Colonel Vortex nodded as he looked to Colonel Lownds.

"What is the ammunition state so far?"

Lownds answered, "The Providers have landed 8,000lbs of ordnance up to this point in time. By tomorrow night we hope to have in about 110 to 130 tons."

"That's good. It's going along well."

One of Lownds' officers standing nearby said to the two Colonels', "I don't understand why the PAVN haven't emplaced more anti-aircraft guns behind the escarpment?"

Colonel Lownds asked, "What do you mean?"

The Major continued, "Well sir. If I were trying to interdict the flow of supplies to this base I would try to hammer the air traffic with everything I had!"

Colonel Vortex agreed, "He's right. The PAVN could have installed their 37mm or 0.51 calibre machine guns all around the approaches to the airstrip."

Colonel Lownds rubbed his chin. He looked worried.

"Well gentlemen! Let's hope that they don't!"

Vortex chuckled, "Yes. We better not give them any bright ideas on how to make life more difficult for us."

Just then Master Sergeant Richter came running up to the group of assembled officers.

"What is it Master Sergeant?" asked Colonel Lownds.

As they were speaking two more C-123's could be seen as they made their final approach towards the *Khe Sanh* airstrip.

Richter replied, "Its Brigadier General William McBride from USAF.

He wants to talk to both of you sirs."

Vortex and Lownds trotted back into the FSCC bunker with Captain Mirza Baig.

"This is Colonel Vortex sir."

The Air Force Brigadier answered, "This is McBride. I am in *Dong Ha* Colonel. I have Colonel William Walker with me. He's my J-2 (Director of Intelligence) for III MAF.

We have received orders from both Lieutenant General Cushman and your immediate superior Major General Rathvon C. Tompkins."

Colonel Lownds picked up another handset, asking, "What are those orders sir?"

Brigadier McBride continued, "Both Generals want additional sensors placed in the *Khe Sanh* area. General Cushman suggested that I place up to 250 additional devices all around the approaches to your base."

Colonel Vortex smiled as Sergeant Major Leonard Crighton handed him a cup of steaming Hungarian coffee.

He said, "That is an excellent idea sir."

Lownds added, "We desperately need more information as to the latest movements of the 325Cth and 304th Divisions. Not to mention what the 320th PAVN Division is doing up near Camp Carroll."

Brigadier McBride replied, "Then I am the man for the job. We are going to place some new sensors using reconnaissance aircraft as well as helicopters.

My Air Force intelligence analysts are pouring over the latest aerial photographs.

We want to make sure that we cover the most likely routes used by the enemy.

For that reason gentlemen, I need your valued input as to what you consider to be the most likely trails used by the Main Force VC/PAVN units around *Khe Sanh*?"

Colonel Lownds was given an area map by an excited Captain Baig.

Baig whispered instructions into Lownds' ear as the Colonel spoke to the USAF Brigadier.

"We consider the jungle area between the DMZ and the Hill outposts at Hills 861/861A, 881S, 881N, 558, 950 and 1015 at *Dong Tri* to be crucial. The PAVN are pouring in masses of men and material in this sector. I am going to make a direct request to General William Momyer to hit these areas with Arc Light strikes from Operation NIAGARA."

Then Colonel Vortex interrupted as he peered at the map held up by Captain Baig.

"In addition to that I would include the whole Laos border area sir," began Vortex, "The PAVN are using the sanctuaries in Laos as well as the DMZ.

The most critical area is that between the South Vietnamese and Laotian border and the town of *Tchepone*.

If you drop in seismic, acoustic and chemical sensors in that *Tchepone* region I am sure you will achieve excellent intelligence results. The PAVN are moving along the axis of the *Xe Pon River* from *Tchepone* to the village of *A Luoi*, which is right on the border.

The northern route from *Khe Sanh* village to *Tabat* is also important."

Colonel Lownds nodded his assent and added to an attentive Brigadier General McBride, "But most important is the staging areas used by the PAVN units within close proximity to *Khe Sanh*. They are the valleys between the major hill outposts I have just mentioned.

Particularly the *'horseshoe'* which is 2,000 yards from Hill 861A, the valley between 881S and 861A where we ran into a full PAVN Regiment on the 20th January. And Brigadier General Davidson, the J-2 for MACV, has informed us of a complex of limestone caves on the Laotian side of the border about 20 miles north-west of *Khe Sanh*…"

Vortex interrupted, "Yes! MACV and I think that this could be an operational headquarters for General Vo Nguyen Giap. If it is true, I am going to make a strong recommendation to COMUSMACV to smash it with a maximum effort B-52 Arc Light strike.

Let's see if we can't kill that criminal son-of-a-bitch once and for all!"

General McBride agreed, "If we could take out the North Vietnamese Defence Minister Giap. That is if he would be stupid enough to expose himself in the field! In an operational headquarters! Then it would be a major coup for COMUSMACV and for Washington!"

Both Vortex and Lownds agreed as they studied the map in front of them.

Finally, Brigadier McBride added, "The seismic sensors we are using have spiked noses. When they are dropped into the ground they dig in deep. Thus we can pick up the vibrations of moving men and vehicles.

I am having a meeting with Major General Tompkins on the 23rd January 1968. We should be able to put the whole operation into full gear by the 24th January and the sensors should be in place by the 27th or 28th at the latest."

Colonel Vortex said with enthusiasm, "That sounds good sir!"

Both commanders then signed off.

Just as Vortex and Lownds were leaving the FSCC bunker, the PAVN artillery bombardment erupted with a throaty roar.

Streaking trails of fire caused by tracer ammunition hurtled down on the scurrying Marines inside the *Khe Sanh* base. This was the Communist revenge bombardment for the B-52 strike a few moments ago.

Despite the barrage the C-123's continued to fly in for their LAPES run.

Every American aircraft that approached *Khe Sanh* had to run the gauntlet of Communist firepower.

Colonel Lownds ordered the fleet of AH-1 *Cobras* and *Huey* gunships to take off immediately while the bombardment was in progress.

Vortex ran over to the 105mm and 155mm howitzer emplacements doing the *'Khe Sanh Shuffle.'*

He personally directed the outgoing fire with the artillery fire control officers.

Soon the US guns were blasting back at all known PAVN positions.

However it was incredibly difficult for the Marines to be sure that their counter barrage was totally effective.

Vortex said to Lieutenant Colonel John A. Hennelly in command of the 1st Battalion 13th Marines (Artillery), "I don't know if our fire does them much damage?"

Lieutenant Colonel Hennelly replied, "Well sir. We might as well fire back. It's better than sitting here like ducks in thunder!"

Both men laughed.

Vortex had to plug his ears with his fingers.

The tremendous concussion blast of the 155mm howitzers was enough to burst his tympanic membrane inside the middle ear.

And blood would have gushed out of his ears otherwise.

All the artillery troopers wore ear protection as they pumped shell after shell into the heavy guns.

The massive artillery duel continued for hours everyday at *Khe Sanh*.

The Communists would pound the Marines with their 130mm and 152mm guns from the *'horseshoe'* and the *'Co Roc'*.

The Americans would answer with their 175mm field pieces at *Camp Carroll* and the 105mm and 155mm howitzers inside the *Khe Sanh* perimeter.

A specialist fourth class gunner came running up to Vortex and the fire control officer.

The Marine had a field phone strapped to his back, the AN/PRC-41.

"What is it soldier?" asked Vortex.

The SP4 offered the handset to the two officers as he said, "Its Captain Dabney calling from Hill 881S. Sir."

The artillery Lieutenant Colonel Hennelly took it quickly and grinned at Vortex.

The calm and clear voice of the commander of India Company rang through.

"Lieutenant Colonel! I've got some more accurate coordinates for you. Regarding the PAVN artillery positions.

One of my forward patrols had spotted the 24th Artillery regiment repositioning its howitzers in the valley floor."

Hennelly asked, "Excellent. Give them to me!"

Colonel Vortex grabbed the handset from Hennelly for a few seconds after he had written down the new fire control coordinates.

"This is Colonel Vortex! Report your current status Dabney!"

The India Company CO answered, "We are receiving pressure all around the 881S perimeter sir. The PAVN have snipers everywhere in the jungle below us.

Also a few of my men have been injured by 'spiked balls' and punji sticks while on patrol."

Vortex coughed into the handset. He wiped the sweat off his brow.

The humidity on the *Khe Sanh* plateau was unbearable.

Rolling mist and damp fog reduced visibility for the AH-1 *Cobras* as they strafed the PAVN positions continuously while executing their SUPERGAGGLE missions to the hill outposts.

"Did you run into any PAVN units on your patrols last night?"

Captain Dabney replied, "Yes sir."

The radio frequency crackled with static due to the weather conditions.

Dabney continued, "One of my 30 man patrols was ambushed about 1,000 yards from the 'horseshoe'.

We killed about 13 gooks but I lost 1 KIA and 4 WIA.

The UH-1E's took the casualties out about 30 minutes ago, sir."

Colonel Vortex clicked his fingers at Master Sergeant Richter who stood behind him.

"Listen Captain Dabney!" continued Colonel Vortex as he whispered to Richter to run to the MATU bunker and get Colonel Lownds.

"You're position on 881S is the most important of our hill outposts.

It is the most westerly position of US Forces in the Republic of Vietnam.

If there is any major PAVN movement. Or even company sized attacks on your hill, I want you to get on the horn to me ASAP! Is that clear? Because you are the end of the line!"

Captain Dabney barked back, "Yes sir!"

Vortex added, "You will give me the coordinates at FSCC and Captain Baig will coordinate the TAC air and B-52 strikes to support you."

Captain Dabney answered, "Will do sir!"

Vortex handed the phone back to the SP4 and slapped the artillery Lieutenant Colonel on the back.

"She's all yours!"

Hennelly nodded as his 450 gunnery Marines manhandled the howitzers into their new positions.

The Vulnerability of Khe Sanh's Water Supply and the *Rao Quan River*

"What is it Vortex?" snapped Colonel Lownds as he emerged from the FSCC bunker, "I am busy coordinating the next Arc Light strike."

Vortex asked, "Where is it going to be applied?"

Lownds answered, "Captain Baig has analysed the sensor information along with our boys at *Nakhon Phanom* in Thailand.

It seems that there is a heavy concentration of PAVN troops from the 304th Division building up in and around the *Khe Sanh* village itself.

Since the village has been evacuated of civilians we are going to pound it with B-52's and declare it a free fire zone.

The next cell should be overhead in approximately 1 hour."

Vortex nodded as he crooked his finger towards Lownds.

"Come! Colonel! I want to show you something."

Lownds asked, "What is it?"

The two men plus a retinue of NCO's and junior officers walked over to the northwestern perimeter of the base.

Vortex asked, "Have you considered where our water supply comes from?"

Colonel Lownds looked through his field glasses towards the water point that was about 500 yards from the outer row of concertina wire.

"It comes from the *Rao Quan River*! Why?"

Vortex giggled and brushed back his light brown hair that was extremely short.

"And who controls the source of the *Rao Quan River*?" asked Vortex.

Lownds stammered for a few seconds.

Both Colonels' watched as a team of about 100 Marines from the 26th drove jeeps and water trucks back and forth from the water point. The *Khe Sanh* base needed at least 50 tons of fresh water per day for its 2,500 men as well as for other applications involving machinery and electric generators.

Then it hit Colonel Lownds like a thunderbolt.

"The bloody PAVN control the source of our water supply!"

Vortex nodded as he placed his hand on Lownds' shoulder.

He asked, "Do you see any problems with that small detail that we have seemed to overlook until now?"

Lownds immediately replied, "The Communists can divert the flow of the *Rao Quan River* and reduce our water access!"

"It's worse than that!" said the commander of the 9th.

Vortex smiled as Master Sergeant Richter and Sergeant Major Leonard Crighton listened avidly to their two commanders.

Either one of them would gladly have laid down their lives for the safety of their Chiefs.

But it was Colonel Richard Vortex who had an almost God-like status with the Marines in his 9th Regiment.

"What do you mean?" asked Colonel Lownds with stupefaction.

Vortex answered, "Well! Don't you see? That bloodsucker, Giap, could order his men to poison and contaminate the source of the *Rao Quan River*! The gooks hold the whole stretch of that waterway right up to the DMZ!"

Colonel Lownds exclaimed, "Jesus Christ!"

Vortex stood with his hands on his hips.

The whole scenario had only come to his mind the night before.

Vortex continued, "Yes! Can you imagine if that fiend did exactly that! Where would we get our water? The C-123's and the C-130's would have to fly in our fresh water supplies from *Quang Tri* or *Nha Trang* or even *Da Nang*. It would be a logistical nightmare!

Then, if Giap massed his 37mm and 0.51 calibre anti-aircraft guns off the *Khe Sanh* airstrip we would be really looking down the barrel!"

Colonel Lownds ordered his aide, a 1st Lieutenant, to take down notes.

"You're absolutely right Vortex. What do you suggest we do?"

Vortex answered, "Nothing!"

Lownds looked mesmerised, and asked, "Nothing?"

"That's right David! Nothing. Nothing until the PAVN make their move. If and when it comes. Then our action will proceed accordingly.

I am not even going to inform Forward MACV or III MAF for the moment."

Colonel Lownds nodded as a platoon of Marines assembled near the north-western perimeter of the base along the 'Blue Sector'.

"Let's hope that that swindler, jackal and imperialist pig, Giap, is not as clever as you are Colonel Vortex.

I mean, to see with such foresight and clarity of vision, the weaknesses of our position here at *Khe Sanh*!"

Richard Vortex replied as he squeezed Lownds' arm affectionately, "I hope so too! Believe me! I hope that the Communists don't take advantage of us using the *Rao Quan River*."

Before Colonel Lownds walked back to the FSCC bunker he asked, "What are these men assembled here for?"

The Colonel pointed to the handpicked platoon of elite Marines from the 1st Battalion 9th Marine Regiment, nicknamed, *'The Walking Dead'* because they had been in Vietnam since the beginning from 1965.

Vortex answered, "These men have all had experience in VLRP (Very Long Range Patrolling).

The concept of VLRP was first devised by Major General Herman J. Nickerson Jr."

Colonel Lownds said, "'Herman the German! He's currently commander of the 1st Marine Division at Con Thien."

Vortex nodded and continued, "General Nickerson is the Godfather of Long-Range Patrolling. These men have all had a stint with the *Second Force Reconnaissance Company*.

I am going to insert them up the *Rao Quan Tributary* under deep cover.

If Giap and his troops are going to poison our water supply then I want to know about it in advance!"

Colonel Lownds agreed and asked with shock, "You're not going with them all the way? Are you?"

Vortex chuckled, "No! I'm just going up as far as Hill 558. The Force RECON Marines – all from my 9th Regiment, will continue on as far as they can go. They will observe any activity in and around the *Rao Quan*.

I'll fly back with a Supergaggle once I've inspected the positions around Hill 558 and conferred with the commander there being, Lieutenant Colonel Francis Heath."

Colonel Lownds was just about to leave for the FSCC bunker when Vortex remembered something.

"Oh! Can you tell Captain Baig to organise a 'DAISY CUTTER'."

The DAISY CUTTER was a 15,000lb high explosive iron bomb used to blast away up to 4 square acres of jungle in a single detonation. The awesome weapon was a quick way and easy way to clear large areas of jungle to create a LZ (landing zone for helicopters) or simply to clear the jungle to provide a better field of fire and clear observation of incoming VC/NVA troops.

Colonel Vortex continued, "I want this foliage wiped clear.

It will give us an easier route to the water point as well as increasing our field of clear vision in which to spot the PAVN assault when it comes."

Lownds replied, "I'll get onto it right away Vortex!"

Colonel Vortex signalled for the elite platoon to move out.

Master Sergeant Richter and Sergeant Major Crighton went with their boss.

"The men tell me that there are a lot of gook snipers out here sir," said Sergeant Major Crighton.

The Sergeant Major carried a Minigun out in front of his waist. The NCO always loved to have the edge in firepower.

Colonel Vortex carried a M79 Grenade launcher and an M16.

Master Sergeant Richter fielded an M60 with extra ammunition belts.

As usual, Vortex and his two NCO's took point while the rest of the elite super commandos followed behind.

Vortex snarled, "Then we shall cut out their hearts!"

They met a group of Marines coming back with water trucks as they approached the Rao Quan River.

The Warrant Officer E13 in charge of the detail informed Vortex that one of his men had been shot through the spine and testicles by an NVA sniper.

Vortex answered, "Get your men back to the perimeter ASAP! I've called in a DAISY CUTTER to fucken wipe the gooks clean out of here!"

The Warrant Officer snarled, "Its about time sir!"

Vortex and Richter took a quick look at the wounded Marine.

His trousers were off. Blood was everywhere.

The right sac of his testicles were missing and the head of his penis was torn completely off. It was a disgusting sight.

"I think it was a VC sniper," began the Warrant Officer, "The PAVN are using Main Force VC in an auxiliary role such as sniping and anti-aircraft activities. I think it was a woman who did this."

Vortex barked out his orders, "Alright! I said get back to the base! And get this man medevacked out to *Dong Ha* ASAP!"

The Warrant Officer saluted and his 50 man detail moved back through the *Blue Sector* and the KSCB concertina wire.

It was now 1549 hours on the 22nd January 1968.

Vortex was seething with a lust for revenge.

"I am going to get that sniper, Richter!"

"Yes sir," answered the NCO as they moved forward in staggered formation.

The elite platoon of Force RECON Marines were experts at moving with stealth and speed. During the night they would find a secure 'harbour site' in which to hunker down. The Force RECON Marines always chose rough, uneven ground in which to stop after dark. This would reduce the possibility of running into NVA patrols which mostly kept to the trails worn through the dense jungles.

Master Sergeant Richter pointed to the east.

Vortex and his troops saw the *Rao Quan River* as it meandered slowly to the south. The peacefulness of the river belied the terrible and vicious human struggle that raged around it.

The Marines had also set up a pump which continually sucked water back into the *Khe Sanh* base through a steel pipe that had been laid down by the Seabee Mobile Construction Unit.

The platoon slithered down to the edge of the river.

Vortex gave hand signals to Richter.

The Master Sergeant crawled over and inspected the pump.

It was still working.

Then one of the RECON Marines, a Sp4, pointed to a dense corner of jungle on the other side of the *Rao Quan* waterway.

Colonel Vortex crawled over to the junior NCO.

"What is it?" he whispered.

The Sp4 whispered back, "A sniper sir! I don't think he's seen us. Otherwise he would have fired."

The Marines were all heavily camouflaged with face paint and leaves in their helmets. They had crawled on their bellies all the way to the river's edge.

Vortex told the Sp4, "You stay here with the platoon. The Master Sergeant and I shall take care of the sniper."

The platoon commander, a 2nd Lieutenant from Vortex's Regiment came over with excitement in his hazel eyes.

"I can get him for you sir!"

Vortex said, "No! Lieutenant! This one is mine. You start moving your platoon up the river. We shall meet you about 1,000 yards further up towards Hill 558."

It took Vortex, Richter and Crighton about 15 minutes of careful manoeuvring to swim across the river to the other embankment. They worked their way around the rear of the sniper until they were only 20 yards away.

Vortex nodded to his two NCO's. He put down his M16 and drew his Marine dagger out of its sheath. The razor sharp steel glistened in the humid air.

Vortex ran the flat edge of the blade over his moist tongue and winked to Richter.

The Master Sergeant grinned with vicious glee. Both NCO's unsheathed their 18 inch knives.

It was pay back time.

The three men moved like phantoms through the jungle. Vortex could see the camouflaged helmet of the VC sniper right in front of him. It was only a few yards now.

With the grace of a tiger the Colonel pounced the last few feet.

He literally floated through the air, catching the head of the gook in his arms. He crushed down on the spine as the Communist body lay on top of him.

With a delicious movement of pure venom he slit open the throat from ear to ear. But the body felt unusually soft as he embraced it. The moans were sweet and soft. Blood poured over the soil of the stinking jungle floor.

Master Sergeant Richter pounced on top of the VC as Vortex lunged his knife for a second time into the kidneys of the sniper.

"Shit! Sir! It's a woman!" cried Sergeant Major Crighton as he kicked off the girl's pith helmet.

Vortex barked, "I thought so!"

Richter screamed, "Sir! Watch out!"

As Colonel Vortex jumped to his feet, a second and then a third VC woman sniper leapt out of the jungle. A rifle shot boomed out into the valley.

Spinning 180 degrees on the balls of his feet, Vortex gripped the long, luxurious hair of the Viet Cong girl as she sprang forward.

Richter tripped over the third girl as she screamed.

Vortex then slammed the second girl's head into the nearest tree. She was dazed but struggled upright. She spat into Vortex's face.

Her eyes were a vision of animal-like hatred. Their black centres seemed like infinity.

The Colonel lunged forward with a vicious head butt that cracked open her forehead and split the septum of her nose. Female blood flowed beautifully and deliciously.

By this time Richter and Crighton had smashed the third girl to her knees. They stripped off her black tunic and pantaloons. Vortex ravaged his VC female until she too was stripped naked. Her soft and round breasts wiggled brazenly at the three men.

Richter held up the sniper rifles used by the VC women and said, "They are Chinese SKS marksmen models with folding stocks."

Vortex gripped the second girl's head in his massively muscular arms and ran his fingers down her naked torso with delicious and vicious seduction.

"When are the PAVN going to attack *Khe Sanh*?" asked Colonel Vortex in fluent Vietnamese.

Sergeant Major Crighton held his Marine dagger to the girl's left ear. At the first word from Vortex he would sever it off her head.

The slim and beautiful body of the Communist girl, who was not more than 22 or 23 years of age, struggled vainly in the Colonel's brutal embrace.

She spat at the Marines in her native tongue, "Fuck you dogs to hell!"

Vortex nodded to Crighton, "The Sergeant Major severed off her left ear easily. He then threw the organ onto the naked breasts of the third girl as Richter held her pelvis to the sodden earth, raping her with quick thrusts in a missionary position.

As the Master Sergeant flipped the girl over after ejaculating into her womb, he proceeded with much aplomb to sodomise her to perfection.

"I said where are the Main VC and North Vietnamese units and where are they going to attack and when?" asked Vortex again.

The second girl, screaming with agony, continued to spit obscenities at Vortex. Sergeant Major Crighton mutilated off her remaining ear. He then inserted the razor sharp point of his Marine dagger inside the raw holes in her head while Vortex penetrated her soft and delicious womb.

Richter found a punji pit nearby. He gripped out one of the punji stakes which was covered in faeces.

As he completed his second ejaculation into the Communist's tight and inviting anus he said, "Let's give back to this bitch some of the treatment she has meted out to our American boys!"

With those words Richter plunged the filthy punji stake directly into the bowels of the Viet Cong girl. He then stabbed her through the heart with his Marine dagger while Sergeant Major Crighton decapitated the VC terrorist with undiluted ferocity.

Vortex finished his interrogation without results and threw the naked body of the girl up against a tree. Picking up his trench spade he stoved in the VC's head until her eyes were dislodged from their sockets and the grey brain matter sprinkled their faces in a gruesome miasma of blood and twitching arteries.

"Let's rejoin the platoon! We can't fuck around here having this fun all day long! As much as we would like to ferret out more of these fucking bitch snipers! We have a more important job to do.

And besides in a couple of days I have to go to BEARCAT Base in *Long Thanh* for a top secret conference."

Crighton asked, "Why BEARCAT? Isn't that the 9th Infantry Division Base? What do you have to do there sir?"

Vortex laughed, "You and Richter will both find out soon enough. Because you are both going with me to BEARCAT! It's the *'In' place to be*. Didn't you know that?"

Richter chuckled, "It's the home of the *'Old Reliables'* in Vietnam, our brothers-in-arms, the 9th Infantry Division."

Vortex said, "I can't tell you anything now but we are going on a fucking deep penetration mission along with a couple of other senior non commissioned officers."

Crighton rubbed his hands with unqualified ecstasy, "A deep penetration mission! Fuck-me-dead! I can't wait! I just want to kill as many Communists as I can get my hands on!"

Vortex ushered them to move out as he kicked the mutilated corpse of the Communist whore sniper out of the way, saying, "Well you sure as cotton-picking hell will get the chance to do that where we are going!"

They found the Force RECON platoon almost at the beginning of the defensive perimeter at Hill 558.

It took Vortex about an hour to slowly patrol his way up to the Marine outpost of the 2/26th of 1,000 Marines. The three men had waded through the river for most of the way with dead bodies floating in and out like so much rubbish and detritus.

Richter could feel that several leeches had wormed their way into his trousers. The blood suckers were already attached to his flesh and gonads. He was in agony. Vortex nearly had one crawl up his nostrils before Crighton pulled it out.

"Report Lieutenant!" shouted Vortex.

The Force RECON officer responded, "We observed a massive build-up of PAVN troops on both sides of the *Rao Quan* River, sir. I also noticed that National Route 9 leading to the east has been cut off by at least two PAVN regiments.

It appears to me that the Communists are going to launch their big push soon."

The Siege of Khe Sanh 1967-1968

Vortex nodded and slapped the Lieutenant on the back, "Well done!"

Then the Colonel looked to Master Sergeant Richter, "Well Max! It's as we suspected. *Khe Sanh* is now totally surrounded. It doesn't make our job any easier."

Sergeant Major Crighton asked, "Do you think they will launch the 1st Cavalry Division (Airmobile) to relieve us sir?"

Vortex shook his head, "No. It's too early yet. General Cushman and COMUSMACV won't risk it. The forces of III MAF are spread too thin from here to *Dong Ha* and *Con Thien*.

Operation NIAGARA will have to soften up Giap's forces a little more before they can launch a relief operation."

Just then Richter noticed a C-130 Hercules flying over the north-eastern edge of the *Khe Sanh* base.

Vortex pointed as the Marines crouched in the thick jungle, "It's the DAISY CUTTER! Watch this!"

The Force RECON Marines of the 9th Regiment had seen the DAISY CUTTER in action before. There was nothing like it.

A few seconds later a huge barrel-like object slid out of the back of the C-130. It was attached to a red and white parachute that allowed the 15,000lb iron bomb to glide gracefully to its target.

The munitions had a long spear at the front which was the detonation spike for contact with the earth.

"Looks like the pilot is right on target!" said Vortex.

The DAISY CUTTER landed exactly halfway between the water point and the *Khe Sanh* perimeter along the 'Blue Sector.' This area was thick with jungle.

The blast was thunderous. Even from 2,000 yards away they could feel the concussion wave as it hit them. It felt like a swift burst of wind.

"Jesus Christ!" sighed one of the Sp4's in the Force RECON unit.

Colonel Vortex chuckled, "Jesus has got nothing to do with it son!"

The DAISY CUTTER blasted away the jungle in an instant. Yellow sheets of fire spread skyward and the smell of cordite was nauseating as it was intermingled with the horrid slush of burning jungle foliage and roasting human flesh.

The DAISY CUTTER had also killed some nearby PAVN personnel." Its finished! Let's go Lieutenant!" began the Colonel.

Just at that instant, as Vortex moved forward to give final instructions to his specialist platoon, the unmistakable roar of AK-47 fire erupted all around them.

"Jesus! The PAVN have spotted us!" said Master Sergeant Richter.

The Marines returned fire as Colonel Vortex told the Lieutenant to slip away up the *Rao Quan* River and get on with his surveillance.

A Pfc standing next to Sergeant Major Crighton was hit. The bullet passed through his midbrain and he died instantly.

Blood gushed out in regular pulses over his eyes and nose as a Corpsman medic ran over.

"Its too late. It's no use," began Vortex feeling the lack of any pulse, "…he's dead!"

The Force RECON Marines moved out and past Hill 558.

Only Vortex, Richter and Crighton headed for the defensive perimeter of the outpost.

Calling up the commander of Hill 558, Vortex identified his position so that the troops manning the perimeter would not fire on them as they approached.

"Those men are catching hell already sir," said Master Sergeant Richter.

Colonel Vortex watched his platoon as it fought its way up the *Rao Quan* tributary.

The PAVN had sandwiched them to the western embankment. But they were tough and professional soldiers and the fire fight went on regardless.

Vortex said, "I doubt whether they will complete their mission successfully. The PAVN are too thick on the ground for them to remain unobserved."

Ten minutes later, Vortex was in the HQ bunker on top of 558.

"Good to see you here sir!" said Lieutenant Colonel Francis Heath the CO of the 2/26th.

"We had a hell of a time getting here, I can tell you!" answered Colonel Vortex as he surveyed the trench lines and recoilless rifle positions on the hill outpost.

The 1,000 Marines on Hill 558 were constantly on the alert. PAVN snipers, 81mm mortar fire and heavy artillery from the 'horseshoe' kept them running, ducking and diving for cover.

"Have you had any major Communist attacks in the last 48 hours?" asked Colonel Vortex.

Lieutenant Colonel Heath grabbed a field map from one of his Captains, answering, "No sir. But I sent out three patrols during the day and two at night. Every time we make a foray down into the valley between here and 861A or east to Hill 950 and 1015, we get bushwhacked. As far as I can see the PAVN have not yet decided to make a full scale ground assault on all our hill strongholds…"

Vortex rubbed his chin, "Yes. I agree Heath. Go on."

Heath added, "The 325thC *Golden Star* Division is just testing and probing our perimeter. They want to determine which axis of attack would give them the best results.

Also, sir, we have been cut off to the east as well. National Route 9 is blocked by at least 2 PAVN Regiments."

Vortex said, "I already know that Heath."

The commander of the 2nd Battalion said, "Also sir. My patrols have discovered numerous caves dug into the hillsides. The PAVN are using them as shelters during our air strikes."

Vortex looked to Master Sergeant Richter with surprise, as he answered, "That! I didn't know!"

As Vortex and the officers from the 2nd Battalion went over the maps in the HQ bunker, the Communist mortar and artillery fire started up yet again.

Several wounded Marines were brought into the bunker. As the medics and Corpsmen started to work on them and the repugnant smell of blood, dirty bandages and cordite filled the damp air, Colonel Vortex wondered when it was all going to end.

Master Sergeant Richter looked at his Colonel and seemed to be able to read his innermost thoughts.

Richter said grimly, "This is only the beginning sir!"

Vortex smiled at one of the two senior non commissioned officers that he had an absolute and unqualified faith in and said, "General Giap started this *Khe Sanh* siege!

But I am going to *FINISH IT*!"

Prelude to the TET OFFENSIVE 1968

Pentagon East as they called it, was bustling with activity. The huge office complex adjacent to the *Tan Son Nhut Air Base* near Saigon was in overdrive.

The MACV Staff felt that something was brewing but they didn't know exactly what – as yet.

General Westmoreland was sitting comfortably in one of the large and luxurious conference rooms inside the Pentagon East HQ. He had just had a meeting with the South Vietnamese JGS (Joint General Staff). They had been discussing the 3rd Brigade base at *Dong Tam* and the increase in strength of the *Mobile Riverine Force* that was sprawling its tentacles across the Mekong Delta. The US 9th Infantry Division based at BEARCAT was primarily responsible for this area of IV Corps Operational Zone. After all, President Thieu's family came from *My Tho* and the President wanted to make sure that his family town did not fall to the Main Force VC that used the *Rung Sat Special Zone* as a logistics hub for their operations in the Delta.

General Westmoreland knew that if you ever wanted a fight and had nothing else going on you could always find it in the *Rung Sat*.

That is why *UDT Team 1* and *UDT Team 2* were permanently assigned to the *Rung Sat*. The Navy Seals cut their teeth in hunting down the murderers and terrorists that lay in wait like black cockroaches in this filthy swamp that lay south-east of Saigon.

Westmoreland knew that the *Rung Sat* was a Communist dagger aimed at the very heart of COMUSMACV in Saigon and he was determined to crush and annihilate it.

If ever, thought General Westmoreland, nuclear weapons were needed then it would be his first choice to blast the *Rung Sat* to bloody hell and back.

The military officers of the Republic of Vietnam were worried. They were apprehensive as to the next move of the Hanoi Government and the COSVN (Central Office South Vietnam: Headquarters controlling all political and military operations in Central and South Vietnam which was subordinate to the North Vietnamese Politburo).

General Ngoi Quang Truong was sitting next to COMUSMACV. They were both studying the latest field reports from action that had erupted in six major provincial cities in South Vietnam.

General Truong was commander of the 1st ARVN Division.

This was the best unit in the entire South Vietnamese Army.

"It doesn't look good sir," said General Truong.

General Westmoreland grunted, "Don't come to any conclusions just yet General! Let's wait and see what develops."

The double mahogany doors of the conference room swung open. Two sturdy military police NCO's held them in place while Brigadier General Phillip B. Davidson entered.

Davidson, the J-2 (senior military intelligence officer for MACV) walked quickly up to COMUSMACV.

The Brigadier had a bundle of teletype messages in his hands. All of which were marked Top Secret.

"I was just about to call for you Davidson!" shouted Westmoreland, "Where have you been?"

Brigadier General Davidson was about to reply when COMUSMACV pounded his fist on the oak table.

"Don't you realise that we have a war on our hands here? Six provincial capitals were attacked last night! You are the intelligence officer for MACV! So what the hell is going on?"

Brigadier General Davidson winced.

However, the senior J-2 kept his composure as he unfolded the latest reports.

It was 0700 hours on the 30th January 1968.

"Sir! During the last 12 hours there have been a series of Main Force VC assaults. The first was a battalion sized attack on the port of *Nha Trang*. The second attack was focused on the provincial capital of *Hoi An* near the coast.

The third attack occurred in the Central Highlands. There the VC launched a rocket and mortar attack on the town of *Ban Me Thuot*.

In *Da Nang* Viet Cong sappers tried to infiltrate the headquarters of the ARVN 1 Corps. Another attack involved two VC battalions which struck *Qui Nhon*. Fortunately the garrison there was on full alert and the attack was beaten back with heavy Communist losses.

Finally an attack by joint VC/PAVN forces was made on *Pleiku*, also in the Central Highlands."

General William Westmoreland asked, "What is the situation now?"

Brigadier General Davidson replied, "All the assaults I have just mentioned have been stopped in their tracks. Sir."

COMUSMACV looked to General Truong, "What do you think?"

The ARVN General shook his head, "It doesn't make sense. It seems like part of something else. Something bigger. More sinister."

Brigadier Davidson nodded, "I agree sir. It is my opinion and the conclusion of my staff that this is the beginning of a full scale assault by COSVN all over the Republic of South Vietnam."

General Westmoreland rubbed his chin thoughtfully.

He realised that if this was the case, he would have to pay a visit to President Thieu immediately, for the purpose of requesting that all ARVN personnel be recalled from the Lunar New Year festivities. Or TET as they called it.

"Go on!" barked back General Westmoreland.

Brigadier General Davidson continued, "It appears to me that the Communist forces have struck in these sectors 24 hours too soon. I come to that conclusion because all of the preliminary assaults were controlled by one particular North Vietnamese HQ complex. The only likely explanation is that there has been some sort of communications and command and control breakdown in the VC/PAVN force structure.

Perhaps the TET holiday dates have been mixed up by the enemy and their COSVN HQ? These units obviously got the timing wrong."

General Westmoreland was in a foul mood as he screamed back, "So what are you saying Brigadier?"

Davidson answered firmly, "I am saying that the main attack is tonight, the 30 to 31st January 1968. Sir."

General Truong added, "I agree!"

Westmoreland said, "Then I shall have to go and see President Thieu. Ask him to recall all ARVN troops immediately."

Then COMUSMACV said, "It is my assessment also, that the main attack is for tonight."

For the next two hours COMUSMACV called in all senior commanders and put all US and ARVN units on full alert.

All the tactical Zones from I corps to IV Corps inclusive were also put on maximum alert status.

Later that day President Thieu, under pressure from General Westmoreland, agreed to recall 50% of the total ARVN strength of 732,000 troops to active duty.

However, only a small proportion of the ARVN made it back to their units before the onslaught began at around midnight on the 30th to 31st January 1968.

Yet President Thieu decided not to remain in Saigon to coordinate his overall command and control of the Republic's forces.

Instead the President and his entourage retired to the Mekong Delta town of *My Tho* to enjoy the festivities with his wife's relatives.

This infuriated and disgusted General Westmoreland who, along with all the other senior American commanders, were trying to hold the whole show together before it would be ripped apart by the VC and the PAVN.

General Vo Nguyen Giap and the Hanoi Politburo had been planning and scheming the TET Offensive since the first quarter of 1967.

The Communists called it the 'TCK-TKN' (*Tong Cong Kich – Tong Khoi Nghia*) or General Offensive, General Uprising.

The North Vietnamese plan was to launch a major offensive, primarily with Main Force VC units on as wide an area as possible.

The strategic objective was to demoralise the ARVN and to severely damage its potential as an effective fighting force.

The second strategic objective was to win over the mass of the South Vietnamese people to the cause of the Viet Cong and the COSVN Communists.

General Giap thought that once the offensive would begin, it would galvanise the South Vietnamese people's support behind the Communists. With the ARVN crushed, the American forces would find themselves isolated and besieged. Their only option then would be withdrawal.

The TCK-TKN failed miserably due to the sycophantic dream world in which the criminals in the Hanoi Politburo lived and worked. They thought and machinated as a coterie of incestuous mental defectives.

The North Vietnamese Politburo believed that the people in the South were ripe for Communism.

They were NOT.

The Communists achieved nothing with their much vaunted TET Offensive of 1968.

The only thing that they did achieve was the virtual destruction of the Main Force Viet Cong who were ripped to pieces by superior American firepower.

Of the 84,000 Viet Cong Main Force and puppet troops and units that initiated the TET attacks, more than 45,000 were killed or captured.

The political leadership cadres of the Viet Cong were the most heavily hit as they surfaced in the provincial towns and cities to make their suicide attacks.

The ARVN did not disintegrate as General Giap thought it would.

The South Vietnamese people did not fall in, *en masse*, behind the Communists and the criminal COSVN lunatics.

The VC/PAVN units were repulsed from every town and village they assaulted with crippling losses.

Only in Saigon and *Hue* did the fighting continue for up to a month before the PAVN were repulsed.

Much to the surprise of both the Communists and the Free World Forces, the ARVN troops of President Thieu fought magnificently against the Communist scourge and pestilence.

The Viet Cong Sapper Attack on the US Embassy Saigon: 30th to 31st January 1968

Susie Ky was resting in her bedroom on the top floor of her parent's palatial villa a few blocks from the Presidential Palace in Saigon.

It was 1830 hours on the evening of the 30th January 1968.

"I can't wait any longer!" said the beautiful Susie to herself.

She jumped out of bed and ran downstairs to the telephone. Her father, a Minister in the Thieu Government, was in an emergency cabinet session with the President and the JGS.

General Westmoreland and his staff were also in attendance at the Presidential Palace, trying to recall ARVN troops to active duty in the middle of the Lunar New Year festivities.

The almost physical pain and mental anguish of Susie Ky was intense. She was deeply worried for her lover, Colonel Richard Vortex.

She missed him terribly. More than she ever thought she could miss anyone.

"Oh! Come on!" admonished Susie Ky as she tried to get through to the communications centre at the III MAF headquarters at either *Phu Bai* or *Quang Tri*.

Finally she managed to hook into the telephone system. The Marine Lieutenant at *Quang Tri* asked who she was when she requested to be put through to the *Khe Sanh* combat base.

Upon identification, the base at *Quang Tri* transferred her call to the VHF tactical frequency which used a very high wavelength. Minutes past as Ms Ky perspired with anticipation.

Her smooth, white skin, luxurious black hair and delicious figure trembled with the hope and the expectation of hearing her lover's voice after more than a week.

Terrible thoughts passed through Susie's mind.

Was Richard injured? Was he sick? Was he missing in action? And that other terrible thought which she dared not even contemplate. The black reaper of death that tugged at her heart and soul, threatening to destroy her life even before it had started.

The crackling and static over the radio link-up was awful. Then Susie's heart jumped as a distant and very faint voice could be heard through the handset.

"Hello! This is the DASC centre at *Khe Sanh*!"

"I want to speak to Colonel Richard Vortex!" screamed Susie into the receiver.

There was a few seconds gap as the signal was transmitted.

The American voice asked, "Did you say Colonel Vortex?"

The voice was so faint that she could hardly hear it.

"Yes! Yes!" screamed Susie, "Colonel Vortex! The commander of the 9th Marine Regiment!"

The male voice at the other end of the line said, "Hold on! I'll see if he is inside the base perimeter."

Minutes seemed like hours as Madame Ky, Susie's mother walked into the lobby and tried to comfort her daughter. She placed her hands on Susie's shoulders and caressed her daughter's back. Finally a voice spoke. It was hardly audible but she could just make it out.

"I am Captain Baig!" the voice began, "You want to speak to Colonel Vortex?"

Susie cried, "Yes! Please! Is he there?" Her voice was almost suffocating with emotion.

"No! Wait! I don't know if he…" there was a pause, crackling static and then…

"Susie? Is that you my darling?"

Susie Ky immediately recognised the voice of her lover.

"Its me! Its me - Susie! I love you! I miss you Richard!"

The powerful voice of Vortex answered, "I miss you too and I love you too my darling Susie! Are you alright? Are your parents safe?"

Susie cried, her tears flowing over her face with joy, "Yes! Yes! We are all fine! Just worried about you at *Khe Sanh*!"

She could hear Richard's voice laughing over the static filled VHF frequency.

"Don't worry about me my darling! I haven't received a scratch. Not yet anyway!"

Susie screamed, her heart at ease, "Stay inside the base my darling! Look after yourself. I would die if anything happened to you!"

Susie waited for a response. The static became worse.

She was afraid that the line had been cut off.

But it wasn't as Vortex said, "Nothing is going to happen to me my love."

Susie cried, "When are they going to let you out of there? We hear terrible things about *Khe Sanh*. The newspapers and the American media tell us that it is going to be another catastrophe! Your newsman, this Walter Cronkite from CBS is telling the whole world that it will be another *Dien Bien Phu*!"

Vortex screamed back through the tenuous line, "That's fucking nonsense Susie! Its rubbish, a croc-of-shit! *Khe Sanh* is not another *Dien Bien Phu*!"

Susie was sobbing hysterically into the handset.

Her mother was also emotional. Madame Ky remembered well the annihilation of the French forces at *Dien Bien Phu* 14 years before. It destroyed her world.

Susie begged as she cried, "Oh! Richard! My darling! Come out of that fucking hole! Leave *Khe Sanh*! Save yourself my darling! And fuck the rest of the world and this stinking, putrid war!

I don't want you to be killed or captured by the filthy Viet Cong puppets!"

Her beautiful body was shaking, convulsing with agony.

She was terrified for her lover. She had been an infant when the French forces were murdered at *Dien Bien Phu*.

"I tell you there is nothing to be worried about!"

Susie persisted, "Get out of there my darling!"

"I can't! I am a Marine first and foremost! I do my duty! *Sempre Fi*!"

Vortex felt his heart breaking into pieces. One for her and one for his love affair with the Marine Corps that was his whole life.

He had never wanted to cause his lover so much pain.

"You will be killed if you don't!" cried Susie.

Her slim and beautiful figure was racked with pain.

"My darling! I love you!" cried Vortex over the static.

The invincible Colonel Vortex felt tears coming to his own eyes.

When he faced his own love he was weak as piss.

He could face the enemy with vigour but he wilted under her infectious love and devotion.

Susie sobbed, "I shall pray to Almighty God to keep you safe! I shall pray to the Lord to spare *Khe Sanh*! From the Communists! God hates Communists!

I shall beseech God to smite down the Viet Cong and deny them another *Dien Bien Phu*! For God and Jesus are on our side! Just as at *Dorylaeum* on 1st July 1097 A.D. God and his Soldiers of Christ were victorious!

The side of the righteous shall always prevail over pernicious evil!"

Vortex's throat was plastered with emotion as he said, "Stay safe my darling! And don't worry about me! I shall be victorious at *Khe Sanh*!

I promise you!

Dorylaeum shall look like a picnic to the Communists once I am finished with them!"

Susie cried, "Return quickly to Saigon my darling! I would much rather you satisfying yourself by killing Communists here than over in that cruddy little base at *Khe Sanh*. There are plenty of those motherfuckers for you to pulverise over here in this fucked city! I love you!"

Ms Ky waited for a response.

There was none. The line had been cut. She was devastated. If only she could hear her lover's voice for a few more seconds, a few minutes more before he went back to what he did best – immolating Communist puppets and whore meisters.

She screamed into the telephone and the terrible thought came back to her. Was this the last time she would hear Richard's voice?

Who would die first? And then she knew that Vortex never would – he was invincible.

He lived for War.

He breathed it, smoked it, ate it and it came out of his ass everyday in the form of Communist hating shit.

Susie half fainted. The phone crashed to the marble floor of the lobby. Madame Ky was just able to grab her daughter before she keeled over with anguish.

Brigadier General Davidson left the meeting with COMUSMACV and returned to his billet in Saigon.

He had never seen Westmoreland so frantic, so suffused with anxiety. He was almost about to tell his chief to take a couple of Zoloft. His chief was under terrible pressure so instead he took a handful of Zoloft instead.

"The populace is really throwing up a great New Year party tonight sir!" exclaimed Brigadier Davidson's driver.

"Fucked if I care!" was the only reply from the J-2.

They were in an army jeep and proceeding past the Presidential Palace [minus the President who was in *My Tho*] towards the upper class residential areas where the rich anti-Communists lived oblivious to the carnage and mayhem around them and not caring about it either.

Brigadier General Davidson lived with three enlisted aides and two other Brigadier Generals in an old French villa in downtown Saigon.

"I'm not much interested in the festivities Sergeant!" barked back Davidson.

Adding, "After this fucking war is over I think I am going to write a complete history of this Vietnam fiasco. Both the French war and the one we inherited from them thanks to the boys back at Langley."

They arrived back at the villa and as Davidson ran up the stairs he met the other two Generals who were planning on getting themselves some whores for the evening for some extra-curricular spooning activities.

"We've borrowed some M16's, an M79 grenade launcher and a crate full of grenades from the MACV armoury. Just in case!" said one of the Generals who was in the USAF 7th Air Force.

"Good idea! But are you sure you've got enough?" asked Davidson as he heard the telephone ring in the spacious lobby.

"You never know what shit will happen tonight!" yelled the second Brigadier.

Davidson waved his hands in agreement as he leapt for the ringing phone, saying, facetiously, "Don't you Air Force boys go shooting yourselves in the ass by accident! Have you ever fired a gun before anyway?"

The Air Force General barked back, "Fuck you Davidson!"

"Hello? This is Brigadier General Phillip Buford Davidson Jr."

The time was 1946 hours on the evening of the 30th January 1968. The eve of the TET Offensive.

A female voice replied, "General Davidson? We have met before. I was wondering if I could come over to your place tonight. I want to talk to you. To ask you a few questions."

General Davidson was stupefied. He had no idea who it was.

"Who's this?" he said sternly.

The soft feminine voice answered, "My name is Susie Ky!"

Then Davidson sighed, "Oh! Susie! Its good to hear your voice. How are you?"

Brigadier Davidson had socialised with Colonel Vortex and Ms Ky on many occasions at the Officer's Club inside Pentagon East.

Then Susie's emotions burst free. She started to cry into the telephone.

"I'm so worried about Richard!"

Davidson tried to comfort her, "Listen Susie! Come over to my place at once. I am sure that Colonel Vortex will be alright. There has not been any major ground assault against *Khe Sanh* so far."

"But I'm terrified that he might be killed or injured General!" she cried.

"When can you come over?" asked Davidson.

"Right now Phillip," answered Susie.

"Good! I'll have my aides prepare dinner and some wine for you. Looking forward to greeting you," said Davidson.

Susie Ky took her father's second car, a supercharged 6.9 litre two door Mercedes sports with bullet proof glass and driver doors.

She hurtled past the US Embassy building with its high white walls and impressive frontage.

As she drove at 90 mph she accidentally knocked over some fruit stalls that crashed into the gutter.

"Oh! Fuck it!" she said to herself.

The Embassy was at the intersection of *Mac Dinh Chi* and *Thong Nhut Boulevard*.

The building was rectangular in shape and had six stories. It was probably the only embassy in the world which had a helicopter landing pad on the roof. The windows were made of shatterproof Plexiglas. The outer walls were rocket proof.

A South Vietnamese Police Station was also nearby on *Mac Dinh Chi Street*.

The United States Embassy was guarded by Military Police from the 527th MP Company of the 716th MP Battalion based in Saigon.

The commander of the 716th was Lieutenant Colonel G.D. 'Doug' Rowe.

He was the Provost Marshal for the whole Saigon area.

The 716th was under the operational command and control of HAC (Headquarters Area Command).

The commander of HAC was Brigadier General Albin F. Irzyk.

General Irzyk controlled all US support units inside Saigon itself. He also had direct access to reinforcements from the US 199th Light Infantry Brigade at *Bien Hoa*. General Irzyk was a no nonsense soldier of the old school and a personal friend of Colonel Vortex. He considered Vortex to be a second non-biological son to him. Irzyk was a veteran of General George Patton's 3rd US Army in World War II and a hero of *Bastogne*. He rode up front on Patton's personal tank in the European Theatre.

There was no finer nor more dedicated soldier than General Albin F. Irzyk.

He was a hero of the United States Army *par excellence*.

A hero of the Nation and of the United States gallant and heroic War Machine.

Colonel Vortex would run through hell itself for General Irzyk.

Susie drove like a maniac through the Saigon streets trying to aim her supercharged car against anyone that she thought looked like a Communist.

She was convulsed with fear and anguish all intermingled. She wished she could go to *Khe Sanh* herself with a *Zippo* flamethrower and assist her lover in incinerating the Communists.

What she needed now was to hear some sort of reassuring voice. This is why she had to see Brigadier General Davidson. The senior J-2 intelligence officer in South Vietnam.

If anyone knew the real situation at *Khe Sanh*, then it would most definitely be him. Perhaps he could soothe her. She would suck his brains out till he could do just that.

"Hello Susie! Come in please!" said Davidson as Susie stood in front of the old but gracious French villa of colonial times.

"Thank you for seeing me General," said Susie.

Davidson ushered her into the dining room which was at the back of the house. A beautiful Japanese garden could be seen through the sliding glass doors.

"Oh! You have a wonderful place here General!" exclaimed Susie Ky.

Davidson winked at the other US aides who were introduced to her.

"Yes thanks! Thanks to the American taxpayer!"

They all laughed. The three NCO's served *Beluga caviar* and *Bollinger R.D.* champagne before dinner.

"I'm so desperately worried about Richard. My only concern is for his safety Phillip!"

Davidson put his palm on Susie's soft and aromatic thigh. He stroked it and said, "I understand. But I can give you my best assurance that the worst is probably over at *Khe Sanh*."

The initial attack has been beaten off."

Susie responded, "But you know Richard! General! He always loves to lead his men into battle personally! I can't think of losing him!"

She started to sob quietly as Davidson explained the best case scenario at *Khe Sanh*.

But even the best case scenario was quite frightening with regards to its ramifications for the besieged Marines.

The three NCOs' looked on sympathetically.

Dinner was served. Onion soup, roast chicken and Vienna Schnitzel along with *gefilte fish* were just some of the delicacies laid on for the delicious repast.

Finally Susie Ky started to regain some of her composure trying to forget the man she had run over in the street on her way to Davidson's house.

The pep-talk with General Davidson had eased her almost panic-like sensitivity.

The three NCOs' were cleaning up in the kitchen while Susie and General Davidson were playing canasta and sipping on some vintage Napoleon Brandy in the luxurious room oblivious to the mounds of shit and suffering outside.

Suddenly Davidson pricked up his ears. The ominous rumble of distant explosions could be heard coming from the *Cholon District* of Saigon. This area was mainly inhabited by Chinese merchants and their families. It was a hotbed of Viet Cong infiltration.

Susie jumped up from the lounge in fright.

"Do you think its started?" asked one of the NCO's, a Master Sergeant who had two Colt 0.45's strapped to each side of his waist.

"It's possible," said Davidson calmly as he walked to the windows.

"What has started?" asked Susie.

Brigadier Davidson sipped on his brandy, "Don't you know?"

Susie laughed, "Know what? What's happening?"

Phillip replied, "We are expecting a big attack by the VC scum inside Saigon."

Then some pistol shots could be heard a few blocks away.

The three NCOs' scurried up to their bedrooms on the second floor and reached for their M16's and M79 grenade launchers.

Davidson said, "Susie! You stay here with one of the Sergeants in the lounge room and fucking kill anything that comes in or out! Here! Take my Colt 0.45 pistol!"

Susie Ky pushed his hand away, "I don't need it Phillip!"

"What do you mean? You need it for personal safety. The Viet Cong may attack this house. They know the billets of every senior American officer in Saigon."

Then, much to Brigadier General Davidson's amazement, Susie pulled out from the folds of her silk Chinese dress a *Smith & Weston 0.45 Magnum*. One of the most powerful handguns in the world.

Davidson smiled, "I see you have come well prepared for this evening's festivities!"

Brigadier Davidson and the other NCO's went outside and patrolled the back of the house. It was from there that the gunshots were coming.

Davidson told the other two Sergeants to keep watch at the front of the French villa and in the driveway.

An hour passed which seemed like half a night.

The young Sergeant and Susie played a hand of poker.

Then a tremendous crack thundered into the room.

"Oh! God! What the fuck is that?" shouted Susie Ky.

Glass was flying everywhere. It hit Susie in the forearm and drew blood. A superficial wound. The glass doors leading into the Japanese garden had been shattered.

Susie was just about to open her mouth to speak to the young Sergeant when she noticed that his body had whiplashed into an awful arch.

His face contorted with horror. A red point grew from the middle of his forehead as he vomited blood over the dining table.

"You're shot!" yelled Susie as she jumped back in fright. The Sergeant crashed on top of the dining table demolishing the cutlery. He spun 90 degrees and collapsed onto the Persian rug, blood and brain tissue sprinkling from his head.

He died seconds later as Susie dived behind the leather lounge, her *Smith & Weston* at the ready.

She tried to think even though she was in a state of shock. Glancing through the broken glass she saw shadows moving swiftly across the Japanese garden.

It must be General Davidson and the other two NCO's, she thought.

Suddenly a figure burst into the lounge through the broken sliding doors. He was not American. He carried an AK-47 assault rifle. He wore black pantaloons and a black-grey tunic.

Viet Cong! Thought Susie.

The VC guerrilla looked frantically about the room as Susie crouched behind the furniture. She had not been spotted yet.

Then a voice said loudly, "Hey! What's going on in here?"

Susie recognised the voice of the other Sergeant who was now walking into the back of the house from the driveway.

He had obviously heard the commotion.

Immediately AK-47 fire erupted from the VC. The Sergeant's body seemed to blow apart sideways as geysers of blood burst from every pore of his body. The NCO whiplashed backwards and crashed into the antique clock in the hallway.

"You fucking Viet Cong pig!" screamed Susie Ky.

She leapt up from behind the leather lounge and aimed her *Smith & Weston Magnum* handgun.

The VC turned his head in surprise. Before he could raise his AK-47 towards Susie's body she fired.

The Magnum literally blew 50% of the man's head away. Brain matter showered the lounge room like an exploding watermelon. Susie could see only one eye and half a mouth left on the skull as the force of the blast, the kick-back, blew her back across the lounge. Then she fell forwards onto the antique clock.

A massive punch had slammed into the back of her neck. She groaned with agony. Her spine felt as if it was paralysed.

"You dirty fucking imperialist slut!" screamed the voice in fluent Vietnamese.

"Ban fucking đế quốc đi."

A second Viet Cong had crept up behind her. He launched himself on top of Susie Ky's body and started to rip her Chinese dress off.

"Tôi sẽ làm tình voi bạn như bạn đã không bao gio được fucked."

Translated to English;

"I am going to make love to you like you've never been fucked before!" screamed the Viet Cong who smelt of repugnant body odour and opium fumes from his obvious addiction to that narcotic mind altering substance.

Susie Ky answered as she spat in the Communist's face, "I would rather die first! Or even be fucked by a non-Communist peasant rather than you!"

She catapulted her knee upwards from the base of the lounge and crushed the Viet Cong's testicles with a powerful blow.

This gave her the few seconds that she needed.

Susie scratched open the VC's eyes and he screamed, falling backwards as he held his gonads with both hands.

Susie picked up her Smith & Weston and fired a round into the Communist's pelvis. The Magnum blew away his gonads and penis as well as splattering his bladder all over the mahogany side table.

Brigadier Davidson burst into the lounge room with the last remaining NCO.

"Jesus Christ!" he screamed as he saw his two dead aides.

Miraculously, the wounded VC still had the strength to raise his AK-47 rifle towards Susie's head.

Brigadier Davidson dropped his M79 grenade launcher and leapt onto the Communist in his fine dress uniform. The senior J-2 intelligence officer drove his 12 inch officer's dagger into the VC's spine from behind.

The other aide yelled, "I've got him!"

Spinning around to place himself between Susie and the Viet Cong the other American lunged his knife into the man's throat until the point of the blade exited through his neck.

As Davidson tore into his organs, his American colleague ripped out the VC's trachea.

The American General threw the cadaver into the garden while the surviving Sergeant checked to see if his buddies were still alive.

"They are both dead sir!" cried the NCO.

Brigadier Davidson was furious, "Damn it! I should have brought additional troops with me tonight!"

The Sergeant asked, "What are we going to do now sir?"

"Fucked if I know?" answered Davidson.

Davidson held Susie's arm gently and soothed her. He said to his aide who stood six foot six inches tall and was a Chief Warrant Officer, "You stay here and guard the villa. Also contact MACV HQ and tell them what happened. I am going to take Ms Ky back to her home."

Susie and Davidson ran out to the driveway and hopped into her supercharged custom built Mercedes that had blood on the front bumper due to Susie's earlier accident.

The throaty roar of 16 cylinders gurgled at them.

"Bloody hell? What kind of a car is this?" asked Brigadier Phillip B. Davidson.

Susie Ky laughed, "It has over 650 horse power!"

"I can't believe it!" chuckled the J-2 Chief as they catapulted into the street and accelerated to over 100 mph on the straight sections of the roadway.

They headed for the *Ben Luc* Bridge.

The festivities that had been proceeding everywhere in Saigon for the Lunar New Year were now replaced with grim and pathetic panic.

Very few Saigon citizens were in the street and those that were ran for cover as explosions and machine gun fire rocked the entire capital.

Davidson said as he wiped the sweat of his brow, "This really is the beginning of the Communist offensive that we had been expecting for so long!"

As he spoke General Davidson took out from a black leather bag an immaculate AK-47 machine gun and started to fire out of his side of the car window. Bullets flew everywhere as they sped past into the Saigon night.

"What the fuck are you firing at?" asked Susie Ky in amazement.

Susie Ky was driving so fast and the huge engine was so loud that it attracted adverse attention.

"I am firing for effect!" said General Davidson calmly.

Susie looked stupefied, "Firing for what...?"

Just as they turned into *Mac Dinh Chi* Street a group of American military police from the 716th MP battalion noticed them as they raced past at over 120 mph.

They were standing at the corner and manning M60 machine gun emplacements. Davidson was careful to hold his fire as they approached the US troops.

The Military Police Sergeant in charge of the squad cried, "Look! That car! It's a Viet Cong gone berserk! Fire! Fire at it!"

General Davidson could feel the 7.62mm slugs hitting the side of the vehicle. The bullets narrowly missed his thigh and testicles.

"For Christ's sake! Slow down!" he screamed to Susie Ky.

But Susie had already lost control of the supercharged Mercedes on a greasy section of the roadway in front of the American Embassy in *Thong Nhut* Boulevard.

The car fish-tailed and slid sideways.

General Davidson hung on for all he was worth as the Mercedes crashed into a group of American jeeps in front of the Embassy building.

As they recovered from their concussion and bruising, Davidson and Susie Ky noticed that they were surrounded by over 100 heavily armed US soldiers.

Every gun was trained on them.

They had smashed directly into an American military police company that had been called to the US Embassy.

An officer screamed, "Hold your fire! They are friendly!"

The forest of muzzles were lowered.

The officer stalked over and swung open the car door.

"Cotton pick'n hell! What the hell do you think you are doing?"

The man who castigated them was Brigadier General Albin F. Irzyk, the commanding officer of HAC.

"I'm sorry about that Brigadier!" exclaimed General Davidson as he was helped out of the car.

"Oh! Jesus! Its you Phillip!" began Brigadier Irzyk, "...what the hell are you doing driving like a madman in the middle of the night? You were this far from being shot by mistake!"

Susie Ky also knew Brigadier Irzyk very well. She had met him on numerous occasions at the Pentagon East Officer's Club with Vortex.

"Miss Ky!" beamed Irzyk, "It's always a pleasure!" The commander of HAC gallantly kissed Susie's outstretched hand.

Irzyk was tall and lean with blue eyes and short black hair that was greying.

Davidson asked as he looked around at all the troops and then heard shooting coming from inside the US Embassy compound itself.

"Irzyk! What the hell is going on here? We were just on our way back to Ms Ky's home!"

Brigadier Irzyk explained. It was now 0357 hours in the early morning of the 31st January 1968.

"Big trouble in little China!" began Irzyk.

"Major General Tran Do, the commander of VC forces in Saigon has sent some sappers into the American Embassy. I think there is about 16 of them but we're not sure yet.

The Communists drove up to the Embassy gates in a taxi cab and a small Peugeot truck. They are armed with AK-47's and RPG rocket launchers. As the taxi came up the VC fired at the two MPs standing just outside the entrance.

The Military Police locked the gate and the VC sappers from the C-10 sapper battalion unloaded their weapons and satchel charges."

Brigadier Davidson shook his head with disbelief as Irzyk continued, "They blew a hole here…"

Irzyk pointed to the southeast wall of the chancery, "…and crawled in killing two of my Military Police troops. They then blew in the embassy doors with RPG's and attacked two more Americans in the lobby.

There is also another Marine guard on the roof. I have been told that one of the wounded Marines was taken up to the roof while the other is still defending the lobby.

We are just about to launch a counterattack on the remaining VC sappers."

General Davidson asked, "Are there any other friendly personnel in the building?"

Brigadier Irzyk replied, "Yes. There is a Mr Wendt. He's a USAID economics officer on the fourth floor. There is a night watchman and a teletype clerk on the ground floor – both Vietnamese. There is also a code clerk, a CIA night duty officer and three other men on the fourth floor.

In addition we have Colonel George Jacobson and Master Sergeant Josephson who are assistants to the Ambassador, Mr Ellsworth Bunker. They are in the French villa behind the Chancery compound to the north."

Brigadier General Davidson rubbed his chin, "I see! I would like a piece of this action, Irzyk. I can't believe that the VC would have the nerve and the gall to attack the US Embassy itself!"

The HAC commander said, "Be my guest!"

Then Brigadier Irzyk sympathised, "Can you imagine what a field day the American press are going to have over this fiasco?

Look!..." pointed Irzyk.

"The vultures are already here! And they are gloating!"

Susie Ky looked over to the corner of *Mac Dinh Chi* Street and *Thong Nhut* Boulevard.

The reporters and newsmen were already gathering and talking excitedly amongst each other.

Then a young MP officer came running up to Brigadier Irzyk.

He saluted and said crisply, "We are ready to go sir!"

The officer was First Lieutenant Frank Ribich. The commander of the 527th MP Company.

Brigadier Irzyk asked, "Are your troops in position?"

Ribich said, "Yes sir. Though we had a hell of a time getting here!

My men had to de-truck near the JFK Square. We then leapfrogged down the *Thong Nhut* Boulevard under heavy VC sniper fire.

The Viet Cong seem to be everywhere! Not just here at the Embassy!"

Irzyk ordered, "Launch the attack!"

He then turned and smiled at Brigadier General Davidson and Susie Ky, saying, "You're joking of course? Aren't you?"

Susie Ky said, "You mean about participating in the attack?"

Irzyk nodded with an expression of sheer amazement.

General Davidson said, "We are not joking Albin."

As the MP troops and some Marine guards ran forward towards the *Norodom* compound, General Davidson and Susie Ky ran behind them.

Susie carried her *Smith & Weston* 0.45 Magnum handgun.

General Davidson carried his M79 grenade launcher in the left hand and his AK-47 in the right.

They scurried forward with the MPs until they burst into an open gate which led into the parking lot of the US Embassy.

Three Marine guards were already exchanging fire with the VC sappers.

Susie cried, "Look! The Viet Cong shit-heads are hiding behind the cars! Get them, fucking kill the bastards!"

As she spoke she jumped to her feet and shot several rounds in the direction of the Communist fire.

The sound of her *Smith & Weston* echoed across the Embassy compound.

Ms Ky was the only person standing while the American troops were all crouching behind any cover they could find.

Lieutenant Ribich exclaimed, "Sir! You should retire back to *Mac Dinh Chi* Street! Its too dangerous here sir! And take this crazy woman with you!

She's liable to get her pretty head blown off with her histrionic antics much as the spirit of her vehemence is appreciated!"

Davidson clapped the young officer on the shoulders, "You just do your job son, and get on with the attack to fuck these VC pigs. We are going to flush those Communist sappers out of here and into the cesspool of hell!"

The Military Police and Marines were laying down a murderous suppressive fire all along the row of cars inside the embassy compound. The vehicles started to explode as the gasoline in them ignited from the veritable hail of bullets.

Then, suddenly, two VC killers started running across the front wall of the Chancery towards the lobby door.

"I've got them," said Susie Ky with calm precision.

Much to the amazement of Lieutenant Ribich, the beautiful South Vietnamese girl rose slowly to her feet and took aim.

The powerful handgun boomed out into the early morning pre-dawn.

One of the scurrying sappers lost an ear and the left side of his cheek.

Brigadier Davidson finished off the other one as he launched a grenade from his M79.

The detonation threw the Communist criminal over several vehicles, one of which exploded as its petrol tank ignited.

A severed arm flew gracefully through the air.

Susie Ky signalled to several Marines on top of the OSA (Office of the Special Assistant) roof.

This roof ran along the inner wall of the Chancery and overlooked the Embassy grounds.

Susie Ky indicated to the Marines on the OSA roof that several VC scum were hiding behind the decorative planters in front of the Chancery.

The troops opened fire as Ms Ky, General Davidson and Lieutenant Ribich worked their way around the planters to attack from behind.

Ribich's Military Police continued to fire from in front thus providing an effective covering fire for their movement.

Suddenly, as Ms Ky had worked up to the planters too quickly, she was hit in the back of the head by a Viet Cong sapper who had leapt out from behind one of the decorative planters.

"Aiiee!" she screamed.

The VC sapper fell on top of Susie and started to beat her breasts and throat.

But Ms Ky managed to knee the Communist's groin as Lieutenant Ribich came up from behind and slit open the man's throat with his 18 inch double-edged Marine dagger of honour.

All three of them had to dive for cover immediately as more VC started firing in their direction.

Lieutenant Ribich screamed, "This is no good! They are covered too well by those concrete walls and the planters!"

RPG-7 rockets screeched across the lawn and exploded behind their position.

"Fuck this shit!" screamed Susie Ky, firing her Magnum in all directions.

"What are you firing at?" asked General Davidson.

Susie answered, "I am firing for effect!"

Some of the Military Police in Ribich's squad were hit by grenade fragments. A Corporal screamed as he received a fragment in his left eye, blood streaming over his face.

As he staggered forward the VC sappers mowed him down with AK-47 fire.

The soldier's body twirled in a deadly quadrille, blood geysers erupting all over his chest.

"Shit!" screamed Brigadier General Davidson.

Lieutenant Ribich said, "There is a group of Communists over there! Behind that decorative planter! But we can't get at them."

Just then another RPG-7 rocket slammed into the OSA rooftop.

It wounded two more Marine Security troops.

"Wait here! I've thought of something!" said Susie Ky.

"Where are you going?" screamed Brigadier General Davidson.

But Ms Ky had already run back to the main gate of the Chancery.

The beautiful fiancée of Colonel Vortex rushed to her car in the middle of *Thong Nhut* Boulevard.

As she turned the ignition key the roar of the supercharged 6.9 litre engine echoed down the wide street as more American Military Police were pouring in from the *International Hotel* in central Saigon.

The *International Hotel Saigon* was the Headquarters of the 716th Military Police Battalion commanded by Lieutenant Colonel Rowe.

As the situation at the US Embassy developed more and more reaction teams were sent into the battle.

Eventually Lieutenant Colonel Rowe would also receive helicopter support from the 101st Airborne Division [*The 'Chicken Men'*] under Major General Olinto Barsanti.

A telephone call from General William Westmoreland to Colonel Rowe and the latter's urgent plea for assistance made this possible.

Brigadier General Irzyk ran over to Susie's car from his command post across the street.

"What the hell do you think you are doing Ms Ky?" asked Irzyk.

"Please get out of my way General!" she answered.

"Please! Ms Ky!" admonished Irzyk, "…there are VC snipers everywhere! You'll get hurt or killed! And that's worse!"

Before Susie could open her mouth a black sedan approached the Military Police checkpoint up on *Thong Nhut* Boulevard.

Brigadier Irzyk glanced around to see what was going on. Then, suddenly, the black sedan started moving rapidly down the Boulevard in their direction.

The Military Police at the checkpoint screamed for the car to stop and then opened fire with a CAR 15.

"What the hell?" screamed Irzyk.

One of Irzyk's Major's shouted to the Military Police, "Stop that car!"

Brigadier Irzyk himself, spun around with his M16 and hosed down the car as it approached. He fired at the driver's door, the engine bay and the left front tyre.

The Marine security troops also opened a deadly stream of M60 fire onto the sedan from the OSA rooftop.

Susie Ky took this opportunity to slam her foot onto the accelerator.

The supercharged Mercedes catapulted forward.

Brigadier Irzyk ran after the car as it crashed into a tree on the left side of the *Thong Nhut* Boulevard.

The General continued to fire at the vehicle, his 7.62mm rounds spraying through the back window.

As the Military Police and their Brigadier approached the car they could see that the driver was a Viet Cong sapper.

There were satchel charges in the back seat along with several brand new AK-47 rifles.

Part of the sapper's head was sprayed across the front dashboard of the car. His intestines were leaking onto the floor of the vehicle.

Brigadier Irzyk ordered, "Check this fucked bastard for any papers and/or any identity documents!"

The Major nodded, "Yes sir!"

The Military Police dragged the half gutted body of the VC out of the vehicle as Irzyk said, "Now what the hell is Ms Ky doing?"

But it was already too late.

Susie Ky had spun her Mercedes around and accelerated it to over 60 mph as she crashed through the main gates of the US Embassy.

The car catapulted into the Chancery grounds speeding past Brigadier General Davidson and Lieutenant Ribich and his troops.

The Military Police were flabbergasted.

Ms Ky steered the car towards the group of Viet Cong who were entrenched behind the decorative planters in the front lawn of the Chancery.

She placed a wooden stick under the accelerator so that it was jammed at full speed.

Ms Ky then threw open the driver's door as she primed a C4 plastic explosive to detonate in 10 seconds.

The beautiful and attractive South Vietnamese girl then leapt out of the speeding car and crawled back to Davidson and Ribich on her hands and knees.

Seconds later, Ribich watched as the Mercedes pulverised the whole concrete planter and knocked down about five VC sappers behind it.

The C4 plastic explosive then went up with a 'Vrooosh!'

Orange-red flames spurted across the lawn as three VC staggered forward burning like torches.

Susie Ky grabbed an M60 machine gun from one of the Military Police and hosed the Communists down in a veritable avalanche of hot steel.

"Beautiful!" exclaimed Brigadier General Davidson.

"I've never seen anything like it!" yelled Lieutenant Ribich.

General Davidson hugged the excited Susie Ky and said, "I am going to recommend you to General Westmoreland for the highest civilian gallantry award available!"

Ribich and Davidson then continued to pump hundreds of rounds towards the few remaining sappers in the Embassy grounds.

The fighting continued until 0830 hours on the 31st January 1968.

A heliborne assault by HU-1E Hueys from the 101st Airborne Division finally finished off the C-10 sapper team.

The final action involved General Davidson and Susie Ky assisting Military Police and Marines to flush out a surviving VC from the white stucco villa behind the Chancery.

This was where Colonel Jacobson lived, who was one of Ellsworth Bunker's aides at the Embassy.

Davidson and Ribich stormed the front of the villa while Ms Ky threw in two tear gas grenades to shake the Communist loose. As the tear gas spread through the ground floor, Susie fired an M60 machine gun into the window at the back of the house. The VC sapper ran upstairs where Colonel Jacobson was waiting.

The Colonel was crouched behind a thin plywood wall.

His only weapon was a Colt 0.45 handgun that had been thrown up to him from the lawn by Brigadier General Davidson.

As the VC sapper burst into the upstairs bedroom, firing his AK-47 rifle from side to side, the rounds missed Colonel Jacobson by mere inches.

As the VC turned the Colonel leapt to his feet and shot the man twice at point blank range.

The Communist's skull blew apart and splashed across the walls of the room.

Seconds later Susie Ky rushed up the stairs followed by the Marines.

The Colonel held his fire when he saw the friendly troops.

"It's all over!" said Susie to Colonel Jacobson.

The fiasco at the United States Embassy in Saigon was over.

The PAVN Attack on Hills 881 South and 861A: 5th February 1968

Colonel Vortex had covered his eyes with his hands after putting down the radio telephone.

His line to Susie Ky had been cut off.

He was in a state of sheer anguish.

But there was nothing he could do at this moment to alleviate his lover's worry and her suffering.

Vortex knew that he had a duty to perform at *Khe Sanh*.

And he was determined to carry it out.

He couldn't give a shit what the maniacal media were saying back in the States.

Their comparison of *Khe Sanh* with *Dien Bien Phu* was absolute nonsense.

The only thing he wanted to do at this moment was to kiss and make love to his gorgeous South Vietnamese girl. His delightful Susie Ky.

His wife could gladly have her divorce. Vortex would present it to her on a silver platter.

"Are you alright sir?" asked Captain Mirza Baig as the junior officer entered the DASC bunker.

Mirza Baig could see that Colonel Vortex's iron disposition had been temporarily shaken.

For the first time Captain Baig actually saw the *human* side of Colonel Vortex and not just the unstoppable military killing machine.

"I'm fine thank you," replied Vortex in a daze.

The constant stress and violent combat of the past few weeks was slowly grinding Colonel Vortex down. But out of the innermost depths of his body, Vortex pulled hidden reserves of strength and a magnificent will to carry on the battle.

His stinging hate of the Viet Cong puppets and their North Vietnamese whore masters renewed his body as the thermonuclear reactions inside the sun by fusion renewed that star's energy.

Vortex retired to bed and slept through the night of the 30th to 31st January 1968 in the 26th Marine HQ bunker.

From the hours of 2300 to 0900 there was sporadic Communist shelling of the *Khe Sanh* base.

But even that was not enough to wake him from an exhausted sleep. The next day Vortex arose and walked into the DASC bunker.

He studied the planned TAC air strikes for the coming 24 hours.

Master Sergeant Richter walked in and said, "There will be another B-52 Arc Light strike in about 30 minutes sir."

Vortex nodded as he fixed himself a cup of jasmine tea.

"We are going to hit the valley between Hill 64 and Hill 881 South," added Captain Baig.

Vortex asked, "Did you detect PAVN troops in that area?"

Baig answered as he pulled out his field map and laid it on the table, "We have sir. We estimate there is at least one Regiment there. We think it is the 24th Regiment of the 304th Division."

Colonel Lownds also appeared in the Direct Air Support Centre. He acknowledged Vortex and the others and then fell into deep conversation with his staff.

Apart from the men at the radar consoles and those manning the Combat SKYSPOT computer there were at least 35 junior officers from the 26th, the 9th and the 37th ARVN Rangers.

Colonel Vortex was wondering why the PAVN had not yet made a full scale ground assault upon the *Khe Sanh* perimeter.

On the 27th January the last men of the 37th ARVN Rangers had arrived with all their heavy equipment.

They had been brought in by CH-54 *Tare Sky Cranes* and Ch-47 Chinooks.

Colonel Lownds and Colonel Vortex had made repeated calls to both III MAF Headquarters and MACV in Saigon.

They were pressuring Lieutenant General Cushman and Major General Tompkins to find out from COMUSMACV whether they were going to be allowed to use atomic munitions at *Khe Sanh*. Specifically the *W48* fission shell for the 155mm howitzers.

But no answer came.

And no answer would come much to Vortex's chagrin.

"I have some new sensor information sir," said Captain Mirza Baig.

"What is it?" asked Vortex as he looked over in Lownds' direction.

The superlative Fire Control Officer pointed to Hill 881 South.

"The boys over at *Nakhon Phanom* believe that the next big ground assault is going to hit Hill 881 South.

They believe, as I do, that the attack will come on the 5th February. Five days from now!"

Vortex's eyes sparkled with renewed fervour.

"Let me see!"

Captain Baig handed Vortex a computer printout. It was the seismic, acoustic and chemical sensor information.

The Colonel spent 15 minutes studying the figures. He noticed the changes in vibrations and the increased noise level around the suspect hill.

"Yes. It definitely looks like something is brewing around 881S!"

Colonel Lownds walked over with his officers.

"What are you two scheming about?"

Vortex laughed, "Who said anything about scheming?"

Captain Baig added, "We are just studying the latest sensor information."

Lownds asked, "What does it point to?"

Baig repeated his analysis to the 26th commander.

"Then we shall have to coordinate all available TAC air, artillery and B-52 strikes to stop that push if and when it happens."

A Marine from communications called out, "Its MACV for you sir!"

Colonel Lownds asked, "For me?"

The Corporal answered, "No sir. For Colonel Vortex."

Vortex grabbed the phone and winked at Lownds.

David E. Lownds was thoroughly pissed of.

As commander of the *Khe Sanh* combat base, KSCB, it was he who should have received the call.

"Hello? Who's this?" asked Vortex.

"It's General Westmoreland!" answered the Supreme Commander.

Vortex went straight to the heart of the matter.

"Are we going to be allowed to use nuclear weapons sir?"

COMUSMACV said, "No!"

"Shit! No?" asked Vortex with disgust permeating his voice.

"No!" repeated COMUSMACV.

There was a pause and then Westmoreland continued.

"I have been instructed by the President to cease all contingency planning regarding the use of nuclear weapons, atomic or fusion devices, at *Khe Sanh*. And that means a definite no to your question."

"I'm sorry to hear that sir," said Vortex.

"But that is not the reason that I called," said COMUSMACV.

The time was now 1100 hours on the morning of the 31st January 1968.

"Have you heard?" asked General Westmoreland.

"Heard what sir?" asked Vortex.

"The General Offensive – General Uprising has started! The Communists call it *Tong Cong Kich – Tong Khoi Nghia*."

Colonel Lownds picked up another handset and interrupted, "You mean a full scale offensive sir?"

COMUSMACV shouted back, "That's exactly what I mean!"

Colonel Vortex asked, "Where is this offensive taking place? Which part of the Republic of Vietnam? Is it the A Shau Valley?"

COMUSMACV said calmly, "The offensive is all over South Vietnam! It caught the ARVN by surprise during their Lunar New Year festivities! They call it TET."

Vortex asked with disbelief, "All over the Republic of Vietnam? It can't be sir?"

Westmoreland said, "It is! We estimate over 84,000 local and Main Force Viet Cong have initiated the offensive. It started at approximately midnight last night!

Over 100 towns and cities have been attacked by the VC and PAVN main forces. Thirty-six provincial capitals have been hit.

The onslaught is so wide spread that we are having difficulty at this early stage to get a clear picture. But the three main assaults have been identified."

Colonel Lownds asked, "Where are they sir?"

COMUSMACV replied, "The 6th PAVN Regiment supported by the 4th PAVN Regiment and 6 Main Force Viet Cong battalions have attacked the ancient Imperial capital of *Hue*."

Colonel Vortex looked at Master Sergeant Richter and screamed, "It can't be sir! *Hue*? The city itself?"

COMUSMACV confirmed what he said and continued, "My MACV staff have determined that the VC are also striking the *Bien Hoa* combat base as well as BEAR-CAT, the home of the US 9th Infantry Division north-east of Saigon. *Bien Hoa* is the headquarters of the 199th Light Infantry Brigade, the 101st Airborne Division and the II Field Force Vietnam (FFV) which are all situated there.

"*Alles ist ein fauler und stinkender Misserfolg!*" exclaimed Sergeant Major Crighton to Vortex.

Vortex nodded and replied back in German, "*Diejenigen, die VC Scheiden bumsen, sind dabei, lieb für dieses Verbrechen zu zahlen.*"

[Vortex's reply translated to English: "Those fucking VC vaginas are going to pay dearly for this outrage."]

Westmoreland, not hearing the German language interchange between Vortex and Crighton which they loved to engage in when particularly angry, continued, "The VC attack force probably consists of two infantry battalions and one reinforced infantry company.

The *Tan Son Nhut Air Base* as well as Pentagon East is also under attack by at least four Main Force VC infantry battalions and one sapper battalion.

Overall as I said, 36 Provincial Capitals out of a total of 44 have been hit.

Five major autonomous cities have also been assaulted.

Twenty-three US and ARVN bases are under Communist fire.

Our CORDS Program and the Strategic Hamlet Program is under dire threat.

The major centres of Communist military activity are *Ben Tre, Can Tho, My Tho, Ban Me Thuot, Kontum City, Qui Nhon, Nha Trang, Da Nang*, your III MAF Headquarters at *Quang Tri City* and *Phu Bai* as well as *Hue* and Saigon itself.

The most vicious attacks in Saigon have been in the *Cholon District* populated mainly by ethnic Chinese."

Both Lownds and Vortex exclaimed, "Its unbelievable sir!"

General Westmoreland grunted and said, "The VC and PAVN forces now have control of 10 Provincial capitals.

I have ordered the US 4th Infantry Division as well as the 25th Tropic Lightning Infantry Division to converge on Saigon and *Bien Hoa* to counter the Communist's thrusts and outrages."

Vortex said, "That is a wise precaution sir. But now more than ever is the time to unleash our nuclear arsenal. To wipe out these rabid interlopers in a spray of atomic weaponry *par excellance*!"

COMUSMACV said, "In the light of this all out attack I order you at *Khe Sanh* to be doubly alert!

The PAVN Divisions surrounding you may launch a major attack at any moment."

Colonel David E. Lownds answered, "Understood sir!"

Colonel Vortex added, "The sensor analysis teams are indicating that another major assault on the hill outposts is imminent. Probably the 4th or 5th February sir."

COMUSMACV acknowledged the information and asked, "What do you think Vortex? Colonel Lownds?

Some of my staff at MACV think that this whole *Khe Sanh* siege is just an elaborate '*diversion*' to draw our attention away from this Lunar New Year offensive they have just unleashed upon us!

I have my opinion on that theory.

But I want to hear yours!"

Colonel Vortex looked at Lownds and then laughed with disgust, "Sir! With all due respect to your MACV staff.

I think that is absolute bullshit! Its pure crap! Sir!"

COMUSMACV chuckled, "Go on Colonel Vortex. I'm listening."

Vortex explained, "I can understand that the North Vietnamese may indeed want to create a diversion before launching this major Lunar New Year offensive. Or TET as they call it.

But not at *Khe Sanh*!

Not with 3 full North Vietnamese Divisions plus two artillery regiments and countless support troops.

This force of three and one half divisions is the bulk of the PAVN strength in and around the DMZ!

You don't create a simple diversion with such a massive force! On the contrary, General Giap intends to assault and take *Khe Sanh* if he is able. But we shall stop him sir! I promise you that!"

Then Colonel Lownds added his comments to the Supreme Commander.

Just then the B-52 Arc Light strike fell like the *hammer of Thor* onto suspected PAVN positions around Hill 564 [aka Hill 64].

The noise, even inside the DASC bunker was deafening.

The tremendous vibrations and earth tremors created a comical sight.

Colonel Vortex and the other officers had difficulty standing on their feet as they swayed like rag dolls in the wind.

The soil under their general purpose combat boots shifted back and forth from the awesome power of the 500lb and 750lb iron bombs that fell like a torrent from hell out of the yawning mouths of the B-52 bomb-bay doors.

The 2,500 Marines inside the *Khe Sanh* perimeter ran for cover even though it was their own firepower that had been unleashed.

Vortex said a silent pray to Almighty God and asked Jesus for victory with a deep sense of religious contemplation. He knew that theirs was the way of the righteous.

COMUSMACV answered through the VHF tactical frequency as the cacophony continued.

"I agree absolutely with you Colonel Vortex. This master stroke by General Vo Nguyen Giap at *Khe Sanh* is not a diversion!

I suspect that he wanted to crush your Marine combat base during the final stages of this current Lunar offensive.

But I have this Communist General where I want him!"

Colonel David E. Lownds asked as he grinned at Vortex and the ever attentive Captain Baig, "What do you mean sir?"

COMUSMACV went on, "I have been waiting and praying! I have been asking God to grant me the beautiful chance!

The opportunity to face the North Vietnamese in a large and meat-grinding set-piece battle!

And it has finally happened!

Now I shall be able to use the full spectrum of our invincible American firepower against a concentrated enemy target!

I shall for once be able to fight the PAVN on our terms! And not on theirs! With their hit and run tactics hitherto employed.

With large units in a traditional set-piece battle.

We shall annihilate the Main Force VC units in this Lunar Offensive and at *Khe Sanh* under a virtual avalanche of bombs directly heaven-sent!"

Vortex, enthused by General Westmoreland's tirade, answered, "I promise you sir! I guarantee with my blood and the blood of my troops that *Khe Sanh* will not fall!

We shall exterminate and decimate the foul and stinking PAVN vermin!

They shall be eradicated sir!

Once our air strikes are completed around *Khe Sanh* the PAVN will be so dazed and rooted that they won't know which way is which when they retreat from this base back into the lousy DMZ sanctuary areas!

I only hope that President Johnson will be advised correctly.

I pray that our forces will be allowed to launch a full scale ground assault into North Vietnam itself. We must interdict the massive Communist base areas inside Laos and the southern portion of North Vietnam above the 17th Parallel.

Only then can we achieve a lasting victory! Sir!"

COMUSMACV was very pleased with Vortex's comments as he said, "You're understanding of the strategic concepts and the larger picture is phenomenal, Vortex!"

"Thank you sir," said the Colonel.

General Westmoreland went on, "I wanted to implement the plan that you have just enunciated.

But no! The President and the civilian administration would not allow it.

These people back in Washington who have no idea about military strategy or tactics are telling me how to fight one of the most complex wars in human history.

They don't know the first thing about logistics, force levels, the movement of military units and the co-ordination of multiple operations involving combined arms on the battlefield!

I wanted to repeat the operations that we carried out in early 1967.

I wanted to emulate attacks such as Operation JUNCTION CITY and Operation CEDAR FALLS inside Cambodia, Laos and North Vietnam! Because that is the only way that we are going to win this war!

We must deal a body blow to the infiltration routes along the *Ho Chi Minh* Trail. The trail has to be cut and remain cut for the flow of Communist materiel and men to be halted."

Colonel Vortex answered, "I agree absolutely sir."

Colonel Lownds came back down to earth and asked General Westmoreland, "Sir? With regards to *Khe Sanh*. When can we expect a relief operation to break the siege?"

COMUSMACV answered, "On the 25th January 1968 I ordered my staff to start preparing plans for Operation PEGASUS.

Operation PEGASUS will involve a thrust by the 1st Cavalry Division (Airmobile) plus elements from the ARVN and Marines along National Route 9 to re-open the *Khe Sanh* base.

But this Lunar offensive means that we shall have to postpone this OP-Plan for the attack temporarily.

Vortex asked, "For how long will it be postponed sir?"

Westmoreland replied that he did not know. That all would depend on how soon they could bring the Lunar Offensive under control.

"I see!" said Vortex.

Then General Westmoreland said, "When this *Khe Sanh* business is over Colonel, I have plans for you.

I consider you to be General Officer material.

You are probably the best tactical field commander in MACV."

Vortex beamed with pride, "Thank you sir."

COMUSMACV added, "There are a number of one star (Brigadier General) billets coming up soon that need filling. I hope you will be interested Vortex?"

Richard Vortex could not believe his ears. He was only 41 years of age having been born in 1926. If he were to be promoted again within the next 6 months, he would be the youngest Brigadier General in the entire United States Marine Corps. Or in the US Army for that matter.

Richard Vortex's father was also an Attorney-at-Law and his mother was a specialist intensive care Nurse who had worked at Bethseda Naval Hospital.

Richard Vortex joined the Marines in 1944 on his 18th birthday and had just missed out on being sent to Okinawa during the final stages of World War 2.

Vortex had seen action in the Korean War from 1950 to 1952.

"I don't know what to say sir?"

Westmoreland laughed, "Don't say anything. Just wait and see."

COMUSMACV signed off as the B-52 strike ended.

Colonel Lownds, Vortex and the other officers emerged from the DASC bunker. The weather was overcast and a thick mist filled the valley surrounding the *Khe Sanh* plateau.

"This abominable mist!" uttered Master Sergeant Crighton as he looked through his Navy Power-20 field binoculars towards the devastated area around Hill 564 (aka 64) and Hill 881 South.

Plumes of black smoke billowed high up into the cloud layer above the Marine combat base (KSCB) and would eventually disperse into the lower stratosphere.

"It's lucky that the B-52's can attack under any weather conditions sir," mentioned Master Sergeant Richter.

The American 105mm and 155mm batteries opened fire as the PAVN started up their artillery and mortars yet again.

It was battery to counter-battery fire on an immense scale.

Explosions rocked the *Khe Sanh* base. Shells fell near the airstrip, the FSCC and MATU bunkers as the siren wailed.

Sergeant Major Crighton had set up an old truck horn that was nailed to a tree. When the signal came in from the men of India Company on Hill 881 South calling, "Arty, Arty, Co Roc!"

One of the Marines inside the *Khe Sanh* perimeter would press two wired beer-can lids together to set off the truck horn.

Then 2,500 men would perform the *'Khe Sanh Shuffle.'*

Running, weaving, scampering and diving for the nearest cover.

Except for Colonel Vortex and his select band of NCO's. They couldn't care less. Most of the time Colonel Vortex remained above ground because he wanted to see what was going on around the 360 degree ambit of the *Khe Sanh* perimeter.

Colonel Vortex told Lownds, "The generally bad weather during these early months of the year has hampered 'Operation ROLLING THUNDER'. That is why we have been so lucky with the increased number of B-52 strikes that have been allocated to the *Khe Sanh* area in Operation NIAGARA."

Colonel Lownds said, "Yes. I know Vortex."

A second later there was a horrific explosion next to the northern end of the airstrip. It was a 152mm Communist shell scorching in from the 'Co Roc.'

Two Marines and one Seabee sailor were blown into the air as they repaired one section of the airstrip.

Not much was left of their bodies to fall back to earth.

A few yards of steel matting along the runway was ripped apart as aluminium planking shot into the air.

"Jesus! Medics! Medics!" screamed Colonel Lownds.

None of the men had survived as plastic body bags were brought up to return them to their families in the States.

Then a follow-up TAC air strike thundered overhead. Six A-6 *Grumman Intruders* from Task Force 77 streaked in over the valley between Hill 64 and 881 South.

Their cluster bombs peeled off the wing racks and smashed the jungle below. The explosive funnels of each detonation erupted skywards. The earth trembled.

But the Communist barrage went on as did the American counter barrage from *Camp Carroll* and from the batteries inside the KSCB Marine base.

It was never ending. Day after relentless day.

Nearly one-tenth of the Marines inside *Khe Sanh* had been either killed or wounded by the middle of February 1968. That was approximately 250 men not counting the casualties on the hill outposts that had been medevacked out.

That night Colonel Vortex lay down exhausted at 0300 hours.

His body felt like lead. When the large black rats scurried around his headquarters bunker he didn't have the energy to raise himself in self defence.

Khe Sanh was infested with rats. These vermin survived off the rubbish and carnage of that human cataclysm.

There was no escaping the *Khe Sanh* rats.

As Vortex lay on his back one of these beasts started to nibble at his toes. The Colonel waited until the animal had moved around to tickle his right hand and wrist.

Then Richard struck. He brought his left hand down on the stinking vermin. In it he wielded a machete. The edge of the blade deliciously sliced off the head of the rodent. Its guts and bloodied intestines spilled over the floor.

The *Khe Sanh* rats were as big as small kittens but much more ferocious. They would usually bite a chunk out of a man's face as he slept if he was stupid enough to leave it uncovered.

At last Colonel Vortex could get to sleep.

Between the 1st day of February 1968 and the night of the 4th February 1968 the Communist shelling intensified.

Colonel Vortex was also informed by Lieutenant Colonel Francis Heath in command of Hill 558 that the Force Recon Marines he had sent out earlier had been ambushed.

Only one mutilated survivor managed to stagger back to Hill 558. The PAVN were everywhere in large numbers. The sole survivor informed his fellow Marines at de-briefing that the PAVN troops were filled with a mad blood lust. He had seen them strip and mutilate to pieces the American bodies after the fire fight. An airstrike allowed him to slip away from the debacle.

At 2030 hours on the 4th February 1968 Colonel Vortex was in the FSCC bunker with Captain Mirza Baig, Colonel Lownds and the usual retinue of staff officers. They were discussing the expected attack against Hill 881 South.

"I better get up to 881 South with a reinforced Company. I'll take two platoons from the 37th ARVN Rangers as well," said Colonel Vortex.

"Then we had better organise a SUPERGAGGLE to helo-lift you in," added Colonel Lownds.

Captain Baig said, "The artillery support from *Camp Carroll* is set to start at 0320 hours this morning. That will give the signal for our artillery here at *Khe Sanh* to commence firing on the PAVN occupied slopes of the hill."

Vortex asked as they studied the field map on the FSCC table, "And what about TAC air and some AC-47 *SPOOKY* gunship support?"

The Fire Support Officer said, "It's all arranged sir. After the artillery finish their softening up preparation on 881 South the TAC air will zero in on the PAVN held slopes of the stronghold.

I've brought in a full squadron of no less than 12 F-4E *Phantoms* from the 'hot pad' at Da Nang. In addition there will be six F-100D *Supersabre's* from *Bien Hoa* and *Tan Son Nhut* and the Navy boys are bringing in eight A-6 *Grumman Intruders* to really plaster those 'dinks.'"

Colonel Lownds said, "Excellent! You should have all the fire support you need Colonel Vortex!"

Richard laughed, "I hope so David!"

Then he turned to Captain Baig and his senior assistant, a 1st Lieutenant who had the face of a cherub, "Are you sure about your sensor information? The PAVN are going to attack where we expect them to attack?"

Baig answered without hesitation, "I am positive sir! No question about it."

Vortex sighed as he said, "Well then! Let's get on with it!"

Captain Baig interrupted just as Vortex, Richter, Crighton and the others were leaving for the waiting choppers.

"Oh! And the AC-47 SPOOKY gunships will be on station after the TAC air is completed. You can call them in for support at anytime within a 3 hour window."

Colonel Vortex nodded as he scurried out of the bunker.

At 0100 hours the SUPERGAGGLE lifted off from the runway with a reinforced Company of 350 men made up of a composite of all three units; the 26th, 9th and the 37th ARVN Rangers. There were 15 UH-1E's and 10 AH-1 *Cobra* gunships in support.

A heavy, almost suffocating mist shrouded the humid air around *Khe Sanh*. The night was moonless and as black as the ace of spades.

Colonel Vortex was in the command chopper as usual, with Richter, Crighton and the ARVN officer, Captain Hoang Pho in charge of the 37th component.

Major Thrush was still over at Hill 861A with a recuperated Captain Jasper.

They had radioed Captain Dabney that they were on their way in. India Company was on full alert.

Suddenly intense 37mm anti-aircraft fire burst into the SUPERGAGGLE. Vortex could see the green light of the Communist tracer fire (one tracer in ten bullets) as it slammed into several of the UH-1E's ahead of his gunship. Many of the choppers were taking severe damage.

"We are almost there sir!" screamed the pilot of Vortex's Cobra gunship.

The Colonel yelled to Master Sergeant Richter, "The gooks must have brought in extra guns since last time!"

As Richter nodded a tremendous impact was felt all along the side fuselage of the *Cobra*. Flames and smoke filled the cabin. It was sheer chaos as one of the door gunners was hit, his skull ripped off his shoulders by the 37mm rounds.

Sergeant Major Crighton reached for the man but his headless body fell out of the helicopter, the mangled skull rolling inside because his safety harness had been cut through by the 37mm rounds.

The gruesome torso was dangling ten feet below the skids by one remaining and half-torn safety harness.

"Shit! Get us the fuck out of this!" screamed Vortex as he jumped into the co-pilot's seat.

The Colonel grabbed the pilot and screamed into his ear. But to his horror he saw that the man had lost his left eye. Blood was streaming out of the face of the aviation Marine as he fell into a coma.

Vortex grabbed the controls. His skill with helicopters was nowhere near as good as his fixed wing piloting.

The chopper took another stream of 37mm rounds in its tail section and started to lurch downwards.

Richter, Crighton and Captain Hoang Pho were rolling all over the interior of the *Cobra*. The machine was going down fast with flames spreading everywhere. There was not enough potential energy left in the rotors to affect a smooth landing. Besides that there was no clear place to land. The jungle was as thick as molasses with its triple layered canopy.

"I can't control it!" screamed Vortex.

The AH-1 was now down to tree top level and the PAVN were blasting it with 0.51 calibre fire (the US troops called the Communist weapon the *51 Cal*) until two RPG's detonated the airframe.

The ARVN Captain, Hoang Pho, next to Richter had both his legs blown sideways below the knee level.

The tail section of the *Cobra* peeled off and Vortex hung onto the cockpit Plexiglas as the rest of the helicopter crashed through the three layers of jungle canopy.

"Jesus! Sir! Are you alright?" yelled Master Sergeant Richter.

Vortex scrambled out of the wrecked machine by kicking his foot through the shattered Plexiglas.

Sergeant Major Crighton and Master Sergeant Richter followed with their weapons.

As they ran away from the burning chopper the other door gunner was cut down by AK-47 fire.

The PAVN were all around them.

"God! Where are we sir? Where are the other choppers!" asked Sergeant Major Crighton as he fired his M60 in a defensive arc all around their position.

Colonel Vortex answered, "We're somewhere between Hill 64 and 881 South! Right in the middle of the PAVN regiments that are going to attack our troops on the hill!"

"Jesus! No!" expostulated Richter, "…what a place to land!"

Colonel Vortex rushed forward to the burning helicopter.

He wanted to save Captain Hoang Pho, the commander of the 37th ARVN Rangers.

Before he could get to the doorway the flaming body crawled out of the wreck. Its legs gone.

The ARVN Captain looked like a human blow torch as he tried to brush the fire off his body.

Vortex picked up a ground sheet and tried to smother the flames out. But it was no use. The charred and mutilated body of the gallant South Vietnamese officer died in his arms.

Sergeant Major Leonard Crighton ran through the thick jungle and checked the front of the burning *Cobra*. The pilot was lying in a ditch with his spine broken in half.

Colonel Vortex also found the other four Marines at the back of the helicopter. They were all dead. Their bodies peppered with 0.51 calibre bullets.

Two of the men had been decapitated. It was a gruesome sight.

"Let's get the fuck out of here!" yelled Vortex as he grabbed the still serviceable M60 machine gun from the door mount.

The three men dived into the jungle and started to make their way north-east towards Hill 861A.

They could sense the PAVN troops moving in all around them.

"The field telephone was destroyed in the chopper sir," mentioned Sergeant Major Crighton.

"That's great!" quipped Vortex, "What a fiasco!"

Major Thrush walked into the headquarters bunker of K Company on Hill 861A just after Colonel Vortex's AH-1 *Cobra* crashed into the jungle.

Lieutenant Donald Shanley called out, "I have Captain Dabney on the horn sir!"

Lieutenant Shanley was one of the platoon commanders in K Company. He was manning the field phone when Major Thrush walked in.

Thrush grabbed the handset from the Lieutenant.

It was 0230 hours. Less than 1 hour to the commencement of the massive American artillery bombardment which was going to attempt to interdict the PAVN assault on Hill 881 South.

"What is it Captain Dabney?" asked Major Thrush impatiently as Captain Jasper stood behind him. His back bandaged up like an Egyptian mummy.

"We've lost the Colonel!" he screamed.

"What? What did you say?" asked back Major Thrush with disbelief.

Captain Dabney repeated, "We've lost Colonel Vortex! His *Cobra* gunship has crashed somewhere between your hill and mine!"

Major Thrush looked devastated. For a few moments he was lost for words.

Captain Dabney continued, "The MIKE Force lead by Colonel Vortex has reinforced our hill. The pilots saw Colonel Vortex's chopper go down under heavy PAVN fire."

Major Thrush asked, "And you have received no radio communication from Colonel Vortex or his men?"

Captain Dabney answered, "No sir. The 37th ARVN Ranger Captain Hoang Pho was with them also."

Major Thrush rubbed his chin, "This is serious Captain. But there is nothing we can do about it at the moment. You have to get the choppers out of there before the artillery fire starts up.

And we can't launch a rescue operation.

Hell! We don't even know if the Colonel and his NCO's survived the crash!"

Captain Dabney agreed and informed Major Thrush that he would communicate the loss of Colonel Vortex to Colonel Lownds back at *Khe Sanh*. He then signed off.

Major Thrush put down the handset and said to the assembled officers of K Company on Hill 861A, "We've just lost the best Marine officer in the whole damn Marine Corps!"

Master Sergeant Richter had his Starlight scope out and was reading his compass in the murky blackness of the jungle.

"What do you think sir?" asked Richter.

Vortex was hacking his way through the tangled foliage as he said, "The only thing we can do is try to make it back to Hill 861A. We can't attempt to climb 881 South. The artillery fire will kill us before we get to the perimeter."

Sergeant Major Crighton agreed and remarked, "I have estimated our position sir. We are 1,500 yards from 861A."

Vortex said as he continued to swipe his machete from side to side, "Well! Let's get a move on gentlemen! Let's see if we can make it to 861A before the TAC air comes in to blast the gooks."

The three Marines had traversed about 250 yards past the point where their *Cobra* had crashed when Master Sergeant Richter observed enemy troops ahead.

The NCO was using his *Starlight Starbright* scope as he lay in a muddy depression upon the stinking, mist covered jungle floor.

"Sir!" he pointed. "Look! Dirty fucking gooks ahead!"

Vortex saw them too. He spat in their direction.

There were two men and three women from a PAVN anti-aircraft battery about 25 yards to the north.

Sergeant Major Crighton whispered, "They were probably one of the 0.51 calibres which shot us down and killed Captain Hoang Pho and our other men."

Colonel Vortex said with vicious lust, "Let's get them! Use your knives to stab their guts and their hearts. We don't want to draw attention to ourselves with too much M16/M60 fire."

The two senior NCO's nodded and worked around the PAVN position.

Then they struck like panthers.

Sergeant Major Crighton leapt out of the jungle foliage to the east and knocked down the two VC women. He immediately stabbed one of them in the buttocks and the other in her throat. Blood sprinkled out in fine, hot streams.

The blood from one girl splashed onto the breasts of the other as they screamed in their death throes.

Colonel Vortex knifed the kidneys of the third girl while Master Sergeant Richter head-butted both men in quick succession.

"Watch out Master Sergeant!" screamed the Colonel.

The PAVN men were regular soldiers from the 304th PAVN Division. They wore camouflage tunics and pith helmets with leaves in them.

One of the PAVN men sprang to his feet and charged the Master Sergeant with his detached AK-47 bayonet.

Richter managed to thrust his dagger into the heart of the other man. He snapped his jaws around the enemies' throat and said, "Die! You motherfucking Communist bastard warmonger!"

As he spoke he twisted the blade viciously to left and right inside the myocardial tissue of the Communist.

Colonel Vortex snapped the neck of the third Communist female by inserting his fingers inside her mouth and then grabbing her skull with his free hand. He then yanked her head around 270 degrees until he could feel the delicious click which indicated that her cervical vertebrae had been torn apart at the level of C3 to C6. [cervical vertebrae number 3 to 6]

The Colonel then did a forward summersault across the jungle mud and kicked the bayonet out of the Communist's hands just before he was about to knife Master Sergeant Richter.

Richter lunged forward and head-butted the PAVN trooper with such force that his nose was crushed right across his face, smearing blood and tissue everywhere.

Sergeant Major Crighton had meanwhile cut out the living hearts of the two VC girls.

The ARVN Captain Hoang Pho who had died in the *Cobra* was a close personal friend of his. His revenge was unbounded and ruthless and beyond the sanctions and circumscribed limits of *public international law.*

Richter finished off the second PAVN by blowing his brains out with his Colt 0.45 pistol.

Colonel Vortex placed a satchel charge under the 0.51 calibre and blew it to hell.

"Let's get going!" ordered the Colonel.

Before they could proceed another 100 yards and just as they were turning around a steep embankment amidst the thick foliage, a squad of PAVN regulars popped out of nowhere right in front of them.

Both groups were so surprised that they just stood there for a few seconds stupidly staring at each other with their mouths wide open. Then the Communists opened fire with RPD light machine guns and numerous AK-47's.

"Shit! Take cover!" screamed Colonel Vortex.

All three men dived simultaneously to the left. But Sergeant Major Crighton was not quick enough. Three rounds from the RPD light machine gun slammed into his left arm, destroying his biceps muscle and shattering his humerus. The white splinters of bone could be seen through the mutilated flesh.

"Aiiee!" he screamed as Vortex crawled on his belly and pulled the Sergeant Major E9, his best friend in Vietnam and his personal assistant into a ditch several yards behind a thick outgrowth of vines.

Master Sergeant Richter was blazing away with his M60 machine gun as the three Americans were forced back by an avalanche of PAVN fire.

"I'm hurt bad sir! You and Richter better get going to 861! Leave me sir! I can take a few of the dinks with me before I die!"

Colonel Vortex frantically put a tourniquet around his Sergeant Major's shattered arm as he yelled, "Shut up Crighton! We are not leaving you anywhere! Do you hear me? We are all in this shit together!

And we are going to come out of it together!"

Crighton nodded as Colonel Vortex gave him seven ampoules of morphine.

Richter was pumping his last belts of 7.62mm munitions into the M60.

In a few minutes he would be out of ammunition. Then they would have only their M79 grenade launchers and their M16's.

PAVN rounds were erupting all around them. The jungle earth flew upwards in a deathly spray.

Vortex cried out as a Communist bullet tore open his flesh right along the left side of his chest. Luckily it was only a superficial wound but it bled profusely.

The Colonel's blood mixed with the Sergeant Major's as Crighton struggled forward with his M16.

He cried to his Colonel, "Let me go out fighting sir!"

The two of them joined Richter in firing everything they had at the gooks from the 304th PAVN Division.

"They're charging us sir!" screamed Richter as he finally exhausted his M60 ammunition.

"Fix bayonets men!" ordered Colonel Vortex.

They could see the yellow pith helmets of the PAVN regulars as they screamed in Vietnamese and charged through the thick foliage of that merciless pre-dawn jungle.

"What are your orders sir?" asked Richter, "…in case we are separated?"

Vortex screamed as he fired his M16, "Fight to the death! Don't let them take you alive! And fuck that bastard Ho Chi Minh!"

The enormously built Richter took the empty M60 machine gun and leapt to his feet as more than a dozen PAVN were practically on top of them.

"Eat this!" screamed the Master Sergeant.

As the first PAVN scrambled into their ditch, Richter rammed the butt end of the M60 into his mouth. Blood and teeth flew everywhere.

The second Communist came up and Richter swung the empty machine gun into the side of his skull. A large chunk of brain tissue and broken skull bone splattered the three Americans as the Communist was decapitated in a gruesome display of unbelievable savagery.

A third Communist leapt over the three Americans and into the ditch.

Colonel Vortex thrust his 18 inch dagger into the man's intestines and then catapulted him over the body of Sergeant Major Crighton.

Richter then blew his chest away with M16 fire.

But the Communists kept charging. They screamed obscenities at the US Marines as they ran forwards with their bayonets gleaming.

"They've got me sir!" cried Richter as two dinks had jumped onto the NCO's back.

Vortex punched one of them in the spine and kidney's and then slit his throat open while ripping the man off his comrade's back.

Richter spat out, "I'll vivisect you! You gook motherfucker!"

The Master Sergeant gripped a handful of the Communist's black hair and swung him over his head into the mud. He then kicked his boot into the Communist's testicles and stuck his Colt 0.45 pistol inside the enemies' mouth, blowing his head apart like a ripe watermelon.

Sergeant Major Crighton had a swarm of PAVN troopers charging at him.

Vortex shot one of them through the left eye.

Crighton punched two in quick succession and fired his M16 quickly killing them. But three more appeared behind him.

"No!" yelled Colonel Vortex.

But it was too late.

As Crighton turned to face them he was shot in the left testicle by an AK-47. The sac was blown clean off, flooding the NCO's trousers with blood and urine.

Two PAVN managed to leap forward and dig their bayonets into him. One pierced his already shattered arm while the other sliced into his throat.

"Sir! Help me!" gurgled Crighton in excruciating agony.

As he reached his arms out to Colonel Vortex, begging for relief, yet another Communist shot him in the lumbar section of his spine.

Blood vomited from Crighton's mouth all over his commanding officer and friend.

At this Vortex went absolutely berserk. The three PAVN were standing in front of him taunting the Sergeant Major as they stabbed him with their bayonets.

"Fuck you!" screamed the Colonel as he loaded his M79 grenade launcher and shot it at point blank range into the group of Communists.

The detonation blasted them away in a mutilated shower of human tissue and excrement.

But the attack went on without pity or mercy.

The badly injured Sergeant Major Crighton staggered to his feet and fell into Colonel Vortex's waiting arms.

"Tell my wife I love her!" cried Crighton.

Vortex was speechless.

Crighton repeated, "Tell her I died fighting for my Beloved United States of America! Home of the Brave! And Land of the Free! I love my country!"

Then Crighton took a last inrush of air into his mutilated lungs and said, "I just want my country to love me as much as I love it! Tell her for me sir! Tell her, my wife, to make sure that none of our children become Communists! I don't want no Domino Effect at home!"

Blood was pulsing out of the Sergeant Major's lungs as he moaned.

"I will tell her! I will make sure that none of your children become Communists! And that they don't marry any Communists! You have my word my dear and trusted friend! I give you my oath! Jesus is witness to it! It is my testament to you Leonard! But it's not over yet! I'll get you out of here somehow!" cried Colonel Vortex as he was overcome with emotion, tears streaming down his eyes so that it caused rivulets to form through the mud and blood that besmeared his agonized face.

Richter punched a large PAVN soldier who tried to wrestle the mortally wounded Crighton away from Colonel Vortex.

Richter grabbed the Communist's groin and ripped it to shreds with his dagger. Richter then crushed the enemies' skull like an egg after head butting the PAVN trooper.

But more enemy troops were pouring into the ditch.

Vortex tried to drag Crighton with him when a slice of AK-47 fire tore open the Sergeant Major's back.

Richter fired his M79 grenade launcher into the advancing enemy as they crawled back out of the ditch and towards a thicker part of the jungle.

The three Americans had killed eleven PAVN scoundrels and wounded nine more as Sergeant Major Leonard Crighton died silently in Colonel Vortex's arms.

"He's gone sir!" screamed Richter in a frenzy.

"He was my friend!" cried Vortex, tears streaming down his face.

"I know sir! But you must let him go!"

"I can't!"

"You must!"

"I can't leave him here!"

"You have to sir!"

Richter grabbed his Colonel's sleeve, "You must come with me sir! Jesus understands your pain! The Lord will forgive you! You did everything you could!"

"I won't! I will die here with my friend! The Lord knows that I did not do enough for him! And for my Beloved United States of America!

I hope God will forgive me! Have mercy on my shortcomings for I am too soft towards the enemies of Christ!"

Richter beseeched his commander, "You have fortitude sir! The Lord knows it!"

"No! I am weak! I lack faith against the Anti-Christ!

So many times I have let the Communist enemy of God slip from my grasp! So many times I have winked at so many indiscretions on the part of the enemy!

I have failed to fully comprehend the gravity of my faith and my will to resist the Communist demon that threatens to devour all of us in a sea of blood and damnation! God will never forgive me!

I have not attained *True Grace*!

The *Grace* as ordained by the great Christian philosopher and martyr *Dietrich Bonhoeffer*! A hero of our faith in Christ!

A true soldier of Christ!"

"You have to leave him sir!" said Richter as he pulled at the large and muscular body of his commander that was trembling like a leaf in a sea of malformation.

Vortex said as he held the dead body of his friend, "For I tell you that unless your righteousness surpasses that of the Pharisees and the teachers of the law, you will certainly not enter the kingdom of heaven!"

Crighton's corpse fell out of the Colonel's hands.

The two Americans hesitated as fresh PAVN troops closed in.

The moment of truth was at hand.

Vortex lunged forward to grab the dead Sergeant Major but Richter pulled him back.

They staggered into the jungle.

"I can't leave his body there to be violated by the Anti-Christ!" anguished Colonel Vortex.

"We have no choice sir!" yelled Master Sergeant Richter.

The 312 lb Richter almost lifted up the 204.6 lb Colonel.

Both men staggered and then ran through the jungle, cutting their faces and arms against the sharp elephant razor grass and the stinking and fucked foliage that was like a stew of detritus amidst their broken faith.

Richard Vortex looked back one last time and saw a frenzied squad of PAVN troops hacking the body of his friend to pieces with machetes and bayonets.

The feeling in Vortex's guts was indescribable.

Vietnamese voices were screaming all around them.

Three Regiments from the 304th PAVN Division were preparing their attack against Hill 881 South.

"What is the time?" asked Vortex as they both dived into a stream that was a tributary of the *Rao Quan River*.

"Its 0310 hours sir!"

"Only 10 minutes until the artillery begins Richter!" said Vortex as he ripped a leech out of his left nostril.

The stream was infested with them.

The Master Sergeant had one burying into his right testicle but could not stop to extricate it. The pain was hideous.

"I know this waterway sir!" whispered Richter as the two Americans waded through the muddy stream with their M16's and M79 grenade launchers above their heads.

"It leads directly to the base of Hill 861A"

Vortex said with intense sorrow in his voice, "We've got to reach that stronghold before the TAC air hits the 304th PAVN Division!"

Meanwhile, Captain Dabney and his staff were looking through their infrared Starlight Scopes when the American artillery opened up in front of their stronghold.

The 175mm howitzers at *Camp Carroll* were the first to begin, followed up by the 105mm and 155mm guns inside *Khe Sanh* itself. The huge shells from *Camp Carroll* streaked in across the night sky from 15 miles to the east.

To Captain Dabney and Major Thrush each one seemed like small stars hurtling to earth.

As they rocketed in they left a red glowing trail of fire that cut open the misty and humid air above the foul and stinking jungle.

It was this jungle that was the prime element of the Main Force VC and the PAVN regulars. It was the perfect cover for their own peculiar specie of guerrilla warfare, hiding them, sustaining them against the overwhelming American firepower and into which they borrowed like moles in the vast complex of tunnels they had created waging war like fucking rats too scared to venture out and meet the Americans head on like men but fighting like murderers and pimps at night striking at the US forces in the blackness when their backs were turned much to their discredit and dishonour.

The noise was like a shrieking from the very pits of hell, followed by a thunderous roar that tore open the bowels of the earth, burying the PAVN bastards in buckets of their own blood.

In addition the 4.2 inch mortars and 106mm recoilless rifles added their weight to the tremendous roar of explosives pulverising the Communist jackal imperialist troops.

"It's awesome!" cried Captain Dabney to the men standing behind him.

More than 1,500 PAVN troops, a whole Regiment, had formed up for the attack.

When the United States artillery hit them by surprise, their heavy weapons were smashed to bits, their trucks incinerated and their men cut to pieces like rotten fuck coming out of their putrid douche-bag Communist hides.

The PAVN attack on Hill 881 South never materialised as the Communists were drowned under a torrent of righteous American firepower sent by Jesus himself.

It was truly a NIAGARA of destructive power and everything that the brilliance of General William Childs Westmoreland had envisaged culminating in the exposition of his designs and the fulfilment of his plans making him one of the true heroes in the annals of the American people and its glorious history.

But what Captain Dabney did not realise, nor Colonel David Lownds nor Colonel Richard Vortex or Major Thrush or any of the other American field commanders at *Khe Sanh*, was that the PAVN were simultaneously launching another attack.

As the Communist forces advanced on Hill 881 South they divided into two attack units.

One Regiment advanced on 881 South while the other reinforced Regiment supported by artillery advanced on Hill 861A.

It was this second force that was just behind Colonel Vortex and Master Sergeant Richter as they struggled through the muddy stream.

Major Thrush and Captain Jasper had no idea that their defensive perimeter was about to be assaulted.

Colonel Vortex clambered up a steep embankment and reached for Richter's M79 grenade launcher as the two men finally emerged from the putrid and unavailing water.

"Here sir! Let me help you!" said Richter as he catapulted onto the embankment and then dragged his Colonel clear.

Vortex could feel the detonation tremors as the approaches to Hill 881 South were blasted mercilessly.

"It is probably the heaviest bombardment so far in this awful siege of *Khe Sanh*," said Vortex.

"Yes sir," answered Richter as he checked their weapons.

"I have to go back for what is left of Sergeant Major Crighton's body!"

Richter too, was filled with emotion, "I understand sir."

"I can't face Crighton's wife without bringing back his body to her!"

"Yes sir. We will accomplish that sir!" added Richter.

Suddenly a stream of AK-47 fire as well as RPD light machine gun rounds slammed into the embankment upon which the two Marines were resting.

Vortex dived for cover and could see the PAVN advancing in large numbers on a wide perimeter.

"What is happening sir?" asked Master Sergeant Richter as both men started to retreat up the gradual slopes of Hill 861A.

"I don't know!" screamed back Colonel Vortex.

When they had climbed to a higher altitude both men peered through their Navy Power-20 field binoculars.

Then Colonel Vortex realised the situation, "Oh! My God! Richter!"

"What is it sir?" asked the beefy Master Sergeant.

"The Communists are attacking 861A in force!"

"It can't be!"

"It is!" repeated Vortex.

Richter yelled, "Then we must get up to Major Thrush and warn him ASAP! Sir!"

Vortex nodded and as they climbed higher they could see the trenches and sand-bags of the Marines in K Company.

With the PAVN fire tickling them from behind the Marines in front of them opened fire down the hillside.

"Shit!" screamed the Colonel.

M60 rounds whizzed past their heads as Vortex screamed, "Its Colonel Vortex! And Master Sergeant Richter! Hold your fire!"

Lieutenant Donald Shanley was manning the forward bunkers and foxholes on the southern slope.

He heard the English language being spoken down the hill.

Just then the F-4E *Phantoms* were hitting the forward slopes of 881 South with napalm and high explosive iron bombs of 500 lb calibre.

"Its friendly forces! Hold your fire! Hold your fire!" ordered Lieutenant Shanley with excitement.

The junior officer looked through his *Starlight* scope and could see the familiar figure of Vortex accompanied by his senior command NCO.

"My God sir!" exclaimed Shanley when Vortex collapsed in front of him inside the foxhole.

"We thought you were dead!"

The Colonel laughed, "I am not that easy to kill Lieutenant!"

Richter added, "But we lost all the other men in the chopper including Sergeant Major Leonard Crighton."

Vortex grabbed Lieutenant Shanley by his camouflage collar, "Quick! Alert your men and open fire! The gooks are attacking here! They are coming straight for you! Thousands of them!"

Lieutenant Shanley nodded and the 200 Marines leapt into their trenches and foxholes as they fired their weapons.

A few minutes later Major Thrush, Captain Jasper and their staff came running down the slopes of 861A.

With them was Lieutenant Colonel James Wilkinson, the overall commander of the 1st Battalion 26th Marines who had been sent over from KSCB to observe and assist Major Thrush.

They had no idea what was going on after Lieutenant Shanley had radioed up to the HQ bunker that Colonel Vortex was still alive.

"Thank God! Oh! Sir! You made it!" cried Major Thrush as he embraced the Colonel in the muddy trench line.

Lieutenant Colonel James Wilkinson added, "A sterling top-notch performance sir in making your way back to friendly forces."

"The PAVN are coming! Thousands of them!" yelled Shanley.

"Here's the VHF/UHF AN/PRC-41 field phone sir!" said Lieutenant Shanley.

Vortex immediately called Colonel David E. Lownds at the FSCC bunker inside KSCB.

"I need more artillery on the approaches to 861A!

I need additional TAC air!

I need howitzer fire from *Camp Carroll* and from the *Rockpile*!

I need *W48* nuclear tactical shells!

I need a DAISYCUTTER dropped on the southern slopes of 861A!

And I mean now! Colonel Lownds!"

The *Khe Sanh* joint commander blurted out with disbelief, "How could we be so wrong?"

"Hell! Fucked if I know? I don't know Lownds! I don't have a motherfucking crystal ball up my asshole!" answered Vortex in a lather.

Vortex was beside himself with rage, fury and a burning sting of revenge that ignited his soul. He was still thinking of the loss of Sergeant Major Crighton.

David E. Lownds deduced correctly, "The bloody Communists must have advanced through an area not covered by our sensors!"

Major Thrush added as he listened in with another handset, "I've just spoken to Captain Dabney. He tells me that no major attack has developed on 881 South. But one of his patrols has been ambushed with heavy losses from the base of Hill 881 North! The Communists now have full control of 881 North!"

Vortex screamed, "Shit! Forget about 881 North! I know that a full battalion of PAVN have dug in tunnels and bunker complexes in 881 North!

Our major concern now is to defend what we have.

And that means 861A."

Colonel Lownds said over the VHF tactical frequency, "I can give you everything you asked for Vortex except the *W48* tactical nuclear ordnance."

Vortex answered, "I know that Lownds!"

"Then why did you ask for them?" asked the 26th Marine commander.

"It sounded good to just hear the words for tactical nuclear weapons even though those pen pushers and desk jockeys in Washington D.C. won't allow us to have them."

Colonel Lownds nodded to Captain Baig who was already calling in additional TAC air and another DAISYCUTTER from all over South Vietnam including Cam Ranh Bay.

"Listen! Colonel Vortex! Hang on! Hold for as long as you can! The FSCC centre is re-directing the artillery fire to your positions!

Captain Baig is also calling in more TAC air."

Vortex signed off saying, "Understood. There will be no retreat! None! I promise you that!

We shall, us Marines! Prove as steadfast in our defence of this Hill as the German 6th Army was in its defence of *Stalingrad* in 1943. No retreat!

No capitulation!

We shall do honour to our German brethren! I promise you that!"

Before Vortex could look at Major Thrush a huge 120mm mortar round from 881 North came streaking into the Marine foxholes. Three Marines were blown out of the earth just as the first wave of PAVN troops approached the southern edge of 861A.

Two of the men lost their arms and the other his left leg and testicles. Pieces of bloodied groin tissue showered the group of dedicated officers who had been deafened by the giant PAVN mortars.

The Marine bunkers at *Khe Sanh* could withstand the standard 81mm round but not the 120mm giant mortars or the 152mm Communist artillery from the 'Co Roc' supplied to the gooks courtesy of the Soviet Imperialist Regime and their Chinese Communist [CHICOM] lickspittles.

Khe Sanh simply did not have the materials at hand to build bunkers of sufficient strength.

Master Sergeant Richter climbed onto a ONTOS M50A1 'PIG' and started to fire like a crazed madman with the six 106mm recoilless rifles and the 0.30 calibre M1919A4 machine gun.

He hosed down the southern slope of 861A in an orgy of fire with rounds filling the air above the ONTOS like a fine mist of fucking mosquitoes. He was still scathing over the death of Sergeant Major Leonard Crighton. Vortex jumped onto the PIG [Nickname for the ONTOS] and fired a Minigun with a passion that defied belief or reason.

The Communists crept forward not by yards but by inches as their flesh was torn apart in beautiful mists of blood.

Every second Marine from the northern perimeter of 861A was brought down to the trench lines facing south to counter the massed PAVN assault.

Then the 304th PAVN Division struck. And they struck hard. Literally hundreds of North Vietnamese regulars dived into the trench lines with the Marines of which there were barely 400.

The Marines of K Company could not load their M16's or M60's fast enough to hose down the advancing enemy.

Master Sergeant Richter was knocked down off the ONTOS by three PAVN as Vortex knifed one in the guts almost immediately. Orange-green intestines poured in a filthy miasma across the Colonel's trousers.

Major Thrush cracked his M16 butt against the head of another. Brain tissue and blood vomited out from the skull cavity.

A young Marine who witnessed it vomited onto the trench floor. But before he could lift his head up to suck in air he was bayoneted by another PAVN who in turn was shot in the forehead by an enraged Lieutenant Shanley.

Master Sergeant Richter screamed, "Suck on this you gook bastard!" As he yelled he viced open the mouth of the remaining PAVN as Colonel Vortex upholstered his Colt 0.45 pistol and rammed it down the Communist's trachea pulling the trigger.

The whole chest cavity exploded outwards in a spray of crimson blood. Little pieces of lung tissue and arteries showered Richter's nostrils and cheeks.

Major Thrush gave frantic orders to his troops to hold the line. Vicious hand to hand fighting erupted all along the defensive perimeter of 861A.

Now the surprise attack intensified as the Main Force Viet Cong and PAVN from Hill 881 North moved in on the lightly defended northern slopes of 861A.

Only four platoons held that northern trench line.

And already they were being pushed back up the hill.

Colonel Vortex was like a demon possessed. He ran up and down the trenches and foxholes screaming orders at the young Marines. Two radio operators and Major Thrush followed him wherever he went. Master Sergeant Richter covered his rear with a Minigun, blasting away across the mud filled trenches and into the Communists.

Vortex stumbled upon a North Vietnamese and a Marine Staff Sergeant strangling each other's throats as they tried to grab a knife on the ground.

"Fuck you!" yelled Vortex as he thrust his dagger deliciously into the enemies' throat. The blade exited through the cervical spine.

The Colonel then smashed his right arm down so that he separated the tangled limbs of the two men.

Suddenly a burst of AK-47 fire ripped into both the Marine and the PAVN trooper just as Vortex slid his knife out of the Asian's flesh.

The Communist died instantly but the Marine Sergeant who was wearing an armoured Kevlar vest survived.

Medics ran up and dragged him away towards the top of the hill. However, one of the Marine medics was caught in the murderous RPD light machine gun fire, the back of his skull being blown away before he walked 10 yards.

Slowly but inexorably the PAVN were getting the upper hand. About a quarter of the Marines in K Company had either been killed or wounded, some horribly.

Limbs were reduced to splinters, ankles blasted off and hands severed from their wrists. Blood ran hot and cold upon the soft and unforgiving earth of that terrible hill.

The fighting was much too close for the use of American firepower which could have turned the tide.

Lieutenant Shanley screamed, "Watch out sir!"

A squad of North Vietnamese had killed all the Marines in the trench in front of them and were now running up the side of the hill towards the apex.

Colonel Vortex and his party were directly in front of them. One of the radio operators was shot through the heart and died instantly.

Vortex grabbed the M16 with bayonet attached from out of the man's lifeless fingers.

As the first PAVN trooper came up the Colonel sliced and diced open his guts and large intestine. The bloody bowels spewed out and mixed with the stench of cordite and sulphur along with napalm petro-jelly that wafted over from 881 South.

"Withdraw! Withdraw to the second defensive line!" ordered Lieutenant Shanley.

The surviving Marines scrambled out of their foxholes and crawled, leapfrogged and stumbled up the hill.

Now the North Vietnamese could shoot them down with greater efficiency.

It was difficult for the Marines to run backwards and shoot forwards at the same time. K Company suffered more horrific casualties during that awful withdrawal.

"Sir! You must get to safety! You must follow us back to the HQ bunker on the crest of the hill!" screamed Major Thrush.

Colonel Vortex looked at him in a daze as Richter dived onto the earth next to his commander.

"No! I'm staying here with Shanley and Richter!

You lead the men back to the last defensive perimeter and hold! Hold on! Do you hear me Major?"

Major Thrush nodded and withdrew as Richter and Shanley both manned an M60 each.

Captain Jasper was also with them. He fired countless grenades from his M79 and blasted away with his CAR 15.

Colonel Vortex watched the Navy *Skyraiders* as they came in with anti-personnel canisters and cluster bombs.

But the air strike was much further down the hill. It had no immediate effect on the current battle for 861A.

Corpses littered that mangled slope as Richter hosed down dozens of oncoming Communists with Shanley and Jasper.

Vortex swung his Starlight scope up the incline and saw the Marines bolting into their last line of defence which was about three quarters of the way up 861A.

"There is no more room for retreat!" yelled Vortex.

Richter nodded as their position was fast becoming untenable.

The PAVN were almost on top of them.

But they had performed their task of covering the retreat of K Company.

The party of four abandoned their weapons and made a run for the apex of 861A.

AK-47 rounds splattered all around them as their bodies ached with fear and trepidation.

Somehow two PAVN had gotten up in front of them, between K Company and their line of retreat.

Both groups blasted away at each other. Vortex head butted one North Vietnamese regular, knocking off his pith helmet and then in the same smooth movement sliced another across the chest.

Captain Jasper was hit in the thigh, the bullet splitting open his *Sartorius* muscle.

The four Marines miraculously extricated themselves from the melee and seconds later dived into the defensive perimeter.

Now the valiant US Marines had the upper hand.

Finally Captain Mirza Baig at FSCC had homed in the heavy guns from *Khe Sanh*, the *Rockpile* and *Camp Carroll*.

The DASC (Direct Air Support Centre) coordinated the TAC air.

The US shells blasted the reserve formations of the PAVN that were now following up the initial attack.

The ascent of 861A was becoming murderous for the Communists.

In addition, the Marines of K Company had the advantage of shooting down a steeper incline. This made their organic weapons fire more deadly.

It also gave them a better overall field of fire. The killing continued but the worst of the hand to hand fighting was over.

It was the arsenal of American artillery fire and TAC air which dictated events now.

The sun was just rising on that blood soaked dawn.

But the mist that wafted across the *Khe Sanh* base, smothering everything in its pale shroud would not evaporate for a few hours yet.

Yet Colonel Vortex wished that its comforting veil would cover him up.

Would cover up *Khe Sanh* forever.

Expunge this terrible battlefield from the face of the earth so that its lost souls would find peace as the spirits of those men who had fought fourteen years before at *Dien Bien Phu*, had also found everlasting peace.

And it was the sanctity of the earth that would embrace them, cover over them and soothe the memories of their violent demise.

He had lost his best friend in Vietnam and his heart ached with sorrow, blistered with remorse.

He felt personally responsible. Every man under his command was his responsibility.

No matter what precautions a commander may take with regards to his troops there was always a pervading sense of guilt when your own men die.

The commander's mind agonises over what more could have been done.

Colonel Richard Vortex remembered the words of **'Sun-Tzu'**;

"Command is, Wisdom, Integrity, Compassion, Courage and Severity. Discipline is; Organisation, Chain of Command and Control of expenditure on the battlefield. Of the Five Fundamentals for a Commander in the Field, He who grasps them Wins, He who fails to grasp them, Fails.

The Way of War is A way of Deception.

When able, Feign inability; When deploying troops, Appear not to be; When near, Appear far; When far, Appear near; Lure with Bait; Strike with Chaos;

If the Enemy is Full, Be prepared.

If strong, Avoid him.
If he is angry, Disconcert him.
If he is weak, Stir him to Pride.
If he is relaxed, Harry Him.
If His men are harmonious, Split them.
Attack where he is unprepared; Appear where you are Unexpected;
And that Victory and its handmaidens cannot be divulged in advance."

Colonel Vortex looked around as he crouched in that blood reeking trench. He saw the contorted faces of these young Marines from all over the United States, from large cities, state capitals and small towns in the Pacific north-west, the South and the Mid-West.

Each feature was etched in horror.

Each grimace hiding the fear that lay within.

God! Thought Colonel Vortex. He was proud of these troops. These young men! The flower of American youth.

They were America's finest sons!

Their steadfastness in defence and their courage in the attack exemplified the magnificence of the American Military Tradition.

Colonel Vortex remembered;

"The Battle of Shiloh."

He remembered 'Seven Pines' and 'Antietam.'

'Chickamauga', 'Spotsylvania' and the 'Battle of the Wilderness'.

In these tempestuous contests was the metal forged that would later transfer into 'Iwo Jima', 'Saipan' and 'Okinawa'.

Colonel Vortex felt his strength renewed.

The battle would be rejoined afresh. The North Vietnamese had not yet felt the full wrath of America's steel nor the invincible hearts of its valiant warriors.

Thunder approached as the waves of PAVN regulars wilted upon the vine.

Their rear was decimated and their forward momentum was crushed. It was then that they started to crumple under the avalanche of rockets, iron bombs and shells.

From out of the dawn blood-glow came the roar of massed jet engines.

It was part screaming, part rumbling.

The flight leaders had been given the exact coordinates by Combat SKYSPOT.

Their payload was brimming with lethal destruction.

The bombs flew gracefully to the winds of Victory.

Sixteen F-105 *Thunderchiefs* and seven F-4E *Phantom II's* swooped in just above the triple layered jungle canopy.

Colonel Vortex realised, as he observed through his field binoculars, that this was perhaps the largest single sortie yet mounted by the Combined American Air Forces in the defence of *Khe Sanh* and its hill outposts.

His young Marines plastered themselves to the walls and floors of their grotesque bunkers, trenches and foxholes.

They knew what was coming.

And it broke over and before them like nothing yet seen in the annals of warfare.

Khe Sanh was the most heavily bombed area per square mile in the history of human conflict.

The advancing PAVN were cut to pieces under high explosive, fragmentation, cluster and folding-fin bombs as well as huge shrouds of napalm.

Their lines pulled back upon the charred slopes of Hill 861A.

Major Thrush asked, "We are ready sir. You just give the word."

Colonel Richard Vortex looked up at the Major and said, his face blackened with grime and dried blood, "Its finished!

All is finished here!"

The Destruction of US Special Forces at Lang Vei: 7th February 1968

After the TAC air had worked over the attackers on Hill 861A the AC-47 SPOOKY Gunships were called in by Colonel Vortex.

Captain Mirza Baig at the DASC bunker inside *Khe Sanh* fine tuned their approach with the latest coordinates which had been radioed to him by the forward spotters and the *'Mightiest Corporal in the World'* Robert J. Arrotta and his aide, *'Pineapple Chunk'* Lance Corporal Molimao Niuatoa as well as the fire control officers not only on 861A but on 881 South as well.

"I think we've broken their back sir!" said a tired but excited Lieutenant Shanley.

Captain Jasper was being treated for his smashed thigh in the K Company bunker by a Corpsman.

Master Sergeant Richter scoffed, "They will be back again Lieutenant! I can promise you that!"

Colonel Vortex shouted, "Shut up! I'm speaking to the AC-47 pilots!

I want them to get their strafing run right on target!"

Everyone fell silent and watched through their field glasses as the last of the supersonic fighter-bombers completed their evisceration of the hated PAVN/VC.

Reports had been received by Colonel Lownds from the *Bru* tribesmen regarding the activities of the Communists. These refugees had told the Americans before being evacuated from *Khe Sanh* that the PAVN and their puppet VC auxiliary troops had murdered mothers and their babies in the village of *Lang Vei*.

The slaughter had been a terror tactic of the Viet Cong in response to the villagers refusing to supply the Communist troops with food and an unsuccessful attempt at tax extortion.

Both Regiments on 881 South and 861A had already been well and truly smashed.

But Colonel Vortex and the other field commanders at *Khe Sanh* were not satisfied with mere 'smashing'.

They wanted pure annihilation.

And they got it.

'PUFF the MAGIC DRAGON' as some Marines called the AC-47 gunship came swooping in low over the mist layer from the southern end of the *Khe Sanh* escarpment.

The Communists had fallen back to the Marines first defensive perimeter on Hill 861A. They were regrouping and resupplying intent on launching another assault.

They were also stripping, mutilating and looting the naked bodies of the Americans. This was their standard practice on the battlefield.

But PUFF the MAGIC DRAGON broke their fucking gook spines.

Colonel Vortex watched with glee and a sense of elation as the three SPOOKY gunships came in tearing up the earth before them.

Master Sergeant Richter who was also peering through his field binoculars exclaimed to Thrush and Vortex, "Look! Sirs! Captain Baig has an extra surprise for us!"

Major Thrush asked, "What is it Master Sergeant?"

From the north-east came three additional aircraft. These machines were cigar-shaped and they had a double tail fin.

Colonel Vortex answered, "These are the new gunships. Just come into service. They are AC-119's."

Major Thrush added, "The troops call them 'SHADOWS'.

The AC-119's and the AC-119K's which are called, 'STINGERS'.

These aircraft are gunship conversions of the Fairchild C-119 transport aircraft.

They have four 7.62mm Miniguns and two 20mm Gatling's."

Master Sergeant Richter admonished, "Jesus! What firepower!"

Colonel Vortex did some calculations in his head as the PAVN troops below them were running helter skelter across the corpse littered slopes of 861A.

Gurgled Vietnamese voices were screaming and crying as the six gunships moved in above them.

"Six gunships with a total of 36 Miniguns!" began Vortex, "…that is 108,000 rounds per minute pouring into those Communist bastards!

Beautiful! Look at them go!"

The survivors watched with awe as the rain of bullets creamed the already smashed PAVN.

The atmosphere was so thick with metal that it looked like 'Black Rain' was falling on the slopes of 861A.

Bodies, pith helmets and limbs were mutilated to pieces in a shower of crimson tissue.

The black soil of the hill was washed red with gore and guts.

Colonel Vortex said aloud to himself, "I am sorry like a motherfucker General Vo Nguyen Giap! You fucking piece of shit!"

Colonel Vortex observed the avalanche of righteous American firepower until 0845 hours.

When the six gunships had expended their ordnance the 175mm howitzers from *Camp Carroll* started up again within seconds.

The PAVN Regiments and their VC puppets and stooges melted away like dirty water down a hill.

The rotten and putrid sewerage had been disposed of.

Vortex spoke to Colonel David E. Lownds on the field phone, saying,

"We have kept 861A."

Vortex headed back to KSCB in a AH-1 *Cobra* gunship.

Lieutenant Colonel Howard M. Dallman (United States Air Force) – AFSN:0-823814
Hero of the United States of America

Lieutenant Colonel Howard M. Dallman was serving with the 345th Tactical Airlift Squadron at *Tuy Hoa* Air Base. He was a C-130E *Hercules* pilot and an exceptionally experienced and adept one at that.

At about the time Colonel Richard Vortex was making the flight back to KSCB from Hill 861A on the morning of the 5th February 1968, Lieutenant Colonel Dallman was taking off in a C-130E from *Da Nang* air base en route to *Khe Sanh*.

Lieutenant Colonel Dallman was carrying 35,000 pounds of much needed ammunition for the *Khe Sanh* base including 4.2 inch mortar rounds, 7.62mm bullets, 106mm recoilless rifle rounds and CS tear gas. He was also carrying a medical evacuation team of Navy Corpsmen and doctors to service the growing number of injured Marines at the base.

The supplies were desperately needed and were sent as part of a multi-faceted request from Colonel David E. Lownds to III MAF.

Colonel Richard Vortex knew of the supply run and approved it as his 9th Marine regiment were suffering, per capita, as many casualties in KIA and WIA as the 26th Marine Regiment.

"So what is the situation on the other hill outposts Lownds?" asked Colonel Vortex as he entered the FSCC bunker straight after coming back from 861A.

Colonel Lownds answered, "The North Vietnamese are pressing all positions, Hills 950, 558 and 64 but we are holding. None of them are going to fall. I have over 1,000 men on Hill 558 and Lieutenant Colonel Francis Heath commander of the 2nd Battalion 26th is doing a sterling top class job over there. He also has the E/2/26th with him as well.

I have men on Hill 689, Hill 552 to the west of KSCB about 1 mile from the perimeter of the 'Gray Sector' and an observation team on Hill 471 which is also about a mile south of the 37th ARVN Ranger Battalion perimeter south of the airstrip. In addition I have placed a reinforced platoon at the *'Old French Fort'* which is about half a mile or less from *Khe Sanh* Village. However the 304th PAVN Division has the Ville and thus Captain Frank Willoughby at *Lang Vei* is effectively cut off and surrounded on all sides by, we estimate at J-2, upwards of 15,000 Communist troops from the 304th and 325th C *Golden Star* Divisions with elements of the 320th PAVN Division as well backed up by artillery regiments. All in all now that we are completely surrounded here at KSCB and Route 9 is cut off and our ground communication with *Camp Carroll* and the *Rockpile* is sealed by General Giap we estimate conservatively that 45,000 Communist troops have enveloped the entire *Khe Sanh* plateau. However General Momyer (USAF) has allocated 25 B-52 bombers to be made available for Arc Light strikes around KSCB on a 90 minute rotational basis in cells of either 3 or 6 aircraft bombing at between 25,000 to 35,000 feet using computer radar controlled guidance."

Vortex asked as Captain Mirza Baig joined the conversation, "And any news of Washington and General Earle Wheeler's decision on releasing to us the *W48* tactical nuclear warheads?"

Colonel David Lownds shook his head, "COMUSMACV has pressed for them but it's a definite no from Washington D.C. and the Pentagon. Sorry Vortex."

Colonel Vortex spat out in a rage, "You don't have to be sorry to me Lownds! But those dunderheads back in Washington will be sorry when the body counts come in and are tallied up after this bloody fiasco at *Khe Sanh* is finally over! They will see then how many American lives could have been saved if we had even the smallest yield nuclear shells released to us!

But it's like talking to a fucking brick wall!

What is President Johnson doing? Why is he so scared about releasing them?

Anyone knows that the Chinese and the Soviets will not risk an all out nuclear war on the strategic level just for this putrid 4th World backwater of North Vietnam.

If I had my way I would as a second option, instead of nuclear weapons, order the immediate and wholesale bombing of the *'Red River Dykes'* in the north of North Vietnam to flood their entire rice bowl and drown the cities and towns of North Vietnam.

That will most effectively curtail their evil and pernicious war effort and clinch us a quick victory.

This TET Offensive is a blessing in disguise.

The Main Force VC puppets think that they have dealt us a body blow.

They need a reality check!

COMUSMACV tells me that the best of the Main Force VC are being right now torn to pieces against a wall of our American firepower and that the guts of their units are being methodically torn out by this TET offensive.

One by one the 36 Provincial Capitals of South Vietnam out of the 44 total are being re-taken by our gallant and magnificent US forces one by one.

TET is fucked!

It has come to nothing!

And Giap is a fucking moron for launching it in the first place!"

Colonel Lownds answered, "I could not agree with you more. However the American people don't see it that way. They just believe whatever Walter Cronkite at CBS tells them. He is their messenger of doom and gloom *par excellance.*

Night after night on national television in the hundreds of thousands of homes, the millions of American families watching and listening believe that *Khe Sanh* is about to fall any day. That it is a repeat of the *Dien Bien Phu* debacle suffered by the French back in 1954. The French Colonial Forces lacking sufficient air assets, without the protection of holding the outlying hill positions and with a vastly inferior Air Force compared to ours still managed to hold out for nearly four months.

How the American people can even remotely equate *Dien Bien Phu* with *Khe Sanh* is beyond my comprehension!"

Vortex grunted his assent as he held out his arm to Master Sergeant Richter who brought up seven ampoules of Morphine and injected them directly into the ante-cubital vein of Vortex's right arm. The Colonel was still bleeding profusely from his chest wound on Hill 861A and was in a significant amount of pain and discomfort.

As he felt the Morphine wash through his blood stream an ordinary man would have sunk to the floor. However Vortex continued to pour over the Combat SKYSPOT reports and tactical charts as Captain Baig had laid them out on the conference table in the FSCC bunker.

Lieutenant Colonel John Mitchell, commander of the 1st Battalion 26th Marines entered the FSCC bunker and handed Colonel Vortex a telex, saying, "From Pentagon East just come in for you sir."

"What's this?" asked Vortex as he struggled to keep on his feet from the effects of the Morphine.

"I don't know sir. I have not read it. It's marked for your eyes only."

Vortex clumsily grabbed the yellow telex sheet.

It was from COMUSMACV ordering him to report to Pentagon East by the afternoon of the 8th February 1968.

Vortex said aloud, "Again? I have to go down there again? I just came back!"

Colonel Lownds asked, "What is it Vortex?"

"I have to report again to COMUSMACV. I think Westmoreland wants me to go down there and hold President Thieu's hand and baby-sit him through this TET offensive smash-up."

Captain Baig answered, "I think its something else sir."

"What do you mean? You haven't read anything that I have haven't seen have you?"

Captain Baig smiled, "No sir. I don't know anything for the reasons nor the requirements for you to travel back to Saigon but I have my eyes and ears open and something is brewing at US Air Force HQ and at Task Force 77 in the Gulf of Tonkin."

Colonel Vortex was perplexed, "Well then you better tell me about it before I leave Baig."

"Will do sir. Something is cooking on the radar screen. And its not Combat SKYSPOT either. Its got nothing to do with Operation NIAGARA."

Vortex's curiosity increased by a factor of ten.

"Sounds intriguing Baig?"

Captain Baig added, "Don't take my word for it but I smell something. And that something has got to do with the suspected headquarters of the war criminal General Vo Nguyen Giap. Increased radio traffic has been picked up by our Air Force boys over at *Nakhon Phanom* coming from about twenty-five miles north-west of *Khe Sanh* just inside the Laotian border in a known 'Kill Zone' where a complex of limestone caves are situated. We have sortied a number of Arc Light raids with B-52's onto that cave complex already from November 1967 to January 1968 but with little affect due to the deep subterranean nature of the stronghold where the geological characteristics do not lend for easy penetration even by our 750 lb and 500 lb H & E iron ordnance.

That is why I suspect that the USAF and Task Force 77 are involved.

Also at the meeting, your meeting on the 8th February 1968 in Saigon, General Ewell, Commanding Officer of the US 9th Infantry Division (the *Old Reliables*) will also be in attendance."

"I know General Ewell! We are good friends," said Vortex with anticipation.

Captain Baig continued, "I have heard that he wants to talk to you about something very important."

"For someone that doesn't know shit from shiola you know a hell of a lot Baig!" said Colonel Vortex.

The Captain answered, "Its my business to know as much as I can. Otherwise I could not keep the bombs flowing in the right direction."

The officers and men in the FSCC bunker chuckled audibly.

At the same time as Colonel Richard Vortex, Captain Mirza Baig and Colonel David E. Lownds were chatting so enjoyably about subjects close to their heart in the FSCC bunker, Lieutenant Colonel Howard M. Dallman of the United States Air Force (Service Number:0-823814) was actually doing some serious work.

Lieutenant Colonel Dallman was making his final descent into *Khe Sanh* over the rugged escarpment of the plateau and then piloting the massive C-130E Hercules transport aircraft towards the KSCB airstrip from the south-east.

On board he had a medical emergency team of Navy Corpsmen and several US Army doctors as well as 35,000 pounds of ammunition.

"This blasted anti-aircraft fire is a pain in the proverbial ass!" shouted Lieutenant Colonel Dallman to his co-pilot over the roar of the C-130E engines.

His co-pilot, a First Lieutenant, also USAF, said nothing but nodded nervously.

Colonel Dallman looked down from his cockpit and could see the outlines and trench positions of the Blue and Gray Sectors of the KSCB perimeter defence line. He was at 500 feet approaching the airstrip fast with shells from the PAVN impacting all around the base.

The C-130E landed at over 155mph. There would be no LAPES delivery on this run.

As the Hercules passed the KSCB control tower and rolled on towards the *'Ponderosa'* the portside second engine was blown away by a 152mm Communist shell from positions around Hill 881 North.

Within seconds the first engine and then the entire portside wing were aflame.

"Christ! I can't control her!" screamed Lieutenant Colonel Howard Dallman as the Hercules ground to a sickening halt.

In the FSCC bunker the air traffic control Marine rushed in yelling, "Sirs! We have a Hercules on fire near the helicopter revetments!"

Vortex shouted, "Fuck those Communists!"

In moments Captain Mirza Baig, Richter, Colonel Lownds and Vortex plus a dozen other officers and NCO's stumbled out of the FSCC bunker and ran pell mell towards the 'Charlie Med' and the aircraft parking area near the edge of the airstrip where the C-130E had stopped its left wing a ball of fire.

Lieutenant Colonel Dallman instinctively opened the hydraulic bay doors at the rear of the Hercules and started to shepherd the medical evacuation team out of the aircraft.

"Go! Move! Save yourselves!" he shouted.

An Army Major and doctor came up to Lieutenant Colonel Dallman saying, "What are you going to do? You need help!"

Dallman answered, "I do but not from you! Take cover! Take your medical team to the Base Exchange and Post Office/PX area at once. We can't afford to lose a single member of the medical team and that includes you Major."

The Major nodded frantically and lead his team along with all the equipment they could carry away from the burning C-130E and towards the centre of KSCB near the Exchange.

At this moment Colonel Vortex and Master Sergeant Richter came running up with about ten other Marines from 1st Battalion 9th Marine Regiment.

"What the deuce is going on Colonel?" asked Vortex to Colonel Dallman.

Dallman looked Vortex up and down, recognised his rank insignia of a full bird eagle on his collar and asked, "Are you in charge of this circus Colonel?"

Vortex grabbed Dallman's arm and answered, "I am the ringmaster! Yes!"

Dallman looked about the airstrip and saw the KSCB ammunition dump, the ONTOS and tank laager, the 1st Battery of 155mm howitzers and the additional helicopter parking area with upwards of six Chinooks and eleven UH-1D's and UH-1E's all sitting within the danger area of the burning C-130E.

"Then help me to back this C-130E away from the main area of the base!"

Looking around frantically Dallman added, "Over there! To the north of the helicopter revetments near the edge of the 'Blue Sector'. If I can generate enough power in the starboard engines I can taxi the Hercules over to that point and then let the aircraft burn at a safe distance from the rest of the base."

Vortex nodded.

Dallman asked, "Colonel! Can you help inside the plane with the fire fighting equipment?"

Colonel Vortex screamed, "Lead the way in!" Turning to Richter he shouted, "Are you game Master Sergeant?"

Richter said in a frenzy, "We are wasting time sirs! Let's get on with it!"

The three Marines entered the C-130E which was now empty of all medical personnel and Vortex followed Dallman into the cockpit.

The Air Force officer cranked up the starboard engines to maximum rpm and turned the C-130E slowly around towards the northern edge of the 'Blue Sector' away from the helicopter revetments.

Richter screamed, "The fire from the engines has spread to the cargo department. Look at this shit! Its stacked with 155mm shells, 7.62mm ammo and mortar rounds. This whole plane is going sky high in a matter of minutes!"

Vortex shouted over the din of both the Communist bombardment outside and the roar of the two remaining engines of the aircraft, "I will help to fight the fire! You, Colonel get the plane moving!"

Dallman managed to crank up the Hercules to about 15mph and yanked the controls to the left causing the plane to move slowly away from the KSCB airstrip.

Within three to four minutes the Hercules was now at a *minimum safe distance* from the rest of the base and the military hardware, aircraft, ammunition, trenches and positions of C Company, 1st Battalion 26th Marines.

Dallman joined in and directed the fire fighting effort inside the cargo department of the plane.

If it was not for Lieutenant Colonel Howard M. Dallman and his expertise in handling aircraft fires the efforts of Colonel Vortex and Master Sergeant Richter would have come to nought.

After the elapsure of ten minutes of frantic fire extinguisher hosing and dousing the immediate threat of an internal explosion of the cargo ammunition had been averted.

"Look like she's under control," said Dallman to Vortex.

"Good work Colonel!" said Vortex.

The fire engine trucks of the KSCB had positioned themselves around the stricken C-130E and were applying a thick white foam of fire control substances around the fuselage.

Outside the aircraft as Dallman inspected the damage to his plane Vortex and Richter were looking through their Navy Power-20 binoculars trying to ascertain the originating position of the Communist fire that was still blasting away at the KSCB airstrip and base.

"Those fucking PAVN cunts! I can see mortar positions over there near Hill 64 past the Rock Quarry and FOB3! Some of the fire that hit this Hercules came from there!" screamed Vortex.

A few moments later Major Lucius J. Campbell, commander of Forward Operations Base 3 came running up with a few of his men. Three of the Major's men were carrying a large weapon of some sort.

"What do you want Major?" asked Vortex.

Lieutenant Colonel Dallman looked with amazement at the weapon that was being manhandled by Major Campbell's troops.

"What the deuce is that? I have never seen anything like it?" said Colonel Dallman.

Vortex walked over to the weapon and inspected it with his expert eye.

"So you have brought me a present Major Campbell?"

"Indeed I have sir," he replied enthusiastically.

"What is this thing again? Remind me Major," asked Colonel Vortex.

Major Lucius Campbell explained, "This, Colonel Vortex, is the *LAHTI L-39* Anti-tank Rifle. Its actually made in Finland but the Special Forces boys have procured some for their use here in Vietnam. The *Lahti L-39* is a 20mm anti-tank rifle. The early models were first used in the Second World War 23 years ago. It has, I am happy to say, excellent accuracy, penetration and range. One disadvantage of the weapon is of course its size. You see three of my boys are needed to carry it over here to you for inspection.

The nickname of the *Lahti L-39* is *'Norsupyssy'* which means, I am told by Captain Frank Willoughby over at *Lang Vei*, 'Elephant Gun'."

Vortex laughed saying, "It sure as hell looks like it could kill an elephant!"

Major Lucius Campbell scoffed, "It can do more than that. I have a crate of 20mm cannon ammunition over here as well."

Colonel Vortex looked to Master Sergeant Richter while Lieutenant Colonel Howard Dallman surveyed the wreckage of his C-130E as the PAVN shells continued to fall uncomfortably close all around the KSCB airstrip and the *'Ponderosa'* area.

"I am itching to try it out! Over there towards Hill 64 from where these Communist turds are firing at us now!"

Major Campbell smiled, "Why do you think I brought it over here sir?"

"But I can't lift the fucking thing!" said Vortex.

"No problem," said Major Campbell.

In the next 3 minutes a half-track was brought up and Major Campbell's FOB3 troops expertly mounted the *Lahti L-39* onto the 4 ton half-track and loaded up the anti-tank rifle with its 20mm cannon shells.

"Ready to go Colonel Vortex," said the Major.

"Oh! Yeah!" was all Colonel Vortex said as he jumped onto the half-track with glee. Richter jumped up behind him as Lieutenant Colonel Dallman just shook his head from side to side asking in a whisper to Major Campbell, "Who is this guy?"

The Major answered, "He's the 9th Marine Regiment Commander."

"Does he ever get tired?" asked Dallman.

"The Colonel is too busy killing imperialist shit-turd gooks to bother about getting tired sir," answered Campbell.

Before Campbell could finish his sentence a crackling, ear-splitting, screeching sound pierced the atmosphere. Colonel Vortex had fired the first 20mm cannon round towards Hill 64 with the *Lahti L-39*.

At that moment a 152mm Communist shell landed 30 yards away and sent a shower of red dusty earth which smothered over Dallman and all the others. They were bathed in the red clay of *Khe Sanh*.

"Bloody fantastic!" shouted Colonel Vortex as he watched the trajectory of the 20mm cannon orbit through the atmosphere and land close to the apex of Hill 64 to the west of the KSCB airstrip about 1.2 miles distant.

"I'm a little bit off target though."

Major Campbell jumped up and helped Colonel Vortex to adjust the sights on the *'Norsupyssy'*.

"That's better," said Vortex.

For the next hour and a half Richter helped Vortex load the *'Norsupyssy'* while his commander poured shell after shell into the Communist positions on Hill 64. It was an orgy of destruction. Vortex used up all the 550 rounds of 20mm ammunition before he finally called it a day. By that time the enemy fire from Hill 64 had been reduced considerably.

Later on back at the MATU bunker Colonels Vortex and Lownds, Lieutenant Colonel Howard Dallman, Captain Mirza Baig, Major Lucius Campbell, Master Sergeant Richter and other officers and NCO's broke open several cartons of *Budweiser*, discussing the days' events.

"So what is your background Lieutenant Colonel," asked Vortex to Dallman.

Dallman advised, "During World War II I flew 45 missions in a *B-17* over Italy and was shot down on 23rd October 1944 when I was interred as a POW. In 1966 I participated in the excellent invasion of the Dominican Republic. During 1967 I flew numerous combat missions in I Corps and in II Corps in support of ground operations. Now I am here flying in supplies to you men at *Khe Sanh*."

Vortex clapped Dallman on the back with approval, "Well you did a hell of a job today Lieutenant Colonel. I am going to, I mean Colonel Lownds and I are going to immediately recommend you for a Decoration to COMUSMACV for saving the C-130E and for preventing a catastrophe with that ammunition you were carrying. It was smart thinking to manoeuvre the craft away from the storage areas and revetments just in case the whole thing blew up in our faces."

Vortex looked to Colonel Lownds, saying, "Isn't that right Dave?"

Colonel Lownds nodded, "A decoration. For sure! I will mark up the paperwork immediately!"

Monica Thang was crouching deep in the jungle about 500 yards from the *Lang Vei Village*.

It was 0035 hours on the early morning of the 7th February 1968.

Captain Frank C. Willoughby and Lieutenant Max Reinhardt of the US Army Green Beret Special Forces were reconnoitring the jungle both west and north of the *Lang Vei* base camp.

The troops under Captain Willoughby's command included 900 *Montagnard* [CIDG] irregulars made up into four ad hoc companies.

There was also a company of *Bru* troops and a Mobile Strike Force of 161 *Hre Montagnards*.

The tip of the spear consisted of the elite platoon of 24 American Green Berets under Captain Willoughby of the 5th Special Forces Group.

The beautiful South Vietnamese girl, Monica Thang was waiting for her *Captain of America*, her commander and her lover to return. She was glad that the Americans were trying to save her country from the Communists.

She despised them and was grateful when Captain Willoughby had assisted her in executing her own father who was discovered to be a Viet Cong political cadre and a Company commander in the regional VC forces.

To Monica Thang and her young sister Susan, that day was the happiest in her life.

Monica's only desire apart from being with Captain Willoughby was to exterminate Viet Cong and North Vietnamese. As she lay low to the earth she could hear the noises of the jungle in its forbidding darkness.

The owls, insects and bats that flew in-between the triple layered jungle canopy. The scent of the foliage around her was like a rotten sweetness. It was heavy and humid.

But unlike her American lover she was used to the crushing humidity, the heat and the virulent, blood-sucking leeches. Monica could feel one of those black leathery parasites approaching her vagina.

She quickly extricated it from out of her black pantaloons with her sharp fingernails. She then crushed the leech in-between her thumb and forefinger. The blood oozing onto the mud next to her feet.

Monica was slim, curvaceous and had a smooth angelic face. Her body was sensuous but strong and agile.

She was in every way as beautiful as Susie Ky though several years younger.

The South Vietnamese girls had their own special beauty. They were small compared to Western women but their delicateness made them superbly feminine.

Monica carried a captured AK-47 rifle. She used this weapon only because the M16 was not as reliable as the Chinese made assault rifle which in turn was copied from the Soviet design. It had a tendency to jam at the worst possible moment. Usually in the heat of battle when your life depended on it.

Monica also wore a web belt upon which hung a claymore mine, an 18 inch dagger and extra clips of 7.62mm ammunition. Behind her were 150 *Montagnard* irregulars from the *Lang Vei* Camp. So far there had been no word or sign from her lover, Captain Willoughby. She only prayed that the PAVN had not ambushed him and the nine other Green Berets that were in his patrol.

Approximately 650 yards in front of Monica's position, Captain Frank Willoughby and Lieutenant Max Reinhardt were lying stomach down in a ditch.

Both men were observing the PAVN through their Starlight Scopes. Their eight Green Beret comrades were all alongside, armed with CAR 15's, M79's and AK-47's.

The US Special Forces reluctantly used AK-47's not because they had no confidence in American technology.

Everyone knew that *'made in America'* meant that the product was second to none.

It was just that Captain Willoughby had found from experience that the AK-47 was far more reliable than the M16 which constantly jammed.

"Those dink bastards are preparing something big sir," whispered Lieutenant Reinhardt.

"It looks like it, doesn't it Max," answered Willoughby as he smiled at his 2-I-C.

The Green Berets could see about six 130mm artillery pieces belonging to the Communists.

These howitzers were being moved into position. Their muzzles were facing *Lang Vei*.

It looked extremely ominous.

Captain Frank Willoughby gave hand signals to his men.

They locked and loaded their weapons.

The PAVN regulars were 50 yards directly north of their position through the dense foliage.

The Communists did not have infrared Starlight scopes like the US Army and Marines. Thus they had not observed the elite commando unit.

Giap's troops also did not know that the Green Berets they were planning to murder had acquired captured RPG rocket launchers or B40's.

The US Special Forces were delighted by the fact that they would be able to use the Communists' own weapons against them.

"Open fire!" said Captain Willoughby calmly.

The elite squad let loose a barrage of RPG's and AK-47 fire into the PAVN artillery battery ahead of them.

Bloodied bits of torso and streams of intestines speckled the foliage as the screaming RPG's blasted into more than 250 North Vietnamese regulars.

Immediately the PAVN returned fire.

"Shit! There's more of them sir!" screamed Lieutenant Reinhardt.

"Where?" asked a frantic Willoughby.

"At eleven,…no! Ten o'clock!" answered Reinhardt.

Captain Willoughby adjusted his Starlight scope in the new direction and saw what looked like at least a full PAVN battalion of regular infantry from the 304th Division.

Perhaps a thousand men were now screaming through the jungle towards them.

The PAVN in this sector were not 'ghosts'.

'Charlie' was on the offensive in I Corps Operational Zone.

Especially in and around the infamous DMZ.

Captain Willoughby gave the signal to withdraw.

Like the movement of a single body, the nine other Green Berets slithered to their feet and were already racing through the jungle.

They easily moved at close to 10mph through the murderously dense foliage and elephant grass that ripped and scratched at their flesh. No other unit in the American forces could match this except for the UDT Teams and the Navy Seals from which they originated. The Green Berets were experts at surprise attack and could disappear from under the PAVN's noses like apparitions.

They had proceeded about 400 yards when a hail of fire hit them from the south-east.

"Jesus!" screamed Captain Willoughby.

"Another gook unit has outflanked us sir!" cried Lieutenant Reinhardt.

The Special Forces troops fired from their hips as they ran. Captain Willoughby called *Lang Vei* base and ordered them to open fire with their 106mm recoilless rifles.

Within seconds the friendly artillery was impacting against the advancing PAVN.

The small band of men were being pursued from three sides.

The soldier next to Willoughby was decapitated by an RPG-7.

Another Green Beret had his chest eviscerated open by AK-47 fire.

Another three men were severely wounded.

And then the PAVN fell upon them en masse.

"We've got to get back to the base sir!" screamed Reinhardt as he thrust his Special Forces dagger into the throat of one Communist while cutting down another with his rifle.

Willoughby shouted, "This is not just a pursuit! The gooks are launching an all out offensive!"

The *Captain of America* watched with horror as another of his supercommandos was gutted open by seven PAVN soldiers who pounced on top of his chest.

They cut out his heart and testicles.

But their victory was short lived as the German born American, Lieutenant Reinhardt, hosed them away with an RPG-7 rocket launcher. The blast intermingled their body parts and blew them across the foliage in clumps of bloodied meat and intestines.

"Retreat! Retreat!" ordered Captain Willoughby.

But it was too late.

Only three other Green Berets had survived the vicious hand to hand combat.

Willoughby dived across a small stream and landed face first in the mud. A leech attached itself to his left eyeball. The commander had no time to pull it out. Then as if he had become delirious, he heard the unmistakable sound of tank tracks.

"Tanks! Tanks!" shouted Willoughby, America's *Captain* in Vietnam.

Just after he screamed, his observation was vindicated by explosions that ripped up in front of them.

It was the shells from those Communist tanks that had struck so unexpectedly.

Captain Willoughby and Lieutenant Reinhardt thought they were finished.

Six of his men lay dead behind him.

He turned and saw his lover approaching with more than a hundred Montagnard irregulars. They were all armed with AK-47's.

Captain Willoughby grabbed Monica and kissed her.

He did not know whether he would ever have the chance to do that again.

"Form a defensive line!" yelled Captain Willoughby.

A shallow ditch ran across the northern approaches to the *Lang Vei* base camp.

The Montagnards dived into it and commenced firing at the several thousand advancing PAVN regulars.

Willoughby knew that he could not hold this line for longer than about 10 to 12 minutes.

The Montagnards were brave and valiant little soldiers. But they were no match for the ruthless PAVN and their superior cunning and savagery.

The Montagnards had previously told Captain Frank Willoughby, whom they admired and trusted, that their only desire was to fight.

They wanted to fight to the death to save their honour. The Viet Cong had raped their wives and daughters, humiliated their village chiefs, murdered their families and plundered what meagre possessions they had.

They despised the North Vietnamese also, whom they saw merely as ruthless and Satanic oppressors and as puppets of the Main Force Viet Cong.

Now Captain Willoughby watched the titanic struggle of these brave little men with their few assault rifles against the awesome power of the North Vietnamese War Machine.

"Oh! My lover! My darling! You are still alive!" cried Monica with tears streaming down her cheeks.

"I have never been so happy at this moment to see you living since the moment that you executed my traitorous father, the Viet Cong pig and interloper!"

The beautiful South Vietnamese patriot blasted away with her AK-47 in the direction of the Communists.

"Take cover Monica!" screamed Willoughby.

Lieutenant Reinhardt held them both and threw them into a deep gulley that ran almost up to the *Lang Vei* defensive perimeter.

"Incoming!" gurgled Lieutenant Reinhardt.

His timely action had just saved them because a huge 152mm shell from the *'Co Roc'* landed where they had previously stood.

The two large Americans lay on top of Monica Thang and shielded her from the blast.

Six more Green Berets came crawling up from the base.

"What are your orders sir?" asked one of the men who was a Warrant Officer 1st Class explosives expert.

Willoughby screamed over the din of battle, "We shall make a fighting withdrawal to the *Lang Vei* defensive perimeter! You call *Khe Sanh* now!

Tell them we want TAC air support, artillery and anything else they can give us! This is the big push against *Lang Vei*!"

It was now 0457 hours on the 7th February 1968.

The Warrant Officer was already crawling on his belly to get back to the COMMO bunker when Willoughby grabbed his sleeve viciously, "And tell *Khe Sanh* that the PAVN have tanks!"

The Warrant Officer was speechless.

"Tanks?"

"Yes! Tanks!" shouted Willoughby as Monica rested on her lover's back and fired her AK-47 into the advancing enemy.

"Are you sure sir? The gooks have never had tanks anywhere in South Vietnam before?"

Captain Willoughby, the United States' *'Captain of America'* in Vietnam kicked at the Warrant Officer with fury without actually making contact, "I told you! They have tanks! Tell Colonel David Lownds and Colonel Richard Vortex!

Hurry! God damn you!"

It was now 0500 hours on the 7th February 1968.

The PAVN had begun their major attack on the *Lang Vei* Special Forces Camp. The tanks spotted by Frank Willoughby were PT-76 tanks which approached from three directions. Five tanks from the south, four from National Route 9 along its western side and two from the eastern causeway of QL9. Eleven tanks were committed by the Communists for the *Lang Vei* assault.

The Green Berets managed to knock out two of the PT-76's with 106mm recoilless rifles but the other nine ran amuck inside the perimeter of Willoughby's command with sappers and PAVN regulars supporting them.

The M72 anti-tank ordnance malfunctioned and the Green Berets cursed under their breath as the counter-attack proved to be a total failure. The LAW M72 was a total disaster of biblical proportions.

The humidity had a deleterious effect on the 66mm high-explosive (HEAT) warhead causing them to misfire. However the magnificent courage of the Green Berets

and their fortitude in battle against overwhelming odds allowed them to crush five more of the PT-76's.

The Soviet made PT-76 light amphibious tank mounted a 7.62mm D-56B main gun with a capacity for 44 rounds. A 7.62mm coaxial machine gun was also mounted beside that. The PT-76 was primarily a reconnaissance tank and not a main force battle tank, weighing only 14 tons. Its armour was only 11 to 14mm thick and could easily be penetrated by a 0.50 calibre machine gun.

The WO1 nodded and scurried away.

The PAVN artillery had found the range and were pounding the Montagnard defensive line.

The rest of the tribal force of 750 Montagnards had now come running up from *Lang Vei*.

They, together with the *Bru* irregulars, made up Captain Willoughby's strike force.

The 12 Green Berets inside the *Lang Vei* perimeter were all firing the M40A1 106mm recoilless rifles and RPG rocket launchers.

Back at *Khe Sanh* Captain Baig was handed the field phone by one of his Corporals in the FSCC bunker.

"Its *Lang Vei* sir. It seems like trouble."

Captain Baig snatched the handset away from the NCO, "Hello? Who am I speaking to?"

The WO1 could hardly make himself heard over the explosions above his head. 130mm and 152mm shells were crashing down on the wood and sandbagged ceiling of the *Lang Vei* Commo bunker.

There were 55 gallon drums filled with rocks protecting the *Lang Vei* 25 feet by 40 feet concrete command bunker. A sandbag-faced concrete observation bunker which was situated at the opposite end of the command bunker was also attacked by the PAVN.

"We need TAC air and artillery! Now! *Khe Sanh*!" screamed the senior NCO.

Baig remained cool and professional, "Just give me the coordinates Warrant Officer."

As the *Khe Sanh* fire control staff fed the information into the Combat SKYSPOT computer, both Colonel Lownds and Colonel Vortex stormed in.

"What's going on?" asked Lownds.

Captain Baig listened to the excited voice of the Green Beret NCO at the other end of the receiver and put his hand up to both Colonel's to wait a second.

Even from where Vortex was standing he could hear the muffled explosions and screams of the Montagnards through the handset.

"Are you sure?" said Baig.

There was an eerie pause.

"But it can't be? It's impossible! We have never had intelligence like that?" repeated Captain Baig.

Colonel Vortex looked with feverish energy at Colonel Lownds.

"What is it?" he asked Baig.

The Fire Control Officer cupped the head of the receiver with one hand, "The *Lang Vei* boys are telling me that the Communists are attacking their perimeter with tanks!"

Colonel Lownds spluttered, "That's impossible!"

"It can't be!" added Colonel Vortex.

Captain Mirza Baig shrugged his shoulders and offered the receiver to the two incredulous commanders.

"Give it here!" screamed Vortex as he wrenched the phone up to his ears.

For the next three minutes the WO1 at *Lang Vei* repeated his message to a flabbergasted Vortex.

Colonel Lownds also spoke to the senior NCO and asked for Captain Willoughby.

The Green Berets were furiously firing their 'BATS' (M40 A1 recoilless rifles) and RPG-7's at the advancing men of the 304th PAVN Division and told Lownds that they did not even know if Captain Frank Willoughby was still alive.

He was right up on the forward defence perimeter.

Before the WO1 signed off he screamed, "Help us *Khe Sanh*! We are being cut to pieces here!"

Colonel Vortex grabbed the sleeve of Captain Baig asking, "What have you got for the *Lang Vei* troops? What's incoming?"

The Fire Support Coordination Officer said, "Seven F-4E's from the 'hot pad' at *Da Nang* have just been scrambled towards *Lang Vei*. Estimated ETA is 12 minutes.

In addition we have nine Navy *Skyraiders* coming in from Task Force 77 in the Gulf of Tonkin. Their ETA is 18 minutes sir. The Navy have also put twelve more F-4's on alert status for the next round of air strikes. I am organising an Arc Light strike for the next 90 minute period after this one."

Colonel Lownds said, "Good man!" He turned to Vortex, "Come with me Richard! We have to start planning a relief operation for *Lang Vei*."

Vortex nodded as he guided Master Sergeant Richter in front of him, "Yes! Its going to take at least a full battalion made up of a composite force from both Regiments to relieve *Lang Vei*! Let's get a move on!"

The Colonels and their staff entourage trooped out of the FSCC bunker and into the DASC complex to begin detailed planning.

Meanwhile the onslaught against *Lang Vei* was intensifying.

General Vo Nguyen Giap had ordered the full weight of the 304th PAVN Division to pulverise the US 5th Special Forces Group at all costs.

Giap had also committed the first Communist PT-76 light amphibious tanks from the Soviet union.

Each weighed about 14 tons and were the first armoured tanks used by the Communist forces in South Vietnam.

The war was escalating at a horrifying rate.

But to Colonel Richard Vortex it was a dream.

Vortex thought that now with Communist tanks thrown in that it may be possible that Washington would come to their senses and allow tactical nuclear weapons to be used at last.

The time was now 0815 hours on the 7th February 1968.

Three hours into the attack the Montagnard and *Bru* irregulars were starting to give way.

Monica Thang gripped her lover's shoulders as she threw several grenades at the oncoming PAVN.

A mutilated Montagnard lay next to them in the trench line.

His colon and spleen were visible as they oozed out of his lacerated stomach flesh.

"Give me water! Please water!" he cried like a child in Vietnamese.

Monica handed Captain Willoughby another AK-47 ammunition clip and then took his army issue water bottle from the webbing over his camouflage uniform.

"Here! Drink this! Be brave my comrade!" said Monica Thang as she held up the head of the agonized tribesman and fed him the precious water.

The Montagnard was already half delirious and most of the water just ran uselessly down his chin.

He gripped Monica's arm until it hurt, spine arching in a weird spasm and then he died with rolls of blood and stomach tissue vomiting from his mouth.

"You should not stay here my darling!" screamed Captain Willoughby as he ran up and down the defensive line encouraging the local troops.

"But it is my duty to fight with you my sweetheart!" admonished the beautiful Monica, her large brown eyes streaming with tears.

"I am a South Vietnamese patriot! I shall stay next to you and fight to the death!"

Captain Willoughby's chest heaved with a surge of terrible passion and love for his native girl.

Monica rushed through a hail of Communist fire.

She threw her arms around the Green Beret Captain and lavished him with sensuous kisses.

Then, grabbing an RPG-7 rocket launcher that was strapped to his back, she aimed it forwards at the screaming PAVN troops who were now engaged in vicious hand to hand fighting with the Montagnards.

Monica was about to depress the trigger when she spotted a large tracked vehicle that looked like a tank. It was crashing through the jungle undergrowth almost at the very edge of the *Lang Vei* concertina wire.

This vehicle was followed by at least nine others.

"Fuck you General Vo Nguyen Giap! And screw you! Ho Chi Minh! Eat this!" yelled the beautiful Monica as she swung the RPG-7 onto the lead tank and fired.

"Unbelievable!" cried Captain Frank Willoughby as he sheltered his lover from the stream of bullets.

Monica Thang had struck the first blow against the Communist tanks.

A huge ball of blue-red flame shot upwards into the air as the tracked PT-76 amphibious vehicle shuddered to a halt.

Several PAVN soldiers climbed out of the burning hulk but were immediately machine gunned to death by Willoughby and his handful of 5th *Special Forces Group* Green Berets and the CIDG [Civilian Irregular Defense Group] Montagnards.

Lieutenant Max Reinhardt had been hit in the left arm by fragmentation debris from an incoming 120mm mortar.

Blood was pouring over his camouflage tunic, his bone shattered but he carried on in a wild frenzy of combat.

"Its time sir!" he screamed.

"To withdraw inside the *Lang Vei* perimeter?" asked Captain Willoughby with shock.

The Lieutenant nodded as a second later the men of the 304th PAVN Division broke the line of Montagnards and *Bru* tribesmen.

The 24th Regiment, 304th Division, led by Colonel Le Cong Phe was the Communist assault force. The regiment was to be supported by the 2nd Battalion (part of the 101D Regiment, 325th Division), the 2nd Artillery Battalion (part of the 675th Artillery Regiment), one tank company (part of the 198th Tank Battalion, 203rd Armored Regiment), two sapper companies, one anti-aircraft gun company, and one flamethrower platoon. One of the most important features of the North Vietnamese formation were the elements of the 203rd Armored Regiment which, with its PT-76 tanks, were the first armored units to be deployed in South Vietnam.

Captain Willoughby swung his machete with gruesome power and hacked off the arm of the nearest PAVN.

The *Captain of America's* face was splattered with blood, some of which he accidentally swallowed.

Willoughby immediately vomited as he fell to the ground.

Reinhardt head butted two Communists in quick succession after they had bayoneted several wounded Montagnards who were trying to crawl away.

"You foul bastards!" yelled Willoughby as he shielded Monica with his muscular body and used his arms to cut to pieces the two PAVN soldiers with a machete.

Lieutenant Reinhardt stabbed them from the left and pushed them towards Willoughby who stabbed them in the buttocks, spine and the back of the neck.

"The PT-76 tanks! Watch out Lieutenant!" screamed Captain Willoughby.

Both officers started to grab the surviving Montagnards and the whole melee of about 500 survivors ran helter skelter into the *Lang Vei* prepared defenses. The Green Berets had claymores and M60's set up. The Montagnards quickly manned them and continued the suppressive fire.

It was a total fiasco.

What had started out to be a routine patrol by Captain Willoughby and his 5th *Special Forces Group* Green Berets now developed into a life and death struggle for the continuation of the whole American position at *Lang Vei*.

Already seven out of the twenty-four Green Berets had been murdered by the attackers.

The butchered and mutilated corpses of several hundred Montagnards and enemy alike littered the approach slopes of *Lang Vei* like a gruesome collage.

"I'll take control of one of those BATS! (M40A1 recoilless rifles)," screamed Monica as she ran to the central position inside *Lang Vei* near the Command and HQ bunker.

Captain Willoughby yelled after her, "Where is your sister, Susan?"

Monica answered that she was safe with the Warrant Officer inside the COMMO bunker.

Willoughby nodded with approval because at least one of his men had to remain in constant contact with *Khe Sanh* at all times. If for no other reason than to coordinate TAC air and the artillery.

"What do you think they are?" asked an agonised Lieutenant Reinhardt as two other Green Berets from Iowa helped the officer to load and fire the M60 that was set up in the forward trenches.

"I think it's a…" began Captain Willoughby as he rubbed his scalp, "…I think it's a Soviet PT-76 light amphibious tank which weighs approximately 14 tons."

Reinhardt nodded and with his uninjured arm he launched an RPG-7 that went screaming into the turret of the light armored vehicle.

This time it did not pierce the hull but bounced off the tank and instead killed three PAVN soldiers from the 101D Regiment of the 325th C *Golden Star* PAVN Division who were standing near it.

"Damn!" screamed Lieutenant Reinhardt.

The Montagnards were putting up a stiff defense as the Communist troops stormed the first defense perimeter of *Lang Vei*.

The PAVN were climbing like excited rats all over the concertina wire. They used the dead bodies of their comrades to throw over the barbed wire so that they could scramble on top of the corpses.

"Detonate the claymores!" ordered Captain Willoughby.

A Green Beret Staff Sergeant dived into the control trench and reached for the arming switches in response to the Captain's orders.

But the 20 Montagnards who had been manning the foxhole had all been killed or mutilated.

Three enemy soldiers fell on the Staff Sergeant and knifed him in the kidneys and the testicles while another tore at his face with a bayonet.

The NCO was close to death but still vainly tried to detonate the pre-set claymores and satchel charges that would have put a temporary dent in the PAVN onslaught.

"Come with me!" screamed Captain Willoughby to ten Montagnards and fifteen *Bru* irregulars from the CIDG force.

They rushed over to the control trench as the insidious Soviet supplied PT-76 tanks blasted the entire expanse of the *5th Special Forces Group* enclave.

Lang Vei was like an island of freedom fighters amidst a sea of rampaging Communists hell bent on destroying them.

Captain Willoughby saw Monica feed round after round into the 'BATS' as he jumped into the trench and knifed and bludgeoned to pieces everything he could lay his hands on.

The Staff Sergeant was already dead as Willoughby and five PAVN regulars from the 198th Tank Battalion, 203rd Armored Regiment tried to strangle each other with only their hands.

Captain Willoughby tore the ear off one Communist with his teeth while head butting another.

A Montagnard knifed in the liver an NVA that had Willoughby in a head lock.

That Montagnard in turn was shot through the heart by another North Vietnamese.

The *Captain of America* finally dived for the arming switches and ripping the skull of one PAVN away from the wires and then stoving it in with a trench spade, he ignited the whole awesome arrangement of munitions.

Claymores and *Phoo Gas* blasted all around the *Lang Vei* perimeter which was now almost fully occupied by the enemy.

The bodies of friend and foe alike erupted in showers of human tissue and severed limbs as the 400 or so remaining Montagnards and *Bru* fought with knives and clubs as well as assault rifles against the hated PAVN and the few Main Force Viet Cong that accompanied them.

Captain Willoughby threw several corpses off his body and killed six oncoming PAVN with his AK-47 as he leapt out of the control trench.

"Retreat to the bunkers and foxholes! Retreat!

And God save the United States of America and its valiant men and women in Vietnam!"

Lieutenant Reinhardt and seven Green Berets who half dragged and half carried the wounded officer before them were making their way to the central redoubt of *Lang Vei*.

This was a final formation of six reinforced bunkers with the HQ and COMMO bunker in the centre.

All the bunkers were connected by deep trench lines with M60 machine guns and 'BATS' on all four corners of the defense perimeter.

Barbed wire and claymores had also been installed around this inner ring.

This was the last ditch defense for *Lang Vei*.

"Everybody into the inner ring! Take positions inside the redoubt!" screamed Captain Frank Willoughby.

Lieutenant Max Reinhardt grabbed Willoughby's arm and snarled, "Don't surrender sir! Fight to the death! I wish John Wayne was here to help us! He would know what to do!"

"Don't worry Lieutenant! I have no intention of surrendering to that mongrel Giap! And I know what John Wayne would say."

Lieutenant Reinhardt asked, "What? What would John Wayne say sir?"

Willoughby answered, "He would advise, you stay here and hold the fort! I will go and head them off at the pass!"

Reinhardt looked puzzled, "Is that tactic relevant in this situation at *Lang Vei* sir?"

Captain Willoughby blurted out, "Fucked if I know Lieutenant! But it sure as hell sounds good to me!"

Then Willoughby pointed to the sky as Monica threw her arms around her lover's waist. She had expended more than 700 rounds of the M40A1 recoilless rifle ammunition.

"*Phantoms*! *Phantoms*!" screamed the *Captain of America*.

The Montagnards could see the incoming TAC air and this gave them a chance to disengage from the ever advancing PAVN.

But to Willoughby's horror he saw a group of about 20 *Bru* irregulars from the CIDG rolled right over in their trench lines.

Horrific screams ushered forth as nearly all of the 20 little warriors were crushed under the tracked wheels of the 14 ton PT-76 monsters.

"Oh! My dear God!" expostulated Monica as she saw their skulls squashed open like ripe grapes in a vat. A lathery spread of wrenched open human intestines slimed the tracks of the tanks as they turned.

Hearts, brain tissue, livers, colons and kidneys were ground up and revolved around the tank treads in a stinking morass.

"Radio controller! Come here! Damn you!" shouted Captain Willoughby.

As they ran to the inner trench line the Captain directed the incoming *Phantoms* after grabbing the handset.

The roar of over a million jet horsepower bore down on the advancing PAVN criminals.

Cluster bombs and napalm softened them up. Then the Navy *Skyraiders* came in and saturated the area with cluster and flechette bombs.

Hundreds of PAVN fell in a bloody heap where they stood.

But hundreds more continued their fanatical and dogged advance. When the Navy A-1 *Skyraiders* had completed their mission they peeled off to the east to allow the *Phantoms* to return for their strafing run.

The 20mm Gatling guns thundered maniacally as Captain Frank Willoughby herded his last troops into the inner ring of *Lang Vei*.

Only 289 Montagnards, 37 *Bru* irregulars from CIDG [one of five CIDG groups in Vietnam] and 16 Green Berets remained alive.

Monica was like a feline tiger as she manned the M60 inside the COMMO bunker.

She pumped away with belt after belt of 7.62mm ammunition into the screaming Communist troops that were now pressing in on all sides of the 'inner ring'.

Her sister, Susan, was huddled in one corner of the foxhole. The 14 year old girl did not cry but sat there with a resolute determination that belied her age.

Hatred of the Communists was not reserved only for adults in South Vietnam.

"Where is the artillery?" screamed Captain Frank Willoughby into the field phone.

"It's coming! Hang on!" answered Colonel Vortex as he spoke from the FSCC bunker at *Khe Sanh*.

Willoughby asked, "Sir! We are almost finished here. Practically annihilated! When are you going to send a relief force?"

Colonel Vortex reassured, "We are working on it Captain. We are gathering a fifty man Mobile Strike Force Company. Lieutenant General Cushman and Major General Norman J. Anderson the commander of the 5th *Special Forces Group* are working on it. They are being gathered here at *Khe Sanh* and another Company Reaction force is being organised at *Da Nang*.

But in the meantime you must hold *Lang Vei*! Do you understand? You must hold to the last man! Remember the heroism of the German 6th Army at Stalingrad and try to emulate that! Don't let those Mongoloids get the better of you! And remember you have Jesus on your side!

The Lord told me in my dreams last night that Jesus is on the side of *Lang Vei*!"

Captain Willoughby answered, "You know sir that I would never surrender.

The Germans in the 6th Army surrendered to the Soviets. But I never will!

Only if the situation became catastrophic would I countenance a strategic withdrawal."

A Green Beret Sergeant was blown into the COMMO bunker by an exploding 152mm shell from the *'Co Roc'*.

Two other Special Forces men grabbed him as he knocked Captain Willoughby off his feet and over the map table.

"Jesus!" screamed the Captain.

The Sergeant reached backwards for his spine as his lungs were visible through his flesh. He wavered in front of Reinhardt and the others with a look of confusion and despair. Then he started to cry like a child and said, "My son!"

Monica Thang ran to him. She wanted to hold him up.

But before the beautiful South Vietnamese patriot could hold the American he fell onto his face in a surge of blood.

The trauma of his wounds caused his stomach lining and intestines to curl in a vomiting mess out of his mouth and nostrils.

He died a few minutes later.

The soldier never saw his son again.

"Sir! There is a forward air controller on the VHF tactical frequency," said another Green Beret who was manning a secondary communications AN/PRC-41 radio.

"What does he want?" asked Willoughby.

Lieutenant Reinhardt answered, "There is an Air Force *Martin B-57 Canberra* bomber making its way in.

The forward spotter plane wants to know where to tell the *B-57* to place its bombs."

Captain Willoughby bolted out of the bunker and into the hail of Communist fire. He took three of his men with him and started to give exact coordinates to the pilot in the *Beach Model A36 Bonanza* Light Reconnaissance aircraft used for guiding in the fighter-bombers to their targets.

The *Beech Bonanza* had originally been designed to be pilotless but during combat operations in Vietnam a pilot was nevertheless essential.

The *Beech Bonanza* had an on-station endurance of about 18 hours flying over the combat zone. The reconnaissance plane automatically relayed information from the sensors to the Infiltration Surveillance Centre both in *Da Nang* and at *Nakhon Phanom* in Thailand.

"I can see the tank coming in to your position Captain!" called in the surveillance pilot.

Lieutenant David Peter EHRLICH

Willoughby was running through the trenches that connected the last six bunkers of the redoubt.

"That's where we want the ordnance Lieutenant!" answered Willoughby as he looked through his field binoculars at the PT-76 light amphibious vehicles.

The PAVN tanks roared into life and their guns smashed through two of the western bunkers.

Sandbags and Montagnard bodies flew through the air as the first North Vietnamese soldiers started to hack their way inside the foxholes.

"We've got to stop them! Come with me!" shouted Willoughby to his three Green Berets.

The Americans were horrified with what they saw in bunker one.

The first of the defensive inner ring.

The North Vietnamese troops had overwhelmed the little Montagnard tribesmen as they cut open their torsos with machetes and bayonets.

As Captain Willoughby bolted into the half demolished underground complex, he shot his M16 around in a wide arc, hosing down the PAVN assassins.

Suddenly he felt a terrible cutting pain behind his right arm. A North Vietnamese had bayoneted him so that the blade pierced the first two inches of his flesh and then exited again.

"Aiiee!" groaned the Captain as he swung around on the balls of his feet.

Willoughby grabbed the neck of the Communist with one hand and the AK-47 with the other.

In a swift and expert movement he slid his wounded arm out of the enemy bayonet, turned it around and thrust it back into the Communist's stomach.

At the same instant Willoughby head butted the soldier and grabbed his skinny buttocks with both hands.

Using this leverage he drove the man's own bayonet through his guts and down into his penis and testicles.

The Green Beret Sergeant behind the two of them smashed his trench axe into the Communist's spine, cutting it in half.

"Well done sir! God wills it!" cried the beefy Sergeant.

Willoughby watched in horror as he realised that these had been the Sergeant's last words on this earth.

The PAVN broke through the line of struggling Montagnards and blew the Green Beret away with a hail of AK-47 fire that dissected the American's chest.

"Oh! My God!" screamed the *Captain of America*. His eyes burned with hate as he turned on the enemy.

Willoughby picked up a fallen *Minigun* and blasted over 700 rounds into every corner of the bunker.

North Vietnamese bodies fell sideways, were blown upwards, decapitated and mutilated by the stream of bullets pouring out at 3,000 rounds per minute.

This fusillade gave just enough time to Captain Willoughby and the army medic next to him, to pull the mortally wounded Sergeant out of bunker one and into the connecting trench line that led up to the HQ and COMMO bunkers.

"He's had it sir. We can't save him," said the army Corporal who was also a paramedic.

"Is there anything you want to say Sergeant?" asked Captain Willoughby as he cradled the Green Beret's head in his arms.

The Sergeant opened his mouth like a goldfish but no sound came out.

Only crimson bubbles of blood frothed as his body shook with violent convulsions.

"Hang on! Hang on Sergeant!" uttered Willoughby.

"My daughter!" moaned the Sergeant.

He thrust an envelope into Captain Willoughby's hands. It was stained with blood and excrement.

Willoughby saw that it was addressed to the Sergeant's daughter.

"Do you want me to give it to her?" asked the Captain as the paramedic fed adrenalin into his veins with a large syringe.

But no answer ushered forth.

Until suddenly in a dying gasp he said, "Tell my daughter that if she marries a Communist then I will disinherit her! That if she even dates anyone who is not a Republican or right wing Democrat I shall disown her!"

Then the Sergeant was dead. His head slumped into Willoughby's arms.

Monica Thang came crawling along the trench line, pushing the Montagnards to one side.

The tremendous roar of mortars and artillery continued to decimate the *Lang Vei* defenders.

"Up there! Its coming in my love!" cried Monica as she pointed skywards.

It was now almost 1000 hours on the 7th February 1968.

The Air Force *Martin B-57* had received its instructions from the *Beach Bonanza* and was diving for the attack.

The cluster bombs and high explosives sailed through the air as Willoughby traced them with his binoculars.

Through the smoke and burning rubble of the Green Beret base he could see that some of the bombs exploded directly onto one of the Communist PT-76's.

One and perhaps two tanks had been put out of action as 15 secondary explosions rocked the perimeter of the *Lang Vei* inner ring.

"Excellent!" screamed Willoughby as he slapped the Montagnard tribal chief on the back with enthusiasm.

This chief was in command of the Montagnard troops, part of the CIDG component at *Lang Vei* responsible for 85 square miles around the vicinity of the camp. He smiled up with a toothless grin and swore obscenities at the North Vietnamese and their Viet Cong puppets.

But Captain Willoughby grabbed his lover, Monica, and raced back into the COMMO bunker.

As they ran hand in hand he said to the ravishing South Vietnamese girl, "I think we are going to lose *Lang Vei*."

Behind them the PT-76 amphibious tanks continued their advance as bunker two exploded in a gruesome inferno.

It was the beginning of the end for *Lang Vei*.

Chapter 12
OPERATION NIAGARA

Captain Frank C. Willoughby's Escape from Lang Vei: 7th to 8th February 1968

At 1534 hours on the 7th February 1968 a special mobile HQ C-130E Hercules transport aircraft touched down on *Khe Sanh's* airstrip.

Inside were Lieutenant General Robert E. Cushman and Major General Rathvon C. Tompkins, along with their III MAF and 3rd Marine Division Staffs comprising in total about 40 officers and senior NCOs.

The two Generals had come to *Khe Sanh* for only one reason.

And that reason was *Lang Vei*.

130mm and 120mm mortar and artillery shells were continuing to explode spasmodically all around the *Khe Sanh* airstrip and base interior.

"They took a big personal risk in coming here at the height of the siege!" said Colonel David E. Lownds as he stood next to Colonel Richard Vortex on the edge of the runway near the TAFDS (Tactical Airfield Fuel Dispensing System).

Master Sergeant Richter had picked up the remains of Sergeant Major Crighton only a few hours before.

At dawn, the senior NCO had taken three heavily armed *Sikorsky* S-65 HH-53B *Super Jolly Green Giants* into the valley between 881 South and 861A.

Two of the *Jolly Green's* remained above the tree line providing massive suppressive fire from their multitude of *Miniguns* and 20mm *Gatlings* as they circled in a 'Wagon Wheel' formation.

Richter had descended with the other chopper to find and extract the Sergeant Major's body.

The corpse had been immediately air lifted back to *Da Nang* in a C-123 *Provider* and from there it was placed on a USAF 707 for the journey back to the United States.

Sergeant Major Crighton would be buried at Arlington National Cemetery with full military honours and would be promoted posthumously to the rank of Captain in the Marine Corps for his outstanding bravery and courage.

A Congressional Medal of Honour and a Purple Heart with clusters would also be awarded to one of America's finest sons.

Colonel Richard Vortex was still mesmerised by the loss of his close personal friend and colleague.

He said to Colonel Lownds, "Well? Its all part of the profession of arms isn't it David?"

Lownds nodded as Vortex added, "Generals are supposed to expose themselves to combat at least as much as the ordinary PFC and perhaps even more than that!

Officers are supposed to set an example to their men!

That is why I always lead my Regiment into battle or any one of my individual battalions.

I relish in taking point duty with my senior NCOs!

Only in that way can you gain the respect of your enlisted men and junior officers."

Colonel Lownds remarked, "It is very admirable Colonel Vortex. But I am afraid you will find that not many senior officers of field rank practice the same unyielding principles."

Vortex snapped back as he saluted the approaching Generals, "I disagree with you Lownds! I think that most of the officers in our magnificent United States Marine Corps have the same devotion to duty as you and I do! That is what makes the American military tradition second to none!"

Lieutenant General Robert Cushman barked out angrily as he approached, "What are you talking about gentlemen?"

Colonel Lownds answered hesitatingly, "Nothing sir!"

Colonel Vortex merely gave a sly grin.

Lieutenant General Cushman turned to Major General Tompkins and laughed, "I always feel safe and secure in my position when two of my senior Colonel's conspire together to talk about nothing!"

The four officers laughed heartily as the 3rd Marine Division staff hurriedly disembarked from the C-130E.

The whole gaggle of officers ran through the foxholes and bunkers of *Khe Sanh* as the Communist shelling seemed to intensify.

Once they were in the relative safety of the FSCC bunker Captain Mirza Baig prepared large scale maps of the *Lang Vei* environs and 5th *Special Forces Group* base.

"Alright! Gentlemen! Give me the current situation [SitRep] at *Lang Vei*!" ordered General Cushman as he lit up a thick Cuban cigar.

Colonel Vortex gently nudged the Fire Control Officer out of the way and began the briefing.

"Sir! Colonel Lownds and I have been in contact with Captain Frank Willoughby at *Lang Vei*. It appears that the bulk of the 304th PAVN Division is engaged at this very moment in a large scale assault on the Special Forces Base.

We can only presume from the sheer magnitude of the attack, involving an estimated 3 to 4 Communist regiments that Giap intends to take *Lang Vei* as a prelude to an all out offensive against *Khe Sanh* itself!"

General Cushman was visibly shaken by this no nonsense report.

The III MAF commander looked to the CG (commanding General) of the 3rd Marine Division.

General Tompkins was rubbing his chin thoughtfully.

"Can it be Rathvon? Is this the prelude to an all out offensive against *Khe Sanh*? The big push that we have been waiting for for so long?"

Major General Tompkins looked apologetically to his superior, "I am afraid so, sir! That yes! It could well be the beginning of a pincer drive by General Giap!"

Colonel Lownds asked incredulously, "Pincer drive? What are you saying sir?"

General Tompkins explained, "Well. It is quite simple."

He pointed with a pearl handled baton at the large map in front of them. He moved with the agility of an orchestra conductor.

"I think that this stinking scoundrel, Giap, wants to drive in the defenses at *Lang Vei* while he keeps the hill outposts at 881 South, 861/861A and 558 pinned down.

With *Khe Sanh* under constant artillery and mortar bombardment he will crush and take *Lang Vei* with the 304th Division.

As this is happening he will strike hard against *Khe Sanh* itself with the 325th C *Golden Star Division* supported by the 320th Division while he continues to 'roll-up' the western front around *Lang Vei* Village."

Colonel Vortex grunted, "I have to agree with Major General Tompkins sir."

General Cushman asked, "Alright then gentlemen! We have a serious situation here! How many TAC air strikes have been launched against the PAVN in and around *Lang Vei*?"

Captain Mirza Baig answered with pride, "I have assigned 379 Combat SKYSPOT sorties against the 304th PAVN Division in the last 24 hours to crush the Communists sir!"

General Cushman was immensely pleased as he day dreamed about the possible body counts, "Three hundred and seventy-nine!"

Captain Baig continued as he checked his watch, "In addition to that sir. I have a B-52 Arc Light strike commencing just about now!"

"What is the target?" asked Major General Rathvon C. Tompkins.

"The supply dumps and lines of communication of the 304th Division which is approximately 3 kilometers from the *Lang Vei* defensive perimeter. Therefore as you can see sir, it is in direct support of Captain Willoughby and his troops."

General Cushman nodded, "That's good! Very fine indeed."

Major General Tomkins ordered, "Listen Captain Baig. In view of the very serious situation at *Lang Vei* I want you to divert every B-52 Arc Light to the Special Forces area until further notice."

Colonel Lownds remarked, "You mean until *Lang Vei* falls?"

General Cushman lost his temper as his face became crimson with fury, "*Lang Vei* will not fall! Do you hear me Lownds and Vortex?"

Colonel Vortex snapped to attention, "You have my word sir! I shall not allow Captain Willoughby to evacuate his position unless it is absolutely necessary."

Colonel Lownds was furious but kept his mouth shut. He knew that it would be impossible for the Green Beret officer of the 5th Special Forces Group and his CIDG troops to hang on to that small base in the face of a full PAVN division.

For all they knew *Lang Vei* could have already fallen. No radio communications had been received from Captain Willoughby for some 2 hours.

Colonel Vortex continued as the 40 or so officers of the III MAF staff stood nervously behind the two Generals taking notes.

"But I have some disturbing news sir," said Vortex.

"What's that?" snapped General Cushman as he was handed a cup of steaming Hungarian coffee by Master Sergeant Richter.

Vortex continued, "The gooks have tanks. We are sure that they are PT-76 light amphibious vehicles weighing about 14 tons each. Captain Willoughby radioed in to tell us."

General Cushman became catatonic, "Tanks? Tanks! That's crazy! The fucking gooks don't have tanks!"

Colonel Lownds nodded sheepishly, "They do sir."

General Tompkins also bobbed his head, "Yes. They do."

Vortex nodded again.

"They do?" asked General Cushman in a state of shock.

"They do," added Vortex.

"Then we shall have to destroy them at once! It is the first time that the North Vietnamese have fielded tanks inside the Republic of South Vietnam!" shouted an agitated General Cushman.

"I know sir! But Captain Baig is trying to pinpoint the PT-76's for immediate B-52 attack," said Vortex.

"Christ! I am the one who has to tell COMUSMACV that Giap has fielded tanks against us. This is indeed an ominous development!" said Cushman.

Colonel Vortex sniggered, "I wouldn't be too alarmed at this stage sir. After all. They are only *light* amphibious vehicles."

General Cushman scoffed and turned to Colonel Lownds, "Is there anything else? Because I have to go to Saigon this evening for a conference with General Westmoreland at *Pentagon East*."

Colonel Lownds answered, "We are readying a fully equipped and reinforced battalion of 400 to 500 men made up of a composite from the 9th and 26th Marine Regiments.

They will be jumping off in about 30 minutes sir.

They are under the command of Major George Quamo.

The helo lift mixture will be 20 UH-1E's and UH-1H's supported by 5 *Cobra* gunships."

Vortex added, "The 25 choppers are en route now from *Phu Bai* and *Dong Ha*, as well as *Qaung Tri* and *Da Nang*. They will rendezvous over the base, pick up the men and then proceed with the mission.

I shall personally brief Major George Quamo."

General Cushman looked flabbergasted, "What mission?"

Colonel Vortex said, "I beg your pardon sir?"

Major General Tompkins was also surprised as Cushman said again, "What mission? I haven't authorised any mission?"

Vortex laughed. He thought General Cushman was joking as he said, "The mission to relieve the Special Forces base at *Lang Vei*, sir."

General Cushman turned livid with anger, "There is not going to be any relief or assault operation for *Lang Vei*! Especially not with 400 or 500 men which is nearly one quarter the strength of the *Khe Sanh* base not including the hill strongholds."

Colonel Lownds felt like he was going to be sick.

Vortex stammered, "Are you joking sir?"

Cushman barked back angrily, "I never joke! Especially not about orders! And this is an order! No relief or assault operation is to be mounted for *Lang Vei*!

Only that Major George Quamo may try to rescue and exfiltrate the survivors if he thinks it is feasible. That's all.

Is that understood gentlemen?"

Colonel Vortex screamed in a high pitched voice, "But why? Sir! I was going to lead with Major George Quamo the battalion sized assault myself! There is no ground action around *Khe Sanh* at the moment. I want to. I must lead that attack to rescue Captain Willoughby and his troops!"

General Cushman slammed his fists on to the table and tore the battle maps as he did so.

"Are you and Major Quamo crazy?" began Cushman as spittle shot from his mouth, "We can't risk a rescue operation for the Green Berets! The danger of ambush is much too high! We will just needlessly waste more Marines for no purpose."

Vortex slumped back against the table as Captain Baig turned away in disgust.

Master Sergeant Richter regretted the fact that he had taken so much care with the General's Hungarian coffee having ground the coffee beans himself manually to perfection for the Lieutenant General.

"Who is this Major George Quamo anyway?" asked General Cushman.

Major General Rathvon Tompkins answered, "Major Quamo is with Command and Control North, Forward Operating Base (FOB) 3 with the 5th Special Forces Group (Airborne), 1st Special Forces Command. He is one of our best Green Beret officers and Captain Willoughby's immediate superior."

Suddenly one of the radio operators along the bunker consoles said, "Its Captain Willoughby sirs! He wants to speak to either Colonel Lownds or Colonel Vortex."

"Give that to me here!" shouted Vortex as he lurched for the handset and fumbled with it so that it nearly fell out of his grasp. Vortex was fuming with anger at Lieutenant General Cushman.

"Hello? This is *Khe Sanh* FSCC! Over!"

Muffled explosions and continuous machine gun fire could be heard through the handset.

The voice of Captain Willoughby was desperate and frantic.

"Who am I speaking to?"

"Don't you recognise my voice yet? Frank? This is Colonel Vortex! Go ahead Captain. Report your current situation."

The Captain screamed, "We are almost annihilated sir! The North Vietnamese are inside the defensive redoubt. I have only 150 men left all up!"

Vortex smiled to General Cushman and said sarcastically, "Would you like to tell Captain Willoughby yourself that there will be no rescue operation mounted."

And then Vortex added, "Sir!"

Lieutenant General Cushman scowled at everyone in the room.

He then walked hesitantly over to the radio.

Picking up the receiver as if it was a snake, General Cushman said in a stern voice, "Listen to me Captain Willoughby!"

"Yes sir," said the Green Beret officer.

Cushman ordered, "You are doing a sterling job out there at *Lang Vei* Captain. I congratulate you! But you must hold out a little bit longer son."

Captain Willoughby asked as Monica fired a 'BAT' above his head, "How much longer sir? We are almost smashed now! I have lost about 800 men killed and wounded. I have only 150 CIDG Montagnards left plus about 15 of my Green Berets! Sir!"

General Cushman looked genuinely sorry as he shrugged his shoulders at a morose General Rathvon Tompkins.

The III MAF commander answered, "Hold on for 4 weeks more! We might be able to launch a rescue operation then."

Captain Willoughby half laughed and half cried, "Four weeks? We will be lucky to hold on for another 4 minutes! Sir!"

General Cushman said, "We can't commence a rescue operation now Captain. The best that I can do is to exfiltrate you and the survivors. Major George Quamo and Colonel Vortex will organise that by helicopter. The danger of ambush and annihilation by the North Vietnamese is too great!"

Then before Captain Willoughby could respond, General Cushman quickly handed the receiver back to Colonel Vortex as if it was contaminated.

Vortex signed off by saying that they would give them every means of air and artillery support from *Khe Sanh* and all over the Republic.

Before Captain Willoughby put down his receiver in disgust he asked, "Sir! What are my orders if *Lang Vei* is about to be overrun? If we are about to be annihilated? Do I have permission to retreat and evacuate the base?"

The radio was on open channel all across the FSCC bunker so that everybody could hear the conversation.

General Cushman rubbed his chin with exasperation and then finally nodded to Colonel Vortex, who said, "You have permission Captain. Good luck."

Captain Willoughby turned to Monica with a look of extreme anguish.

"There will be no relief operation from *Khe Sanh*. Just evacuation with the help of Major George Quamo and Colonel Vortex."

Monica held her sister Susan to her bosom and cried, "But it can't be my love!"

"It is!" said Willoughby in disgust. Then he added as he kissed both Monica and Susan deliciously, "If it was up to my friend Colonel Vortex and Colonel Lownds there would be an attack to save us. But Vortex, Quamo and Lownds have been thwarted by General Cushman."

Just at that second the seriously wounded Lieutenant Max Reinhardt screamed as he peered out of one of the bunker gun sights.

"Sir! The gook tanks have crashed into bunkers 2, 3 and 4! We are wide open!"

Captain Willoughby climbed up the sandbagged wall and thrust his head into the gun sight. To his horror he could see the whole inner ring of *Lang Vei* crumbling. There were no more clear defensive lines. The Communists were intermingled with the Montagnards in a struggle to the death.

It was Vietnamese against Vietnamese as they killed, slashed, cut and bludgeoned each other to pieces in an orgy of hate. An ear splitting crash rocked the entire COMMO bunker.

"Fuck! What was that?" cried Captain Willoughby.

A Corporal and a SP4 standing on the firing boom were knocked to the floor of the bunker.

A primed grenade rolled out of the SP4's hand. He had intended to throw it at the advancing Communists before the impact.

"Grenade!" screamed a Sergeant who raced up behind them. Two seconds after the Green Beret NCO had picked up the grenade it exploded before he could toss it out of the bunker.

A shower of blood covered everybody there as his chest was ripped open revealing his pulsing heart, ribcage and pink lungs.

Lieutenant Reinhardt smashed the mutilated body out of the way and held up a rocket launcher.

"What the Jesus are you doing?" shouted Willoughby.

But it was too late.

The RPG-7 screamed forward just as the PT-76 tank bowled over the whole western wall of the COMMO bunker. The roof collapsed and the handful of Montagnards and Green Berets were covered in dust, blood, smoke and excrement.

The beautiful Monica screamed as she dragged her young sister away from the tank, "He's crushed! Oh! Dear God!"

The Communist machine gunner inside the PT-76 was hosing down nearly all the men in the underground complex.

To Captain Willoughby's horror he saw Lieutenant Reinhardt under a pile of dislodged sandbags. But what was worse his legs from the knees down were under the tracks of the tank itself.

His screams pierced the bowels of hell itself.

"Hold on Lieutenant! I'll get you out!" screamed Captain Willoughby.

He rushed forwards but was confronted by the first PAVN soldier who jumped through the broken wall.

Without thinking, Willoughby head butted the Communist and whipped his dagger out of its sheath, burying it inside the Communist's right eyeball.

The Captain then crushed his knee into the Communist's testicles and shot his Colt 0.45 *pistola* through the man's eardrum. Half the skull was sheared off in a bloody and delicious shower.

The tank driver was trying to fire up the diesel engine of the PT-76 because Reinhardt's' RPG-7 had caused it to stall temporarily.

"Oh! Dear God!" screamed the Captain as he kneeled down next to the shrieking Lieutenant.

The feet and shins up to the knee had been completely crushed under 14 tons of Communist steel. A pool of blood oozed out from every side of the mangled limbs.

Lieutenant Reinhardt's lower legs had been compressed to the thickness of a piece of cardboard.

But miraculously he was still conscious.

"No! Stop! Stop!" shouted Captain Willoughby with extreme horror.

The PT-76 tank started to roll forward into the COMMO bunker. The driver had succeeded in re-starting the engine of the PT-76. As the tank moved forward it progressively crushed the half naked body of Lieutenant Max Reinhardt.

"Aiiee!" shrieked the doomed Green Beret officer.

Now his legs and been completely crushed up to the groin. His testicles and penis vanished under the 14 tons of metal. They popped open like ripe grapes. His pelvis was flattened, his lumbar spine destroyed. The stomach burst open and smashed, his lungs collapsed, the arms twisted to nothing.

Lieutenant Reinhardt vomited his intestines into Captain Willoughby's face as the tank tracks crushed his neck and finally his skull until there was nothing left.

"You bastards!" screamed Willoughby.

Monica threw her lover a bag full of C4 plastic explosives.

"My lover! Fuck them up the ass with this!" shrieked Monica as she started to drag the crying Susan out of the ruined COMMO bunker and along the trench line.

"I'll kill you gook Communist bastards!" shouted Captain Willoughby.

The commander of the Green Berets was crestfallen at the loss of his faithful Lieutenant Max Reinhardt.

As the PT-76 inside the COMMO bunker rolled forward crushing yet more CIDG Montagnards in its path, Willoughby attached the magnetic satchel charges to the steel underbelly and sides of the tank.

"Everyone out! Get out!" ordered the Captain.

The Special Forces and CIDG troops at *Lang Vei* were extremely well trained. They were the crème de la crème of the US Army and its magnificent, righteous and valorous history.

They knew exactly what to do in case the base was about to fall to the enemy. The procedure had been well drilled and rehearsed. The fifteen American survivors and about 90 Montagnards and *Bru* irregulars moved backwards to a secret escape tunnel that had been built at the same time as the base itself.

It was the brainchild of Colonel Vortex who told Willoughby that he must have an escape option in case the worst possible scenario came to pass.

There was no chance of helicopter extraction because all the LZ's (landing zones) had been occupied by the enemy.

"Beautiful!" screamed Captain Willoughby as the satchel charges on the lead PT-76 tank ignited the hull and blew the whole machine to pieces.

Two PAVN crewmen, one of which was actually a female Viet Cong, tried to scramble out of the top turret.

"No you don't you dirty VC slut!" admonished Captain Willoughby.

Like a raving tiger the junior officer leapt onto the ruined PT-76 and dragged the VC girl out by her long and luxurious black hair.

Monica, who held the M60, blew away the second tank crewman.

"I'm going to fuck your guts out you stinking VC bitch! You killed my best friend!" screamed Captain Willoughby.

The attractive looking Viet Cong girl spat viciously into Willoughby's face and still had the strength to smash his testicles with her upraised knee.

"Aiiee!" moaned Willoughby as he clutched his groin in sheer agony.

The testicles were always the weakest point in any man who had them.

And women could achieve great destructive potential against a physically superior man by always trying to crush or mutilate a man's gonads.

The *Captain of America* swung his arm in a brutal arc and slapped the Viet Cong girl across the face with such power that the red imprint of his hand remained on her smooth and delicious flesh like an involuntary marking.

Despite his better judgment, Captain Willoughby could see that the North Vietnamese girl was quite beautiful.

"You mongrel American imperialist cowboy and murderer!" shouted back the VC girl in Vietnamese.

Translated she said, "Bạn mongrel Mỹ Đế quốc cowboy và kẻ giết người."

She then slapped the *Captain of America* across the face with equal force.

Willoughby answered, also in fluent Vietnamese, "I am going to tear out your living womb! You filthy VC slut!"

The Captain then punched the girl in her stomach and slapped her twice across the face and the breasts which were not insubstantial.

She reeled backwards screaming and fell into the arms of Monica Thang who had come running up from behind.

The gorgeous Monica ripped her nails into the VC girl's face as the Communist girl tore at Monica's breasts which were slightly less substantial but nevertheless of faultless form and texture.

"You are a disgrace to our nation and you are a stinking traitor! You whore!" accused Monica.

The two girls started to cat-fight like she-devils without restraint nor even a modicum of dignity.

Even Captain Willoughby was slightly taken aback by the sheer ferocity of their hatred for each other's succulent flesh.

Here was one beautiful girl representing the South, fighting another attractive female warrior of the North.

It epitomized the whole situation of the civil war in Vietnam.

"She's mine Monica!" said Captain Frank Willoughby as he dragged the VC girl away from his lover.

But just at that second the advancing PAVN troops poured into the devastated bunker and around the burning PT-76 tank.

As the Captain held the VC girl in his arms he saw that one of the North Vietnamese troops was about to bayonet him in the back at the level of Thoracic 4 to 8.

So Willoughby quickly swung the VC girl's body around in the direction of her Communist comrade.

To the Green Beret's delight the bayonet intended for him went instead into the VC girl's voluptuous breasts and through her chest at the level of the *manubrium*.

With expert skill and viciousness, the Captain unsheathed his own Marine dagger of honour and fidelity and thrust it into the throat of the PAVN soldier. At the same time he grabbed hold of the VC girl's neck and started to jam her into the PAVN soldier while using his Marine dagger to push the Communist man into the girl at the same time with expert synchronicity.

In this way Captain Willoughby drove the two Communists together on their own bayonet in a death embrace.

It titillated Captain Willoughby's senses to the point of sexual excitement.

"And fuck you for killing my friend!" screamed Willoughby.

The Captain then slid out his dagger from the man's throat and deliciously sliced it into the VC girl's vagina until it tickled her abdomen and eviscerated her womb.

A Sergeant from Willoughby's outfit smashed in both their skulls with his trench spade while the dagger was still inside them both.

Captain Willoughby thought it was beautiful to watch and almost forgot about the fall of *Lang Vei*.

"We better get out of here sir!"

"Yes! Everyone to the tunnel!" ordered the Captain.

Willoughby looked at the carnage behind him as he ran with Monica and Susan.

The heavy artillery from *Khe Sanh* and *Camp Carroll* was continuing to pound the Regiments of the 304th PAVN Division.

But it was already too late as the entire expanse of *Lang Vei* was strewn with mangled corpses and the bodies of squirming wounded who would soon be tortured and put to death by the North Vietnamese which was their normal *modus operandi*. It was also contrary to *public international law*.

The Special Forces survivors and their CIDG irregulars ran helter skelter to the escape location. But when they reached the tunnel, four PT-76 tanks burst in upon them. The tanks fired and the detonations erupted with indescribable force.

One of the blasts caved in the entrance to the escape tunnel which was about 250 yards from the edge of the jungle. Once inside the jungle canopy it was about 6.5 miles to *Khe Sanh* which lay to the east.

It was only 1 mile to the *Lang Vei* village but that was now completely dominated by the PAVN. The refugee civilians having fled along National Route 9.

"Shit!" admonished Captain Willoughby, "What are we going to do now?"

The Green Beret Warrant Officer said, as he scratched his head, "I don't know sir?"

Just then the PT-76 tanks of which there were about 5 left out of an initial 11, started to pound the Americans and their CIDG's.

The Montagnards had set up six M60 positions and were firing everything they had at the relentless foe.

The PAVN advanced only a yard at a time but still they came.

"We need some sort of a distraction in order to slip away into the jungle!" shouted Captain Willoughby over the tremendous din of battle.

"I think we have that distraction sir!" said the Warrant officer.

"Where?" asked the Captain.

A roar of jet engines could be heard rumbling closer.

"There! Sir!" pointed the senior NCO.

"Good! Just in the nick of time too!" said Willoughby excitedly.

Willoughby grabbed the field radio from the back of one of the radio operators who was firing his M16 as the Captain spoke to the flight leader above through the FSCC bunker at *Khe Sanh*.

"Listen! This is the *Lang Vei* commander! We need you to lay down a screen of suppressive fire in order for my surviving troops to slip into the jungle. Can you arrange that Tango Five?"

The voice of the Marine aviation officer answered, "No problem! When do you want it and where? I've got 12 birds with napalm, cluster bombs and HE."

The flight of *Phantoms* thundered directly over them and strafed the oncoming PAVN with their 20mm Gatling's as a prelude.

Captain Willoughby answered, "When – is in 2 minutes from now. Where – is directly to the west of our position and right on top of the *Lang Vei* base!

We don't have it anymore! The gooks are in control! Do you copy?"

The Marine Major above laughed, "Understood! Get ready to move in 120 seconds!"

Captain Willoughby watched with horror as a PT-76 tank rolled over a group of 10 Montagnards, crushing them into a bloodied pulp of ruined flesh.

"Everybody retreat! Retreat! Pull back!" screamed the *Captain of America*.

Monica Thang ran up and down the line of *Bru* tribesmen and Montagnards telling them that they were going to withdraw into the jungle.

She told them they were going to head east towards *Khe Sanh* and that they would be picked up en route by helo-extraction.

The first rippling explosions detonated in front of them as Willoughby, his handful of Special Forces troops and the CIDG irregulars made a mad rush for the jungle.

Susan was hanging onto the neck of the Captain as the *Phantoms* pulverized the 304th PAVN Division just long enough for them to escape.

A wall of flame and petroleum jelly ignited over the advancing PAVN.

The Montagnards ran on their skinny little legs firing their assorted mixture of M16's, captured AK-47's and CAR 15's backwards as they retreated.

Unbelievably, the Communist troops still managed to kill about 20 Montagnards during the insane dive for the relative safety of the triple canopied jungle.

"Are you alright my darling?" asked Captain Willoughby.

Monica and Susan were the first to reach the dense foliage of the jungle followed by the Green Berets.

"Oh! My dear God! Watch out!" screamed the Warrant Officer.

A solitary North Vietnamese soldier leaped in front of the two girls and Captain Willoughby as they had already penetrated about 100 yards into the undergrowth.

It was so dark in the jungle under its triple layered canopy that only fractured beams of sunlight penetrated that stinking and leech infested morass of vegetation crawling with Communist vermin.

Monica swung her 12 inch dagger across her chest. The Communist stumbled backwards in surprise, firing his AK-47. He missed.

Willoughby continued to run like a madman.

Pushing in-between the two sisters he smashed a powerful head butt into the forehead of the enemy soldier who was still off balance.

The Warrant Officer did a forward summersault and knifed the PAVN in the kidney as he fell backwards from the Captain's skull butt.

It was a quick, expertly executed maneuver which demonstrated the superlative hand to hand combat skills of the Green Berets.

It was also a credit to President John F. Kennedy who originated the initial establishment of the Green Beret Special Forces and a testament to the superlative fighting prowess of the American soldier.

"Come on men!" encouraged Captain Willoughby in fluent Vietnamese.

The marvelous little Montagnard and *Bru* tribesmen fought their way into the jungle as they saw a new flight of Navy A-1 *Skyraiders* come in to support the F-4E *Phantoms*.

The unbelievable roar of explosions on top of the *Lang Vei* base and its accompanying destruction wrought on the enemy was the only reason that Willoughby and his men had been able to slip away.

"Look at that sir!" pointed the Warrant Officer.

Captain Willoughby saw the red streak of huge artillery shells from *Camp Carroll* as they hurtled the 20 miles from east to west, landing directly on the evacuated Special Forces Camp. It was awesome in the orange-humid glow of dusk. The time was now 1834 hours.

In the forbidding and eerie darkness of the jungle eve, the survivors crawled another 2 miles to the east before hunkering down in a night harbor encampment.

Claymores, trip flares and M60's were placed in a defensive ring. Only 60 Montagnards and 13 Green Berets had survived the catastrophic battle.

Monica held Willoughby's arm as the young Susan slept with utter exhaustion next to them.

"Come! Love me one more time Frank! I am scared! I don't know if we shall live to see another sunset!"

Captain Willoughby stretched the beautiful and sensuous body of the South Vietnamese girl on the wet ground sheet that was their only comfort.

The *Captain of America* said flippantly, "You are right. Let's live for the moment. If we can't fuck the North Vietnamese at least we can still fuck each other."

As they performed their extracurricular sexual intercourse in the middle of that cursed battlefield they could hear the gentle moans and terrible whimpering cries of the wounded CIDG Montagnards.

Willoughby released his exhausted seed into the girl's womb and said as he cried with anger and bitterness, "I am sorry for losing *Lang Vei*!"

Monica held her lover's head to her ample bosom as she spoke.

"Screw that! You can't afford the luxury of a conscience on the field of battle. Let the brass in Saigon worry about that shit! We've fucked them as much as we could and we have fucked each other. All in all it turned out as best as it could.

Anyway it could not be helped because that asshole Colonel Vortex did not come and save us as he said he would.

Fuck the lot of them! Those morons in *Pentagon East* and their manic obsession with meaningless body counts!"

Willoughby said with sorrow, "Don't judge my superiors so harshly. After all they are only human. Everybody makes mistakes. Even though they have seemed to have made more than their fair share.

This war should have been won already. But we Americans are pussing-footing around fighting with one hand tied behind our backs with all these moronic *Rules of*

Engagement and this fucked *public international law* and the *laws of war*! They should keep lawyers out of the battlefield!"

The Battle for Lang Vei was over.

Conference at MACV FORWARD

At the same time that the Special Forces Camp at *Lang Vei* was being attacked General William Childs Westmoreland convened a top level meeting at the Marine Headquarters in *Da Nang* at precisely 1900 hours on the 7th February 1968.

It was attended by all the senior commanders including; Deputy COMUSMACV and now the commander of MACV Forward at *Phu Bai* and *Quang Tri*, General [Four Star] Creighton Abrams; Admiral Ulysses S. Grant Sharp Jr. who represented CinCPAC at the US 7th Fleet; Brigadier General Joseph A. McChristian of the J-2 Section; Brigadier General Phillip B. Davidson [who in 1988 would write an excellent and well researched History of both the French Indochina War (1948 to 1954) and the American involvement in Vietnam from 1959 to 1973]; Lieutenant General Robert E. Cushman; Major General Rathvon C. Tompkins [Colonel Vortex's superior], [the latter two officers having flown in with COMUSMACV from Saigon a few hours earlier after returning from *Khe Sanh* for their own meeting with the junior field commanders, Colonel David E. Lownds and Colonel Richard Vortex); Brigadier General William McBride who commanded the sensor operations; Colonel William Walker of the United States Air Force Intelligence section; Major General Norman J. Anderson, the commanding General of the 1st Marine Air Wing; Brigadier General Burl McLaughlin of the United States Air Force in charge of aerial supply by LAPES [*Low Altitude Parachute Extraction System*] and GPES [*Ground Proximity Extraction System*]; Colonel Kenneth Houghton, the G-2 Intelligence officer for III MAF; Major General John J. Tolson, the commanding General of the 1st Air Cavalry (Airmobile) Division, (who wrote an excellent study entitled, *"Airmobility 1961 -1971 Vietnam Studies"): Department of the Army: Washington D.C.* with a Foreword by Major General Verne L. Bowers, the Adjutant General of the US Army); this study being to trace the evolution of airmobility in the US Army and the integration of aircraft into the organic structure of ground forces; Major General William DePuy, the commanding General of the US 1st Infantry Division (The Big Red One); Lieutenant General Fred Weyand, the commanding General of II FFV (2nd Field Force Vietnam); Brigadier General Ellis W. Williamson, strategic planning division of MACV and General William W. Momyer, the commanding General of the United States superlative 7th Air Force.

Also in attendance was Air Marshal Nguyen Cao Ky, the Vice President of South Vietnam (still wearing his pilot's G suit with purple scarf around his neck and constantly smoking Pal Mals).

President Thieu was still enjoying his holiday with his wife and her relatives (oblivious to the catastrophic mayhem that was tearing his country apart), in their opulent bungalow protected by an entire Battalion from the 9th Infantry Division in the Mekong Delta provincial capital of *My Tho*.

When everyone was assembled COMUSMACV put his hands on his hips and screamed at the top of his voice, "This whole situation is a bloody fiasco!"

As he spoke COMUSMACV pounded his fists against the marble and gold edged table of the conference room.

His face was livid with anger and frustration.

Deputy COMUSMACV, General Creighton Abrams was so taken aback that the huge Cuban cigar in his mouth fell onto the table.

Its glowing embers singed some of the large scale maps much to the annoyance of Brigadier General Phillip B. Davidson.

"I am sick to death of the stupid and idiotic interservice bickering!" shouted General Westmoreland as he handed the Cuban cigar back to his Deputy saying, "Abe! Get rid of those fucking Communist cigars for Christ sake! Can't you smoke Jamaican cigars? They are just as good you know!"

General Abrams nervously stuck it back in his lips and puffed on it like a bullfrog.

"That is why I have created the post of Forward MACV! With my Deputy 'Abe' as its boss!

Now I want some co-operation here!" screamed General Westmoreland and then he added, scowling at Lieutenant General Cushman, "…and that means the Marines as well!"

General Cushman was not intimidated as he said, "Sir! With all due respect. I must protest at the setting up of this quasi-Corps Headquarters under General Abrams. I have been in consultation with General Chapman, the Commandant of the Marine Corps. And we are both in agreement that this step is unprecedented and cannot be conducive to the proper functioning of our Marine and Army units in the I Corps Operational Zone!"

General Westmoreland barked back, "There will be no argument General! One of the reasons that made me embark on this drastic step was the fact that your III MAF Headquarters seems to be having trouble co-ordinating all our land and air units in the I Corps Operational Zone."

Brigadier General Davidson winced at COMUSMACV's remark and looked suspiciously at Vice-President Nguyen Cao Ky.

Brigadier Davidson knew that this comment would infuriate the Marine commanders who were presently assembled.

General Cushman turned crimson with rage as his chest heaved up and down like a steam train.

"Sir!" he began, "That is simply not true! It is not accurate! The Marines are well able to handle their own units and co-ordinate the TAC air and aerial supply schedules for *Khe Sanh*, *Camp Carroll* and the other Marine fire support bases such as *Phu Bai* and *Dong Ha*."

General Abrams said angrily as he puffed on his enormous zeppelin shaped cigar, "You cannot!"

General Cushman answered, "We can so!"

"No you can't!" snapped back General Abrams.

"We can too!" interrupted Major General Tompkins.

Suddenly, much to everybody's amazement, Vice-President Nguyen Cao Ky stepped forward in-between the American generals and said, "I don't care about any of this!"

And then Ky looked to General Westmoreland, "All I want to know is when will you use nuclear weapons in the defence of *Khe Sanh*?"

COMUSMACV rolled his eyes upwards to the ceiling.

It seemed like General Westmoreland was going to take a swipe at the much smaller Ky.

Brigadier Davidson could see that the Supreme Commander's body was shaking with adrenalin.

"Not now! I don't have any time for this nonsense now Air Marshal Ky! Please!"

The Vice-President sulked and stepped back behind the bickering American generals.

Then General William Momyer asked, "What I don't understand is why there has been no relief operation in support of our troops and the irregular CIDG forces with them at *Lang Vei*?"

General Cushman waved his hands flippantly at the Air Force General, "I've explained all that before!"

General Momyer said sarcastically, "Then explain it to me again."

General Cushman grunted angrily, "It's simply too dangerous to send a relief force from *Khe Sanh*. The chance of ambush and total annihilation is very high. Besides the Communists have fielded tanks against us for the first time inside South Vietnam."

General Momyer said, "But I could have guaranteed full air support for such a mission!"

General Westmoreland added, "Anyway gentlemen. Our latest reports from *Khe Sanh* indicate that *Lang Vei* has just fallen."

Then COMUSMACV turned to the commanding General of the US 7th Air Force, "Do you think that you can increase the sortie rate for TAC missions over *Khe Sanh*? To help those boys out?"

General Momyer answered that he could and that he would implement those increased attacks immediately in cooperation with Major General Norman Anderson, the commander of the 1st Marine Air Wing.

General Westmoreland then said, "In view of the continuing pressure on *Khe Sanh* and its hill outposts as well as the fall of *Lang Vei*, I am going to reorganise our forces."

General Creighton Abrams asked, "How sir?"

COMUSMACV smiled and informed the host of senior commanders, "For starters I am going to move one Brigade of the 101st Airborne Division from Saigon to Northern I Corps."

Major General Olinto Barsanti, the commander of the 101st shifted uneasily in his chair.

"Is that alright with you Olinto?" asked Westmoreland.

Major General Barsanti looked around the conference room and nodded to the Vice-President Ky, with who he was particularly friendly.

Both General Barsanti and Vice-President Ky had had some fun times together in upper Tu Do Street in Saigon. They enjoyed the night life there and were frequent revellers at some of the more salubrious establishments providing female entertainment.

"I suppose so sir," answered Barsanti and then he asked, "But why don't you allow my whole Division to drop directly onto *Khe Sanh*!

We can then smash those fucking gooks once and for all!"

General Westmoreland thanked Barsanti for his suggestion but said nothing more about it.

Brigadier General Davidson asked COMUSMACV, "Sir? What about the 25th Tropic Lightning Division?"

General Creighton Abrams asked, "What about it Davidson?"

"Are we going to send any of its units up to Northern I Corps?" asked the chief of the J-2 section.

Lieutenant General Cushman sniggered to Major General Tompkins.

This was his chance to get back at the Army as he said facetiously, "Hell! No! The Tropic Lightning Division has been in Vietnam for 2 years and it still hasn't even secured its own Headquarters at *Cu Chi* yet! Nor cleaned out those fucking tunnels in the IRON TRIANGLE and War Zone C!"

Everybody in the conference room started to howl with laughter.

Everybody, that is, except General Westmoreland.

He did not like to have his large units rubbished in this way. And any failing of a Division in the field ultimately rests with his own responsibility and was a reflection on his own competence or rather, lack of it.

"Anyway gentlemen," began COMUSMACV, "That is enough about the 25th Tropic Lightning Division for the moment."

General Abrams said, "Now that I am in *Phu Bai* with MACV Forward what are your specific orders sir?"

General Westmoreland informed his Deputy that his mission was to make sure that *Khe Sanh* received all the air support it needed. He was also to begin detailed planning for OPERATION PEGASUS which was the relief operation for *Khe Sanh*.

Westmoreland then turned to Major General John J. Tolson.

"You're 1st Cavalry Division (Airmobile) will lead the attack to raise the siege of *Khe Sanh*."

General Tolson answered with pride, "We shall perform a first rate job for you sir! We have cashed in our horses for choppers and we know how to execute a fluid airborne response."

Westmoreland continued, "You will have the assistance of 3 ARVN Airborne Battalions.

General Abrams will coordinate the exact details and fine tune the operation with you over the coming weeks."

Brigadier General Davidson said, "There is one more thing sir. We need to put together a composite force to interdict the PAVN/Main Force VC threat against the *Da Nang* air base and also *Hue*, the imperial city on the *Perfume River*."

General Westmoreland asked, "Are your units in position yet, General Nickerson?"

General Nickerson was the commander of the magnificent 1st Marine Division which made up part of III MAF.

"Yes sir. I have 7 Battalions, 2 Artillery Regiments and the 173rd Airborne Brigade ready to go."

COMUSMACV said, "Then launch the operation to secure the approaches to *Da Nang*. There will be no *"Street Without Joy"* under my watch! National Route One will be secured properly!"

Westmoreland then looked at his watch and said, "I shall reconvene this meeting at 0700 hours tomorrow morning.

Then we shall discuss the situation at *Hue*, the imperial city.

I want to smash the PAVN forces around the Imperial City of *Hue* once and for all!"

With those words the meeting ended.

Major George Quamo [ASN:0-5307391] FOB3, 5th Special Forces Group (Airborne), 1st Special Forces Command.

And

Captain Edward Kufeldt [MCSN:0-89361] VMO-6, Marine Aircraft Group Sixteen, First Marine Aircraft Wing, United States Marine Corps

'Two Heroes of the United States of America'

Colonel Richard Vortex and Colonel David E. Lownds were in the MATU bunker at *Khe Sanh* along with Major George Quamo from FOB3 [Forward Operating Base 3].

Major George Quamo was a Green Beret officer attached to the 5th Special Forces Group, 1st Special Forces Command. He was *'hell on wheels'* and a superlative Communist killing machine well respected by his Green Beret commandos. Already highly decorated in Vietnam with the *Silver Star* on the 27th March 1963. He had, in fact, more experience in Vietnam than even Colonel Richard Vortex.

Vortex asked, "It's good to have you with us Major Quamo. I heard you have seen a lot of action in this civil war."

Major Quamo was about five feet ten inches tall and weighed a lean 185 lbs. He had a youthful appearance and was born on 10th June 1940 at Lynn, Massachusetts. He was a career Army officer.

Major Quamo answered, "You are talking about the time when I was a Captain serving as Assistant Battalion Advisor to the 3rd Battalion, 33rd Regiment, 21st Infantry Division of the Army of the Republic of Vietnam. The 27th March 1963 incident?"

Colonel Vortex asked, "Yes. I heard about that. Could you tell me what happened?"

Major Quamo continued, "It's very simple and nothing much really. Just another day on the job."

Vortex smiled, "But I would like to know anyway Major Quamo."

"If you insist Colonel. But before I start could I have some medicine please. I hurt my right femur jumping out of a CH-47 Chinook a couple of days ago."

"Of course!" interrupted Colonel Lownds.

Master Sergeant Richter asked, "What can I get for you sir?"

Major George Quamo looked at the massive frame of Richter and asked, "Could I have two glasses of cold water and seventeen Codeine tablets. Also I would like six injections of Morphine and a shot of whisky to wash it all down with."

Vortex looked at Colonel David E. Lownds in amazement and then nodded to Richter.

The Master Sergeant said, "Of course Major! I'll get on to it asap! I'll be back in a jiffy!"

"Now! The story of the 27th March 1963 sir. Very well," began Major Quamo, "On 27th March 1963 during the 21st Infantry Division Operation DUC THANG-8/42 I accompanied the lead left company which was part of the battalion task force

attacking south with our position to close and destroy the Viet Cong. The Main Force VC had been forced into a holding position by the attacking 3rd Battalion plus Division troops that were blocking as well as interdicting from the west and the south. We were forced to hold the two Viet Cong battalions plus a new and partially reorganised battalion in an attempt to draw the 3rd battalion into the area and encircle, crush, kill, annihilate and destroy it. Closing in to the area I lead my 2nd Company but we were pinned down by heavy Communist fire. I ordered a 0.30 calibre machine gun into a forward position which thus gave supporting fire for all the other manoeuvring companies of the 21st ARVN Infantry Division. However the bloody thing jammed and my crew could not render it operational again. I realised that unless I did something we and the other ARVN companies would be cut to pieces by the Viet Cong. So I moved through the heavy Communist suppressive fire and to that 0.30 calibre and remedied its malfunctioning status. We could then continue to dispatch the gooks to exactly where they belonged – to death and into hell where these Communists heathens belong. The attack order finally came but the ARVN battalion commander was too scared and did not carry out the order from divisional headquarters because of the said heavy Communist fire. So I persuaded this South Vietnamese officer to rally the 2nd Company and seeing me charge forward our gallant and meritorious South Vietnamese allies moved forward behind me as the example. The battle lasted four to five hours and we achieved a more than satisfactory outcome for Operation DUC THANG-8/42 which was recognised by the Joint Command back in Saigon at *Pentagon East*. Later I was awarded the *Silver Star* for my modest efforts in that engagement."

Colonel Vortex whistled, "I would not call it modest! Major Quamo. You did an excellent job! I heartily concur with the decision to award you that decoration of which I have a couple myself."

"Magnificent Major," was all that Colonel David E. Lownds said as he puffed on a cigar. (Not Cuban).

At that moment, Captain Mirza Baig, Captain Dabney, Lieutenant Colonel John A. Hennelly commanding the 1st Battalion, 13th Marines (Artillery) and Major Thrush (Vortex's 2-IC) came in to the MATCU [Marine Air Traffic Control Unit] or MATU bunker.

Thrush and Dabney had come in from Hill 881 South and 861/861A.

All of them had heard that Major George Quamo was going to launch a rescue operation by helicopters and a SUPERGAGGLE to the Old Lang Vei Fort to rescue the survivors of the CIDG irregular forces of Montagnards and Bru tribesmen as well as the handful of US Army Green Berets which hopefully would include Captain Frank Willoughby.

Vortex said to Major Quamo, "You had a very eventful year of 1963 in Vietnam then? I was still back at *Camp Lejeune* on an assignment there for advanced infantry training in 1963."

Major Quamo laughed, saying, "Oh! Colonel. That was just the foretaste of what I did during 1963 and 1964. I was involved in a lot more operations than just Operation DUC THANG-8/42!"

Colonel Lownds and Colonel Vortex were taken aback, Lownds asking, "Weren't you rotated back to the States at the end of 1963 after your first 12 month tour as an advisor?"

"Hell no Colonel!"

Master Sergeant Richter interrupted just as Colonel Vortex was about to ask Quamo a question.

"I have your medicine sir! The Codeine tablets, morphine and the remedial spirits," said Richter.

"Great Sergeant! You are a life saver! I am in a lot of pain. Besides I have developed arthritis in my right femur as I told you and I need constant pain killers. Especially before running into combat which I shall do in a couple of hours."

"A pleasure sir," said Richter as he carefully laid two large glasses of cold water onto the map table in the MATU bunker along with nearly twenty tablets of 30mg Codeine. As he did so he prepared the injections of morphine and stood at the ready. Injections in one hand and the glass of whisky in the other.

Vortex, Lownds, Baig, Dabney, Hennelly and Thrush watched in amazement as Major Quamo scoffed down all the Codeine in about four of five gulps of water.

Master Sergeant Richter then carefully wiped down Quamo's right arm with antiseptic and injected seven ampoules of Morphine into his blood stream.

"Now the whisky please," asked Quamo.

He took the spirits neat without ice and finished the whole half glass.

"Ah! That's much better! Thanks!"

"Jesus Christ! Quamo!" exclaimed Vortex, "Are you sure that's enough pain killers? I thought I was a Codeine junky but you take the cake!"

Everybody in the MATU bunker laughed hysterically except for Colonel Lownds who thought the whole display was totally ridiculous and that field officers like Quamo should not be taking such copious quantities of drugs before going into combat as it might slow down his judgment and reflexes.

"Now what were you asking me Colonel Lownds?"

The Colonel repeated, "You didn't ask to go back to the States after one tour?"

Major Quamo seemed in a daze, "What was that?"

"Going back after 12 months in 1963?"

"Oh? No. I didn't feel like it. I wanted to stay in Vietnam."

"Stay? Why?" asked Vortex, adding, "I thought you would be glad to get the hell out."

"I enjoy it here!" expostulated Major Quamo.

"Christ! Talk about reckless enthusiasm for duty," commented Captain Mirza Baig.

Major Quamo shook his head from side to side as if he was trying to shake his brains loose from their stem to the cervical spinal cord, his eyes were glazed over and he seemed slightly groggy as he lifted up his right leg and started to massage his thigh.

Major George Quamo then recited the rest of what happened to him in 1963 and 1964.

All the officers gathered around and listened with avid attention while Vortex whispered to Master Sergeant Richter to also go and get him a couple of tablets of Codeine.

"After that incident we, the US Advisors, were involved in organising and overseeing Operation FARM GATE. It was an Air Force mission in Vietnam under the Kennedy Administration. In the early 1960's the US Armed Forces were developing units specifically designed to counter the VC guerrilla insertion activities. The first unit I was an advisor for was the 4400th Combat Crew Training Squadron codenamed 'JUNGLE JIM'. That was later renamed the 1st Air Commando Group. This squadron specialised in supporting friendly ground forces in small brush-fire insurgent operations such as what was going on in the South Vietnamese countryside during the early 1960's. The 4400th CCTS was organised at Eglin Air Force Base and was then let loose into South Vietnam by President Kennedy. The mission was to train the VNAF in the use of older style aircraft against the Viet Cong. I was a principal advisor to Operation Farm Gate. We flew the T-28 Trojan, C-47 Dakota and B-26 Invader. It was required under public international law and the Geneva Accords that at least one South Vietnamese military person be onboard these flight missions in case we were shot down by the VC terrorists. This way we would not be in violation of the Geneva Accords. But after the Gulf of Tonkin Resolution under President Johnson this was no longer necessary and the missions were flown on the most part only by US Air Force personnel plus Army advisors such as myself. That's when we became the 1st Air Commando Squadron."

Colonel Lownds asked, "Did you prove successful in Operation Farm Gate in assisting the ARVN?"

Major Quamo answered, "It was a mixed big. But yes, we had a modicum of success in thwarting a few of the VC terrorist conspiracies in those early days."

Vortex waved his hand, "Please continue Quamo."

The Major went on, "On the 22nd November 1963 I was involved in the Battle of Hiep Hoa. About 500 FNL fighters had attacked and taken over the Hiep Hoa

Special Forces Camp. We lost 4 American MIA. I was part of the US Special Operations Forces and we were supported by South Vietnamese commandos but after fierce resistance we were overpowered by the arrival of a VC mortar unit.

Isaac Camacho was one of the four MIA. It was the first time that a Special Forces Camp [CIDG Forces Camp] had been overrun by the enemy.

I also had a hand in OP-PLAN 34A. This plan involved covert operations against the DRV [North Vietnam]. We launched naval sabotage operations and agent team insertions along the coast of North Vietnam. It was begun by the CIA in 1961 but was then transferred to the control of Military Assistance Command Vietnam. We formed the SOG [Vietnam Studies and Operation Group] primarily for Operation PARASOL and Operation SWITCHBACK.

SOG under the command of the Pentagon was a multi-service unconventional warfare group that used fast patrol boats to land agents into North Vietnam along its coast above the 17th Parallel. I was in some of those operations. It was quite exciting."

Vortex asked incredulously, "Exciting?"

Major Quamo continued, "Yes Colonel. Exciting. It gave me the opportunity to kill Communists on their home ground. I was itching to take the war into the Communist's own backyard.

When the *big red dog* is in your own backyard you have every right to shoot it. But when you jump into the enemies' backyard and shoot their dog it gives you much greater satisfaction as you know that you initiated the attack and not them. Not as now, where we simply react to what they do. We should be making them react to what we do! That is why we should launch a full scale invasion of Laos and Cambodia and North Vietnam for that matter and finish this fucked war once and for all with total victory for the American people!"

Colonel Vortex exclaimed, "I could not agree with you more! Major Quamo! That is what I have been pestering General Westmoreland to do all along. But its like talking to a brick wall!"

Major Quamo went on, "Staring in mid-1962 the US Navy started electronic surveillance operations conducted by a division of ocean going minesweepers. These were equipped with portable vans containing highly sophisticated electronic surveillance equipment. The minesweepers fuelled at a coastal village near Da Nang on the stealth. They took on intelligence from CIA operatives that the war mongering states and pariah of the imperialist Chinese and Bolshevik Soviets were clandestinely supplying the North Vietnamese terrorists with arms and equipment contrary to the Laws of Humanity. Usually between midnight and 3am in the morning the DRV would approach the minesweepers at high speed and then peel off and return to the DRV naval base from which they came. Usually a North Vietnamese naval base on a small island operating north of the 30th Parallel. The Communist gunboats made threaten-

ing manoeuvres but never actually had the courage to attack the minesweepers. You see what fucking cowards they are, the Communists. These manoeuvres were reported to CinC PAC Fleet and the Pentagon in nightly top secret cryptograph messages. Our minesweepers were defenceless should an actual attack occur. In early 1963 the minesweepers were relieved by a Division of destroyers called the DESOTO Patrols which carried out the same electronic surveillance operations against the Communist terrorist state. The North Vietnamese could not distinguish the attacks made by the gunboats and the surveillance of the minesweepers. The DESOTO patrols monitored the naval operations of the DRV and thus were able to glean some very important information on the capabilities, or lack thereof, of the Communist navy. The DRV then employed heavy gunboats and torpedo equipped frigates to monitor the minesweepers. Thus on 24th August 1964, the Gulf of Tonkin incident occurred. This was a reaction to the attack by US Special Forces on a radio transmitter on an offshore island. The USS destroyers; USS *Maddox* and USS *C Turner Joy* returned fire on the DRV vessels in response to the Communist naked aggression and terrorist activities. President Johnson then took this opportunity to pass through Congress the South East Asia Resolution or Gulf of Tonkin Resolution on 7th August 1964. In any case prior to the Gulf of Tonkin Resolution I participated in some of these clandestine raids into the naval shore installations of North Vietnam. That was very edifying for me."

Colonel Vortex exclaimed, "Wow! You have seen a lot of action haven't you?"

Colonel David E. Lownds remarked, "I am surprised Major Quamo that you don't have even more decorations."

Captain Mirza Baig asked, "What did you do in 1964?"

"Yes. What did you get up to on your second tour of Vietnam?" asked Colonel Vortex.

Major Quamo continued as everybody in the MATCU bunker could hear the PAVN shelling of the base start up again.

"I was part of the US helicopter gunship force that flew out of Vung Tau airbase during the Battle of BINH GIA which took place from 28th December 1964 to 1st January 1965. This battle took place in Phuoc Tuy Province which is now under the control of Australian forces. As a military advisor I understood that following the assassination of President Ngo Dinh Diem in 1963 the South Vietnamese government was still in turmoil. Following the coup against Diem the military situation worsened. The National Liberation Front (NLF) known as the Viet Cong gained significant ground in the countryside because the Military Revolutionary Council which then governed South Vietnam lacked direction in both policy and planning as they were too busy amongst each other trying to vie control over the reins of power. General Duong Van Minh as the Chairman of the Military Revolutionary Council

and the civilian Prime Minister, Nguyen Ngoc Tho, favoured a political solution to the insurgency rather than a course which resulted in the use of force. This was contrary to United States policy which was being groomed to smash the Communists with overwhelming firepower. Both of these men became increasingly unpopular with the Generals in Saigon who held the real power behind the scenes. On 30th January 1964 General Nguyen Khanh successfully ousted General Duong Van Minh and spent most of 1964 consolidating his own power rather than concentrating on smashing the growing NLF insurgency that was threatening to rip his country apart. On 11th October 1964 the NLF were given orders by the politburo in Hanoi to carry out a series of attacks against the South as part of the winter-spring offensive. The NLF Nam Bo which stands for Mekong Delta region established a military command or regional command/sub-command under the leadership of Tran Dinh Xu with Nguyen Hoa as the Deputy Commander and Le Van Tuong as the political commissar. Their mission was to inflict damage on the regular units of the South Vietnamese Army (ARVN). Also to destroy the strategic hamlets created by the previous regime under Ngo Dinh Diem. The NLF targeted the regions of Binh Long-Phuoc and Baria-Long Khanh along National Route 14 as the main targets for their dastardly offensive. While this was happening the Central Military Commission in Hanoi appointed General Nguyen Chi Thanh as the commander of the North Vietnamese military operations in South Vietnam along with Major Generals Le Trong Tan and Tran Do and Colonel Hoang Cam who were sent to South Vietnam to supervise the military build-up for the winter-spring offensive.

In July 1964 the 271st and 272nd Regiments of the PLAF (People's Liberation Armed Forces) began moving in to the provinces of Binh Duong, Binh Long and Phuoc Long. Various strategic hamlets were overrun such as; Xan Sang, Cam Xe, Dong Xa and Thai Kai. Between August and September 1964 the PLAF made deep thrusts into Binh Duong and Chau Thanh to apply additional pressure on the ARVN situated along National Route 14. During Phase Two of the campaign the PLAF ambushed two companies of the ARVN and five M24 armoured vehicles. These were the Chaffee light tanks and the M-113 APC's. The strategic hamlets of Binh My and Binh Co were also struck heavily. The actual Battle of Binh Gia which I was involved in started in the early hours of 28th December 1964 when elements of the PLAF 271st Regiment and the 445th Company thereof signalled their main attack on Binh Gia by attacking from the east of the village. They ran into the South Vietnamese Popular Force Militia but these 65 troops were no match for the Viet Cong. They retreated to their underground bunkers and immediately called for help. Colonel Ta Minh Kham, the Viet Cong commander established his headquarters in the village church. Here he waited for reinforcements such as recoilless rifles, mortars and heavy machine guns. The ARVN launched

helicopter assaults but Colonel Kham set up defensive fields of fire all around the village. He also set up trenches and bunkers protected by mines and barbed wire. Two Vietnamese Ranger Battalions were sent to retake Binh Gia. On the 29th December 1964 two companies from the 33rd Ranger Battalion and one from the 30th Ranger Battalion were airlifted to the west of Binh Gia by helicopters from the US 118th Aviation Company to thwart the Communist foe.

But these three companies were bushwhacked by the Viet Cong in a dastardly ambush and decimated by the rotten VC Colonel Ta Minh Kham. More ARVN Rangers were thrown against the VC pimps and the company from the 33rd ARVN Rangers attacked from the north-east but were unable to break the siege. One company was lured into a VC 'kill zone' near a coffee plantation and they were obliterated by two battalions of VC gangsters with heavy weapons and mortars. Our gallant South Vietnamese allies lost 70% dead and wounded and were forced to retreat to a nearby Catholic church. But the 30th ARVN Rangers managed to break into the village assisted by the loyal freedom loving local residents who despised the Communist pigs and marauders. The American advisor was severely wounded while the valiant local peasants recouped the weapons from the dead ARVN as well as the Communist thugs and hid them to continue the fight. At this point the 38th ARVN Ranger Battalion landed near the village unopposed by the Communists. They advanced on Binh Gia from the south. Yet after a whole day of ferocious hand to hand fighting they could not break through to the survivors in the Catholic Church. They called in suppressive mortar fire to push back the PLAF goons and drive them back to their headquarters. On the morning of the 30th December 1964 a South Vietnamese Marine Battalion was called in from the Bien Hoa base. The 1/4th Battalion was the first to arrive. I was with the 38th ARVN Battalion as an advisor. When the main body of the 1/4th Marine Battalion arrived they forced their way to the Catholic Church to link up with the besieged 30th, 33rd and 38th ARVN Ranger Battalions. The VC started to withdraw to the north-east and the 4th Marine Battalion recaptured the village of Binh Gia. I personally killed three Viet Cong terrorists in gruesome hand to hand fighting by slicing them open with my US Army issued bayonet. I always prefer to kill close-up as it gives me much greater satisfaction to see the bloodied guts of the enemy spill out in front of my feet than shoot them from a distance. I heard that you like knife combat as well Colonel Vortex."

Vortex ignored this remark but asked, "So tell me what happened then Major?"

Quamo continued as he sipped on his remedial whisky, "The VC had withdrawn during the night like slippery eels and were nowhere to be seen. But on the evening of the 30th December 1964 the PLAF returned to attack Binh Gia from the south-eastern perimeter. The local peasants caught wind of this and sounded the alarm to the valiant South Vietnamese Rangers and Marines. This Communist

murdering attack was driven back by US Air Support and helicopter gunships from the Vung Tau airbase. While the pursuit by the US choppers were in progress one aircraft from the 68th Assault helicopter company was shot down and crashed into the rubber plantation at Quang Giao which was four kilometres from Binh Gia. Unfortunately all four crew members were killed. On the 31st December the US Advisory Team which I was attached to sent four NCOs and officers led by Captain Donald G. Cook. The 4th Marine Battalion was ordered to locate the crashed helicopter and recover the bodies of the dead US service personnel. Major Nguyen Van Nho, commander of the 4th Marine Battalion, against our advice sent the 2/4th Marine Company out to reconnoitre the Quang Giao rubber plantation. But the 271st Viet Cong Regiment had assembled in that plantation for regrouping and re-supply. The 2/4th Marines found the downed helicopter and the four dead US servicemen but were immediately fired upon by the Communist Regiment. The 2/4th Marine Company was forced to pull back but the entire 4th Marine Battalion was sent out in an attempt to rescue their comrades. As they approached the Quang Giao rubber plantation they were beset by accurate PLAF artillery fire from the 271st Viet Cong Regiment which was followed by human wave attacks. The 2/4th Marine Company had to fight their way out of the plantation with bayonets and knives and the slaughter was heavy and prolonged. The batteries of our 105mm howitzers at Baria and Phuoc Tuy were out of range and could not support the 4th Marine Battalion and specifically its 2nd Company that was in desperate straits. But our US helicopters and fixed wing aircraft came in with rocket attacks and managed to assist in their exfiltration from the battlefield around the rubber plantation. The next morning on the 1st January 1965 the entire 4th ARVN Marine Battalion returned to the helicopter crash site and dug up the graves of the four dead US soldiers. A US helicopter was sent to evacuate the four dead Americans but the rest of the South Vietnamese wounded and dead had to wait for further airlift until 4pm that afternoon. Major Nguyen Van Nho decided not to wait for the evacuation choppers but instead march back to the Binh Gia village through the plantation. While they were en route three VC battalions supported by heavy artillery fire attacked the withdrawing column of Marines. The PLAF attacked from three sides and the Major and his XO [Executive Officer] were killed almost immediately. Two of the ARVN Marine companies managed to fight their way out and back to Binh Gia. I was with those two companies and the conflict was unrelenting and merciless. It was a real experience for me I can tell you. I was shooting around rubber trees in every direction. I don't know how many Communist foes I dispatched. However the third company was overrun and almost totally wiped out by the 271st Viet Cong Regiment. The fourth ARVN

company held out on a hilltop near the rubber plant and withstood withering artillery fire and human wave assaults until dawn of the 2nd January 1965 when they managed to slip away from the battlefield.

The entire operation was a bloody and unmitigated fiasco!

The 4th ARVN Marine Battalion lost 117 troops killed, 71 wounded and 13 missing out of a total force of 426 men. No less than 35 officers were killed. Also four American advisors attached to the unit, of which I was one were wounded. I suffered a 7.62mm round that pierced my brachialis muscle but it was only a flesh wound and I recovered after three weeks. On the 1st January 1965 three more ARVN Airborne Battalions arrived at Binh Gia backed up by US Air Force fighter-bombers but the VC had already slipped away.

This whole debacle indicated to MACV the growing strength and veracity of Main Force PLAF/VC forces in the Mekong Delta. This illustrated that when the PLAF were backed with heavy weapons from their masters in the North Vietnamese Main Force Army they could take on even the best ARVN units despite them being supported by US air and artillery firepower. It was a sobering development indeed. It was a wake-up call for me as well.

After the Battle of Binh Gia I knew that this war would be a long and tenacious one and that I was not going home to the United States anytime soon.

Nor did I want to.

My primary desire after Binh Gia was to kill Communists without pity or remorse, without hesitation and with the faith and the wherewithal of our righteous cause and our trust in the Lord and Jesus Christ. For I prayed every night after that and I was told that Jesus was on our side!"

Vortex asked, "Who told you?"

Major Quamo answered, "The spirits of my dead father of course! He was a very pious and religious man of high ecclesiastical station having been a Preacher in Salt Lake City for over 10 years! Whatever his spirit conveys to me in my dreams is certainly the will of God. Just as it his will that my mission be only to exterminate and rid the world of these Communist anti-Christs!"

"Oh! I see!" began Colonel Vortex, adding, "I can see that you and I are going to get on famously Major Quamo."

"Are you a religious man Colonel Vortex?"

"I am indeed. I pray that my faith will survive to see this war through to its rightful conclusion – which is victory for the God fearing and righteous heroism of our beloved United States of America – Land of the Free and Home of the Brave."

Major George Quamo put his hands together as if praying and said simply, "Amen! Amen to that!"

Captain Mirza Baig was still intrigued and asked, "After the Battle of Binh Gia what major action did you take part in while you entered your third tour of duty in Vietnam?"

Major Quamo answered, "Actually as 1965 rolled around I was already starting my fifth tour of duty in Vietnam. Consecutive tours mind you."

"Oh! Sorry," said Captain Baig.

"Yes I would like to know what you were doing in 1965?" asked Captain Dabney.

Major Quamo put his feet up on a nearby chair and went on with his most entertaining dissertation of his colourful experiences in the second Indochina War.

"Well. As I said in 1965 I took part in the first major regimental size action conducted purely by American forces in Vietnam. It was here in the I Corps Operational Zone. The whole operation was based on intelligence provided by Major General Nguyen Chanh Thi who was the commander of the ARVN in the I Corps area. Based on this INTEL Lieutenant General Lewis W. Walt concocted a plan to launch a pre-emptive strike against a Viet Cong Main Force Regiment to nullify that enemy force's threat to the vital base at *Chu Lai* which was super important to you Marine boys because of its powerful radio antenna tower that was situated there. The operation was conducted as a combined arms assault involving ground, air and naval units – our units, not the South Vietnamese. This was a big step forward in the war as previously we always acted as shepherd for the ARVN and their Local Force Militia boys. US Marines were inserted by helicopter infiltration into a designated landing zone while there was also an amphibious landing to deploy additional Marine units.

The Operation was called 'STARLITE'.

On the 18th August 1965 some 5,500 Marines from the 2nd Battalion, 4th Marines, 1st Battalion, 7th Marines, 3rd Battalion, 3rd Marines and 3rd Battalion, 7th Marines were given the go-ahead by CinCPAC Admiral Sharp to assault the Viet Cong base near Van Tuong. Also involved were the US Navy ships, USS *Galveston* (CLG-3), USS *Cabildo* (LSD-16) as well as 3rd Battalion, 12th Marines to provide artillery support along with the USS *Vernon County* (LST-1161). The USS *Vernon County* embarked the 3rd Battalion, 3rd Marines designated Battalion Landing Team under Lieutenant Colonel Joseph E. Muir at *Chu Lai* and these forces sailed south to *An Thuong* where the troops were put ashore as Phase One of Operation STARLITE.

The Viet Cong forces opposing us were the 1st VC Regiment made up of the 60th and 80th VC Battalions, the 52nd VC Company and a company of the 45th VC Weapons Battalion. The total enemy strength was approximately 1,500 men backed up by several mortar units.

The 3rd Battalion, 3rd Marines (MIKE Force) was designated as the blocking force and was deployed on the 18th August 1965 using the LVT-5s. When landed the battalion marched 4 miles to establish their blocking positions. They were

tasked with driving the Viet Cong towards the 2nd Battalion, 4th Marines who were to be lifted by helicopter to three separate landing zones. These LZ's had been previously cleared using DAISY CUTTER's dropped by the US Air Force. These LZ's were west of Van Tuong. Because we had to keep the whole thing quiet we did not inform the ARVN High Command because as you know the South Vietnamese forces are impregnated with dirty fucking Communist spies and saboteurs. Initially the US Marines met light resistance and used suppressive machine gun fire to push back probing assaults by the insidious Viet Cong criminals. The 2nd Battalion, 4th Marines spotted VC units out in the open and called in artillery fire to blast these pigs to hell. The 3rd Battalion, 12th Marines launched the artillery assault and about 90 Viet Cong were killed which put paid to their mortar capabilities. The 2nd Battalion, 4th Marines then launched a thrust towards the 60th Viet Cong Battalion who put up stiff resistance which was only overcome by the use of helicopter rocket assaults and Minigun fire. During this phase about 40 weapons were captured. The 3rd Battalion, 3rd Marines drove deep towards the ville of *An Cuong* after taking a lot of mortar fire from that village. Several companies of the 3rd Marines were then directed to *Nam Yen Dan Hill* 30 and came under an intense cross-fire. A supply column to the west was ambushed by the VC. The Communists used 37mm recoilless rifle fire to damage five LVT's and three flame tanks. I was in the attack to take *Nam Yen Dan Hill* 30. I organised the counter fire against the tanks. Heavy losses were incurred."

"Fascinating!" exclaimed Colonel Vortex, "What happened then?"

Major Quamo looked at Vortex and the others, "Well I am getting to that – if you give me a chance!"

Quamo continued, "During the counter-attack to assist the LVT's and the flame units we came under ferocious assault and lost 5 KIA and 17 WIA. It was a fucking nightmare.

We called in F-4 fighter-bombers to drop cluster bombs on the gooks. This happily caused an avalanche on the hillside which wiped out many of the Communist scum as well as counter-battery fire and mortar fire that was called in by the Marines. The fighting was so fierce that Lima Company was called in from the USS *Iwo Jima* to join the affray and to assist the extraction of the ambushed supply column. These troops were from the 3rd Battalion, 7th Marines. But the 3/7th were caught in a 'horseshoe ambush' while trying to save a downed LVT and we lost a further 4 KIA and 10 WIA. I was extremely pissed off at that! During the night we hunkered down into defensive positions and prepared for a morning assault of the VC regiment. But as usual the Viet Cong had slipped away from the encirclement intended for them though pockets of resistance continued from Communist pimps that cowered in holes and caves in the side of Hill 30 *Nam Yen Dan*.

The fighting ceased at nightfall on that following day but we tallied up more than 600 VC dead as a body count. Lieutenant General Lewis W. Walt loved his body counts. Nine Communist prisoners were taken along with 42 suspected Communist sympathisers. I asked, and was given permission to personally interrogate them by physical means of persuasion that was not entirely subtle."

Vortex was shocked, "I hope you abided my the 1949 *Geneva Convention on the Treatment of Prisoners of War* and their proper handling?"

Major Quamo asked with annoyance, "What are you sir? Some fucking lawyer or something?"

Vortex and Colonel Lownds burst out laughing as they looked at each other, Vortex answering, "In fact I am a lawyer Major Quamo."

Quamo was nonchalant, "Well yes I did abide by the 1949 Convention or whatever! – I tortured the piss out of their bowels!"

Vortex slapped him affectionately on the back, "Good! As long as you used only reasonable force to elicit the required INTEL out of them."

"I did exactly that," answered Major Quamo.

"Then you are perfectly within your rights under the Law," said Vortex.

"Excuse me Colonel, but fucked if I know? And fuck the Law that is supposed to know."

Quamo waited until everybody in the MATU bunker had stopped laughing and said, "We considered Operation STARLITE to be a great success for the American forces. We proved again that the forces of good will always overcome the forces of evil – the Communist forces.

But the PLAF in their state of delirious insanity claimed that they had won a victory and quoted some preposterous figure of 900 US WIA and KIA and 22 tanks destroyed which is total bullshit. However I admit that the 1st VC Regiment was not totally wiped out as we had planned for and hoped and they still controlled some hamlets on the peninsula.

Corporal Robert E. O'Malley and Lance Corporal Joe C. Paul received the Medal of Honour each for their valiant efforts against the forces of the anti-Christ."

Colonel Lownds remarked, "You performed admirably as usual Major Quamo."

Captain Mirza Baig interrupted, "Sirs! Its time. The rescue SUPERGAGGLE is on the airstrip waiting for you. There are twenty CH-47 Chinooks and 5 AH-1 *Cobras* in support."

Colonel Lownds asked, "Have we heard from the survivors at *Lang Vei*? Where are they?"

Captain Baig replied, "We think they are now approaching the *Old Lang Vei* Special Forces Camp to the east of the overrun *New Lang Vei* Special Forces Camp. The

Old Lang Vei Camp is about half a mile from the main camp now crawling with Communists."

Major George Quamo screamed, "Give me that AN/PRC-41 radio here!"

Master Sergeant Richter dutifully handed it to the Major who was now feeling a lot better after the powerful effects of the Codeine/Morphine surge in his bloodstream.

Vortex remarked, "Thank God that we upgraded our radios from what the poor French martyrs and gallant troops of the Colonial French Foreign Legion used at *Dien Bien Phu*! They only had the ancient and unreliable AN/PRC-10 radio sets which kept cutting out."

Colonel Lownds was on another radio telling the SUPERGAGGLE on the *Khe Sanh* airstrip outside to start their engines and get the rotor blades spinning as every minute idle on the KSCB runway was increasing the chance of PAVN mortar and artillery fire blowing the helicopters into hundreds of burning pieces of scrap metal.

"Shit!" said Captain William Dabney, "The gooks have started up from the 'Co Roc' again. Tell Corporal Robert J. Arrotta on Hill 881 South to hone in on the coordinates so we can launch a TAC air strike on those unfriendly Communist gentlemen."

A First Lieutenant immediately jumped at the orders from Captain Dabney and called up the 'Mightiest Corporal in the World.'

"Hill 881 South! I want to speak to Corporal Arrotta! Asap!"

As the First Lieutenant in the MATCU bunker called in a voice answered, "This is Lance Corporal Molimao Niuatoa speaking."

"Captain Dabney and Colonel Lownds want you to pinpoint that PAVN fire coming in. We have a SUPERGAGGLE ready to take off and we don't want them blown to hell," said the Lieutenant.

Pineapple Chunk, as Lance Corporal Niuatoa was known replied, "We are already one step ahead of you sir. Corporal Arrotta has already located the source of the fire and is right now relaying the Intel to the FSCC and MATU fire control personnel."

Colonel Vortex listened in and said, "Major Quamo. We better get going now."

Quamo was on his AN/PRC-41 and was speaking to one of the surviving Sergeants from the Green Beret Special Forces.

Everybody in the MATCU bunker listened in to what the Green Beret revealed as to his position and the survivors with him.

"I don't know where Captain Frank Willoughby is sir," he began.

"What the fuck do you mean you don't know where Willoughby is? What the bloody deuce is going on there? This whole thing is a debacle. I am charged with your exfiltration. How can I coordinate anything if your Commanding Officer has pissed off somewhere for a leak?" screamed Major Quamo.

"I don't think that he has gone for a leak sir," answered the Green Beret Sergeant who sounded quite stressed.

"What then?" asked Major Quamo.

"The last time I saw Captain Willoughby was when he gave me orders to take all the troops, the CIDG survivors, Montagnards and Bru warriors and the 5th Special Forces we have left and go to our current position. We are hunkered down inside the shambles of the *Old Lang Vei* fort, sir."

"So where did Captain Willoughby go after giving you those orders?" asked Major Quamo.

The Sergeant answered, "The last time I saw Captain Willoughby was when he finished relaying his orders to me a couple of hours ago. I asked him where he was going. I mentioned to my superior officer that he should not be leaving his main body of troops at a time like this. After all the *Lang Vei* camp had just fallen thanks to those bloody Soviet-supplied PT-76 amphibious tanks. Anyway Captain Willoughby left with his two girlfriends and told me that he had to go and see Father Poncet at his school in the *Khe Sanh* Village. He headed off with his girls and headed north towards Hill 471 as he said that he wanted to cut around and flank to the north of the village and then make a dash towards Reverend Loc's Chapel School to try to find both Father Poncet and the Reverend."

Major Quamo was furious as Colonel Vortex put his ear next to the Major's as he wanted to know everything that was being said.

"This is fucking ridiculous!" shouted Vortex.

"Girlfriends? What girlfriends! I did not authorise Captain Frank Willoughby to mess about with exotic local pussy in the middle of a battlefield! What girls are you talking about Sergeant?"

The senior NCO tried to explain, "Well with all due deference to the Captain they were not exactly girlfriends. They were more like co-combatants."

"But you said girlfriends? Did you not Sergeant?" asked Major Quamo.

"I did sir."

"So was the Captain fooling around with them or not?" asked Vortex as he joined the conversation ramming is mouth next to Quamo's in front of the AN/PRC-41 handset.

"I would not call it fooling around. The Captain was giving them on the job training and instruction sir."

"Yeah! I bet he was!" said Quamo.

"What the hell was Willoughby doing with women on the battlefield?" asked Vortex in a lather.

The Sergeant continued as he minced his words not wanting to get his CO into more trouble, "Well sir, this Monica Thang told Captain Willoughby that there were VC spies hiding out in Reverend Loc's Chapel School on the eastern side of the *Khe*

Sanh ville. His girls suggested to the Captain that on their way back to KSCB they should root out and assassinate these local VC traitors."

Major Quamo asked, "Who the fuck is Monica Thang? Is that one of Willoughby's girlfriends?"

"I bet it is," added Vortex.

"As I said sirs. It is not exactly a girlfriend in the normal meaning of that colloquial term. I would put it rather like women that Captain Willoughby picked up in the ville to assist him with Intel gathering. And besides Major Quamo, I would reconsider my distaste for them especially if you would have seen how they assisted the Special Forces last night and this morning in defending the *Lang Vei* camp against overwhelming odds. I personally saw them kill at least five or six VC and North Vietnamese troops with AK-47's and recoilless rifle fire. They are, these two girls, expert marksmen. Or should I say, markswomen."

"Are you serious?" asked Major Quamo trying to suspend his disbelief.

"I am sir! Deadly serious! Pardon the pun."

Vortex grabbed a couple of Codeine tablets brought up by Richter as he felt another headache coming on, saying, "Well that puts a whole new light on the situation doesn't it Major?"

"How Vortex?" asked Quamo.

"Well they are not merely showpieces for Willoughby's nocturnal amusement but actual combat personnel assisting the ARVN and MACV."

"Hardly that Colonel? Surely?"

"But I do think that is the case. That is what the case law on public international law provides and the Laws of War."

Major Quamo was furious, "Not again with this law claptrap Colonel. Why do you put so much weight on the Law? We are in a war here! If you haven't noticed! We're not in some frigging law school back at the *Joint Forces Staff College* in Norfolk, Virginia."

Colonel Richard Vortex became slightly agitated, "Have you ever attended the *Joint Forces Staff College* Major?"

"No. Why?"

"Well if you don't know anything about – don't rubbish it Quamo!"

Major Quamo was feeling nauseated.

"Master Sergeant Richter!" yelled Vortex.

"Yes sir!"

"Did you pack my law books before we left for *Khe Sanh* a few weeks ago?"

Master Sergeant Richter replied, "You know sir that I never leave behind the most important tools of the trade. Your M16, your Colt 0.45 pistol and your law books in that order."

"Well then go and fetch the book entitled, *"Handbook of Humanitarian Law in Armed Conflicts" by D. Fleck, Oxford University Press*. And hurry up about it."

"I know exactly where it is sir! Its next to your Milkor MGL-140 Grenade Launcher and your box of 40mm grenades! I'll be back in a second!"

"And bring me my reading spectacles and some of those yellow post-it-notes also!"

Richter nodded and ran out of the MATU/MATCU bunker as if his life depended on it.

"Are you still there Sergeant?" asked Vortex as he spoke into the handset.

The Green Beret at the *Old Lang Vei* camp was trying to make himself understood over heavy machine gun fire that could be heard through the AN/PRC-41.

"I am sir? But I have to run for cover in a minute. The PAVN are getting closer."

Vortex ordered calmly, "Just stay where you are for a few minutes more until I can refer to my international law texts about this planned assassination by Willoughby."

The Sergeant's voice sounded mesmerised, "You're what sir?"

"Never mind Sergeant! Now tell us what exactly Captain Willoughby is planning to do and why he has wandered off to this Chapel School in the ville?" asked Major Quamo.

The senior NCO explained as best as he could, "Monica Thang mentioned to Captain Willoughby that the owner of a coffee plantation in the *Khe Sanh* ville was a spy for the Communists. His name is Felix Poilane. Monica observed over the last few months as preparations were made by your 5th Special Forces Group as well as the Seabee Naval Mobile Construction Battalion 5, 10 and 53 and Unit 301 that cleared the ville for defence against the coming onslaught that Poilane was bitter that his coffee groves were being bulldozed away to the military needs of the Marines and US Army. Tanks and bulldozers as well as heavy trucks were grinding his farm roads and coffee trees to mangled piles of waste and thus destroying his business and livelihood. Willoughby ordered power saws to clear fields of fire around the ville that had a deleterious effect on his coffee crops. The Marines also had filled one of his gullies on the plantation with garbage and refuse from their terra-forming activities in the attempt to yield nothing to the unyielding Communists. For Captain Willoughby always argued to us that we must do over and above that which was necessary or expected by the Communists in the defence of freedom and democracy from their hideous tyranny, murder, intimidation and stand-over tactics. But this Felix Poilane seemed not to appreciate the efforts being made for his own constituency nor the lighter realms of those ideals for which it now appears that he had no understanding nor compunction to acknowledge. It was then explained and advised by Susan, the attractive sister of Monica Thang, that she had overheard in the dead of night when Felix Poliane was conversing with unidentified persons dressed in the black pantaloons of the VC specie. She watched and heard the unforgiveable and the unmentionable. That this

Poilane was agreeing to a pact with the Main Force VC to provide information and local coordinates which would pinpoint the locale of Marine and 5th Special Forces Group activities in return for an undertaking by the Viet Cong that once the area of *Khe Sanh* Village would be retaken by the Communists then they would allow the free enterprise arrangements of the coffee plantation to go unhindered.

It slowly came to Captain Willoughby's realisation that some type of *'arrangement'* must then have been made between Felix Poilane and the Communists. Felix, though, would be treated with respect as a leader and a man of local import as he was, his coffee plantation provided the economic mainstay for the entire area including the *Khe Sanh* Village itself.

The Miller household were good friends with Captain Frank Willoughby and Carolyn Miller mentioned on numerous occasions that she thought that Poilane was 'paying off' the Communists as well as providing the aforementioned information. In other words, Captain Willoughby admitted to me that Felix Poilane was a 'spy' for the Viet Cong.

Until this entire fiasco began and before the Hill Fights around *Khe Sanh* in April and May 1967 most of the western civilians and the French missionaries such as Reverend Loc and Father Poncet and his nuns had never caught a glimpse of enemy soldiers.

It was well known and Monica Thang told me herself that Madame Poilane was becoming increasingly worried and anxious as to the whole situation and particularly the 'accommodations' being made by her husband in return for unhindered economic activity in the event of a Communist takeover. It was, she said, a very tempting opportunity for the Viet Cong to illicit concessions via means of their traditional stand-over tactics from her husband, Felix Poilane, and that he had fallen for the bait without realising the immense gravity of his own situation and the predicament that he was unwittingly placing the entire village of *Khe Sanh*. For retribution was guaranteed. It was only a question from whence it would come – the Americans or the Communists. All would come crashing down, eventually, onto his traitorous head. Madame Poilane was so disturbed that she was planning to decamp the coffee plantation and leave her husband to the consequences of his own devices.

Monica Thang, one evening while we were having drinks in the COMMO bunker at *Lang Vei*, confessed to us all of these details and persuaded Captain Willoughby that Felix Poilane was a traitor and a spy and must therefore be killed. It appeared to me that the Captain our CO heeded her advice. He advised that if ever *Lang Vei* would fall then Felix Poilane would fall with it in a sea of retributive blood at his own hands and that of Monica Thang and her sister, Susan.

So that is where Captain Frank Willoughby is going. He is marching to the drums of war and to the tune of vengeance to ferret out and kill Felix Poilane. I am sure of it!

As sure as I know that we cannot hold out here at the *Old Lang Vei* Camp unless you come and rescue us at once!"

Both Colonel Vortex and Major George Quamo were completely flabbergasted.

There were a few moments of stunned silence before any utterance ushered forth.

"That is one hell of a story!" admonished Major Quamo.

Master Sergeant Richter scrambled in with Colonel Vortex's international law textbooks on the Laws of War. A couple of minutes passed while the Colonel referred to his notes and checked on the combat status of civilians giving aid to the enemy *de facto* forces.

"As far as I know sir, its all accurate just as I have related it to you," answered the Sergeant under siege.

"Its alright. You can do it." said Vortex seemingly to himself.

Major Quamo remarked, "Now that you put it that way Sergeant, then, yes, I understand now. It is part of the Standing Operational Orders of the 5th Special Forces Group to liquidate terrorists and traitors that give aid, sustenance or information to the Communists. It thus appears that Captain Willoughby's assassination escapade with these two women would come within combat operation parameters."

Captain Baig interjected, "Colonel Vortex has found an answer for you Major Quamo."

"What? What is that you are saying?"

Colonel Vortex grabbed the radio handset from Quamo's hands ordering, "Forget about Captain Frank Willoughby. If I know him he'll make his way back some how. We are coming to your position at the *Old Lang Vei* fort to extract you. Be ready and get your CIDG troops in order."

The Sergeant confirmed the orders and signed off.

"So what does the Law say?" asked Major Quamo.

Vortex answered, "It is sanctioned by international law and the rules of engagement."

Quamo laughed, "That's what I just told the Sergeant! Haven't you be listening Colonel?"

"I listen to everything. But the Law overrides your so-called standing orders! I follow the Law."

Major Quamo grabbed his M16 saying, "Whatever Colonel. Let's get on with it then!"

Vortex riposted, "Don't you want to know what the law says?"

Colonel David Lownds looked with amusement at Major George Quamo who answered, "Should I want to?"

Vortex said seriously, "I think you should Major."

"Do we really have time for this Colonel – I mean with all due respect sir."

Colonel Vortex was becoming agitated with the highly proficient and decorated Special Forces officer.

"There is always time for the Law. That is what we are here in Vietnam for after all. To teach the Communist gooks the meaning of the *'law'* and that they just can't run roughshod over it whenever or wherever they like. That's what separates the United States of America from every other country in the world. Every sickening tin-pot dictatorship and banana style republic that plays lip service to the law but heeds none of its precepts, doctrines nor precedents.

As a United States Marine I was taught at the *Joint Forces Staff College* at Norfolk that over and above the exigencies of military necessity nor even that of tactical expediency we must adhere at all times to the maxims of law and the *Jus Cogens*."

Major Quamo asked, scratching his head, "The what?"

"The *Jus Cogens*!"

"What the devil incarnate is that Colonel? Speak English please."

Vortex laughed, "You really are a simpleton aren't you Major. Despite all your *'he-man'* bravado and gusty wherewithal you appear sadly and shockingly mentally deficient in vital aspects of the legality of your command."

Major Quamo was dumbfounded as Colonel Vortex continued, "The *Jus Cogens* is 'A mandatory or peremptory norm of general international law accepted and recognised by the international community as a norm from which no derogation is permitted. A peremptory norm can be modified only by a later norm that has the same character. This is called *Jus Dispositivum* and under the civil law a mandatory rule of law that is not subject to the disposition of the parties, such as an absolute limitation on the legal capacity of minors below a certain age. This can also be couched in terms of the phrase a *'peremptory norm'*."

Major George Quamo loaded his M16 and said with bewilderment, "Its all double-Dutch to me Colonel. I just want to go out of here and kill Communists. I don't have the time nor the inclination to enter into a sophisticated and convoluted debate about it. You know that we have a war going on here don't you Colonel Vortex?"

Richard Vortex laughed, "But that's just my point Major Quamo! I am trying to explain to you why Captain Frank Willoughby of your 5th *Special Forces Group* is completely exonerated and pre-destined to be vindicated in whatever form or specie of action or group of mechanistic operational parameters that he chooses to undertake because of the principles of *'Jus Cogens'* that I have just explained to you. There are fifty shades of grey between black and white and the 'Law' is the personification of those varied hues of grey that sit quite comfortably between the two polar opposites of white, what is permissible, and black being what, under the crystallisation of public international law and the sources of that international code of conduct, is clearly inadmissible and wrong in the eyes of international humanitarian law. But Captain Frank

Willoughby is not privy to any wrongdoing as far as I can ascertain. Especially in this particular fact situation regarding Felix Poilane and his traitorous accommodations, shall we say, with the dreaded Viet Cong and their puppet masters the North Vietnamese rogue State of sycophantic, toady and servile mental defectives."

Major Quamo asked, "How can that then possibly be the case? As you say, fitting within the fifty shades of permissible grey that the Law provides for?"

Colonel Vortex loaded up his M60 machine gun as Master Sergeant Richter made ready with his M79 grenade launcher and rallied up men from both the 9th Marine Regiment and the 26th Marine Regiment to board the waiting SUPERGAGGLE of helicopters on the *Khe Sanh* airstrip assembled near the 'Ponderosa' and the helicopter revetments.

"It is really quite simple Major. The answer to your question is explained by *Article 51* of the United Nations Charter."

"Never heard of it Colonel," said the Major impatiently.

"Well if you give me a chance I am going to explain it to you now!"

Vortex continued, "A sovereign State is entitled to defend itself. To protect its territorial integrity. The right of self-preservation in other words. This is an absolute right and *ipso facto* the right of the United States to its territorial sovereignty goes hand-in-hand with our right to defend and to honour South Vietnam's territorial sovereignty. For it is the State of South Vietnam that has asked us to protect its sovereignty which relates to the territory of one to the other, so that by necessary implication anything that threatens the territorial sanctity of South Vietnam automatically threatens that of the United States and comes therefore under the auspices of *Article 51* of the UN Charter protection. This right of self-defence on the international level is the fabric of a sovereign States existence lying at the foundation of all the other rights of States. Subject as it is, only to rare instances of the Resolutions of the Security Council of the United Nations.

Article 51 provides; *'Nothing in the present Charter shall impair the inherent right of individual or collective self-defence if an armed attack occurs against a Member of the United Nations."*

South Vietnam being at the relevant time in 1959 upon its prior creation a member of the United Nations, the United States, having taken the initiative to protect this fledgling State now invokes *Article 51* to provide an umbrella of 'collective self-defence' against the aggressor State being, in this case, North Vietnam. Also I might add, Major, concomitant with *Article 51's* right to self-defence is *Article 2(4)*'s prohibition against 'the threat or use of force against the territorial integrity or political independence of any State.'

The *1933 Montevideo Convention on the Rights and Duties of States* provides that 'no State or States has the right to intervene (in this case North Vietnam) in the internal or external affairs of another (South Vietnam).

In the United Nations *General Assembly Resolution 2131* Part XX, Article 21 on 21st December 1965 it was decided [with only one abstaining vote] that it was to be condemned on the part of any member nation to use 'armed intervention and all other forms of interference or attempted threats against the personality of the State or against its political, economic and cultural elements.'

This is what Robert Komer and the PHOENIX Program and the *Strategic Hamlet Program* are trying to achieve for South Vietnam without which this friendly government could not withstand the internal implosive forces that threaten to render it out of existence. These measures, such as the PHOENIX Program fall squarely within the sanctioned limits of the operation of *Article 51* and *Article 2(4)* of the United Nations Charter, being as they are and as they were designed by our government in Washington D.C. to be measures conducive to the implementation of the Doctrine of 'collective self-defence'.

The internal affairs of South Vietnam are its own domain. North Vietnam has no standing under the United Nations Charter nor under public international law to unilaterally interfere with the sovereign affairs of our client, South Vietnam.

Its aggressive actions in supporting, nurturing, feeding, indoctrinating, sustaining, motivating, propelling, coercing, handling, transporting and clandestinely infiltrating the territory of South Vietnam with aggressor troops and armaments of its own foreign army the PAVN [so-called People's Army of Vietnam] is tantamount to one of the most flagrant breaches of the collective international peace and security of the world since the 1956 invasion of the State of Hungary by the aggressor Communist armies of the Bolshevik gangsters and the Soviet Supreme Command that have inherited the mantle of despotism from Lenin and the Bolshevik precursor State that overthrew the Kerensky Government in 1917 and murdered the Tsar (Nicholas II & all his family at Yekaterinburg in the Ural Soviet).

These crimes cannot and will not be allowed to go unpunished.

It is the right and the duty of the United States of America under the *'Law'* to come to the aid of South Vietnam when that friendly State invokes the 'Doctrine of Collective self-defence.'

We, the United States have the power and we have the moral obligation, the duty, to defend weaker States with free and democratic institutions such as South Vietnam from mongrel, lawless, aggressor and sadistic States such as North Vietnam.

The general prohibition against the intervention by one State in the internal or external affairs of another does not apply to the situation here in South Vietnam. There are many exceptions to the rule of law laid down in *Article 2(4)* of the United Nations Charter. South Vietnam and the United States assistance to our client State falls within one of these exceptions in so far as it is not illegal to intervene to send armed forces into a foreign State in order to support that government when, in this

case, the South Vietnamese government has asked and requested assistance in that form. In other words the necessary aid to combat a local and internal insurgency within its borders exemplified by the activities of the PLAF and the Main Force Viet Cong that are the puppets of their North Vietnamese masters and the cronies in the Communist cabal in Hanoi. There is thus overwhelming legal justification for the collective self-defence actions of the United States and its Allies, such as Australia, New Zealand, South Korea and Thailand to name but a few in the aid both military and economic sent to President Thieu's government. I would refer you, Major Quamo, to the Department of State Bulletin No:54 Vol 56 entitled: 'Vietnam and the International Law of Self-Defence' as well as the excellent work about to be released for publication by Mr Falk entitled: *'The Vietnam War and International Law' Volume 1*.

It is clear that the *Corfu Channel* case which can be found in the 1949 Edition of I.C.J. Reports 4, page 35 is clearly wrong. In that case the International Court of Justice [as it was then known] held that the alleged right of intervention was a manifestation of a policy of force and the excuse to use force, such as has, in the past, given rise to most serious abuses and such as cannot, whatever be the current defects in international organization and the community of States, find a place in international law and thus the *Jus Cogens*. In my opinion that finding in the Corfu Channel matter of 1949 is clearly wrong and the reasoning unsound. There is always a ground for intervention that is covered by both *Article 51* and *Article 2(4)* in the situation of humanitarian reasons as we have here in South Vietnam.

International Law is now moving towards the doctrine of justifiable pre-emptive military action which is necessary when the usual avenues of addressing rogue States such as North Vietnam and its masters, the CHICOMS and the Bolshevik Imperialists give rise to unacceptable instances of aggravated interference and military lawlessness in the affairs of free and democratic peoples such as the South Vietnamese. When recourse to international diplomacy proves to be futile the United States of America has the inherent right and the moral obligation that it has inherited from the peace-loving members of the international community to use and to exercise pre-emptive military intervention when, how and where it sees fit in consultation with other responsible States in the World Order and the General Assembly of States in the United Nations. The right of self-defence embodied in *Article 51* extrapolates itself to the use of this pre-emptive intervention both economically and militarily even if the time and place of the rogue States attacks or aggravating actions are as yet unknown nor specified with accurate intelligence. When the consequences of allowing such actions by rogue States would prove so de-stabilising, so destructive and so dangerous as to upset the balance of peaceful nations then the pre-emptive use of force is fully legitimate. This is the duty of the United States in South Vietnam. The pre-emptive use of force that I speak of is the dismantling and removal of the North Vietnamese

threat by direct ground, air and naval actions inside the borders of that country – it is fully justified and the international laws of war under the present circumstances would condone such operations. The procedure for such action will always be deliberate to the nth degree, rational and fully weighing the consequences of such action. The reasons for the actions will be unequivocal, clear and obvious, the force used measured and just and similarly for a just cause as we have here in South Vietnam.

Thus in light of all of the above the assassination by Captain Frank Willoughby of this Communist traitor, Felix Poilane, is in terms of this pre-emptive action, fully justified."

Major George Quamo shook his head even though he was quite impressed with Colonel Vortex's explanations of a topic he knew very little about.

"If you are willing to take personal responsibility for Captain Frank C. Willoughby's actions after the fall of *Lang Vei* then I have nothing to say about the actions of my officer," began Major Quamo, "I don't understand most of what you said Colonel but I can at least comprehend that the liquidation of traitors, 5th Columnists and saboteurs falls within Green Beret Standing Orders and thus Captain Willoughby's command parameters."

Captain Mirza Baig was quite agitated as he said to the two field grade officers, "Sirs! Please! The SUPERGAGGLE can't wait any longer on the KSCB runway. The PAVN shells are going to make a mess of them if they just sit there like 'ducks-in-thunder' outside of their revetments."

Colonel Vortex grabbed his gear, M16 and stuffed six 40mm Grenades into his webbing, ordering, "Let's get on with it then Major! Richter you're with me."

The 40mm Grenade that was Vortex's preferred choice was a high velocity weapon that could either be launched by hand or by a grenade launcher. There were two types of 40mm grenade. The 40mm by 46mm grenade was a low velocity round used in hand held launchers and the 40mm by 53mm grenade was a high velocity round. The cartridges were not inter-changeable. These grenades used the high-low propulsion system. Colonel Vortex preferred to use the multi-shot grenade launcher designated M32 MGL but there were also other types such as; M79, M203 and M320 grenade launcher. Colonel Vortex's command jeep had the special tripod mounted Mk 19 grenade launcher with the automatic firing option. Vortex also packed with him the M47 'Striker' 40mm grenade launcher which was in fact a grenade machine gun or designated as (GMG's) made by the master craftsmanship of the equally supreme Armed Forces in the World next to the United States Army which was of course the German Army [designated in World War 2 as the Wehrmacht]. The Germans had a genius for almost everything, from cars to space rockets such as the Saturn V designed and built by Werner Von Braun who was the German father of space flight and who had worked on the V-1 and the V-2 project for the German government in World War 2,

to electronic equipment and scientific medical instruments. Whatever you wanted the supreme intelligence of the German citizen and/or scientists to build for you – they could build it and they built it with accuracy, precision and durability. The German Nation was second-to-none in brilliance and ingenuity.

The 40mm by 53mm grenade machine gun was also mounted on Vortex's command and control helicopter which was the Hughes OH-6A *Cayuse Loach* (Light Observation) helicopter which had a maximum speed of 150mph with a weight of 2,700 lbs and a range of 380 miles. Its usual armament was a 7.62mm Minigun mounted on the portside and one 40mm (GMG) mounted starboard. But Colonel Richard Vortex was itching to eviscerate as many Communists as he could on this mission and he had ordered Captain Mirza Baig to fit especially for him, two 7.62mm Miniguns on both sides plus two GMG's also on starboard and portside to give that extra bit of firepower.

"Have you launched the five DAISYCUTTER's onto the *Lang Vei* Base?" asked Colonel Vortex to Colonel David E. Lownds.

Colonel Lownds was a gasp, "But that would destroy whatever was left of the infrastructure of the camp?"

Vortex screamed, "I don't give a fucking hoot-and-hell rat's fucking ass! Drop them now Lownds!"

"Will do," answered Colonel David Lownds as he turned to his 2-IC, Lieutenant Colonel James B. Wilkinson, the commander of the 1st Battalion, 26th Marine Regiment saying, "See to it!"

"Yes sir."

Then the light Colonel asked, "What about the SPOOKY gunships?"

Colonel Vortex interjected, "Coordinate the flechette attack and Minigun hose down of the two SPOOKY's so that they finish their attack run just before Major Quamo and our MIKE Force hit the dirt at the *Old Lang Vei* Camp."

Colonel Lownds asked, "Do you realise Vortex that if you drop DAISYCUTTER's onto *Lang Vei* it might impact on the survivors now heading for the *Old Lang Vei* camp which is barely half a mile to the east?"

Major Quamo answered for Vortex, "It's a chance that we shall have to take – I am afraid Colonel Lownds. Our primary mission is to annihilate the Communists. The second priority is to rescue the 5th Special Forces Group and CIDG survivors."

"Well that is as it is then. Be it on your heads. I am not taking responsibility for any 'friendly fire' incidents!"

Colonel Vortex scoffed and waved his hands at Colonel Lownds in a gesture of exasperation and with that the MIKE Force commanders and their NCO's scrambled out of the MATU/MATCU bunker to the KSCB airstrip and the waiting SUPER-GAGGLE whose rotor blades were spinning at pre-launch maximum rpm.

It was 5 air miles from the 'Ponderosa' and the *Khe Sanh* airstrip to the *Lang Vei* camp and slightly less to the *Old Lang Vei* base half a mile to the east. The SUPERGAGGLE travelling at the speed of the slowest helicopter which was the CH-47 Chinook double rotor aircraft being approximately 150mph (even though the maximum speed of this aircraft was 189mph) took just over two minutes.

The CH-47 Chinook used to rescue the survivors of the 5th Special Forces Group and the *Bru* and *Hre* Tribesmen of the CIDG forces was properly designated as the Boeing-Vertol CH-47A Chinook Medium Transport helicopter. Its weight was 33,000lbs and it had an operational range of 115 miles. The standard armament was two 40mm grenade launchers; 2.75 inch rockets; two 20mm cannon and five 0.50 calibre machine guns which were usually locally fitted inside South Vietnam after transportation by the US Navy from the United States. The carrying capacity of the CH-47A was a maximum of 20 to 25 men and there were 20 CH-47A's in Vortex's SUPERGAGGLE. The Colonel thus had a capacity to rescue about 500 troops which were more than the number of actual survivors. The unused Chinooks would be used along with the five AH-1 *Cobra's* to lay down a heavy suppressive fire on the Communists to keep them at bay while the exfiltration was in progress.

The whole concept of this awesome air mobility originated with the previous Secretary of Defence of the United States of America, Robert McNamara.

Mr McNamara, who had an intellect as sharp as an IBM [International Business Machines Corporation] super-computer and who used to be President of the Ford Motor Company, had expressed dissatisfaction with the US Army's apparent inability to think beyond the 'square'. As a result the Secretary of Defence as he then was under President John F. Kennedy, had set up the *'Army Tactical Mobility Requirements Board'* under Lieutenant General Hamilton Howze. The function of the Board was to examine with a minutiae of detail the full range of military capability and logistical enhancements that would arise from tactical air mobility brought about by the advent of the modern helicopter.

The Korean War from 1950 to 1953 had seen the first use of limited helicopter capacities mainly in evacuating the wounded. But it was the Vietnam War and the exigencies that this conflict brought to bear that necessitated a revolution in doctrinal thinking, command and control on both the tactical and the strategic level. Never before in the history of human conflict had one army being the United States Army in Vietnam possessed such an enormous arsenal and wherewithal of lethal firepower. The problem for Robert McNamara was how to effectively deliver that firepower to crush the criminal Communists and their war mongering lackeys.

The solution to this dilemma was the advent of 'Air Mobility' first tried and tested in Vietnam from 1959 to 1973. The result was the use of one heli-borne formation or SUPERGAGGLE that could at a speed determined by its slowest craft deliver

effectively and simultaneously an entire Army formation into the field of battle within a matter of hours or even less. The Howze Board recommended that a unit be created which was designated the 11th Air Assault Division (Test) under the command of Brigadier General Harry W.O. Kinnard.

This formation was the origin of the superlative and magnificent freedom fighters in Vietnam against Communist tyranny and wanton aggression that became the famous 1st Cavalry Division (Airmobile) which would later be commanded by General John J. Tolson.

Major General Tolson would enunciate the lessons learned in Vietnam with his own thesis published by the Army entitled; *"Air Mobility & Vietnam Studies"* or *"Air Mobility 1961 -1971 Vietnam Studies":* Department of the Army: Washington D.C.

As the SUPERGAGGLE approached the *Old Lang Vei* base camp they passed over *Khe Sanh* Village on National Route 9 which was a fancy name for a dirt track strewn with pot holes, mud slides and the debris of war.

"Look that's Reverend Loc's Chapel School! And over there. That's the Miller's house and Howard Johnson's house," said Colonel Vortex as he manned the GMG machine grenade launcher and pumped round after round of high velocity 40mm grenades into the ville.

Major Quamo asked above the din of the rotor blades of the OH-6A *Cayuse Loach* they were travelling in, "Are you sure that all friendly personnel have been evacuated from the ville? You sure are reaping an avalanche of carnage on top of those schools and residential huts?"

Colonel Vortex answered, "The place is crawling with Communists and VC rats! We are going to have to dig those rats out of their stinking holes and cut them apart like we were in a high school biology class with specimens."

Master Sergeant Richter laughed as he sat beside the Colonel and Major Quamo on his helmet so that his ass would not be blown off by a stray 7.62mm round from the assassins below.

Richter screamed, "We are coming up on the *Old Lang Vei* base now sirs! What are your orders?"

Colonel Vortex spoke through the microphone which was patched in to the helicopter pilots of the other 24 aircraft of the SUPERGAGGLE. He gave orders for eight Chinooks to circle anti-clockwise the perimeter of the *Old Lang Vei* camp while the other 12 CH-47A's would slowly descend for exfiltration. He ordered the supporting five AH-1 *Cobra's* to do the same but to circumvent the area in a wider locus and with a larger diameter field of fire but in a clock-wise direction. This bi-rotational field of fire would create a lethal cross-fire on the Communists and cut them to bloody pieces.

"There are the two SPOOKY's!" yelled Master Sergeant Richter, adding, "Looks like they just finished their attack sortie."

"Good!" said Colonel Richard Vortex, "Let's get in there and kick some fucking, putrid Communist backsides! Those disagreeable little monkeys as they are."

Major Quamo laughed as he locked and loaded his special weapon. It was the *H & K UMP 0.45 Submachine Gun* arguably the most powerful submachine gun in the world.

The *H & K UMP* or Universal Machine Pistol is a very high velocity and high impact submachine gun made in Germany. The UMP is chambered for larger cartridges than other submachine guns to provide more stopping power against unarmoured targets such as Communist infantrymen. It is not standard issue for US forces in Vietnam but Major George Quamo managed to purchase a fully operational unit from a German colleague of his who is currently serving in the French Foreign Legion as a Captain and who was a veteran of *Dien Bien Phu* from 13th March to 7th May 1954 during the valiant and heroic defence of that base by the honoured French Colonial Forces of the *French Union*.

"Where on earth did you get that weapon?" asked Colonel Vortex incredulously as he fired a full five 40mm grenades into Monsieur Sinard's village house as they whizzed past the *Khe Sanh* ville blowing at least three PAVN troops into a bloody shambles of splintered bone and mangled, blood washed flesh.

"I won't tell you Colonel. Sorry. But if you like I can get you one if you like it," answered Major Quamo as he fired into the hot LZ (Landing Zone) near the *Old Lang Vei* base.

The force of the *H & K UMP* rounds were devastating as they shredded the jungle foliage all around them.

"Yes please Major. Much obliged," answered Colonel Vortex.

The MIKE Force de-planned from the CH-47A Chinooks and immediately took up a defensive circle around the wreckage of what was left of *Old Lang Vei*.

It was now mid-afternoon on the 7th February 1968.

The *Khe Sanh* siege was in its bloody and heroic 18th day.

Just then, as Major Quamo and Colonel Vortex hit the ground running after having jumped six feet from the moving *Cayuse Loach* a UH-1E helicopter from *Khe Sanh* landed next to the CH-47A's.

Captain Edward Kufeldt of the United States Marine Observation Squadron SIX [VMO-6] being part of Marine Aircraft Group Sixteen, First Marine Aircraft Wing jumped out and ran up to the Colonel's eagles that he saw on Vortex's collars.

"How do you wish me to assist sir?" asked Captain Edward Kufeldt.

Vortex looked the Captain up and down, smiling as he did so and said, "Glad to have you with us Captain. You can help round up the CIDG survivors. I am going to talk to the ranking Green Beret here if I can find him."

"Yes sir," replied Captain Kufeldt.

Colonel Vortex and Major Quamo ran to the centre of *Old Lang Vei* where they saw a group of US Army Special Forces troops in a sorry state of exhaustion. Most of the commandos were smeared with blood and grime and most of them were wounded.

Without having to say anything Lieutenant Longgrear ran up to Colonel Vortex saying, "Thank God you have come at last sir! We are almost finished. The gooks attacked with PT-76 tanks! We lost most of our forces either killed or wounded."

"I know all of that Lieutenant!" answered Vortex as 152mm shells pounded the jungle surrounds of their LZ from the 'Co Roc' mountain just over the border in Laos.

"But I am not going to let anymore of your men nor the CIDG forces perish! Not on my watch! You understand that Lieutenant?"

Lieutenant Longgrear barked back, "Yes sir! Your orders sir?"

Major Quamo took the Lieutenant by the arm and screamed into his ear to make himself heard over the din of PAVN mortar and artillery fire.

"Get your survivors into the choppers in groups of ten at a time."

Lieutenant Longgrear said, "But we have only 11 wounded commandos left and the three of us left," he pointed to Sergeant Phillips and Sergeant Early and SP5 Fragos.

"Damn it then! Get whoever you have in to the choppers!"

Lieutenant Longgrear answered in the affirmative and shepherded his motley band of wounded and bedraggled commandos into the machines on the LZ.

Colonel Vortex felt a mortar round screeching past his head from the PAVN held jungle around them.

"Christ!" he shouted to Major Quamo, "We are surrounded."

Just then a mortar round hit the tailfin of one of the CH-47 Chinooks and the back half of the aircraft burst into flames. The troops inside threw themselves out as the Chinook started to spin on the ground and was threatening to career into another CH-47 landed next to it.

Master Sergeant Richter ran up as he fired his M16 in a rampage into the Communist positions from where the incoming fire was originating.

"Sirs! Bad news I am afraid."

"What is it Sergeant?" asked Major Quamo.

"Not all the CIDG survivors are here sir!"

"What do you mean Richter?" asked Colonel Vortex.

Richter explained, "This *Hre* CIDG mercenary has just informed me that more than half of the *Bru* and *Hre* Montagnards are pinned down about 200 yards from here in a gulley and are surrounded by what appears to be a battalion strength force of PAVN. They can't get to us here at the LZ."

Major Quamo screamed, "Then we'll have to go and extract them the hell out!"

The Major looked at Colonel Vortex in a state of extreme agitation.

Vortex threw down a couple of empty 40mm grenade canisters in a steaming fury, "Fuck it! To hell with it! I am going to smash these VC bastards!"

"The only thing to do is to divide the MIKE Force in half sir. If you are agreeable. I'll take about 80 men and head towards the CIDG cut off. You stay here with the rest of the troops and hold the LZ till I get back."

Vortex pondered only for a few seconds as he looked about as men were running and weaving in all directions under withering small arms and mortar fire from the Communists.

"Yes. It's the only thing to do."

Major Quamo gathered two platoons of the MIKE Force and headed to the north-west away from *Old Lang Vei*.

Colonel Vortex, Master Sergeant Richter and Captain Kufeldt gathered their group of survivors and saw six of the CH-47A's lift off and head back towards *Khe Sanh* fully loaded with the CIDG men and the 11 wounded Green Berets.

Suddenly the green uniforms and pith helmets of the PAVN could be seen by the hundreds emerging from all around their perimeter at the *Old Lang Vei* camp as Major Quamo and his half of the MIKE Force had already disappeared into the jungle fighting their way through to the remaining troops that had been cut off.

"Looks like we are in for one hell of a fight!" exclaimed Captain Kufeldt.

"They can come Captain and we shall be ready for them!" answered Colonel Vortex.

Master Sergeant Richter gathered fifty of the MIKE Force and followed Colonel Vortex to the perimeter of *Old Lang Vei*.

"We are going to attack!" ordered Vortex.

Captain Kufeldt was ordered to lift off with two more CH-47A's while the remaining 12 kept circling overhead laying down a heavy suppressive fire.

The battle to rescue the CIDG forces was in full gear.

Vortex ran into the jungle followed by Richter firing his GMG into the tree line like a man gone berserk.

He saw about twenty or thirty PAVN through the foliage and threw himself onto his belly firing the 40mm grenades. Body parts were flying everywhere as the fire and mortar explosions ripped the jungle apart. Master Sergeant Richter and his men threw themselves into battle trying to support their commanding officer.

At once Vortex was set upon by at least a dozen VC/PAVN troops after having expended his last rounds of 40mm ordnance.

"Damn it I'm out!" screamed Vortex to his men.

One large Communist trooper came out of the stinking and putrid jungle morass firing his AK-47 as he went.

"Watch out sir!" screamed Richter.

But the Colonel, spying from his superb peripheral vision could see the enemy approaching. Taking out his 18 inch dagger of Marine honour he spat at the PAVN NCO who was almost as tall as him, "Come on then! You rat fucking Communist pimping bastard!"

The North Vietnamese trooper seemed to understand English as his face turned crimson over his yellow skin with unadulterated fury.

He charged Colonel Vortex with his bayonet gleaming from the end of his AK-47.

"Give me all you've got – you cunt-sucking Ho Chi Minh dog!" yelled Vortex.

As the North Vietnamese soldier from the 304th PAVN Division lunged forward with bayonet streaking through the air, Vortex easily side-stepped the lunge with the swift elegance of a panther. As the Communist stumbled past the Colonel slashed out with his dagger across the back of the enemy's neck causing blood to spurt in a stream from a cut that was about one quarter of an inch thick.

This only seemed to enrage the soldier even further as he swung around one hundred and eighty degrees on the balls of his feet to try another stabbing lunge at Vortex with his bayonet.

"Not so tough now are you? Without your PT-76 tanks you insidious and pernicious malcontent!" screamed Vortex.

Master Sergeant Richter was a few yards away firing with ten more of the MIKE Force into the advancing Communists.

As the PAVN trooper fired a clip of 7.62mm bullets in the Colonel's direction Vortex could feel the turbulence in the air as the ordnance narrowly missed the left side of his body. Side-swiping the Communist with his dagger the Colonel cut open the carotid artery and then fell to his knees jamming his knife into the enemies' kidneys, spleen and then one final thrust between the septum of his testicles. As the Communist shrieked Vortex tore upwards from the groin splitting open the man's ribcage causing his intestines to leak out over his Marine uniform discolouring his camouflage design.

At that instant Master Sergeant Richter appeared from behind and cleaved open the NVA trooper's head with a trench spade and then fired a full clip of his M16 rounds into the back of his head blowing it apart.

Vortex screamed, "Let's get these men forward to Major Quamo's group!"

"Yes sir!" answered Richter.

As Vortex and Richter left Captain Kufeldt, who was now back in the air and flying towards KSCB with some of the CIDG survivors and the 11 wounded Green Berets, a group of about 20 Marines remained at the LZ to supervise any more stragglers that would make their way back from *Lang Vei* to the *Old Lang Vei* camp running, as they had to at that time, a ferocious gauntlet of fire from both incoming PAVN

mortar fire now coming from *Lang Vei* itself as the Communists had all but overrun the base except for the emergency medical bunker as well as AK-47 and small arms fire. The PAVN also rained down upon the *Old Lang Vei* base and the LZ a heavy dose of artillery fire from the D74 122mm howitzers that had a range of 24,000 metres. Most of this fire was coming from the 'Co Roc' mountain inside the Laotian border.

The PAVN also used the triple-mounted DKB single-tube rocket launcher which could be barrage fired from a simple bamboo tripod. These DKB rockets could be set up quickly and the NVA troopers could fire them and quickly depart the area without the need to carry any excess equipment.

Colonel Vortex ordered to Master Sergeant Richter, "Tell the men to slowly withdraw and disengage from the north and the north-east away from *Old Lang Vei* and head towards Major Quamo's position to our west. He's not far away – just a few hundred yards. I don't know what's happening over there."

Richter answered, "Your intentions sir, are to aid in the extraction by Major Quamo of the other half of the survivors?"

The Colonel answered, "That's right."

Everyone in Colonel Vortex's group had taken cover and were firing in what seemed like multiple directions. It was hard to tell exactly what the axis of attack of the PAVN was as the jungle around the MIKE Force was buzzing with bullets and the wet jungle earth spewing upwards with constant mortar explosions.

Colonel Vortex yelled over the din to Lieutenant Longgrear, "I thought you were supposed to have been on one of those evacuation choppers?"

"I was," began the Special Forces Lieutenant, "…but my wounds are only slight. I thought it would be better to stay at the LZ and assist with getting out the rest of the CIDG."

"Good man!" said Vortex.

Slowly but inexorably Vortex's group of about 30 Marines fought their way in a retrograde motion to the west where they thought Major George Quamo's portion of the MIKE Force was situated.

Colonel Vortex had no idea how many of the remaining CIDG would link up with the Major.

Suddenly a figure came running from the direction of the northern perimeter concertina wire of the overrun *Lang Vei* base that lay approximately to the south-west about half a mile away.

"Hold your fire!" screamed Master Sergeant Richter.

Vortex blew the head off two PAVN troopers who had instantaneously emerged from out of nowhere through a clearing in the jungle foliage using his M79 grenade launcher that was resupplied to him by one of the Staff Sergeants in his MIKE Force.

Brain matter and a shower of blood coursed through the air.

Three of his Marines hosed down a further four Communists that had set up a machine gun nest about 30 yards away.

"Christ!" screamed Vortex, "Where did you come from?"

The figure was that of Lieutenant Todd who was covered in mud, blood and dust.

"I must be one of the last to leave the *Lang Vei* base sir!" began Lieutenant Todd.

Vortex asked as they all dived for cover as a 152mm Communist shell came screeching overhead from the west. The explosion seconds later made the earth shake under their bellies.

"What happened Lieutenant? How the hell did you get out?" asked Vortex as he lifted up his M16 and fired backwards over his head as he spoke in the general direction of the PAVN onslaught.

Master Sergeant Richter asked the Lieutenant, "Have you seen Captain Frank Willoughby?"

Lieutenant Todd replied, "The last time I saw the Captain was in the COMMO bunker and he was wounded quite badly. He was still mobile though. I think that he gathered what was left of our boys and some of the CIDG and made it out through the northern concertina wire."

Vortex asked, "Do you know where he went?"

Lieutenant Todd said surprised, "Isn't he here?"

"No!" answered Vortex.

"Are there any troops left at *Lang Vei*?" asked Richter.

Lieutenant Todd explained, "I was in the medical bunker. I could hear firing outside and I did not know if anyone was left alive in the base perimeter or if a defence was still being mounted. I decided to make a run for it and check out the Operations Centre. As I left the medical bunker I came under a hail of automatic weapons fire. I also saw at least six or seven knocked out PT-76 tanks. Bodies were strewn all around – ours and theirs. When I got to the Operations centre I found Sergeant Moreland badly injured and almost dead, buried under a pile of rubble. I tried to resuscitate him. It looks like a 152mm shell had made a direct impact on the roof of the bunker. I made my way out but I could not carry Sergeant Moreland with me. I made my way through the northern concertina wire and as I went I avoided the land mines that we had placed all around the base. I knew exactly where each one was. Now I could see the CH-47's coming in and I made my way here. Captain Willoughby, the last I saw him, said he was going to evacuate all of the men. I only arrived at *Lang Vei* from Da Nang on the 5th February. My job was to fix the base defences that had been torn apart by the preliminary PAVN mortar and artillery barrage. I saw the first of the PT-76 tanks as I was searching for grenades in the emergency medical bunker. The bloody thing stopped right in front of the entrance to the bunker and fired at point blank range. As I fired back I saw a second PT-76 tank following up behind with at least a hundred NVA all attacking and taking

cover behind the armoured vehicle. I was lucky and only suffered a few flesh wounds. I am an engineer officer you know Colonel. I was ordered into *Lang Vei* to rebuild the base and now its totally destroyed. I am just sorry I could not bring Sergeant Moreland out with me!"

Colonel Vortex nodded as he gave orders to his men to continue the sweep west towards Major Quamo and his group from the MIKE Force.

"If you ask me sir! The whole thing is an unmitigated fiasco!"

Vortex rebuffed, "Nobody's asking you Lieutenant Todd. But you did well to get yourself out."

Lieutenant Todd added, "I know that all these air strikes were called in by Colonel Schungel."

Vortex had heard of this officer asking, "Where is he?"

Todd answered, "He should also be here at the *Old Lang Vei* base. Have you seen him?"

Vortex turned to Richter, "Have you seen Colonel Schungel?"

The Master Sergeant looked around the force with them. Each man was running, then diving to the ground, firing his M16 or M79 grenade launcher, then squirming on his belly in the mud, standing up again, running a few more yards and then hitting the dirt again to repeat the process. Colonel Vortex's small portion of the MIKE Force already had a few wounded but they were still mobile.

Richter passed the word around. In the mayhem and the confusion of the LZ operation to evacuate the wounded some of the officers like Lieutenant Longgrear had decided to stay behind and fight until the last man was exfiltrated.

A few moments passed and as if by some miracle another set of Light Colonel's silver leafs worn by a soldier on his helmet came running up to Colonel Vortex's command group.

It was Lieutenant Colonel Schungel.

"So there you are Colonel!" said Vortex with surprise and some elation.

Lieutenant Colonel Daniel Schungel was the commander of Company C of the 5th Special Forces Group. In December 1967 Schungel had ordered a mobile strike force to *Lang Vei* to assist Captain Willoughby's A-Team. The strike force consisted of six Green Berets and a company of *Hre* Montagnards totalling about 160 men. It was this force that was Lieutenant Longgrear's command with Schungel supervising. The team leaders were; heavy weapons specialist SFC Harvey G. Brande; SFC Charles Lindewald; senior medic SFC Earl Burke; another weapons expert by the name of SFC John Early and the mortally wounded medic SP4 James L. Moreland that Lieutenant Todd and Captain Willoughby had been forced to leave behind in the Operations Centre.

The *Hre* Montagnard troops with them were in fact mercenaries and were paid by the number of enemy weapons that they managed to capture in battle.

The Green Beret team leaders were elite troops and were also, like Colonel Vortex and Master Sergeant Richter, airborne qualified as well as being explosives and demolition experts. Colonel Vortex was also a highly qualified Marine aviation pilot as he had flown the F-100D *Super Sabre* of the *416th Tactical Fighter Squadron* into *Khe Sanh* before the siege proper had begun on the early morning of the 21st January 1968.

"Ah! Yes! Colonel Vortex! I have heard of you. And I am happy to say all of it high with praise for your efforts. General Norman J. Anderson speaks highly of your endeavours at *Khe Sanh*," said Lieutenant Colonel Daniel Schungel.

"Never mind that now Colonel! What have you been doing?" asked Vortex.

"What do you think Vortex?" Schungel held a AN/PRC-41 radio handset and a Marine radio operator was right next to him with the unit on his back while firing like everybody else into the jungle infested with PAVN troops who kept biting at the heels of the small force.

"I have been calling in for TAC air from the FSCC and the MATCU at KSCB! Also asking for Arc Light from *Da Nang*. I have heard that COMUSMACV is right at this moment in *Da Nang* for a conference and he's ordered all available NIAGARA air assets to assist with our exfiltration."

Vortex yelled back over the din of battle, "We are not leaving here until we reach Major Quamo and the MIKE Force and get every single one of the CIDG and Special Forces survivors out of this debacle and back to *Khe Sanh*!"

Lieutenant Colonel Schungel nodded, "I agree with you Colonel!"

As they spoke an ear-drum-splitting roar could be heard from the east and then the sonic boom of the cone-shaped air shockwave hit them as six F-105E *Thunderchiefs* came out of supersonic transit to drop their 500 lb iron H&E bombs on the *New Lang Vei* base camp.

"Did you order that?" asked Vortex as he pointed to the flock of *Thunderchiefs*.

"I sure did!" answered Lt. Colonel Schungel.

"Good! That should keep those Communist monkey's heads down for awhile as we try to link up with Major Quamo."

Richter asked Lt. Colonel Schungel, "Is it true that after Captain Willoughby organised the escape of the survivors from *New Lang Vei* camp through the northern perimeter – that he went on some sort of mission on his own volition?"

Vortex knew that his trusty aid was trying to ferret out information on what Captain Willoughby was really up to.

"Willoughby went in search of that mongrel dog and traitor Felix Poilane that has been giving intelligence of our dispositions to the enemy and our troop strengths," answered Lt. Colonel Schungel seemingly without compunction nor hesitation.

"So its true then?" asked Vortex.

"He told me so himself," added Schungel, "…just before the attack began on the night of the 6th February Willoughby mentioned that he was going to track down and extra-judicially execute this Poilane fellow. I couldn't care less. I am his superior but he has my total confidence as he has responsibility for the actual field command at *Lang Vei* – not I."

"I fully support it." said Vortex nonchalantly.

"Anyway let's get the hell over to Major Quamo! I want to extract everyone and get the blazes out of here!" ordered Colonel Vortex.

While Colonel Richard Vortex, Master Sergeant Richter, Lieutenant Todd, Lieutenant Longgrear and Lieutenant Colonel Daniel Schungel were chatting so enjoyably about the exploits of Captain Frank Willoughby, Major George Quamo had managed to fight his way through with half the MIKE Force sent from *Da Nang* to the CIDG survivors cut off from the designated LZ near *Old Lang Vei* camp. They were mostly comprised of *Bru* and *Hre* Montagnards and were armed with CAR 15's and M1 and M2 carbines. Back at the *New Lang Vei* camp the CIDG troops had available 250,000 rounds of 7.62mm and other assorted ammunition (enough for 3 basic loads per man) plus 1,000 fragmentation grenades, 390 Claymore mines (front towards the enemy ordnance) and 250 12-gauge shotgun shells for the few pump action shotguns available. This was all now lost to the Communists.

The CIDG survivors who could not make it out through the northern perimeter concertina wire with Captain Willoughby's group managed to get through the Company 104 Compound at *New Lang Vei* and Major Quamo found them about 400 yards to the north of the base where he now linked up with them.

Unfortunately they were now totally surrounded by elements of the 304th PAVN Division and were being pressed on all sides.

The TAC Air and the supporting CH-47A's and AH-1's were doing as best they could overhead to keep the Communist foe from overrunning their positions at this alternate LZ. In addition some four UH-1E Huey gunships had joined the heli-borne assault support force to cover Major Quamo and Colonel Vortex's groups as they struggled to rejoin into a single cohesive formation prior to the planned exfiltration.

Meanwhile Captain Kufeldt had made one trip to *Khe Sanh* depositing his CIDG and wounded Green Beret survivors at the KSCB medical centre designated 'Charlie Med' which was just behind the aircraft parking area and next to graves registration and the Logistics Support Unit and the Motor Pool.

Hearing from Captain Mirza Baig (soon to be promoted Major) that Colonel Vortex and Major Quamo were still fighting to extract the remaining CIDG survivors, he unhesitatingly accompanied two of the CH-47A's back to the original LZ and started to lay down skilful rocket and machine gun fire to support the platoon of Marines that Colonel Vortex had left there as a back-up.

Captain Kufeldt hammered several North Vietnamese anti-aircraft emplacements and moved on to Major Quamo's position where he landed his UH-1E. Two of the evaluation aircraft with Kufeldt were damaged by the ferocious PAVN fire and were forced to lift off after having picked up one more US military advisor from Captain Willoughby's command. Three of Kufeldt's crew onboard the UH-1E were injured during the manoeuvres to extract the Green Beret but the Captain assisted the other supporting CH-47A's and AH-1's in laying down enough suppressive fire on the masses of North Vietnamese so that more of the CIDG troops could be evacuated. The gunship that Captain Kufeldt piloted was struck by tracer and mortar fragmentation debris and lost power. However with expert skill the Captain managed to fly the craft back to *Khe Sanh* with his group of survivors.

"Where is Colonel Vortex?" asked Major Quamo to his Staff Sergeant.

"He can't be that far away sir," answered the NCO.

"Shit-a-brick! We're totally surrounded. Give me that AN/PRC-41 radio! I need to call *Khe Sanh* and the MATCU command centre," said Major George Quamo.

A few moments later he was listening to Captain Mirza Baig.

"We have another SPOOKY coming in to your position in about four to five minutes sir," said Baig.

Major Quamo acknowledged and gathered a squad of ten men from his force.

"You see that machine gun nest about forty yards to the north-east?" he asked the Staff Sergeant.

"Yes sir."

"Well, we have to take it out. Otherwise the choppers can't land to extract us once Colonel Vortex gets here. Wherever the deuce has he got to?"

The Staff Sergeant nodded and took five men and swung around to the east while Major Quamo and another five Marines and a couple of Green Berets from his 5th Special Forces Group moved around to the west north-west in a double envelopment manoeuvre.

Major Quamo's plan was to take out the machine gun positions of the PAVN and destroy whatever force was immediately to the north and the north-east of them.

As the rest of the MIKE Force were all pinned down and returning devastating fire Major Quamo ran into the jungle and then dived for cover while firing his M60 machine gun. Slowly but inexorably both small groups of five and six managed to crawl and slither their way yard by painful yard towards the PAVN machine gun positions.

The rumble of turbo-prop propellers could be heard overhead as Quamo looked skywards. The SPOOKY gunship, that the Major had asked Captain Baig for was making its attack sortie in an arc around their position with tracer fire and high-velocity Miniguns tearing up the thick concentrations of surrounding North Vietnamese troops.

Lieutenant David Peter EHRLICH

The concentration of firepower was lethal and devastating for close-in ground air support such as that now needed by the MIKE Force at *Old Lang Vei*. The AC-47 SPOOKY was based on a military version of the DC-3 Dakota aircraft. The US troops in Vietnam also nicknamed it *'Puff, The Magic Dragon'*. It provided more firepower than could be delivered by light and medium ground-attack aircraft. The AC-47 was modified by mounting three 7.62mm *General Electric Miniguns* to fire through two rear window openings and the side cargo door of the craft. All three Miniguns were on the portside. The guns were actuated by a remote control on the pilot's yoke where the weapons could be controlled either individually or together for simultaneous fire. The main function of 'SPOOKY/PUFF The MAGIC DRAGON' was to circle the battlefield on the ground which it could do for several hours (depending on fuel) providing a wherewithal of suppressive fire. The coverage of the AC-47 was delineated by an elliptical area of approximately 52 yards placing one 7.62mm round in every 2.4 yards during a 3 second burst of fire. The AC-47 was also capable of dropping illumination star shells to aid the friendly forces on the ground during night battles against the North Vietnamese and Main Force Viet Cong. Some of the converted AC-47 were fitted with AN/M2 machine guns of World War 2 and Korean War vintage. However it was found in practice over the skies of Vietnam that these weapons were far less effective and a lot less dispensing of firepower than even one single Minigun and they had a severe problem of jamming and producing excessive gases within the fuselage of the aircraft. The mountings used for the Miniguns were the SUU-11/A gun pods but these were later replaced by the ones manufactured by *Emerson Electric Corporation* designated MXU-470/A.

Major Quamo and Colonel Vortex, the latter now closing rapidly onto the former's position were delighted to have the support of the AC-47.

Colonel Vortex remembered that it was Captain Ron W. Terry, who, as part of the Air Force Systems Command Team in Vietnam had developed the AC-47 from the original C-47 design. Captain Terry's task was to examine options for improved air support in ground counter-insurgency operations and it was this officer that revived the concept of side-firing gunship support. In October 1964 a C-47D was provided to Captain Terry and Operation *'Project Gunship'* was launched under his command and control. The rationale of this Project was similar to *Project Tailchaser* and the craft had three *General Electric Miniguns* installed portside. On 2nd December 1964 Captain Terry and his team arrived at Bien Hoa Air Base near Saigon with the necessary equipment to modify two C-47's. The two modified craft were assigned to the 1st Air Commando Squadron. Originally the planes were designated FC-47 with the call sign of *'Puff'* and hence the nickname of *'Puff The Magic Dragon'*. Initially they were used to protect villages, hamlets and friendly forces from large-scale ground attacks by Main Force VC. Colonel Vortex recalled with satisfaction as he advanced

with his party, Colonel Schungel on his left and Master Sergeant Richter and Lieutenants Todd and Longgrear on his right providing covering fire, that the first successful use of the FC-47 occurred on the 23rd to 24th December 1964 when they were called in to the Special Forces Outpost at Tranh Yend in the Mekong Delta. The aircraft having reached their fail-safe points within 37 minutes of the US force commander requesting them. The FC-47 fired 4,500 rounds of ammunition and broke the impetus of the VC attack. The second sortie was directed at Trung Hung approximately 20 miles away and again the Communist attack was thwarted. In the week of 15th to 26th December 1964 the FC-47's flew 16 combat sorties and were successful in decimating the criminal attacks of the VC insurgents. On 8th February 1965 an FC-47 flying over the Bong Son area in the Central Highlands fired 25,000 rounds into a Viet Cong concentration on an elevated position and succeeded brilliantly in liquidating 300 of the Communist gangsters. In July 1965 a TAC air Squadron designated the 4th Air Commando Squadron was established with five FC-47's. By the end of 1965 there were 26 AC-47's in service in South Vietnam spewing death upon the heads of the rambunctious VC vermin.

The 26 AC-47's of the 4th Air Commando Squadron (4th ACS) were primarily based at Tan Son Nhut Air Base in Saigon with the call sign SPOOKY.

Each of these aircraft fitted with three of the *General Electric Miniguns* on the portside could fire one 7.62mm bullet into every square yard of a football field sized target flying in a left-hand orbit at 120 knots at an altitude of 3,000 feet with tracers intermixed being every 5th bullet expended from the aircraft and all within 3 seconds. The basic load of each AC-47 was 24,000 rounds and 45 illumination flares and as long as its ammunition lasted it could loiter over the battlefield for several hours (fuel depending) bringing heaven-sent death and destruction raining down upon the heads of the Communist war criminals.

As Colonel Richard Vortex looked skywards and watched the stream of red tracers gliding down like angels of death upon the heads of the North Vietnamese he prayed silently to himself asking Jesus to grant them victory over the Communist Anti-Christ.

Before Operation NIAGARA would be over and the 77 day siege of *Khe Sanh* concluded with absolute and unqualified victory for the heroic forces of the United States of America and its Free World Allies, the awesome power of the United States War Machine would pump 110,000 tons of bombs and rockets in 24,000 tactical sorties (over 300 sorties per day) together with 2,700 B-52 Arc Light sorties in a constant rain of death, day and night regardless of the weather, all guided in part by the FSCC and MATCU command centres in *Khe Sanh* and Captain Mirza Baig, to achieve the overwhelming vindication of righteous firepower against the Communist aggressors in Hanoi and their CHICOM masters. Colonel Vortex and all the others fighting at

Khe Sanh could hear each night the constant chatter of high-velocity 7.62mm *Minigun* fire raining down upon the stinking hides of the PAVN.

For Colonel Richard Vortex it was his lullaby serenade to help him catch a few hours of sleep before the next day's fighting at *Khe Sanh* would begin.

The time was now nearly 1630 hours as Major Quamo and his two detached groups crept towards the PAVN machine gun positions. The light was fading through the triple layered jungle canopy. As the US Army Special Forces and Marines advanced they moved past the stench of many dead bodies of North Vietnamese soldiers killed by the TAC air and the AC-47 gunships. At one point they passed a series of enormous holes in the earth with indescribable human waste and body parts strewn within it and hanging from the foliage of the jungle. Bits of brain tissue, blood, broken pieces of human bones, parts of internal organs and severed limbs crawling with insects. As Major Quamo crawled through the mud he realised that the Communists were paying a high price for their concerted yet futile attacks. Their only success so far had been the *New Lang Vei* base and this only as a result of overwhelming superiority in numbers and their use of the PT-76 amphibious tanks for the first time in South Vietnam against a largely indigenous force of relatively inexperienced *Bru* and *Hre* Montagnards with only 13 US Special Forces to provide the stiffening mortar to hold the shaky command structure in place. It had been too much to expect native tribesmen to withstand an attack from two and perhaps three elite North Vietnamese Battalions from the 304th Division with reinforced anti-air and artillery units in support.

Major Quamo used hand signals to his group indicating that there were three more machine gun nests on their left as they approached the main PAVN position from where the interdicting fire onto the alternate LZ would make the planned extraction impossible.

Tracers and 7.62mm rounds were flying in all directions in deadly cross-fire.

Major Quamo whispered to the Sergeant with him, "Christ! There's more machine gun positions than I had first thought."

"And there is a mortar position up ahead sir," answered the NCO as 4.2 inch shells were exploding to their front and rear.

The Communist 7.62mm RPD Light Machine guns were light weight and compact. They sported a drum magazine and held 50 round belts of ammunition that was now spewing forth 650 to 750 rounds per minute onto Major Quamo's portion of the MIKE Force. The Communists had also used *Bangalore* torpedoes to blast holes in the *New Lang Vei* base perimeter made up of concertina wire/sandbagged barriers and improvised 55 gallon drums filled with rocks and sand before overrunning it.

Major Quamo threw several 'frags' (40mm grenades) into the RPD machine gun nest immediately in front of their position. A few seconds later he charged the position and as he ran threw his special forces knife into the face of the nearest PAVN

trooper from the 8th Battalion, 66th Regiment of the 304th PAVN Division. The blade sliced through his neck and exited out from the opposite side of his right cheek. Major Quamo twirled on his feet picking up a nearby AK-47 from a dead North Vietnamese and rammed the bayonet through the back of the enemies' spine, then twisted it anti-clockwise as he ripped upwards cleaving the body into two distinct pieces. Using his right foot he kicked the still breathing body in front of him and then sliced open the cranium of the next North Vietnamese who was stumbling dazed from the grenade blasts.

The Sergeant with Major Quamo hosed down another six PAVN as they struggled to return to their feet, blood oozing from most of them with his M60 machine gun. The M60 was nicknamed *'The Pig'* in Vietnam. It was a robust and reliable weapon which was gas-operated. Thus as the first round travels down the chromium-plated barrel it pushes gas into a special cylinder which forces a piston down the chamber to bring the next 7.62mm round into firing position. It weighed 23 lbs and 39.6 lbs with the tripod; was 43.3 inches in length; had a rate of fire of 550 rpm (cyclic) and 200 rpm (automatic) and an effective range of 984 yards or 1,968 yards with tripod attached. Like the M16 the M60 did occasionally have a tendency to jam or misfire when unclean or compromised with dirt or dust particles. However the M60 was not too heavy and could be carried into battle easily producing sustained and lethal fire. It could be mounted on a M122 tripod or its own in-built tripod. The Sergeant used neither as he shot up the Communists while screaming to the other section that was approaching from the north-east to finish off the next RPD nest about 20 yards away.

As Major Quamo moved on to the next RPD nest he was suddenly jumped on by three large North Vietnamese troopers from the 3rd Company, 198th Tank Battalion, 24th Regiment of the 304th PAVN Division who had joined the fight after *New Lang Vei* had fallen. One Communist placed Major Quamo in a head-lock and was about to stab his heart with a detached bayonet. Instinctively the Major grabbed the soldier's left arm and shifting the weight of his body to the point of least resistance catapulted the enemy over his head in a summersault and like swift winds of retribution unsheathed his machete from his webbing. As he twisted the left arm and wrenched it out of its sockets he brought his machete down and severed off the Communist's arm with a single slicing blow splashing blood and nerve endings over both attacker and defender.

The Sergeant came running up behind with his Colt 0.45 pistol and blew off the right side of the second Communist's brain leaving one eye on what was left of the skull and the other flying through the air with the left cheek totally detached. Simultaneously Major Quamo wielded the severed arm in his right hand as if it was a weapon and head-smacked the third PAVN trooper with the body part of his mutilated comrade.

"Fuck Ho Chi Minh! You gook miscreants!" shouted Quamo.

As he spoke he belted the third trooper left and right, up and down the sides of his head and chest with the severed arm that was still wearing the sleeve of its shirt.

The Sergeant dived down and gripped both ankles of the enemy bringing the body to the ground while inserting his US Army knife into the crevice of the man's anal rectum slicing the buttocks apart like a succulent turkey at Thanks-giving dinner.

"Die! You rotten rat-fucker!" screamed the NCO.

The Major now seeing that his Sergeant had floored the Communist proceeded with deliberate and enjoyable abandonment to the erotic senses to crush the man's head to a bloody pulp with the severed arm he was holding as a trouncing tool.

Picking up the body of the second North Vietnamese they covered themselves with it, both the Major and the Sergeant, using it is a human shield from the bullets fired by the third attacker.

"Take this!" screamed Quamo. With those words Major Quamo assisted by his Sergeant lifted up the body and threw it at the third North Vietnamese trooper. A Marine running up from behind, saw what was happening and emptied a whole clip from his M16 into the two figures shredding them to pieces.

At the time this was happening Colonel Vortex, Lieutenants Todd, Longgrear and Lieutenant Colonel Daniel Schungel finally managed to break into and rejoin Major Quamo's group of about fifty Army and combined Marine MIKE Force. This assisted the rescue package in consolidating their positions not too far away from *Old Lang Vei*.

"You see that 37mm M1939 40mm Bofor anti-air gun and its crew?" asked Major Quamo to Lieutenant Colonel Schungel and Colonel Vortex.

Vortex replied as Master Sergeant Richter launched an RPG-7 rocket towards another group of PAVN about 40 yards to their north.

"We have to take it out! The Huey's and CH-47's can't insert into the LZ until it is destroyed!" answered Vortex.

"That's right Colonel," said Quamo as he re-grouped about fifteen men and with Vortex and Richter following they fired their weapons furiously at the Communists with deadly accuracy while the rest of the MIKE Force formed a circular defensive perimeter and lay down heavy suppressive fire to support their advance.

From behind a dense thicket of jungle vines and foliage Major Quamo spotted a North Vietnamese advancing behind them with *Kalashnikov* at the ready.

"No you don't!" screamed Vortex.

Before the Colonel could gun the assailant down Major Quamo flung his army knife with incredible force and velocity at the Communist which penetrated through the torso so completely that it pinned the enemy soldier to a tree impaling the body to the trunk.

"Stick around!" yelled Quamo hoarsely as he kept running and then used the butt end of his M16 to crush the skull of the impaled, yet still breathing carcass of the enemy soldier.

"Surprising to say the least," exclaimed Lieutenant Colonel Schungel as he gripped what was left of the skull revealing long black hair.

"Its not uncommon for female soldiers to be intermixed into the North Vietnamese regular army units," said Vortex calmly as he tossed three grenades towards the 37mm Bofor anti-aircraft gun. The PAVN panicked and abandoned their weapon.

Master Sergeant Richter had picked up a surplus M2 flamethrower from *Old Lang Vei* left behind by one of the 5th Special Forces survivors from *New Lang Vei* after having been exfiltrated out by chopper a couple of hours previously. The M2 flamethrower was the successor to the M1 and M1A1 flamethrower used by American forces in World War 2 and Korea. The M2 was a man-portable backpack flamethrower which used fire thickened fuel jelly which was a variant of napalm.

Richter screamed, "Time for a barbecue!"

With those words he leapt forward as Quamo, Vortex and Schungel fired their M16's and M79 grenades into the fleeing PAVN.

When he was within the 45 metre range of the M2 flamethrower Richter let loose and a stream of golden searing flame that dribbled from the edges like a babies' drooling saliva shot forth as if a load of juice from a man's loins had been released causing shrieks of horrific suffering and agony to be heard over the continuous din of the battle now in its deadly stage of culmination.

Colonel Vortex had a feeling of deep elation and almost orgasmic satisfaction as he could feel the heat of and smell the burning stench of the napalm enhanced fire engulfing the North Vietnamese troops.

Their bodies were charred beyond recognition as they now ran like glowing torches hither and thither in front of them as at least twenty-five North Vietnamese were incinerated in an orgy of destruction.

Ten of Major Quamo's troops ran in pursuit and pumped hundreds of 7.62mm rounds into their withering, glowing, melting and deforming bodies while Vortex ran after the stragglers and sliced open their intestines with his machete while they were still on fire.

Master Sergeant Richter felt immensely satisfied at his endeavours as three Navy A-1 *Skyraiders* swooped in with flechette bombs to annihilate the North Vietnamese concentrations to their north, north-west and north-east.

Vortex launched an M79 40mm grenade into the 37mm Bofor anti-aircraft gun which totally destroyed it just in case additional Communists came back to operate it while they were in the process of exfiltration by helicopter.

The time, Colonel Vortex realised, was now ripe for the entire MIKE Force and the CIDG survivors to evacuate back to *Khe Sanh* leaving no-one behind.

Major Quamo, Vortex, Schungel, Richter, Longgrear and now Todd who had joined the party executed a tactical withdrawal back to the main body of the MIKE Force not far from *Old Lang Vei*.

Within the next twenty minutes with the pressure slightly reduced from the latest TAC air by the Navy *Skyraiders* the entire force managed to circumvent slight resistance on the axis of advance from their current position about 400 yards north-west of *Old Lang Vei* back to that abandoned base and rejoined the 20 man platoon sized force that Colonel Vortex had left there to protect the LZ about 2 hours earlier. All the CIDG *Bru* and *Hre* Montagnards and other assorted native allies from the surrounding area were with them and ready for exfiltration.

There were many wounded CIDG troops and also several wounded from the MIKE Force. The CH-47's now began their extraction supported by the UH-1E Huey's and AH-1 *Cobra's* circling above laying down a withering and blasting suppressive fire in a 360 degree circular locus of attack around the LZ. The air support was intense, unceasing, relentless and accurate. Without Operation NIAGARA it is quite possible that *Khe Sanh may* have fallen to the Communists even despite the artillery support from Camp Carroll and the Rockpile with its 175mm *Long Tom* artillery. Even now the shells of the US M107 175mm (Self-Propelled) Gun which weighed 57,690 lbs; rate of fire of 1 round per 2 minutes with a crew of 13 and a range of 35,760 yards was raining down on the PAVN positions around and inside the *New Lang Vei* base from Camp Carroll.

Without artillery support the American and Free World Allied Forces would simply be unable to operate in large tracts of South Vietnam away from major towns and cities. The positioning of Fire Support Bases was a new concept in counter-insurgency warfare. Each Fire Support Base was placed close enough but at the same time not too close in proximity to the next so that each base could support the other with its long range artillery such as the US M114A1 155mm Medium Howitzer (Towed); US M101/M102 105mm Light Howitzer (Towed) and the US M107 with interlocking fields of fire. Each Fire Support Base was part of an umbrella of suppressive fire that covered the next in the line and so on all the way up and down the length and breadth of South Vietnam from the Mekong Delta and the *Rung Sat* all the way up to the DMZ.

The M114A1 155mm Medium Howitzer inside *Khe Sanh* weighed 12,950 lbs with a sustained rate of fire of 1 round per minute, crew of 12 men and a range of 15,967 yards. The US M101/M102 105mm Light Howitzer also at *Khe Sanh* weighed 4,466 lbs and had a rate of fire of 3 rounds per minute with a crew of 8 men and a range of 12,325 yards.

The Siege of Khe Sanh 1967-1968

The North Vietnamese man-handled down the treacherous *Ho Chi Minh* Trail their own Soviet/ChiCom supplied artillery such as the Soviet M46/Chinese Type 59 130mm Gun-Howitzer (Towed) with a weight of 16,978 lbs, rate of fire of 5 to 6 rounds per minute, crew of 9 men and a range of 27,150 yards. These artillery pieces were mostly dismantled into smaller segments for easier transport down the *'Trail'* as the infrastructure of the *Ho Chi Minh* supply route was rudimentary at best.

As the CH-47's landed two at a time onto the LZ at *Old Lang Vei* and stayed on the ground for the absolute minimum amount of time that it would take to load the wounded on first and then the able-bodied troops who would literally throw themselves inside the fuselage they took off again with the pilot making sure that maximum power and revolutions per minute of the rotor blades on the double-rotor aircraft were kept so as to dust-off instantaneously the aircraft had been loaded to capacity.

Colonel Vortex, Richter, Lieutenant Colonel Schungel who was in fact quite severely wounded from the earlier fight defending *New Lang Vei* but who refused to acknowledge it along with Major George Quamo who was the prime-mover of the entire operation organised the semi-orderly exfiltration.

"I am not going to leave until every last man is out of here!" screamed Major Quamo to Colonel Vortex and Lieutenant Colonel Schungel.

"That's as it should be Major," said Vortex, adding, "Its your overall command – not mine this time."

The Major assented as Lieutenant Quy came up to assist in organising the small contingent of ARVN Rangers who had survived the deadly assault by the PT-76 tanks at *New Lang Vei*.

"We're nearly done here sir," said Quy, "The last two Chinooks are coming in now. You better get ready to leave and you too sir." He turned to Colonel Vortex with his last words.

Schungel advised, "I have ordered Captain Kufeldt to come in with his UH-1E Huey to take the last of us out. Once we are gone then I am afraid that our positions at *Old* and *New Lang Vei* have been lost to the Communists."

Master Sergeant Richter commented as he fired his M2 flamethrower into the tree line from whence PAVN fire was emanating, "We shall be back!"

Then Colonel Vortex said holding his two palms together in a gesture of solemnity, "And in that time between the going and the coming we shall be beholden unto our faith in God and the cause of righteousness that he has bequeathed unto us. So that when we return we shall do so like a hammer from heaven and smite those that are dead to the faith that we have in him and in our Saviour Jesus Christ!"

"Amen," said Major Quamo as he bowed his head.

Lieutenant Quy who shepherded the last of his ARVN troops and the few remaining CIDG into the final dust-off of two Chinooks was the operations

officer of the ARVN Special Forces unit who had fought in support of Captain Willoughby's command at *New Lang Vei*. Lieutenant Quan was the commander of the unit and had been evacuated earlier. It was Lieutenant Quy who had brought up a jeep to the northern concertina wire of *New Lang Vei* to collect Sergeant Phillips and the wounded Sergeant Earley along with Lieutenant Longgrear and all of them made it back to *Old Lang Vei*. It was at this point that Captain Frank Willoughby left the group and was last seen heading into the jungle in the direction of Hill 471 and the BREH hamlet inhabited by *Bru* tribesmen. Hill 471 was about 900 yards north of *Khe Sanh* Village and only 500 yards north of the Miller's House who were white settlers that ran several schools in the area for local villagers in the surrounding hamlets. Colonel Lownds had even made a couple of trips to Carolyn Miller's house to warn them of the dangers of the increasing PAVN presence in the area and to deliver fresh groceries for their household. Colonel David Lownds often spoke to Colonel Vortex about his admiration and respect for the work being done by the Millers to educate the local children. Even General Hochmuth, the then commander of the 3rd Marine Division preceding General Rathvon C. Tompkins back in the first half of 1967 had been sending food packages to Carolyn Miller as a sign of support.

Major Quamo watched as the last two CH-47 Chinooks lifted off leaving only Vortex, Richter, Schungel, Todd and Longgrear with him.

The six men continued to fire their M16's and M79 grenade launchers into the jungle around *Old Lang Vei*.

The situation was becoming desperate and Captain Kufeldt's Huey was nowhere to be seen.

"Maybe he's forgotten that we are still here!" screamed Lieutenant Todd in a panic, his eyes in a state of frenzied bewilderment.

"Get a grip on yourself Lieutenant!" shouted Major Quamo.

Vortex shook the Lieutenant by the shoulders, "Nobody has forgotten anybody!"

A few moments later the familiar thudding sound of the UH-1E could be heard approaching above them from the east and the direction of *Khe Sanh*.

It was the dependable and heroic Captain Kufeldt with his two door gunners blasting away with their *General Electric* 7.62mm *Miniguns*.

The final helicopter had arrived.

The time was now 1730 hours on the 7th February 1968.

The North Vietnamese seeing the small group of officers realised that this was their last chance to kill Americans at the LZ. They launched a human wave attack coming out of the tree line by their hundreds from every direction.

"You get into the chopper and I'll hold them for as long as possible!" screamed Major George Quamo.

Vortex gathered the others as Master Sergeant Richter emptied what was left in the twin tanks of his M2 backpack flamethrower into the Communists.

Burning bodies silhouetted against the afternoon sun as Captain Kufeldt landed about 10 yards behind the group.

The Captain was waving through the plexiglass cockpit window frantically for them to get in the aircraft before it was too late or before the Huey's engines would be hit by machine gun or mortar fire.

Longgrear, Todd and Lt. Colonel Schungel jumped in almost throwing themselves onto the metal deck of the chopper.

"Come on Richter!" shouted Colonel Vortex, "Its finished here! You're out of gas!"

As he spoke the searing stream of golden flame spluttered out and Vortex ripped the tanks off Master Sergeant Richter's back.

Major Quamo was a few yards away blasting away at the PAVN with his M60.

About fifteen North Vietnamese were either incinerated or cut to pieces by the automatic weapons fire from both the officers on the ground and the two *Miniguns* on the Huey.

Colonel Vortex and Master Sergeant Richter dropped their spent M16's and M2 and dived into the Huey that was already lifting off the ground.

Captain Kufeldt simply could not loiter over the LZ any longer.

"What the deuce is the Major doing?" screamed Kufeldt to Vortex.

The Colonel said nothing as he jumped into the cockpit and wrenched the controls away from the Captain.

He pressed down on the control yoke and the helicopter lurched forward spasmodically throwing Todd, Longgrear and Schungel to the back of the craft.

As the gunship thrust forward about six feet off the ground Major Quamo was suddenly shot by a stream of 7.62mm rounds one of which gashed open his right knee.

Vortex threw himself from the control seat of the craft and hung half his body out of the door-hatch pushing one of the door gunners sideways away from his *Minigun*. Master Sergeant Richter grabbed hold of the Colonel's ankles and legs up to his thighs in an attempt to hold the field rank officer inside the craft.

"For heaven's sake Major! Get in! Move yourself before its too late!" screamed Vortex.

Captain Kufeldt was expertly maintaining the hover about six feet off the dirt.

Two North Vietnamese troopers from the 8th Battalion, 66th Regiment of the 304th PAVN Division broke through the suppressive fire and were running towards Major George Quamo who was now the last man with his feet on the dirt at *Old* or *New Lang Vei*.

Vortex was hanging like some huge upside down monkey from the hatch of the UH-1E.

All the troops inside watched as Major Quamo now totally out of bullets picked up his M60 by the butt-end and started to swing it around like a maniac at the two North Vietnamese assailants.

One of them lunged forward with his bayonet as the Major gracefully side-stepped the axis of the man's attack and swung the M60 so hard across the back of his skull that his brains flew out and the cranium sweetly cracked into two pieces with a thick and viscous suction sound. He then kicked the body in the buttocks and smashed it to the ground with another blow from the M60 using it as a sledgehammer.

Without slowing down or breaking the flow of his movements the Major swung his knife out from his webbing and sliced open the top two inches of the scalp of the second attacker.

Lurching down he then picked up the fallen bayonet of the first assailant and thrust it into the intestines of the second. Ripping anti-clockwise and tearing as he rotated the bayonet, Major Quamo emptied the guts of the Communist trooper in a miasma onto the dirt of *Old Lang Vei*.

"Give me your hand!" screamed Vortex.

Major Quamo threw himself towards the helicopter as dozens more PAVN troops rushed towards them.

Be-slimed with perspiration and grime Vortex desperately clung on to Major Quamo's hand and the whole party – with Vortex and Quamo swinging and hanging loosely from the side of the craft lifted into the air.

"It's time to fuck this place off!" screamed Quamo.

Richter and Schungel gripped the legs of Vortex and pulled him back into the chopper and as Quamo's head was within reach they grabbed his shoulders yanking both field-grade officers into the Huey.

The evacuation and exfiltration was completed.

Major George Quamo was the last man to leave the LZ at *Old Lang Vei*.

The Battle for Lang Vei was over.

Of the original force of 500 CIDG troops Captain Frank Willoughby lost 200 killed or missing and 75 wounded. Out of 24 Americans, 10 were killed or missing and 11 wounded. Nearly all the camp's weapons and equipment were lost or destroyed.

The fall of *New Lang Vei* was one of the few and very rare defeats of US forces by the Communists in the conflict to date.

As Major Quamo, Colonel Vortex and the others flew back to *Khe Sanh* they wondered about the whereabouts of Captain Frank Willoughby.

But as Vortex watched another flight of F-105's streak in for a tactical air strike on the now abandoned *Old Lang Vei* position deep down in the pit of his guts he knew that he would see Willoughby again.

There would be another 59 days of siege for *Khe Sanh* to endure.

[Postscript: By US Army General Orders No:56 dated 31st December 1974; Major George Quamo was awarded the 'Distinguished Service Cross' for his; 'dedication to his men, his coolness in battle and his extraordinary courage which are in keeping with the highest traditions of the United States Army and which reflected great credit upon himself and the military service.']

[Postscript: Captain Edward Kufeldt, Marine Observation Squadron 6 (VMO-6) was awarded the 'Silver Star' for his; 'courage, superb airmanship and unwavering devotion to duty in the face of great personal danger which inspired all who served with him and upheld the highest traditions of the Marine Corps and of the United States Naval Service.']

The 304th PAVN Division Attack the 1st Battalion 9th Marines on Hill 64: 8th February 1968

It was 0456 hours on the morning of the 8th February 1968.

Lance Corporal Robert Wiley was one of 217 Marines of A Company 1st Battalion, 9th Marine Regiment. [part of Colonel Richard Vortex's command]

He was in a foxhole on the outer defensive perimeter of Hill 64.

Hill 64 (aka Hill 564) was a little less than half a mile from the 'Rock Quarry' on the top north-western edge of KSCB and approximately 1 mile from the FOB3 [Forward Operating Base 3] commanded by Major Lucius J. Campbell who was later replaced by Major David C. Smith who took command at the end of February 1968.

His hands were seeping blood from a fragmentation wound that he had suffered in fighting on Hill 861A/861 a few days before.

But he did not want to be medevacked out.

He had a great sense of pride and *'élan vital'* at being in Colonel Richard Vortex's Regiment.

During the brutal engagement on Hill 861A at the beginning of the *Khe Sanh* siege, Colonel Vortex had helped him up after he had fallen into a ditch from the effects of a Communist 120mm mortar blast.

To Lance Corporal Wiley it was like being helped up by God himself.

All the men in the 9th Marine Regiment looked to Colonel Vortex with awe and reverence.

Lance Corporal Wiley was joking and laughing with his comrades from A Company. They manned a long trench line that was almost circular. It was at the base of Hill 64.

The remnants of Vortex's 1st Battalion, some 678 men, had moved out of the *Khe Sanh* perimeter and onto Hill 64 at their commander's direct instructions.

This hill was only 500 to 600 yards from the outer ring of concertina wire that delineated the main base. It was situated to the north-west.

Colonel Vortex had thought it prudent to place his battalion there as a buffer between any PAVN attack and the *Khe Sanh* airstrip.

The 105mm and 155mm howitzers inside *Khe Sanh* could give powerful support to Hill 64 when needed.

Similarly, Colonel David E. Lownds had ordered the 37th ARVN Rangers to take up positions south-west of the base.

The sun had not yet risen as Lance Corporal Wiley clutched his M60 machine gun and waited.

The mist and fog over the *Khe Sanh* plateau was as thick as ever. The constantly bad weather made it very difficult for the spotter planes to guide the fighter-bombers in to their targets.

The Marine, Air Force or Navy pilots had to make instantaneous decisions on whether or not to hit a potential target from the cabins of their light reconnaissance aircraft.

It was an extremely tricky business.

The dangers of 'friendly fire' were always in the back of every soldier's mind.

Lance Corporal Wiley thought he was dreaming.

But he wasn't.

A black canvas bag came flying through the air above his head.

It had come from outside the defensive perimeter!

The other Marines in the trench line also saw it.

"Satchel charge!" screamed someone from A Company.

Lance Corporal Wiley bolted out of the trench and ran for the explosive bag.

It had not yet detonated. He lunged into the mud.

Grabbing the Communist ordnance he threw it with all his might over the American positions and back down the hill.

M16 and M60 fire had already erupted all over the 1st Battalion positions.

Lance Corporal Wiley was scurrying back to his M60 when another and then another satchel charge came gliding down on top of A Company like a terrible mana from heaven. He dived for the nearest one and then felt his eardrums explode. A blood-red flash of light seared his eyeballs. The camouflage tunic and trousers of Lance Corporal Wiley were blackened as he was thrown 10 yards across the earth. Wiley landed on his spine with a sickening thud. He was still conscious and could hear the screams and shouts of his comrades as the PAVN attack on Hill 64 began.

He tried to move his arm but couldn't. Neither his legs nor head could move. Wiley realised that he had been paralysed by the satchel explosion.

All he could do now was wait to be killed either by an artillery round or a North Vietnamese bayonet.

In the joint 9th/26th Marine HQ bunker inside *Khe Sanh*, Colonel Vortex was resting on his bunk and talking to John T. Wheeler of the Associated Press.

John Wheeler was a top ranking correspondent who had been sent to *Khe Sanh* to cover one of the biggest, if not *'the'* biggest story of the Vietnam War to date.

"So? Colonel Vortex," began Wheeler, "You know that you and Colonel David Lownds have become virtual celebrities back in the States.

Both your names are in nearly every daily newspaper every day."

Colonel Vortex laughed, "I am not interested in being a celebrity. My only concern is for the defence of *Khe Sanh* and the annihilation of the Communist forces besieging it."

As they spoke Wheeler wrote down everything that Vortex said. And even some things that he didn't say.

Wheeler continued, "Do you think that *Khe Sanh* will hold out? If not, for how much longer can the Marines remain in possession of the base?"

Vortex jumped to his feet and shrieked at the top of his voice, "*Khe Sanh* will hold out! I promise you that!"

Wheeler laughed, "How can you be so sure Colonel?"

Vortex admonished, "Because we are Marines! That's why!"

The Associated Press journalist sniggered, "Is that the only reason that you can give me?"

Vortex snapped back as he started to become infuriated with the smugness of the man, "That should be reason enough for anyone! Mister!"

John Wheeler was unperturbed, "And what about this obvious similarity between *Khe Sanh* and *Dien Bien Phu*?"

"What are you talking about?" asked Vortex.

"The very clear and precise similarities between the two battles," added Wheeler.

Vortex scoffed, "There is no similarity!"

"Oh! Come on! Of course there is!" said the journalist.

"Its bullshit!" began Vortex, "The two battles are completely different! Our forces at *Khe Sanh* are in a far better position than the French were in the *Nam Yum River Valley*!"

Wheeler was just about to disagree when Master Sergeant Richter came tumbling down the sandbagged stairs of the bunker room.

"What is it Master Sergeant?" asked the Colonel with surprise.

"It's Hill 64! Sir! It's under full scale attack!" spluttered an excited NCO.

Vortex had already jumped to his feet, grabbing his webbing and field binoculars.

The Associated Press journalist scooped up his notes and cameras and followed the two men out to the *Khe Sanh* airstrip.

Colonel Lownds and Lieutenant Colonel Tran of the ARVN Rangers, were already at the MATU (Marine Air Traffic Control) centre.

"You've heard?" asked Lownds.

"I have!" answered Vortex.

The 1st battalion HQ Staff came running in two's and three's towards the senior officers including Lieutenant Colonel John F. Mitchell (commanding officer of the 1st/9th Marines).

"I'm going to drop in to Hill 64 with about seven AH-1 *Cobra* gunships. It's my battalion and I want to direct them in battle," said Vortex.

"Suit yourself," answered Lownds, and then he added, "I'll arrange artillery support and TAC air with Captain Baig."

Ten minutes later Colonel Vortex, Master Sergeant Richter and about 20 staff officers were in the air.

The formation of *Cobra* gunships could see that the Communist troops were digging trenches closer and closer to the *Khe Sanh* perimeter and concertina wire barrier.

"This is what they did at *Dien Bien Phu*!" said the Colonel to Richter.

The Master Sergeant answered, "It would be a good idea to launch some sort of mission to disrupt those siege works sir!"

Colonel Vortex nodded as the *Cobras* fired their 20mm Gatling's and folding-fin rockets into the pulverised earth between Hill 64 and *Khe Sanh*.

The previous B-52 Arc Light strikes had virtually flattened the jungle into burning molasses. The sight was incredible. There was nowhere for the NVA and VC to hide as they approached the concertina wire. That is why their only recourse was to dig trenches to move in closer to the defenders. However the steep gullies all around *Khe Sanh* made this job very difficult and arduous.

Colonel Vortex and his staff were dropped off at the main HQ bunker on the apex of Hill 64.

This hill was not as high or as large as 861A or 881 South. But because of its close proximity to *Khe Sanh*, barely 500 yards, it was crucially important.

Vortex said to Master Sergeant Richter and Major Thrush who had come over from K Company on 861A, "Can you imagine gentlemen! What would happen if the PAVN captured this hill?"

Major Thrush answered with concern, "The gooks could bring up their 130mm M46 Soviet-designed howitzers, their 37mm anti-aircraft guns and their 81mm and 120mm giant mortars and pound the shit out of us down at the main KSCB base!"

"That's absolutely right! *Khe Sanh's* airstrip would almost certainly be put out of action. That's why we can't afford to lose this stronghold!" began Vortex, "Now listen up! Listen up everybody!"

The assembled officers and platoon leaders on Hill 64 crowded around their stalwart commander. Every man's eyes gleamed with admiration and a sense of awe when they gazed upon Colonel Richard Vortex.

Their commander had been at the forefront of every major engagement so far in the epic *Khe Sanh* siege. Every man in the Regiment, Vortex's 9th Marine Regiment of the 3rd Marine Division knew that their commander was going to receive a swathe of medals and decorations when this was over.

Some thought that he would even be promoted to Brigadier General and made Assistant Division Commander of the 3rd Marine Division. That would make him, at 41 years, the youngest Brigadier General in the entire United States Marine Corps. He was already the youngest 'full bird' Colonel in the Corps.

"What's the position of A Company?" asked Colonel Vortex.

The Captain who was in temporary command of Hill 64 before the attack answered, "The NVA have launched a massive assault sir. Our men have not yet fallen back but I don't know for how long they can hold out."

A 130mm Communist shell came streaming in to where Vortex and his staff were standing.

The blast was so horrific that the Captain who had just spoken was launched into the air minus his feet and ankles which had been severed off as well as his right arm. The junior officer was also decapitated by the blast.

The headless cadaver, trailing a stream of blood, fell onto Master Sergeant Richter who kicked it off with horror.

Three other junior officers were killed and five wounded.

The Communists had found the range on the main position of the Marine bunker complex on Hill 64.

"Jesus! Shit!" screamed Major Thrush, "Medics! Medics!"

Master Sergeant Richter asked, "Are you alright sir?"

Colonel Vortex was bleeding along the front of his left shin.

"It's nothing! Just a superficial flesh wound," answered the Colonel.

The dazed staff officers picked themselves out of the mud. The dead and wounded were lying all around. Their mangled limbs twisted and forlorn.

A radio operator crawled up to Vortex as the Colonel looked through his field binoculars at the A Company position.

"We've got to go down there and reinforce those men!" shouted Vortex.

"Its Captain Mirza Baig on the horn sir," said the signals Corporal.

Vortex snatched the handset and instructed, "Listen Captain. These are the new artillery coordinates."

Colonel Vortex read out the latitude and longitude over the horrendous cacophony of battle, while Master Sergeant Richter held up the map in front of Vortex's face.

"You've got it sir!" answered the Fire Control Officer.

Seconds later the huge American 155mm and 175mm shells from the Rockpile and Camp Carroll came hurtling down onto the base of Hill 64.

It was here that the main concentrations of PAVN forces were massing for the attack.

Vortex estimated that General Giap was throwing in upwards of 5 battalions.

"As I was saying. We've got to go down there and save what's left of A Company!" began Colonel Vortex.

"I'm with you sir!" beamed the ever faithful Master Sergeant Richter.

Vortex turned to Major Thrush, "You stay here with the other Companies and hold. Do you hear me Major?"

Major Thrush nodded as the Colonel turned to Master Sergeant Richter and placed his hands on the senior NCOs massive shoulders.

Even at Vortex's six foot two and a half inches he was only two thirds the size of Richter in overall body mass.

The Master Sergeant, though only six foot five inches tall, weighed in at 151 kg [332.2 lbs] of solid muscle. There was not one ounce of fat anywhere on the NCOs body. He was superbly fit. And like Vortex he was an expert in Karate and other forms of martial arts such as Akido and Kendo as well as Judo.

A pure and vicious Communist killing machine.

Dedicated to the destruction of all enemies of the United States be they foreign or domestic, the Marine Corps and the American way of life which epitomised, 'freedom, justice and democracy' that was an example to all the world.

America, knew Vortex and Richter, was the 'Peacemaker.'

And the Marine Corps was a magnificent instrument of that Peace and Security that America brought so unselfishly to the World. The peace and security that America was trying to bring to the world out here on these dismal hills surrounding *Khe Sanh*.

All these thoughts crossed Colonel Vortex's mind as he said to Richter, "By the authority granted to me as Commanding Officer of the 9th Marine Regiment and as Joint Commander of the *Khe Sanh* Fire Support and Combat Base.

I hereby award you a 'battlefield commission.'

And a battlefield promotion!'"

Master Sergeant Richter was flabbergasted as he repeated, "A battlefield promotion sir?"

"Yes!" said Vortex excitedly.

In fact the Colonel had already been arranging the paperwork for Master Sergeant Richter's promotion with III MAF staff personnel since before the *Khe Sanh* siege got underway.

The Colonel clapped Richter on the shoulders and then shook his hand, "You are hereby promoted to the rank of Captain in the Marine Corps! Such promotion to take effect immediately!"

Captain Richter was overcome with emotion as he thanked his commander with great enthusiasm.

Colonel Vortex pulled out of his trouser pocket a pair of brilliantly shined 'Captain's bars' which he pinned on Richter's camouflage shirt collar.

Vortex then grabbed hold of the Master Sergeant's stripes that were sown onto both his sleeves and ripped them off with brutal force.

"This promotion is in my opinion long overdue!" added the Colonel.

Then Vortex added as he shook Captain Richter's hand with both his own, "Welcome to the Officer Corps! And I would like you to know that these Captain's bars were my very own that I cherished when I was a Captain back from 1955 to 1959. I was promoted to Major on 6th August 1959. I have kept these Captain's bars to give to a fellow Marine some day who I thought would be worthy to wear them. Until this day, since 6th August 1959, I have never met such a man until I have had the privilege and the honour to serve with you my dear friend and colleague!"

Captain Richter said with great pride and yet also with humility, "Sir! May I prove worthy to wear your honoured and sacred 'Captain's bars' and may I live up to your great expectations both on and off the battlefield! I pray to Jesus Christ every night and every day for Victory in Vietnam! For I know that the United States and its mission here is sacred, true, honest and righteous in the eyes of God! May we be guided by the Grace of his eternal Son to smite the evil Communist Anti-Christ!"

Colonel Richard Vortex put his hands together and said solemnly, "Amen!"

But there was no time for any further pleasantries as Vortex took about 100 Marines with him to reinforce A Company further down Hill 64.

It was a mad scramble to the foxholes of A Company. Vortex's men fired their M16's and M60's as they ran from hip level. Yet eight of them were shot down by the heavy PAVN assault fire.

Vortex, Captain Richter and the survivors hurled themselves into the devastated trench line.

A brutal and uncompromising hand to hand fight was in full progress.

The PAVN troops were everywhere, hacking, shooting, slashing and looting the dead bodies of the Marines.

Captain Richter, imbued with a new surge of energy from his recent commission, drove his double-edged knife into the spine of a large Communist who was strangling a Pfc. The tip of the blade pierced through the abdominal aorta and the man died as he vomited up his own blood.

Colonel Vortex caught two PAVN soldiers with his M60, the rounds ripped open their chests to reveal their heart muscle. A third Communist soldier jumped onto Vortex's back inside the trench. With a textbook Judo manoeuvre, the Colonel grabbed a handful of the man's black hair and ripped him over his body like a catapult.

Once the Communist was flat on his back in front of Vortex, the Colonel slashed a knife hand strike to the man's trachea, breaking it open. Then with his huge and immensely powerful hands, the Colonel dug into the raw flesh of the man's throat and used his dagger to make quick penetrating incisions. Vortex then clasped his hands around the bloody oesophagus and trachea itself and wrenched out the whole incredible organ. It was as if Vortex had completely gutted the man's throat with a single horrible tear.

"Watch out sir!" cried Captain Richter.

Vortex threw the organs into the face of an oncoming Communist and ducked. The enemy bullets missed him but Captain Richter hosed the attacker down with M60 fire.

But the remnants of A Company were already climbing out of their foxholes and trenches and making their way up to the last defence line on Hill 64.

Seeing the inevitable, Colonel Vortex screamed, "Withdraw! Withdraw to the HQ bunker!"

At that second a flight of five A-1 *Skyraiders* came screeching in from the east. With their napalm and high explosive loads they smothered the PAVN drive for a few minutes. Just enough time for the Marines to successfully retire up to the apex of the hill.

But Lance Corporal Robert Wiley, paralysed but still conscious, was lying on his back in exactly the same position that he had originally fallen.

His eyes were open and he could see the smoke, the explosions and the pith helmets of the North Vietnamese as they advanced all around him. But his body was hopelessly paralysed. He could not budge an inch.

Lance Corporal Robert Wiley looked up at that dirty, mist shrouded *Khe Sanh* sky and he knew that these were his last moments on earth.

Suddenly he felt three pairs of heavy boots trampling over his chest and abdomen. He wanted to scream but there was no air or power in his lungs to groan with the agony.

Then Wiley became scared. He knew that despite the absolute terror of his situation he must try to stay alive. Even if the North Vietnamese decided to stick a bayonet into his intestines.

Perhaps the wound may not prove to be fatal, he thought.

Then Lance Corporal Wiley realised that if the PAVN approached him he must close his eyes and play dead.

There was only a slim chance for life but he must utilise it. The junior NCO lay there for what seemed like hours.

It was in fact only minutes.

Then suddenly he saw out of his peripheral vision, two Viet Cong females carrying AK-47's and a host of North Vietnamese regulars.

The enemy was running and screaming and firing all the way up Hill 64.

Before Corporal Wiley closed his eyes he thought he saw the pair of VC female irregulars come towards him. Then a pair of soft hands searched his body roughly.

He had managed to close his eyes just in time.

The VC women ripped off his camouflage shirt and trousers and removed his webbing. They stole his grenades, his spare clips of 7.62mm ammunition and his M16 that was lying near by.

The terror was indescribable as he heard the babbling Vietnamese voices only inches from his face.

Wiley could feel the Viet Cong women as they took his identity papers, his dog tag and worst of all the wallet in his back trouser pocket which contained the seven pictures of his beautiful wife whom he had left in Atlantic City.

Lance Corporal Wiley had only six weeks left to complete his tour of duty in Vietnam. And the only thing he wanted to do was to go back to his wife in their modest suburban home in Atlantic City.

And now the filthy Communist North Vietnamese were taking even the sacred pictures of his gentle wife.

He wanted to spit in the VC women's faces, to rip at their reproductive organs, tear them to shreds. But his body was paralysed and he was doomed to suffer the indignity and humiliation of these shameless North Vietnamese sluts.

All these thoughts passed through Lance Corporal Wiley's mind as he was finally stripped naked of his underwear and boots as well.

The PAVN/VC vermin left nothing when they looted their enemies. And General Vo Nguyen Giap never attempted to control the excesses and murderous barbarity of his troops. Just as he did not care about how many of his own men died in fruitless and idiotic assaults against a vastly superior American war machine, both in firepower and in the quality and leadership of its men.

Lance Corporal Robert Wiley knew that his great nation would prevail in the end because it was fighting for a just cause and not the subjugation of a free and democratic government in Saigon.

Miraculously, Lance Corporal Wiley was not killed by the VC female irregulars but left for dead on the grim slopes of Hill 64.

He was nevertheless surrounded by his dead and dying Marine comrades.

Meanwhile Colonel Vortex had regrouped what was left of his battered 1st Battalion as he spoke to Captain Henry Radcliffe at the entrance to the HQ bunker. Captain Radcliffe was the 2-I-C of the stronghold being slightly junior in seniority to the Captain who was killed by the PAVN bombardment about an hour previously.

"I have good news sir!" shouted Captain Radcliffe with enthusiasm.

"And what is that Captain?" asked Colonel Vortex.

Major Thrush and Captain Richter were also curious as they manned two quad 0.50 calibre machine guns and blasted the PAVN as they continued to scramble up the slope of Hill 64.

Captain Radcliffe pointed in the direction of *Khe Sanh*.

Everyone looked in the direction of the western perimeter. Through the fog and mist of the early morning they could make out large objects moving at speed towards them.

"Jesus is praised!" expostulated Colonel Vortex.

"I don't believe it!" added Captain Richter.

"Its true!" screamed Captain Radcliffe.

Major Thrush turned around from his quad 0.50 calibre and said, "Its M48 Patton tanks!"

Colonel Vortex said with surprise as he swung his field binoculars from the advancing PAVN to the approaching medium tanks from *Khe Sanh*, "I didn't know about this? I thought the tanks were at the 'Rock Quarry'."

Captain Radcliffe chuckled, "Colonel Lownds has been keeping a few in reserve sir!"

"Excellent!" beamed Colonel Vortex.

The M48 Patton tanks came lumbering up the eastern slope of Hill 64, churning up the mud, smashed jungle and debris from past B-52 strikes.

When they arrived Vortex ordered, "You! Major Thrush! You are in command here at the HQ bunker. Captain Richter and I are getting on one of those beauties! Its time to peel these PAVN motherfuckers off our hill!"

The Major nodded as the two officers jumped onto the lead M48. There were twelve tanks in all making up the strike force.

The M48 was a medium tank weighing about 47 metric tons. It had a road speed of 30 mph and a range of 288 miles.

Its armament consisted of a 90mm gun and an M73 7.62mm MG co-axial machine gun.

It had been some time since Colonel Vortex was inside one of these. He immediately took over the controls and lurched the behemoth down the hill towards the PAVN who were now balanced somewhere between advance and retreat.

The air strikes that had hit them so far had been devastating. Over 45% of their initial strength had been smashed. And now Colonel Vortex would give them the *coup*

de grace on that misty, wet and humid morning in that fuck-rooted, slime and leech infested shit hole of a jungle that surrounded *Khe Sanh*.

Major Thrush watched the sky to the east.

He thought at first that it was early morning thunder.

But it wasn't.

It was a massive TAC air strike forming up at 20,000 feet. Captain Mirza Baig had orchestrated an enormous NIAGARA of firepower as the equivalent of 5 Air Force squadrons, a whole Wing, came in for the final attack.

The 155mm and 175mm guns fell silent as the first wave of fighter-bombers descended from the clouds after having been given their attack coordinates by the *Beech Bonanza* spotter planes.

There were four waves of attack aircraft with over 5,000 tons of napalm, high explosives and cluster bombs.

Before the first wave descended, Captain Baig had arranged a softening up B-52 Arc Light raid on the PAVN around Hill 64.

The unseen, unheard *Stratofortress* unleashed their 750 lb bombs. It was an incredible and joyous sight as Colonel Vortex saw the actual landscape around Hill 64 changing with the gigantic eruptions that were God sent and righteous in the name of the United States and its heroic troops.

The first wave of 18 F-4E *Phantoms* came in and wiped out the tip or spearhead of the PAVN advance on Hill 64. This was the signal for Colonel Vortex to move his M48 Patton tanks forward. And he did so at high speed, firing the 90mm guns all the way in.

"Listen up!" he shouted into the handset of the command tank as he spoke to the other eleven tank commanders.

"I want all of you to follow me! We are going in full bore! I'm going to cut the gooks down the middle until we reach and rescue A Company!"

The other tank drivers acknowledged the command as they fired their 90mm guns down the corpse littered slope.

Vortex accelerated the M48 tank to a downhill speed of some 45 mph. He saw a group of PAVN regulars ahead of him. They were firing their AK-47's and RPG's at his oncoming machine. One of the rocket launchers pierced the armour plating next to the driver's compartment.

"You bastards!" screamed Captain Richter.

"Eat this!" roared Colonel Vortex.

He quickly caught up with the group of Communists and steered his tank directly at the main group.

"Beautiful sir! Oh! Magnificent!" cried Captain Richter as he fired his M73

co-axial machine gun from the turret.

The M48 tank caught about six North Vietnamese soldiers in its front tracks. The steel belts whizzed around and the 47 tons of steel ground over their bodies and squashed them like grapes. Blood and entrails were intermixed with the steel belts of the tank tracks.

"Fuck you Charlie!" shrieked Colonel Vortex as an unexpected bonus occurred.

About fifteen PAVN soldiers were so surprised at what had just happened to their comrades they froze for a few seconds near the base of Hill 64.

This was just enough time for Vortex's tank and those behind him to smash them down and crush them all to a bloodied pulp at over 35 mph. At this precise moment the second wave of 12 A-6 *Grumman Intruders* unloaded their ordnance on the decimated PAVN Regiments. It was the beginning of the end for General Giap's latest attack.

Hill 64 had been saved.

Colonel Vortex's armoured column reached the trench line of A Company. His machines had cut the PAVN spearhead in half. Shortly after, Captain Radcliffe and the rest of the 1st Battalion came streaming down the hill.

The Marines from *Khe Sanh* held off the artillery support until the third and fourth waves of fighter-bombers had completed their sortie.

The third wave consisted of twenty-two F-105 *Thunderchiefs*.

The fourth formation of jets consisted of an assortment of *Skyhawks, Crusaders, Intruders* and *Skyraiders* from the US 7th Fleet. It was an avalanche of destruction that followed the PAVN in a rolling barrage as they retreated from Hill 64.

Meanwhile Captain Radcliffe picked over what was left of A Company.

Once the artillery had rolled forward into the PAVN held valleys and gullies between Hills 64, 881 South, 861A, 861, 558 and 881 North, the UH-1E's and CH-47's came in to evacuate the wounded.

"Sir! Come here! This one is still alive!" said a Sergeant in the paramedic team.

Colonel Vortex and Captain Radcliffe came running over.

"I know this man. He's Lance Corporal Robert Wiley," noted the Captain.

Colonel Vortex watched Wiley as the wounded NCO opened his eyes. Wiley moved his mouth to speak but only groans ushered forth.

"This man has had a lucky escape!" cried Colonel Vortex.

"He sure has!" added Captain Richter.

Captain Radcliffe quickly arranged for Lance Corporal Wiley to be loaded onto the nearest Chinook for medivac to the *Da Nang* 37th EVAC field hospital.

"It's over Captain!" said Colonel Vortex as he inspected the forward defence lines.

"Thank God for that!" admonished Captain Radcliffe.

OPERATION S.L.I.C.E. [8th & 9th February 1968] (Search. Locate. Identify. Crush. & Exterminate.)

Immediately after the North Vietnamese assault on Hill 64 had been crushed and thrown back on the early morning of the 8th February 1968 Colonel Richard Vortex left on a CH-47 Chinook for Da Nang and then by C-130E Hercules arrived at Bien Hoa Air Base from whence he was transported by a UH-1E to BEARCAT Base the home of the US 9th Infantry Division *('The Old Reliables')*.

Colonel Vortex took Captain Richter with him as they were driving by jeep to the main gates of the BEARCAT base.

The meeting had originally been scheduled for Pentagon East but General William C. Westmoreland had ordered the venue to be changed due to the time constraints.

Colonel Vortex had absolutely no idea why he was being called to Long Binh Post 16 kilometres south-east of Bien Hoa to meet General Julian J. Ewell the soon to be commander of the 9th US Infantry Division.

The time was just before 1030 hours on the 8th February 1968.

"These 9th Division boys sure have a sense of humour!" exclaimed Colonel Vortex to Captain Richter as they drove into the base.

Richter laughed when he saw the welcoming sign to the 9th Division's home in Vietnam.

The sign showed a comic cartoon drawing of a bear and a cat with dialogue.

The bear was lying on his back with one leg crossed over the other wearing a green jacket and beret and smoking a cigarette. Next to him was a plate of fruit and an iced drink of some description that looked like a cocktail. The bear was saying; "This must be the place!"

Next to the bear and standing up in beach sandals was a cat wearing a red beret and sporting a black moustache. The cat was holding up a sign in its paws saying; "Welcome to BEARCAT".

Colonel Vortex glanced at the Disneyland sign and smiled, "I am afraid Richter that our mission here – whatever it turns out to be will not be so amusing. Vietnam is definitely not Disneyland!"

Captain Richter nodded as they approached the main 9th US Division Headquarters Building at BEARCAT.

BEARCAT and the adjacent base Camp Martin/Cox was situated alongside the eastern boundary of National Route 15 [QL-15] approximately 6 kilometres south-east of Long Binh Post and 16 kilometres south-east of Bien Hoa, 25 kilometres east north-east of Saigon and 30 kilometres west north-west of BLACKHORSE Base Camp. The site of BEARCAT was originally a French base prior to World War

2. It was occupied by the Japanese Imperial Army during that conflict. At the beginning of United States involvement in Vietnam the site was originally established as a Special Forces camp Tri Quyet Thang. It was then named after a radio call-sign of the 1st Special Forces unit situated there which was quite prominently painted on the roof of the main building for aerial identification. BEARCAT was home to the US 9th Infantry Division as well as Dong Tam which became the additional base for the 9th in 1967.

Long Thanh North Air Force base was also situated there.

BEARCAT was also home to the Royal Thai Army Expeditionary Force called the 'Black Panthers' which was later renamed the RTA Volunteer Force which arrived at BEARCAT in 1968 and eventually built up into the entire 3rd Brigade Divisional Force consisting of 1st, 2nd and 3rd Brigades, four battalions of Royal Thai Army artillery and an Armoured Cavalry Squadron with attached Aviation, Military Police units, Divisional Headquarters unit and a Long Rang Patrol Company [LRP Co].

In addition the 9th US Infantry Division was the host to the Royal Thai Brigades.

The BEARCAT heliport was part of the complex and was situated 6 kilometres south-east of Long Binh Post. The heliport was divided into two nearly equivalent (in area) heliports by a large complex of Quonset huts and woods with an artillery advisory team from Bien Hoa also in residence.

In April 1970 the XXIV Corps took over the BEARCAT complex for its headquarters and it was also used as the HQ for the 101st Airborne Division which was currently commanded by Colonel Vortex's colleague and friend, Major General Olinto Barsanti.

Captain Richter commented, "Sir, the 9th US Infantry Division has had a long and illustrious history. It is quite a privilege to be attending a meeting here and especially with Major General Julian J. Ewell."

Vortex looked around the massive base. There were fuel storage tanks and helicopter revetments, hundreds of troops marching back and forth, M48 Patton tanks parked in row after row and an entire artillery park with at least 170 pieces of both the 105mm and 155mm Light and Medium howitzers which was part of the Divisional artillery and organic to the unit.

"Yes! The 9th Division is a superb outfit Richter. My second choice back in 1944 when I joined the Marines at age 18 years was the Army. I told myself back then that I wanted more than anything to kill and exterminate the enemies of the United States of America. I couldn't care less which unit I was in as long as they gave me guns to shoot with. After I had a punch-up outside a nightclub in New York near Times Square in 1944 somebody in the crowd told me that I should join the Marines. I asked this guy why? He said that somebody as large and as vicious as I was at the time. You see now

that I am 41 years of age I have softened in my old age and mellowed a lot. He said – this guy, whoever the fuck he was, that I should join the Marines and kill the Communists. I said that I had already made up my mind to join the forces but I had no idea which branch. So that's why I joined the Marines. Otherwise I would have joined the US Army – their guns are just as big if not bigger than the Marines."

Captain Richter laughed, "Shit sir! If you have mellowed now I can't imagine what you were like back in the 1940's and 1950's!"

Both men laughed and then Colonel Richard Vortex explained the history of the US 9th Division in Vietnam to his erstwhile Captain.

"The 9th arrived in Vietnam in 1966. The main elements of the unit are the; 6th/31st; 2nd/39th; 3rd/39th; 4th/39th; 2nd/47th Mechanized; 3rd/47th Riverine; 4th/47th Riverine; 2nd/60th, 3rd/60th Riverine; 5th/60th Mechanized; 3rd Squadron of the 5th Cavalry; E Company of the 50th Infantry Battalion being Long Range Patrol [LRP]; E Company of the 75th Rangers; 9th Aviation Battalion; 2nd/4th, 1st/11th, 3rd/34th, 1st/84th and H Battery of the 29th Artillery Regiment.

The first Vietnam Operation of the 9th Division was Operation PALM BEACH from January 1966 to May 1967. This was a sweep through Dinh Tuong and Log An provinces.

Beginning in 1967 the 2nd Brigade was assigned to the Mobile Riverine Force and its operations with the United States Navy. This was the first time since the Civil War from 1861 to 1865 that an Army unit became amphibious and totally afloat. The 2nd Brigade trained in the Rung Sat swamps south-east of Saigon. Then in 1967 it moved its headquarters to Dong Tam near My Tho where President Thieu has his family and created a base by building a 600 acre Island in the Mekong River. The Mobile Riverine Force operated also with the SVN Marines, the Navy Seals [Seal Team One and Two], the ARVN 7th Infantry Division and River Assault Groups. Elements of the 2nd Brigade participated in the ferocious III Corps fighting with the Communists in the vicinity of Saigon just this month as this TET offensive is in progress.

The 2nd Brigade of the 9th was also part of the joint Army/Navy Task Force known as the 'Mobile Riverine Force'. The 2nd Brigade mostly operated from water craft and its dry-land bases in the Mekong Delta of IV Corps Operational Zone.

The 9th's 1st and 3rd Brigades were also comprised of 7 other Infantry Battalions.

Up in I Corps the 3rd Squadron of the 5th Cavalry consisting of 3 mechanized ground reconnaissance Troops assisted the III MAF in its operations near the DMZ. This 3rd Squadron of the 5th Cavalry less its air cavalry troop also operated in support of the 101st Airborne Division in the dreaded A Shau Valley.

During 1967 the 4th/39th Infantry operated for a short while in II Corps Operational Zone while the main elements of the division being the 1st and 3rd Brigades

were based here at BEARCAT. Now the 3rd Brigade has moved to Tan An Base in Long An province south-east of Saigon. The 3rd/39th was assigned for a short period to the south-west coast of SVN at Rach Gia. During most of 1967 the 2nd BDE/USN MRF was headquartered at Dong Tam in Dinh Tuong province while also operating from naval vessels further south in the Mekong Delta.

Now the 1st Brigade is in the process of moving to Dong Tam while the 2nd Brigade and USN MRF set up a land base at Mo Cay which is further south in the Delta."

Captain Richter was amazed, "You are a walking encyclopaedia sir! How do you remember all this stuff?"

Vortex replied, "Its part of my legal training Captain. When you go to Law School you learn to pick up an eye for detail and you acquire the ability to retain those facts which are most important."

A Sergeant opened the jeep door for the two officers and saluted smartly, saying, "The General is waiting to see you sirs."

A few moments later they were ushered into a large conference room complete with ducted air conditioning and plush velvet chairs. A large oval conference table was in the middle of the expansive room and at the northern end was a mahogany office table behind which was a red leather armchair that had a back that was so tall that you could not tell if anyone was sitting in it or not.

"Its good to see that General Officers here in Vietnam know how to work in comfort," said Colonel Vortex sarcastically.

Outside it was 98 degrees Fahrenheit in the shade and almost 100% humidity.

When Vortex and Richter walked into the enormous conference room at the headquarters of the US 9th Infantry Division at BEARCAT the temperature was a pleasant 68 degrees with a humidity of no more than 55% at most.

All the air conditioners were running at full blast courtesy of the American taxpayer.

"Hhm! Rather chilly in here sir!" said Captain Richter as he deposited himself in one of the twelve chairs at the table and started to twirl himself around 360 degrees on the swivel seating.

"Stop fooling around Captain," said Vortex, adding, "Major General Ewell could walk in at any moment and what would he think of us Marines horse-playing around on his expensive furniture?"

"I am sure there is a good reason for all this opulence sir," said Captain Richter.

Suddenly to the amazement of Vortex and Richter the enormous red leather chair at the far end of the room moved and swung around just as Richter was swinging and revolving childishly on his.

"Gentlemen! Glad to see you!"

Colonel Vortex nearly jumped out of his skin as he thought that nobody else was in the room.

Immediately Captain Richter grabbed the edge of the conference table and brought his revolutions to a grinding halt.

"Sir!" barked out Colonel Vortex as he snapped to attention and brought up a salute so fast to his face that his Colt 0.45 pistol almost fell out of its holster.

Captain Richter was so stunned that as he jumped to his feet and stretched to his full six foot five inches he practically fell over sideways across the surface of the conference table.

"Colonel Richard Vortex! It is indeed a pleasure to see you at last. How was your trip down from *Khe Sanh*?"

Vortex stammered a few words out of his mouth trying to collect himself from the surprise appearance of Major General Julian J. Ewell.

"Uneventful sir," replied Vortex, adding, "It was quite a surprise to receive orders from COMUSMACV to see you here at BEARCAT. I have never had the pleasure of visiting the 9th Division's HQ before."

"The pleasure is all mine Colonel. I hear great things about you from General Westmoreland – our illustrious leader in this jungle swamp of a place. You have performed miracles at *Khe Sanh* so far."

"I wouldn't say that sir."

General Ewell asked half-seriously, "Ever thought of transferring to the US Army?"

Vortex quickly replied, "No sir. The Marines are my life. But that is not taking anything away from the great and superlative boys that we have in the US Army."

General Ewell laughed as he rushed forward and shook Colonel Vortex's hands and then Captain Richter's.

"And glad to meet you Captain. I also receive many interesting reports of your unit's activities in I Corps. Its good to have you with Colonel Vortex and with us for the next couple of days."

Richter beamed with pride, "Thank you sir." He could not believe where he was and with whom he was speaking, now an officer after all, he thought, only a day ago he was a mere Sergeant. Now he was conferring with Generals.

Major General Julian J. Ewell was to be the 9th Division's third commanding general in Vietnam starting from 25th February 1968. The general had arrived from Fort Belvoir, Virginia where he was stationed as Deputy Commander and Chief of Staff for Combat Developments-in-Command.

Major General Ewell was a highly decorated general in both US and foreign matters. His decorations included; the Distinguished Service Cross, Silver Star with Oak Leaf Cluster, Legion of Merit with Oak Leaf Cluster, Bronze Star, Air Medal with

Four Oak Leaf Clusters, Combat Infantryman's Badge, Master Parachutist's Badge and the Purple Heart. Just before leaving as Deputy Commander and Chief of Staff for Combat Developments Command he had received the Distinguished Service Medal, the second highest award for service in the United States military for his services in the study on the future of and the deployment of artillery in warfare now and into the future.

Major General Ewell graduated from the US Military Academy at West Point [just as General William Childs Westmoreland] and took his first assignment with the 29th Infantry at Fort Benning, Georgia and became part of the 501st Parachute Infantry in 1942. This was, at the time, a new type of service used in the Normandy assault on D Day on 6th June 1944. General Ewell jumped into Normandy on D Day with great bravery and distinction – the year that Colonel Vortex first joined the US Marines but narrowly missed out on action at Okinawa. After World War 2, Ewell returned to the United States as a student and later took a position as instructor at the Command and General Staff College at Fort Leavenworth, Kansas. The general was later assigned to Berlin as executive officer to the US Commander, Berlin, and became chief planner of the Seventh Army there at Stuttgart.

After his tour with US NATO Forces, General Ewell was sent to Korea in 1952 as the commander of the 9th *"Manchu"* Infantry Regiment of the Eighth Army and he attended the Army War College at Carlisle Barracks in Pennsylvania.

After Korea Ewell spent four years at West Point as commander of a cadet regiment and in 1958 to 1959 attended the National War College where he served on the Army General Staff as a planner for two years after graduation. He was then transferred to the White House as Executive Assistant to the Military Representative of the President, General Maxwell D. Taylor.

After this stint at the White House in Washington D.C. Ewell moved to the Pentagon as executive to the Chairman of the Joint Chiefs of Staff [CJCS] and in 1963 went again to Germany as Assistant Division Commander of the 8th Infantry Division.

In June of 1965 Major General Ewell was transferred to Frankfurt as Chief of Staff of the V Corps and assumed his final posting before being sent to Vietnam as the Commander of the US 9th Infantry Division which before arriving in-country was based at Fort Belvoir.

Colonel Vortex asked, "Sir. I would like to ask you why General Westmoreland and yourself need me down here in Long Binh when Colonel David E. Lownds and my boys in the 9th Marine Regiment need me so badly up at *Khe Sanh* to put paid to the dastardly plans of that leech and blood-sucking parasite, General Vo Nguyen Giap?"

Major General Ewell chuckled audibly, "I am glad that you mention Giap – Colonel." Then Ewell turned to Captain Max Richter, "And of course you want to know as well, don't you Captain?"

Max Richter answered, "Yes sir."

Major General Ewell rubbed his chin and paced a few steps up and down the enormous room in front of the two Marine officers.

With great circumspection and thoughtfulness he began to speak, "Colonel. Captain. Before I can go any further I have to warn you that you have been asked and should I say hand-picked by General Westmoreland himself for a Top Secret mission. Now, I have to tell you that if you accept this mission I am afraid there is a high probability of both of you being killed or wounded. Now I must ask, and of course you are volunteers. There is no order here. You are not ordered to go on the mission. I am, COMUSMACV is asking you both whether you would volunteer for this mission. All I can tell you is that if successful it could have a devastating affect on the capability of the North Vietnamese enemy to wage war in the South. So think now – carefully, about your answer. Because whatever answer you give now is final before I can reveal to you anything more about this Top Secret mission."

Colonel Vortex looked to Captain Richter and asked General Ewell, "May I smoke sir?"

Ewell nodded as he sipped a glass of red wine that was on the conference table next to him, saying, "As long as its not Cuban cigars! I don't want to breathe in any of that fucking putrid Communist smoke."

Colonel Vortex drew Captain Max Richter aside and Ewell could see that they wanted to have a moment of privacy so he stepped a few paces back.

As Vortex took a puff on his cigarette he offered one to Max and asked in a low voice, almost a whisper, "Also, was denken Sie?"

Max scratched his head and looked around the vast room. Out of one of the shaded windows he saw an M48 Patton tank roll by.

"Ich bin nicht sicherer Herr," answered Richter.

[Translated: I am not sure – sir.]

Vortex replied, "Ich kann nicht wirklich entscheiden, ohne mehr darüber zu wissen."

[Translated: I cannot decide now without knowing more about it.]

Richter said, "Unsere Männer brauchen uns zurück an Khe Sanh."

[Translated: Our men need us back at Khe Sanh.]

"Ja weiß ich. Jede Minute weg von meinem Regiment ist für meine Jungen schlecht," commented Vortex.

[Translated: Yes I know. Every minute away from my regiment is bad for my boys.]

Both Richter and Vortex reverted to their second language of German after their mother tongue of English as they did not want Major General Ewell to hear or understand their deliberations before deciding whether or not to embark on what now seemed like a suicide mission.

Max said, "Diese ganze Situation und diese Kategorie, in der sie uns gebracht haben, werden gebumst."

[Translated: This whole situation and predicament in which we have been brought is fucked.]

"Ja!" said Vortex, and added, "Sie werden uns nicht erlauben, Atomwaffen zu verwenden, um diese motherfucking Kommunisten wegzuwischen, aber jetzt bitten sie uns, eine Selbstmordmission weiterzugehen."

[Translated: They will not permit us to use nuclear weapons to wipe out these motherfucking communists, but now they ask us to go on a suicide mission.]

Max replied, "Alles stinkt, wenn Sie mich fragen."

[Translated: It stinks, if you ask me.]

Vortex said, "Ich will nicht auf einem kranken vorgestellt sterben, und Hälfte buk Plan der Operation."

[Translated: I do not want to die on an ill-conceived plan and half-baked operation.]

Max scoffed, "Ich wette, dass ich weiß, wer diese Mission präsentierte."

[Translated: I bet that I know who came up with this mission.]

Vortex asked, "Wer? General Westmoreland?"

"No Davon muss der neue Verteidigungssekretär Clark Clifford gewesen sein," guessed Max.

[Translated: No. It must have been the idea of the Secretary of Defence, Clark Clifford.]

"Ich höre, dass dieser Clark Clifford jetzt weich auf den Kommunisten geht," said Vortex.

[Translated: I hear that this Clark Clifford is soft on Communists.]

"Das würde mich nicht überraschen," answered Max.

[Translated: That would not surprise me.]

"Wir müssen diesen Akademikern zurück in Washington sagen, dass dieser Krieg nicht gewonnen werden kann, wenn Sie Seidenhandschuhe tragen," said Vortex as he lit up another cigarette.

[Translated: We must tell these civilian operators back in Washington that you cannot win this war if you wear silk gloves.]

Captain Richter walked over to the conference table and helped himself to a glass of red wine after pouring one for Vortex as well from a beautiful crystal decanter.

"Dieser Wein ist gut," said Max finishing half the glass in a single swipe.

"Ja brauche ich ein Getränk. Ich kann nicht gerade ohne einen in Momenten wie diese denken," said the Colonel.

[Translated: Yes the wine is good. I cannot think clearly without a drink at times like this.]

"Wir kämpfen mit diesem Krieg mit einer hinter unseren Rücken gebundener Hand," said Max with disgust.

[Translated: We are expected to fight this war with one hand tied behind our backs.]

"Ja weiß ich. Wenn ich die Macht hätte - wenn sie mir die Macht geben würden, dass Reinhard Heydrich die Kommunisten hatte, würde bereits in Vietnam vereitelt," commented Vortex.

[Translated: Yes I know. If I had the power – if they gave me the power that *Reinhard Heydrich* had against the Communists, this war in Vietnam would already have been won.]

"So was tun wir?" asked Max.

[Translated: So what do you think?]

"Ich sehe nicht, dass wir wirklich jede Wahl haben," answered Vortex.

[Translated: I do not see that we really have any choice.]

"Ich stimme zu. Wenn wir zurück aus dieser Mission - was dafür ist - wir wie Feiglinge aussehen warden," said Max.

[Translated: I agree. If we back out of this mission we look like cowards. There is no turning back.]

"Dann gehen wir und Erlaubnis es in den Händen des allmächtigen Gottes," Vortex decided.

[Translated: Then we must go and accept and leave it in the hands of almighty God.]

"Natürlich Herr. Ich bin mit Ihnen den ganzen Weg," agreed Richter.

[Translated: Of course sir. I am with you all the way.]

Colonel Vortex put his glass of red wine down on the table as Captain Richter walked up behind him towards Major General Ewell.

"We have decided sir. We are in. You can count on us!"

Captain Richter added, "I am ready for the mission sir."

Major General Ewell smiled as he puffed on his Jamaican cigar, saying, "Good on you boys! I knew I could count on you."

Colonel Vortex commented, "I am sorry sir for talking in private with the Captain. We were just conferring. Also for speaking in another language."

Major General Ewell said, "Überhaupt nicht. Vollkommen ganz richtig Herren. Ich verstand alles, dass Sie irgendwie sagten."

[Translated: Not at all. Its completely alright. I understood everything that you said anyway.]

As Major General Ewell spoke in German also the mouths of both Vortex and Richter fell open. They were both flabbergasted.

Seeing the enormity of their surprise General Ewell said, "You forget gentlemen that I completed two tours of duty for NATO in Germany. First in Stuttgart in the late 1940's and then in Berlin and Frankfurt as Assistant Division Commander of the 8th Infantry Division and then as Chief of Staff for the V Corps. I speak German fluently. I made a point while I was over there to learn a second language. And what better language is there for an English person to speak after his mother tongue than German?"

"I agree with you absolutely sir!" said Colonel Vortex.

General Ewell asked, "And how did you come to learn German Captain?"

Richter answered, "We spoke it at home sir. After all my father was also a World War 2 veteran."

Ewell asked, "So he fought in the American Army on the Western Front as I did?"

"No sir. He fought on the Western Front but in the Wehrmacht. In the 17th Army in fact – on the Siegfried Line."

Major General Ewell smiled as Colonel Vortex winced at this revelation. He did not want the commander of the 9th Infantry Division to think that he was hiring a couple of German sympathisers.

"That is very interesting Captain. As you know I was in the 29th Infantry and we came up against the German 17th Army. They were a tough nut to crack!"

"Yes, my father told me that the German soldier does not surrender lightly."

"That is bloody true! I can vouch for that!"

"*General der Infanterie Friedrich Schulz* was my father's commander," added Captain Richter.

"That is fascinating Captain, but time is of the essence and now that you have accepted the mission I must get on with the briefing," said General Ewell.

"Of course sir," said Colonel Vortex.

"Do you remember Captain Steven Pless?" asked Ewell.

"Of course I do," answered Vortex. Then adding, "I was there at the award ceremony when General Westmoreland awarded him the Medal of Honour plus other decorations for rescuing some of our wounded boys just a couple of months ago."

General Ewell said, "That's right. However, in addition to that, on 2nd June 1967 Captain Steven Pless led a flight of Marine UH-1E helicopter gunships escorting 14 transport helicopters being Marine CH-46's and Vietnamese Air Force H-34's, on a secret "Prairie Fire" mission into Laos for MACVSOG. His mission was to insert a

Hatchet Force of about one hundred men into the heart of the main North Vietnamese Command Centre for the *Ho Chi Minh Trail*, known to American Intelligence and special operations forces as 'TARGET OSCAR EIGHT.'

The troops and supporting air units were told that the objective of the raid was to do a bomb damage assessment immediately following a large bombing raid on the logistical and command centre at OSCAR EIGHT. The real objective of the raid, however, was to be the capture or killing of General Vo Nguyen Giap. Giap was the commander of the North Vietnamese Army and chief architect of the war strategy and as you know, still is."

Vortex spat out, "Obviously the mission was a total failure."

"Yes, it was," said Ewell, adding, "But we are going to have another try."

"Was this General Westmoreland's idea sir?" asked Vortex.

"No!"

"Then whose?"

"It was the brainchild of Robert Komer," said Ewell.

"*Blowtorch*! Excellent! If you would have fucking told me from the beginning that it was *Blowtorch* Komer's idea then I would not have hesitated in taking on the mission – sir," said Vortex angrily.

"And me too!" interrupted Captain Richter.

"Whatever Robert Komer and the PHOENIX Operation wants done, then I am the man to do it sir," said the Colonel.

"I am glad that you have such unbounded confidence in Komer," said Ewell somewhat surprised at Colonel Vortex's reaction.

"What is the Operation designated?" asked Vortex.

The General answered, "Komer has called it Operation SLICE."

"And what the fuck does that mean sir? I'd like to know at least that if I am going to risk my life and that of my aide Captain Max Richter."

"It stands for Search, Locate, Identify, Crush and Exterminate."

"Komer sure has a sense of humour! That's what we should do with some of those bleeding heart politicians back in Washington D.C. Don't you think so sir?" asked Vortex getting his steam up.

"Hmm! Well I wouldn't exactly go as far as that Colonel."

"Well I sure as hell bloody would." Then Vortex ranted, "I'd like to take a blowtorch to some of those Democrats on the Hill. Their fucking policies here in Vietnam with us pussy-footing around like a bunch of pansies with these Communists has cost us the lives of thousands of American soldiers."

"You may well be right Colonel."

"I know I am fucking right!"

Captain Richter asked, "So what are we supposed to do sir. I mean how in the frigging hell are we going to get anywhere near this pimping, cocksucking, murdering parasite of a bastard, Giap? He's surrounded by battalions of regular North Vietnamese Army troops. He never goes to the front line and fights heroically and as an example to his men like American generals do!"

"Yes Captain. You also are quite correct in what you say. I have read your service files and I note that both of you are – like me, certified in advance parachuting."

Vortex replied, "That's right. Both Captain Richter here and I have made hundreds of jumps. And we have done so from all types of aircraft both high altitude and low altitude."

Ewell said, "Good!"

Vortex asked, "So what is this Operation SLICE?"

Major General Ewell answered without hesitation, "Operation SLICE is an OP-PLAN to assassinate General Vo Nguyen Giap."

"Then I am glad that I agreed to this mission," said Vortex as Captain Richter looked to the Colonel and nodded with glee and a sense of almost erotic excitement.

"Can we get to use flamethrowers?" asked Richter to the general.

"You will have available to you all the utmost advances in destructive technology that our armed forces can provide and more," answered Ewell.

Vortex asked, "But how are we going to get anywhere close to Giap?"

Ewell answered Vortex's question with another question, saying, "Explain to me Colonel Vortex what you know about HALO."

Richter repeated, "HALO?"

Vortex commenced his dissertation, "HALO is a method of delivering personnel, equipment and supplies from a transport aircraft at a high altitude via free-fall parachute insertion and hence the acronym 'High Altitude Low Opening' or HALO. It is also known as MFF which means 'Military Free Fall.' In this procedure the parachutist opens his or her parachute at a low altitude after free-falling for a certain predetermined amount of time. The origins of the HALO technique were first envisaged and developed by Colonel John Stapp from the late 1940's to the 1950's. In these first tests it was used for pilots flying at high altitude to be able to safely eject from their aircraft at those elevated altitudes. The normal operating range for HALO insertions is between 15,000 feet to 35,000 feet. Colonel Stapp was a research biophysicist and medical doctor who used himself as a 'guinea pig' in rocket sled tests at Edwards Air Force Base to study the effects of very high G forces on the human body. Colonel Stapp actually jumped from altitudes as high as 45,000 feet. He also developed flight pressure suits and ejector seats which today can be found in almost all jet fighters. On 16th August 1960 Colonel Joseph Kittinger performed the first high altitude jump of

19.5 miles above the ground. This technique has already been used here in Vietnam by the MACV-SOG SEAL TEAM 6 when they inserted into Laos. The technique of HALO has since been refined to include insertion of equipment such as boats and weapons packages. The whole idea of HALO is to avoid Surface-to-Air batteries by flying at high altitude above the range of these ground-to-air weapons. When you are using a plane such as the C-130E Hercules the cargo airdrops are cut free and then roll out of the plane as a result of the aircraft deck angle or AOA. The load then falls under canopy to its designated drop zone. For personnel the parachutist will free-fall from the plane at terminal velocity and then open the chute at the designated low altitude.

Thus HALO is an excellent insertion technique as the combination of high downward speed or velocity and minimal metal and forward air-speed serves to defeat most of the radar detection capabilities of the enemy which thus enables a stealthy insertion into occupied territory of the foe.

However, I must add, General Ewell, that this type of insertion has health risks. At the higher altitudes above 22,000 feet the partial pressure of Oxygen which is required for human respiration is low. The lack of pressure for the parachutist can lead to hypoxia and because of the rapid descent without the Nitrogen first being released or flushed out from the human bloodstream can lead to decompression sickness. This is known as Caisson Disease or the Bends as we all know. All of us being superlative experts in parachuting. We all have the USASOC Military Free Fall Parachute Badge as well as the HALO/HAHO Badge for the other technique of High Altitude High Opening which I am sure we are not going to use in Operation SLICE.

The typical HALO exercise will require about 35 to 40 minutes of pre-breathing prior to a jump where we must take in and breathe 100% Oxygen in order to flush out as much Nitrogen from our bloodstream as possible. Also we normally use an oxygen bottle during the jump. It is also advised not to smoke, drink or take mind-altering narcotic substances before a HALO insertion and this includes histamine antagonists, sedatives and analgesics. Because if these substances are not avoided then fatigue, anxiety, anemia and carbon monoxide poisoning can result. Also hypoxia. There is also the problem of changing over from the pre-breather to the Oxygen bottle as the Nitrogen levels can creep back into the blood stream of the jumper and thus increase the chance of the Bends or Caisson disease and decompression sickness. It is so serious that a single breath of atmospheric air may elevate the jumper's arterial Nitrogen level to dangerous levels. The dangers are obvious in that hypoxia can cause unconsciousness and thus the parachutist will not be awake to open his or her parachute thus resulting in almost certain death. Also you can become permanently disabled from Nitrogen bubbles in the bloodstream which causes inflammation of the joints.

The other problem is the low ambient temperature at high altitudes so that if we jump at say 35,000 feet the temperature outside the fuselage would be of the order of negative 45 degrees Celsius which can result in frostbite. We normally wear polypropylene knit undergarments and other warm battle suits to prevent that. And of course there is always the chance of canopy malfunction which at these extremely high insertion altitudes of 35,000 to 45,000 feet will almost certainly result in death.

So that is everything that I know about HALO General Ewell."

Captain Richter asked both Vortex and General Ewell, "But sirs. If we are going to HALO insert then we need all the special equipment such as; an altimeter, an automatic parachute with the activation device or AAD; a high tensile titanium knife; special helmet; pair of thermo-gloves; pair of military free-fall boots of the highest quality; Oxygen available on the aircraft plus bailout Oxygen and either a 50 lb or 100 lb pack with all our combat gear and sustenance gear such as rations and a high yield 40mm grenade set plus the most durable and most destructive weapons that you have available."

General Ewell said simply as he waved his hand at the Captain in a dismissive gesture, "Don't worry Max! We have all that plus much more! You will have everything you need."

Vortex asked, "So where do you think Giap is at the moment? And how are we going to get close to him? Also, you don't seriously think the Captain and I, by ourselves, can take him out single-handedly? Do you general?"

Ewell laughed, "Of course not. Have patience Richard. Let me first introduce you to all the other officers that will assist you in this Operation SLICE. Once all the men are here I shall then go into the specifics of the mission proper."

"Sounds good to me," said Vortex as he too helped himself to a glass of red wine.

"Do you think sir we can have some lobster mornay and caviar brought in? I am famished and I'm sick of the *C Ration* shit that I have to swallow everyday. Its worse than pig's swill!"

Ewell said, "Of course Colonel! I am here to please after all."

Major General Ewell pressed an intercom button on his expansive desk and an orderly NCO answered. Ewell ordered in some refreshments and added, "Can you send the Air Force Captain in now."

A few moments later a smartly dressed Captain in his US Air Force dress blues entered the large conference room. He wore his ceremonial sword and a *Luger Pistole Parabellum* 1908 which is a toggle-locked recoil-operated semi-automatic pistol. The design was patented by George J. Luger in 1898 and produced by the German arms manufacturer *Deutsche Waffen –und Munitionsfabriken* (DWM) starting in 1900. It was an evolution of the 1893 *Hugo Borchardt* designed C-93. It was succeeded by the *Walther P38* in caliber 9 by 19.

Vortex was surprised to see the Air Force Captain wearing the Luger as it was not standard US Air Force or Army issue.

Major General Ewell said, "May I introduce you to Captain John R. Ehrlich of the United States Air Force. He is one of the most experienced pilots we have and an expert in these types of Top Secret missions. He's based at *Da Nang* and is checked out on almost every type of aircraft we have in both the Air Force and the Marine air wing. If anyone can fly you to your destination for covert insertion then Captain Ehrlich can."

[Postcript: Captain John R. Ehrlich USAF would, on the 22nd March 1972 be awarded the 'Distinguished Flying Cross' for his action in flying a EC-47 on a top secret mission in support of friendly ground forces at a time when America, under President Richard Nixon, was already in full scale retreat from Vietnam.]

"I have heard so much about you Colonel Vortex," said Captain John Ehrlich as he extended his hand.

Vortex shook it and Captain Richter also.

"I am sorry but I haven't heard of you Captain Ehrlich. How long have you been in Vietnam?" asked Vortex.

Ehrlich replied, "Only 9 months. This is my first 1 year tour soon to be over. But I volunteered for this mission just as you."

"Good man. Ready to kick some Communist butt are we?" asked Vortex.

"Sure am!" replied the Air Force Captain.

Captain John Ehrlich was about five feet eight inches tall and had hazel eyes and light brown hair. He was of medium built and looked surprisingly young even for a Captain.

Richter asked, "How long have you been in the Air Force?"

Ehrlich replied that he had joined in 1958 and thus almost 10 years.

"So you can fly most of our aircraft?" asked Colonel Vortex.

"That's right Vortex."

"Do you specialize in ELINT [Electronic Intelligence Gathering] missions?"

"Yes," answered Captain Ehrlich.

"Can you fly the EWR VJ 101C V/STOL fighter?"

Ehrlich smiled, "Of course. I first tested it out in Stuttgart on my tour of duty in 1964 with US Air Forces in NATO. It's a German experimental jet fighter VTOL tiltjet aircraft or *"Versuchsjäger"* and it was the basis for the successor to the F-104G Starfighter but was cancelled this year after a five year test program. It had the potential for Mach 2 flight. Quite a nice piece of equipment and it's a pity development was scrapped."

"I'm impressed Captain," said Colonel Vortex.

Major General Ewell remarked, "I told you that the Captain can fly practically everything we've built and even some craft that we haven't even finished developing yet!"

Vortex laughed, "I bet you can't fly the *Dassault Mirage IV*?"

Captain Ehrlich chuckled, "Sure I can! It's a French supersonic strategic bomber and deep reconnaissance aircraft introduced in 1964. It is part of the *Force de Frappe* and thus part of France's nuclear deterrent striking force. While in NATO in Europe I tested out and became qualified on that beauty. It set in 1960 the world speed record of 1,822 kmph or 1,132 mph on a 1,000 kilometer closed circuit. Later that year it increased the record to 1,225 mph on a 500 kilometer closed circuit around Paris and the Melun air force base. It was piloted by Captain Rene Bigand of the French Air Force.

"Remarkable," said Colonel Vortex and then turning to Major General Ewell said, "This guy can fly me anywhere you like."

General Ewell said, "He's going to fly you into some serious shit. But God willing the job will be done and you'll all come home safely."

Captain Richter prayed, "Amen to that!"

Vortex asked, "Your name is German. It means honour or honesty."

"That's right Colonel," said Ehrlich.

"What's your background Captain?"

"Born in Los Angeles but parents from Bavaria. Both of them from Munchen. Father was in World War 2."

Vortex asked, "In the Wehrmacht?"

"No, in the *Sicherheitsdienst* or SD under Gruppenfuhrer Reinhard Heydrich which was part of the Reich Main Security Office [RSHA] or *Reichssicherheitshauptamt*."

"Fascinating," said Colonel Vortex.

"After the war my parents emigrated to the United States. During the war my father was a Sturmbahnfuhrer (Major) in the Ausland-SD in Department E (Espionage in Eastern Europe). He told me a lot of stories about his exploits against the Communists that would make your hair curl."

Major General Ewell interrupted, "Gentlemen please! This is all wonderful cocktail party chit-chat but I am afraid I'm going to have to cut you short as we have a mission to undertake and I need to introduce you to the other members of your highly professional and dedicated team."

Richter, Vortex and Ehrlich nodded sheepishly.

Vortex asked, "So müssen Sie im Stande sein, Deutsch zu sprechen?"

Captain John Ehrlich replied, "Natürlich Oberst."

General Ewell pressed the intercom on his desk again and ordered, "Could you send the Sergeant in now from the 8th Cavalry, 1st Airborne Divison."

A few moments later three orderly Corporals brought in a huge repast of fish, meats and salads plus copious quantities of white and red wine and laid out the feast on the conference table. Immediately following them the Sergeant from the 1st Airborne Division entered the room.

Before General Ewell could saying anything by way of introductions Colonel Vortex exclaimed, "I know you! Your *Mad Dog* Dave Dolby! You won the Medal of Honour for your actions at An Khe back in May 1966."

Sergeant David Charles Dolby (ASN: RA-13844628) was awarded the highest decoration of the United States for his actions on 21st May 1966 at An Khe while serving in B Company, 1st Battalion, 8th Cavalry Regiment, 1st Cavalry Division being the Medal of Honour presented to him by President Lyndon B. Johnson on 28th September 1967.

Sergeant David Dolby was known by every combat soldier in South Vietnam and his nickname was 'Mad Dog' as he showed no fear under fire. He was a superlative combat soldier.

"What is this sir?" asked Mad Dog Dave, "The last supper?"

Everyone in the room laughed as they helped themselves to the food and wine.

General Ewell explained, "I thought you guys must be hungry after your long trips here to BEARCAT."

Captain John Ehrlich corrected, "I am more thirsty than hungry." The Captain then poured himself two glasses of wine, one white and the other red and drank them in quick succession.

"I suppose you all know about Sergeant Dolby's exploits back in 1966 at An Khe for which he was awarded the Medal of Honour."

Vortex, Richter and Ehrlich nodded.

Sergeant David Dolby was six foot tall and solidly built. He enlisted in the US Army at age 18 and became an Army Ranger and Green Beret. Mad Dog as he was known to his colleagues always scouted ahead of his men holding an M60 machine gun at the ready as if it was a light pistol. On 21st May 1966 at An Khe his platoon walked into a Viet Cong ambush and six Americans were immediately killed by machine gun fire. Second Lieutenant Robert H. Crum Jr was the platoon leader but he was wounded and covered with blood along with several others of the other survivors in the platoon and he handed over command of the remaining troops to Sergeant David Dolby. Mad Dog proceeded to attack the VC machine gun nests until he had exhausted all of his ammunition from the M60. He reloaded his weapons and killed three enemy soldiers on the ridge where the VC positions were located ahead of the platoon.

Other platoons on the right and left flanks of Dolby's unit then were able to launch a flank attack on the VC redoubt.

Lieutenant David Peter EHRLICH

He then carried one of his wounded platoon members to the rear for medical evacuation and treatment. Advancing again to within 50 meters of the VC positions which were concealed with camouflage mats and jungle fronds he lobbed several smoke grenades into the machine gun nests to mark them for TAC air and artillery strikes which soon eventuated killing most of the VC insurgents. The engagement lasted some 4 hours in which Sergeant Dolby organised the tactical withdrawal of his men under the protective umbrella of friendly artillery fire. The other platoon Sergeant, Alonzo Peoples, was also wounded. The body count listed 55 VC killed and over 100 wounded. Sergeant Dolby served a total of four more tours [one tour is 12 months service in Vietnam] after his initial tour in 1966.

"You did not advise me, sir, that the best combat soldier in the whole of South Vietnam will be accompanying us on this mission," said Colonel Vortex.

General Ewell said, "Well I am telling you now."

Sergeant Dolby remarked, "I have heard of you also, sir. You are no slouch either when it comes to tactical engagements."

Vortex said, "I just want to put it on the record right now. That it will be a privilege and an honour to serve and to lead you, Sergeant David Dolby, into battle. A great vindication it is of the confidence that COMUSMACV and General Ewell have in me as a field officer that he assigns men of the very first rank to me such as you and Captain John Ehrlich."

"Thank you for those kind words of felicitation and *elan vital* Colonel," commented General Ewell.

"So can the briefing begin now," asked Captain Richter.

General Ewell said, "No. We are not all here yet. There are two other men assigned to this mission and they have already volunteered."

With those words the general again activated his desk intercom, "Could you kindly ask the other two officers to come in now for the situation conference."

"Yes sir!" barked back the Warrant Officer who sat at the reception outside.

In less than a minute two more field ranking officers entered the room.

Vortex, Richter, Ehrlich and Dolby were quite surprised as everyone had thought that Colonel Richard Vortex was the ranking officer on the mission. But this was not the case as they now were to discover.

"May I introduce Colonel Egon Pohl of the 1st Brigade, 101st Airborne Division which as you all know is a modular light infantry division trained for air assault operations and which arrived in Vietnam in 1965. Colonel Egon Pohl is a graduate of the US Army Air Assault School and a superlative veteran parachutist who has had extensive experience in World War 2. He used to be a member of the 7th Flieger Division which along with the 22nd Air Landing Division formed the bulk of the Wehrmacht forces responsible for the invasion of Crete on 20th May 1941. General Alexander

Lohr was the German Theatre commander for Operation Mercury or as the Germans say, *Unternehmen Merkur.*"

Colonel Vortex and the others were astounded.

Major General Ewell continued, "Also please meet Brigadier General Manfred Laubscher who is also attached to the 101st Airborne Division under the command of Major General Olinto Barsanti. Brigadier General Laubscher is also a veteran of the airborne invasion of Crete in 1941 and was part of the forces lead by Major-General Kurt von Student being assigned to Group West.

Brigadier General Laubscher after World War Two ended decided to join the French Foreign Legion and took part in the French campaign to recover its colonial possessions in French Indochina. He was part of the paratroop forces of the French at *Dien Bien Phu*. Colonel Egon Pohl also joined the French Foreign Legion after the war and was also at *Dien Bien Phu*. So you see gentlemen I have organised a very well experienced and expert parachuting team for this assignment."

There were handshakes and greetings all around and a lot of chit chat in German as everybody could speak the language except Sergeant David Dolby.

"I did not know that there were any veterans of your immense stature and caliber in the 101st?" said Vortex with amazement to Brigadier Laubscher.

"I am here with pleasure Herr Oberst! Or as we say in German to, "Rausschmeißen Sie die Eingeweide und das Herz aus dem Kommunistischen Schaum."

Richter, Ehrlich, Vortex and Ewell roared with laughter. Sergeant Dolby just stood there dumbfounded not understanding what Brigadier Laubscher had just said.

Major General Ewell added, "Brigadier Laubscher is also a recipient of the *Medaille Militaire* for his actions in the French Indochina War against the hated Viet Minh and their coterie of mad psychopaths in Hanoi which includes our target for today's mission designated Operation SLICE and I am talking about General Vo Nguyen Giap."

Brigadier Laubscher said, "Its now time for some pay-back for what this scoundrel and disagreeable gentleman did to our French Foreign Legion troops at *Dien Bien Phu*."

Colonel Vortex asked both Colonel Egon Pohl and Brigadier Manfred Laubscher, "Is it true Brigadier that more than half the French Legionnaires in Indochina were either ex-Wehrmacht or ex-Waffen-SS?"

Colonel Pohl answered, "That is complete rubbish Colonel. I wish we did have more of our comrades in the French military service from 1948 to 1954 but unfortunately there were only a handful of us in the Legion. Brigadier Laubscher and I were amongst a very small minority of Germans in the French Foreign Legion."

Colonel Vortex remarked, "Thank you for enlightening me Colonel. That was a misconception that I had which has been promulgated by the subversive leftist and

Communist press in Europe, particularly the French Communists under the Presidency of Charles de Gaulle in the 1950's and 1960's."

Brigadier General Laubscher explained, "After the war most of Germany lay in ruins. Many of our comrades decided to go overseas to South America and some few were accepted into the French Foreign Legion due to their special military skills. We just wanted to escape the chaos and the rubble of post-war Europe. I would estimate that approximately 35,000 Germans served in the eight year conflict in French Indochina. Many of the German volunteers were ex-Wehrmacht and Waffen-SS it is true, some younger comrades were only born just before the war started in 1939 and were in the *Hitler Jugend*. It was the promise of a new start and a new adventure as well as good food and pay. The French had a high regard for German soldiers after the war and the prejudice having diminished somewhat. They appreciated our high efficiency and discipline in combat. It is true that German personnel made up about half the Foreign Legion units and we bore a lot of the heavy fighting against the Communist Viet Minh forces of Ho Chi Minh. More than 10,000 of the total of 70,000 Legionnaires were killed from 1946 to 1954 in the first brutal Indochina war where the French government was trying to hold on to its colonial prestige and possessions after the debacle of World War 2 and the Vichy Era. In fact the French Foreign Legion had helped to conquer the Vietnamese French Empire back in 1883. I personally won the *Medaille Militaire* for my exploits in the Plain of Jars and at Battles such as Cox Xa Gorge in October 1950, the battle of Vinh Yen in 1951, the Day River Battles from 29th May to 18th June 1951, the Hoa Binh battle on 14th November 1951, the First Laotian Campaign in April 1953 when we defended the Plain of Jars and Pak Seng from Giap's offensive operations, the battle of Lang Son on 17th July 1953, the battle of Camarque on 28th July 1953 and Mouette on 22nd September 1953 and of course *Dien Bien Phu* from 20th November 1953 to 13th March 1954. I was under Major Bigeard of the 6th BPC or 6th Bataillon de Parachutistes. The other unit to land that first day at *Dien Bien Phu* was the 2nd Battalion, 1st Regiment of Chasseurs Parachutistes II/1RCP commanded by Major Brechignac.

Anyway, I will not elaborate on that battle which ended the first Indochina war as you already know all about it.

Suffice it to say that there were 1,600 Germans at the battle of *Dien Bien Phu*.

Colonel Christian de Castries's forces were outgunned and outmatched by the tenacious Viet Minh. I am a close personal friend of the Colonel. We also had Algerian, Moroccan and Senegalese troops fighting in the Legion and the regular French units. Most of us spoke our native German and only learnt enough French to follow and obey and give commands. There was also a mixed bag of Eastern Europeans in the Legion as well. The tradition of the Legion was upheld by ferocious discipline and ruthless punishment for those of us who failed to keep up with the demanding

timetable of training and field exercises. We had good French wine though and fine French cuisine plus an *espirit de corps* that was priceless. I enjoyed my time in the French Foreign Legion. After that I emigrated to the United States became a citizen and joined the US Army. So I know what it means to wage war on the Viet Minh, Viet Cong or PAVN or whatever you want to call these people but I must warn you not to underestimate them but of course you all know that already.

You might have heard of the old song *"Der Legionaer"* which was top of the music charts in Europe back in the 1950's. Well that was because of the strong fascination that conformist Germany had with the Legion in those days and those few of us that actually joined its ranks.

Finally, I would say that nobody who was in the Legion would regret it today. I certainly do not! It was like a new home to me from 1946 to 1955 when I resigned and went to the United States."

"What an incredible history you have had sir," remarked Colonel Vortex. Then adding, "I insist that you must lead this mission sir."

Major General Ewell answered, "Yes. It has already been decided Vortex that Brigadier General Manfred Laubscher will lead this Operation designated SLICE. But you and Colonel Egon Pohl will be joint second-in-command. Captain Richter and Sergeant Dolby will support you as they are both weapons and explosives experts and Captain John Ehrlich will just fly you in by C-130E Hercules. He will not participate in the actual ground mission. We chose Captain Ehrlich because he has had extensive experience in flying behind the enemy lines above the DMZ and knows every trick in the book when it comes to evasive flying and how to avoid the SAM-1, SAM-2 and SAM-3 anti-aircraft sites and the heavy concentrations of anti-air that will be encountered when you approach the insertion point just inside the Laotian border.

Captain Ehrlich will then fly back to Da Nang and will have nothing further to do with your ground mission which is to, as the acronym suggests, search for, locate, identify, crush and exterminate this most unfriendly gentleman, Vo Nguyen Giap. Brigadier Laubscher has a score to settle with this Giap fellow but he assures me that his subjective distaste for the man will not interfere with his solid and precision-like objective execution by the book and by the numbers of this operation which is so tender to the heart for COMUSMACV and also our boys in the 9th Division. As you know we lost a lot of men from the 9th in the Michelin Rubber Plantation ambush last year and my boys are itching for some kick-ass pay-back against these Communist aggressors and criminals."

"It all sounds good to me sir," said Colonel Vortex.

"I have been waiting for this opportunity since 1954," said Brigadier General Manfred Laubscher.

"Me too," began Colonel Egon Pohl, "I have had some very bad experiences at *Dien Bien Phu*. In February 1954 while the battle was reaching its climax in the *Nam Yum River* Valley I called for my fiancée to come and join me at Dominique one of the bastions of the base next to Eliane and Huguette and Claudine and near the Sparrowhawk. Normally this would not be allowed but my fiancée was a Lieutenant in the nursing staff at Hanoi and thus flew in with the much needed medical team. Anyway she was killed by Viet Minh artillery fire on 3rd April 1954 during the *'Battle for the Five Hills'* when we were almost finished at *Dien Bien Phu*. From that day I have been thirsting for revenge against the architect of that very unfortunate French defeat of its glorious arms and the heroic sacrifices made by the French Colonial Forces who were surfeit with honour and prestige in every action that they took against the aggressor forces of the insurgent Communist lickspittles. Now I am ready to avenge my fiancée's death at the hands of Giap by bringing death down upon him and his!"

Colonel Vortex asked, "What was your fiancée's name Colonel Pohl?"

"Juliette," answered the Colonel.

"I am sure she was very attractive," said Vortex.

"She was radiant like a summer's twilight dream with blue eyes and long blonde hair. She was a member of the Vichy Government when we supported our French allies in World War 2. She was then a Colonel in the Medical Services and I met her originally back in 1944 when we were defending Paris from the British 1st Army under Field Marshal Sir Bernard Montgomery."

"So you served on the Western Front after Crete? Is that right Colonel Egon Pohl?"

"I served on both the Eastern Front and the Western, yes, that's correct. On the Western Front I was an Oberst (Colonel) in command of a Panzer Regiment of Panther tanks in the German 7th Army under General Oberst von Stulpnagel."

"Excuse me for asking you Colonel Pohl but in 1944 you must have been at least in your thirties?"

Pohl answered, "I was 35 years old and born in 1909 in Nuremburg. I joined the Wehrmacht in 1927 when I was 18 years old."

"I also joined the US Marines at 18 years," said Vortex with great admiration.

"And I was 41 years old in 1944 and born in 1903," answered Brigadier General Manfred Laubscher. I too served on both the Eastern and Western Front. In 1943 I commanded a Panzergrenadier Regiment at the battle of Kursk as part of the 3rd Panzer Corps under Wiking SS Commander SS Obergruppenführer Felix Steiner. So you see I have had plenty of experience in fighting the Communist aggressors be they Russian or these little yellow motherfuckers that we have here in this jungle swamp."

"Very impressive!"

Sergeant David Dolby remarked, "I am sorry sirs! But that makes you Colonel Pohl 59 years old and you sir, Brigadier Laubscher, 65 years old. Do you think you are physically up to this mission? Begging your pardon sirs. And no disrespect intended on either of you sirs."

Colonel Pohl and Brigadier Laubscher laughed as Pohl answered, "I am fighting fit and itching for action. Ready for it! I want to see some Communist blood flow! And when I am through with these little cunt-suckers they will wish they never ventured out of their whore of a mother's rotten womb!"

"Excellent!" cried Colonel Richard Vortex, "That is what I like to see in General Officers! Real gumption and some serious kick-ass *elan vital*!"

Brigadier Laubscher said as he took out his combat dagger and waved it around the room and then playfully aiming it at Colonel Vortex's face, "Ich bin dabei, ein Chirurg zu sein und die lebenden Eingeweide aus diesen kleinen zwergenhaften gelben Kommunistischen Scheide-Schößlingen zu schneiden!"

[Translated:- 'I am going to be a surgeon and cut the living guts out of these little dwarfish yellow Communist cunt suckers!]

Captain Richter interjected, "Yes! Don't talk nonsense Sergeant Dolby! Its not the Colonel and the Brigadier that will have to keep up with us but it is us who will have trouble keeping pace with them. If I know anything about the German Army in World War 2 and that is it is the most valiant and ferocious fighting force the world has ever seen and these two officers will demonstrate to us how a war should be fought and the tactics to employ to achieve our designated goals in this Operation SLICE!"

"Well said! Gentlemen! Well done! I see that we are all imbued with the requisite degree of enthusiasm for this Operation!" said Major General Ewell.

"I think we should get on with the specifics of this mission," asked Colonel Vortex as he with mock tom-foolery side-stepped the fake knife strike to his face that Brigadier Laubscher was play-acting with him.

"Yes! Now listen-up gentlemen!" began Major General Julian Ewell, "We have received some interesting intelligence reports from General Phillip Davidson who as you know is J-2 for COMUSMACV. As I mentioned a few minutes ago the *Hatchet Force* that we inserted with Captain Stephen Pless last year failed to locate and assassinate this mongrel dog, Giap. But now we have received Intel which came to us shortly after the beginning of this TET offensive on 30th January 1968 that the North Vietnamese have set up shop in a series of limestone caves inside the DMZ just a few miles north-west of the *Khe Sanh* combat base. We have received this Intel, or rather should I say that General Davidson's office has received both seismic and photographic evidence by our U-2 Spy planes and the F-111 high altitude reconnaissance missions that a major enemy headquarters is situated there only recently. We have seen in that locale vastly increased vehicular traffic and also the photographs show a whole

range and battery of radio antennas which have been set up near the limestone cave entrance. The prisoners-of-war that we have so subtly interrogated,…."

Colonel Vortex interrupted, "I hope that you abided by the *1949 Geneva Convention on the Treatment of Prisoners of War in Armed Conflicts* sir?"

General Ewell continued, "Yes Vortex. I know you are worried about the legal niceties of the rules of engagement and all that croc being a lawyer and all. Now, what was I saying,…Oh! Yes! These prisoners have reported to us that a large multi-divisional headquarters has been set up in this aforesaid cave complex in the DMZ. Shit Vortex! Now you even have me talking like a lawyer! The officers that we captured told us under examination by physical persuasion that Giap himself was directing operations there. In the first few days of this month we began, the US 7th Air Force commenced, B-52 Arc Light strikes against these limestone caves where these people were hiding out. In one such attack we succeeded in bringing down a pile of rocks and debris onto the cave entrance which sealed it. But these industrious little gooks managed to clear the entrance again within 48 hours. We are still picking up a lot of traffic and other goings on at this site. Now we think that General Giap may be there himself to take command of his futile attacks on *Khe Sanh*. One point against this is that it would be deleterious for Giap to absent himself from the main hub of command-and-control which of course is Hanoi. And if the TET offensive was to have been successful which it is not then it may have come out that Giap was in fact located in these limestone cave headquarters. But we think, I think and COMUSMACV thinks that General Giap is in fact there hiding in those caves because as Colonel Pohl and Brigadier Laubscher can confirm for you, Giap at *Dien Bien Phu* did in fact set up his headquarters near the battlefield in the *Nam Yum* River Valley. He personally directed operations there in 1953 to 1954. Also we have reliable evidence that Giap so far has not been seen in Hanoi for some time now, from the 2nd September 1967 to at least 5th February 1968 and today is the 8th February. Thus Giap's absence from Hanoi for this long period points to him being now in those cave headquarters. My reckoning is that Giap is going to plan his so-called Phase III Offensive from there being the main PAVN/VC attack on the major cities and US bases in South Vietnam. However he is not having much luck at *Khe Sanh* which in no small part is due to your efforts Colonel Vortex and of course Colonel Lownds. We believe that General Giap had intended *Khe Sanh* to be the climactic conflict in this TET offensive from which all other actions may spring. Since it is not going his way as far as KSCB is concerned we think that now is the right time to try to assassinate this fiend if he is in fact situated in the cave complex. So you men are the ones chosen for this task. You are stealthy and secretive and you have superlative combat skills and experience. If any small team can do the job then you can and rid us and the world once and for all of this impudent and obscene maggot."

The Siege of Khe Sanh 1967-1968

Colonel Egon Pohl commented, "Sir. If Vortex, Dolby, Richter, Laubscher and I are going in to those limestone caves as a hit-squad of just five men we are going to need some serious and state-of-the-art firepower. You can't expect us to go in there with just M16's and M60's. General Giap, knowing the coward that he is, will probably be surrounded by at least two crack battalions of North Vietnamese troops from either the 325th C *Golden Star Division* or the 304th PAVN Division. We need some type of edge over the enemy and we need to avoid hand-to-hand combat as much as possible. So what have you got for us in terms of lethal weaponry?"

Major General Julian Ewell raised his hands above his head as if to pacify everyone in the room, saying, "I understand your concerns. Just give me a chance and I shall reveal to you the equipment that we have so painstakingly prepared for you for this Operation SLICE. You will have much more firepower than the Hatchet Team that we inserted with Captain Stephen Pless last year. So don't worry. But suffice it to say that officially this mission is to either capture General Vo Nguyen Giap in these limestone caves just inside the Laos border north-west of *Khe Sanh* and bring him back to Da Nang for interrogation, - or, if capture is not possible due to the exigencies of the situation, then your mission is to liquidate, take-out, snuff, exterminate or otherwise kill this most unsavory gentleman. I hereby authorize that as leader of the five man team it will be Brigadier Manfred Laubscher's decision on the ground as to whether to try to capture this fiend from hell or to exterminate him where he stands. Capture may not always be possible as you well know. But now I would like to hand this briefing over to Captain John Ehrlich of the US 7th Air Force whose job it is to fly you in and insert you by HALO infiltration."

Major General Ewell nodded to Captain John Ehrlich to take over.

Ehrlich finished stuffing a salami sandwich into his mouth and took a copious swill of red wine from his glass and began.

"Gentlemen! Just let me say from the outset what a privilege it is to be here and to take part in this Operation SLICE, which, if successful, may assist in forcing this unfortunate conflict to a speedy conclusion, or it may force the North Vietnamese to consider a 'negotiated peace' with the United States and the free and democratic government of South Vietnam and President Thieu, who, I might add is a man of impeccable moral standards and integrity and a beacon of freedom and righteousness in the whole of South East Asia."

"Hallaluya! To that!" exclaimed Sergeant David Dolby.

Captain Ehrlich continued, "The 7th Air Force has, since the beginning of January this year been running reconnaissance missions with the F-111 jet-bomber which has been specially modified for ELINT warfare with high resolution cameras and acoustic sensors built into its nose cone. We also have the advantage of U-2 Spy Plane intelligence of the area situated approximately north-west of *Khe Sanh* by some 18 to 25

miles. As I said just across the border in Laos and not far from the 17th Parallel and the DMZ.

The limestone caves and their entrance as Major General Ewell has indicated have been precisely located just inside the Laotian border."

Captain Ehrlich motioned to Ewell who pressed his desk intercom yet again and ordered to the Sergeant outside in the reception to bring in the Intel.

"At once sir," answered the voice on the other end of the line.

A few moments later two corporals carried in a very large relief map of the I Corps Operational Zone and the surrounding areas of bordering North Vietnam and Laos.

Colonel Vortex and the others were surprised at the sheer immensity and detail of the meticulously prepared map. Each Corporal had to hold the top and bottom ends of the map that was laminated and was 10 feet high by 7 feet wide while a third 9th Division trooper brought in a tripod to stand it upright for easy viewing by the assembled officers. It took about 2 minutes to set it up properly to the left of General Ewell's desk that had a large bronze eagle statue in the front middle of its surface clutching seven arrows in its talons.

Before leaving one of the 1st Brigade, 9th Division Corporals handed Captain John Ehrlich a wooden pointing baton of approximately four feet in length.

Colonel Egon Pohl thought that Ehrlich looked like an English Grammar School headmaster about to give a lecture on geography.

The Air Force Captain continued, "We have pinpointed the exact coordinates of the limestone cave entrance which are; 16 degrees: 49 minutes: 11.39 seconds North; and 106 degrees: 27 minutes: 06.65 seconds East. The elevation of the caves and the entrance is 637 meters above sea level and the limestone structure is built into a small mountain approximately 6.69 miles as the crow flies from the north-south border between North Vietnam and Laos. If you travel directly east for more than 6.69 miles you are in the DMZ Zone and the nearest town or ville is Huong Viet which is to the east of the main complex of trails called the *Ho Chi Minh Trail* as you well know.

Our intelligence has also identified several small villages or villes around the cave complex. Now I must mention also that it is believed that these limestone caves are the main headquarters of not only the 304th PAVN Division but also the 325th C *Golden Star Division* and the 320th PAVN Division even though the 320th is believed to be concentrated to the east of the *Cua Viet River* and north of Camp Carroll. It appears that the 320th PAVN Division and the 324th PAVN Division which in fact is more akin to the strength of a reinforced Brigade, are being held in reserve to exploit any success that General Vo Nguyen Giap might have at *Khe Sanh* and if the plan to take KSCB fails then it is believed that Giap may swing these two divisions plus elements of the 325th C Division to the south-east to strike Hue and assist the Main Force VC units already fighting there at the Imperial Capital.

Our intelligence reports that the entire area between the DMZ and the limestone caves are crawling with PAVN troops and patrols. You must also assume that the native population inside Laos around the cave complex is also hostile and if you come into contact with any of the 'indigenous' then you exterminate them out of hand. The villages in Laos are providing aid and sustenance to both the North Vietnamese and the Pathet Lao Communist guerillas.

Of course the Pathet Lao are hostile to US forces. They are a Communist political movement organised in the late 1940's and 1950's and are closely associated with the North Vietnamese aggressor Communists. In fact the Pathet Lao are organised and fully equipped and sustained by the North Vietnamese Army. So be wary of coming into contact with them. Kill them without compunction, hesitation or remorse for they are a peculiar and particularly evil brand of imperialistic Communism. They also have links to the Main Force Viet Cong cadre in South Vietnam as well as the Khmer Rouge in Cambodia. The original name of these insurgents was the Lao People's Party from 1955 onwards. The main leaders of the Pathet Lao are; *Souphanouvong, Kaysone Phomvihane, Phoumi Vongvichit, Nouhak Phoumsavanh* and *Khamtay Siphandone*. If you open your Classified Briefs that have been placed on the conference table in front of you, you will find the latest photographs of these sycophantic goons and a brief dossier of information as to their criminal activities both inside and outside the confines of their decrepit little country of Laos. If you meet them on the way in to the limestone caves or during your exfiltration then your orders are to – 'take-them-out' with extreme prejudice. In other words kill the fucking motherfuckers. They are the secondary target after the primary objective which is General Vo Nguyen Giap. You will also find in your dossier pictures of Giap which we believe to be the latest plus a short Brief as to his habits, idiosyncrasies and particular penchants. Make no mistake about it, this guy – is about as evil and as tenacious as they come. And that is even by North Vietnamese standards!"

Sergeant David Dolby (who was proudly wearing his Medal of Honour ribbon) said, "So what you are saying is that these guys are better off dead?"

Captain Ehrlich nodded as Brigadier Manfred Laubscher asked General Ewell, "Is that really the orders set down for this mission? To kill these Pathet Lao and their leaders? Are we to be pro-active in ferreting them out? Because I thought and what I was lead to believe by General William Childs Westmoreland when I spoke to him at Bien Hoa just 24 hours ago was that all our efforts on this escapade were to be concentrated on liquefying General Giap?"

Major General Ewell rubbed his chin and grabbed the pointing baton away from Captain John Ehrlich of the 7th Air Force, saying, "You are absolutely correct Brigadier Laubscher! The primary aim and maximum ground effort is to be unwaveringly concentrated on getting into those limestone caves, penetrating the North Vietnamese headquar-

ters, compromising their communications and sabotaging their command-and-control apparatus with the pre-eminent goal of taking-out General Giap."

"I just wanted to be clear on that point," said Laubscher.

Colonel Vortex asked, "How are we going to be inserted within striking distance of those caves and how, hopefully, if all goes well, are we going to be exfiltrated when the mission is completed. We are going to be as you say, 6.69 miles inside Lao enemy territory surrounded by hostile forces of both the PAVN and the Pathet Lao?"

Major General Ewell nodded to Captain John Ehrlich saying, "Please complete your briefing Captain."

Ehrlich explained, "You will be inserted by HALO drop from a C-130E Hercules aircraft that has also been specially modified for ELINT operations.

The C-130E variant of the Hercules is now at Da Nang airfield waiting for you.

All your parachute equipment is on board and fully checked-out. You will each have a Ground Positioning System or GPS transponder to identify your exact position on the earth's grid by latitude and longitude. You will also have an altimeter to assist with the HALO procedure. The extended range C-130E that we are going to use and which I shall fly you in with entered service in 1962 after it was developed as an interim long-range transport for the Military Air Transport Service. The craft is essentially the old B-model but with the installation of 1,360 US gallon tanks called Sargent Fletcher external fuel tanks under each wing's mid-section and more powerful Allison T56-A-7A turboprops. The hydraulic boost pressure to the ailerons was reduced back to 2050 psi as a consequence of the external tanks' weight in the middle of the wingspan. This E model also has structural improvements, avionics upgrades and a higher gross weight. The model I am going to fly you in with is the MC-130E Combat Talon version of the Hercules used primarily for special operations such as this.

The performance of the MC-130E is 366 mph at 20,000 feet; a cruising speed of 336 mph; a range of 2,360 miles; a service ceiling of 33,000 feet; rate of climb of 1,830 feet per minute or 9.3 meters per second and a take-off distance of 3,586 feet with maximum gross weight. Hence their extreme importance for LAPES and GPES re-supply at *Khe Sanh* as you well know.

You will parachute/HALO out at 33,000 feet being the maximum ceiling of the Hercules and thus as you reach terminal velocity over the target area you will be silent, unseen, unheard and hopefully undetected to the Communist radar. The MC-130E will be escorted as far as the Laotian border by three F-105E Thunderchiefs also from Da Dang. This is just in case any Mig-19's or Mig 21's of the North Vietnamese Air Force are in the vicinity. Once we cross the border into Laos the Thunderchief's will peel off and take up their fail-safe points just inside the US/South Vietnam side of the DMZ buffer zone in case they are needed. However, our main problem or worry is

not the possible appearance of Mig's but the SAM-2 sites that the North Vietnamese ground-to-air defence units might have installed to protect the limestone cave headquarters complex. This is a real worry!"

Colonel Egon Pohl asked, "What are the capabilities of the SAM-2's? I would just like to know in case we all get our asses blown out of the sky even before we reach the insertion point for HALO drop!"

Everybody laughed except for Major General Ewell who was nonchalantly sweeping the pointing baton up and down the laminated map as if in a trance.

Captain Ehrlich explained, "The SAM-2 is actually the Soviet designed S-72 Dvina which is a portable system with very high performance. It is a high-altitude, command guided surface-to-air missile. It is the most widely deployed air-defence missile in history. You will remember that the newer S-75 Dvina which we do not believe the North Vietnamese have at the moment in this area, was responsible for the shooting down of the U-2 spy plane piloted by Francis Gary Powers over the Soviet Union on 1st May 1960. The North Vietnamese use the S-75 as far as we know only around Hanoi and Haiphong but we do not believe there to be any in the Operation SLICE area. The firing range of the S-72 is 7 to 29 kilometers; firing altitude of 3 to 25,000 meters or about 75,000 feet; the warhead weight is 190 kg and this deadly weapon can reach speeds of anywhere from Mach 1 up to Mach 3.5.

The MC-130E has heat flares to divert any SAM-2 but these are not particularly effective. Let's just hope and pray that there are no SAM-2 sites anywhere near us or the limestone caves, otherwise we are toast!"

Captain Max Richter scoffed, "That is very reassuring Captain – Thanks!"

Colonel Vortex added, "Its just another risk that we have to calculate into the plan."

Ehrlich advised, "You will begin HALO drop when we reach 4 miles from the cave co-ordinates that I have just given you. The US Navy weather boys have calculated the jet-stream force and direction at 33,000 feet and have provided us with their calculations that you can HALO drift about 3 further miles towards the caves bringing you approximately within 1 to 1.5 miles of the headquarters where General Giap is expected to be.

When you hit the ground – well then, its all in your hands."

Brigadier Manfred Laubscher asked, "And how will I get my team out? I am assuming you are not going to just leave us stranded in the middle of the Laos jungle after attacking their HQ with the retribution that will follow. We need to get the hell out of there and fast!"

Vortex said, "Yes! You don't expect us to run 6.69 miles to the DMZ border and even when we get there we must be at least a further 20 miles from *Lang Vei* which has fallen and then another 7 miles to *Khe Sanh*? Its suicide!"

Lieutenant David Peter EHRLICH

Major General Ewell took over the briefing, "In fact its 22 miles from the caves to *Lang Vei* and about 29 miles to *Khe Sanh* and safety. But of course Colonel you will not have to traverse that distance."

Ewell pointed to a spot on the large map marked LZEXF. The acronym stood for Landing Zone Exfiltration.

The 9th Division commander continued, "All you have to do after you have finished the attack at the limestone cave complex is to traverse on foot 3.84 miles or 6.56 kilometers exactly due South of the position of the cave entrance. You have 36 hours to accomplish your mission once you drop by HALO out of the MC-130E to penetrate the NVA headquarters, neutralize enemy forces guarding the cave approaches, infiltrate the interior of the caves, search for and locate and identify General Giap and then crush and exterminate him, after which you will fight your way back to the surface, then proceeding on foot with all your equipment, traverse through the triple-layered jungle canopy and pass over two small mountains in your due south line to the exfiltration point. The two hills or passes that you will have to climb over are 836 meters and 730 meters respectively. In-between these two high points are two deep valleys and then the final run down to the exfiltration landing zone is a gradual slope descending from 730 meters to only 473 meters. Once at the exact point here, designated LZEXF which you can see on the map which has co-ordinates; 16 degrees: 46 minutes; 01.67 seconds North; 106 degrees: 27 minutes: 00.99 seconds East – you should be almost at the time of expiration of the 36 hours allotted. To meet you will be two HH-53C *Sikorsky Jolly Green Giants*. One will lay down suppressive fire in an ellipse around the LZEXF and the other will be used to hoist you up and to safety. In addition there will be two *AC-47 "SPOOKY" Gunships* that will take up a left-hand orbit at 120 knots at an altitude of 3,000 feet with tracers intermixed being every 5th bullet expended from the aircraft and with a load of 24,000 rounds each to support you with further suppressive fire at 3 second bursts. This should keep the North Vietnamese and any Pathet Lao at bay while you extract. The two HH-53C's with, hopefully all of you in them, will head straight back to *Khe Sanh* at which point in time the mission – Operation SLICE, will be over."

"Oh!" began Vortex, "Is that all we have to do? I thought that this mission was going to be a tad difficult. But now that you have explained it to us in such simple terms, sir, it sounds easy! A walk in the park!"

Brigadier Manfred Laubscher said, his blue eyes bulging out of his head, "Es ist dabei, ein Spaziergang im Irrenhaus-Park für geistigen defectives zu sein."

"What was that? What–? What did the Brigadier say?" asked Sergeant David Dolby who could not speak a word of German.

Colonel Vortex laughed as he answered Dolby, "He said, 'It is going to be a walk in the lunatic asylum park for mental defectives.'"

Sergeant Dolby just put both his hands up to his face and shook his head slowly from side-to-side, moaning softly as he did so.

"I am glad that you are all so enthused by the mission! I am positive that your confidence will meet with total and unqualified success!" exclaimed Major General Julian Ewell.

Captain Richter asked, "Sir? Do you think there are any of your 1st Brigade, 9th Division boys here at BEARCAT that could do this job just as well as us? We really need to get back to the relative safety of *Khe Sanh*!"

Colonel Egon Pohl playfully slapped Richter across the back of his head, "Don't be ridiculous Captain!"

Richter answered back, "Nur die tollkühnen sterben jung!"

[Translated: 'Only the foolhardy die young.']

"OK! That's enough gentlemen! Sir!" addressing Major General Ewell Colonel Vortex asked, "I assume sir, that you are not going to send us into this unholy meat-grinder with just our cruddy and unreliable M16's and M60's? Otherwise you better tell those boys flying the *Jolly Green Giants* to bring five good quality body bags with them to keep in the pieces of our mangled dead bodies!"

Ewell laughed, "The briefing is over! Now its time to issue you with some real special goodies we have managed to scavenge-up from the Experimental Weapons Division of the US Army back at Fort Bragg. I am sure you will like these big-boy toys we have for you!"

"Ja! Ja! Ich kann nicht warten!" said Brigadier Laubscher.

"Come on then! Follow me boys!" said Major General Ewell.

The six officers and Sergeant David Dolby trooped out of the conference room and headquarters building and walked a few hundred yards to the adjacent armoury of the US 9th Division at BEARCAT. It was a huge warehouse-type structure like a gigantic *Quonset* hut the size of a football field.

Inside the armoury were a row of steel fabricated tables and shelves with a variety of large and small weaponry and other unidentified devices, some of which, even Colonel Vortex had never seen before.

Major General Ewell led them to the first steel table and began, "Now! Listen-up gentlemen!

We have for your delectation in terms of side-arms the Model 500 Smith & Weston Magnum Revolver the most, arguably, powerful handgun in the world in production. The Smith & Weston Model 500 is a five-shot, double-action revolver firing the 0.500 calibre cartridges. This calibre is suitable for hunting the biggest game even large rodents like General Vo Nguyen Giap. It is built on the X-frame which is Smith & Weston's largest frame. The *Zeliska* Revolver is more powerful but it is not a 'production' revolver and being as you are such staunch anti-Communists I did not think

that you would want to carry into battle some Czechoslovakian Warsaw Pact shit. The Model 500 can fire a bullet weighing 350 grams at 602 metres per second generating muzzle energy of over 3,030 foot-pounds of force or 4.1 Kilo joules!"

Colonel Pohl exclaimed, "If only I had one of these at the Battle of Kursk in 1943!"

"Bloody fantastic!" cried Colonel Richard Vortex, "I can blow Giap's entire head clean off with a single shot from one of these beauties!"

"I thought you would like it," said Ewell with a cheesy smile on his face.

"So that means we can throw these Colt 0.45's in the garbage tin?" said Richter.

Sergeant Dolby admonished, "Hey! That's United States property you are talking about!"

"Just kidding!" answered Richter.

Ewell advised, "You will each be issued with one of these Model 500's plus 1,000 rounds of ammunition each."

The Operation SLICE team then moved on to the next steel table in the line as the 9th Division CO continued, "Next we have the AA12 Shotgun which is again, arguably, the most powerful shotgun in the world. This Auto-Assault-12 (AA-12) is a very powerful shotgun developed by Maxwell Atchisson. It is selective firing operating as a semi-automatic or fully automatic weapon capable of 300 rounds per minute. It is fed from either an 8 shell box magazine or a 20 or 32 shell drum magazine. The AA12 is the only shotgun that has ever been developed entirely from scratch for military use. So you will be issued with two of these remarkable tools-of-the-trade. One for you Sergeant Dolby and one for you Captain Richter. You will each have 600 rounds of ammunition to go with it."

Vortex said to Brigadier Laubscher, "Das wird vor der Minute besser!"

[Translated: This is getting better by the minute!]

Ewell continued as they moved to the third set of shelves in the vast *Quonset* hut armoury building, "Colonel Pohl and Colonel Vortex, you will be issued each with one of these MGL/M-32 Grenade Launchers plus 400 rounds of 40mm ordnance which will have a mix of HE (high explosive), HEAT, irritant and pyrotechnic. The MGL/M-32 is a multiple shot grenade launcher. It is light-weight and semi-automatic with a 6-shot circular magazine developed by Milkor Ltd of South Africa. It is simple, rugged and reliable and can be fired as fast as you can pull the trigger. The cylinder can be loaded or unloaded rapidly to maintain a high rate of fire. I would suggest that you use this weapon to blow open the entrances to the limestone cave complex. Also to take-out masses of North Vietnamese troops in the stone caverns inside the caves while they are concentrated against you."

"I have used this weapon before and found it highly conducive to a successful cleansing of the Communist disease and pestilence," mentioned Colonel Vortex.

"Good! Then you won't mind carrying one into battle," said Ewell.

"Certainly not!" answered Vortex.

The SLICE team moved on to the 'sniper' table as Ewell explained, "Here we have the RT-20 anti-material sniper rifle. It is a hand-cannon 20mm designed to pierce light armour. It is one of the most powerful anti-material rifles currently in use and its not standard US Army or Marines issue obviously. A unique feature of the weapon is that it is recoilless. There is a counter-recoil reactive tube above the barrel which funnels gases from the cartridge out the back end and thus similar to the recoilless rifle or rocket launcher. It is so powerful that it cannot be fired in confined places with anything in the rear of the back-blast which would injure the person firing it, like a wall for example. The optics and the bolt lever are positioned on the left side of the rifle itself. The chambering is 20mm by 110mm Hispano and it fires a 130 gram projectile at a muzzle velocity of 850 metres per second producing a massive muzzle energy of 46,962 Joules. It can penetrate the armour of any APC or light-armoured tank out to a range of 800 metres. Thus you can blow up tanks and jeeps by igniting their fuel tanks or taking off the front side of any enemy vehicle with a single shot. I also order you on this mission to blow up any fuel storage facilities that you encounter in or near the limestone caves to create an inferno."

"Sir! Please! Now you have me quite worked up and in a state of feverish excitement!" said Vortex, "All this talk about fires and blowing things up in flames."

Ewell continued ignoring Colonel Vortex's penchant for pyromania, "Its weight is 42.33 lbs, length 52.4 inches and the barrel length is 36.2 inches."

There were a few moments of silence as Dolby and the four officers assigned to the ground extermination mission picked up the RT-20 hand-cannon and felt its weight and dimensions. They were like excited school boys with a new fangled toy. Then Ewell asked, "Who is the best shot here?"

Vortex looked to Richter who shrugged his shoulders. Dolby looked to Laubscher who immediately glanced over to Egon Pohl who answered, "I am sir!"

"And how is that Colonel?" asked Ewell.

"I was a student of SS Standartenfuhrer Erwin Konig at the Zossen Sniper School in 1942 for 3 months before I went back to the Eastern Front to fight at Kursk. I can attest to liquidating at least 13 Russian soldiers with my Mauser 98K rifle. The best sniper in the whole of the Waffen SS or Wehrmacht was probably Erwin Konig. But that is debatable."

Colonel Vortex asked, "But wasn't Oberst Konig killed by the Russian sniper Vasily Zaytsev at the Stalingrad train yard in early 1943 before the German 6th Army surrendered?"

Colonel Egon Pohl riposted, "That is why I said 'debatable' Colonel Vortex! I believe that if I would have had the good fortune of coming up against Vasily Zaytsev then I would have defeated him. But I was in the 3rd Panzer Corps which was part

of Army Group Centre. The 6th Army under Field Marshal von Paulus was in Army Group South or Army Group Don as we called it then. I never had the chance to kill that particular individual. But I am good friends with the daughter of Oberst Konig who I first met at the Berlin Olympic Stadium. We still keep in touch to this day."

"Yes that's all very interesting Colonel Pohl but totally irrelevant. Alright then. You shall be the team sniper with this RT-20 and you shall have 200 rounds of the 130 gram bullets to take with you. Kick some proverbial Communist ass with this hand cannon! I am counting on you! And tell me how it works in combat. Give me your expert appraisal of this weapon because I may recommend that it be employed in the US Army sniper teams and also for the UDT teams as well."

At the fifth table Major General Ewell revealed the H & K UMP 0.45 Submachine Gun.

"Each of you will be issued with the UMP 0.45 calibre submachine gun. Nothing can beat it in terms of stopping power. It's of German manufacture which I know will please all of you. It is chambered for the larger cartridges which provides it with plenty of stopping power against unarmored targets. You will each be issued with 5,000 rounds."

Captain Richter asked, "And how about a flamethrower sir? This weapon would be very effective in cleansing out that nest of vipers and rats that infest the limestone caves where Giap is hunkered down."

Major General Ewell laughed, "That's what I am coming to next Captain!"

The SLICE Team walked over to the final display table and were amazed at what they saw. Captain Richter was expecting to see the M2A1-7 flamethrower that he had just used at the *Lang Vei* extraction. But to everybody's surprise they were showed what looked like an RPG-7 rocket launcher.

"This gentlemen," began Ewell, "…and don't ask me how we came by them because I can't tell you, is the *RPO-A Shmel* rocket-propelled flamethrower which is Soviet designed and made. Now I don't want to hear any shit from you guys about your delicate sensibilities in stooping to the use of Communist weaponry and all that crap-turd!"

Richter exclaimed, "You'll have no protest from me sir! Bloody fantastic!"

Ewell continued, "The RPO-A *Shmel* is a single shot, self-contained tube shaped launcher which operates similar to the LAW and RPG rocket launchers and the launcher is in a sealed tube. It can be carried in a man-pack two at a time. I am going to give you, Captain Richter, two of these beauties and two for you also Sergeant Dolby. By yourselves you can easily remove the tube, place it in the firing position and launch the weapon without assistance. You can then throw away the tube once fired. There are three types of ordnance that you can use. I am giving you two each of the thermobarbic warhead and the incendiary warhead. The thermobarbic is used for attacking

soft targets under moderate cover and the incendiary is designed for, and don't get excited on me Vortex, for spreading fires and igniting targets. The other is the smoke producing warhead but you will not need any of those. But just in case, you Colonel Pohl will carry one warhead just in case. You might need it at the LZEXF to divert attention away from your getaway and to cover the area with thick camouflage smoke. The thermobarbic and incendiary warheads weigh 2.1 kilograms each, the weight of the entire unit is 11 kilograms and the length is 0.92 metres. It has a 93mm calibre chamber and the muzzle velocity is approximately 125 metres per second with an effective range of 20 metres out to 1 kilometre. So you only have 9 of these warheads which means that you have to use them judicially to create the maximum destruction when the opportunities present themselves to you."

Brigadier Manfred Laubscher remarked, "It is an excellent weapon to give that little extra punch to our RT-20 hand-cannon. We should be able to ignite the interior of the cave complex with this *RPO-A Shmel*."

Sergeant David Dolby added, "I want to incinerate as many Communists as I can find in those fucked caves! They can't hide from me down there like putrid rats!"

Colonel Vortex ordered, "That's enough Sergeant. Can't you see it is difficult enough for me to control myself as it is with all this flame producing equipment around me?"

"Right then! That's it then in terms of your weaponry and equipment," said Major General Ewell.

"What about explosives to blow open any steel doors or barriers to the limestone cave complex sir?" asked Colonel Vortex, adding, "That's if we can get that far – to the entrance of the caves after neutralising the enemy troops outside. For I envisage that the North Vietnamese will have stationed a considerable number of men guarding the jungle surrounds and the cave entrance, possibly as many as battalion strength. Our only chance of getting inside the caves is to hope that the North Vietnamese will take time to react and that we can get in and out of the limestone structure before they can concentrate their full battalion sized force or multi-regimental sized troop concentrations against us. Once back into the jungle we have a chance of evading them and/or holding them off until we can get within range of the ellipse of murderous suppressive fire of the two SPOOKY gunships. That should hold the PAVN forces just long enough for us to be extracted by the HH-53C *Sikorsky Jolly Green Giants*."

"Oh! Yes! Thanks for reminding me Colonel Vortex."

Ewell waved his hands and a Warrant Officer Specialist in explosives walked over with what looked like a steel serving table on wheels.

Ewell picked up one of the devices on the table explaining, "You will also be issued with these. This is the latest technology in portable laser ignited plastic explosives with inbuilt timers. It is the Semtex plastic explosive comprising of PETN or Pentaeryth-

ritol Tetranitrate. PETN is one of the most powerful explosives known to man. It has a relative effectiveness factor of 1.66. When mixed with a plasticizer it forms a plastic explosive. It can be used as Pentolite when mixed with TNT can penetrate up to 5 inches of armor. PETN can be initiated by laser which is what you have here, as you can see the miniature clock and timer. Once the timer is set by this clock turning it clockwise to the desired time-delay there is a laser pulse with a duration of 25 nanoseconds and 0.5 to 4.2 joules of energy being released from a Q-Switched ruby laser which initiates the detonation of the PETN which is surface coated with 100nm thick aluminium and the explosion results in less than half a microsecond. It has an explosive velocity of 8,400 metres per second and an autoignition temperature of 190 degrees Celsius. Each of you will be equipped with three of these devices."

Brigadier Manfred Laubscher asked, "And when is Operation SLICE scheduled to begin General?"

Ewell said with a poker face, "Now!"

Vortex laughed, "You are joking sir, surely?"

"Do I ever joke about anything Vortex?"

"I wouldn't know sir? I never served under you - so I am not familiar with the idiosyncrasies of your own peculiar brand of *'black humour'*."

"Don't be facetious Colonel Vortex," said Ewell as he started to get agitated.

"I fucking don't have the time nor the inclination to be funny or engage in comical scenarios when everything that we are doing here and all that we are propelling into motion with our plans and operations is of the utmost importance to our military assistance and our duties under *public international law* to assist our client state of South Vietnam with repelling the Communist imperialist aggressors, sir!"

"Enough said," said Ewell, as he continued, "Captain John Ehrlich will lead you to the BEARCAT airstrip where a C-130E is waiting to take you to Da Nang. When you arrive another specially equipped C-130E fitted out for ELINT operations is waiting for you at the Da Nang air base. It has all these weapons onboard ready to go plus your HALO parachute gear, altimeters and your Oxygen re-breathers. So the Briefing is completed. The 36 hour duration of the mission will commence once you leave the Hercules at 33,000 feet being the maximum ceiling of the aircraft. You will have time to suit-up when you reach Da Nang. The time is now 1425 hours. It is estimated that you will reach insertion point over Laos within 4 miles of the limestone caves sometime around 1800 hours tonight and thus you will be in HALO descent at night to give you the best cover. The AC-47 SPOOKY support and the two HH-53C's will be coordinated exactly 36 hours from the time you infiltrate. So, any questions gentlemen?"

Brigadier General Manfred Laubscher attached to the 'Screaming Eagles'/101st Airborne Division asked, "As I am the Operation SLICE leader what are your orders

in case the following happen or any combination of the circumstances that I now ask clarification for. First, if we fail to locate and liquefy General Giap. Second, if the defences of the limestone caves are too great and we cannot infiltrate the primary objective. And third, if we manage to insert ourselves into the caves and whether or not we locate, crush and exterminate Giap the possibility that we cannot make it back the 3.84 miles to the exfiltration point?"

Major General Julian Ewell scratched his head and advised, "The answers, Brigadier, to your questions are simple and unequivocal. First, if you fail to kill the war criminal and mass murderer General Vo Nguyen Giap you inflict the maximum amount of damage and carnage on the North Vietnamese and Pathet Lao guerrillas as possible including the leadership figures I have already identified which are in your Briefs that you hold in your hands. You will also exterminate any Laotian villagers or village structures that you encounter. You are in Laos. You will treat every human excluding the five members of your SLICE team as the enemy to be executed and shot down on sight – no questions asked. We are in a state of *de facto* war with not only North Vietnam but Laos also. They are the enemy to be annihilated with maximum force, without pity or remorse. Second, if you cannot enter the limestone caves because the entire battalion or multi-regimental PAVN forces in the vicinity are too strong to overcome you exfiltrate immediately back to the rescue coordinates 3.84 miles to the south. While doing so you destroy everything in sight and anything that gets in your way, whether it be human, animal, plant life or structures of whatever description. Third, if you are not at the LZEXF point within 36 hours you are to attempt to make it back to the Laos/South Vietnam border just below the DMZ. From there the US 7th Air Force and the 1st Marine Air Wing will make another attempt to exfiltrate you approximately 72 hours after the mission commencement time. Of course, we shall continue to give you as much support as we can until you are all back at the nearest Fire Support Base, which in this case is *Khe Sanh*, *Lang Vei* having fallen yesterday."

"Sounds good to me," said Colonel Egon Pohl as he caressed his Model 500 Smith & Weston.

"And you said sir, begging your pardon that this mission is feasible? I mean do we really have a chance to get Giap?" asked Sergeant David Dolby.

"COMUSMACV certainly thinks so Sergeant, otherwise he would not have authorised SLICE."

Everyone looked at each other and then at Major General Ewell. Outside the 9th Division Quonset Warehouse they could see five M48 Patton tanks roll by. Distant artillery fire could also be heard to the West in the direction of War Zone C near the Cambodian border and *Black Virgin Mountain*.

Colonel Richard Vortex spoke, "I would like us to remember what we are fighting for. I would like to recite a passage from the *Book of Luke*. We should take a few

moments of silence and reflection before we undertake this most righteous mission of God."

Major General Ewell and the others nodded, Ewell said, "Go ahead please Colonel Vortex."

The seven men, including Captain John Ehrlich stood to attention as Vortex spoke.

"Jesus and his followers sailed across the lake from Galilee to the area of the Gerasene people. When Jesus got out on the land, a man from the town who had demons inside him came to Jesus. For a long time he had worn no clothes and had lived in the burial caves, not in a house. When he saw Jesus, he cried out and fell down before him. He said with a loud voice, 'What do you want with me, Jesus, Son of the Most High God? I beg you, don't torture me!'

He said this because Jesus was commanding the evil spirit to come out of the man. Many times it had taken hold of him. Though he had been kept under guard and chained hand and foot, he had broken his chains and had been forced by the demon out into a lonely place.

Jesus asked him, 'What is your name?'

He answered, 'Legion,' because many demons were in him. The demons begged Jesus not to send them into eternal darkness. A large herd of pigs was feeding on a hill, and the demons begged Jesus to allow them to go into the pigs. So Jesus allowed them to do this. When the demons came out of the man, they went into the pigs, and the herd ran down the hill into the lake and was drowned.

When the herdsmen saw what had happened, they ran away and told about this in the town and the countryside. And people went to see what had happened. When they came to Jesus, they found the man sitting at Jesus' feet, clothed and in his right mind, because the demons were gone."

[Luke 8:31]

When Vortex had finished reciting the passage the other six men looked at each other in bewilderment not comprehending the import of the words spoken that were so clear to Vortex.

The Colonel then explained, "This man whom Jesus had met in Gerasene is diseased with the devil. But it was the Son of God that exculpated the evil forces within this man to set him free from the Anti-Christ. South Vietnam is like this man possessed. Riddled with the 'Legion' of demons that lurk in the depths of the limestone caves. Jesus calls upon us to liberate the man and the nation from the Devil incarnate. It is God that calls upon us to venture down into the pits of hell, into these caves and exterminate the Legion of evil that lurks there. Only then will the man and the nation of South Vietnam be set free into the Light of God and into everlasting Peace."

The other six men said, "Amen!"

Colonel Richard Vortex said with solemnity, "Let us pray."

He then recited as everybody bowed their heads there amidst the tools of God and of the Crusade commanded by the Almighty; **[Psalm 143]:-**

"Hear my prayer, O Lord, give ear to my supplications: in thy faithfulness answer me, and in thy righteousness. And enter not into judgment with thy servant: for in thy sight shall no man living be justified. For the enemy hath persecuted my soul; he hath smitten my life down to the ground; he hath made me to dwell in darkness, as those that have been long dead. Therefore is my spirit overwhelmed within me; my heart within me is desolate. I remember the days of old; I meditate on all thy works; I muse on the work of thy hands. I stretch forth my hands unto thee: my soul thirsteth after thee, as a thirsty land. Hear me speedily, O Lord: my spirit faileth: hide not thy face from me, lest I be like unto them that go down into the pit. Cause me to hear thy lovingkindness in the morning; for in thee do I trust: cause me to know the way wherein I should walk; for I lift up my soul unto thee. Deliver me, O Lord, from mine enemies: I flee unto thee to hide me. Teach me to do thy will; for thou art my God: thy spirit is good; lead me into the land of uprightness. Quicken me, O Lord, for thy name's sake: for thy righteousness' sake bring my soul out of trouble. And of thy mercy cut off mine enemies, and destroy all them that afflict my soul: for I am thy servant."

Ten minutes later the six men were in the air and heading the 387 air miles from Long Binh (BEARCAT) to Da Nang air base. Captain Ehrlich was piloting.

The SLICE Team arrived approximately 1.5 hours later and immediately boarded the ELINT C-130E and suited up in their HALO parachute gear and adorned the weaponry of God's righteousness for the mission against what Colonel Vortex saw as a sacred trust from God to exterminate the human form of the Anti-Christ and bring freedom and democracy to the people's of South Vietnam. The religious feeling amongst the members of the SLICE Team was profound.

There was little talk amongst the officers and Medal of Honour recipient, Sergeant David Dolby. The orders and directives were precise. Each man withdrew into himself for the final 133 mile flight of 30 minutes to the HALO insertion point. The sun was soon to sink below the horizon and the devils from hell would be unleashed upon them in the jungles and pits of Laos.

They were entering the domain of *'Legion.'*

"We are now over the village of Huong Phung which is 9 miles from the HALO insertion point!" screamed Captain John Ehrlich from the cockpit as he made himself heard over the roar of the four Allison T56-A-7A turboprops of the Hercules MC-130E ELINT.

Colonels Vortex and Pohl were with him in the co-pilot and engineer's seat.

"Wish us luck Ehrlich!" said Egon Pohl.

"My best wishes are with you always," said the 7th Air Force Captain.

"I'm going to do Jesus' work down there!" screamed Vortex.

The five men were all completing their Oxygen re-breathing.

There were also three US Air Force crew personnel assisting them with their weaponry and survival gear.

The Operation SLICE Team were going to HALO drop out of the rear cargo door of the Hercules.

Brigadier Manfred Laubscher remembered the moments just before, as a young man in his late thirties he dropped over Crete to fight the British and Australians. How times had changed he thought to himself. Now the Australians were the stalwart partners of the US Forces and on his side.

"Sixty seconds!" shouted Captain Ehrlich, "Get ready!"

Brigadier Manfred Laubscher said silently to himself the Lord's Prayer in German;

Vater unser im Himmel,
geheiligt werde dein Name;
dein Reich komme;
dein Wille geschehe,
wie im Himmel so auf Erden.
Unser tägliches Brot gib uns heute.
Und vergib uns unsere Schuld,
wie auch wir vergeben unsern Schuldigern;
und führe uns nicht in Versuchung,
sondern erlöse uns von dem Bösen.

Denn dein ist das Reich und die Kraft
und die Herrlichkeit in Ewigkeit.
Amen.

The load-master of the MC-130E signalled to the SLICE Team to make their way to the cargo bay doors which seconds later opened. All the men switched from their onboard pre-breather to their Oxygen bottles to avoid Nitrogen contamination in their bloodstream which could cause Caisson Disease or the Bends and decompression sickness.

Colonel Vortex nodded to Brigadier Laubscher and the five men lined up as the cargo doors opened and the icy blast of freezing air at 33,000 feet hit them like a sledgehammer. They waited for the red light on the Hercules control panel that indicated they were over the drop coordinates.

Three seconds later the red flash greeted their eyes and all five men dropped out of the MC-130E as one smooth unit destined for 36 hours of hell.

Operation SLICE had commenced.

Colonel Vortex could see Laubscher and Pohl to his left and Richter and Dolby slightly below and to his right as they reached terminal velocity of a human body

through air. Each terminal velocity of the five men was slightly different due to their individual body weights. For Vortex at 93 kilograms his terminal velocity was approximately 117 to 125 mph but he wanted a quick insertion and began to posture his whole body plus gear and weaponry that were attached to his webbing in a bullet posture. Vortex had also instructed the other four members of the SLICE team to take similar postures.

In the bullet posture with legs together and arms held closely to the sides of the torso a person's terminal velocity can reach up to 210 mph. Vortex knew that terminal velocity is achieved when the gravity force upon an object is equal to that of the wind resistance. In other words down force equals up force being wind resistance. The aerodynamics or surface area of the human body is thus critical to the terminal velocity.

Sergeant Dolby and Richter had trouble assuming the bullet posture as Vortex saw them disappear above them his velocity being greater but Laubscher and Pohl were superlative skydivers and they were approximately at a level with his descent as they looked at their altimeter. Seconds had passed and they were already passing through the 20,000 feet barrier. At 10,000 feet they could dispense with their Oxygen bottles and prepare for imminent release of their HALO chutes.

All the men were trying to maintain a north-west axis of descent to land somewhere within a 1.5 mile radius of the limestone caves. Colonel Vortex knew that a southerly landing would suit their mission rather than overshooting and landing north of the cave complex at the designated coordinates provided by Captain John Ehrlich of the US 7th Air Force.

It was 6.25 miles from the Hercules jump to the ground. Travelling at 170 mph which is what Vortex guesstimated was his rate of descent he knew that he would hit the dirt in about 2.2 minutes. One and a half minutes had passed and Dolby and Richter were high above the other three field officers. Suddenly everything went black as they passed through the Cumulus cloud layer which consisted of high moisture formations which were dark and which were undergoing the condensation process of rising thermals or air bubbles which was at the condensation level of the atmosphere. Colonel Vortex realised that the thick Cumulus and Stratocumulus cloud cover would assist in preventing their detection by North Vietnamese patrols on the ground which, with the added cover of night and the dead silent descent at over 125 mph would almost ensure an insertion that would go unnoticed by the Communist troops, both North Vietnamese and Pathet Lao.

Colonel Vortex had made previous HALO jumps in Vietnam and he was confident that he could hit the ground without injury despite the fact that each man was carrying an arsenal of weapons and a battle-field pack of over 110 pounds each with which to carry the ammunition necessary.

Brigadier Manfred Laubscher had also instructed his team to empty their digestive systems of faeces and urine for once on the ground any passing of waste would leave an odour for the Pathet Lao or PAVN to pick up. The North Vietnamese were known to distinguish the human waste that was left by their own troops and those of the American forces. The rich and high fat diet of the Americans left a slightly different aroma of human shit which would be discerned quite easily by the regular forces of North Vietnam. Laubscher had instructed that if any man 'had to' shit open his bowels then it must be done down wind from the Communist positions.

Vortex glanced at his altimeter which read 6,000 feet and descending. Orders had been given to open the HALO parachutes at precisely 3,000 feet just enough time for the chutes to deploy and to arrest their descent to the jungle floor.

Wearing protective goggles Vortex could see the dark contours of the triple layered jungle canopy below. He just hoped that he would not become entangled in either the second or third layer of that morass of vegetation, vines, trees and fronds.

Laubscher and Egon Pohl were still within visual range but about 500 feet above him as his altimeter read 3,000 feet. Vortex activated the ripcord and the parachute that was jet black and designed not to reflect even moon-light reflections opened with a crisp thud. He felt his body whiplashed upwards as the terminal velocity was arrested. Guiding his chute by left and right hand toggles Vortex steered himself to what he perceived as a slight aperture in the jungle cover. The slow descent for the last 2,500 feet was the most dangerous for the SLICE team because if they were spotted they could be shot to shreds by the Communists before they touched the ground and could deploy their arsenal of firepower.

Brigadier Laubscher remembered that this was exactly what had happened to the *Polish 1st Independent Parachute Brigade* under Major General Sosabowski when they were dropped south of the Rhine near the village of Driel during the miserable failure that was *'Operation Market Garden'* from 17th to 25th September 1944 when the British and American forces had tried to recapture the Arnhem Bridge from the 2nd SS Panzer Corps under General Wilhelm Bittrich and Field Marshal Model. The failed operation was the brainchild of the over-cautious and pompous British Field Marshal Sir Bernard Montgomery in his attempt to open a 'highway' direct into the heart of the Ruhr and the interior of Germany to bring the war to a speedy conclusion. However the fighting prowess and resilience of the Wehrmacht and their valiant associated Waffen-SS units scotched that preposterous plan with very heavy allied casualties of approximately 17,200 killed and wounded mostly from the 1st British Airborne Division that was out-maneuvered and out-performed by the disciplined German soldier who still had a lot of resistance left from which to draw upon in the face of the Allied juggernaut on the Western Front.

Finally Colonel Richard Vortex watched as his feet hit the slush and mud of the Laotian jungle floor. Immediately he ripped away the parachute webbing and the canvas of the device rolling it up and burying it in under a mass of leaves and vines. Laubscher and Pohl landed next in that order and did the same. The three men were less than 100 yards from each other and quickly rejoined into one group.

Laubscher whispered to Vortex, "Have you seen the others?"

Pohl pointed to the north north-east without saying a word. The three officers could see two figures silently drifting downwards about 400 yards away. One descended below the foliage but the other fouled in the upper branches of the jungle foliage.

"Shit!" said Vortex, "Let's get him out of there!"

The field officers ran as best they could with their considerable load of weaponry and ammunition towards Richter's and Dolby's location.

The night was black and only the sound of insects could be heard.

Colonel Egon Pohl thought they were indeed lucky not to have been detected by the Communists up to this point.

Vortex was wearing infrared goggles while Laubscher was using his 'Starlight Starbright' scopes. They soon located Captain Max Richter who had just finished concealing his parachute.

"Up there!" whispered Richter to the trees above him.

Colonel Vortex motioned to Colonel Egon Pohl to deploy the RT-20 sniper rifle and keep watch in a 360 degree field of fire while they tried to extricate Sergeant David Dolby from his position.

Brigadier Laubscher took out the MGL/M-32 Grenade Launcher and loaded it up with High Explosive 40mm rounds. Richter already had his H & K UMP 0.45 Submachine gun at the ready as did Vortex and all the others.

"I am going to get him down. You cover me with Laubscher and Pohl," ordered Vortex to Richter.

The officers could see that Dolby was flailing his legs in the air and trying to wiggle his way clear of a mass of jungle vines and cords that had become entangled in his webbing. Vortex could also see that he was trying to unsheathe his machete to cut himself loose but could not reach the weapon that was hooked onto his back webbing.

With silence and speed Colonel Vortex divested himself of his field-pack and weapons except for his 18 inch Marine dagger and machete. Slowly and carefully he began to ascend the group of trees from which Dolby was dangling like a rag doll making a very enticing target for any passing Pathet Lao or PAVN patrol.

Colonel Vortex was taking one branch at a time and realised that the heavy duty combat boots that he was wearing was not conducive to climbing moist tree surfaces. Several times he lost his footing while standing on near horizontal branches and it was only the sheer power of his arms and hands that prevented him from falling the

8 yards to the ground. He estimated that Dolby was at least 15 yards into the air and was hanging from a large branch that shot out and joined another set of trees to the north of their position.

Pohl, Laubscher and Richter were on high alert with their array of weaponry at the ready as Vortex proceeded with his painstaking and arduous ascent to the Sergeant.

Suddenly Egon Pohl used the military hand signals etiquette to alert Vortex and Dolby that there was movement below.

Richter and Pohl had picked up the sounds of human footsteps and rustling leaves coming from the south.

Brigadier Laubscher had ordered that only knives and the Model 500 pistol with silencer were to be used before they reached the limestone cave entrance. Otherwise the sounds of heavy weaponry would alert the multi-battalion size force that US enemy forces were approaching and the game would be up as General Giap would undoubtedly be evacuated by his troops to a more secure location (if in fact he was actually in the caves).

Colonel Vortex froze balancing precariously on the two branches of the tree, hanging like an enormous and awkward baboon while he nodded upwards to Dolby that movement was afoot below and to be still. The Sergeant stopped his flailing about and relinquished his body to simply hanging in mid-air, helpless and silhouetted against the night sky. The perfect target.

A monkey hanging from a ten cent balloon from a distance of a hundred yards could have put a bullet in him with ease.

Richter and Pohl got down on their knees and trained their Model 500 pistols at the direction of the sound while Laubscher stood behind them at the ready with his MGL/M-32 covering behind a thick copse of foliage as back-up in case everything went to hell.

Vortex strained his eyes downwards and could hear only the buzz of mosquitoes and the soft rustle of the leaves from a hot and moist wafting breeze that passed through the jungle.

To Richter and Pohl it seemed like half an hour that they waited crouching in the dark with their heavy packs when in reality it was just over a minute until they saw the figures of what appeared to be one man and a woman with two large animals in tow.

To Colonel Egon Pohl it was obvious that they were Laotian peasants with their livestock making it back to their ville from some water source for the animals.

Richter discerned a dirt track about 10 yards south of their position and the tree that Vortex and Dolby were hanging so ridiculously from was immediately adjacent to that mud path. To the three officers below it was almost certain that the two men would be spotted by the peasants as they were obviously using this path to wherever they were heading.

Slowly and cautiously Egon Pohl turned around to Laubscher and without saying a word indicated by his head as to what the Brigadier's orders were to be.

Laubscher nodded slowly.

Pohl knew what he had to do and touched Richter's arm who also understood implicitly.

The two peasants had to be liquidated in order to prevent their presence being detected. All indigenous, as Major General Julian Ewell had ordered were assumed to be hostile inside Laos.

A few moments passed as the villagers walked onwards until they were barely 10 yards from the three officers. They were guiding along two large cows which plodded behind them.

Pohl nodded and gave the military hand signals to Richter to kill them with the Model 500 silenced pistol. And to do so with extreme prejudice.

[Pohl's hand signals were as follows as per the: *'Military C.R.E (Close Range Engagement) Standardized Operation Procedures'*] [First Pohl raised his left arm and placed his left hand over his right wrist and hand which held the handgun with fingers of the left hand slightly raised. This indicated the immediate presence of the enemy.]

[Next, Pohl raised his left arm with his left hand pointing upwards. The left forefinger and left thumb were perpendicular to each other with the other three fingers of the left hand folded down at the interphalangeal joints. The forefinger and the thumb of the left hand were thus in the shape of an imaginary gun. This indicated that they were to use pistols to take-out the target.]

As the two peasants and their cows were now almost upon them Colonel Egon Pohl gave the final C.R.E. Standardized Hand Signal. This was to extend the right arm with the right hand parallel to the ground, palm facing downwards and pointing to the left and then supinate the arm out as it was extended to the right of the body with the right hand pointing away from the torso and palm still facing downwards to the ground. This was the kill signal.

In a fraction of second after the last C.R.E. command from Pohl both men leapt out into the centre of the mud path and fired simultaneously the most powerful production handgun in the world. The heads of the two peasants blew apart and left their shoulders flying backwards from the point blank range. The headless cadavers wavered in the air for a few seconds before Richter and Pohl brutally kicked them to the dirt.

The two cows bolted backwards and let out noises. The animals were turning in the mud path away from Richter and Pohl.

Laubscher nodded to Richter and Pohl. The stray animals could alert any nearby villagers that something was amiss.

Pohl aimed his Model 500 and blew away the rear left leg of one of the cows.

Richter stepped up for the *coup de grace* and blew the cows head off with a single shot from the immensely powerful 0.500 caliber cartridges which had a muzzle energy of 3,030 foot-pounds of force. The effect was devastating.

However to the officers' horror the second cow had bolted into the jungle and out of sight with terror. Captain Richter ran after it in a northerly direction.

Brigadier Laubscher ran up to the tree from which Colonel Vortex and Sergeant Dolby were hanging so precariously.

"Kommen Sie von dort sofort herunter!" whispered the Brigadier as he looked up. Colonel Pohl scanned the darkness of the surrounding jungle with his 'Starlight' scope.

Vortex took another two minutes to claw his way up to Dolby.

"We don't have time to fuck around in trees Sergeant!" said the Colonel as he swiped his machete across the tangle of vines that had immobilized Dolby.

Immediately Dolby fell seven yards to the next large branch below. Grabbing hold of jungle fronds and vines he managed to lower himself to the jungle floor. Vortex followed moving downwards like a black panther.

When the four men were back on the ground Vortex asked, "Where the fuck is Richter?"

Pohl pointed north, "One of the cows got away from him. He went after it."

"Fuck that!" began Vortex, adding, "It must be a damned Communist cow going to alert the Pathet Lao!"

Brigadier Laubscher whispered with disbelief, "Seien Sie nicht das lächerliche Bumsen!"

[Translated: Don't be fucking ridiculous!]

Vortex asked incredulously, "What do you mean sir?"

Laubscher answered, "Tiere sind zu dumm, um politische Ansichten zu haben!"

[Translated: Animals are too stupid to have political persuasions!]

Vortex scoffed, "Not where I come from Laubscher. Haven't you heard of the *House Un-American Activities Committee*, the HUAC from 1950 to 1954 and the activities of Senator Joseph McCarthy of Wisconsin? The Second Red Scare? It was proven by the FBI and J. Edgar Hoover that Communist sympathies can be found almost anywhere and in anything. The rule of law is used to make accusations of disloyalty, subversion or treason based on circumstantial evidence or in the absence of such evidence when it is likely that such material facts may indeed be found by further investigation. Even if you are not a Communist it is equally sinful to be a Communist sympathizer or a co-conspirator in things that may not amount to outright Communism but which are *prima facie* un-American and hence the setting up of the *'Un-American Activities Committee'*. So even if this cow is not a Communist it may be willing to alert

any nearby indigenous of our presence which is the same thing as if it were in fact a Socialist subversive."

Sergeant Dolby looked at Pohl who simply shrugged while Laubscher remarked, "Colonel! You are suffering from delusions! Did you take any medication before you embarked on this mission?"

Vortex ignored the question as Captain Richter came running back from the blackness beyond the dirt track.

"Don't worry! I neutralised the cow that got away."

"Good!"

Laubscher shook his head and said jokingly, "Did it admit as being a spy for the *Animal Farm*?"

"I'm sorry sir? What are you asking me?" said Richter.

Vortex rolled his eyes upwards in their sockets as obviously the Brigadier's remark went right over Richter's head.

Colonel Vortex took out his Ground Positioning System transponder and checked their coordinates.

"We have landed too far west."

"Where are we then?" asked Laubscher.

Vortex read out the exact latitude and longitude from the transponder, "16 degrees: 47 minutes and 42.09 seconds North and 106 degrees: 28 minutes and 59.57 seconds East. By my reckoning we are just over 3 miles from the limestone caves."

Colonel Pohl advised, "Then we better move fast. Time is of the essence. We are already 1.5 hours into the mission."

"We stuffed-up the HALO descent. We should not be more than 1.5 miles from the caves and the primary target," mentioned Brigadier Laubscher.

"A tributary of the *Cua Viet River* is about 2 miles east of us and by this map there is a village or rather a very small ville by the name of *Ta Loi* about 1 mile to the west of here. We need to head north north-west to reach the cave complex," said Colonel Vortex.

Laubscher said, "Then I suggest we skirt north of this *Ta Loi* ville and approach the PAVN headquarters through those low hills,…." He pointed to the map, "There."

"I agree," said Vortex.

For the next twenty minutes the five members of the SLICE team proceeded through the dense jungle with their heavy loads of advanced weaponry and weighed down by their thousands of rounds of exotic and lethal ordnance.

It was now 2045 hours on 8th February 1968.

Vortex continued to monitor their positions with the GPS transponder every 5 minutes. All the men knew that the chances of running into a PAVN or Pathet Lao

patrol was better than 50%. If that would occur before they reached the limestone caves the mission was doomed to failure.

A myriad of thoughts fleeted through Brigadier Laubscher's mind as they struggled onwards. In Russia over 45 years ago he had remembered that the Ukrainian summer could be just as hot as the Vietnamese one but albeit with less humidity. All the SLICE team were soon dripping with perspiration. Even at night the temperature in the tropics did not fall much more than 5 to 7 degrees Fahrenheit.

Colonel Vortex and Brigadier Laubscher knew that their only advantage was surprise. The North Vietnamese would never expect that a small LRRP team would be inserted so deep into Communist controlled territory and into Laos. Major General Ewell advised them that if they were captured the US Government would disavow any knowledge of their mission and not recognise their operation in any way. Vortex understood that this meant that if they were captured it was a *de facto* death sentence for all of them.

Colonel Egon Pohl was on point with Vortex immediately behind, Laubscher and Dolby in the centre and Captain Richter covering the rear with his MGL/M-32.

The terrain was difficult to pass with numerous hills whose slopes were steep and covered in thick vegetation.

As the SLICE team ascended a 50 degree incline after traversing a ravine they were half way up the slope when Egon Pohl lost his footing in the mud and commenced to slither out-of-control down the hill. He passed Vortex by a few inches but slammed into Laubscher who also lost his footing and the two ex-Wehrmacht officers tumbled like bowling pins towards Richter further down.

Seeing that the two men were heading to a ledge after which there was a 20 foot drop into the ravine below Richter threw off his pack and whipped out a length of rope which he tied to a nearby sapling strong enough to support the weight. At the same time he threw out the rope to the falling officers who managed to grab hold as they careered towards the ravine crevasse. It was just in time as Pohl and Laubscher arrested their downward spiral just before falling off the edge which would have been an ignominious embarrassment for both of them.

"Scheiße Herren! Können wir unsere Taten oder was zusammenbringen? "said Colonel Vortex with annoyance as he looked backwards down the slope.

[Translated: 'Shit sirs! Can we get our acts together or what?']

Laubscher and Pohl dragged themselves back up the stinking Laotian hill. They were covered in mud and several leeches that had attached themselves to their camouflage uniforms.

Colonel Vortex lit up a cigarette and with the glowing end of which he incinerated the bugs first on Laubscher's uniform and then on Pohl's.

"Sorry about that Vortex," said Colonel Egon Pohl.

Vortex watched the slimy bugs curl up in their death agony.

"Fuck this shit Colonel! I think I better take point now. You go back with the Brigadier and Sergeant Dolby."

Dolby whispered, "I want to kill anything! I'm getting impatient sirs!"

Laubscher smiled, "Don't worry Sergeant. You will have plenty of opportunities for immolating these little bow-legged, yellow Communist swine soon enough!"

"Stop the chit-chat!" whispered Colonel Richard Vortex.

The SLICE team reached the top of the hill and started to make their way back down to yet another ravine with another hilltop in the distance. In the darkness it was extremely difficult to make out the contours of the slopes without their Starlight scopes and infrared goggles. Wearing the night-vision aids however reduced their visual acuity to spot the PAVN or any Pathet Lao in the vicinity.

As Vortex picked his way down the reverse slope he had heard nothing. Laubscher, Pohl and Dolby were seven yards behind him and Richter another five yards beyond that bringing up the rear.

To his amazement as he jumped over a fallen log Vortex slammed straight into an object that was crossing his path from north to south.

To his horror he realised it was a Pathet Lao guerilla armed with an AK-47. The two bodies tumbled to the ground and then scrambled to their feet. Vortex and the Pathet Lao soldier looked at each other for some seconds in utter amazement.

The Communist thought that Vortex was another Laotian while the Colonel was so taken aback by the sheer suddenness of it all and the virtual impossibility of colliding with another human in the middle of such a vast jungle that he too froze stupefied into inaction.

"Bạn là ai?" said the Pathet Lao as he could speak Vietnamese.

Vortex shook his mind out of its paralysis and expertly kicked the AK-47 machine gun out of the Communist's hands.

Fortunately for Vortex the Laotian was not carrying any other weapons.

With the same movement as he kicked the Colonel unsheathed his 18 inch Marine dagger and with its razor sharp double-edged blade rammed the implement upwards and into the Pathet Lao's jaw and mandible so that it pierced upwards through his tongue and then into the interior of his skull through the midbrain.

As the blood spurted over Vortex's camouflage fatigues he twisted around to the rear of the man so that he had him in a head-lock and then with the dagger still imbedded in his cranium Vortex used his immense upper body strength to crack the skull free from the cervical spinal cord and with one last movement drove the dagger out from the skull and directly into the man's anus so that the tip of the blade exited through his penis from the front, upon which he brutally kicked the body into the mud and stamped on the skull once more for good measure.

"Das ist für Sie dieser Weg besser," said Colonel Vortex to himself.

As the others made their way down the reverse slope Brigadier Laubscher whispered with agitation, "Was das Bumsen das ist?"

"Was denkt das Bumsen von Ihnen?" answered Vortex in a lather.

[Translated: 'What the fuck do you think? (In response to the question: What the fuck is this?)]

"Ich habe Zeit für diese Scheiße nicht!" said Laubscher getting quite angry.

"Denken Sie, dass ich ihn bat, mit mir zu kollidieren?" answered Vortex.

[Translated: 'Do you think I asked him to collide with me? (In response to the statement: 'I don't have time for this shit.')]

Laubscher riposted, "Haben Sie Ihren Dauerauftrag-Obersten vergessen?"

"Ich habe nichts vergessen," answered Vortex looking around him in the darkness.

[Translated: 'Have you forgotten your standing orders Colonel?' Answer: "I have forgotten nothing.']

Colonel Egon Pohl used the C.R.E. hand signals to tell everyone to be still and quiet.

The five members of the SLICE team heard the distinct babble of Vietnamese voices less than 20 yards away coming from below them on the reverse slope and near to the ravine.

The team took out their Model 500 handguns and hit the deck.

As luck would have it the voices were heading directly for their position.

Colonel Vortex knew it was the rest of the Pathet Lao patrol.

Already the mission was in danger of being compromised.

Egon Pohl gave the C.R.E. signal for the enemy and then for the order to commence firing at will.

Vortex could see two figures coming out of the low scrub directly in front of him. Jumping to his feet he shot at the two Communist's in quick succession with his silencer attached. One shot blew off the side of the head of the Communist to the left while the second tore off the right arm of the second assailant on the right.

Laubscher and Pohl scurried forward and finished the two Pathet Lao aggressors by burying their combat knives deeply into their heart tissue.

"What do you think sir?" asked Sergeant Dolby as the five men continued to run down to the bottom of the ravine.

Captain Richter answered, "If there are three then you can bet there are plenty more."

Colonel Vortex checked his transponder and realised that they had not stayed far enough north of the village on the map which was *Ta Loi* as the slopes had forced them to take an approach of less resistance that meandered its way further south-west than they would have liked.

"Blast!" began Vortex, "It looks like we stumbled onto this decrepit village after all."

"How can that be?" asked Colonel Pohl, "You are supposed to be the navigator on this mission."

Vortex shrugged his shoulders as he asked, "What are your orders Brigadier Laubscher?"

The Brigadier said nothing at first and waved for the team to ascend the next slope in front of them.

After five minutes of arduous climbing and clawing with their substantial battle packs and field-gear through the mud and slush the SLICE team hunkered down on the apex of the hill that was 579 meters above sea level. It was the highest point in the immediate surroundings.

Silence ensued as Laubscher and Vortex examined the entire area that lay before them with Starlight scopes.

Richter, Pohl and Dolby loaded up their UMP's and Pohl chambered one round into the RPO-A *Shmel*. He also loaded the RT-20 anti-material sniper rifle.

"That shit of a place is directly in our path. If we maneuver around it – it will add at least 2 hours onto the mission time which we cannot afford," said Vortex to Brigadier Laubscher.

"This is a fine state of affairs I must say!"

"Sorry Brigadier but the terrain is more difficult than we had first anticipated."

"Fuck the anticipation. And fuck all your carefully laid preparations. We are fucked!"

"I wouldn't jump to any solid conclusions as yet sir. The three aggressors we dispatched seemed to have been alone. So, as far I can tell by the inactivity down there – nobody else has been alerted to our presence as yet."

"Very comforting Colonel," said Laubscher facetiously.

Colonel Pohl advised, "I don't see any other option other than to neutralize the entire ville and everything in it."

Richter asked Sergeant Dolby, "Did you hear that Sergeant?"

"I did. And I like it! I'm ready for action."

"It's your job to keep as accurate a body count as possible Dolby," said Vortex.

"I understand sir," said the Medal of Honour recipient.

Before leaving BEARCAT Major General Julian Ewell had impressed upon the SLICE team that an accurate 'body count' was absolutely necessary as General Westmoreland was eager to include their tally with this month's statistics that would go back to Secretary of Defence Clark Clifford's desk in the Pentagon. A high 'body count' would be another feather in the cap for COMUSMACV and would begin to negate the negative impact of the TET offensive that was going on. It would also take

attention away from the ongoing siege of *Khe Sanh* some 25 miles down the road on QL9 (National Route 9).

The US forces, said General Ewell needed a morale boosting statistical body count even though the mission would of course not be revealed as the statistics would be added onto the *Khe Sanh* kill ratios and force requirement levels and their outcomes. In many ways the body count ratios were more important even than the primary objective of neutralizing General Giap as his death would count for just one kill like everybody else that was incinerated in the magnificent application of American offensive firepower (as Major General Ewell had described it).

"Well to hell with it then," began Brigadier Manfred Laubscher, "We shall fucking kill them all!"

"With extreme prejudice?" asked Colonel Pohl.

"Yes! With extreme prejudice and leave nothing standing. That's an order gentlemen!"

Vortex remarked, "Good! I am sick of all this pussy-footing around in the dead of night with daggers! We are not Jack the fucking Ripper after all. And this is not White Chapel! This is Laos which is free for extermination as we see fit! For it is the Grace of God that wills it!"

"Amen to that!" said Brigadier Laubscher.

Colonel Pohl said in Latin, "*Deus Vult*!"

Laubscher and Vortex reconnoitered the entire village of *Ta Loi* that lay, unsuspecting, before them with cold and calculating eyes that were trained to pick up the points of least resistance. They were looking through their infrared scopes for all objects, machinery, structures and fuel sources that could be combustible for the RPO-A *Shmel* rocket propelled flamethrower to be operated by Sergeant David Dolby. As he was the Congressional Medal of Honour winner, Vortex thought that it would be appropriate for him to open-up the initial assault on *Ta Loi*.

"Look! Over there!" said Laubscher, "A fuel storage tank. It must be part of the Pathet Lao set-up in this location."

"And there is a Soviet made ZIL 130 truck.

[*ZIL truck: Zavod imeni Likhachova (Russian): Soviet made truck weighing 9,500 lbs; 5.9 litre ZIL engine carbureted: 170 hp; 5 speed manual; Supplied in large numbers to the North Vietnamese Army by their Puppet Masters the Soviet & Chinese Imperialist Aggressors.*]

We can ignite the petrol tanks. Also the huts are thatched and wooden structures which are highly combustible. If we set the whole ville ablaze most of the protagonists will be incinerated in their slumber."

"Das ist ausgezeichnet," answered Laubscher to Colonel Vortex.

[Translated: That is excellent.]

Colonel Pohl gave the C.R.E. standardized hand signals to the SLICE team to lock-and-load their weapons.

"You will have the privilege of the first kills Sergeant Dolby," said Laubscher.

"Yes! Since you have been pestering us for your gratuitous need for action. Then action you shall most surely have!" quipped Vortex.

Captain Richter sniggered as he prepared his MGL/M-32. He was determined not to be outdone on the 'body count' scale by Sergeant David Dolby – Medal of Honour recipient or not.

"Get ready then!" ordered Laubscher.

Vortex spotted three men standing next to the ZIL-130 truck that looked like PAVN troopers because they had the green tunics and pith helmets of the North Vietnamese regular forces.

He had also brought with him the M40A3 Standard Issue Marine Corps Sniper Rifle which was 7.62 by 51 mm. Taking careful aim he shot the first PAVN trooper in the head. Quickly reloading manually because the M40A3 was bolt-action he let off a second round which went straight through the heart of the second enemy soldier who crumpled to the dirt. By this time 6 seconds had passed and the third Communist started to fire the AK-47 he was holding in all directions as he could not discern in the night where the killing shots had come from.

"Scheißen Sie!" said Vortex audibly. His failure to kill the third man who had started to expend his ammunition would alert the entire village of *Ta Loi*.

He took careful aim and with the third shot blew the top of the man's skull off from the level of the eyes. But it was too late now for a full surprise attack.

"Now we are fucked!" said Brigadier Laubscher, criticizing, "I thought you were a faster shot than that Vortex!"

Pohl added, "Since I was a graduate of the Zossen Sniper School I should have killed those men."

"It's too damned late now! The game is afoot," said Laubscher.

Pohl handed the RPO-A *Shmel* to David Dolby who took aim and fired one round of High Explosive directly at the ZIL-130 truck. An enormous explosion lifted the truck 10 yards into the air and it exploded into a ball of fire.

The burning debris scattered over the village of *Ta Loi* and set the thatched roofs on fire. Within 60 seconds the entire ville was a blazing inferno.

More than twenty men and women ran screaming from a large building in the centre of the ville some of whom we carrying AK-47's.

Colonel Pohl with deliberate and calm movements took the RT-20 mm anti-material sniper rifle and started to pick them off.

First he killed the five men that ran towards their position blowing various parts of their bodies off so that limbs and intestines were splaying over the burning area of

the village in a grotesque mess. Some of the Pathet Lao were bunched together as they ran hither and thither not knowing how to counter-attack.

Pohl took great relish in blowing the 20mm ordnance of the RT-20 through three bodies at a time.

One bullet took the head off one man, continued to the person behind and cut his torso in two and then ended up in a third person, a woman, whose both arms were sheared off.

"Now is the time!" screamed Colonel Vortex.

The five member SLICE team stood up and commenced firing with their H & K UMP 0.45 caliber submachine gun.

Bullets rained down on men, women and children alike as they ran from their burning huts. The SLICE team cut them down in an orgy of destructive power.

The fertile ground of *Ta Loi* was made more so by the many quarts of blood that washed over the killing ground that was such a pure vindication of America's righteous firepower against the Communist aggressor forces be they Pathet Lao or North Vietnamese for to Colonel Vortex they were all the same. Vermin to be eradicated by any and all means at their disposal. And eradicate them they did with extreme prejudice.

The stupid failures, as Vortex perceived them, were somewhat atoned and negated by the heavy toll of successful evisceration that they were now dispensing to the vicious foe. (as Colonel Vortex perceived them)

"Look there!" shouted Sergeant Dolby.

The Medal of Honour recipient pointed to a small jeep with four Laotian guerillas inside making its way towards the north-west and away from the village.

"Take them out!" ordered Laubscher.

Colonel Pohl nodded and aimed the RT-20 cannon at the jeep's fuel tank. Pressing the trigger the 20mm 130 gram caliber round flew at 850 meters per second and erupted the small vehicle into thousands of metal shards and burning splinters which added combustible force to the already raging fires that engulfed *Ta Loi*.

"Move in to mop-up!" ordered Brigadier Laubscher.

The five men ran into the centre of the village and fired their UMP's in a full 360 degree circumference of heavy suppressive fire. Women, children and Lao troopers continued to pour out of their burning dwellings but were immediately mutilated to pieces by five of the most powerful submachine guns in the world.

Dolby relished in the mayhem. As he fired he had his left hand clutching his machete so that when the bullet ridden bodies of the villagers hurtled past within striking distance of his locus of attack he decapitated them with a brutal blow from the razor sharp implement.

Captain Richter had the UMP in his right hand, firing, and the Model 500 pistol in the left. Anything that escaped the carnage of the submachine gun was bludgeoned apart by the powerful handgun.

Brigadier Laubscher had also brought with him a M2 standard US Army issue flamethrower in addition to the *Shmel*. The double tanks were strapped to his back and he let loose with a stream of napalm mixed aluminum jell fire that tore open the village structures and caused multiple secondary explosions.

As per Major General Ewell's orders Sergeant Dolby was keeping a 'body count' but it was hard to get an accurate figure as so many people were dying and so quickly.

Some of the bodies fused together with flesh burning into flesh so that it became arduous to distinguish whether it was one corpse or two.

Colonel Pohl rushed into the nearest hut from where a few rounds had been fired in the direction of the SLICE team.

"Exterminate those hostile forces!" shouted Laubscher to his ex-Wehrmacht comrade.

Pohl kicked in the burning shit of a door (as he perceived it to be) and rushed in to find three women and two children lying terrified in a corner of the structure and hiding behind a makeshift stove which had boiling rice upon it.

"No eating and no dinner for you!" screamed Pohl as he peppered all five women and children with his UMP tearing their flesh apart so that their bodies fell into each other in hot and sickly sweet streams of blood.

A bullet was fired from behind a flimsy partition and narrowly missed Egon's head.

Seeing that it was an old man over 70 years of age Pohl wanted to take time in the dispatching of this geriatric foe that was so impecunious in his attitude.

"Wie Sie herausordern, zurück alten Mann zu schießen?"

[Translated: 'How dare you shoot back old man?']

To his surprise the Pathet Lao understood German.

Egon Pohl could hardly believe his ears when the elderly man said, "Sie Scheiß-cowboy-Amerikaner-Schwein! Warum lassen Sie unser Land nicht allein?"

[Translated: You fucking cowboy American swine! Why don't you leave our country alone?]

Egon said overcome with amazement, "Ich bin nicht amerikanisch."

The old villager said, "Aber Sie tragen die Uniform der 101. Bordabteilung."

His face wrinkled and decaying was a vision of pure and unadulterated hatred.

[Translated: "But you are wearing the uniform of the 101st Airborne Division?"]

Colonel Pohl rushed forward and grabbed the old man by his throat and rammed him up against the bloody and mutilated bodies of his family so that the blood and intestines of that orgy of destruction seeped into his leathery skin, "I am a German! And that is all you have to know you cunt-sucking motherfucking Communist pig!"

With those words Egon ripped his US combat knife directly into the geriatric's gonads and twisted the knife in, first clockwise and then anti-clockwise until he had ripped open the scrotal sacs.

The elderly gentleman howled in agony as Egon then withdrew the knife and buried it first into his left eyeball and then into his right eye, gouging both organs free from their cranial cavity. With the skill and aplomb of a qualified surgeon he then inserted his blade with deliberate tardiness into the carotid artery of the neck severing the tissues back to the level of the cervical spine.

Like a stupid rag-doll the old man's head collapsed backwards as it was now in a state of semi-decapitation.

"I am going to fuck your ass with this knife!" screamed the Colonel.

He swung the man around and drove his blade into the man's anus so that it pierced through his gluteus maximus and into his pelvis making a crushing mess of his lower intestines.

Kicking the elderly Communist on top of his dead family he then bludgeoned his skull to a bloody pulp with the butt end of his UMP submachine gun.

Brigadier Laubscher burst into the burning hut shouting, "Was geht hier weiter?"

Pohl smiled and said, "I was just finishing the mopping up sir."

"Good! Vortex wants to get moving before the North Vietnamese are alerted to this minor disturbance."

The five member SLICE team re-grouped in the centre of the ravaged and burning village with bodies strewn in every direction around their positions.

"I think that we have successfully accounted for the entire population of this hive of traitors," said Vortex calmly.

Sergeant David Dolby reported, "I have a body count of 137 dead. So with the three that we killed back up the slope plus the two peasants that makes a total body count of 142."

Captain Richter asked, "You forgot about the cows?"

Dolby corrected himself, "Sorry sir. Yes, 142 human dead plus two Communist cows!"

Vortex chuckled, "This is fucking absurd! Who asked for these body counts anyway?"

Dolby replied, "General Ewell impressed upon me the absolute importance of registering accurate body counts, sir."

"But he didn't say anything about counting-up the dead livestock did he?"

"He said everything living sir."

"Oh? He did?"

'Yes sir!" replied the Sergeant.

"Oh! Well then! That's different! Good work Dolby!"

Pohl remarked, "Keep your notebook handy. The real statistics haven't even started yet!"

Brigadier Laubscher said, "I hope Clark Clifford will be pleased when the report lands on his desk at the Pentagon."

Vortex smiled and the SLICE team moved out as quickly as they could and traversed the remaining 2 miles to the entrance of the limestone caves as they worried that the PAVN forces might have been alerted to the minor altercation at *Ta Loi*.

Within two hours they had reached to within 500 yards of the entrance to the limestone caves as Colonel Vortex checked his GPS transponder.

The SLICE team took up positions on a ridge overlooking the cave complex that was buried in the side of a small mountain which had an elevation of 1,032 meters above sea level.

"This is it," whispered Colonel Vortex as he double-checked his transponder coordinates.

The transponder that Vortex was using emits an identifying signal in response to an interrogating received signal coming from US satellites in geosynchronous orbit around the Earth. It was a client of one of many such satellites used by the United States Air Force and the Strategic Air Command or SAC. In these communication satellites a transponder gathers signals over a range of uplink frequencies and retransmits them on a different set of downlink frequencies to receivers on the surface of the Earth. This is done without changing the content of the received signals. The term 'transponder' is a portmanteau for Transmitter-Responder and it can be variably abbreviated to; XPDR; XPNDR; TPDR or simply TP. The channels used by the US military satellites that Colonel Vortex was relying on to pinpoint the limestone cave complex where General Vo Nguyen Giap was suspected and hoped to be currently situate was an XPDR because each is a separate transceiver or repeater. With the latest digital video data compression techniques and multiplexing several video and audio channels may travel through a single XPDR transponder on a single wideband carrier. Analog video only has one channel per transponder with subcarriers for audio and automatic transmission identification services (ATIS). Non-multiplexed radio stations can also travel in a single channel per carrier (SCPC) mode, with multiple carriers (analog or digital) per transponder.

The XPDR that Colonel Vortex was using was a multiplexed digital transponder that was hooked up to both the Pentagon in Washington D.C. and the MACV HQ in Saigon or Pentagon East. There were also subsidiary channels to BEARCAT where the communications unit of the US 9th Infantry Division was monitoring the digital signals. This system allows each channel to communicate directly with the US Military satellites in low Earth orbit. This had advantages over the old landline system that was limited by its physical characteristics of having a solid connection in order to function. The XPDR was similar to the RACON device or radar identification systems used by the US Navy. RACON is a portmanteau of Radar and Beacon. The coordinates that Captain John Ehrlich of the US 7th Air Force had provided were now confirmed by Colonel Richard Vortex on his XPDR.

The battle proper was about to commence.

"Hail to the Chief!" whispered Brigadier Manfred Laubscher.

[He was referring to the President of the United States of America].

Colonel Egon Pohl whispered back, "In our previous uniforms we would have been hailing to a different chief."

Colonel Vortex answered the two ex-Wehrmacht officers, "I wish I would have been old enough to serve with you then."

The men chuckled.

"Yes, the war was not entirely successful for our previous organisation," said Brigadier Laubscher.

Vortex quipped, "That's because you were up against the US Armed Forces."

Egon asked, "You said you met Gruppenfuhrer *Mohnke*?"

"Yes I did. I actually met Wilhelm when I was stationed at *Ramstein* for a few months back in 1963."

"Oh? Really? That's wonderful Richard. I was a good friend of his back in the old days. What does Wilhelm do these days now that he is out of *that*, or I should say *'our'* old uniform?" asked Egon.

Vortex smiled, "He has gone into the trucking business in West Germany Egon."

"I have lost touch with him since I immigrated to America. I tried to persuade him to come with me and start a new life in New York. But he refused. I told him the US recruiters would accept us with open arms due to our considerable military experience. But Wilhelm did not believe me. He said that because he was in the *Schierheitsdienst* he would never be accepted by the US Army. I told him that it was not true. I said look at Wernher Von Braun. He was a much higher ranking defence civilian working for our government [National Socialist Government] on secret weapons of mass destruction or WMD's as you now so amusingly call them. And look where that got him. He virtually ran the technological side of the National Aeronautics and Space Administration [NASA] right through this decade of the 1960's. Hell! They are just about to launch Wernher's rocket for Apollo 8 due on 21st December this year. Not only Wernher but his whole team of German World War 2 scientists were carried off by the US Military and installed at *White Sands* Air Force Base to develop the United States Space Program. It was a combination of American money and power and German scientific prowess that is going to make this Moon landing a possibility. I explained all this to Wilhelm but he just refused to believe me."

"Yes I know," began Vortex. "The American military draws heavily on captured technology of the German *Reich* after the Second World War. Its common knowledge. Look at what we did at *Nordhausen*! We shipped the entire German experimental rocket the *'Mittelwerk'* V-2 rocket back to *White Sands* testing grounds for operations such as *Operation Sandy, Operation Blossom* and the *Hermes Project* at *White*

Sands in New Mexico. Most of the *Operation Paperclip* scientists had worked at *Nordhausen* for the Reich. Operation Paperclip was the program of the OSS [Office of Strategic Services] to recruit the scientists of Germany back to the United States for employment and was conducted by the JIOA [Joint Intelligence Objectives Agency]. The purpose was primarily to deny German scientific expertise to both the Soviets and even the United Kingdom. The JIOA 'bleached' these scientists of their National Socialist affiliations in order to *'sanitise'* them for American classified work on military and space applications."

Brigadier Laubscher interrupted, "Gentlemen please. Yes, I knew Gruppenfuhrer Mohnke also but I think we better dispense with this chit-chat for we have a mission to complete and time is of the essence here!"

Sergeant Dolby said impatiently, "I am going to fuck these Communist pigs good and proper!"

"Thank you for that erudite statement Sergeant," said Captain Max Richter sarcastically.

Brigadier Laubscher and Colonel Vortex planned the imminent attack. As they peered through their Starlight scopes they surveyed the North Vietnamese Regular Army positions in detail. Their brains clicked over and analysed everything that they saw with their expert eye trained for battle.

"Fuck! There are more PAVN troops than I thought! These units are from the 304th PAVN Division. The same unit that fucked-us-up at *Lang Vei*. Boy! Oh! Boy! I am itching to give them a bruising!" whispered Vortex to the SLICE team.

"Yeah! Fuck their guts out the motherfuckers!" said Sergeant Dolby.

Colonel Vortex observed at least 200 North Vietnamese troops deployed before them. These, thought Vortex were only those enemy troops that were visible to him. He had no idea how many more PAVN were in the surrounding jungle on their right and left flanks. There were three watch-towers each approximately 20 yards high with the Chinese made *Type 24 7.92mm* heavy machine guns. Each tower had four troopers in them. Around the three watch-towers there were seven anti-aircraft guns which were the Soviet 37mm M1939 40mm Bofors. The ones that the North Vietnamese were using in front of the limestone cave complex was the Chinese Type 55 which had a rate of fire of 80 rounds per minute. In addition there were 12 ZIL-130 trucks parked in two parallel rows in front of the entrance of the caves with PAVN troops milling about and talking. Vortex estimated at least 100 Communist soldiers directly in front of the entrance at the base of the small mountain plus 100 more in the watch-towers and manning the Type 55 anti-air weapons.

"What do you think sir? How should we open the attack?" asked Vortex to Laubscher.

"We need to clear an axis of advance to the entrance of the limestone cave complex. I think we should start with a bombardment of high explosive and incendiary ordnance from the MGL/M-32. Colonel Pohl, at the same time, can work on the ZIL's with his RT-20 anti-material rifle. If he can blow enough of them to smithereens that should place the PAVN in a state of confusion. Then all five of us can go in with our UMP's and the M2 flamethrower. I can't see from here. Is the entrance to the caves accessible?"

Vortex looked carefully with his Starlight Scope as Laubscher added, "You are younger than me and your eyes are better."

Colonel Vortex took several minutes to peer into the night that was moonless. He could see a large bunker door that appeared to be manufactured from steel or iron. It appeared to be semi-open just wide enough for two men to pass through.

"If we can't get to the entrance fast enough the North Vietnamese will seal the base tight. We shall then have to blow the entrance with our Semtex plastic explosives."

Laubscher nodded to Vortex as he spoke.

Suddenly to the east they saw a formation of additional Communist troops approaching that hitherto had not been observed by Colonel Vortex nor Brigadier Laubscher.

"Scheißen Sie!" swore Vortex.

"What is it?" asked Laubscher.

"Mehr Truppen nähern sich! Vom Osten."

"How many?" asked the Brigadier.

"Mindestens Firmenkraft. Wahrscheinlich zweihundert," answered Vortex.

[Translated: At least Company strength. Probably two hundred.]

"This is getting better by the minute!" exclaimed Laubscher as he was overcome with exasperation.

"This is a fucking suicide mission! I know we are good but not *that* good!"

Vortex nodded as he put down the Starlight scope and sank back in the dirt of the ridge overlooking the limestone cave entrance.

"We're screwed."

Laubscher remarked, "I won't accept defeat even before we have begun this escapade. I would like to get General Westmoreland down here so that he can see the pickle that he has placed us in regarding this unenviable predicament."

Richard Vortex did not know what to say.

Silence ensued for several minutes.

The clock was ticking and time was in short supply.

It was now 2345 on the 8th February 1968.

"This war is fucked!" said Vortex finally.

"Ja. Erzählen Sie mir darüber."

[Translated: Yes. Tell me about it.]

"I see no option but to advance and attack!" said Colonel Egon Pohl who joined in the conversation.

"Why is that?" asked Colonel Vortex.

"Why?" asked Pohl.

"Yes. Please explain," asked Laubscher.

"Because we are traitors to the mission if we do not attack. Renegades to our righteous and sacred mission here in Vietnam and we have an oath of allegiance to our new masters and protectors – the United States of America. If we renege on our mission we will be ostracised in the face of the Joint Chiefs of Staff and General Earle Wheeler, disgraced by General Westmoreland and become toxic pariahs to the United States Army that has been so kind to us in allowing us to join its ranks after the fiasco that was the experiment of National Socialism and its ideals of purity that never came to fruition!"

Colonel Vortex said calmly, "I assume that you are talking about Manfred and yourself. Just because I speak German does not mean that I am German. I am not. I was born American and my ancestors fought in the Revolutionary Wars against Britain when the United States was struggling for its independence from that Colonial Superpower – as it then was in the 19th Century. Now it is but a mere shadow of its former self."

Laubscher laughed, "Yes! That Phoenix never managed to arise from its own ashes!"

Pohl added, "And neither did Germany! Militarily today – Germany is totally emasculated and just one cog in the giant wheel of NATO!"

"So, was Sie sagen, ist - werden wir gebumst, wenn wir nicht und doppelt gebumst tun, wenn wir tun?" asked Vortex.

[Translated: So what you are saying is – we are fucked if we don't and double fucked if we do?]

"We have no other option but to attack," said Captain Max Richter.

"I don't even understand why we are entering into a debate about it," said David Dolby, adding, "Of course we must attack! Its our orders! Our duty!"

Laubscher said to Pohl, "He's right! Imagine what would happen to us if we failed deliberately to carry out orders in the *Wehrmacht*? We would have been executed on the spot for treason. It would have made the *Wehrmacht* no better than our allies in World War 2 , the *Regio Esercito* (Royal Italian Army)."

"I agree," said Colonel Pohl.

"Me too," added Colonel Vortex.

"Then I shall give the order to attack and complete our mission. If we can't locate, identify, crush and exterminate General Vo Nguyen Giap here in these putrid fucking

limestone caves then at least we can inflict substantial damage on the nerve-centre of the Imperialist aggressor North Vietnamese puppet forces of the Soviet Union and the CHICOMS," said Brigadier Laubscher.

"Amen to that!" said Colonel Vortex as he made the sign of the cross across his upper torso.

"Let's do it then!" said Colonel Pohl.

"Now Vortex! What do you suggest?" asked the Brigadier and commander of the SLICE team.

The 9th Marine Commander continued to peer through his Starlight scope for several minutes more. Vortex's trained eye passed on the information to his calculative mind. The only method to create enough confusion and mayhem within the ranks of the PAVN was, according to Vortex, to incinerate them in one massive and almighty orgy of destructive suppressive fire using all the wherewithal at their disposal. Colonel Pohl knew that they would have to expend a considerable amount of their ammunition even before they were able to enter the limestone cave complex. As Vortex examined, perused, reconnoitred, surveyed, deduced, watched, listened and formulated the axis and method of attack he suddenly saw a large jeep drive up to the entrance of the caves from the west along a makeshift dirt road. The track appeared to form just one path of the many fingered *Ho Chi Minh* trail in this area of Laos. Vortex knew that the main series of roads that made up the north-south pipeline of the *Ho Chi Minh* trail passed through the strategic town of *Tchepone*. Even Brigadier Laubscher knew that as *Tchepone* was some 18.31 miles to the south-west of their location there was no logical reason for seeing what they were currently observing.

"Blast! Do you see what I am seeing?" asked Vortex to Laubscher.

"I do indeed," answered the Brigadier as he peered through his infrared telescopic sights that were attached to the RT-20 sniper rifle.

"Its some heavy North Vietnamese brass rolling up. From what I can see and I am not certain but it appears the troops disembarking from that vehicle are officers of General Staff rank. COSVN officers and what appears to be commissioned personnel of the rank of Colonel and General as well as what looks like political cadre or Communist Commissars! Looks like we are in luck Manfred! General Giap - that reptilian slime of evil may well be inside these putrid and fucked-up limestone caves! Otherwise, why would officers of such rank be visiting these headquarters out in the middle of this rancid and malodorous jungle shit-hole of a swamp?"

Brigadier Laubscher ordered, "We must attack now! Jetz!"

Colonel Pohl confirmed, "I recognise the insignia of the Communist Party and of COSVN. There are definitely Commissars amongst the group. We need to liquidate those toxic vermin before they even enter the underground bolt-hole of that coward and pimp Giap who may or may not be hunkered down within."

"The Colonel is right," said Captain Richter.

Sergeant Dolby was becoming extremely restless as he fidgeted with his RPO-A *Shmel* rocket propelled flamethrower.

The SLICE team gathered together in the darkness atop the ridge that overlooked the headquarters of the PAVN forces that had surrounded and besieged *Khe Sanh*.

After conferring with Vortex, Brigadier Laubscher gave the orders.

"Ganz richtig dann!"

Dolby immediately asked, "What?"

Laubscher corrected, "Oh! Yes! Sorry Sergeant. I forgot that you are the only one here that does not speak German."

Pohl looked at the Medal of Honour winner and grinned as Laubscher handed out the stratagem for the imminent assault.

"You Sergeant and you Captain Richter shall eliminate those three watch-towers with the *Shmel*. Its important to kill everyone of those gooks up there. Because if any of those Type 24 machine guns are left operative they will, from that high vantage point, rip us to pieces before we get anywhere near the limestone cave entrance.

You, my friend, Egon shall attempt to render inoperative as many of those ZIL-130's as you possibly can with your RT-20 sniper rifle. I suggest going for the fuel tanks. Vortex and I shall lay down suppressive fire with high explosive and incendiary ordnance with our MGL/M-32's. Once you have finished Richter and you too, Dolby, you join in with the multiple grenade launchers to incinerate as many of the infantry now before you guarding the cave entrance.

When I give the word, and not before mind you, the whole team shall advance from this ridge to those large steel doors that you see to the north of us being the main entrance to the lair of General Giap. If the North Vietnamese activate some automatic switch or control to close that steel barrier then Colonel Vortex and I shall use the Semtex plastic explosives to pry them open once more.

Any questions?"

Richter looked to Dolby who nodded excitedly and licked his lips. Egon looked to Richter who looked expectantly to Richard Vortex. Colonel Vortex then glanced over to Laubscher and commented, "You are forgetting one thing sir."

"I don't claim to be infallible Vortex. What is it?"

Vortex pointed to the large fuel storage tanks that he had observed to the western side of the limestone cave entrance.

"What about those fuel depository's sir? Igniting them would create an avalanche of destructive and beneficent secondary explosions that would assist in burning alive the PAVN infantry that now number in excess of 500 by my reckoning."

"So you mean what we do not neutralise by our weapons should be sent to the netherworld by the burning fuel?" asked the Brigadier.

"That's exactly correct sir. Also I shall take charge of the M2 flamethrower and burn to death anyone or anything that gets in the way of the entrance."

"Good then," said Laubscher.

Colonel Pohl asked, "But Manfred? What do we do once we are inside? We have no structural blueprints for the interior of those caves. General Giap and his lickspittles could be anywhere inside those rancid subterranean vaults of evil perniciousness? How the deuce to we find him once inside? That is if he is in reality even there?"

Colonel Vortex answered for Laubscher, "Its simple Egon! We proceed from room-to-room and exterminate with extreme prejudice everything that moves, lives or breathes inside that kettle of Communist deception and intrigue, killing as fast as we can pump the bullets out of our weapons so kindly supplied by the ordnance section of the US 9th Infantry Division."

"Well! That sounds simple enough to me!" expostulated Sergeant Dolby.

Richter added, "It is usually the simplest of plans that prove to be the most effective in battle and in which we may safely lodge our absolute and unqualified trust."

Brigadier Laubscher said finally, "Let us begin this enterprise with our faith in God for I know that Jesus looks down upon us with full and enthusiastic blessings. And may the providence of those angels of light accompany us in our scared mission to strike yet one more resounding blow against the forces of evil and repugnant trickery that assail all our efforts here in the free and democratic nation of South Vietnam that has proven to be such a stalwart and reliable ally of our great United States of America!"

"Amen! Amen to that Brigadier!" said Colonel Vortex as he said a few silent words of prayer to steel his soul in the face of the imminent conflagration that was soon to test their mettle as men and as representatives of the Free World that America represented and for which it was its pre-eminent champion.

The members of the SLICE team took up their allotted positions and prepared their weapons for battle against what Laubscher perceived as the forces of the Communist anti-Christ.

The time was now 0230 hours on 9th February 1968.

It was thus 8.5 hours into the assigned timeframe for the completion of Operation SLICE.

Laubscher said to Vortex, "Wir können nicht länger warten."

Vortex replied, "Ja. Wir müssen jene Allgemeinen Offiziere ausrotten, bevor sie in die Höhle eingehen. Das würde eine andere Feder in unseren jeweiligen Hüten sein."

[Translated: We cannot wait any longer.

Answer: Yes. We must exterminate those General Officers before they enter the cave. That would be another feather in our respective hats.]

The jackals of retribution were now to be unleashed as Colonel Richard Vortex steeled his 6 foot 2 and a half inch frame for stupendous battle. He knew that he

would need to gather all the finer machinery of his considerable battle prowess to see this operation through. As he gripped his MGL/M-32 semi-automatic grenade launcher he felt privileged to be fighting with soldiers from World War 2 who had seen action in the most splendiferous environments while he was still an infant suckling at his mother's teats back in California and relaxing in the opulent luxury of the American way-of-life that had been earned by the inhabitants of that country by conquering the mid-west and the Pacific coast from the chaotic groupings of itinerant savages that had brought the evolutionary time-line of that continent to a standstill for over 5,000 years. Just as the Spanish conquistadores had brought civilisation and order to the Latin Americas to the south.

"This is pay-back time for *Lang Vei* you vile and insidious Communist imperialists!" said Colonel Vortex under his breath.

Brigadier Laubscher raised his hand and the attack was launched.

Sergeant David [Maddog] Dolby and Captain Max Richter raised themselves on their knees and aimed their RPO-A *Shmel's* at the watch-towers – their fingers primed on the trigger.

Seconds later the thermobarbic incendiary rockets streaked like a flash of brilliant fire towards their targets. Dolby knew that as soon as he fired the first rocket he would have to fire another at the third watch-tower to take all of them out simultaneously.

At approximately 300 yards the thermobarbic warheads reached their targets in just over one second.

The eruption of human flesh, steel, wooden structures and ammunition on the towers was deafening. The power of the *Shmel* was far greater than that needed for obliterating the structures in front of them.

Immediately the entire framework of the watch-towers came apart in an inferno of outward explosive force sending debris as far as the ridge that they were positioned on.

Colonel Vortex and Laubscher watched as the several hundred North Vietnamese troops were stunned as many hit the dirt for cover.

"Bumsen Sie Sie zu Tode! Kommunistische Ratte-Ficker!" screamed Brigadier Laubscher as he started to hose down the burning bodies that fell from the watch-towers with his H & K UMP submachine gun. The heavy calibre rounds tore the bodies into ever smaller pieces of human waste and organic debris.

Simultaneously Colonel Egon Pohl started to work on the ZIL-130's pouring round after round of the 20mm ordnance into the trucks' fuel tanks igniting them like towers of orange–red flame.

Burning PAVN troops were running hither and thither like human torches as the ZIL trucks flew through the air colliding with others that had not been hit yet by the suppressive fire.

Colonel Vortex and Brigadier Laubscher then commenced to launch the H&E and incendiary grenades into the high ranking staff officers that were still out in the open. As fast as they could pull the trigger from the circular chamber the 40mm grenades cut a swathe of unparalleled destruction into the PAVN brass and lofty and conceited big-shots ripping them into their constituent parts of shit and human garbage.

Vortex revelled in the site of so much death wrought upon the heads of the NVA who were now at the receiving end of *their* surprise after always having been at their initiative hitherto in the fucked war that was Vietnam according to Vortex's thoughts as he continued unabated with his deliverance of come-back for the *Lang Vei* fiasco.

Sergeant Dolby screamed, "I am go to fuck out your living guts!"

With those words the Sergeant started to use the *Shmel* against the new formation of 200 PAVN troops who had recently arrived cutting down scores of them with each detonation from the thermobarbic warheads.

Colonel Pohl had finished with the ZIL's which were now all obliterated and started to work on the seven Type 55 anti-air emplacements reducing them to rubble.

The North Vietnamese were so shocked and disorientated that they did not know how to react and were flabbergasted that they were the one's that were on the receiving end of an unsuspected ambush and un-planned for skirmish. So many times, thought Colonel Vortex, it had been the valiant forces of the United States that had been constantly caught off guard by the sly, slinking and deviously devised rear echelon attacks mounted by the 'Army of Moles' [as General William Childs Westmoreland had anointed them] when caught out in the open in places such as *Cu Chi* and War Zone C as well as the Parrot's Beak on the border with Cambodia which was then an off-limits sanctuary for the main force Viet Cong slime-soldiers that used the tunnel complexes of Cu Chi to launch assassination attacks against the regular American Infantry Divisions.

Now Vortex could see the tables turned.

Egon Pohl was using his RT-20 to pick off the high ranking generals and colonels of the COSVN High Command as a first priority.

"There goes another one!" he screamed.

The 20mm by 110mm Hispano chambering and the 130 gram projectile shot out at a muzzle velocity of 850 metres per second producing a massive muzzle energy of 46,962 Joules had an effect on the human body which cannot be described but only observed.

One of the 130 gram rounds hit a general officer in the head and evaporated not only the skull but half the upper torso with it. The force of the impact threw the rest of the carcass into five other ranking North Vietnamese and bowled them over like nine-pins while the bullet from the RT-20 ricocheted off the burning hulk of one of the ZIL-130's and came back ripping the legs off three other commissioned PAVN at the level of the upper thighs.

"Beautiful shot Egon!" screamed Laubscher as he stood up and let loose with his UMP 0.45 submachine gun. The Brigadier ripped to pieces the Communist flesh that was vomiting blood and leaking intestines over the jungle floor in front of the limestone cave complex.

Sergeant Dolby observed more than 50 PAVN troopers making a run for the entrance to the cave headquarters.

"No! You fucking don't!" he yelled as he launched a thermobrabic *Shmel* round into the entire platoon size force igniting them like the combustible pieces of human shit-turd that the Sergeant believed them to be.

Colonel Pohl then launched the MGL/M-32 grenades into that group plus more than 100 other Communist troops using the pyrotechnic warheads that melted the yellow flesh of the imperialist Vietnamese aggressor forces.

It was an orgy of blood and satisfying and heart-warming destruction that overcame the delicate sensibilities of Brigadier Manfred Laubscher and Colonel Richard Vortex.

The battle for the axis of advance to the limestone cave entrance was now in full overdrive.

Suddenly Captain Richter observed ten North Vietnamese struggling up the reverse slope of the ridge upon which they were situated. It appeared to the Captain that these soldiers, most of whom were severely wounded and suffering second and third degree flash and incendiary burns to their flesh, were trying to decamp the entire area and make a run for it into the jungle towards the south and away from their own headquarters. The screams of the burnt men alerted Captain Richter to their presence.

"No you don't! Trying to scamper away are we! What about your sacrosanct Communist ideals comrades?" shouted Max Richter as he launched himself off the edge of the ridge and scrambled down to meet the oncoming *Krankenhaus* (Hospital) brigade of deserters to their beloved General Vo Nguyen Giap.

"So you would like to escape up the top of this ridge would you?" asked Richter to one of the startled NVA troopers who he recognised was a senior lieutenant in the 304th PAVN Division.

The NVA officer was so surprised that he placed his burnt arms high into the air and shouted something in Vietnamese which to Richter sounded like a surrender supplication.

"So you want to surrender do you?" asked the Captain.

The Lieutenant seemed to understand some English and nodded his head frantically up and down with his arms now lurched to an even higher elevation above his head despite the fact that Richter could see strips of blackened flesh were oozing free from the bone surfaces of the limbs due to the conflagration below.

Richter smiled as he withdrew from his holster the Model 500 S&W 0.500 calibre handgun. Being the most powerful production hand pistol in the world the NVA officer looked at it in bewilderment.

"I shall surrender you then to the pits of hell!" shouted Richter as he aimed the Model 500 at the Communist's skull and fired.

The force of the blast force-fed both eyes of the enemy officer through the back of his skull so that they were catapulted onto the dirt behind them. The lower portion of the mouth was still visible but the nose, upper lip, eyebrows, eyes and left and right mandibles were obliterated by the kinetic force of the exploding 50 calibre round.

"Ha! Ha!" smiled Captain Richter as he looked into a hollow space through which he could place his entire forearm which was the cavity that had evacuated more than half the skull.

Lowering his Model 500 Richter blew out the gonads of the officer as well as the pelvis almost cutting the body into two pieces.

Colonel Egon Pohl observed the heart-warming spectacle but did not approve of Captain Richter's economy of force as he scrambled down the reverse slope after having shouldered his RT-20 hand-cannon.

"This is a waste of bullets Captain!" shouted Egon Pohl.

"Whatever do you mean Colonel? Do you not wish me to dispatch these perfidious hounds from the North?" asked Richter.

"Natürlich tue ich!"

"What then?" asked Richter.

"You are wasting bullets Max," answered Egon.

"It's the quickest way is it not sir?"

"I know a method that is equally punctilious and rapid but which avoids the expenditure of ordnance that we may be required to call upon once we begin the assault proper within the interior of these limestone caves," answered Colonel Pohl.

"Dann erleuchten Sie mich Herr Oberst."

"Knives Captain! Use your cutting implements! Its just as timely and commodious," answered Colonel Pohl.

Captain Richter watched as Colonel Pohl began to pirouette like a courtesan at a Viennese Waltz with his custom-made 18 inch dagger in one hand and his machete in the other slicing and dicing from one locus of movement to the other upon the balls of his feet.

With a single slash of his machete the Colonel decapitated the next Communist that struggled to make his way up the reverse slope to the ridge. Using the revolutions and momentum of his body he twirled the double-edged dagger and the machete like a virtuoso in a continuous circular motion.

With the third PAVN soldier he thrust his knife into the intestines and simultaneously cut off the left arm from the trapezium muscle, then the right leg was hacked asunder, then the right arm and finally Pohl severed off both feet as he kicked the carcass into the mud.

Without halting or arresting his advance from one target to the next, Colonel Pohl sliced open the carotid artery of a fourth and fifth NVA while digging deliciously into their innards with his dagger twisting clockwise and then counter-clockwise to achieve the maximum disruptive effect to the organs and viscera of the victim that was, in his eyes, so richly deserving of the immolation bequeathed unto them.

"Now you try it!" said Colonel Pohl calmly as he stepped backwards so that he was facing away from another PAVN soldier and as he did so he brought his machete down between his own legs striking upwards and outwards so that the blade sliced open the chest of the enemy.

Captain Richter could not equal the finesse of Pohl's extermination ballet but simply hacked away like an in-opportunistic butcher at a flea market, gouging, hammering and hacking to death his way through the seventh, eighth, ninth and tenth Communist soldier attempting to flee the debacle of their imminent defeat to protect the penetration of the cave entrance by the SLICE team.

"That is enough fooling around with your kitchen implements! We have serious business to attend to gentlemen. We can't spend all our valuable time dissecting these nefarious specimens from the North as if we were medical students in an anatomy laboratory!" excoriated Colonel Vortex.

Colonel Pohl said nothing and returned to his position next to Brigadier Laubscher on the ridge.

The SLICE team now watched as they surveyed the destruction below.

Sergeant David Dolby was finding it impossible to maintain an accurate body count as he peered through his Starlight scope.

Of the initial force of upwards of 400 to 500 NVA troops there were hardly any alive to be seen. The ground in front of the cave entrance was littered with burning corpses and mutilated body parts.

One group of about 80 PAVN had taken cover directly in front of two Type 55 anti-air guns which had been put out of action as had the other five.

These forces amounting to two reinforced platoons were firing their AK-47 rifles in random and tell-tale directions. It appeared that their commanding officers had been killed in the initial onslaught from the SLICE team with their heavy weaponry.

"What do you think?" asked Brigadier Manfred Laubscher to Colonels Pohl and Vortex.

"The time is ripe for penetration," said Vortex calmly as he continued to fire his MGL/M-32 at the bunched up survivors near the limestone cave entrance.

Colonel Pohl said facetiously, "Are you talking about your mistress or this mission Colonel?"

Vortex scoffed as he spat back, "Egon! I don't have a mistress! I am not a Colonial. I am an officer in the United States Marine Corps! We have standards to uphold even though you may not concur with that. I have a girlfriend. Not a mistress."

Pohl grimaced with amusement.

"Alright! Alright! Now let us see what General Vo Nguyen Giap is made of. I hope he is made of sterner stuff than these lickspittles and lackeys that have failed so miserably to defend his sanctimonious and sacred bolt-hole from which he has derived such a false sense of self-ingratiating security! We begin the main attack now for full penetration and begin Phase 2 of Operation SLICE which is Locate and Identify. After that we shall move onto Phase 3 for the Crushing and Exterminating of this slithery leech from wherever he is hiding," said Brigadier Manfred Laubscher.

Sergeant David [Maddog] Dolby was finishing up with another six NVA soldiers who had tried to crawl up the reverse slope and away from the battlefield. He was using the standard issue M2 flamethrower and as he activated the weapon a long finger of orange-red flame that dripped from its edges shot down to engulf the bodies that attempted to elevate themselves to safety.

The human torches careered down the slope with their entire bodies, including their hair on fire and stumbled back into the 'killing zone' where Captain Richter mowed them down with the UMP submachine gun.

The atmosphere around the entire area of the caves was suffused with the stench of burning flesh and exposed raw intestines. It was enough even to turn the iron-clad stomach of Colonel Egon Pohl who had witnessed similar spectacles on the Eastern Front from 1942 to 1945.

"Make ready gentlemen!" shouted Brigadier Laubscher, adding, "We shall move forward now!"

The SLICE team carefully picked their way down the reverse slope and towards the limestone cave entrance taking what cover there was available from the remaining PAVN forces.

A siren was still sounding from above the steel door of the headquarters subterranean entrance.

Colonel Vortex took out his Model 500 handgun and blew it to pieces as the noise was irritating to him.

The only thing that could be heard now was the automatic rifle fire and the screams and moaning of dying Communists.

When the SLICE team reached within 50 yards of the remaining PAVN forces blocking the cave entrance they took cover behind the hulks of two burning ZIL-130

trucks. Richter and Dolby were on the left and Vortex, Pohl and Laubscher on the right.

The weapons fire was fast and furious as the 80 or so surviving Communists put up a staunch resistance.

"How do we get them the fuck out of there and away from the cave entrance?" asked Captain Richter.

Sergeant Dolby crawled forward and screamed as he held the nozzle of the M2 flamethrower, "Like this!"

Maddog Dave manoeuvred within 20 yards of the opposing forces and then let loose with the M2 shooting a long dripping shard of flame directly into the centre of the enemy formation.

Brigadier Laubscher shouted, "Give the Sergeant supporting and covering fire!"

Vortex and Pohl lobbed 40mm high explosive grenades from their MGL/M-32's in an inverse parabolic arc over Dolby's head and into the North Vietnamese troops blowing away and obliterating their bunched-up positions.

Some of the 304th Division troops whose uniforms were on fire ran backwards and through the cave entrance into the interior of the subterranean vault. Others simply ran to the left and right flanks which allowed Brigadier Laubscher to pick them off one by one with the RT-20 hand-cannon.

"Die! You Communist interlopers!" yelled Sergeant Dolby as he released yet more and more of the aluminium jelly-induced flame from the M2 onto the positions of the PAVN that was now beginning to crumple under the relentless attack.

As the offensive continued one North Vietnamese broke ranks and ran directly towards the SLICE team as they blasted away from behind the two ZIL-130 trucks. Vortex recognised him as a senior sergeant of the 304th Division in the artillery corps. The man, to the astonishment of the SLICE team was firing his AK-47 and shouting what appeared to be obscenities and derogatory remarks as to the professionalism of the United States forces in his indigenous language.

Colonel Vortex could not make out everything that the man said but he understood enough to discern that this particular PAVN NCO was displeased with the entire attack being launched at them and also was more than a trifle upset with the surprise presence of a United States commando squad (as he described them) within the borders of Laos.

Laubscher asked, "Was sagt dieser feindliche Sergeant?"

Pohl answered, "Ich weiß nicht. Aber was jemals es es ist, klingt allzu schmeichelhaft nicht."

[Translated: What is this enemy Sergeant saying?
Answer: I don't know. But what ever it is it does not sound overly complimentary.]

Richard Vortex interrupted, "I have an idea what he is going on about."

"What?" asked Pohl and Laubscher speaking in unison so that their gravelly voices sounded like some bizarre chorus from a Wagnerian Opera.

"He is commenting on the illegality of American forces being present in the territory of Laos. He says that it is unheard of and contrary to the rules of law and of war. He also points out that we should not interfere with the free flow of Communist supplies and equipment down the complex of trails and streams known as the *Ho Chi Minh* trail. He makes references while saying all of this to the purity of essence of our respective mother's reproductive organs and he also makes reference to our mother's sexual practices and penchants which I must inform you are of a highly offensive nature. While explaining all the military niceties of how North Vietnam is the only country that has the moral right to invade other countries territory as it is now doing, such as Laos and Cambodia not to mention South Vietnam itself, he also describes the unhealthy surroundings in which we were born, that is, he is referring to you and me and all of us, likening our upbringing to that of swine being kept in pig-sty's. He says also that our mother's fornicate with sheep and other wild animals, our father's are no better than pimps and itinerant drunkards and that we are all Texas cowboy's with ten gallon hats and that we should turn around and march straight back to fucking Texas where we came from.

He also mentions that our society (that is I think the American society and community he is alluding to) are weak, insipid, vacillating, decadent with opulent luxury, corrupted with narcotics and that we are all slaves to perversions of every kind and specie calling us sexual degenerates and low-life of the highest order."

Egon Pohl looked with incredulity to Colonel Vortex as he translated, asking, "He said all that?"

"Yes," began Vortex, adding, "Oh! Yes! I forgot one thing. He also mentioned that we shall never penetrate the cave complex. That General Giap is not there in any case. And he added a qualifier, namely that he would personally see to it that our testicles would be removed with a blunt and rusty knife and that he would force us to watch as his dog ate what had once been an integral part of our bodies and our manhood, which he then explains, that we lack. Oh! And that after that he is going to kill all of us himself."

Egon Pohl stopped firing his UMP submachine gun for a few seconds trying to digest all the insults and assertions relating to his family's pedigree and quality of worth.

Brigadier Laubscher was incensed saying, "I don't care about the rest of what he said but nobody insults my mother!"

Vortex laughed, "Sir! I would not worry about it too much. After all he is not in a position to make threats in the current situation."

Laubscher ignored Vortex's supplication and dived forward from out of the cover of the ZIL-130 wreck with his eyes burning like torches from a National Socialist parade at the *Prinz Albert Strasse*.

As Maddog Dave Dolby continued to fire-up the remaining PAVN troops in an ever increasing conflagration Brigadier Laubscher hurled himself like a lunatic at the North Vietnamese Sergeant oblivious of the AK-47 in his hand.

Both Egon and Richard watched with baited breath as the leader of the SLICE team dove towards the Communist Sergeant.

As the enemy NCO fired his Kalashnikov the rounds whizzed barely two inches above Laubscher's head as the *ex-Wehrmacht* officer snapped both his feet and legs downwards kicking the boots of the PAVN soldier. At the same instant Laubscher drove his combat knife upwards into the ass-cheeks of the Sergeant and ripped forwards and then backwards with all his upper body strength.

The enemy NCO fell to the ground dropping his AK-47 as Laubscher did a backflip and piston'd himself back on his feet.

Laubscher looked down at the Communist with his knife still imbedded in the man's asshole, saying, "Now you listen here! I did not take all the trouble of fighting an entire world war, then spending a year in an American POW camp, and struggling in the ruins of my own country for 2 years to listen to you now insulting my mother! You do not have any idea how difficult it was to come over here to your shit-box little country back in 1953 and have to fight you gooks at *Dien Bien Phu*. I have heard enough insults about my mother from the Russians back in the Ukraine so I don't have to take that shit from you little yellow dwarf moles here in your tunnels and caves in Vietnam! If I could barely tolerate it from the Russians I sure as hell can't abide it from you little midget cunt-suckers!"

The PAVN Sergeant had no idea what Brigadier Laubscher was talking about and simply said in Vietnamese, "Fuck off! Do your worst you American dog!"

Vortex yelled out, "Sir! Take cover! Don't worry about that miserable piece of slime-turd!"

Laubscher ignored Vortex as the PAVN troops at the cave entrance started to direct and intensify their fire towards the Brigadier.

In an instant and ignoring the warnings from Vortex, Laubscher swung his machete and cut off first the right foot and then the left of the screaming Communist below him.

Bending down he gripped the North Vietnamese Sergeant's head in a vice and brought the machete across his neck in a sawing action. Slowly and deliberately and inch by inch Laubscher decapitated the Communist caring nothing for the copious quantities of blood that was staining his camouflage uniform.

Lieutenant David Peter EHRLICH

When he had finished he ordered Maddog Dave to burn the body with his M2.

"Shit sir!" said Dolby, "I need to replenish the flamethrower!"

"Don't worry about that now Sergeant! Get to the cave entrance," said the Brigadier.

Vortex, Pohl and Richter ran towards the limestone cave entrance firing their UMP's and MGL/M-32's.

Laubscher took out a Semtex plastic explosive and set the Q-switched ruby laser to initiate detonation in 10 seconds. Running forward he threw the Pentaerythritol Tetranitrate explosive into the remaining PAVN troops blocking their path to the headquarters of General Giap in Laos.

Vortex screamed, "Take cover!"

An enormous explosion lifted the two wrecked Type 55 anti-air guns into the sides of the mountain face and obliterated the remaining Communist troopers.

The way was now clear to initiate penetration of the limestone cave complex and to begin Phase 2 of the SLICE mission.

The time was now 0645 hours on 9th February 1968.

The first rays of light were splintering through the viperous morass that was the jungles of Laos.

The SLICE team cautiously made their way to the steel doors of the caves that had been sheared away from their hinges as a result of the force of the Semtex blast. There was no obstacle in their path other than the mutilated remains of the North Vietnamese troops that had been defending the defile into the headquarters of the 304th, 325th and 320th PAVN Divisions.

Colonel Vortex had a deep sense of religious elation almost like an epiphany from Jesus as he realised that he was now in the heart of the beast's lair – a beast that had so beset and bothered his Marine troops at *Khe Sanh*.

As Vortex prayed he promised to accomplish the inspiration that Jesus had given him to create as much irreversible destruction and cleansing amidst the forces of the anti-Christ as he could possibly bring to bear.

The first section of the interior of the limestone cave complex that greeted the SLICE team was a long circular tunnel whose walls had been buttressed by steel girders and upon which iron matting had been placed on the surface. Electric lights were strung at intervals of 5 yards from the ceiling and positioned there by hooks. This indicated to Laubscher that an internal generator of some description was supplying the power for the NVA headquarters.

"This is no ordinary tunnel and cave complex," said Colonel Egon Pohl.

"Yes, you are correct. Its nothing like I have ever seen in the maze of tunnel hideouts at *Cu Chi* or War Zone C near the Cambodian border. The sophistication, organisation and meticulous depth of preparation of these corridors and bunkers is something

that is unparalleled in my experience of the *'Army of Moles'* that hitherto we have had to contend with," answered Colonel Vortex.

"I suggest that we remain as a single unit and move methodically from each bunker, each room, each bolt-hole and every recess and facility here in these subterranean vaults of secretive and dastardly intrigue so that we can flush out the stench of the vermin that infest it with a single-minded and unique purpose that will be effectuated by our deliberate thoroughness and professionalism," ordered Brigadier Manfred Laubscher.

"I don't know shit from shiola sirs! But if I think you said what I was thinking then you are ordering me to kill every fucking gook that we can lay our hands on?" asked Maddog Dave Dolby.

"That is correct Sergeant," said the Brigadier.

"And with *extreme prejudice*," added Colonel Vortex.

"Are you sure about that?" asked Egon Pohl.

"Of course! I checked my Law texts about military operations in foreign countries outside the *de facto* area of hostilities. We are perfectly within the limits of *public international law*."

"I am glad to hear it!" said Laubscher.

"So you can rest your mind easy sir - confident in the knowledge that everything that we do here, all the personnel that we neutralise and the machinery of aggression that we render inoperative is fully within the sanctions, legislation and purview of the legal and abiding community of nations and their concomitant policies of Peace. After all we are here for that reason only.

For Peace are we not?" asked Vortex.

"Yes indeed! And that's coming from a lawyer! Is that not so Richard?" asked Laubscher.

"It is indeed sir," said Vortex.

"Then truly I can relax for I have great faith in the legal profession and whatever a lawyer tells me in the solicitor/client relationship I can be sure of it being accurate to the nth degree with total veracity."

"Thank you sir," answered the Colonel.

The conversation was interrupted by gunfire coming from the other end of the long tubular subterranean corridor.

"Shit! Take cover!" screamed Colonel Pohl.

7.62mm rounds were buzzing all around the SLICE team as they plastered themselves to the sides of the conduit leading deeper into the cave complex.

Laubscher, Pohl and Vortex used the dead bodies of the North Vietnamese troops who had retreated inside and then succumbed to their burns from the Semtex explosion and the *Shmel* ordnance as human shields.

Maddog Dave and Richter dived behind 50 gallon fuel barrels that lay strewn across the surface of the long corridor.

As the cross-fire continued all five of the SLICE team opened up with their UMP's and a deadly contest for supremacy of the thoroughfare ensued for some ten minutes.

"They are advancing!" shouted Laubscher.

Approximately 25 PAVN troops armed with AK-47's and RPG-7's launched a human wave attack down the far end of the walkway.

Maddog Dave had already re-loaded his M2 flamethrower and was ready for them.

"Hold until the last second!" screamed Colonel Vortex.

The SLICE team waited until the Communists were less than 10 yards from their positions. Then Sergeant Dolby opened fire with a stream of burning napalm derivative from his M2.

Horrendous screams and shouts in Vietnamese greeted their acoustic senses.

The bedlam and excoriating sounds of human agony were amplified in the cocooned surroundings of the underground thoroughfare.

"Burn! Burn! You dink slime-shits!" screamed Maddog Dave Dolby as he worked the M2 as if it were a garden hose and he was sprinkling his lawn on a lazy Sunday afternoon in the suburb of Brentwood in the Hollywood Hills.

Vortex looked at Sergeant Dolby and was mesmerised by the NCOs' total lack of fear and his relentless drive and enthusiasm for annihilating the enemy forces that had been such a bane to the efforts of MACV and to the technology of the US War Machine that was designed to bring peace and security to South Vietnam.

Vortex thought that in many ways Dolby was the quintessential essence of what the American fighting man should have been in South Vietnam against an adversary that showed no compunction to abide by the rules of law nor the conduct set down for armed forces in the field. Sergeant Dave Dolby showed a surfeit of tenacity, resilience, stamina, wherewithal, punctuality, forbearance, aptitude, expertise in delivery, staying-power in application and fortitude in execution of his orders all tempered by a full appreciation of the humane standards and time-honoured methods of showing mercy and compassion to the enemy regardless of the nefarious characteristics of the hostile forces arrayed against him and the whole apparatus of Peace and Security that was the United States Armed Forces much to their credit, honour and steadfastness to uphold the Community of Nations since the creation of the *League of Nations* after World War 1.

Vortex looked at the burning carcasses of the hated *Vietminh* and felt proud to be serving with men such as these – America's finest sons.

A quality that exemplified the entire nation of the United States of America which was the Lawmaker and the Peacemaker for the entire world as no other country

had the courage to take on such an immense and unenviable task. A testament to the honour and integrity of the *American People* – Colonel Vortex thought, as the action reached a crescendo of ferocity hitherto not seen even by the Colonel himself.

As the fighting continued Brigadier Laubscher and Colonel Pohl brought up the rear and positioned themselves behind Sergeant Dolby to deal with any of the North Vietnamese that managed to escape the inferno or while burnt managed to slip past the industrious and dutiful Sergeant.

As the enemy passed, Pohl and Laubscher used their 18 inch combat knives and machete's to cut to pieces the flesh, burning or not, of anyone that managed to proceed beyond a pre-defined point in the narrow confines of the battle-conduit.

Richter and Vortex acted as a last line of defence behind the other three with their Model 500 handguns at the ready, more than able to obliterate that yellow Communist flesh that was lucky enough to reach their positions as they were filled with a sense of élan vital and *espirit de corps*.

Colonel Richard Vortex was ready to die if necessary but he wanted to take as many of the Communist bandits and aggressors with him before he checked out from the Vietnam War Episode 2, with all its failures and shortcomings that had been brought about by the vacillation, double-talk and inane prevarication of the powers that be, excluding the United States Joint Chiefs of Staff, who knew how to win the war but were hog-tied by the civilian leadership and the Johnson Administration that had no conception of military strategy nor tactics and who meddled in matters that were best left to the Generals in the Pentagon in Washington D.C.

[With the exception of the counsel of wise men such as; **Walt Rostow, Richard Perle** *and* **Dean Acheson.**

Dean Acheson: *Born:11th April 1893: Death:12th October 1971: United States Secretary of State in the Truman Administration 1949-1953. Responsible for defining American Foreign Policy towards the Communist Aggressor nations during the Cold War. Devised the Marshall Plan to help Europe back onto its feet to stem the tide of Communist subversion and supplantation. Was a prime architect in the creation of the North Atlantic Treaty Organisation (NATO) – the Most successful Military Alliance in the History of Mankind and of the World to date. Gave sound and excellent advice to President Harry S. Truman to intervene in the Korean War (1950 to 1953) to stem the pernicious aggression and lawlessness of both North Korea and the CHICOMS (Bolshevik-Communist China). Also advised President Truman to intervene and support the gallant and heroic French Forces and the Republic of France in Vietnam War Episode 1 (The First Indochina War (1948 -1954). Was called upon by President John F. Kennedy to advise and to give guidance as part of XCOMM (Executive Committee of the National Security Council) in the Cuban Missile Crisis against the Soviet Union's deployment of intermediate range strategic nuclear warheads in Cuba. Was instrumental in advising President Truman on*

the appropriate policies to be taken against the increasing militarism of Communist China and the threat that this country posed to world peace then and now. Defended anti-Communists such as Alger Hiss wrongfully accused during the Red Scare and the McCarthy Congressional Hearings. Responsible for advising President Truman to provide aide to the anti-Communist forces in Greece and Turkey in 1947. Helped to formulate the Truman Doctrine. Believed and rightly so that the best method to contain the virulent disease that is Communism is to bring economic prosperity back to Europe, including the Warsaw Pact countries under the yoke of Bolshevism. Received on 30th June 1947 the 'Medal of Merit' from President Truman. With George Kennan was responsible for developing the Policy of Containment. One of the authors of the 'White Paper' dealing with Sino-American Relations which discouraged direct American military ground intervention in Communist China. That the spread of Communism in China was irreversible. Advocated the defence and assistance of South Korea and the ROK (South Korea's Armed Forces). Briefed President Charles de Gaulle on the Cuban Missile Crisis and was a pre-eminent Lawyer and Legal Scholar.]

If Colonel Richard Vortex had had his way he would give open slather to the Joint Chiefs to conduct the war in Vietnam in any manner and by any means that they sought fit to prosecute it. If that had been the case, thought Vortex, this fucked war would already have been over by 1966 at the latest and North Vietnam crushed back into the Stone Age.

As one North Vietnamese non-commissioned officer succeeded in slipping past the flames of Sergeant Dolby's M2 he reacted with swift expertise and decapitated the assailant with a single but efficient blow from his machete. The head of the Communist, its lips still spouting invectives against the Americans was kicked backwards by Colonel Pohl whereupon Maddog Dave hosed it in a sea of cleansing fire. The headless body weirdly kept walking towards Colonel Vortex who not satisfied with the current state of immolation drove his 18 inch combat knife into the intestines of the trunk spilling its guts in a filthy miasma across the bunker floor.

"Fuck this shit! Kill them all! Don't let any of them get away! Our mission is to create as much discomfort and mental trauma for these Communists as possible!" screamed Colonel Vortex.

Captain Richter intercepted two PAVN soldiers that tried to rip the M2 fuel tanks from off the back of Sergeant Dolby.

"No you don't!" he remarked as he gripped the head of one NVA trooper and using it much like a soccer ball he rammed it into the steel fuel tank that was trying to be displaced from its rightful owner.

With his other hand Richter tore into the second trooper's neck with his machete and then blasted off his testicles with his Model 500 pistol that tore out the entire pelvis as well as the reproductive organs.

Laubscher and Pohl advanced chasing the half dozen Communists that now dropped their weapons and tried to decamp the scene.

Colonel Pohl threw his combat knife into the back of one PAVN while Laubscher shot dead the others in quick succession with his UMP 0.45 calibre submachine gun. The bullets tore the flesh of the enemy off in great swathes as Colonel Vortex kicked past the dead bodies of the fallen North Vietnamese to the first steel bunker door to their right.

The SLICE team was now deep inside the interior of General Giap's bolt-hole.

The Vietnamese lettering on the bunker door was explained to the team by Vortex.

"What does it say?" asked Brigadier Manfred Laubscher.

"It says, *"Communications and Radar Room"* – it's the control centre for the 304th, 325th and 320th North Vietnamese Divisions," advised Vortex.

"Then we must force entry and render it in-operational!" ordered Laubscher.

Sergeant Dolby rushed up and pushed the officers aside letting loose with his flame-producing M2.

The point-blank range of the inferno caused the finger of flame to bounce off the steel door and almost incinerated Laubscher and the others as part of Richter's own uniform caught fire.

"What the fuck do you think you are doing Sergeant?" asked Colonel Pohl.

Dolby looked at the 101st Airborne Division field officer and blurted out, "I am trying to open this fucked door for you sir."

"Not like that! You dolt! Don't you know that steel has a much higher melting point than ever those flames can produce!" advised Vortex in a lather as he shook his head.

Captain Richter was furious as he said, "Scheiße-Dolby! Sie verbrannt durch die Tarnung trouser Hosen! Ich hatte sie gerade gestärkt vor dieser Mission!"

[Translated: Shit Dolby! You burnt by camouflage trouser pants! I just had them starched before this mission!]

Vortex shouted, "Forget about your fucking pants will you! Stand back and let me do it!"

The SLICE team retreated away from the steel door as Colonel Vortex aimed the RT-20 hand-cannon directly at the hinges to the steel barrier.

Firing the 130 gram projectile at incredible speed the bullet penetrated two inches of solid armor plating and tore off the top hinge.

Vortex fired again and again as the entire door was cleaved off its support structure and came crashing down almost onto their heads.

"Fuck-this-shit! Watch what you are doing Richard!" shouted Pohl as a steel splinter ricocheted off the surface and pierced his thigh causing blood to flow from a superficial flesh wound.

Sergeant Dolby applied bandages to Egon's leg from the medical kit that he had with him.

"There! Are you better now," asked Maddog Dave.

"Much! But I don't appreciate this friendly-fire shit you are putting me through Vortex. Be more careful next time!" admonished Pohl.

The SLICE team rushed into the room firing their UMP's in a wide arc of suppressive fire. Two North Vietnamese signal troops tried to rush for their *Kalashnikov's* but Laubscher shot them down as they leapt across a nearby table for their weapons with his Model 500 pistol that turned their heads into ripe watermelons.

More automatic weapons fire erupted from the far end of the communications bunker as three PAVN soldiers were shooting from the cover of a steel radar console.

Egon Pohl took three standard high explosive 40mm grenades from his webbing and lobbed them over towards the opposing troops. The detonation flung all three clear of the radar console killing one and wounding the other two.

Laubscher rushed up and pumped three bullets into each Communist with his Model 500 pistol.

"Look at this shit!" said Richter.

"Its enough communications equipment to control the entire North Vietnamese Corps around *Khe Sanh* and the DMZ!" said Colonel Vortex excitedly.

"We must incapacitate it at once," ordered Brigadier Laubscher.

The SLICE team surveyed the large array of radar stations and consoles that were placed on steel racks and tables in three parallel rows. There were radio sets, antenna relay devices and even Ground Positioning System controls and surface-to-air interface units.

"Most of this shit is Chinese and Soviet designed and produced," said Vortex.

"Then we shall have to deprive General Giap and his three divisions of the use of it! Won't we?" said Egon.

"Yes, we will indeed," answered Laubscher.

Suddenly as they were discussing the contents of the enormous underground vault of communications equipment that was 50 yards wide by 30 yards long the SLICE team heard movement coming from a doorway that they had not yet noticed at the extreme northerly end of the bunker.

Shots were fired at them and Maddog Dave and Captain Richter returned fire with their UMP's. Laubscher and Vortex saw one North Vietnamese officer firing at them as he dived from the doorway and took cover behind one of the radar consoles.

"Surrender! You are surrounded!" shouted Colonel Pohl.

Four more shots rang out from the enemy and then silence.

Nearly a minute passed as Pohl asked the Communist a second time to surrender.

Suddenly two hands appeared high above the electronic equipment behind which the solider was taking cover.

"Come out! Get out of there! And I promise we shall not shoot you!" said Vortex in a loud voice.

Brigadier Laubscher whispered to Colonel Vortex as they peered over a steel rack while the other three SLICE members were also hunkered down behind desks and steel containers that were strewn around the communications room.

"What do you think you are doing Richard? You know that our orders are not to take prisoners. We can't hold this man hostage. He's a liability and a hindrance to our mission. We have to find Giap and we can't drag along prisoners while doing so."

Vortex answered as they watched the North Vietnamese man whom the Colonel recognised as a Major in the 304th PAVN Division slowly crawl to his feet and walk out into the open and into the centre of the COMMO bunker.

"Sir! Don't you see? He's a field ranking officer. If we can get him to talk he may reveal the whereabouts of General Vo Nguyen Giap. If indeed he is here hiding out in this limestone maze of bunkers."

Laubscher looked bewildered as his deep blue eyes peered at the Colonel, "You don't seriously think he will spill his guts to us – do you? You know better than anyone how intransigent and impecunious these little Communist bastards are? He won't tell us diddly-squat!"

Vortex laughed, "For a German sir, you've picked up our American colloquialisms quite well!"

The Brigadier sniggered, "I spent three years living in Mississippi in Hattiesburg with my first American girlfriend back in the mid-1950's after I came back from French Indochina. She taught me all the intricacies of southern slang." Then Manfred ran his hands through his black hair that had been dyed to hide the grey and said, "Alright! But make it quick! We don't have the time to be pussy-footing around with these Communist jerks! And if he makes so much as a sneeze in the wrong direction then kill him!"

Vortex nodded and watched as the NVA Major stood with hands in the air in front of them, his pistol in his left hand.

"Drop the fucking gun! Now!" yelled Vortex.

Maddog Dave grew impatient, "This is fucking ridiculous! Just take him out! And let's get on with the mission!"

To everyone's mild surprise the NVA Major immediately relinquished his weapon to the floor.

The NVA Major then said in Vietnamese, "Bạn biết rằng bạn đang đi để chết tại đây."

Vortex laughed as Laubscher asked, "What did this Communist say?"

Vortex informed the Brigadier that the PAVN officer had advised that they were all going to die in the cave complex.

Laubscher told Vortex to tell the NVA Major to tell him where General Giap was or the only person that was going to die would be him and in a most uncomfortable and leisurely fashion.

Vortex sniggered and said to the North Vietnamese officer in Vietnamese, "Listen you fucking gook! Tell us where General Vo Nguyen Giap is or else!"

The PAVN soldier answered, "Hoặc khác những gì? Bạn mảnh của Đế quốc shit turd?"

"What! What's this I hear about shit and turds?" asked Brigadier Laubscher starting to get himself into a heated lather of excitement.

Colonel Vortex advised, "He said or else what? Then he called us pieces of imperialistic shit."

"How dare he say that? What did you ask him Vortex for him to say or else what?" asked Laubscher.

"I said tell us where General Giap is or *else*."

Maddog Dave Dolby interrupted the line of impolite verbal exchanges with his own rhetoric, "Tell this gook that or else I am going to dismantle his joints and bones from his flesh in a most unseemly manner! What cheek!"

Laubscher ordered, "Listen Vortex! We don't have time for this shit! Tell him that unless he answers our questions he'll be in big trouble!"

Vortex looked puzzled, "Which questions are you referring to sir? The reason he called us imperialists and pieces of shit? Or the whereabouts of General Giap?"

Maddog Dave rolled his eyes up into the upper lids of his sockets as Laubscher was becoming distraught, "No! The question of when does he think that we will find intelligent life on Mars! Of course about General Giap! For Christ's sake Vortex!"

The Colonel turned to the Communist always speaking in fluent Vietnamese, "If you don't answer us about Giap then I am going to have to proceed to interrogate you by means of rendition here from the authority of that Brigadier General over there."

As Vortex spoke he pointed to Brigadier Laubscher.

The Major asked a question, saying, "Điều gì làm bạn có nghĩa là bởi Rendition bạn motherfucker?"

Laubscher walked up to the North Vietnamese prisoner and prodded his back with his UMP submachine gun, asking Vortex, "What is this I heard? He said something about a 'mother' with a rude connotation? Was he talking about *my* mother?"

"I don't think so sir. He was talking about all of our mothers. He asked what I meant by 'rendition'."

Laubscher ignored the latter reference to the threat by Vortex of rendition and said, "If he's talking about all mothers – our mothers, then that means *my* mother also! Does it not?"

"Logically yes sir. You are correct," answered Vortex.

"Then fuck him! He has ten seconds to answer the question about Giap or I personally will beat the crap out of him!"

Laubscher peered into the Communist's eyes' with unabated fury, adding, "Now you tell him exactly what I said Vortex!"

Vortex complied and repeated the comments of the Brigadier to the Major before them.

The enemy Major responded, "Ông không thể đánh bại các crap ra khỏi một em bé tã cát túi."

Vortex looked annoyed as he told Laubscher, "He said that you could not beat the crap out of a baby's nappy san bag. Sir."

Colonel Pohl was exasperated, "Why are we fooling around with this guy? This is not like you Vortex! I have heard that you are an expert in stringent interrogation techniques. So interrogate this goon and find out where Giap is."

Laubscher was beside himself, "He said what? Is he calling me weak?"

"Yes, it appears so, sir," answered Vortex.

"Tell this son-of-a-bitch that he has no more time left. If he doesn't tell us where Giap is in this putrid shit-hole of a cave I'm going to personally crucify him." As Laubscher spoke he pointed his finger at the North Vietnamese and then raised his forefinger to his face in the *'up-yours'* position.

Before anybody could respond the PAVN officer stepped forward and head-butted Laubscher so hard that he bloodied his nose.

"What the fuck!" screamed Maddog Dave Dolby.

Vortex stepped forward and head-butted the North Vietnamese in turn. The force of the blow sent the enemy soldier reeling backwards so that he crashed into a radar console on the desk behind where he was standing.

"What do you wish me to do here sir? I am trying to be accommodating with this Communist gentleman but he is providing me with no reason to continue my civility towards him. In fact I am starting to get more than a little agitated."

"So you're agitated are you?" asked Laubscher as he clutched his face in agony.

Captain Richter brought out his medical kit and applied some Betadine to the wound of the Brigadier.

"Bạn đang mẹ là một con điếm fucking sucks hai pimps' tinh ranh của cùng một lúc," said the enemy Major.

"I have had enough of this!" screamed Vortex.

"What did he say now?" asked Laubscher.

"I don't think I should tell you sir," said Vortex.

"Tell me!"

"Are you sure? Sir?"

"Yes! I am going to let this guy have it!"

"He said that your mother is a whore. He also made mention of the fact that she has the ability to perform fellatio with more than one gentleman at the same time. And that these individuals ply her services shall we say on the streets for a monetary compensation part of which they render unto themselves as a commission."

Laubscher rushed forward and took a swing with his right fist directly at the North Vietnamese officer. The blow struck heavily just below the right eye but seemed to have no effect as the Major hardly moved nor even winced at the impact.

The Brigadier felt as if his metacarpal joints had been smashed as he nursed his hand.

"Sir?" asked Vortex.

"What?"

"Do you wish me to go to the next level and try physical persuasion with this guy? It seems that threats and our constant cajoling do not in any way move him into revealing anything. Also time is of the essence. The longer we wait here the more time Giap has to escape and the greater the chance that the North Vietnamese are preparing a counter-reaction force. They know we are here. Hell! The rest of this subterranean headquarters must be still crawling with enemy troops."

"Do it then!" screamed Laubscher.

"Why don't you belt the crap out of this douche-bag?" asked Egon to Laubscher.

"I have hurt my hand! That's why! Let Richard hoe into this prick," answered Laubscher.

"But he insulted your mother?" asked Egon. Then adding, "You never took that shit from the Bolsheviks on the Eastern Front. What's the matter? Have you gone soft in your old age!"

"Fuck off Egon! I am not old! I want Richard to take care of him. That's it. I could if I wanted to. But I have to remain fit for the rest of this mission. Vortex can handle him easily!"

Colonel Egon Pohl laughed and threw his hands up in the air dismissively.

Then Maddog Dave asked, "Do you want any help Colonel sir?"

"Its alright Sergeant. I can handle this recalcitrant hyena."

"Suit yourself sir. But he looks pretty fucking big to me," answered Maddog Dave as he looked the Communist up and down with more than a little begrudged admiration.

Colonel Vortex also noticed that the PAVN Major was very sturdy even by American standards let alone Vietnamese standards. The average Vietnamese man was no

more than 5 feet five inches at best and weighed on average approximately 136 lbs. This compared to the average Anglo Saxon American was quite small.

Vortex at 6 feet two and a half inches and 204.6 lbs was bigger and taller than the average American white male. However, as the Colonel surveyed his opponent he was quite amazed at looking at a Vietnamese who was an even 6 feet tall. Yet what was even more striking was the sheer size and girth of the man. Vortex estimated that he must have weighed at least 280 lbs to 300 lbs and it was all solid muscle. His neck was like that of a prize bull at a Spanish tauromachia spectacle (bullfighting). His biceps were nearly 50% larger than those of Vortex as were his thighs and forearms.

In addition the man appeared to be, at least, superbly fit and resilient.

"You have this one last chance to tell us where General Vo Nguyen Giap is hiding before I dismantle you into your constituent pieces, you slime-dog piece of shit!" screamed Colonel Vortex.

"Nhận được nhồi bạn chó Đế quốc Mỹ!"

"You are the imperialist! Not us! And we are not dogs but lions of peace!" shouted back Vortex in response to the Communist's taunts.

Captain Richter said calmly, "Sir. Take him apart. I've got you covered."

Richter and Maddog Dave were holding their UMP's in one hand and the Model 500's in the other. They were standing back to cover Vortex just in case the North Vietnamese antagonist got the better of the 9th Marine Regiment Commander.

Colonel Vortex took one step closer to the Major and then with a speed that was difficult to track he launched a punch directly at the Communist's face.

Equally fast the Major caught Vortex's entire fist in his right hand and stopped it inches in front of his nose.

There was no impact.

The two large men just stood there with Vortex trying to press his entire arm forward while the Major was pushing Vortex's entire momentum back while at the same time crushing with ever increasing force the fingers, knuckles and palm of the Colonel's fist that was immobilised.

"Did you see that?" shouted Maddog Dave.

Slowly but inexorably the Communist's massive frame of nearly 300 lbs pushed Vortex's entire 204.6 lb body backwards so that the Colonel's feet were sliding across the floor.

Vortex then remembered his Judo training and decided to flow to the point of least resistance.

With lightning speed he unclenched his fist gripping his hand around the wrist of the Major and added his force to the direction of the opposing force. This resulted in him flinging the Communist forward and off his feet through the air and crashing into a radio communications set near the entrance to the COMMO bunker.

"That's more like it Vortex!" shouted Laubscher with encouragement still nursing both his hand and his nose.

Seeing a North Vietnamese flag hanging from the far wall Vortex leaped over and ripped the emblem off its hooks twisting one end around his right wrist.

[The North Vietnamese flag had an all bright red background with a five pointed yellow star placed directly in the middle]

"What is this piece of shit?" said Vortex in Vietnamese.

The Colonel playfully swung the flag in a ricochet action snapping its loose end at the Communist's buttocks.

The sound of the material made a swishing and then whiplash sound as it struck the enemy's backside.

Laubscher, Pohl and the others laughed as they too taunted Vortex's adversary with jibes and intermittent cat-calls.

This infuriated the PAVN Major to a new level of viciousness.

"I feel like wiping my ass with this putrid rag!" shouted Vortex to the Communist.

The Colonel was like a delinquent schoolboy at a beach party as he whiplashed the North Vietnamese flag back and forth across the Major's face, arms, cheeks, buttocks and legs. Each snapping action brought a deeper hue of red fury to the NVA's face.

The Communist shouted to Vortex to put the flag down.

In response Vortex held out the piece of cloth in front of the Major and with tremendous power he tore the fabric down the middle into two pieces. Taking one piece he pretended to wipe his backside with it bringing the cloth up and down the crevice of his ass-cheeks.

"Tôi sẽ giết bạn!" shouted the Major.

"What did he say now?" asked Laubscher.

Vortex smiled as he flicked the torn half of the flag at the Communist's heels making him jump.

"He said he's going to kill me."

"Fat chance!" added Maddog Dave.

In an instant the Communist lashed forward with a knife-hand Karate strike directly at Vortex's left temple.

The Colonel was too quick and ducked just before impact.

However Sergeant Dolby, who was standing behind the Colonel was not so lucky.

The textbook manoeuvre flew past Vortex's skull by less than a quarter of an inch and impacted with deadly force onto the chest of Dolby who careered backwards from the impact knocking over Egon who fell onto his knees.

"You bastard!" shouted the Sergeant.

Vortex flung a right-hook that smashed the Major's nose and broke it at the septum.

In the same instant Dolby recovered and kicked the Communist with devastating force in the testicles.

As the Major bent over double in agony Vortex rushed forward to execute some follow-up punches but was surprised as the Communist straightened out his enormous body and lashed his arms around the Colonel starting to crush him in a bear-hug embrace of death.

"Shit!" screamed Richter.

Vortex was lifted clear off the floor of the COMMO bunker as the Communist used his incredible power to crush the spine and the ribs of his opponent.

The Colonel's head was nearly touching the low ceiling of the bunker and he felt the air being squashed out of his lungs. His legs flailed in the air helplessly.

Then Vortex brought both his arms back and across to the level of his shoulder twisting and at the same time he squirmed them free of the embrace bringing both fists simultaneously crashing into the left and right temples of the Major.

The death-grip loosened somewhat.

Next, Vortex commenced to press his two thumbs into both eyes of the Communist as Maddog Dave moved around to the rear and smashed a vicious punch into the lumbar spine of the enemy soldier.

This finally broke the hug-of-death.

Colonel Vortex swept across the face of the man and delivered a series of seven left and right-hooks that brought blood sprinkling across not only himself but Egon and Manfred who were standing behind him, cheering him on in a juvenile fashion.

Sergeant Dolby then slashed his combat knife across the NVA's back ripping open his shirt.

"No! Sergeant! Let me have him! He's mine!"

At the order from Vortex, Dolby backed off.

The Major let loose with his right-hook that smashed Vortex's face sideways causing blood to squirt across the ripped flag.

Vortex countered with his own left-hook that brought teeth flying in all directions.

The Communist and Colonel Vortex then started to trade punches one at a time.

Each man was so powerful and strongly built that each blow sounded like a pistol shot.

"Show him your pugilistic skills Vortex! We are counting on you! Teach this gook recalcitrant a lesson he shall never forget!" shouted Brigadier Laubscher.

Each man staggered forward at first and delivered a right or left hook which was followed by another blow from his adversary upon which he careered backwards. The slug-fest continued for some five minutes until both men were utterly exhausted and bleeding from a profusion of flesh wounds.

Maddog Dave threw the ripped North Vietnamese flag to Vortex while the other half of the emblem was on the floor covered in blood.

As the Communist lurched forward swinging his arms to contact with Vortex the Colonel quickly side-stepped and locked the NVA in a head-vice.

As he did so Vortex wrapped the North Vietnamese flag around the Major's neck several times and then started to strangle him with it.

"Happy now! Have you had enough?" asked Vortex.

The Communist officer gurgled back only further unseemly obscenities.

"Tell me where General Giap is hiding!"

Colonel Vortex repeated the question seven times over.

There was no response other than a lot of blood spitting, swearing and gurgling as the PAVN officer was being methodically strangled to death.

"I have never seen anybody so obstinate," commented Captain Max Richter.

"Sie sind alle wie das," answered Vortex.

[Translated: They are all like that.]

"Fuck him then. If he's of no use to us then get rid of him. We've wasted enough time already!" ordered Laubscher.

As the Brigadier spoke Vortex was caught off guard as the Communist suddenly swung both his legs up and head-locked the Colonel throwing him over his head and onto the COMMO bunker floor.

Vortex was so surprised that he had all the wind gutted from his lungs.

From a concealed pocket in his military tunic the NVA officer swung out a razor sharp barber's knife and slashed Maddog Dave across the chest as he moved forward to assist Colonel Vortex.

The Colonel scrambled to his feet panting and spitting globules of blood from out of his mouth as his tongue had been lacerated earlier when the Major had bitten into it.

Grabbing Dolby by the hair he yanked the Sergeant away screaming, "Leave him! I have had just about enough of this unbending aggressor terrorist!"

"I told you you were all going to die in this cave!" screamed the PAVN officer in Vietnamese.

From outside the COMMO bunker the SLICE team heard noises and shots being fired at the secondary steel door (still intact) which Egon had slammed and bolted after their entry.

"Damn! The NVA are trying to break in!" shouted Laubscher.

Vortex stepped forward and kicked the razor out of the Communist's hands and then did a back-flip across the floor picking the weapon up.

With only a minute or two before the PAVN troops would break in or either they would have to force their way out, Vortex knew that he must dispatch the enemy in front of him.

"Get the bastard!" shouted Sergeant Dolby, "He's cut me!"

As he spoke Maddog Dave ran his hands across his chest and felt a substantial and deep wound that ran from just under his left nipple across his sternum and to his right arm-pit. Blood was flowing freely.

Like a man gone out of his mind with maniacal frenzy Colonel Vortex slashed out at the Major first right in a sweeping arc and then from below aiming at the man's gonads. The third swipe neatly severed off the Communist's left testicle and penis.

Sergeant Dolby watched as the Communist bent over double in excruciating pain and drove his combat knife into the man's jugular. The point of the blade went from right to left straight through the neck and exited just below the left ear.

Colonel Vortex grabbed the Major's right arm and cut down with vicious force ripping open his entire forearm and cutting the ulna artery.

Maddog Dave sliced the NVA's throat open as he withdrew the knife and then reinserted it with a sawing action.

Brigadier Laubscher stepped up and shot the Communist in both feet with his Model 500 pistol blowing the entire flesh off right up to the ankles.

Gripping the North Vietnamese flag that was covered in the blood of American and Communist protagonists Vortex sliced open the Major's stomach so that the lower and upper intestines spilled out onto the COMMO bunker floor.

"If you want your fucking rag back you can have it!" screamed Vortex.

With those words Vortex stuffed the blood drenched flag of North Vietnam back into the internal organs of the Communist to which it belonged.

"Amen to that!" said Colonel Egon Pohl.

"Well that was a total waste of time!" said Brigadier Laubscher as he stepped up and with two powerful shots from his Model 500 he blew the entire skull off what was left of the Communist's torso.

The head splattered across the COMMO bunker floor with pieces of brain tissue strewn all over the SLICE team's uniforms.

"If I had had more time I could have properly and methodically elicited the information out of this gook," said Vortex.

"What do you mean? If you had more time. You could see that he wasn't going to divulge anything anyway!" shouted Laubscher.

"Don't be too sure about that sir. I have my methods. Tried, true and tested," answered back Vortex with indignation.

"Well we shall never know shall we?"

"No sir," answered Vortex.

"We have to get the deuce out of here and find General Giap otherwise this whole ill-conceived mission will be a total failure and an unmitigated fiasco of the highest order!" screamed Egon.

"We shall be lucky if we extricate ourselves from these caves in time to escape," said Captain Richter as he trained his MGL/M-32 towards the steel door of the COMMO bunker.

Loud noises that sounded like machinery or electrical generators could be heard on the other side of the barrier.

"The element of surprise has eluded us," said Laubscher.

"What do you suggest we do now sir?" asked Vortex as he collected himself and re-loaded his UMP, Model 500 pistol and the RT-20 hand-cannon.

"We blast ourselves out of here and continue the search for Giap. That's the orders. I always follow my directives to the letter. I am a perfectionist!" said Laubscher.

Sergeant Dolby and Colonel Pohl took up positions behind the steel COMMO bunker door while the others hunkered down at the far end of the room.

The Brigadier gave the order and both Dolby and Egon fired their RPO-A-*Shmel* simultaneously which were armed with the high explosive ordnance. Immediately they too dived for cover and covered their ears while opening their mouths wide to diffuse the air compression blast.

The explosion was horrendous and more powerful than required to rip the steel frame barrier free from its underpinnings.

The blast tore the two inch thick armor plating clear down the corridor that they had just traversed.

As it hurtled through the atmosphere it crushed five PAVN soldiers from the 304th Division and splattered their bodies across the walls and upper surface of the tubular corridor.

The mayhem and gunfire that now erupted was uncontrolled and ferocious.

Colonel Vortex and Maddog Dave Dolby led the charge back down the thoroughfare shooting as they went.

The PAVN troops withered on the vine as they were decimated in swathes by the SLICE team's superior heavy weaponry.

Forking to the right half-way down the corridor they had navigated through earlier the SLICE team came up against a group of PAVN troops manning a 12.7 mm DShKM38/46 machine gun which the US troops in the 'Nam' called the 0.51 cal. It was a Type 54 Chinese made machine gun which was usually used for anti-air engagements.

"Take it out!" screamed Laubscher.

Colonel Vortex signalled for Maddog Dave to move forward with his M2 flamethrower as bullets whizzed around their heads bouncing off the limestone walls of the seemingly endless cavern.

The Sergeant engulfed the ten enemy soldiers in a veritable bath of yellow-orange fire that shot like a laser beam from his fuel tanks that were still strapped to his back and held in place by his battle webbing.

Horrendous screams and shouts ushered forth from the Communist forces as they scurried from their weapon like comical spectres or fire-flies in the darkness of the subterranean battlefield.

The destruction was continuous and unrelenting as the SLICE team crushed and exterminated their way from one corridor to another, destroying one bolt-hole until they had to deal with another and so on down the line of what appeared to be a vast network of underground control rooms and storage facilities.

The time was now 1015 hours on the 9th February 1968.

It was 16 and a quarter hours into Operation SLICE and the team had only 19.75 hours left in which to locate, crush and exterminate General Vo Nguyen Giap, traverse the 3.84 miles to the LZEXF (exfiltration point due south) rendezvous with the *Sikorsky's* and the two AC-47 SPOOKY gunships and make it back to *Khe Sanh* for the drop off to conclude the enterprise.

"Kill that machine!" shouted Laubscher.

Colonel Vortex fired his MGL/M-32 and disintegrated an electrical generator that was in their path. Pieces of shrapnel flew in a multitude of directions and tore into further squads of Communist troops as they proceeded ever deeper into the furthest bowels of the headquarters complex.

"Fuck this! There is no sign of General Giap."

Colonel Pohl answered in response to Vortex's statement, "I haven't seen any officer in here higher than the rank of Colonel."

Maddog Dave remarked, "Looks like we blew it!"

"Don't be too sure about that yet!" answered Brigadier Laubscher.

Colonel Pohl nodded and said, "I was in the glider-borne attack on *Fort Eben-Emael* on the 10th May 1940 as part of Operation YELLOW for the German invasion of France. We thought that the mission had failed when we failed to penetrate the first line of defences. However, with solid and unflinching perseverance we prevailed against insurmountable odds."

Sergeant Dolby asked, "What is *Eben-Emael*, sir?"

Colonel Egon Pohl answered, "Fort *Eben-Emael* is a now inactive Belgian Fortress located between *Liege* and *Maastricht* on the Dutch-Belgian border near the *Albert Canal*. It was designed to defend Belgium from a German attack across the narrow expanse of territory that was the Dutch border. It was constructed from 1931 to 1935 and was reputed by many to be impregnable. It was also the largest Fort in the world at the time. The Wehrmacht-Fallschirmjäger (paratroopers) of which I was a part of, successfully destroyed that myth of invincibility. We used a glider-borne assault to crush that fort. It was a great success. I was part of the *1st Fallschirmjäger Division* and there were 78 of us. We used the DFS 230 gliders and carried special high explosive ordnance. We destroyed all the main guns on the surface of the fortress

such as the 120 mm gun turrets and the 75 mm guns but we could not penetrate into the lower galleries of the underground fortress bunker complex. However the 1,200 man Belgian force could not come up to the surface either as we exterminated them if they tried. The taking of Fort *Eben-Emael* proves what a few dedicated men can do against an overwhelmingly superior force!"

Vortex asked, "You were decorated for that were you not – Egon?"

Colonel Pohl answered, "The Iron Cross First Class with oak leave cluster!"

"Excellent work Egon!" said Vortex as the SLICE team now moved down to the 2nd Level of the limestone cave complex after exterminating all the Communist troops on the first level.

The surface of the cave complex was so awash with human blood and body parts that their boots started to develop congealed blood on their heels and leggings.

"This is sticky, messy business," said Captain Max Richter.

Vortex replied smugly, "War usually is Max!"

The steel staircase leading down to the second level was blocked by an iron gate which Captain Richter easily blew open with his RT-20 hand-cannon.

As they proceeded down into the subterranean vaults of the lower level they were fired upon by about twenty PAVN troops who were at the other end of a long tubular limestone corridor illuminated by electric lights strung on the roof similar to the corridor above.

"Let them have it!" ordered Laubscher.

Richter and Sergeant Dolby launched five MGL/M-32 incendiary grenades from their semi-automatic launchers and blew the force to smithereens.

As Colonel Vortex and the team passed by the wounded survivors they used their Marine and combat daggers to cut into the still living and by doing so they ripped open their throats and penetrated their heart tissues to put a finish to them.

Major General Julian Ewell had ordered back at BEARCAT that no wounded were to be spared. Everyone in the limestone cave complex was to be ruthlessly exterminated.

Colonel Vortex was at ease with these orders as it was totally legitimate under the rules of *public international law*. The opposing forces were aggressor terrorists and thus were deserving of no quarter. The entire State that they represented was under International Law a Criminal-Terrorist Organisation of the first magnitude. It was thus open slather as far as Colonel Vortex was concerned.

The SLICE team moved deeper into Level 2 of the limestone cave headquarters and came up against another solid steel door of two inches armor plating.

"Blow it open!" ordered Brigadier Laubscher.

Captain Richter attached the Semtex plastic explosive comprising of PETN or Pentaerythritol Tetranitrate. He set the Q-switched ruby laser timer for 20 seconds.

"Take cover!" screamed the Captain.

Seconds later an enormous shock-wave hurtled down the confined spaces of the corridor and the armor barrier was sheared off.

The SLICE team bolted inside and found seven North Vietnamese officers struggling to their feet with blast and shrapnel wounds.

All five Americans lined up with their UMP's and Model 500's at the ready aimed directly at the PAVN brass who had had no time to react or to reach for their weapons which had been blown out of their hands by the Semtex penetration of their vault.

"Looks like a central headquarters of some kind. Probably the Command Centre for the NVA Divisions around *Khe Sanh*," commented Colonel Vortex.

Colonel Pohl who knew only a few words of Vietnamese said, "Good morning Vietnam!"

The PAVN officers bloodied and bedraggled as they were immediately shot up their hands in the air above their heads in a gesture of unconditional surrender.

"What was that? What did you say?" asked Vortex.

One of the Communist's said in his language that he wanted to surrender and that they should spare their lives.

"I can't hear you! Say that again?" asked the Colonel.

Again the most senior of the PAVN brass said that he wanted to surrender with his officers.

Vortex asked in Vietnamese, "Where is General Vo Nguyen Giap?"

Immediately and without hesitation the PAVN Colonel replied, "Bạn phải tin rằng tôi. Anh ta không ở đây. Ông còn cho phía bắc ngày hôm qua."

Vortex nodded, and looked to Laubscher.

The Brigadier asked not understanding a word of the language, "Well? What the fuck did he say? Does he know where General Giap is?"

Vortex replied, "He said that Giap is not here and that he left for the north yesterday – sir."

"He's a fucking liar!"

"I think he is telling the truth," answered Vortex.

"And why do you think that?" asked Laubscher.

"Because I have a gut feeling that Giap is indeed absent from these headquarters. If he was here we would have found him by now."

"Oh! Is that so?"

"Yes, I believe so."

"And what makes you an expert Vortex on the movements of this slimy character?"

"It's just that if Giap *was* really here the opposition would have been a lot stiffer, sir. I think we better abort the mission and return to the exfiltration point before they bring the entire 304th PAVN Division down on our heads."

Brigadier Laubscher ran his hands through his thinning hair with exasperation and looked to Colonel Egon Pohl asking, "And what do you think Egon?"

Pohl looked at the PAVN officers and stared deeply into their eyes.

Finally he said, "I agree with Colonel Vortex. I don't think that Giap is here Manfred."

Laubscher took a minute to think it over as he paced back and forth while the other four continued to train their weapons on the enemy brass.

"Alright then!" began Laubscher finally and after much deliberation, "We shall return to the surface after sweeping what's left of this lower level and then make our way post haste to the exfiltration point."

Vortex nodded as he said to the Communists, "Sorry gentlemen. But I am afraid that we have to leave. Nice to have known you!"

As he spoke Vortex slowly walked up to the senior officer that had been doing all the talking and lifted his Model 500 Smith & Weston to his head blowing his brains out like an exploding shower-head.

The rest of the SLICE team immediately thereafter opened fire with their UMP submachine guns and liquidated the other six in a grotesque orgy of destruction as their bodies were literally torn apart by the heavy calibre bullets.

"Good then! Let's go!" ordered Laubscher as he collected all the maps and other North Vietnamese secret military correspondence and documents that were lying on the conference table in front of them and stuffed it all into his back-pack.

Sergeant Dolby asked in a whisper as they made their way further into the depths of Level 2 of the limestone cave complex, "Do you think its right Max? To just give-up so easily? Who knows? – Giap might be here somewhere?"

Captain Richter answered, "Its not my call! And certainly not yours either. I just do what I am told. I follow Colonel Vortex's orders to the letter and carry them out with a minutiae of detail just as he desires his directives to be executed."

Maddog Dave just shook his head from side to side.

The SLICE team were running now with all their heavy weaponry down the last Level 2 subterranean corridor which forked to the north-east from the one where they had found the seven North Vietnamese staff officers.

Suddenly as they passed a stairwell a PAVN soldier came out of nowhere and started firing his AK-47. One 7.62mm round grazed Colonel Egon Pohl's right upper arm causing a superficial flesh wound.

"Bloody hell!" shouted Laubscher.

The team dived to the floor except for Vortex who returned fire with his UMP.

Chasing the enemy Vortex ran down a flight of steel fabricated ladders into another sub-corridor and hosed down the Communist who was running backwards and firing.

The 0.45 calibre slugs from the UMP tore his left arm off and then decapitated the soldier who fell with a thump.

As the rest of the team followed-up Laubscher said, "Keep a close watch! This place is still crawling with hidden NVA troops!"

"I think I have found something sir," said Vortex as they continued down the sub-corridor and came upon a massive steel door in the shape of an ellipse.

"What do you think is inside there?" asked Maddog Dave Dolby.

"Fucked if I know?" said Captain Richter.

"I have an idea," answered Vortex.

"Well? What is this hunch that you have? You seem to have premonitions for everything now!" said Brigadier Laubscher sarcastically.

"I think it's the armoury!"

Colonel Pohl said, "Well the door is too massive! Just leave it and let's get back to the surface and out of this rat-hole!"

Laubscher shouted, "No! Egon! No!"

Colonel Vortex advised, "We can't just leave this intact – if indeed it is the main armoury of the PAVN forces in this area. That would be negligent and a dereliction of our duties and a failure in our mission objectives!"

Brigadier Laubscher remarked, "Yes! I agree with Colonel Vortex. After all we don't want to be accused of failing in one our primary objectives. I remember the total fiasco and failure of Operation PASTORIUS!"

Captain Richter asked, "What? What is Operation PASTORIUS?"

Colonel Vortex corrected, "You mean – what *was* Operation PASTORIUS?"

Laubscher smiled, "So you have heard about it then Vortex?"

"I have sir."

Brigadier Laubscher explained, "Operation PASTORIUS – Captain Richter, is a scheme that was dreamt up by the German Military Intelligence forces or *Abwehr* which was headed by Admiral Wilhelm Canaris and General Hans Oster. The operation was named after Franz Daniel Pastorius who led the first German settlement in America. The plan came under the auspices of *Abwehr II* which was in charge of sabotage and four German agents were involved. All of them had grown up in the United States and thus spoke English perfectly with very little discernible accent to give them away. The four agents were equipped with $175,200 US currency, numerous crates of explosive devices and a comprehensive list of targets in the United States. They were ordered not to come back to Germany until the war had been won which was estimated by Admiral Canaris to be at the end of 1944. The targets for Operation PASTORIUS included; aluminium factories, power plants, railroad stations and water supplies amongst others. There were to be two teams of Abwehr saboteurs. One team would land in Long Island, New York State and the other in Jacksonville, Flor-

ida. The teams were also put in touch with a group of current German operatives in the United States to assist them in their errands of destruction and general mayhem. The Long Island group was led by George John Dasch. The aim was to rendezvous with the second team in Chicago to begin their missions to thwart the US war effort against the *Tri-Partite Pact*."

"So what happened sir?" asked Richter with amazement.

"George Dasch and his three men were discovered by US coast guard personnel just after they landed ashore at the Hamptons on Long Island after leaving U-Boat 202. To his discredit, Dasch gave himself up to the US authorities and provided the details of the other teams who were all rounded up within 2 weeks and executed, - except for George Dasch who was given clemency by President Harry S. Truman in April 1948."

"Yes it is most fortunate for the United States Manfred," began Richard Vortex, "Or, as you *then* were, for you and Egon – most unfortunate in terms of the uniform that you were *then* wearing."

Laubscher rubbed his chin, "Yes! Indeed! But now, just like Werner Von Braun, I owe my allegiance and loyalty to the United States that has so graciously provided me with employment in its armed forces. Therefore – I don't want any Operation PASTORIUS fuck-up here! We are going to blow to hell whatever is inside that bunker vault! I don't care if its cartons of milk or ladies underwear – I am going to destroy it and blow it to hell!"

Colonel Vortex saluted, "Yes! Of course sir! Thy will shall be done!"

Captain Richter commenced to set the Semtex charges.

When they were all in place he asked, "How long should I set the timer for sir? We need to get to the other end of this corridor because the blast is going to be a big one!"

"Two minutes should give us enough time," said Laubscher.

Captain Richter set the Pentaerythritol Tetranitrate charges as ordered and the SLICE team ran and hauled themselves and their equipment to a position which was approximately 40 yards away and underneath the stairwell from which Vortex had descended in pursuit of the lone NVA trooper.

Covering their ears and opening their mouths wide to dissipate the concussion blast as the air shock-wave would pass with tremendous concussive force they waited for the explosion.

Colonel Vortex was in a dream and only slowly awoke as he found himself lying on top of Maddog Dave. With his ears echoing and his nose bleeding he slowly dragged himself and Sergeant Dolby up from the cave floor. Pohl, Laubscher and Richter had been thrown back against the stairwell and he noticed that Max had one leg caught in a sheared-off piece of metal girding.

All of them had nose bleeds from the stupendous shockwave that had emanated from the Semtex explosion.

"Christ! Max!" shouted Vortex as he could hardly hear himself speak, thinking that he had gone deaf, "How much of that stuff did you use?"

Richter pulled himself out of his entanglements asking, "What? I can't hear you?"

Vortex walked over giddily still reeling from the blast and grabbed Richter's left ear shouting at the top of his lungs, "How much of that shit did you use!"

"What? What did you say?" answered Richter as he could only see Vortex's lips moving but the noises he heard coming from his commanding officer's mouth sounded garbled.

"Fuck-this-shit!" shouted Laubscher, "…that crazy son-of-a-bitch Captain of yours used too much of that explosive ordnance!"

"We are still alive!" comforted Colonel Pohl as he brought a tissue up to his nose trying to stem the flow of blood that had covered the entire frontage of his military tunic.

"Bloody hell! Look what you did to my precious *101st Airborne Division* shoulder flashes! They are all soaked in blood thanks to you Richter!"

Vortex laughed as his hearing slowly recovered, "I'll make sure that the Captain buys you a new set sir!"

Laubscher was more than a little displeased, saying, "From now on let Sergeant Dolby set the charges! He's supposed to be the demolition expert in this team."

Vortex nodded as he looked at the embarrassed Richter.

"A monkey could have done better hanging from a banana skin!"

The SLICE team scurried back to where the elliptical steel armor plated barrier had been.

There was nothing left except a gaping hole and part of the limestone superstructure around the entrance had been blown away leaving large chunks of stone strewn around for more than 20 yards.

"We are in!" said Vortex.

"Oh! Mein geliebter und lieber Gott!" said Brigadier Laubscher in wondrous amazement.

As the SLICE team moved cautiously inside they feasted their eyes on one of the largest stockpiles of ammunition, explosive ordnance and weaponry that they had ever seen.

"Major General Ewell never told us anything about this!" exclaimed Colonel Vortex.

"It's a stupendous find!" began Colonel Pohl, "…this alone will justify and condone the expediency of our mission even if we do not find General Giap!"

Laubscher added, "This must be one of the main supply dumps for the entire North Vietnamese Corps in and around the DMZ and *Khe Sanh*."

The subterranean vault in which they found themselves was approximately 20 yards high by 60 yards long by 30 yards in width.

Inside the bolt-hole was in addition to what seemed like millions of rounds of 7.62mm ammunition were row upon row of AK-47 assault rifles standing butt-end up in steel racks that extended the entire length of the armoury. In addition they saw at least 10,000 rounds of 12.7mm ammunition for the DShKM38/46 anti-air Type 54 machine gun, about 15 complete sets of the Soviet-made 37mm M1939 40mm Bofor guns in what appeared to be full working order and in mint condition, also 5 pieces of the D74 heavy howitzer with its 122mm shells stacked up to the ceiling, at least 20 sets of the DKB single-tube 122mm rocket launchers which were sitting there complete with their tripod mounts and countless handguns and 40mm grenades. There was also at the extreme northerly end of the vault two of the D20 152mm heavy artillery pieces that were being used to bombard *Khe Sanh* from the Communist held 'Co Roc' position.

"Fuck-me-dead! What a stash! Those dastardly, deceptive and unnaturally cunning little Communist shits! They have all this shit right under our noses barely 6 to 7 miles from the DMZ! Fuck them to hell!" screamed Brigadier Laubscher. Then he added, "Wait till I tell Major General Olinto Barsanti! And Major General Ewell! They are going to go ape-shit! That's iff'n we don't blow this fuck-shit'n pile of goodies to hell and back!"

"All I can say sir – is that reptile and sneaking fuck-faced piece of turd – General Giap has been thumbing his noses at III MAF and our Marine boys in I Corps Operational Zone! Captain Mirza Baig has been telling me all along that the J-2 Section knew that there must be an enormous mother-of-all fucking ammunition dumps somewhere close to *Khe Sanh* which has escaped our air strikes and Operation NIAGARA. The little dinks fucking knew that they couldn't store this humongous pile of shit above ground otherwise we would blow it to pieces within 48 hours! So the bloody stuff is right here!"

"Does that mean we get to blow it up?" asked Maddog Dave Dolby.

Laubscher laughed, "What the fuck do you think? – Sergeant. Do you want us to just leave it here with a thank you note for the little bow-legged Communist motherfuckers to use it against us and our boys at *Khe Sanh* and Camp Carroll?"

Sergeant Dolby looked embarrassed, "Sorry sir. I was just asking."

Colonel Pohl added, "*If* and when I get back to 101st Airborne Division HQ I am going to make a strong recommendation to our CO – General Barsanti."

"And what pray tell is that Egon?" asked Laubscher with curiosity.

"This entire area between Laos, Tchepone and *Khe Sanh/Lang Vei* must be doused with a massive quantity of *Agent Orange*."

"And how the fuck is that going to help Egon? We want to kill the Communists not the fucking flowers and the fauna and wildlife! Who gives a flying-shit about whether the grass is too long in Laos! Is that going to make one iota of difference in this fucking fiasco that is called the Vietnam War Episode 2. The fucking Pilot Show with the French who we fought for didn't turn out too well either!" screamed Brigadier Laubscher.

"Yeah! I am surprised that we Americans agreed to make Episode 2. We should have learnt from the Pilot!" said Vortex.

"Let's get our asses into gear. I want all this ordnance blown to hell! And not by Captain Richter this time!" said Laubscher in feverish excitement.

Then he added, "No offense Max."

"None taken sir," replied Richter.

"I know that we have copious quantities of Semtex and a plentiful supply of detonators but for some unfathomable reason it appears that the Captain here has a penchant for the over-application of destructive force more that what is required to do the job. I don't want a repetition of the fireworks circus we just enjoyed a few minutes ago. So I want Sergeant Dolby to set the place up for imminent destruction and obliteration – just go easy on the Pentaerythritol Tetranitrate charges, - …will you Sergeant?" ordered Laubscher.

Vortex laughed as he pocketed half a dozen 40mm grenades and a couple of Zeliska Revolvers from the gigantic stash of weapons, along with a bucket full of 0.600 rounds.

[The Zeliska Revolver is not a Production handgun as the Model 500: But it is the most powerful handgun in the world which is not mass-produced. The 0.600 Nitro Express Zeliska Revolver is an Austrian made single action revolver and is manufactured on a demand-only basis by the Pfeifer Firearms Factory Ltd. GmBh. The Zeliska is a heavyweight handgun which is 6.001 kilograms with a length of 55 centimetres. It produces muzzle energy of over 6 kilojoules. The weight of the gun helps control the recoil, making controlled shooting possible. The capacity of the Zeliska is five 0.600 Nitro Express or 0.458 Win Mag rounds. The Zeliska fires a slug at 462 metres per second or 1,663 km per hour. The average purchase price in 1968 dollars (US) is $16,000.00 and each 0.600 round costs $40.00 (US). It has a gold-plated hammer and cylinder port and the Pfeifer's address is also indicated with a gold-filled inscription. Every part of the Zeliska is hand-made and each weapon is matched individually to the owner.]

"What the flying-fuck do you want that pistol for Vortex? We all have the Model 500. Isn't that good enough for you?" asked Colonel Pohl.

"I always dreamt about having a Zeliska but I could never afford one because I spent all my money on codeine tablets, booze and cigarettes!" exclaimed Colonel Vortex.

"Bloody hell Vortex! You're nuts!" said Egon.

"Why? What do you mean?"

"I can understand the booze and the cigarettes, but what's the story with the pain killers, - the Codeine? Do you have perpetual headaches or something?" asked Egon.

Vortex threw one of the Zeliska revolvers he had confiscated up into the air so that it spun 360 degrees and then expertly caught it in his right hand on the way down and then whipped it out in the direction of Egon as if he was Doc Holliday at the OK Corral, pretending he was a 19th Century cowboy, saying, "Of course I have perpetual headaches! Wouldn't you!"

"Whatever do you mean?"

Vortex answered as he loaded five 0.600 Nitro rounds into the Zeliska and replaced the Model 500 with it neatly in his holster, "If you thought just a bit about how this fucked-up war is being run it would give you perpetual headaches as well! We have to fight according to these ridiculous Rules of Engagement (ROE) dreamt up by President Johnson and his NSC boys over their daily luncheon at the White House that have no basis nor validity under international law. We should be taking the offensive here in Laos and launching a full-scale invasion of Cambodia through the Parrot's Beak and War Zone C to interdict and cut off the supply lines of the Main Force Viet Cong and PAVN forces! Instead we are merely posturing as a reactive force that only responds at the instigation of Giap's strategic movements. If you really ponder carefully and with circumspection the whole issue, I am sure that you would have a humongous headache as well. And I am not criticising General Westmoreland or Earle Wheeler either. Its not their fault! They are hog-tied by the ridiculous policies coming out of the NSC [*National Security Council*] the majority of which, like Clark Clifford, try to impede the valid advice from the Joint Chiefs. And you ask me why I have perpetual headaches!"

Laubscher interrupted, "That's enough of that idle banter and chit-chat! We have a job to do. You can argue strategy all you want when and *if* we get the fuck out of this stinking Communist rat-hole!"

Turning to Maddog Dave Laubscher asked, "Have you set the charges yet?"

"Just about done sir!" answered Sergeant Dolby.

As Vortex and Egon Pohl were discussing the pharmaceutical needs of each other and their expenditure on luxury items, Sergeant Dolby was frantically laying out the Semtex charges. He placed charges on the 122mm artillery shells, the 152mm ordnance and the bulk of the explosives he sat right on top of a huge pile of 40mm grenades. He then prepared the Q-switched ruby laser timer for setting.

"That should do it then," said Maddog Dave.

"Good!" said Laubscher.

"Sir. Do you want me to set the timer for 10 minutes?"

"Are you crazy Dolby! Do you want to blow us all to Valhalla?" screamed Vortex.

"No you dolt! Set it for exactly 1 hour from now. That should give us enough time to fight our way out of here and back to the surface and to reach minimum safe distance," answered the Brigadier.

"Are you sure that's enough time sir?" asked Captain Richter scratching his head.

"Of course I am not sure! It's a guesstimate. If its not - then we are all fucked. But two hours is too risky. The dinks might have time to disarm the Semtex after we are out of here," answered Laubscher.

"Let's go then!" said Colonel Vortex.

The SLICE team made their way back down the series of three long corridors from whence they had come and were just about to ascend the steel fabricated stairwell back to Level 1 of the limestone cave complex when as they were two-thirds of the way up they were caught in a ferocious hail of 7.62mm fire from an unknown number of PAVN troops at the top of the stairwell.

"Take cover!" shouted Sergeant Dolby.

Pohl was hanging from the side of a steel girder with his left hand and holding the RT-20 hand-cannon in the other. He started to pick-off the Communist attackers one by one.

Blood and entrails showered down from above.

Colonel Vortex and Captain Richter fired their MGL/M-32 grenades upwards and blew swathes into the NVA ranks.

The Communists retreated as the SLICE team scrambled onto the first corridor on Level 1 from which they had first entered the headquarters of the 304th, 325th and 320th PAVN Divisions.

"We have to continue the attack! Forward! Vortex - and you Egon! Take point!" ordered Laubscher.

However the five men did not get far down the corridor and their path to the surface when an enormous hail of heavy calibre rounds showered the confines of the passage.

The SLICE team took cover behind a large block of concrete that had fallen from the roof as a result of Vortex's MGL/M-32 grenade attack.

"I don't believe it!" screamed Colonel Pohl to Laubscher and Vortex.

Laubscher peered over the edge of the masonite and pieces of stone from the cave structure and was mesmerised by what he saw.

Egon said, "The gooks have managed to wheel in a *Vladimirov KPV-14.5 Heavy Machine gun* on a *Kharanin* wheel mount."

Laubscher added, "I saw the early version of this weapon on the Eastern Front at Voronhez and at Kursk. It's the *ZPU-4 quad mounted - KPVT-14.5 heavy machine guns*! Shit! These monster-mothers can fire 600 rounds per minute!"

"What do we do?" asked Captain Richter.

"Attack!" said Colonel Vortex.

"How the fuck do you propose to do that?" asked Laubscher.

As they were yelling at each other over the din of the KPVT fusillade that rained the 14.5 by 115 mm rounds in their direction the entire concrete slab was being torn to pieces around them as the shower of steel literally tore it apart.

"We are dead meat in less than a second if we don't do something fast," said Colonel Pohl.

"I have an idea," said Colonel Vortex, saying to Maddog Dave, "Give me some of that Semtex!"

Vortex set the timer on the Pentaerythritol Tetranitrate charge for 20 seconds and threw it at the *KPVT-14.5 quad mounted heavy machine gun.*

They waited and an enormous explosion blew the weapon its crew and 20 other PAVN troops into a shower of mutilated flesh.

The SLICE team advanced down the corridor killing, hacking and shooting everything in their path.

Vortex shot three wounded NVA with his newly acquired Zeliska revolver that dismembered their bodies beyond recognition.

Maddog Dave brought up the rear and hosed the entire area down with what fuel he had left in the M2 flame thrower. Burning bodies ran comically hither and thither in the inferno while the rest of the team steam-rolled their way out into the open and through the main entrance to the limestone cave headquarters with their UMP's.

Waiting outside was the first elements of the reaction force being sent in from surrounding Communist base areas in Laos including transport troops who were manning the *Ho Chi Minh Trail* and who were thrown into battle with only AK-47's.

Approximately 200 NVA were opposing the SLICE team as Vortex said, "This is only the forward elements sir. We have to get to the LZEXF at once before they seal the entire area off!"

"Agreed Vortex!" said Laubscher.

Using their MGL/M-32 grenades as an umbrella of suppressive fire the SLICE team looked around for a fast way to decamp the area.

As they pressed forward Colonel Pohl discovered an abandoned PT-76 tank that had been brought up.

"We can commandeer that tank!"

Vortex nodded as they scrambled onto and inside the tracked vehicle.

Captain Richter started up the engine and they rolled forward.

Richter and Maddog Dave were inside the tank while Vortex manned the 76.2mm D-56T rifled tank gun that had a range of 1,500 metres.

Meanwhile Laubscher and Pohl jumped onto another ZIL-130 truck that had been brought up by the NVA troops killing the driver with a machete as they decapitated him and threw his cadaver in front of the truck. Driving forward they crushed the body plus two other Communist troops directly in front of them firing their AK-47's.

Using the C.R.E. hand signals Vortex signalled to Brigadier Laubscher to start rolling at full speed. The PT-76 and the ZIL-130 sped off in a southerly direction heading into the jungle and making their way the 3.84 miles to the exfiltration point. About 150 North Vietnamese troops ran after the vehicles yelling and firing their light weapons.

The two heavy vehicles crashed into the jungle undergrowth and were now under the triple canopied jungle which offered some protection.

"We are being followed!" shouted Richter to Vortex as they spotted four army jeeps and three ZIL trucks full of PAVN troops bludgeoning their way through the jungle morass behind them.

"I'll fuck them off with this tank's armament!" screamed Vortex.

Maddog Dave rammed a shell into the 76.2mm D-56T gun and Vortex used the hydraulic controls swinging the gun turret around 180 degrees to the rear.

"Fire!" shouted Captain Richter.

The 76.2mm shell detonated through three large trees and into the lead three NVA jeeps killing all 12 men onboard in a withering explosion.

The remaining jeep and three ZIL's accelerated out of the firing line of the PT-76.

"Faster! Faster!" shouted Laubscher in the ZIL-130 as Egon was launching MGL/M-32 grenades with one hand and holding the steering wheel with the other trying to keep onto a small dirt track that wound its way south to the approximate location of their exfiltration point.

One of the enemy ZIL's moved fast and managed to get ahead of Vortex's PT-76 on the dirt track as they positioned themselves in-between Laubscher's ZIL and the tank.

"No you don't! You dink shits!" screamed Colonel Vortex.

Rotating the gun turret of the tank back around to the front Maddog Dave reloaded the magazine.

Laubscher looked backwards and could see about 15 NVA soldiers firing their AK-47's wildly at the PT-76 tank. The Brigadier fired backwards with his Model 500 handgun blowing the brains out of one and then another Communist trooper in his attempt to reduce the odds against Vortex.

"Fire the fucking gun!" shouted Vortex as he saw that the gun turret was now aimed directly at the enemy ZIL in front of them with all three vehicles travelling at about 35 miles per hour down the dirt road.

Maddog Dave took aim through the gun sights while Richter worked the controls of the PT-76.

"Now!" yelled Vortex as the enemy ZIL was directly in front of them with at least twenty NVA troopers standing up in the back of the truck and peppering the tank hull steel plating with a hail of automatic machine gun fire.

Vortex felt the recoil as the 76.2mm shell burst forth and detonated the ZIL in front. It lifted the hefty vehicle high into the air and body parts, severed limbs, blood and pieces of human tissue came down like a sun-shower.

"Watch it! Steer clear!" shouted Colonel Vortex as he could see his tank careering directly for the enemy truck as it came back to earth.

The truck was tilted ninety degrees and the PT-76 tank caught the vehicle in mid-air with the D-56T tank turret impaling through the centre of the truck as the two speeding vehicles impacted.

Brigadier Laubscher looking back from his ZIL with Egon could hardly believe what he was seeing. If the whole situation was not so deadly serious it could almost have been comical. There he saw Vortex's tank carrying the enemy ZIL truck along with its gun turret sticking directly through the centre of the vehicle and protruding out of the undercarriage. Dead NVA soldiers were crushed inside and body parts hanging from the sides of the two vehicles.

Laubscher gave C.R.E. hand signals to Colonel Vortex to try to catch up as they were approaching the exfiltration point.

Meanwhile Colonel Vortex had to retreat back into the PT-76 as the truck, when it collided with them, had almost decapitated him.

Vortex looked down to Richter and shouted, "Schießen Sie den Lastwagen von dieser Zisterne. Schießen Sie es davon."

[Translated: Shoot the truck off this tank. Shoot it off.]

"Jawhol Herr Oberst!" answered Richter as Maddog Dave reloaded another shell into the gun and fired.

Brigadier Laubscher was standing at the back of his ZIL when Sergeant Dolby fired. To his horror he saw the enemy ZIL thrust off the PT-76 in a ball of fire and fly through the air. It thereupon crashed into the back of Laubscher's truck almost killing him.

Vortex, peeping up from out of the gun hatch could see what had happened and ordered Richter to speed up. The PT-76 then caught up with Laubscher's ZIL and crashed into it. The force of the collision rammed the burning enemy ZIL clear and free from Colonel Pohl and Brigadier Laubscher's vehicle.

The SLICE team then accelerated away from the two remaining NVA ZIL's and jeep that continued the pursuit.

Suddenly Vortex and the others heard a tremendous explosion from the direction of the limestone cave complex. A few seconds later they felt an earth tremor and then a few seconds after that a blast of air as the shock-wave hit them travelling close to the speed of sound.

"Its done!" cried Laubscher to Colonel Pohl.

The Semtex charges that they had prepared inside the Communist armoury had detonated and they were now feeling the effects of the larger and more devastating secondary explosions as the entire stash of ammunition and weapons were ignited.

Colonel Vortex looked back and could see an enormous mushroom cloud ascending into the atmosphere behind them with huge chunks of rock and debris flying majestically through the air, crashing into the triple-layered jungle canopy.

Captain Richter laughed, "We could not find General Giap but at least we have deprived the North Vietnamese of that massive reserve of ordnance."

Colonel Vortex smiled as he looked down through the gun hatch of the PT-76 at Sergeant Dolby and Captain Richter saying, "This will have a flow-on affect on the Communist's ability to continue the siege around *Khe Sanh*! It should assist us greatly!"

Both Richter and Dolby agreed.

Meanwhile Brigadier Laubscher checked the GPS transponder and confirmed that they were now arriving at the exact coordinates of the LZEXF (exfiltration point) for the conclusion of the mission.

"We have made it!" he shouted to Colonel Pohl.

"But not alone sir! Look!" said Egon.

As Vortex's PT-76 manoeuvred up and stopped alongside Laubscher's ZIL they saw the remaining Communist vehicles crashing through the jungle towards them with about 35 PAVN troops yelling and firing their AK-47's and even some RPG-7 rocket launchers.

"Take up defensive positions around the vehicles!" ordered the Brigadier from the 101st Airborne Division.

"You! Vortex and Richter! Stay in the tank and work the main armament!" yelled Laubscher.

Colonel Pohl, Sergeant Dolby and the Brigadier took cover behind the PT-76 and started firing a furious barrage of suppressive fire against the oncoming vehicles.

Meanwhile Vortex gave directions to Richter who fired the 76.2mm gun. It missed the lead ZIL-130.

"Load up! And try again!" shouted Colonel Vortex.

"We have only one shell left in this hulk!" cried back Max Richter.

"Then we better make it count!" answered Colonel Vortex.

As the Captain was reloading the last remaining PAVN jeep careered out of the jungle and collided with the abandoned ZIL of Brigadier Laubscher.

Immediately the SLICE team outside the tank fired their UMP's and MGL/M-32's at the enemy.

The jeep exploded in a massive fireball killing four NVA but two had jumped out and were now rushing towards the Americans.

Stepping out from behind the cover of the PT-76 tank Egon walked calmly forward and oblivious of the automatic weapons fire buzzing around his body lifted up his Model 500 pistol and carefully took aim.

In less than five seconds he had killed both Communist soldiers. The first was decapitated by the powerful handgun and the second was almost torn in half by the powerful muzzle force of the pistol.

"That takes care of that!" said Colonel Pohl calmly.

Laubscher smiled and said, "Looks like you haven't lost your touch from the training at Zossen Sniper School - Egon!"

Colonel Pohl looked over his shoulder to check if any more of the enemy were approaching and said, "Let the bastards come! I am ready for them!"

Vortex saw the enemy ZIL about 100 yards away as it was bombarded with UMP machine gun fire from the SLICE team.

"Fire!"

Captain Richter let loose with the last 76.2mm shell that streaked past the burning jeep, ripped open two trees and impacted with the NVA truck just as about 20 enemy troops were disembarking. The explosion ripped the truck apart and most of the soldiers were either blown apart and killed while the others struggled to take cover while returning fire against the Americans.

"Where the hell is our support and the two *Sikorsky's* to get us the hell out of here?" asked Laubscher to Vortex as he looked up to the gun turret.

"You're prayers have been answered sir! Look! Up there!"

The five SLICE members peered through the jungle canopy and saw two AC-47 SPOOKY gun ships flying in a left-hand orbit around the LZEXF each with three *General Electric* miniguns.

As each minute passed more and more PAVN forces from both the 304th Division and the 325thC *Golden Star Division* were deploying into the jungle in pursuit of the five Americans.

However the AC-47 SPOOKY's now kept up a withering and deadly concentration of fire that kept what now amounted to about 450 Communist troops at bay.

Three minutes later the two HH-53C *Sikorsky's* arrived on the scene. One descended right next to the abandoned PT-76 and ZIL while the other *Sikorsky*

circled in a tighter orbit than the AC-47 SPOOKY's to provide a more intimate ring of protective suppressive fire for the SLICE team.

Nothing could now get through to threaten the five team members.

All were exhausted with slight superficial flesh wounds suffered by Brigadier Laubscher, Colonel Egon Pohl and Captain Richter. Colonel Vortex and Sergeant David Dolby were relatively unscathed apart from bruising and nose bleeds suffered by the explosions and torn muscles from their altercation with the Communist Major in the limestone cave complex.

The primary SLICE Mission was a total failure.

General Vo Nguyen Giap was nowhere to be found.

The secondary objectives of destroying as much of the cave complex as possible and inflicting the maximum amount of damage on North Vietnamese Regular Forces (PAVN) had been a *'qualified success.'*

"Its time to go," said Brigadier Laubscher to the others as Vortex hurled himself down from the gun turret of the PT-76 tank.

As he jumped Vortex tripped on one of the dead bodies strewn around the evacuation point and did a summersault landing heavily on his backside.

"Shit! That hurt!" said Vortex.

"Don't die on us now Richard! Not when the mission is just about over!" laughed Colonel Egon Pohl.

The pilot of the HH-53C *Jolly Green Giant* was frantically waving at the SLICE team to get into the large helicopter.

"Let's move! Now!" screamed Laubscher.

All the team scrambled into the evacuation aircraft as the two door gunners fired their own *General Electric* Miniguns at the enemy.

Just as the *Sikorsky* was about to lift off to join the other aircraft Colonel Vortex screamed, "Wait!"

"What the fuck is it now Colonel?" screamed Laubscher.

"I dropped my Zeliska! My beautiful Zeliska!"

Colonel Vortex jumped out of the *Sikorsky* that was already lifting off the dirt and scrambled for his Austrian made handgun.

Egon and Max grabbed hold of his head as he stumbled back to the edge of the hatchway and pulled him in.

"I've got it! I saved it! Thank God!"

Brigadier Laubscher just shook his head with disbelief as the *Jolly Green Giant* rose high into the air and re-joined the other chopper.

In less than a minute both helicopters were travelling in excess of 145mph back in the direction of *Khe Sanh* and into South Vietnamese air space.

Lieutenant David Peter EHRLICH

B-52 Arc Light Raids on General Vo Nguyen Giap's Suspected Headquarters in Laos: 10th to 18th February 1968

Captain Mirza Baig was reading over some very interesting intelligence reports from the Surveillance and Reconnaissance Centre at Nakhon Phanom in Thailand.

It appeared that since the beginning of February there had been a significant increase in the volume of radio traffic coming from just inside the Laotian border.

Captain Baig was informed by the intelligence people in the USAF that the enemy radio traffic was situated in a complex of limestone caves some twenty miles north-west of *Khe Sanh*.

It was now the 10th February 1968.

The time was 1845 hours and even from the depths of the FSCC bunker, Baig could hear the incoming NVA artillery and mortars as the explosions ripped into the flimsy foxholes and corrugated iron buildings of the fire support base.

The PX was a shambles and there were rats everywhere.

Colonel David E. Lownds had told the Captain only the night before that a large black rat had bitten a small piece of flesh out of his left cheek.

Captain Baig was disgusted. But he told Colonel Lownds that he should always keep his face and body covered while he slept.

Colonel David Lownds had laughed at the Fire Control Officer, saying, "How can I sleep when my face is smothered by a blanket?"

Baig realised it was difficult but there was nothing else you could do to protect yourself from the *'real'* inhabitants of *Khe Sanh*.

Captain Richter and Colonel Richard Vortex were in the officer's accommodation section of the 9th/26th Marine HQ bunker complex at the foot of the *Khe Sanh* airstrip.

Just a few minutes earlier the *Sikorsky* had landed them back at *Khe Sanh*.

They were of course under strict orders not to divulge nor speak about anything relating to Operation SLICE with anyone at *Khe Sanh* or anywhere else for that matter.

They both kept their lips sealed despite the fact that they knew that Operation NIAGARA was continuing to bombard the limestone cave headquarters where they were unsuccessful in locating General Vo Nguyen Giap.

Brigadier Manfred Laubscher, Colonel Egon Pohl and Sergeant David Dolby had all returned to BEARCAT for a thorough de-briefing by Major General Julian Ewell and Brigadier General Phillip B. Davidson the J-2 for COMUSMACV. They would give the full details of the failed mission to execute the war criminal, General Giap.

There had been no further ground assault on *Khe Sanh* or its hill outposts since the vicious attack on Hill 64 two days earlier.

Captain Richter handed his chief a can of Budweiser.
Colonel Vortex drank it thirstily and started to speak.
"I really miss Sergeant Major Crighton," he began.
Vortex's voice was choked with emotion.
Captain Richter nodded, "He was my friend too, sir."
Both officer's fell silent and finished their beer.
Even though they were, resourceful, cunning, resilient and supremely fit men, both Vortex and Richter were utterly exhausted.
Especially after just completing Operation SLICE.
They had been in nearly every major fire fight and ground assault at *Khe Sanh* since the beginning. And it was beginning to show.
Cracks were appearing on the surface of Colonel Vortex's diamond hard exterior.
Captain Richter's muscles bulged with bruises and contusions. He couldn't even remember how many Communists he had killed since the beginning of the *Khe Sanh* siege.
"I am going to make sure that the Sergeant Major is awarded the decorations that are due to him," added Vortex.
"Right you are sir," answered Captain Richter with surprising emotion for such a tough and vicious professional soldier.
"And the promotion too!" said the Colonel, "…even if it is only posthumous."
"It would mean a great deal to his family sir," said Richter, and then he added, "As an officer the family will obtain greater privileges from the Veterans legislation."
Colonel Vortex nodded as he was deep in thought.
The thunder of Communist artillery could be heard in the distance followed by the destructive eruptions all around the *Khe Sanh* base.
"I wonder what the American people think is going on here at *Khe Sanh*?" asked Vortex to himself.
Captain Richter cracked open another two cans of Budweiser and said, "I don't think anyone really knows what the people back home think sir."
Colonel Vortex laughed, "You are right. But I know that the domestic media is painting quite an inaccurate picture of events here at *Khe Sanh*."
Richter asked as he offered a plate of savouries to the Colonel, "You mean that ridiculous comparison with *Dien Bien Phu*?"
"Yes Captain. Preposterous isn't it?" asked Vortex.
"Absolutely sir! It just shows you the incredible ignorance of laymen when they try to create a *'big story'* just for the sake of getting themselves on the front page."
*[Peter Braestrup, a Journalist and News Reporter wrote: **"Big Story: How the American Press & Television Reported and Interpreted the Crisis of TET in Vietnam and Washington D.C."** Published by Garden City, New York: Anchor Press/ Doubleday, First Edition 1978.]*

Vortex sighed, "I have a feeling that the worst is over Richter."

*[See also: **Bernard B. Fall**: The world's leading expert on the two Vietnam Wars: His book titled: "**The Two Vietnams**" Revised edition. New York, Washington and London: Frederick A. Praeger, 1966: Publisher]*

*[For an Account of the Vietnam War Episode 1: The Pilot of this long running sitcom and fiasco: See also the book by Bernard Fall on the Siege of Dien Bien Phu; "**Hell in a Very Small Place; the Siege of Dien Bien Phu,**" New York: Vintage Books, 1968.]*

The Captain asked, "Do you really think so sir?"

"I do. And do you know why?" asked the Colonel.

"No. Why?" asked a curious Captain Richter.

Vortex explained, "The NVA are having trouble hanging on to those parts of Hue that they have captured since the start of the TET or Lunar Offensive at the end of January 1968. I think that that cockroach, General Giap, is going to transfer some of his units around *Khe Sanh* to reinforce his troops at Hue."

Richter said, "That is an interesting theory sir. But all of us here are still expecting the '*big push.*'"

Colonel Vortex arose from his chair and stretched to his full 191 cm frame.

Richter smiled as he could hear the cracking noises of Vortex's spine as it realigned itself after the incredible fatigue.

"There is not going to be any '*big push*' Richter. I was not so sure a week ago. But now I am convinced."

The Captain breathed easily as he had absolute confidence in his commander.

"You know sir? You are going to be promoted for your work here at *Khe Sanh*," said Richter.

Vortex smiled, "I am looking forward to the command of a full Brigade. Or perhaps a billet as an Assistant Division Commander. But I would rather go over to General Nickerson's outfit."

Richter said, "Yes. The 1st Marine Division is a great unit. I am sure they will be proud to have you as their ADC (assistant division commander).

"You know something else Richter?"

"What's that sir?" asked the Captain as he watched the Colonel's hazel eyes shimmer with a glassy stare in the artificial light.

"Once I get Ms Ky safely back to the States and fix up my divorce, I'm going to volunteer for my 3rd tour of duty in Vietnam!"

Richter whistled, "I thought this tour was your first sir?"

"No! It's my second. I didn't tell you but I was here from January 1965. I was in a Marine Battalion that had been attached to the US 25th Tropic Lightning Division.

The Tropic Lightning Division was setting up its main headquarters complex around the town of *Cu Chi* just a few miles north-west of Saigon.

I was only a Major then and Executive Officer of the battalion. We had to assist the 25th in digging the VC cadres out of the massive tunnel complexes they have at *Cu Chi* and the "Iron Triangle."

Richter was overawed, "It sounds fascinating sir!"

Vortex continued, "At the end of my tour in 1965 I was promoted to Lieutenant Colonel. In that year I saw incredible action inside War Zone C and War Zone D as well as the 'Iron Triangle.' More than half my battalion had been either KIA or WIA during that awful 12 months.

During my tour I took over the 9th Marine Regiment and have been holding it ever since."

Suddenly there was a knock on the door to the bunker bedroom.

Richter swivelled his chair away from the entrance.

"Come!" answered Colonel Vortex.

Major Thrush walked in like an automaton and saluted the Colonel. Then he relaxed.

Vortex thought that Thrush's grey hair had become even more pronounced since the beginning of the *Khe Sanh* fiasco.

"Have a Budweiser Major!" said Vortex as he slapped his 2IC affectionately on the shoulders.

The three officers talked on for most of the late afternoon. They talked about their wives, their families, and their previous service in the Corps.

But the most interesting topic was when Colonel Vortex told Richter and Thrush about his part in 'Operation CRIMP.'

Vortex explained, "Operation CRIMP was a joint US and ARVN thrust to clear the Viet Cong terrorists out of the tunnel complexes in and around the Iron Triangle.

It was the first major assault on the Communist's elaborate base areas in that region around the north and west of Saigon which the gooks called 'Military Region IV.'

So, in January 1965 the shit really started to hit the fan. The 25th Tropic Lightning Division supported by the 1st Division, the *Big Red One* and the Australians moved in along all three sides of the Iron Triangle. We thought we had '*Charlie*' in a vice from which he could not escape. We were soon to be proved wrong.

At that stage of the war we only had a vague idea about the VC using tunnels for communications purposes. We had no idea that they also used them to live in, work in and store their weapons and ammunition therein! As you know, '*Charlie*' also fought very effectively and viciously from them and that included their women cadres as well. Operation CRIMP would definitely give us a further education on the effective use of tunnels.

Over 10,000 allied troops moved in from their bases at *Cu Chi*, *Tay Ninh* and *Dau Tieng*. We surrounded the village of *Ben Suc* which was the 'hub' of the Iron Triangle.

The village was evacuated of civilians. Then it was wiped off the face of the earth with napalm and high explosives.

Our units then closed in on the *Ho Bo Woods* and the *Boi Loi Woods* as well as the *Filhol Plantation* which bordered on the massive Saigon River system (Song Saigon).

The Australians and the US 1st Infantry Division swept the *Michelin Rubber Plantation* to the north. At first the VC seemed to just melt away. But we continued to take casualties from sniper fire. We didn't know where it was coming from until we realised that we were walking right on top of the Communist strongholds.

Well! I can tell you gentlemen! We did not clear out all the VC tunnels in Operation CRIMP! Neither did we smash the VC there during Operations CEDAR FALLS and JUNCTION CITY in early 1967.

The gooks would always melt back into those tunnels a few weeks after we had finished our operations."

Major Thrush interrupted, "But what I don't understand sir, is…"

Suddenly the door to Vortex's room burst open.

Colonel David E. Lownds stumbled in. The officer was out of breath as he screamed, "You won't believe this!"

"What?" asked Vortex.

Lownds continued, "Captain Frank Willoughby, some of his Green Berets and 60 Montagnard survivors have broken through to *Khe Sanh*!"

"That's incredible!" shouted Major Thrush.

The four officers scrambled out of the bunker and ran down past the MATU (marine air traffic control unit) and the FSCC centre to the western perimeter of the base.

The 105mm and 155mm guns were continuing to fire into the dense jungle around the 'Horseshoe.' The *Khe Sanh* artillery batteries were always trying to silence the enemy howitzers. But they were seldom successful in scoring a direct hit on one of Giap's 130mm artillery pieces.

The North Vietnamese always withdrew their guns into a prepared camouflage emplacement after firing. This made it incredibly difficult for the spotter planes to locate them and the ground fire control observers were never close enough to see the enemy artillery.

A ragged but happy looking Captain Frank Willoughby staggered up to Colonels Lownds and Vortex.

"Good to see you again sirs!"

Vortex held the Captain up as he almost fell over.

"My God! Captain! How did you make it back?" asked Colonel Lownds.

Captain Willoughby laughed, "Don't ask!"

Susan and Monica Thang were close behind. The few Green Berets were immediately taken to the Medivac centre. They would be flown out that night to the Da Nang field hospital.

Captain Willoughby pointed to his lover of sorts and her satellite sister, "Can you arrange for them to be airlifted to *Quang Tri?*"

Colonel Vortex answered with a sly and winking smile that he would see to it immediately.

Captain Willoughby told the assembled officers how they had evaded numerous PAVN patrols between *Lang Vei* and *Khe Sanh*.

(He said nothing about his other mission)

The officer recounted the horrible fire fights where his group had almost been annihilated by vastly superior Communist formations deep in the jungle.

"It's a miracle that we survived at all Colonel Lownds!" said an exhausted Captain Willoughby.

Vortex and Richter threw a blanket across Willoughby's shoulders and helped him to the medical centre.

A few minutes later Captain Baig came running up. He greeted the tired survivors and then whispered to Lownds and Vortex, "Can I see you, sirs, in the FSCC bunker right away?"

The two Colonels nodded and trooped along with the Combat SKYSPOT personnel.

Once inside the Fire Support Coordination Centre, Captain Baig explained the latest intelligence.

"We think that General Giap set up some sort of field headquarters in a series of limestone caves about 20 miles north-west of here on the Laotian side of the border."

Colonel Vortex was intensely interested and asked, "I assume then, that you and the boys at *Nakhon Phanom* in Thailand have picked up a large quantity of radio traffic?"

"That's absolutely right sir," said Baig. "How did you know that sir?"

Vortex ignored the question saying nothing about Operation SLICE.

"If it is the headquarters of General Giap then we should try to take it out with everything we have!" added Colonel Lownds.

Captain Baig smiled, "General William Momyer has already ordered a massive series of B-52 strikes for that limestone cave complex. And it will start tonight!"

Vortex asked as he winked to Richter playing along as if he knew nothing, "Are they preparing something special for this son-of-a-bitch motherfucker?"

Baig chuckled, "They sure are sir! Tonight's raid will be by a maximum effort of 36 B-52's with delayed action 750lb bombs to smash those caves in once and for all. We are also using the conventional warhead version of the B61 ROBUST EARTH

PENETRATING Bomb. We have now devised the technology to build a warhead that can penetrate 30 metres into solid concrete before detonating. This bomb that we are going to use now has better components that can withstand larger stresses, is made of better penetrator materials and is delivered with higher impact velocities! Of course we have available the nuclear version of the B61 ROBUST EARTH PENETRATING Bomb – but we are fucking not allowed to use it here in South Vietnam, Laos nor anywhere else as you well know! It is designed specifically to destroy deeply buried targets."

"Excellent!" cried Colonel Vortex.

"When is the attack for?" asked Lownds.

"Exactly 2200 hour's sir. If all goes well," answered Captain Baig.

"Let's hope it does!" added Colonel Vortex.

Colonel Lownds remarked, "Let's also hope that General Giap is inside those headquarters tonight so that we can nail his ass!"

Captain Baig chuckled as he flicked his fingers over the position on the map, "That's the whole idea Colonel."

A Warrant Officer on the Combat Skyspot team interrupted, "Radio telephone for you sir."

Both Colonel Lownds and Vortex turned in the NCOs' direction.

"For Colonel Vortex," added the Warrant Officer.

Vortex thanked the Marine and took the handset away from the map table. Walking over to the radar consoles and the *Khe Sanh* computer that controlled both air strikes and aerial supply of the base, he cupped one ear and started talking.

"Hello?" asked Vortex, "This is the FSCC at *Khe Sanh*."

"Are you alright my darling?" asked a smooth feminine voice.

Immediately he recognised the soft voice of Susie Ky.

"Oh! Susie! I should be asking you that question!" said Vortex with joy.

"Don't worry about me Richard. I love you. And I'm fine," answered Susie as she started to cry into the phone.

Vortex could hear her anguish.

But there was nothing he could say to soothe her.

"I'm sure that it won't be long before they relieve us here at *Khe Sanh* my darling," said Colonel Vortex, his voice also shaking with emotion.

Susie cried, "When? Richard? When will it be? When will they let you out of there?"

"I don't know Susie. National Route 9 is still closed. The North Vietnamese have *Khe Sanh* almost completely surrounded. But don't panic my darling! The base is strong. We have massive air support. The aerial resupply is going well with LAPES and GPES.

They are even talking about starting parachute drops soon. And most importantly Jesus is on our side! He told me himself in my dreams! In an epiphany!"

Susie Ky said, "I'm not interested in any of that my darling. I just want you to come back safe and well.

I love you Richard! Please don't be a hero!"

Colonel Vortex laughed softly as Colonel Lownds and the other officers continued to discuss the NIAGARA air strikes on General Giap's suspected headquarters.

"I promise you that I will be back in Saigon soon Susie. And in one piece."

The beautiful South Vietnamese girl said, "I heard about the death of Sergeant Major Crighton – Richard. I am very sorry. He was my friend also."

Vortex's throat choked with emotion, "Yes. Thank you my sweetheart. His loss is something that we shall all have to bear. He died valiantly for his country."

"Come back to me as soon as you can Richard! I miss you so much!"

"I will Susie!"

"The fighting is almost over here in Saigon. My parents are safe. The house is fine. Don't worry about me Richard."

Susie Ky dared not tell her lover about the fire fight at the US Embassy compound on the night of the 30th to 31st January. There would be enough time to tell him later.

Much later, when *Khe Sanh* was finally over.

Then Susie said angrily, "Can't they give you a posting at Pentagon East? Or somewhere close to me? It's ridiculous Richard! They always give you the most dangerous, the most lethal combat duties!"

"Perhaps they think I'm a pretty good field commander Susie?"

The beautiful South Vietnamese girl scoffed with disdain.

Colonel Vortex spoke softly to his lover for another 5 minutes. The line was crackling with static but they could understand each other.

"I'll try to call you again next week my darling!" said Susie, "I love you! And may God keep you safe!"

Vortex could hear her gentle sobs, her cries and his heart went out to her.

"I love you Susie!"

Then the line was cut off.

Vortex said nothing to anyone and returned to his makeshift bedroom in the 9th/26th Marine bunker. He had a fitful sleep filled with macabre images of his struggle in Vietnam which seemed like a circus fiasco.

Vortex also dreamt about his daughter, Peggy, and his new love, Susie Ky. He also dreamt about crushing General Vo Nguyen Giap's skull in with his bare hands.

It was at that point in his sleep that his nightmare became a blissful dream.

The Colonel had no idea for how long he had slept.

Captain Richter decided not to wake him. He knew that his commander was on the edge of utter exhaustion especially after the rigours of the SLICE mission. Vortex was both mentally and physically drained.

Just on 2200 hours on the 10th February 1968 it was Captain Mirza Baig himself who knocked on Vortex's door and walked in.

"What is it Captain?" asked the still groggy Colonel Vortex.

"You've got to come and see this Colonel!"

Captain Baig was extremely excited, almost joyous in his appearance.

"It better be important!" grumbled Colonel Vortex.

"Oh! It is! It is Colonel!" exclaimed Captain Baig.

Colonel Vortex picked up Captain Richter along the way and they were told to join Colonel Lownds and his staff up on the *Khe Sanh* control tower.

"So what is it?" asked Vortex.

Colonel Lownds and Captain Baig said with one voice as they pointed to the north-east, "Look!"

The mouths of Richter and Vortex fell open with astonishment.

"Oh! My God! It's unbelievable!" said Vortex.

Even from this distance they could feel the trembling of the impact vibrations as the ground shuddered with each new detonation.

"It's the Arc Light strike against the suspected HQ of Giap!" exclaimed Captain Baig.

Vortex added, "It looks like the whole earth is opening up! It's primeval in its ferocity and heaven-sent savagery! Praise be to our Lord Jesus!"

The thirty staff officers crammed into the *Khe Sanh* control tower and watched with awe as the 36 B-52 *Stratofortresses* unleashed their harvest of death.

Every Arc Light strike during Operation NIAGARA was a new experience.

Tonight, even from 20 plus miles away the cataclysm was awesome to behold.

Vortex watched as towers of red-orange flame ignited the night sky. Each spike of the detonations was like a heartbeat towards America's eventual victory in Vietnam.

Colonel Vortex wanted to get down on his knees like a choir boy and pray to almighty God that the 'fiend' was actually there – even though he knew that he was not. There in the middle of that hellish maelstrom of man-made destruction.

He prayed for Giap's death wherever he was.

"What do you think sir?" asked Captain Baig as Colonel Lownds grinned with smug delight at Vortex.

Vortex answered, "I think it is the cleansing fire of heaven! I think that Jesus has heard my supplications and my prayers. I think that all of us – all our efforts shall be

vindicated by the Lord our God and that victory shall shine upon all our most sincere endeavours here in Vietnam!"

As Vortex watched on, he knew one thing and one thing only that would secure America's final victory in Vietnam.

And that was the overwhelming industrial might of his nation.

The *'Atlas would not Shrug'* on Colonel Vortex's watch.

[See: Ayn Rand: 'Atlas Shrugged' (1957) Random House:ISBN: 0-452-28636-0]

CHAPTER 13
THE STORM ABATES

The Hazards of Aerial Supply at Khe Sanh

Colonel Vortex knew that it would be impossible to ascertain immediately whether General Giap had been killed or injured in the previous night's Arc Light. Just because, thought Vortex, he was absent during Operation SLICE does not mean that he was also absent from the limestone cave complex at the time of the subsequent air attack.

But he smiled to himself, there was always hope and a judicious exercise of positive thinking.

Now that Master Sergeant Richter was Captain Richter he could sit down with Colonel Vortex and Colonel Lownds for a cosy breakfast in the Officer's Mess at KSCB.

It was now 0700 hours but the officers had been up since 0458 hours on the 11th February 1968.

"I'm concerned about the increase in the number of anti-aircraft guns being set up by the North Vietnamese to the south of the airstrip," began Colonel David E. Lownds.

Lownds was tucking into a plate of fried eggs and bacon. The commander was in a particularly good mood this misty morning of the 11th February 1968.

Lownds' wife had radio telephoned him from their home in Florida. His family was fine and she wished him luck as well as extending her love.

Colonel Lownds was very much the 'family man' apart from being a career soldier and a superlative one at that.

Colonel Lownds was undoubtedly the greatest hero of the Siege of *Khe Sanh*.

"Yes David!" answered Vortex, "I think those 37mm's and 0.51 calibre guns are going to need some quick and expeditious eliminating."

Colonel Lownds informed, "I wouldn't try it today Richard. The weather is particularly lousy and you wouldn't get the full spectrum of TAC air."

Vortex nodded as a Sergeant from the Officer's Mess brought up his meal.

Colonel Vortex always had the same every morning. Two cups of piping hot black coffee, extremely strong. Two slices of toast with cheese and a plate of Hungarian cheese pockets.

The *Khe Sanh's* Officer's Mess had to do a lot of improvising with the cheese cakes.

A group of officers from the Combat Controller's Section of the USAF 8th Aerial Port Squadron came running into the Officer's Mess.

They went straight up to Colonel Lownds who was chewing on a mouthful of bacon and eggs.

"Sir! Sir! Come quickly!" screamed a youthful looking 2nd Lieutenant.

Vortex grinned at Captain Richter and examined one of his Hungarian cheese cakes. It was not the real *McCoy*. Nevertheless he shrugged his shoulders and took a hearty bite.

Colonel Lownds put down his knife and fork and swivelled in his breakfast chair to examine the officers from the 8th Aerial Port Squadron.

These combat controllers were going to supervise the para-drops of supplies to *Khe Sanh* over the coming weeks.

Colonel Lownds felt helpless as he fought with his leather hard bacon and eggs that didn't seem to want to be digested.

"There's an emergency sir!" added another junior officer.

Finally Colonel Lownds gulped down what was infesting his mouth.

He spluttered, "What emergency?"

"On the airstrip sir!" cried the 2nd Lieutenant.

The Captain in command of the USAF 8th Aerial Port Squadron was more coherent.

In a clam and measured tone he told both Colonels that a Marine KC-130 Hercules transport had been hit by PAVN anti-aircraft fire as it was making its final approach to *Khe Sanh* along the southern escarpment.

"The plane is in big trouble sir! The pilot has requested an emergency landing!" added the Captain.

Colonel Lownds jumped to his feet and was already running to the *Khe Sanh* airstrip.

Vortex, Richter and the others followed post haste.

As soon as they emerged into the open air they could hear the clatter of Communist 37mm and 0.51 calibre fire in the distance.

A few sporadic artillery and mortar shells were also landing inside the base perimeter.

"You see! I told you about those anti-aircraft guns *'Charlie'* has set up!" admonished Colonel Lownds.

"I believe you!" replied Vortex.

Both commanders looked through their field binoculars.

Captain Baig came up in a jeep with a radio set for communication with the pilot of the KC-130.

"We're losing fuel fast!" screamed the Marine aviator.

"I don't think I can hold it steady," he added.

Colonel Vortex grabbed the handset from Captain Baig, "Do your best! We have the rescue boys standing by."

The KC-130 Hercules was now visible through the fog. It was 0745 hours.

The large nose of the aircraft cut a swathe through the mist as it lumbered over the 800 foot escarpment.

"You see that!" pointed Vortex to Richter and Lownds.

"We see it," answered the commander of *Khe Sanh's* 26th Marine Regiment.

The officers were talking about a rich blue plume of leaking helicopter fuel that was trailing from the KC-130's right wing.

"How many men are onboard?" asked Captain Richter.

"Fourteen," answered Captain Baig.

The noise from the 105mm and 155mm howitzers was so deafening that they could hardly hear the engines of the KC-130 as it touched down on the aluminium planking of the runway.

"Jesus! That fuel could ignite any second from the enemy incoming!" screamed Colonel Vortex.

As the KC-130 lurched forward towards the TAFDS and the northern end of the airstrip, it was pouring helicopter fuel all along the *Khe Sanh* runway.

A highly dangerous situation.

"I think we made it!" said the voice of the Marine pilot through Baig's radio.

Colonel Lownds ordered the KC-130 pilot, "Steer your aircraft away from the MATU centre and the control tower! Do you hear me? We don't want that leaking fuel blowing up in our faces! And get your crew off as soon as the plane stops."

The pilot acknowledged the orders as Vortex, Lownds and the others piled onto their jeeps for the drive down to the airstrip's northern end.

The Hercules seemed to be alright as it taxied down the runway past the huge piles of pallets, crates, half-unloaded boxes and enormous mounds of food, ammunition, building materials and fuel that kept *Khe Sanh* running in the midst of overwhelming Communist aggressor forces attacking it around the clock.

The whole aerial re-supply of *Khe Sanh* was an enormous logistical achievement.

But sometimes it would come unstuck.

The convoy of jeeps was almost at the TAFDS station and the rescue trucks and personnel were getting into position.

It appeared the Marine pilot was trying to steer the KC-130 towards the concrete revetments at the eastern side of the airstrip.

There were a number of parked C-123's, HH-53 helicopters and UH-1E's all along the length of the airstrip. But fortunately none were in close proximity to the Marine Hercules.

Colonel Vortex screamed, "Oh! No!"

The jeeps ground to a halt and the officers jumped out running forwards to the runway.

The KC-130 was rolling forward when its starboard wing exploded into a ball of brilliant flame.

"Christ! I was afraid this would happen!" screamed Colonel Lownds.

Vortex said quickly, "Richter! Come with me!"

The Colonel jumped back into one of the jeeps and raced towards the stricken aircraft.

The fire had now spread to the main fuselage and was quickly engulfing the Hercules. The transport had been carrying fuel for *Khe Sanh's* helicopter strike force.

Colonel Vortex and Captain Richter were joined by the airstrip rescue teams. They started to spray foam all over the plane as best they could.

By this time the Hercules had slid off the edge of the runway and had come to an indelicate stop.

Vortex screamed to the Warrant Officer in charge of the fire control team, "Did you see any of the crew disembark?"

"No sir," screamed back the NCO over the roar and heat of the fire.

"Those men are going to fry in there if we don't help them!" shouted Captain Richter.

Vortex grabbed Richter's arm and the two of them rushed around the tail end of the KC-130 dodging the flames as they went.

The Warrant Officer couldn't believe his eyes.

The Hercules had already started to crumple from the intense heat and the main fuselage rolled over so that one of the cabin doors near the cockpit could be reached from ground level.

Vortex screamed, "Help me!"

Using a steel lever both men tried to prise open the cabin door but without success.

They could hear screams and shouts inside the aircraft.

"We've got to get those men out!" shrieked Colonel Vortex.

Richter threw the Colonel an axe and Vortex started to hack and chop away at the cabin release handle while the Captain continued to wrench away with the steel lever.

Finally the cabin door burst open.

Immediately two cargo handlers came falling out. They jumped onto the ground, their lungs filled with smoke.

Vortex bolted into the burning wreck and pulled out the pilot and co-pilot by their shirt collars.

Captain Richter managed to reach four other men.

He dragged them out one by one as they were dazed by the intense smoke and fire. That was eight men in all.

Vortex wanted to go back inside the fuselage to continue the search but the intensity of the flames increased.

"No sir! You can't!" screamed Captain Richter as he tried to pull the heroic commander away from the smouldering aircraft.

Vortex lashed his arm free of Richter, "I've got to Captain!"

I have to save anyone else in there!"

Captain Richter shrieked, "But why sir?"

"Because it's my duty as an officer! A Marine officer!"

Captain Richter watched helplessly as Colonel Vortex disappeared once again into the hellish bowels of the incinerated KC-130.

Vortex could see nothing as he groped his way along the hull of the plane.

"Aiiee!" he screamed.

The steel surface of the Hercules was red hot and almost glowing. The thick black smoke from melting rubber and burning wood assailed his nostrils.

Then Colonel Vortex stumbled over something about half way down the burning fuselage.

He reached out and felt something soft. It smelled like burning human flesh.

Then Colonel Vortex realised that that was exactly what he was touching.

He reeled back in horror.

Outside, the Warrant Officer in charge of the airstrip rescue detachment came running up to Captain Richter.

"Where is Colonel Vortex?" he asked.

"Inside!" barked back Richter.

The Captain was just about to jump back into the blazing wreckage when Colonel Vortex practically fell out of the fuselage.

"Are you alright sir?" asked Richter.

Vortex was covered in black soot. He was coughing up blood and black grime violently.

"Jesus! Come on!" yelled the Warrant Officer, "We've got to get him away from the plane. It's going to blow any minute!"

Captain Richter and the senior NCO dragged Colonel Vortex more than 100 yards away from the wreck.

"Incoming!" yelled Colonel Lownds as he came running up with his staff.

A giant 120mm Communist mortar shell came screeching down onto the airstrip. Unbelievably it hit the mid-section of the KC-130 and the whole burning mess exploded into the morning sky like a firebomb.

"I'm alright now. I'm OK!" spluttered Colonel Vortex as he staggered to his feet in front of the group of officers.

"You did a marvellous job! Both of you!" congratulated Colonel Lownds.

Captain Richter grinned as Vortex turned around and watched the eight injured men from the KC-130 being stretchered away to the Medivac centre near the MATU bunker.

Colonel Vortex looked at Colonel Lownds and Captain Mirza Baig and shook his head with frustration.

"I could not save the others! They were burnt to a crisp before I could reach them!"

Colonel Lownds nodded sympathetically and helped the other Colonel and Captain Richter back to the Medivac centre.

The PAVN artillery and mortar barrage went irrepressibly on.

The Heaviest PAVN Artillery Barrage of the Siege: 1,307 Incoming Rounds on the 23rd February 1968

The first major parachute drops which were made to the *Khe Sanh* base started from the second week of February 1968.

The C-123 *Provider's* came in low and deposited their loads over a special drop zone that had been set up just outside the main perimeter.

The disadvantages of the parachute delivery system were that it was unsuitable for large or bulky items and it exposed the Marines to Communist fire when they retrieved the supplies from the drop zone.

The PAVN shelling of the *Khe Sanh* base also increased steadily during the period from the 10th to the 23rd February 1968.

In the days up to the 23rd February there were sometimes 500, 700, 900 and then nearly 1,000 enemy rounds exploding inside the concertina wire.

Colonel Vortex awoke from his bunker before dawn on the 23rd February 1968.

All the hill outposts were still in the possession of the Marines except for Hill 881 North which had been lost to the 325th C *Golden Star Division* just before the *Khe Sanh* siege began.

But Colonel Vortex had other matters on his mind.

He walked over to the western perimeter of the base with Major Thrush, Captain Richter and Captain Mirza Baig.

The officers stood in a line and surveyed the devastated terrain with high powered Power-20 Navy field binoculars.

The continuous B-52 Arc Light raids had reduced the jungle around *Khe Sanh* to a virtual lunar landscape.

The jungle had been obliterated completely. The ground, once fertile had been reduced to a fine pulverised dust from the 750lb and 500lb bombs.

There was nowhere above ground for the PAVN soldiers to hide or to concentrate for the attack. They were like sitting ducks to the American artillery and machine gun fire.

The Communists had only one option left with which to manoeuvre closer to *Khe Sanh*.

The *Khe Sanh* artillery was already answering Giap's gunners at the 'Horseshoe' and at the 'Co Roc' in Laos.

In addition the avalanche of 175mm shells from Camp Carroll were screeching overhead like the German *V-1 weapons* of World War Two.

Colonel Vortex could feel the atmosphere being ripped apart as the huge rounds travelled at several times the speed of sound [Mach 1 plus] to crash into the Communist troops, their supply dumps, storage areas and hopefully their artillery pieces.

"What exactly are we looking for?" asked Captain Mirza Baig.

Before Vortex could answer, Colonel Lownds also arrived in front of the 155mm artillery pieces. He mimicked his colleagues and peered through his field binoculars.

"Look at that line along the crest of the hill just past the concertina wire," instructed Colonel Vortex.

"I can't see anything except a deep gulley," answered Captain Baig.

"Look slightly forward of the gullies," barked back Vortex.

"I think I can see what you are talking about," said Colonel Lownds.

There was some sort of activity going on just in front of the deep gullies that bordered the *Khe Sanh* plateau.

A few moments of silence ensued which was punctuated only by the roar of American and North Vietnamese artillery.

Then Colonel Vortex said in a slow and deliberate voice.

"The Communists are digging trenches!"

"Trenches?" asked Colonel David Lownds.

"Trenches!" repeated Vortex.

"It's impossible!" admonished Captain Richter.

"And why so?" asked Vortex with a bemused grin on his face.

"Because sir, the Communist bastards always like to dig tunnels and not trenches," answered Richter.

Colonel Lownds scanned the horizon with his binoculars and nodded his head.

"Colonel Vortex is right! The gook scum are indeed digging trenches."

Colonel Vortex turned to Captain Richter and explained, "Remember Richter! This is not the 'Iron Triangle.' Neither is it War Zone C or War Zone D near the Cambodian border.

We are at *Khe Sanh*. And as I have said before the deep gullies all around this plateau make the digging of tunnels very difficult."

Captain Baig added, "Yes. We found only one tunnel. And that was near Hill 861A. It has since been destroyed using high explosives and *Sarin* nerve gas."

Colonel Vortex asked, "Captain Baig? Can you organise a napalm strike in the next few minutes while we are all here and observing the PAVN trenches?"

The energetic Captain beamed with delight," No problem sir!"

The Fire Control officer clicked his fingers and a radio operator came running up with the communication set strapped to his back. Mirza Baig spoke to the FSCC bunker at *Khe Sanh* and they in turn spoke to the 'hot pad' at Da Nang airbase.

"I see! Well! That's even better then!" cried Captain Baig.

Fighter control at Da Nang informed Baig that there was already a full squadron of F-4D's over the infamous A Shau Valley.

The fighter bombers were, however, unable to find their target over the A Shau Valley in a mission to support the 173rd Airborne Brigade operating there in a classic *'search and destroy'* mission.

Thus the TAC air assets still had a full load of ordnance, including napalm and flechette bombs. It would take only 5 minutes for the fighter bombers to reach *Khe Sanh* from the A Shau Valley.

Captain Baig informed the others who nodded and continued their surveillance of the PAVN trench preparations.

"I can't believe that I didn't spot this activity earlier," said Colonel Vortex.

"All that matters is that we know about it now," added Colonel Lownds.

"Look! Do you see that rotten dink over there? About 350 yards past the wire," shouted Major Thrush.

"I see the bastard!" screamed Colonel Vortex.

The NVA soldier was just above the berm of the nearest gully.

Not far from the positions of the 1st Battalion 9th Marines.

"Quick! Give me a sniper's rifle!" ordered Colonel Vortex.

A Staff Sergeant standing behind Major Thrush gave Vortex a large, powerful sporting rifle with telescopic sights.

Vortex quickly took aim, focusing carefully on the Communist soldier's heart and/or head.

Vortex pulled back on the trigger. He was a superlative marksman. The loud cracking noise of the extremely powerful hunting rifle could hardly be heard over the roar

of artillery fire that seemed to be getting louder and to be increasing in intensity from both sides.

Captain Richter watched as the North Vietnamese soldier lost the top section of his skull. The powerful hunting rifle blew away a chunk of his brain matter as well as his left eye and nose.

"Excellent shot!" congratulated Colonel Lownds.

In that second a tremendous explosion rocked the concrete and steel revetments on the eastern side of the *Khe Sanh* airstrip. A Communist 152mm shell from the 'Co Roc' had found the body of a UH-1E helicopter.

Unfortunately the Huey was full of gas as it was getting ready for a medivac mission back to Quang Tri and then Phu Bai.

"Jesus!" screamed Major Thrush as all the officers instinctively ducked as the huge, searing fireball etched skywards.

In the next five minutes more than three dozen heavy calibre Communist shells rocked the *Khe Sanh* base.

152mm, 130mm and 120mm rounds landed near the MATU bunker, along the artillery emplacements, at the eastern end of the airstrip, on top of the ceiling of the DASC (Direct Air Support Centre) killing one Marine and wounding seven others and right in the middle of the runway blowing aluminium planking into the air like showers of silver debris.

"The PAVN are up to something!" said Colonel Vortex.

"It's the heaviest bombardment I've seen so far!" added Colonel Lownds.

"Do you think this could be the prelude to the *'big push'* that we have all been waiting for?" asked Major Thrush as he looked to the south-west.

"It could very well be. Could be…," mentioned Captain Baig.

A giant 120mm PAVN mortar shell exploded only 25 yards from the group of officers.

The force of the explosion was so great that a 155mm artillery piece rocked sideways off its wheels for about 3 to 4 feet before crashing down in the upright position again.

The *Khe Sanh* artillery were now undertaking *H & I Missions* [Harassment & Interdiction Fire missions] to the west of *Lang Vei* and also along an arc from Hill 861/861A and north to Hill 881 North.

An artillery crewman had his right leg blown off and three more received fragmentation wounds.

The wounded men ran screaming away from their positions with blood streaming down their agonised faces. They were all in a panic.

"Stop! It's alright! Calm down men!" beseeched Colonel Vortex as he grabbed one of the injured Marines by his shoulders.

Colonel Lownds ordered the medics up and they carried the wounded away in stretchers.

"The TAC air is coming!" said Captain Baig excitedly.

Vortex, Lownds and the others watched the F-4E *Phantoms* come rolling in from the south-west.

"Jesus! That was quick!" exclaimed Vortex as he looked at his watch. It had taken the fighter bombers less than 4.5 minutes to reach them from the A Shau Valley at supersonic speed.

The *Phantoms* routinely travelled in excess of Mach 2.1 (1,560 mph).

It was a magnificent sight. The roar of the jet engines was even louder than the stiffening barrage.

"It's a big sortie Captain!" said Colonel Lownds.

From 8,000 feet up the line abreast formation of F-4E's peeled off one by one for the attack run on the Communist trenches.

The PAVN could see and hear the planes come in and they started to run for cover.

But there was no cover to be had in that devastated lunar landscape.

Seeing this Colonel Vortex rushed to the Marine trench line on the *Khe Sanh* perimeter and ordered the 106mm recoilless rifles to blast the enemy from the ground while they were being hit from the air.

The Marines from the 2nd and 3rd Battalions of the 26th Marines also opened fire with M60's and 0.50 cals.

The firepower was lethal.

The first fighter bombers came in low and parallel to the Communist trenches. The cigar shaped petro-jelly bombs glided peacefully through the air and then erupted like an inferno from hell.

The screams and gurgled cries of the NVA could be faintly heard over the cacophony of artillery and mortar fire.

Jet after jet streaked in with flechette and cluster bombs as well as napalm. There were 18 *Phantoms* in all. A massive air strike.

"You can smell the petroleum jelly from here!" cried Colonel Lownds as he covered his nose with a handkerchief.

Thick black clouds of nauseating smoke wafted across the *Khe Sanh* plateau.

But the air strike didn't stop the Communist artillery.

For the remainder of that day the shelling became more and more frantic.

The 2,500 Marines inside the main perimeter of *Khe Sanh* scurried for their lives.

It was truly a marvellous day for the *'Khe Sanh' shuffle*.

Everybody was doing it.

At 1500 hours there was a full staff meeting in the FSCC bunker. The DASC bunker had been badly damaged in the morning by a 152mm shell from the PAVN artillery in Laos. The whole ceiling had caved-in with several Marines being wounded.

"I don't quite understand it," said Captain Mirza Baig as the meeting began.

"What don't you understand?" asked Colonel Lownds as he rubbed his chin and sipped on a cup of very strong black coffee.

Captain Baig leafed through his sensor intelligence reports, both from III MAF headquarters and from *Nakhon Phanom* in Thailand.

The Fire Control Officer scratched his head and began, "Well sir. We are expecting the big attack any moment are we not?"

"We are," answered Colonel Vortex.

Baig continued, "Well. The enemy bombardment has been extremely heavy today and we saw them digging trench lines closer and closer to the *Khe Sanh* concertina wire such as they did at *Dien Bien Phu* back in 1954. But my sensor information for the period from the 10th February up until today, the 23rd February has indicated movement of the PAVN *away* from *Khe Sanh*."

Everybody in the room was flabbergasted.

There was stony silence.

"It can't be!" screamed Colonel Lownds.

"Are you sure you're sensor information is correct?" asked Colonel Vortex.

"There is no question about it sirs! The PAVN have definitely moved some of their battalions away from *Khe Sanh*!"

Major Thrush whistled with awe and surprise.

"Which battalions? How many? When?" asked Colonel Lownds in a frenzy of excitement.

Captain Baig continued, "I have been discussing the intelligence with Brigadier General Phillip B. Davidson and Colonel Kenneth Houghton, the G-2 for III MAF. I wanted to be sure before I informed you of the developments. But it is apparently clear from the network of seismic, acoustic, chemical and electronic sensors that we have emplaced that large formations of Communist troops have left *Khe Sanh* and have headed east.

Our intelligence reports indicate that no less than 5 battalions have left *Khe Sanh*, quite possibly to reinforce the beleaguered Communist forces at the imperial city of Hue."

Colonel Lownds sank back in his chair, "That's incredible."

Colonel Vortex looked at Captain Richter and smiled.

Both men could smell victory like a welcome odour of spring after a terrible winter.

Major Thrush moved closer to the map table as Captain Baig continued, "Two battalions from the 29th PAVN Regiment of the 325th C *Golden Star Division* and three battalions from the 24th Regiment of the 304th PAVN Division have moved to Hue as far as we can ascertain."

Colonel Vortex chuckled, "What is the logic of that foul bastard General Giap? It doesn't make any sense? If he wants to take *Khe Sanh* and its airstrip and repeat another *Dien Bien Phu* on the Americans why weaken his forces at the critical moment?"

A figure walked into the FSCC bunker as everyone turned around in surprise.

The voice of the newcomer said, "There is no logic to that motherfucking Communist douche-bag!"

Colonels Lownds and Vortex spun on their heels with anger.

Then their faces softened as they saw Captain Frank Willoughby walk in.

The Special Forces commander of *Lang Vei* had decided to stay on at *Khe Sanh* while all the rest of his Green Berets had been evacuated to Quang Tri.

The heroic *Captain of America* wanted to be in at the finish of the *Khe Sanh* siege however it worked out.

"Captain Willoughby! Please come in and join us!" beamed Colonel David Lownds.

John Wheeler, the war correspondent from Associated Press was also allowed to attend the conference. Colonel Vortex hated that man's guts because he constantly misinformed the American public as to what was really happening at *Khe Sanh*.

Without any apologies Vortex brutally shoved his elbow into John Wheeler's kidneys, pushing the newsman out of his way to make room for Captain Willoughby in front of the map table. Vortex knew that the Captain was more deserving of a chair than that agent of misinformation and falsehoods.

The Green Beret Captain had his left arm in a sling because his humerus was broken with compound fractures in three separate locations. Willoughby also had four cracked ribs and cerebral contusions.

"You can sit here Frank!" said Vortex as he ushered his friend alongside.

Colonel David Lownds continued as he shrugged his shoulders nonchalantly, "Well gentlemen? We can debate the logic or otherwise of the reasons for Giap's troop withdrawal for as long as we like until we are blue in the face. But the only thing I am grateful for is the fact that we have less Communist troops facing us than we had earlier in the siege. And that is good news!"

All the officers and NCOs' in the conference bunker grunted their approval except for John Wheeler - he knew that this was *not* good news for the American media that wanted to create a sensation for the public back at home and thus continue to undermine America's peace efforts in Vietnam.

The split second after Colonel Lownds had finished speaking a massive detonation rocked the FSCC bunker. That eruption was followed by a string of others all over the *Khe Sanh* base.

Colonel Vortex wiped the dust off his camouflage uniform and picked Captain Willoughby up from the floor.

"Giap may have withdrawn some of his infantry battalions from *Khe Sanh* but his artillery regiments are still all here!"

The officers broke up the meeting and walked outside.

The 2,500 Marines inside the main perimeter and their gallant and courageous ARVN allies were in a frenzy of activity as they scurried helter skelter through the deadly rain of enemy fire.

Billows of black, turgid smoke were rising like deadly and sinister plumes all over the Marine base.

Incoming rounds crashed into parked helicopters sending their rotor blades flying through the air like daggers, holes were blasted into the above ground buildings so that they began to resemble Swiss cheese, aluminium planking from the battered runway was spewing into the air and sandbagged walls exploded in huge, ugly showers of red earth.

The red sand and dust of *Khe Sanh*.

The whole *Khe Sanh* plateau was covered in this red earth. Red like the colour of dried or clotted blood. It was eerie, thought Colonel Vortex as he watched the continuing and merciless enemy barrage and their counter-barrage.

The whole air reeked of cordite as the American guns fired back three or four rounds for every Communist incoming shell.

"This is the worst artillery attack of the siege Vortex!" mentioned Colonel Lownds as he frantically gave instructions to his junior officers.

"You're right David. I have not seen it like this before. Its definitely more than a thousand rounds today! A lot more!" answered Vortex.

Captain Frank Willoughby told both Colonels as he watched the blood drenched sun go down on the 34th day of the siege, "We still have a hell of a fight on our hands!"

But Colonel Richard Vortex knew that the righteous and God-sanctioned industrial might of the United States of America would guarantee eventual victory over the Communist scum.

The PAVN's Last Major Ground Assault Against Khe Sanh: 29th February to 1st March 1968

The Chairman of the Joint Chiefs of Staff, General Earle Wheeler arrived in Saigon on the 23rd February 1968.

General William Childs Westmoreland went out to the Tan Son Nhut airfield to meet his old pal, *'Bus'* Wheeler.

The USAF command 707 jet landed smoothly and taxied along the vast amphitheatre of concrete revetments that housed squadron after squadron of America's massive air armada in South Vietnam that was like the wings of peace upon which South Vietnam would eventually fly.

General Earle Wheeler's 707 had arrived from Washington D.C. via the Kadena Air base in Okinawa, Japan.

The Chairman of the Joint Chiefs of Staff had a lot of troubling matters on his mind as he peered out of the cabin window of the 707. The portable stairway was rolled up to the cabin door by three United States Air Force personnel.

General Wheeler collected his attaché case and walked out of the plane.

A 35 piece brass band was playing *'Hail-to-the-Chief'* as his feet touched South Vietnamese soil.

"Welcome to the Republic of Vietnam *'Bus'*," beamed General Westmoreland as he saluted the CJCS briskly.

The first thing that hit General Earle Wheeler was the stifling heat and rancid humidity. He hated it.

Even though he was wearing his summer khaki dress fatigues the intense tropical weather caused his body to drip with sweat.

"Jesus! *Westy*!" began Earle Wheeler.

"Its damned hot isn't it?"

COMUSMACV laughed and placed his hand on General Wheeler's shoulder, "I'm sure you'll get used to it! We all have here!"

'Bus' Wheeler barked back, "I don't think I'll ever get used to this rotten heat! And Jesus *Westy*! It stinks here!"

General Westmoreland grinned, "Listen *'Bus'*, it stinks everywhere in this God-forsaken place. It's a third world country after all. And what makes it smell worse is that you can pick up the putrid odour of Communists from over one hundred miles away! Especially the dead ones."

General Wheeler went to meet the other senior officers who were standing nearby with expectant smiles on their otherwise grim faces.

They knew what Vietnam was really like.

"It's a fucking fifth world country, William, not a third world country!

This place makes Tijuana look like Palm Springs!"

General William DePuy, the commander of the 1st Infantry Division (*the Big Red One*) overheard the comment of the CJCS and chuckled to himself. He wished he could get General Wheeler to go down into one of the Viet Cong tunnels in the Iron Triangle.

That, he thought, would be a real education for him.

General Westmoreland began the introductions, "Firstly 'Bus', I would like you to meet General Ngoi Quang Truong, the commander of the elite 1st ARVN Division."

General Wheeler nodded and shook hands smartly with the South Vietnamese general.

"Next,…" began COMUSMACV, "You know General Phillip Davidson my J-2 Chief?"

"Of course! How are you Phillip?" asked General Wheeler.

"Very good sir. Thank you sir," answered Brigadier Davidson.

"Are you going to write a history of this war someday General Davidson?" asked Wheeler.

"I have been thinking about it – yes sir. Someday," answered the Brigadier.

COMUSMACV went on, "And here is Major General William DePuy, Major General Fillmore Mearns, the commander of the 25th Tropic Lightning Division based at Cu Chi, and…"

General Earle Wheeler interrupted sarcastically, "Oh! Yes! General Mearns! How are you?"

Major General Mearns smiled, "Very well thank you sir!"

Then General Wheeler asked facetiously, "Have you secured your headquarters yet? Do you need any other units to help you secure your command installations?"

General Westmoreland winced with embarrassment.

Major General Mearns turned beetroot red and scowled with undiluted anger at the remark.

COMUSMACV went on regardless, "General William Momyer the commander of the 7th Air Force, Brigadier General Burl McLaughlin the commander of aerial supply at *Khe Sanh* and Major General Norman J. Anderson, the Commandant of the 1st Marine Air Wing, Brigadier General William McBride in charge of sensor operations at *Khe Sanh*, Lieutenant General Robert Cushman the III MAF commander, Major General Rathvon Tompkins of the 3rd Marine Division, Major General Herman Nickerson Jr. of the 1st Marine Division, Lieutenant General Frederick Weyand the commander of the 2nd Field Force Vietnam [II FFV] and of course my Deputy and Commander of MACV Forward, General Creighton Abrams."

General Earle Wheeler greeted all the senior officers and the whole entourage clambered into air conditioned limousines for the short drive to the massive Pentagon East Headquarters close to the air base.

Once luxuriously installed in the main conference room with cocktails served all round, the conference commenced.

General Earle Wheeler would have to be back in Washington D.C. within 48 hours to report to the President on the TET offensive and the situation at the

The Siege of Khe Sanh 1967-1968

beleaguered combat base at *Khe Sanh* in I Corps Operational Zone as well as the intense fighting at the imperial city of Hue.

When General William Westmoreland began speaking to open the conference, Major General William DePuy was shocked at the physical appearance of the Chairman of the Joint Chiefs of Staff.

Wheeler was worn out, he looked frazzled, nervous and on edge and was slightly obese with a large belly that hung like a sack of potatoes from his waist.

General William DePuy thought that the four star supreme commander looked disgusting. It was not how he had remembered him at all, from his earlier service in the army.

"First I would like to say, General Wheeler, that there is no immediate danger of the *Khe Sanh* base falling to the enemy. And that is the case despite the wildly exaggerated and pessimistic not to mention irresponsible press and media reports!"

General Wheeler sipped on his dry martini and asked, "Who is the field commander in charge at *Khe Sanh*?"

Lieutenant General Cushman interrupted with an answer, "Its one of my boy's sir. A Colonel David E. Lownds. He's an excellent tactical commander."

General Westmoreland chipped in for his favourite, "And I have also sent in the *exterminator*, Colonel Richard Vortex, the commander of the 9th Marine Regiment."

General Wheeler pricked up his ears, "Colonel Vortex?"

"Yes sir," replied COMUSMACV.

"Then you were expecting one of the most savage attacks from the North Vietnamese to date?" asked General Wheeler.

"I was sir," said COMUSMACV.

"I have been told that Colonel Vortex can just about handle anything that is thrown in his face," mentioned the CJCS.

Major General Rathvon Tompkins beamed with pride. Colonel Vortex was after all one of the officers in his Division and thus he had to expect some of the credit.

General Wheeler continued, "I want to speak to you later General Westmoreland about Colonel Vortex's promotion to Brigadier General. We also have to find an appropriate billet for him after he has completed the Army's advanced General Staff College."

"Yes sir," answered COMUSMACV.

Then General Westmoreland continued the briefing, "The Lunar or TET offensive has been a complete disaster for the Main Force Viet Cong and the PAVN forces in South Vietnam! There is only a small pocket of resistance remaining in the Cholon District of Saigon which we are crushing to pieces at this very moment. I estimate the fight there will be finalised in the next 72 hours.

The only other area of continuing PAVN/VC activity is in the imperial capital of Hue. But the enemy has been thrown onto the defensive there too. And we are going to crush them with the 3rd and 1st Marine Divisions as well as the 1st ARVN Infantry Division and massive air assaults.

I can say with certainty that we have achieved a great victory against the Communist forces in this aborted attempt by them to dislocate the ARVN troops and their insane plan to win the general population over to their insidious cause.

The vast bulk of the South Vietnamese peasantry hate and despise the Viet Cong criminals and their North Vietnamese masters in Hanoi.

Of the estimated 84,000 Viet Cong military and political cadres that were thrown into this farcical TET offensive, Brigadier General Davidson has reported that at least 45,000 have been killed or captured from the period 31st January 1967 to 23rd February 1968."

"That is excellent William!" smiled General Wheeler, "At least I have some good news to tell the President when I get back."

General Westmoreland continued, "With regards to the *Khe Sanh* situation I have to report that no major ground offensive has been launched against the base so far. Only regimental size probing assaults have been experienced around the hill outposts and against the main perimeter. The *Khe Sanh* airstrip is also still fully operational as a Seabee Mobile Construction unit is constantly repairing it.

The Air Force and Marine air assets are using the Ground Proximity Extraction System [GPES] as well as the Low Altitude Parachute Extraction System [LAPES] to keep the base fully supplied with whatever it requires.

We are also employing parachute drops but this, as you know, is not suitable for bulky or heavier items."

General William Momyer interrupted as he spoke directly to General Earle Wheeler.

"Sir. I can say with a considerable degree of accuracy that the main reason why *Khe Sanh* has not been attacked in force until now is the effects of Operation NIAGARA.

This operation has been the largest air assault and bombardment in the history of human warfare.

We have six B-52's over *Khe Sanh* every 90 minutes, 24 hours a day, day or night, seven days a week and 30 to 31 days a month for as long as it is required.

Strategic Air Command (SAC) is dropping 1,800 tons of bombs per day on the *Khe Sanh* surrounding area and environs.

It is magnificent and heart-warming to watch the sincere efforts of SAC.

The Arc Light strikes are crushing enemy men and women, pulverising storage areas and annihilating the enemy units as they form up for the attack.

Using Operation Combat SKYSPOT and the on-base computer at *Khe Sanh*. Captain Mirza Baig, the Fire Support and Coordination officer is using both computer power and sensor information to coordinate massive air strikes against the evil and degenerate Communist forces and their douche-bag VC puppets.

In addition to Arc Light raids I am pleased to announce that we have lifted our Tactical Air sortie rate from 350 missions per day to over 470."

General Wheeler was truly flabbergasted, "Over 470 sorties per day! That's incredible!"

General Westmoreland answered, "It's incredible but it is true sir."

"Wonderful! Now I can finally sleep easy at night!" was all that the CJCS could say.

General William DePuy, the commander of the US 1st Infantry Division and one of the most brilliant and charming officers in the entire United States Army added, "By the time this *Khe Sanh* siege is successfully over sir, we will have dropped more bombs on the North Vietnamese imperialist aggressors in that sector alone than in the entire course of the Second World War."

There was stunned silence in the conference room for a few seconds.

Then General Westmoreland asked, "Sir! I want you to ask the President to allow me to go over to the strategic offensive including the release of battlefield tactical nuclear weapons!

We have been on the strategic defensive for much too long. The only thing that we do is to react to PAVN/VC thrusts! They are the ones who always choose the place and time of battle which invariably suites them and not us! We must launch a massive ground assault into Cambodia, Laos and North Vietnam and north of the DMZ to dislocate their supply lines and throw their logistical system into chaos. Only then can we bring this pitiful war to a quick and righteous conclusion."

General Wheeler answered, "I can sympathise with you William. And I wish there was something I could do. But I really don't think that the President or the Secretary of Defence want to go over to the strategic offensive.

Clark Clifford, the lawyer from the boon-docks, does not like us to be too aggressive in the way that we wage this war.

It is my opinion that the President wants to remain in the defensive posture here in Vietnam until it is time to pull the plug and withdraw our troops altogether.

He wants to get back to creating his *Great Society* for social welfare and rights."

General Westmoreland scratched his head, "But sir? What is the logic of remaining in the defensive posture when you have over 550,000 American troops in Vietnam as at the beginning of March 1968?"

General Wheeler said quite seriously, "Well, there is no logic to it. The National Security Council (NSC) cannot agree on which logic is the best logic so there is no logic. But they are very keen on *'body counts.'*"

General Westmoreland asked with stupefaction, "But then why, *'Bus'*, is the President following such a policy here in Vietnam which amounts to no policy? And which is clearly so devoid of any logic simply because the NSC cannot agree on one? Especially military logic?"

General Wheeler laughed and winked at Major General DePuy, "You must understand that the President is driven by other factors besides mere logic!

For example he has to think of political considerations as well. And as you know, politics has nothing to do with logic!"

General Westmoreland persisted, "I know that. But when you have more than half a million American troops here in a foreign country, facing a vicious and Godless enemy intent on murdering every last one of them and us, you are forced to use some sort of logical framework to ensure that those men are not annihilated by constantly being on the defensive."

Wheeler took another sip of his dry martini and watched the overhead ceiling fans which were not really necessary because the plush conference room was fully air-conditioned.

Finally General Wheeler had a suggestion to the impasse.

"Perhaps, General Westmoreland, you could draw up a plan to go on the strategic offensive without such plan appearing to be too logical. Maybe then the President will consider it."

Westmoreland looked at General DePuy and then at General Abrams.

The commander of MACV Forward was speechless.

"I don't understand what you mean? You want me to draw up an illogical plan?" asked COMUSMACV.

General Wheeler beamed, "Yes! Precisely! If you devise a plan that appears to be more of the same in terms of inconclusive military results, the Secretary of Defence, Clark Clifford and the President might just go for it. Then, if it happens that this plan produced a stunning military victory in Vietnam! Well then!

You could just tell the President that it was an accident!"

General Westmoreland had a sudden craving for a stiff drink.

But he knew that he couldn't afford such a luxury because he was trying to discuss logically something that did not require any logic at all.

COMUSMACV asked, "Are you telling me *Bus*, that President Johnson and Clark Clifford don't want a speedy victory in Vietnam? They don't want to defeat the North Vietnamese?"

General Wheeler said with a sigh, "It is my opinion General Westmoreland, that the President and his advisers have not yet decided whether they want to defeat the North Vietnamese.

That is why they are asking you to maintain the defensive line while they continue their deliberations.

I am sure that you can understand the logic in that!"

"No! I don't!" screamed back General Westmoreland.

With that the conference broke up.

The senior officers retired to their billets in Saigon for the evening to partake of the usual delicious culinary enjoyments.

A smaller group of MACV senior generals went to General Westmoreland's billet near upper Tu Do Street in Saigon.

Apart from General Wheeler and General Westmoreland the following Generals were also present; Abrams, Davidson, Barsanti, DePuy, Weyand, Momyer, Cushman, Tompkins and Anderson.

General William Westmoreland lived in a lovely and spacious French villa from the Colonial period.

He had three butlers, seven cooks and twenty-three housemaids.

But COMUSMACV was hardly ever there to enjoy the opulence as he was either at Pentagon East or in the field overseeing combat operations.

"Now Westy! Why I really came to Saigon for was to ask you what you need," began General Wheeler.

"That's easy *Bus*!" quipped Westmoreland, "I told you I need 206,000 additional troops to go on the strategic offensive."

General Wheeler put down his plate of oysters Kilpatrick, "Alright then! The President has authorised me to give you the 82nd Airborne Division and the other half of the 2nd Marine Division."

COMUSMACV smiled at General Olinto Barsanti, the 101st Airborne commander, "Good! I'll take them as soon as you can give them to me."

Suddenly tremendous explosions could be heard coming from the Cholon District of Saigon.

"Hell! Are we safe here General Westmoreland?" asked Wheeler as he wiped the sweat off his brow with his table napkin.

"Perfectly safe! I assure you *Bus*!" beamed Westmoreland as he added, "I guarantee you that not a single Communist bullet will come within 3 miles of this house while you are here."

General Wheeler nodded and smiled nervously as the roast chicken and Beluga caviar was served with succulent steamed vegetables and lobster mornay.

The party of Generals were about half way through their main course.

Lieutenant David Peter EHRLICH

General Wheeler was sitting at the head of the huge mahogany dining table. Westmoreland was on his right, Abrams on the left and the other generals down both sides.

Suddenly, as General Wheeler had a fork full of delicious chicken in his mouth, a terrible screeching noise came at them from out of the sky above the French villa.

Before any of them could speak an RPG-7 anti-tank missile launcher exploded in the garden adjacent to the dining room. The glass doors leading out to the garden were splintered into a thousand pieces and General Wheeler was blasted off his chair backwards by the concussion wave.

Another RPG rocket slammed into the left side of the house bringing down a large crystal chandelier above the dining table which smashed the mahogany wood into several large pieces.

"Are you alright sir?" asked Major General Barsanti as he helped General Wheeler to his feet. The CJCS had bruised his scalp against a piece of furniture and he was covered in glass.

Shrieks and screams could be heard coming from both outside and inside the French villa.

Now rocket and artillery fire could be heard only 2 or 3 blocks away.

General Wheeler was livid with fury as he shrieked at the top of his voice, "You said that not a single bullet would come within 3 miles of this place!

You said that I would be safe!"

General Westmoreland brushed the glass off Wheeler's uniform and tried to soothe him, "That's right sir! I said a bullet! This was not a bullet. It was a rocket propelled grenade from an RPG launcher!"

General Wheeler rolled his eyes up to the ceiling with exasperation.

The only thing he wanted to do now was to get the hell out of Vietnam as soon as possible.

Colonel Vortex was awakened at 0530 hours on the 28th February 1968 by Captain Richter.

The PAVN bombardment on the 23rd February had been the heaviest but in the last 5 days the Communists had given *Khe Sanh* a tremendous pounding as well.

"I don't understand it Richter?" began Vortex, "Why are they hitting us so hard if they have withdrawn five battalions of infantry?"

Captain Richter handed his Colonel a cup of steaming black coffee.

"I don't know sir? But I have a feeling that we are going to get an education and pretty soon at that!"

"Yes!" laughed Colonel Vortex.

The two officers walked out of the 9th/26th HQ complex and went over to the Forward Operating Base 3 [FOB3] which was near the *Khe Sanh* drop zone on the western perimeter.

The Siege of Khe Sanh 1967-1968

Colonel Lownds had decided to keep as many of his men occupied as he could. There had been no major ground assault since the attack on Hill 64 on the 8th February and the problem of boredom and a slackening of alertness in the men was ever present.

To this end, Lownds had decided to form teams of 'tunnel ferrets' to combat the danger of the PAVN digging tunnels under the base.

He tried to frighten the men by telling them that the Communist hordes could emerge from these tunnels in the middle of the base and slaughter them all by surprise.

Even though this threat was extremely remote, it was decided by both Vortex and Lownds that the men had to be kept busy.

"No like this!" said Colonel Lownds as he showed a group of Marines how to drive metal stakes into the earth and then press stethoscopes against them.

"What are we listening for sir?" asked a SP4.

Colonel Lownds explained as Vortex and Richter strolled up with their own staff from the 9th Regiment as well as Major Thrush.

"We are listening for any unusual vibrations or clanking noises coming from under the earth. That is a sure sign that the Communists are trying to dig vast tunnels under the base. If you hear any such noises you must report it to your team commander who will then report it to me or to one of the other senior officers."

"Yes sir! I understand sir," answered the SP4.

All the other Marines in the ferret teams nodded grimly but with unbounded enthusiasm. "How are we going to destroy these tunnels sir, if and when they are found?" asked a senior Warrant Officer from the 3rd Battalion 26th Marines.

Colonel Vortex stepped up and answered, "We are going to use *Bangalore* torpedoes."

Colonel Lownds explained, "The *Bangalore* torpedoes will be driven into the earth directly above where we find the tunnels. When we have inserted a sufficient length of these high explosives we will detonate them and hope and pray that the gook tunnels will collapse."

The Warrant Officer nodded, "I see sir."

Colonel Vortex grabbed Colonel Lownds' arm and pulled him aside.

He also called over Major Thrush, Captain Richter and a few other junior officers from both the 9th and 26th Marines.

"I am going to launch a night raid on those PAVN trenches," informed Vortex.

Colonel Lownds ran his fingers through his hair, "Are you sure that is a good idea?"

Vortex continued, "Captain Baig has received advice that the Communists are getting closer to the *Khe Sanh* concertina wire. The *Beech Bonanza* spotter planes have indicated to him that the nearest trench line is only 100 yards away from here!"

Vortex pointed directly across from the wire where they stood at Forward Operating Base 3.

"My God!" screamed Colonel Lownds, "I had no idea that the North Vietnamese had dug in that close."

A voice behind them cried, "Its true sir!"

The officers turned around with surprise. It was Captain Mirza Baig with a bundle of relief maps in his hands.

For the next 30 minutes the Fire Control and Coordination Captain showed them exactly where the North Vietnamese trenches were.

Colonel Lownds was deeply disturbed by the proximity of the PAVN siege works.

"I can't understand why the massive air strikes haven't been able to destroy the trenches?" asked Colonel Lownds.

Captain Baig answered, "They have sir. But we can't destroy all of them."

Vortex added, "The PAVN do most of their digging at night. I can hear the bastards digging towards us in the dark. That's what they did to the French at *Dien Bien Phu*! They can repair up to 1,000 feet of trenches in a single 12 hour period!"

Colonel Lownds admonished, "It's unbelievable!"

"Its true sir!" added Captain Baig as he rolled up his maps.

"So when are you going to launch this attack?" asked Lownds.

Vortex answered, "I'm taking 400 men in my strike force. We'll cross the perimeter here at Forward Operating Base 3 and try to kill as many as we can and disrupt the PAVN siege operation as much as possible. We'll go at precisely 2300 hours tonight and be back by 0400 hours on the 29th February.

Captain Baig has organised a series of massive TAC air sorties on the gook trenches here after we return. Unfortunately we can't use the B-52's because it is too close to the *Khe Sanh* wire. They are limited to within 1 mile of the base perimeter otherwise we could suffer *friendly fire* casualties."

Lownds said, "It sounds excellent Vortex. Good luck!"

Suddenly sniper fire erupted unexpectedly from the direction of the Communist trenches. The several hundred Marines in Forward Operating Base 3 ducked for cover but it was too late.

The Warrant Officer who had asked Colonel Lownds some questions just a few minutes earlier had been shot directly through the brain.

A thin trickle of sweet red blood rolled over his nose and mouth.

He had died instantly as the 7.62mm round entered his skull.

Major Thrush caught him before he collapsed into the red mud of *Khe Sanh*.

"Jesus! You see what I mean about those damned trenches?" asked Vortex as he picked up an M60 and started firing like a maniac into the Communist forces beyond the concertina wire.

Colonel Lownds nodded and said, "I'll keep the rest of the men working on these *tunnel ferret* teams. At least it will keep them busy."

Vortex informed Lownds that he thought that was a good idea.

When 2300 hours arrived, Vortex took one company from the 9th Marines and one from the 26th Marines.

Major Thrush led the men from Colonel Lownds' unit.

Crossing over the concertina wire on the western perimeter of the *Khe Sanh* base adjacent to Forward Operating Base 3 and in the 'Red Sector' next to *Ta Con Village* and the Rock Quarry, the advance went smoothly for the first

80 yards.

All 400 Marines crawled on their bellies in the dark and the mud.

There had been no activity on Hills 861A or 881 South in the previous 48 hours.

No activity had been reported on Hill 558 either.

So the night was unusually quiet.

"Over there!" whispered Colonel Vortex to Captain Richter and Captain Radcliffe.

"Do you see the enemy troops?"

"I do sir," answered Radcliffe.

Vortex licked his lips as they crawled closer and closer to the Communist trench lines.

"We haven't been spotted yet sir," whispered Richter.

"We've been lucky!" answered the Colonel.

Major Thrush and his 200 men were approaching from the left flank. Situated there was a dirt track that ran parallel with both the PAVN trenches and Forward Operating Base 3.

Colonel Vortex took out his AN/PVS-2 Starlight Scope and scanned the trenches just a few yards in front of them.

All the Marines had their weapons trained on the enemy.

With his expertly trained military eye, Colonel Vortex could see the spades and trench tools rising and falling into the earth as hundreds of North Vietnamese worked frantically to extend and enlarge the siege works.

General Vo Nguyen Giap had ordered his troops to inch as close to the *Khe Sanh* concertina wire for a surprise attack as they possibly could, regardless of casualties – for that meant nothing to general Giap as he never did any of the digging himself.

Vortex thought to himself that it was the same fucked-up strategy he had used at *Dien Bien Phu* but this time he was up against United States Marines who didn't take shit from anyone, while the French lacked air power to locate the position of the trenches that the '*Army of Moles*' loved to dig.

"Have you got it?" asked Vortex as he looked around in the dark and the stinkingly foul *Khe Sanh* mist.

"Its here sir," said Captain Richter excitedly.

"Then give it to me! Quickly! We are going to attack. Signal Major Thrush to coordinate our assault," ordered Vortex.

"Yes sir," answered Captain Radcliffe as he got onto the field phone.

Three Marines crawled up with a large circular object and handed it to Colonel Vortex.

Vortex strapped it on his back with the help of Captain Richter and Captain Radcliffe.

"My God sir!" laughed Richter, "Are you really going to use this thing?"

The handsome and rugged looking Vortex, his azure blue eyes flashing in the eerie darkness, chuckled, "Why not? The Marines used it at *Iwo Jima*, *Saipan* and *Okinawa*. We just used it on the SLICE Mission. So let's use it at *Khe Sanh!*"

Colonel Vortex had an extremely powerful M2 flamethrower on his back which was the same as that used by Sergeant David [Maddog] Dolby on 8th to 9th February 1968 during their failed Operation SLICE mission at the limestone cave complex. It weighed more than 45 kilograms.

"Attack!" screamed the Colonel.

The North Vietnamese were taken completely by surprise as the 400 Marines stormed the enemy trench line.

Colonel Lownds ordered the pre-arranged artillery barrage to open up.

As Vortex and his troops leapt into the enemy trenches the 105mm and 155mm guns pounded the PAVN positions behind the trench lines.

This would prevent any Communist reinforcements from reaching the trenches while Colonel Vortex's attack was in progress.

Captain Richter jumped into the trench first and head-butted a NVA soldier who had raised his spade to crush the American's skull.

Radcliffe kicked the man in the testicles so that he fell backwards onto two more North Vietnamese.

"Eat this!" screamed Vortex.

The Colonel depressed the lever on the flamethrower nozzle and a huge yellow-orange sheet of flame lit up the night sky around the trenches.

Swirls of flame engulfed half a dozen enemy soldiers and their screams were horrific as they danced around in the mud stupidly trying to brush the fire off their skinny bodies.

Colonel Vortex laughed as he could see their flesh blacken and turn crispy from the petro-jelly fire laced with aluminium combustible chemical compounds.

"You gook douche-bags!" screamed Captain Richter as he snatched a trench spade away from one Communist and stoved in his skull with vicious force.

The head of the soldier crumpled and grey brain matter mixed with blood sprinkled inside Vortex's nose and lips as he plunged onwards with the flamethrower almost igniting himself as well as the Communist criminals.

Major Thrush and his troops were shooting their way up one end of the trench line while Vortex burned his way up the other.

This particular trench, the closest yet to the *Khe Sanh* perimeter was more than 400 yards long.

The North Vietnamese were screaming and firing their AK-47's at the advancing Marines.

But they had nowhere to retreat to. They couldn't run out of the trench because of the American artillery behind them. They couldn't run forwards in the direction of the *Khe Sanh* base as they would be shot to pieces by the Marines manning the concertina wire and they couldn't run to the right or left flanks because of the advancing Marines in the double pincer'd strike force.

A few hundred PAVN in this particular trench were trapped.

"I am going to exterminate them all!" shouted Colonel Vortex as he saw about 20 enemy soldiers scramble out of the trench in front of them.

Vortex took aim with the M2 flamethrower as he leaned against the trench wall and hosed all of them down in an orgy of fire and heat. Their burning bodies were then machine gunned to pieces by the Marines as they advanced.

The PAVN troops were being pressed closer and closer together between the two Marine assault groups.

Now the fighting became a vicious hand-to-hand contest.

Captain Richter drove his bayonet through the intestines of two North Vietnamese who stood one behind the other.

Colonel Vortex ran forward with his troops and shot his flamethrower into a Communist pile of ammunition further up the trench. It exploded like a bomb. PAVN bodies were flying through the air due to the concussion blast.

Major Thrush ordered, "Attack! Attack!"

The Major fired his M60 from the hip as he bolted through the dark depths of the earthen siege works.

An NVA grabbed Thrush's neck from behind and pulled him to the mud.

"You gook bastard!" yelled the Major as he kicked the Communist's face viciously with his boots. The man's left ear was shorn off.

One of the Sergeants from his company drove his bayonet into the man's chest splitting the heart in two.

Captain Radcliffe moved forward ahead of Colonel Vortex firing his M16 wildly in every direction.

In sheer desperation the PAVN were tumbling out the sides of the trench trying to get away.

"No you don't!" yelled Vortex as he sprayed the flamethrower at the retreating bodies.

The yellow flesh of the North Vietnamese turned crimson and then as black as soot. They contorted like puppets or rag dolls in a wild gyration of frenzied agony.

Their hands patted, stroked, beat and pummelled their blazing bodies.

"Look at that!" laughed Colonel Vortex.

"Watch out sir! Behind you!" warned Captain Radcliffe.

Captain Richter swivelled on the balls of his feet and punched viciously two enemy soldiers who tried to bayonet Colonel Vortex from the rear.

"No you don't!" said Vortex as he kicked them out of the way and then washed their bodies over with flame.

Suddenly, several PAVN soldiers bolted out from a side trench.

Richter machine gunned most of them but Captain Radcliffe, who had his back turned, caught an AK-47 bayonet in the spine.

Vortex dropped the nozzle of his flamethrower and rushed towards the Captain who had his arms splayed out in agony.

"I've got you Radcliffe!" called out the Colonel.

But it was too late.

Captain Radcliffe gripped Colonel Vortex's shoulders as if beseeching him to take him away from the trench.

Vortex dragged the Captain for a few yards as his Marines were advancing slowly under increasing Communist machine gun fire.

But without any warning, several dozen North Vietnamese soldiers who had been hiding behind the berm that ran parallel to the trench dropped back into it.

A vicious hand-to-hand battle ensued as the Marines were almost overcome by the sheer numbers of enemy troops and their ferocity.

Captain Radcliffe was knifed in the testicles by one PAVN and shot through the lungs by another.

He stumbled forwards and vomited blood all over Vortex and Richter.

It also appeared that some of his small intestines were coming up through his nostrils.

"Save me!" he cried.

But these words were his last as the Communist troops fired into his body. Radcliffe died moments later, choking on his own tongue.

Colonel Vortex stepped over the dead junior officer and screamed, "You filthy Communist pigs!"

The Colonel let loose in a wild frenzy with everything he had left in the twin storage tanks of the M2 flamethrower.

Captain Richter stood next to his commander with a huge *General Electric* Minigun and sprayed the North Vietnamese with bullets as Vortex shot out a continuous stream of fire that melted everything in its path.

Whole ranks of NVA troops went down in hideous balls of fire.

Twisted limbs, charred faces, burnt genitals and roasted flesh.

Captain Richter thought that it smelt like *Bergen Belsen*, Vietnam style.

Minutes passed as the Marines punched, kicked and shot their way through the enemy.

The flamethrower was exhausted. There was no more ignitable fuel in the twin tanks strapped to Vortex's back.

"What do we do now sir?" asked Richter with dismay as he saw the fire dwindle to nothingness.

Colonel Vortex screamed, "We do this!"

The Colonel eased the twin flamethrower tanks off his back and held it high over his head.

As a Communist soldier rushed forward Vortex smashed the steel tanks on top of the man's skull splitting it open in a disgusting mess of blood and broken brain tissue.

Captain Richter shot the man in the testicles and brutally kicked the carcass away.

"We've done it sir!" cried Major Thrush as he broke through the last group of enemy troops to join up with Colonel Vortex.

"Good work Major!" said Vortex.

"Look sir!" pointed Captain Richter, "The PAVN are forming a counterattack."

Vortex looked through his infrared Starlight scope. The ground behind the Communist trench was littered with corpses. Smoke and cordite filled the air as the American artillery continued to fire in a steady rolling barrage.

But now the Communist artillery was answering with shells falling onto Vortex's men.

"I think we better withdraw," mentioned Colonel Vortex.

It was now 0307 hours on the 29th February 1968.

Major Thrush added, "The planned air strikes will be hitting this trench system in about 50 minutes sir."

Vortex nodded and the surviving Marines picked up their wounded, including the body of Captain Radcliffe and made their way under intense fire back to the *Khe Sanh* perimeter and Forward Operating Base 3 [FOB3].

But before the strike force could get 50 yards after crawling out of the devastated trench line, the PAVN reinforcements opened fire with terrible effect. More than 20 Marines were shot in the back and the legs as they crumpled to the earth.

In addition the 130mm PAVN artillery from the *'Horseshoe'* was punching huge holes through Vortex's retreating formation.

"Jesus!" screamed the Colonel, "How did they bring up reinforcements so fast?"

"I don't know sir! But we better get onto redirecting the artillery," said Major Thrush.

Captain Richter handed Vortex the field phone and the Colonel spoke to Captain Baig and one of the artillery commanders.

"I want you to lay down some 'NAILS' on top of the trench line we just attacked!" screamed Vortex into the handset.

'NAILS' was the modern day equivalent of the old fashioned 'grapeshot' that armies used in their 19th century artillery.

It was extremely destructive flechette type howitzer ammunition that was designed primarily to cut to pieces human flesh in vast and indiscriminate quantities.

Captain Mirza Baig instructed excitedly, "Then you better get back into Forward Operating Base 3. Because that ammunition is going to tear the whole place apart!"

"Roger that Captain!" answered the Colonel as he signed off.

7.62mm rounds were flying everywhere as the much reduced strike force scrambled back over the *Khe Sanh* concertina wire.

Of the original 400 Marines in the attack Vortex had suffered 27 KIA (killed in action) and 159 WIA (wounded in action).

Captain Richter shook his head with dismay. It had been an expensive bloodbath.

But then Richter smiled and thought it had been well worth it just to see Colonel Vortex in action with a flamethrower.

However many of the dead Marines were still lying in that dismal trench and there was nothing that Colonel Lownds or Colonel Vortex could do about it.

The 175mm howitzers from the Rockpile and Camp Carroll were now also homing in on the Communist trench lines just as the last Marines leapt back into the *Khe Sanh* trenches and foxholes.

Enormous eruptions of earth sprang skywards as the first faint shimmers of dawn broke through the blackness of that murderous night.

Mist and fog also rolled in from the mountain tops around *Tiger Peak* and *Tchepone* in Laos.

Vortex said with disgust, "Its going to be another one of those damned awful fog covered days at *Khe Sanh*!"

Captain Richter patted his Colonel on the back as Captain Frank Willoughby came rushing up.

"What is it Frank?" asked Vortex.

The Green Beret officer said, "Colonel Lownds, Captain Baig and the whole staff want an emergency meeting immediately! Lieutenant Colonel Tran and Captain Hoang Pho's replacement, the commander of the 37th ARVN Ranger Battalion will also be there. There is something very big brewing!"

"OK! Frank!" began Vortex, "But for God's sake take cover! It's just on 0400 hours!"

The Marines inside Forward Operating Base 3 on the western perimeter of *Khe Sanh* had been taking the brunt of the Communist thrusts for the last couple of weeks.

Nobody knew it, but now was to be the turn of the 37th ARVN Ranger Battalion that was set up in the deep defensive positions along the 'Gray Sector' on the south-eastern and south-western perimeters of *Khe Sanh*.

The ARVN Rangers were just outside the main defence line but they had created their own defensive enclave that was a type of buffer zone between the enemy and the *Khe Sanh* base proper. It was not clear why the South Vietnamese forces had been placed just outside the main locus of the base.

Some thought, including the two Colonels at *Khe Sanh* that it was as a result of a direct order from General Creighton Abrams, the MACV Forward.

It was possible that General Abrams did not have complete confidence in the elite ARVN Rangers and so he had placed them outside the main base perimeter and away from the Americans.

Vortex and Lownds, in private and secret discussions had decided that this was insulting to their gallant and professional South Vietnamese allies. But they would not dare to reposition the Rangers in contravention of Abrams' instructions.

Colonel Vortex would have preferred these elite troops to be spread out in a fan to protect the 105mm and 155mm artillery pieces inside the base concertina wire.

Like clockwork the USAF and Marine Corps fighter bombers swooped in from the east to attack the PAVN trenches.

The artillery fire was pulverising the Communist positions but it had to stop temporarily for the TAC air to begin its work over. Otherwise flying artillery rounds could impact against the fuselage of the jets as they flew in for their attack runs.

"Look at that!" praised Colonel Vortex, "…right on target!"

The exhausted Marines watched as 3 *Phantoms* and 4 *Skyhawks* swooped in with their 20mm Gatling guns blazing.

The napalm cigars flew gracefully into the narrow trench lines.

Captain Richter noticed, "The pilots are so good at this now, they can drop their bombs directly into the narrow slits of the trenches!"

Colonel Vortex nodded, "Thank God that we have total air superiority at *Khe Sanh*! Otherwise this whole thing would be much closer! Much deadlier!"

The Marines standing next to their Colonel all nodded glumly. Most men had cuts, bruises and contusions all over their grime caked torsos from scrambling through the filthy trenches.

But at least this attack was now over as the fighter bombers continued their deadly rain of napalm, high explosives, cluster bombs, folding fin rockets and especially delayed action bombs, which first penetrated the walls of the trenches and then after a few seconds blew them apart.

"We better get going," mentioned Colonel Vortex.

The Colonel and his entourage ran through the interior of the *Khe Sanh* base towards the FSCC bunker where Colonel Lownds and the others were waiting for them.

As they moved past the TAFDS station they saw three AH-1 *Cobra* gunships fly in just as the sun was rising over the mist covered hills around *Khe Sanh*.

"Who's that?" asked Captain Richter.

The officers watched a group of Marines disembark and run across the airstrip towards them.

"I don't know?" answered Colonel Vortex.

Before the *Cobra* gunships lifted off for their return trip to Quang Tri and then Phu Bai, the medical personnel loaded on some seriously wounded Marines for a quick and expeditious medivac.

Colonel Vortex couldn't believe his eyes as his Executive Officer (the second-in-command of the entire 9th Marine Regiment and the commander of the 1st Battalion 9th Marines) came running up with his hand on his helmet.

The remainder of Colonel Vortex's Regiment comprising the 2nd and 3rd Battalions had been positioned first at Dong Ha and then at Quang Tri with his Executive Officer in temporary command while Vortex was at *Khe Sanh*.

Lieutenant Colonel John J. Cahill came striding up to his superior. He was six feet tall, muscular and only about 15 kilograms lighter than Colonel Vortex.

Lieutenant Colonel Cahill was also an expert in the Hungarian style of sabre fencing and he hated and despised all types of Communists even more than Colonel Vortex and Major Thrush.

Cahill also relished in killing the North Vietnamese with a more personal and intense style. The Executive officer of the 9th Marines liked to see the eyes of the enemy as he plunged in a knife or a long double-edged dagger into their steaming and rancid guts. He loved to watch as the life quivered out of their skinny bodies.

"What a fabulous surprise! Lieutenant Colonel Cahill!" screamed Colonel Vortex as the other officers ducked when a NVA 152mm shell from the 'Co Roc' exploded next to one of the concrete revetments.

Huge pieces of shattered concrete and steel girding flew through the air and crashed into the rotor blades of a *Jolly Green*.

Lieutenant Colonel Cahill gave a super quick and alert looking salute to his commander.

"Thank you sir! Its good to see you!" barked Cahill.

Vortex grabbed Cahill's shoulders and they walked towards the FSCC bunker where Lownds was patiently awaiting.

"What's the situation along the DMZ?" asked Captain Richter.

"It's very intense. The North Vietnamese are applying probing attacks all along the line from Con Thien to Ca Lu," answered the Lieutenant Colonel.

"And what about Operation PEGASUS?" asked Vortex with concern.

Cahill laughed, "Don't worry sir! General Tolson's 1st Cavalry Division (Airmobile) is already moving into position with its heavy equipment and its battalion of sappers and engineers to repair National Route 9 for the offensive thrust. There are also 7 ARVN Airborne battalions that will support the drive by the air cavalry and the Marines. But I don't think that we can get it underway until the beginning of April 1968."

Vortex asked, "We are still expecting the *'big push'* here at the base. Come! Colonel Lownds wants us for a very urgent meeting. This could be it. Maybe Captain Baig has received some sensor information which will indicate that *Charlie* is massing for the big attack against *Khe Sanh*."

When the officers trooped into the underground conference room inside the FSCC bunker Captain Baig immediately began the briefing.

"Gentlemen! Listen up please!"

There was a murmur of excitement across the bunker. All the staff officers from the 9th and 26th Regiments were there, including Lieutenant Colonel Tran, Captain Hoang Pho's replacement and his officers and the artillery commanders at *Khe Sanh*.

"Before you begin Captain Baig," interrupted Colonel Vortex, "I would like to introduce my Executive Officer who has just arrived."

Colonel Lownds stepped forward and shook Cahill's hand, "Glad to have you with us at *Khe Sanh*."

When the introductions were finished Captain Baig continued.

The First Attack Against the 37th ARVN Rangers: 2130 hours, 29th February 1968

"As I was saying gentlemen. We have received some very interesting and disturbing sensor information concerning the movements of the 304th PAVN Division. It appears

that large formations of troops have moved down along Route 9 and are concentrating for the attack on *Khe Sanh's* south-eastern perimeter."

Captain Baig pulled out some large coloured maps. Three of his fire control Warrant Officers helped him lay them out on the table in front of Lownds, Vortex, Cahill and the others.

"What is the size of this enemy troop concentration?" asked Colonel Lownds as he nervously wrung his hands together.

Captain Baig answered, "It is Regimental size at least sir."

Vortex deduced, "Then that could be the biggest assault on *Khe Sanh* so far?"

"Very possibly!" answered Captain Baig excitedly.

Lieutenant Colonel Tran spoke up, "Captain! You said they are concentrating to the south-east?"

"That's right sir," said Baig.

"Then that would place the PAVN directly facing my Ranger battalion."

Captain Baig nodded, "That is correct sir. But don't worry! I have already begun preparations for the largest B-52 Arc Light, TAC air and artillery support strike ever seen by *Khe Sanh*!"

Colonel Vortex looked to Lieutenant Colonel Cahill and then to Colonel Lownds and scoffed, "But we've seen some pretty big ones so far?"

Captain Baig chuckled and said, "Believe me sirs! This air and artillery strike that I am preparing will be the most colossal demonstration of firepower the world has ever witnessed!"

Colonel Lownds seemed very pleased as he ran his fingers around the thick black texted line that marked the *Khe Sanh* area on the map.

Colonel Lownds asked, "So the big question is, when?"

"Ah! Sir! Yes! It is expected tonight! The attack is expected tonight!" shouted the Fire Control and Coordination officer.

Lieutenant Colonel Tran said, "But I wish I could have given my men more notice! Many of them will die tonight if the attack you predict will eventuate."

Colonel Vortex shook his head, "I don't think so Colonel Tran!"

"And why not?" asked the ARVN officer.

"Well! You heard what Captain Baig said?" screamed back Vortex.

The South Vietnamese officer scoffed.

Captain Baig interrupted as he looked sympathetically to Lieutenant Colonel Tran, "Sir. My planned air strikes will be so devastating, so intense and so destructive that I doubt whether any North Vietnamese troops will even reach your outer defensive wire!"

There was stunned silence in the whole conference room.

Then a smile slowly started to spread across Lieutenant Colonel Tran's relieved face.

"Really?" he asked with bemusement.

"Yes really," answered Captain Baig.

Colonel Lownds asked in a loud voice, "For the benefit of us Infantry Officers here. Can you please explain exactly how the firepower will be coordinated?"

"Certainly sir!" barked back Captain Baig.

The Fire Control officer took out a large piece of paper and started to draw a diagram as he explained the mechanics of Operation NIAGARA.

Captain Richter and Major Thrush were fascinated as they watched and listened with avid attention.

"OK! Here is how it works!" began Mirza Baig, "…here is the main *Khe Sanh* defensive wire. In this case it will be the defensive perimeter of the 37th ARVN Rangers. Here are the artillery pieces inside the base. Now! Here are the Communist PAVN troops. They usually advance in a column for the attack. We will allow them to advance until the head of their column is almost up to the defensive wire…"

Lieutenant Colonel Tran cried out, "Is that wise?"

"Let him finish!" screamed Colonel Lownds.

Captain Baig continued, "…when the PAVN are almost up to the defensive perimeter then we open fire with our 155mm and 105mm howitzers at almost point blank range. We arrange the artillery fire so that it forms three sides of a box with the open side facing the base…"

Captain Baig drew a sketch to illustrate and continued, "…then, when the fixed concentrations of fire forming the three sides of the box are in full swing we let loose with a reserve battery of 155mm's. This extra battery of guns will pound the North Vietnamese inside the box as we orchestrate a walking barrage or *creeping barrage* up and down the length of the box surrounded by fire. This first step should really soften up the enemy quite a bit!"

Colonel Vortex cried, "Boy! It sounds devastating!"

"It is!" laughed Captain Baig and then he said, "Any enemy troops that manage to survive that and who emerge from the open end of the box towards the base are dealt with by you gentlemen in the infantry battalions. You crush them down with M60, 106mm recoilless rifles and M79 grenade fire – the organic weapons of a standing US Infantry Battalion.

Then!" Captain Baig lifted up his fingers like an orchestra conductor, "Then! The 175mm howitzers from the Rockpile and Camp Carroll open fire with fixed linear concentrations about 550 yards outside the inner box of fire.

This will smother any enemy troops who have managed to stagger out of the inner box of firepower.

That is step two!

And now for the *coup de grace*!"

Captain Baig was really enjoying himself and Colonel Vortex relished his soul in the unbelievable and righteous American firepower that he had at his disposal.

Captain Baig explained, "Then, while this is going on I simultaneously order the B-52 Arc Light strikes and the large formations of radar-equipped fighter-bombers to drop a rolling barrage of ordnance on the rear of the PAVN advance behind the inner and outer boxes of fire. This final attack will crush and smother the Communists reserves preventing them from supporting the floundering initial attack!

And that! Gentlemen! Is that!"

Captain Baig smacked his hands together like a satisfied school boy.

"Its fantastic!" screamed Lieutenant Colonel Tran with joy.

"Its all part and parcel of American ingenuity and firepower," added Colonel Vortex.

Lieutenant Colonel John J. Cahill asked, "Sir?"

Both Colonel Lownds and Colonel Vortex looked in his direction.

"Yes?" they both answered.

Lieutenant Colonel Cahill continued, "I request to be allowed to join the 37th ARVN Rangers in their defensive enclave on the eastern side of the *Khe Sanh* perimeter."

Colonel Vortex chuckled, "Permission granted. Because we are all going to be there to observe the immolation of the stinking North Vietnamese Army of Moles!"

Colonel Lownds smiled to Captain Richter and Captain Mirza Baig, "Yes! Normally I would remain here in the FSCC bunker to coordinate all combat operations. But on this occasion I want to see for myself the fabulous destructive effect of our technology on a brutish, foul, stinking and primitive Communist Army!"

All the officers grunted with approval.

The entire *Khe Sanh* operational staff hated the despised PAVN with pure and undiluted venom.

At 2030 hours the elite South Vietnamese 37th Rangers were on full alert.

Every M16, every M60 and M79 grenade launcher, all the *Khe Sanh* batteries of 105mm and 155mm guns as well as the 175mm's from Camp Carroll and the Rockpile were all on full alert.

The B-52's were already airborne and en route to the *Khe Sanh* area.

An unprecedented force of 36 *Stratofortresses* were to be used to crush and exterminate the expected PAVN attack.

The new B-52D models now in use were the *'Big Belly'* configuration which allowed the *Stratofortresses* to carry a much larger bomb load.

The B-52D carried 42 750lb bombs internally and 24 500lb bombs on the external wing racks.

Thus each plane carried 43,500lbs of high explosive ordnance.

The total strike package that Captain Mirza Baig had organised from the Strategic Air Command bases at *Guam* and *U-Tapao* thus amounted to 1,566,000 lbs of bombs.

Colonels Vortex and Lownds, Major Thrush, Captain Dabney (who had come down from Hill 861/861A), Captains Richter and Baig, Lieutenant Colonels Tran and Cahill and Chaplain Ray Stubbe as well as a host of other junior officers and senior NCOs' were all crowded into the forward command bunker inside the 37th ARVN Rangers defensive enclave in the 'Gray Sector.'

The main *Khe Sanh* perimeter was just a few hundred yards behind them and the secondary road that branched off National Route 9 and which cut straight through the *Khe Sanh* base was on their left flank as they faced south-east.

All the senior officers held AN/PVS-2 Starlight infrared night vision scopes to their eyeballs.

The tension both inside *Khe Sanh* and at the 37th ARVN Ranger position was electric. Everybody knew that this could be the *'big push'* that MACV had been waiting for.

"Jesus! The night is as black as the ace of spades!" said Colonel Vortex nervously.

"It sure is Richard!" began Colonel David Lownds as he continued to scan the gullies and low hills ahead of them for any sign of the PAVN advance.

Captain Baig looked at his watch and said as he stood behind the two Colonels, "The B-52D's are already in the air. We expect the attack within the next 60 minutes."

Major Thrush asked the Fire Control and Coordination officer, "What is the payload that Arc Light is bringing in?"

Captain Baig answered with joy, "More than one and a half million pounds of high explosives."

Captain Richter lowered his Starlight scope, "That's unbelievable!"

"Are the howitzers ready inside the main base and at Camp Carroll?" asked Lieutenant Colonel Cahill as he stood on the balls of his feet, peering over the sandbagged wall of the foxhole with his infrared scope.

Lieutenant Colonel Tran answered, "All the guns are trained onto their expected targets!"

Colonel Vortex walked forwards and briefly inspected the South Vietnamese troops with Colonel Lownds and their commander. Vortex spoke in perfect Vietnamese to the elite Ranger troops from the 37th Battalion.

"Are you ready?" he asked one of the ARVN Sergeants manning an M60.

"Sir! I am ready to kill the foul and putrid Communist scum!" shouted back the NCO.

"Good! Good man! God bless you!" beamed Vortex as he patted the soldier on his arm.

All the way up and down the stalwart ranks of South Vietnamese troops, Vortex, Lownds and Tran were greeted with grim and fanatical determination to crush and exterminate the enemy. Some of the Rangers briefly told the officers how their families, their daughters and mothers had been raped and mutilated by the North Vietnamese army and the Viet Cong guerrillas.

From every village and town across the gallant democracy of South Vietnam there were horrible revelations of brutal atrocities committed by the Viet Cong forces and their hypocritical North Vietnamese masters.

Colonel Vortex and Chaplain Ray Stubbe tried to console the anger and fury of the South Vietnamese troops.

But it was useless. It was like being in the eye of a hurricane.

When Colonel Vortex heard the stories from, *Ban Me Thuot, Ninh Hoa, Dong Ba Thin, Da Lat, Phan Thiet, Quan Loi, Lai Khe, Di An, Cu Chi, Tay Ninh, Dong Tam, Tan An, Nui Dat, Ba Tri* and *Can Tho* his eyes filled with the sulphuric tears of maniacal fury and revenge.

Chaplain Ray Stubbe, the Marine Chaplain at *Khe Sanh*, gave the men absolution for what they were about to inflict on the Godless and pitiless enemy and agents of the Anti-Christ on earth.

When the two Colonels and the chaplain returned to the command bunker, Vortex needed a few moments to regain his composure and whip himself up into a psychological fury of action and dedication. He slapped his own face with his fists to bring the blood-flow up to his face and screamed at the top of his lungs with filthy invectives against the Communist shit-turds that he was about to exterminate.

He shouted to himself, "I am the *Exterminator*! I am the *Exterminator*! And nothing can stop me!"

Colonel Lownds looked at him with expectation and a slight degree of apprehension, asking, "Are you still in command of your faculties? – Richard?"

Vortex replied, "Fuck-off Lownds and leave me alone! Can't you see I am working myself up into a frenzy so that I may be able to do God's work and kill the Communist Anti-Christ more efficiently! Fuck off!"

The time was now 2120 hours on the 29th February 1968.

Vortex said, "Now listen up! I know what is in your hearts but I can assure you that each man will do his duty!"

The officers and NCOs' gathered around the two Colonels in the command bunker.

Vortex continued, "Let us bow our heads in prayer!"

All the men looked to the red earth of *Khe Sanh* as the commander of the 9th Marine Regiment began.

"Oh! God! We ask you on this foul and foreboding night to give us the strength and the wherewithal possessed by your mighty angels!

Allow us to triumph in the name of the righteous and the free.

Give us the power to extinguish the evil forces that are arrayed against you on this earth.

Bequeath unto us a lasting victory here on these hills around *Khe Sanh*!

We are your servants to command and we shall obey you in this great and righteous enterprise.

Have mercy on your children as we prepare to combat the evil and treacherous minions that have arisen from the stinking and putrid pits of hell!

Place in our hands the mighty axe of retribution so that we may exterminate the murdering criminals of North Vietnam and annihilate in a vortex of fire their Satanic leaders and the putrid edifice that they have designed to be a monstrosity in the face of our saviour Jesus Christ!

All this we pray to you our Lord!

Amen!"

The officers and NCOs' said with solemn reverence, "Amen!"

Colonel Vortex's prayer was followed by a few moments of silence.

Chaplain Ray Stubbe was delighted and moved by the priestly supplications which had his full support.

Each man prepared his soul for the coming cataclysm.

Each asked for the strength and gift of absolution.

And each knew that God was on their side *exclusively*.

The side of the United States of America and its *Soldiers of Christ*.

Suddenly Lieutenant Colonel Cahill observed something through his Starlight scope.

"Over there! Look!" cried the 1st Battalion commander.

"What is it? Is it the figure of our gracious Mother Mary?" asked Colonel Vortex, asking, "Do you see a miracle?"

"No! The enemy is advancing sir!" cried the Lieutenant Colonel.

As in a single row the officers jumped onto the sandbagged wall of the forward COMMO bunker.

A maze of Starlight scopes were trained forward into the inky black darkness that seemed like the gaping jaws of hell itself.

The men of the 37th ARVN Ranger Battalion as well as the 700 Marines from the 9th and 26th Regiments that stood with them locked and loaded their forest of bristling weapons.

"Are the howitzers ready?" whispered Colonel Vortex as he saw the dark shapes of countless *mole men* slowly moving forward directly in front of the defensive enclave.

Captain Baig spoke slowly and professionally into his radio handset to the artillery command officers inside *Khe Sanh*.

All the guns were ready behind them in the main base and in front of them with the Rangers.

"All howitzers are in position sir. They have spotted the enemy and are lined up for the commencement of fire support," answered Captain Baig.

Colonels Vortex and Lownds nodded as the first PAVN artillery shells crashed into the forward trench lines.

Already some ARVN Rangers were blown out of their foxholes and trenches.

Severed limbs and crushed flesh flew through the air in bloody swathes.

"Hold! Hold! Until my orders!" screamed Colonel Lownds.

Captain Baig watched the arm of Colonel David Lownds.

He knew that when that arm would fall he would call into his handset to the artillery officers to commence fire.

The PAVN were firing wildly with their AK-47's and RPD light machine guns as they started to run helter skelter towards the ARVN position.

"What do you think is their attack strength?" asked Major Thrush as he manned a 0.50 calibre on top of the command bunker.

"It must be over 1,300 men! A full battalion!" screamed back Colonel Vortex.

The PAVN troops were only about 200 yards from the outer defensive wire.

The 37th Rangers had already opened up with their M16's and M60's. The South Vietnamese poured an avalanche of small arms fire into the attackers.

Colonel Lownds could see PAVN bodies falling in large numbers.

But still they came.

"Now! Now! Open fire now!" screamed Colonel Vortex as he grabbed Colonel Lownds' arm.

The PAVN were only 150 yards from their position. They came on like screaming devils.

"Not yet!" shrieked back Lownds. Captain Baig hesitated with the radio handset.

At that instant all the men inside and outside *Khe Sanh* heard an enormous and continuous growl of thunder coming from the heavens.

"Jesus! What's that?" asked Lieutenant Colonel Cahill.

Captain Baig answered, "It's the radar-equipped fighter-bombers!"

"How many jets have you called in?" asked Captain Richter as his knuckles were bled white from holding the Minigun.

Baig answered, "Over 70 in the first wave and more than 35 in the second assault."

"Oh! My God!" screamed Lieutenant Colonel Tran.

Never in the history of modern aerial warfare has such a massive tactical air strike been called in support of ground troops.

Even though the night was dark the 6,000 Marines in and around *Khe Sanh* and the Hill positions could see the glow of the jet's afterburners as row after row of attack planes swooped around at 20,000 feet preparing for the first wave of high explosive strikes and cluster bomb runs.

The PAVN were only 100 yards from the ARVN position at the 'Gray Sector.'

"Now!" screamed Colonel Lownds, "Fire! Fire! Fire!"

Colonel Vortex shouted in Captain Baig's ear over the roar of the jets above and the PAVN fire in front of them, "Shoot! Shoot!"

Captain Baig shouted, "Shoot! And Fire!"

With that one word there came a tremendous screeching wail that smothered the screams of the attacking PAVN battalion.

The 105mm and 155mm howitzers crashed their shells forward with devastating power and accuracy.

A sheet of flame towered into the atmosphere 300 feet above the heads of the defending ARVN Rangers and the supporting Marines.

The PAVN attackers could no longer be seen through the smoke and eruptions of high explosive ordnance.

This was Operation NIAGARA at its best.

The three sides of the inner box of firepower were being formed with annihilating effect.

The North Vietnamese spearhead was already wilting on the vine even before they had reached the concertina wire.

"It's incredible!" shouted Colonel Vortex.

Captain Baig shouted above the cacophony, "The guns from Camp Carroll and the Rockpile are due in now! They will commence the walking/creeping barrage up and down within the inner box of fire!"

As soon as the words left Baig's mouth a thundering howl could be heard overhead as the 175mm shells rained in like parcels of death.

The devastation was awesome. The shrieks and moans of terror could be heard like a ghastly chorus coming up from the blood soaked earth in front of the Americans and South Vietnamese.

"Look at that!" screamed Colonel David Lownds,"…it looks like a nuclear explosion!"

The creeping barrage ripped up the earth inside the box of fire.

The PAVN battalion was smothered in a veil of high explosive and flechette ordnance.

Colonel Vortex looked through his Starlight scope with Captain Richter on his left and Major Thrush on his right, as he observed, "Not a single North Vietnamese bastard has reached our defensive perimeter! Congratulations Captain Baig!"

The Fire Control officer beamed with pride as he spoke into the VHF tactical frequency, "You may begin your attack run Octopus 7!"

Captain Baig was speaking to the flight leader of the first group of 24 F-105 *Republic Thunderchiefs* that were manoeuvring 20,000 feet far above them in the clouds.

The first and second waves of fighter-bombers to be used over *Khe Sanh* on that fateful night consisted of everything in the United States colossal air arsenal.

There were dozens of F-4E *Phantoms*, F-105 *Thunderchiefs*, *Sky Hawks*, A-6 *Grumman Intruders*, *Skyraiders*, *Crusaders* and even OV-10 *Bronco's* with folding fin rockets and 20mm Gatling guns.

And thundering above all this, unseen and unheard by the men on the ground, were the 36 B-52D *Stratofortresses* that would belch forth a deadly stream of death upon the North Vietnamese attackers of the 304th PAVN Division.

"The outer box of fire is starting to form!" screamed Colonel Vortex as the *Thunderchiefs* or THUD's as they were affectionately called by the troops started to swoop in for the attack.

The noise of the five million combined jet horsepower was unimaginable.

And there were still several squadrons of fighter-bombers above *Khe Sanh* that could be called in within seconds by Captain Mirza Baig if needed.

Vortex and Lownds watched with awe as the sheets of flame and towers of erupting earth blanketed any view of the North Vietnamese soldiers that they had earlier.

The outer box of 175mm fixed linear fire was pulverising the PAVN into mounds of bloodied flesh and crushed bones.

The *Thunderchiefs* hit the rear of the attacking PAVN column, killing, smashing trucks, obliterating Communist artillery pieces, decapitating Viet Cong women irregulars and causing massive and continuous secondary explosions as the PAVN supply dumps ignited like an uncontrollable inferno.

The men of the 37th ARVN Ranger Battalion had no choice but to stop firing.

There was nothing for them to unload on. Even the incoming Communist artillery had trickled to a few sporadic detonations as the second wave of 18 *Phantoms* struck the rear of the Communist formations.

The Second Attack Against the 37th ARVN Rangers: 2330 hours On 29th February 1968

Approximately one hour after the initial attack began the smoke and flames started to clear from the minced terrain in front of the ARVN Rangers.

"Oh! My God!" cried Colonel Lownds as he witnessed the spectacle in front of him.

Vortex was also surprised and overjoyed by the extent of the delicious carnage that he surveyed with almost sexual excitement.

"Our defence has been successful," he said calmly.

An enormous field of broken corpses littered the expanse before the *Khe Sanh* base in the 'Gray Sector.'

It was heart-warming and edifying.

"A whole battalion has been wiped out!" whistled Captain Richter as he saw body parts, limbs and streams of blood pulsing over the red earth in hot and cold spasms.

As Richter spoke he walked around the battlefield and thrust his M16 bayonet into the throats and skulls of any moving Communists.

"I want no pity for these mongrels!" screamed Vortex to the officers behind him.

But out in front the troops of the South Vietnamese Rangers were beside themselves with ecstasy.

The ARVN officers were spotting moving or crawling PAVN bodies that were still alive with their infrared scopes. They then ordered the men to fire their M60's into the Communist flesh to finish them off.

This, the men of the 37th ARVN Rangers did with relish and great enthusiasm. For them it was 'pay back time.'

"It looks like the first PAVN assault has failed!" beamed Captain Baig with satisfaction.

Overhead the constant roar of American fighter-bombers could be heard as they traversed the sky above *Khe Sanh* between Ta Con Village and Hill 861/861A.

Colonel Lownds ordered in some ancillary air strikes around the bases of the Communist held valleys that surrounded Hills 881 South and 861A while they were waiting for any further developments in front of the ARVN position.

At 2330 hours it was Colonel Vortex who first noticed a second attack forming as he grabbed Captain Baig's arm with one hand and Colonel Lownds' with the other.

"I don't believe it!" screamed Vortex.

"What is it?" asked Lownds and Cahill in unison.

"The stupid bastards are trying it all over again!"

"Here! Let me see!" barked Colonel Lownds who could not believe that even the North Vietnamese could be stupid enough to waste more men on a pure suicide attack against the razor sharp teeth of the magnificent American firepower arrayed against them.

"You're right Vortex!" groaned Lownds as he stepped back from the sandbagged wall with utter bewilderment.

Lieutenant Colonel Tran and his ARVN officers were wringing their hands with glee.

The first PAVN artillery shells again began to pound the *Khe Sanh* base. But this fusillade was nowhere near as powerful as that experienced in the first attack at 2130 hours.

Colonel Vortex thought to himself that many of the PAVN 130mm M46 Soviet-designed field pieces must have been destroyed in the first assault.

"We are ready for them sirs!" began Captain Baig as four of his senior NCOs' came running up with the VHF radios to coordinate the deadly NIAGARA of streaming explosives that would answer this latest assault.

Colonel Lownds scratched his head as he looked to his field commanders, "This rogue, General Giap, has no consideration for his troops and the horrendous losses they are suffering as a result of these suicide attacks!"

Colonel Vortex said with brutal viciousness, "Who gives a fuck what that bastard General Giap thinks or does! And who gives a fuck as to how many of these murdering PAVN scum-shits and vermin-dogs are killed by our gallant troops and their stalwart and courageous South Vietnamese allies."

Colonel Lownds seemed rather pleased and relieved by Vortex's comments as it lifted the responsibility for the carnage from his shoulders.

"I would not exactly put it like that!" admonished Lownds.

"Well I would Colonel!" barked back Vortex.

Captain Richter was watching the PAVN advance with Lieutenant Colonel Cahill.

"The gooks are close sir!" said Richter.

Vortex watched with his Starlight. He could see the second attack wave that appeared to be about the same strength as the first.

Nearly a whole battalion of over 1,300 men.

The North Vietnamese were having more difficulty in advancing this time because of the piles of shattered corpses in their path and the huge bomb craters that had been formed by the swarms of fighter-bombers.

"Open fire!" screamed Vortex as the enemy reached to within 100 yards of the 'Gray sector' perimeter.

The inner box of fire erupted with just as much force as the first demonstration two hours earlier.

The 175mm howitzers from Camp Carroll and the Rockpile applied the walking/creeping barrage with devastating effect.

This time the North Vietnamese started to waver even sooner than the first battalion sent in.

Captain Baig mentioned as he put down the handset of his radio telephone, "I have just spoken to the boys in the FSCC bunker. They tell me that half the B-52D force is now over *Khe Sanh*.

I have just ordered them to attack!

You'll see something in a few seconds!"

"Excellent!" screamed Vortex as the outer box of fixed linear concentrations of fire erupted with earth shattering devastation.

The PAVN soldiers were blown apart in every conceivable direction. Intestines splayed everywhere in a revolting miasma of human destruction.

"They are retreating!" shrieked Captain Richter with excitement.

The troops of the 37th ARVN fired into the mangled remains of the second assault.

The fighter-bombers with their onboard radar pounded the Communists without mercy.

A-6 *Grumman Intruders* and *Skyraiders* came in at over 400mph. They plastered the area with cluster bombs, napalm and flechette ordnance.

Whole PAVN platoons were wiped out within seconds. The attack wave floundered, stopped, collapsed within itself and then disintegrated in an orgy of blood.

Then the B-52D's struck with devilish surprise.

From a distance, as Vortex and Lownds watched with their field binoculars, it seemed like the 750lb bombs were like rain drops falling to the earth to cleanse the soil of the Communist festering corruption.

It was truly a deadly cascade from heaven. Vortex knew that Jesus sent it.

"My dear Jesus!" was all that Colonel Vortex could say.

Even his hatred of the North Vietnamese was mellowed somewhat at the mind numbing catastrophe wrought upon the enemy scum by the B-52D's.

These superlative instruments of Peace and Security could strike without warning in any weather conditions.

At that moment Colonel Vortex wished that Strategic Air Command (SAC) was an attractive woman so that he could kiss her.

They flew in excess of 30,000 feet high which made them impervious to SAM -2's (surface-to-air) missiles possessed by the North Vietnamese Army/Air Defence Forces.

They were unseen and unheard by the troops on the ground immediately before an attack.

Now Colonel David Lownds held his hands up to his ears and mouth as the rippling concussion of the multiple explosions cut through the night sky.

Captain Baig slowly nodded his head in approval as the blast effect shuddered the earth underneath which they stood.

"Oh! My God!" expostulated Lieutenant Colonel Cahill as the sandbagged wall in front of them leapt into the air.

Each individual sandbag was separated by a few inches from the next one as they all jumped up in a type of hysteria of action.

Colonel Vortex staggered from side to side with his field binoculars as the earth trembled from the Arc Light offensive.

He didn't need the Starlight scope because the detonation fires from the 750lb iron bombs lit up the whole area around *Khe Sanh*. The PAVN reserves were being annihilated in a tornado of ordnance.

Several of the Marines standing next to Major Thrush and Lieutenant Colonel Cahill started vomiting.

Colonel Lownds looked at them and yelled, "Hey! What's the matter with you men?"

Vortex explained, "I've seen this sort of thing before. The tremendous concussion blast and shock of the Arc Light explosions puts men into a state of neural paralysis. Their entire nervous system is traumatised causing vomiting and nausea."

Captain Richter added, "It's a well documented medical phenomena sir."

Vortex glanced sideways and looked at Colonel Lownds' left ear.

"What is it? What are you looking at?" asked the commander of the 26th Marines.

"You're ears are bleeding David!" said Vortex.

Colonel Lownds clapped his hands to his ears.

When he removed them and brought them in front of his face they were covered in blood from the middle ear. The tympanic membrane had been traumatised.

"It's the concussion blast from the Arc Light explosions!" informed Colonel Vortex.

Colonel Lownds simply shook his head with disbelief as several medics ran up to attend to the commander of *Khe Sanh*.

The Third Attack Against the 37th ARVN Rangers: 0315 hours On 1st March 1968

A new month dawned upon the embattled troops at *Khe Sanh*.

But the Marines had a feeling that the worst was just about over.

Colonel Lownds had recovered from his minor injury as the 105mm and 155mm artillery pieces inside the base continued a steady stream of fire onto the ground in front of the ARVN Ranger position in the 'Gray Sector.'

The sight was indescribable. Mangled corpses and broken PAVN vehicles littered the moonscape terrain.

Secondary explosions continued to erupt a few kilometres back where the Communist supply dumps and storage area had been devastated.

It was Lieutenant Colonel Cahill who spotted the third battalion sized PAVN attack against the ARVN Ranger position.

"I'm going to hit them now!" ordered Vortex.

"But sir? The dinks are still 300 yards from the concertina wire," answered Captain Baig.

"Does it make any difference?" asked back Vortex.

"Not really sir," said the Fire Control officer.

Colonel Vortex grabbed the handset and called up the flight leaders of the large formations of fighter-bombers circling over *Khe Sanh*.

"I want you to hit the PAVN with everything you have! I think this is their last attack! So make it a good one!" screamed Colonel Vortex.

"I will incinerate the bastards for you!" replied a United States Navy Commander who was in command of the A-6's and *Skyraiders* from Task Force 77 in the Gulf of Tonkin.

Captain Baig also got on the VHF tactical frequency and coordinated the spotter planes to go in before the main TAC air strikes.

As the PAVN battalion picked their way through the mountain of mutilated corpses towards the 37th Ranger Battalion enclave a shrieking roar echoed across the *Khe Sanh* plateau.

Seven Rockwell OV-10 *Bronco* aircraft screamed in at 350mph directly over the *Khe Sanh* airstrip.

The turbo-prop planes swooped over the heads of Vortex, Lownds and the others as they supervised the softening up fire from the heavy artillery.

The Rockwell OV-10 *Bronco* was primarily used as a forward air control platform, even though it was armed with 20mm Gatling guns.

"They are going to mark the target for the fighter-bombers," mentioned Captain Baig.

Colonel Lownds watched as the OV-10's flew over the multitude of Communist pith helmets firing white phosphorous rockets into the mass of advancing human flesh.

Seconds later the fighter-bombers dived in and smothered the third assault with a massive application of cluster and flechette bombs, napalm, high explosives and delayed action bombs.

The annihilation was complete.

Vortex winced with pain at the sonic boom that crashed over the *Khe Sanh* combat base.

"Jesus! My ears! Christ! They hurt!" he screamed.

Richter, Tran, Cahill, Lownds, Thrush, Captain Dabney, Captain Mirza Baig, Captain Hoang Pho's replacement of the 37th ARVN plus the entourage of junior officers and NCOs' dived to the earth as 35 F-105 *Thunderchiefs* screamed over them at Mach 1.1 (817mph).

It was an unbelievable display of tactical jet power from the *Century Fighters*.

More than 20,000,000 horsepower descended on top of the Communist aggressor and imperialist troops.

Colonel Vortex was handed twelve 10mg Codeine tablets and his water flask by Captain Richter.

The Colonel had a terrible migraine from all the excitement. The pain killers would take the edge off, thought Vortex.

Captain Max Richter could not give a fuck about the medicine but just felt like killing more Communists.

The Navy A-6's and *Skyraiders* had finished their attack run when the next wave of B-52D's in their Arc Light strikes hit the rear formations once again of the North Vietnamese Imperialist Aggressor Army.

It was at this moment that the wave of THUD's came in with napalm and flechette bombs.

A sea of burning jellied flame arose from the flesh of the already retreating PAVN.

Colonel Lownds could hardly believe his eyes as the few hundred survivors of the third attack dropped their weapons and fled in disorder.

The remaining F-4E *Phantoms* came in behind the *Thunderchiefs* and cut these men down as well.

It was all over.

The 37th ARVN Ranger position in the 'Gray Sector' was secure.

Both Colonels watched the enormous mountains of fire erupt only 2.5 miles from the *Khe Sanh* base as the Arc Light strike was nearing completion.

The radar-equipped fighter-bombers streamed into a vertical climb back to their patrol altitude of 20,000 feet.

What was left of the 304th PAVN Division's regiment crawled away into the depths of the blood-fucked triple canopy jungle. Its logistics smashed, its transport incinerated and its troops vivisected into oblivion by the greatest tactical application of airpower the world has ever seen.

Colonel Lownds watched the American Machine of Peace and Security go into overdrive that was such a heart-warming demonstration of General Westmoreland's Operation NIAGARA.

As soon as the fighter-bombers were clear, Colonel Vortex ran with Captain Max Richter and Lieutenant Colonel Cahill to the *Khe Sanh* airstrip where 8 *Sikorsky* S-65 HH-53B *Jolly Green Giants* were waiting in line abreast formation for take-off.

Each *Sikorsky* was armed with three *General Electric* Miniguns.

As the officers jumped into the command HH-53B the whole formation leapt into the air and streamed over to the 37th ARVN position.

"I want you to hose down the entire area!" screamed Colonel Vortex to the commander of the helicopter gunships.

Then Colonel Vortex himself manned one of the powerful 7.62mm Miniguns and commenced firing into the mass of dead and wounded flesh below him as he leaned out of the hatch of the huge chopper.

Captain Richter asked his Colonel, "What do you think sir?"

Colonel Vortex looked back as he fired away like a man possessed – doing God's work to bring peace and salvation to America's loyal South Vietnamese allies.

"I think the North Vietnamese Imperialist Army has just suffered its death throes here at *Khe Sanh*!"

CHAPTER 14
OPERATION PEGASUS

It was 0645 hours on the morning of the 1st March 1968.

The field grade officers of the Marine combat base at *Khe Sanh* (KSCB) were having a conference inside the MATU bunker.

They were weary but well pleased with that morning's events.

"I think we have crushed them!" exclaimed Colonel Lownds.

"I agree. They are finished," added Colonel Vortex.

A few moments later Major General Rathvon C. Tompkins arrived inside the bunker complex.

The commander of the 3rd Marine Division had just arrived from Dong Ha aboard a C-123K *Provider* that was unloading ammunition.

"Good morning sir!" saluted both Colonels.

"And good morning to you gentlemen," said Major General Tompkins as the entourage of officers in the bunker stiffened to attention.

"Relax! Please!" beamed the General.

"Last night's assault by the 304th PAVN Division has been annihilated sir," said Vortex with grim pride.

For the next two hours Major General Tompkins went over the emerging plans for Operation PEGASUS.

General Westmoreland was going to commit more than 30,000 troops to the offensive along National Route 9.

Spearheading the attack was the 1st Cavalry Division (Airmobile) under Major General John J. Tolson.

When the planning session was over both Colonels and their staff accompanied the 3rd Division commander out to the airstrip.

When Major General Tompkins was safely airborne in a *Sikorsky* HH-53B, this time heading for a meeting with General Creighton Abrams and Lieutenant

General Cushman at MACV Forward headquarters in Phu Bai, a tremendous explosion rocked the airstrip.

The officers looked around with surprise.

A PAVN mortar shell had exploded adjacent to the *Khe Sanh* control tower.

It landed right next to another C-123K *Provider* as it was gathering speed for takeoff.

The effects were disastrous.

The starboard engine of the *Fairchild Provider* shrieked as metal grinded on metal and then it exploded with a roar at over 103mph.

"Hell! Look at that!" shouted Vortex as he grabbed Captain Richter and Major Thrush.

The transport plane was already veering off the runway as the three officers jumped into a nearby jeep and raced towards the stricken and out of control aircraft.

The fuselage was already burning from the starboard wing down to the tail fin.

The whole scene was a catastrophe as more Communist artillery exploded all around the base perimeter of KSCB.

As he drove like a madman with Captain Richter hanging on to his shoulders, Vortex thought that the PAVN may have been stopped on the ground for the moment but their artillery continued with the incessant pounding of *Khe Sanh* creating the concomitant havoc and mayhem.

Colonel Lownds and his staff watched helplessly as the huge plane careered wildly off the airstrip at over 90mph crashing into a steel corner of one of the revetments.

The fuselage spun 180 degrees in a mad twirl so that the nose was facing where the tail had been.

The whole undercarriage system of the plane was sheared off with the stench of blue rubber smoke belching into the air from the burning tyres.

"We've got to get the crew out!" shrieked Colonel Vortex as he spun the jeep alongside the C-123.

Just as the three officers leapt out of the vehicle the whole plane burst into flames.

Some secondary explosions inside the *Provider* burst open the portside cabin door. The metal frame was catapulted through the air missing Captain Richter's head by mere inches.

"For heaven's sake!" cried the officer with annoyance.

Colonel Vortex grabbed the first crew members as they literally jumped from the burning wreck.

The 17 foot drop was not easy on the knees and ankles and three out of the twelve crew suffered severe leg injuries from the mad jump for life.

However, and much to the relief of Colonel Vortex, none of the Americans inside the plane had been killed.

At noon on the same day the Communist artillery fire was intensifying.

Lieutenant Colonel Cahill and Colonel Lownds were supervising an incoming parachute drop near Forward Operating Base 3.

They were working with the United States Air Force 8th Aerial Port Squadron when the C-130 Hercules and C-123 *Providers* came gliding in under low power.

The huge chutes opened like roses in spring and the life giving supplies wafted to the red and rat infested soil of *Khe Sanh*.

The huge black and brown rats were everywhere.

There was nowhere in the *Khe Sanh* base where you could sleep or even rest without the rats attempting to eat you alive as you slumbered.

Chaplain Ray Stubbe hated and despised the vermin but there was nothing he could do about it.

[See: "Valley of Decision: The Siege of Khe Sanh" by Ray Stubbe & John Prados; 1st Naval Institute Press. (1991)": Originally Published by Houghton Mifflin (New York) 1991. ISBN 1-59114-696-8; Naval Institute Press: 291 Wood Road, Annapolis, MD 21402]

Inside the makeshift church that had been set up at the base, the rats always interrupted the religious services.

Colonel Vortex was with Major Thrush and Captain Richter as they looked over the artillery emplacements.

Vortex had ordered counter-battery fire and H & I missions (harassment and interdiction fire) against the PAVN held 'Horseshoe'.

The huge 155mm guns bounced back on their wheels with each firing. The velocity of the high explosive rounds created an opposite kinetic energy which could move such an enormous mass of steel with ease.

The Fire Control officers used a computer inside the FSCC bunker as well as trigonometry to calculate the angle of fire for any given target.

Everyone near the field pieces had to wear ear protection and Colonel Vortex was no exception.

"You know something Major?" asked Colonel Vortex as Captain Richter gave instructions to the howitzer crews.

"What's that sir?" asked Major Thrush.

"Our biggest failure here at *Khe Sanh* will be the inability of our guns and air power to smash the Communist artillery!"

Major Thrush nodded glumly as suddenly a huge explosion could be heard ripping into the aluminium planking of the *Khe Sanh* airstrip.

A parked C-123K *Provider* was damaged by an incoming 130mm artillery round from the 'Horseshoe.'

"There goes another one of our transport aircraft!" shrugged Colonel Vortex.

For the rest of that humid day of the 1st March 1968 the enemy shelling continued at *Khe Sanh*.

On the 2nd March 1968 Colonel Vortex was in the control tower when yet another PAVN mortar round completely destroyed the C-123K *Provider* that had been damaged the day before.

The air force repair crews had ordered in replacement parts but now that was useless as the fuselage detonated into a charred heap of burning wreckage.

Vortex shook his head with dismay and walked back to one of the bunkers near the FSCC complex. This particular bunker was occupied by the men of his own 1st Battalion 9th Marines.

"Are you going to visit some of our wounded?" asked Lieutenant Colonel Cahill.

"That's right," answered Vortex as he stepped down into the foxhole.

Some of the lightly wounded Marines were inside and Colonel Vortex started to give out battlefield promotions as was his duty.

He promoted several Lance Corporals to Corporals, some Corporals to Sergeants and a few more Sergeants to Warrant Officers ranging from SP1 to SP4.

The men were in high spirits as they could feel that *Khe Sanh* was no longer in imminent danger.

Unknown to Vortex and the rest of the Marines inside the bunker, a C-130 Hercules was making its final approach to the airstrip.

It was going to use the LAPES (Low Altitude Parachute Extraction System) to drop a container carrying heavy timber beams for bunker construction at *Khe Sanh*.

The C-130 made a smooth landing but then the pilot saw the wrecked C-123K ahead of him near the concrete and steel revetments.

"Jesus! Hell!" he exclaimed inside the cockpit.

The Marine pilot swerved the huge aircraft to portside just as the rear wheels touched the tarmac.

Colonel Lownds and his staff were up in the control tower and could see everything that was about to unfold.

"Abort! Abort the parachute extraction!" screamed the pilot of the C-130 to the cargo handler's further back in the fuselage.

But it was too late.

The loadmaster released the pallet locks on the container just as the Hercules swerved to avoid the wrecked plane ahead.

The huge 2,000lb container rolled from the rear hatch and the small parachute billowed open to slow it down.

The pilot, cursing with foul obscenities had no choice but to throttle up the Hercules and take off again. He was fast running out of runway.

But the swerve of the landing caused the metal container to career out of control across the aluminium planking that the Seabees were constantly repairing.

The 2,000lb juggernaut slid right off the left side of the runway as Colonel Lownds screamed, "Oh! No! No!"

The steel mass jumped a few feet into the air past the MATU complex and bunker and slammed into the very bunker containing Colonel Vortex and his Marines.

Inside Vortex was just stepping to the exit when the steel container burst through the sandbagged walls.

Several Marines were knocked across the floor but one unfortunate Lance Corporal caught the full impact of 2,000lbs of deadweight crashing into his skull at over 60mph.

The Lance Corporal died instantly as his body was crushed between the wall of the bunker and the container that finally came to a halt.

So ended another day at the Marine combat base of *Khe Sanh* (KSCB).

By the 6th March 1968 the Communist shelling was becoming noticeably less frequent.

Captain Mirza Baig had called a full staff meeting for all officers inside the FSCC bunker at precisely 1300 hours on the 6th March 1968.

The Fire Control and Coordination Officer had some very good news to report.

When the *Khe Sanh* command structure had filed into the underground conference room, Colonel Lownds asked, "So what have you for us today?"

Captain Baig grinned like a Cheshire cat and said simply, "The North Vietnamese Imperialist Army is leaving *Khe Sanh en masse*."

Colonel Vortex felt almost disappointed as he cried, "Are you fucking sure? Damn it! Fuck it!"

"Positive!" answered the Captain.

"How do you know?" asked Colonel Lownds as Lieutenant Colonel Cahill studied the relief map of *Khe Sanh* on the conference table.

"All our seismic, electronic, acoustic and chemical sensors are indicating large scale movement away from the *Khe Sanh* area.

Some of the units are heading towards the imperial capital of Hue. But most of the remaining battalions and regiments of the 304th PAVN Division as well as the 325th C *Golden Star Division* and the 320th PAVN Division are withdrawing back into their border sanctuaries in Laos and North Vietnam proper."

Colonel Vortex pointed with an ivory baton that had been given to him by his great-grandfather who had participated in the American Civil War on the side of the Confederacy under General Robert E. Lee.

"What precisely are the movements of both the 304th and the 325thC?" asked the Colonel as he waved the antique baton around like a performing prima donna.

"Well," began Captain Baig as Colonel Lownds leaned over his shoulder, "…the 304th PAVN Division, or what is left of it!.."

There was a burst of laughter coming from all the officers in the conference room at those last words.

"…the 304th is withdrawing along an axis from *Khe Sanh* village/*Lang Vei/Tchepone* and into Laos. Presumably they are in the process of refitting and regrouping after the beating they have received from us and Operation NIAGARA.

However some of their units, approximately 2 regiments are remaining within the vicinity of *Khe Sanh* as, presumably, a covering force for the rest of the withdrawing divisions.

The intelligence boys at *Nakhon Phanom* in Thailand believe that about 30% of the Division is remaining behind. They also believe, after a thorough computer analysis of the sensor information that these troops are dug in along National Route 9 to the west as well as on Hill 471 which is astride the highway intended for our relief forces."

Colonel Lownds interrupted, "This elevation, Hill 471, could cause serious problems when Operation Pegasus is launched. It is a critical outpost that commands a view of the entire *Khe Sanh* Valley."

Vortex added, "You are absolutely right! I think we are going to have to take Hill 471 with the Pegasus assault."

Captain Baig informed as he held up some aerial surveillance photographs to the artificial light of the bunker.

"It's not going to be easy sirs! The PAVN are entrenched in multiple bunker and tunnel complexes that are interlocking and self-supporting."

Vortex smiled, "With all due respect Captain! My boys can handle them!" Colonel Lownds added, "You won't be able to flush them off Hill 471 with just the 9th Marines and some of my 26th. You are going to need the help of the 1st Cavalry Division (Airmobile)."

Vortex nodded as one of the 2nd Lieutenant's from the 8th Aerial Port Squadron came running down the sandbagged steps into the conference room.

Colonel Lownds held up his hand to signal him to wait.

"Continue with your briefing Captain."

The Fire Control Officer added, "The 325th C *Golden Star Division*, on the other hand is withdrawing northwards back across the DMZ into their sanctuaries there. They are taking up positions along the *Benttai River* with the 320th and 324th PAVN Divisions.

Some of the units of these latter two divisions have participated in the attacks on Hue."

Colonel Lownds nodded, "Thank you Captain."

The 26th commander turned to the USAF Lieutenant and asked, "Now. What is it?"

The air force officer seemed quite excited, "You better come out to the airstrip sir!"

Vortex asked, "What's wrong?"

"The MATU centre has had an emergency call from a C-123K *Provider*! The aircraft has been hit by Communist 37mm anti-aircraft fire. It's in trouble sir!"

Without another word Colonels Vortex and Lownds rushed out of the FSCC bunker to the runway. They were closely followed by the others as the officers streamed out in a long and madcap line.

Once atop the control tower Colonel Vortex called the MATU bunker.

"What's going on?"

The Marine air traffic control unit informed the Colonels that as a C-123 were making its final approach across the 800 foot escarpment to the south of *Khe Sanh* it had been hit by 37mm anti-aircraft fire and was trailing black smoke from its portside engine.

"There it is sir!" screamed Captain Richter as he lowered his field glasses and pointed to the hills east of the combat base.

"Shit!" screamed Vortex, "It doesn't look good!"

The C-123 *Provider* was clearly visible about 3,000 yards east of the airstrip.

It was losing altitude very fast and its nose was down. Thick clouds of black smoke were pouring from its portside wing.

The undercarriage was not yet down or locked for landing.

"What can we do?" asked Colonel Lownds helplessly.

"There is nothing we can do," answered Vortex as he followed the stricken aircraft with his field binoculars.

Major Thrush said with a tinge of horror in his voice, "Mary Mother of God! It's going to crash! We have to go out to those men and save them! They are crashing right into PAVN held hills to the east of the airstrip!"

Colonel Lownds nodded, "You're right Major."

Vortex grabbed both Major Thrush and Lieutenant Colonel Cahill as he said to Colonel Lownds, "I'm taking a small force with three *Cobra* gunships and a *Jolly Green*! I'm going out there to bring in any survivors!"

Colonel David Lownds said, "Good luck Vortex! I'll give you as much suppressive fire as I can."

The officers were watching the C-123K *Provider* as it used up the last moments of its existence.

The transport plane seemed to literally drop out of the sky.

It crashed into the side of a heavily forested hill about 3,000 yards from the *Khe Sanh* airstrip not far from the dreaded Hill 471 where units of the 304th PAVN Division were dug-in.

Both wings were sheared off and the fuselage burst into flames.

"It looks bad!" screamed Vortex as he ran with his entourage to the waiting *Cobra* gunships.

Captain Richter piled into the *Sikorsky* HH-53B with 50 elite Marines from the (VLRP) Very Long Range Patrolling India Company of the 1st Battalion, 9th Marines.

Vortex, Cahill and Thrush scrambled into the three AH-1's with another 50 Marines from the same unit.

Within seconds they were airborne and jumping the short 3,000 yards to their stricken C-123K.

"Jesus!" screamed Major Thrush.

The PAVN had opened up on the four choppers with heavy concentrations of 37mm and 0.51 calibre anti-aircraft fire.

The 37mm guns were highly mobile and were placed on large wheels. This allowed the Communists to quickly change the position of the guns as it suited them.

"Now listen up!" screamed Colonel Vortex to the Marine Lieutenant who flew the lead AH-1 *Cobra*.

The roar of the spinning rotor blades was deafening.

"I don't want you to fire anywhere near the downed C-123. Our wounded and dead boys are down there. I can't risk having any of our men wounded by *'friendly fire.'* Do you copy?"

The aviation Lieutenant shouted back briskly, "Understood sir! I will only fire upon your express orders sir!"

Vortex slapped him on the back as he leaned into the tight cockpit of the AH-1 and continued, "I want you to circle the *Jolly Green* as we land near the *Provider*. When I tell you that all our boys are loaded up – then you can hose down the entire area with your folding-fin rockets and 20mm Gatling guns. OK?"

"OK, sir!" answered the pilot above the drone of the *Cobra* engines.

The *Jolly Green* swooped in to the starboard side of the burning *Provider*. Captain Richter and his troops from the VLRP unit leapt out, followed by Vortex, Cahill and Thrush from the AH-1 *Cobras*.

Immediately the AH-1's powered back to a patrol altitude of about 2,000 feet and circled the area with large scythe-like sweeps.

The *Jolly Green* remained on station about 15 yards off the jungle floor.

"Shit!" screamed Vortex to Captain Richter, "The plane could not have crashed in a worse piece of jungle!"

The officers nodded as the VLRP Recon Marines spread out in a fan shape to encompass the aircraft.

They began to methodically sweep the area around the *Provider* for any bodies and/or survivors.

The C-123 had crashed on a steep incline of about 45 degrees. The wreckage was smouldering over more than 2 acres of triple canopy jungle.

It was an unmitigated disaster for Marine aviation.

"We're going to have a lot of trouble getting the bodies out sir!" said Lieutenant Colonel Cahill.

"That we are. That we are," sighed Vortex.

As usual, Colonel Vortex took point duty and advanced through some tall elephant grass with razor sharp edges.

"Cahill! You take half the force and move around the plane above us so that you come down on the wreckage from the apex of this hill. Scoop up any wounded or dead that have been thrown clear."

Lieutenant Colonel Cahill nodded and moved off to the left with his troops to reconnoitre the higher ground.

Vortex pressed on ahead. But he had an uneasy feeling about the whole operation.

The Recon Marines started to spread out around the bits and pieces of burning fuselage. They also found charred and mutilated American bodies.

The *Sikorsky* was hovering a little further down the hill as the body bags were brought out and the dead were hoisted into the chopper.

Major Thrush pointed to the tail section of the plane that was buried in a dense portion of the jungle.

Vortex and Richter moved forward with him. Their M16's in the firing position at their hips.

Suddenly Vortex dropped to the ground. He could see several Viet Cong females stripping and looting the corpses of some of the dead aircrew.

"I want to take one of these sluts alive. For interrogation," whispered Vortex to Richter.

The officers moved forward on their bellies through the rancid and stinking jungle on that desolate hill near *Khe Sanh*.

A twig crunched under Major Thrush's foot.

The Viet Cong females looked up.

Vortex saw to his horror that one of the women had slit open the throat of a still living Master Sergeant who had been the loadmaster for the C-123K.

The Colonel could see the black eyes of the Viet Cong girls as they scanned the jungle.

Then Colonel Vortex sprang forward like a Bengal tiger.

The VC girls leapt to their feet and started running.

With his initial movement Vortex could not grab one of them as he had hoped to.

The enemy opened fire with their AK-47's.

Captain Richter returned fire and caught two of the women across their breasts. Geysers of blood erupted from their flesh like crimson fountains.

The VC bodies fell to the ground.

Yet several more were still running higher up the slope.

Vortex scrambled after them as he pulled out his Marine dagger and placed it in his teeth.

He lunged again and caught one slim VC girl by the ankle.

Smashing his arm across the girl's face he kicked the AK-47 rifle out of her hands as she fired wildly. The bullets missed him as Major Thrush ran past trying to grab another enemy woman. The girl underneath Vortex reached up with her nails and scratched open three deep gashes in his face.

"You foul VC bitch! You slut!" screamed Vortex as he head-butted the enemy female. His own facial blood dripping onto her naked breasts.

She shouted in her native tongue, "You warmongering American pig! You are all going to die!"

Much to the girl's surprise, Vortex answered back in fluent Vietnamese, "You are the one who is going to feel the suffering of humiliation and defeat! You whoring VC bitch!"

The girl spat in Vortex's face as he stripped off all her clothes revealing a smooth, slim and delicious body that shivered in its nakedness.

Meanwhile Captain Richter and Major Thrush had each caught themselves a Viet Cong female by shooting at their ankles as they ran through the jungle thus immobilising them.

Vortex smashed his fist into the girl's breasts, thighs and vagina with vicious and pitiless force.

He reminded himself that he must have no remorse for these people.

This girl, who could have been no more than 19 years of age, had just murdered one of his fellow Americans in the most callous and unthinking manner.

Lowering his face to that of the VC girl, Vortex gripped open her mouth and inserted his tongue therein. He lavished inside that attractive face for some moments, savouring the sweet saliva of the enemy fluid force of evil.

His fingers probed that soft mound of the *mons pubis* while exploring the she-devil's vagina. He would have liked to possess that girl now in the middle of that stinking jungle of decay. To see her juices flow under the violent thrusts of his ramming pelvis.

But it was not to be. With mad rage Vortex licked, sucked and kissed the flesh that he had just beaten.

Then he intermingled his punches with lewd caresses.

The girl screamed until Richter and Major Thrush burst through the jungle foliage with their own female prisoners.

Meanwhile, Lieutenant Colonel Cahill had swept up the hill collecting dead Americans as he went. It appeared to him that there were indeed no survivors of that

awful and ill-fated plane crash. All 48 Marine and Air Force personnel onboard had been killed.

Cahill shook his head with dismay as he approached Vortex from above the wreckage.

Just as the Lieutenant Colonel's head turned around to speak to one of his Warrant Officer's who was taking point, a tremendous fusillade of small arms fire opened up all around them.

"Hit the dirt!" shrieked Cahill.

But the murderous crossfire of innumerable AK-47's and RPD light machine guns had already wounded four Recon Marines.

The Americans returned fire with great savagery as their blood was up from the air crash debacle.

Colonel Vortex grabbed the radio handset from off the back of one of the signal operators.

"Everyone back to the choppers! It's an ambush!"

Dragging the three naked VC girl-soldiers back to the *Jolly Green* the door gunners on the *Sikorsky*, who manned 7.62mm *General Electric* Miniguns grabbed the females by their breasts and long and luxurious hair and brutally catapulted them inside like pieces of toxic garbage.

One of the aviation Sergeants placed the three women on their stomachs and then sat on their naked asses with two other crew members.

Major Thrush chuckled as he followed Vortex back to the scene of the ambush.

A tremendous fire fight was in progress all around the burning C-123K *Provider*. The North Vietnamese had obviously withdrawn while the Marines had landed, waiting for the appropriate time to strike.

Calling the *Cobra* gunships Vortex ordered, "As soon as we are clear you pound the gook bastards to hell!"

Lieutenant Colonel Cahill was having trouble extricating his men from the ambush. Large formations of North Vietnamese had swung in from both the left and right flanks. They were laying down a carpet of savage fire that had the Recon Marines pinned with their backs to the burning aircraft.

Most of the American bodies had by this time been loaded onto the *Sikorsky*.

Before Colonel Vortex and his men had reached Cahill the PAVN decided to charge the whole American position in one massive assault.

The multitude of pith helmets burst out of the steep jungle from every direction. Swinging around with an M60 Captain Richter hosed down several attackers. Major Thrush found himself in the middle not only of his own troops but those of the enemy as well.

The combat became a vicious hand-to-hand contest as more and more PAVN literally swamped the Marine defensive perimeter.

"Watch out Captain!" shouted Thrush to Richter.

Two bigger than average PAVN imperialist soldiers had leapt onto Richter with their bayonets.

Catching one North Vietnamese by the hair, the Captain ripped the man over his back and drove his own knife through the man's right eyeball so that the blade vivisected his brain matter behind the optic chiasm.

It was wonderful to watch, thought Major Thrush.

A Corporal behind Richter stabbed the second PAVN aggressor soldier through his lower abdomen with his M16 bayonet. Blood gushed out onto the moist jungle earth accompanied by snake-like intestines. Slicing the bayonet free Richter caught hold of the enemies' skinny ass and held him still while the Corporal reinserted his bayonet into the man's penis and testicles almost ripping them off in the horrible mutilation.

When it was finished Captain Richter smashed the man's head sideways into the jungle dirt while shooting another PAVN who was about to stab Colonel Vortex in the spine from behind.

"Thank you!" shouted the Colonel.

Lieutenant Colonel Cahill had shot three PAVN terrorists through the heart with his Colt 0.45 pistol after his M16 rifle jammed (which they often did under battlefield conditions).

Unfortunately the M16 was not as reliable as the AK-47 which resulted in a Congressional enquiry later on. (But too late for the hundreds of American lives lost in Vietnam from 1962 to 1973 because of the failure of the M16 as a reliable weapon).

Major Thrush was struck on the back of his skull by the butt of an AK-47. Five of his Marines pulled him back to his feet. However several of those men were blown away by an RPG-7 rocket launcher.

The Marines were now in a desperate situation. Vortex could not call in an air strike from the *Cobras* because they were totally intermingled with the PAVN who kept pouring in reinforcements from all around the downed C-123K from their heavily fortified position on Hill 471.

Colonel Vortex knew that if they did not extricate themselves quickly they would be annihilated down to the last man.

Staggering forward over his dead and wounded men, Major Thrush opened up with his M60. He succeeded in knocking down several more PAVN when another RPG detonation sent hot steel fragments into his left cheek and both eyes.

"Aiiee!" shrieked Major Thrush. His face was blinded with blood as the mutilation of his eyes rendered him totally blind.

The Recon Marines behind Cahill could see the Major and they tried to make their way towards him as they fired at the advancing North Vietnamese.

With his arms outstretched as if begging for help, Major Thrush thought he was staggering towards his own Marines.

Instead he walked into the sharp edge of a Communist bayonet.

"Oh! No! Major!" shouted Colonel Vortex who was fighting from about 20 yards away.

A PAVN trooper had driven his weapon straight through the Major's guts. Long, thin trails of blood soaked intestines snaked out of the American's torso as a second North Vietnamese rushed up from behind and bayoneted Major Thrush in the back of his neck. The point of the knife exited through his throat as more bullets hit the officer.

Vortex ran towards the mortally wounded Major and killed the PAVN attackers with a burst of fire from his CAR 15.

Captain Richter caught hold of Thrush's blood soaked collar after pulling out both bayonets.

In the next few minutes the surviving Marines managed to run helter skelter down the heavily foliaged hill to the waiting choppers.

Once airborne the AH-1's launched everything they had at the Communists. The whole area was turned into a charred wasteland. The *Jolly Green* belched forth Minigun fire cutting to pieces the hordes of PAVN on the ground.

"Hang on Major!" screamed Vortex as he held his friend's head in his arms. Both men were covered in blood.

Seconds later Major Thrush died without saying a word except for, "Fuck those Communist turds!"

His injuries had been massive and critical.

"I've lost another friend!" cried Colonel Vortex.

Captain Richter and Lieutenant Colonel Cahill bowed their heads with genuine sorrow as the gunships wrecked their revenge, vomiting out a deadly stream of fire as they headed back to *Khe Sanh*.

"Sir!" said one of the Sergeants in the *Sikorsky*.

"What is it?" asked Vortex.

"Two of these gook bitches have committed suicide! I think they had cyanide ampoules in their mouths."

"Shit! You fucking moron! I told you to watch them! I wanted them for interrogation!" screamed Vortex, his face livid with fury.

He pushed the Sergeant out of the way and felt the pulse of two of the naked VC girls. They were indeed dead as white foam frothed from their lips.

Colonel Vortex picked up the naked corpses and kicked them out of the *Sikorsky* at an altitude of 1,500 feet. Their naked breasts bobbed up and down as they flew through the air.

Grabbing the third girl Vortex and Richter started to punch and kick her ass and vagina with savage force.

"Why are the Communists leaving *Khe Sanh*?" questioned the Colonel.

The female spat into Vortex's face.

Captain Richter head-butted her to the metal floor of the *Sikorsky* and copulated with the enemy woman so savagely that her womb was torn apart in a miasma of blood and ripped internal tissues.

Finally she revealed that the PAVN were indeed leaving *Khe Sanh*.

But she did not know why.

Lieutenant Colonel Cahill severed off both her ears.

Vortex also copulated with the VC murderess as did Lieutenant Colonel Cahill and some of the other Marines.

The *Jolly Green* was circling *Khe Sanh* while the lewd action was in progress.

The 105mm and 155mm guns opened up on the hill they had just left.

When the gross fornication had been completed to the satisfaction of the regulations relating to interrogation, Vortex and Richter dismembered the girl with machetes. They cut off her arms and legs and dumped them on top of Hill 471 after relinquishing them from the confines of the helicopter.

With the torso of the girl still living, Vortex unpinned a grenade and rammed it into her mouth. In the next second he picked up the bleeding trunk and threw it out of the *Sikorsky* at over 2,000 feet over Ta Con Village to the cheers of the Marines both inside the helicopter and also at *Khe Sanh* as they watched from below.

Colonel Vortex felt elated as a spring of joy had unpinned itself from the subterranean caverns of his mental anguish at the loss of the soldier of Peace, Major Thrush.

The WITHDRAWAL of the PAVN (North Vietnamese) from KHE SANH: 6th to 31st March 1968

Captain Mirza Baig had several meetings with the *Khe Sanh* staff. On the 12th March 1968 he reported to both Colonel Vortex and Colonel Lownds that at least 20,000 North Vietnamese Imperialist troops had left the *Khe Sanh* area.

However the intermittent fire from the PAVN artillery and mortars continued to harass the base.

The PAVN were also holding on to Hill 881 North with a full battalion. And they had no intention of moving from that strategic locale.

Hill 471 which was astride National Route 9 was also held by two battalions of the 304th PAVN Division which had remained behind to cover the withdrawal of the bulk of the 304th and 325thC PAVN Divisions. In other words as a rearguard.

Colonel Vortex made several visits to Hill 881 South on the 13th March 1968 and also the 15th, 21st and 25th March 1968.

He directed fire from *Khe Sanh*, the Rockpile and Camp Carroll against the PAVN held stronghold.

With Captain Richter he organised Company sized patrols to probe the defences of Hill 881 North.

Colonel Lownds was now replenishing his troops and evacuating the last of the wounded to base hospitals in Da Nang and Quang Tri City.

The commander of the 26th Marines also started to make offensive patrols into the hills around *Khe Sanh*.

The tide had turned and the siege was slowly coming to an end. It was now the Americans and the gallant ARVN Rangers who were doing all the attacking.

The Communists had also ceased to repair their trenches as of the 10th March 1968.

Colonel Vortex said to Colonel David E. Lownds, "They have fucking left to rot those motherfucking trenches that they tried to dig like moles – the bastard rats that they are! It worked at *Dien Bien Phu* but we taught them at *Khe Sanh* not to dig like cowards inside their underground trenches. For we are the teachers and they, - the fucked Communists are the students when it comes to warfare on a massive scale – that they are no match for us! We showed them the utter futility of their hopes and dreams of ever defeating the United States forces on the battlefield!"

The Lunar or TET Offensive had been crushed.

Only at Hue did the PAVN continue to hold out during March 1968.

Operation NIAGARA, however, did not wind down.

General William Childs Westmoreland, one of the greatest and most successful generals in the history of the prestigious Armed Forces of the United States of America wanted to kick and grind the Communists down even further while they withdrew from *Khe Sanh*. To this desire we owe him our greatest thanks and reverence. This is what Colonel Vortex realised and the majority of the troops in Vietnam.

Arc Light strikes continued to pound the North Vietnamese as they withdrew into their border sanctuaries.

The losses suffered by the 304th PAVN Division and the 325thC *Golden Star* Division were colossal.

What was the North Vietnamese Strategy at Khe Sanh?

As Colonel Vortex boarded an HH-53B *Jolly Green Giant* his mind crunched through all the different possibilities.

What had been General Vo Nguyen Giap's real aim in attacking *Khe Sanh*?

Had he really hoped to defeat the American War Machine in a large set-piece battle?

Was General Giap really that stupid? That moronic?

Didn't Giap know about the incredible weight and destructive power of the American air arsenal?

Had he not realised that his two elite North Vietnamese Divisions (the 304th and 325thC supported by the 320th and the 324th Divisions) would be virtually smothered and incinerated under an avalanche of high explosives and napalm?

And even if Giap had managed to capture *Khe Sanh*?

So fucking what? Thought Colonel Richard Vortex.

The US forces were strong everywhere in the South. It would only be a matter of weeks before the KSCB (*Khe Sanh*) base would be recaptured again.

Was Giap's plan to attack *Khe Sanh* in order to create a diversion for the planned TET offensive?

Did General Giap want to employ almost three reinforced divisions amounting to some 45,000 troops to pin down only 6,000 Marines?

It was completely crazy?

Why create a mere diversion to hold down only one reinforced Marine regiment with three of your first rate Divisions? This was a force which amounted to the bulk of the VC/PAVN strength in the whole of Northern I Corps.

It was ludicrous and idiotic strategy, thought Colonel Vortex.

If it had been a feint to draw US troops away from the TET offensive and their attacks it failed miserably. There were only 6,000 Marines and air men at *Khe Sanh*. A very small force compared to the total strength of over half a million American troops in South Vietnam.

Even the air power used at *Khe Sanh* was only a small fraction of that possessed by the US forces in the Republic of South Vietnam.

Whatever that bastard's plan was, thought Colonel Vortex, it had failed miserably.

General Westmoreland had achieved a brilliant victory not only at *Khe Sanh* but during the whole of the abortive and farcical TET offensive where the Main Force VC cadre had been almost annihilated *in toto* as an effective force.

Vortex pondered that if General Giap had hoped to draw major US combat units to the borders of Cambodia, Laos and North Vietnam by a series of diversionary attacks in order to attack the interior of South Vietnam and mainly its cities, then his strategy had failed again.

Vortex imagined that that fiend, Giap, must have forgotten about the US Army's incredible mobility.

A mobility which would allow 400 to 500 helicopters to transport half an entire Division with all its supporting arms from one side of South Vietnam to the other in less than six hours.

The Colonel also imagined that the coterie of mental defectives and criminals in the Hanoi Politburo were trying to recreate a 'magical' *Dien Bien Phu* from the ashes (*their ashes*) of *Khe Sanh*.

In that mad adventure of their minds they had been totally out of touch with reality.

The American Army in 1968 was not the French Army of 1954.

The American Machine of Peace and Security was the most powerful juggernaut on the face of the Earth.

The Americans were fighting for Freedom and Democracy.

They were not fighting to enslave and subjugate a free and independent people of South Vietnam who wanted nothing to do with the foul and rancid Viet Cong scum.

Robert Komer, the head of the Pacification Program in the Republic was having brilliant successes before the eruption of the TET offensive.

Robert Komer, thought Colonel Vortex, was one of the most brilliant and charming American officials ever employed by the Johnson Administration and he was doing a marvellous job in Vietnam along with William E. Colby who was in charge of the PHOENIX Program to root out suspected Viet Cong political cadres and operatives.

These cadres being responsible for the torture, intimidation, rape, murder and pillage of innocent South Vietnamese peasants who did not want to cooperate with the criminal organisation that made up the Viet Cong.

The only thing that Colonel Vortex regretted as he pondered all these questions was the fact that they had been unable to use tactical nuclear weapons against the PAVN at *Khe Sanh*.

Colonel Vortex would have loved to have seen the expression on the faces of Giap and Pham Van Dong if nuclear weapons had been used against Hanoi or *Khe Sanh*.

It was now noon on the 30th March 1968 and he was on his way to Ca Lu flying over National Route 9 for a meeting with COMUSMACV and MACV Forward.

Ca Lu was approximately 15 miles north-east of *Khe Sanh*.

It was to be the jumping off point for the much vaunted Operation PEGASUS involving 30,000 US and ARVN elite troops.

Colonel Vortex helped Captain Richter and Lieutenant Colonel Cahill into the hatch of the *Jolly Green* as the pain of his experiences at *Khe Sanh* racked his tired body.

He had lost Sergeant Leonard Crighton and Major Thrush and Major Lansdale.

His personal aide and his two best battalion commanders were dead.

Colonel Vortex tried to hold back the fury and ravaging lust for revenge and he did not want his men to see the weaknesses of his uncontrolled impulses to utterly destroy the Communists during Operation PEGASUS. But he could not pass a veil over the tumultuous hell-fire burning within.

The Siege of *Khe Sanh* had extracted a terrible price from him personally and physically.

Vortex also thought of Colonel David E. Lownds as he personally manned a 7.62mm Minigun in the hatch of the helicopter as it lifted into the air above the 800 foot escarpment to the south of the *Khe Sanh* airstrip.

Despite his early differences with the other Colonel he was grateful for Lownds' professional and expert defence of the crucial combat base.

"Sir! Look! The gooks have a 37mm set up over there!" cried Captain Richter as they flew to the east gathering speed. Immediately Colonel Vortex opened up with the Minigun while Lieutenant Colonel Cahill fired his M60 from the hatchway.

A stream of bullets came down upon the heads of the PAVN anti-aircraft crew.

"Circle around one more time!" screamed Vortex to the pilot of the *Jolly Green*. As the *Sikorsky* made a wide sweeping arc the other door gunner opened fire with the Colonel. Then the pilot fired rockets into the Communist gun position. A series of secondary explosions indicated that the ammunition dump next to the weapon had been hit.

"Do you see that?" asked Colonel Vortex over the roar of the huge rotor blades.

"Yes! Yes sir!" answered Lieutenant Colonel Cahill.

Two Viet Cong female irregulars were running through the jungle foliage away from the explosions.

"Take us down to 200 feet!" screamed Vortex at the pilot.

"I can't sir! It's too dangerous! We could be hit by gook machine gun fire!" shouted the pilot.

Vortex was livid with rage, "I said take us down to 200! That's an order!"

Reluctantly the pilot guided the massive chopper down to that low and highly dangerous altitude as three escorting UH-1E Huey's swung in behind Vortex's machine.

The rotor blades were skimming the top layer of the jungle canopy, blasting leaves everywhere in the up wash.

A roar could be heard to the starboard side of the four helicopters. It was six F-105D *Republic Thunderchiefs* coming in at Mach 1 to attack PAVN units around Hill 881 North.

Colonel Vortex aimed directly at the heads of the two young VC girls.

Then he opened fire with the Minigun.

"Jesus sir! Good shot!" said Captain Richter as he added his M16 to the fusillade.

Vortex continued to fire as the brains of one girl were literally scooped out of her skull by the hail of bullets. Blood, pieces of grey matter and broken arteries splashed through the air.

The other girl was cut down at her knees. Her spine was peeled open by the fire, revealing her blood-soaked and heaving lung tissue.

Vortex fired into both cadavers as the *Sikorsky* completed its final pass and they headed off to Ca Lu for a meeting with COMUSMACV and the mandatory succulent repast that was waiting for them as they would talk about Operation PEGASUS.

As the Sikorsky sped off at a higher altitude Colonel Vortex said laughing, "Fuck-me-dead! That makes me feel a lot fucking better!"

The Creation of Landing Zone STUD: 25th March 1968

When Colonel Vortex and his entourage landed at Ca Lu he could hardly believe his eyes.

The last time Colonel Vortex had been at Ca Lu was back in January 1968 before the siege of *Khe Sanh* had begun.

Now he could hardly recognise the place.

Since the middle of March the Marine and Army engineers, along with the Navy Seabees had converted the primitive base at Ca Lu into a premier installation. It was equal to anything in the Northern I Corps sector.

"My God!" exclaimed Captain Richter as they piled out of the *Sikorsky*.

"Its unbelievable how much they have done," added Lieutenant Colonel Cahill.

"Look at this 1,000 yard airstrip they've built," said Colonel Vortex.

Richter added, "…and the massive bunker complexes, the ammunition storage areas, the communication bunkers and radio reception facilities, the fuel bladders and maintenance depots!"

Colonel Vortex smiled at his men, "You know what this is for?"

Colonel Cahill nodded, "Operation PEGASUS."

As Colonel Vortex and his staff walked slowly across the aluminium planking of the newly constructed airstrip at Ca Lu they saw more than 150 UH-1E's and 1H's swoop in and land in rows for refuelling from the fat petroleum bladders that had been laid out.

The service crew on the ground were making ready to '*earth*' the aircraft to avoid a build-up of electrical charge which might ignite the helicopter into a ball of fire while taking on gas.

This technique was called, '*Hot-Refuelling*' and it was perfected in Vietnam. This permitted the UH-1E's and other craft from keeping their engines on while replenishing

their fuel so as to save time from a total shut-down and re-start of the main turbines. This meant the choppers could get back in the air faster as the down-time for re-firing the engines was about 20 minutes for a Huey-1D, Huey-1E or Huey-1H, as well the basic Huey-1B model – called *'The Thumper'* by the troops in Vietnam.

These helicopters were from the 1st Battalion, 7th Cavalry of the 1st Cavalry Division (Airmobile) under Major General John J. Tolson.

This unit was to spearhead the attack that would launch Operation PEGASUS.

Suddenly the 20 or so officers and NCOs' with Colonel Vortex saw the unmistakable figure of Major General Rosson walking towards them from the TAFDS station at the Ca Lu runway.

"Congratulations Colonel Vortex!" beamed General Rosson.

Colonel Vortex saluted his superior like a pistol shot.

General Rosson returned the salute and shook Colonel Vortex's hand with genuine enthusiasm.

Major General Rosson was over six foot tall with sparkling blue eyes and he had a supremely fit and athletic build.

Rosson was second-in-command of the III MAF under General Robert E. Cushman.

"How are you sir? We have just come in from *Khe Sanh*," informed Colonel Vortex.

"I know! I want to express my great appreciation for the magnificent job both you and Colonel David Lownds have performed for us at *Khe Sanh*! It was a superb performance and a skilful defence!" said General Rosson with great pride.

"Thank you sir," answered Colonel Vortex as they made their way to the Ca Lu communications complex in the middle of Landing Zone Stud.

Emerging from the bunker as they approached was Lieutenant General Robert Cushman and Major General Rathvon C. Tompkins.

Both Generals greeted Vortex and his officers with great warmth.

Also present was Major General Norman J. Anderson, the commander of the 1st Marine Air Wing.

"Richard! Are you alright? Are you hurt in any way?" asked Lieutenant General Cushman as he literally grasped both hands in a warm handshake which Vortex reciprocated by placing his hands on the General's shoulders. It was an unusual greeting for Marine general officers and field officers.

Vortex chuckled and smiled at Cushman, "I'm fine thanks! Sir! I am itching to take part in this relief attack! This Operation PEGASUS! Do I get a command for PEGASUS?"

General Cushman slapped his thighs with amazement and looked to Major General Tompkins, saying, "Jesus! Rathvon! You're boy never stops for even a second! He's

just come out of the meat-grinder at *Khe Sanh*! and he wants an attack force for PEGASUS!"

General Tompkins clapped Vortex on the shoulders, "Only the best officers are allowed into my 3rd Division!"

Everybody laughed as a swarm of helicopters from the 1st Cavalry Division passed by overhead.

"Listen Richard!" began General Cushman, "Are you hungry?"

"I'm famished sir," said Vortex.

"Good! Then let's have lunch. The Seabee boys have built a magnificent buffet restaurant for all field grade officers here at LZ Stud. But we're just waiting for COMUSMACV and the other big boys to arrive."

Vortex looked to Captain Richter.

Field Grade officers were those of the rank of Major and above.

This would allow Lieutenant Colonel Cahill to attend the top level luncheon conference with General Westmoreland but not Captain Richter.

"Sir! I request that an exception be made with respect to Captain Richter. The Captain is also the nominal adjutant of my 9th Marine Regiment."

General Cushman looked to General Tompkins and Anderson, both of whom nodded without hesitation.

"Of course! The Captain can also attend the high level luncheon briefing for Operation PEGASUS."

Just then a specially fitted HH-53B *Sikorsky* came in from the east.

"This must be COMUSMACV and Major General Tolson," exclaimed General Cushman with anticipation.

Five minutes later, as the enormous rotor blades of the *Jolly Green* were slowing their rotation, General Westmoreland stepped off the chopper.

A Marine brass band was lined up three deep and playing, *"Hail-to-the-Chief."*

COMUSMACV had arrived fresh from Phu Bai where he had had discussions with General Creighton Abrams.

MACV Forward was right behind COMUSMACV as was Major General Tolson, Colonel Kenneth Houghton (G-2 for III MAF), Brigadier General Phillip B. Davidson (J-2 for MACV), General William Momyer (Commanding General of the US 7th Air Force) and Brigadier General William McBride, the Chief of Sensor Operations in and around *Khe Sanh* and the DMZ.

The salutes and introductions were completed as General Westmoreland placed his hand on Colonel Vortex's shoulder.

COMUSMACV said, with all the other General Officers listening, "I can't express to you my satisfaction, the deep gratitude and heartfelt thanks that all of us owe you

Colonel Vortex! Your attention to duty, your super-excellent command of the troops at *Khe Sanh*, your vigour and aggressiveness in the attack plus your rock hard stubbornness in the defence has saved all of us at *Khe Sanh*! The same goes for Colonel David E. Lownds and I shall tell him likewise as soon as I see him in person.

Indeed, in the whole of Vietnam during this TET Offensive, you and Colonel Lownds have performed the execution of your duties to the utmost satisfaction of all concerned and to the highest standards of the Marine Corps bringing great credit upon yourselves and the Marine Corps and US Army and Air Force.

Congratulations! And again congratulations to you and of course to Colonel David E. Lownds!

It was a sterling and top-notch performance!"

All the generals clapped enthusiastically as did Captain Richter and Lieutenant Colonel Cahill.

"When I see Colonel Lownds," continued General Westmoreland, "...the same congratulations will be bestowed upon him together with decorations for both of you which I cannot yet reveal."

Colonel Vortex said, "Thank you sir. I hope that I can continue to perform to my utmost in this upcoming PEGASUS Operation. My only wish now is to totally exterminate the North Vietnamese criminal aggressor forces in I Corps without any inkling of pity, remorse or mercy! No quarter is asked for by them and no quarter shall be bequeathed unto them – for they are deserving of none!"

General Creighton Abrams smiled as the whole entourage, now some 150 officers, made their way to the luxurious officer's buffet restaurant behind the communications centre at Landing Zone STUD.

"You will go in with the 3rd Brigade of the 1st Cavalry Division to spearhead Operation PEGASUS," informed General Abrams.

Colonel Vortex was overcome with joy. His whole body trembled with delight at the prospect of continuing the fight against the Communists and the chance so graciously given to him to continue his extermination of the infestation, as he said, "Thank you sir!"

Operational Plans for PEGASUS

Ten minutes later the high ranking party were installed in their comfortable lounge chairs before an enormous mahogany dining table.

General William Westmoreland was seated at the head of the table with General Abrams on his right and General Tolson on his left. The other officers were placed down both sides of the table.

A late lunch was served starting with Russian eggs, garlic bread, onion soup and Beluga caviar for entrée.

"Can you please begin the briefing Major General Tolson?" asked COMUSMACV as he was served a succulent plate of Vienna Schnitzel with Caesar salad, onions and fresh steamed vegetables.

"Certainly sir!" said the commander of the 1st Cavalry Division (Airmobile).

General John J. Tolson put down his fork that was covered in delicious lobster Mornay and raised his left hand above his head clicking his fingers as he did so.

Immediately the door to the buffet restaurant opened and four NCOs' carried in a large map stand with a beautiful colour relief map of the whole DMZ area from Tchepone in Laos to Quang Tri City on the coast bordering the South China Sea.

Standing up Major General Tolson clicked the fingers of his right hand.

Seconds later another Staff Sergeant brought him his pearl handled and ivory shafted pointing baton.

Colonel Vortex thought it was even more beautiful than his own.

Tolson waved the baton around like an orchestra conductor.

"Now! If you please gentlemen! And sirs!" Tolson nodded his head towards Westmoreland, Abrams and Cushman.

General Momyer reluctantly interrupted his consumption of a plate of two dozen delicious oysters *Kilpatrick*.

Tolson commenced his highly detailed briefing as he placed the tip of his baton against the spot marked Landing Zone STUD.

"Operation PEGASUS is a highly integrated top to bottom operation that requires split second timing and faultless logistical support.

The attack will begin here at Ca Lu with the advance by the 2nd Battalion,

1st Marines and the 2nd Battalion, 3rd Marines. These two battalions will push forward along the Ca Lu/Route 9 axis of advance towards *Khe Sanh*.

They will be closely followed by the 11th Marine Engineers who will bring up bulldozers, trucks, repair machinery such as graders and cranes to fix up the quality of the highway that has suffered so much damage during the siege of *Khe Sanh*.

My 3rd Brigade of the 1st Cavalry Division will launch the spearhead of our air assault to directly support the two Marine battalions."

Colonel Vortex interrupted, "So I will be with the 3rd Brigade then?"

General Tolson nodded, "You will. Now can I please continue?"

Vortex nodded glumly as he fingered his plate of Devil's chicken and French fries with chilli sauce.

"Then, as the 3rd Brigade and the two Marine battalions continue their advance on D Day, which as you know is 48 hours from now on the 1st April 1968, the precise locus of attack will come into operation.

The 2nd Battalion of the 1st Marine Regiment will detach 2 Marine Companies late in the day on the 1st April. The objective of these two Companies will be to reach and secure Landing Zone ROBIN.

Landing Zone ROBIN has already been built. It is a small LZ just west of Ca Lu on the northern side of National Route 9.

The remainder of the 2nd/1st Marines will press on westward just south of LZ ROBIN.

The 2nd/3rd Marines will also push west just south of the highway.

Now! The 3rd Brigade, once airborne on D Day will split up into two assault forces. The whole force will have 350 UH-1E's and 1H's plus escorting firepower from 150 AH-1 *Cobra* gunships and two squadrons of Navy *Skyraiders* from Task Force 77.

In addition there will be massive B-52D Arc Light strikes all along Route 9 from the *Old French Fort* just south-east of *Khe Sanh* right up to Ca Lu.

The first prong of the 3rd Brigade will be made up of the 5th Battalion of the 7th Cavalry Regiment. This unit will helo-assault onto Landing Zone CATES, which is further west of LZ ROBIN and slightly further north of Route 9.

The 5th/7th Cavalry will then spread out in a concentric attack around LZ CATES to seek and destroy any PAVN in the area. This assault will take place on the 2nd April which is D plus 1. The second prong of the 3rd Brigade spearhead will be made up of the 1st Battalion, 7th Cavalry Regiment and the 2nd Battalion, 7th Cavalry. These two battalions will helo-assault onto Landing Zone MIKE on the 1st April.

LZ MIKE has been constructed just south of Route 9 and approximately on the same north-south axis as LZ CATES.

On D plus 1, the 1st/7th Cavalry will make a concentric attack around LZ MIKE to sweep away any PAVN forces in that area.

Simultaneously on the 2nd April, the 2nd/7th Cavalry will helo-assault onto Landing Zone THOR which is more than half way from Ca Lu to *Khe Sanh*.

LZ THOR will be reinforced later in Operation PEGASUS.

That completes the operations for D Day and D plus 1."

Brigadier General Davidson interrupted, "What will be the TAC air support for PEGASUS?"

General Momyer cut in and answered that question.

"The 7th Air Force will make sure that there will be at least 300 sorties launched in support of Operation PEGASUS in every 24 hour period."

Major General Anderson added as he sipped on a glass of wine, "I will commit every available Marine jet and chopper to the offensive. Probably 250 sorties per day."

Tolson exclaimed, "Excellent! Now! Let us proceed to the 3rd of April 1968 which will be D plus 2.

Colonel Lownds and the 26th Marines at *Khe Sanh* will launch an attack against Hill 471 which commands a strategic view of Route 9 as well as the whole *Khe Sanh* plateau.

The 26th Marines assisted by what is left of Colonel Vortex's 1st Battalion, 9th Marines will also thrust forward and clear the PAVN from their bunkers between *Khe Sanh* and Hills 881 South and 861A in preparation for a later assault against Hill 881 North."

General Westmoreland interrupted as he took another piece of garlic bread, "I want you to make sure that Colonel Lownds knows how crucial it is for us to take Hill 471. This is not only a major stronghold for the PAVN but it is critical for the Communist's resupply effort along Route 9."

Colonel Vortex munched on his Devil's chicken, "Don't worry sir! I'll get Lownds on the horn as soon as this briefing is concluded!"

COMUSMACV nodded as Major General Tolson continued with his highly detailed and intricate briefing while all the officers in the room took notes.

"Thus on D plus 2, the 3rd April 1968, I will send in my 2nd Brigade.

The 3rd Brigade should by then be fully engaged by the enemy at LZ CATES, MIKE and THOR.

The 1st Battalion, 5th Cavalry Regiment and the 2nd Battalion, 12th Cavalry Regiment will helo-assault onto Landing Zone WHARTON which is just south of the *Old French Fort*.

Simultaneously, the 2nd Battalion, 5th Cavalry will be carried by a gunship armada to Landing Zone TOM which is further south below LZ WHARTON.

On D plus 3, the 4th April, the 1st Battalion, 5th Cavalry will attack and hopefully secure the *Old French Fort*. It will also make a concentric attack around LZ WHARTON with the 2nd/12th Cavalry.

As you know the *Old French Fort* is only 2.5 miles south of *Khe Sanh* itself, below Route 9.

Also on D plus 3 the 2nd/5th Cavalry will attack north-west towards LZ WHARTON thus rolling up any PAVN in that sector.

The 2 Marine Battalions, namely the 2nd/1st Marines and the 2nd/3rd Marines will continue with their advance along Route 9. Hopefully by D plus 3 they will have reached LZ MIKE and smashed up the enemy forces along the highway.

On D plus 4, the 5th April 1968, I will unleash the final prong of Operation PEGASUS to crush the North Vietnamese and relieve *Khe Sanh* at last!"

There was a murmur of approval and relief coming from all the officers in the banquet room.

General Tolson explained, "On D plus 4 I will launch my elite 1st Brigade of the 1st Cavalry Division. The 1st Battalion of the 8th Cavalry Regiment and the 1st Battalion of

the 12th Cavalry Regiment will helo-assault onto Landing Zone SNAPPER which is about 2.5 miles south-east of *Lang Vei* (Old and New *Lang Vei*). At the same time the 5th/7th Cavalry will attack south-westwards from LZ CATES and the 2nd/7th Cavalry will attack north-westwards from LZ THOR. The 2 Marine battalions on Route 9 with their supporting engineers should have reached LZ MIKE.

Now! On D plus 5, which will be the 6th April 1968, the final scene to this great act will be concluded.

The 2nd/5th Cavalry will attack from LZ TOM to LZ WHARTON. The 2nd/12th Cavalry will move up to Hill 471 to reinforce Colonel Lownds and his 26th Marine Regiment and then move out further west from *Khe Sanh*.

The 1st/8th and the 1st/12th Cavalry Battalions will attack west from LZ SNAPPER.

And for the *coup de grace!*" shouted General Tolson as he waved his baton around in the air so that it almost touched General Creighton Abrams' nose.

"For the *coup de grace* I will send in the 84th Company of the 8th Airborne Battalion of the ARVN! Thus when the 84th Company land by choppers into the Marine Combat base the siege of *Khe Sanh* will be over!"

Colonel Vortex repeated, "The siege will be over!"

General Westmoreland looked with approval at the map and said, "Let's hope that the North Vietnamese resistance along Route 9 will not be too severe."

In that second there was a loud crashing noise and the double doors to the buffet restaurant swung open violently.

Everyone whiplashed their heads around.

It was Major General Olinto Barsanti, the commander of the 101st Airborne Division that almost stumbled across the room in his crazy haste.

"Glad you could make the briefing General!" shouted COMUSMACV.

General Barsanti swaggered over to the table and nodded to General Tolson, even though he didn't like the man.

"Thank you sir!" said Barsanti.

"But the briefing is over!" shouted General Creighton Abrams.

"Oh!" was all that the 101st Airborne commander said.

Then Barsanti smiled at Colonel Vortex and leaned over the table to shake his hand, "Bloody good work son!"

Vortex snapped to his feet and saluted the eccentric but capable Division commander.

"Thank you sir. We tried our best," replied Vortex.

"Oh! You did more than that! You and Colonel Lownds were bloody magnificent! My G-2 section in the 101st Division have estimated that no less than 17,000 gooks have been killed around *Khe Sanh*."

"I had no idea that it was that many sir?" said Vortex as he grinned to Lieutenant Colonel Cahill.

Brigadier Davidson laughed, "I think you are exaggerating General Barsanti."

The Division commander's face turned red with rage as he slammed his fist down on the table in front of a startled Brigadier Davidson.

"When my G-2 section tells me that 17,000 gooks have been killed at *Khe Sanh* then 17,000 gooks have been killed!" screamed Barsanti.

Brigadier Davidson's wine glass had been knocked over due to the General's antics and two NCOs' hurried up to clean the mess away.

"Alright! That's enough General Barsanti!" shouted COMUSMACV, who was starting to lose his temper.

"You can pick up all the operational details from General Tolson's staff. Now please sit down and listen!

Do you think that you can do that?"

General Barsanti nodded but then said, "Sir! I had a plan to relieve *Khe Sanh*!"

Vortex looked to Westmoreland as the Supreme Commander raised his eyes to the ceiling in a look of despair, saying, "And what was that General?"

Barsanti said enthusiastically, "We can parachute in my entire 101st Airborne Division right on top of *Khe Sanh*! Just like the French parachuted into *Dien Bien Phu*! Then me and my boys will spread out and kill those motherfucking North Vietnamese by the bushel!"

Westmoreland ran his hands over his face in a gesture of annoyance, "Is that your whole plan?"

General Barsanti said that it was and COMUSMACV said flippantly, "Well! I think we can forget about that Cockaigne Plan!"

There was hilarious laughter throughout the room as General Westmoreland said, "Now I want to discuss the plans for Operation SCOTLAND II to begin on the 15th April 1968 to push the enemy forces away from *Khe Sanh* and back into Laos.

I am going to relieve the four Marine battalions at *Khe Sanh* [26th Marine Regiment (1st, 2nd and 3rd Battalions) and the 1st Battalion, 9th Marine Regiment; plus the 1st Battalion, 13th Marines (artillery) & 37th ARVN Ranger Battalion] and insert three fresh Marine battalions plus two battalions from the 1st Brigade of the 1st Cavalry Division."

The conference went on for another 90 minutes as all the intricate logistical planning and TAC air was worked out for both PEGASUS and SCOTLAND II.

After the meeting, when all the officers were assembled outside on the airstrip of Landing Zone STUD, General Westmoreland drew Colonel Vortex aside to speak to him privately.

"I have been processing your papers myself Colonel Vortex," began Westmoreland.

"What papers sir?" asked Vortex with bewilderment.

General Westmoreland smiled and said, "Your promotion to Brigadier General."

CHAPTER 15
The RELIEF of KHE SANH

D DAY: 1st April 1968: The 3rd Brigade, 1st Cavalry Division (Airmobile) Attacks West of CA LU

After the incredible news from General Westmoreland, Vortex walked along the Ca Lu airstrip at LZ STUD in a sort of weird daydream.

Captain Richter and Lieutenant Colonel Cahill were on either side of their commander when a C-130E *Hercules* landed after coming in from Da Nang.

A small but beautiful South Vietnamese girl stepped off the *Hercules*.

Colonel Vortex could hardly believe his eyes.

It was his fiancée, Susie Ky.

The two lovers ran across the tarmac and embraced for what seemed like hours.

They were oblivious to the masses of troops, the jeeps, the M48 Patton tanks, helicopters, paraphernalia of war and the large transport planes that swirled around them spraying *Agent Orange* like a cleansing bath to wipe clean the filth and stench of the Communist scum-rats infesting the jungle about them, all in the huge concentration of unstoppable military power that was the magnificent and righteous United States Freedom Forces.

"I love you my sweetheart!" whispered Vortex into the delicate ear of the gorgeous girl.

"I'm so glad that you are unhurt Richard! Oh! I love you my darling! I love you more than I love *even* to kill the Communist douche-bags! And that *really* means that I do love you!" cried Susie Ky.

Captain Richter looked on with satisfaction from a respectable distance. He was convinced that Colonel Vortex had the immortality of an Achilles Hero in Vietnam. There was nothing that could harm his commander.

Everyman in the 9th Marine Regiment came to know their CO as;

'*The Exterminator.*'

Captain Richter smiled at Lieutenant Colonel Cahill and they walked away for a short rest in the officer's quarters at Ca Lu after Colonel Vortex told them politely to 'bugger off.'

Susie Ky and Vortex retreated to a sumptuous complex of senior officer's living quarters behind the LZ STUD airstrip.

"Do you want to hear some good news?" asked Vortex as he undressed and kissed Susie passionately.

"What is it my darling?" asked the delicious South Vietnamese beauty, the flower of anti-Communist womanhood in the Republic.

"I am going to be promoted to Brigadier General!" he cried.

"No? Fuck-me-dead! It's fucking not true! – Is it?"

"Yes! It sure as fuck'n is true! I get to command more men and bigger formations to exterminate the Communist vermin!"

"Oh! It's wonderful!" began Susie as they commenced to make passionate copulatory embraces under the whirling ceiling fan. The satin sheets underneath them caressed their naked and co joined flesh as Vortex still dreamed of killing the enemy even as he engaged in fornication. He was obsessed with cleansing the entire planet Earth of the Bolshevik pestilence.

"First God brings you back to me in one piece. And now you are going to be promoted!" cried Susie as she sucked on Vortex's ear.

"Now I have some good news for you Richard," she laughed.

Susie Ky told her lover that her Green Card permanent residency papers for the United States had just come in from the Embassy in Saigon.

They drank a few glasses of whisky to celebrate as Vortex said, "I have bought a small two storey house in Georgetown for us to live in."

Susie asked, "Where the fuck is Georgetown my darling?"

Vortex told her that it was right next to Washington D.C. and mentioned that it was a cool, crisp and clean city in which to live and he mentioned that most importantly it was largely free of Communists except for the Soviet and other Warsaw Pact spies at the Embassy and their staffs.

Susie was beside herself with joy.

Vortex said, "I got a really good deal on the house because I used to engage in discreet sexual intercourse with the Real Estate Agent that arranged the conveyance. Also I was not charged any estate agent commission fees."

Susie asked, "Was she a good root then?"

"Not as good as you my precious flower of Vietnam!"

Then she asked, "Your tour of duty as the 9th Marine Regiment commander ends in May 1968. Are you going to volunteer for another tour in Vietnam?"

Vortex told Susie that he must. As a Brigadier General he was sure to become an Assistant Division Commander or the Chief-of-Staff for a Marine Division.

She was not very pleased at that revelation but Susie realised that even though her lover and soon to be husband had to come back to South Vietnam to continue the struggle for freedom and democracy she would accompany him no matter what as long as he promised to supply her with a surfeit of guns and bullets. It would also give her a chance to be with her parents in Saigon.

After another intense bout of fornication and drinking they dressed and proceeded outside. There were a few people in the village of Ca Lu that Susie Ky wanted to visit. She also wanted to ferret out some Communist sympathisers in that locale so as to report them to the South Vietnamese Military Police so that they could be arrested, tortured and executed which, she thought, would give her great satisfaction.

"Colonel Vortex! What a surprise!"

The Colonel turned around and saw the familiar face of Captain Frank Willoughby, the Green Beret commander of *Lang Vei*.

Beside the junior officer was his lover, Monica Thang and her sister Susan. The trio had a miraculous escape from *Lang Vei* when it was overrun by Giap's forces on the 7th February 1968.

"Frank Willoughby! How are you? You son of a gun!" cried Vortex as he shook the Captain's hand.

Vortex asked, "Did you manage to exterminate that bastard Felix Poilane?"

Captain Willoughby asked, "How the fuck did you know about that?"

Vortex laughed, "A little anti-Communist bird on a tree at *Khe Sanh* told me all about your justified execution of that traitorous dog."

Willoughby answered that he had indeed done so with extreme prejudice.

Vortex introduced Susie Ky and kissed Monica and Susan Thang on their cheeks.

"The Colonel has told me so much about you," began Captain Willoughby as he kissed Susie's hand, "But your beauty far exceeds the descriptions that Colonel Vortex could give us!"

Susie Ky pretended to blush, "Why! Thank you Frank. You are too kind."

"So what are you up to now?" asked Vortex.

Willoughby shrugged his shoulders, "I have been ordered to get some R & R but I'd rather get back and screw those mongrel PAVN bastards! I'm itching for more action!"

Colonel Vortex stroked his chin thoughtfully and said, "How would you like to ride along with me? I'm going in with the 3rd Brigade of the 1st Cavalry Division in less than 48 hours. It will be good to have you along. Captain Richter and Lieutenant Colonel Cahill are with me also."

The Green Beret Captain needed no time to say yes. And he did so with relish in his voice.

Monica Thang pinched Willoughby's backside cheekily and laughed, "Frank! You're incorrigible!"

Everyone laughed and the happy group of five went off to dinner in the village of Ca Lu.

It was the calm before the final storm.

On the 1st April 1968 Operation PEGASUS Phase One began.

The day previously President Johnson had given his *'peace address'* to the American people.

Vortex had listened to it while interrogating and viciously beating some PAVN prisoners who had been caught murdering and raping innocent peasants outside Hue on the *Perfume River*. The Colonel thought that it was all double-talk and pure bullshit of the highest order. There could be no peace in Vietnam as far as he was concerned.

Colonel Vortex believed, as did a lot of other officers, that America's aim should be nothing less than the total extermination of the North Vietnamese Imperialist Army and the entire infrastructure of North Vietnam itself.

Vortex, Cahill, Richter and Willoughby flew over the 2nd/1st and the 2nd/3rd Marines as they were preparing to launch the initial ground attack. The 11th Marine Engineers were close behind the two elite battalions.

Also with Colonel Vortex was the commander of the 3rd Brigade of the 1st Cavalry Division, a Colonel Hubert Campbell.

"Are you ready?" asked Colonel Campbell who was about five feet ten inches tall, with a muscular build, brown eyes and hair and whose face was wrinkled with the strain and pressure of many months of combat in the 'NAM.'

"We are all ready Colonel!" answered Vortex.

The group of five officers were riding in a specially supercharged AH-1 *Cobra* gunship. They were accompanied by a squadron of the 1st Battalion, 7th Cavalry consisting of 40 UH-1E's and AH-1's.

The entire sky was filled with spinning rotor blades.

The noise was absolutely deafening.

Before flying in to Landing Zone STUD Colonel Vortex and his entourage touched down on National Route 9 to speak to the two battalion commanders.

"We are due to commence our attack at precisely 0700 hours sir," said the commander of the 2nd/1st Marines.

At that second the pre-arranged artillery bombardment commenced from the Rockpile and Camp Carroll.

The huge 175mm howitzers obliterated both sides of Route 9 but were careful not to impact on the highway itself as the 11th Marine Engineers would have to repair it

for the relief of *Khe Sanh*. Next stop for Colonels Campbell and Vortex was the airstrip at LZ STUD.

The sight, thought Captain Richter, was absolutely fantastic. The 1st Cavalry Division (Airmobile) had more helicopters than the entire Marine force in Vietnam which amounted to almost 3 Divisions.

There were 550 assorted helicopters at Landing Zone STUD for the beginning of Operation PEGASUS.

They included; HH-53B *Sikorsky's*; CH-54 *SkyCranes*; UH-34's; UH-1's; UH-1E's; UH-1H's; AH-1 *Cobras*; Ch-37's and CH-47 *Chinooks* as well as a host of other models like the '*Erector Set*' midget helicopters used by the PHOENIX Program Operatives as well as the CIA [Central Intelligence Agency] which had a very sizeable presence in Vietnam to assist in the extermination of the Communist political cadres and also for intelligence gathering so that the Operation PHOENIX personnel could locate, identify, interrogate and then liquidate the Main Force VC and their coterie of psychopathic sympathisers.

Major General John J. Tolson walked up with his divisional headquarters staff and gave a final briefing to Colonel Campbell. The time was now 0705 hours on the 1st April 1968 and the two Marine battalions had already moved in for the attack.

"Listen-up gentlemen!" began Major General Tolson,"…I want you to remember that we are conducting a bottom to top operation! This means that you must press the attack against the PAVN in a continuous and fluid stream. If you run into any pockets of stiff Communist resistance along Route 9 or in the boondocks then you go around it! Understood?"

Colonel Campbell shouted, "Understood sir!"

Colonel Vortex asked, "Do we know of any PAVN activity around the two Landing Zones at CATES and MIKE?"

General Tolson answered, "Latest intelligence from III MAF indicates that there are substantial remnants of the 304th PAVN Division in the area. So be on your guard. I shall remain here at LZ STUD in the Command and Operations Centre.

Good luck gentlemen!"

Both Colonels saluted and clambered into their AH-1 *Cobra* gunship.

All three airmobile battalions were lined up on LZ STUD. Rows upon rows upon countless rows of helicopters both large and small.

The 5th/7th was on the left, the 1st/7th in the middle and the 2nd/7th on the right of the Ca Lu airstrip. The choppers were lined up in huge rows that stretched for the full mile of LZ STUD's runway.

Nothing could be heard except the staccato whump-whump-whump of the endless forest of rotor blades.

Colonel Vortex was going to lead the biggest attack yet staged in Northern I Corps.

With a cool and professional voice, Colonel Campbell spoke into his microphone communications set under the helmet visor. Colonel Vortex sat next to him. The two pilots were in front and Richter, Cahill and Willoughby plus two door gunners were in the rear of the *Cobra*.

The command went out.

"Commence the attack!"

Each battalion lifted off in turn. Both Colonels would go in with the 1st/7th. This regiment had been General George Armstrong Custer's old command. But Vortex was determined that there would be no cock-up as had happened at the Battle of the *'Little Big Horn'* in June 1876 when Major Reno screwed up the orders because he was drunk while on duty.

Colonel Vortex only wanted to taste the sweet aroma of victory in his mouth.

The three cavalry battalions roared over the two Marine battalions on the ground.

Colonel Campbell was in constant communication with his three battalion commanders as the air armada of over 500 helicopters bore down on the vicious PAVN foe.

Even though the 304th PAVN Division had been decimated they were still capable of fanatical and determined resistance.

Fighting had already broken out just west of Ca Lu along Route 9.

The 2nd/1st Marines had run into 3 Companies of Main Force VC troops who were blocking the highway to *Khe Sanh*.

As the 2nd/1st worked slowly forwards taking the enemy fire the 2nd/3rd Battalion moved around in a flanking attack and dislodged the VC troops after vicious fighting.

Both sides had suffered numerous casualties.

Colonel Vortex could hear over the VHF tactical frequency that the 2nd/3rd Battalion had now run into a full battalion of the 66th Regiment of the 304th PAVN Division.

"It looks like progress is going to be quite slow with the ground assault," mentioned Vortex to Colonel Campbell.

The commander of the 3rd Brigade answered, "I know! But I can't detach any of my forces to help the Marine ground assault. I need all my troops for LZ MIKE and CATES."

Vortex nodded as both door gunners started to open fire with their Miniguns.

The 1st/7th was starting to receive Communist 37mm and 0.51 calibre anti-aircraft fire. Some of the choppers had already taken hits and casualties.

The 5th/7th battalion was approaching LZ CATES under heavy ground fire from an assorted mixture of PAVN/VC troops.

The 2nd/7th Battalion was blasting the entire jungle between Ca Lu and LZ MIKE with rocket and 20mm cannon fire intermixed with tracers while the infantry laid down white phosphorous to mark the targets for TAC air.

Within minutes both battalions were hovering over LZ MIKE.

F-105D *Thunderchiefs* were called in by Colonel Campbell. The choppers of the 3rd Brigade rotated within a 1.2 mile diameter of LZ MIKE as the fighter-bombers equipped with onboard radar worked the area over.

Sixteen THUDs came in at tree top level with anti-personnel flechette canisters and napalm.

The fighter-bombers turned the whole jungle around LZ MIKE into a charred molasses of smouldering vegetation.

"You see that?" asked Vortex, "…secondary explosions! The THUDS have hit their targets!"

Colonel Campbell nodded and ordered in the first wave of gunships from the 2nd/7th Cavalry.

The cavalry troops swooped in and detonated a small village next to LZ MIKE from where PAVN fire had been spotted.

The village was utterly destroyed as the first Hueys and *Cobras* landed onto MIKE, disgorging their troops.

When the 2nd/7th Cavalry were all unloaded the 1st/7th Cavalry remained in the air and swept forward to LZ THOR.

Colonel Vortex took over one of the Miniguns and blasted enemy troops on the ground as he spotted them from the hatchway.

Vortex killed anything and everything that was in range of his *General Electric* Minigun be they human or animal life. The cleansing fire of annihilation would prove to the Communists that it was utterly futile for them to hope for any victory on the battlefield against American arms.

Colonel Vortex knew that the cows, chickens, roosters, pigs and other animals had to die so as not to give sustenance to the Communist human-vermin.

Meanwhile, the 5th/7th Cavalry had made a successful landing against LZ CATES but had now run into a full PAVN battalion that was blocking any further advance to the west and towards *Khe Sanh*.

The vicious fighting continued for the rest of the 1st April 1968 – D Day for Operation PEGASUS.

D Plus 2: 2nd/3rd April 1968: The 2nd Brigade, 1st Cavalry Division (Airmobile) Attacks Towards LZ TOM and LZ Wharton

On D plus 1, the 2nd April 1968, Colonel Vortex called in B-52 Arc Light strikes against 2 mile diameter SLAM (Seek, Locate, Annihilate, Monitor) target zones around LZ CATES and MIKE.

There were still plenty of enemy troops stretched all the way from Ca Lu to *Khe Sanh*. Vortex also knew that mopping them up was not going to be a cakewalk.

The two Marine battalions were advancing only slightly behind schedule after calling in a massive series of TAC air strikes. They were now approaching LZ MIKE with the 2nd/1st Battalion taking point.

Colonel Vortex and his entourage spent a chilling night of the 1st April on LZ MIKE as the fighting raged all around them. Operation PEGASUS had taken the North Vietnamese completely by surprise. They had never expected such a concentrated and massive attack along their lines of communication and supply with the imperial city of Hue.

The Communists were now trapped in what is called an *'inverted front.'*

An inverted front folds the enemies' supply and logistical apparatus in on itself. The PAVN now had to fight hard from both directions and as a result their defensive perimeter started to crumble rapidly.

On D plus 1 Colonel Vortex and the 3rd Brigade commander flew into Landing Zone THOR with the 2nd/7th Cavalry.

After vicious fighting with the loss of 35 KIA and 138 WIA plus the destruction of 6 helicopters, the LZ was taken.

LZ THOR was only 3.5 miles south-east of *Khe Sanh*.

"Is that you Colonel Lownds?" asked Vortex as he radioed *Khe Sanh*.

"Its Captain Baig sir!" came back the familiar voice.

"Get me Colonel Lownds," asked Vortex.

A few seconds past and Lownds asked, "Is the 2nd Brigade of the 1st Cavalry Division (Airmobile) going to launch the second prong tomorrow as planned?"

"It is," answered Vortex as he asked, "What's the situation at *Khe Sanh*?"

The 26th commander answered, "My battalions and your 1st/9th Marines are preparing to attack Hill 471 in about 48 hours from now. We are also going to make a thrust towards Hills 861A and 881 South to clear the enemy bunkers that are dug into the valleys and hillsides on the low ground."

Colonel Vortex answered that that was good and signed off after informing Colonel Lownds that he was going to lead his 1st Battalion in their assault against Hill 471.

On the 3rd April, D Plus 2, the 2nd Brigade of the Cavalry launched itself from LZ STUD in another enormous air armada. This time the troops called in AC-119's which were another variant of the SPOOKY called SHADOWS.

These aerial gunship platforms called 'SHADOWS' had unbelievable firepower. The model used for PEGASUS contained four 7.62mm *General Electric* Miniguns and 3 20mm Gatling machine guns which sprayed out a veritable rain of death upon the heads of the PAVN and Main Force VC criminal aggressors.

Six SHADOWS took off from Phu Bai and Da Nang and were over LZ TOM and LZ Wharton before the 2nd Brigade arrived. The second prong of Operation PEGASUS involved in excess of 600 helicopters.

Colonel Vortex and Colonel Campbell joined the commander of the 2nd Brigade as his three battalions went into the attack.

The 1st/5th Cavalry and the 2nd/12th Cavalry landed onto LZ WHARTON after the SHADOWS had finished working the jungle surrounds over with deadly and accurate fire. But Communist resistance was still heavy as the Americans were now very close to *Khe Sanh* itself.

LZ WHARTON was barely 1 mile from the *Old French Fort*, the next objective of the 1st/5th Cavalry.

The 2nd/5th Cavalry Battalion swooped in on LZ TOM to the south of the main action around WHARTON.

Fighting was vicious and sustained as the 304th PAVN Division curled in its flanks to concentrate its remaining strength south and south-east of *Khe Sanh*.

The intention of the 304th PAVN Divisional commander was to block the American thrust to relieve *Khe Sanh* with everything he had left at his disposal. For awhile the Communist counter-attack worked.

But after a series of B-52D Arc Light strikes plus TAC air on the night of the 3rd to 4th April 1968, the PAVN started to crumple again.

The 304th PAVN Division was being attacked on so many fronts and all at once that this elite unit started to cave in.

The Communist troops were retreating everywhere in a rout.

The 1st Battalion, 5th Cavalry Attack the Old French Fort

At noon on the 4th April 1968, Vortex, Campbell and their entourage scrambled into their *Cobra* and Huey gunships for the assault on the Old French Fort.

The 1st/5th Cavalry was to lead the charge.

Two hundred and fifty helicopters that made up the battalion punched into the jungle south of National Route 9. The attack was preceded by a massive air assault from 12 THUDS and 16 F-4E *Phantoms* dropping 'iron bombs.' The smell of the petroleum-jelly reeked through the atmosphere as a hail of rockets descended upon the PAVN positions in and around the *Old French Fort*.

The colonial fort itself was a mass of broken masonry. But the rubble made for good hiding positions for the Communists as they fired up at the advancing helicopters.

"Land us over there! To the right of the Fort!" ordered Colonel Vortex.

The rest of the 1st/5th Cavalry were surrounding the Fort with multiple landings in a rough circle that stretched out to 500 yards from the entrenched PAVN. As soon as the Cavalry troopers disgorged from the helicopters they started to take casualties.

An RPG-7 rocket hit one UH-1E and burst it into a ball of flame. The troops inside were burnt to death. Two more gunships were shot down by 37mm fire and crashed into the rubble of the French Fort.

"Let's go sir!" screamed Captain Richter as he fired his M60 from the hip level.

Colonel Vortex had equipped himself with a M2 flamethrower while Captain Willoughby and Lieutenant Colonel Cahill carried M79 grenade launchers and M16's.

The four officers charged through the line of hesitant cavalry troopers and straight into the teeth of the enemy defence around the colonial fort.

It was sheer madness from the beginning.

Vortex was screaming, "Get out of the way! Get the fuck out of the way! I'm coming through with a flamethrower!"

The men of the 1st/5th Cavalry watched with awe as this mad Colonel started to spray fire into the concrete ruins.

Suddenly RPD light machine gun fire burst all around them from the enemies' direction.

Lieutenant Colonel Cahill screamed, "Aiiee!" as he held his bleeding face. But it was only a superficial flesh wound as a PAVN round had sliced off a chunk of his left cheek and fractured his mandible.

The Lieutenant Colonel ignored the excruciating pain and pressed on with the attack right behind Vortex and the two Captains. Watching the incredible action the cavalry troopers were impressed by the courage of these senior officers and by the example they set to the rank and file. So they got to their feet and scrambled after Colonel Vortex giving him as much suppressive fire as they could. There were ruthless NVA snipers dug in all over the ruins of the French Fort.

The 2nd Brigade commander helicopter'd in 155mm howitzers which he slung under CH-54 *Tarhe SkyCranes*. The artillery pieces were set up at LZ WHARTON and they had already started to fire behind the French Fort to block any Communist retreat from the area.

Colonel Vortex screamed as he shot huge sheets of flame from his twin M2 flamethrower tanks that were strapped to his back, "Die! Die you gook bastards! Fucking die! *Khe Sanh* will be saved!"

"Look sir!" shouted Captain Willoughby as he pointed and fired his M16.

About six North Vietnamese soldiers who had been hiding behind a partially collapsed wall of the Fort suddenly broke cover and ran away from the advancing US troops.

"Motherfuckers!" screamed Vortex as he took a few hurried steps forward and aimed his flamethrower nozzle right at them. He then depressed the lever and the burning arrow of flame engulfed the six PAVN bodies.

The shrieks and screams of the Communist soldiers were Satanic. Their bodies spun, writhed, contorted, danced and crawled with agony. Their skin turned from yellow to red to a crispy black as their eyes were liquefied by the intense heat.

"I've got them sir!" shouted Captain Frank Willoughby.

As the charred bodies started to collapse to the earth, the Green Beret Captain blasted his M60 into them.

The bullets broke apart the burnt flesh in a bloody orgy of filth.

Blood, intestines and limbs erupted everywhere.

Slowly the attack by the 1st/5th Cavalry was gaining the upper hand. The US troops were combing the ruined interior of the Fort. Snipers killed many of the cavalry soldiers before being killed themselves by M60 fire and M79 grenade launchers.

Vortex and his party had reached what appeared to be the central staircase of the colonial fort. Suddenly a group of NVA opened fire with their AK-47's. As the bullets whizzed past Vortex sprayed the staircase with flame. The fire licked at the crumbling edifice and one enemy soldier who looked no more than 15 years of age came screaming out from behind cover with his hair on fire.

"Ha! Ah! Ha!" laughed Vortex as he pointed to the enemy teenager. Captain Willoughby chuckled as he drew out his razor sharp throwing knife. As a Green Beret he was an expert in knife combat.

The boy was running his hands through his burning black hair and screaming horrifically.

Captain Willoughby threw his dagger with expert precision so that it impaled the young boy's throat and cut open his jugular. Blood sprayed out in crimson sheets as the Captain rushed forward and head-butted the boy. He then grabbed hold of the boy's testicles in his huge hands and crushed them to a pulp. The mangled flesh and blood vessels seeped through the black Viet Cong pantaloons.

At the same time he withdrew the dagger from the boy's throat and plunged it into his penis.

"Here! Catch this!" laughed Captain Willoughby to Captain Richter.

The junior Green Beret officer threw the mutilated body of the Communist over to the enormous Richter.

As the boy screamed with the knife embedded in his groin, Richter grabbed the boy's skull and with a vicious twist rotated it around more than 270 degrees. The face of the enemy was almost pointing backwards as the spinal cord was ripped free of the brainstem.

Captain Richter then kicked the bloodied mess into the mud.

By this time Vortex had manoeuvred around to the back of the ruined staircase. He caught the group of PAVN soldiers by surprise and tickled them with sheets of vomiting fire.

As Giap's troops dropped their weapons in agony trying to brush the incinerating fire off their flesh, Vortex rushed forward and started to savagely knife and cut them to pieces with his 18 inch Marine dagger.

In moments the earth was covered with mutilated bodies. Colonel Vortex met with Colonel Campbell at the rear of the *Old French Fort*.

"We've almost secured the area Vortex!" said Colonel Campbell.

"Good! I want to finish up here quickly! We have to be ready for tomorrow's assault on Hill 471," answered Colonel Vortex.

The 1,000 men of the 1st/5th Cavalry were now flushing out the few remaining pockets of PAVN resistance in and around the *Old French Fort*.

A roar came from overhead as a flight of 6 F-4E *Phantoms* streaked in heading towards Hill 471. They were to make a preliminary air strike against that PAVN stronghold in preparation for *Khe Sanh's* attack.

Just as Colonel Campbell looked skyward, bullets whizzed past his head. All the staff officers at the rear of the *Old French Fort* ducked for cover.

"It's more bloody gooks!" shouted Captain Richter, "…they are behind that broken wall next to the berm sir!"

Vortex leapt forward followed by Richter, Willoughby and Cahill.

Without waiting for suppressive fire from the cavalry troopers, Vortex jumped over the wall and caught several North Vietnamese soldiers crouching between the wall and the berm, firing their AK-47's.

The Colonel depressed his flamethrower lever and a shot of fire engulfed a couple of NVA. He pressed the lever again but no fire ushered forth.

To Vortex's horror he realised that the twin tanks on his back were empty.

Three PAVN soldiers saw this and turned their automatic weapons on the Colonel. They were just about to blow him away when Captain Richter and Captain Willoughby emerged from the back of the berm and shot two of them down. The remaining North Vietnamese soldier had time to press his trigger but the AK-47 did not fire.

Colonel Vortex saw this and ran forward towards the enemy. As the man tried desperately to fire his weapon at Vortex, the Colonel screamed, "Eat this! You fucking douche-bag Communist bastard!"

With a swift sliding action, Vortex peeled off the heavy steel tanks from his back and raised them high above his head. The PAVN soldier cringed and Vortex smashed the tanks down upon the man's head, stoving it in.

"Beautiful sir!" cried Lieutenant Colonel Cahill who leapt up from behind and knifed the man in the buttocks as Vortex lifted up the empty tanks and crushed them into the NVA's brain again.

Blood and brain matter sprayed everywhere in a revolting miasma.

"Whew!" sighed Vortex as he wiped the sweat off his brow.

"That was a close escape!"

The 1ˢᵗ Battalion, 9ᵗʰ Marines Attack Hill 471 : 4ᵗʰ to 5ᵗʰ April 1968

Colonel Vortex's battalion had already reached the approaches to Hill 471 which was about 1 mile south of *Khe Sanh*, on the morning of the 4ᵗʰ April 1968.

At 0400 hours on the morning of the 5ᵗʰ April, Vortex and his staff arrived back at the *Khe Sanh* airstrip. In only 24 hours from now, the epic siege of *Khe Sanh* would be officially lifted when the 84ᵗʰ Company of the 8ᵗʰ ARVN Airborne Battalion would be helo-assaulted onto the *Khe Sanh* airstrip.

This would be the first relief unit to directly fly into the Marine combat base since the beginning of the siege on the 21ˢᵗ January 1968.

Colonel Lownds was waiting for Colonel Vortex outside the MATU bunker complex adjacent to the runway.

The Communist shelling had all but stopped. For the moment anyway.

"Good to see you back so soon!" smiled Colonel David E. Lownds. Colonel Vortex clapped his fellow officer on the back, "We are nearly finished here Lownds! The 84ᵗʰ ARVN Airborne Company is due in tomorrow. Your outfit and mine are going to be rotated out of *Khe Sanh*. We have earned a break haven't we?"

Colonel Lownds offered Vortex a glass of water, "You bet we deserve a break Vortex!"

"We are going to be relieved starting from the 14ᵗʰ April 1968. General Cushman and General Tolson are sending in three fresh Marine battalions plus two battalions from the 1ˢᵗ Brigade of the 1ˢᵗ Cavalry Division," informed Vortex.

"Believe me! I'm glad to hear it!" cried Lownds.

Captain Baig interrupted, "This is Sergeant William Lanier from the 1ˢᵗ/9ᵗʰ."

Vortex and Richter stepped up to the Staff Sergeant and shook his hands.

"Of course! I know Sergeant Lanier!" began Captain Richter, "…he's in my company."

Captain Mirza Baig continued the outdoor briefing as C-130 Hercules transports flew in to the *Khe Sanh* airstrip with thousands of pounds of fresh supplies.

"I've ordered in massive TAC air and B-52 strikes on Hill 471. We've softened up the PAVN that are dug in on the crest of the hill. But only ground troops can dislodge them completely.

Sergeant Lanier will take you gentlemen up to Hill 471."

Colonel Vortex asked as they moved across the tarmac's aluminium planking, "What is the current situation on Hill 471?"

The NCO answered, "Sir. Your 1st Battalion has moved only about one third of the way up the hill. The air strikes could not destroy the enemy bunkers which are on the forward face of the hill. Only a direct hit by high explosives can knock out these elaborate bunker systems.

Your men are pinned down by heavy PAVN fire coming from these bunkers. There are also considerable numbers of North Vietnamese troops hiding on the apex of the elevation inside the massive bomb craters caused by our B-52 Arc Light strikes."

Vortex looked at Lieutenant Colonel Cahill and screamed, "Jesus! What's the matter with your men? They should have taken that hill by now! This is not how we are going to end the siege of *Khe Sanh*!

I am going out there to kick some butt!

I'm going to exterminate those fucking motherfucking rat bastard Communist douche-bags on Hill 471!"

Then Captain Richter turned around to the Quartermaster who was standing behind Captain Mirza Baig, "Get me some *Bangalore* torpedoes! I want you to load them onto these two *Sikorsky's*! Get a move on!"

The Quartermaster scurried away.

Colonel Lownds said, "We'll give you as much fire support as we can."

Vortex nodded as Captain Baig said, "If you need any additional TAC air just ask me."

"We must clear the PAVN off Hill 471 before tomorrow when the ARVN relief force arrives!" warned Vortex as he added, "The 1st Brigade of the Cavalry has already started its attack. The final phase of Operation PEGASUS has begun!"

Captain Frank Willoughby added as he looked at Colonel Lownds, "The 1st Battalion, 8th Cavalry and the 1st Battalion, 12th Cavalry are already in the air and heading towards LZ SNAPPER which is just south of *Lang Vei*. General Tolson has planned to retake *Lang Vei* by the 14th April!"

"Excellent!" cried Lownds as he slapped his palms together.

Ten minutes later the *Bangalore* torpedoes as well as satchel charges, C4 plastic explosives and detonation caps had been loaded onto the waiting HH-53B *Sikorskys*.

Colonel Vortex and his entourage clambered onto the *Jolly Greens* for the short 1 mile hop to Hill 471.

Colonel Lownds and the 26th Marine Regiment were launching its own aggressive patrols into the area around Hills 881 South and 861A. This was a preparatory move to clear the PAVN out of the immediate vicinity of those critical hills before the big attack against Hill 881 North would be launched. It was here that a full PAVN battalion of the 325th C *Golden Star Division* was still dug in and mortaring the US positions inside *Khe Sanh*.

The Major in temporary command of the 1st Battalion on Hill 471 saluted Vortex and Cahill as the *Jolly Greens* were unloaded at the base of the elevation. A platoon scurried up and unloaded the *Bangalore* torpedoes.

"I want the choppers to dust off immediately!" began Colonel Vortex, "…then I want them to blast the crest of the hill with their Miniguns!"

The Marine pilot saluted and the two huge gunships roared skyward to commence their attack.

Lieutenant Colonel Cahill grabbed the handset from a radio operator and called in an AC-47 SPOOKY gunship which vomited out a deadly rain of fire on the forward slopes of Hill 471.

"Let's get a move on!" screamed Colonel Vortex as the air strike was underway.

The commander of the 9th Marines picked his way up the hill to the forward position in front of the enemy bunkers. Sniper fire from the Communists was intense as three Marines were wounded and two killed in the last 6 hours.

"Attack! Get up! You are United States Marines! Get up! The battle is almost won! Just a few yards more!" screamed Colonel Vortex as he grabbed one Marine after the other and pulled them out of their trenches by their camouflage collars.

Vortex and Richter stood side by side in full view of the enemy fire and launched RPG-7 shoulder rockets at the PAVN which had been captured from them.

They had captured the RPGs and other Communist weapons from the *Old French Fort* the day before.

The RPGs slammed into the bunker entrances as the three Companies of Marines from the 1st Battalion stormed up the slope.

Cahill, Richter and Vortex lead the way as they leapt into the bunkers through the dirt holes in the rugged slopes of Hill 471. Immediately the fighting became a vicious hand-to-hand contest.

Vortex could feel a pair of skinny hands grip his throat in an attempt to strangle him.

It was almost pitch black inside the bunkers.

Taking out his double edged Marine knife the Colonel sliced it into the unseen testicles of the Communist. At the same time he head-butted the NVA trooper.

Vortex could feel the warm blood over his trousers as he lashed his throat free and crushed the man's trachea with a vicious grip of steel.

Captain Richter took two platoons and fired his way into the bunkers on the southern side of the hill.

Lieutenant Colonel Cahill led another four platoons to the right flank.

Vortex grabbed the *Bangalore* torpedoes from Captain Frank Willoughby and with about 50 demolition specialists from his battalion started to insert the long

hollow metal tubes into the earthworks of the Communist bunker system. The high explosives were then fed into the *Bangalore* tubes as the NVA sniped at the American sappers, killing and wounding many of them.

The machine gun fire was horrendous as the enemy put up a stiff battle to retain Hill 471.

A thundering roar sent the entire hill reverberating from the detonation of the *Bangalore* torpedoes.

"Take cover!" shouted Colonel Vortex as a wall of black earth spouted into the atmosphere above their heads.

Nine hundred men of the battalion dived for cover as the rippling series of explosions continued to break apart the enemy strongholds. A swarm of North Vietnamese troops scurried out into the open as their subterranean hideouts fell in on their heads.

Colonel Vortex knifed one in the guts as the man ran straight into the Marine positions.

Captain Willoughby caught a group of enemy soldiers as they tried to run further up the hill. He decimated them with his Minigun and then ran after the wounded hacking them to pieces with a large machete.

Blood flowed hot and soft through the putrid jungle earth.

Captain Richter screamed, "Watch out Lieutenant Colonel Cahill!"

Three NVA soldiers had charged up behind Cahill and were about to shoot him in the back.

Richter hosed all of them down with his M60. But two Marines nearby were cut to pieces by AK-47 fire.

Vortex ordered, "Hand me those satchel charges!"

Sergeant William Lanier threw the canvas bags full of explosives over to the Colonel.

Vortex grabbed a handful and rushed into the ruined bunkers followed by his other officers and troops.

The whole battalion was now sweeping up the hill. The Marines were more than 70% of the way to the apex, their final objective. As Captain Richter followed Vortex into the dark and stinking recesses of the PAVN's mud holes they discovered that more than a whole company of North Vietnamese were still hiding in the bowels of the earth.

Colonel Vortex thought that the North Vietnamese were nothing but an 'army of treacherous moles.'

Lieutenant Colonel Cahill turned over a dead Communist with the point of his bayonet and recognised the insignia on the uniform.

"Sir! These gooks are from the 66th North Vietnamese Army Regiment. It is an elite unit of the 304th PAVN Division."

Colonel Vortex scoffed as he fired his M60 into the dark vaults before them, "I don't care how elite these mongrels are! I'll fucken slaughter every last one of them! Its pay back time!"

Captain Richter shouted to his men, "Be alert! Be on guard! Don't touch the dink corpses! They might be booby-trapped!"

Just as the Captain spoke he was blown sideways as metal fragments tore into the flesh of his buttocks almost cutting his scrotal sacs.

"Jesus! Bloody Christ!" screamed Vortex as he was knocked over by the airborne Richter.

An SP4 had leant down to turn over a dead North Vietnamese contrary to the Captain's instructions. There was a grenade with a trip wire attached to the underside of his body. The movement set it off and killed the SP4 as well as wounding three other Marines.

"For heaven's sake!" shouted Colonel Vortex as he helped his close friend and comrade-at-arms, Captain Richter back to his feet.

"I'm telling you again! Don't touch the dink bodies in this bunker system! Just shoot a few rounds into their skulls if you think the mongrels are still alive and use a length of rope tied around their feet if you want to move them or drag them anywhere," ordered Colonel Vortex.

The 350 Marines behind the Colonel shouted their confirmation of the orders.

As they spread out through the dark recesses of the underground foxholes, firing erupted everywhere as the Americans flushed out sniper after NVA sniper.

No prisoners were taken as the Communist's usually always fought to the death.

Each bunker system was joined to the one above it on Hill 471 in an interlocking complex of defences.

The PAVN had been quite skilled in linking the bunkers to each other so that they were mutually supporting with overlapping fields of fire.

As Vortex advanced doggedly forward, Lieutenant Colonel Cahill was nearing the crest of that battered hill with the remaining strength of the 1st Battalion, some 550 men, which included the aggressive and gung-ho A Company.

"Jesus! Look at this sir!" screamed Captain Frank Willoughby as he prodded a huge cache of rice.

Colonel Vortex stepped forward and was amazed to see what looked like a mountain of rice under the roof of the bunker.

In addition the Communists had stored vast quantities of 7.62mm rounds, 81mm mortar shells, blasting caps, fuses, wires, C4 plastic explosives, AK-47 rifles and at least 200 RPG-7 rocket launchers.

"There must be at least 700 tons of rice here."

Captain Richter clicked his fingers and ordered, "You men! Get some gasoline and pour it over this food!"

Thirty Marines took about 20 minutes to douse the rice with oil and then Colonel Vortex blew it to hell with a grenade. The weapons were carried to the surface and airlifted back to *Khe Sanh* for Colonel Lownds and Major General Tolson's inspection.

Suddenly an enemy soldier jumped onto Captain Frank Willoughby as the officer took point while rounding a corner in the next bunker up the hill.

The Green Beret was an expert in unarmed combat and pugilistic techniques.

Captain Willoughby was a pure Communist killing machine. He had no pity, no remorse and no regret when it came to enemies of the United States of America and he willingly dispatched them to the netherworld.

Willoughby was one of the finest soldiers ever produced by the US Special Forces. And he was looking forward to getting back to the Northern Force Command Group for further action in the *A Shau Valley* for the rest of 1968.

With the movement of a slippery eel, Captain Willoughby crushed his fist inside the man's mouth and tore out his tongue. As the NVA blood poured over his camouflage tunic the Captain whiplashed the enemies body under his own and drove his Special Forces dagger deliciously into the man's heart, twisting the steel to right and left thus mutilating the myocardial muscle.

"Boy!" exclaimed Colonel Vortex, "You don't do anything at half measure, do you Captain Willoughby?"

The Green Beret officer kicked the corpse off his body and jumped to his feet as he wiped his blood stained dagger across the dead NVA's pants.

"No sir! My job is to kill these scum Communist pricks anyway I can."

A few of the Marines who passed by laughed as they threw grenades into the rear of the bunker.

Finally, as Vortex's two Companies were emerging from the last of the subterranean hideouts they were greeted by a hail of AK-47 and RPD light machine gun fire coming from the top of Hill 471.

Lieutenant Colonel Cahill's three Companies were also pinned down just 100 yards from the summit and their final objective.

"How many of them do you think there are sir?" asked Captain Richter as he picked the razor sharp steel fragments out of his bleeding ass.

"Fucked if I know!" screamed Colonel Vortex.

Then Vortex looked at his friend, "Jesus! Don't you think you better get back to *Khe Sanh* and have those buttock wounds looked to? You've done enough today Richter."

The Captain shook his head and used a handkerchief to staunch the flow of blood from his ass and legs, saying, "No sir! I want to see this miserable fucking hill taken! I want to see the gooks die in a total cohesive mass of death!"

The Colonel nodded as he grinned widely.

"Very well my friend," said Vortex as he called in the AC-47 SPOOKY gunship that was circling in a left hand orbit around Hill 471. It was flying out to a radius of 1.5 miles from Hill 471.

The flying Minigun platform swooped in and blasted the crest of Hill 471 with a renewed shower of death.

The screams and shrieks of the North Vietnamese could be heard coming out of the bomb craters at the top of the elevation.

The PAVN jumped, scurried, dived, crawled, ran and died under the stream of Minigun fire.

Their back was already broken.

Now it was time for the 1st Battalion, 9th Marines to move in for the kill.

Sergeant William Lanier led the charge of A Company with Lieutenant Colonel Cahill right next to him. As Lanier dived headfirst into the first bomb crater he crashed into four young PAVN soldiers.

The four NVA were merely teenagers of about 13 to 15 years of age. They screamed like girls as their voices had not yet broken.

Sergeant Lanier lunged on the nearest two.

He gripped their black hair and smashed two of their skulls together.

Small pieces of brain matter and sprinkles of blood splashed onto Lanier's face as both boys suffered compression fractures. One of the bigger boys behind punched Lanier in the spine causing him to fall face forward into the mud and excrement at the bottom of the B-52D bomb crater.

Lieutenant Colonel Cahill cut his fist loose into the neck of the boy who had punched Lanier.

The fourth boy swung at the Lieutenant Colonel but missed.

"You dirty young cur!" screamed Cahill as he kicked the boy in the testicles with his steel-capped army boots crushing one of the scrotal sacs in an orgy of fine sprinkling blood.

Lanier scrambled back to his knees and head-butted the third NVA teenager.

Colonel Vortex had just scrambled over the crest of the crater when he saw the vicious hand-to-hand contest between the two huge men and the four skinny Asian boys.

He was furious that Cahill had not killed them yet.

"What the fuck is the matter with you? Can't you dispatch these second-rate enemy troops! Fucking kill all of them now!" screamed Colonel Vortex as he was trembling with undiluted rage and venom.

Captain Richter scurried along the bottom of the crater like an enormous 265lb cockroach with a huge dagger between his teeth. Before Sergeant Lanier knew what was happening, Richter had stabbed the first NVA boy through the kidneys. Lanier

followed suite by knifing the same boy through his left eyeball. The stab was so powerful that Lanier's blade slid deliciously through the entire brain of the child and punched a bloody hole through the back of the skull.

Captain Richter re-plunged his dagger into the boy's penis and testicles, as well as his asshole and his heart as he saw the tip of Lanier's Marine knife spurt through the blood washed skull.

Colonel Vortex approached the fracas with a steel garrotte in his hands.

[Garrotte: Definition: Strangulation device used by the Spanish Inquisition to execute criminals by throttling them to death.]

The third NVA teenage soldier had gripped Lieutenant Colonel Cahill from behind and was pressing his fingers into the officer's eyes trying to gouge them out.

"Aiiee!" shrieked the light Colonel.

Vortex kicked the second boy in the guts as Lanier pistol whipped him. In the same easy, swift movement, Vortex noosed the garrotte around the third boy's neck, the steel wire already cutting into the soft flesh like a hot knife through butter. This was the signal for Captain Richter and Colonel Cahill to pounce on the second boy while Lanier executed the fourth according to the Rules of Engagement and with the full sanctions of the *Laws of War*.

The Captain and the Lieutenant Colonel threw the 13 year old NVA soldier between their massive bodies.

Richter crunched a Karate blow to the boy's nose, crushing it flat into his face.

Colonel Cahill caught the body as it flung towards him and viced his huge hands around the boy's penis and testicles. The gonads were slowly crushed under immense power, the blood and mashed groin tissue spilling out of the NVA's pantaloons.

Colonel Vortex was savagely ripping into the neck and spine of the child-soldier under his care.

The garrotte had stripped away all the flesh right back to the cervical spine.

"I'm going to decapitate you!" screamed the Colonel.

Lanier kicked the boy in the heart as Colonel Vortex finally tore off the child's head in a gruesome display of physical strength and prowess.

Sergeant Lanier then gripped the skull of the last PAVN soldier and rammed it into Vortex's fist which was held out in front for just that purpose.

"Jesus Mary!" laughed Colonel Vortex, "Do you see that?"

Vortex's fist almost stoved-in the entire skull of the teenage Communist as Cahill and Richter lunged over to knife the body that Sergeant Lanier was holding.

The officers performed more than 87 stab wounds into the reeking carcass of the PAVN soldier.

The mutilated corpses of the four boys were left where they had been killed as the men of the 1st Battalion trod right over them in the relentless advance to take and crush Hill 471.

The 66th North Vietnamese Army Regiment Launch a Counter-Attack Against Hill 471 on 5th April 1968

One hour after reaching the apex of Hill 471 the 1st Battalion, 9th Marine Regiment was victorious in taking the hill.

Colonel Vortex and his officers manoeuvred the battalion around the PAVN held bomb craters and showered the Communists with grenades, 106mm recoilless rifles and M60 fire.

"Take this and eat it!" screamed Captain Richter as he drove his bayonet through the open mouth of one North Vietnamese soldier who was lying in the blood and filth of the crater with half his intestines hanging out.

Lieutenant Colonel Cahill cornered three NVA soldiers who had run out of ammunition. He hosed them down with his M60 severing their legs off from above the knees.

"Look at this sir," said Captain Frank Willoughby, "…it's finished here. We have the hill!"

Colonel Vortex nodded as five *Sikorsky Jolly Green* helicopters swooped in to medivac out the American wounded and to collect the dead. (USA dead)

There were only a handful of PAVN prisoners out of a whole enemy battalion.

The famous rats from *Khe Sanh*, in all their varying colours and sizes came out to devour the mutilated remains of the North Vietnamese 'mole' soldiers.

Hill 471 looked like a vast unburied cemetery.

To their surprise an elegant and smart looking officer jumped out of the hatch of one of the HH-53B's.

It was Captain Mirza Baig.

"Captain!" cried Vortex with surprise, "I didn't know that you occasionally get your hands dirty in the field? I thought you were a REMF!

[REMF: Rear Echelon Motherfucker]

I thought you were confined to the comfort and security of the FSCC and MATU bunkers?"

Captains Richter and Willoughby chuckled as they wiped their blood drenched daggers across the bodies of some dead PAVN carcasses.

Captain Baig also smiled as he saluted Colonel Vortex crisply, "I wanted to take some fresh air and see some of the action for myself sir."

Colonel Vortex slapped his thighs and laughed, "Captain! You won't find any fresh air out here! Just the reeking stench of these fucking filthy gook bodies!

And besides you are too fucking late to see any action! We just finished here on this fucked piece of shit-turd called Hill 471!"

The Marines standing around laughed along with the senior officers.

There was a wonderful feeling in the air (stinking air according to Colonel Vortex) that the *'Agony of Khe Sanh'* was just about over.

It was almost a sense of bizarre elation that swept through the ranks mixed with the feeling of an enormous anti-climax.

But the agony of *Khe Sanh* was not quite over – not yet.

"Why are you really here Captain Baig?" asked Colonel Vortex as Cahill offered the Fire Control Officer a cigarette.

"Because of that!" said Baig with concern in his voice.

The Captain's hand was pointing to the south-east from the direction of the *Perfume River* and the imperial city of Hue.

"I can't see anything!" shouted Colonel Vortex as he strained his eyes in the stipulated direction.

"Have my field binoculars sir!" offered Captain Willoughby.

Captain Richter and Lieutenant Colonel Cahill were already standing on the highest point of Hill 471 and looking through their eye pieces.

Richter placed his two feet on top of the skull of a dead enemy soldier to give himself a few inches of extra height.

Then Vortex could see what Captain Baig was talking about.

A whole group of junior officers and NCOs' from the 1st Battalion now walked up excitedly and looked into the distance behind their stalwart commander.

"When did you spot them?" he asked the Fire Control and Coordination Officer.

"A few hours ago sir," answered Baig.

"How many?"

"Probably two full battalions."

"Where did they come from?"

"From their camp near the imperial city of Hue on the *Perfume River*."

Captain Richter nudged his Colonel's shoulder, "Its trouble sir!"

Colonel Vortex smiled back at his friend, "I know!"

"Colonel Lownds has been informed," added Captain Baig.

"Good," was all that Vortex commented.

There were a few minutes of eerie silence.

Foreboding filled the air. The hundreds of Marines standing with their commander prepared their weapons afresh as they looked to the south-east.

"I've planned a hot reception for the putrid motherfuckers!"

Vortex grinned at Captain Baig's last colourful metaphor.

In that immediate second illumination shells shot out from the artillery at *Khe Sanh*.

Three AC-47's and two AC-119G's or SHADOWS as they were called, glided in from the direction of Da Nang and started to blast the North Vietnamese battalions as they advanced towards Hill 471.

The rain of bullets from the five SPOOKY and SHADOW gunships was absolutely incredible. Already one of the PAVN battalions was being pulled apart.

"Intelligence from the G-2 section at III MAF has identified these units to be two battalions from the 66th North Vietnamese Army Regiment. We also think that they have been ordered to attack and retake this hill. Aerial reconnaissance has been following them since they left the banks of the *Perfume River* about 36 hours ago in a forced march."

Lieutenant Colonel Cahill admonished, "That's just great! What the fuck are we supposed to do now? One tired under strength battalion against two fresh ones!"

Colonel Vortex interrupted, "Don't worry! Our fine Captain Mirza Baig has some goodies in store for them."

The Fire Control Officer said, "You remember sir, the way we crushed the Communist thrust against the 37th ARVN Rangers on the 29th February 1968?"

"How can I forget it!" cried the Colonel.

"Well! That is exactly what is going to happen now sir," answered Captain Baig.

Immediately the screeching sound of the atmosphere being ripped apart was heard over Hill 471 and at *Khe Sanh*.

The heavy batteries of 175mm guns were opening up from their positions at the Rockpile and Camp Carroll.

The point enemy battalion was already approaching the slopes of Hill 471 from the far side.

They caught the full fury of the American artillery as the computer at *Khe Sanh* worked out the exact trigonometrical trajectory coordinates and pre-arranged defensive fields of fire. The FSCC bunker then wired them to the batteries at Camp Carroll.

Captain Baig pointed upwards as a deep thunder rolled over Hills 861A, 861, 881 South and Hill 558 where nearly 1,000 Marines of the 26th Regiment were still dug in blocking the northern approaches to *Khe Sanh*.

As the SHADOWS and SPOOKY gunships peeled off after their mission, the radar-equipped fighter-bombers bolted into the attack.

Colonel Vortex could see with his field glasses, the PAVN troops caught right out in the open to the south-east of Hill 471. The landscape in this area was more desolate than the moon.

"There is nowhere for the fucking PAVN to hide!" laughed Captain Willoughby as the first wave of F-4E's, F-105's and A-6's jettisoned their napalm and flechette canisters.

A rolling swirl of petroleum jelly flame engulfed the point battalion.

Hundreds of men screamed as their lungs were incinerated, their flesh charred and their bones crushed.

The survivors joined the second enemy battalion as the fighter-bombers dropped their ordnance then went vertical to reach their patrol altitude of 20,000 feet. The 105mm, 155mm and 175mm artillery from *Khe Sanh* and Camp Carroll did the rest of the work.

"They are still advancing over that dead lunar landscape!" cried Vortex.

"They won't get far sir," said Captain Baig.

The 1st Battalion had set up their M60's and 106mm recoilless rifles from the summit of Hill 471.

Now it was they who had the advantage of the elevated position.

The downward angle of fire was to prove devastating to the PAVN attack.

The Marines vomited out tens of thousands of rounds as the artillery ripped apart the second PAVN battalion belonging to the much vaunted 66th PAVN Regiment, 304th Division.

"They are about to crumble sir!" said Lieutenant Colonel Cahill with great relish.

The North Vietnamese bodies were falling one atop the other in a grotesque orgy of death. Body limbs and intestines were splattered through the air.

It was the end of the abortive Communist attack on Hill 471.

The Relief of Khe Sanh : 6th April 1968 84th Company, 8th ARVN Airborne Battalion Lands at Khe Sanh

"Fire at the bastards!" screamed Colonel Vortex, "Kill them in rows before they get to the perimeter!"

The 1st Battalion, 9th Marines poured everything they had into the Communists. But still they staggered forward.

The *Khe Sanh* artillery had orchestrated a rolling barrage to keep pace with the advancing PAVN battalions.

The first battalion had already melted away.

The second PAVN battalion was about to become ancient history.

"The dinks are only 100 yards from the wire!" screamed Captain Willoughby who pumped M79 grenades into the foe with devilish fanaticism.

"They won't reach the wire at all," said Captain Baig calmly as he spoke to the FSCC bunker through his AN/PRC-41 field radio.

"Are you so sure?" asked Colonel Vortex.

"I am sir," repeated the handsome and youthful looking Captain Mirza Baig. [Soon to be promoted to Major and decorated for his super-excellent work during Combat SKYSPOT and in the organisation of numerous SUPERGAGGLE Missions in support of *Khe Sanh*.]

Colonel Vortex lowered his binoculars for only a few seconds as the 66th PAVN Regiment, or what was left of it, staggered towards the perimeter now only 50 yards away.

Captain Richter listened to what his commander was saying as he fired his M60 like a madman but with a pure purpose that smacked of sanity.

"You know something Captain Baig?" asked Colonel Vortex.

"What sir?"

"These Communist troops are incredible!"

"How do you mean sir?" asked Captain Baig with astonishment in his voice.

"I mean,…" hesitated Vortex, "I mean they never give up! They just keep coming! What drives them? Surely not the *'Communist Manifesto'* by Karl Marx and Friedrich Engels?"

[See: *'Communist Manifesto'*; by Karl Marx & Friedrich Engels; First Published 21st February 1848 (United Kingdom); contains the authors views about the nature of society and politics, and in their own words;

"The history of all hitherto existing society is the history of class struggles."

Also expostulates on how the Capitalistic Society of their times being the 19th Century would eventually succumb to the regime of Socialism and then Communism. The Book was first published in German.]

Colonel Vortex was racked with a sudden avalanche of doubt.

Could the United States really win the war in Vietnam?

Did it have the morale to carry the fight through?

As Richard Vortex watched the two battalions of the 66th PAVN Regiment being cut to pieces he wondered whether such fanaticism could ever *really* be defeated.

Maybe the whole struggle of the United States in Vietnam would in total be another *Dien Bien Phu*?

Not in terms of just one battle like *Khe Sanh*.

But in terms of the entire fiasco and debacle that America found itself in while attempting to prop-up the decaying regime of South Vietnam.

Vortex did not know anymore – not for certain.

His heart was filled with terror for his beloved country.

The country that he had served and would continue to serve for the rest of his life.

"I don't know sir?" answered Captain Baig as the artillery from *Khe Sanh* itself intensified.

Vortex looked to the Captain and then observed that only a few dozen of the NVA had managed to get within 15 to 20 yards of the defensive positions of his 1st Battalion.

The Communists received massive Minigun fire from a renewed assault by the SPOOKY gunship platforms.

This broke their forward momentum.

The two pulverised battalions fled back down Hill 471.

The engagement was over.

Then Captain Baig smiled and said, "They are like you sir! Because you never give up either!"

On the morning of the 6th April 1968 the entire *Khe Sanh* operational staff stood behind their two Colonels at the edge of the KSCB airstrip.

Every Marine and Seabee inside the perimeter as well as the artillery boys from the 13th Marine Regiment watched the horizon to the east.

Each man knew in his own heart the fears he had vanquished during the 77 day siege of *Khe Sanh* and what fears still remained to be unleashed upon him.

Colonel Vortex looked at Colonel David E. Lownds and started to speak. His voice was strained with emotion.

There were tears in Colonel Richard Vortex's eyes.

David Lownds could see those tears. He understood.

More than any other man, it had been Vortex who had carried through the heroism and gut wrenching determination of the *Khe Sanh* defence.

Lownds knew that he had been the guiding brain, the cool intellect and the command authority on the ground that had saved *Khe Sanh*.

But he also realised that he could not have saved the combat base without the magnificent performance of Colonel Richard Vortex.

Vortex had been the raw and undiluted energy which had galvanised the men into an indestructible bulwark against the savage and relentless Communist forces.

Lownds looked at this enormous man, this Marine par excellence.

Despite their early disagreements Lownds had nothing but admiration for this remarkable warrior.

America, thought Lownds, should be proud to have such sons.

There are none finer, thought Colonel Lownds.

Vortex began to speak as the staccato whump-whump-whump of many helicopters could be heard approaching *Khe Sanh* from the east.

"Operation PEGASUS LAM SON 207A is a classic example of airmobile operations.

Its inception was brilliant. Its execution faultless.

LAM SON 207A has shown how a large Divisional force can be moved with speed, surprise, manoeuvrability and devastating firepower to smother the enemies'

lines of communication, turn his flanks and bewilder his troops that are simultaneously being ripped apart from the air and engulfed by
multi-directional attacks."

Colonel Lownds nodded, "Yes! We have totally thrown the 304th PAVN Division and the 325th C PAVN Division off balance."

Vortex added, "This Operation PEGASUS could not have succeeded without the combined and efficient team work of all four services. It is a credit to all the staffs and personnel of the United States Navy, Army, Air Force and Marines!"

Lieutenant Colonel Cahill nodded his approval and pointed to the hills that lay east of *Khe Sanh*.

"They are coming sir!"

There was intense excitement from the more than 2,500 Marines and airmen in the *Khe Sanh* perimeter.

The Marines on the hill outposts could also see the relief force swooping in.

"The 84th Company of the 8th ARVN Airborne Battalion is on schedule!" exclaimed Colonel Lownds.

Fifty UH-1E's and AH-1's started to land in rows upon the battered aluminium planking of the now famous KSCB runway.

A tremendous cheer went up from all over the base.

Some of the Marines started to dance on the huge CONEX containers [large metal boxes] that were used to build the bunkers.

Colonel Lownds and Vortex ran up to the command chopper and greeted the ARVN Captain commanding the 84th Company.

The South Vietnamese officer was short but powerfully built at only five feet seven inches.

He saluted both Colonels as his airborne rangers started to disembark from the choppers.

"Good to see you! Captain!" said Colonel Lownds.

"The siege is lifted sir!" answered the ARVN officer.

Colonel Vortex asked, "Has the 2nd Battalion, 12th Cavalry commenced its attack from LZ WHARTON to us here on Hill 471? My men up there need to be relieved as soon as possible."

The ARVN Captain informed, "Yes sir! I've just been in touch with Major General Tolson at operational headquarters Landing Zone STUD.

The General has informed me that the 2nd/12th Cavalry is already en route to Hill 471. They should arrive in about 30 minute's sir. The Cavalry is shooting up all the stray PAVN units that they can find between LZ WHARTON and *Khe Sanh*."

Elements of the 3rd Brigade, 1st Cavalry Division (Airmobile) Arrive at Khe Sanh on 8th April 1968

"Excellent!" cried Colonel Vortex.

"Captain! I want your men to join my 26th Marines in clearing out the enemy bunkers around Hills 861A and Hill 881 South in preparation for our attack on the PAVN Battalion that is entrenched on Hill 881 North.

Only when we recapture 881 North will the *Khe Sanh* base be completely secure."

The commander of the 84th ARVN Company saluted smartly and joined one of Lownds' battalion commanders.

The South Vietnamese troops went into the attack that very afternoon.

This clearing of Hills 881 South and 881 North would be the culmination to Operation SCOTLAND I.

[Operation Scotland I: Defence of the Khe Sanh/Lang Vei area: Commenced: 1st November 1967: Terminated 31st March 1968: US Casualties: 205 killed in action; 1,668 wounded and 25 missing presumed dead; does not include losses at Lang Vei suffered by the 5th Special Forces group under Captain Frank Willoughby's command nor the losses of Marine aircrew lost from downed aircraft nor the losses of Marines exiting or entering the base while leaving or boarding US aircraft. Communist losses; (estimated); 1,602 killed according to body counts; 7 prisoners captured; but US J-2 for MACV estimate that between 10,000 to 15,000 PAVN troops were killed during the defence of Khe Sanh, which is 90% of the attacking aggressor forces of 17,200 men. The claim by the North Vietnamese that they lost only 2,500 killed during the Khe Sanh/Operation Scotland I operations is totally ludicrous and preposterous. But then what else do you expect from Communist disinformation techniques.]

The fighting inside the Communist bunkers around *Khe Sanh* was just as vicious as at the height of the siege.

Also that afternoon, the 1st Battalion, 9th Marines returned to *Khe Sanh* from Hill 471 after the 2nd Battalion, 12th Cavalry relieved them from that position to the south of *Khe Sanh*.

The 1st Battalion, 8th Cavalry and the 1st Battalion, 12th Cavalry both from the elite 1st Brigade, 1st Cavalry Division (Airmobile) began their attack towards *Lang Vei* from LZ SNAPPER.

This assault was a vital preparatory move for the planned retaking of the ruined US 5th Special Forces group Camp at *Lang Vei*.

As on the 6th April 1968 both Colonel Lownds and Colonel Vortex greeted Colonel Hubert Campbell as he arrived with a vast force of over 300 helicopters on the afternoon of the 8th April 1968.

The commander of the 3rd Brigade had brought with him the entire 2nd Battalion, 7th Cavalry.

"Gentlemen!" began Colonel Campbell, "The 84th ARVN Company was just the spearhead of your relief!

I now have the pleasure to formally relieve the *Khe Sanh* Marine combat base in the name of MACV Forward, III MAF headquarters and Major General Tolson, the commander of the 1st Cavalry Division (Airmobile)."

Colonel Vortex looked to Colonel Lownds and Lieutenant Colonel Cahill with joy and relief in his eyes.

"Congratulations! Gentlemen!" beamed Colonel Campbell.

"It has been a magnificent and stupendous performance against overwhelming odds!"

Captain Max Richter lost his composure and fell into Colonel Vortex's arms.

The two enormous Marine warriors gave each other an unashamed bear hug.

"Well done Richter!" cried Vortex as he slapped the beefy Captain on the back.

"And thank you sir for your unyielding support, your understanding and your compassion for our troops!" cried Richter.

"You are a good man Captain!" said Vortex, "Will you stay with me in our service to the Marine Corps?"

Richter almost suffocated with emotion as he said, his voice choking with tears, "I shall stay with you sir even if you are assigned as a fucking toilet attendant in the Pentagon!"

Despite the emotionality of the moment there was a burst of hilarious laughter from both Colonel Lownds and Colonel Campbell.

Captain Frank Willoughby stepped forward and embraced Colonel Vortex with genuine warmth and enthusiasm.

"As for my part sir, let me say that it has been an honour and a privilege to serve with you in these difficult but exciting times! I feel obligated to say that your example to the men not only in the Marine Corps but in the Army Special Forces and the Air Force has been a foundation of courage and devotion to duty that is seldom exceeded!

I only wish sir, that you were with us in the Green Berets! The Marine Corps of our great and beloved United States of America cannot imagine what a fine officer it has in its ranks!"

Colonel Vortex was stunned by the appreciation shown to him.

He had imagined that he was only doing his duty like every other Marine in the Corps.

He said, "Thank you for those kind words Captain Willoughby! But if I fuck-up enough in the Corps I might very well find myself in the Green Berets!"

Cahill, Lownds and Campbell drew closer as Vortex continued, "But let me say this to you gentlemen. I believe that senior officers such as ourselves are only the guiding hand for our troops in the field. The real credit, the real glory and the real honour for our victory here at *Khe Sanh* against an evil and pernicious enemy, goes entirely to the young men and women who make up our command. It is the young men from Iowa, from Arkansas, from Kentucky, from the hamlets of Virginia, the towns and cities of New Jersey and California and Washington State! And all the other towns and counties of America. These are the real heroes of *Khe Sanh*!

I salute every one of them.

I love each man as if he were my own son!

Never has America had such fine sons! Such men that are willing to sacrifice their all, their very lives! In this nasty and confusing war in Vietnam.

All my thanks and heartfelt gratitude goes out to them!"

Colonel Lownds was mesmerised by Vortex's heretofore unrevealed sensitivity.

He had thought that the Colonel was simply a brutish killing machine.

'An Exterminator.'

How wrong had he been.

Now Lownds could see that underneath the diamond hard surface was a sensitive and honourable man that followed the rules and *Laws of War*.

A man full of passionate emotion for everything American.

A man of feeling and empathy for the men and women of the United States.

"Well said Colonel! Well said!" approved Colonel Campbell.

A vast crowd of over 300 officers and senior NCOs' greeted the men of the 2nd Battalion, 7th Cavalry as they poured off their UH-1E's, UH-1H's, Ch-47's and AH-1's being over 1,500 strong.

The siege of *Khe Sanh* was truly over.

Immediately 3 Companies of the 2nd/7th went into action north-west of *Khe Sanh*.

The cavalry troopers attacked the remnants of the 325th *C Golden Star Division* with a vengeance.

The *Cobra* gunships of the 2nd/7th, fresh and devastating, massacred any PAVN soldier caught out in the open around Hills 861A and 881 South.

What was left of the North Vietnamese forces retreated to their last remaining stronghold at *Khe Sanh*.

This was the formidable Hill 881 North.

The Communists had 130mm and M46 artillery, 81mm and giant 120mm mortars dug into firing positions on that hill.

The battle for Hill 881 North was destined to be the last action of Operation PEGASUS – LAM SON 207A.

Lieutenant David Peter EHRLICH

1st Battalion, 8th Cavalry Regiment, 1st Airborne Brigade Recapture the US Special Forces Camp at LANG VEI : 10th April 1968

Between the 8th and the 10th April 1968 the men of the 2nd Battalion, 26th Marines and the 2nd Battalion, 7th Cavalry continued their assault north-west of *Khe Sanh*.

Captain Dabney of India Company welcomed Colonel Vortex and Colonel Lownds to Hill 881 South on the early pre-dawn morning of the 10th April 1968.

"Is the TAC air ready?" asked Lownds to Captain Baig.

"Its coming in now sir!" began the Fire Control officer, "…eighteen F-105's from the 'hot pad' at Da Nang."

Colonel Vortex was looking through his Starlight scope with Captain Richter. They were on the summit of Hill 881 South which commanded a good view of the valley below.

It was still semi-dark in the pre-dawn atmosphere.

The air was humid and the reeking stench of the jungle was all around them.

There was also the rancid odour of rotting human flesh mixed in with cordite.

The infamous *Khe Sanh* rats had abandoned their cosy home amongst the Marines and were busy devouring the dead and mutilated flesh of hundreds, perhaps thousands of North Vietnamese bodies strewn all over the hills around *Khe Sanh*.

Under the catastrophic air bombardment the PAVN had been unable to bury all their dead. They were suffering too many casualties in the burial squads.

"Well? Captain Dabney!" began Colonel Lownds, "It's almost over for you."

Captain Dabney smiled and said with exhaustion in his voice, "It's been a hard contest sir!"

"That it has been," added Vortex as a roar of jet thunder could be heard coming in over the distant Hill 471.

The *Republic Thunderchiefs* came in line abreast.

Then each fighter-bomber peeled off for its napalm and H & E run.

Colonel Lownds said, "There are only a few remaining bunkers on the reverse slope of this hill and that of Hill 861A.

We'll finish the enemy off with this air strike and then I've ordered the 2nd/7th and my 2nd/26th to move into the slopes for the final kill.

We are going to root them out and destroy them!"

Vortex said to Richter, Cahill, Willoughby and the others, "Gentlemen! More than anything else it is our airpower that has saved us at *Khe Sanh*. I have just received information from III MAF headquarters which states that never in the history of warfare has there been such a massive application of air power upon one specific operational target.

The daily average for tactical air sorties exceeds 360.

The Strategic Air Command [SAC] has been able to provide an average of 45 B-52 and B-52D Arc Light sorties per day.

The concentration of air power has been unprecedented!

Approximately 1,800 tons of high explosive, napalm and flechette ordnance has been dropped on the positions around *Khe Sanh* per day for the entire 77 day siege.

Huge swathes of jungle have been obliterated into charred molasses and the enemy has suffered hundreds of secondary explosions as his supply dumps, storage areas, communication centres and vehicular assets have been incinerated under an avalanche of bombs.

Over 100,000 tons of bombs have been dropped during the siege of *Khe Sanh* which is more than double that dropped by the US *Army Air Force* [as it then was] in the Pacific Theatre during the whole of World War Two for the years 1942 and 1943!"

Captain Richter wrung his hands together with supreme relish and enthusiasm, "Its beautiful sir! What a magnificent effort by our fly boys!"

All the officers nodded gratefully as Vortex continued.

"But it was the B-52 and B-52D Arc Light strikes that provided the biggest punch. Thanks to Captain Baig's brilliant fire control and coordination almost all the Arc Light sorties were right on target.

The psychological effect of these awesome machines on the enemy was absolutely devastating from start to finish!"

Lieutenant Colonel Cahill pointed, "Look at our air power now!"

All the officers peered through their AN/PVS-2 Starlight Scopes, penetrating the dark that was immediately ignited by a fireball of exploding munitions.

The THUDS were wonderful to watch.

The jets screamed towards the lower slopes of the enemy held terrain at over 500mph. When their ordnance glided gracefully out of the bomb racks the planes climbed into the vertical to regain their patrol altitude.

THUD after THUD pounded the jungle slopes. Everywhere the eye could see the jungle was burning like a roast from hell itself. Now the *Cobra* and Huey gunships poured their folding-fin rockets and delayed action ordnance into the slopes as they worked the entire area over with Minigun and 20mm Gatling gun fire.

It was sheer chaos for the PAVN.

For the next two hours Colonel Lownds and Colonel Vortex watched the relentless operation.

Vortex thought that this was indeed the sweet taste and smell of revenge that he felt in his mouth and olfactory senses.

Revenge for Sergeant Major Leonard Crighton.

Revenge for the deaths of Majors Lansdale and Thrush.

Later in the day as the clearing of the PAVN bunkers continued, Vortex asked Captain Frank Willoughby, "How would you like to take back what you have lost?"

Willoughby looked slightly bewildered, "I don't understand sir?"

Vortex smiled, "To take back *Lang Vei*! Captain!"

The Green Beret officer took out his 18 inch army knife and brandished it in the air, "You don't even have to ask sir!"

His voice shrieked with devilish savagery.

Vortex explained, "The 3rd Army of the Republic of Vietnam Airborne Task Force plus our 1st Battalion, 8th Cavalry are already en route to *Lang Vei*.

They should reach the perimeter of the camp in about an hour for the final assault."

Captain Willoughby had already picked up his M60, claymores and satchel charges. A few of his Green Beret specialists were also standing behind him including; Colonel Schungel, Lieutenant Longgrear, Lieutenant Todd (all being the original defenders of *New Lang Vei* with Captain Willoughby on the 7th February 1968 when the PAVN attacked the camp with PT-76 amphibious tanks) as well as the ARVN Special Forces Ranger commander, Lieutenant Quy.

"Then let's go sir! Its pay back time!" screamed the Captain.

Colonel Vortex, Captain Richter, Lieutenant Colonel Cahill and Frank Willoughby plus the others, jumped into a waiting AH-1 *Cobra* for the quick 6 mile hop to *New Lang Vei*.

They would rendezvous with the 1st/8th Cavalry in a few minutes.

As they approached the heavily canopied jungle area around *New Lang Vei* and the *Lang Vei Village* they could see the ground littered with the dead bodies of murdered South Vietnamese peasants as well as *Bru* Tribesmen and Montagnards.

The only crime of the innocent *Bru* and Montagnards was that they wanted nothing to do with the Communist agenda and about 80 to 90% of them were loyal to the US and ARVN forces.

Death at the hands of the North Vietnamese Imperialist Aggressor Army was their reward for this loyalty to the Free World thought Colonel Vortex as he surveyed the carnage.

The North Vietnamese 304th Division had raped and murdered as many of the native tribesmen as well as women and children as they could find in retaliation for the Montagnards fighting alongside the heroic and gallant Green Berets.

It was a gruesome and disgusting sight that pays little tribute to the harsh and immodest polices of General Vo Nguyen Giap *vis a vis* his treatment of the indigenous population that he was trying to convert to the psychotic, inane and puerile policies and dogma of Marx and Engels.

Naked mothers clutching their mutilated children.

The bodies of violated teenage girls that had been nailed to trees upside down, their wombs torn out with steel pincers. And decapitated men strewn around the earth like pebbles at a seashore.

Colonel Vortex looked at the obscene carnage and said with tears in his eyes, "This is North Vietnamese justice!"

Captain Richter shook his head with violent horror, saying, "We always try to evacuate the civilian population before an operation to avoid collateral damage and casualties!

But the stinking fiend and jackal, General Vo Nguyen Giap simply butchers them if they get in the way!"

Captain Willoughby added, "This is what we are fighting for here in the Republic of South Vietnam! To stop this slaughter by the VC political cadres. I hope and pray that Operation PHOENIX is proceeding well under Robert *'Blowtorch'* Komer."

Vortex said, his voice full of venom, "I should grab that bastard Giap's skull and ram it into a copy of the *1949 Geneva Convention IV Relative to the Protection of Civilian Persons in Time of War!*

Article 3(1)(a) of that Convention provides that persons who take no part in hostilities, including members of armed forces who have laid down their arms or are *'hors de combat'* should not be; murdered, mutilated, treated cruelly or tortured. Also there must be no taking of hostages or outrages upon personal dignity such as humiliating or degrading treatment."

Lieutenant Colonel Cahill nodded as the 300 helicopters of the 1st/8th Cavalry and the 3rd Army of Vietnam Airborne Task Force came into sight.

"Why are the cavalry boys holding back from the *Lang Vei* camp?" asked Colonel Vortex as he got Captain Baig on the VHF tactical frequency at the *Khe Sanh* FSCC bunker.

"Stay back to at least 2.5 miles sir!" shouted Captain Baig, "A B-52D Arc Light strike is due in now!"

"Copy that!" clipped back Vortex.

In the next few seconds a tremendous cacophony of noise erupted ahead of them.

The very molecular structure of the jungle was being ripped apart with horrendous power.

The 750lb bombs of the *'Big Belly'* B-52D's tore the PAVN troops at *Lang Vei* apart.

The Cavalry battalion joined Vortex's lone *Cobra* so that he was now surrounded by a vast air armada. There were even *Sikorskys* and CH-54 *Tarhe Sky Cranes* in the assault force carrying massive 155mm howitzers in their slings.

It was a magnificent mobilisation of firepower by the 1st Cavalry Division (Airmobile).

The PAVN forces at *New Lang Vei* were about to be annihilated as Captain Willoughby licked his lips with sensuous anticipation.

The B-52D's were unseen and unheard as they disgorged their deadly load at over 30,000 feet.

The commander of the 1st/8th Cavalry and the 3rd Army of Vietnam Airborne Task Force watched with satisfaction as the ruined Special Forces Camp was ruined a little bit more.

The explosions sent colossal towers of smoke and earth into the sky, uprooting trees and smothering the triple canopy jungle into burning jelly.

"We are moving in for the attack," informed the Lieutenant Colonel of the 1st/8th Cavalry.

"Roger that!" answered Vortex, "Hit them hard!"

The armada of helicopters landed 500 yards to the east of *New Lang Vei* with part of its force and 400 yards to the west of the Special Forces Camp with its remaining strength.

The 1,300 men of the elite 8th Cavalry Regiment plus 900 ARVN troops moved forward for the attack.

Unbelievably, the *Cobra* and Huey gunships that circled the target still received 37mm anti-aircraft fire.

The PAVN were masters at the art of camouflage and digging in against American air strikes of whatever force and magnitude.

Colonel Vortex and his entourage jumped off their *Cobra* and rushed into the ruins of the 5th Special Forces Camp.

There were PAVN snipers everywhere as bullets whizzed past them. Captain Willoughby took point and headed straight for the Command and Communication bunkers. He wanted to see if Lieutenant Reinhard's body was still in the ruins. Even though he knew that the chance of that was almost zero.

Captain Richter sneaked up on one PAVN soldier as he was firing at the cavalry troopers and knifed him in the buttocks. The Communist turned around screaming and Colonel Vortex plunged his M16 with bayonet attached into the man's groin while Richter cut open his chest with a machete.

"Stop that fooling around sir!" screamed Captain Willoughby as he half laughed, "Help me to retake the COMMO bunker!"

Colonel Vortex nodded as the officers picked their way through the destruction of the recent B-52D strike.

Decapitated and rotting NVA bodies were everywhere. The stench was nauseating even to hardened veterans like Colonel Vortex. Wherever you walked you trod on unravelled intestines and pieces of bloodied flesh. That was the awesome power of the B-52 and B-52D.

"Quick! Get that bastard!" screamed Colonel Vortex.

A Pith helmeted PAVN trooper ran out of the ruins of the COMMO bunker.

Lieutenant Colonel Cahill took careful aim and shot the man through the heart with his CAR 15.

"There's another one!" admonished Captain Willoughby who saw a Main Force VC female irregular running over the mass of broken timber and burning metal.

The Green Beret bolted after her and managed to pull her to the earth by grabbing her breasts with vicious force.

"You foul VC fucking bitch of a whore!" screamed the Captain.

The Communist woman spat into Willoughby's face and ripped her nails across his face creating deep flesh wounds.

"Take this you murdering slut!" said Willoughby as he sliced his dagger into the VC's womb through the slit in her vagina.

Even Colonel Vortex was slightly taken aback at the ferocity of the Green Beret as he positioned himself near the entrance to the COMMO bunker.

Additional cavalry troopers took up positions to both the left and right of the doorway. Others climbed onto the roof to fire down at the enemy.

"Finish up with that stinking VC whore!" ordered Colonel Vortex as he threw a canvas bag satchel charge into the command bunker.

"Yes sir!" shouted back Willoughby as he deliciously sliced the soft womb apart with powerful strokes of his 18 inch army combat knife.

The Green Beret dismembered and disembowelled the VC female leaving her still alive to try to gather her guts and womb back into her mutilated carcass.

Vortex jumped through the door firing.

He was followed by Lieutenant Colonel Cahill and Captain Richter.

A madcap shoot out developed as about 20 PAVN soldiers were still living inside the ruined COMMO bunker.

Vortex shot one man through the foot.

Cahill head-butted an NVA who stumbled before him. The man swung at the Lieutenant Colonel with his machete but Richter blew his brains out from behind with his Colt 0.45 pistol.

A row of cavalry troopers faced a row of NVA in the cramped confines of the command bunker. Their AK-47's and M16's spitted to life. The bullets tore both sides up simultaneously.

Every man on each side was either killed or wounded.

It was a stand-up Bergheim fight.

One cavalry trooper had his left hand blown off. He shrieked as he stumbled across the room with jets of blood pumping from the mangled stump.

At that second Captain Willoughby who had climbed onto the roof of the COMMO bunker spotted two VC females as they crouched behind a 55 gallon

petrol drum. They were sniping at the men of the 1st/ 8th Cavalry Regiment as they came through the bunker entrance.

The Green Beret killing machine jumped the 5 yards to the ground with the agility of a gazelle and landed directly onto one of the VC girls. He plunged his 18 inch army knife directly through the bone of her skull.

The tip of the blade cut the brain in half and exited through her jaw.

"Oh! My God!" exclaimed Vortex as he saw what had happened.

Willoughby then held the second girl in front of him by grabbing her breasts from behind and Captain Richter screamed, "Hold the dirty rapacious slut still! I am going to stick her one!"

With those words Richter drove his bayonet through her womb and then re-plunged it into the soft and moist slit of her promiscuous vagina.

Blood poured out onto both officers.

Then amazingly, they all saw a tiny foetus ooze out of the mutilated stomach flesh.

The VC female guerrilla had been pregnant.

At this moment the ARVN troops from the 3rd Airborne Army burst into the bunker. They saluted Colonel Vortex and executed the remaining PAVN soldiers by applying water torture first to extract any information and then by disembowelling them as their bones were smashed to a pulp with iron bars.

"Who is this dirty VC bitch?" asked the ARVN Major in command.

Colonel Vortex screamed as he grabbed the ARVN Major by the collar of his camouflage shirt almost lifting him off the ground.

"When you address me Major! You use the word – *Sir*! I am your superior officer! And when you ask me questions you do so with a more polite and respectful tome of voice!

Is that understood Major!"

Colonel Vortex's face was crimson with fury as he pushed the Major away from his body with a vicious punch.

"I'm sorry sir! No disrespect intended!" cried the ARVN Major in Vietnamese.

Colonel Vortex grunted and informed the ARVN Major in his own language that the VC female was probably a spy used in the nearby *Lang Vei Village* to intimidate and terrorise the population before they were callously murdered by the North Vietnamese.

The ARVN Major saluted with a pistol-like action and asked Vortex if he could deal with the VC operative before she expired.

"Do whatever the fuck you like with her!" answered the Colonel in Vietnamese, "She is a degenerate war criminal and a filthy Communist spy! None of the international treaties protect spies!

And I follow the strict letter of the Law and of *Public International Law* at all times! There is no Convention neither Geneva nor Hague that protects this person who is not a combatant and not a civilian either of the Republic of South Vietnam. So International Law has washed its hands of such individuals!

The Law is clear on that point and as a Lawyer with a capital 'L' I obey the Law to the nth degree!"

The ARVN Major gloated with evil relish as he proceeded to torture the VC female to death by introducing red hot steel pokers into her anal and vaginal orifices before dismembering her with slow and deliberate strokes.

The ARVN Special Airborne Rangers were experts at gathering information from the VC political cadres that murdered and terrorised the innocent South Vietnamese population of agrarian peasants.

The ARVN Special Forces Rangers had a ferocious and feared reputation in South Vietnam even as far as the US forces were concerned and not only with their own people. They were the elite of the elite.

Colonel Vortex and the others combed through the wreckage of the forlorn 5th Special Forces Camp that had been *New Lang Vei*.

No American or Montagnard bodies could be found. They had all been violated and destroyed by the PAVN as the Vietminh had desecrated the bodies of those gallant and heroic French troops which had died after the horrific defeat of the proud French Colonial Forces at Dien Bien Phu in March 1954.

"Jesus! Look at this!" exclaimed Vortex as he showed Cahill and Richter a bundle of operational plans that had been left behind by the PAVN.

Captain Richter examined them for a few moments and said, "These are General Giap's plans for crushing *Khe Sanh* and the Hill positions around it! What a find!"

"We shall take them back to MACV Forward for a thorough analysis," remarked Colonel Vortex.

For the remainder of the 10th April 1968 the 1st/ 8th Cavalry and the 3rd ARVN Army Airborne quickly crushed all remaining pockets of PAVN resistance in and around *New* and *Old Lang Vei*.

"It's a pity we can't continue the attack into the Communist's stinking border sanctuaries in Laos and Cambodia and across the DMZ!" said Vortex.

Captain Willoughby nodded, "That is the only way we are going to win this war sir! But it's off-limits! Fuck it!"

The Final Act of Khe Sanh
3rd Battalion, 26th Marines Attack Hill 881 North: 14th April 1968

On the 12th April 1968 National Route 9 was reopened by the 1st Battalion of the 7th Cavalry Regiment, 1st Cavalry Division (Airmobile).

It was the first time that vehicular traffic could use the road to directly resupply *Khe Sanh* base since September 1967.

Operation PEGASUS had been a magnificent success.

An NCO in the 1st/ 7th Cavalry had put up a small placard on Route 9 to show that the road had been opened by the 7th Cavalry.

His name was Garry Owens.

Colonel Vortex met with Lieutenant General Cushman, Major General Rathvon C. Tompkins and Major General Norman J. Anderson at the *Khe Sanh* FSCC bunker on the afternoon of the 13th April 1968.

General Cushman was beaming with satisfaction as he embraced both Vortex and Lownds.

"Gentlemen! Your ordeal is about to come to an end! In fact you can now rotate out of *Khe Sanh* with your troops."

Colonel Vortex smiled as he placed his fists firmly on the conference table and said, "No sir. Not yet!"

General Cushman was flabbergasted as he asked, "What do you mean Richard?"

Colonel Lownds smiled, "I know what the Colonel is talking about."

Vortex explained to the three Generals, "Colonel Lownds and I are not leaving *Khe Sanh* until we crush the PAVN battalion that is dug in stubbornly on Hill 881 North! That hill was the scene of the start of this *Khe Sanh* siege. Well!"

Vortex cracked his knuckles and drew in a deep breath, "The bloody North Vietnamese started it at Hill 881 North but I am going to finish them on Hill 881 North! So help me God!"

Major General Tompkins said with pride, "Colonel! Your devotion to duty is an example to the entire Marine Corps!"

Vortex elucidated his plans to the Generals.

"I am going to attack Hill 881 North tomorrow before dawn.

I shall use what is left of my 1st Battalion, 9th Marines together with Colonel Lownds' 3rd Battalion, 26th Marines.

We shall strike hard after launching massive air strikes and artillery bombardments from Camp Carroll, the Rockpile and from *Khe Sanh*.

I shall lead the attack myself and relentlessly kill the Communists until we have captured that vital and strategic hill which belongs to us! As does the rest of South Vietnam for that matter! For we have paid for every square inch of this fucked real estate with American blood!"

"Its sounds good to me," said Major General Anderson, the commander of the 1st Marine Air Wing, "I shall give you all available air assets."

Colonel Lownds spoke softly, "I must be in on this last attack at *Khe Sanh*! I want revenge against the criminal aggressor forces of the North Vietnamese Army – the puppets of the CHICOMS and the Bolsheviks."

General Cushman clapped his hands together with delight, "Then it shall be thus! You have my approval! And you have my blessings! I know, Colonel Vortex, that you are a deeply religious man.

May Almighty God be with you and guide you in tomorrow's enterprise!"

Vortex clapped his hand on David Lownds' shoulder and said to the General, "Thank you sir. I greatly appreciate it."

Suddenly Captain Mirza Baig opened the doors to the FSCC bunker and Major General Tolson walked in.

The commander of the 1st Cavalry Division (Airmobile) had just arrived from a conference at *Hue-Phu Bai* with Deputy COMUSMACV and MACV Forward, General Creighton Abrams.

"Good news gentlemen!" began General Tolson, "The last pockets of PAVN resistance at Hue and along the *Perfume River* have been annihilated in an orgy of destruction by the 1st Brigade of Major General Olinto Barsanti's 101st Airborne Division! Together with elements from the elite 1st Marine Division. The operation was a classic pincer thrust followed by a 'cauldron battle' which extinguished the Communist's logistical and support apparatus in Military Region 6."

There was a murmur of relief and approval throughout the conference room.

"Well! That doesn't make the job of the 325thC *Golden Star Division* or the 304th PAVN Division any easier," said Major General Anderson.

Colonel Vortex laughed, "Fuck the 304th and 325th Communist motherfucker cunt-sucking divisions! Fuck them to hell!"

General Tomkins added, "With Hue gone the Communists have no choice but to retreat back into Laos to lick their wounds."

"Yes. The entire strategic plan of General Giap has failed miserably with a capital 'F' for fuck him! And fuck his putrid stinking plans!" shouted Colonel Vortex in a fury of relief.

The meeting continued for another two hours. The senior officers began to discuss the planning and logistics for the upcoming Operation SCOTLAND II, which was to begin on the 15th April 1968. The day that Colonel Lownds' troops would be rotated out of *Khe Sanh*.

On the humid and desolate slopes of Hill 881 South, Colonel Vortex and Colonel Lownds looked through their Starlight scopes in the pre-dawn darkness. It was the morning of the 14th April 1968. The final dramatic act of the *Khe Sanh* saga was about to unfold. The entire 3rd Battalion of the 26th Marines plus the stalwart 1st Battalion of the 9th Marines had positioned themselves at the base of Hill 881 South facing Hill 881 North.

They were manoeuvring themselves for the attack, almost 1,900 strong.

Cahill, Richter, Willoughby and Captain Baig were in attendance.

The Fire Control officer had cooked up an unbelievable cocktail of lethal firepower to begin the attack.

Captain Baig had made a special effort for his last operation at *Khe Sanh* for he too was going to be relieved on the 15th April 1968.

Colonel Vortex asked Captain Baig, "Is everything ready?"

The Fire Support and Coordination maestro said, "I've covered us for every eventuality sir. The two batteries at Camp Carroll and the Rockpile have stored up more than 70,000 rounds of 175mm artillery shells just for this parting exercise.

The bombardment will begin in exactly two minutes from now. Illumination star shells will light up the gooks. It is now 0343 hours sir."

Colonel Lownds looked through his Starlight scope at the enemy bunkers on the hill opposite and nodded with approval as Captain Baig continued, "I have coordinated more than 4 squadrons of fighter-bombers to lead in the assault.

Using computer analysis of sensor information gained on Hill 881 North I have given the pilots the latest positions of the enemy bunkers. They are going to use 2,000lb B1 BLOCKBUSTER Bombs with delayed action fuses."

Colonel Vortex looked to Captain Max Richter who was aiming his quad 0.50cal at the enemy held terrain and commented, "Yes! The delayed action bombs are the best for this sort of thing."

"They are indeed sir! The metal casing of the bombs penetrate the PAVN bunkers, burying deep within the vaults of the enemy redoubt. About 15 seconds later they explode. The effect on human flesh is indescribable! I have also ordered in antipersonnel flechette canisters and napalm. There will also be high explosive bombs in the package."

A few minutes later the F-4E *Phantoms*, F-105 *Republic Thunderchiefs* and A-6 *Grumman Intruders* from Task Force 77 in the Gulf of Tonkin screamed in for the attack.

Colonel Vortex could see the jet up wash as it burned the atmosphere in slices. The *Phantoms* came in first and ignited the forward slopes of Hill 881 North.

Captain Baig had taken great care to analyse the sensor information and the napalm and delayed action ordnance seemed to detonate within the very bowels of the hill itself.

The THUDS came in dropping multiple flechette canisters after the *Phantoms* peeled off.

"What are they doing over there?" asked Lieutenant Colonel Cahill as he pointed to a formation of about 25 low flying Marine F-4's.

Captain Baig answered, "That is an additional squadron from Bien Hoa. As the PAVN try to make a run for it later on, these fighters will take them out. The only possible escape route for the remnants of the North Vietnamese battalion on 881 North

is either up this secondary road from *Khe Sanh* to the DMZ or west, across the jungle to *Tchepone* and Laos."

Captain Richter picked up his webbing and laughed, "You think of everything Captain! Nothing escapes your meticulous planning!"

Baig chuckled, "I wanted the last act of PEGASUS and NIAGARA to be a great one."

Colonel David E. Lownds beamed, "And so it shall be! So it shall!"

"I think its time we got going Colonel," said Vortex as the THUDS roared in for strike after devastating strike against the enemy bunkers on that famous hill. The hill where on the 20th January 1968, Captain Dabney and I Company had fought a vicious preliminary action with elements of the 325thC *Golden Star Division* that signalled the start of the *Khe Sanh* siege.

Both Colonels and their staffs proceeded down the slopes of Hill 881 South and into the low saddle of ground between the two hills. They were accompanied by most of Vortex's battalion which then joined the 3rd/ 26th Marines.

"Open fire with the 106mm recoilless rifles and the 4.2 inch mortars!" cried Vortex as the Marines scrambled into their attack positions.

Already AK-47 fire was erupting all along the low saddle of ground before the defiant enemy hill.

Second Lieutenant Charles King came running up with his radio operator.

He was the commander of the point platoon in L Company that would spearhead the horrific climb up Hill 881 North.

"We are ready when you are sir!" shouted Lieutenant King over the cacophony of mortars and machine gun fire.

"Let's go!" said Vortex as he clapped King on the shoulder, "I'm taking point with you!"

Lieutenant King expected as much. They were all aware of Colonel Vortex's fearsome reputation and his habit of leading from the front.

The junior officers at *Khe Sanh* regarded Colonel Vortex as almost a raw phenomenon of unstoppable PAVN crushing power.

"I'll coordinate the advance of the rest of the troops," began Colonel Lownds.

"We'll spread out around the base of the hill and then advance concentrically up to the summit," added Lieutenant Colonel Cahill.

The roar of the Marine F-4's and USAF THUDS could be heard as the radar-equipped fighter-bombers continued to circle 881 North like hornets around a viper's nest.

The sun had just risen over the shrouds and mists of the infamous *Khe Sanh* fog, its red-orange glow penetrating the gloom of that violent and battle scared plateau,

glowing like the hot brilliance of the blood that would be spilt on that final day of PEGASUS.

It was the blood of *Khe Sanh* – red like its dirt and dust.

Its agony and its triumph.

The attack began with L Company scrambling up the slopes of that heavily layered jungle terrain.

Colonel Vortex, Captain Richter and Captain Willoughby were out on point with a squad from Lieutenant King's platoon. Giving C.R.E. hand signals, Vortex pointed to the first enemy bunker that was heavily camouflaged into the side of the hill.

The men spread out firing.

"Jesus! I'm hit!" cried a Sergeant behind Captain Richter.

Communist fire had ripped open the man's face, his palate visible through his cheeks as the blood pulsed out in crimson streams. Two more Marines were cut down by RPD light machine gun fire coming from inside the bunkers.

"Incoming!" screamed Captain Frank Willoughby.

The Green Beret could hear the lethal swoosh! of an RPG-7 rocket being launched. It impacted into the centre of the platoon and blew away three more Marines.

"Fuck this! It's becoming a rout!" screamed Vortex as he scowled at Charles King, "What's the matter with your men Lieutenant?"

The Second Lieutenant was bewildered and in a state of shock as he fumbled around in the mud of that treacherous hill.

"We haven't come this far to be beaten back by the bloody dinks now!" shrieked Captain Richter.

Richter pulled the 2nd Lieutenant to his feet and shook his whole body from side to side, saying, "Gather your men for the attack! We have to clear this bunker before the rest of the 3rd Battalion move up!"

King had hardly turned around to obey when a shower of Chinese made grenades came cascading out of the PAVN bunker. Seven more Marines were seriously wounded. Two men lost their legs which were blown off above the knee. Disgusting sprinkles of lacerated flesh splashed across Colonel Vortex's camouflage uniform. The shining eagles on his collar, the insignia of his rank, were shrouded in the blood of his fellow Americans.

Captain Willoughby could see the Colonel's eyes turn white hot with an avenging rage.

The time for killing was at hand. The final act of *Khe Sanh* would be the bloodiest.

"Richter! Willoughby!" screamed Vortex, "Follow me!"

The two Captains watched their Colonel as he grabbed an M60 and a handful of satchel charges.

To their amazement Vortex ran up the stinking jungle slope of Hill 881 North straight into the mouth of the PAVN bunker.

"Sir! No! Wait!" cried Richter with anguish.

But Colonel Vortex had already thrown himself against the logs that made up the left side of the bunker entrance. In the next second he threw in the first canvas satchel bag followed by two more. A plume of thick black smoke vomited out of the bunker slits as massive explosions thudded the enemy hideout mingled with dull screams.

Lieutenant King's platoon were still mesmerised at the bottom of the hill as Richter and Willoughby threw their bodies against the right side of the burning bunker.

Vortex nodded to them as he bolted head first into the enemy bunker complex.

"Oh! My God!" was all that the Green Beret Captain could say.

He had never seen such bravery or foolishness or both.

Colonel Vortex scrambled over several bleeding bodies in the cordite reeking bowels of that devilish PAVN hideout.

Shots rang out as the two Captains leapt in after their commander.

Captain Willoughby could hardly see a thing due to the smoke and fires inside as he kept a hold on Richter's arm so that they would not accidentally shoot each other in the confusion.

As Vortex scrambled around in the subterranean bunker it reminded him of January 1967 when he had taken part in Operation CEDAR FALLS to clear the Main Force Viet Cong out of the tunnels that infested like a scourge the infamous 'Iron Triangle' area around the *Ho Bo Woods* and the *Michelin Rubber Plantation*.

"Come out you dirty gook bastards! Come out! Come out wherever you are! Boo! Hoo!" taunted and screamed Colonel Vortex in Vietnamese as he tried to infuriate the North Vietnamese with their own guttural sounding language that sounded like a person choking to the Western ear.

"I am going to fuck your brains out with this machete! You motherfucking douchebags! Don't hide behind General Giap's apron skirts you fucking putrid Communist cowards!"

AK-47 7.62mm bullets whizzed past his ears. Then he felt a pair of coarse hands grip him around the neck from behind as they tried to garrotte him.

Colonel Vortex was furious because this was *his* personal method of dispatching Communists to the netherworld.

With a cat-like movement Vortex reached back and grabbed the NVA's hair while dropping his body forwards to the ground in a textbook Judo manoeuvre.

The Colonel catapulted the enemy onto his back and slid his dagger into the Communist's guts.

Before he could withdraw the blade from the chunk of intestines which enclosed it, another Communist soldier body knocked him sideways against the wall of the bunker.

The reeking smoke started to clear a little and to Vortex's horror he saw a large North Vietnamese soldier standing before him with his AK-47 pointed directly at his chest.

The black, callous eyes of Giap's minion met his own.

Vortex's stare was fathomless. It was a bottomless pit of vicious hate.

The Communist's eyes weakened under the animal-like ferocity of the American Colonel.

But then the North Vietnamese soldier gave a hideous smile, his finger pulling down on the trigger of the AK-47 *Kalashnikov*.

Vortex knew that this time he was dead. His M60 was on the floor beside him and out of reach.

A shot rang out but Vortex's eyes remained open.

The Colonel was convinced that he was dying.

He saw in disbelief the body of the Communist trooper fall onto his outstretched legs.

Captain Max Richter was revealed standing behind the enemy with his smoking Colt 0.45 pointed where the enemies' skull had been.

Vortex was extremely thankful as he winked at Richter while gripping the head of the North Vietnamese and plunging his Marine dagger into the man's right eyeball so that the sleek shaft of the weapon sliced beautifully into the midbrain.

"That was close sir!" cried Captain Richter as Willoughby caught a Viet Cong woman hiding behind a cache of ammunition and tore out her bowels with his machete.

"I owe you my life Captain!" said Vortex as he kicked the mutilated North Vietnamese off his torso.

"It's my pleasure sir!" answered the beefy Captain.

The fight raged on as the three officers's led the point platoon through the ruined bunker and onto the next one further up the slope.

The lone Communist battalion put up an extremely stiff resistance.

Lieutenant King's platoon was almost entirely wiped out due to casualties from enemy sniper fire. Another platoon rotated up to replace it on point duty.

While Vortex and the 1st Battalion fought their way up the south-western slope of 881 North, Colonel Lownds and Lieutenant Colonel Cahill were tackling the south-eastern side.

The Marine fighters kept up a constant suppressive fire on the summit of Hill 881 North as they circled it at subsonic speed. This was the final objective of the two Marine battalions.

Corporal Eldridge was taking point with his seven man squad about 100 yards in front of Colonel Lownds and the 3rd Battalion, 26th Marines.

Suddenly AK-47 fire burst all around them. The Communist soldiers were pulling back in a fan shape as the Marines doggedly advanced up the slope.

The further up the hill they went the stiffer became the PAVN resistance as their troops concentrated into a smaller expanse of ground.

"This bloody elephant grass!" cried Lieutenant Colonel Cahill, "Its edges are so sharp it can cut you to pieces!"

Colonel Lownds nodded as he was followed by 35 officers and NCOs' of his regimental staff. They had all volunteered for this final action of the *Khe Sanh* siege.

Corporal Patterson fired his M60 as his point team hit the dirt. Bullets erupted the soil all around the advancing Marines.

Corporal Patterson could see the Pith helmeted silhouettes of the PAVN as they ran through the vines, undergrowth and trees.

They were like ghosts even in daytime. There was something magical about the evil tenacity of the North Vietnamese soldier.

They were indeed experts at jungle warfare. And they never gave up without a bloody and prolonged fight.

Then Corporal Patterson felt a numbing blow to his skull. He fell to the ground just as he was about to stand up. The 7.62mm round sliced off a layer of his scalp but it was only a superficial wound.

When Patterson awoke he was covered in his own blood and the 3rd Battalion were almost at the summit of Hill 881 North.

The Corporal picked up his M16 and ran after the enemy soldier who had shot him. He had seen the vicious and uncompromising face for a second through the jungle canopy.

Marines were scurrying and firing all around him.

Corporal Patterson reached the summit of Hill 881 North and the enemy soldier shot at him a second time. But the AK-47 round whizzed past his left ear.

"You dink bastard!" cried Patterson as he fired off a whole clip from his M16 at hip level.

The PAVN's chest was cleaved open by eruptions of blood. He gurgled in his own fluids and fell to the earth.

Three *Sikorsky's* swooped in to the top of Hill 881 North and sprayed that section still held by the enemy with relentless Minigun fire.

Secondary explosions detonated several command bunkers that had been set up by the defending PAVN battalion.

It was now mid-afternoon. The assault had been going on for more than 10 hours.

As Colonel Vortex approached the apex of 881 North from the south-west his 1st Battalion overran a PAVN mortar position.

"Kill them! Don't let them get away!" screamed the Colonel as the Marines charged up the final sections of 881 North.

Captain Richter threw several grenades into the mortar pit blowing the tubes skyward with pieces of the enemy crew's flesh.

Vortex knelt down and took aim with his CAR 15 blowing the top of an NVA head off so that half the man's eyeballs were free to the air from above.

Captain Frank Willoughby lunged forward and bayoneted two North Vietnamese who tried to scramble into one of the ruined command bunkers.

Another enemy soldier attempted to dive into a small tunnel at the summit of 881 North.

Colonel Vortex caught him before he slipped away like a greasy eel.

"Do you need a hand sir?" asked Richter as he grabbed the other ankle. Together they pulled the NVA rat dweller out of his burrow.

Vortex kicked a Chinese grenade out of the enemies' hand and threw it down the tunnel just before it exploded.

The Communist whipped out his knife and was about to stick it into the Colonel's thigh when Captain Willoughby bolted up from behind and stoved in the NVA's skull with the butt end of his M16.

"Welcome this into your putrid guts!" said Vortex as he sliced his 18 inch Marine combat knife into the man's trachea.

Using both hands the Colonel tore out the man's throat while Captain Richter blew his brains out with his Colt 0.45 calibre pistol.

The gallant men of the 1st/ 9th and the 3rd/ 26th Marines detonated nearly all the 130mm M46 Soviet designed howitzers that they found on the summit of Hill 881 North.

As Vortex and Colonel Lownds linked up in victory the commander of the 26th Marines said as he wiped the sweat off his brow, "We've done it Colonel Vortex!"

"Yes! These artillery pieces have been pestering us at *Khe Sanh* since the beginning of the siege!"

"I've ordered in a CH-54 *Tarhe Sky Crane* to sling one away for examination by III MAF headquarters," added Captain Richter as he signalled the several hundred Marines around them to continue the mopping-up operation on Hill 881 North.

"Good idea!" said Captain Willoughby as he wiped the blood off his dagger by reaching down and brushing it through the mangled hair of a dead Communist.

One of the HH-53B *Jolly Green's* landed on the summit and Captain Mirza Baig jumped out. He shook his head with horror as he saw the carnage of the assault's aftermath.

"I'm glad I'm not in the infantry!" he said to both Colonels.

Suddenly the Marine F-4E *Phantoms* roared into life as they used their 20mm cannon to pulverise those North Vietnamese who had managed to escape the noose around 881 North.

Intermittent machine gun fire clattered all around the group of officers as they surveyed the view of *Khe Sanh* below them.

The Marine combat base looked strangely serene without the PAVN artillery and mortar fire.

"I wonder what they will say of this battle 45 years from now?" asked Colonel David E. Lownds.

Colonel Vortex shrugged his shoulders as he looked at Captain Richter, "I don't know. But I do know that it will be remembered as America's finest hour in Vietnam!"

Colonel David Lownds nodded and said, "We better get back to *Khe Sanh*. Operation SCOTLAND II is due to start tomorrow and our regiments are transferring out."

About 50 yards from Colonel Vortex's position, Lance Corporal Dennis Mannion pulled down his camouflage pants and shit all over the exalted North Vietnamese summit of Hill 881 North.

A Sergeant next to him laughed and asked, "What the fuck do you think you are doing Corporal?"

Mannion answered, "I want to show these North Vietnamese bastards that everything they hold sacred and sacrosanct will be destroyed by us!

America will win this war!

And I shit on those murdering scum!"

And so saying he continued with his personal business.

Colonel David E. Lownds turned into the blood-red sunset and said softly to Vortex, "I've just been wishing…, wishing that I could have come face-to-face with the man who was running their side.

I would have liked to compare notes with him."

Captain Richter smiled.

Frank Willoughby sat down exhausted and placed his head between his legs. The Green Beret Captain was mesmerised with fatigue.

Colonel Lownds turned to Richard Vortex and could see his face being illuminated by the crimson colours of the sunset.

The man seemed suddenly at peace. His features composed into serenity.

"What are you going to do now?" asked Colonel Lownds.

Colonel Richard Vortex said as he sighed deeply, "It's time to go home."

CHAPTER 16
PRESIDENTIAL UNIT CITATIONS

Farewell Gathering at MACV Headquarters, Pentagon East

Colonel Richard Vortex flew out of *Khe Sanh* on the 16th April 1968.

He briefly reviewed the 2nd and 3rd Battalions of his 9th Marine Regiment at Dong Ha and placed Lieutenant Colonel John J. Cahill in temporary command.

Vortex received orders to return to the United States.

Decorations were to be awarded to certain individuals who had taken part in the defence of *Khe Sanh*.

In addition the Head of State had decided to award, upon the recommendation of the Joint Chiefs of Staff and the subordinate commands including MACV, Presidential Unit Citations to the defenders.

The Citations were to go to;

1st Battalion, 9th Marine Regiment of the 3rd Marine Division.

1st, 2nd and 3rd Battalions of the 26th Marine Regiment of the 3rd Marine Division.

Seabee Mobile Construction Battalion attached to Task Force 77 being Naval Mobile Construction Battalions 5, 10 and 53 and Detachment Bravo, Naval Mobile Construction Battalion Unit 301.

Command & Control North (Forward Operating Base 3); MACV-SOG: Detachment A-101 & Company C, 5th Special Forces Group (Airborne).

Susie Ky was at the Tan Son Nhut Air Base to join her partner, Colonel Vortex as he touched down in a C-130E Hercules ELINT from Quang Tri.

As Vortex looked out of the plane the city of Saigon below looked strangely serene. It was as if there had been no TET Offensive, no glorified;

TCK-TKN [TONG CONG KICH – TONG KHOI NGHIA] – General Offensive, General Uprising.

Tu Do Street was alive and humming with activity and the fires in the Cholon District had been extinguished.

"It's been a long tour of duty sir," said Captain Max Richter as he sat alongside his commander sipping on a cup of Earl Grey tea.

Colonel Vortex smiled and sipped on something a little stronger than tea as he patted Richter on the knee, "We've earned a rest. That is for sure!"

Colonel David E. Lownds was sitting on the aisle opposite and Captain Frank Willoughby was in front of them.

The four officers had enjoyed a pleasant 50 minute flight from I Corps Operational Zone.

Needless to say they were all exhausted.

"You know something Vortex?" asked Colonel Lownds as he leaned across the middle of the C-130E.

"What's that?"

"My wife is going to be waiting for me in Washington D.C. I haven't seen her for more than a year!"

Colonel Vortex laughed, "Well! Lownds! My wife sure as hell won't be waiting for me in Washington or anywhere else for that matter!"

Colonel Lownds looked stunned as Captain Willoughby handed him a glass of Budweiser, "And why not?"

"Because we are in the process of getting divorced!"

Lownds shook his head, "I'm sorry Vortex."

"Don't be! It's for the best. Besides, I have a new fiancée."

This time Colonel Lownds laughed and pointed out the cabin window of the C-130E, "Yes! I know! And she's waiting for you just over there!"

The enormous C-130E shuddered to a halt near the main hangar complex of Tan Son Nhut.

A Marine brass band was playing martial music outside. Captain Richter grinned and thought that they were being treated like returning heroes.

But as far as Richter was concerned they were just doing their duty for;

Unit, Corps, God and Country.

Colonel Vortex fell into the beautiful arms of Susie Ky in the middle of the tarmac and right in front of the Marine band.

"I love you my darling!" she cried as she smothered the Colonel with kisses.

"It's all over Susie!" said Vortex as he gathered her up like a rare flower.

"You promise!" she teased.

"I promise my sweetheart! At least for the moment anyway! We are going to Washington!"

They both laughed as Captain Richter carried his Colonel's bags to the line of jeeps that would take them to Pentagon East.

"I'm going to show you our new home in Georgetown," added Richard.

"Will we have a peaceful life in the United States?" asked Susie, her large moonlike eyes shining with warmth and love.

Vortex hesitated for a few seconds as he held Susie's hand and they climbed into one of the army jeeps.

"When final victory has been achieved – then, then we shall have peace."

Susie Ky looked a little forlorn, "Not before?"

Vortex kissed his fiancée and said, "I can smell victory in the air my darling.

I saw victory approaching in the incredible performance of our logistical apparatus at *Khe Sanh*.

I smelt victory in the 110,000 tons of napalm and high explosives that we dropped on the criminal forces of North Vietnam during the magnificent siege of *Khe Sanh*!

I grasped victory in the 159,000 rounds that our artillery fired at the enemy during the siege for H & I missions.

I revel in the prospect of final victory when our air armada performed more than 24,000 tactical sorties against PAVN positions around *Khe Sanh*.

And more than 2,700 B-52 and B-52D Arc Light sorties that smothered the enemy in a veil of utter destruction.

I marvel at the economic power and industrial might of my glorious country which supplied its troops at *Khe Sanh* with 12,400 tons of life-giving supplies during the deadly siege!

All this points to victory my darling!

Victory in Vietnam is coming! Be assured!"

Susie Ky had tears in her eyes as she hugged her lover.

The jeeps were already in motion towards Pentagon East.

Colonel Vortex looked forwards without blinking as the humid air assailed their bodies, the stench and the raw effluent rot of the Vietnam surroundings as a constant challenge.

"And I am going to be a part of that final victory!" said Vortex as Colonel David Lownds looked back from the front seat, wondering whether America ever had such a fine son as this, or would have again.

General William Childs Westmoreland greeted the small party as they arrived inside the main conference room of the Pentagon East headquarters which was the nerve centre for MACV.

Colonels Lownds and Vortex saluted COMUSMACV like two pistol shots, their bodies rigidly at attention.

"Relax gentlemen! This is an informal occasion designed to give you thanks!" beamed General Westmoreland.

Deputy COMUSMACV, General Creighton Abrams stepped up and shook hands with Vortex, Lownds, Richter and Willoughby, saying, "You can't imagine gentlemen

how much we appreciate the stupendous performance of you and your troops at *Khe Sanh*! You held on at a critical time for the whole of the Military Assistance Command. If the North Vietnamese had managed to overrun *Khe Sanh* and then move both the 304th and 325thC Divisions into the battles for Hue…"

General Westmoreland interrupted swiftly, "Then it could have been a disaster for all of us! With incalculable consequences!"

"Thank you sir," said Colonel Lownds.

Holding Susie's hand, Vortex spotted General William W. Momyer the commanding General of the US 7th Air Force. He made straight for him.

"I want to thank you sir," began Vortex, "…for the magnificent air support our troops received at *Khe Sanh*. Without the sterling dedication of the air crews and of Strategic Air Command that supplied us with devastating B-52 strikes every 90 minutes, I think the battle for our Marine combat base would have been much bloodier, much tougher and more heartbreaking for the American people as a whole."

General William Momyer embraced Vortex around the shoulders with genuine affection, "I shall certainly pass your appreciation on to the boys at SAC!"

The conference room at Pentagon East had been laid out with a sumptuous buffet table. Stewards were serving drinks to all the guests and Captain Richter and Captain Willoughby joined Vortex and Lownds to mingle with Generals; William DePuy (Commander 1st Infantry Division), Major General Norman J. Anderson (Commander 1st Marine Air Wing), Brigadier General Burl McLaughlin (Aerial Supply for *Khe Sanh*), Brigadier General William McBride (Sensor Operations for *Khe Sanh*), Major General Rathvon C. Tompkins (Commander 3rd Marine Division), Lieutenant General Robert Cushman (Commander III Marine Amphibious Force), Major General Herman Nickerson Jr. (Commander 1st Marine Division), Major General William Rosson (Deputy III MAF), Major General Olinto Barsanti (Commander 101st Airborne Division), Brigadier General Phillip B. Davidson (J-2 for MACV), Brigadier General Joseph A. McChristian (CG of G-2), Major General Fillmore K. Mearns (Commander 25th Tropic Lightning Division), General Ngoi Quang Truong (Commander 1st ARVN Infantry Division), Lieutenant General Fred C. Weyand (Commander 2nd Field Force Vietnam [II FFV]), Brigadier General Ellis Williamson (Commander 173rd Airborne Brigade), Nguyen Cao Ky (Air Vice-Marshal South Vietnamese Air Force & Vice-President of the Republic of South Vietnam), Admiral Ulysses S. Grant Sharp (Commander of the US 7th Fleet & CincPAC), Major General Julian Ewell (Commander 9th Infantry Division), Brigadier General Manfred Laubscher (Deputy Assistant Division Commander 101st Airborne Division), Colonel Egon Pohl (G-2 Section, 101st Airborne Division) plus many others.

"Colonel Lownds! Colonel Vortex!" shouted a voice with a thick South Vietnamese accent.

Both Colonels trotted up and saluted while the host of Generals, Colonels and civilian officials such as Robert *'Blowtorch'* Komer enjoyed the cocktail banquet.

It was President Thieu of the Republic of Vietnam.

"I have been following the *Khe Sanh* battle closely! You did a marvellous job up there. My country and I thank you!" beamed President Thieu.

"No thanks are necessary Mr President!" said Colonel Lownds.

President Thieu looked the Colonel up and down with a light hearted grin and laughed, "You American Marines! You are always so serious. So dedicated."

Colonel Vortex smiled and said, "Dedication is the *modus operandi* of all our undertakings Mr President."

Thieu laughed and said, "Come! Let us eat!"

The feasting continued and as the party moved into full swing, General Westmoreland drew Colonel Vortex aside.

"Richard," he began, "I am almost sorry to see you promoted to Brigadier General so soon."

Susie Ky and Vortex laughed, "Why is that sir?"

General Westmoreland wrung his hands together in an agonised gesture, "Because where am I going to find another Regimental grade tactical commander like you?"

Vortex chuckled as he sipped on a glass of Bollinger R.D., "I am sure you will find plenty of commanders as good as or even better than me. After all…" Vortex looked to Susie, "I am not infallible!"

Westmoreland added, "It's a pity I can't give you your own Division. But that is up to the Commandant of the Marine Corps, General Chapman. In my opinion you deserve it. But I suppose you have to serve your time as an Assistant Division Commander first."

"I am grateful for your support sir, your confidence and above all your faith in me," began Vortex as he put down his champagne glass and straightened up his body like a ramrod.

"It is the faith and support from my Supreme Commander that has given me the strength to endure the unendurable during this momentous siege of *Khe Sanh*!"

General Westmoreland congratulated Colonel David E. Lownds as he stepped up with Vice-President Nguyen Cao Ky who was still talking about using tactical nuclear weapons in Northern I Corps.

COMUSMACV ignored the Vice-President and instead kissed Susie Ky's hand with reverence.

Colonel Vortex felt a strange elation come over his body.

He was going home.

Next stop was Washington D.C.

The Tomb of the Unknown Soldier : Arlington National Cemetery

It was already the middle of May 1968 when Colonel Vortex and Susie Ky arrived in Washington D.C.

The flight from Saigon had been quite smooth and enjoyable.

Vortex had not been back to the States since March 1967, just before the start of his 3rd tour in Vietnam.

The cool and invigorating air of Washington was a Godsend after the stinking heat and humidity of the Vietnam jungle.

"Oh! Daddy! Daddy! I love you!" cried Peggy Vortex.

The Colonel heard the voice of his beloved 19 year old daughter as he stepped off a Boeing C-135 *Stratolifter* at Andrews Air Force Base.

He could not find the words to speak but rushed into his daughter's arms kissing her with tender affection and heartfelt longing.

"It's been too long Peggy!" he cried.

Vortex's daughter was in a state of joyous excitement at seeing her father again after a long year of absence.

"Is this the friend you have been telling me about?" asked Peggy as she pointed at Susie Ky.

Vortex introduced the two women to each other and they immediately built up an instant rapport.

"How's your mother?" asked Vortex.

Peggy smiled, "She's fine Dad. She actually asked me how you were."

Richard smiled, "Oh! Really?"

Peggy added as she hooked her arms around both her father and Susie, "But she still wants the divorce!"

Vortex nodded as they headed off to downtown Washington.

A week after their arrival, Colonel Vortex took his daughter and his fiancée to the Arlington National Cemetery to pay their respects to his grandfather and great-grandfather who were both buried there.

As they drove over to the Virginia side of the Potomac River Vortex could see the lush green fields wherein the heroes lay. The Lincoln Memorial was clearly visible from across the Potomac. The air was cool and clear. Its crispness gave Vortex an inner strength, a perseverance that would ready his soul for the struggles yet to come.

For he knew that he would have to leave the serenity of the nation's heroes and return to that charnel hell they called Vietnam.

But for now he was in the arena of the Gods as the three of them stepped out of the black limousine hire car.

Colonel Vortex was in his Class A Dress uniform.

His Marine sword, polished to perfection, was hanging from his *Sam Browne* belt. He had two shoe-like mirrors on his feet that reflected the cool sunshine of Arlington.

This was the place where Vortex could renew his soul. This place of honour and love and duty. The eternal resting place for those that have made the ultimate sacrifice for their country.

With Susie Ky on his left and his daughter Peggy on the right, the three walked arm-in-arm to the spot near Arlington House where Vortex's great-grandfather lay.

Colonel Vortex placed a garland of flowers upon the grave of Colonel Thackeray Hubert Vortex of the Confederate Army.

Kneeling at the foot of the grave, Colonel Vortex prayed silently for five minutes with his daughter and Susie Ky standing behind.

He remembered the Battle of Antietam in September 1862 when his great-grandfather, an officer in the army of General Ambrose Hill had helped to save the Confederate Army of Northern Virginia under General Robert E. Lee.

Moving on to his grandfather's grave a few hundred yards away, Vortex paid the same respects. His grandfather had been a Brigadier General in the US 90th Infantry Division of the United States First Army at the Battle of St. Mihiel in France during the 1917-1918 period of American involvement in World War I.

As they moved away towards the Arlington Memorial Amphitheatre, Colonel Vortex thought of his fallen comrades at *Khe Sanh*.

Of Sergeant Major Leonard Crighton and Majors Lansdale and Thrush.

He wished for them the peace that he found here at Arlington.

For they too were now the fallen heroes of the past.

Khe Sanh would join the memories of Iwo Jima, Saipan, Guadalcanal and Bastogne as a symbol of the dedication and prowess of the American military tradition.

It would be, thought Colonel Vortex, another glorious chapter in the minds of present and future generations of Americans.

Khe Sanh would take its place alongside *Inchon* and *Okinawa* as symbols of American tenacity and courage against a pitiless and criminal foe.

Upon reaching the *Tomb of the Unknown Soldier* in front of the Arlington Memorial Amphitheatre, Colonel Vortex held the hand of his daughter and fiancée and started to pray.

"Almighty God! Give us the strength and the courage to obey your dictates! Allow us the wisdom to see what is right and give us the fortitude to carry out your works as we perceive that they should be done.

Let us not stumble or falter in our path but through your guiding hand, Oh! Lord! We shall walk out of the dark tunnels of tyranny and into the bright sunshine of freedom!

Let us not shirk our responsibilities to the free people of the world but let us combat with ever greater strength, ever greater power the evil forces that try to expunge the light of your Son Jesus Christ from the world!

Give us your Blessings Oh! Lord! So that we may continue to bring Peace and Security to the world! As we are doing in Vietnam! Amen!"

Susie Ky looked up to Vortex and could see the determination in his eyes as he saluted to the Tomb of the Unknown Soldier.

Presidential Unit Citations The White House

A great throng of people belonging to the Washington Press Corps were already outside on the White House Lawn when Colonel Vortex, Colonel David E. Lownds, Captain Max Richter and Captain Frank Willoughby arrived in a black Cadillac limousine.

All four officers were in their immaculate Class A Dress uniforms with swords.

"They really put on a hell of a show for us!" exclaimed Colonel Lownds.

"They did indeed!" laughed Vortex.

Colonel Lownds had his wife and two daughters with him.

Captain Frank Willoughby had left Monica and Susan Thang in Saigon in safe hands.

Captain Richter was unmarried but his parents were at the White House gathering. They were very excited.

"Look who's coming," whispered Colonel Vortex to Susie Ky and his daughter Peggy.

The Commandant of the Marine Corps, General Chapman came up to them as he descended from the White House steps.

"Gentlemen! Welcome!" said General Chapman in a cheerful voice.

The four officers saluted as the Commandant continued, "I would like you all to come and see the President before the awards and decorations are given out."

They started walking into the White House as the press photographers ran in front and behind taking dozens of pictures.

"President Johnson himself has asked to see the senior commanders at *Khe Sanh* and their families," added General Chapman.

"It's an honour!" cried Colonel Vortex as he held Susie's hand.

The party made their way into the White House and up to the Oval Office where the President was having a small reception for members of the National Security Council and the Joint Chiefs of Staff.

One of the President's secretaries ushered them inside the famous room.

The room where *'The Buck Finally Stops.'*

Immediately President Lyndon B. Johnson stepped forward with his arms outstretched.

The officers saluted and then shook hands with the President.

"Well done gentlemen!" began President Johnson, "I am so glad at being able to thank you personally for the fine service that you have rendered our country!"

Colonel Vortex smiled at the President's thick Texan accent.

Peggy and Susie Ky were mesmerised at actually being in the Oval Office.

"Your valour and devotion to duty at *Khe Sanh* has literally saved our Vietnam policy at a time of great crisis and at a crucial point in the war!" added President Johnson.

Colonel Lownds said, "Mr President. We are glad that your Administration has so much faith in the professionalism of the United States Marine Corps."

Vortex said, "Sir. I would repeat the entire performance tomorrow if necessary! If you so ordered!

For you are the Supreme Commander. You make Government policy sir! But we are the instruments of that policy!

The United States Marine Corps is an unflinching bulwark against Communism and a force to be wielded by the President as he sees fit."

President Johnson responded, "Well said Colonel Vortex. I have heard a lot about you from General Earle Wheeler and General Chapman. You know I have been following every move of your men on a scale model of *Khe Sanh* in the White House basement!"

Colonel Vortex and Colonel Lownds smiled as they glanced over to the Chairman of the Joint Chiefs of Staff.

"And I am sure that it is a very fine model too sir!" said Vortex flippantly.

There was laughter in the Oval Office at that remark.

Also present with President Johnson were; Clark Clifford (Secretary of Defence), Henry Kissinger (Special Adviser to the President), Robert *'Blowtorch'* Komer (Chief of the Pacification Program [CORDS]), Walt Rostow (National Security Adviser), Dean Rusk (Secretary of State), General Earle Wheeler (CJCS), George Christian (Press Secretary to the President) and Lady Bird Johnson.

Vortex, Lownds and the others mingled with the high ranking officials as cocktails were served.

Walt Rostow grabbed Vortex's arm and pulled him across to one side of the Oval Office.

The National Security Adviser said in a serious tone of voice, "I have heard from various sources that you were a strong advocate for the use of tactical nuclear weapons at *Khe Sanh*? Is that right?"

Colonel Vortex looked Walt Rostow directly in the eye, "It is sir."

"And why is that?"

"Because it is my opinion sir," answered Vortex defiantly.

"Don't you think that is a little bit drastic in a largely conventional war?" asked Walt Rostow.

"No."

"No?"

"I don't think that the Vietnam War should or even can any longer remain conventional! Sir!

We must be prepared at some point in time, and not very far in the future, to use tactical nuclear weapons in Vietnam."

Then Vortex paused and added, "It would be better for them."

There were a few moments of silence as Walt Rostow rubbed his chin and smiled, "I agree with you Colonel Vortex! Or should I say, Brigadier General Vortex! I am going to urge the President to reconsider the use of atomic munitions in Vietnam."

Colonel Vortex nodded, "The North Vietnamese are not fighting a conventional war anymore! So why should we? I suggest that you should go after the infrastructure and the rail and road system of North Vietnam sir! In tandem with our military operations in South Vietnam, Operation ROLLING THUNDER should be vastly increased. We must blow up the dykes on the *Red River* and flood the coastal plains of North Vietnam.

We must mine Haiphong and all the other major harbours. Our B-52's should level their cities with low-yield atomic munitions. That will teach the coterie of criminals and mental defectives in Hanoi to make peace with the United States of America. The greatest country on the face of this planet!"

Walt Rostow chuckled and sipped on a glass of champagne, saying, "Boy! And I thought I was a Hawk! Whew!"

President Lyndon B. Johnson and Lady Bird Johnson walked over to Vortex who was now joined by Colonel Lownds.

"Its time for the ceremony gentlemen!" exclaimed President Johnson.

All the officials and military men of the Executive arm of government started to move out of the Oval Office and towards the White House Reception area.

Lady Bird Johnson extended her hand to both Lownds and Vortex.

As they shook hands with the First Lady, Vortex said, "It is a pleasure to meet you Mam!"

"Likewise Madame," added Colonel Lownds.

"I want to thank you gentlemen for the wonderful service you have performed for our great nation. We are indeed indebted to you always," said Lady Bird.

"Why thank you Mam!" replied Vortex with obvious delight.

"You have no idea how worried Lyndon was about the horrid situation at *Khe Sanh*," continued Lady Bird Johnson.

"Is that so?" asked Colonel Lownds as Captains Richter and Willoughby stepped up behind him.

"It is! It is indeed Colonel!" replied Lady Bird, "My husband continually stalked the White House corridors in the middle of the night going up and down from the basement to look at that sand-table model!"

Vortex said respectfully, "The President's concern was a great inspiration and morale booster to the troops Mam!"

Suddenly the Commandant of the Marine Corps, General Chapman came up, "Its time gentlemen! Please!"

Vortex nodded graciously to Lady Bird Johnson, "It's been a pleasure Mam!"

Ten minutes later the Armed Forces Personnel who were to receive decorations and commendations were lined up in immaculate linear formations.

The President himself was to hand out the decorations with the Secretary of Defence, Clark Clifford and General Earle Wheeler.

The White House was packed to overflowing with the Press Corps, foreign dignitaries, members of the United States Congress and Senate and the families of the service men and women who were to be honoured.

Colonel Vortex and Colonel Lownds were at the head of the line.

They were to be the first to be decorated.

Susie Ky and Peggy Vortex watched on with excitement and pride.

The Master of Ceremonies read out the names of the decorations and the persons to whom they were to be awarded to, to the huge crowd of dignitaries assembled in the White House.

General Earle Wheeler held up a large silver tray containing the colourful medals.

The Master of Ceremonies began in an officious voice, "Ladies and Gentlemen! The first award goes to Colonel Richard Vortex, Commander of the 9th Marine Regiment.

For his gallant actions on Hill 861A the *Purple Heart* with clusters.

For actions on Hill 881 South and Hill 471 the *Congressional Medal of Honour* and the *Distinguished Service Cross*.

For actions above and beyond the call of duty inside the Marine Combat Base at *Khe Sanh*, two *Silver Stars* and three *Bronze Medallions*."

President Johnson pinned the decorations on Vortex's Class A uniform and shook hands warmly with the Colonel.

"Well done! Excellent job! A magnificent and sterling performance Colonel Vortex!" beamed the President.

Next was Colonel David E. Lownds.

The Siege of Khe Sanh 1967-1968

The Master of Ceremonies said, "Colonel David E. Lownds, Commander of the 26th Marine Regiment, receives the *Purple Heart* and the *Congressional Medal of Honour* for his defence of the Marine Combat Base at *Khe Sanh*."

Over the next 30 minutes decorations were handed out to more than 50 officers and NCOs' who had taken part in the Siege of *Khe Sanh*.

Finally the Unit Flags were brought up by the Sergeant Majors of each Regiment and of the other formations to be honoured.

The President pinned the Presidential Unit Citations and their corresponding Ribbons onto the flags one by one.

Both the 1st Battalion, 9th Marines and all the Battalions of the 26th Marines received the highest Unit Citations of all.

When the award part of the ceremony was over the Master of Ceremonies waited a few moments until there was hushed silence in the White House.

President Lyndon B. Johnson walked up to the podium and began his speech.

The President said;

"This is a decisive time in Vietnam!
The eyes of the nation and the eyes of the entire world!
The eyes of all of history itself! Were on that little brave band of defenders who held the pass at Khe Sanh!
And the area that is around it.
Some have asked what the gallantry of these Marines and Airmen accomplished?
Why did we choose to pay the price to defend those dreary hills?
By pinning down and by decimating two North Vietnamese Divisions, the few thousand Marines and their gallant South Vietnamese Allies prevented those Divisions from entering other major battles.
I believe that our initiative towards talks with North Vietnam was greatly strengthened by what these men did at Khe Sanh!
For they vividly demonstrated to the enemy the utter futility of his attempts to win a military victory in the South!"

When the proceedings were over and a fresh round of cocktails was served, President Johnson walked up to Colonel Vortex and drew him aside for a few seconds.

The President told Colonel Vortex that he was halting the bombing of the North for the time being.

He also expressed great concern and consternation over the entire policy of the Administration with regards to the conduct of the war.

Finally President Johnson asked Colonel Vortex as to his opinion regarding America's prospects in the war.

"Tell me Colonel? I don't know what to do anymore? General Westmoreland is constantly asking for massive troop increases which would be political suicide for my government," began President Johnson.

Then the President took a deep sigh. The exhalation of a very tired and confused man, asking,

"Can we win in Vietnam?"

Colonel Vortex stiffened his body like a ramrod, his eyes glowing with purpose and an uncompromising *élan vital* as he answered his President.

"Victory in Vietnam is just around the corner Mr President!

I am sure of it!"

THE END

Further Suggested Reading

I have short listed 12 military histories, eye witness accounts and autobiographies that I found particularly useful while researching this dramatisation of the siege of Khe Sanh. I would respectfully recommend them to the general reader or student of military history that wishes to delve deeper into this momentous engagement fought by the United States Marines and Airmen and their South Vietnamese allies during those 77 days of sacrifice and heroism by the forces of Military Assistance Command Vietnam (MACV) & (Studies & Observations Group, Military Assistance Command Vietnam) MACV-SOG.

We should never forget the great service and dedication to duty of these men and women who served with distinction in both MACV and MACV-SOG.

"Vietnam at War: The History 1946 – 1975" by Phillip B. Davidson (1988); First Published by Presidio Press, 31 Pamaron Way, Novato CA 94949

"Close Air Support and The Battle for Khe Sanh" by Lieutenant Colonel Shawn P. Callahan (USMC); History Division, United States Marine Corps: Quantico, Virginia; (2009) Published by Books Express Publishing

"A Patch of Ground Khe Sanh Remembered" by Michael Archer (2004): Published by Hellgate Press (2004) (2005) (Personal Narrative account)

"The End of the Line The Siege of Khe Sanh" by Robert Pisor (1982): Published by W.W. Norton & Company New York & London

Peter Braestrup, *a Journalist and News Reporter wrote:* "Big Story: How the American Press & Television Reported and Interpreted the Crisis of TET in Vietnam and

Washington D.C." Published by Garden City, New York: Anchor Press/ Doubleday, First Edition 1978

Bernard B. Fall: The world's leading expert on the two Vietnam Wars: His book titled: "The Two Vietnams" Revised edition. New York, Washington and London: Frederick A. Praeger, 1966: Publisher]

For an Account of the First Indochina War, See also the book by Bernard Fall on the Siege of Dien Bien Phu; "Hell in a Very Small Place; the Siege of Dien Bien Phu," New York: Vintage Books, 1968

"The Vantage Point" by Lyndon Baines Johnson, New York: Holt, Rinehart & Winston, 1971.

"Dien Bien Phu" by John Keegan, New York: Random House, 1974

"The Pentagon Papers: The Secret History of the Vietnam War. New York Times Edition" New York: Bantam Books, 1971.

"Battle of Dien Bien Phu" by Jules Roy, New York: Pyramid Books, 1966.

"A Soldier Reports" by William Childs Westmoreland, Garden City, N.Y: Doubleday & Co., 1976 (Soldier)

www.ingramcontent.com/pod-product-compliance
Lightning Source LLC
Chambersburg PA
CBHW060306240426
43661CB00059B/2676